LITERATURE

Structure, Sound, and Sense

Second Edition

LITERATURE

Structure, Sound, and Sense

Second Edition

LAURENCE PERRINE
Southern Methodist University

HARCOURT BRACE JOVANOVICH, INC.
New York Chicago San Francisco Atlanta

ISBN: 0-15-551102-5

Library of Congress Catalog Card Number: 73-15237

Printed in the United States of America

COVER PHOTO Belzeaux, Rapho Guillumette Pictures.

COPYRIGHTS AND ACKNOWLEDGMENTS

SAMUEL ALLEN for "To Satch" from *American Negro Poetry* by Samuel Allen.

ATHENEUM PUBLISHERS, INC. for "More Light! More Light!" from *The Hard Hours* by Anthony Hecht. Copyright © 1961 by Anthony E. Hecht. Reprinted by permission of Atheneum Publishers. Appeared originally in *Hudson Review*.

DONALD W. BAKER for "Formal Application," *Saturday Review*, May 11, 1963.

BARRIE & JENKINS LTD. for "The Guitarist Tunes Up" by Frances Cornford.

D. C. BERRY for "On Reading Poems to a Senior Class at South High" by D. C. Berry from *Poet Lore 66*, Autumn 1971.

THE BODLEY HEAD, LTD. for "Cha Till Maccruimein" from *A Highland Regiment* by E. A. Mackintosh.

WILLIAM BURFORD for "A Christmas Tree" from *Man Now* by William Burford.

JANET BURROWAY for "The Scientist."

JONATHAN CAPE LIMITED for "The Villain" from *The Collected Poems of W. H. Davies;* "Naming of Parts" and "Judging Distances" from *A Map of Verona* by Henry Reed. Reprinted by permission of the publisher. "The Villain" also reprinted by permission of Mrs. H. M. Davies; "Naming of Parts" and "Judging Distances" also by permission of the author.

CHATTO & WINDUS LTD. for "Anthem for Doomed Youth," "Dulce et Decorum Est," and "The Send-Off" from *The Collected Poems of Wilfred Owen* edited by C. Day Lewis. By permission of Chatto & Windus Ltd. and the executors of the Estate of Harold Owen.

CHILMARK PRESS, INC. for "John Anderson" from *Collected Poems* by Keith Douglas.

COLLINS-KNOWLTON-WING for "The Troll's Nosegay" from *The Pier Glass* by Robert Graves. Reprinted by permission of Collins-Knowlton-Wing, Inc. Copyright © 1921 by Robert Graves.

MALCOLM COWLEY for "The Long Voyage" from *The Dry Season,* copyright 1941 by Malcolm Cowley.

THE CRESSET PRESS for "The Guitarist Tunes Up" from *On a Calm Shore* by Frances Cornford.

CURTIS BROWN LTD. (New York) for "Six Poets in Search of a Lawyer" from *Exiles and Marriages* by Donald Hall. Copyright © 1955 by Donald Hall. Reprinted by permission of Curtis Brown Ltd.

CURTIS BROWN LTD. (London) for "A Bookshop Idyll" from *A Case of Samples* by Kingsley Amis.

THE JOHN DAY COMPANY INC. PUBLISHERS for "The Griesly Wife" Copyright © 1946 by The John Day Co., Inc. Reprinted from *Selected Verse* by John Manifold by permission of The John Day Company, Inc., an Intext publisher.

J. M. DENT & SONS LTD. for "Poem in October" and "Do not go gentle into that good night" from *The Collected Poems of Dylan Thomas*. By permission of J. M. Dent and the Trustees for the Copyrights of the late Dylan Thomas.

DOUBLEDAY & COMPANY, INC. for "The Rich Man" copyright 1911 and renewed by Doubleday & Company, Inc. from the book *Tobogganing on Parnassus* by Franklin P. Adams. Reprinted by permission of Doubleday & Company, Inc. For two haiku, "Fallen flowers rise" and "A lightning gleam," from *An Introduction to Haiku* by Harold G. Henderson. Copyright © 1958 by Harold G. Henderson. Reprinted by permission of Doubleday & Company, Inc. For "I Knew a Woman" and "The Waking" copyright 1954 by Theodore Roethke from *The Collected Poems of Theodore Roethke*. Reprinted by permission of Doubleday & Company, Inc.

GERALD DUCKWORTH & CO. LTD. for "The Changeling" from *Collected Poems* by Charlotte Mew, published by Gerald Duckworth & Co. Ltd., 1953.

ALAN DUGAN for "Love Song: I and Thou" from *Poems* by Alan Dugan (Yale University Press, 1961).

E. P. DUTTON & CO. LTD. for "The Hunt" from *Declensions of the Air* by Louis Kent. Copyright 1950, by E. P. Dutton & Co., Inc. Reprinted by permission of the publisher.

EDITIONS POETRY LONDON for "Vergissmeinicht" from *Collected Poems* by Keith Douglas.

MARI EVANS for "When In Rome," from *I Am a Black Woman,* published by William Morrow and Company, 1970, by permission of the author.

FABER & FABER LTD. for "The Unknown Citizen" and "That night when joy began" from *Collected Shorter Poems 1927–1957* by W. H. Auden. For "The Shield of Achilles" from *The Shield of Achilles* by W. H. Auden. For "John Anderson" from *Collected Poems* (1966) by Keith Douglas. For "The Love Song of J. Alfred Prufrock" from *Collected Poems 1909–1962* by T. S. Eliot. For "The Forge" from *Door Into The Dark* by Seamus Heaney. For "View of a Pig" from *Lupercal* by Ted Hughes. For "A Study of Reading Habits" from *The Whitsun Weddings* by Philip Larkin. For "The Horses" from *Collected Poems 1921–1958* by Edwin Muir. For "Base Details" from *Collected Poems* by Siegfried Sassoon. Reprinted by permission of Faber & Faber Ltd.

PADRAIC FALLON for "Mary Hynes."

FARRAR, STRAUS & GIROUX for "The Ball Poem," reprinted with the permission of Farrar, Straus & Giroux, Inc. from *Short Poems* by John Berryman, copyright 1948 by John Berryman.

FUNK AND WAGNALLS for haiku by Moritake, "The falling flower." Reprinted from *Poetry Handbook; A Dictionary of Terms* by Babette Deutsch. By permission of the publishers, Funk & Wagnalls, New York.

VICTOR GOLLANCZ, LTD. for "A Bookshop Idyll" from *A Case of Samples* by Kingsley Amis.

GROVE PRESS, INC. for "The Horses" from *One Foot in Eden* by Edwin Muir.

HARCOURT BRACE JOVANOVICH, INC. for "A Bookshop Idyll" from *A Case of Samples* © 1956 by Kingsley Amis. Reprinted by permission of Harcourt Brace Jovanovich, Inc. For "if everything happens that can't be done" and "what if a much of a which of a wind" by e. e. cummings. Copyright, 1944, by e. e. cummings; copyright, 1972, by Nancy Andrews; for "when serpents bargain for the right to squirm" by e. e. cummings. Copyright, 1950 by e. e. cummings. Reprinted from his volume *Poems 1923–1954* by permission of Harcourt Brace Jovanovich, Inc. For "the greedy the people" from *73 Poems* by e. e. cummings. © 1960 by e. e. cummings. For "in heavenly realms of Hellas" by e. e. cummings. © 1963 by Marion Morehouse Cummings. Reprinted from *73 Poems* by e. e. cummings by permission of Harcourt Brace Jovanovich, Inc. For "The Love Song of J. Alfred Prufrock" by T. S. Eliot, from *Collected Poems 1909–1962* by T. S. Eliot copyright, 1936, by Harcourt Brace Jovanovich Inc.; copyright, © 1963, 1964, by T. S. Eliot. Reprinted by permission of the publisher.

ALFRED A. KNOPF, INC. for "Dream Deferred" from *The Panther and the Lash* by Langston Hughes. Copyright © 1951 by Langston Hughes. Reprinted by permission of Alfred A. Knopf, Inc. For "Cross," copyright 1926 by Alfred A. Knopf, Inc. and renewed 1954 by Langston Hughes. Reprinted from *Selected Poems* by Langston Hughes, by permission of Alfred A. Knopf, Inc. For "Devil, Maggot and Son." Copyright 1949, © 1959 by Frank O'Connor. Reprinted from *Kings, Lords and Commons,* by Frank O'Connor, by permission of Alfred A. Knopf, Inc. For "Parting Without a Sequel" by John Crowe Ransom. Copyright 1927 by Alfred A. Knopf, Inc. and renewed 1955 by John Crowe Ransom. Reprinted from *Selected Poems,* Third Edition, Revised and Enlarged by John Crowe Ransom, by permission of Alfred A. Knopf, Inc. For "Bells for John Whiteside's Daughter" by John Crowe Ransom. Copyright 1924 by Alfred A. Knopf, Inc. and renewed 1952 by John Crowe Ransom. Reprinted from *Selected Poems,* Third Edition, Revised and Enlarged, by John Crowe Ransom, by permission of Alfred A. Knopf, Inc. For "Peter Quince at the Clavier" and "A High-Toned Old Christian Woman" by Wallace Stevens. Copyright 1923 and renewed 1951 by Wallace Stevens. Reprinted from *The Collected Poems of Wallace Stevens,* by permission of Alfred A. Knopf, Inc. For "Winter Ocean," copyright © 1960 by John Updike. Reprinted by permission of Alfred A. Knopf, Inc. from *Telephone Poles* by John Updike.

J. B. LIPPINCOTT COMPANY for "The Barrel-Organ." Copyright 1906, 1909, renewed 1934, 1937 by Alfred Noyes. From the book *Collected Poems,* Volume I by Alfred Noyes. Copyright 1913 by Frederick A. Stokes Company. Copyright renewed 1941 by Alfred Noyes. Reprinted by permission of J. B. Lippincott Company.

LITTLE, BROWN AND COMPANY for "My life had stood, a loaded gun" from *The Complete Poems of Emily Dickinson* edited by Thomas H. Johnson. Copyright 1929, © 1957 by Mary L. Hampson. Reprinted by permission of Little, Brown and Co. For "The Turtle" from *Verses From 1929 On* by Ogden Nash. Copyright 1940 by Ogden Nash. Reprinted by permission of Little, Brown and Co. For "Portrait of the Artist as a Prematurely Old Man" from *Verses From 1929 On* by Ogden Nash. Copyright, 1934, by The Curtis Publishing Company. For "The Sea-Gull" from *Verses From 1929 On* by Ogden Nash. Copyright, 1940 by Ogden Nash. Reprinted by permission of Little, Brown and Co.

MCGRAW-HILL BOOK COMPANY, INC. for "Enticer" from *Light Amour* by Richard Armour. Copyright © 1954 by Richard Armour. Used with permission of McGraw-Hill Book Company.

GEORGE MACBETH for "Bedtime Story" from *The Broken Places* by George Macbeth (Scorpion Press, 1963). Reprinted by permission of the author.

THE MACMILLAN COMPANY (NEW YORK) for "Eve," reprinted with permission of The Macmillan Company from *Poems* by Ralph Hodgson. Copyright 1917 by The Macmillan Company, renewed 1945 by Ralph Hodgson. For "A Carriage from Sweden," reprinted with permission of The Macmillan Company from *Collected Poems* by Marianne Moore. Copyright 1944 by Marianne Moore, renewed 1972 by Marianne Moore. For "Mr. Flood's Party," reprinted with permission of The Macmillan Company from *Collected Poems* by Edwin Arlington Robinson. Copyright 1921 by Edwin Arlington Robinson, renewed 1949 by Ruth Nivison. For "The Mill," reprinted with permission of The Macmillan Company from *Collected Poems* by Edwin Arlington Robinson. Copyright 1920 by The Macmillan Company, renewed 1948 by Ruth Nivison. For "A Glass of Beer," reprinted with permission of The Macmillan Company from *Collected Poems* by James Stephens. Copyright 1918 by The Macmillan Company, renewed 1946 by James Stephens. For "Barter," reprinted with permission of The Macmillan Company from *Collected Poems* by Sara Teasdale. Copyright 1917 by The Macmillan Company, renewed 1945 by Mamie T. Wheless. For "Down By the Salley Gardens," reprinted with permission of The Macmillan Company from *Collected Poems* by William Butler Yeats Copyright 1906 by The Macmillan Company, renewed 1934 by William Butler Yeats. For "The Coming of Wisdom with Time," reprinted with permission of The Macmillan Company from *Collected Poems* by William Butler Yeats. Copyright 1912 by The Macmillan Company, renewed 1940 by Bertha Georgie Yeats. For "A Prayer for My Daughter," reprinted with permission of The Macmillan Company from *Collected Poems* by William Butler Yeats. Copyright 1924 by The Macmillan Company, renewed 1952 by Bertha Georgie Yeats. For "Among School Children," "Sailing to Byzantium," and "Leda and the Swan," reprinted with permission of The Macmillan Company from *Collected Poems* by William Butler Yeats. Copyright 1928 by The Macmillan Company, renewed 1956 by Georgie Yeats. For "Fragment," reprinted with permission of The Macmillan Company from *Collected Poems* by William Butler Yeats. Copyright 1933 by The Macmillan Company, renewed 1961 by Bertha Georgie Yeats. For "The Spur," reprinted with permission of The Macmillan Company from *Collected Poems* by William Butler Yeats. Copyright 1940 by Bertha Georgie Yeats, renewed 1968 by Bertha Georgie Yeats, Anne Yeats, Michael Butler Yeats. For "To A Young Girl," reprinted with permission of The Macmillan Company from *Collected Poems* by William Butler Yeats. Copyright 1919 by The Macmillan Company, renewed 1947 by Bertha Georgie Yeats.

MACMILLAN & CO. LTD. (LONDON) for "A Glass of Beer" from *Collected Poems* by James Stephens, by permission of Mrs. Iris Wise; Macmillan London & Basingstoke; and The Macmillan Company of Canada Limited.

THE MACMILLAN COMPANY OF CANADA LTD. for "Afterwards," "The Darkling Thrush," and "The Man He Killed" from *Collected Poems* of Thomas Hardy by permission of the Estate of Thomas Hardy. For "Eve" from *Poems* by Ralph Hodgson, by permission of Macmillan & Co. Ltd. London, and The Macmillan Company of Canada Limited. For "A Glass of Beer" from *Collected Poems* by James Stephens, by permission of Mrs. Iris Wise; Macmillan London & Basingstoke; and The Macmillan Company of Canada Limited.

THE MARVEL PRESS for "Church Going" by Philip Larkin from *The Less Deceived* by permission of The Marvel Press, England.

HAROLD MATSON COMPANY, INC. for "Sheepdog Trials in Hyde Park" from *The Gate* by C. Day Lewis. Copyright C. Day Lewis. Reprinted by permission of The Harold Matson Company, Inc.

WILLIAM MORROW & COMPANY, INC. for "Love Poem" from *The Iron Pastoral* by John Frederick Nims. Copyright © 1947 by John Frederick Nims. Reprinted by permission of William Morrow and Company, Inc.

JOHN MURRAY for "The Barrel-Organ" by Alfred Noyes from *Collected Poems of Alfred Noyes,* John Murray (Publishers) Ltd.

NEW DIRECTIONS for "Constantly risking absurdity" from *A Coney Island of the Mind* by Lawrence Ferlinghetti Copyright © 1958 by Lawrence Ferlinghetti. Reprinted by permission of New Directions Publishing Corporation. For "Portrait d'une Femme" from *Personae* by Ezra Pound. For "Poem in October" and "Do not go gentle into that good night" from *The Poems of Dylan Thomas*. Copyright 1946 by New Directions Publishing Corporation, copyright 1952 by Dylan Thomas. Reprinted by permission of New Directions Publishing Corporation. For "This Is Just to Say" from *Collected Earlier Poems* by William Carlos Williams. Copyright 1938 by William Carlos Williams. For "The Dance" from *Collected Later Poems* by William Carlos Williams. Copyright 1944 by William Carlos Williams. Reprinted by permission of New Directions Publishing Corporation. For "Anthem for Doomed Youth," "Dulce et Decorum Est" and "The Send Off" by Wilfred Owen, from *Collected Poems*. Copyright Chatto & Windus, Ltd. 1946, © 1963. Reprinted by permission of New Directions Publishing Corporation. For "Losing Track" by Denise Levertov, from *O Taste and See*. "Losing Track" was first published in *Poetry*. Copyright © 1963 by Denise Levertov Goodman. Reprinted by permission of New Directions Publishing Corporation.

HAROLD OBER ASSOCIATES, INC. for "Southern Mansion" by Arna Bontemps. Copyright © 1963 by Arna Bontemps. Reprinted by permission of Harold Ober Associates Incorporated. For "Epigram" by Langston Hughes. Copyright 1957 by Langston Hughes. Reprinted by permission of Harold Ober Associates Incorporated.

OHIO STATE UNIVERSITY PRESS for "Spectrum" by William Dickey. Reprinted from *Interpreter's House,* published by the Ohio State University Press and copyright © 1962, 1963 by William Dickey. All rights reserved. Used by permission of the author and the publisher.

OXFORD UNIVERSITY PRESS (NEW YORK) for "Morning Song from 'Senlin'" from *Collected Poems* by Conrad Aiken. Copyright © 1953, 1970 by Conrad Aiken. Reprinted by permission of Oxford University Press, Inc. For "The Forge" from *Door Into the Dark* by Seamus Heaney. © 1969 by Seamus Heaney. Reprinted by permission of Oxford University Press, Inc. For "The Horses" from *Collected Poems* by Edwin Muir. Copyright © 1960 by Willa Muir. Reprinted by permission of Oxford University Press, Inc.

OXFORD UNIVERSITY PRESS (LONDON) for "Elegy for Alfred Hubbard" from *With Love Somehow* by Tony Connor. © Oxford University Press 1962.

A. D. PETERS & CO. for "Devil, Maggot and Son" from *Fountain of Youth* by Frank O'Connor. For "Lines for a Christmas Card" by Hilaire Belloc. Reprinted by permission of A. D. Peters and Company.

PRINCETON UNIVERSITY PRESS for haiku by Bashō, "The lightning flashes!" translated by Earl Miner, reprinted from *Encyclopedia of Poetry and Poetics* by A. Preminger, F. Warnke, & O. Hardison (Princeton University Press, 1965).

RANDOM HOUSE, INC. for "That night when joy began" by W. H. Auden. Copyright 1937 and renewed 1965 by W. H. Auden. Reprinted from *Collected Shorter Poems 1927–1957,* by W. H. Auden, by permission of Random House, Inc. For "The Unknown Citizen" by W. H. Auden. Copyright 1940 and renewed 1968 by W. H. Auden. Reprinted from *Collected Shorter Poems 1927–1957,* by W. H. Auden, by permission of Random House, Inc. For "The Shield of Achilles" by W. H. Auden. Copyright 1952 by W. H. Auden. Reprinted from *Collected Shorter Poems 1927–1957,* by W. H. Auden, by permission of Random House, Inc. For "An Old Photo in an Old Life" from *The Center of Attention* by Daniel Hoffman. Copyright © 1970, 1971, 1972, 1973, 1974 by Daniel Hoffman. Reprinted by permission of Random House, Inc. For "A Study of Reading Habits" from *The Whitsun Weddings* by Philip Larkin. Copyright © 1964 by Philip Larkin. Reprinted by permission of Random House, Inc. For "Boy-Man" by Karl Shapiro. Copyright 1947 by Karl Shapiro. Reprinted from *Selected Poems,* by Karl Shapiro, by permission of Random House, Inc. Originally appeared in *The New Yorker.*

G. T. SASSOON for "Base Details" from *Collected Poems* by Siegfried Sassoon. Reprinted by permission of G. T. Sassoon.

SATURDAY REVIEW for "Formal Application" by Donald W. Baker from *Saturday Review,* May 11, 1963.

MICHAEL SCHMIDT for "Underwater" from *Desert of the Lions,* 1972, Carcanet Press, 266 Councillor Lane, Cheadle Hulme, Cheadle, Cheshire SK 8 S P N England. Used by permission of the author. First published in *Poetry,* June 1971.

CHARLES SCRIBNER'S SONS for "Hunting Song," copyright © 1959 by Donald Finkel, reprinted with the permission of Charles Scribner's Sons from *The Clothing's New Emperor* by Donald Finkel (*Poets of Today VI*). "Feel Like a Bird" is reprinted with the permission of Charles Scribner's Sons from *To Mix With Time* by May Swenson. Copyright © 1963 by May Swenson. "America for Me" is reprinted by permission of Charles Scribner's Sons from *The Poems of Henry van Dyke,* Copyright 1911 Charles Scribner's Sons; renewal copyright 1939 Tertius van Dyke. "Earth" is reprinted by permission of Charles Scribner's Sons from *The Gardener and Other Poems* by John Hall Wheelock. Copyright © 1961 John Hall Wheelock.

THE SOCIETY OF AUTHORS for "Reveille," "When smoke stood up from Ludlow," "To an Athlete Dying Young," "The New Mistress," "Is my team ploughing," "Loitering with a vacant eye," "Stars I have seen them fall," "On Moonlit Heath and Lonesome Bank," "Terence, this is stupid stuff," and "The Carpenter's Son," by permission of The Society of Authors as the literary representative of the Estate of A. E. Housman, and Jonathan Cape Ltd., publishers of A. E. Housman's *Collected Poems*. For "The Listeners" from *The Collected Poems of Walter de la Mare* (1970), by permission of the Literary Trustees of Walter de la Mare, and the Society of Authors as their representative.

WOLE SOYINKA for "Telephone Conversation."

WILLIAM STAFFORD for "At the Un-National Monument along the Canadian Border" by William Stafford, from *The Ladies' Home Journal*.

THE UNIVERSITY OF MASSACHUSETTS PRESS for "The Hound" by Robert Francis. Reprinted by permission of Robert Francis and the University of Massachusetts Press from *Come Out Into the Sun: New and Selected Poems* by Robert Francis, 1965.

THE VIKING PRESS, INC. for "The Long Voyage" from *Blue Juniata: Collected Poems* by Malcolm Cowley. Copyright 1939, copyright © renewed 1967 by Malcolm Cowley. All rights reserved. Reprinted by permission of The Viking Press, Inc. For "Agony Column" by A. D. Hope from *Collected Poems 1930–1965* by A. D. Hope. Copyright 1963, 1966 in all countries of the International Copyright Union by A. D. Hope. All rights reserved. Reprinted by permission of The Viking Press, Inc. For "Advice to Young Ladies" from *Collected Poems 1930–1965* by A. D. Hope. Copyright 1963, 1966 in all countries of the International Copyright Union by A. D. Hope. All rights reserved. Reprinted by permission of The Viking Press, Inc. For "On the Beach at Fontana" by James Joyce. From *Collected Poems* by James Joyce. Copyright 1927 by James Joyce. All rights reserved. Reprinted by permission of The Viking Press, Inc. For "All Day I Hear" (XXXV—"Chamber Music"). From *Collected Poems* by James Joyce. Copyright 1918 by B. W. Huebsch, Inc., 1946 by Nora Joyce. All rights reserved. Reprinted by permission of The Viking Press, Inc. For "City Life" from *The Complete Poems of D. H. Lawrence* ed. by Vivian de Sola Pinto and F. Warren Roberts. Copyright © 1964, 1971 by Angelo Ravagli and C. M. Weekley, Executors of the Estate of Frieda Lawrence Ravagli. All rights reserved. Reprinted by permission of The Viking Press, Inc. For "I May, I Might, I Must" by Marianne Moore from *The Complete Poems of Marianne Moore*. All rights reserved. Reprinted by permission of The Viking Press, Inc. For "Base Details" from *Collected Poems* by Siegfried Sassoon. Copyright 1918 by E. P. Dutton Co., 1946 by Siegfried Sassoon. All rights reserved. Reprinted by permission of The Viking Press, Inc.

A. P. WATT & SON for "Fragments," "Down by the Salley Gardens," "To a Young Girl," "Among School Children," "Sailing to Byzantium," "Leda and the Swan," "The Coming of Wisdom with Time," "A Prayer for My Daughter," "The Spur," and "The Folly of Being Comforted," from *The Collected Poems of William Butler Yeats,* reprinted by permission of Mr. M. B. Yeats and the Macmillan Company of Canada Ltd. For "The Troll's Nosegay" and "The Naked and the Nude" from *Collected Poems 1965* by Robert Graves. By permission of Mr. Robert Graves and A. P. Watt & Son.

WESLEYAN UNIVERSITY PRESS for "The Bee," copyright © 1966 by James Dickey. Reprinted from *Poems 1957–1967* by James Dickey by permission of Wesleyan University Press. For "The Villain" copyright © 1963 by Jonathan Cape Limited. Reprinted from *The Complete Poems of W. H. Davies* by permission of Wesleyan University Press (and Jonathan Cape Limited). For "A Blessing" by James Wright. Copyright © 1961 by James Wright. Reprinted from *The Branch Will Not Break,* by James Wright, by permission of Wesleyan University Press. This poem first appeared in *Poetry*.

JOHN WOLFERS for "Curiosity" from *Passwords* by Alastair Reid. Copyright © 1959 by Alastair Reid. Originally published in *The New Yorker*. Reprinted by permission of John Wolfers and the author.

Preface

Literature: Structure, Sound, and Sense is intended for the student who is beginning a serious study of imaginative literature. It provides a comprehensive introduction to the principal forms of fiction, poetry, and drama. Each section begins with a simple discussion of the elements of the form and is illustrated, throughout, by carefully chosen stories, poems, and plays. Each section also includes additional selections for further reading. The book seeks to give the student a sufficient grasp of the nature and variety of literary works, some reasonable means for reading them with appreciative understanding, and some basic principles for making literary judgments. Its objective is to help the student to understand, enjoy, and prefer good works of literature.

Each of the three sections has been revised for this Second Edition: thirteen of the forty-three stories, almost one-fourth of the nearly three hundred poems, and three of the twelve plays are new. The number of selections by black authors has been increased. (The fiction section is the Fourth Edition of *Story and Structure;* the poetry section is the Fourth Edition of *Sound and Sense.*)

A book of this kind inevitably owes something to all who have thought or written about literature. It would be impossible to express all indebtedness, but for personal advice, criticism, and assistance I wish especially to thank my wife, Catherine Perrine; Margaret Morton Blum and Marshall Terry, Southern Methodist University; Maynard Mack and David Thorburn, Yale University; Mark Schorer, University of California; Charles S. Holmes, Pomona College; Donald Peet, Indiana University; James W. Byrd, East Texas State University; Calvin L. Skaggs, Drew University; and Willis Glover, Mercer University.

L. P.

Southern Methodist University
Dallas, Texas

Contents

Stories for Further Reading

POETRY

The Elements of Poetry

Catch Falling Star

Poems for Further Reading

Plays for Further Reading

FICTION

The Elements of the Short Story

CHAPTER ONE

Escape and Interpretation

The first question to ask about fiction is: Why bother to read it? With life as short as it is, with so many pressing demands on our time, with books of information, instruction, and discussion waiting to be read, why should we spend precious time on works of imagination? The eternal answers to this question are two: enjoyment and understanding.

Since the invention of language, men have taken pleasure in following and participating in the imaginary adventures and imaginary experiences of imaginary people. Whatever—without causing harm—serves to make life less tedious, to make the hours pass more quickly and pleasurably, surely needs nothing else to recommend it. Enjoyment—and ever more enjoyment—is the first aim and justification of reading fiction.

But, unless fiction gives something more than pleasure, it hardly justifies itself as a subject of college study. Unless it expands or refines our minds or quickens our sense of life, its value is not appreciably greater than that of miniature golf, bridge, or ping-pong. To have a compelling claim on our attention, it must yield not only enjoyment but understanding.

The experience of men through the ages is that literature may furnish such understanding and do so effectively—that the depiction of imagined experiences can provide authentic insights. "The truest history," said Diderot of the novels of Samuel Richardson, "is full of falsehoods, and your romance is full of truths." But the bulk of fiction does not present such insights. Only some does. Initially, therefore, fiction may be classified into two broad categories: literature of escape and literature of interpretation.

Escape literature is that written purely for entertainment—to help us pass the time agreeably. Interpretive literature is written to broaden and deepen and sharpen our awareness of life. Escape literature takes us *away* from the real world: it enables us temporarily to forget our troubles. Interpretive literature takes us, through the imagination, deeper *into* the real world: it enables us to understand our troubles. Escape literature has as its only object pleasure. Interpretive literature has as its object pleasure *plus* understanding.

Having established a distinction, however, we must not exaggerate or oversimplify it. Escape and interpretation are not two great bins, into one or the other of which we can toss any given story. Rather, they are opposite ends of a scale, the two poles between which the world of fiction spins. The difference between them does not lie in the absence or presence of a "moral." The story which in all of its incidents and characters is shallow may have an unimpeachable moral, while the interpretive story may have no moral at all in any conventional sense. The difference does not lie in the absence or presence of "facts." The historical romance may be full of historical information and yet be pure escape in its depiction of human behavior. The difference does not lie in the presence or absence of an element of fantasy. The escape story may have a surface appearance of everyday reality, while the tale of seeming wildest fancy may press home on us some sudden truth. The difference between the two kinds of literature is deeper and more subtle than any of these distinctions. A story becomes interpretive as it illuminates some aspect of human life or behavior. An interpretive story presents us with an insight—large or small—into the nature and conditions of our existence. It gives us a keener awareness of what it is to be a human being in a universe sometimes friendly, sometimes hostile. It helps us to understand our neighbors and ourselves.

Perhaps we can clarify the difference by suggestion. The escape writer is like an inventor who devises a contrivance for our diversion. When we push the button, lights flash, bells ring, and cardboard figures move jerkily across a painted horizon. The interpretive writer is a discoverer: he takes us out into the midst of life and says, "Look, here is the world!" The escape writer is full of tricks and surprises: he pulls rabbits out of hats, saws a beautiful woman in two, and snatches brightly colored balls out of the air. The interpretive writer takes us behind the scenes, where he shows us the props and mirrors and seeks to make clear the illusions. This is not to say that the interpretive writer is merely a reporter. More surely than the escape writer he shapes and gives form to his materials.

But he shapes and forms them always with the intent that we may see and feel and understand them better, not for the primary purpose of furnishing entertainment.

Now, just as there are two kinds of fiction, there are also two kinds of reader. The immature or inexperienced reader seeks only escape. Even when he thinks he is reading for interpretation or some useful moral, he insists that what he reads return him always some pleasant or exciting image of the world or some flattering image of himself. We all begin with fairy tales. Our early reading experiences are likely to be with stories such as that of Cinderella, whose fairy godmother transforms a pumpkin and mice into a coach-and-four, whose slim foot is the only one that fits the crystal slipper, who rises superior to her cruel stepmother and taunting step-sisters to marry and "live happily ever after" with the charming prince, and who, never for a moment anything but sweet and virtuous, forgives her former tormentors who tried to keep her a cinder girl.

Though most people move on from fairy tales into a seemingly more adult kind of reading, they may well be mistaken in thinking that they have progressed. The element of unreality does not lie primarily in magic wands and fairy godmothers but in a superficial treatment of life. The story of a shopgirl who is lifted from the painful conditions of her work and home life by a handsome young suitor from the upper classes may be as truly a Cinderella story as the one we read in childhood, though its setting is Hoboken rather than a kingdom by the sea. Unfortunately many readers—indeed most—never grow beyond the fairy tale except in the most elementary of senses. In some ways, perhaps, their movement is backward, for it involves a loss of that sense of wonder which marks the child's vision.

There are many signs of the inexperienced reader. He makes fixed demands of every story he reads, and he feels frustrated and disappointed unless these demands are satisfied. Often he sticks to one type of subject matter. Instead of being receptive to any story that puts human beings in human situations, he reads only sports stories, Western stories, love stories, or crime stories. If he is willing to accept a wider range of experience, he still wishes every story to conform at bottom to several strict though perhaps unconsciously formulated expectations. Among the most common of these expectations are: (1) a sympathetic hero (or heroine)—one with whom the reader can in imagination identify himself as he reads and whose adventures and triumphs he can share; (2) a plot in which something exciting is always happening and in

experience, felt in the emotions as well as apprehended by the mind. The aim of this book is to aid in the growth of understanding and judgment.

Richard Connell

THE MOST DANGEROUS GAME

"Off there to the right—somewhere—is a large island," said Whitney. "It's rather a mystery—"

"What island is it?" Rainsford asked.

"The old charts call it 'Ship-Trap Island,' " Whitney replied. "A suggestive name, isn't it? Sailors have a curious dread of the place. I don't know why. Some superstition—"

"Can't see it," remarked Rainsford, trying to peer through the dank tropical night that was palpable as it pressed its thick warm blackness in upon the yacht.

"You've good eyes," said Whitney, with a laugh, "and I've seen you pick off a moose moving in the brown fall bush at four hundred yards, but even you can't see four miles or so through a moonless Caribbean night."

"Nor four yards," admitted Rainsford. "Ugh! It's like moist black velvet."

"It will be light in Rio," promised Whitney. "We should make it in a few days. I hope the jaguar guns have come from Purdey's. We should have some good hunting up the Amazon. Great sport, hunting."

"The best sport in the world," agreed Rainsford.

"For the hunter," amended Whitney. "Not for the jaguar."

"Don't talk rot, Whitney," said Rainsford. "You're a big-game hunter, not a philosopher. Who cares how a jaguar feels?"

"Perhaps the jaguar does," observed Whitney.

"Bah! They've no understanding."

"Even so, I rather think they understand one thing—fear. The fear of pain and the fear of death."

"Nonsense," laughed Rainsford. "This hot weather is making you soft, Whitney. Be a realist. The world is made up of two classes—the hunters and the huntees. Luckily, you and I are hunters. Do you think we've passed that island yet?"

"I can't tell in the dark. I hope so."

"Why?" asked Rainsford.

"The place has a reputation—a bad one."

"Cannibals?" suggested Rainsford.

"Hardly. Even cannibals wouldn't live in such a God-forsaken place. But it's gotten into sailor lore, somehow. Didn't you notice that the crew's nerves seemed a bit jumpy to-day?"

"They were a bit strange, now you mention it. Even Captain Nielsen—"

"Yes, even that tough-minded old Swede, who'd go up to the devil himself and ask him for a light. Those fishy blue eyes held a look I never saw there before. All I could get out of him was: 'This place has an evil name among sea-faring men, sir.' Then he said to me, very gravely: 'Don't you feel anything?'—as if the air about us was actually poisonous. Now, you mustn't laugh when I tell you this—I did feel something like a sudden chill.

"There was no breeze. The sea was as flat as a plate-glass window. We were drawing near the island then. What I felt was a—a mental chill; a sort of sudden dread."

"Pure imagination," said Rainsford. "One superstitious sailor can taint the whole ship's company with his fear."

"Maybe. But sometimes I think sailors have an extra sense that tells them when they are in danger. Sometimes I think evil is a tangible thing—with wave lengths, just as sound and light have. An evil place can, so to speak, broadcast vibrations of evil. Anyhow, I'm glad we're getting out of this zone. Well, I think I'll turn in now, Rainsford."

"I'm not sleepy," said Rainsford. "I'm going to smoke another pipe up on the after deck."

"Good night, then, Rainsford. See you at breakfast."

"Right. Good night, Whitney."

There was no sound in the night as Rainsford sat there, but the muffled throb of the engine that drove the yacht swiftly through the darkness, and the swish and ripple of the wash of the propeller.

Rainsford, reclining in a steamer chair, indolently puffed on his favorite brier. The sensuous drowsiness of the night was on him. "It's so dark," he thought, "that I could sleep without closing my eyes; the night would be my eyelids—"

An abrupt sound startled him. Off to the right he heard it, and his ears, expert in such matters, could not be mistaken. Again he heard the sound, and again. Somewhere, off in the blackness, some one had fired a gun three times.

Rainsford sprang up and moved quickly to the rail, mystified. He strained his eyes in the direction from which the reports had come, but it was like trying to see through a blanket. He leaped upon the rail and balanced himself there, to get greater elevation; his pipe, striking a rope, was knocked from his mouth. He lunged for it; a short, hoarse cry came from his lips as he realized he had reached too far and had lost his balance. The cry was pinched off short as the blood-warm waters of the Caribbean Sea closed over his head.

He struggled up to the surface and tried to cry out, but the wash from the speeding yacht slapped him in the face and the salt water in his open mouth made him gag and strangle. Desperately he struck out with strong strokes after the receding lights of the yacht, but he stopped before he had swum fifty feet. A certain cool-headedness had come to him; it was not the first time he had been in a tight place. There was a chance that his cries could be heard by some one aboard the yacht, but that chance was slender, and grew more slender as the yacht raced on. He wrestled himself out of his clothes, and shouted with all his power. The lights of the yacht became faint and ever-vanishing fireflies; then they were blotted out entirely by the night.

Rainsford remembered the shots. They had come from the right, and doggedly he swam in that direction, swimming with slow, deliberate strokes, conserving his strength. For a seemingly endless time he fought the sea. He began to count his strokes; he could do possibly a hundred more and then—

Rainsford heard a sound. It came out of the darkness, a high screaming sound, the sound of an animal in an extremity of anguish and terror.

He did not recognize the animal that made the sound; he did not try to; with fresh vitality he swam toward the sound. He heard it again; then it was cut short by another noise, crisp, staccato.

"Pistol shot," muttered Rainsford, swimming on.

Ten minutes of determined effort brought another sound to his ears—the most welcome he had ever heard—the muttering and growling of the sea breaking on a rocky shore. He was almost on the rocks before he saw them; on a night less calm he would have been shattered against them. With his remaining strength he dragged himself from the swirling waters. Jagged crags appeared to jut into the opaqueness, he forced himself upward, hand over hand. Gasping, his hands raw, he reached a flat place at the top. Dense jungle came down to the very edge of the cliffs. What perils that tangle of trees and underbrush might hold for him did not concern Rainsford just then. All he knew was that he was safe from his enemy, the sea, and that utter weariness was on him. He flung himself down at the jungle edge and tumbled headlong into the deepest sleep of his life.

When he opened his eyes he knew from the position of the sun that it was late in the afternoon. Sleep had given him new vigor; a sharp hunger was picking at him. He looked about him, almost cheerfully.

"Where there are pistol shots, there are men. Where there are men, there is food," he thought. But what kind of men, he wondered, in so forbidding a place? An unbroken front of snarled and ragged jungle fringed the shore.

He saw no sign of a trail through the closely knit web of weeds and trees; it was easier to go along the shore, and Rainsford floundered along by the water. Not far from where he had landed, he stopped.

Some wounded thing, by the evidence a large animal, had thrashed about in the underbrush; the jungle weeds were crushed down and the moss was lacerated; one patch of weeds was stained crimson. A small, glittering object not far away caught Rainsford's eye and he picked it up. It was an empty cartridge.

"A twenty-two," he remarked. "That's odd. It must have been a fairly large animal too. The hunter had his nerve with him to tackle it with a light gun. It's clear that the brute put up a fight. I suppose the first three shots I heard was when the hunter flushed his quarry and wounded it. The last shot was when he trailed it here and finished it."

He examined the ground closely and found what he had hoped to find—the print of hunting boots. They pointed along the cliff in the direction he had been going. Eagerly he hurried along, now slipping on a rotten log or a loose stone, but making headway; night was beginning to settle down on the island.

Bleak darkness was blacking out the sea and jungle when Rainsford sighted the lights. He came upon them as he turned a crook in the coast line, and his first thought was that he had come upon a village, for there were many lights. But as he forged along he saw to his great astonishment that all the lights were in one enormous building—a lofty structure with pointed towers plunging upward into the gloom. His eyes made out the shadowy outlines of a palatial château; it was set on a high bluff, and on three sides of it cliffs dived down to where the sea licked greedy lips in the shadows.

"Mirage," thought Rainsford. But it was no mirage, he found, when he opened the tall spiked iron gate. The stone steps were real enough; the massive door with a leering gargoyle for a knocker was real enough; yet about it all hung an air of unreality.

He lifted the knocker, and it creaked up stiffly, as if it had never before been used. He let it fall, and it startled him with its booming loudness. He thought he heard steps within; the door remained closed. Again Rainsford lifted the heavy knocker, and let it fall. The door opened then, opened as suddenly as if it were on a spring, and Rainsford stood blinking in the river of glaring gold light that poured out. The first thing Rainsford's eyes discerned was the largest man Rainsford had ever seen—a gigantic creature, solidly made and black-bearded to the waist. In his hand the man held a long-barreled revolver, and he was pointing it straight at Rainsford's heart.

Out of the snarl of beard two small eyes regarded Rainsford.

"Don't be alarmed," said Rainsford, with a smile which he hoped was disarming. "I'm no robber. I fell off a yacht. My name is Sanger Rainsford of New York City."

The menacing look in the eyes did not change. The revolver pointed as rigidly as if the giant were a statue. He gave no sign that he understood

Rainsford's words, or that he had even heard them. He was dressed in uniform, a black uniform trimmed with gray astrakhan.

"I'm Sanger Rainsford of New York," Rainsford began again. "I fell off a yacht. I am hungry."

The man's only answer was to raise with his thumb the hammer of his revolver. Then Rainsford saw the man's free hand go to his forehead in a military salute, and he saw him click his heels together and stand at attention. Another man was coming down the broad marble steps, an erect, slender man in evening clothes. He advanced to Rainsford and held out his hand.

In a cultivated voice marked by a slight accent that gave it added precision and deliberateness, he said: "It is a very great pleasure and honor to welcome Mr. Sanger Rainsford, the celebrated hunter, to my home."

Automatically Rainsford shook the man's hand.

"I've read your book about hunting snow leopards in Tibet, you see," explained the man. "I am General Zaroff."

Rainsford's first impression was that the man was singularly handsome; his second was that there was an original, almost bizarre quality about the general's face. He was a tall man past middle age, for his hair was a vivid white; but his thick eyebrows and pointed military mustache were as black as the night from which Rainsford had come. His eyes, too, were black and very bright. He had high cheek bones, a sharp-cut nose, a spare, dark face, the face of a man used to giving orders, the face of an aristocrat. Turning to the giant in uniform, the general made a sign. The giant put away his pistol, saluted, withdrew.

"Ivan is an incredibly strong fellow," remarked the general, "but he has the misfortune to be deaf and dumb. A simple fellow, but, I'm afraid, like all his race, a bit of a savage."

"Is he Russian?"

"He is a Cossack," said the general, and his smile showed red lips and pointed teeth. "So am I."

"Come," he said, "we shouldn't be chatting here. We can talk later. Now you want clothes, food, rest. You shall have them. This is a most restful spot."

Ivan had reappeared, and the general spoke to him with lips that moved but gave forth no sound.

"Follow Ivan, if you please, Mr. Rainsford," said the general. "I was about to have my dinner when you came. I'll wait for you. You'll find that my clothes will fit you, I think."

It was to a huge, beam-ceilinged bedroom with a canopied bed big enough for six men that Rainsford followed the silent giant. Ivan laid out an evening suit, and Rainsford, as he put it on, noticed that it came from a London tailor who ordinarily cut and sewed for none below the rank of duke.

The dining room to which Ivan conducted him was in many ways remarkable. There was a medieval magnificence about it; it suggested a baronial hall of feudal times with its oaken panels, its high ceiling, its vast refectory table where twoscore men could sit down to eat. About the hall were the mounted heads of many animals—lions, tigers, elephants, moose, bears; larger or more perfect specimens Rainsford had never seen. At the great table the general was sitting, alone.

"You'll have a cocktail, Mr. Rainsford," he suggested. The cocktail was surpassingly good; and, Rainsford noted, the table appointments were of the finest—the linen, the crystal, the silver, the china.

They were eating *borsch,* the rich, red soup with whipped cream so dear to Russian palates. Half apologetically General Zaroff said: "We do our best to preserve the amenities of civilization here. Please forgive any lapses. We are well off the beaten track, you know. Do you think the champagne has suffered from its long ocean trip?"

"Not in the least," declared Rainsford. He was finding the general a most thoughtful and affable host, a true cosmopolite. But there was one small trait of the general's that made Rainsford uncomfortable. Whenever he looked up from his plate he found the general studying him, appraising him narrowly.

"Perhaps," said General Zaroff, "you were surprised that I recognized your name. You see, I read all books on hunting published in English, French, and Russian. I have but one passion in my life, Mr. Rainsford, and it is the hunt."

"You have some wonderful heads here," said Rainsford as he ate a particularly well cooked filet mignon. "That Cape buffalo is the largest I ever saw."

"Oh, that fellow. Yes, he was a monster."

"Did he charge you?"

"Hurled me against a tree," said the general. "Fractured my skull. But I got the brute."

"I've always thought," said Rainsford, "that the Cape buffalo is the most dangerous of all big game."

For a moment the general did not reply; he was smiling his curious red-lipped smile. Then he said slowly: "No. You are wrong, sir. The Cape buffalo is not the most dangerous big game." He sipped his wine. "Here in my preserve on this island," he said in the same slow tone, "I hunt more dangerous game."

Rainsford expressed his surprise. "Is there big game on this island?"

The general nodded. "The biggest."

"Really?"

"Oh, it isn't here naturally, of course. I have to stock the island."

"What have you imported, general?" Rainsford asked. "Tigers?"

The general smiled. "No," he said. "Hunting tigers ceased to interest me some years ago. I exhausted their possibilities, you see. No thrill left in tigers, no real danger. I live for danger, Mr. Rainsford."

The general took from his pocket a gold cigaret case and offered his guest a long black cigaret with a silver tip; it was perfumed and gave off a smell like incense.

"We will have some capital hunting, you and I," said the general. "I shall be most glad to have your society."

"But what game—" began Rainsford.

"I'll tell you," said the general. "You will be amused, I know. I think I may say, in all modesty, that I have done a rare thing. I have invented a new sensation. May I pour you another glass of port, Mr. Rainsford?"

"Thank you, general."

The general filled both glasses, and said: "God makes some men poets. Some He makes kings, some beggars. Me He made a hunter. My hand was made for the trigger, my father said. He was a very rich man with a quarter of a million acres in the Crimea, and he was an ardent sportsman. When I was only five years old he gave me a little gun, specially made in Moscow for me, to shoot sparrows with. When I shot some of his prize turkeys with it, he did not punish me; he complimented me on my marksmanship. I killed my first bear in the Caucasus when I was ten. My whole life has been one prolonged hunt. I went into the army—it was expected of noblemen's sons—and for a time commanded a division of Cossack cavalry, but my real interest was always the hunt. I have hunted every kind of game in every land. It would be impossible for me to tell you how many animals I have killed."

The general puffed at his cigaret.

"After the debacle in Russia I left the country, for it was imprudent for an officer of the Czar to stay there. Many noble Russians lost everything. I, luckily, had invested heavily in American securities, so I shall never have to open a tea room in Monte Carlo or drive a taxi in Paris. Naturally, I continued to hunt—grizzlies in your Rockies, crocodiles in the Ganges, rhinoceroses in East Africa. It was in Africa that the Cape buffalo hit me and laid me up for six months. As soon as I recovered I started for the Amazon to hunt jaguars, for I had heard they were unusually cunning. They weren't." The Cossack sighed. "They were no match at all for a hunter with his wits about him, and a high-powered rifle. I was bitterly disappointed. I was lying in my tent with a splitting headache one night when a terrible thought pushed its way into my mind. Hunting was beginning to bore me! And hunting, remember, had been my life. I have heard that in America business men often go to pieces when they give up the business that has been their life."

"Yes, that's so," said Rainsford.

The general smiled. "I had no wish to go to pieces," he said. "I must do something. Now, mine is an analytical mind, Mr. Rainsford. Doubtless that is why I enjoy the problems of the chase."

"No doubt, General Zaroff."

"So," continued the general, "I asked myself why the hunt no longer fascinated me. You are much younger than I am, Mr. Rainsford, and have not hunted as much, but you perhaps can guess the answer."

"What was it?"

"Simply this: hunting had ceased to be what you call 'a sporting proposition.' It had become too easy. I always got my quarry. Always. There is no greater bore than perfection."

The general lit a fresh cigaret.

"No animal had a chance with me any more. That is no boast; it is a mathematical certainty. The animal had nothing but his legs and his instinct. Instinct is no match for reason. When I thought of this it was a tragic moment for me, I can tell you."

Rainsford leaned across the table, absorbed in what his host was saying.

"It came to me as an inspiration what I must do," the general went on.

"And that was?"

The general smiled the quiet smile of one who has faced an obstacle and surmounted it with success. "I had to invent a new animal to hunt," he said.

"A new animal? You're joking."

"Not at all," said the general. "I never joke about hunting. I needed a new animal. I found one. So I bought this island, built this house, and here I do my hunting. The island is perfect for my purposes—there are jungles with a maze of trails in them, hills, swamps—"

"But the animal, General Zaroff?"

"Oh," said the general, "it supplies me with the most exciting hunting in the world. No other hunting compares with it for an instant. Every day I hunt, and I never grow bored now, for I have a quarry with which I can match my wits."

Rainsford's bewilderment showed in his face.

"I wanted the ideal animal to hunt," explained the general. "So I said: 'What are the attributes of an ideal quarry?' And the answer was, of course: 'It must have courage, cunning, and, above all, it must be able to reason.'"

"But no animal can reason," objected Rainsford.

"My dear fellow," said the general, "there is one that can."

"But you can't mean—" gasped Rainsford.

"And why not?"

"I can't believe you are serious, General Zaroff. This is a grisly joke."

"Why should I not be serious? I am speaking of hunting."

"Hunting? Good God, General Zaroff, what you speak of is murder."

The general laughed with entire good nature. He regarded Rainsford quizzically. "I refuse to believe that so modern and civilized a young man as you seem to be harbors romantic ideas about the value of human life. Surely your experiences in the war—"

"Did not make me condone cold-blooded murder," finished Rainsford stiffly.

Laughter shook the general. "How extraordinarily droll you are!" he said. "One does not expect nowadays to find a young man of the educated class, even in America, with such a naïve, and, if I may say so, mid-Victorian point of view. It's like finding a snuff-box in a limousine. Ah, well, doubtless you had Puritan ancestors. So many Americans appear to have had. I'll wager you'll forget your notions when you go hunting with me. You've a genuine new thrill in store for you, Mr. Rainsford."

"Thank you, I'm a hunter, not a murderer."

"Dear me," said the general, quite unruffled, "again that unpleasant word. But I think I can show you that your scruples are quite ill founded."

"Yes?"

"Life is for the strong, to be lived by the strong, and, if need be, taken by the strong. The weak of the world were put here to give the strong pleasure. I am strong. Why should I not use my gift? If I wish to hunt, why should I not? I hunt the scum of the earth—sailors from tramp ships—lascars, blacks, Chinese, whites, mongrels—a thorobred horse or hound is worth more than a score of them."

"But they are men," said Rainsford hotly.

"Precisely," said the general. "That is why I use them. It gives me pleasure. They can reason, after a fashion. So they are dangerous."

"But where do you get them?"

The general's left eyelid fluttered down in a wink. "This island is called Ship-Trap," he answered. "Sometimes an angry god of the high seas sends them to me. Sometimes, when Providence is not so kind, I help Providence a bit. Come to the window with me."

Rainsford went to the window and looked out toward the sea.

"Watch! Out there!" exclaimed the general, pointing into the night. Rainsford's eyes saw only blackness, and then, as the general pressed a button, far out to sea Rainsford saw the flash of lights.

The general chuckled. "They indicate a channel," he said, "where there's none: giant rocks with razor edges crouch like a sea monster with wide-open jaws. They can crush a ship as easily as I crush this nut." He dropped a walnut on the hardwood floor and brought his heel grinding down on it. "Oh, yes," he said, casually, as if in answer to a question, "I have electricity. We try to be civilized here."

"Civilized? And you shoot down men?"

A trace of anger was in the general's black eyes, but it was there for but a second, and he said, in his most pleasant manner: "Dear me, what a righteous young man you are! I assure you I do not do the thing you suggest. That would be barbarous. I treat these visitors with every consideration. They get plenty of good food and exercise. They get into splendid physical condition. You shall see for yourself to-morrow."

"What do you mean?"

"We'll visit my training school," smiled the general. "It's in the cellar. I have about a dozen pupils down there now. They're from the Spanish bark San Lucar that had the bad luck to go on the rocks out there. A very inferior lot, I regret to say. Poor specimens and more accustomed to the deck than to the jungle."

He raised his hand, and Ivan, who served as waiter, brought thick Turkish coffee. Rainsford, with an effort, held his tongue in check.

"It's a game, you see," pursued the general blandly. "I suggest to one of them that we go hunting. I give him a supply of food and an excellent hunting knife. I give him three hours' start. I am to follow, armed only with a pistol of the smallest caliber and range. If my quarry eludes me for three whole days, he wins the game. If I find him"—the general smiled—"he loses."

"Suppose he refuses to be hunted?"

"Oh," said the general, "I give him his option, of course. He need not play that game if he doesn't wish to. If he does not wish to hunt, I turn him over to Ivan. Ivan once had the honor of serving as official knouter to the Great White Czar, and he has his own ideas of sport. Invariably, Mr. Rainsford, invariably they choose the hunt."

"And if they win?"

The smile on the general's face widened. "To date I have not lost," he said.

Then he added, hastily: "I don't wish you to think me a braggart, Mr. Rainsford. Many of them afford only the most elementary sort of problem. Occasionally I strike a tartar. One almost did win. I eventually had to use the dogs."

"The dogs?"

"This way, please. I'll show you."

The general steered Rainsford to a window. The lights from the windows sent a flickering illumination that made grotesque patterns on the courtyard below, and Rainsford could see moving about there a dozen or so huge black shapes; as they turned toward him, their eyes glittered greenly.

"A rather good lot, I think," observed the general. "They are let out at seven every night. If anyone should try to get into my house—or out of it—something extremely regrettable would occur to him." He hummed a snatch of song from the Folies Bergère.

"And now," said the general, "I want to show you my new collection of heads. Will you come with me to the library?"

"I hope," said Rainsford, "that you will excuse me to-night, General Zaroff. I'm really not feeling at all well."

"Ah, indeed?" the general inquired solicitously. "Well, I suppose that's only natural, after your long swim. You need a good, restful night's sleep. To-morrow you'll feel like a new man, I'll wager. Then we'll hunt, eh? I've one rather promising prospect—"

Rainsford was hurrying from the room.

"Sorry you can't go with me to-night," called the general. "I expect rather fair sport—a big, strong black. He looks resourceful—Well, good night, Mr. Rainsford; I hope you have a good night's rest."

The bed was good, and the pajamas of the softest silk, and he was tired in every fiber of his being, but nevertheless Rainsford could not quiet his brain with the opiate of sleep. He lay, eyes wide open. Once he thought he heard stealthy steps in the corridor outside his room. He sought to throw open the door; it would not open. He went to the window and looked out. His room was high up in one of the towers. The lights of the château were out now, and it was dark and silent, but there was a fragment of sallow moon, and by its wan light he could see, dimly, the courtyard; there, weaving in and out in the pattern of shadow, were black, noiseless forms; the hounds heard him at the window and looked up, expectantly, with their green eyes. Rainsford went back to the bed and lay down. By many methods he tried to put himself to sleep. He had achieved a doze when, just as morning began to come, he heard, far off in the jungle, the faint report of a pistol.

General Zaroff did not appear until luncheon. He was dressed faultlessly in the tweeds of a country squire. He was solicitous about the state of Rainsford's health.

"As for me," sighed the general, "I do not feel so well. I am worried, Mr. Rainsford. Last night I detected traces of my old complaint."

To Rainsford's questioning glance the general said: "Ennui. Boredom."

Then, taking a second helping of Crêpes Suzette, the general explained: "The hunting was not good last night. The fellow lost his head. He made a straight trail that offered no problems at all. That's the trouble with these sailors; they have dull brains to begin with, and they do not know how to get about in the woods. They do excessively stupid and obvious things. It's most annoying. Will you have another glass of Chablis, Mr. Rainsford?"

"General," said Rainsford firmly, "I wish to leave this island at once."

The general raised his thickets of eyebrows; he seemed hurt. "But, my dear fellow," the general protested, "you've only just come. You've had no hunting—"

"I wish to go to-day," said Rainsford. He saw the dead black eyes of the general on him, studying him. General Zaroff's face suddenly brightened.

He filled Rainsford's glass with venerable Chablis from a dusty bottle.

"To-night," said the general, "we will hunt—you and I."

Rainsford shook his head. "No, general," he said. "I will not hunt."

The general shrugged his shoulders and delicately ate a hothouse grape. "As you wish, my friend," he said. "The choice rests entirely with you. But may I not venture to suggest that you will find my idea of sport more diverting than Ivan's?"

He nodded toward the corner to where the giant stood, scowling, his thick arms crossed on his hogshead of chest.

"You don't mean—" cried Rainsford.

"My dear fellow," said the general, "have I not told you I always mean what I say about hunting? This is really an inspiration. I drink to a foeman worthy of my steel—at last."

The general raised his glass, but Rainsford sat staring at him.

"You'll find this game worth playing," the general said enthusiastically. "Your brain against mine. Your woodcraft against mine. Your strength and stamina against mine. Outdoor chess! And the stake is not without value, eh?"

"And if I win—" began Rainsford huskily.

"I'll cheerfully acknowledge myself defeated if I do not find you by midnight of the third day," said General Zaroff. "My sloop will place you on the mainland near a town."

The general read what Rainsford was thinking.

"Oh, you can trust me," said the Cossack. "I will give you my word as a gentleman and a sportsman. Of course you, in turn, must agree to say nothing of your visit here."

"I'll agree to nothing of the kind," said Rainsford.

"Oh," said the general, "in that case—But why discuss that now? Three days hence we can discuss it over a bottle of Veuve Cliquot, unless—"

The general sipped his wine.

Then a businesslike air animated him. "Ivan," he said to Rainsford, "will supply you with hunting clothes, food, a knife. I suggest you wear moccasins; they leave a poorer trail. I suggest too that you avoid the big swamp in the southeast corner of the island. We call it Death Swamp. There's quicksand there. One foolish fellow tried it. The deplorable part of it was that Lazarus followed him. You can imagine my feelings, Mr. Rainsford. I loved Lazarus; he was the finest hound in my pack. Well, I must beg you to excuse me now. I always take a siesta after lunch. You'll hardly have time for a nap, I fear. You'll want to start, no doubt. I shall not follow till dusk. Hunting at night is so much more exciting than by day, don't you think? Au revoir, Mr. Rainsford, au revoir."

General Zaroff, with a deep, courtly bow, strolled from the room.

From another door came Ivan. Under one arm he carried khaki hunting clothes, a haversack of food, a leather sheath containing a long-bladed hunting knife; his right hand rested on a cocked revolver thrust in the crimson sash about his waist. . . .

Rainsford had fought his way through the bush for two hours. "I must keep my nerve. I must keep my nerve," he said through tight teeth.

He had not been entirely clear-headed when the château gates snapped shut behind him. His whole idea at first was to put distance between himself and General Zaroff, and, to this end, he had plunged along, spurred on by the sharp rowels of something very like panic. Now he had got a grip on himself, had stopped, and was taking stock of himself and the situation.

He saw that straight flight was futile; inevitably it would bring him face to face with the sea. He was in a picture with a frame of water, and his operations, clearly, must take place within that frame.

"I'll give him a trail to follow," muttered Rainsford, and he struck off from the rude paths he had been following into the trackless wilderness. He executed a series of intricate loops; he doubled on his trail again and again, recalling all the lore of the fox hunt, and all the dodges of the fox. Night found him leg-weary, with hands and face lashed by the branches, on a thickly wooded ridge. He knew it would be insane to blunder on through the dark, even if he had the strength. His need for rest was imperative and he thought: "I have played the fox, now I must play the cat of the fable." A big tree with a thick trunk and outspread branches was nearby, and, taking care to leave not the slightest mark, he climbed up into the crotch, and stretching out on one of the broad limbs, after a fashion, rested. Rest brought him new confidence and almost a feeling of security. Even so zealous a hunter as General Zaroff could not trace him there, he told himself; only the devil himself could follow that complicated trail through the jungle after dark. But, perhaps, the general was a devil—

An apprehensive night crawled slowly by like a wounded snake, and sleep did not visit Rainsford, altho the silence of a dead world was on the jungle. Toward morning when a dingy gray was varnishing the sky, the cry of some startled bird focused Rainsford's attention in that direction. Something was coming through the bush, coming slowly, carefully, coming by the same winding way Rainsford had come. He flattened himself down on the limb, and through a screen of leaves almost as thick as tapestry, he watched. The thing that was approaching was a man.

It was General Zaroff. He made his way along with his eyes fixed in utmost concentration on the ground before him. He paused, almost beneath the tree, dropped to his knees and studied the ground. Rainsford's impulse was to hurl himself down like a panther, but he saw that the general's right hand held something metallic—a small automatic pistol.

The hunter shook his head several times, as if he were puzzled. Then he straightened up and took from his case one of his black cigarets; its pungent incense-like smoke floated up to Rainsford's nostrils.

Rainsford held his breath. The general's eyes had left the ground and were traveling inch by inch up the tree. Rainsford froze there, every muscle tensed for a spring. But the sharp eyes of the hunter stopped before they reached the limb where Rainsford lay; a smile spread over his brown face. Very deliberately he blew a smoke ring into the air; then he turned his back on the tree and walked carelessly away, back along the trail he had come. The swish of the underbrush against his hunting boots grew fainter and fainter.

The pent-up air burst hotly from Rainsford's lungs. His first thought made him feel sick and numb. The general could follow a trail through the woods at night; he could follow an extremely difficult trail; he must have uncanny powers; only by the merest chance had the Cossack failed to see his quarry.

Rainsford's second thought was even more terrible. It sent a shudder of cold horror through his whole being. Why had the general smiled? Why had he turned back?

Rainsford did not want to believe what his reason told him was true, but the truth was as evident as the sun that had by now pushed through the morning mists. The general was playing with him! The general was saving him for another day's sport! The Cossack was the cat; he was the mouse. Then it was that Rainsford knew the full meaning of terror.

"I will not lose my nerve. I will not."

He slid down from the tree, and struck off again into the woods. His face was set and he forced the machinery of his mind to function. Three hundred yards from his hiding place he stopped where a huge dead tree leaned precariously on a smaller, living one. Throwing off his sack of food, Rainsford took his knife from its sheath and began to work with all his energy.

The job was finished at last, and he threw himself down behind a fallen log a hundred feet away. He did not have to wait long. The cat was coming again to play with the mouse.

Following the trail with the sureness of a bloodhound, came General Zaroff. Nothing escaped those searching black eyes, no crushed blade of grass, no bent twig, no mark, no matter how faint, in the moss. So intent was the Cossack on his stalking that he was upon the thing Rainsford had made before he saw it. His foot touched the protruding bough that was the trigger. Even as he touched it, the general sensed his danger and leaped back with the agility of an ape. But he was not quite quick enough; the dead tree, delicately adjusted to rest on the cut living one, crashed down and struck the general a glancing blow on the shoulder as it fell; but for his alertness, he must have been smashed beneath it. He staggered, but he did not fall; nor did he drop his revolver. He stood there, rubbing his injured shoulder, and Rainsford, with fear again gripping his heart, heard the general's mocking laugh ring through the jungle.

"Rainsford," called the general, "if you are within sound of my voice, as I suppose you are, let me congratulate you. Not many men know how to make a Malay man-catcher. Luckily, for me, I too have hunted in Malacca. You are proving interesting, Mr. Rainsford. I am going now to have my wound dressed; it's only a slight one. But I shall be back. I shall be back."

When the general, nursing his bruised shoulder, had gone, Rainsford took up his flight again. It was flight now, a desperate, hopeless flight, that carried him on for some hours. Dusk came, then darkness, and still he pressed on. The ground grew softer under his moccasins; the vegetation grew ranker, denser; insects bit him savagely. Then, as he stepped forward, his foot sank into the ooze. He tried to wrench it back, but the muck sucked viciously at his foot as if it were a giant leech. With a violent effort, he tore his foot loose. He knew where he was now. Death Swamp and its quicksand.

His hands were tight closed as if his nerve were something tangible that some one in the darkness was trying to tear from his grip. The softness of the earth had given him an idea. He stepped back from the quicksand a dozen feet or so and, like some huge prehistoric beaver, he began to dig.

Rainsford had dug himself in in France when a second's delay meant death. That had been a placid pastime compared to his digging now. The pit grew deeper; when it was above his shoulders, he climbed out and from some hard saplings cut stakes and sharpened them to a fine point. These stakes he planted in the bottom of the pit with the points sticking up. With flying fingers he wove a rough carpet of weeds and branches and with it he covered the mouth of the pit. Then, wet with sweat and aching with tiredness, he crouched behind the stump of a lightning-charred tree.

He knew his pursuer was coming; he heard the padding sound of feet on the soft earth, and the night breeze brought him the perfume of the general's cigaret. It seemed to Rainsford that the general was coming with unusual swiftness; he was not feeling his way along, foot by foot. Rainsford, crouching there, could not see the general, nor could he see the pit. He lived a year in a minute. Then he felt an impulse to cry aloud with joy, for he heard the sharp crackle of the breaking branches as the cover of the pit gave way; he heard the sharp scream of pain as the pointed stakes found their mark. He leaped up from his place of concealment. Then he cowered back. Three feet from the pit a man was standing, with an electric torch in his hand.

"You've done well, Rainsford," the voice of the general called. "Your Burmese tiger pit has claimed one of my best dogs. Again you score. I think, Mr. Rainsford, I'll see what you can do against my whole pack. I'm going home for a rest now. Thank you for a most amusing evening."

At daybreak Rainsford, lying near the swamp, was awakened by a sound that made him know that he had new things to learn about fear. It was a distant sound, faint and wavering, but he knew it. It was the baying of a pack of hounds.

Rainsford knew he could do one of two things. He could stay where he was and wait. That was suicide. He could flee. That was postponing the inevitable. For a moment he stood there, thinking. An idea that held a wild chance came to him, and, tightening his belt, he headed away from the swamp.

The baying of the hounds drew nearer, then still nearer, nearer, ever nearer. On a ridge Rainsford climbed a tree. Down a watercourse, not a quarter of a mile away, he could see the bush moving. Straining his eyes, he saw the lean figure of General Zaroff; just ahead of him Rainsford made out another figure whose wide shoulders surged through the tall jungle weeds;

it was the giant Ivan, and he seemed pulled forward by some unseen force; Rainsford knew that Ivan must be holding the pack in leash.

They would be on him any minute now. His mind worked frantically. He thought of a native trick he had learned in Uganda. He slid down the tree. He caught hold of a springy young sapling and to it he fastened his hunting knife, with the blade pointing down the trail; with a bit of wild grapevine he tied back the sapling. Then he ran for his life. The hounds raised their voices as they hit the fresh scent. Rainsford knew now how an animal at bay feels.

He had to stop to get his breath. The baying of the hounds stopped abruptly, and Rainsford's heart stopped too. They must have reached the knife.

He shinnied excitedly up a tree and looked back. His pursuers had stopped. But the hope that was in Rainsford's brain when he climbed died, for he saw in the shallow valley that General Zaroff was still on his feet. But Ivan was not. The knife, driven by the recoil of the springing tree, had not wholly failed.

Rainsford had hardly tumbled to the ground when the pack took up the cry again.

"Nerve, nerve, nerve!" he panted, as he dashed along. A blue gap showed between the trees dead ahead. Ever nearer drew the hounds. Rainsford forced himself on toward that gap. He reached it. It was the shore of the sea. Across a cove he could see the gloomy gray stone of the château. Twenty feet below him the sea rumbled and hissed. Rainsford hesitated. He heard the hounds. Then he leaped far out into the sea. . . .

When the general and his pack reached the place by the sea, the Cossack stopped. For some minutes he stood regarding the blue-green expanse of water. He shrugged his shoulders. Then he sat down, took a drink of brandy from a silver flask, lit a perfumed cigaret, and hummed a bit from "Madame Butterfly."

General Zaroff had an exceedingly good dinner in his great paneled dining hall that evening. With it he had a bottle of Pol Roger and half a bottle of Chambertin. Two slight annoyances kept him from perfect enjoyment. One was the thought that it would be difficult to replace Ivan; the other was that his quarry had escaped him; of course the American hadn't played the game—so thought the general as he tasted his after-dinner liqueur. In his library he read, to soothe himself, from the works of Marcus Aurelius. At ten he went up to his bedroom. He was deliciously tired, he said to himself, as he locked himself in. There was a little moonlight, so, before turning on his light, he went to the window and looked down at the courtyard. He could see the great hounds, and he called: "Better luck another time," to them. Then he switched on the light.

A man, who had been hiding in the curtains of the bed, was standing there.

"Rainsford!" screamed the general. "How in God's name did you get here?"

"Swam," said Rainsford. "I found it quicker than walking through the jungle."

The general sucked in his breath and smiled. "I congratulate you," he said. "You have won the game."

Rainsford did not smile. "I am still a beast at bay," he said, in a low, hoarse voice. "Get ready, General Zaroff."

The general made one of his deepest bows. "I see," he said. "Splendid! One of us is to furnish a repast for the hounds. The other will sleep in this very excellent bed. On guard, Rainsford. . . ."

He had never slept in a better bed, Rainsford decided.

QUESTIONS

1. On what simple ironical reversal is the plot of the story based? What two meanings has the title?

2. How important is suspense in the story? In what ways is it aroused and sustained? What part do chance and coincidence play in the story?

3. Discuss the characterizations of Rainsford and General Zaroff. Which one is more fully characterized? Are both characters plausible?

4. What purpose is served by the "philosophical" discussion between Whitney and Rainsford at the beginning of the story (page 24)? What limitation does it show Rainsford to have? To what extent is his character illuminated during the course of the story? Does he change his ideas?

5. In what ways is the discussion between Whitney and Rainsford paralleled by the after-dinner discussion between Rainsford and Zaroff (pages 15–16)? In these discussions, is Rainsford more like Whitney or Zaroff? How does he differ from Zaroff? Does the end of the story resolve that difference?

6. Is the principal emphasis of the story on plot, character, or theme? On escape or interpretation? Support your answer.

Thomas Wolfe

THE CHILD BY TIGER

Tiger, tiger, burning bright
In the forests of the night,
What immortal hand or eye
Could frame thy fearful symmetry?

One day after school, twenty-five years ago, several of us were playing with a football in the yard at Randy Shepperton's. Randy was calling signals and handling the ball. Nebraska Crane was kicking it. Augustus Potterham was too clumsy to run or kick or pass, so we put him at center, where all he'd have to do would be to pass the ball back to Randy when he got the signal.

It was late in October and there was a smell of smoke, of leaves, of burning in the air. Nebraska had just kicked to us. It was a good kick, too —a high, soaring punt that spiraled out above my head, behind me. I ran back and tried to get it, but it was far and away "over the goal line"—that is to say, out in the street. It hit the street and bounded back and forth with that peculiarly erratic bounce a football has.

The ball rolled away from me down toward the corner. I was running out to get it when Dick Prosser, Shepperton's new Negro man, came along, gathered it up neatly in his great black paw and tossed it to me. He turned in then, and came on down the alleyway, greeting us as he did. He called all of us "Mister" except Randy, and Randy was always "Cap'n"—"Cap'n Shepperton." This formal address—"Mr." Crane, "Mr." Potterham, "Mr." Spangler, "Cap'n" Shepperton—pleased us immensely, gave us a feeling of mature importance and authority.

"Cap'n Shepperton" was splendid! It had a delightful military association, particularly when Dick Prosser said it. Dick had served a long enlistment in the United States Army. He had been a member of a regiment of crack Negro troops upon the Texas border, and the stamp of the military man was evident in everything he did. It was a joy, for example, just to watch him split up kindling. He did it with a power, a kind of military order, that was astounding. Every stick he cut seemed to be exactly the same length and shape as every other one. He had all of them neatly stacked against the walls of the Shepperton basement with such regimented fault-

THE CHILD BY TIGER From *The Web and the Rock* by Thomas Wolfe. This version originally appeared in the *Saturday Evening Post,* and is reprinted by permission of Harper & Row, Publishers.

lessness that it almost seemed a pity to disturb their symmetry for the use for which they were intended.

It was the same with everything else he did. His little whitewashed basement room was as spotless as a barracks room. The bare board floor was always cleanly swept, a plain bare table and a plain straight chair were stationed exactly in the center of the room. On the table there was always just one object: an old Bible almost worn out by constant use, for Dick was a deeply religious man. There was a little cast-iron stove and a little wooden box with a few lumps of coal and a neat stack of kindling in it. And against the wall, to the left, there was an iron cot, always precisely made and covered cleanly with a coarse gray blanket.

The Sheppertons were delighted with him. He had come there looking for work just a month or two before, and modestly presented his qualifications. He had, he said, only recently received his discharge from the Army and was eager to get employment, at no matter what wage. He could cook, he could tend the furnace, he knew how to drive a car—in fact, it seemed to us boys that there was very little that Dick Prosser could not do. He could certainly shoot. He gave a modest demonstration of his prowess one afternoon, with Randy's .22, that left us gasping. He just lifted that little rifle in his powerful black hands as if it were a toy, without seeming to take aim, pointed it toward a strip of tin on which we had crudely marked out some bull's-eye circles, and he simply peppered the center of the bull's-eye, putting twelve holes through a space one inch square, so fast we could not even count the shots.

He knew how to box too. I think he had been a regimental champion. At any rate, he was as cunning and crafty as a cat. He never boxed with us, of course, but Randy had two sets of gloves, and Dick used to coach us while we sparred. There was something amazingly tender and watchful about him. He taught us many things—how to lead, to hook, to counter and to block—but he was careful to see that we did not hurt each other.

He knew about football, too, and today he paused, a powerful, respectable-looking Negro man of thirty years or more, and watched us for a moment as we played.

Randy took the ball and went up to him. "How do you hold it, Dick?" he said. "Is this right?"

Dick watched him attentively as he gripped the ball, and held it back above his shoulder. The Negro nodded approvingly and said, "That's right, Cap'n Shepperton. You've got it. Only," he said gently, and now took the ball in his own powerful hand, "when you gits a little oldah yo' handses gits biggah and you gits a bettah grip."

His own great hand, in fact seemed to hold the ball as easily as if it were an apple. And, holding it so a moment, he brought it back, aimed over his outstretched left hand as if he were pointing a gun, and rifled it in a beautiful, whizzing spiral thirty yards or more to Gus. He then showed us how to kick, how to get the ball off of the toe in such a way that it would rise and spiral cleanly. He knew how to do this too. He must have got off kicks there, in the yard at Shepperton's, that traveled fifty yards.

He showed us how to make a fire, how to pile the kindling so that the flames shot up cone-wise, cleanly, without smoke or waste. He showed us how to strike a match with the thumbnail of one hand and keep and hold the flame in the strongest wind. He showed us how to lift a weight, how to tote a burden on our shoulders in the easiest way. There was nothing that he did not know. We were all so proud of him. Mr. Shepperton himself declared that Dick was the best man he'd ever had, the smartest darky that he'd ever known.

And yet? He went too softly, at too swift a pace. He was there upon you sometimes like a cat. Looking before us, sometimes, seeing nothing but the world before us, suddenly we felt a shadow at our backs and, looking up, would find that Dick was there. And there was something moving in the night. We never saw him come or go. Sometimes we would waken, startled, and feel that we had heard a board creak, and the soft clicking of a latch, a shadow passing swiftly. All was still.

"Young white fokes, oh, young white gent'mun,"—his soft voice ending in a moan, a kind of rhythm in his hips—"oh, young white fokes, Ise tellin' *you*"—that soft low moan again—"you gotta love each othah like a brothah." He was deeply religious and went to church three times a week. He read his Bible every night. It was the only object on his square board table.

Sometimes Dick would come out of his little basement room, and his eyes would be red, as if he had been weeping. We would know, then, that he had been reading his Bible. There would be times when he would almost moan when he talked to us, a kind of hymnal chant that came from some deep and fathomless intoxication of the spirit, and that transported him. For us, it was a troubling and bewildering experience. We tried to laugh it off and make jokes about it. But there was something in it so dark and strange and full of a feeling that we could not fathom that our jokes were hollow, and the trouble in our minds and in our hearts remained.

Sometimes on these occasions his speech would be made up of some weird jargon of Biblical phrases, of which he seemed to have hundreds, and which he wove together in this strange pattern of his emotion in a sequence that was meaningless to us, but to which he himself had the coherent clue. "Oh, young white fokes," he would begin, moaning gently, "de dry bones in de valley. I tell you, white fokes, de day is comin' when He's comin' on dis earth again to sit in judgment. He'll put de sheep upon de right hand and de goats upon de left. Oh, white fokes, white fokes, de Armageddon day's a-comin', white fokes, an' de dry bones in de valley."

Or again, we could hear him singing as he went about his work, in his deep rich voice, so full of warmth and strength, so full of Africa, singing hymns that were not only of his own race but familiar to us all. I don't know where he learned them. Perhaps they were remembered from his Army days. Perhaps he had learned them in the service of former masters. He drove the Sheppertons to church on Sunday morning, and would wait for them throughout the morning service. He would come up to the side door of the church while the service was going on, neatly dressed in his good dark suit, holding his chauffeur's hat respectfully in his hand, and stand there humbly and listen during the course of the entire sermon.

And then, when the hymns were sung and the great rich sound would swell and roll out into the quiet air of Sunday, Dick would stand and listen, and sometimes he would join in quietly in the song. A number of these favorite Presbyterian hymns we heard him singing many times in a low rich voice as he went about his work around the house. He would sing Who Follows in His Train? or Alexander's Glory Song, or Rock of Ages, or Onward, Christian Soldiers!

And yet? Well, nothing happened—there was just "a flying hint from here and there," and the sense of something passing in the night. Turning into the square one day as Dick was driving Mr. Shepperton to town, Lon Everett skidded murderously around the corner, sideswiped Dick and took the fender off. The Negro was out of the car like a cat and got his master out. Shepperton was unhurt. Lon Everett climbed out and reeled across the street, drunk as a sot at three o'clock. He swung viciously, clumsily, at the Negro, smashed him in the face. Blood trickled from the flat black nostrils and from the thick liver-colored lips. Dick did not move. But suddenly the whites of his eyes were shot with red, his bleeding lips bared for a moment over the white ivory of his teeth. Lon smashed at him again. The Negro took it full in the face again; his hands twitched slightly, but he did not move. They collared the drunken sot and hauled him off and locked him up. Dick stood there for a moment, then he wiped his face and turned to see what damage had been done the car. No more now, but there were those who saw it who remembered later how the eyes went red.

Another thing: Sheppertons had a cook named Pansy Harris. She was a comely Negro wench, young, plump, black as the ace of spades, a good-hearted girl with a deep dimple in her cheeks and faultless teeth, bared in a most engaging smile. No one ever saw Dick speak to her. No one ever saw her glance at him, or him at her, and yet that smilingly good-natured wench became as mournful-silent and as silent-sullen as midnight pitch. She went about her work as mournfully as if she were going to a funeral. The gloom deepened all about her. She answered sullenly now when spoken to.

One night toward Christmas she announced that she was leaving. In response to all entreaties, all efforts to find the reason for her sudden and unreasonable decision, she had no answer except a sullen repetition of the assertion that she had to leave. Repeated questionings did finally wring from her a sullen statement that her husband needed her at home. More than this she would not say, and even this excuse was highly suspect, because her husband was a Pullman porter, only home two days a week and well accustomed to do himself such housekeeping tasks as she might do for him.

The Sheppertons were fond of her. They tried again to find the reason for her leaving. Was she dissatisfied? "No'm"—an implacable monosyllable, mournful, unrevealing as the night. Had she been offered a better job elsewhere? "No'm"—as untelling as before. If they offered her more wages, would she stay with them? "No'm," again and again, sullen and unyielding, until finally the exasperated mistress threw her hands up in a gesture of defeat and said, "All right then, Pansy. Have it your own way, if that's the way you feel. Only for heaven's sake don't leave us in the lurch until we get another cook."

This, at length, with obvious reluctance, the girl agreed to. Then, putting on her hat and coat and taking the paper bag of "leavings" she was allowed to take home with her at night, she went out the kitchen door and made her sullen and morose departure.

This was on Saturday night, a little after eight o'clock. That afternoon Randy and I had been fooling around the basement and, seeing that Dick's door was slightly ajar, we looked in to see if he was there. The little room was empty, swept and spotless, as it had always been.

But we did not notice that! We saw it! At the same moment, our breaths caught sharply in a gasp of startled wonderment. Randy was the first to speak. "Look!" he whispered. "Do you see it?"

See it! My eyes were glued upon it. Squarely across the bare board table, blue-dull, deadly in its murderous efficiency, lay a modern repeating rifle. Beside it was a box containing one hundred rounds of ammunition, and behind it, squarely in the center, face downward on the table, was the familiar cover of Dick's worn old Bible.

Then he was on us like a cat. He was there like a great dark shadow before we knew it. We turned, terrified. He was there above us, his thick lips bared above his gums, his eyes gone small and red as rodents'.

"Dick!" Randy gasped, and moistened his dry lips. "Dick!" he fairly cried now.

It was all over like a flash. Dick's mouth closed. We could see the whites of his eyes again. He smiled and said softly, affably, "Yes, suh, Cap'n Shepperton. Yes, suh! You gent'mun lookin' at my rifle?" he said, and moved into the room.

I gulped and nodded my head and couldn't say a word, and Randy whispered, "Yes." And both of us still stared at him, with an expression of appalled and fascinated interest.

Dick shook his head and chuckled. "Can't do without my rifle, white fokes. No, suh!" he shook his head good-naturedly again. "Ole Dick, he's —he's—he's an ole Ahmy man, you know. If they take his rifle away from him, why, that's jest lak takin' candy from a little baby. Yes, suh!" he chuckled, and picked the weapon up affectionately. "Ole Dick felt Christmas comin' on—he-he—I reckon he must have felt it in his bones"—he chuckled—"so I been savin' up my money. I just thought I'd hide this heah and keep it as a big surprise fo' the young white fokes untwil Christmas morning. Then I was gonna take the young white fokes out and show 'em how to shoot."

We had begun to breathe more easily now and, almost as if we had been under the spell of the Pied Piper of Hamelin, we had followed him, step by step, into the room.

"Yes, suh," Dick chuckled, "I was just fixin' to hide this gun away twill Christmas Day, but Cap'n Shepperton—hee!" He chuckled heartily and slapped his thigh. "You can't fool ole Cap'n Shepperton. He just must've smelled this ole gun right out. He comes right in and sees it befo' I has a chance to tu'n around. . . . Now, white fokes"—Dick's voice fell to a tone of low and winning confidence—"now that you's found out, I'll tell you what I'll do. If you'll just keep it a supprise from the other white fokes twill Christmas Day, I'll take all you gent'mun out and let you shoot it. Now, cose," he went on quietly, with a shade of resignation, "if you want to tell on me, you can, but"—here his voice fell again, with just the faintest, yet most eloquent shade of sorrowful regret—"ole Dick was looking fahwad to this; hopin' to give all the white fokes a supprise Christmas Day."

We promised earnestly that we would keep his secret as if it were our own. We fairly whispered our solemn vow. We tiptoed away out of the little basement room as if we were afraid our very footsteps might betray the partner of our confidence.

This was four o'clock on Saturday afternoon. Already, there was a somber moaning of the wind, gray storm clouds sweeping over. The threat of snow was in the air.

Snow fell that night. It came howling down across the hills. It swept in on us from the Smokies. By seven o'clock the air was blind with sweeping snow, the earth was carpeted, the streets were numb. The storm howled on, around houses warm with crackling fires and shaded light. All life seemed to have withdrawn into thrilling isolation. A horse went by upon the streets with muffled hoofs. Storm shook the houses. The world was numb. I went to sleep upon this mystery, lying in the darkness, listening to that exultancy of storm, to that dumb wonder, that enormous and attentive quietness of snow, with something dark and jubilant in my soul I could not utter.

A little after one o'clock that morning I was awakened by the ringing of a bell. It was the fire bell of the city hall, and it was beating an alarm—a hard fast stroke that I had never heard before. Bronze with peril, clangorous through the snow-numbed silence of the air, it had a quality of instancy and menace I had never known before. I leaped up and ran to the window to look for the telltale glow against the sky. But almost before I looked, those deadly strokes beat in upon my brain the message that this was no alarm for fire. It was a savage clangorous alarm to the whole town, a brazen tongue to warn mankind against the menace of some peril, secret, dark, unknown, greater than fire or flood could ever be.

I got instantly, in the most overwhelming and electric way, the sense that the whole town had come to life. All up and down the street the houses were beginning to light up. Next door, the Shepperton house was ablaze with light from top to bottom. Even as I looked, Mr. Shepperton, wearing an overcoat over his pajamas, ran down the snow-covered steps and padded out across the snow-covered walk toward the street.

People were beginning to run out of doors. I heard excited shouts and questions everywhere. I saw Nebraska Crane come pounding down the middle of the street. I knew that he was coming for me and Randy. As he ran by Shepperton's, he put his fingers to his mouth and whistled piercingly. It was a signal we all knew.

I was all ready by the time he came running down the alley toward our cottage. He hammered at the door; I was already there.

"Come on!" he said, panting with excitement, his black eyes burning with an intensity I'd never seen before. "Come on!" he cried. We were half-way out across the yard by now. "It's that nigger. He's gone crazy and is running wild."

"Wh-wh-what nigger?" I gasped, pounding at his heels.

Even before he spoke, I had the answer. Mr. Crane had already come out of his house, buttoning his heavy policeman's overcoat as he came. He had paused to speak for a moment to Mr. Shepperton, and I heard Shepperton say quickly, in a low voice, "Which way did he go?"

Then I heard somebody cry, "It's that nigger of Shepperton's!"

Mr. Shepperton turned and went quickly back across his yard toward the house. His wife and two girls stood huddled in the open doorway, white, trembling, holding themselves together, their arms thrust into the wide sleeves of their kimonos.

The telephone in Shepperton's house was ringing like mad, but no one was paying any attention to it. I heard Mrs. Shepperton say quickly, as he ran up the steps, "Is it Dick?" He nodded and passed her brusquely, going toward the phone.

At this moment, Nebraska whistled piercingly again upon his fingers and Randy Shepperton ran past his mother and down the steps. She called sharply to him. He paid no attention to her. When he came up, I saw that his fine thin face was white as a sheet. He looked at me and whispered, "It's—it's Dick!" And in a moment, "They say he's killed four people."

"With——" I couldn't finish.

Randy nodded dumbly, and we both stared there for a minute, aware now of the murderous significance of the secret we had kept, with a sudden sense of guilt and fear, as if somehow the crime lay on our shoulders.

Across the street a window banged up in the parlor of Suggs' house, and Old Man Suggs appeared in the window, clad only in his nightgown, his brutal old face inflamed with excitement, his shock of silvery white hair awry, his powerful shoulders, and his thick hands gripping his crutches.

"He's coming this way!" he bawled to the world in general. "They say he lit out across the square! He's heading out in this direction!"

Mr. Crane paused to yell back impatiently over his shoulder, "No, he went down South Dean Street! He's heading for Wilton and the river! I've already heard from headquarters!"

Automobiles were beginning to roar and sputter all along the street. Across the street I could hear Mr. Potterham sweating over his. He would whirl the crank a dozen times or more; the engine would catch for a moment, cough and sputter, and then die again. Gus ran out-of-doors with a kettle of boiling water and began to pour it feverishly down the radiator spout.

Mr. Shepperton was already dressed. We saw him run down the back steps toward the carriage house. All three of us, Randy, Nebraska and myself, streaked down the alleyway to help him. We got the old wooden doors open. He went in and cranked the car. It was a new one, and started up at once. Mr. Shepperton backed out into the snowy drive. We all clambered up on the running board. He spoke absently, saying, "You boys stay here. . . . Randy, your mother's calling you," but we all tumbled in and he didn't say a word.

He came backing down the alleyway at top speed. We turned into the street and picked up Mr. Crane at the corner. We lit out for town, going at top speed. Cars were coming out of alleys everywhere. We could hear people shouting questions and replies at one another. I heard one man shout, "He's killed six men!"

I don't think it took us over five minutes to reach the square, but when we got there, it seemed as if the whole town was there ahead of us. Mr. Shepperton pulled the car up and parked in front of the city hall. Mr. Crane leaped out and went pounding away across the square without another word to us.

From every corner, every street that led into the square, people were streaking in. One could see the dark figures of running men across the white carpet of the square. They were all rushing in to one focal point.

The southwest corner of the square where South Dean Street came into it was like a dog fight. Those running figures streaking toward that dense crowd gathered there made me think of nothing else so much as a fight between two boys upon the playgrounds of the school at recess time. The way the crowd was swarming in was just the same.

But then I *heard* a difference. From that crowd came a low and growing mutter, an ugly and insistent growl, of a tone and quality I had never heard before. But I knew instantly what it meant. There was no mistaking the blood note in that foggy growl. And we looked at one another with the same question in the eyes of all.

Only Nebraska's coal-black eyes were shining now with a savage sparkle even they had never had before. "Come on," he said in a low tone, exultantly. "They mean business this time, sure. Let's go." And he darted away toward the dense and sinister darkness of the crowd.

Even as we followed him we heard coming toward us now, growing, swelling at every instant, one of the most savagely mournful and terrifying sounds that night can know. It was the baying of the hounds as they came up upon the leash from Niggertown. Full-throated, howling deep, the savagery of blood was in it, and the savagery of man's guilty doom was in it too.

They came up swiftly, fairly baying at our heels as we sped across the snow-white darkness of the square. As we got up to the crowd, we saw that it had gathered at the corner where my uncle's hardware store stood. Cash Eager had not yet arrived, but, facing the crowd which pressed in on them so close and menacing that they were almost flattened out against the glass, three or four men were standing with arms stretched out in a kind of chain, as if trying to protect with the last resistance of their strength and eloquence the sanctity of private property.

Will Hendershot was mayor at that time, and he was standing there, arm to arm with Hugh McNair. I could see Hugh, taller by half a foot than anyone around him, his long gaunt figure, the gaunt passion of his face, even the attitude of his outstretched bony arms, strangely, movingly Lincolnesque, his one good eye blazing in the cold glare of the corner lamp with a kind of cold inspired Scotch passion.

"Wait a minute! You men wait a minute!" he cried. His words cut out above the clamor of the mob like an electric spark. "You'll gain nothing, you'll help nothing if you do this thing!"

They tried to drown him out with an angry and derisive roar. He shot his big fist up into the air and shouted at them, blazed at them with that cold single eye, until they had to hear. "Listen to me!" he cried. "This is no time for mob law! This is no case for lynch law! This is a time for law and order! Wait till the sheriff swears you in! Wait until Cash Eager comes! Wait ——"

He got no farther. "Wait, hell!" cried someone. "We've waited long enough! We're going to get that nigger!"

The mob took up the cry. The whole crowd was writhing angrily now, like a tormented snake. Suddenly there was a flurry in the crowd, a scattering. Somebody yelled a warning at Hugh McNair. He ducked quickly, just in time. A brick whizzed past him, smashing the plate-glass window into fragments.

And instantly a bloody roar went up. The crowd surged forward, kicked the fragments of jagged glass away. In a moment the whole mob was storming into the dark store. Cash Eager got there just too late. He arrived in time to take out his keys and open the front doors, but as he grimly remarked it was like closing the barn doors after the horse had been stolen.

The mob was in and helped themselves to every rifle they could find. They smashed open cartridge boxes and filled their pockets with the loose cartridges. Within ten minutes they had looted the store of every rifle, every cartridge in the stock. The whole place looked as if a hurricane had hit it. The mob was streaming out into the street, was already gathering round the dogs a hundred feet or so away, who were picking up the scent at that point, the place where Dick had halted last before he had turned and headed south, downhill along South Dean Street toward the river.

The hounds were scampering about, tugging at the leash, moaning softly with their noses pointed to the snow, their long ears flattened down. But in that light and in that snow it almost seemed no hounds were needed to follow Dick. Straight as a string right down the center of the sheeted car tracks, the Negro's footsteps led away until they vanished downhill in the darkness.

But now, although the snow had stopped, the wind was swirling through the street and making drifts and eddies in the snow. The footprints were fading rapidly. Soon they would be gone.

The dogs were given their head. They went straining on softly, sniffing at the snow; behind them the dark masses of the mob closed in and followed. We stood there watching while they went. We saw them go on down the street and vanish. But from below, over the snow-numbed stillness of the air, the vast low mutter of the mob came back to us.

Men were clustered now in groups. Cash Eager stood before his shattered window, ruefully surveying the ruin. Other men were gathered around the big telephone pole at the corner, pointing out two bullet holes that had been drilled cleanly through it.

And swiftly, like a flash, running from group to group, like a powder train of fire, the full detail of that bloody chronicle of night was pieced together.

This was what had happened. Somewhere between nine and ten o'clock that night, Dick Prosser had gone to Pansy Harris' shack in Niggertown. Some said he had been drinking when he went there. At any rate, the police had later found the remnants of a gallon jug of raw corn whisky in the room. What happened, what passed between them, was never known. And, besides, no one was greatly interested. It was a crazy nigger with "another nigger's woman."

Shortly after ten o'clock that night, the woman's husband appeared upon the scene. The fight did not start then. According to the woman, the real trouble did not come until an hour or more after his return.

The men drank together. Each was in an ugly temper. Shortly before midnight, they got into a fight. Harris slashed at Dick with a razor. In a second they were locked together, rolling about and fighting like two madmen on the floor. Pansy Harris went screaming out-of-doors and across the street into a dingy little grocery store.

A riot call was telephoned at once to police headquarters on the public square. The news came in that a crazy nigger had broken loose on Gulley Street in Niggertown, and to send help at once. Pansy Harris ran back across the street toward her little shack.

As she got there, her husband, with blood streaming from his face, staggered out into the street, with his hands held up protectively behind his head in a gesture of instinctive terror. At the same moment, Dick Prosser appeared in the doorway of the shack, deliberately took aim with his rifle and shot the fleeing Negro squarely through the back of the head. Harris dropped forward on his face into the snow. He was dead before he hit the ground. A huge dark stain of blood-soaked snow widened out around him. Dick Prosser seized the terrified Negress by the arm, hurled her into the shack, bolted the door, pulled down the shades, blew out the lamp and waited.

A few minutes later, two policemen arrived from town. They were a young constable named Willis, and John Grady, a lieutenant of police. The policemen took one look at the bloody figure in the snow, questioned the frightened keeper of the grocery store and, after consulting briefly, produced their weapons and walked out into the street.

Young Willis stepped softly down on to the snow-covered porch of the shack, flattened himself against the wall between the window and the door, and waited. Grady went around to the side and flashed his light through the window, which, on this side, was shadeless. Grady said in a loud tone: "Come out of there!"

Dick's answer was to shoot him cleanly through the wrist. At the same moment Willis kicked the door in and, without waiting, started in with pointed revolver. Dick shot him just above the eyes. The policeman fell forward on his face.

Grady came running out around the house, rushed into the grocery store, pulled the receiver of the old-fashioned telephone off the hook, rang frantically for headquarters and yelled out across the wire that a crazy nigger had killed Sam Willis and a Negro man, and to send help.

At this moment Dick stepped out across the porch into the street, aimed swiftly through the dirty window of the little store and shot John Grady as he stood there at the phone. Grady fell dead with a bullet that entered just below his left temple and went out on the other side.

Dick, now moving in a long, unhurried stride that covered the ground with catlike speed, turned up the long snow-covered slope of Gulley Street and began his march toward town. He moved right up the center of the street, shooting cleanly from left to right as he went. Halfway up the hill, the second-story window of a two-story Negro tenement flew open. An old

Negro man stuck out his ancient head of cotton wool. Dick swiveled and shot casually from his hip. The shot tore the top of the old Negro's head off.

By the time Dick reached the head of Gulley Street, they knew he was coming. He moved steadily along, leaving his big tread cleanly in the middle of the sheeted street, shifting a little as he walked, swinging his gun crosswise before him. This was the Negro Broadway of the town, but where those poolrooms, barbershops, drugstores and fried-fish places had been loud with dusky life ten minutes before, they were now silent as the ruins of Egypt. The word was flaming through the town that a crazy nigger was on the way. No one showed his head.

Dick moved on steadily, always in the middle of the street, reached the end of Gulley Street and turned into South Dean—turned right, uphill, in the middle of the car tracks, and started toward the square. As he passed the lunchroom on the left, he took a swift shot through the window at the counter man. The fellow ducked behind the counter. The bullet crashed into the wall above his head.

Meanwhile, at police headquarters, the sergeant had sent John Chapman out across the square to head Dick off. Mr. Chapman was perhaps the best-liked man upon the force. He was a pleasant florid-faced man of forty-five, with curling brown mustaches, congenial and good-humored, devoted to his family, courageous, but perhaps too kindly and too gentle for a good policeman.

John Chapman heard the shots and ran. He came up to the corner by Eager's hardware store just as Dick's last shot went crashing through the lunchroom window. Mr. Chapman took up his post there at the corner behind the telephone post that stood there at that time. Mr. Chapman, from his vantage point behind this post, took out his revolver and shot directly at Dick Prosser as he came up the street.

By this time Dick was not more than thirty yards away. He dropped quietly upon one knee and aimed. Mr. Chapman shot again and missed. Dick fired. The high-velocity bullet bored through the post a little to one side. It grazed the shoulder of John Chapman's uniform and knocked a chip out of the monument sixty yards or more behind him in the center of the square.

Mr. Chapman fired again and missed. And Dick, still coolly poised upon his knee, as calm and steady as if he were engaging in a rifle practice, fired again, drilled squarely through the center of the post and shot John Chapman through the heart. Then Dick rose, pivoted like a soldier in his tracks and started down the street, straight as a string, right out of town.

This was the story as we got it, pieced together like a train of fire among the excited groups of men that clustered there in trampled snow before the shattered glass of Eager's store.

But now, save for these groups of talking men, the town again was silent. Far off in the direction of the river, we could hear the mournful baying of the hounds. There was nothing more to see or do. Cash Eager stooped, picked up some fragments of the shattered glass and threw them in the window. A policeman was left on guard, and presently all five of us—Mr. Shepperton, Cash Eager and we three boys—walked back across the square and got into the car and drove home again.

But there was no more sleep, I think, for anyone that night. Black Dick had murdered sleep. Toward daybreak, snow began to fall again. The snow continued through the morning. It was piled deep in gusting drifts by noon. All footprints were obliterated; the town waited, eager, tense, wondering if the man could get away.

They did not capture him that day, but they were on his trail. From time to time throughout the day, news would drift back to us. Dick had turned east along the river and gone out for some miles along the Fairchilds road. There, a mile or two from Fairchilds, he crossed the river at the Rocky Shallows.

Shortly after daybreak, a farmer from the Fairchilds section had seen him cross a field. They picked the trail up there again and followed it across the field and through a wood. He had come out on the other side and got down into the Cane Creek section, and there, for several hours, they lost him. Dick had gone right down into the icy water of the creek and walked upstream a mile or so. They brought the dogs down to the creek, to where he broke the trail, took them over to the other side and scented up and down.

Toward five o'clock that afternoon they picked the trail up on the other side, a mile or more upstream. From that point on, they began to close in on him. The dogs followed him across the fields, across the Lester road, into a wood. One arm of the posse swept around the wood to head him off. They knew they had him. Dick, freezing, hungry and unsheltered, was hiding in that wood. They knew he couldn't get away. The posse ringed the wood and waited until morning.

At 7:30 the next morning he made a break for it. He got through the line without being seen, crossed the Lester road and headed back across the field in the direction of Cane Creek. And there they caught him. They saw him plunging through the snowdrift of a field. A cry went up. The posse started after him.

Part of the posse were on horseback. The men rode in across the field. Dick halted at the edge of the wood, dropped deliberately upon one knee and for some minutes held them off with rapid fire. At two hundred yards he dropped Doc Lavender, a deputy, with a bullet through the throat.

The posse came in slowly, in an encircling, flankwise movement. Dick got two more of them as they closed in, and then, as deliberately as a trained soldier retreating in good order, still firing as he went, he fell back through the wood. At the other side he turned and ran down through a sloping field that bordered on Cane Creek. At the creek edge, he turned again, knelt once more in the snow and aimed.

It was Dick's last shot. He didn't miss. The bullet struck Wayne Foraker, a deputy, dead center in the forehead and killed him in his saddle. Then the posse saw the Negro aim again, and nothing happened. Dick snapped the breech open savagely, then hurled the gun away. A cheer went up. The posse came charging forward. Dick turned, stumblingly, and ran the few remaining yards that separated him from the cold and rock-bright waters of the creek.

And here he did a curious thing—a thing that no one ever wholly understood. It was thought that he would make one final break for freedom, that he would wade the creek and try to get away before they got to him. Instead, he sat down calmly on the bank and, as quietly as if he were seated on his cot in an Army barracks, he unlaced his shoes, took them off, placed them together neatly at his side, and then stood up like a soldier, erect, in his bare bleeding feet, and faced the mob.

The men on horseback reached him first. They rode up around him and discharged their guns into him. He fell forward in the snow, riddled with bullets. The men dismounted, turned him over on his back, and all the other men came in and riddled him. They took his lifeless body, put a rope around his neck and hung him to a tree. Then the mob exhausted all their ammunition on the riddled carcass.

By nine o'clock that morning the news had reached the town. Around eleven o'clock, the mob came back along the river road. A good crowd had gone out to meet it at the Wilton Bottoms. The sheriff rode ahead. Dick's body had been thrown like a sack and tied across the saddle of the horse of one of the deputies he had killed.

It was in this way, bullet-riddled, shot to pieces, open to the vengeful and the morbid gaze of all, that Dick came back to town. The mob came back right to its starting point in South Dean Street. They halted there before an undertaking parlor, not twenty yards away from where Dick knelt to kill John Chapman. They took that ghastly mutilated thing and hung it in the window of the undertaker's place, for every woman, man and child in town to see.

And it was so we saw him last. We said we wouldn't look. But in the end we went. And I think it has always been the same with people. They protest. They shudder. And they say they will not go. But in the end they always have their look.

At length we went. We saw it, tried wretchedly to make ourselves believe that once this thing had spoken to us gently, had been partner to our confidence, object of our affection and respect. And we were sick with nausea and fear, for something had come into our lives we could not understand.

We looked and whitened to the lips, and craned our necks and looked away, and brought unwilling, fascinated eyes back to the horror once again, and craned and turned again, and shuffled in the slush uneasily, but could not go. And we looked up at the leaden reek of day, the dreary vapor of the sky, and, bleakly, at these forms and faces all around us—the people come to gape and stare, the poolroom loafers, the town toughs, the mongrel conquerors of earth—and yet, familiar to our lives and to the body of our whole experience, all known to our landscape, all living men.

And something had come into life—into our lives—that we had never known about before. It was a kind of shadow, a poisonous blackness filled with bewildered loathing. The snow would go, we knew; the reeking vapors of the sky would clear away. The leaf, the blade, the bud, the bird, then April, would come back again, and all of this would be as it had ever been. The homely light of day would shine again familiarly. And all of this would vanish as an evil dream. And yet not wholly so. For we would still remember the old dark doubt and loathing of our kind, of something hateful and unspeakable in the souls of men. We knew that we should not forget.

Beside us, a man was telling the story of his own heroic accomplishments to a little group of fascinated listeners. I turned and looked at him. It was Ben Pounders, of the ferret face, the furtive and uneasy eye, Ben Pounders of the mongrel mouth, the wiry muscles of the jaw, Ben Pounders, the collector of usurious lendings to the blacks, the nigger hunter. And now Ben Pounders boasted of another triumph. He was the proud possessor of another scalp.

"I was the first one to git in a shot," he said. "You see that hole there?" He pointed with a dirty finger. "That big hole right above the eye?" They turned and goggled with a drugged and feeding stare.

"That's mine," the hero said, turned briefly to the side and spat tobacco juice into the slush. "That's where I got him. Hell, after that he didn't know what hit him. He was dead before he hit the ground. We all shot him full of holes then. We sure did fill him full of lead. Why, hell, yes," he declared, with a decisive movement of his head, "we counted up to two hundred and eighty-seven. We must have put three hundred holes in him."

And Nebraska, fearless, blunt, outspoken as he always was, turned abruptly, put two fingers to his lips and spat between them, widely and contemptuously.

"Yeah—*we!*" he grunted. "*We* killed a big one! We—we killed a b'ar, we did! . . . Come on, boys," he said gruffly. "Let's be on our way!"

And, fearless and unshaken, untouched by any terror or any doubt, he moved away. And two white-faced, nauseated boys went with him.

A day or two went by before anyone could go into Dick's room again. I went in with Randy and his father. The little room was spotless, bare and tidy as it has always been. But even the very austerity of that little room now seemed terribly alive with the presence of its black tenant. It was Dick's room. We all knew that. And somehow we all knew that no one else could ever live there again.

Mr. Shepperton went over to the table, picked up Dick's old Bible that still lay there, open and face downward, held it up to the light and looked at it, at the place that Dick had marked when he last read in it. And in a moment, without speaking to us, he began to read in a quiet voice:

"The Lord is my shepherd; I shall not want.

"2. He maketh me to lie down in green pastures: he leadeth me beside the still waters.

"3. He restoreth my soul: he leadeth me in the paths of righteousness for his name's sake.

"4. Yea, though I walk through the valley of the shadow of death, I will fear no evil: for thou art with me ——"

Then Mr. Shepperton closed the book and put it down upon the table, the place where Dick had left it. And we went out the door, he locked it, and we went back into that room no more forever.

The years passed, and all of us were given unto time. We went our ways. But often they would turn and come again, these faces and these voices of the past, and burn there in my memory again, upon the muted and immortal geography of time.

And all would come again—the shout of the young voices, the hard thud of the kicked ball, and Dick moving, moving steadily, Dick moving, moving silently, a storm-white world and silence, and something moving, moving in the night. Then I would hear the furious bell, the crowd a-clamor and the baying of the dogs, and feel the shadow coming that would never disappear. Then I would see again the little room that we would see no more, the table and the book. And the pastoral holiness of that old psalm came back to me and my heart would wonder with perplexity and doubt.

For I had heard another song since then, and one that Dick, I know, had never heard, and one perhaps he might not have understood, but one whose phrases and whose imagery it seemed to me would suit him better:

What the hammer? What the chain?
In what furnace was thy brain?
What the anvil? What dread grasp
Dare its deadly terrors clasp?

When the stars threw down their spears,
And water'd heaven with their tears,
Did He smile His work to see?
Did He who made the lamb make thee?

"*What* the hammer? *What* the chain?" No one ever knew. It was a mystery and a wonder. There were a dozen stories, a hundred clues and rumors; all came to nothing in the end. Some said that Dick had come from Texas, others that his home had been in Georgia. Some said that it was true that he had been enlisted in the Army, but that he had killed a man while there and served a term at Leavenworth. Some said he had served in the Army and had received an honorable discharge, but had later killed a man and had served a term in a state prison in Louisiana. Others said that he had been an Army man, but that he had gone crazy, that he had served a period in an asylum when it was found that he was insane, that he had escaped from this asylum, that he had escaped from prison, that he was a fugitive from justice at the time he came to us.

But all these stories came to nothing. Nothing was ever proved. Men debated and discussed these things a thousand times—who and what he had been, what he had done, where he had come from—and all of it came to nothing. No one knew the answer. But I think that I have found the answer. I think I know from where he came.

He came from darkness. He came out of the heart of darkness, from the dark heart of the secret and undiscovered South. He came by night, just as he passed by night. He was night's child and partner, a token of the other side of man's dark soul, a symbol of those things that pass by darkness and that still remain, a symbol of man's evil innocence, and the token of his mystery, a projection of his own unfathomed quality, a friend, a brother and a mortal enemy, an unknown demon, two worlds together—a tiger and a child.

QUESTIONS

1. Discuss the setting of the story. How important is it? How much do we learn about the town and its people? On what implicit premise are the black-white relationships in this town based?

2. The story begins and ends with stanzas from William Blake's poem, "The Tiger." How does this poem relate to the theme of the story? If you are not familiar with it, look it up and read the whole poem. How is it related to the passage in the Bible to which Dick's Bible is left open (page 40)?

3. The second sentence in "The Most Dangerous Game" is, "It's rather a mystery" (page 8). Are there any "mysteries" in this story? With what kind of mystery is each story concerned? To what extent is the mystery in each resolved?

4. Dick Prosser's character, like that of General Zaroff, consists of many contradictions. Discuss. In his contradictions, is Dick completely unlike the people of the white community? Why does he "go crazy"? Is his character more or less plausible than General Zaroff's?

5. Compare the man-hunt in this story with that in "The Most Dangerous Game." How is it similar? How is it different?

6. What feelings and considerations motivate the whites in tracking Dick

down? What meaning has Dick's final gesture of removing his shoes and awaiting the posse? How does this action contrast with the way his body is treated by the whites?

7. "The Most Dangerous Game" ends with General Zaroff's death. "The Child by Tiger" continues for several pages after Dick Prosser's death. Why? In what element of the story is each author most interested?

8. The narrator tells this story twenty-five years after its events took place. What importance does this removal in time have for the meaning of the story?

9. Discuss the conflict of good and evil as it is presented in this story and in "The Most Dangerous Game." Which story has greater moral significance? Why?

Plot

PLOT is the sequence of incidents or events of which a story is composed. When recounted by itself, it bears about the same relationship to a story that a map does to a journey. Just as a map may be drawn on a finer or grosser scale, so a plot may be recounted with lesser or greater detail. It may include what a character says or thinks, as well as what he does. But it leaves out description and analysis and concentrates ordinarily on major happenings.

Because plot is the easiest element in fiction to comprehend and put into words, the beginning reader tends to equate it with the content of the work. When asked what a story is about, he will say that it is about a person to whom particular events happen, not that it is about a certain kind of person or that it presents a particular insight into life. The immature reader reads chiefly for plot; the mature reader reads for whatever revelations of character or life may be presented by means of plot. Because he reads chiefly for plot, the beginning reader may put a high valuation on intricacy of plot or on violent physical action. On the one hand, he may want schemes and intrigues, mixed identities, disguises, secret letters, hidden passages, and similar paraphernalia. On the other, he may demand fights by land and sea, dangerous missions, hazardous journeys, hair-breadth escapes. There is nothing improper in liking such things, of course, and sometimes the greatest fiction provides them. But, if a reader can be satisfied *only* with stories having these elements, he is like a person who can enjoy only highly spiced food. Physical action by itself, after all, is meaningless. In a good story a minimum of physical action may be used to yield a maximum of insight. Every story must have some action, but for a worthwhile story it must be *significant* action. For a discerning reader there may be as much significant action in the way a man greets a friend as in how he handles a sword.

Conceivably a plot might consist merely of a sequence of related actions. Ordinarily, however, both the excitement craved by the beginning reader and the meaningfulness demanded by the mature reader arise out of some sort of CONFLICT—a clash of actions, ideas, desires, or wills. The main character may be pitted against some other person or group of persons (man against man); he may be in conflict with some external force—physical nature, society, or "fate" (man against environment); or he may be in conflict with some element in his own nature (man against himself). The conflict may be physical, mental, emotional, or moral. There is conflict in a chess game, where the competitors sit quite still for hours, as surely as in a wrestling match; emotional conflict may be raging within a person sitting quietly in an empty room. The central character in the conflict, whether he be a sympathetic or an unsympathetic person, is referred to as the PROTAGONIST; the forces arrayed against him, whether persons, things, conventions of society, or traits of his own character, are the ANTAGONISTS.[1] In some stories the conflict is single, clear-cut, and easily identifiable. In others it is multiple, various, and subtle. A person may be in conflict with other persons, with society or nature, and with himself, all at the same time, and sometimes he may be involved in conflict without being aware of it.

"The Most Dangerous Game" illustrates most of these kinds of conflict. Rainsford, the protagonist, is pitted first against other men—against Zaroff and Whitney in the discussions preceding the man-hunt and against General Zaroff and Ivan during the man-hunt. Near the beginning of the story, he is pitted against nature when he falls into the sea and is unable to get back to the yacht. At the beginning of the man-hunt, he is in conflict with himself when he tries to fight off his panic by saying to himself, over and over, "I must keep my nerve. I must keep my nerve." The various conflicts illuminated in this story are physical—Rainsford against the sea and against Zaroff—mental—Rainsford's initial conflict of ideas with Whitney and his battle-of-wits with Zaroff during the man-hunt (which Zaroff refers to as "Outdoor chess")—emotional—Rainsford's efforts to control his terror—and moral—Rainsford's refusal to "condone cold-blooded murder" in contrast with Zaroff's contempt for "romantic ideas about the value of human life."

Excellent interpretive fiction has been written utilizing all four of

[1] The technical term PROTAGONIST is preferable to the popular term "hero" because it is less ambiguous. The protagonist is simply the central character, the one whose struggles we follow with interest, whether he or she be good or bad, sympathetic or repulsive. A "hero" or "heroine" may be *either* a person of heroic qualities *or* simply the main character, heroic or unheroic.

these major kinds of conflict. The cheaper varieties of commercial fiction, however, emphasize the conflict between man and man, depending on the element of physical conflict to supply the main part of their excitement. It is hard to conceive of a Western story without a fist fight or a gun fight. Even in the crudest kinds of fiction, however, something more will be found than mere physical combat. Good men will be arrayed against bad men, and thus the conflict will also be between moral values. In cheap fiction this conflict is usually clearly defined in terms of white versus black, hero versus villain. In interpretive fiction, the contrasts are likely to be less marked. Good may be opposed to good or half-truth to half-truth. There may be difficulty in determining what *is* the good, and internal conflict tends therefore to be more frequent than physical conflict. In the world in which we live, significant moral issues are seldom sharply defined, judgments are difficult, and choices are complex rather than simple. The interpretive writer is aware of this complexity and is more concerned with catching its endless shadings of gray than with presenting glaring contrasts of black and white.

SUSPENSE is the quality in a story that makes the reader ask "What's going to happen next?" or "How will this turn out?" and impels him to read on to find the answers to these questions. Suspense is greatest when the reader's curiosity is combined with anxiety about the fate of some sympathetic character. Thus in the old serial movies—often appropriately called "cliffhangers"—a strong element of suspense was created at the end of each episode by leaving the hero hanging from the edge of a cliff or the heroine tied to the railroad tracks with the express train rapidly approaching. In murder mysteries—often called "who-dun-its"—suspense is created by the question of who committed the murder. In love stories it is created by the question "Will the boy win the girl?" or "Will the lovers be re-united, and how?" In more sophisticated forms of fiction the suspense often involves not so much the question *what* as the question *why*—not "What will happen next?" but "How is the protagonist's behavior to be explained in terms of human personality and character?" The forms of suspense range from crude to subtle and may concern not only actions but psychological considerations and moral issues. Two common devices for achieving suspense are to introduce an element of MYSTERY—an unusual set of circumstances for which the reader craves an explanation, or to place the hero or heroine in a DILEMMA—a position in which he must choose between two courses of action, both undesirable. But suspense can be readily created for most readers by placing *anybody* on a seventeenth-story window ledge or simply by bringing together a physically attractive young woman and a man.

In "The Most Dangerous Game," suspense is initiated in the opening sentences with Whitney's account of the mystery of "Ship-Trap Island," of which sailors "have a curious dread"—a place that seems to emanate evil. The mystery grows when, in this out-of-the-way spot, Rainsford discovers an enormous château with a leering gargoyle knocker on its massive door and is confronted by a bearded giant pointing a long-barreled revolver straight at his heart. A second mystery is introduced when General Zaroff tells Rainsford that he hunts "more dangerous game" on this island than the Cape buffalo. He then puts off Rainsford's (and the reader's) curiosity for some thirty-six paragraphs before revealing what that game is. Meanwhile, by placing the hero in physical danger, a second kind of suspense is introduced. Initiated by Rainsford's fall into the sea and his confrontation with Ivan, this kind of suspense becomes the principal suspense device in the second half of the story. Will Rainsford escape—and how?—are the questions that keep the reader going. The man-hunt itself begins with a dilemma. Rainsford must choose between three undesirable courses of action: he can hunt men with Zaroff; he can let himself be hunted; or he can submit to being tortured by Ivan. During the hunt, he is faced with other lesser dilemmas. For instance, on the third day, pursued by Zaroff's hounds, "Rainsford knew he could do one of two things. He could stay where he was and wait. That was suicide. He could flee. That was postponing the inevitable."

Suspense is usually the first quality mentioned by a young reader when asked what makes a good story—and, indeed, unless a story makes us eager to keep on reading it, it can have little merit at all. Nevertheless, the importance of suspense is often overrated. After all, we don't listen to a Beethoven symphony to discover how it will turn out. A good story, like a good dinner, should furnish its pleasure as it goes, because it is amusing or well-written or morally penetrating or because the characters are interesting to live with. One test of a story is whether it creates a desire to read it again. Like the Beethoven symphony, a good story should be as good or better on a second or third encounter—when we already know what is going to happen—as on the first. The discriminating reader, therefore, while he does not *disvalue* suspense, may be suspicious of stories in which suspense is artificially created—by the simple withholding of vital information, for instance—or in which suspense is all there is. He will ask whether the author's purpose has been merely to keep him guessing what will happen next or to reveal something about experience. He will be less interested in whether the man on the seventeenth-story window ledge will jump than in the reasons that impel him to jump. When a reader's primary interest is shifted from "What happens next?" to "*Why* do things happen as they do?" or "What is the significance of this series of events?" he has taken his most important step forward.

Closely connected with the element of suspense in a short story is the element of SURPRISE. If we know ahead of time exactly what is going to happen in a story and why, there can be no suspense; as long as we do not know, whatever happens comes with an element of surprise. The surprise is proportional to the unexpectedness of what happens; it becomes pronounced when the story departs radically from our expectation. In the short story such radical departure is most often found in a surprise ending: one that reveals a sudden new turn or twist.

As with physical action and suspense, the inexperienced reader makes a heavier demand for surprise than does the experienced reader. The escape story supplies a surprise ending more frequently than does the interpretive. There are two ways by which the legitimacy and value of a surprise ending may be judged: (1) by the fairness with which it is achieved; (2) by the purpose that it serves. If the surprise is brought about as the result of an improbable coincidence or an unlikely series of small coincidences or by the planting of false clues—details whose only purpose is to mislead the reader—or through the withholding of information that the reader ought to have been given earlier in the story or by manipulation of the point of view (see Chapter Five), then we may well dismiss it as a cheap trick. If, on the other hand, the ending that comes at first as a surprise seems perfectly logical and natural as we look back over the story, we may grant it as fairly achieved. Again, a surprise ending may be judged as trivial if it exists simply for its own sake—to shock or to titillate the reader. We may judge it as a fraud if it serves, as it does in much routine commercial fiction, to conceal earlier weaknesses in the story by giving the reader a shiny bauble at the end to absorb and concentrate his attention. Its justification comes when it serves to open up or to reinforce the meaning of the story. The worthwhile surprise is one that furnishes illumination, not just a reversal of expectation.

Whether or not a story has a surprise ending, the beginning reader usually demands that it have a HAPPY ENDING: the protagonist must solve his problems, defeat the villain, win the girl, "live happily ever after." A common obstacle confronting the reader who is making his first attempts to enjoy interpretive stories is that they often, though by no means always, end unhappily. He is likely to label such stories as "depressing" and to complain that "real life has troubles enough of its own" or, conversely, that "real life is seldom as unhappy as all that."

Two justifications may be made for the UNHAPPY ENDING. First, many situations in real life have unhappy endings; therefore, if fiction is to illuminate life, it must present defeat as well as triumph. The commercial sports-story writer usually writes of how an individual or a team achieves victory against odds. Yet, if one team wins the pennant, eleven others must lose it, and, if a golfer wins a tournament, fifty or a hundred others must fail to win it. In situations like these, at least, success is much less frequent than failure. Sometimes the sports writer, for a variant, will tell how an individual lost the game but learned some important moral lesson—good sportsmanship, perhaps, or the importance of fair play. But here again, in real life, such compensations are gained only occasionally. Defeat, in fact, sometimes embitters a person and makes him less able to cope with life than before. Thus we need to understand and perhaps expect defeat as well as victory.

Second, the unhappy ending has a peculiar value for the writer who wishes us to ponder life. The story with a happy ending has been "wrapped up" for us: the reader is sent away feeling pleasantly if vaguely satisfied with the world and ceases to think about the story searchingly. The unhappy ending, on the other hand, may cause him to brood over the results, to go over the story in his mind, and thus by searching out its implications to get more from it. Just as we can judge men better when we see how they behave in trouble, so we can see deeper into life when it is pried open for inspection. The unhappy endings are more likely to raise significant issues. Shakespeare's tragedies reverberate longer and more resonantly than his comedies.

The discriminating reader evaluates an ending not by whether it is happy or unhappy but by whether it is logical in terms of what precedes it[2] and by the fullness of revelation it affords. He has learned that an ending that meets these tests can be profoundly satisfying, whether happy or unhappy. He has learned also that a story, to be artistically satisfying, need have no ending at all in the sense that its central conflict is resolved in favor of protagonist or antagonist. In real life some problems are never solved and some contests never permanently won. A story, therefore, may have an INDETERMINATE ENDING, one in which no defini-

[2] The movies frequently make a book with an unhappy ending into a film with a happy ending. Such an operation, if the book was artistically successful, sets aside the laws of logic and the expectations we naturally build on them.

tive conclusion is arrived at. Conclusion of some kind there must of course be: the story, if it is to be an artistic unit, cannot simply stop. But the conclusion need not be in terms of a resolved conflict. We never learn in Faulkner's "That Evening Sun" (page 271) the outcome of the conflict between Nancy and Jesus. But the story is more effective without a resolution, for this individual conflict merely symptomizes a larger social conflict that has no easy solution.

ARTISTIC UNITY is essential to a good plot. There must be nothing in the story that is irrelevant, that does not contribute to the total meaning, nothing that is there only for its own sake or its own excitement. A good writer exercises a rigorous selection: he includes nothing that does not advance the central intention of the story. But he must not only select; he must also arrange. The incidents and episodes should be placed in the most effective order, which is not necessarily the chronological order, and, when rearranged in chronological order, should make a logical progression. In a highly unified story each event grows out of the preceding one in time and leads logically to the next. The various stages of the story are linked together in a chain of cause and effect. With such a story one seldom feels that events might as easily have taken one turn as another. One feels not that the author is managing the plot but rather that the plot has a quality of inevitability, given a certain set of characters and an initial situation.

When an author gives his story a turn unjustified by the situation or the characters involved, he is guilty of PLOT MANIPULATION. Any unmotivated action furnishes an instance of plot manipulation. We suspect an author of plot manipulation also if he relies too heavily upon chance or upon coincidence to bring about a solution to his story. In Poe's famous story "The Pit and the Pendulum," when the victim of the Spanish Inquisition is rescued by the outstretched arm of the commanding general of the invading French army just at the moment when the converging fiery walls of his torture chamber have caused him to fall fainting into the abyss, we have a famous example of such a manipulated ending.[3]

Chance cannot be barred from fiction, of course, any more than it can be barred from life. But, if an author uses an improbable chance to

[3] This kind of coincidental resolution is sometimes referred to as *deus ex machina* ("god from the machine") after the practice of some ancient Greek dramatists in having a god descend from heaven (in the theater by means of a stage-machine) to rescue their protagonist at the last minute from some impossible situation. The general in Poe's story is clearly the modern counterpart of such a supernatural deliverer.

effect a resolution to his story, the story loses its sense of conviction and inevitability. The objections to such a use of coincidence[4] are even more forcible, for coincidence is chance compounded. Coincidence may be justifiably used to initiate a story, and occasionally to complicate it, but not to resolve it. It is objectionable in proportion to its improbability, its importance to the story, and its nearness to the end. If two characters in a story both start talking of the same topic at once, it may be a coincidence but hardly an objectionable one. If they both decide suddenly to kill their mothers at the same time, we may find the coincidence less acceptable. But the use of even a highly improbable coincidence may be perfectly appropriate at the start of a story. Just as a chemist may wonder what will happen if certain chemical elements are placed together in a test tube, an author may wonder what will happen if two former lovers accidentally meet long after they have married and in Majorca where they longed as young lovers to go. The improbable initial situation is justified because it offers a chance to observe human nature in conditions that may be particularly revealing, and the good reader demands only that the author develop his story logically from that initial situation. But if the writer uses a similar coincidence to resolve his story, then we feel that he has been avoiding the logic of life rather than revealing it. It is often said that fact is stranger than fiction: it *should* be stranger than fiction. In life almost any concatenation of events is possible; in a story the sequence of events should be probable.

There are various approaches to the analysis of plot. We may, if we wish, draw diagrams of different kinds of plots or trace the development of rising action, climax, and falling action. Such procedures, however, if they are concerned with the examination of plot *per se*, are not likely to take us far into the story. Better questions will concern themselves with the *function* of plot—with the relationship of each incident to the total meaning of the story. Plot is important, in interpretive fiction, for what it reveals. The analysis of a story through its central conflict is likely to be especially fruitful, for it rapidly takes us to what is truly at issue in the story. In testing a story for quality, it is useful to examine how the

[4] CHANCE is the occurrence of an event that has no apparent cause in antecedent events or in predisposition of character. In an automobile accident in which a drunk, coming home from a party, crashes into a sober driver from behind, we say that the accident was a chance event in the life of the sober driver but that it was a logical consequence in the life of the drunk. COINCIDENCE is the chance concurrence of *two* events that have a peculiar correspondence. If the two drivers involved in the accident had been brothers and were coming from different places, it would be coincidence.

incidents and episodes are connected, for such an examination is a test of the story's probability and unity. We can never get very far, however, by analysis of plot alone. In any good story plot is inextricable from character and total meaning. Plot by itself gives little more indication of the total story than a map gives of the quality of a journey.

Graham Greene

THE DESTRUCTORS

I

It was on the eve of August Bank Holiday that the latest recruit became the leader of the Wormsley Common Gang. No one was surprised except Mike, but Mike at the age of nine was surprised by everything. "If you don't shut your mouth," somebody once said to him, "you'll get a frog down it." After that Mike had kept his teeth tightly clamped except when the surprise was too great.

The new recruit had been with the gang since the beginning of the summer holidays, and there were possibilities about his brooding silence that all recognised. He never wasted a word even to tell his name until that was required of him by the rules. When he said "Trevor" it was a statement of fact, not as it would have been with the others a statement of shame or defiance. Nor did anyone laugh except Mike, who finding himself without support and meeting the dark gaze of the newcomer opened his mouth and was quiet again. There was every reason why T., as he was afterwards referred to, should have been an object of mockery—there was his name (and they substituted the initial because otherwise they had no excuse not to laugh at it), the fact that his father, a former architect and present clerk, had "come down in the world" and that his mother considered herself better than the neighbours. What but an odd quality of danger, of the unpredictable, established him in the gang without any ignoble ceremony of initiation?

The gang met every morning in an impromptu car-park, the site of the last bomb of the first blitz. The leader, who was known as Blackie, claimed to have heard it fall, and no one was precise enough in his dates to point out that he would have been one year old and fast asleep on the down platform of Wormsley Common Underground Station. On one side of the car-park leant the first occupied house, No. 3, of the shattered Northwood Terrace—literally leant, for it had suffered from the blast of the bomb and the side walls were supported on wooden struts. A smaller bomb and some incendiaries had fallen beyond, so that the house stuck up like a jagged tooth and carried on the further wall relics of its neighbour, a dado, the remains of a fireplace. T., whose words were almost confined to voting "Yes" or "No" to the plan of operations proposed each day by Blackie, once startled the whole gang by saying broodingly, "Wren built that house, father says."

"Who's Wren?"

"The man who built St. Paul's."

"Who cares?" Blackie said. "It's only Old Misery's."

Old Misery—whose real name was Thomas—had once been a builder and decorator. He lived alone in the crippled house, doing for himself: once a week you could see him coming back across the common with bread and vegetables, and once as the boys played in the car-park he put his head over the smashed wall of his garden and looked at them.

"Been to the loo," one of the boys said, for it was common knowledge that since the bombs fell something had gone wrong with the pipes of the house and Old Misery was too mean to spend money on the property. He could do the redecorating himself at cost price, but he had never learnt plumbing. The loo was a wooden shed at the bottom of the narrow garden with a star-shaped hole in the door: it had escaped the blast which had smashed the house next door and sucked out the window-frames of No. 3.

The next time the gang became aware of Mr. Thomas was more surprising. Blackie, Mike and a thin yellow boy, who for some reason was called by his surname Summers, met him on the common coming back from the market. Mr. Thomas stopped them. He said glumly, "You belong to the lot that play in the car-park?"

Mike was about to answer when Blackie stopped him. As the leader he had responsibilities. "Suppose we are?" he said ambiguously.

"I got some chocolates," Mr. Thomas said. "Don't like 'em myself. Here you are. Not enough to go round, I don't suppose. There never is," he added with sombre conviction. He handed over three packets of Smarties.

The gang were puzzled and perturbed by this action and tried to explain it away. "Bet someone dropped them and he picked 'em up," somebody suggested.

"Pinched 'em and then got in a bleeding funk," another thought aloud.

"It's a bribe," Summers said. "He wants us to stop bouncing balls on his wall."

"We'll show him we don't take bribes," Blackie said, and they sacrificed the whole morning to the game of bouncing that only Mike was young enough to enjoy. There was no sign from Mr. Thomas.

Next day T. astonished them all. He was late at the rendezvous, and the voting for that day's exploit took place without him. At Blackie's sugges-

loo: outdoor toilet

tion the gang was to disperse in pairs, take buses at random and see how many free rides could be snatched from unwary conductors (the operation was to be carried out in pairs to avoid cheating). They were drawing lots for their companions when T. arrived.

"Where you been, T.?" Blackie asked. "You can't vote now. You know the rules."

"I've been *there,*" T. said. He looked at the ground, as though he had thoughts to hide.

"Where?"

"At Old Misery's." Mike's mouth opened and then hurriedly closed again with a click. He had remembered the frog.

"At Old Misery's?" Blackie said. There was nothing in the rules against it, but he had a sensation that T. was treading on dangerous ground. He asked hopefully, "Did you break in?"

"No. I rang the bell."

"And what did you say?"

"I said I wanted to see his house."

"What did he do?"

"He showed it to me."

"Pinch anything?"

"No."

"What did you do it for then?"

The gang had gathered round: it was as though an impromptu court were about to form and to try some case of deviation. T. said, "It's a beautiful house," and still watching the ground, meeting no one's eyes, he licked his lips first one way, then the other.

"What do you mean, a beautiful house?" Blackie asked with scorn.

"It's got a staircase two hundred years old like a corkscrew. Nothing holds it up."

"What do you mean, nothing holds it up. Does it float?"

"It's to do with opposite forces, Old Misery said."

"What else?"

"There's panelling."

"Like in the Blue Boar?"

"Two hundred years old."

"Is Old Misery two hundred years old?"

Mike laughed suddenly and then was quiet again. The meeting was in a serious mood. For the first time since T. had strolled into the car-park on the first day of the holidays his position was in danger. It only needed a single use of his real name and the gang would be at his heels.

"What did you do it for?" Blackie asked. He was just, he had no jealousy, he was anxious to retain T. in the gang if he could. It was the word "beautiful" that worried him—that belonged to a class world that you could still see parodied at the Wormsley Common Empire by a man wearing a top hat and a monocle, with a haw-haw accent. He was tempted to say, "My dear Trevor, old chap," and unleash his hell hounds. "If you'd broken in," he said sadly—that indeed would have been an exploit worthy of the gang.

"This was better," T. said. "I found out things." He continued to stare at his feet, not meeting anybody's eye, as though he were absorbed in some dream he was unwilling—or ashamed—to share.

"What things?"

"Old Misery's going to be away all tomorrow and Bank Holiday."

Blackie said with relief, "You mean we could break in?"

"And pinch things?" somebody asked.

Blackie said, "Nobody's going to pinch things. Breaking in—that's good enough, isn't it? We don't want any court stuff."

"I don't want to pinch anything," T. said. "I've got a better idea."

"What is it?"

T. raised eyes, as grey and disturbed as the drab August day. "We'll pull it down," he said. "We'll destroy it."

Blackie gave a single hoot of laughter and then, like Mike, fell quiet, daunted by the serious implacable gaze. "What'd the police be doing all the time?" he said.

"They'd never know. We'd do it from inside. I've found a way in." He said with a sort of intensity, "We'd be like worms, don't you see, in an apple. When we came out again there'd be nothing there, no staircase, no panels, nothing but just walls, and then we'd make the walls fall down—somehow."

"We'd go to jug," Blackie said.

"Who's to prove? and anyway we wouldn't have pinched anything." He added without the smallest flicker of glee, "There wouldn't be anything to pinch after we'd finished."

"I've never heard of going to prison for breaking things," Summers said.

"There wouldn't be time," Blackie said. "I've seen housebreakers at work."

"There are twelve of us," T. said. "We'd organise."

"None of us know how . . ."

"I know," T. said. He looked across at Blackie, "Have you got a better plan?"

"Today," Mike said tactlessly, "we're pinching free rides . . ."

"Free rides," T. said. "You can stand down, Blackie, if you'd rather . . ."

"The gang's got to vote."

"Put it up then."

Blackie said uneasily, "It's proposed that tomorrow and Monday we destroy Old Misery's house."

"Here, here," said a fat boy called Joe.

"Who's in favour?"

T. said, "It's carried."

"How do we start?" Summers asked.

"He'll tell you," Blackie said. It was the end of his leadership. He went away to the back of the car-park and began to kick a stone, dribbling it this way and that. There was only one old Morris in the park, for few cars were left there except lorries: without an attendant there was no safety. He took a flying kick at the car and scraped a little paint off the rear mudguard. Beyond, paying no more attention to him than to a stranger, the gang had gathered round T.; Blackie was dimly aware of the fickleness of favour. He thought of going home, of never returning, of letting them all discover the hollowness of T.'s leadership, but suppose after all what T. proposed was possible—nothing like it had ever been done before. The fame of the Wormsley Common car-park gang would surely reach around London. There would be headlines in the papers. Even the grown-up gangs who ran the betting at the all-in wrestling and the barrow-boys would hear with respect of how Old Misery's house had been destroyed. Driven by the pure, simple and altruistic ambition of fame for the gang, Blackie came back to where T. stood in the shadow of Misery's wall.

T. was giving his orders with decision: it was as though this plan had been with him all his life, pondered through the seasons, now in his fifteenth year crystallised with the pain of puberty. "You," he said to Mike, "bring some big nails, the biggest you can find, and a hammer. Anyone else who can better bring a hammer and a screwdriver. We'll need plenty of them. Chisels too. We can't have too many chisels. Can anybody bring a saw?"

"I can," Mike said.

"Not a child's saw," T. said. "A real saw."

Blackie realised he had raised his hand like any ordinary member of the gang.

"Right, you bring one, Blackie. But now there's a difficulty. We want a hacksaw."

"What's a hacksaw?" someone asked.

"You can get 'em at Woolworth's," Summers said.

The fat boy called Joe said gloomily, "I knew it would end in a collection."

"I'll get one myself," T. said. "I don't want your money. But I can't buy a sledge-hammer."

Blackie said, "They are working on No. 15. I know where they'll leave their stuff for Bank Holiday."

"Then that's all," T. said. "We meet here at nine sharp."

"I've got to go to church," Mike said.

"Come over the wall and whistle. We'll let you in."

2

On Sunday morning all were punctual except Blackie, even Mike. Mike had had a stroke of luck. His mother felt ill, his father was tired after

Saturday night, and he was told to go to church alone with many warnings of what would happen if he strayed. Blackie had had difficulty in smuggling out the saw, and then in finding the sledge-hammer at the back of No. 15. He approached the house from a lane at the rear of the garden, for fear of the policeman's beat along the main road. The tired evergreens kept off a stormy sun: another wet Bank Holiday was being prepared over the Atlantic, beginning in swirls of dust under the trees. Blackie climbed the wall into Misery's garden.

There was no sign of anybody anywhere. The loo stood like a tomb in a neglected graveyard. The curtains were drawn. The house slept. Blackie lumbered nearer with the saw and the sledge-hammer. Perhaps after all nobody had turned up: the plan had been a wild invention: they had woken wiser. But when he came close to the back door he could hear a confusion of sound, hardly louder than a hive in swarm: a clickety-clack, a bang bang bang, a scraping, a creaking, a sudden painful crack. He thought: it's true, and whistled.

They opened the back door to him and he came in. He had at once the impression of organisation, very different from the old happy-go-lucky ways under his leadership. For a while he wandered up and down stairs looking for T. Nobody addressed him: he had a sense of great urgency, and already he could begin to see the plan. The interior of the house was being carefully demolished without touching the outer walls. Summers with hammer and chisel was ripping out the skirting-boards in the ground floor dining-room: he had already smashed the panels of the door. In the same room Joe was heaving up the parquet blocks, exposing the soft wood floor-boards over the cellar. Coils of wire came out of the damaged skirting and Mike sat happily on the floor, clipping the wires.

On the curved stairs two of the gang were working hard with an inadequate child's saw on the banisters—when they saw Blackie's big saw they signalled for it wordlessly. When he next saw them a quarter of the banisters had been dropped into the hall. He found T. at last in the bathroom—he sat moodily in the least cared-for room in the house, listening to the sounds coming up from below.

"You've really done it," Blackie said with awe. "What's going to happen?"

"We've only just begun," T. said. He looked at the sledge-hammer and gave his instructions. "You stay here and break the bath and the wash-basin. Don't bother about the pipes. They come later."

Mike appeared at the door. "I've finished the wire, T.," he said.

"Good. You've just got to go wandering round now. The kitchen's in the basement. Smash all the china and glass and bottles you can lay hold of. Don't turn on the taps—we don't want a flood—yet. Then go into all the rooms and turn out drawers. If they are locked get one of the others to break them open. Tear up any papers you find and smash all the ornaments. Better take a carving-knife with you from the kitchen. The bedroom's opposite here. Open the pillows and tear up the sheets. That's enough for the moment. And you, Blackie, when you've finished in here crack the plaster in the passage up with your sledge-hammer."

"What are you going to do?" Blackie asked.

"I'm looking for something special," T. said.

It was nearly lunch-time before Blackie had finished and went in search of T. Chaos had advanced. The kitchen was a shambles of broken glass and china. The dining-room was stripped of parquet, the skirting was up, the door had been taken off its hinges, and the destroyers had moved up a floor. Streaks of light came in through the closed shutters where they worked with the seriousness of creators—and destruction after all is a form of creation. A kind of imagination had seen this house as it had now become.

Mike said, "I've got to go home for dinner."

"Who else?" T. asked, but all the others on one excuse or another had brought provisions with them.

They squatted in the ruins of the room and swapped unwanted sandwiches. Half an hour for lunch and they were at work again. By the time Mike returned, they were on the top floor, and by six the superficial damage was completed. The doors were all off, all the skirtings raised, the furniture pillaged and ripped and smashed—no one could have slept in the house except on a bed of broken plaster. T. gave his orders—eight o'clock next morning, and to escape notice they climbed singly over the garden wall, into the car-park. Only Blackie and T. were left: the light had nearly gone, and when they touched a switch, nothing worked—Mike had done his job thoroughly.

"Did you find anything special?" Blackie asked.

T. nodded. "Come over here," he said, "and look." Out of both pockets he drew bundles of pound notes. "Old Misery's savings," he said. "Mike ripped out the mattress, but he missed them."

"What are you going to do? Share them?"

"We aren't thieves," T. said. "Nobody's going to steal anything from this house. I kept these for you and me—a celebration." He knelt down on the floor and counted them out—there were seventy in all. "We'll burn them," he said, "one by one," and taking it in turns they held a note upwards and lit the top corner, so that the flame burnt slowly towards their fingers. The grey ash floated above them and fell on their heads like age. "I'd like to see Old Misery's face when we are through," T. said.

"You hate him a lot?" Blackie asked.

"Of course I don't hate him," T. said. "There'd be no fun if I hated him." The last burning note illuminated his brooding face. "All this hate and love," he said, "it's soft, it's hooey. There's only things, Blackie," and he looked round the room crowded with the unfamiliar shadows of half things, broken things, former things. "I'll race you home, Blackie," he said.

3

Next morning the serious destruction started. Two were missing—Mike and another boy whose parents were off to Southend and Brighton in spite of the slow warm drops that had begun to fall and the rumble of thunder in the estuary like the first guns of the old blitz. "We've got to hurry," T. said.

Summers was restive. "Haven't we done enough?" he said. "I've been given a bob for slot machines. This is like work."

"We've hardly started," T. said. "Why, there's all the floors left, and the stairs. We haven't taken out a single window. You voted like the others. We are going to *destroy* this house. There won't be anything left when we've finished."

They began again on the first floor picking up the top floor-boards next the outer wall, leaving the joists exposed. Then they sawed through the joists and retreated into the hall, as what was left of the floor heeled and sank. They had learnt with practise, and the second floor collapsed more easily. By the evening an odd exhilaration seized them as they looked down the great hollow of the house. They ran risks and made mistakes: when they thought of the windows it was too late to reach them. "Cor," Joe said, and dropped a penny down into the dry rubble-filled well. It cracked and span among the broken glass.

"Why did we start this?" Summers asked with astonishment; T. was already on the ground, digging at the rubble, clearing a space along the outer wall. "Turn on the taps," he said. "It's too dark for anyone to see now, and in the morning it won't matter." The water overtook them on the stairs and fell through the floorless rooms.

It was then they heard Mike's whistle at the back. "Something's wrong," Blackie said. They could hear his urgent breathing as they unlocked the door.

"The bogies?" Summers asked.

"Old Misery," Mike said. "He's on his way." He put his head between his knees and retched. "Ran all the way," he said with pride.

"But why?" T. said. "He told me . . ." He protested with the fury of the child he had never been, "It isn't fair."

"He was down at Southend," Mike said, "and he was on the train coming back. Said it was too cold and wet." He paused and gazed at the water. "My, you've had a storm here. Is the roof leaking?"

"How long will he be?"

"Five minutes. I gave Ma the slip and ran."

"We better clear," Summers said. "We've done enough, anyway."

"Oh no, we haven't. Anybody could do this—" "this" was the shattered hollowed house with nothing left but the walls. Yet walls could be preserved. Façades were valuable. They could build inside again more beautifully than before. This could again be a home. He said angrily, "We've got to finish. Don't move. Let me think."

"There's no time," a boy said.

"There's got to be a way," T. said. "We couldn't have got thus far . . ."

"We've done a lot," Blackie said.

"No. No, we haven't. Somebody watch the front."

"We can't do any more."

"He may come in at the back."

"Watch the back too." T. began to plead. "Just give me a minute and I'll fix it. I swear I'll fix it." But his authority had gone with his ambiguity. He was only one of the gang. "Please," he said.

"Please," Summers mimicked him, and then suddenly struck home with the fatal name. "Run along home, Trevor."

T. stood with his back to the rubble like a boxer knocked groggy against the ropes. He had no words as his dreams shook and slid. Then Blackie acted before the gang had time to laugh, pushing Summers backward. "I'll watch the front, T.," he said, and cautiously he opened the shutters of the hall. The grey wet common stretched ahead, and the lamps gleamed in the puddles. "Someone's coming, T. No, it's not him. What's your plan, T.?"

"Tell Mike to go out to the loo and hide close beside it. When he hears me whistle he's got to count ten and start to shout."

"Shout what?"

"Oh, 'Help,' anything."

"You hear, Mike," Blackie said. He was the leader again. He took a quick look between the shutters. "He's coming, T."

"Quick, Mike. The loo. Stay here, Blackie, all of you till I yell."

"Where are you going, T.?"

"Don't worry. I'll see to this. I said I would, didn't I?"

Old Misery came limping off the common. He had mud on his shoes and he stopped to scrape them on the pavement's edge. He didn't want to soil his house, which stood jagged and dark between the bomb-sites, saved so narrowly, as he believed, from destruction. Even the fanlight had been left unbroken by the bomb's blast. Somewhere somebody whistled. Old Misery looked sharply round. He didn't trust whistles. A child was shouting: it seemed to come from his own garden. Then a boy ran into the road from the car-park. "Mr. Thomas," he called, "Mr. Thomas."

"What is it?"

"I'm terribly sorry, Mr. Thomas. One of us got taken short, and we thought you wouldn't mind, and now he can't get out."

"What do you mean, boy?"

"He's got stuck in your loo."

"He'd no business . . . Haven't I seen you before?"

"You showed me your house."

"So I did. So I did. That doesn't give you the right to . . ."

"Do hurry, Mr. Thomas. He'll suffocate."

"Nonsense. He can't suffocate. Wait till I put my bag in."

"I'll carry your bag."

"Oh no, you don't. I carry my own."

"This way, Mr. Thomas."

"I can't get in the garden that way. I've got to go through the house."

"But you *can* get in the garden this way, Mr. Thomas. We often do."

"You often do?" He followed the boy with a scandalised fascination. "When? What right? . . ."

"Do you see . . .? the wall's low."

"I'm not going to climb walls into my own garden. It's absurd."

"This is how we do it. One foot here, one foot there, and over." The boy's faced peered down, an arm shot out, and Mr. Thomas found his bag taken and deposited on the other side of the wall.

"Give me back my bag," Mr. Thomas said. From the loo a boy yelled and yelled. "I'll call the police."

"Your bag's all right, Mr. Thomas. Look. One foot there. On your right. Now just above. To your left." Mr. Thomas climbed over his own garden wall. "Here's your bag, Mr. Thomas."

"I'll have the wall built up," Mr. Thomas said, "I'll not have you boys coming over here, using my loo." He stumbled on the path, but the boy caught his elbow and supported him. "Thank you, thank you, my boy," he murmured automatically. Somebody shouted again through the dark. "I'm coming, I'm coming," Mr. Thomas called. He said to the boy beside him, "I'm not unreasonable. Been a boy myself. As long as things are done regular. I don't mind you playing round the place Saturday mornings. Sometimes I like company. Only it's got to be regular. One of you asks leave and I say Yes. Sometimes I'll say No. Won't feel like it. And you come in at the front door and out at the back. No garden walls."

"Do get him out, Mr. Thomas."

"He won't come to any harm in my loo," Mr. Thomas said, stumbling slowly down the garden. "Oh, my rheumatics," he said. "Always get 'em on Bank Holiday. I've got to go careful. There's loose stones here. Give me your hand. Do you know what my horoscope said yesterday? 'Abstain from any dealings in first half of week. Danger of serious crash.' That might be on this path," Mr. Thomas said. "They speak in parables and double meanings." He paused at the door of the loo. "What's the matter in there?" he called. There was no reply.

"Perhaps he's fainted," the boy said.

"Not in my loo. Here, you, come out," Mr. Thomas said, and giving a great jerk at the door he nearly fell on his back when it swung easily open. A hand first supported him and then pushed him hard. His head hit the opposite wall and he sat heavily down. His bag hit his feet. A hand whipped the key out of the lock and the door slammed. "Let me out," he called, and heard the key turn in the lock. "A serious crash," he thought, and felt dithery and confused and old.

A voice spoke to him softly through the star-shaped hole in the door. "Don't worry, Mr. Thomas," it said, "we won't hurt you, not if you stay quiet."

Mr. Thomas put his head between his hands and pondered. He had noticed that there was only one lorry in the car-park, and he felt certain that the driver would not come for it before the morning. Nobody could hear him from the road in front, and the lane at the back was seldom used. Anyone who passed there would be hurrying home and would not pause for what they would certainly take to be drunken cries. And if he did call "Help," who, on a lonely Bank Holiday evening, would have the courage to investigate? Mr. Thomas sat on the loo and pondered with the wisdom of age.

After a while it seemed to him that there were sounds in the silence—they were faint and came from the direction of his house. He stood up and peered through the ventilation-hole—between the cracks in one of the shutters he saw a light, not the light of a lamp, but the wavering light that a candle might give. Then he thought he heard the sound of hammering and scraping and chipping. He thought of burglars—perhaps they had employed the boy as a scout, but why should burglars engage in what sounded more and more like a stealthy form of carpentry? Mr. Thomas let out an experimental yell, but nobody answered. The noise could not even have reached his enemies.

4

Mike had gone home to bed, but the rest stayed. The question of leadership no longer concerned the gang. With nails, chisels, screwdrivers, anything that was sharp and penetrating they moved around the inner walls worrying at the mortar between the bricks. They started too high, and it was Blackie who hit on the damp course and realised the work could be halved if they weakened the joints immediately above. It was a long, tiring, unamusing job, but at last it was finished. The gutted house stood there balanced on a few inches of mortar between the damp course and the bricks.

There remained the most dangerous task of all, out in the open at the edge of the bomb-site. Summers was sent to watch the road for passers-by, and Mr. Thomas, sitting on the loo, heard clearly now the sound of sawing. It no longer came from his house, and that a little reassured him. He felt less concerned. Perhaps the other noises too had no significance.

A voice spoke to him through the hole. "Mr. Thomas."

"Let me out," Mr. Thomas said sternly.

"Here's a blanket," the voice said, and a long grey sausage was worked through the hole and fell in swathes over Mr. Thomas's head.

"There's nothing personal," the voice said. "We want you to be comfortable to-night."

"To-night," Mr. Thomas repeated incredulously.

"Catch," the voice said. "Penny buns—we've buttered them, and sausage-rolls. We don't want you to starve, Mr. Thomas."

Mr. Thomas pleaded desperately. "A joke's a joke, boy. Let me out and I won't say a thing. I've got rheumatics. I got to sleep comfortable."

"You wouldn't be comfortable, not in your house, you wouldn't. Not now."

"What do you mean, boy?" but the footsteps receded. There was only the silence of night: no sound of sawing. Mr. Thomas tried one more yell, but he was daunted and rebuked by the silence—a long way off an owl hooted and made away again on its muffled flight through the soundless world.

At seven next morning the driver came to fetch his lorry. He climbed into the seat and tried to start the engine. He was vaguely aware of a voice shouting, but it didn't concern him. At last the engine responded and he backed the lorry until it touched the great wooden shore that supported Mr. Thomas's house. That way he could drive right out and down the street without reversing. The lorry moved forward, was momentarily checked as though something were pulling it from behind, and then went on to the sound of a long rumbling crash. The driver was astonished to see bricks bouncing ahead of him, while stones hit the roof of his cab. He put on his brakes. When he climbed out the whole landscape had suddenly altered. There was no house beside the car-park, only a hill of rubble. He went round and examined the back of his car for damage, and found a rope tied there that was still twisted at the other end round part of a wooden strut.

The driver again became aware of somebody shouting. It came from the wooden erection which was the nearest thing to a house in that desolation of broken brick. The driver climbed the smashed wall and unlocked the door. Mr. Thomas came out of the loo. He was wearing a grey blanket to which flakes of pastry adhered. He gave a sobbing cry. "My house," he said. "Where's my house?"

"Search me," the driver said. His eye lit on the remains of a bath and what had once been a dresser and he began to laugh. There wasn't anything left anywhere.

"How dare you laugh," Mr. Thomas said. "It was my house. My house."

"I'm sorry," the driver said, making heroic efforts, but when he remembered the sudden check to his lorry, the crash of bricks falling, he became convulsed again. One moment the house had stood there with such dignity between the bomb-sites like a man in a top hat, and then, bang, crash, there wasn't anything left—not anything. He said, "I'm sorry. I can't help it, Mr. Thomas. There's nothing personal, but you got to admit it's funny."

QUESTIONS

1. Who is the protagonist in this story—Trevor, Blackie, or the gang? Who or what is the antagonist? Identify the conflicts of the story.
2. How is suspense created?
3. This story uses the most common basic formula of commercial fiction: protagonist aims at a goal, is confronted with various obstacles between himself and his goal, overcomes the obstacles and achieves his goal. Comment on the differences. Does this story have a happy ending?
4. Discuss the gang's motivations, taking into account (a) the age and beauty of the house, (b) Blackie's reasons for not going home after losing his position of leadership, (c) the seriousness with which the gang work at their task, and their loss of concern over their leadership, (d) the burning of the banknotes, (e) their consideration for Old Misery, (f) the lorry driver's reaction. What characteristics do the gang's two named exploits—pinching free rides and destroying the house—have in common?
5. Of what significance, if any, is the setting of this story in blitzed London? Does the story have anything to say about the consequences of war? about the causes of war?
6. Explain as fully as you can the causes of the gang's delinquency, taking into account (a) their reaction to the name Trevor, (b) their reaction to Old Misery's gift of chocolates, (c) Blackie's reaction to the word "beautiful," (d) Trevor's comments on "hate and love," (e) Summers' reaction to the word *Please*, (f) the setting.
7. What good qualities do the delinquents in this story have? Do they differ as a group from other delinquent gangs you have read or know about? If so, account for these differences.
8. On the surface this is a story of action, suspense, and adventure. At a deeper level it is about delinquency, war, and human nature. Try to sum up what the story says about human nature in general.

John Galsworthy

THE JAPANESE QUINCE

As Mr. Nilson, well known in the City, opened the window of his dressing room on Campden Hill, he experienced a peculiar sweetish sensation in the back of his throat, and a feeling of emptiness just under his fifth rib. Hooking the window back, he noticed that a little tree in the Square Gardens had come out in blossom, and that the thermometer stood at sixty. "Perfect morning," he thought; "spring at last!"

THE JAPANESE QUINCE Reprinted from *Caravan* by permission of William Heinemann, Ltd., London. First published in 1910.

Resuming some meditations on the price of Tintos, he took up an ivory-backed handglass and scrutinised his face. His firm, well-coloured cheeks, with their neat brown moustaches, and his round, well-opened, clear grey eyes, wore a reassuring appearance of good health. Putting on his black frock coat, he went downstairs.

In the dining room his morning paper was laid out on the sideboard. Mr. Nilson had scarcely taken it in his hand when he again became aware of that queer feeling. Somewhat concerned, he went to the French window and descended the scrolled iron steps into the fresh air. A cuckoo clock struck eight.

"Half an hour to breakfast," he thought; "I'll take a turn in the Gardens."

He had them to himself, and proceeded to pace the circular path with his morning paper clasped behind him. He had scarcely made two revolutions, however, when it was borne in on him that, instead of going away in the fresh air, the feeling had increased. He drew several deep breaths, having heard deep breathing recommended by his wife's doctor; but they augmented rather than diminished the sensation—as of some sweetish liquor in course within him, together with a faint aching just above his heart. Running over what he had eaten the night before, he could recollect no unusual dish, and it occurred to him that it might possibly be some smell affecting him. But he could detect nothing except a faint sweet lemony scent, rather agreeable than otherwise, which evidently emanated from the bushes budding in the sunshine. He was on the point of resuming his promenade, when a blackbird close by burst into song, and, looking up, Mr. Nilson saw at a distance of perhaps five yards a little tree, in the heart of whose branches the bird was perched. He stood staring curiously at this tree, recognising it for that which he had noticed from his window. It was covered with young blossoms, pink and white, and little bright green leaves both round and spiky; and on all this blossom and these leaves the sunlight glistened. Mr. Nilson smiled; the little tree was so alive and pretty! And instead of passing on, he stayed there smiling at the tree.

"Morning like this!" he thought; "and here I am the only person in the Square who has the—to come out and—!" But he had no sooner conceived this thought than he saw quite near him a man with his hands behind him, who was also staring up and smiling at the little tree. Rather taken aback, Mr. Nilson ceased to smile, and looked furtively at the stranger. It was his next-door neighbour, Mr. Tandram, well known in the City, who had occupied the adjoining house for some five years. Mr. Nilson perceived at once the awkwardness of his position, for, being married, they had not yet had occasion to speak to one another. Doubtful as to his proper conduct, he decided at last to murmur: "Fine morning!" and was passing on, when Mr. Tandram answered: "Beautiful, for the time of year!" Detecting a slight nervousness in his neighbour's voice, Mr. Nilson was emboldened to regard him openly. He was of about Mr. Nilson's own height, with firm, well-coloured cheeks, neat brown moustaches, and round, well-opened, clear grey eyes; and he was wearing a black frock coat. Mr. Nilson noticed that he had his morning paper clasped behind him as he looked up at the little tree. And, visited somehow by the feeling that he had been caught out, he said abruptly:

"Er—can you give me the name of that tree?"

Mr. Tandram answered:

"I was about to ask you that," and stepped towards it. Mr. Nilson also approached the tree.

"Sure to have its name on, I should think," he said.

Mr. Tandram was the first to see the little label, close to where the blackbird had been sitting. He read it out.

"Japanese quince!"

"Ah!" said Mr. Nilson, "thought so. Early flowerers."

"Very," assented Mr. Tandram, and added: "Quite a feelin' in the air today."

Mr. Nilson nodded.

"It was a blackbird singin'," he said.

"Blackbirds," answered Mr. Tandram. "I prefer them to thrushes myself; more body in the note." And he looked at Mr. Nilson in an almost friendly way.

"Quite," murmured Mr. Nilson. "These exotics, they don't bear fruit. Pretty blossoms!" and he again glanced up at the blossom, thinking: "Nice fellow, this, I rather like him."

Mr. Tandram also gazed at the blossom. And the little tree, as if appreciating their attention, quivered and glowed. From a distance the blackbird gave a loud, clear call. Mr. Nilson dropped his eyes. It struck him suddenly that Mr. Tandram looked a little foolish; and, as if he had seen himself, he said: "I must be going in. Good morning!"

A shade passed over Mr. Tandram's face, as if he, too, had suddenly noticed something about Mr. Nilson.

"Good morning," he replied, and clasping their journals to their backs they separated.

Mr. Nilson retraced his steps toward his garden window, walking slowly so as to avoid arriving at the same time as his neighbour. Having seen Mr. Tandram mount his scrolled iron steps, he ascended his own in turn. On the top step he paused.

With the slanting spring sunlight darting and quivering into it, the Japanese quince seemed more living than a tree. The blackbird had returned to it, and was chanting out his heart.

Mr. Nilson sighed; again he felt that queer sensation, that choky feeling in his throat.

The sound of a cough or sigh attracted his attention. There, in the shadow of his French window, stood Mr. Tandram, also looking forth across the Gardens at the little quince tree.

Unaccountably upset, Mr. Nilson turned abruptly into the house, and opened his morning paper.

QUESTIONS

1. Although we are given only a brief glimpse of Mr. Nilson's life, there are many clues as to what the whole of his life is like. What kind of house and district does he live in? To what social class does he belong? What kind of existence does he lead? What clues enable us to answer these questions? (In the opening sentence "the City" refers to the financial and commercial section of London; the term has roughly the meaning for Englishmen that "Wall Street" has for Americans.)

2. Mr. Nilson at first thinks something is wrong with his health. What really is troubling him? How do the terms in which his symptoms are described (paragraphs 1 and 5) help to define his "ailment"?

3. In what ways might Mr. Nilson's fragmentary sentence at the beginning of paragraph 6 be completed? Why doesn't Mr. Nilson complete it?

4. How are Mr. Nilson and Mr. Tandram alike in appearance, manner, and situation? Of what significance are these similarities?

5. Mr. Nilson's meeting of Mr. Tandram at the tree might be described as a coincidence. Is it pure coincidence or does it have antecedent causes? Is it a legitimate device in terms of the story? Why or why not?

6. The quince tree is what we shall later refer to as a *symbol* (see Chapter Six). What qualities or abstractions does it seem to you to represent?

7. Although this story contains little action, it dramatizes a significant conflict. What are the opposed forces? How can the conflict be stated in terms of protagonist and antagonist? Is the conflict external or internal? How is it resolved—that is, which force wins?

8. This story demonstrates how a very slight plot may be used to provide a considerable illumination of life. How would you describe, in a sentence, the purpose of the story?

CHAPTER THREE

Character

In the last chapter plot was considered apart from character, as if the two were separable. Actually, like the ends of a seesaw, the two are one substance; there can be no movement at one end without movement at the other. The two ends of the seesaw may be talked about separately, however, and we can determine which element in any story is being emphasized—which end is up and which is down. As fiction passes from escape to interpretive, the character end is likely to go up. The good reader is less interested in actions done by characters than in characters doing actions.

Reading for character is more difficult than reading for plot, for character is much more complex, variable, and ambiguous. Anyone can repeat what a person has done in a story, but considerable skill may be needed to describe what a person *is*. Even the puzzles posed by the detective story are less complex and put less strain on comprehension than does human nature. Hence, escape fiction tends to emphasize plot and to present characters that are relatively simple and easy to understand. The limited reader demands that the characters be easily identifiable and clearly labeled as good or bad; they must not be so complex as to tax his understanding.

The limited reader also demands that the main character always be an attractive one. Though he need not be perfect, he must ordinarily be fundamentally decent—honest, good-hearted, and preferably good-looking. If he is not virtuous, he must have strong compensatory qualities—he must be daring, dashing, or gallant. He may defy law and order only if he has a tender heart, a great love, or a gentleman's code. The reader who makes these demands does so because for him the story is not a vehicle for understanding but material for a daydream. Identifying himself as he reads with the main character, he vicariously shares that character's adventures and escapes and triumphs. The main character must therefore return him a pleasing image of self. He must be someone such as the reader imagines himself to be or such as he would like to be. In this way the story subtly flatters the reader, who forgets his own inadequacies and satisfies his ego. If the hero has vices, they must be such as the reader himself would not mind or would enjoy having. Some escape fiction has been about the man or girl who is appealing but sexually easy. The reader has thus been able to indulge imaginatively in forbidden pleasures without losing a flattering self-image.

Interpretive fiction does not necessarily renounce the attractive central character. It simply furnishes a greater variety of central characters, characters that are less easily labeled and pigeonholed, characters that are sometimes unsympathetic. Human nature is not often either black or white, and interpretive fiction deals usually with characters that are neither.

Once we get past the need of a mechanical opposition between hero and villain, we discover that fiction offers an unparalleled opportunity to observe human nature in all its complexity and multiplicity. It enables us to know people, to understand them, and to learn compassion for them, as we might not otherwise do. In some respects we can know fictional characters even better than we know real people. For one thing, we are enabled to observe them in situations that are always significant and that serve to bring forth their character as the ordinary situations of life only occasionally do. For another, we can view their inner life in a way that is impossible to us in ordinary life. An author can tell us, if he wishes, exactly what is going on in a character's mind and exactly what the character feels. In real life we can only guess at these inner thoughts and feelings from a person's external behavior, which may be designed to conceal what is going on inside. In limited ways, therefore, we can know people in fiction more thoroughly than we can know them in real life, and by knowing fictional characters we can also understand people in real life better than we otherwise could do.

An author may present his characters either directly or indirectly. In DIRECT PRESENTATION he tells us straight out, by exposition or analysis, what a character is like, or has someone else in the story tell us what he is like. In INDIRECT PRESENTATION the author *shows* us the character in action; we infer what he is like from what he thinks or says or does. Graham Greene uses direct presentation when he tells us about Blackie: "He was just, he had no jealousy." He uses indirect presentation when he shows Blackie allowing the gang to vote on Trevor's project, accepting the end of his leadership fairly calmly, taking orders from Trevor without resentment, burning banknotes with Trevor, and racing him home. In this story, of course, the word "just" has a slight ironical twist—it applies only to behavior within the gang—and Greene presents this indirectly. John Galsworthy relies entirely on indirect presentation to show us that Mr. Nilson is a man of regulated habit who lives a life that is ordered and convention-bound.

The method of direct presentation has the advantages of being clear and economical, but it can never be used alone. The characters must act, if there is to be a story; when they do not act, the story approaches the condition of an essay. The direct method, moreover, unless supported by the indirect, will not be emotionally convincing. It will give us not a character but an explanation. The reader must be shown as well as told. He needs to see and hear and overhear. A story will be successful only when the characters are DRAMATIZED—shown speaking and acting, as in a drama. If we are really to believe in the selfishness of a character, we must see him acting selfishly. The successful writer must therefore rely mainly upon indirect presentation and may use it entirely.

To be convincing, characterization must also observe three other principles. First, the characters must be CONSISTENT in their behavior: they must not behave one way on one occasion and a different way on another unless there is a clearly sufficient reason for the change. Second, the characters must be clearly MOTIVATED in whatever they do, especially when there is any change in their behavior: we must be able to understand the reasons for what they do, if not immediately, at least by the end of the story. Third, the characters must be PLAUSIBLE or lifelike. They must be neither paragons of virtue nor monsters of evil nor an impossible combination of contradictory traits. Whether we have observed anyone like them in our own experience or not, we must feel that they have come from the author's experience—that they could appear somewhere in the normal course of events.

In proportion to the fullness of their development, the characters in a story are relatively flat or round.[1] The FLAT CHARACTER is characterized by one or two traits; he can be summed up in a sentence. The ROUND CHARACTER is complex and many-sided; he might require an essay for full analysis. Both types of character may be given the vitality that good fiction demands. Round characters live by their very roundness, by the many points at which they touch life. Huck Finn, in all respects an

[1] These terms were originated by the novelist E. M. Forster, who discussed them in *Aspects of the Novel* (New York: Harcourt Brace Jovanovich, 1927), pp. 103–18.

individual, lives vigorously in the imagination of the reader, while scholars and critics debate his moral development. Flat characters, though they touch life at only one or two points, may be made memorable in the hands of an expert author through some individualizing detail of appearance, gesture, or speech. Ebenezer Scrooge, in Dickens' "Christmas Carol," can be summed up and fully expressed in the two words "miserly misanthropy," but his "Bah! Humbug!" makes him live vividly in every reader's memory.

The requirement of good fiction is that each character be characterized fully enough to justify his role in the story and make it convincing. Most short stories will hardly have room for more than one or two very fully developed characters. Minor characters must necessarily remain flat. If the primary intention of a story is something other than the exhibition of character, none of the characters need be fully developed. Inferior fiction, however, is often developed with characters who are insufficiently characterized to justify their roles. The essential nature and motivations of the protagonist may be so vaguely indicated that we are neither shocked nor convinced by any unusual action he performs or change of nature he undergoes. If a thief suddenly reforms and becomes an honest man, we must obviously know a great deal about him if the change is to be truly convincing. It is easier, however, for the writer to leave the characterization shadowy and hope that this weakness will slip by his readers unnoticed—as with uncritical readers it well may do.

A special kind of flat character is the STOCK CHARACTER—the stereotyped figure who has occurred so often in fiction that his nature is immediately known: the strong silent sheriff, the brilliant detective of eccentric habits, the mad scientist who performs fiendish experiments on living human beings, the beautiful international spy of mysterious background, the comic Englishman with a monocle and an exaggerated Oxford accent, the handsome brave hero, the beautiful modest heroine, the cruel stepmother, the sinister villain with a waxed black mustache. Such stock characters are found very often in inferior fiction because they require neither imagination nor observation on the part of the writer and are instantly recognizable to the reader. Like interchangeable parts, they might be transferred from one story to another with little loss of efficiency. The really good writer, however, may take a conventional type and by individualizing touches create a new and memorable figure. Conan Doyle's Sherlock Holmes is constructed on a pattern often imitated since, but he outlives the imitations and remains in our imaginations long after we have forgotten the details of his adventures. In proportion as an author gives his characters such individualizing touches, they become less flat and accordingly less stock.

All fictional characters may be classified as static or developing. The STATIC CHARACTER is the same sort of person at the end of the story as he was at the beginning. The DEVELOPING (or dynamic) CHARACTER undergoes a permanent change in some aspect of his character, personality, or outlook. The change may be a large or a small one; it may be for better or for worse; but it is something important and basic: it is more than a change in condition or a minor change in opinion. Cinderella is a static character, though she rises from cinder girl to princess. The boy Frederick in "Tears, Idle Tears" (page 95) is a dynamic character, for at the end he is cured of his fits of irrational crying. Paul in "Paul's Case" (page 190) is likewise dynamic, for his need to escape from everyday reality grows progressively stronger.

Obviously, we must not expect many developing characters in *any* piece of fiction: in a short story there is not usually room for more than one. A not infrequent basic plan of short stories, however, is to show change in the protagonist as the result of a crucial situation in his life. When this is done in an interpretive story, the change is likely to be the surest clue to the story's meaning. To state and explain the change will be the best way to get at the point of the story. In escape fiction, changes in character are likely to be more superficial, intended merely to ensure a happy ending. Such changes will necessarily be less believable. To be convincing, a change must meet three conditions: (1) it must be within the possibilities of the character who makes it, (2) it must be sufficiently motivated by the circumstances in which the character finds himself, and (3) it must be allowed sufficient time for a change of its magnitude believably to take place. Basic changes in human character seldom occur suddenly. The interpretive writer does not present bad men who suddenly reform at the end of the story and become good or drunkards who jump on the wagon at a moment's notice. He is satisfied with smaller changes that are carefully prepared for.

Human life began, we are told, when God breathed life into a handful of dust and created Adam. Fictional life begins when an author breathes life into his characters and convinces us of their reality. Though fullness of characterization need not be his aim, soundness of characterization is a test by which he stands or falls. The reader of good fiction lives in a world where the initial act of creation is repeated again and again by the miracle of imagination.

Sherwood Anderson

I'M A FOOL

It was a hard jolt for me, one of the most bitterest I ever had to face. And it all came about through my own foolishness, too. Even yet sometimes, when I think of it, I want to cry or swear or kick myself. Perhaps, even now, after all this time, there will be a kind of satisfaction in making myself look cheap by telling of it.

It began at three o'clock one October afternoon as I sat in the grand stand at the fall trotting and pacing meet at Sandusky, Ohio.

To tell the truth, I felt a little foolish that I should be sitting in the grand stand at all. During the summer before I had left my home town with Harry Whitehead and, with a nigger named Burt, had taken a job as swipe with one of the two horses Harry was campaigning through the fall race meets that year. Mother cried and my sister Mildred, who wanted to get a job as a schoolteacher in our town that fall, stormed and scolded about the house all during the week before I left. They both thought it something disgraceful that one of our family should take a place as a swipe with race horses. I've an idea Mildred thought my taking the place would stand in the way of her getting the job she'd been working so long for.

But after all I had to work, and there was no other work to be got. A big lumbering fellow of nineteen couldn't just hang around the house and I had got too big to mow people's lawns and sell newspapers. Little chaps who could get next to people's sympathies by their sizes were always getting jobs away from me. There was one fellow who kept saying to everyone who wanted a lawn mowed or a cistern cleaned that he was saving money to work his way through college, and I used to lay awake nights thinking up ways to injure him without being found out. I kept thinking of wagons running over him and bricks falling on his head as he walked along the street. But never mind him.

I got the place with Harry and I liked Burt fine. We got along splendid together. He was a big nigger with a lazy sprawling body and soft, kind eyes, and when it came to a fight he could hit like Jack Johnson. He had Bucephalus, a big black pacing stallion that could do 2.09 or 2.10 if he had to, and I had a little gelding named Doctor Fritz that never lost a race all fall when Harry wanted him to win.

We set out from home late in July, in a box car with the two horses and after that, until late November, we kept moving along to the race meets and the fairs. It was a peachy time for me, I'll say that. Sometimes now I think that boys who are raised regular in houses, and never have a fine nigger like

Burt for best friend, and go to high schools and college, and never steal anything, or get drunk a little, or learn to swear from fellows who know how, or come walking up in front of a grand stand in their shirt sleeves and with dirty horsy pants on when the races are going on and the grand stand is full of people all dressed up—What's the use of talking about it? Such fellows don't know nothing at all. They've never had no opportunity.

But I did. Burt taught me how to rub down a horse and put the bandages on after a race and steam a horse out and a lot of valuable things for any man to know. He could wrap a bandage on a horse's leg so smooth that if it had been the same color you would think it was his skin, and I guess he'd have been a big driver, too, and got to the top like Murphy and Walter Cox and the others if he hadn't been black.

Gee whizz! it was fun. You got to a county-seat town, maybe say on a Saturday or Sunday, and the fair began the next Tuesday and lasted until Friday afternoon. Doctor Fritz would be, say, in the 2.25 trot on Tuesday afternoon and on Thursday afternoon Bucephalus would knock 'em cold in the "free-for-all" pace. It left you a lot of time to hang around and listen to horse talk, and see Burt knock some yap cold that got too gay, and you'd find out about horses and men and pick up a lot of stuff you could use all the rest of your life, if you had some sense and salted down what you heard and felt and saw.

And then at the end of the week when the race meet was over, and Harry had run home to tend up to his livery-stable business, you and Burt hitched the two horses to carts and drove slow and steady across country, to the place for the next meeting, so as to not overheat the horses, etc., etc., you know.

Gee whizz! Gosh amighty! the nice hickory-nut and beechnut and oaks and other kinds of trees along the roads, all brown and red, and the good smells, and Burt singing a song called "Deep River," and the country girls at the windows of houses and everything. You can stick your colleges up your nose for all me. I guess I know where I got my education.

Why, one of those little burgs of towns you came to on the way, say now on a Saturday afternoon, and Burt says, "Let's lay up here." And you did.

And you took the horses to a livery stable and fed them, and you got your good clothes out of a box and put them on.

And the town was full of farmers gaping, because they could see you were racehorse people, and the kids maybe never see a nigger before and was afraid and run away when the two of us walked down their main street.

And that was before prohibition and all that foolishness, and so you went into a saloon, the two of you, and all the yaps come and stood around, and there was always some one pretended he was horsy and knew things and spoke up and began asking questions, and all you did was to lie and lie all you could about what horses you had, and I said I owned them, and then some fellow said, "Will you have a drink of whisky?" and Burt knocked his eye out the way he could say, offhand like, "Oh, well, all right, I'm agreeable to a little nip. I'll split a quart with you." Gee whizz!

But that isn't what I want to tell my story about. We got home late in November and I promised mother I'd quit the race horses for good. There's a lot of things you've got to promise a mother because she don't know any better.

And so, there not being any work in our town any more than when I left there to go to the races, I went off to Sandusky and got a pretty good place taking care of horses for a man who owned a teaming and delivery and storage and coal and real-estate business there. It was a pretty good place with good eats, and a day off each week, and sleeping on a cot in a big barn, and mostly just shoveling in hay and oats to a lot of big good-enough skates of horses that couldn't have trotted a race with a toad. I wasn't dissatisfied and I could send money home.

And then, as I started to tell you, the fall races come to Sandusky and I got the day off and I went. I left the job at noon and had on my good clothes and my new brown derby hat I'd bought the Saturday before, and a stand-up collar.

First of all I went downtown and walked about with the dudes. I've always thought to myself, "Put up a good front," and so I did it. I had forty dollars in my pockets and so I went into the West House, a big hotel, and walked up to the cigar stand. "Give me three twenty-five-cent cigars," I said. There was a lot of horsemen and strangers and dressed-up people from other towns standing around in the lobby and in the bar, and I mingled amongst them. In the bar there was a fellow with a cane and a Windsor tie on, that it made me sick to look at him. I like a man to be a man and dressed up, but not to go put on that kind of airs. So I pushed him aside, kind of rough, and had me a drink of whisky. And then he looked at me, as though he thought maybe he'd get gay, but he changed his mind and didn't say anything. And then I had another drink of whisky, just to show him something, and went out and had a hack out to the races, all to myself, and when I got there I bought myself the best seat I could get up in the grand stand, but didn't go in for any of these boxes. That's putting on too many airs.

And so there I was, sitting up in the grand stand as gay as you please and looking down on the swipes coming out with their horses, and with their dirty horsy pants on and the horseblankets swung over their shoulders, same as I had been doing all the year before. I liked one thing about the same as the other, sitting up there and feeling grand and being down there and looking up at the yaps and feeling grander and more important, too.

One thing's about as good as another, if you take it just right. I've often said that.

Well, right in front of me, in the grand stand that day, there was a fellow with a couple of girls and they was about my age. The young fellow was a nice guy, all right. He was the kind maybe that goes to college and then comes to be a lawyer or maybe a newspaper editor or something like that, but he wasn't stuck on himself. There are some of that kind are all right and he was one of the ones.

He had his sister with him and another girl and the sister looked around over his shoulder, accidental at first, not intending to start anything—she wasn't that kind—and her eyes and mine happened to meet.

You know how it is. Gee, she was a peach! She had on a soft dress, kind of a blue stuff and it looked carelessly made, but was well sewed and made and everything. I knew that much. I blushed when she looked right at me and so did she. She was the nicest girl I've ever seen in my life. She wasn't stuck on herself and she could talk proper grammar without being like a schoolteacher or something like that. What I mean is, she was O.K. I think maybe her father was well-to-do, but not rich to make her chesty because she was his daughter, as some are. Maybe he owned a drug store or a dry-goods store in their home town, or something like that. She never told me and I never asked.

My own people are all O.K. too, when you come to that. My grandfather was Welsh and over in the old country, in Wales he was— But never mind that.

The first heat of the first race come off and the young fellow setting there with the two girls left them and went down to make a bet. I knew what he was up to, but he didn't talk big and noisy and let everyone around know he was a sport, as some do. He wasn't that kind. Well, he come back and I heard him tell the two girls what horse he'd bet on, and when the heat trotted they all half got to their feet and acted in the excited, sweaty way people do when they've got money down on a race, and the horse they bet on is up there pretty close at the end, and they think maybe he'll come on with a rush, but he never does because he hasn't got the old juice in him, come right down to it.

And then, pretty soon, the horses came out for the 2.18 pace and there was a horse in it I knew. He was a horse Bob French had in his string but Bob didn't own him. He was a horse owned by a Mr. Mathers down at Marietta, Ohio.

This Mr. Mathers had a lot of money and owned some coal mines or something and he had a swell place out in the country, and he was stuck on race horses, but was a Presbyterian or something, and I think more than likely his wife was one, too, maybe a stiffer one than himself. So he never raced his horses hisself, and the story round the Ohio race tracks was that when one of his horses got ready to go to the races he turned him over to Bob French and pretended to his wife he was sold.

So Bob had the horses and he did pretty much as he pleased and you can't blame Bob, at least, I never did. Sometimes he was out to win and sometimes he wasn't. I never cared much about that when I was swiping a horse. What I did want to know was that my horse had the speed and could go out in front, if you wanted him to.

And, as I'm telling you, there was Bob in this race with one of Mr.

Mathers' horses, was named "About Ben Ahem" or something like that, and was fast as a streak. He was a gelding and had a mark of 2.21, but could step in .08 or .09.

Because when Burt and I were out, as I've told you, the year before, there was a nigger Burt knew, worked for Mr. Mathers and we went out there one day when we didn't have no race on at the Marietta Fair and our boss Harry was gone home.

And so everyone was gone to the fair but just this one nigger and he took us all through Mr. Mathers' swell house and he and Burt tapped a bottle of wine Mr. Mathers had hid in his bedroom, back in a closet, without his wife knowing, and he showed us this Ahem horse. Burt was always stuck on being a driver but didn't have much chance to get to the top, being a nigger, and he and the other nigger gulped the whole bottle of wine and Burt got a little lit up.

So the nigger let Burt take this About Ben Ahem and step him a mile in a track Mr. Mathers had all to himself, right there on the farm. And Mr. Mathers had one child, a daughter, kinda sick and not very good looking, and she came home and we had to hustle to get About Ben Ahem stuck back in the barn.

I'm only telling you to get everything straight. At Sandusky, that afternoon I was at the fair, this young fellow with the two girls was fussed, being with the girls and losing his bet. You know how a fellow is that way. One of them was his girl and the other his sister. I had figured that out.

"Gee whizz," I says to myself, "I'm going to give him the dope."

He was mighty nice when I touched him on the shoulder. He and the girls were nice to me right from the start and clear to the end. I'm not blaming them.

And so he leaned back and I give him the dope on About Ben Ahem. "Don't bet a cent on this first heat because he'll go like an oxen hitched to a plow, but when the first heat is over go right down and lay on your pile." That's what I told him.

Well, I never saw a fellow treat any one sweller. There was a fat man sitting beside the little girl, that had looked at me twice by this time, and I at her, and both blushing, and what did he do but have the nerve to turn and ask the fat man to get up and change places with me so I could set with his crowd.

Gee whizz, craps amighty. There I was. What a chump I was to go and get gay up there in the West House bar, and just because that dude was standing there with a cane and that kind of a necktie on, to go and get all balled up and drink that whisky, just to show off.

Of course she would know, me setting right beside her and letting her smell of my breath. I could have kicked myself right down out of that grand stand and all around that race track and made a faster record than most of the skates of horses they had there that year.

Because that girl wasn't any mutt of a girl. What wouldn't I have give right then for a stick of chewing gum to chew, or a lozenger, or some licorice, or most anything. I was glad I had those twenty-five-cent cigars in my pocket and right away I give that fellow one and lit one myself. Then that fat man got up and we changed places and there I was, plunked right down beside her.

They introduced themselves and the fellow's best girl, he had with him, was named Miss Elinor Woodbury, and her father was a manufacturer of barrels from a place called Tiffin, Ohio. And the fellow himself was named Wilbur Wessen and his sister was Miss Lucy Wessen.

I suppose it was their having such swell names that got me off my trolley. A fellow, just because he has been a swipe with a race horse, and works taking care of horses for a man in the teaming, delivery, and storage business isn't any better or worse than any one else. I've often thought that, and said it too.

But you know how a fellow is. There's something in that kind of nice clothes, and the kind of nice eyes she had, and the way she had looked at me, awhile before, over her brother's shoulder, and me looking back at her, and both of us blushing.

I couldn't show her up for a boob, could I?

I made a fool of myself, that's what I did. I said my name was Walter Mathers from Marietta, Ohio, and then I told all three of them the smashingest lie you ever heard. What I said was that my father owned the horse About Ben Ahem and that he had let him out to this Bob French for racing purposes, because our family was proud and had never gone into racing that way, in our own name, I mean, and Miss Lucy Wessen's eyes were shining, and I went the whole hog.

I told about our place down at Marietta, and about the big stables and the grand brick house we had on a hill, up above the Ohio River, but I knew enough not to do it in no bragging way. What I did was to start things and then let them drag the rest out of me. I acted just as reluctant to tell as I could. Our family hasn't got any barrel factory, and since I've known us, we've always been pretty poor, but not asking anything of any one at that, and my grandfather, over in Wales—but never mind that.

We set there talking like we had known each other for years and years, and I went and told them that my father had been expecting maybe this Bob French wasn't on the square, and had sent me up to Sandusky on the sly to find out what I could.

And I bluffed it through I had found out all about the 2.18 pace, in which About Ben Ahem was to start.

I said he would lose the first heat by pacing like a lame cow and then he would come back and skin 'em alive after that. And to back up what I said I took thirty dollars out of my pocket and handed it to Mr. Wilbur Wessen and asked him, would he mind, after the first heat, to go down and place it on About Ben Ahem for whatever odds he could get. What I said was that I didn't want Bob French to see me and none of the swipes.

Sure enough the first heat come off and About Ben Ahem went off his stride, up the back stretch, and looked like a wooden horse or a sick one, and come in to be last. Then this Wilbur Wessen went down to the betting place under the grand stand and there I was with the two girls, and when that Miss Woodbury was looking the other way once, Lucy Wessen kinda, with her shoulder you know, kinda touched me. Not just tucking down, I don't mean. You know how a woman can do. They get close, but not getting gay either. You know what they do. Gee whizz.

And then they give me a jolt. What they had done, when I didn't know, was to get together, and they had decided Wilbur Wessen would bet fifty dollars, and the two girls had gone and put in ten dollars each, of their own money, too. I was sick then, but I was sicker later.

About the gelding, About Ben Ahem, and their winning their money, I wasn't worried a lot about that. It came out O.K. Ahem stepped the next three heats like a bushel of spoiled eggs going to market before they could be found out, and Wilbur Wessen had got nine to two for the money. There was something else eating at me.

Because Wilbur come back, after he had bet the money, and after that he spent most of his time talking to that Miss Woodbury, and Lucy Wessen and I was left alone together like on a desert island. Gee, if I'd only been on the square or if there had been any way of getting myself on the square. There ain't any Walter Mathers, like I said to her and them, and there hasn't ever been one, but if there was, I bet I'd go to Marietta, Ohio, and shoot him tomorrow.

There I was, big boob that I am. Pretty soon the race was over, and Wilbur had gone down and collected our money, and we had a hack downtown, and he stood us a swell supper at the West House, and a bottle of champagne beside.

And I was with that girl and she wasn't saying much, and I wasn't saying much either. One thing I know. She wasn't stuck on me because of the lie about my father being rich and all that. There's a way you know . . . Craps amighty. There's a kind of girl you see just once in your life, and if you don't get busy and make hay, then you're gone for good and all, and might as well go jump off a bridge. They give you a look from inside of them somewhere, and it ain't no vamping, and what it means is—you want that girl to be your wife, and you want nice things around her like flowers and swell clothes, and you want her to have the kids you're going to have, and you want good music played and no ragtime. Gee whizz.

There's a place over near Sandusky, across a kind of bay, and it's called Cedar Point. And after we had supper we went over to it in a launch, all by ourselves. Wilbur and Miss Lucy and that Miss Woodbury had to catch a ten o'clock train back to Tiffin, Ohio, because, when you're out with girls like that you can't get careless and miss any trains and stay out all night, like you can with some kinds of Janes.

And Wilbur blowed himself to the launch and it cost him fifteen cold plunks, but I wouldn't never have knew if I hadn't listened. He wasn't no tin horn kind of a sport.

Over at the Cedar Point place, we didn't stay around where there was a gang of common kind of cattle at all.

There was big dance halls and dining places for yaps, and there was a beach you could walk along and get where it was dark, and we went there.

She didn't talk hardly at all and neither did I, and I was thinking how glad I was my mother was all right, and always made us kids learn to eat with a fork at table, and not swill soup, and not be noisy and rough like a gang you see around a race track that way.

Then Wilbur and his girl went away up the beach and Lucy and I sat down in a dark place, where there was some roots of old trees the water had washed up, and after that the time, till we had to go back in the launch and they had to catch their trains, wasn't nothing at all. It went like winking your eye.

Here's how it was. The place we were setting in was dark, like I said, and there was the roots from that old stump sticking up like arms, and there was a watery smell, and the night was like—as if you could put your hand out and feel it—so warm and soft and dark and sweet like an orange.

I most cried and I most swore and I most jumped up and danced, I was so mad and happy and sad.

When Wilbur come back from being alone with his girl, and she saw him coming, Lucy she says, "We got to go to the train now," and she was most crying too, but she never knew nothing I knew, and she couldn't be so all busted up. And then, before Wilbur and Miss Woodbury got up to where we was, she put her face up and kissed me quick and put her head up against me and she was all quivering and—Gee whizz.

Sometimes I hope I have cancer and die. I guess you know what I mean. We went in the launch across the bay to the train like that, and it was dark, too. She whispered and said it was like she and I could get out of the boat and walk on the water, and it sounded foolish, but I knew what she meant.

And then quick we were right at the depot, and there was a big gang of yaps, the kind that goes to the fairs, and crowded and milling around like cattle, and how could I tell her? "It won't be long because you'll write and I'll write to you." That's all she said.

I got a chance like a hay barn afire. A swell chance I got.

And maybe she would write me, down at Marietta that way, and the letter would come back, and stamped on the front of it by the U.S.A. "there ain't any such guy," or something like that, whatever they stamp on a letter that way.

And me trying to pass myself off for a big-bug and a swell—to her, as decent a little body as God ever made. Craps amighty—a swell chance I got!

And then the train come in, and she got on it, and Wilbur Wessen, he come and shook hands with me, and that Miss Woodbury was nice too and bowed to me, and I at her, and the train went and I busted out and cried like a kid.

Gee, I could have run after that train and made Dan Patch look like a freight train after a wreck but, socks amighty, what was the use? Did you ever see such a fool?

I'll bet you what—if I had an arm broke right now or a train had run over my foot—I wouldn't go to no doctor at all. I'd go set down and let her hurt and hurt—that's what I'd do.

I'll bet you what—if I hadn't a drunk that booze I'd a never been such a boob as to go tell such a lie—that couldn't never be made straight to a lady like her.

I wish I had that fellow right here that had on a Windsor tie and carried a cane. I'd smash him for fair. Gosh darn his eyes. He's a big fool—that's what he is.

And if I'm not another you just go find me one and I'll quit working and be a bum and give him my job. I don't care nothing for working, and earning money, and saving it for no such boob as myself.

QUESTIONS

1. This story is told by an uneducated boy who is handicapped in the telling by bad grammar, an inadequate vocabulary, ignorance, and a digressive story-telling method. Find a good exemplification of each. Why do these handicaps advance rather than hinder the story? What is the story's main purpose?

2. What kind of moral standards does the swipe have? Is he mean? Where does he get his moral standards?

3. What is the swipe's attitude toward education? Can you reconcile "You can stick your colleges up your nose for all me" with "The young fellow was a nice guy, all right. He was the kind maybe that goes to college and then comes to be a lawyer . . ."? What is an *ambivalent* attitude? What is *rationalization*? Explain the swipe's attitude.

4. The main tenet of the swipe's rather rudimentary philosophy of life is "Put up a good front." On what occasions in the story does the swipe put up a good front? Is this the philosophy of a mature individual? What is the difference between "putting up a good front" and "putting on airs"?

5. Another tenet of the swipe's philosophy is that "A fellow, just because he has been a swipe with a race horse, and works taking care of horses for a man in the teaming, delivery, and storage business, isn't any better or worse than any one else." Why has the swipe "often thought that, and said it too"? Why is he so impressed by the "swell names" and good clothes of

the Wessens and Miss Woodbury? What is his attitude toward being a swipe? What does he like about being a swipe?

6. Why does the swipe resent the man in the Windsor tie? Why does he like Burt and the Wessens and Miss Woodbury? Why does he refer to most people as "yaps"?

7. Evaluate the swipe's emotional maturity in the light of his reactions to the little chap who got jobs away from him, what he would do to the real Walter Mathers if there were one, his behavior toward the man in the Windsor tie, what he would like to happen to himself at the end of the story.

8. What psychological term might be used to explain the swipe? Account for his behavior in terms of his size, his social and economic background, his success in school, his earning ability.

9. The swipe blames his whopper at the race track on the whisky, and he blames the whisky on the man in the Windsor tie. What is the real reason for his behavior?

10. How is your attitude toward the swipe affected by the fact that you hear his story from himself? How would it be different if you had heard it from, say, a high school principal?

Anton Chekhov

THE KISS

On the twentieth of May, at eight o'clock in the evening, six batteries of the N Artillery Brigade arrived at the village of Miestetchki to spend the night, before going to their camp.

The confusion was at its height—some officers at the guns, others in the church square with the quartermaster—when a civilian upon a remarkable horse rode from the rear of the church. The small cob with well-shaped neck wobbled along, all the time dancing on its legs as if someone were whipping them. Reaching the officers, the rider doffed his cap with ceremony and said—

"His Excellency, General von Rabbek, requests the honor of the officers' company at tea in his house near by . . ."

The horse shook its head, danced, and wobbled backwards; its rider again took off his cap, and turning around disappeared behind the church.

"The devil!" the general exclaimed, the officers dispersing to their quarters. "We are almost asleep, yet along comes this von Rabbek with his tea! That tea! I remember it!"

THE KISS First published in 1887.

The officers of the six batteries had vivid recollections of a past invitation. During recent maneuvers they had been asked, with their Cossack comrades, to tea at the house of a local country gentleman, a Count, retired from military service; and this hearty old Count overwhelmed them with attentions, fed them like gourmands, poured vodka into them and made them stay the night. All this, of course, was fine. The trouble was that the old soldier entertained his guests too well. He kept them up till daybreak while he poured forth tales of past adventures and pointed out valuable paintings, engravings, arms, and letters from celebrated men. And the tired officers listened, perforce, until he ended, only to find out that the time for sleep had gone.

Was von Rabbek another old Count? It might easily be. But there was no neglecting his invitation. The officers washed and dressed, and set out for von Rabbek's house. At the church square they learnt that they must descend the hill to the river, and follow the bank till they reached the general's gardens, where they would find a path direct to the house. Or, if they chose to go uphill, they would reach the general's barns half a *verst* from Miestetchki. It was this route they chose.

"But who is this von Rabbek?" asked one. "The man who commanded the N Cavalry Division at Plevna?"

"No, that was not von Rabbek, but simply Rabbe—without the von."

"What glorious weather!"

At the first barn they came to, two roads diverged; one ran straight forward and faded in the dusk; the other, turning to the right, led to the general's house. As the officers drew near they talked less loudly. To right and to left stretched rows of red-roofed brick barns, in aspect heavy and morose as the barracks of provincial towns. In front gleamed the lighted windows of von Rabbek's house.

"A good omen, gentlemen!" cried a young officer. "Our setter runs in advance. There is game ahead!"

On the face of Lieutenant Lobuitko, the tall stout officer referred to, there was not one trace of hair though he was twenty-five years old. He was famed among comrades for the instinct which told him of the presence of women in the neighborhood. On hearing his comrade's remark, he turned his head and said—

"Yes. There are women there. My instinct tells me."

A handsome, well-preserved man of sixty, in mufti, came to the hall door to greet his guests. It was von Rabbek. As he pressed their hands, he explained that though he was delighted to see them, he must beg pardon for not asking them to spend the night; as guests he already had his two sisters, their children, his brother, and several neighbors—in fact, he had not one spare room. And though he shook their hands and apologized and smiled, it was plain that he was not half as glad to see them as was the last year's Count, and that he had invited them merely because good manners demanded it. The officers climbing the soft-carpeted steps and listening to their host understood this perfectly well; and realized that they carried into the house an atmosphere of intrusion and alarm. Would any man—they asked themselves—who had gathered his two sisters and their children, his brother and his neighbors, to celebrate, no doubt, some family festival, find pleasure in the invasion of nineteen officers whom he had never seen before?

A tall elderly lady, with a good figure, and a long face with black eyebrows, who resembled closely the ex-Empress Eugénie, greeted them at the drawing-room door. Smiling courteously and with dignity, she affirmed that she was delighted to see the officers, and only regretted that she could not ask them to stay the night. But the courteous, dignified smile disappeared when she turned away, and it was quite plain that she had seen many officers in her day, that they caused not the slightest interest, and that she had invited them merely because an invitation was dictated by good breeding and by her position in the world.

In a big dining room, at a big table, sat ten men and women, drinking tea. Behind them, veiled in cigar smoke, stood several young men, among them one, red-whiskered and extremely thin, who spoke English loudly with a lisp. Through an open door the officers saw into a brightly lighted room with blue wallpaper.

"You are too many to introduce singly, gentlemen!" said the general loudly, with affected joviality. "Make one another's acquaintance, please—without formalities!"

The visitors, some with serious, even severe faces, some smiling constrainedly, all with a feeling of awkwardness, bowed, and took their seats at the table. Most awkward of all felt Staff-Captain Riabovitch, a short, round-shouldered, spectacled officer, whiskered like a lynx. While his brother officers looked serious or smiled constrainedly, his face, his lynx whiskers, and his spectacles seemed to explain: "I am the most timid, modest, undistinguished officer in the whole brigade." For some time after he took his seat at the table he could not fix his attention on any single thing. Faces, dresses, the cut-glass cognac bottles, the steaming tumblers, the molded cornices—all merged in a single, overwhelming sentiment which caused him intense fright and made him wish to hide his head. Like an inexperienced lecturer he saw everything before him, but could distinguish nothing, and was in fact the victim of what men of science diagnose as "psychical blindness."

But, slowly conquering his diffidence, Riabovitch began to distinguish and observe. As became a man both timid and unsocial, he remarked first of all the amazing temerity of his new friends. Von Rabbek, his wife, two elderly ladies, a girl in lilac, and the red-whiskered youth (who, it appeared, was a young von Rabbek) sat down among the officers as unconcernedly as if they had held rehearsals, and at once plunged into various heated arguments in which they soon involved their guests. That artillerists have a much better time than cavalrymen or infantrymen was proved conclusively by the lilac girl while von Rabbek and the elderly ladies affirmed the converse. The conversation became desultory. Riabovitch listened to the lilac girl fiercely debating themes she knew nothing about and took no interest in, and watched the insincere smiles which appeared on and disappeared from her face.

While the von Rabbek family with amazing strategy inveigled their guests into the dispute, they kept their eyes on every glass and mouth. Had everyone tea, was it sweet enough, why didn't one eat biscuits, was another fond of cognac? And the longer Riabovitch listened and looked, the more pleased he was with this disingenuous, disciplined family.

After tea the guests repaired to the drawing room. Instinct had not cheated Lobuitko. The room was packed with young women and girls, and ere a minute had passed the setter-lieutenant stood beside a very young, fair-haired girl in black, and, bending down as if resting on an invisible sword, shrugged his shoulders coquettishly. He was uttering, no doubt, most unentertaining nonsense, for the fair girl looked indulgently at his sated face, and exclaimed indifferently, "Indeed!" And this indifferent "Indeed!" might have quickly convinced the setter that he was on a wrong scent.

Music began. As the notes of a mournful valse throbbed out of the open window, through the heads of all flashed the feeling that outside that window it was springtime, a night of May. The air was odorous of young poplar leaves, of roses and lilacs—and the valse and the spring were sincere. Riabovitch, with valse and cognac mingling tipsily in his head, gazed at the window with a smile; then began to follow the movements of the women; and it seemed that the smell of roses, poplars, and lilacs came not from the gardens outside, but from the women's faces and dresses.

They began to dance. Young von Rabbek valsed twice round the room with a very thin girl; and Lobuitko, slipping on the parqueted floor, went up to the girl in lilac, and was granted a dance. But Riabovitch stood near the door with the wallflowers, and looked silently on. Amazed at the daring of men who in sight of a crowd could take unknown women by the waist, he tried in vain to picture himself doing the same. A time had been when he envied his comrades their courage and dash, suffered from painful heart-searchings, and was hurt by the knowledge that he was timid, round-shouldered, and undistinguished, that he had lynx whiskers, and that his waist was much too long. But with years he had grown reconciled to his own insignificance, and now looking at the dancers and loud talkers, he felt no envy, but only mournful emotions.

At the first quadrille von Rabbek junior approached and invited two nondancing officers to a game of billiards. The three left the room, and Riabovitch, who stood idle, and felt impelled to join in the general movement, followed. They passed the dining room, traversed a narrow glazed corridor and a room where three sleepy footmen jumped from a sofa with a start; and after walking, it seemed, through a whole houseful of rooms, entered a small billiard room.

Von Rabbek and the two officers began their game. Riabovitch, whose only game was cards, stood near the table and looked indifferently on, as the players, with unbuttoned coats, wielded their cues, moved about, joked, and shouted obscure technical terms. Riabovitch was ignored, save when one of the players jostled him or nudged him with the cue, and turning towards him said briefly, "Pardon!" so that before the game was over he was thoroughly bored, and, impressed by a sense of his superfluity, resolved to return to the drawing room and turned away.

It was on the way back that his adventure took place. Before he had gone far he saw that he had missed his way. He remembered distinctly the room with the three sleepy footmen; and after passing through five or six rooms entirely vacant, he saw his mistake. Retracing his steps, he turned to the left, and found himself in an almost dark room which he had not seen before; and after hesitating a minute, he boldly opened the first door he saw, and found himself in complete darkness. Through a chink of the door in front peered a bright light; from afar throbbed the dullest music of a mournful mazurka. Here, as in the drawing room, the windows were open wide, and the smell of poplars, lilacs, and roses flooded the air.

Riabovitch paused in irresolution. For a moment all was still. Then came the sound of hasty footsteps; then, without any warning of what was to come, a dress rustled, a woman's breathless voice whispered "At last!" and two soft, scented, unmistakably womanly arms met round his neck, a warm cheek impinged on his, and he received a sounding kiss. But hardly had the kiss echoed through the silence when the unknown shrieked loudly, and fled away—as it seemed to Riabovitch—in disgust. Riabovitch himself nearly screamed, and rushed headlong towards the bright beam in the door chink.

As he entered the drawing room his heart beat violently, and his hands trembled so perceptibly that he clasped them behind his back. His first emotion was shame, as if everyone in the room already knew that he had just been embraced and kissed. He retired into his shell, and looked fearfully around. But finding that hosts and guests were calmly dancing or talking, he regained courage, and surrendered himself to sensations experienced for the first time in his life. The unexampled had happened. His neck, fresh from the embrace of two soft, scented arms, seemed anointed with oil; near his left mustache, where the kiss had fallen, trembled a slight, delightful chill, as from peppermint drops; and from head to foot he was soaked in new and extraordinary sensations, which continued to grow and grow.

He felt that he must dance, talk, run into the garden, laugh unrestrainedly. He forgot altogether that he was round-shouldered, undistinguished, lynx-whiskered, that he had an "indefinite exterior"—a description from the lips of a woman he had happened to overhear. As Madame von Rabbek passed him he smiled so broadly and graciously that she came up and looked at him questioningly.

"What a charming house you have!" he said, straightening his spectacles.

And Madame von Rabbek smiled back, said that the house still belonged to her father, and asked were his parents still alive, how long he had been in the Army, and why he was so thin. And hearing his answers she departed. But though the conversation was over, he continued to smile benevolently, and think what charming people were his new acquaintances.

At supper Riabovitch ate and drank mechanically what was put before him, heard not a word of the conversation, and devoted all his powers to the unraveling of his mysterious, romantic adventure. What was the explanation? It was plain that one of the girls, he reasoned, had arranged a meeting in the dark room, and after waiting some time in vain had, in her nervous tension, mistaken Riabovitch for her hero. The mistake was likely enough, for on entering the dark room Riabovitch had stopped irresolutely as if he, too, were waiting for someone. So far the mystery was explained.

"But which of them was it?" he asked, searching the women's faces. She certainly was young, for old women do not indulge in such romances. Secondly, she was not a servant. That was proved unmistakably by the rustle of her dress, the scent, the voice . . .

When at first he looked at the girl in lilac she pleased him; she had pretty shoulders and arms, a clever face, a charming voice. Riabovitch piously prayed that it was she. But, smiling insincerely, she wrinkled her long nose, and that at once gave her an elderly air. So Riabovitch turned his eyes on the blonde in black. The blonde was younger, simpler, sincerer; she had charming kiss-curls, and drank from her tumbler with inexpressible grace. Riabovitch hoped it was she—but soon he noticed that her face was flat, and bent his eyes on her neighbor.

"It is a hopeless puzzle," he reflected. "If you take the arms and shoulders of the lilac girl, add the blonde's curls, and the eyes of the girl on Lobuitko's left, then—"

He composed a portrait of all these charms, and had a clear vision of the girl who had kissed him. But she was nowhere to be seen.

Supper over, the visitors, sated and tipsy, bade their entertainers good-by. Both host and hostess apologized for not asking them to spend the night.

"I am very glad, gentlemen!" said the general, and this time seemed to speak sincerely, no doubt because speeding the parting guest is a kindlier office than welcoming him unwelcomed. "I am very glad indeed! I hope you will visit me on your way back. Without ceremony, please! Which way will you go? Up the hill? No, go down the hill and through the garden. That way is shorter."

The officers took his advice. After the noise and glaring illumination within doors, the garden seemed dark and still. Until they reached the wicket gate all kept silence. Merry, half tipsy, and content, as they were, the night's obscurity and stillness inspired pensive thought. Through their brains, as through Riabovitch's, sped probably the same question: "Will the time ever come when I, like von Rabbek, shall have a big house, a family, a garden, the chance of being gracious—even insincerely—to others, of making them sated, tipsy, and content?"

But once the garden lay behind them, all spoke at once, and burst into causeless laughter. The path they followed led straight to the river, and then ran beside it, winding around bushes, ravines, and overhanging willow trees. The track was barely visible; the other bank was lost entirely in gloom. Sometimes the black water imaged stars, and this was the only indication of the river's speed. From beyond it sighed a drowsy snipe, and beside them in a bush, heedless of the crowd, a nightingale chanted loudly. The officers gathered in a group, and swayed the bush, but the nightingale continued his song.

"I like his cheek!" they echoed admiringly. "He doesn't care a *kopek!* The old rogue!"

Near their journey's end the path turned up the hill, and joined the road not far from the church enclosure; and there the officers, breathless from climbing, sat on the grass and smoked. Across the river gleamed a dull red light, and for want of a subject they argued the problem, whether it was a bonfire, a window light, or something else. Riabovitch looked also at the light, and felt that it smiled and winked at him as if it knew about the kiss.

On reaching home, he undressed without delay, and lay upon his bed. He shared the cabin with Lobuitko and a Lieutenant Merzliakoff, a staid, silent little man, by repute highly cultivated, who took with him everywhere *The Messenger of Europe* and read it eternally. Lobuitko undressed, tramped impatiently from corner to corner, and sent his servant for beer. Merzliakoff lay down, balanced the candle on his pillow, and hid his head behind *The Messenger of Europe*.

"Where is she now?" muttered Riabovitch, looking at the soot-blacked ceiling.

His neck still seemed anointed with oil, near his mouth still trembled the speck of peppermint chill. Through his brain twinkled successively the shoulders and arms of the lilac girl, the kiss-curls and honest eyes of the girl in black, the waists, dresses, brooches. But though he tried his best to fix these vagrant images, they glimmered, winked, and dissolved; and as they faded finally into the vast black curtain which hangs before the closed eyes of all men, he began to hear hurried footsteps, the rustle of petticoats, the sound of a kiss. A strong, causeless joy possessed him. But as he surrendered himself to this joy, Lobuitko's servant returned with the news that no beer was obtainable. The lieutenant resumed his impatient march up and down the room.

"The fellow's an idiot," he exclaimed, stopping first near Riabovitch and then near Merzliakoff. "Only the worst numbskull and blockhead can't get beer! *Canaille!*"

"Everyone knows there's no beer here," said Merzliakoff, without lifting his eyes from *The Messenger of Europe.*

"You believe that!" exclaimed Lobuitko. "Lord in heaven, drop me on the moon, and in five minutes I'll find both beer and women! I will find them myself! Call me a rascal if I don't!"

He dressed slowly, silently lighted a cigarette, and went out.

"Rabbek, Grabbek, Labbek," he muttered, stopping in the hall. "I won't go alone, devil take me! Riabovitch, come for a walk! What?"

As he got no answer, he returned, undressed slowly, and lay down. Merzliakoff sighed, dropped *The Messenger of Europe,* and put out the light. "Well?" muttered Lobuitko, puffing his cigarette in the dark.

Riabovitch pulled the bedclothes up to his chin, curled himself into a roll, and strained his imagination to join the twinkling images into one coherent whole. But the vision fled him. He soon fell asleep, and his last impression was that he had been caressed and gladdened, that into his life had crept something strange, and indeed ridiculous, but uncommonly good and radiant. And this thought did not forsake him even in his dreams.

When he awoke the feeling of anointment and peppermint chill was gone. But joy, as on the night before, filled every vein. He looked entranced at the windowpanes gilded by the rising sun, and listened to the noises outside. Someone spoke loudly under the very window. It was Lebedietsky, commander of his battery, who had just overtaken the brigade. He was talking to the sergeant-major, loudly, owing to lack of practice in soft speech.

"And what next?" he roared.

"During yesterday's shoeing, your honor, *Golubtchik* was pricked. The regimental doctor ordered clay and vinegar. And last night, your honor, mechanic Artemieff was drunk, and the lieutenant ordered him to be put on the limber of the reserve gun carriage."

The sergeant-major added that Karpoff had forgotten the tent pegs and the new lanyards for the friction tubes, and that the officers had spent the evening at General von Rabbek's. But here at the window appeared Lebedietsky's red-bearded face. He blinked his short-sighted eyes at the drowsy men in bed, and greeted them.

"Is everything all right?"

"The saddle wheeler galled his withers with the new yoke," answered Lobuitko.

The commander sighed, mused a moment, and shouted—

"I am thinking of calling on Alexandra Yegorovna. I want to see her. Good-by! I will catch you up before night."

Fifteen minutes later the brigade resumed its march. As he passed von Rabbek's barns, Riabovitch turned his head and looked at the house. The Venetian blinds were down; evidently all still slept. And among them slept she—she who had kissed him but a few hours before. He tried to visualize her asleep. He projected the bedroom window opened wide with green branches peering in, the freshness of the morning air, the smell of poplars, lilacs, and roses, the bed, a chair, the dress which rustled last night, a pair of tiny slippers, a ticking watch on the table—all these came to him clearly with every detail. But the features, the kind, sleepy smile—all, in short, that was essential and characteristic—fled his imagination as quicksilver flees the hand. When he had covered half a *verst* he again turned back. The yellow church, the house, gardens, and river were bathed in light. Imaging an azure sky, the green-banked river specked with silver sunshine flakes was inexpressibly fair; and, looking at Miestetchki for the last time, Riabovitch felt sad, as if parting forever with something very near and dear.

By the road before him stretched familiar, uninteresting scenes; to the right and left, fields of young rye and buckwheat with hopping rooks; in front, dust and the napes of human necks; behind, the same dust and faces. Ahead of the column marched four soldiers with swords—that was the advance guard. Next came the bandsmen. Advance guard and bandsmen, like mutes in a funeral procession, ignored the regulation intervals and marched too far ahead. Riabovitch, with the first gun of Battery No. 5, could see four batteries ahead.

To a layman, the long, lumbering march of an artillery brigade is novel, interesting, inexplicable. It is hard to understand why a single gun needs so many men; why so many, such strangely harnessed horses are needed to drag it. But to Riabovitch, a master of all these things, it was profoundly dull. He had learned years ago why a solid sergeant-major rides beside the officer in front of each battery; why the sergeant-major is called the *unosni,* and why the drivers of leaders and wheelers ride behind him. Riabovitch knew why the near horses are called saddle horses, and why the off horses are called led horses—and all of this was uninteresting beyond words. On one of the wheelers rode a soldier still covered with yesterday's dust, and with a cumbersome, ridiculous guard on his right leg. But Riabovitch, knowing the use of this leg guard, found it in no way ridiculous. The drivers, mechanically and with occasional cries, flourished their whips. The guns in themselves were unimpressive. The limbers were packed with tarpaulin-covered sacks of oats; and the guns themselves, hung round with teapots and satchels, looked like harmless animals, guarded for some obscure reason by men and horses. In the lee of the gun tramped six gunners, swinging their arms, and behind each gun came more *unosniye,* leaders, wheelers; and yet more guns, each as ugly and uninspiring as the one in front. And as every one of the six batteries in the brigade had four guns, the procession stretched along the road at least half a *verst.* It ended with a wagon train, with which, its head bent in thought, walked the donkey Magar, brought from Turkey by a battery commander.

Dead to his surroundings, Riabovitch marched onward, looking at the napes ahead or at the faces behind. Had it not been for last night's event, he would have been half asleep. But now he was absorbed in novel, entrancing thoughts. When the brigade set out that morning he had tried to argue that the kiss had no significance save as a trivial though mysterious adventure; that it was without real import; and that to think of it seriously was to behave himself absurdly. But logic soon flew away and surrendered him to his vivid imaginings. At times he saw himself in von Rabbek's dining room, *tête-à-tête* with a composite being, formed of the girl in lilac and the blonde in black. At times he closed his eyes, and pictured himself with a different, this time quite an unknown, girl of cloudy feature; he spoke to her, caressed her, bent over her shoulders; he imagined war and parting . . . then reunion, the first supper together, children . . .

"To the brakes!" rang the command as they topped the brow of each hill.

Riabovitch also cried "To the brakes!" and each time dreaded that the cry would break the magic spell, and recall him to realities.

They passed a big country house. Riabovitch looked across the fence into the garden, and saw a long path, straight as a ruler, carpeted with yellow sand, and shaded by young birches. In an ecstasy of enchantment, he pictured little feminine feet treading the yellow sand; and, in a flash, imagination restored the woman who had kissed him, the woman he had visualized after supper the night before. The image settled in his brain and never afterward forsook him.

The spell reigned until midday, when a loud command came from the rear of the column.

"Attention! Eyes right! Officers!"

In a *calèche* drawn by a pair of white horses appeared the general of the brigade. He stopped at the second battery, and called out something which no one understood. Up galloped several officers, among them Riabovitch.

"Well, how goes it?" The general blinked his red eyes, and continued, "Are there any sick?"

Hearing the answer, the little skinny general mused a moment, turned to an officer, and said—

"The driver of your third-gun wheeler has taken off his leg guard and hung it on the limber. *Canaille!* Punish him!"

Then raising his eyes to Riabovitch, he added—

"And in your battery, I think, the harness is too loose."

Having made several other equally tiresome remarks, he looked at Lobuitko, and laughed.

"Why do you look so downcast, Lieutenant Lobuitko? You are sighing for Madame Lopukhoff, eh? Gentlemen, he is pining for Madame Lopukhoff!"

Madame Lopukhoff was a tall, stout lady, long past forty. Being partial to big women, regardless of age, the general ascribed the same taste to his subordinates. The officers smiled respectfully; and the general, pleased that he had said something caustic and laughable, touched the coachman's back and saluted. The *calèche* whirled away.

"All this, though it seems to me impossible and unearthly, is in reality very commonplace," thought Riabovitch, watching the clouds of dust raised by the general's carriage. "It is an everyday event, and within everyone's experience . . . This old general, for instance, must have loved in his day; he is married now, and has children. Captain Wachter is also married, and his wife loves him, though he has an ugly red neck and no waist . . . Salmanoff is coarse, and a typical Tartar, but he has had a romance ending in marriage . . . I, like the rest, must go through it all sooner or later."

And the thought that he was an ordinary man, and that his life was ordinary, rejoiced and consoled him. He boldly visualized *her* and his happiness, and let his imagination run mad.

Towards evening the brigade ended its march. While the other officers sprawled in their tents, Riabovitch, Merzliakoff, and Lobuitko sat round a packing case and supped. Merzliakoff ate slowly, and, resting *The Messenger of Europe* on his knees, read on steadily. Lobuitko, chattering without cease, poured beer into his glass. But Riabovitch, whose head was dizzy from uninterrupted daydreams, ate in silence. When he had drunk three glasses he felt tipsy and weak; and an overmastering impulse forced him to relate his adventure to his comrades.

"A most extraordinary thing happened to me at von Rabbek's," he began, doing his best to speak in an indifferent, ironical tone. "I was on my way, you understand, from the billiard room. . . ."

And he attempted to give a very detailed history of the kiss. But in a minute he had told the whole story. In that minute he had exhausted every detail; and it seemed to him terrible that the story required such a short time. It ought, he felt, to have lasted all the night. As he finished, Lobuitko, who as a liar himself believed in no one, laughed incredulously. Merzliakoff frowned, and, with his eyes still glued to *The Messenger of Europe,* said indifferently—

"God knows who it was! She threw herself on your neck, you say, and didn't cry out! Some lunatic, I expect!"

"It must have been a lunatic," agreed Riabovitch.

"I, too, have had adventures of that kind," began Lobuitko, making a frightened face. "I was on my way to Kovno. I traveled second-class. The carriage was packed, and I couldn't sleep. So I gave the guard a *rouble,* and he took my bag, and put me in a *coupé*. I lay down, and pulled my rug over me. It was pitch dark, you understand. Suddenly I felt someone tapping my shoulder and breathing in my face. I stretched out my hand, and felt an elbow. Then I opened my eyes. Imagine! A woman! Coal-black eyes, lips red as good coral, nostrils breathing passion, breasts—buffers!"

"Draw it mild!" interrupted Merzliakoff in his quiet voice. "I can believe about the breasts, but if it was pitch dark how could you see the lips?"

By laughing at Merzliakoff's lack of understanding, Lobuitko tried to shuffle out of the dilemma. The story annoyed Riabovitch. He rose from the box, lay on his bed, and swore that he would never again take anyone into his confidence.

Life in camp passed without event. The days flew by, each like the one before. But on every one of these days Riabovitch felt, thought, and acted as a man in love. When at daybreak his servant brought him cold water, and poured it over his head, it flashed at once into his half-awakened brain that something good and warm and caressing had crept into his life.

At night when his comrades talked of love and of women, he drew in his chair, and his face was the face of an old soldier who talks of battles in which he has taken part. And when the rowdy officers, led by setter Lobuitko, made Don Juanesque raids upon the neighboring "suburb," Riabovitch, though he accompanied them, was morose and conscience-struck, and mentally asked *her* forgiveness. In free hours and sleepless nights, when his brain was obsessed by memories of childhood, of his father, his mother, of everything akin and dear, he remembered always Miestetchki, the dancing horse, von Rabbek, von Rabbek's wife, so like the ex-Empress Eugénie, the dark room, the chink in the door.

On the thirty-first of August he left camp, this time not with the whole brigade but with only two batteries. As an exile returning to his native land, he was agitated and enthralled by daydreams. He longed passionately for the queer-looking horse, the church, the insincere von Rabbeks, the dark room; and that internal voice which so often cheats the lovelorn whispered an assurance that he should see *her* again. But doubt tortured him. How should he meet her? What must he say? Would she have forgotten the kiss? If it came to the worst—he consoled himself—if he never saw her again, he might walk once more through the dark room, and remember . . .

Towards evening the white barns and well-known church rose on the horizon. Riabovitch's heart beat wildly. He ignored the remark of an officer who rode by, he forgot the whole world, and he gazed greedily at the river glimmering afar, at the green roofs, at the dove-cote, over which fluttered birds dyed golden by the setting sun.

As he rode towards the church, and heard again the quartermaster's raucous voice, he expected every second a horseman to appear from behind the fence and invite the officers to tea. . . . But the quartermaster ended his harangue, the officers hastened to the village, and no horseman appeared.

"When von Rabbek hears from the peasants that we are back he will send for us," thought Riabovitch. And so assured was he of this, that when he entered the hut he failed to understand why his comrades had lighted a candle, and why the servants were preparing the samovar.

A painful agitation oppressed him. He lay on his bed. A moment later he rose to look for the horseman. But no horseman was in sight. Again he lay down; again he rose; and this time, impelled by restlessness, went into the street and walked towards the church. The square was dark and deserted. On the hill stood three silent soldiers. When they saw Riabovitch they started and saluted, and he, returning their salute, began to descend the well-remembered path.

Beyond the stream, in a sky stained with purple, the moon slowly rose. Two chattering peasant women walked in a kitchen garden and pulled cabbage leaves; behind them their log cabins stood out black against the sky. The river bank was as it had been in May; the bushes were the same; things differed only in that the nightingale no longer sang, that it smelt no longer of poplars and young grass.

When he reached von Rabbek's garden Riabovitch peered through the wicket gate. Silence and darkness reigned. Save only the white birch trunks and patches of pathway, the whole garden merged in a black, impenetrable shade. Riabovitch listened greedily, and gazed intent. For a quarter of an hour he loitered; then hearing no sound, and seeing no light, he walked wearily towards home.

He went down to the river. In front rose the general's bathing box; and white towels hung on the rail of the bridge. He climbed on to the bridge and stood still; then, for no reason whatever, touched a towel. It was clammy and cold. He looked down at the river which sped past swiftly, murmuring almost inaudibly against the bathing-box piles. Near the left bank glowed the moon's ruddy reflection, overrun by ripples which stretched it, tore it in two, and, it seemed, would sweep it away as twigs and shavings are swept.

"How stupid! How stupid!" thought Riabovitch, watching the hurrying ripples, "How stupid everything is!"

Now that hope was dead, the history of the kiss, his impatience, his ardor, his vague aspirations and disillusion appeared in a clear light. It no longer seemed strange that the general's horseman had not come, and that he would never again see *her* who had kissed him by accident instead of another. On the contrary, he felt, it would be strange if he did ever see her again . . .

The water flew past him, whither and why no one knew. It had flown past in May; it had sped a stream into a great river; a river, into the sea; it had floated on high in mist and fallen again in rain; it might be, the water of May was again speeding past under Riabovitch's eyes. For what purpose? Why?

And the whole world—life itself—seemed to Riabovitch an inscrutable, aimless mystification . . . Raising his eyes from the stream and gazing at the sky, he recalled how Fate in the shape of an unknown woman had once caressed him; he recalled his summer fantasies and images—and his whole life seemed to him unnaturally thin and colorless and wretched . . .

When he reached the cabin his comrades had disappeared. His servant informed him that all had set out to visit "General Fonrabbkin," who had sent a horseman to bring them . . . For a moment Riabovitch's heart thrilled with joy. But that joy he extinguished. He cast himself upon his bed, and wroth with his evil fate, as if he wished to spite it, ignored the invitation.

QUESTIONS

1. What details of circumstance and setting serve as preparation for the romantic effect the kiss has on Riabovitch?

2. In his story the author does not attempt to make a complete characterization but to delineate and trace a psychological reaction. The story is nevertheless necessarily grounded in character. How is Riabovitch characterized? How does his behavior at the party support his initial characterization?

3. How does the presence in the story of Lobuitko and Merzliakoff enhance the characterization of Riabovitch?

4. Describe the effect of the kiss on Riabovitch. How irrational does he become? Is he completely irrational or does he have moments of realism? What exactly does he expect to happen on his return to Miestetchki? What effect does his fruitless visit to the darkened house have on him? Why does he not take advantage of the invitation when his servant tells him of it?

5. Riabovitch's reaction to the kiss is preposterously disproportionate to its cause. How is it made plausible? Could it have occurred in a different kind of person? Would it have been the same if he had known which girl kissed him?

6. Why does Lobuitko's story (page 91) annoy Riabovitch? Had such an incident as described by Lobuitko happened to Riabovitch, would it have had the same effect on him as the kiss?

7. Of what relevance is Riabovitch's touching the general's bathing towel (page 93)?

8. What is the function in the story of such realistic details of army life as the morning reports to the battery commander on page 88 (e.g., "The saddle wheeler galled his withers with the new yoke"), the description of the battery on the march (page 89), the appearance of the general in his *calèche* (page 90), and the account of Lieutenant Merzliakoff who eternally reads *The Messenger of Europe* (page 87)?

9. Von Rabbek is a minor character; nevertheless, he is more than simply an agent of the plot. What details of characterization serve to make him and his family real? What other incidental characters also seem sharply though briefly drawn? How are they made so?

Elizabeth Bowen

TEARS, IDLE TEARS

Frederick burst into tears in the middle of Regent's Park. His mother, seeing what was about to happen, had cried: "Frederick, you *can't*—in the middle of Regent's Park!" Really, this was a corner, one of those lively corners just inside a big gate, where two walks meet and a bridge starts across the pretty winding lake. People were passing quickly; the bridge rang with feet. Poplars stood up like delicate green brooms; diaphanous willows whose weeping was not shocking quivered over the lake. May sun spattered gold through the breezy trees; the tulips though falling open were still gay; three girls in a long boat shot under the bridge. Frederick, knees trembling, butted towards his mother a crimson convulsed face, as though he had the idea of burying himself in her. She whipped out a handkerchief and dabbed at him with it under his grey felt hat, exclaiming meanwhile in fearful mortification: "You really haven't got to be such a *baby*!" Her tone attracted the notice of several people, who might otherwise have thought he was having something taken out of his eye.

He was too big to cry: the whole scene was disgraceful. He wore a grey flannel knickerbocker suit and looked like a schoolboy; though in fact he was seven, still doing lessons at home. His mother said to him almost every week: "I don't know what they will think when you go to school!" His tears were a shame of which she could speak to no one; no offensive weakness of body could have upset her more. Once she had got so far as taking her pen up to write to the Mother's Advice Column of a helpful woman's weekly about them. She began: "I am a widow; young, good tempered, and my friends all tell me that I have great control. But my little boy—" She intended to sign herself "Mrs. D., Surrey." But then she had stopped and thought no, no: after all, he is Toppy's son . . . She was a gallant-looking, correct woman, wearing to-day in London a coat and skirt, a silver fox, white gloves and a dark-blue toque put on exactly right—not the sort of woman you ought to see in a Park with a great blubbering boy belonging to her. She looked a mother of sons, but not of a son of this kind, and should more properly, really, have been walking a dog. "Come on!" she said, as though the bridge, the poplars, the people staring were to be borne no longer. She began to walk on quickly, along the edge of the lake, parallel with the park's girdle of trees and the dark, haughty windows of Cornwall Terrace looking at her over the red may. They had meant to go to the Zoo, but now she had changed her mind: Frederick did not deserve the Zoo.

Frederick stumbled along beside her, too miserable to notice. His mother seldom openly punished him, but often revenged herself on him in small ways. He could feel how just this was. His own incontinence in the matter of tears was as shocking to him, as bowing-down, as annulling, as it could be to her. He never knew what happened—a cold black pit with no bottom opened inside himself; a red-hot bellwire jagged up through him from the pit of his frozen belly to the caves of his eyes. Then the hot gummy rush of tears, the convulsion of his features, the terrible square grin he felt his mouth take all made him his own shameful and squalid enemy. Despair howled round his inside like a wind, and through his streaming eyes he saw everything quake. Anyone's being there—and most of all his mother—drove this catastrophe on him. He never cried like this when he was alone.

Crying made him so abject, so outcast from other people that he went on crying out of despair. His crying was not just reflex, like a baby's; it dragged up all unseemliness into view. No wonder everyone was repelled. There is something about an abject person that rouses cruelty in the kindest breast. The plate-glass windows of the lordly houses looked at him through the may-trees with judges' eyes. Girls with their knees crossed, reading on the park benches, looked up with unkind smiles. His apathetic stumbling, his not seeing or caring that they had given up their trip to the Zoo, became more than Mrs. Dickinson, his mother, could bear. She pointed out, in a voice tense with dislike: "I'm not taking you to the Zoo."

"Mmmph-mmph-mmph," sobbed Frederick.

"You know, I so often wonder what your father would think."

"Mmmph-mmph-mmph."

"He used to be so proud of you. He and I used to look forward to what you'd be like when you were a big boy. One of the last things he ever said was: 'Frederick will take care of you.' You almost make me glad he's not here now."

"Oough-oough."

"What do you say?"

"I'm t-t-trying to stop."

"Everybody's looking at you, you know."

She was one of those women who have an unfailing sense of what not to say, and say it: despair, perversity or stubborn virtue must actuate them. She had a horror, also, of the abnormal and had to hit out at it before it could hit at her. Her husband, an R.A.F. pilot who had died two days after a ghastly crash, after two or three harrowing spaces of consciousness, had never made her ashamed or puzzled her. Their intimacies, then even his death, had had a bold naturalness.

"Listen, I shall walk on ahead," said Frederick's mother, lifting her chin with that noble, decided movement so many people liked. "You stay here and look at that duck till you've stopped that noise. Don't catch me up till you have. No, I'm really ashamed of you."

She walked on. He had *not* been making, really, so very much noise. Drawing choppy breaths, he stood still and looked at the duck that sat folded into a sleek white cypher on the green grassy margin of the lake. When it rolled one eye open over a curve, something unseeing in its expression calmed him. His mother walked away under the gay tree-shadows; her step quickened lightly, the tip of her fox fur swung. She thought of the lunch she had had with Major and Mrs. Williams, the party she would be going to at five. First, she must leave Frederick at Aunt Mary's, and what would Aunt Mary say to his bloated face? She walked fast; the gap between her and Frederick widened: she was a charming woman walking by herself.

Everybody had noticed how much courage she had; they said: "How plucky Mrs. Dickinson is." It was five years since her tragedy and she had not remarried, so that her gallantness kept on coming into play. She helped a friend with a little hat shop called *Isobel* near where they lived in Surrey, bred puppies for sale and gave the rest of her time to making a man of Frederick. She smiled nicely and carried her head high. Those two days while Toppy had lain dying she had hardly turned a hair, for his sake: no one knew when he might come conscious again. When she was not by his bed she was waiting about the hospital. The chaplain hanging about her and the doctor had given thanks that there were women like this; another officer's wife who had been her friend had said she was braver than could be good for anyone. When Toppy finally died the other woman had put the unflinching widow into a taxi and driven back with her to the Dickinsons' bungalow. She kept saying: "Cry, dear, cry: you'd feel better." She made tea and clattered about, repeating: "Don't mind me, darling: just have a big cry." The strain became so great that tears streamed down her own face. Mrs. Dickinson looked past her palely, with a polite smile. The empty-feeling bungalow with its rustling curtains still smelt of Toppy's pipe; his slippers were under a chair. Then Mrs. Dickinson's friend, almost tittering with despair, thought of a poem of Tennyson's she had learnt as a child. She said: "Where's Frederick? He's quiet. Do you think he's asleep?" The widow, rising, perfectly automatic, led her into the room where Frederick lay in his cot. A nursemaid rose from beside him, gave them one morbid look and scurried away. The two-year-old baby, flushed, and drawing up his upper lip in his sleep as his father used to do, lay curved under his blue blanket, clenching one fist on nothing. Something suddenly seemed to strike his mother, who, slumping down by the cot, ground her face and forehead into the fluffy blanket, then began winding the blanket round her two fists. Her convulsions, though proper, were fearful: the cot shook. The friend crept away into the kitchen, where she stayed an half-hour, muttering to the maid. They made more tea and waited for Mrs. Dickinson to give full birth to her grief. Then extreme silence drew them back to the cot. Mrs. Dickinson knelt asleep, her profile pressed to the blanket, one arm crooked over the baby's form. Under his mother's arm, as still as an image, Frederick lay wide awake, not making a sound. In conjunction with a certain look in his eyes, the baby's silence gave the two women the horrors. The servant said to the friend: "You would think he knew."

Mrs. Dickinson's making so few demands on pity soon rather alienated her women friends, but men liked her better for it: several of them found in her straight look an involuntary appeal to themselves alone, more exciting than coquetry, deeply, nobly exciting: several wanted to marry her. But courage had given her a new intractable kind of virgin pride: she loved it too much; she could never surrender it. "No, don't ask me that," she would say, lifting her chin and with that calm, gallant smile. "Don't spoil things. You've been splendid to me: such a support. But you see, there's Frederick. He's the man in my life now. I'm bound to put him first. That wouldn't be fair, would it?" After that, she would simply go on shaking her head. She became the perfect friend for men who wished to wish to marry but were just as glad not to, and for married men who liked just a little pathos without being upset.

Frederick had stopped crying. This left him perfectly blank, so that he stared at the duck with abstract intensity, perceiving its moulded feathers and porcelain-smooth neck. The burning, swirling film had cleared away from his eyes, and his diaphragm felt relief, as when retching has stopped. He forgot his focus of grief and forgot his mother, but saw with joy a quivering bough of willow that, drooping into his gaze under his swollen eyelids, looked as pure and strong as something after the Flood. His thought clutched at the willow, weak and wrecked but happy. He knew he was now qualified to walk after his mother, but without feeling either guilty or recalcitrant did not wish to do so. He stepped over the rail—no park keeper being at hand to stop him—and, tenderly and respectfully, attempted to touch the white duck's tail. Without a blink, with automatic uncoyness, the duck slid away from Frederick into the lake. Its lovely white china body balanced on the green glass water as it propelled itself gently round the curve of the bank. Frederick saw with a passion of observation its shadowy webbed feet lazily striking out.

"The keeper'll eat you," said a voice behind him.

Frederick looked cautiously round with his bunged-up eyes. The *individual* who had spoken sat on a park bench; it was a girl with a despatch case beside her. Her big bony knee-joints stuck out through her thin crepe-de-chine dress; she was hatless and her hair made a frizzy, pretty outline, but she wore spectacles, her skin had burnt dull red: her smile and the cock of her head had about them something pungent and energetic, not like a girl's at all. "Whatcher mean, eat me?"

"You're on his grass. And putting salt on his duck's tail."

Frederick stepped back carefully over the low rail. "I haven't got any salt." He looked up and down the walk: his mother was out of sight but from the direction of the bridge a keeper was approaching, still distant but with an awesome gait. "My goodness," the girl said, "what's been biting *you*?" Frederick was at a loss. "Here," she said, "have an apple." She opened her case, which was full of folded grease-paper that must have held sandwiches, and rummaged out an apple with a waxy, bright skin. Frederick came up, tentative as a pony, and finally took the apple. His breath was still hitching and catching; he did not wish to speak.

"Go on," she said, "swallow: it'll settle your chest. Where's your mother gone off to? What's all the noise about?" Frederick only opened his jaws as wide as they would go, then bit slowly, deeply into the apple. The girl re-crossed her legs and tucked her thin crepe-de-chine skirt round the other knee. "What had you done—cheeked her?"

Frederick swept the mouthful of apple into one cheek. "No," he said shortly. "Cried."

"I should say you did. Bellowed. I watched you all down the path." There was something ruminative in the girl's tone that made her remark really not at all offensive; in fact, she looked at Frederick as though she were meeting an artist who had just done a turn. He had been standing about, licking and biting the apple, but now he came and sat down at the other end of the bench. "How do you do it?" she said.

Frederick only turned away: his ears began burning again.

"What gets at you?" she said.

"Don't know."

"Someone coming it over you? I know another boy who cries like you, but he's older. He knots himself up and bellows."

"What's his name?"

"George."

"Does he go to school?"

"Oh, lord, no; he's a boy at the place where I used to work." She raised one arm, leaned back, and watched four celluloid bangles, each of a different colour, slide down it to her elbow joint, where they stuck. "He doesn't know why he does it," she said, "but he's got to. It's as though he saw something. You can't ask him. Some people take him that way: girls do. I never did. It's as if he knew about something he'd better not. I said once, well what just *is* it, and he said if he *could* tell me he wouldn't do it. I said, well, what's the *reason,* and he said, well, what's the reason not to? I knew him well at one time."

Frederick spat out two pips, looked round cautiously for the keeper, then dropped the apple-core down the back of the seat. "Where's George live?"

"I don't know now," she said, "I often wonder. I got sacked from that place where I used to work, and he went right off and I never saw him again. You snap out of that, if you can, before you are George's age. It does you no good. It's all in the way you see things. Look, there's your mother back. Better move, or there'll be *more* trouble." She held out her hand to Frederick, and when he put his in it shook hands so cheerfully, with such tough decision, that the four celluloid bangles danced on her wrist. "You and George," she said. "Funny to meet two of you. Well, good-bye, Henry: cheer up."

"I'm Frederick."

"Well, cheer up, Freddie."

As Frederick walked away, she smoothed down the sandwich papers inside her despatch case and snapped the case shut again. Then she put a finger under her hair at each side, to tuck her spectacles firmly down on her ears. Her mouth, an unreddened line across her harsh-burnt face, still wore the same truculent, homely smile. She crossed her arms under the flat chest, across her stomach, and sat there holding her elbows idly, wagging one foot in its fawn sandal, looking fixedly at the lake through her spectacles wondering about George. She had the afternoon, as she had no work. She saw George's face lifted abjectly from his arms on a table, blotchy over his clerk's collar. The eyes of George and Frederick seemed to her to be wounds in the world's surface, through which its inner, terrible, unassuageable, necessary sorrow constantly bled away and as constantly welled up.

Mrs. Dickinson came down the walk under the band of trees, carefully unanxious, looking lightly at objects to see if Frederick were near them; he had been a long time. Then she saw Frederick shaking hands with a sort of girl on a bench and starting to come her way. So she quickly turned her frank, friendly glance on the lake, down which, as though to greet her, a swam came swimming. She touched her fox fur lightly, sliding it up her shoulder. What a lovely mother to have. "Well, Frederick," she said, as he came into earshot, "coming?" Wind sent a puff of red mayflowers through the air. She stood still and waited for Frederick to come up. She could not think what to do now: they had an hour to put in before they were due at Aunt Mary's. But this only made her manner calmer and more decisive.

Frederick gave a great skip, opened his mouth wide, shouted: "Oo, I say, mother, I nearly caught a duck!"

"Frederick, dear, how silly you are: you couldn't."

"Oo, yes, I could, I could. If I'd had salt for its tail!" Years later, Frederick could still remember, with ease, pleasure and with a sense of lonely shame being gone, that calm white duck swimming off round the bank. But George's friend with the bangles, and George's trouble, fell through a cleft in his memory and were forgotten soon.

QUESTIONS

1. By what means is Mrs. Dickinson characterized? What kind of person is she? What are her chief motivations? Does she love her son?

2. Explain Mrs. Dickinson's behavior after her husband's death. Why has she not remarried?

3. In what respect are Frederick and his mother character foils? In what ways are Frederick's mother and the girl on the park bench character foils?

4. Why cannot Frederick cure himself of his habit of crying? In what way does his mother attempt to cure him? How does he feel toward his mother?

5. Is there any suggestion as to the origin of Frederick's crying?

6. Is Frederick a static or a dynamic character? What effect does his conversation with the girl have on him? Why? Why does he remember the duck years later?

7. The title is a literary allusion. If you are unable to explain it, look up the famous poem of Tennyson's that begins with those words. Literary allusions are a kind of literary shorthand: what does knowledge of this poem add to the meaning of the title and of the story?

8. On page 97 the "poem of Tennyson's" that Mrs. Dickinson's friend remembers is probably "Home they brought her warrior dead," another lyric from the same long work (*The Princess*) that contains the poem referred to in the title. Look it up. How does it relate to the situation in the story?

CHAPTER FOUR

Theme

"Daddy, the man next door kisses his wife every morning when he leaves for work. Why don't you do that?"

"Gracious, little one, I don't even know the woman."

"Daughter, your young man stays until a very late hour. Hasn't your mother said anything to you about this habit of his?"

"Yes, father. Mother says men haven't altered a bit."

For the reader who contemplates the two jokes above, a significant difference emerges between them. The first joke depends only upon a reversal of expectation. We expect the man to explain why he doesn't kiss his wife; instead he explains why he doesn't kiss his neighbor's wife. The second joke, though it contains a reversal of expectation, depends as much or more for its effectiveness on a truth about human life; namely, that *men tend to grow more conservative as they grow older,* or that *fathers often scold their children for doing exactly what they did themselves when young*. This truth, which might be stated in different ways, is the *theme* of the joke.

The THEME of a piece of fiction is its controlling idea or its central insight. It is the unifying generalization about life stated or implied by the story. To derive the theme of a story, we must ask what its central *purpose* is: what view of life it supports or what insight into life it reveals.

Not all stories have theme. The purpose of a horror story may be simply to scare the reader, to give him gooseflesh. The purpose of an adventure story may be simply to carry the reader through a series of exciting escapades. The purpose of a murder mystery may be simply to pose a problem for the reader to try to solve (and to prevent him from solving it, if possible, until the last paragraph). The purpose of some stories may be simply to provide suspense or to make the reader laugh or to surprise him with a sudden twist at the end. Theme exists only (1) when an author has seriously attempted to record life accurately or to reveal some truth about it or (2) when he has mechanically introduced some concept or theory of life into it that he uses as a unifying element and that his story is meant to illustrate. Theme exists in all interpretive fiction but only in some escape fiction. In interpretive fiction it is the purpose of the story; in escape fiction it is merely an excuse, a peg to hang the story from.

In many stories the theme may be equivalent to the revelation of human character. If a story has as its central purpose to exhibit a certain kind of human being, our statement of theme may be no more than a concentrated description of the person revealed, with the addition, "Some people are like this." Frequently, however, a story through its portrayal of specific persons in specific situations will have something to say about the nature of all men or about the relationship of human beings to each other or to the universe. Whatever central generalization about life arises from the specifics of the story constitutes theme.

The theme of a story, like its plot, may be stated very briefly or at greater length. With a simple or very brief story, we may be satisfied to sum up the theme in a single sentence. With a more complex story, if it is successfully unified, we can still state the theme in a single sentence, but we may feel that a paragraph—or occasionally even an essay—is needed to state it adequately. A rich story will give us many and complex insights into life. In stating the theme in a sentence, we must pick the *central* insight, the one that explains the greatest number of elements in the story and relates them to each other. For theme is what gives a good story its unity. In any story at all complex, however, we are likely to feel that a one-sentence statement of theme leaves out a great part of the story's meaning. Though the theme of *Othello* may be expressed as "Jealousy exacts a terrible cost," such a statement does not begin to suggest the range and depth of Shakespeare's play. Any successful story is a good deal more and means a good deal more than any one-sentence statement of theme that we may extract from it, for the story will modify and expand this statement in various and subtle ways.

We must never think, once we have stated the theme of a story, that the whole purpose of the story has been to yield up this abstract statement. If this were so, there would be no reason for the story: we could stop with the abstract statement. The function of the interpretive writer is not to state a theme but to vivify it. He wishes to deliver it not simply to our intellects but to our emotions, our senses, and our imaginations. The theme of a story may be little or nothing except as it is embodied and vitalized by the story. Unembodied, it is a dry backbone, without flesh or life.

Sometimes the theme of a story is explicitly stated somewhere in the story, either by the author or by one of the characters. In "Youth" the narrator Marlow makes several statements that, with slight editorial changes, would serve admirably as statements of theme. More often, however, the theme is implied. The story writer, after all, is a story writer, not an essayist or a philosopher. His first business is to reveal life, not to comment on it. He may well feel that unless the story somehow expresses its own meaning, without his having to point it out, he has not told the story well. Or he may feel that if the story is to have its maximum emotional effect, he must refrain from interrupting it or making remarks about it. He is also wary of spoiling a story for the perceptive reader by "explaining" it as some people ruin jokes by explaining them. For these reasons theme is more often left implicit than stated explicitly. The good writer does not ordinarily write a story to "illustrate" a theme, as does the writer of parables or fables. He writes the story to bring alive some segment of human existence. When he does so searchingly and coherently, theme arises naturally out of what he has written. The good reader may state the generalizations for himself.

Some readers—especially student readers—look for a "moral" in everything they read—some rule of conduct that they regard as applicable to their lives. They consider the words "theme" and "moral" to be interchangeable. Sometimes the words are interchangeable. Occasionally the theme of a story may be expressed as a moral principle without doing violence to the story. More frequently, however, the word "moral" is too narrow to fit the kind of illumination provided by a first-rate story. It is hardly suitable, for instance, for the kind of story that simply displays human character. Such terms as "moral" and "lesson" are therefore best avoided in the discussion of fiction. The critical term THEME is preferable for several reasons. First, it is less likely to obscure the fact that a story is not a preachment or a sermon: a story's *first* object is enjoyment. Second, it should keep us from trying to wring from every story a didactic pronouncement about life. The person who seeks a moral in every story is likely to oversimplify and conventionalize it—to reduce it to some dusty platitude like "Be kind to animals" or "Look before you leap" or "Crime does not pay." The purpose of the interpretive story writer is to give us a greater awareness and a greater understanding of life, not to inculcate a code of moral rules for regulating daily conduct. In getting at the theme of the story it is better to ask not *What does this story teach?*

but *What does this story reveal?* The reader who interprets Anderson's "I'm a Fool" as being merely a warning against lying has missed nine-tenths of the story. It is really a marvelously penetrating exploration of a complex personality. The theme is *not* "Honesty is the best policy" but something more like this: "A young man of respectable background who fails in various enterprises may develop ambivalent or contradictory values as well as feelings of inferiority. Consciously or unconsciously he will adopt various stratagems to compensate for these feelings by magnifying his importance both in his own eyes and in the eyes of others. If these stratagems backfire, he may recognize his folly but not the underlying reasons for it." Obviously, this dry statement is a poor thing beside the living reality of the story. But it is a more faithful abstracting of the content of the story than any "moral."

The revelation offered by a good story may be something fresh or something old. The story may bring us some insight into life that we had not had before, and thus expand our horizons, or it may make us *feel* or *feel again* some truth of which we have long been merely intellectually aware. We may know in our minds, for instance, that "War is horrible" or that "Old age is often pathetic and in need of understanding," but these are insights that need to be periodically renewed. *Emotionally* we may forget them, and, if we do, we are less alive and complete as human beings. The story writer performs a service for us—interprets life for us—whether he gives us new insights or refreshes and extends old ones.

The themes of commercial and quality stories may be identical, but frequently they are different. Commercial stories, for the most part, confirm their readers' prejudices, endorse their opinions, ratify their feelings, and satisfy their wishes. Usually, therefore, the themes of such stories are widely accepted platitudes of experience which may or may not be supported by the life around us. They represent life as we would like it to be, not always as it is. We should certainly like to believe, for instance, that "Motherhood is sacred," that "True love always wins through," that "Virtue and hard work are rewarded in the end," that "Cheaters never win," that "Old age brings a mellow wisdom that compensates for its infirmity," and that "Every human being has a soft spot in him somewhere." The interpretive writer, however, being a thoughtful observer of life, is likely to question these beliefs and often to challenge them. His ideas about life are not simply taken over ready-made from what he was taught in Sunday school or from the books he read as a child; they are the formulation of a sensitive and independent observer who has collated all that he has read and been taught with life itself. The themes of his stories therefore do not often correspond to the pretty little sentiments we find inscribed on candy valentines. They may sometimes represent rather somber truths. Much of the process of maturing as a reader lies in the discovery that there may be more nourishment and deeper enjoyment in assimilating these somber truths than in licking the sugar off of candy valentines.

We do not, however, have to accept the theme of an interpretive story any more than we do that of a commercial story. Though we should never summarily dismiss it without reflection, we may find that the theme of a story represents a judgment on life with which, on examination, we cannot agree. If it is the reasoned view of a seasoned and serious artist, nevertheless, it cannot be without value to us. There is value in knowing what the world looks like to other men, and we can thus use a judgment to expand our knowledge of human experience even though we cannot ourselves accept it. A genuine artist and thoughtful observer, moreover, can hardly fail to present us with partial insights along the way although we disagree with his total view. A good reader, therefore, will not reject a story because he rejects its theme. He can enjoy any story that arises from sufficient depth of observation and reflection and is artistically composed, though he disagrees with its theme; and he will prefer it to a shallower, less thoughtful, or less successfully integrated story that presents a theme he endorses.

Discovering and stating the theme of a story is often a delicate task. Sometimes we will *feel* what the story is about strongly enough and yet find it difficult to put this feeling into words. If we are skilled readers, it is perhaps unnecessary that we do so. The bare statement of the theme, so lifeless and impoverished when abstracted from the story, may seem to diminish the story to something less than it is. Often, however, the attempt to state a theme will reveal to us aspects of a story that we should otherwise not have noticed and will thereby lead to more thorough understanding. The ability to state theme, moreover, is a test of our understanding of a story. Beginning readers often think they understand a story when in actuality they have misunderstood it. They understand the events but not what the events add up to. Or, in adding up the events, they arrive at an erroneous total. People sometimes miss the point of a joke. It is not surprising that they should frequently miss the point of a good piece of fiction, which is many times more complex than a joke.

There is no prescribed method for discovering theme. Sometimes we can best get at it by asking in what way the main character has changed in the course of the story and what, if anything, he has learned before its end. Sometimes the best approach is to explore the nature of the central conflict and its outcome. Sometimes the title will provide an important clue. At all times we should keep in mind the following principles:

1. Theme must be expressible in the form of a statement with a subject and a predicate. It is insufficient to say that the theme of a story is motherhood or loyalty to country. Motherhood and loyalty are simply subjects. Theme must be a statement *about* the subject. For instance, "Motherhood sometimes has more frustrations than rewards" or "Loyalty to country often inspires heroic self-sacrifice." If we express the theme in the form of a phrase, the phrase must be convertible to sentence form. A phrase such as "the futility of envy," for instance, may be converted to the statement "Envy is futile": it may therefore serve as a statement of theme.

2. The theme must be stated as a *generalization* about life. In stating theme we do not use the names of the characters in the story, for to do so is to make a specific rather than a general statement. The theme of "Tears, Idle Tears" is not that "Frederick is cured of his irrational fits of crying after talking with the girl on the park bench." Rather, it is something like this: "A boy whose irrational behavior is only aggravated by attempts to make him feel guilty and ashamed may be cured when his behavior is accepted calmly and he learns that it is not unique."

3. We must be careful not to make the generalization larger than is justified by the terms of the story. Terms like *every, all, always* should be used very cautiously; terms like *some, sometimes, may* are often more accurate. The theme of "The Japanese Quince" is not that "Spring stirs vague longings in the hearts of all people," for we are presented with only two instances in the story. In this particular story, however, the two people, by their similarity in appearance, dress, and manner, are clearly meant to be representative of a social class, and, when we come to speak of how they respond to these stirrings, we may generalize a little more broadly. The theme might be expressed thus: "In springtime there occasionally comes to those upper-middle-class people whose lives are bound by respectability and regulated by convention a peculiar impulse toward life, freedom, and beauty; but the impulse is seldom strong enough to overcome the deep-seated forces of habit and convention." Notice that we have said *seldom,* not *never*. Only occasionally will the theme of a story be expressible as a universal generalization. In "Youth," since all four of Marlow's auditors nod affirmatively in answer to his final ques-

tion, we may well accept the theme of this story as having, if not universal, at least widespread application.

4. Theme is the *central* and *unifying* concept of the story. Therefore (a) it must account for all the major details of the story. If we cannot explain the bearing of an important incident or character on the theme, either in exemplifying it or modifying it in some way, it is probable that our interpretation is partial and incomplete, that at best we have got hold only of a subtheme. Another alternative, though it must be used with caution, is that the story itself is imperfectly constructed and lacks entire unity. (b) The theme must not be contradicted by any detail of the story. If we have to overlook or blink at or "force" the meaning of some significant detail in order to frame our statement, we may be sure that our statement is defective. (c) The theme must not rely upon supposed facts—facts not actually stated or clearly implied by the story. The theme must exist *inside,* not *outside,* the story. It must be based on the data of the story itself, not on assumptions supplied from our own experience.

5. There is no *one* way of stating the theme of a story. The story is not a guessing game or an acrostic that is supposed to yield some magic verbal formula that won't work if a syllable is changed. It merely presents a view of life, and, as long as the above conditions are fulfilled, that view may surely be stated in more than one way. Here, for instance, are three possible ways of stating the theme of "The Kiss." (a) "The emotions of a shy young man may spring almost entirely from fancy rather than from fact." (b) "A shy man who builds a romance upon a trifling incident may find that the return to reality disillusions and embitters him." (c) "A shy man is capable in his imagination of building up out of some trivial incident a fantastically absurd romantic dream life that he emotionally mistakes for reality at the same time that he intellectually knows it to be false; when the romantic bubble is pricked, he may plunge from the heights of ecstasy to the depths of despair, though in reality there has been no basis for either emotion." The third of these statements is fuller and therefore more precise than the first two, but each is a valid formulation.

6. We should avoid any statement that reduces the theme to some familiar saying that we have heard all our lives, such as "You can't judge a book by its cover" or "A stitch in time saves nine." Although such a statement *may* express the theme accurately, too often it is simply the lazy man's shortcut, which impoverishes the essential meaning of the story in order to save mental effort. When a reader forces every new

experience into an old formula, he loses the chance for a fresh perception. Instead of letting the story expand his knowledge and awareness of the world, he falls back dully on a cliché. To come out with "Honesty is the best policy" as the theme of "I'm a Fool" is almost to lose the whole value of the story. If the impulse arises to express the meaning of a story in a ready-made phrase, it should be suppressed.

Joseph Conrad

YOUTH

This could have occurred nowhere but in England, where men and sea interpenetrate, so to speak—the sea entering into the life of most men, and the men knowing something or everything about the sea, in the way of amusement, of travel, or of bread-winning.

We were sitting round a mahogany table that reflected the bottle, the claret glasses, and our faces as we leaned on our elbows. There was a director of companies, an accountant, a lawyer, Marlow, and myself. The director had been a *Conway* boy, the accountant had served four years at sea, the lawyer—a fine crusted Tory, High Churchman, the best of old fellows, the soul of honor—had been chief officer in the P. & O. service in the good old days when mail-boats were square-rigged at least on two masts, and used to come down the China Sea before a fair monsoon with stun'-sails set alow and aloft. We all began life in the merchant service. Between the five of us there was the strong bond of the sea, and also the fellowship of the craft, which no amount of enthusiasm for yachting, cruising, and so on can give, since one is only the amusement of life and the other is life itself.

Marlow (at least I think that is how he spelt his name) told the story, or rather the chronicle, of a voyage:

"Yes, I have seen a little of the Eastern seas; but what I remember best is my first voyage there. You fellows know there are those voyages that seem ordered for the illustration of life, that might stand for a symbol of existence. You fight, work, sweat, nearly kill yourself, sometimes do kill yourself, trying to accomplish something—and you can't. Not from any fault of yours. You simply can do nothing, neither great nor little—not a thing in the world—not even marry an old maid, or get a wretched 600-ton cargo of coal to its port of destination.

"It was altogether a memorable affair. It was my first voyage to the East, and my first voyage as second mate; it was also my skipper's first command.

YOUTH Reprinted from *Youth: A Narrative and Two Other Stories* by Joseph Conrad. Reprinted by permission of J. M. Dent and Sons, Ltd., London. Written in 1898.

You'll admit it was time. He was sixty if a day; a little man, with a broad, not very straight back, with bowed shoulders and one leg more bandy than the other, he had that queer twisted-about appearance you see so often in men who work in the fields. He had a nutcracker face—chin and nose trying to come together over a sunken mouth—and it was framed in iron-gray fluffy hair, that looked like a chin strap of cotton-wool sprinkled with coal dust. And he had blue eyes in that old face of his, which were amazingly like a boy's, with that candid expression some quite common men preserve to the end of their days by a rare internal gift of simplicity of heart and rectitude of soul. What induced him to accept me was a wonder. I had come out of a crack Australian clipper, where I had been third officer, and he seemed to have a prejudice against crack clippers as aristocratic and high-toned. He said to me, 'You know, in this ship you will have to work.' I said I had to work in every ship I had ever been in. 'Ah, but this is different, and you gentlemen out of them big ships; . . . but there! I dare say you will do. Join tomorrow.'

"I joined tomorrow. It was twenty-two years ago; and I was just twenty. How time passes! It was one of the happiest days of my life. Fancy! Second mate for the first time—a really responsible officer! I wouldn't have thrown up my new billet for a fortune. The mate looked me over carefully. He was also an old chap, but of another stamp. He had a Roman nose, a snow-white, long beard, and his name was Mahon, but he insisted that it should be pronounced Mann. He was well connected; yet there was something wrong with his luck, and he had never got on.

"As to the captain, he had been for years in coasters, then in the Mediterranean, and last in the West Indian trade. He had never been round the Capes. He could just write a kind of sketchy hand, and didn't care for writing at all. Both were thorough good seamen of course, and between those two old chaps I felt like a small boy between two grandfathers.

"The ship also was old. Her name was the *Judea*. Queer name, isn't it? She belonged to a man Wilmer, Wilcox—some name like that; but he has been bankrupt and dead these twenty years or more, and his name don't matter. She had been laid up in Shadwell basin for ever so long. You can imagine her state. She was all rust, dust, grime—soot aloft, dirt on deck. To me it was like coming out of a palace into a ruined cottage. She was about 400 tons, had a primitive windlass, wooden latches on the doors, not a bit of brass about her, and a big square stern. There was on it, below her name in big letters, a lot of scroll work, with the gilt off, and some sort of a coat of arms, with the motto 'Do or Die' underneath. I remember it took my fancy immensely. There was a touch of romance in it, something that made me love the old thing—something that appealed to my youth!

"We left London in ballast—sand ballast—to load a cargo of coal in a northern port for Bankok. Bankok! I thrilled. I had been six years at sea, but had only seen Melbourne and Sydney, very good places, charming places in their way—but Bankok!

"We worked out of the Thames under canvas, with a North Sea pilot on board. His name was Jermyn, and he dodged all day long about the galley drying his handkerchief before the stove. Apparently he never slept. He was a dismal man, with a perpetual tear sparkling at the end of his nose, who either had been in trouble, or was in trouble, or expected to be in trouble—couldn't be happy unless something went wrong. He mistrusted my youth, my common sense, and my seamanship, and made a point of showing it in a hundred little ways. I dare say he was right. It seems to me I knew very little then, and I know not much more now; but I cherish a hate for that Jermyn to this day.

"We were a week working up as far as Yarmouth Roads, and then we got into a gale—the famous October gale of twenty-two years ago. It was wind, lightning, sleet, snow, and a terrific sea. We were flying light, and you may imagine how bad it was when I tell you we had smashed bulwarks and a flooded deck. On the second night she shifted her ballast into the lee bow, and by that time we had been blown off somewhere on the Dogger Bank. There was nothing for it but go below with shovels and try to right her, and there we were in that vast hold, gloomy like a cavern, the tallow dips stuck and flickering on the beams, the gale howling above, the ship tossing about like mad on her side; there we all were, Jermyn, the captain, everyone, hardly able to keep our feet, engaged on that gravedigger's work, and trying to toss shovelfuls of wet sand up to windward. At every tumble of the ship you could see vaguely in the dim light men falling down with a great flourish of shovels. One of the ship's boys (we had two), impressed by the weirdness of the scene, wept as if his heart would break. We could hear him blubbering somewhere in the shadows.

"On the third day the gale died out, and by-and-by a north-country tug picked us up. We took sixteen days in all to get from London to the Tyne! When we got into dock we had lost our turn for loading, and they hauled us off to a tier where we remained for a month. Mrs. Beard (the captain's name was Beard) came from Colchester to see the old man. She lived on board. The crew of runners had left, and there remained only the officers, one boy, and the steward, a mulatto who answered to the name of Abraham. Mrs. Beard was an old woman, with a face all wrinkled and ruddy like a winter apple, and the figure of a young girl. She caught sight of me once, sewing on a button, and insisted on having my shirts to repair. This was something different from the captains' wives I had known on board crack clippers. When I brought her the shirts, she said: 'And the socks? They want mending, I am sure, and John's—Captain Beard's—things are all in order now. I would be glad of something to do.' Bless the old woman. She overhauled my outfit for me, and meantime I read for the first time 'Sartor Resartus' and Burnaby's 'Ride to Khiva.' I didn't understand much of the first then; but I remember I preferred the soldier to the philosopher at the time; a preference which life has only confirmed. One was a man, and the other was either more—or less. However, they are both dead, and Mrs.

Beard is dead, and youth, strength, genius, thoughts, achievements, simple hearts—all die . . . No matter.

"They loaded us at last. We shipped a crew. Eight able seamen and two boys. We hauled off one evening to the buoys at the dock-gates, ready to go out, and with a fair prospect of beginning the voyage next day. Mrs. Beard was to start for home by a late train. When the ship was fast we went to tea. We sat rather silent through the meal—Mahon, the old couple, and I. I finished first, and slipped away for a smoke, my cabin being in a deck-house just against the poop. It was high water, blowing fresh with a drizzle; the double dock-gates were opened, and the steam colliers were going in and out in the darkness with their lights burning bright, a great plashing of propellers, rattling of winches, and a lot of hailing on the pier-heads. I watched the procession of headlights gliding high and of green lights gliding low in the night, when suddenly a red gleam flashed at me, vanished, came into view again, and remained. The fore-end of a steamer loomed up close. I shouted down the cabin, 'Come up, quick!' and then heard a startled voice saying afar in the dark, 'Stop her, sir.' A bell jingled. Another voice cried warningly, 'We are going right into that bark, sir.' The answer to this was a gruff 'All right,' and the next thing was a heavy crash as the steamer struck a glancing blow with the bluff of her bow about our fore-rigging. There was a moment of confusion, yelling, and running about. Steam roared. Then somebody was heard saying, 'All clear, sir.' . . . 'Are you all right?' asked the gruff voice. I had jumped forward to see the damage, and hailed back, 'I think so.' 'Easy astern,' said the gruff voice. A bell jingled. 'What steamer is that?' screamed Mahon. By that time she was no more to us than a bulky shadow maneuvering a little way off. They shouted at us some name—a woman's name, Miranda or Melissa—or some such thing. 'This means another month in this beastly hole,' said Mahon to me, as we peered with lamps about the splintered bulwarks and broken braces. 'But where's the captain?'

"We had not heard or seen anything of him all that time. We went aft to look. A doleful voice arose hailing somewhere in the middle of the dock, '*Judea* ahoy!' . . . How the devil did he get there? . . . 'Hallo!' we shouted. 'I am adrift in our boat without oars,' he cried. A belated waterman offered his services, and Mahon struck a bargain with him for half-a-crown to tow our skipper alongside; but it was Mrs. Beard that came up the ladder first. They had been floating about the dock in that mizzly cold rain for nearly an hour. I was never so surprised in my life.

"It appears that when he heard my shout 'Come up,' he understood at once what was the matter, caught up his wife, ran on deck, and across, and down into our boat, which was fast to the ladder. Not bad for a sixty-year-old. Just imagine that old fellow saving heroically in his arms that old woman—the woman of his life. He set her down on a thwart, and was ready to climb back on board when the painter came adrift somehow, and away they went together. Of course in the confusion we did not hear him shouting. He looked abashed. She said cheerfully, 'I suppose it does not matter my losing the train now?' 'No, Jenny—you go below and get warm,' he growled. Then to us: 'A sailor has no business with a wife—I say. There I was, out of the ship. Well, no harm done this time. Let's go and look at what that fool of a steamer smashed.'

"It wasn't much, but it delayed us three weeks. At the end of that time, the captain being engaged with his agents, I carried Mrs. Beard's bag to the railway station and put her all comfy into a third-class carriage. She lowered the window to say, 'You are a good young man. If you see John—Captain Beard—without his muffler at night, just remind him from me to keep his throat well wrapped up.' 'Certainly, Mrs. Beard,' I said. 'You are a good young man; I noticed how attentive you are to John—to Captain—' The train pulled out suddenly; I took my cap off to the old woman: I never saw her again . . . Pass the bottle.

"We went to sea next day. When we made that start for Bankok we had been already three months out of London. We had expected to be a fortnight or so—at the outside.

"It was January, and the weather was beautiful—the beautiful sunny winter weather that has more charm than in the summertime, because it is unexpected, and crisp, and you know it won't, it can't, last long. It's like a windfall, like a godsend, like an unexpected piece of luck.

"It lasted all down the North Sea, all down Channel; and it lasted till we were three hundred miles or so to the westward of the Lizards: then the wind went round to the sou'west and began to pipe up. In two days it blew a gale. The *Judea,* hove to, wallowed on the Atlantic like an old candlebox. It blew day after day: it blew with spite, without interval, without mercy, without rest. The world was nothing but an immensity of great foaming waves rushing at us, under a sky low enough to touch with the hand and dirty like a smoked ceiling. In the stormy space surrounding us there was as much flying spray as air. Day after day and night after night there was nothing round the ship but the howl of the wind, the tumult of the sea, the noise of water pouring over her deck. There was no rest for her and no rest for us. She tossed, she pitched, she stood on her head, she sat on her tail, she rolled, she groaned, and we had to hold on while on deck and cling to our bunks when below, in a constant effort of body and worry of mind.

"One night Mahon spoke through the small window of my berth. It opened right into my very bed, and I was lying there sleepless, in my boots, feeling as though I had not slept for years, and could not if I tried. He said excitedly—

" 'You got the sounding-rod in here, Marlow? I can't get the pumps to suck. By God! it's no child's play.'

"I gave him the sounding-rod and lay down again, trying to think of various things—but I thought only of the pumps. When I came on deck they were still at it, and my watch relieved at the pumps. By the light of the lantern brought on deck to examine the sounding-rod I caught a glimpse of their weary, serious faces. We pumped all the four hours. We pumped all night, all day, all the week,—watch and watch. She was working herself loose, and leaked badly—not enough to drown us at once, but enough to kill us with the work at the pumps. And while we pumped the ship was going from us piecemeal: the bulwarks went, the stanchions were torn out, the ventilators smashed, the cabin door burst in. There was not a dry spot in the ship. She was being gutted bit by bit. The longboat changed, as if by magic, into matchwood where she stood in her gripes. I had lashed her myself, and was rather proud of my handiwork, which had withstood so long the malice of the sea. And we pumped. And there was no break in the weather. The sea was white like a sheet of foam, like a caldron of boiling milk; there was not a break in the clouds, no—not the size of a man's hand—no, not for so much as ten seconds. There was for us no sky, there were for us no stars, no sun, no universe—nothing but angry clouds and an infuriated sea. We pumped watch and watch, for dear life; and it seemed to last for months, for years, for all eternity, as though we had been dead and gone to a hell for sailors. We forgot the day of the week, the name of the month, what year it was, and whether we had ever been ashore. The sails blew away, she lay broadside on under a weather-cloth, the ocean poured over her, and we did not care. We turned those handles, and had the eyes of idiots. As soon as we had crawled on deck I used to take a round turn with a rope about the men, the pumps, and the mainmast, and we turned, we turned incessantly, with the water to our waists, to our necks, over our heads. It was all one. We had forgotten how it felt to be dry.

"And there was somewhere in me the thought: By Jove! this is the deuce of an adventure—something you read about; and it is my first voyage as second mate—and I am only twenty—and here I am lasting it out as well as any of these men, and keeping my chaps up to the mark. I was pleased. I would not have given up the experience for worlds. I had moments of exultation. Whenever the old dismantled craft pitched heavily with her counter high in the air, she seemed to me to throw up, like an appeal, like a defiance, like a cry to the clouds without mercy, the words written on her stern: '*Judea,* London. Do or Die.'

"O youth! The strength of it, the faith of it, the imagination of it! To me she was not an old rattletrap carting about the world a lot of coal for a freight—to me she was the endeavor, the test, the trial of life. I think of her with pleasure, with affection, with regret—as you would think of someone dead you have loved. I shall never forget her . . . Pass the bottle.

"One night when, tied to the mast, as I explained, we were pumping on, deafened with the wind, and without spirit enough in us to wish ourselves dead, a heavy sea crashed aboard and swept clean over us. As soon as I got my breath I shouted, as in duty bound, 'Keep on, boys!' when suddenly I felt something hard floating on deck strike the calf of my leg. I made a grab at it and missed. It was so dark we could not see each other's faces within a foot—you understand.

"After that thump the ship kept quiet for a while, and the thing, whatever it was, struck my leg again. This time I caught it—and it was a saucepan. At first, being stupid with fatigue and thinking of nothing but the pumps, I did not understand what I had in my hand. Suddenly it dawned upon me, and I shouted, 'Boys, the house on deck is gone. Leave this, and let's look for the cook.'

"There was a deckhouse forward, which contained the galley, the cook's berth, and the quarters of the crew. As we had expected for days to see it swept away, the hands had been ordered to sleep in the cabin—the only safe place in the ship. The steward, Abraham, however, persisted in clinging to his berth, stupidly, like a mule—from sheer fright I believe, like an animal that won't leave a stable falling in an earthquake. So we went to look for him. It was chancing death, since once out of our lashings we were as exposed as if on a raft. But we went. The house was shattered as if a shell had exploded inside. Most of it had gone overboard—stove, men's quarters, and their property, all was gone; but two posts, holding a portion of the bulkhead to which Abraham's bunk was attached, remained as if by a miracle. We groped in the ruins and came upon this, and there he was, sitting in his bunk, surrounded by foam and wreckage, jabbering cheerfully to himself. He was out of his mind; completely and for ever mad, with this sudden shock coming upon the fag-end of his endurance. We snatched him up, lugged him aft, and pitched him head-first down the cabin companion. You understand there was no time to carry him down with infinite precautions and wait to see how he got on. Those below would pick him up at the bottom of the stairs all right. We were in a hurry to go back to the pumps. That business could not wait. A bad leak is an inhuman thing.

"One would think that the sole purpose of that fiendish gale had been to make a lunatic of that poor devil of a mulatto. It eased before morning, and next day the sky cleared, and as the sea went down the leak took up. When it came to bending a fresh set of sails the crew demanded to put back—and really there was nothing else to do. Boats gone, decks swept clean, cabin gutted, men without a stitch but what they stood in, stores spoiled, ship strained. We put her head for home, and—would you believe it? The wind came east right in our teeth. It blew fresh, it blew continuously. We had to beat up every inch of the way, but she did not leak so badly, the water keeping comparatively smooth. Two hours' pumping in every four is no joke—but it kept her afloat as far as Falmouth.

"The good people there live on casualties of the sea, and no doubt were glad to see us. A hungry crowd of shipwrights sharpened their chisels at the sight of that carcass of a ship. And, by Jove! they had pretty pickings off us before they were done. I fancy the owner was already in a tight place. There were delays. Then it was decided to take part of the cargo out and calk her topsides. This was done, the repairs finished, cargo reshipped; a new crew came on board, and we went out—for Bankok. At the end of a week we were back again. The crew said they weren't going to Bankok—a hundred and fifty days' passage—in a something hooker that wanted pumping eight hours out of the twenty-four; and the nautical papers inserted again the little paragraph: '*Judea.* Bark. Tyne to Bankok; coals; put back to Falmouth leaky and with crew refusing duty.'

"There were more delays—more tinkering. The owner came down for a day, and said she was as right as a little fiddle. Poor old Captain Beard looked like the ghost of a Geordie skipper—through the worry and humiliation of it. Remember he was sixty, and it was his first command. Mahon said it was a foolish business, and would end badly. I loved the ship more than ever, and wanted awfully to get to Bankok. To Bankok! Magic name, blessed name. Mesopotamia wasn't a patch on it. Remember I was twenty, and it was my first second mate's billet, and the East was waiting for me.

"We went out and anchored in the outer roads with a fresh crew—the third. She leaked worse than ever. It was as if those confounded shipwrights had actually made a hole in her. This time we did not even go outside. The crew simply refused to man the windlass.

"They towed us back to the inner harbor, and we became a fixture, a feature, an institution of the place. People pointed us out to visitors as 'That 'ere bark that's going to Bankok—has been here six months—put back three times.' On holidays the small boys pulling about in boats would hail, '*Judea,* ahoy!' and if a head showed above the rail shouted, 'Where you bound to?—Bankok?' and jeered. We were only three on board. The poor old skipper mooned in the cabin. Mahon undertook the cooking, and unexpectedly developed all a Frenchman's genius for preparing nice little messes. I looked languidly after the rigging. We became citizens of Falmouth. Every shopkeeper knew us. At the barber's or tobacconist's they asked familiarly, 'Do you think you will ever get to Bankok?' Meantime the owner, the underwriters, and the charterers squabbled amongst themselves in London, and our pay went on . . . Pass the bottle.

"It was horrid. Morally it was worse than pumping for life. It seemed as though we had been forgotten by the world, belonged to nobody, would get nowhere; it seemed that, as if bewitched, we would have to live for ever and ever in that inner harbor, a derision and a byword to generations of longshore loafers and dishonest boatmen. I obtained three months' pay and a five days' leave, and made a rush for London. It took me a day to get there and pretty well another to come back—but three months' pay went all the same. I don't know what I did with it. I went to a music hall, I believe, lunched, dined, and supped in a swell place in Regent Street, and was back to time, with nothing but a complete set of Byron's works and a new railway rug to show for three months' work. The boatman who pulled me off to the ship said: 'Hallo! I thought you had left the old thing. *She* will never get to Bankok.' 'That's all *you* know about it,' I said scornfully—but I didn't like that prophecy at all.

"Suddenly a man, some kind of agent to somebody, appeared with full powers. He had grog blossoms all over his face, an indomitable energy, and was a jolly soul. We leaped into life again. A hulk came alongside, took our cargo, and then we went into dry dock to get our copper stripped. No wonder she leaked. The poor thing, strained beyond endurance by the gale, had, as if in disgust, spat out all the oakum of her lower seams. She was recalked, new coppered, and made as tight as a bottle. We went back to the hulk and reshipped our cargo.

"Then on a fine moonlight night, all the rats left the ship.

"We had been infested with them. They had destroyed our sails, consumed more stores than the crew, affably shared our beds and our dangers, and now, when the ship was made seaworthy, concluded to clear out. I called Mahon to enjoy the spectacle. Rat after rat appeared on our rail, took a last look over his shoulder, and leaped with a hollow thud into the empty hulk. We tried to count them, but soon lost the tale. Mahon said: 'Well, well! don't talk to me about the intelligence of rats. They ought to have left before, when we had that narrow squeak from foundering. There you have the proof how silly is the superstition about them. They leave a good ship for an old rotten hulk, where there is nothing to eat, too, the fools! . . . I don't believe they know what is safe or what is good for them, any more than you or I.'

"And after some more talk we agreed that the wisdom of rats had been grossly overrated, being in fact no greater than that of men.

"The story of the ship was known, by this, all up the Channel from Land's End to the Forelands, and we could get no crew on the south coast. They sent us one all complete from Liverpool, and we left once more—for Bankok.

"We had fair breezes, smooth water right into the tropics, and the old *Judea* lumbered along in the sunshine. When she went eight knots everything cracked aloft, and we tied our caps to our heads; but mostly she strolled on at the rate of three miles an hour. What could you expect? She was tired—that old ship. Her youth was where mine is—where yours is—you fellows who listen to this yarn; and what friend would throw your years and your weariness in your face? We didn't grumble at her. To us aft, at least, it seemed as though we had been born in her, reared in her, had lived in her for ages, had never known any other ship. I would just as soon have abused the old village church at home for not being a cathedral.

"And for me there was also my youth to make me patient. There was all the East before me, and all life, and the thought that I had been tried in that ship and had come out pretty well. And I thought of men of old who, centuries ago, went that road in ships that sailed no better, to the land of palms, and spices, and yellow sands, and of brown nations ruled by kings more cruel than Nero the Roman and more splendid than Solomon the Jew. The old bark lumbered on, heavy with her age and the burden of her cargo, while I lived the life of youth in ignorance and hope. She lumbered on through an interminable procession of days; and the fresh gilding flashed back at the setting sun, seemed to cry out over the darkening sea the words painted on her stern, '*Judea,* London. Do or Die.'

"Then we entered the Indian Ocean and steered northerly for Java Head. The winds were light. Weeks slipped by. She crawled on, do or die, and people at home began to think of posting us as overdue.

"One Saturday evening, I being off duty, the men asked me to give them an extra bucket of water or so—for washing clothes. As I did not wish to screw on the fresh-water pump so late, I went forward whistling, and with a key in my hand to unlock the forepeak scuttle, intending to serve the water out of a spare tank we kept there.

"The smell down below was as unexpected as it was frightful. One would have thought hundreds of paraffin lamps had been flaring and smoking in that hole for days. I was glad to get out. The man with me coughed and said, 'Funny smell, sir.' I answered negligently, 'It's good for the health, they say,' and walked aft.

"The first thing I did was to put my head down the square of the midship ventilator. As I lifted the lid a visible breath, something like a thin fog, a puff of faint haze, rose from the opening. The ascending air was hot, and had a heavy, sooty, paraffiny smell. I gave one sniff, and put down the lid gently. It was no use choking myself. The cargo was on fire.

"Next day she began to smoke in earnest. You see it was to be expected, for though the coal was of a safe kind, that cargo had been so handled, so broken up with handling, that it looked more like smithy coal than anything else. Then it had been wetted—more than once. It rained all the time we were taking it back from the hulk, and now with this long passage it got heated, and there was another case of spontaneous combustion.

"The captain called us into the cabin. He had a chart spread on the table, and looked unhappy. He said, 'The coast of West Australia is near, but I mean to proceed to our destination. It is the hurricane month too; but we will just keep her head for Bankok, and fight the fire. No more putting back anywhere, if we all get roasted. We will try first to stifle this 'ere damned combustion by want of air.'

"We tried. We battened down everything, and still she smoked. The smoke kept coming out through imperceptible crevices; it forced itself through bulkheads and covers; it oozed here and there and everywhere in slender threads, in an invisible film, in an incomprehensible manner. It made its way into the cabin, into the forecastle; it poisoned the sheltered places on the deck; it could be sniffed as high as the mainyard. It was clear that if the smoke came out the air came in. This was disheartening. This combustion refused to be stifled.

"We resolved to try water, and took the hatches off. Enormous volumes of smoke, whitish, yellowish, thick, greasy, misty, choking, ascended as high as the trucks. All hands cleared out aft. Then the poisonous cloud blew away, and we went back to work in a smoke that was no thicker now than that of an ordinary factory chimney.

"We rigged the force pump, got the hose along, and by-and-by it burst. Well, it was as old as the ship—a prehistoric hose, and past repair. Then we pumped with the feeble head-pump, drew water with buckets, and in this way managed in time to pour lots of Indian Ocean into the main hatch. The bright stream flashed in sunshine, fell into a layer of white crawling smoke, and vanished on the black surface of coal. Steam ascended mingling with the smoke. We poured salt water as into a barrel without a bottom. It was our fate to pump in that ship, to pump out of her, to pump into her; and after keeping water out of her to save ourselves from being drowned, we frantically poured water into her to save ourselves from being burnt.

"And she crawled on, do or die, in the serene weather. The sky was a miracle of purity, a miracle of azure. The sea was polished, was blue, was pellucid, was sparkling like a precious stone, extending on all sides, all round to the horizon—as if the whole terrestrial globe had been one jewel, one colossal sapphire, a single gem fashioned into a planet. And on the luster of the great calm waters the *Judea* glided imperceptibly, enveloped in languid and unclean vapors, in a lazy cloud that drifted to leeward, light and slow: a pestiferous cloud defiling the splendor of sea and sky.

"All this time of course we saw no fire. The cargo smoldered at the bottom somewhere. Once Mahon, as we were working side by side, said to me with a queer smile: 'Now, if she only would spring a tidy leak—like that time when we first left the Channel—it would put a stopper on this fire. Wouldn't it?' I remarked irrelevantly, 'Do you remember the rats?'

"We fought the fire and sailed the ship too as carefully as though nothing had been the matter. The steward cooked and attended on us. Of the other twelve men, eight worked while four rested. Everyone took his turn, captain included. There was equality, and if not exactly fraternity, then a deal of good feeling. Sometimes a man, as he dashed a bucketful of water down the hatchway, would yell out, 'Hurrah for Bankok!' and the rest laughed. But generally we were taciturn and serious—and thirsty. Oh! how thirsty! And we had to be careful with the water. Strict allowance. The ship smoked, the sun blazed . . . Pass the bottle.

"We tried everything. We even made an attempt to dig down to the fire. No good, of course. No man could remain more than a minute below. Mahon, who went first, fainted there, and the man who went to fetch him out did likewise. We lugged them out on deck. Then I leaped down to show how easily it could be done. They had learned wisdom by that time, and contented themselves by fishing for me with a chain-hook tied to a broom handle, I believe. I did not offer to go and fetch up my shovel, which was left down below.

"Things began to look bad. We put the longboat into the water. The second boat was ready to swing out. We had also another, a fourteen-foot thing, on davits aft, where it was quite safe.

"Then behold, the smoke suddenly decreased. We redoubled our efforts to flood the bottom of the ship. In two days there was no smoke at all. Everybody was on the broad grin. This was on a Friday. On Saturday no work, but sailing the ship of course was done. The men washed their clothes and their faces for the first time in a fortnight, and had a special dinner given them. They spoke of spontaneous combustion with contempt, and implied *they* were the boys to put out combustions. Somehow we all felt as though we each had inherited a large fortune. But a beastly smell of burning hung about the ship. Captain Beard had hollow eyes and sunken cheeks. I had never noticed so much before how twisted and bowed he was. He and Mahon prowled soberly about hatches and ventilators, sniffing. It struck me suddenly poor Mahon was a very, very old chap. As to me, I was as pleased and proud as though I had helped to win a great naval battle. O! Youth!

"The night was fine. In the morning a homeward-bound ship passed us hull down—the first we had seen for months; but we were nearing the land at last, Java Head being about 190 miles off, and nearly due north.

"Next day it was my watch on deck from eight to twelve. At breakfast the captain observed, 'It's wonderful how that smell hangs about the cabin.' About ten, the mate being on the poop, I stepped down on the main deck for a moment. The carpenter's bench stood abaft the mainmast: I leaned against it sucking at my pipe, and the carpenter, a young chap, came to talk to me. He remarked, 'I think we have done very well, haven't we?' and then I perceived with annoyance the fool was trying to tilt the bench. I said curtly, 'Don't, Chips,' and immediately became aware of a queer sensation, of an absurd delusion—I seemed somehow to be in the air. I heard all round me like a pent-up breath released—as if a thousand giants simultaneously had said Phoo!—and felt a dull concussion which made my ribs ache suddenly. No doubt about it—I was in the air, and my body was describing a short parabola. But short as it was, I had the time to think several thoughts in, as far as I can remember, the following order: 'This can't be the carpenter—What is it?—Some accident—Submarine volcano?—Coals, gas!—By Jove! we are being blown up—Everybody's dead—I am falling into the afterhatch—I see fire in it.'

"The coal dust suspended in the air of the hold had glowed dull red at the moment of the explosion. In the twinkling of an eye, in an infinitesimal fraction of a second since the first tilt of the bench, I was sprawling full length on the cargo. I picked myself up and scrambled out. It was quick like a rebound. The deck was a wilderness of smashed timber, lying crosswise like trees in a wood after a hurricane; an immense curtain of soiled rags waved gently before me—it was the mainsail blown to strips. I thought, The masts will be toppling over directly; and to get out of the way bolted on all fours towards the poop-ladder. The first person I saw was Mahon, with eyes like saucers, his mouth open, and the long white hair standing straight on end round his head like a silver halo. He was just about to go down when the sight of the main deck stirring, heaving up, and changing into splinters before his eyes, petrified him on the top step. I stared at him in unbelief, and he stared at me with a queer kind of shocked curiosity. I did not know that I had no hair, no eyebrows, no eyelashes, that my young mustache was burnt off, that my face was black, one cheek laid open, my nose cut, and my chin bleeding. I had lost my cap, one of my slippers, and my shirt was torn to rags. Of all this I was not aware. I was amazed to see the ship still afloat, the poop-deck whole—and, most of all, to see anybody alive. Also the peace of the sky and the serenity of the sea were distinctly surprising. I suppose I expected to see them convulsed with horror . . . Pass the bottle.

"There was a voice hailing the ship from somewhere—in the air, in the sky—I couldn't tell. Presently I saw the captain—and he was mad. He asked me eagerly, 'Where's the cabin-table?' and to hear such a question was a frightful shock. I had just been blown up, you understand, and vibrated with that experience—I wasn't quite sure whether I was alive. Mahon began to stamp with both feet and yelled at him, 'Good God! don't you see the deck's blown out of her?' I found my voice, and stammered out as if conscious of some gross neglect of duty, 'I don't know where the cabin-table is.' It was like an absurd dream.

"Do you know what he wanted next? Well, he wanted to trim the yards. Very placidly, and as if lost in thought, he insisted on having the foreyard squared. 'I don't know if there's anybody alive,' said Mahon, almost tearfully. 'Surely,' he said gently, 'there will be enough left to square the foreyard.'

"The old chap, it seems, was in his own berth, winding up the chronometers, when the shock sent him spinning. Immediately it occurred to him—as he said afterwards—that the ship had struck something, and he ran out into the cabin. There, he saw, the cabin-table had vanished somewhere. The deck being blown up, it had fallen down into the lazarette of course. Where we had our breakfast that morning he saw only a great hole in the floor. This appeared to him so awfully mysterious, and impressed him so immensely, that what he saw and heard after he got on deck were mere trifles in comparison. And, mark, he noticed directly the wheel deserted and his bark off her course—and his only thought was to get that miserable, stripped, undecked, smoldering shell of a ship back again with her head pointing at her port of destination. Bankok! That's what he was after. I tell you this quiet, bowed, bandy-legged, almost deformed little man was immense in the singleness of his idea and in his placid ignorance of our agitation. He motioned us forward with a commanding gesture, and went to take the wheel himself.

"Yes: that was the first thing we did—trim the yards of that wreck! No one was killed, or even disabled, but everyone was more or less hurt. You should have seen them! Some were in rags, with black faces, like coal-heavers, like sweeps, and had bullet heads that seemed closely cropped, but were in fact singed to the skin. Others, of the watch below, awakened by being shot out from their collapsing bunks, shivered incessantly, and kept on groaning even as we went about our work. But they all worked. That crew of Liverpool hard cases had in them the right stuff. It's my experience they always have. It is the sea that gives it—the vastness, the loneliness surrounding their dark stolid souls. Ah! Well! we stumbled, we crept, we fell, we barked our shins on the wreckage, we hauled. The masts stood, but we did not know how much they might be charred down below. It was nearly calm, but a long swell ran from the west and made her roll. They might go at any moment. We looked at them with apprehension. One could not foresee which way they would fall.

"Then we retreated aft and looked about us. The deck was a tangle of planks on edge, of planks on end, of splinters, of ruined woodwork. The masts rose from that chaos like big trees above a matted undergrowth. The interstices of that mass of wreckage were full of something whitish, sluggish, stirring—of something that was like a greasy fog. The smoke of the invisible fire was coming up again, was trailing, like a poisonous thick mist in some valley choked with dead wood. Already lazy wisps were beginning to curl upwards amongst the mass of splinters. Here and there a piece of timber, stuck upright, resembled a post. Half of a fife-rail had been shot through the foresail, and the sky made a patch of glorious blue in the ignobly soiled canvas. A portion of several boards holding together had fallen across the rail, and one end protruded overboard, like a gangway leading upon nothing, like a gangway leading over the deep sea, leading to death—as if inviting us to walk the plank at once and be done with our ridiculous troubles. And still the air, the sky—a ghost, something invisible was hailing the ship.

"Someone had the sense to look over, and there was the helmsman, who had impulsively jumped overboard, anxious to come back. He yelled and swam lustily like a merman, keeping up with the ship. We threw him a rope, and presently he stood amongst us streaming with water and very crestfallen. The captain had surrendered the wheel, and apart, elbow on rail and chin in hand, gazed at the sea wistfully. We asked ourselves, What next? I thought, Now, this is something like. This is great. I wonder what will happen. O youth!

"Suddenly Mahon sighted a steamer far astern. Captain Beard said, 'We may do something with her yet.' We hoisted two flags, which said in the international language of the sea, 'On fire. Want immediate assistance.' The steamer grew bigger rapidly, and by-and-by spoke with two flags on her foremast, 'I am coming to your assistance.'

"In half an hour she was abreast, to windward, within hail, and rolling slightly, with her engines stopped. We lost our composure, and yelled all together with excitement, 'We've been blown up.' A man in a white helmet, on the bridge, cried, 'Yes! All right! all right!' and he nodded his head, and smiled, and made soothing motions with his hand as though at a lot of frightened children. One of the boats dropped in the water, and walked towards us upon the sea with her long oars. Four Calashes pulled a swinging stroke. This was my first sight of Malay seamen. I've known them since, but what struck me then was their unconcern: they came alongside, and even the bowman standing up and holding to our main-chains with the boat-hook did not deign to lift his head for a glance. I thought people who had been blown up deserved more attention.

"A little man, dry like a chip and agile like a monkey, clambered up. It was the mate of the steamer. He gave one look, and cried, 'O boys—you had better quit.'

"We were silent. He talked apart with the captain for a time—seemed to argue with him. Then they went away together to the steamer.

"When our skipper came back we learned that the steamer was the *Sommerville,* Captain Nash, from West Australia to Singapore via Batavia with mails, and that the agreement was she should tow us to Anjer or Batavia, if possible, where we could extinguish the fire by scuttling, and then proceed on our voyage—to Bankok! The old man seemed excited. 'We will do it yet,' he said to Mahon, fiercely. He shook his fist at the sky. Nobody else said a word.

"At noon the steamer began to tow. She went ahead slim and high, and what was left of the *Judea* followed at the end of seventy fathom of tow-rope—followed her swiftly like a cloud of smoke with mastheads protruding above. We went aloft to furl the sails. We coughed on the yards, and were careful about the bunts. Do you see the lot of us there, putting a neat furl on the sails of that ship doomed to arrive nowhere? There was not a man who didn't think that at any moment the masts would topple over. From aloft we could not see the ship for smoke, and they worked carefully, passing the gaskets with even turns. 'Harbor furl—aloft there!' cried Mahon from below.

"You understand this? I don't think one of those chaps expected to get down in the usual way. When we did I heard them saying to each other, 'Well, I thought we would come down overboard, in a lump—sticks and all—blame me if I didn't.' 'That's what I was thinking to myself,' would answer wearily another battered and bandaged scarecrow. And, mind, these were men without the drilled-in habit of obedience. To an onlooker they would be a lot of profane scallywags without a redeeming point. What made them do it—what made them obey me when I, thinking consciously how fine it was, made them drop the burnt of the foresail twice to try and do it better? What? They had no professional reputation—no examples, no praise. It wasn't a sense of duty; they all knew well enough how to shirk, and laze, and dodge—when they had a mind to it—and mostly they had. Was it the two pounds ten a month that sent them there? They didn't think their pay half good enough. No; it was something in them, something inborn and subtle and everlasting. I don't say positively that the crew of a French or German merchantman wouldn't have done it, but I doubt whether it would have been done in the same way. There was a completeness in it, something solid like a principle, and masterful like an instinct—a disclosure of something secret—of that hidden something, that gift, of good or evil that makes racial difference, that shapes the fate of nations.

"It was that night at ten that, for the first time since we had been fighting it, we saw the fire. The speed of the towing had fanned the smoldering destruction. A blue gleam appeared forward, shining below the wreck of the deck. It wavered in patches, it seemed to stir and creep like the light of a glowworm. I saw it first, and told Mahon. 'Then the game's up,' he said. 'We had better stop this towing, or she will burst out suddenly fore and aft before we can clear out.' We set up a yell; rang bells to attract their attention; they towed on. At last Mahon and I had to crawl forward and cut the rope with an ax. There was no time to cast off the lashings. Red tongues could be seen licking the wilderness of splinters under our feet as we made our way back to the poop.

"Of course they very soon found out in the steamer that the rope was gone. She gave a loud blast of her whistle, her lights were seen sweeping in a wide circle, she came up ranging close alongside, and stopped. We were all in a tight group on the poop looking at her. Every man had saved a little bundle or a bag. Suddenly a conical flame with a twisted top shot up forward and threw upon the black sea a circle of light, with the two vessels side by side and heaving gently in its center. Captain Beard had been sitting on the gratings still and mute for hours, but now he rose slowly and advanced in front of us, to the mizzen-shrouds. Captain Nash hailed: 'Come along! Look sharp. I have mail bags on board. I will take you and your boats to Singapore.'

" 'Thank you! No!' said our skipper. 'We must see the last of the ship.'

" 'I can't stand by any longer,' shouted the other. 'Mails—you know.'

" 'Ay! ay! We are all right.'

" 'Very well! I'll report you in Singapore . . . Good-by!'

"He waved his hand. Our men dropped their bundles quietly. The steamer moved ahead, and passing out of the circle of light, vanished at once from our sight, dazzled by the fire which burned fiercely. And then I knew that I would see the East first as commander of a small boat. I thought it fine; and the fidelity to the old ship was fine. We should see the last of her. Oh the glamour of youth! Oh the fire of it, more dazzling than the flames of the burning ship, throwing a magic light on the wide earth, leaping audaciously to the sky, presently to be quenched by time, more cruel, more pitiless, more bitter than the sea—and like the flames of the burning ship surrounded by an impenetrable night.

"The old man warned us in his gentle and inflexible way that it was part of our duty to save for the underwriters as much as we could of the ship's gear. Accordingly we went to work aft, while she blazed forward to give us plenty of light. We lugged out a lot of rubbish. What didn't we save? An old barometer fixed with an absurd quantity of screws nearly cost me my life: a sudden rush of smoke came upon me, and I just got away in time. There were various stores, bolts of canvas, coils of rope; the poop looked like a marine bazaar, and the boats were lumbered to the gunwales. One would have thought the old man wanted to take as much as he could of his first command with him. He was very, very quiet, but off his balance evidently. Would you believe it? He wanted to take a length of old stream-cable and a kedge-anchor with him in the longboat. We said, 'Ay, ay, sir,' deferentially, and on the quiet let the thing slip overboard. The heavy medicine chest went that way, two bags of green coffee, tins of paint—fancy, paint!—a whole lot of things. Then I was ordered with two hands into the boats to make a stowage and get them ready against the time it would be proper for us to leave the ship.

"We put everything straight, stepped the longboat's mast for our skipper, who was to take charge of her, and I was not sorry to sit down for a moment. My face felt raw, every limb ached as if broken, I was aware of all my ribs, and would have sworn to a twist in the backbone. The boats, fast astern, lay in a deep shadow, and all around I could see the circle of the sea lighted by the fire. A gigantic flame arose forward straight and clear. It flared fierce, with noises like the whir of wings, with rumbles as of thunder. There were cracks, detonations, and from the cone of flame the sparks flew upwards, as man is born to trouble, to leaky ships, and to ships that burn.

"What bothered me was that the ship, lying broadside to the swell and to such wind as there was—a mere breath—the boats would not keep astern where they were safe, but persisted, in a pig-headed way boats have, in getting under the counter and then swinging alongside. They were knocking about dangerously and coming near the flame, while the ship rolled on them, and, of course, there was always the danger of the masts going over the side at any moment. I and my two boat-keepers kept them off as best we could with oars and boat-hooks; but to be constantly at it became exasperating, since there was no reason why we should not leave at once. We could not see those on board, nor could we imagine what caused the delay. The boat-keepers were swearing feebly, and I had not only my share of the work, but also had to keep at it two men who showed a constant inclination to lay themselves down and let things slide.

"At last I hailed 'On deck there,' and someone looked over. 'We're ready here,' I said. The head disappeared, and very soon popped up again. 'The captain says, All right, sir, and to keep the boats well clear of the ship.'

"Half an hour passed. Suddenly there was a frightful racket, rattle, clanking of chain, hiss of water, and millions of sparks flew up into the shivering column of smoke that stood leaning slightly above the ship. The catheads had burned away, and the two red-hot anchors had gone to the bottom, tearing out after them two hundred fathom of red-hot chain. The ship trembled, the mass of flame swayed as if ready to collapse, and the fore top-gallant-mast fell. It darted down like an arrow of fire, shot under, and instantly leaping up within an oar's-length of the boats, floated quietly, very black on the luminous sea. I hailed the deck again. After some time a man in an unexpectedly cheerful but also muffled tone, as though he had been trying to speak with his mouth shut, informed me, 'Coming directly, sir,' and vanished. For a long time I heard nothing but the whir and roar of the fire. There were also whistling sounds. The boats jumped, tugged at the painters, ran at each other playfully, knocked their sides together, or, do what we would, swung in a bunch against the ship's side. I couldn't stand it any longer, and swarming up a rope, clambered aboard over the stern.

"It was as bright as day. Coming up like this, the sheet of fire facing me was a terrifying sight, and the heat seemed hardly bearable at first. On a settee cushion dragged out of the cabin, Captain Beard, with his legs drawn up and one arm under his head, slept with the light playing on him. Do you know what the rest were busy about? They were sitting on deck right aft, round an open case, eating bread and cheese and drinking bottled stout.

"On the background of flames twisting in fierce tongues above their heads they seemed at home like salamanders, and looked like a band of desperate pirates. The fire sparkled in the whites of their eyes, gleamed on patches of white skin seen through the torn shirts. Each had the marks as of a battle about him—bandaged heads, tied-up arms, a strip of dirty rag round a knee—and each man had a bottle between his legs and a chunk of cheese in his hand. Mahon got up. With his handsome and disreputable head, his hooked profile, his long white beard, and with an uncorked bottle in his hand, he resembled one of those reckless sea-robbers of old making merry amidst violence and disaster. 'The last meal on board,' he explained solemnly. 'We had nothing to eat all day, and it was no use leaving all this.' He flourished the bottle and indicated the sleeping skipper. 'He said he couldn't swallow anything, so I got him to lie down,' he went on; and as I stared, 'I don't know whether you are aware, young fellow, the man had no sleep to speak of for days—and there will be dam' little sleep in the boats.' 'There will be no boats by-and-by if you fool about much longer,' I said, indignantly. I walked up to the skipper and shook him by the shoulder. At last he opened his eyes, but did not move. 'Time to leave her, sir,' I said, quietly.

"He got up painfully, looked at the flames, at the sea sparkling round the ship, and black, black as ink farther away; he looked at the stars shining dim through a thin veil of smoke in a sky black, black as Erebus.

" 'Youngest first,' he said.

"And the ordinary seaman, wiping his mouth with the back of his hand, got up, clambered over the taffrail, and vanished. Others followed. One, on the point of going over, stopped short to drain his bottle, and with a great swing of his arm flung it at the fire. 'Take this!' he cried.

"The skipper lingered disconsolately, and we left him to commune alone for awhile with his first command. Then I went up again and brought him away at last. It was time. The ironwork on the poop was hot to the touch.

"Then the painter of the longboat was cut, and the three boats, tied together, drifted clear of the ship. It was just sixteen hours after the explosion when we abandoned her. Mahon had charge of the second boat, and I had the smallest—the 14-foot thing. The longboat would have taken the lot of us; but the skipper said we must save as much property as we could—for the underwriters—and so I got my first command. I had two men with me, a bag of biscuits, a few tins of meat, and a beaker of water. I was ordered to keep close to the longboat, that in case of bad weather we might be taken into her.

"And do you know what I thought? I thought I would part company as soon as I could. I wanted to have my first command all to myself. I wasn't going to sail in a squadron if there were a chance for independent cruising. I would make land by myself. I would beat the other boats. Youth! All youth! The silly, charming, beautiful youth.

"But we did not make a start at once. We must see the last of the ship. And so the boats drifted about that night, heaving and setting on the swell. The men dozed, waked, sighed, groaned. I looked at the burning ship.

"Between the darkness of earth and heaven she was burning fiercely upon a disc of purple sea shot by the blood-red play of gleams; upon a disc of water glittering and sinister. A high, clear flame, an immense and lonely flame, ascended from the ocean, and from its summit the black smoke poured continuously at the sky. She burned furiously, mournful and imposing like a funeral pile kindled in the night, surrounded by the sea, watched over by the stars. A magnificent death had come like a grace, like a gift, like a reward to that old ship at the end of her laborious days. The surrender of her weary ghost to the keeping of stars and sea was stirring like the sight of a glorious triumph. The masts fell just before daybreak, and for a moment there was a burst and turmoil of sparks that seemed to fill with flying fire the night patient and watchful, the vast night lying silent upon the sea. At daylight she was only a charred shell, floating still under a cloud of smoke and bearing a glowing mass of coal within.

"Then the oars were got out, and the boats forming in a line moved round her remains as if in procession—the longboat leading. As we pulled across her stern a slim dart of fire shot out viciously at us, and suddenly she went down, head first, in a great hiss of steam. The unconsumed stern was the last to sink; but the paint had gone, had cracked, had peeled off, and there were no letters, there was no word, no stubborn device that was like her soul, to flash at the rising sun her creed and her name.

"We made our way north. A breeze sprang up, and about noon all the boats came together for the last time. I had no mast or sail in mine, but I made a mast out of a spare oar and hoisted a boat-awning for a sail, with a boat-hook for a yard. She was certainly overmasted, but I had the satisfaction of knowing that with the wind aft I could beat the other two. I had to wait for them. Then we all had a look at the captain's chart, and, after a sociable meal of hard bread and water, got our last instructions. These were simple: steer north, and keep together as much as possible. 'Be careful with that jury rig, Marlow,' said the captain; and Mahon, as I sailed proudly past his boat, wrinkled his curved nose and hailed, 'You will sail that ship of yours under water if you don't look out, young fellow.' He was a malicious old man—and may the deep sea where he sleeps now rock him gently, rock him tenderly to the end of time!

"Before sunset a thick rain-squall passed over the two boats, which were far astern, and that was the last I saw of them for a time. Next day I sat steering my cockle-shell—my first command—with nothing but water and sky around me. I did sight in the afternoon the upper sails of a ship far away, but said nothing, and my men did not notice her. You see I was afraid she might be homeward bound, and I had no mind to turn back from the portals of the East. I was steering for Java—another blessed name—like Bankok, you know. I steered many days.

"I need not tell you what it is to be knocking about in an open boat. I remember nights and days of calm when we pulled, we pulled, and the boat seemed to stand still, as if bewitched within the circle of the sea horizon. I remember the heat, the deluge of rain-squalls that kept us bailing for dear life (but filled our water cask), and I remember sixteen hours on end with a mouth dry as a cinder and a steering-oar over the stern to keep my first command head on to a breaking sea. I did not know how good a man I was till then. I remember the drawn faces, the dejected figures of my two men, and I remember my youth and the feeling that will never come back any more—the feeling that I could last for ever, outlast the sea, the earth, and all men; the deceitful feeling that lures us on to joys, to perils, to love, to vain effort—to death; the triumphant conviction of strength, the heat of life in the handful of dust, the glow in the heart that with every year grows dim, grows cold, grows small, and expires—and expires, too soon, too soon—before life itself.

"And this is how I see the East. I have seen its secret places and have looked into its very soul; but now I see it always from a small boat, a high outline of mountains, blue and afar in the morning; like faint mist at noon; a jagged wall of purple at sunset. I have the feel of the oar in my hand, the vision of a scorching blue sea in my eyes. And I see a bay, a wide bay, smooth as glass and polished like ice, shimmering in the dark. A red light burns far off upon the gloom of the land, and the night is soft and warm. We drag at the oars with aching arms, and suddenly a puff of wind, a puff faint and tepid and laden with strange odors of blossoms, of aromatic wood, comes out of the still night—the first sigh of the East on my face. That I can never forget. It was impalpable and enslaving, like a charm, like a whispered promise of mysterious delight.

"We had been pulling this finishing spell for eleven hours. Two pulled, and he whose turn it was to rest sat at the tiller. We had made out the red light in that bay and steered for it, guessing it must mark some small coasting port. We passed two vessels, outlandish and high-sterned, sleeping at anchor, and, approaching the light, now very dim, ran the boat's nose against the end of a jutting wharf. We were blind with fatigue. My men dropped the oars and fell off the thwarts as if dead. I made fast to a pile. A current rippled softly. The scented obscurity of the shore was grouped into vast masses, a density of colossal clumps of vegetation, probably—mute and fantastic shapes. And at their foot the semicircle of a beach gleamed faintly, like an illusion. There was not a light, not a stir, not a sound. The mysterious East faced me, perfumed like a flower, silent like death, dark like a grave.

"And I sat weary beyond expression, exulting like a conqueror, sleepless and entranced as if before a profound, a fateful enigma.

"A splashing of oars, a measured dip reverberating on the level of water, intensified by the silence of the shore into loud claps, made me jump up. A boat, a European boat, was coming in. I invoked the name of the dead; I hailed: *Judea* ahoy! A thin shout answered.

"It was the captain. I had beaten the flagship by three hours, and I was glad to hear the old man's voice again, tremulous and tired. 'Is it you, Marlow?' 'Mind the end of that jetty, sir,' I cried.

"He approached cautiously, and brought up with the deep-sea lead-line which we had saved—for the underwriters. I eased my painter and fell alongside. He sat, a broken figure at the stern, wet with dew, his hands clasped in his lap. His men were asleep already. 'I had a terrible time of it,' he murmured. 'Mahon is behind—not very far.' We conversed in whispers, in low whispers, as if afraid to wake up the land. Guns, thunder, earthquakes would not have awakened the men just then.

"Looking around as we talked, I saw away at sea a bright light traveling in the night. 'There's a steamer passing the bay,' I said. She was not passing, she was entering, and she even came close and anchored. 'I wish,' said the old man, 'you would find out whether she is English. Perhaps they could give us a passage somewhere.' He seemed nervously anxious. So by dint of punching and kicking I started one of my men into a state of somnambulism, and giving him an oar, took another and pulled towards the lights of the steamer.

"There was a murmur of voices in her, metallic hollow clangs of the engine room, footsteps on the deck. Her ports shone, round like dilated eyes.

Shapes moved about, and there was a shadowy man high up on the bridge. He heard my oars.

"And then, before I could open my lips, the East spoke to me, but it was in a Western voice. A torrent of words was poured into the enigmatical, the fateful silence; outlandish, angry words, mixed with words and even whole sentences of good English, less strange but even more surprising. The voice swore and cursed violently; it riddled the solemn peace of the bay by a volley of abuse. It began by calling me Pig, and from that went crescendo into unmentionable adjectives—in English. The man up there raged aloud in two languages, and with a sincerity in his fury that almost convinced me I had, in some way, sinned against the harmony of the universe. I could hardly see him, but began to think he would work himself into a fit.

"Suddenly he ceased, and I could hear him snorting and blowing like a porpoise. I said—

" 'What steamer is this, pray?'

" 'Eh? What's this? And who are you?'

" 'Castaway crew of an English bark burnt at sea. We came here tonight. I am the second mate. The captain is in the longboat, and wishes to know if you would give us a passage somewhere.'

" 'Oh, my goodness! I say . . . This is the *Celestial* from Singapore on her return trip. I'll arrange with your captain in the morning . . . and . . . I say . . . did you hear me just now?'

" 'I should think the whole bay heard you.'

" 'I thought you were a shore boat. Now, look here—this infernal lazy scoundrel of a caretaker has gone to sleep again—curse him. The light is out, and I nearly ran foul of the end of this damned jetty. This is the third time he plays me this trick. Now, I ask you, can anybody stand this kind of thing? It's enough to drive a man out of his mind. I'll report him . . . I'll get the Assistant Resident to give him the sack, by . . . See—there's no light. It's out, isn't it? I take you to witness the light's out. There should be a light, you know. A red light on the—'

" 'There was a light,' I said, mildly.

" 'But it's out, man! What's the use of talking like this? You can see for yourself it's out—don't you? If you had to take a valuable steamer along this God-forsaken coast you would want a light too. I'll kick him from end to end of his miserable wharf. You'll see if I don't. I will—'

" 'So I may tell my captain you'll take us?' I broke in.

" 'Yes, I'll take you. Good night,' he said, brusquely.

"I pulled back, made fast again to the jetty, and then went to sleep at last. I had faced the silence of the East. I had heard some of its languages. But when I opened my eyes again the silence was as complete as though it had never been broken. I was lying in a flood of light, and the sky had never looked so far, so high, before. I opened my eyes and lay without moving.

"And then I saw the men of the East—they were looking at me. The whole length of the jetty was full of people. I saw brown, bronze, yellow faces, the black eyes, the glitter, the color of an Eastern crowd. And all these beings stared without a murmur, without a sigh, without a movement. They stared down at the boats, at the sleeping men who at night had come to them from the sea. Nothing moved. The fronds of palms stood still against the sky. Not a branch stirred along the shore, and the brown roofs of hidden houses peeped through the green foliage, through the big leaves that hung shining and still like leaves forged of heavy metal. This was the East of the ancient navigators, so old, so mysterious, resplendent and somber, living and unchanged, full of danger and promise. And these were the men. I sat up suddenly. A wave of movement passed through the crowd from end to end, passed along the heads, swayed the bodies, ran along the jetty like a ripple on the water, like a breath of wind on a field—and all was still again. I see it now—the wide sweep of the bay, the glittering sands, the wealth of green infinite and varied, the sea blue like the sea of a dream, the crowd of attentive faces, the blaze of vivid color—the water reflecting it all, the curve of the shore, the jetty, the high-sterned outlandish craft floating still, and the three boats with tired men from the West sleeping unconscious of the land and the people and of the violence of sunshine. They slept thrown across the thwarts, curled on bottom-boards, in the careless attitudes of death. The head of the old skipper, leaning back in the stern of the longboat, had fallen on his breast, and he looked as though he would never wake. Farther out old Mahon's face was upturned to the sky, with the long white beard spread out on his breast, as though he had been shot where he sat at the tiller; and a man, all in a heap in the bow of the boat, slept with both arms embracing the stem-head and with his cheek laid on the gunwale. The East looked at them without a sound.

"I have known its fascinations since: I have seen the mysterious shores, the still water, the lands of brown nations, where a stealthy Nemesis lies in wait, pursues, overtakes so many of the conquering race, who are proud of their wisdom, of their knowledge, of their strength. But for me all the East is contained in that vision of my youth. It is all in that moment when I opened my young eyes on it. I came upon it from a tussle with the sea—and I was young—and I saw it looking at me. And this is all that is left of it! Only a moment; a moment of strength, of romance, of glamour—of youth! . . . A flick of sunshine upon a strange shore, the time to remember, the time for a sigh, and—good-by!—Night—Good-by . . . !"

He drank.

"Ah! The good old time—the good old time. Youth and the sea. Glamour and the sea! The good, strong sea, the salt, bitter sea, that could whisper to you and roar at you and knock your breath out of you."

He drank again.

"By all that's wonderful, it is the sea, I believe, the sea itself—or is it youth alone? Who can tell? But you here—you all had something out of life:

money, love—whatever one gets on shore—and, tell me, wasn't that the best time, that time when we were young at sea; young and had nothing, on the sea that gives nothing, except hard knocks—and sometimes a chance to feel your strength—that only—that you all regret?"

And we all nodded at him: the man of finance, the man of accounts, the man of law, we all nodded at him over the polished table that like a still sheet of brown water reflected our faces, lined, wrinkled; our faces marked by toil, by deceptions, by success, by love; our weary eyes looking still, looking always, looking anxiously for something out of life, that while it is expected is already gone—has passed unseen, in a sigh, in a flash—together with the youth, with the strength, with the romance of illusions.

QUESTIONS

1. On the surface an adventure story, "Youth" has a deeper meaning that is made explicit in its title and the comments of the narrator, Marlow. State the theme precisely and indicate the passages where Marlow states it.

2. The story utilizes a number of contrasts between youth and age. List them. Does Conrad oversimplify the contrast? For instance, are the old Captain and the First Mate any less brave or heroic than Marlow? What *is* the difference between their response to the voyage and Marlow's?

3. What is the purpose of having a forty-two-year-old Marlow tell this story to a group of men around a mahogany table some twenty years after the voyage it describes? Why is not the story told directly to the reader, beginning in London and ending in Java? Why are Marlow's listeners identified so precisely?

4. If all of Marlow's comments about youth were removed from the story, would it then be without theme? If not, what would the theme be?

5. Marlow says (page 109) that the voyage was a symbol of existence. Develop this comparison.

6. A number of omens at the beginning of the story foreshadow the vicissitudes and fatal end of the *Judea*. What are they?

7. This story conforms to the popular formula "A sympathetic protagonist is confronted with obstacles and overcomes them." It contains a great deal of action. Is this, therefore, an escape story, or would it be if the comments on youth were removed?

8. To what extent are the events of the voyage due to chance rather than to cause-and-effect relationship? Is the use of chance too great to make a plausible story? Why or why not?

9. Find examples of what seem to you especially effective writing and explain their effectiveness. How does Marlow's description of the explosion differ from the way an ordinary writer would describe it (page 120)?

Bernard Malamud

THE SILVER CROWN

Gans, the father, lay dying in a hospital bed. Different doctors said different things, held different theories. There was talk of an exploratory operation but they thought it might kill him. One doctor said cancer.

"Of the heart," the old man said bitterly.

"It wouldn't be impossible."

The young Gans, Albert, a high school biology teacher, in the afternoons walked the streets in sorrow. What can anybody do about cancer? His soles wore thin with walking. He was easily irritated; angered by the war, atom bomb, pollution, death, obviously the strain of worrying about his father's illness. To be able to do nothing for him made him frantic. He had done nothing for him all his life.

A female colleague, an English teacher he had slept with once, a girl who was visibly aging, advised, "If the doctors don't know, Albert, try a faith healer. Different people know different things; nobody knows everything. You can't tell about the human body."

Albert laughed mirthlessly but listened. If specialists disagree who do you agree with? If you've tried everything what else can you try?

One afternoon after a long walk alone, as he was about to descend the subway stairs somewhere in the Bronx, still burdened by his worries, uneasy that nothing had changed, he was accosted by a fat girl with bare meaty arms who thrust a soiled card at him that he tried to avoid. She was a stupefying sight, retarded at the very least. Fifteen, he'd say, though she looks thirty and probably has the mentality of age ten. Her skin glowed, face wet, fleshy, the small mouth open and would be forever; eyes set wide apart on the broad unfocused face, either washed-out green or brown, or one of each—he wasn't sure. She seemed not to mind his appraisal, gurgled faintly. Her thick hair was braided in two ropelike strands; she wore bulging cloth slippers, bursting at seams and soles; a faded red skirt down to massive ankles; and a heavy brown sweater vest, buttoned over blown breasts, though the weather was still hot September.

The teacher's impulse was to pass by her outthrust plump baby hand. Instead he took the card from her. Simple curiosity—once you had learned to read you read anything? Charitable impulse?

Albert recognized Yiddish and Hebrew but read in English: "Heal The Sick. Save The Dying. Make A Silver Crown."

"What kind of silver crown would that be?"

She uttered impossible noises. Depressed, he looked away. When his eyes turned to hers she ran off.

He studied the card. "Make A Silver Crown." It gave a rabbi's name and address no less: Jonas Lifschitz, close by in the neighborhood. The silver crown mystified him. He had no idea what it had to do with saving the dying but felt he ought to know. Although at first repelled by the thought, he made up his mind to visit the rabbi and felt, in a way, relieved.

The teacher hastened along the street a few blocks until he came to the address on the card, a battered synagogue in a store, Congregation Theodor Herzl, painted in large uneven white letters on the plate-glass window. The rabbi's name, in smaller, gold letters, was A. Marcus. In the doorway to the left of the store the number of the house was repeated in tin numerals, and on a card under the vacant name plate under the mezuzah, appeared in pencil, "Rabbi J. Lifschitz. Retired. Consultations. Ring The Bell." The bell, when he decided to chance it, did not work—seemed dead to the touch—so Albert, his heartbeat erratic, turned the knob. The door gave easily enough and he hesitantly walked up a dark flight of narrow wooden stairs. Ascending, assailed by doubts, peering up through the gloom, he thought of turning back but at the first-floor landing compelled himself to knock loudly on the door.

"Anybody home here?"

He rapped harder, annoyed with himself for being there, engaging in the act of entrance—who would have predicted it an hour ago? The door opened a crack and that broad, badly formed face appeared. The retarded girl, squinting one bulbous eye, made noises like two eggs frying, and ducked back, slamming the door. The teacher, after momentary reflection, thrust it open in time to see her, bulky as she was, running swiftly along the long tight corridor, her body bumping the walls before she disappeared into a room at the rear.

Albert entered cautiously, with a sense of embarrassment, if not danger, warning himself to depart at once; yet stayed to peek curiously into a front room off the hallway, darkened by lowered green shades through which thread-like rivulets of light streamed. The shades resembled faded maps of ancient lands. An old gray-bearded man with thickened left eyelid, wearing a yarmulke, sat heavily asleep, a book in his lap, on a sagging armchair. Someone in the room gave off a stale odor, unless it was the armchair. As Albert stared, the old man awoke in a hurry. The small thick book on his lap fell with a thump to the floor, but instead of picking it up, he shoved it with a kick of his heel under the chair.

"So where were we?" he inquired pleasantly, a bit breathless.

The teacher removed his hat, remembered whose house he was in, and put it back on his head.

mezuzah: a Biblical scroll in a case that many Jewish families affix to their doorposts
yarmulke: skull cap

He introduced himself. "I was looking for Rabbi J. Lifschitz. Your—ah—girl let me in."

"Rabbi Lifschitz; this was my daughter Rifkele. She's not perfect, though God who made her in His image is Himself perfection. What this means I don't have to tell you."

His heavy eyelid went down in a wink, apparently involuntarily.

"What does it mean?" Albert asked.

"In her way she is also perfect."

"Anyway she let me in and here I am."

"So what did you decide?"

"Concerning what if I may ask?"

"What did you decide about what we were talking about—the silver crown?"

His eyes roved as he spoke; he rubbed a nervous thumb and forefinger. Crafty type, the teacher decided. Him I have to watch myself with.

"I came here to find out about this crown you advertised," he said, "but actually we haven't talked about it or anything else. When I entered here you were sound asleep."

"At my age—" the rabbi explained with a little laugh.

"I don't mean any criticism. All I'm saying is I am a stranger to you."

"How can we be strangers if we both believe in God?"

Albert made no argument of it.

The rabbi raised the two shades and the last of daylight fell into the spacious high-ceilinged room, crowded with at least a dozen stiff-back and folding chairs, plus a broken sofa. What kind of operation is he running here? Group consultations? He dispensed rabbinic therapy? The teacher felt renewed distaste for himself for having come. On the wall hung a single oval mirror, framed in gold-plated groupings of joined metal circles, large and small; but no pictures. Despite the empty chairs, or perhaps because of them, the room seemed barren.

The teacher observed that the rabbi's trousers were a week from ragged. He was wearing an unpressed worn black suit-coat and a yellowed white shirt without a tie. His wet grayish-blue eyes were restless. Rabbi Lifschitz was a dark-faced man with brown eye pouches and smelled of old age. This was the odor. It was hard to say whether he resembled his daughter; Rifkele resembled her species.

"So sit," said the old rabbi with a light sigh. "Not on the couch, sit on a chair."

"Which in particular?"

"You have a first-class humor." Smiling absently he pointed to two kitchen chairs and seated himself in one.

He offered a thin cigarette.

"I'm off them," the teacher explained.

"I also." The old man put the pack away. "So who is sick?" he inquired.

Albert tightened at the question as he recalled the card he had taken from the girl: "Heal The Sick, Save The Dying."

"To come to the point, my father's in the hospital with a serious ailment. In fact he's dying."

The rabbi, nodding gravely, dug into his pants pocket for a pair of glasses, wiped them with a large soiled handkerchief and put them on, lifting the wire earpieces over each fleshy ear.

"So we will make then a crown for him?"

"That depends. The crown is what I came here to find out about."

"What do you wish to find out?"

"I'll be frank with you." The teacher blew his nose and slowly wiped it. "My cast of mind is naturally empiric and objective—you might say non-mystical. I'm suspicious of faith healing but I've come here, frankly, because I want to do anything possible to help my father recover his former health. To put it otherwise, I don't want anything to go untried."

"You love your father?" the rabbi clucked, a glaze of sentiment veiling his eyes.

"What I feel is obvious. My real concern right now mainly is how does the crown work. Could you be explicit about the mechanism of it all? Who wears it, for instance? Does he? Do you? Or do I have to? In other words, how does it function? And if you wouldn't mind saying, what's the principle, or rationale, behind it? This is terra incognita for me, but I think I might be willing to take a chance if I could justify it to myself. Could I see a sample of the crown, for instance, if you have one on hand?"

The rabbi, with an absent-minded start, seemed to interrupt himself about to pick his nose.

"What is the crown?" he asked, at first haughtily, then again, gently. "It's a crown, nothing else. There are crowns in Mishna, Proverbs, Kabbalah; the holy scrolls of the Torah are often protected by crowns. But this one is different, this you will understand when it does the work. It's a miracle. A sample doesn't exist. The crown has to be made individual for your father. Then his health will be restored. There are two prices—"

"Kindly explain what's supposed to cure the sickness," Albert said. "Does it work like sympathetic magic? I'm not nay-saying, you understand. I just happen to be interested in all kinds of phenomena. Is the crown supposed to draw off the illness like some kind of poultice, or what?"

"The crown is not a medicine, it is the health of your father. We offer the crown to God and God returns to your father his health. But first we got to make it the way it must be made—this I will do with my assistant, a retired jeweler. He has helped me to make a thousand crowns. Believe me, he knows silver—the right amount to the ounce according to the size you wish. Then I will say the blessings. Without the right blessings, exact to each word, the crown don't work. I don't have to tell you why. When the crown is finished your father will get better. This I will guarantee you. Let me read you some words from the mystic book."

"The Kabbalah?" the teacher asked respectfully.

"Like the Kabbalah."

The rabbi rose, went to his armchair, got slowly down on his hands and knees and withdrew the book he had shoved under the misshapen chair, a thick small volume with faded purple covers, not a word imprinted on it. The rabbi kissed the book and murmured a prayer.

"I hid it for a minute," he explained, "when you came in the room. It's a terrible thing nowadays, goyim come in your house in the middle of the day and take away that which belongs to you, if not your life itself."

"I told you right away that your daughter had let me in," Albert said in embarrassment.

"Once you mentioned I knew."

The teacher then asked, "Suppose I am a non-believer? Will the crown work if it's ordered by a person who has his doubts?"

"Doubts we all got. We doubt God and God doubts us. This is natural on account of the nature of existence. Of this kind doubts I am not afraid so long as you love your father."

"You're putting it as sort of a paradox."

"So what's so bad about a paradox?"

"My father wasn't the easiest man in the world to get along with, and neither am I for that matter, but he has been generous to me and I'd like to repay him in some way."

"God respects a grateful son. If you love your father this will go in the crown and help him to recover his health. Do you understand Hebrew?"

"Unfortunately not."

The rabbi flipped a few pages of his thick tome, peered at one closely and read aloud in Hebrew which he then translated into English. " 'The crown is the fruit of God's grace. His grace is love of creation.' These words I will read seven times over the silver crown. This is the most important blessing."

"Fine. But what about those two prices you mentioned a minute ago?"

"This depends how quick you wish the cure."

"I want the cure to be immediate, otherwise there's no sense to the whole deal," Albert said, controlling anger. "If you're questioning my sincerity, I've already told you I'm considering this recourse even though it goes against the grain of some of my strongest convictions. I've gone out of my way to make my pros and cons absolutely clear."

"Who says no?"

The teacher became aware of Rifkele standing at the door, eating a

goyim: gentiles

slice of bread with lumps of butter on it. She beheld him in mild stupefaction, as though seeing him for the first time.

"Shpeter, Rifkele," the rabbi said patiently.

The girl shoved the bread into her mouth and ran ponderously down the passageway.

"Anyway, what about those two prices?" Albert asked, annoyed by the interruption. Every time Rifkele appeared his doubts of the enterprise rose before him like warriors with spears.

"We got two kinds crowns," said the rabbi. "One is for 401 and the other is 986."

"Dollars, you mean, for God's sake?—that's fantastic."

"The crown is pure silver. The client pays in silver dollars. So the silver dollars we melt—more for the large-size crown, less for the medium."

"What about the small?"

"There is no small. What good is a small crown?"

"I wouldn't know, but the assumption seems to be the bigger the better. Tell me, please, what can a 986 crown do that a 401 can't? Does the patient get better faster with the larger one? It hastens the reaction?"

The rabbi, five fingers hidden in his limp beard, assented.

"Are there any other costs?"

"Costs?"

"Over and above the quoted prices?"

"The price is the price, there is no extra. The price is for the silver and for the work and for the blessings."

"Now would you kindly tell me, assuming I decide to get involved in this, where am I supposed to lay my hands on 401 silver dollars? Or if I should opt for the 986 job, where can I get a pile of cartwheels of that amount? I don't suppose that any bank in the whole Bronx would keep that many silver dollars on hand nowadays. The Bronx is no longer the Wild West, Rabbi Lifschitz. But what's more to the point, isn't it true the mint isn't making silver dollars all silver any more?"

"So if they are not making we will get wholesale. If you will leave with me the cash I will order the silver from a wholesaler, and we will save you the trouble to go to the bank. It will be the same amount of silver, only in small bars, I will weigh them on a scale in front of your eyes."

"One other question. Would you take my personal check in payment? I could give it to you right away once I've made my final decision."

"I wish I could, Mr. Gans," said the rabbi, his veined hand still nervously exploring his beard, "but it's better cash when the patient is so sick, so I can start to work right away. A check sometimes comes back, or gets lost in the bank, and this interferes with the crown."

Albert did not ask how, suspecting that a bounced check, or a lost one,

Shpeter: later

wasn't the problem. No doubt some customers for crowns had stopped their checks on afterthought.

As the teacher reflected concerning his next move—should he, shouldn't he?—weighing a rational thought against a sentimental, the old rabbi sat in his chair, reading quickly in his small mystic book, his lips hastening along silently.

Albert at last got up.

"I'll decide the question once and for all tonight. If I go ahead and commit myself on the crown I'll bring you the cash after work tomorrow."

"Go in good health," said the rabbi. Removing his glasses he wiped both eyes with his handkerchief.

Wet or dry? thought the teacher.

As he let himself out of the downstairs door, more inclined than not toward trying the crown, he felt relieved, almost euphoric.

But by the next morning, after a difficult night, Albert's mood had about-faced. He fought gloom, irritation, felt flashes of hot and cold anger. It's throwing money away, pure and simple. I'm dealing with a clever confidence man, that's plain to me, but for some reason I am not resisting strongly. Maybe my subconscious is telling me to go along with a blowing wind and have the crown made. After that we'll see what happens—whether it rains, snows, or spring comes. Not much will happen, I suppose, but whatever does, my conscience will be in the clear.

But when he visited Rabbi Lifschitz that afternoon in the same roomful of empty chairs, though the teacher carried the required cash in his wallet, he was still uncomfortable about parting with it.

"Where do the crowns go after they are used and the patient recovers his health?" he cleverly asked the rabbi.

"I'm glad you asked me this question," said the rabbi alertly, his thick lid drooping. "They are melted and the silver we give to the poor. A mitzvah for one makes a mitzvah for another."

"To the poor you say?"

"There are plenty poor people, Mr. Gans. Sometimes they need a crown for a sick wife or a sick child. Where will they get the silver?"

"I see what you mean—recycled, sort of, but can't a crown be re-used as it is? I mean do you permit a period of time to go by before you melt them down? Suppose a dying man who recovers gets seriously ill again at a future date?"

"For a new sickness you will need a new crown. Tomorrow the world is not the same as today, though God listens with the same ear."

"Look, Rabbi Lifschitz," Albert said impatiently, "I'll tell you frankly that I am inching toward ordering the crown, but it would make my decision a whole lot easier all around if you would let me have a quick look at one of

mitzvah: good deed

them—it wouldn't have to be for more than five seconds—at a crown-in-progress for some other client."

"What will you see in five seconds?"

"Enough—whether the object is believable, worth the fuss and not inconsequential investment."

"Mr. Gans," replied the rabbi, "this is not a showcase business. You are not buying from me a new Chevrolet automobile. Your father lays now dying in the hospital. Do you love him? Do you wish me to make a crown that will cure him?"

The teacher's anger flared. "Don't be stupid, rabbi, I've answered that. Please don't sidetrack the real issue. You're working on my guilt so I'll suspend my perfectly reasonable doubts of the whole freaking business. I won't fall for that."

They glared at each other. The rabbi's beard quivered. Albert ground his teeth.

Rifkele, in a nearby room, moaned.

The rabbi, breathing emotionally, after a moment relented.

"I will show you the crown," he sighed.

"Accept my apologies for losing my temper."

The rabbi accepted. "Now tell me please what kind of sickness your father has got."

"Ah," said Albert, "nobody is certain for sure. One day he got into bed, turned to the wall and said, 'I'm sick.' They suspected leukemia at first but the lab tests didn't confirm it."

"You talked to the doctors?"

"In droves. Till I was blue in the face. A bunch of ignoramuses," said the teacher hoarsely. "Anyway, nobody knows exactly what he has wrong with him. The theories include rare blood diseases, also a possible carcinoma of certain endocrine glands. You name it, I've heard it, with complications suggested, like Parkinson's or Addison's disease, multiple sclerosis, or something similar, alone or in combination with other sicknesses. It's a mysterious case, all in all."

"This means you will need a special crown," said the rabbi.

The teacher bridled. "What do you mean special? What will it cost?"

"The cost will be the same," the rabbi answered dryly, "but the design and the kind of blessings will be different. When you are dealing with such a mystery you got to make another one but it must be bigger."

"How would that work?"

"Like two winds that they meet in the sky. A white and a blue. The blue says, 'Not only I am blue but inside I am also purple and orange.' So the white goes away."

"If you can work it up for the same price, that's up to you."

Rabbi Lifschitz then drew down the two green window shades and shut the door, darkening the room.

"Sit," he said in the heavy dark, "I will show you the crown."

"I'm sitting."

"So sit where you are, but turn your head to the wall where is the mirror."

"But why so dark?"

"You will see light."

He heard the rabbi strike a match and it flared momentarily, casting shadows of candles and chairs amid the empty chairs in the room.

"Look now in the mirror."

"I'm looking."

"What do you see?"

"Nothing."

"Look with your eyes."

A silver candelabrum, first with three, then five, then seven burning bony candlesticks appeared like ghostly hands with flaming fingertips in the oval mirror. The heat of it hit Albert in the face and for a moment he was stunned.

But recalling the games of his childhood, he thought, who's kidding who? It's one of those illusion things I remember from when I was a kid. In that case I'm getting the hell out of here. I can stand maybe mystery but not magic tricks or dealing with a rabbinical magician.

The candelabrum had vanished, although not its light, and he now saw the rabbi's somber face in the glass, his gaze addressing him. Albert glanced quickly around to see if anyone was standing at his shoulder, but nobody was. Where the rabbi was hiding at the moment the teacher did not know; but in the lit glass appeared his old man's lined and shrunken face, his sad eyes, compelling, inquisitive, weary, perhaps even frightened, as though they had seen more than they had cared to but were still looking.

What's this, slides or home movies? Albert sought some source of projection but saw no ray of light from wall or ceiling, nor object or image that might be reflected by the mirror.

The rabbi's eyes glowed like sun-filled clouds. A moon rose in the blue sky. The teacher dared not move, afraid to discover he was unable to. He then beheld a shining crown on the rabbi's head.

It had appeared at first like a braided mother-of-pearl turban, then had luminously become—like an intricate star in the night sky—a silver crown, constructed of bars, triangles, half-moons and crescents, spires, turrets, trees, points of spears; as though a wild storm had swept them up from the earth and flung them together in its vortex, twisted into a single glowing interlocked sculpture, a forest of disparate objects.

The sight in the ghostly mirror, a crown of rare beauty—very impressive, Albert thought—lasted no longer than five short seconds, then the reflecting glass by degrees turned dark and empty.

The shades were up. The single bulb in a frosted lily fixture on the ceiling shone harshly in the room. It was night.

The old rabbi sat, exhausted, on the broken sofa.

"So you saw it?"

"I saw something."

"You believe what you saw—the crown?"

"I believe I saw. Anyway, I'll take it."

The rabbi gazed at him blankly.

"I mean I agree to have the crown made," Albert said, having to clear his throat.

"Which size?"

"Which size was the one I saw?"

"Both sizes. This is the same design for both sizes, but there is more silver and also more blessings for the $986 size."

"But didn't you say that the design for my father's crown, because of the special nature of his illness, would have a different style, plus some special blessings?"

The rabbi nodded. "This comes also in two sizes—the $401 and $986."

The teacher hesitated a split second. "Make it the big one," he said decisively.

He had his wallet in his hand and counted out fifteen new bills—nine one hundreds, four twenties, a five and a single—adding to $986.

Putting on his glasses, the rabbi hastily counted the money, snapping with thumb and forefinger each crisp bill as though to be sure none had stuck together. He folded the stiff paper and thrust the wad into his pants pocket.

"Could I have a receipt?"

"I would like to give you a receipt," said Rabbi Lifschitz earnestly, "but for the crowns there are no receipts. Some things are not a business."

"If money is exchanged, why not?"

"God will not allow. My father did not give receipts and also my grandfather."

"How can I prove I paid you if something goes wrong?"

"You have my word, nothing will go wrong."

"Yes, but suppose something unforeseen did," Albert insisted, "would you return the cash?"

"Here is your cash," said the rabbi, handing the teacher the packet of folded bills.

"Never mind," said Albert hastily. "Could you tell me when the crown will be ready?"

"Tomorrow night before Shabbos, the latest."

"So soon?"

"Your father is dying."

Shabbos: Sabbath

"That's right, but the crown looks like a pretty intricate piece of work to put together out of all those odd pieces."

"We will hurry."

"I wouldn't want you to rush the job in any way that would—let's say—prejudice the potency of the crown, or for that matter, in any way impair the quality of it as I saw it in the mirror—or however I saw it."

Down came the rabbi's eyelid, quickly raised without a sign of self-consciousness.

"Mr. Gans, all my crowns are first-class jobs. About this you got nothing to worry about."

They then shook hands. Albert, still assailed by doubts, stepped into the corridor. He felt he did not, in essence, trust the rabbi; and suspected that Rabbi Lifschitz knew it and did not, in essence, trust him.

Rifkele, panting like a cow for a bull, let him out the front door, perfectly.

In the subway, Albert figured he would call it an investment in experience and see what came of it. Education costs money but how else can you get it? He pictured the crown as he had seen it established on the rabbi's head, and then seemed to remember that as he had stared at the man's shifty face in the mirror the thickened lid of his right eye had slowly dropped into a full wink. Did he recall this in truth, or was he seeing in his mind's eye and transposing into the past something that had happened just before he left the house? What does he mean by his wink?—not only is he a fake but he kids you? Uneasy once more, the teacher clearly remembered, when he was staring into the rabbi's fish eyes in the glass, after which they had lit in visionary light, that he had fought a hunger to sleep; and the next thing there's the sight of the old boy, as though on the television screen, wearing this high-hat magic crown.

Albert, rising, cried, "Hypnosis! The bastard magician hypnotized me! He never did produce a silver crown, it's out of my imagination—I've been suckered!"

He was outraged by the knavery, hypocrisy, fat nerve of Rabbi Jonas Lifschitz. The concept of a curative crown, if he had ever for a moment believed in it, crumbled in his brain and all he could think of were 986 blackbirds flying in the sky. As three curious passengers watched, Albert bolted out of the car at the next stop, rushed up the stairs, hurried across the street, then cooled his impatient heels for twenty-two minutes till the next train clattered into the station, and he rode back to the stop near the rabbi's house. Though he banged with both fists on the door, kicked at it, "rang" the useless bell until his thumb was blistered, the boxlike wooden house, including dilapidated synagogue store, was dark, monumentally starkly still, like a gigantic, slightly tilted tombstone in a vast graveyard; and in the end unable to arouse a soul, the teacher, long past midnight, had to head home.

He awoke next morning cursing the rabbi and his own stupidity for having got involved with a faith healer. This is what happens when a man

—even for a minute—surrenders his true beliefs. There are less punishing ways to help the dying. Albert considered calling the cops but had no receipt and did not want to appear that much a fool. He was tempted, for the first time in six years of teaching, to phone in sick; then take a cab to the rabbi's house and demand the return of his cash. The thought agitated him. On the other hand, suppose Rabbi Lifschitz was seriously at work assembling the crown with his helper; on which, let's say, after he had bought the silver and paid the retired jeweler for his work, he made, let's say, a hundred bucks clear profit—not so very much; and there really *was* a silver crown, and the rabbi sincerely and religiously believed it would reverse the course of his father's illness? Although nervously disturbed by his suspicions, Albert felt he had better not get the police into the act too soon because the crown wasn't promised—didn't the old gent say—until before the Sabbath, which gave him till sunset tonight.

If he produces the thing by then, I have no case against him even if it's a piece of junk. So I better wait. But what a dope I was to order the $986 job instead of the $401. On that decision alone I lost $585.

After a distracted day's work Albert taxied to the rabbi's house and tried to rouse him, even hallooing at the blank windows facing the street; but either nobody was home or they were both hiding, the rabbi under the broken sofa, Rifkele trying to shove her bulk under a bathtub. Albert decided to wait them out. Soon the old boy would have to leave the house to step into the shul on Friday night. He would speak to him, warn him to come clean. But the sun set; dusk settled on the earth; and though the autumn stars and a sliver of moon gleamed in the sky, the house was dark, shades drawn; and no Rabbi Lifschitz emerged. Lights had gone on in the little shul, candles were lit. It occurred to Albert, with chagrin, that the rabbi might be already worshipping; he might all this time have been in the synagogue.

The teacher entered the long, brightly lit store. On yellow folding chairs scattered around the room sat a dozen men holding worn prayer books, praying. The Rabbi A. Marcus, a middle-aged man with a high voice and a short reddish beard, was dovening at the Ark, his back to the congregation.

As Albert entered and embarrassedly searched from face to face, the congregants stared at him. The old rabbi was not among them. Disappointed, the teacher withdrew.

A man sitting by the door touched his sleeve.

"Stay awhile and read with us."

"Excuse me, I'd like to but I'm looking for a friend."

"Look," said the man, "maybe you'll find him."

Albert waited across the street under a chestnut tree losing its leaves. He waited patiently—till tomorrow if he had to.

shul: synagogue

Shortly after nine the lights went out in the synagogue and the last of the worshippers left for home. The red-bearded rabbi then emerged with his key in his hand to lock the store door.

"Excuse me, rabbi," said Albert, approaching. "Are you acquainted with Rabbi Jonas Lifschitz, who lives upstairs with his daughter Rifkele—if she is his daughter?"

"He used to come here," said the rabbi with a small smile, "but since he retired he prefers a big synagogue on Mosholu Parkway, a palace."

"Will he be home soon, do you think?"

"Maybe in an hour. It's Shabbat, he must walk."

"Do you—ah—happen to know anything about his work on silver crowns?"

"What kind of silver crowns?"

"To assist the sick, the dying?"

"No," said the rabbi, locking the shul door, pocketing the key, and hurrying away.

The teacher, eating his heart, waited under the chestnut tree till past midnight, all the while urging himself to give up and go home but unable to unstick the glue of his frustration and rage. Then shortly before 1 a.m. he saw some shadows moving and two people drifting up the shadow-encrusted street. One was the old rabbi, in a new caftan and snappy black Homburg, walking tiredly. Rifkele, in sexy yellow mini, exposing to above the big-bone knees her legs like poles, walked lightly behind him, stopping to strike her ears with her hands. A long white shawl, pulled short on the right shoulder, hung down to her left shoe.

"On my income their glad rags."

Rifkele chanted a long "boooo" and slapped both ears with her pudgy hands to keep from hearing it.

They toiled up the ill-lit narrow staircase, the teacher trailing them.

"I came to see my crown," he told the pale, astonished rabbi, in the front room.

"The crown," the rabbi said haughtily, "is already finished. Go home and wait, your father will soon get better."

"I called the hospital before leaving my apartment, there's been no improvement."

"How can you expect so soon improvement if the doctors themselves don't know what is the sickness? You must give the crown a little more time. God Himself has trouble to understand human sickness."

"I came to see the thing I paid for."

"I showed you already, you saw before you ordered."

"That was an image of a facsimile, maybe, or something of the sort. I

Shabbat: Sabbath

insist on seeing the real thing, for which I paid close to one thousand smackers."

"Listen, Mr. Gans," said the rabbi patiently, "there are some things we are allowed to see which He lets us see them. Sometimes I wish He didn't let us. There are other things we are not allowed to see—Moses knew this—and one is God's face, and another is the real crown that He makes and blesses it. A miracle is a miracle, this is God's business."

"Don't you see it?"

"Not with my eyes."

"I don't believe a word of it, you faker, two-bit magician."

"The crown is a real crown. If you think there is magic, it is on account those people that they insist to see it—we try to give them an idea. For those who believe, there is no magic."

"Rifkele," the rabbi said hurriedly, "bring to Papa my book of letters."

She left the room, after a while, a little in fright, her eyes evasive; and returned in ten minutes, after flushing the toilet, in a shapeless long flannel nightgown, carrying a large yellowed notebook whose loose pages were thickly interleaved with old correspondence.

"Testimonials," said the rabbi.

Turning several loose pages, with trembling hand he extracted a letter and read it aloud, his voice husky with emotion.

" 'Dear Rabbi Lifschitz: Since the miraculous recovery of my mother, Mrs. Max Cohen, from her recent illness, my impulse is to cover your bare feet with kisses. Your crown worked wonders and I am recommending it to all my friends. Yours truly and sincerely, (Mrs.) Esther Polatnik.' "

"This is a college teacher."

He read another. " 'Dear Rabbi Lifschitz, Your $986 crown totally and completely cured my father of cancer of the pancreas, with serious complications of the lungs, after nothing else had worked. Never before have I believed in miraculous occurrences, but from now on I will have less doubts. My thanks to you and God. Most sincerely, Daniel Schwartz.' "

"A lawyer," said the rabbi.

He offered the book to Albert. "Look yourself, Mr. Gans, hundreds of letters."

Albert wouldn't touch it.

"There's only one thing I want to look at, Rabbi Lifschitz, and it's not a book of useless testimonials. I want to see my father's silver crown."

"This is impossible. I already explained to you why I can't do this. God's word is God's law."

"So if it's the law you're citing, either I see the crown in the next five minutes, or the first thing tomorrow morning I'm reporting you and your activities to the Bronx County District Attorney."

"Booo-ooo," sang Rifkele, banging her ears.

"Shut up!" Albert said.

"Have respect," cried the rabbi. "Grubber yung!"

"I will swear out a complaint and the D.A. will shut you down, the whole freaking plant, if you don't at once return the $986 you swindled me out of."

The rabbi wavered in his tracks. "Is this the way to talk to a rabbi of God?"

"A thief is a thief."

Rifkele blubbered, squealed.

"Sha," the rabbi thickly whispered to Albert, clasping and unclasping his gray hands. "You'll frighten the neighbors. Listen to me, Mr. Gans, you saw with your eyes what it looks like the real crown. I give you my word that nobody of my whole clientele ever saw this before. I showed you for your father's sake so you would tell me to make the crown which will save him. Don't spoil now the miracle."

"Miracle," Albert bellowed, "it's a freaking fake magic, with an idiot girl for a come-on and hypnotic mirrors. I was mesmerized, suckered by you."

"Be kind," begged the rabbi, tottering as he wandered amid empty chairs. "Be merciful to an old man. Think of my poor child. Think of your father who loves you."

"He hates me, the son-of-a-bitch, I hope he croaks."

In an explosion of silence the girl slobbered in fright.

"Aha," cried the wild-eyed rabbi, pointing a finger at God in heaven.

"Murderer," he cried, aghast.

Moaning, father and daughter rushed into each other's arms, as Albert, wearing a massive, spike-laden headache, rushed down the booming stairs.

An hour later the elder Gans shut his eyes and expired.

QUESTIONS

1. What contradictory approaches to experience are represented by the professions of Gans and Rabbi Lifschitz? What is Gans's "cast of mind"? What dilemma does he face in his interviews with the rabbi? How do the questions he asks of the rabbi reflect his cast of mind? How do the rabbi's answers reflect a different approach?

2. Gans has three interviews with the rabbi. What is the major function of each?

3. What are Gans's feelings toward his father? What is the explanation of his final outburst against his father? Is it sufficiently prepared for by what we have previously learned about him?

Grubber yung: coarse young man
Sha: be quiet

4. Is the rabbi genuine or fraudulent? That is, is he (a) an authentic faith-healer, (b) a man who sincerely believes himself to possess mystical powers, though he does not, or (c) "a clever confidence man" (page 139)? Examine the evidence for each possibility. Does the story answer the question?

5. What is Rifkele's function in the story? How does her existence affect Gans's attitude toward the rabbi? How does the rabbi's relationship with her compare or contrast with Gans's relationship with his father?

6. Comment on the following details: (a) Gans's relationship with the English teacher (page 133); (b) Gans's motivation in taking a card from the fat girl (page 133). Are there other places in the story where motivations are ambiguous? What does the story say about human motivations in general? (c) the rabbi's "wink"; (d) the rabbi's two prices for his crowns; (e) "You're putting it as sort of a paradox." "So what's so bad about a paradox?" (page 137); (f) Gans's reasons for not calling the police (page 144).

7. Did Gans cause his father's death?

8. Explore the implications of the metaphor in the next-to-the-last paragraph.

9. Frame a statement of the story's theme.

Philip Roth

DEFENDER OF THE FAITH

In May of 1945, only a few weeks after the fighting had ended in Europe, I was rotated back to the States, where I spent the remainder of the war with a training company at Camp Crowder, Missouri. Along with the rest of the Ninth Army, I had been racing across Germany so swiftly during the late winter and spring that when I boarded the plane, I couldn't believe its destination lay to the west. My mind might inform me otherwise, but there was an inertia of the spirit that told me we were flying to a new front, where we would disembark and continue our push eastward—eastward until we'd circled the globe, marching through villages along whose twisting, cobbled streets crowds of the enemy would watch us take possession of what, up till then, they'd considered their own. I had changed enough in two years not to mind the trembling of the old people, the crying of the very young, the uncertainty and fear in the eyes of the once arrogant. I had been fortunate enough to develop an infantryman's heart, which, like his feet, at first aches and swells but finally grows horny enough for him to travel the weirdest paths without feeling a thing.

DEFENDER OF THE FAITH From *Goodbye Columbus* by Philip Roth. Reprinted by permission of Houghton Mifflin Company, Boston. First published in 1959.

Captain Paul Barrett was my C.O. in Camp Crowder. The day I reported for duty, he came out of his office to shake my hand. He was short, gruff, and fiery, and—indoors or out—he wore his polished helmet liner pulled down to his little eyes. In Europe, he had received a battlefield commission and a serious chest wound, and he'd been returned to the States only a few months before. He spoke easily to me, and at the evening formation he introduced me to the troops. "Gentlemen," he said, "Sergeant Thurston, as you know, is no longer with this company. Your new first sergeant is Sergeant Nathan Marx, here. He is a veteran of the European theater, and consequently will expect to find a company of soldiers here, and not a company of *boys*."

I sat up late in the orderly room that evening, trying half-heartedly to solve the riddle of duty rosters, personnel forms, and morning reports. The Charge of Quarters slept with his mouth open on a mattress on the floor. A trainee stood reading the next day's duty roster, which was posted on the bulletin board just inside the screen door. It was a warm evening, and I could hear radios playing dance music over in the barracks. The trainee, who had been staring at me whenever he thought I wouldn't notice, finally took a step in my direction.

"Hey, Sarge—we having a G.I. party tomorrow night?" he asked. A G.I. party is a barracks cleaning.

"You usually have them on Friday nights?" I asked him.

"Yes," he said, and then he added, mysteriously, "that's the whole thing."

"Then you'll have a G.I. party."

He turned away, and I heard him mumbling. His shoulders were moving, and I wondered if he was crying.

"What's your name, soldier?" I asked.

He turned, not crying at all. Instead, his green-speckled eyes, long and narrow, flashed like fish in the sun. He walked over to me and sat on the edge of my desk. He reached out a hand. "Sheldon," he said.

"Stand on your feet, Sheldon."

Getting off the desk, he said, "Sheldon Grossbart." He smiled at the familiarity into which he'd led me.

"You against cleaning the barracks Friday night, Grossbart?" I said. "Maybe we shouldn't have G.I. parties. Maybe we should get a maid." My tone startled me. I felt I sounded like every top sergeant I had ever known.

"No, Sergeant." He grew serious, but with a seriousness that seemed to be only the stifling of a smile. "It's just—G.I. parties on Friday night, of all nights."

He slipped up onto the corner of the desk again—not quite sitting, but not quite standing, either. He looked at me with those speckled eyes flashing, and then made a gesture with his hand. It was very slight—no more than a movement back and forth of the wrist—and yet it managed to exclude from our affairs everything else in the orderly room, to make the two of us the center of the world. It seemed, in fact, to exclude everything even about the two of us except our hearts.

"Sergeant Thurston was one thing," he whispered, glancing at the sleeping C.Q., "but we thought that with you here things might be a little different."

"We?"

"The Jewish personnel."

"Why?" I asked, harshly. "What's on your mind?" Whether I was still angry at the "Sheldon" business, or now at something else, I hadn't time to tell, but clearly I was angry.

"We thought you—Marx, you know, like Karl Marx. The Marx Brothers. Those guys are all—M-a-r-x. Isn't that how *you* spell it, Sergeant?"

"M-a-r-x."

"Fishbein said—" He stopped. "What I mean to say, Sergeant—" His face and neck were red, and his mouth moved but no words came out. In a moment, he raised himself to attention, gazing down at me. It was as though he had suddenly decided he could expect no more sympathy from me than from Thurston, the reason being that I was of Thurston's faith, and not his. The young man had managed to confuse himself as to what my faith really was, but I felt no desire to straighten him out. Very simply, I didn't like him.

When I did nothing but return his gaze, he spoke, in an altered tone. "You see, Sergeant," he explained to me, "Friday nights, Jews are supposed to go to services."

"Did Sergeant Thurston tell you you couldn't go to them when there was a G.I. party?"

"No."

"Did he say you had to stay and scrub the floors?"

"No, Sergeant."

"Did the Captain say you had to stay and scrub the floors?"

"That isn't it, Sergeant. It's the other guys in the barracks." He leaned toward me. "They think we're goofing off. But we're not. That's when Jews go to services, Friday night. We have to."

"Then go."

"But the other guys make accusations. They have no right."

"That's not the Army's problem, Grossbart. It's a personal problem you'll have to work out yourself."

"But it's un*fair*."

I got up to leave. "There's nothing I can do about it," I said.

Grossbart stiffened and stood in front of me. "But this is a matter of *religion,* sir."

"Sergeant," I said.

"I mean 'Sergeant,' " he said, almost snarling.

"Look, go see the chaplain. You want to see Captain Barrett, I'll arrange an appointment."

"No, no. I don't want to make trouble, Sergeant. That's the first thing they throw up to you. I just want my rights!"

"Damn it, Grossbart, stop whining. You have your rights. You can stay and scrub floors or you can go to shul—"

The smile swam in again. Spittle gleamed at the corners of his mouth. "You mean church, Sergeant."

"I mean shul, Grossbart!"

I walked past him and went outside. Near me, I heard the scrunching of a guard's boots on gravel. Beyond the lighted windows of the barracks, young men in T shirts and fatigue pants were sitting on their bunks, polishing their rifles. Suddenly there was a light rustling behind me. I turned and saw Grossbart's dark frame fleeing back to the barracks, racing to tell his Jewish friends that they were right—that, like Karl and Harpo, I was one of them.

The next morning, while chatting with Captain Barrett, I recounted the incident of the previous evening. Somehow, in the telling, it must have seemed to the Captain that I was not so much explaining Grossbart's position as defending it. "Marx, I'd fight side by side with a nigger if the fella proved to me he was a man. I pride myself," he said, looking out the window, "that I've got an open mind. Consequently, Sergeant, nobody gets special treatment here, for the good *or* the bad. All a man's got to do is prove himself. A man fires well on the range, I give him a weekend pass. He scores high in P.T., he gets a weekend pass. He *earns* it." He turned from the window and pointed a finger at me. "You're a Jewish fella, am I right, Marx?"

"Yes, sir."

"And I admire you. I admire you because of the ribbons on your chest. I judge a man by what he shows me on the field of battle, Sergeant. It's what he's got *here*," he said, and then, though I expected he would point to his chest, he jerked a thumb toward the buttons straining to hold his blouse across his belly. "Guts," he said.

"O.K., sir. I only wanted to pass on to you how the men felt."

"Mr. Marx, you're going to be old before your time if you worry about how the men feel. Leave that stuff to the chaplain—that's his business, not yours. Let's us train these fellas to shoot straight. If the Jewish personnel feels the other men are accusing them of goldbricking—well, I just don't know. Seems awful funny that suddenly the Lord is calling so loud in Private Grossman's ear he's just got to run to church."

"Synagogue," I said.

"Synagogue is right, Sergeant. I'll write that down for handy reference. Thank you for stopping by."

shul: synagogue

That evening, a few minutes before the company gathered outside the orderly room for the chow formation, I called the C.Q., Corporal Robert LaHill, in to see me. LaHill was a dark, burly fellow whose hair curled out of his clothes wherever it could. He had a glaze in his eyes that made one think of caves and dinosaurs. "LaHill," I said, "when you take the formation, remind the men that they're free to attend church services *whenever* they are held, provided they report to the orderly room before they leave the area."

LaHill scratched his wrist, but gave no indication that he'd heard or understood.

"LaHill," I said, "*church*. You remember? Church, priest, Mass, confession."

He curled one lip into a kind of smile; I took it for a signal that for a second he had flickered back up into the human race.

"Jewish personnel who want to attend services this evening are to fall out in front of the orderly room at 1900," I said. Then, as an afterthought, I added, "By order of Captain Barrett."

A little while later, as the day's last light—softer than any I had seen that year—began to drop over Camp Crowder, I heard LaHill's thick, inflectionless voice outside my window: "Give me your ears, troopers. Toppie says for me to tell you that at 1900 hours all Jewish personnel is to fall out in front, here, if they want to attend the Jewish Mass."

At seven o'clock, I looked out the orderly-room window and saw three soldiers in starched khakis standing on the dusty quadrangle. They looked at their watches and fidgeted while they whispered back and forth. It was getting dimmer, and, alone on the otherwise deserted field, they looked tiny. When I opened the door, I heard the noises of the G.I. party coming from the surrounding barracks—bunks being pushed to the walls, faucets pounding water into buckets, brooms whisking at the wooden floors, cleaning the dirt away for Saturday's inspection. Big puffs of cloth moved round and round on the windowpanes. I walked outside, and the moment my foot hit the ground I thought I heard Grossbart call to the others, " 'Ten-*hut!*" Or maybe, when they all three jumped to attention, I imagined I heard the command.

Grossbart stepped forward, "Thank you, sir," he said.

" 'Sergeant,' Grossbart," I reminded him. "You call officers 'sir.' I'm not an officer. You've been in the Army three weeks—you know that."

He turned his palms out at his sides to indicate that, in truth, he and I lived beyond convention. "Thank you anyway," he said.

"Yes," a tall boy behind him said. "Thanks a lot."

And the third boy whispered, "Thank you," but his mouth barely fluttered, so that he did not alter by more than a lip's movement his posture of attention.

"For what?" I asked.

Grossbart snorted happily. "For the announcement. The Corporal's announcement. It helped. It made it—"

"Fancier." The tall boy finished Grossbart's sentence.

Grossbart smiled. "He means formal, sir. Public," he said to me. "Now it won't seem as though we're just taking off—goldbricking because the work has begun."

"It was by order of Captain Barrett," I said.

"Aaah, but you pull a little weight," Grossbart said. "So we thank you." Then he turned to his companions. "Sergeant Marx, I want you to meet Larry Fishbein."

The tall boy stepped forward and extended his hand. I shook it. "You from New York?" he asked.

"Yes."

"Me, too." He had a cadaverous face that collapsed inward from his cheekbone to his jaw, and when he smiled—as he did at the news of our communal attachment—revealed a mouthful of bad teeth. He was blinking his eyes a good deal, as though he were fighting back tears. "What borough?" he asked.

I turned to Grossbart. "It's five after seven. What time are services?"

"Shul," he said, smiling, "is in ten minutes. I want you to meet Mickey Halpern. This is Nathan Marx, our sergeant."

The third boy hopped forward. "Private Michael Halpern." He saluted.

"Salute officers, Halpern," I said. The boy dropped his hand, and, on its way down, in his nervousness, checked to see if his shirt pockets were buttoned.

"Shall I march them over, sir?" Grossbart asked. "Or are you coming along?"

From behind Grossbart, Fishbein piped up. "Afterward, they're having refreshments. A ladies auxiliary from St. Louis, the rabbi told us last week."

"The chaplain," Halpern whispered.

"You're welcome to come along," Grossbart said.

To avoid his plea, I looked away, and saw, in the windows of the barracks, a cloud of faces staring out at the four of us. "Hurry along, Grossbart," I said.

"O.K., then," he said. He turned to the others. "Double time, *march!*"

They started off, but ten feet away Grossbart spun around and, running backward, called to me, "Good *shabbus,* sir!" And then the three of them were swallowed into the alien Missouri dusk.

Even after they had disappeared over the parade ground, whose green was now a deep blue, I could hear Grossbart singing the double-time cadence, and as it grew dimmer and dimmer, it suddenly touched a deep memory—

shabbus: Sabbath

as did the slant of the light—and I was remembering the shrill sounds of a Bronx playground where, years ago, beside the Grand Concourse, I had played on long spring evenings such as this. It was a pleasant memory for a young man so far from peace and home, and it brought so many recollections with it that I began to grow exceedingly tender about myself. In fact, I indulged myself in a reverie so strong that I felt as though a hand were reaching down inside me. It had to reach so very far to touch me! It had to reach past those days in the forests of Belgium, and past the dying I'd refused to weep over; past the nights in German farmhouses whose books we'd burned to warm us; past endless stretches when I had shut off all softness I might feel for my fellows, and had managed even to deny myself the posture of a conqueror—the swagger that I, as a Jew, might well have worn as my boots whacked against the rubble of Wesel, Münster, and Braunschweig.

But now one night noise, one rumor of home and time past, and memory plunged down through all I had anesthetized, and came to what I suddenly remembered was myself. So it was not altogether curious that, in search of more of me, I found myself following Grossbart's tracks to Chapel No. 3, where the Jewish services were being held.

I took a seat in the last row, which was empty. Two rows in front of me sat Grossbart, Fishbein, and Halpern, holding little white Dixie cups. Each row of seats was raised higher than the one in front of it, and I could see clearly what was going on. Fishbein was pouring the contents of his cup into Grossbart's, and Grossbart looked mirthful as the liquid made a purple arc between Fishbein's hand and his. In the glaring yellow light, I saw the chaplain standing on the platform at the front; he was chanting the first line of the responsive reading. Grossbart's prayer book remained closed on his lap; he was swishing the cup around. Only Halpern responded to the chant by praying. The fingers of his right hand were spread wide across the cover of his open book. His cap was pulled down low onto his brow, which made it round, like a yarmulke. From time to time, Grossbart wet his lips at the cup's edge; Fishbein, his long yellow face a dying light bulb, looked from here to there, craning forward to catch sight of the faces down the row, then of those in front of him, then behind. He saw me, and his eyelids beat a tattoo. His elbow slid into Grossbart's side, his neck inclined toward his friend, he whispered something, and then, when the congregation next responded to the chant, Grossbart's voice was among the others. Fishbein looked into his book now, too; his lips, however, didn't move.

Finally, it was time to drink the wine. The chaplain smiled down at them as Grossbart swigged his in one long gulp, Halpern sipped, meditating, and Fishbein faked devotion with an empty cup. "As I look down amongst the congregation"—the chaplain grinned at the word—"this night, I see

yarmulke: skull cap

many new faces, and I want to welcome you to Friday-night services here at Camp Crowder. I am Major Leo Ben Ezra, your chaplain." Though an American, the chaplain spoke deliberately—syllable by syllable, almost—as though to communicate, above all, with the lip readers in his audience. "I have only a few words to say before we adjourn to the refreshment room, where the kind ladies of the Temple Sinai, St. Louis, Missouri, have a nice setting for you."

Applause and whistling broke out. After another momentary grin, the chaplain raised his hands, palms out, his eyes flicking upward a moment, as if to remind the troops where they were and Who Else might be in attendance. In the sudden silence that followed, I thought I heard Grossbart cackle, "Let the goyim clean the floors!" Were those the words? I wasn't sure, but Fishbein, grinning, nudged Halpern. Halpern looked dumbly at him, then went back to his prayer book, which had been occupying him all through the rabbi's talk. One hand tugged at the black kinky hair that stuck out under his cap. His lips moved.

The rabbi continued. "It is about the food that I want to speak to you for a moment. I know, I know, I know," he intoned, wearily, "how in the mouths of most of you the *trafe* food tastes like ashes. I know how you gag, some of you, and how your parents suffer to think of their children eating foods unclean and offensive to the palate. What can I tell you? I can only say, close your eyes and swallow as best you can. Eat what you must to live, and throw away the rest. I wish I could help more. For those of you who find this impossible, may I ask that you try and try, but then come to see me in private. If your revulsion is so great, we will have to seek aid from those higher up."

A round of chatter rose and subsided. Then everyone sang "Ain Kelohainu"; after all those years, I discovered I still knew the words. Then, suddenly, the service over, Grossbart was upon me. "Higher up? He means the General?"

"Hey, Shelly," Fishbein said, "he means God." He smacked his face and looked at Halpern. "How high can you go!"

"Sh-h-h!" Grossbart said. "What do you think, Sergeant?"

"I don't know," I said. "You better ask the chaplain."

"I'm going to. I'm making an appointment to see him in private. So is Mickey."

Halpern shook his head. "No, no, Sheldon—"

"You have rights, Mickey," Grossbart said. "They can't push us around."

"It's O.K.," said Halpern. "It bothers my mother, not me."

goyim: gentiles
trafe: non-kosher food
"Ain Kelohainu": "There's no God like our God"

Grossbart looked at me. "Yesterday he threw up. From the hash. It was all ham and God knows what else."

"I have a cold—that was why," Halpern said. He pushed his yarmulke back into a cap.

"What about you, Fishbein?" I asked. "You kosher, too?"

He flushed. "A little. But I'll let it ride. I have a very strong stomach, and I don't eat a lot anyway." I continued to look at him, and he held up his wrist to reinforce what he'd just said; his watch strap was tightened to the last hole, and he pointed that out to me.

"But services are important to you?" I asked him.

He looked at Grossbart. "Sure, sir."

" 'Sergeant.' "

"Not so much at home," said Grossbart, stepping between us, "but away from home it gives one a sense of his Jewishness."

"We have to stick together," Fishbein said.

I started to walk toward the door; Halpern stepped back to make way for me.

"That's what happened in Germany," Grossbart was saying, loud enough for me to hear. "They didn't stick together. They let themselves get pushed around."

I turned. "Look, Grossbart. This is the Army, not summer camp."

He smiled. "So?"

Halpern tried to sneak off, but Grossbart held his arm.

"Grossbart, how old are you?" I asked.

"Nineteen."

"And you?" I said to Fishbein.

"The same. The same month, even."

"And what about him?" I pointed to Halpern, who had by now made it safely to the door.

"Eighteen," Grossbart whispered. "But like he can't tie his shoes or brush his teeth himself. I feel sorry for him."

"I feel sorry for all of us, Grossbart," I said, "but just act like a man. Just don't overdo it."

"Overdo what, sir?"

"The 'sir' business, for one thing. Don't overdo that," I said.

I left him standing there. I passed by Halpern, but he did not look at me. Then I was outside, but, behind, I heard Grossbart call, "Hey, Mickey, my *leben,* come on back. Refreshments!"

"Leben!" My grandmother's word for me!

One morning a week later, while I was working at my desk, Captain Barrett shouted for me to come into his office. When I entered, he had his

leben: darling

helmet liner squashed down so far on his head that I couldn't even see his eyes. He was on the phone, and when he spoke to me, he cupped one hand over the mouthpiece. "Who the hell is Grossbart?"

"Third platoon, Captain," I said. "A trainee."

"What's all this stink about food? His mother called a goddam congressman about the food." He uncovered the mouthpiece and slid his helmet up until I could see his bottom eyelashes. "Yes, sir," he said into the phone. "Yes, sir. I'm still here, sir. I'm asking Marx, here, right now—"

He covered the mouthpiece again and turned his head back toward me. "Lightfoot Harry's on the phone," he said, between his teeth. "This congressman calls General Lyman, who calls Colonel Sousa, who calls the Major, who calls me. They're just dying to stick this thing on me. Whatsa matter?" He shook the phone at me. "I don't feed the troops? What is this?"

"Sir, Grossbart is strange—" Barrett greeted that with a mockingly indulgent smile. I altered my approach. "Captain, he's a very orthodox Jew, and so he's only allowed to eat certain foods."

"He throws up, the congressman said. Every time he eats something, his mother says, he throws up!"

"He's accustomed to observing the dietary laws, Captain."

"So why's his old lady have to call the White House?"

"Jewish parents, sir—they're apt to be more protective than you expect. I mean, Jews have a very close family life. A boy goes away from home, sometimes the mother is liable to get very upset. Probably the boy mentioned something in a letter, and his mother misinterpreted."

"I'd like to punch him one right in the mouth," the Captain said. "There's a war on, and he wants a silver platter!"

"I don't think the boy's to blame, sir. I'm sure we can straighten it out by just asking him. Jewish parents worry—"

"*All* parents worry, for Christ's sake. But they don't get on their high horse and start pulling strings—"

I interrupted, my voice higher, tighter than before. "The home life, Captain, is very important—but you're right, it may sometimes get out of hand. It's a very wonderful thing, Captain, but because it's so close, this kind of thing . . ."

He didn't listen any longer to my attempt to present both myself and Lightfoot Harry with an explanation for the letter. He turned back to the phone. "Sir?" he said. "Sir—Marx, here, tells me Jews have a tendency to be pushy. He says he thinks we can settle it right here in the company . . . Yes, sir . . . I *will* call back, sir, soon as I can." He hung up. "Where are the men, Sergeant?"

"On the range."

With a whack on the top of his helmet, he crushed it down over his eyes again, and charged out of his chair. "We're going for a ride," he said.

The Captain drove, and I sat beside him. It was a hot spring day, and under my newly starched fatigues I felt as though my armpits were melting down onto my sides and chest. The roads were dry, and by the time we reached the firing range, my teeth felt gritty with dust, though my mouth had been shut the whole trip. The Captain slammed the brakes on and told me to get the hell out and find Grossbart.

I found him on his belly, firing wildly at the five-hundred-feet target. Waiting their turns behind him were Halpern and Fishbein. Fishbein, wearing a pair of steel-rimmed G.I. glasses I hadn't seen on him before, had the appearance of an old peddler who would gladly have sold you his rifle and the cartridges that were slung all over him. I stood back by the ammo boxes, waiting for Grossbart to finish spraying the distant targets. Fishbein straggled back to stand near me.

"Hello, Sergeant Marx," he said.

"How are you?" I mumbled.

"Fine, thank you. Sheldon's really a good shot."

"I didn't notice."

"I'm not so good, but I think I'm getting the hang of it now. Sergeant, I don't mean to, you know, ask what I shouldn't—" The boy stopped. He was trying to speak intimately, but the noise of the shooting forced him to shout at me.

"What is it?" I asked. Down the range, I saw Captain Barrett standing up in the jeep, scanning the line for me and Grossbart.

"My parents keep asking and asking where we're going," Fishbein said. "Everybody says the Pacific. I don't care, but my parents—If I could relieve their minds, I think I could concentrate more on my shooting."

"I don't know where, Fishbein. Try to concentrate anyway."

"Sheldon says you might be able to find out."

"I don't know a thing, Fishbein. You just take it easy, and don't let Sheldon—"

"*I'm* taking it easy, Sergeant. It's at home—"

Grossbart had finished on the line, and was dusting his fatigues with one hand. I called to him. "Grossbart, the Captain wants to see you."

He came toward us. His eyes blazed and twinkled. "Hi!"

"Don't point that rifle!" I said.

"I wouldn't shoot you, Sarge." He gave me a smile as wide as a pumpkin, and turned the barrel aside.

"Damn you, Grossbart, this is no joke! Follow me."

I walked ahead of him, and had the awful suspicion that, behind me, Grossbart was *marching,* his rifle on his shoulder as though he were a one-man detachment. At the jeep, he gave the Captain a rifle salute. "Private Sheldon Grossbart, sir."

"At ease, Grossman." The Captain sat down, slid over into the empty seat, and, crooking a finger, invited Grossbart closer.

"Bart, sir. Sheldon Gross*bart*. It's a common error." Grossbart nodded at me; *I* understood, he indicated. I looked away just as the mess truck pulled up to the range, disgorging a half-dozen K.P.s with rolled-up sleeves. The mess sergeant screamed at them while they set up the chowline equipment.

"Grossbart, your mama wrote some congressman that we don't feed you right. Do you know that?" the Captain said.

"It was my father, sir. He wrote to Representative Franconi that my religion forbids me to eat certain foods."

"What religion is that, Grossbart?"

"Jewish."

" 'Jewish, *sir,*' " I said to Grossbart.

"Excuse me, sir, Jewish, sir."

"What have you been living on?" the Captain asked. "You've been in the Army a month already. You don't look to me like you're falling to pieces."

"I eat because I have to, sir. But Sergeant Marx will testify to the fact that I don't eat one mouthful more than I need to in order to survive."

"Is that so, Marx?" Barrett asked.

"I've never seen Grossbart eat, sir," I said.

"But you heard the rabbi," Grossbart said. "He told us what to do, and I listened."

The Captain looked at me. "Well, Marx?"

"I still don't know what he eats and doesn't eat, sir."

Grossbart raised his arms to plead with me, and it looked for a moment as though he were going to hand me his weapon to hold. "But, Sergeant—"

"Look, Grossbart, just answer the Captain's questions," I said sharply.

Barrett smiled at me, and I resented it. "All right, Grossbart," he said. "What is it you want? The little piece of paper? You want out?"

"No, sir. Only to be allowed to live as a Jew. And for the others, too."

"What others?"

"Fishbein, sir, and Halpern."

"They don't like the way we serve, either?"

"Halpern throws up, sir. I've seen it."

"I thought *you* throw up."

"Just once, sir. I didn't know the sausage was sausage."

"We'll give menus, Grossbart. We'll show training films about the food, so you can identify when we're trying to poison you."

Grossbart did not answer. The men had been organized into two long chow lines. At the tail end of one, I spotted Fishbein—or, rather, his glasses spotted me. They winked sunlight back at me. Halpern stood next to him, patting the inside of his collar with a khaki handkerchief. They moved with the line as it began to edge up toward the food. The mess sergeant was still screaming at the K.P.s. For a moment, I was actually terrified by the thought that somehow the mess sergeant was going to become involved in Grossbart's problem.

"Marx," the Captain said, "you're a Jewish fella—am I right?"

I played straight man. "Yes, sir."

"How long you been in the Army? Tell this boy."

"Three years and two months."

"A year in combat, Grossbart. Twelve goddam months in combat all through Europe. I admire this man." The Captain snapped a wrist against my chest. "Do you hear him peeping about the food? Do you? I want an answer, Grossbart. Yes or no."

"No, sir."

"And why not? He's a Jewish fella."

"Some things are more important to some Jews than other things to other Jews."

Barrett blew up. "Look, Grossbart. Marx, here, is a good man—a goddam hero. When you were in high school, Sergeant Marx was killing Germans. Who does more for the Jews—you, by throwing up over a lousy piece of sausage, a piece of first-cut meat, or Marx, by killing those Nazi bastards? If I was a Jew, Grossbart, I'd kiss this man's feet. He's a goddam hero, and *he* eats what we give him. Why do you have to cause trouble is what I want to know! What is it you're buckin' for—a discharge?"

"No, sir."

"I'm talking to a wall! Sergeant, get him out of my way." Barrett swung himself back into the driver's seat. "I'm going to see the chaplain." The engine roared, the jeep spun around in a whirl of dust, and the Captain was headed back to camp.

For a moment, Grossbart and I stood side by side, watching the jeep. Then he looked at me and said, "I don't want to start trouble. That's the first thing they toss up to us."

When he spoke, I saw that his teeth were white and straight, and the sight of them suddenly made me understand that Grossbart actually did have parents—that once upon a time someone had taken little Sheldon to the dentist. He was their son. Despite all the talk about his parents, it was hard to believe in Grossbart as a child, an heir—as related by blood to anyone, mother, father, or, above all, to me. This realization led me to another.

"What does your father do, Grossbart?" I asked as we started to walk back toward the chow line.

"He's a tailor."

"An American?"

"Now, yes. A son in the Army," he said, jokingly.

"And your mother?" I asked.

He winked. "A *ballabusta*. She practically sleeps with a dustcloth in her hand."

"She's also an immigrant?"

ballabusta: housewife

"All she talks is Yiddish, still."

"And your father, too?"

"A little English. 'Clean,' 'Press,' 'Take the pants in.' That's the extent of it. But they're good to me."

"Then, Grossbart—" I reached out and stopped him. He turned toward me, and when our eyes met, his seemed to jump back, to shiver in their sockets. "Grossbart—you were the one who wrote that letter, weren't you?"

It took only a second or two for his eyes to flash happy again. "Yes." He walked on, and I kept pace. "It's what my father *would* have written if he had known how. It was his name, though. *He* signed it. He even mailed it. I sent it home. For the New York postmark."

I was astonished, and he saw it. With complete seriousness, he thrust his right arm in front of me. "Blood is blood, Sergeant," he said, pinching the blue vein in his wrist.

"What the hell *are* you trying to do, Grossbart?" I asked. "I've seen you eat. Do you know that? I told the Captain I don't know what you eat, but I've seen you eat like a hound at chow."

"We work hard, Sergeant. We're in training. For a furnace to work, you've got to feed it coal."

"Why did you say in the letter that you threw up all the time?"

"I was really talking about Mickey there. I was talking *for* him. He would never write, Sergeant, though I pleaded with him. He'll waste away to nothing if I don't help. Sergeant, I used my name—my father's name—but it's Mickey, and Fishbein, too, I'm watching out for."

"You're a regular Messiah, aren't you?"

We were at the chow line now.

"That's a good one, Sergeant," he said, smiling. "But who knows? Who can tell? Maybe you're the Messiah—a little bit. What Mickey says is the Messiah is a collective idea. He went to Yeshiva, Mickey, for a while. He says *together* we're the Messiah. Me a little bit, you a little bit. You should hear that kid talk, Sergeant, when he gets going."

"Me a little bit, you a little bit," I said. "You'd like to believe that, wouldn't you, Grossbart? That would make everything so clean for you."

"It doesn't seem too bad a thing to believe, Sergeant. It only means we should all *give* a little, is all."

I walked off to eat my rations with the other noncoms.

Two days later, a letter addressed to Captain Barrett passed over my desk. It had come through the chain of command—from the office of Congressman Franconi, where it had been received, to General Lyman, to Colonel Sousa, to Major Lamont, now to Captain Barrett. I read it over twice. It was dated May 14, the day Barrett had spoken with Grossbart on the rifle range.

Yeshiva: seminary

Dear Congressman:

First let me thank you for your interest in behalf of my son, Private Sheldon Grossbart. Fortunately, I was able to speak with Sheldon on the phone the other night, and I think I've been able to solve our problem. He is, as I mentioned in my last letter, a very religious boy, and it was only with the greatest difficulty that I could persuade him that the religious thing to do—what God Himself would want Sheldon to do—would be to suffer the pangs of religious remorse for the good of his country and all mankind. It took some doing, Congressman, but finally he saw the light. In fact, what he said (and I wrote down the words on a scratch pad so as never to forget), what he said was "I guess you're right, Dad. So many millions of my fellow-Jews gave up their lives to the enemy, the least I can do is live for a while minus a bit of my heritage so as to help end this struggle and regain for all the children of God dignity and humanity." That, Congressman, would make any father proud.

By the way, Sheldon wanted me to know—and to pass on to you—the name of a soldier who helped him reach this decision: SERGEANT NATHAN MARX. Sergeant Marx is a combat veteran who is Sheldon's first sergeant. This man has helped Sheldon over some of the first hurdles he's had to face in the Army, and is in part responsible for Sheldon's changing his mind about the dietary laws. I know Sheldon would appreciate any recognition Marx could receive.

Thank you and good luck. I look forward to seeing your name on the next election ballot.

Respectfully,
Samuel E. Grossbart

Attached to the Grossbart communiqué was another, addressed to General Marshall Lyman, the post commander, and signed by Representative Charles E. Franconi, of the House of Representatives. The communiqué informed General Lyman that Sergeant Nathan Marx was a credit to the U.S. Army and the Jewish people.

What was Grossbart's motive in recanting? Did he feel he'd gone too far? Was the letter a strategic retreat—a crafty attempt to strengthen what he considered our alliance? Or had he actually changed his mind, via an imaginary dialogue between Grossbart *père* and Grossbart *fils*? I was puzzled, but only for a few days—that is, only until I realized that, whatever his reasons, he had actually decided to disappear from my life; he was going to allow himself to become just another trainee. I saw him at inspection, but he never winked; at chow formations, but he never flashed me a sign. On Sunday, with the other trainees, he would sit around watching the noncoms' softball team, for which I pitched, but not once did he speak an unnecessary word to me. Fishbein and Halpern retreated, too—at Grossbart's command,

I was sure. Apparently he had seen that wisdom lay in turning back before he plunged over into the ugliness of privilege undeserved. Our separation allowed me to forgive him our past encounters, and, finally, to admire him for his good sense.

Meanwhile, free of Grossbart, I grew used to my job and my administrative tasks. I stepped on a scale one day, and discovered I had truly become a noncombatant; I had gained seven pounds. I found patience to get past the first three pages of a book. I thought about the future more and more, and wrote letters to girls I'd known before the war. I even got a few answers. I sent away to Columbia for a Law School catalogue. I continued to follow the war in the Pacific, but it was not my war. I thought I could see the end, and sometimes, at night, I dreamed that I was walking on the streets of Manhattan—Broadway, Third Avenue, 116th Street, where I had lived the three years I attended Columbia. I curled myself around these dreams and I began to be happy.

And then, one Sunday, when everybody was away and I was alone in the orderly room reading a month-old copy of the *Sporting News,* Grossbart reappeared.

"You a baseball fan, Sergeant?"

I looked up. "How are you?"

"Fine," Grossbart said. "They're making a soldier out of me."

"How are Fishbein and Halpern?"

"Coming along," he said. "We've got no training this afternoon. They're at the movies."

"How come you're not with them?"

"I wanted to come over and say hello."

He smiled—a shy, regular-guy smile, as though he and I well knew that our friendship drew its sustenance from unexpected visits, remembered birthdays, and borrowed lawnmowers. At first it offended me, and then the feeling was swallowed by the general uneasiness I felt at the thought that everyone on the post was locked away in a dark movie theater and I was here alone with Grossbart. I folded up my paper.

"Sergeant," he said, "I'd like to ask a favor. It is a favor, and I'm making no bones about it."

He stopped, allowing me to refuse him a hearing—which, of course, forced me into a courtesy I did not intend. "Go ahead."

"Well, actually, it's two favors."

I said nothing.

"The first one's about these rumors. Everybody says we're going to the Pacific."

"As I told your friend Fishbein, I don't know," I said. "You'll just have to wait to find out. Like everybody else."

"You think there's a chance of any of us going East?"

"Germany?" I said. "Maybe."

"I meant New York."

"I don't think so, Grossbart. Offhand."

"Thanks for the information, Sergeant," he said.

"It's not information, Grossbart. Just what I surmise."

"It certainly would be good to be near home. My parents—you know." He took a step toward the door and then turned back. "Oh, the other thing. May I ask the other?"

"What is it?"

"The other thing is—I've got relatives in St. Louis, and they say they'll give me a whole Passover dinner if I can get down there. God, Sergeant, that'd mean an awful lot to me."

I stood up. "No passes during basic, Grossbart."

"But we're off from now till Monday morning, Sergeant. I could leave the post and no one would even know."

"I'd know. You'd know."

"But that's all. Just the two of us. Last night, I called my aunt, and you should have heard her. 'Come—come,' she said. 'I got gefilte fish, *chrain*—the works!' Just a day, Sergeant. I'd take the blame if anything happened."

"The Captain isn't here to sign a pass."

"You could sign."

"Look, Grossbart—"

"Sergeant, for two months, practically, I've been eating *trafe* till I want to die."

"I thought you'd made up your mind to live with it. To be minus a little bit of heritage."

He pointed a finger at me. "You!" he said. "That wasn't for you to read."

"I read it. So what?"

"That letter was addressed to a congressman."

"Grossbart, don't feed me any baloney. You *wanted* me to read it."

"Why are you persecuting me, Sergeant?"

"Are you kidding!"

"I've run into this before," he said, "but never from my own!"

"Get out of here, Grossbart! Get the hell out of my sight!"

He did not move. "Ashamed, that's what you are," he said. "So you take it out on the rest of us. They say Hitler himself was half a Jew. Hearing you, I wouldn't doubt it."

"What are you trying to do with me, Grossbart?" I asked him. "What are you after? You want me to give you special privileges, to change the food, to find out about your orders, to give you weekend passes."

gefilte fish: seasoned chopped fish
chrain: horseradish

"You even talk like a goy!" Grossbart shook his fist. "Is this just a weekend pass I'm asking for? Is a Seder sacred, or not?"

Seder! It suddenly occurred to me that Passover had been celebrated weeks before. I said so.

"That's right," he replied. "Who says no? A month ago—and I was in the field eating hash! And now all I ask is a simple favor. A Jewish boy I thought would understand. My aunt's willing to go out of her way—to make a Seder a month later . . ." He turned to go, mumbling.

"Come back here!" I called. He stopped and looked at me. "Grossbart, why can't you be like the rest? Why do you have to stick out like a sore thumb?"

"Because I'm a Jew, Sergeant. I *am* different. Better, maybe not. But different."

"This is a war, Grossbart. For the time being *be* the same."

"I refuse."

"What?"

"I refuse. I can't stop being me, that's all there is to it." Tears came to his eyes. "It's a hard thing to be a Jew. But now I understand what Mickey says—it's a harder thing to stay one." He raised a hand sadly toward me. "Look at *you*."

"Stop crying!"

"Stop this, stop that, stop the other thing! *You* stop, Sergeant. Stop closing your heart to your own!" And, wiping his face with his sleeve, he ran out the door. "The least we can do for one another—the least . . ."

An hour later, looking out of the window, I saw Grossbart headed across the field. He wore a pair of starched khakis and carried a little leather ditty bag. I went out into the heat of the day. It was quiet; not a soul was in sight except, over by the mess hall, four K.P.'s sitting around a pan, sloped forward from their waists, gabbing and peeling potatoes in the sun.

"Grossbart!" I called.

He looked toward me and continued walking.

"Grossbart, get over here!"

He turned and came across the field. Finally, he stood before me.

"Where are you going?" I asked.

"St. Louis. I don't care."

"You'll get caught without a pass."

"So I'll get caught without a pass."

"You'll go to the stockade."

"I'm *in* the stockade." He made an about-face and headed off.

I let him go only a step or two. "Come back here," I said, and he followed

goy: gentile
Seder: ceremonial dinner on first day of Passover

me into the office, where I typed out a pass and signed the Captain's name, and my own initials after it.

He took the pass and then, a moment later, reached out and grabbed my hand. "Sergeant, you don't know how much this means to me."

"O.K.," I said. "Don't get in any trouble."

"I wish I could show you how much this means to me."

"Don't do me any favors. Don't write any more congressmen for citations."

He smiled. "You're right. I won't. But let me do something."

"Bring me a piece of that gefilte fish. Just get out of here."

"I will!" he said. "With a slice of carrot and a little horseradish. I won't forget."

"All right. Just show your pass at the gate. And don't tell *anybody*."

"I won't. It's a month late, but a good Yom Tov to you."

"Good Yom Tov, Grossbart," I said.

"You're a good Jew, Sergeant. You like to think you have a hard heart, but underneath you're a fine, decent man. I mean that."

Those last three words touched me more than any words from Grossbart's mouth had the right to. "All right, Grossbart," I said. "Now call me 'sir,' and get the hell out of here."

He ran out the door and was gone. I felt very pleased with myself; it was a great relief to stop fighting Grossbart, and it had cost me nothing. Barrett would never find out, and if he did, I could manage to invent some excuse. For a while, I sat at my desk, comfortable in my decision. Then the screen door flew back and Grossbart burst in again. "Sergeant!" he said. Behind him I saw Fishbein and Halpern, both in starched khakis, both carrying ditty bags like Grossbart's.

"Sergeant, I caught Mickey and Larry coming out of the movies. I almost missed them."

"Grossbart—did I say to tell no one?" I said.

"But my aunt said I could bring friends. That I should, in fact."

"*I'm* the Sergeant, Grossbart—not your aunt!"

Grossbart looked at me in disbelief. He pulled Halpern up by his sleeve. "Mickey, tell the Sergeant what this would mean to you."

Halpern looked at me and, shrugging, said, "A lot."

Fishbein stepped forward without prompting. "This would mean a great deal to me and my parents, Sergeant Marx."

"No!" I shouted.

Grossbart was shaking his head. "Sergeant, I could see you denying me, but how you can deny Mickey, a Yeshiva boy—that's beyond me."

"I'm not denying Mickey anything," I said. "You just pushed a little too hard, Grossbart. *You* denied him."

Yom Tov: holiday (literally, good day)

"I'll give him my pass, then," Grossbart said. "I'll give him my aunt's address and a little note. At least let him go."

In a second, he had crammed the pass into Halpern's pants pocket. Halpern looked at me, and so did Fishbein. Grossbart was at the door, pushing it open. "Mickey, bring me a piece of gefilte fish, at least," he said, and then he was outside again.

The three of us looked at one another, and then I said, "Halpern, hand that pass over."

He took it from his pocket and gave it to me. Fishbein had now moved to the doorway, where he lingered. He stood there for a moment with his mouth slightly open, and then he pointed to himself. "And me?" he asked.

His utter ridiculousness exhausted me. I slumped down in my seat and felt pulses knocking at the back of my eyes. "Fishbein," I said, "you understand I'm not trying to deny you anything, don't you? If it was my Army, I'd serve gefilte fish in the mess hall. I'd sell *kugel* in the PX, honest to God."

Halpern smiled.

"You understand, don't you, Halpern?"

"Yes, Sergeant."

"And you, Fishbein? I don't want enemies. I'm just like you—I want to serve my time and go home. I miss the same things you miss."

"Then, Sergeant," Fishbein said, "why don't you come, too?"

"Where?"

"To St. Louis. To Shelly's aunt. We'll have a regular Seder. Play hide-the-matzoh." He gave me a broad, black-toothed smile.

I saw Grossbart again, on the other side of the screen.

"Pssst!" He waved a piece of paper. "Mickey, here's the address. Tell her I couldn't get away."

Halpern did not move. He looked at me, and I saw the shrug moving up his arms into his shoulders again. I took the cover off my typewriter and made out passes for him and Fishbein. "Go," I said. "The three of you."

I thought Halpern was going to kiss my hand.

That afternoon, in a bar in Joplin, I drank beer and listened with half an ear to the Cardinal game. I tried to look squarely at what I'd become involved in, and began to wonder if perhaps the struggle with Grossbart wasn't as much my fault as his. What was I that I had to *muster* generous feelings? Who was I to have been feeling so grudging, so tight-hearted? After all, I wasn't being asked to move the world. Had I a right, then, or a reason, to clamp down on Grossbart, when that meant clamping down on Halpern, too? And Fishbein—that ugly, agreeable soul? Out of the many

kugel: noodle pudding
matzoh: unleavened bread eaten at Passover

recollections of my childhood that had tumbled over me these past few days I heard my grandmother's voice: "What are you making a *tsimmes*?" It was what she would ask my mother when, say, I had cut myself while doing something I shouldn't have done, and her daughter was busy bawling me out. I needed a hug and a kiss, and my mother would moralize. But my grandmother knew—mercy overrides justice. I should have known it, too. Who was Nathan Marx to be such a penny pincher with kindness? Surely, I thought, the Messiah himself—if He should ever come—won't niggle over nickles and dimes. God willing, he'll hug and kiss.

The next day, while I was playing softball over on the parade ground, I decided to ask Bob Wright, who was noncom in charge of Classification and Assignment, where he thought our trainees would be sent when their cycle ended, in two weeks. I asked casually, between innings, and he said, "They're pushing them all into the Pacific. Shulman cut the orders on your boys the other day."

The news shocked me, as though I were the father of Halpern, Fishbein, and Grossbart.

That night, I was just sliding into sleep when someone tapped on my door. "Who is it?" I asked.

"Sheldon."

He opened the door and came in. For a moment, I felt his presence without being able to see him. "How was it?" I asked.

He popped into sight in the near-darkness before me. "Great, Sergeant." Then he was sitting on the edge of the bed. I sat up.

"How about you?" he asked. "Have a nice weekend?"

"Yes."

"The others went to sleep." He took a deep, paternal breath. We sat silent for a while, and a homey feeling invaded my ugly little cubicle; the door was locked, the cat was out, the children were safely in bed.

"Sergeant, can I tell you something? Personal?"

I did not answer, and he seemed to know why. "Not about me. About Mickey. Sergeant, I never felt for anybody like I feel for him. Last night I heard Mickey in the bed next to me. He was crying so, it could have broken your heart. Real sobs."

"I'm sorry to hear that."

"I had to talk to him to stop him. He held my hand, Sergeant—he wouldn't let it go. He was almost hysterical. He kept saying if he only knew where we were going. Even if he knew it *was* the Pacific, that would be better than nothing. Just to know."

Long ago, someone had taught Grossbart the sad rule that only lies can get the truth. Not that I couldn't believe in the fact of Halpern's crying; his

tsimmes: a to-do

eyes *always* seemed red-rimmed. But, fact or not, it became a lie when Grossbart uttered it. He was entirely strategic. But then—it came with the force of indictment—so was I! There are strategies of aggression, but there are strategies of retreat as well. And so, recognizing that I myself had not been without craft and guile, I told him what I knew. "It is the Pacific."

He let out a small gasp, which was not a lie. "I'll tell him. I wish it was otherwise."

"So do I."

He jumped on my words. "You mean you think you could do something? A change, maybe?"

"No, I couldn't do a thing."

"Don't you know anybody over at C. and A.?"

"Grossbart, there's nothing I can do," I said. "If your orders are for the Pacific, then it's the Pacific."

"But Mickey—"

"Mickey, you, me—everybody, Grossbart. There's nothing to be done. Maybe the war'll end before you go. Pray for a miracle."

"But—"

"Good night, Grossbart." I settled back, and was relieved to feel the springs unbend as Grossbart rose to leave. I could see him clearly now; his jaw had dropped, and he looked like a dazed prizefighter. I noticed for the first time a little paper bag in his hand.

"Grossbart." I smiled. "My gift?"

"Oh, yes, Sergeant. Here—from all of us." He handed me the bag. "It's egg roll."

"Egg roll?" I accepted the bag and felt a damp grease spot on the bottom. I opened it, sure that Grossbart was joking.

"We thought you'd probably like it. You know—Chinese egg roll. We thought you'd probably have a taste for—"

"Your aunt served egg roll?"

"She wasn't home."

"Grossbart, she invited you. You told me she invited you and your friends."

"I know," he said. "I just reread the letter. *Next* week."

I got out of bed and walked to the window. "Grossbart," I said. But I was not calling to him.

"What?"

"What are you, Grossbart? Honest to God, what are you?"

I think it was the first time I'd asked him a question for which he didn't have an immediate answer.

"How can you do this to people?" I went on.

"Sergeant, the day away did us all a world of good. Fishbein, you should see him, he *loves* Chinese food."

"But the Seder," I said.

"We took second best, Sergeant."

Rage came charging at me. I didn't sidestep. "Grossbart, you're a liar!" I said. "You're a schemer and a crook. You've got no respect for anything. Nothing at all. Not for me, for the truth—not even for poor Halpern! You use us all—"

"Sergeant, Sergeant, I feel for Mickey. Honest to God, I do. I *love* Mickey. I try—"

"You try! You feel!" I lurched toward him and grabbed his shirt front. I shook him furiously. "Grossbart, get out! Get out and stay the hell away from me. Because if I see you, I'll make your life miserable. *You understand that?*"

"Yes."

I let him free, and when he walked from the room, I wanted to spit on the floor where he had stood. I couldn't stop the fury. It engulfed me, owned me, till it seemed I could only rid myself of it with tears or an act of violence. I snatched from the bed the bag Grossbart had given me and, with all my strength, threw it out the window. And the next morning, as the men policed the area around the barracks, I heard a great cry go up from one of the trainees, who had been anticipating only his morning handful of cigarette butts and candy wrappers. "Egg roll!" he shouted. "Holy Christ, Chinese goddam egg roll!"

A week later, when I read the orders that had come down from C. and A., I couldn't believe my eyes. Every single trainee was to be shipped to Camp Stoneman, California, and from there to the Pacific—every trainee but one. Private Sheldon Grossbart. He was to be sent to Fort Monmouth, New Jersey. I read the mimeographed sheet several times. Dee, Farrell, Fishbein, Fuselli, Fylypowycz, Glinicki, Gromke, Gucwa, Halpern, Hardy, Helebrandt, right down to Anton Zygadlo—all were to be headed West before the month was out. All except Grossbart. He had pulled a string, and I wasn't it.

I lifted the phone and called C. and A.

The voice on the other end said smartly, "Corporal Shulman, sir."

"Let me speak to Sergeant Wright."

"Who is this calling, sir?"

"Sergeant Marx."

And, to my surprise, the voice said, *"Oh!"* Then, "Just a minute, Sergeant."

Shulman's *"Oh!"* stayed with me while I waited for Wright to come to the phone. Why *"Oh!"*? Who was Shulman? And then, so simply, I knew I'd discovered the string that Grossbart had pulled. In fact, I could hear Grossbart the day he'd discovered Shulman in the PX, or in the bowling alley, or maybe even at services. "Glad to meet you. Where you from? Bronx? Me, too. Do you know So-and-So? And So-and-So? Me, too! You work at C. and A.? Really? Hey, how's chances of getting East? Could you do something? Change something? Swindle, cheat, lie? We gotta help each other, you know. If the Jews in Germany . . ."

Bob Wright answered the phone. "How are you, Nate? How's the pitching arm?"

"Good. Bob, I wonder if you could do me a favor." I heard clearly my own words, and they so reminded me of Grossbart that I dropped more easily than I could have imagined into what I had planned. "This may sound crazy, Bob, but I got a kid here on orders to Monmouth who wants them changed. He had a brother killed in Europe, and he's hot to go to the Pacific. Says he'd feel like a coward if he wound up Stateside. I don't know, Bob—can anything be done? Put somebody else in the Monmouth slot?"

"Who?" he asked cagily.

"Anybody. First guy in the alphabet. I don't care. The kid just asked if something could be done."

"What's his name?"

"Grossbart, Sheldon."

Wright didn't answer.

"Yeah," I said. "He's a Jewish kid, so he thought I could help him out. You know."

"I guess I can do something," he finally said. "The Major hasn't been around here for weeks. Temporary duty to the golf course. I'll try, Nate, that's all I can say."

"I'd appreciate it, Bob. See you Sunday." And I hung up, perspiring.

The following day, the corrected orders appeared: Fishbein, Fuselli, Fylypowycz, Glinicki, Gromke, Grossbart, Gucwa, Halpern, Hardy . . . Lucky Private Harley Alton was to go to Fort Monmouth, New Jersey, where, for some reason or other, they wanted an enlisted man with infantry training.

After chow that night, I stopped back at the orderly room to straighten out the guard-duty roster. Grossbart was waiting for me. He spoke first.

"You son of a bitch!"

I sat down at my desk, and while he glared at me, I began to make the necessary alterations in the duty roster.

"What do you have against me?" he cried. "Against my family? Would it kill you for me to be near my father, God knows how many months he has left to him?"

"Why so?"

"His heart," Grossbart said. "He hasn't had enough troubles in a lifetime, you've got to add to them. I curse the day I ever met you, Marx! Shulman told me what happened over there. There's no limit to your anti-Semitism, is there? The damage you've done here isn't enough. You have to make a special phone call! You really want me dead!"

I made the last few notations in the duty roster and got up to leave. "Good night, Grossbart."

"You owe me an explanation!" He stood in my path.

"Sheldon, you're the one who owes explanations."

He scowled. "To *you*?"

"To me, I think so—yes. Mostly to Fishbein and Halpern."

"That's right, twist things around. I owe nobody nothing. I've done all I could do for them. Now I think I've got the right to watch out for myself."

"For each other we have to learn to watch out, Sheldon. You told me yourself."

"You call this watching out for me—what you did?"

"No. For all of us."

I pushed him aside and started for the door. I heard his furious breathing behind me, and it sounded like steam rushing from an engine of terrible strength.

"*You'll* be all right," I said from the door. And, I thought, so would Fishbein and Halpern be all right, even in the Pacific, if only Grossbart continued to see—in the obsequiousness of the one, the soft spirituality of the other—some profit for himself.

I stood outside the orderly room, and I heard Grossbart weeping behind me. Over in the barracks, in the lighted windows, I could see the boys in their T shirts sitting on their bunks talking about their orders, as they'd been doing for the past two days. With a kind of quiet nervousness, they polished shoes, shined belt buckles, squared away underwear, trying as best they could to accept their fate. Behind me, Grossbart swallowed hard, accepting his. And then, resisting with all my will an impulse to turn and seek pardon for my vindictiveness, I accepted my own.

QUESTIONS

1. More use of dilemma is made in this story than in any other in this text. Identify some of the dilemmas the protagonist finds himself in. Are they used primarily to create suspense, to reveal character, or to illuminate theme? Might all of these dilemmas be classified as specific applications of one general dilemma? If so, how might this general dilemma be described? (One suggestion for an answer is contained in the terms used by Nathan Marx's grandmother on page 168.)

2. Sergeant Marx finds himself in so many dilemmas because he is trying to reconcile three roles—top sergeant, Jew, and human being. To what extent do these roles conflict? Point out places where Marx is thinking or acting primarily as a sergeant, as a Jew, as a human being.

3. The plot has four major episodes, centering in conflicts over (a) attendance at Friday night services, (b) company food, (c) pass to St. Louis,

(d) shipping orders. Insofar as these involve external conflict between Sergeant Marx and Grossbart, which is the victor in each?

4. "What are you, Grossbart? Honest to God, what are you?" asks Sergeant Marx. Answer this question as precisely as possible. What is Grossbart's philosophy? Catalogue the various methods he uses to achieve his goals.

5. Even more important to Sergeant Marx is the question, Who is Sergeant Marx? What does the fact that he asks this question (page 167) tell us about him? By what principles does he try to govern his conduct? On page 169, Marx speaks of "strategies of aggression" and "strategies of retreat"; on what occasions does *he* use strategies similar to Grossbart's?

6. What are Sergeant Marx's motivations in his final decision? In which of his roles—sergeant, Jew, human being—is he acting at this point? Is his decision right?

7. What is meant by Sergeant Marx's final statement that he accepted his fate? What *is* his fate?

8. Describe as precisely as possible Captain Barrett's attitude toward Jews.

9. Differentiate Grossbart, Fishbein, and Halpern. How would you rank these three, Captain Barrett, and Sergeant Marx on a scale of human worth?

10. To what character (or characters) does the title refer? Is it used straightforwardly or ironically?

11. This story—by a Jewish author about Jewish characters—has a complex theme. Does the theme at its most general level necessarily involve the idea of Jewishness? Is it more crucial to the story that Nathan Marx is a Jew or a top sergeant? Try stating the theme without mentioning the idea of Jewishness. Now expand it to include the idea of Jewishness. Can it be stated without mentioning the idea of responsibility for command and judgment?

CHAPTER FIVE

Point of View

The primitive storyteller, unbothered by considerations of form, simply spun a tale. "Once upon a time," he began, and proceeded to narrate the story to his listeners, describing the characters when necessary, telling what they thought and felt as well as what they did, and interjecting comments and ideas of his own. The modern fiction writer is artistically more self-conscious. He realizes that there are many ways of telling a story; he decides upon a method before he begins and may even set up rules for himself. Instead of telling the story himself, he may let one of his characters tell it for him; he may tell it by means of letters or diaries; he may confine himself to recording the thoughts of one of his characters. With the growth of artistic consciousness, the question of POINT OF VIEW, of who tells the story, and, therefore, of how it gets told, has assumed especial importance.

To determine the point of view of a story we ask, "Who tells the story?" and "How much is he allowed to know?" and, especially, "To what extent does the author look inside his characters and report their thoughts and feelings?"

Though many variations and combinations are possible, the basic points of view are four, as follows:

1. Omniscient
2. Limited omniscient
   - (a) Major character
   - (b) Minor character
3. First person
   - (a) Major character
   - (b) Minor character
4. Objective

1. In the OMNISCIENT POINT OF VIEW, the story is told by the author, using the third person, and his knowledge and prerogatives are unlimited. He is free to go wherever he wishes, to peer inside the minds and hearts of his characters at will and tell us what they are thinking or feeling. He can interpret their behavior, and he can comment, if he wishes, on the significance of the story he is telling. He knows all. He can tell us as much or as little as he pleases.

The following version of Aesop's fable "The Ant and the Grasshopper" is told from the omniscient point of view. Notice that in it we are told not only what both characters do and say, but also what they think and feel; also, that the author comments at the end on the significance of his story. (The phrases in which the author enters into the thoughts or feelings of the ant and the grasshopper have been italicized; the comment by the author is printed in small capitals.)

> *Weary in every limb,* the ant tugged over the snow a piece of corn he had stored up last summer. *It would taste mighty good at dinner tonight.*
>
> A grasshopper, *cold and hungry,* looked on. *Finally he could bear it no longer.* "Please, friend ant, may I have a bite of corn?"
>
> "What were you doing all last summer?" asked the ant. He looked the grasshopper up and down. *He knew its kind.*
>
> "I sang from dawn till dark," replied the grasshopper, *happily unaware of what was coming next.*
>
> "Well," said the ant, *hardly bothering to conceal his contempt,* "since you sang all summer, you can dance all winter."
>
> HE WHO IDLES WHEN HE'S YOUNG
>
> WILL HAVE NOTHING WHEN HE'S OLD.

Stories told from the omniscient point of view may differ widely in the amount of omniscience the author allows himself. In "Tears, Idle Tears," we share the thoughts and perceptions of Frederick, Frederick's mother, the girl on the park bench, and, fleetingly, of the mother's friends, a chaplain, and a doctor—almost everyone, indeed, except the duck. In "The Destructors," though we are taken into the minds of Blackie, Mike, the gang as a group, Old Misery, and the lorry driver, we are not taken into the mind of Trevor—the most important character. In "The Most Dangerous Game," we are confined to the thoughts and feelings of Rainsford, except for the brief passage between Rainsford's leap into the sea and his waking in Zaroff's bed, during which the point of view shifts to General Zaroff. In "The Kiss," we are confined to the responses of the officers of the regiment in general, and to those of Riabovitch in particular; in effect, then, this story actually belongs in our next category.

The omniscient is the most flexible point of view and permits the widest scope. It is also the most subject to abuse. It offers constant danger that the author may come between the reader and the story, or that the continual shifting of viewpoint from character to character may cause a breakdown in coherence or unity. Used skillfully it enables the author to achieve simultaneous breadth and depth. Unskillfully used, it can destroy the illusion of reality that the story attempts to create.

2. In the LIMITED OMNISCIENT POINT OF VIEW, the author tells the story in the third person, but he tells it from the viewpoint of one character in the story. The author places himself at the elbow of this character, so to speak, and looks at the events of the story through his eyes and through his mind. He moves both inside and outside this character but never leaves his side. He tells us what this character sees and hears and what he thinks and feels; he possibly interprets the character's thoughts and behavior. He knows everything about this character—more than the character knows about himself—but he shows no knowledge of what *other* characters are thinking or feeling or doing, except for what his chosen character knows or can infer. The chosen character may be either a major or a minor character, a participant or an observer, and this choice also will be a very important one for the story. "The Japanese Quince" and "The Storm" are told from the limited omniscient point of view, from the viewpoint of the main character. The use of this viewpoint with a minor character is rare and is not illustrated in this book. Here is "The Ant and the Grasshopper" told, in the third person, from the point of view of the ant. Notice that this time we are told nothing of what the grasshopper thinks or feels. We see and hear and know of him only what the ant sees and hears and knows.

> *Weary in every limb,* the ant tugged over the snow a piece of corn he had stored up last summer. *It would taste mighty good at dinner tonight. It was then that he noticed the grasshopper, looking cold and pinched.*
>
> "Please, friend ant, may I have a bite of your corn?" asked the grasshopper.
>
> He looked the grasshopper up and down. "What were you doing all last summer?" he asked. *He knew its kind.*

"I sang from dawn till dark," replied the grasshopper.

"Well," said the ant, *hardly bothering to conceal his contempt,* "since you sang all summer, you can dance all winter."

The limited omniscient point of view, since it acquaints us with the world through the mind and senses of only one person, approximates more closely than the omniscient the conditions of real life; it also offers a ready-made unifying element, since all details of the story are the experience of one person. At the same time it offers a limited field of observation, for the reader can go nowhere except where the chosen character goes, and there may be difficulty in having him naturally cognizant of all important events. A clumsy writer will constantly have his focal character listening at keyholes, accidentally overhearing important conversations, or coincidentally being present when important events occur.

3. In the FIRST-PERSON POINT OF VIEW, the author disappears into one of the characters, who tells the story in the first person. This character, again, may be either a major or minor character, protagonist or observer, and it will make considerable difference whether the protagonist tells his own story or someone else tells it. In "I'm a Fool," "Defender of the Faith," and, in effect, in "Youth," the protagonist tells the story in the first person. In "The Child By Tiger," "That Evening Sun" and, technically, in "Youth," the story is told by an observer. The story below is told in the first person from the point of view of the grasshopper. (The whole story is italicized, because it all comes out of the grasshopper's mind.)

Cold and hungry, I watched the ant tugging over the snow a piece of corn he had stored up last summer. My feelers twitched, and I was conscious of a tic in my left hind leg. Finally I could bear it no longer. "Please, friend ant," I asked, "may I have a bite of your corn?"

He looked me up and down. "What were you doing all last summer?" he asked, rather too smugly it seemed to me.

"I sang from dawn till dark," I said innocently, remembering the happy times.

"Well," he said, with a priggish sneer, "since you sang all summer, you can dance all winter."

The first-person point of view shares the virtues and limitations of the limited omniscient. It offers, sometimes, a gain in immediacy and reality, since we get the story directly from a participant, the author as middleman being eliminated. It offers no opportunity, however, for *direct* interpretation by the author, and there is constant danger that the narrator may be made to transcend his sensitivity, his knowledge, or his powers of language in telling the story. "Youth" avoids this danger, for the narrator is a highly literate, educated man who reads books like Carlyle's *Sartor Resartus* during his off-hours; but "I'm a Fool" may not altogether escape it. A good author, however, can make tremendous literary capital out of the very limitations of his narrator. The first-person point of view offers excellent opportunities for dramatic irony and for studies in limited or blunted human perceptivity. Often, as in "I'm a Fool," the very heart of the story may lie in the difference between what the narrator perceives and what the reader perceives. In such stories the author offers an interpretation of his materials *indirectly,* through the use of irony. He may also indicate his own judgment, more straightforwardly though still indirectly, by expressing it through the lips of a discerning and sympathetic narrator. In "Defender of the Faith" the reader is disposed to accept Sergeant Marx's interpretation of characters and events as being largely the author's own. Such identifications of a narrator's attitude with the author's, however, must always be undertaken with extreme caution; they are justified only if the total material of the story supports them. In "Defender of the Faith" the moral sensitivity and intelligence of the narrator reflects the author's own; nevertheless, much of the interest of the story arises from Marx's own uncertainty about his judgments—the nagging apprehension that he may be mistaken.

4. In the OBJECTIVE POINT OF VIEW, the author disappears into a kind of roving sound camera. This camera can go anywhere but can record only what is seen and heard. It cannot comment, interpret, or enter a character's mind. With this point of view (sometimes called also the DRAMATIC POINT OF VIEW) the reader is placed in the position of a spectator at a movie or play. He sees what the characters do and hears what they say but can only infer what they think or feel and what they are like. The author is not there to explain. The purest example of a story told from the objective point of view would be one written entirely in dialogue, for as soon as the author adds words of his own, he begins to interpret through his very choice of words. Actually, few stories using this point of view are antiseptically pure, for the limitations it imposes on the author are severe. "Hills Like White Elephants" is an excellent example, however, and "The Lottery" is essentially objective in its narration. The following version of "The Ant and the Grasshopper" is

also told from the objective point of view. (Since we are nowhere taken into the thoughts or feelings of the characters, none of this version is printed in italics.)

> The ant tugged over the snow a piece of corn he had stored up last summer, perspiring in spite of the cold.
>
> A grasshopper, its feelers twitching and with a tic in its left hind leg, looked on for some time. Finally he asked, "Please, friend ant, may I have a bite of your corn?"
>
> The ant looked the grasshopper up and down. "What were you doing all last summer?" he snapped.
>
> "I sang from dawn till dark," replied the grasshopper, not changing his tone.
>
> "Well," said the ant, and a faint smile crept into his face, "since you sang all summer, you can dance all winter."

The objective point of view has the most speed and the most action; also, it forces the reader to make his own interpretations. On the other hand, it must rely heavily on external action and dialogue, and it offers no opportunities for interpretation by the author.

Each of the points of view has its advantages, its limitations, and its peculiar uses. Ideally the choice of the author will depend on his story materials and his purpose. He should choose the point of view that enables him to present his particular materials most effectively in terms of his purpose. If he is writing a murder mystery, he will ordinarily avoid using the point of view of the murderer or the brilliant detective: otherwise he would have to reveal at the beginning the secrets he wishes to conceal till the end. On the other hand, if he is interested in exploring criminal psychology, the murderer's point of view might be by far the most effective. In the Sherlock Holmes stories, A. Conan Doyle effectively uses the somewhat imperceptive Dr. Watson as his narrator, so that the reader may be kept in the dark as long as possible and then be as amazed as Watson is by Holmes's deductive powers. In Dostoevsky's *Crime and Punishment,* however, the author is interested not in mystifying and surprising but in illuminating the moral and psychological operations of the human soul in the act of taking life; he therefore tells the story from the viewpoint of a sensitive and intelligent murderer.

For the reader, the examination of point of view may be important both for understanding and for evaluating the story. First, he should know whether the events of the story are being interpreted by the author or by one of the characters. If the latter, he must ask how this character's mind and personality affect his interpretation, whether the character is perceptive or imperceptive, and whether his interpretation can be accepted at face value or must be discounted because of ignorance, stupidity, or self-deception. Often, as in "I'm a Fool" and "That Evening Sun," an author achieves striking and significant effects by using a narrator not aware of the full import of the events he is reporting.

Next, the reader should ask whether the writer has chosen his point of view for maximum revelation of his material or for another reason. The author may choose his point of view mainly to conceal certain information till the end of the story and thus maintain suspense and create surprise. He may even deliberately mislead the reader by presenting the events through a character who puts a false interpretation on them. Such a false interpretation may be justified if it leads eventually to more effective revelation of character and theme. If it is there merely to trick the reader, it is obviously less justifiable.

Finally, the reader should ask whether the author has used his selected point of view fairly and consistently. Even with the escape story, we have a right to demand fair treatment. If the person to whose thoughts and feelings we are admitted has pertinent information which he does not reveal, we legitimately feel cheated. To have a chance to solve a murder mystery, we must know what the detective knows. A writer also should be consistent in his point of view; or, if he shifts it, he should do so for a just artistic reason. The serious interpretive writer chooses and uses point of view so as to yield ultimately the greatest possible insight, either in fullness or in intensity.

Ring Lardner

HAIRCUT

I got another barber that comes over from Carterville and helps me out Saturdays, but the rest of the time I can get along all right alone. You can see for yourself that this ain't no New York City and besides that, the most of the boys works all day and don't have no leisure to drop in here and get themselves prettied up.

You're a newcomer, ain't you? I thought I hadn't seen you round before. I hope you like it good enough to stay. As I say, we ain't no New York City or Chicago, but we have pretty good times. Not as good, though, since Jim Kendall got killed. When he was alive, him and Hod Meyers used to keep this town in an uproar. I bet they was more laughin' done here than any town its size in America.

Jim was comical, and Hod was pretty near a match for him. Since Jim's gone, Hod tries to hold his end up just the same as ever, but it's tough goin' when you ain't got nobody to kind of work with.

They used to be plenty fun in here Saturdays. This place is jam-packed Saturdays, from four o'clock on. Jim and Hod would show up right after their supper, round six o'clock. Jim would set himself down in that big chair, nearest the blue spittoon. Whoever had been settin' in that chair, why they'd get up when Jim come in and give it to him.

You'd of thought it was a reserved seat like they have sometimes in a theayter. Hod would generally always stand or walk up and down, or some Saturdays, of course, he'd be settin' in this chair part of the time, gettin' a haircut.

Well, Jim would set there a w'ile without openin' his mouth only to spit, and then finally he'd say to me, "Whitey,"—my right name, that is, my right first name, is Dick, but everybody round here calls me Whitey—Jim would say, "Whitey, your nose looks like a rosebud tonight. You must of been drinkin' some of your aw de cologne."

So I'd say, "No, Jim, but you look like you'd been drinkin' somethin' of that kind or somethin' worse."

Jim would have to laugh at that, but then he'd speak up and say, "No, I ain't had nothin' to drink, but that ain't sayin' I wouldn't like somethin'. I wouldn't even mind if it was wood alcohol."

Then Hod Meyers would say, "Neither would your wife." That would set everybody to laughin' because Jim and his wife wasn't on very good terms. She'd of divorced him only they wasn't no chance to get alimony and she didn't have no way to take care of herself and the kids. She couldn't never understand Jim. He *was* kind of rough, but a good fella at heart.

Him and Hod had all kinds of sport with Milt Sheppard. I don't suppose you've seen Milt. Well, he's got an Adam's apple that looks more like a mushmelon. So I'd be shavin' Milt and when I'd start to shave down here on his neck, Hod would holler, "Hey, Whitey, wait a minute! Before you cut into it, let's make up a pool and see who can guess closest to the number of seeds."

And Jim would say, "If Milt hadn't of been so hoggish, he'd of ordered a half a cantaloupe instead of a whole one and it might not of stuck in his throat."

All the boys would roar at this and Milt himself would force a smile, though the joke was on him. Jim certainly was a card!

There's his shavin' mug, settin' on the shelf, right next to Charley Vail's. "Charles M. Vail." That's the druggist. He comes in regular for his shave, three times a week. And Jim's is the cup next to Charley's. "James H. Kendall." Jim won't need no shavin' mug no more, but I'll leave it there just the same for old time's sake. Jim certainly was a character!

Years ago, Jim used to travel for a canned goods concern over in Carterville. They sold canned goods. Jim had the whole northern half of the State and was on the road five days out of every week. He'd drop in here Saturdays and tell his experiences for that week. It was rich.

I guess he paid more attention to playin' jokes than makin' sales. Finally the concern let him out and he come right home here and told everybody he'd been fired instead of sayin' he'd resigned like most fellas would of.

It was a Saturday and the shop was full and Jim got up out of that chair and says, "Gentlemen, I got an important announcement to make. I been fired from my job."

Well, they asked him if he was in earnest and he said he was and nobody could think of nothin' to say till Jim finally broke the ice himself. He says, "I been sellin' canned goods and now I'm canned goods myself."

You see, the concern he'd been workin' for was a factory that made canned goods. Over in Carterville. And now Jim said he was canned himself. He was certainly a card!

Jim had a great trick that he used to play w'ile he was travelin'. For instance, he'd be ridin' on a train and they'd come to some little town like —well, like—we'll say, like Benton. Jim would look out the train window and read the signs on the stores.

For instance, they'd be a sign, "Henry Smith, Dry Goods." Well, Jim would write down the name and the name of the town and when he got to wherever he was goin' he'd mail back a postal card to Henry Smith at Benton and not sign no name to it, but he'd write on the card, well, somethin' like "Ask your wife about that book agent that spent the afternoon last week," or "Ask your Missus who kept her from gettin' lonesome the last time you was in Carterville." And he'd sign the card, "A Friend."

Of course, he never knew what really come of none of these jokes, but he could picture what *probably* happened and that was enough.

Jim didn't work very steady after he lost his position with the Carterville people. What he did earn, doin' odd jobs round town, why he spent pretty near all of it on gin and his family might of starved if the stores hadn't of carried them along. Jim's wife tried her hand at dressmakin', but they ain't nobody goin' to get rich makin' dresses in this town.

As I say, she'd of divorced Jim, only she seen that she couldn't support herself and the kids and she was always hopin' that some day Jim would cut out his habits and give her more than two or three dollars a week.

They was a time when she would go to whoever he was workin' for and ask them to give her his wages, but after she done this once or twice, he beat her to it by borrowin' most of his pay in advance. He told it all round town, how he had outfoxed his Missus. He certainly was a caution!

But he wasn't satisfied with just outwittin' her. He was sore the way she had acted, tryin' to grab off his pay. And he made up his mind he'd get even. Well, he waited till Evans's Circus was advertised to come to town. Then he told his wife and two kiddies that he was goin' to take them to the circus. The day of the circus, he told them he would get the tickets and meet them outside the entrance to the tent.

Well, he didn't have no intentions of bein' there or buyin' tickets or nothin'. He got full of gin and laid round Wright's poolroom all day. His wife and the kids waited and waited and of course he didn't show up. His wife didn't have a dime with her, or nowhere else, I guess. So she finally had to tell the kids it was all off and they cried like they wasn't never goin' to stop.

Well, it seems, w'ile they was cryin', Doc Stair came along and he asked what was the matter, but Mrs. Kendall was stubborn and wouldn't tell him, but the kids told him and he insisted on takin' them and their mother in the show. Jim found this out afterwards and it was one reason why he had it in for Doc Stair.

Doc Stair come here about a year and a half ago. He's a mighty handsome young fella and his clothes always look like he has them made to order. He goes to Detroit two or three times a year and w'ile he's there he must have a tailor take his measure and then make him a suit to order. They cost pretty near twice as much, but they fit a whole lot better than if you just bought them in a store.

For a w'ile everybody was wonderin' why a young doctor like Doc Stair should come to a town like this where we already got old Doc Gamble and Doc Foote that's both been here for years and all the practice in town was always divided between the two of them.

Then they was a story got round that Doc Stair's gal had throwed him over, a gal up in the Northern Peninsula somewheres, and the reason he come here was to hide himself away and forget it. He said himself that he thought they wasn't nothin' like general practice in a place like ours to fit a man to be a good all round doctor. And that's why he'd came.

Anyways, it wasn't long before he was makin' enough to live on, though they tell me that he never dunned nobody for what they owed him, and the folks here certainly has got the owin' habit, even in my business. If I had all that was comin' to me for just shaves alone, I could go to Carterville and put up at the Mercer for a week and see a different picture every night. For instance, they's old George Purdy—but I guess I shouldn't ought to be gossipin'.

Well, last year, our coroner died, died of the flu. Ken Beatty, that was his name. He was the coroner. So they had to choose another man to be coroner in his place and they picked Doc Stair. He laughed at first and said he didn't want it, but they made him take it. It ain't no job that anybody would fight for and what a man makes out of it in a year would just about buy seeds for their garden. Doc's the kind, though, that can't say no to nothin' if you keep at him long enough.

But I was goin' to tell you about a poor boy we got here in town—Paul Dickson. He fell out of a tree when he was about ten years old. Lit on his head and it done somethin' to him and he ain't never been right. No harm in him, but just silly. Jim Kendall used to call him cuckoo; that's a name Jim had for anybody that was off their head, only he called people's head their bean. That was another of his gags, callin' head bean and callin' crazy people cuckoo. Only poor Paul ain't crazy, but just silly.

You can imagine that Jim used to have all kinds of fun with Paul. He'd send him to the White Front Garage for a left-handed monkey wrench. Of course they ain't no such a thing as a left-handed monkey wrench.

And once we had a kind of a fair here and they was a baseball game between the fats and the leans and before the game started Jim called Paul over and sent him way down to Schrader's hardware store to get a key for the pitcher's box.

They wasn't nothin' in the way of gags that Jim couldn't think up, when he put his mind to it.

Poor Paul was always kind of suspicious of people, maybe on account of how Jim had kept foolin' him. Paul wouldn't have much to do with anybody only his own mother and Doc Stair and a girl here in town named Julie Gregg. That is, she ain't a girl no more, but pretty near thirty or over.

When Doc first come to town, Paul seemed to feel like here was a real friend and he hung round Doc's office most of the w'ile; the only time he wasn't there was when he'd go home to eat or sleep or when he seen Julie Gregg doin' her shoppin'.

When he looked out Doc's window and seen her, he'd run downstairs and join her and tag along with her to the different stores. The poor boy was crazy about Julie and she always treated him mighty nice and made him feel like he was welcome, though of course it wasn't nothin' but pity on her side.

Doc done all he could to improve Paul's mind and he told me once that he really thought the boy was gettin' better, that they was times when he was as bright and sensible as anybody else.

But I was goin' to tell you about Julie Gregg. Old Man Gregg was in the lumber business, but got to drinkin' and lost the most of his money and when he died, he didn't leave nothin' but the house and just enough insurance for the girl to skimp along on.

Her mother was a kind of a half invalid and didn't hardly ever leave the house. Julie wanted to sell the place and move somewheres else after the old man died, but the mother said she was born here and would die here. It was tough on Julie, as the young people round this town—well, she's too good for them.

She's been away to school and Chicago and New York and different places and they ain't no subject she can't talk on, where you take the rest of the young folks here and you mention anything to them outside of Gloria Swanson or Tommy Meighan and they think you're delirious. Did you see Gloria in *Wages of Virtue*? You missed somethin'!

Well, Doc Stair hadn't been here more than a week when he come in one day to get shaved and I recognized who he was as he had been pointed out to me, so I told him about my old lady. She's been ailin' for a couple years and either Doc Gamble or Doc Foote, neither one, seemed to be helpin' her. So he said he would come out and see her, but if she was able to get out herself, it would be better to bring her to his office where he could make a completer examination.

So I took her to his office and w'ile I was waitin' for her in the reception room, in come Julie Gregg. When somebody comes in Doc Stair's office, they's a bell that rings in his inside office so as he can tell they's somebody to see him.

So he left my old lady inside and come out to the front office and that's the first time him and Julie met and I guess it was what they call love at first sight. But it wasn't fifty-fifty. This young fella was the slickest lookin' fella she'd ever seen in this town and she went wild over him. To him she was just a young lady that wanted to see the doctor.

She'd came on about the same business I had. Her mother had been doctorin' for years with Doc Gamble and Doc Foote and without no results. So she'd heard they was a new doc in town and decided to give him a try. He promised to call and see her mother that same day.

I said a minute ago that it was love at first sight on her part. I'm not only judgin' by how she acted afterwards but how she looked at him that first day in his office. I ain't no mind reader, but it was wrote all over her face that she was gone.

Now Jim Kendall, besides bein' a jokesmith and a pretty good drinker, well, Jim was quite a lady-killer. I guess he run pretty wild durin' the time he was on the road for them Carterville people, and besides that, he'd had a couple little affairs of the heart right here in town. As I say, his wife could of divorced him, only she couldn't.

But Jim was like the majority of men, and women, too, I guess. He wanted what he couldn't get. He wanted Julie Gregg and worked his head off tryin' to land her. Only he'd of said bean instead of head.

Well, Jim's habits and his jokes didn't appeal to Julie and of course he was a married man, so he didn't have no more chance than, well, than a rabbit. That's an expression of Jim's himself. When somebody didn't have no chance to get elected or somethin', Jim would always say they didn't have no more chance than a rabbit.

He didn't make no bones about how he felt. Right in here, more than once, in front of the whole crowd, he said he was stuck on Julie and anybody that could get her for him was welcome to his house and his wife and kids included. But she wouldn't have nothin' to do with him; wouldn't even speak to him on the street. He finally seen he wasn't gettin' nowheres with his usual line so he decided to try the rough stuff. He went right up to her house one evenin' and when she opened the door he forced his way in and grabbed her. But she broke loose and before he could stop her, she run in the next room and locked the door and phoned to Joe Barnes. Joe's the marshal. Jim could hear who she was phonin' to and he beat it before Joe got there.

Joe was an old friend of Julie's pa. Joe went to Jim the next day and told him what would happen if he ever done it again.

I don't know how the news of this little affair leaked out. Chances is that Joe Barnes told his wife and she told somebody else's wife and they told their husband. Anyways, it did leak out and Hod Meyers had the nerve to kid Jim about it, right here in this shop. Jim didn't deny nothin' and kind of laughed it off and said for us all to wait; that lots of people had tried to make a monkey out of him, but he always got even.

Meanw'ile everybody in town was wise to Julie's bein' wild mad over the Doc. I don't suppose she had any idear how her face changed when him and her was together; of course she couldn't of, or she'd of kept away from him. And she didn't know that we was all noticin' how many times she made excuses to go up to his office or pass it on the other side of the street and look up in his window to see if he was there. I felt sorry for her and so did most other people.

Hod Meyers kept rubbin' it into Jim about how the Doc had cut him out. Jim didn't pay no attention to the kiddin' and you could see he was plannin' one of his jokes.

One trick Jim had was the knack of changin' his voice. He could make you think he was a girl talkin' and he could mimic any man's voice. To show you how good he was along this line, I'll tell you the joke he played on me once.

You know, in most towns of any size, when a man is dead and needs a shave, why the barber that shaves him soaks him five dollars for the job; that is, he don't soak *him,* but whoever ordered the shave. I just charge three dollars because personally I don't mind much shavin' a dead person. They lay a whole lot stiller than live customers. The only thing is that you don't feel like talkin' to them and you get kind of lonesome.

Well, about the coldest day we ever had here, two years ago last winter, the phone rung at the house w'ile I was home to dinner and I answered the phone and it was a woman's voice and she said she was Mrs. John Scott and her husband was dead and would I come out and shave him.

Old John had always been a good customer of mine. But they live seven miles out in the country, on the Streeter road. Still I didn't see how I could say no.

So I said I would be there, but would have to come in a jitney and it might cost three or four dollars besides the price of the shave. So she, or the voice, it said that was all right, so I got Frank Abbott to drive me out to the place and when I got there, who should open the door but old John himself! He wasn't no more dead than, well, than a rabbit.

It didn't take no private detective to figure out who had played me this little joke. Nobody could of thought it up but Jim Kendall. He certainly was a card!

I tell you this incident just to show you how he could disguise his voice and make you believe it was somebody else talkin'. I'd of swore it was Mrs. Scott had called me. Anyways, some woman.

Well, Jim waited till he had Doc Stair's voice down pat; then he went after revenge.

He called Julie up on a night when he knew Doc was over in Carterville. She never questioned but what it was Doc's voice. Jim said he must see her that night; he couldn't wait no longer to tell her somethin'. She was all excited and told him to come to the house. But he said he was expectin' an important long distance call and wouldn't she please forget her manners for once and come to his office. He said they couldn't nothin' hurt her and nobody would see her and he just *must* talk to her a little w'ile. Well, poor Julie fell for it.

Doc always keeps a night light in his office, so it looked to Julie like they was somebody there.

Meanw'ile Jim Kendall had went to Wright's poolroom, where they was a whole gang amusin' themselves. The most of them had drank plenty of gin, and they was a rough bunch even when sober. They was always strong for Jim's jokes and when he told them to come with him and see some fun they give up their card games and pool games and followed along.

Doc's office is on the second floor. Right outside his door they's a flight of stairs leadin' to the floor above. Jim and his gang hid in the dark behind these stairs.

Well, Julie come up to Doc's door and rung the bell and they was nothin' doin'. She rung it again and she rung it seven or eight times. Then she tried the door and found it locked. Then Jim made some kind of a noise and she heard it and waited a minute, and then she says, "Is that you, Ralph?" Ralph is Doc's first name.

They was no answer and it must of came to her all of a sudden that she'd been bunked. She pretty near fell downstairs and the whole gang after her. They chased her all the way home, hollerin', "Is that you, Ralph?" and "Oh, Ralphie, dear, is that you?" Jim says he couldn't holler it himself, as he was laughin' too hard.

Poor Julie! She didn't show up here on Main Street for a long, long time afterward.

And of course Jim and his gang told everybody in town, everybody but Doc Stair. They was scared to tell him, and he might of never knowed only for Paul Dickson. The poor cuckoo, as Jim called him, he was here in the shop one night when Jim was still gloatin' yet over what he'd done to Julie. And Paul took in as much of it as he could understand and he run to Doc with the story.

It's a cinch Doc went up in the air and swore he'd make Jim suffer. But it was a kind of a delicate thing, because if it got out that he had beat Jim up, Julie was bound to hear of it and then she'd know that Doc knew and of course knowin' that he knew would make it worse for her than ever. He was goin' to do somethin', but it took a lot of figurin'.

Well, it was a couple days later when Jim was here in the shop again, and so was the cuckoo. Jim was goin' duck-shootin' the next day and had came in lookin' for Hod Meyers to go with him. I happened to know that Hod went over to Carterville and wouldn't be home till the end of the week. So Jim said he hated to go alone and he guessed he would call it off. Then poor Paul spoke up and said if Jim would take him he would go along. Jim thought a w'ile and then he said, well, he guessed a half-wit was better than nothin'.

I suppose he was plottin' to get Paul out in the boat and play some joke on him, like pushin' him in the water. Anyways, he said Paul could go. He asked him had he ever shot a duck and Paul said no, he'd never even had a gun in his hands. So Jim said he could set in the boat and watch him and if he behaved himself, he might lend him his gun for a couple of shots. They made a date to meet in the mornin' and that's the last I seen of Jim alive.

Next mornin', I hadn't been open more than ten minutes when Doc Stair come in. He looked kind of nervous. He asked me had I seen Paul Dickson. I said no, but I knew where he was, out duck-shootin' with Jim Kendall. So Doc says that's what he had heard, and he couldn't understand it because Paul had told him he wouldn't never have no more to do with Jim as long as he lived.

He said Paul had told him about the joke Jim had played on Julie. He said Paul had asked him what he thought of the joke and the Doc had told him that anybody that would do a thing like that ought not to be let live.

I said it had been a kind of a raw thing, but Jim just couldn't resist no kind of a joke, no matter how raw. I said I thought he was all right at heart, but just bubblin' over with mischief. Doc turned and walked out.

At noon he got a phone call from old John Scott. The lake where Jim and Paul had went shootin' is on John's place. Paul had came runnin' up to the house a few minutes before and said they'd been an accident. Jim had shot a few ducks and then give the gun to Paul and told him to try his luck. Paul hadn't never handled a gun and he was nervous. He was shakin' so hard that he couldn't control the gun. He let fire and Jim sunk back in the boat, dead.

Doc Stair, bein' the coroner, jumped in Frank Abbott's flivver and rushed out to Scott's farm. Paul and old John was down on the shore of the lake. Paul had rowed the boat to shore, but they'd left the body in it, waitin' for Doc to come.

Doc examined the body and said they might as well fetch it back to town. They was no use leavin' it there or callin' a jury, as it was a plain case of accidental shootin'.

Personally I wouldn't never leave a person shoot a gun in the same boat I was in unless I was sure they knew somethin' about guns. Jim was a sucker to leave a new beginner have his gun, let alone a half-wit. It probably served Jim right, what he got. But still we miss him round here. He certainly was a card!

Comb it wet or dry?

QUESTIONS

1. The barber makes much of the unique quality of his town. "We ain't no New York City or Chicago," he says, "but we have pretty good times. . . . When [Jim Kendall] was alive, I bet they was more laughin' done here than in any town its size in America." Evaluate the barber's opinion.

2. How good are the jokes made in Whitey's barbershop? Do they have any characteristics in common? In addition to the jokes that are "made," the story concerns jokes that are "played." What is that kind of joke called? What is its chief characteristic? Does it have anything in common with the jokes "made" in the barbershop? What are Jim Kendall's motivations for playing these jokes? Does he have just cause?

3. What kind of person is Jim Kendall? Make a thorough characterization.

4. Explain the circumstances of Jim Kendall's death. Was it "a plain case of accidental shootin' "? Does Doc Stair think so? Does the barber?

5. What kind of person is the barber? As a narrator, how reliable is he? Study him thoroughly, taking into consideration such things as (a) his evaluations of and attitude toward Jim Kendall, (b) his delight with Jim Kendall's "expressions" and his admiration of Jim's "jokes"—"They wasn't nothin' in the way of gags that Jim couldn't think up, when he put his mind to it," (c) his idea of a good time, (d) his remark, "they's old George Purdy—but I guess I shouldn't ought to be gossipin'," (e) his explanation that "Jim used to travel for a canned goods concern over in Carterville. They

sold canned goods." (Find other examples of the same characteristic), and (f) his evaluation of the circumstances of Jim's death.

6. Who is the most important character in the story?
7. What is the story fundamentally about?

Willa Cather

PAUL'S CASE

It was Paul's afternoon to appear before the faculty of the Pittsburgh High School to account for his various misdemeanors. He had been suspended a week ago, and his father had called at the Principal's office and confessed his perplexity about his son. Paul entered the faculty room suave and smiling. His clothes were a trifle outgrown, and the tan velvet on the collar of his open overcoat was frayed and worn; but for all that there was something of the dandy about him, and he wore an opal pin in his neatly knotted black four-in-hand, and a red carnation in his buttonhole. This latter adornment the faculty somehow felt was not properly significant of the contrite spirit befitting a boy under the ban of suspension.

Paul was tall for his age and very thin, with high, cramped shoulders and a narrow chest. His eyes were remarkable for a certain hysterical brilliancy, and he continually used them in a conscious, theatrical sort of way, peculiarly offensive in a boy. The pupils were abnormally large, as though he were addicted to belladonna, but there was a glassy glitter about them which that drug does not produce.

When questioned by the Principal as to why he was there, Paul stated, politely enough, that he wanted to come back to school. This was a lie, but Paul was quite accustomed to lying; found it, indeed, indispensable for overcoming friction. His teachers were asked to state their respective charges against him, which they did with such a rancour and aggrievedness as evinced that this was not a usual case. Disorder and impertinence were among the offences named, yet each of his instructors felt that it was scarcely possible to put into words the real cause of the trouble, which lay in a sort of hysterically defiant manner of the boy's; in the contempt which they all knew he felt for them, and which he seemingly made not the least effort to conceal. Once, when he had been making a synopsis of a paragraph at the blackboard, his English teacher had stepped to his side and attempted to guide his hand. Paul had started back with a shudder and thrust his hands violently behind him. The astonished woman could scarcely have been more hurt and embarrassed had he struck at her. The insult was so involuntary and definitely personal as to be unforgettable. In one way and another, he had made all his teachers, men and women alike, conscious of the same feeling of physical aversion. In one class he habitually sat with his hand shading his eyes; in another he always looked out of the window during the recitation; in another he made a running commentary on the lecture, with humorous intent.

His teachers felt this afternoon that his whole attitude was symbolized by his shrug and his flippantly red carnation flower, and they fell upon him without mercy, his English teacher leading the pack. He stood through it smiling, his pale lips parted over his white teeth. (His lips were continually twitching, and he had a habit of raising his eyebrows that was contemptuous and irritating to the last degree.) Older boys than Paul had broken down and shed tears under that ordeal, but his set smile did not once desert him, and his only sign of discomfort was the nervous trembling of the fingers that toyed with the buttons of his overcoat, and an occasional jerking of the other hand which held his hat. Paul was always smiling, always glancing about him, seeming to feel that people might be watching him and trying to detect something. This conscious expression, since it was as far as possible from boyish mirthfulness, was usually attributed to insolence or "smartness."

As the inquisition proceeded, one of his instructors repeated an impertinent remark of the boy's, and the Principal asked him whether he thought that a courteous speech to make to a woman. Paul shrugged his shoulders slightly and his eyebrows twitched.

"I don't know," he replied. "I didn't mean to be polite or impolite, either. I guess it's a sort of way I have, of saying things regardless."

The Principal asked him whether he didn't think that a way it would be well to get rid of. Paul grinned and said he guessed so. When he was told that he could go, he bowed gracefully and went out. His bow was like a repetition of the scandalous red carnation.

His teachers were in despair, and his drawing-master voiced the feeling of them all when he declared there was something about the boy which none of them understood. He added: "I don't really believe that smile of his comes altogether from insolence; there's something sort of haunted about it. The boy is not strong, for one thing. There is something wrong about the fellow."

The drawing-master had come to realize that, in looking at Paul, one saw only his white teeth and the forced animation of his eyes. One warm afternoon the boy had gone to sleep at his drawing-board, and his master had noted with amazement what a white, blue-veined face it was; drawn and wrinkled like an old man's about the eyes, the lips twitching even in his sleep.

His teachers left the building dissatisfied and unhappy; humiliated to have felt so vindictive toward a mere boy, to have uttered this feeling in cutting terms, and to have set each other on, as it were, in the gruesome game of intemperate reproach. One of them remembered having seen a miserable street cat set at bay by a ring of tormentors.

As for Paul, he ran down the hill whistling the Soldiers' Chorus from "Faust," looking behind him now and then to see whether some of his teachers were not there to witness his light-heartedness. As it was now late in the afternoon and Paul was on duty that evening as usher at Carnegie Hall, he decided that he would not go home to supper.

When he reached the concert hall, the doors were not yet open. It was chilly outside, and he decided to go up into the picture gallery—always deserted at this hour—where there were some of Raffelli's gay studies of Paris streets and an airy blue Venetian scene or two that always exhilarated him. He was delighted to find no one in the gallery but the old guard, who sat in the corner, a newspaper on his knee, a black patch over one eye and the other closed. Paul possessed himself of the place and walked confidently up and down, whistling under his breath. After a while he sat down before a blue Rico and lost himself. When he bethought him to look at his watch, it was after seven o'clock, and he rose with a start and ran downstairs, making a face at Augustus Caesar, peering out from the cast-room, and an evil gesture at the Venus of Milo as he passed her on the stairway.

When Paul reached the ushers' dressing-room, half a dozen boys were there already, and he began excitedly to tumble into his uniform. It was one of the few that at all approached fitting, and Paul thought it very becoming—though he knew the tight, straight coat accentuated his narrow chest, about which he was exceedingly sensitive. He was always excited while he dressed, twanging all over to the tuning of the strings and the preliminary flourishes of the horns in the music-room; but tonight he seemed quite beside himself, and he teased and plagued the boys until, telling him that he was crazy, they put him down on the floor and sat on him.

Somewhat calmed by his suppression, Paul dashed out to the front of the house to seat the early comers. He was a model usher. Gracious and smiling he ran up and down the aisles. Nothing was too much trouble for him; he carried messages and brought programmes as though it were his greatest pleasure in life, and all the people in his section thought him a charming boy, feeling that he remembered and admired them. As the house filled, he grew more and more vivacious and animated, and the colour came to his cheeks and lips. It was very much as though this were a great reception and Paul were the host. Just as the musicians came out to take their places, his English teacher arrived with cheques for the seats which a prominent manufacturer had taken for the season. She betrayed some embarrassment when she handed Paul the tickets, and a hauteur which subsequently made her feel very foolish. Paul was startled for a moment, and had the feeling of wanting to put her out; what business had she here among all these fine people and gay colours? He looked her over and decided that she was not appropriately dressed and must be a fool to sit downstairs in such togs. The tickets had probably been sent her out of kindness, he reflected, as he put down a seat for her, and she had about as much right to sit there as he had.

When the symphony began, Paul sank into one of the rear seats with a long sigh of relief, and lost himself as he had done before the Rico. It was not that symphonies, as such, meant anything in particular to Paul, but the first sight of the instruments seemed to free some hilarious spirit within him; something that struggled there like the Genius in the bottle found by the Arab fisherman. He felt a sudden zest of life; the lights danced before his eyes and the concert hall blazed into unimaginable splendour. When the soprano soloist came on, Paul forgot even the nastiness of his teacher's being there, and gave himself up to the peculiar intoxication such personages always had for him. The soloist chanced to be a German woman, by no means in her first youth, and the mother of many children; but she wore a satin gown and a tiara, and she had that indefinable air of achievement, that world-shine upon her, which always blinded Paul to any possible defects.

After a concert was over, Paul was often irritable and wretched until he got to sleep—and to-night he was even more than usually restless. He had the feeling of not being able to let down; of its being impossible to give up this delicious excitement which was the only thing that could be called living at all. During the last number he withdrew and, after hastily changing his clothes in the dressing-room, slipped out to the side door where the singer's carriage stood. Here he began pacing rapidly up and down the walk, waiting to see her come out.

Over yonder the Schenley, in its vacant stretch, loomed big and square through the fine rain, the windows of its twelve stories glowing like those of a lighted cardboard house under a Christmas tree. All the actors and singers of any importance stayed there when they were in Pittsburgh, and a number of the big manufacturers of the place lived there in the winter. Paul had often hung about the hotel, watching the people go in and out, longing to enter and leave schoolmasters and dull care behind him forever.

At last the singer came out, accompanied by the conductor, who helped her into her carriage and closed the door with a cordial *auf wiedersehen*—which set Paul to wondering whether she were not an old sweetheart of his. Paul followed the carriage over to the hotel, walking so rapidly as not to be far from the entrance when the singer alighted and disappeared behind the swinging glass doors which were opened by a Negro in a tall hat and a long coat. In the moment that the door was ajar, it seemed to Paul that he, too, entered. He seemed to feel himself go after her up the steps, into the warm, lighted building, into an exotic, a tropical world of shiny, glistening surfaces and basking ease. He reflected upon the mysterious dishes that were brought into the dining-room, the green bottles in buckets of ice, as he had seen them in the supper-party pictures of the Sunday supplement. A quick gust of wind brought the rain down with sudden vehemence, and Paul was startled to find that he was still outside in the slush of the gravel driveway; that his boots were letting in the water and his scanty overcoat was clinging wet about him; that the lights in front of the concert hall were out, and that the rain was driving in sheets between him and the orange glow of the windows above him. There it was, what he wanted—tangibly before him, like the fairy world of a Christmas pantomime; as the rain beat in his face, Paul wondered whether he were destined always to shiver in the black night outside, looking up at it.

He turned and walked reluctantly toward the car tracks. The end had to come sometime; his father in his night-clothes at the top of the stairs, explanations that did not explain, hastily improvised fictions that were forever tripping him up, his upstairs room and its horrible yellow wallpaper, the creaking bureau with the greasy plush collar-box, and over his painted wooden bed the pictures of George Washington and John Calvin, and the framed motto, 'Feed my Lambs,' which had been worked in red worsted by his mother, whom Paul could not remember.

Half an hour later, Paul alighted from the Negley Avenue car and went slowly down one of the side streets off the main thoroughfare. It was a highly respectable street, where all the houses were exactly alike, and where business men of moderate means begot and reared large families of children, all of whom went to Sabbath School and learned the shorter catechism, and were interested in arithmetic; all of whom were as exactly alike as their homes, and of a piece with the monotony in which they lived. Paul never went up Cordelia Street without a shudder of loathing. His home was next the house of the Cumberland minister. He approached it to-night with the nerveless sense of defeat, the hopeless feeling of sinking back forever into ugliness and commonness that he had always had when he came home. The moment he turned into Cordelia Street he felt the waters close above his head. After each of these orgies of living, he experienced all the physical depression which follows a debauch; the loathing of respectable beds, of common food, of a house permeated by kitchen odours; a shuddering repulsion for the flavourless, colourless mass of every-day existence; a morbid desire for cool things and soft lights and fresh flowers.

The nearer he approached the house, the more absolutely unequal Paul felt to the sight of it all: his ugly sleeping chamber; the old bathroom with the grimy zinc tub, the cracked mirror, the dripping spigots; his father, at the top of the stairs, his hairy legs sticking out from his nightshirt, his feet thrust into carpet slippers. He was so much later than usual that there would certainly be enquiries and reproaches. Paul stopped short before the door. He felt that he could not be accosted by his father to-night; that he could not toss again on that miserable bed. He would not go in. He would tell his father that he had no car-fare, and it was raining so hard he had gone home with one of the boys and stayed all night.

Meanwhile, he was wet and cold. He went around to the back of the house and tried one of the basement windows, found it open, raised it cautiously, and scrambled down the cellar wall to the floor. There he stood, holding his breath, terrified by the noise he had made; but the floor above him was silent, and there was no creak on the stairs. He found a soap-box, and carried it over to the soft ring of light that streamed from the furnace door, and sat down. He was horribly afraid of rats, so he did not try to sleep, but sat looking distrustfully at the dark, still terrified lest he might have awakened his father.

In such reactions, after one of the experiences which made days and nights out of the dreary blanks of the calendar, when his senses were deadened, Paul's head was always singularly clear. Suppose his father had heard him getting in at the window and had come down and shot him for a burglar? Then, again, suppose his father had come down, pistol in hand, and he had cried out in time to save himself, and his father had been horrified to think how nearly he had killed him? Then again, suppose a day should come when his father would remember that night, and wish there had been no warning cry to stay his hand? With this last supposition Paul entertained himself until daybreak.

The following Sunday was fine; the sodden November chill was broken by the last flash of autumnal summer. In the morning Paul had to go to church and Sabbath School, as always. On seasonable Sunday afternoons the burghers of Cordelia Street usually sat out on their front "stoops," and talked to their neighbours on the next stoop, or called to those across the street in neighbourly fashion. The men sat placidly on gay cushions placed upon the steps that led down to the sidewalk, while the women, in their Sunday "waists," sat in rockers on the cramped porches, pretending to be greatly at their ease. The children played in the streets; there were so many of them that the place resembled the recreation grounds of a kindergarten. The men on the steps, all in their shirt-sleeves, their vests unbuttoned, sat with their legs well apart, their stomachs comfortably protruding, and talked of the prices of things, or told anecdotes of the sagacity of their various chiefs and overlords. They occasionally looked over the multitude of squabbling children, listened affectionately to their high-pitched, nasal voices, smiling to see their own proclivities reproduced in their offspring, and interspersed their legends of the iron kings with remarks about their sons' progress at school, their grades in arithmetic, and the amounts they had saved in their toy banks.

On this last Sunday of November, Paul sat all the afternoon on the lowest step of his "stoop," staring into the street, while his sisters, in their rockers, were talking to the minister's daughters next door about how many shirtwaists they had made in the last week, and how many waffles someone had eaten at the last church supper. When the weather was warm, and his father was in a particularly jovial frame of mind, the girls made lemonade, which was always brought out in a red-glass pitcher, ornamented with forget-me-nots in blue enamel. This the girls thought very fine, and the neighbours joked about the suspicious colour of the pitcher.

To-day Paul's father, on the top step, was talking to a young man who shifted a restless baby from knee to knee. He happened to be the young man who was daily held up to Paul as a model, and after whom it was his father's dearest hope that he would pattern. This young man was of a ruddy complexion, with a compressed, red mouth, and faded, nearsighted eyes, over which he wore thick spectacles, with gold bows that curved about his ears. He was clerk to one of the magnates of a great steel corporation, and was looked upon in Cordelia Street as a young man with a future. There was a story that, some five years ago—he was now barely twenty-six—he had been a trifle "dissipated," but in order to curb his appetites and save the loss of time and strength that a sowing of wild oats might have entailed, he had taken his chief's advice, oft reiterated to his employees, and at twenty-one had married the first woman whom he could persuade to share his fortunes. She happened to be an angular schoolmistress, much older than he, who also wore thick glasses, and who had now borne him four children, all near-sighted like herself.

The young man was relating how his chief, now cruising in the Mediterranean, kept in touch with all the details of the business, arranging his office hours on his yacht just as though he were at home, and "knocking off work enough to keep two stenographers busy." His father told, in turn, the plan his corporation was considering, of putting in an electric railway plant at Cairo. Paul snapped his teeth; he had an awful apprehension that they might spoil it all before he got there. Yet he rather liked to hear these legends of the iron kings, that were told and retold on Sundays and holidays; these stories of palaces in Venice, yachts on the Mediterranean, and high play at Monte Carlo appealed to his fancy, and he was interested in the triumphs of cash-boys who had become famous, though he had no mind for the cash-boy stage.

After supper was over, and he had helped to dry the dishes, Paul nervously asked his father whether he could go to George's to get some help in his geometry, and still more nervously asked for car-fare. This latter request he had to repeat, as his father, on principle, did not like to hear requests for money, whether much or little. He asked Paul whether he could not go to some boy who lived nearer, and told him that he ought not to leave his school work until Sunday; but he gave him the dime. He was not a poor man, but he had a worthy ambition to come up in the world. His only reason for allowing Paul to usher was that he thought a boy ought to be earning a little.

Paul bounded upstairs, scrubbed the greasy odour of the dishwater from his hands with the ill-smelling soap he hated, and then shook over his fingers a few drops of violet water from the bottle he kept hidden in his drawer. He left the house with his geometry conspicuously under his arm, and the moment he got out of Cordelia Street and boarded a downtown car, he shook off the lethargy of two deadening days, and began to live again.

The leading juvenile of the permanent stock company which played at one of the downtown theatres was an acquaintance of Paul's, and the boy had been invited to drop in at the Sunday-night rehearsals whenever he could. For more than a year Paul had spent every available moment loitering about Charley Edwards's dressing-room. He had won a place among Edwards's following not only because the young actor, who could not afford to employ a dresser, often found him useful, but because he recognized in Paul something akin to what churchmen term "vocation."

It was at the theatre and at Carnegie Hall that Paul really lived; the rest was but a sleep and a forgetting. This was Paul's fairy tale, and it had for him all the allurement of a secret love. The moment he inhaled the gassy, painty, dusty odour behind the scenes, he breathed like a prisoner set free, and felt within him the possibility of doing or saying splendid, brilliant things. The moment the cracked orchestra beat out the overture from "Martha," or jerked at the serenade from "Rigoletto," all stupid and ugly things slid from him, and his senses were deliciously, yet delicately fired.

Perhaps it was because, in Paul's world, the natural nearly always wore the guise of ugliness, that a certain element of artificiality seemed to him necessary in beauty. Perhaps it was because his experience of life elsewhere was so full of Sabbath-School picnics, petty economies, wholesome advice as to how to succeed in life, and the unescapable odours of cooking, that he found this existence so alluring, these smartly clad men and women so attractive, that he was so moved by these starry apple orchards that bloomed perennially under the limelight. It would be difficult to put it strongly enough how convincingly the stage entrance of that theatre was for Paul the actual portal of Romance. Certainly none of the company ever suspected it, least of all Charley Edwards. It was very like the old stories that used to float about London of fabulously rich Jews, who had subterranean halls, with palms, and fountains, and soft lamps and richly apparelled women who never saw the disenchanting light of London day. So, in the midst of that smoke-palled city, enamoured of figures and grimy toil, Paul had his secret temple, his wishing-carpet, his bit of blue-and-white Mediterranean shore bathed in perpetual sunshine.

Several of Paul's teachers had a theory that his imagination had been perverted by garish fiction; but the truth was he scarcely ever read at all. The books at home were not such as would either tempt or corrupt a youthful mind, and as for reading the novels that some of his friends urged upon him—well, he got what he wanted much more quickly from music; any sort of music, from an orchestra to a barrel-organ. He needed only the spark, the indescribable thrill that made his imagination master of his senses, and he could make plots and pictures enough of his own. It was equally true that he was not stage-struck—not, at any rate, in the usual acceptation of that expression. He had no desire to become an actor, any more than he had to become a musician. He felt no necessity to do any of these things; what he wanted was to see, to be in the atmosphere, float on the wave of it, to be carried out, blue league after league, away from everything.

After a night behind the scenes, Paul found the schoolroom more than ever repulsive; the bare floors and naked walls; the prosy men who never wore frock coats, or violets in their buttonholes; the women with their dull gowns, shrill voices, and pitiful seriousness about prepositions that govern the dative. He could not bear to have the other pupils think, for a moment, that he took these people seriously; he must convey to them that he considered it all trivial, and was there only by way of a joke, anyway. He had autographed pictures of all the members of the stock company which he showed his classmates, telling them the most incredible stories of his familiarity with these people, of his acquaintance with the soloists who came to Carnegie Hall, his suppers with them and the flowers he sent them. When these stories lost their effect, and his audience grew listless, he would bid all the boys goodbye, announcing that he was going to travel for a while; going to Naples, to California, to Egypt. Then, next Monday, he would slip back, conscious and nervously smiling; his sister was ill, and he would have to defer his voyage until spring.

Matters went steadily worse with Paul at school. In the itch to let his instructors know how heartily he despised them, and how thoroughly he was appreciated elsewhere, he mentioned once or twice that he had no time to fool with theorems; adding—with a twitch of the eyebrows and a touch of that nervous bravado which so perplexed them—that he was helping the people down at the stock company; they were old friends of his.

The upshot of the matter was that the Principal went to Paul's father, and Paul was taken out of school and put to work. The manager at Carnegie Hall was told to get another usher in his stead; the doorkeeper at the theatre was warned not to admit him to the house; and Charley Edwards remorsefully promised the boy's father not to see him again.

The members of the stock company were vastly amused when some of Paul's stories reached them—especially the women. They were hard-working women, most of them supporting indolent husbands or brothers, and they laughed rather bitterly at having stirred the boy to such fervid and florid inventions. They agreed with the faculty and with his father, that Paul's was a bad case.

The east-bound train was ploughing through a January snowstorm; the dull dawn was beginning to show grey when the engine whistled a mile out of Newark. Paul started up from the seat where he had lain curled in uneasy slumber, rubbed the breath-misted window-glass with his hand, and peered out. The snow was whirling in curling eddies above the white bottom lands, and the drifts lay already deep in the fields and along the fences, while here and there the tall dead grass and dried weed stalks protruded black above it. Lights shone from the scattered houses, and a gang of labourers who stood beside the track waved their lanterns.

Paul had slept very little, and he felt grimy and uncomfortable. He had made the all-night journey in a day coach because he was afraid if he took a Pullman he might be seen by some Pittsburgh business man who had noticed him in Denny and Carson's office. When the whistle woke him, he clutched quickly at his breast pocket, glancing about him with an uncertain smile. But the little, clay-bespattered Italians were still sleeping, the slatternly women across the aisle were in open-mouthed oblivion, and even the crumby, crying babies were for the time stilled. Paul settled back to struggle with his impatience as best he could.

When he arrived at the Jersey City station, he hurried through his breakfast, manifestly ill at ease and keeping a sharp eye about him. After he reached the Twenty-Third Street station, he consulted a cabman, and had himself driven to a men's furnishing establishment which was just opening for the day. He spent upward of two hours there, buying with endless reconsidering and great care. His new street suit he put on in the fitting-room; the frock coat and dress clothes he had bundled into the cab with his new shirts. Then he drove to a hatter's and a shoe house. His next errand was at Tiffany's, where he selected silver-mounted brushes and a scarf-pin. He would not wait to have his silver marked, he said. Lastly, he stopped at a trunk shop on Broadway, and had his purchases packed into various travelling-bags.

It was a little after one o'clock when he drove up to the Waldorf, and, after settling with the cabman, went into the office. He registered from Washington; said his mother and father had been abroad, and that he had come down to await the arrival of their steamer. He told his story plausibly and had no trouble, since he offered to pay for them in advance, in engaging his rooms; a sleeping-room, sitting-room, and bath.

Not once, but a hundred times Paul had planned this entry into New York. He had gone over every detail of it with Charley Edwards, and in his scrapbook at home there were pages of description about New York hotels, cut from the Sunday papers.

When he was shown to his sitting-room on the eighth floor, he saw at a glance that everything was as it should be; there was but one detail in his mental picture that the place did not realize, so he rang for the bell-boy and sent him down for flowers. He moved about nervously until the boy returned, putting away his new linen and fingering it delightedly as he did so. When the flowers came, he put them hastily into water, and then tumbled into a hot bath. Presently he came out of his white bathroom, resplendent in his new silk underwear, and playing with the tassels of his red robe. The snow was whirling so fiercely outside his windows that he could scarcely see across the street; but within, the air was deliciously soft and fragrant. He put the violets and jonquils on the tabouret beside the couch, and threw himself down with a long sigh, covering himself with a Roman blanket. He was thoroughly tired; he had been in such haste, he had stood up to such a strain, covered so much ground in the last twenty-four hours, that he wanted to think how it had all come about. Lulled by the sound of the wind, the warm air, and the cool fragrance of the flowers, he sank into deep, drowsy retrospection.

It had been wonderfully simple; when they had shut him out of the theatre and concert hall, when they had taken away his bone, the whole thing was virtually determined. The rest was a mere matter of opportunity. The only thing that at all surprised him was his own courage—for he realized well enough that he had always been tormented by fear, a sort of apprehensive dread which, of late years, as the meshes of the lies he had told closed about him, had been pulling the muscles of his body tighter and tighter. Until now, he could not remember a time when he had not been dreading something. Even when he was a little boy, it was always there—behind him, or before, or on either side. There had always been the shadowed corner, the dark place into which he dared not look, but from which something seemed always to be watching him—and Paul had done things that were not pretty to watch, he knew.

But now he had a curious sense of relief, as though he had at last thrown down the gauntlet to the thing in the corner.

Yet it was but a day since he had been sulking in the traces; but yesterday afternoon that he had been sent to the bank with Denny and Carson's deposit, as usual—but this time he was instructed to leave the book to be balanced. There was above two thousand dollars in cheques, and nearly a thousand in the banknotes which he had taken from the book and quietly transferred to his pocket. At the bank he had made out a new deposit slip. His nerves had been steady enough to permit of his returning to the office, where he had finished his work and asked for a full day's holiday to-morrow, Saturday, giving a perfectly reasonable pretext. The bank book, he knew, would not be returned before Monday or Tuesday, and his father would be out of town for the next week. From the time he slipped the banknotes into his pocket until he boarded the night train for New York, he had not known a moment's hesitation.

How astonishingly easy it had all been; here he was, the thing done; and this time there would be no awakening, no figure at the top of the stairs. He watched the snowflakes whirling by his window until he fell asleep.

When he awoke, it was four o'clock in the afternoon. He bounded up with a start; one of his precious days gone already! He spent nearly an hour in dressing, watching every stage of his toilet carefully in the mirror. Everything was quite perfect; he was exactly the kind of boy he had always wanted to be.

When he went downstairs, Paul took a carriage and drove up Fifth Avenue toward the Park. The snow had somewhat abated; carriages and tradesmen's wagons were hurrying soundlessly to and fro in the winter twilight; boys in woollen mufflers were shovelling off the doorsteps; the Avenue stages made fine spots of colour against the white street. Here and there on the corners whole flower gardens blooming behind glass windows, against which the snowflakes stuck and melted; violets, roses, carnations, lilies-of-the-valley—somehow vastly more lovely and alluring that they blossomed thus unnaturally in the snow. The Park itself was a wonderful stage winter-piece.

When he returned, the pause of the twilight had ceased, and the tune of the streets had changed. The snow was falling faster, lights streamed from the hotels that reared their many stories fearlessly up into the storm, defying the raging Atlantic winds. A long, black stream of carriages poured down the Avenue, intersected here and there by other streams, tending horizontally. There were a score of cabs about the entrance of his hotel, and his driver had to wait. Boys in livery were running in and out of the awning stretched across the sidewalk, up and down the red velvet carpet laid from the door to the street. Above, about, within it all, was the rumble and roar, the hurry and toss of thousands of human beings as hot for pleasure as himself, and on every side of him towered the glaring affirmation of the omnipotence of wealth.

The boy set his teeth and drew his shoulders together in a spasm of realization; the plot of all dramas, the text of all romances, the nerve-stuff of all sensations was whirling about him like the snowflakes. He burnt like a fagot in a tempest.

When Paul came down to dinner, the music of the orchestra floated up the elevator shaft to greet him. As he stepped into the thronged corridor, he sank back into one of the chairs against the wall to get his breath. The lights, the chatter, the perfumes, the bewildering medley of colour—he had, for a moment, the feeling of not being able to stand it. But only for a moment; these were his own people, he told himself. He went slowly about the corridors, through the writing-rooms, smoking-rooms, reception-rooms, as though he were exploring the chambers of an enchanted palace, built and peopled for him alone.

When he reached the dining-room he sat down at a table near a window. The flowers, the white linen, the many-coloured wine-glasses, the gay toilettes of the women, the low popping of corks, the undulating repetitions of the "Blue Danube" from the orchestra, all flooded Paul's dream with bewildering radiance. When the roseate tinge of his champagne was added—that cold, precious, bubbling stuff that creamed and foamed in his glass—Paul wondered that there were honest men in the world at all. This was what all the world was fighting for, he reflected; this was what all the struggle was about. He doubted the reality of his past. Had he ever known a place called Cordelia Street, a place where fagged-looking business men boarded the early car? Mere rivets in a machine they seemed to Paul—sickening men, with combings of children's hair always hanging to their coats, and the smell of cooking in their clothes. Cordelia Street—Ah, that belonged to another time and country! Had he not always been thus, had he not sat here night after night, from as far back as he could remember, looking pensively over just such shimmering textures, and slowly twirling the stem of a glass like this one between his thumb and middle finger? He rather thought he had.

He was not in the least abashed or lonely. He had no especial desire to meet or to know any of these people; all he demanded was the right to look on and conjecture, to watch the pageant. The mere stage properties were all he contended for. Nor was he lonely later in the evening, in his loge at the Opera. He was entirely rid of his nervous misgivings, of his forced aggressiveness, of the imperative desire to show himself different from his surroundings. He felt now that his surroundings explained him. Nobody questioned the purple; he had only to wear it passively. He had only to glance down at his dress coat to reassure himself that here it would be impossible for anyone to humiliate him.

He found it hard to leave his beautiful sitting-room to go to bed that night, and sat long watching the raging storm from his turret window. When he went to sleep, it was with the lights turned on in his bedroom; partly because of his old timidity, and partly so that, if he should wake in the night, there would be no wretched moment of doubt, no horrible suspicion of yellow wallpaper, or of Washington and Calvin above his bed.

On Sunday morning the city was practically snowbound. Paul breakfasted late, and in the afternoon he fell in with a wild San Francisco boy, a freshman at Yale, who said he had run down for a "little flyer" over Sunday. The young man offered to show Paul the night side of the town, and the two boys went off together after dinner, not returning to the hotel until seven o'clock the next morning. They had started out in the confiding warmth of a champagne friendship, but their parting in the elevator was singularly cool. The freshman pulled himself together to make his train, and Paul went to bed. He awoke at two o'clock in the afternoon, very thirsty and dizzy, and rang for ice-water, coffee, and the Pittsburgh papers.

On the part of the hotel management, Paul excited no suspicion. There was this to be said for him, that he wore his spoils with dignity and in no way made himself conspicuous. His chief greediness lay in his ears and eyes, and his excesses were not offensive ones. His dearest pleasures were the grey winter twilights in his sitting-room; his quiet enjoyment of his flowers, his clothes, his wide divan, his cigarette, and his sense of power. He could not remember a time when he had felt so at peace with himself. The mere release from the necessity of petty lying, lying every day and every day, restored his self-respect. He had never lied for pleasure, even at school; but to make himself noticed and admired, to assert his difference from other Cordelia Street boys; and he felt a good deal more manly, more honest, even, now that he had no need for boastful pretensions, now that he could, as his actor friends used to say, "dress the part." It was characteristic that remorse did not occur to him. His golden days went by without a shadow, and he made each as perfect as he could.

On the eighth day after his arrival in New York, he found the whole affair exploited in the Pittsburgh papers, exploited with a wealth of detail which indicated that local news of a sensational nature was at a low ebb. The firm of Denny and Carson announced that the boy's father had refunded the full amount of his theft, and that they had no intention of prosecuting. The Cumberland minister had been interviewed, and expressed his hope of yet reclaiming the motherless lad, and Paul's Sabbath-School teacher declared that she would spare no effort to that end. The rumour had reached Pittsburgh that the boy had been seen in a New York hotel, and his father had gone East to find him and bring him home.

Paul had just come in to dress for dinner; he sank into a chair, weak in the knees, and clasped his head in his hands. It was to be worse than jail, even; the tepid waters of Cordelia Street were to close over him finally and forever. The grey monotony stretched before him in hopeless, unrelieved years;—Sabbath-School, Young People's Meeting, the yellow-papered room, the damp dish-towels; it all rushed back upon him with sickening vividness. He had the old feeling that the orchestra had suddenly stopped, the sinking sensation that the play was over. The sweat broke out on his face, and he sprang to his feet, looked about him with his white, conscious smile, and winked at himself in the mirror. With something of the childish belief in miracles with which he had so often gone to class, all his lessons unlearned, Paul dressed and dashed whistling down the corridor to the elevator.

He had no sooner entered the dining-room and caught the measure of the music than his remembrance was lightened by his old elastic power of claiming the moment, mounting with it, and finding it all-sufficient. The glare and glitter about him, the mere scenic accessories had again, and for the last time, their old potency. He would show himself that he was game, he would finish the thing splendidly. He doubted, more than ever, the existence of Cordelia Street, and for the first time he drank his wine recklessly. Was he not, after all, one of these fortunate beings? Was he not still himself, and in his own place? He drummed a nervous accompaniment to the music and looked about him, telling himself over and over that it had paid.

He reflected drowsily, to the swell of the violin and the chill sweetness of his wine, that he might have done it more wisely. He might have caught an outbound steamer and been well out of their clutches before now. But the other side of the world had seemed too far away and too uncertain then; he could not have waited for it; his need had been too sharp. If he had to choose over again, he would do the same thing to-morrow. He looked affectionately about the dining-room, now gilded with a soft mist. Ah, it had paid indeed!

Paul was awakened next morning by a painful throbbing in his head and feet. He had thrown himself across the bed without undressing, and had slept with his shoes on. His limbs and hands were lead-heavy, and his tongue and throat were parched. There came upon him one of those fateful attacks of clear-headedness that never occurred except when he was physically exhausted and his nerves hung loose. He lay still and closed his eyes and let the tide of realities wash over him.

His father was in New York; "stopping at some joint or other," he told himself. The memory of successive summers on the front stoop fell upon him like a weight of black water. He had not a hundred dollars left; and he knew now, more than ever, that money was everything, the wall that stood between all he loathed and all he wanted. The thing was winding itself up; he had thought of that on his first glorious day in New York, and had even provided a way to snap the thread. It lay on his dressing-table now; he had got it out last night when he came blindly up from dinner—but the shiny metal hurt his eyes, and he disliked the look of it, anyway.

He rose and moved about with a painful effort, succumbing now and again to attacks of nausea. It was the old depression exaggerated; all the world had become Cordelia Street. Yet somehow he was not afraid of anything, was absolutely calm; perhaps because he had looked into the dark corner at last, and knew. It was bad enough, what he saw there; but somehow not so bad as his long fear of it had been. He saw everything clearly now. He had a feeling that he had made the best of it, that he had lived the sort of life he was meant to live, and for half an hour he sat staring at the revolver. But he told himself that was not the way, so he went downstairs and took a cab to the ferry.

When Paul arrived at Newark, he got off the train and took another cab, directing the driver to follow the Pennsylvania tracks out of the town. The snow lay heavy on the roadways and had drifted deep in the open fields. Only here and there the dead grass or dried weed stalks projected, singularly black, above it.

Once well into the country, Paul dismissed the carriage and walked, floundering along the tracks, his mind a medley of irrelevant things. He seemed to hold in his brain an actual picture of everything he had seen that morning. He remembered every feature of both his drivers, the toothless old woman from whom he had bought the red flowers in his coat, the agent from whom he had got his ticket, and all of his fellow-passengers on the ferry. His mind, unable to cope with vital matters near at hand, worked feverishly and deftly at sorting and grouping these images. They made for him a part of the ugliness of the world, of the ache in his head, and the bitter burning on his tongue. He stooped and put a handful of snow into his mouth as he walked, but that, too, seemed hot. When he reached a little hillside, where the tracks ran through a cut some twenty feet below him, he stopped and sat down.

The carnations in his coat were drooping with the cold, he noticed; their red glory over. It occurred to him that all the flowers he had seen in the show windows that first night must have gone the same way, long before this. It was only one splendid breath they had, in spite of their brave mockery at the winter outside the glass. It was a losing game in the end, it seemed, this revolt against the homilies by which the world is run. Paul took one of the blossoms carefully from his coat and scooped a little hole in the snow, where he covered it up. Then he dozed awhile, from his weak condition, seeming insensible to the cold.

The sound of an approaching train woke him and he started to his feet, remembering only his resolution, and afraid lest he should be too late. He stood watching the approaching locomotive, his teeth chattering, his lips drawn away from them in a frightened smile; once or twice he glanced nervously sidewise, as though he were being watched. When the right moment came, he jumped. As he fell, the folly of his haste occurred to him with merciless clearness, the vastness of what he had left undone. There flashed through his brain, clearer than ever before, the blue of Adriatic water, the yellow of Algerian sands.

He felt something strike his chest—his body was being thrown swiftly through the air, on and on, immeasurably far and fast, while his limbs gently relaxed. Then, because the picture-making mechanism was crushed, the disturbing visions flashed into black, and Paul dropped back into the immense design of things.

QUESTIONS

1. Technically we should classify the author's point of view as omniscient, for she enters into the minds of characters at will. Nevertheless, early in the story the focus changes rather abruptly. Locate the point where the change occurs. Through whose eyes do we see Paul prior to this point? Through whose eyes do we see him afterward? What is the purpose of this shift? Does it offer any clue to the purpose of the story?

2. What details of Paul's appearance and behavior, as his teachers see him, indicate that he is abnormal?

3. Explain Paul's behavior. Why does he lie? What does he hate? What does he want? Contrast the world of Cordelia Street with the worlds that Paul finds at Carnegie Hall, at the Schenley, at the stock theater, and in New York.

4. Is Paul artistic? Describe his reactions to music, to painting, to literature, and to the theater. What value does he find in the arts?

5. Is Paul a static or a developing character? If the latter, at what points does he change? Why?

6. What do Paul's clandestine trips to the stock theater, his trip to New York, and his suicide have in common?

7. Compare Paul and the college boy he meets in New York. Are they two of a kind? If not, how do they differ?

8. What are the implications of the title? What does the last sentence of the story do to the reader's focus of vision?

9. Are there any clues to the causes of Paul's abnormality? How many? In what is the author chiefly interested?

10. In what two cities is the story set? Does this choice of settings have any symbolic value? Could the story have been set as validly in Cleveland and Detroit? in San Francisco and Los Angeles? in New Orleans and Birmingham?

Ernest Hemingway

HILLS LIKE WHITE ELEPHANTS

The hills across the valley of the Ebro were long and white. On this side there was no shade and no trees and the station was between two lines of rails in the sun. Close against the side of the station there was the warm shadow of the building and a curtain, made of strings of bamboo beads, hung across the open door into the bar, to keep out flies. The American and the girl with him sat at a table in the shade, outside the building. It was very hot and the express from Barcelona would come in forty minutes. It stopped at this junction for two minutes and went on to Madrid.

"What should we drink?" the girl asked. She had taken off her hat and put it on the table.

"It's pretty hot," the man said.

"Let's drink beer."

"Doz cervezas," the man said into the curtain.

"Big ones?" a woman asked from the doorway.

"Yes. Two big ones."

The woman brought two glasses of beer and two felt pads. She put the felt pads and the beer glasses on the table and looked at the man and the girl. The girl was looking off at the line of hills. They were white in the sun and the country was brown and dry.

"They look like white elephants," she said.

"I've never seen one," the man drank his beer.

"No, you wouldn't have."

"I might have," the man said. "Just because you say I wouldn't have doesn't prove anything."

The girl looked at the bead curtain. "They've painted something on it," she said. "What does it say?"

"Anis del Toro. It's a drink."

"Could we try it?"

The man called "Listen" through the curtain. The woman came out from the bar.

"Four reales."

"We want two Anis del Toro."

"With water?"

"Do you want it with water?"

"I don't know," the girl said. "Is it good with water?"

"It's all right."

"You want them with water?" asked the woman.

"Yes, with water."

"It tastes like licorice," the girl said and put the glass down.

"That's the way with everything."

"Yes," said the girl. "Everything tastes of licorice. Especially all the things you've waited so long for, like absinthe."

"Oh, cut it out."

"You started it," the girl said. "I was being amused. I was having a fine time."

"Well, let's try to have a fine time."

"All right. I was trying. I said the mountains looked like white elephants. Wasn't that bright?"

"That was bright."

"I wanted to try this new drink. That's all we do, isn't it—look at things and try new drinks?"

"I guess so."

The girl looked across at the hills.

"They're lovely hills," she said. "They don't really look like white elephants. I just meant the coloring of their skin through the trees."

"Should we have another drink?"

"All right."

The warm wind blew the bead curtain against the table.

"The beer's nice and cool," the man said.

"It's lovely," the girl said.

"It's really an awfully simple operation, Jig," the man said. "It's not really an operation at all."

The girl looked at the ground the table legs rested on.

"I know you wouldn't mind it, Jig. It's really not anything. It's just to let the air in."

The girl did not say anything.

"I'll go with you and I'll stay with you all the time. They just let the air in and then it's all perfectly natural."

"Then what will we do afterward?"

"We'll be fine afterward. Just like we were before."

"What makes you think so?"

"That's the only thing that bothers us. It's the only thing that's made us unhappy."

The girl looked at the bead curtain, put her hand out and took hold of two of the strings of beads.

"And you think then we'll be all right and be happy."

"I know we will. You don't have to be afraid. I've known lots of people that have done it."

"So have I," said the girl. "And afterward they were all so happy."

"Well," the man said, "if you don't want to you don't have to. I wouldn't have you do it if you didn't want to. But I know it's perfectly simple."

"And you really want to?"

"I think it's the best thing to do. But I don't want you to do it if you don't really want to."

"And if I do it you'll be happy and things will be like they were and you'll love me?"

"I love you now. You know I love you."

"I know. But if I do it, then it will be nice again if I say things are like white elephants, and you'll like it?"

"I'll love it. I love it now but I just can't think about it. You know how I get when I worry."

"If I do it you won't ever worry?"

"I won't worry about that because it's perfectly simple."

"Then I'll do it. Because I don't care about me."

"What do you mean?"

"I don't care about me."

"Well, I care about you."

"Oh, yes. But I don't care about me. And I'll do it and then everything will be fine."

"I don't want you to do it if you feel that way."

The girl stood up and walked to the end of the station. Across, on the other side, were fields of grain and trees along the banks of the Ebro. Far away, beyond the river, were mountains. The shadow of a cloud moved across the field of grain and she saw the river through the trees.

"And we could have all this," she said. "And we could have everything and every day we make it more impossible."

"What did you say?"

"I said we could have everything."

"We can have everything."

"No, we can't."

"We can have the whole world."

"No, we can't."

"We can go everywhere."

"No, we can't. It isn't ours any more."

"It's ours."

"No, it isn't. And once they take it away, you never get it back."

"But they haven't taken it away."

"We'll wait and see."

"Come on back in the shade," he said. "You mustn't feel that way."

"I don't feel any way," the girl said. "I just know things."

"I don't want you to do anything that you don't want to do———"

"Nor that isn't good for me," she said. "I know. Could we have another beer?"

"All right. But you've got to realize———"

"I realize," the girl said. "Can't we maybe stop talking?"

They sat down at the table and the girl looked across at the hills on the dry side of the valley and the man looked at her and at the table.

"You've got to realize," he said, "that I don't want you to do it if you don't want to. I'm perfectly willing to go through with it if it means anything to you."

"Doesn't it mean anything to you? We could get along."

"Of course it does. But I don't want anybody but you. I don't want any one else. And I know it's perfectly simple."

"Yes, you know it's perfectly simple."

"It's all right for you to say that, but I do know it."

"Would you do something for me now?"

"I'd do anything for you."

"Would you please please please please please please please stop talking?"

He did not say anything but looked at the bags against the wall of the station. There were labels on them from all the hotels where they had spent nights.

"But I don't want you to," he said, "I don't care anything about it."

"I'll scream," said the girl.

The woman came out through the curtains with two glasses of beer and put them down on the damp felt pads. "The train comes in five minutes," she said.

"What did she say?" asked the girl.

"That the train is coming in five minutes."

The girl smiled brightly at the woman, to thank her.

"I'd better take the bags over to the other side of the station," the man said. She smiled at him.

"All right. Then come back and we'll finish the beer."

He picked up the two heavy bags and carried them around the station to the other tracks. He looked up the tracks but could not see the train.

Coming back, he walked through the barroom, where people waiting for the train were drinking. He drank an Anis at the bar and looked at the people. They were all waiting reasonably for the train. He went out through the bead curtain. She was sitting at the table and smiled at him.

"Do you feel better?" he asked.

"I feel fine," she said. "There's nothing wrong with me. I feel fine."

QUESTIONS

1. The main topic of discussion between the man and the girl is never named. What is the "awfully simple operation"? Why is it not named? What different attitudes are taken toward it by the man and the girl? Why?

2. What is indicated about the past life of the man and girl? How? What has happened to the quality of their relationship? Why? How do we know? How accurate is the man's judgment about their future?

3. Though the story consists mostly of dialogue, and though it contains strong emotional conflict, it is entirely without adverbs indicating the tone of the remarks. How does Hemingway indicate tone? At what points are the characters insincere? self-deceived? ironic or sarcastic? To what extent do they give open expression to their feelings? Does either want an open conflict? Why or why not? Trace the various phases of emotion in the girl.

4. How sincere is the man in his insistence that he would not have the girl undergo the operation if she does not want to and that he is "perfectly willing to go through with it" (what is "it"?) if it means anything to the girl? How many times does he repeat these ideas? What significance has the man's drinking an Anis by himself before rejoining the girl at the end of the story?

5. Much of the conversation seems to be about trivial things (ordering drinks, the weather, and so on). What purposes does this conversation serve? What relevance has the girl's remarks about absinthe?

6. What is the point of the girl's comparison of the hills to white elephants? Does the remark assume any significance for the reader beyond its significance for the characters? Why does the author use it for his title?

7. What purpose does the setting serve—the hills across the valley, the treeless railroad tracks and station? What is contributed by the precise information about time at the end of the first paragraph?

8. Which of the two characters is more "reasonable"? Which "wins" the conflict between them? The point of view is objective. Does this mean that we cannot tell whether the sympathy of the author lies more with one character than with the other? Explain your answer.

CHAPTER SIX

Symbol and Irony

Most successful stories are characterized by compression. The writer's aim is to say as much as possible as briefly as possible. This does not mean that most good stories are brief. It means only that nothing is wasted and that each word and detail are chosen for maximum effectiveness. The force of an explosion is proportionate to the strength and amount of powder used and the smallness of the space it is confined in.

The writer achieves compression by exercising a rigid selectivity. He chooses the details and incidents that contribute most to the meaning he is after; he omits those whose usefulness is minimal. As far as possible he chooses details that are multi-valued—that serve a variety of purposes at once. A detail that expresses character at the same time that it advances the plot is more useful than a detail that does only one or the other.

This chapter will discuss two contributory resources of the writer for gaining compression: symbol and irony. Both of them may increase the explosive force of a story, but both demand awareness and maturity on the part of the reader.

A literary SYMBOL[1] is something that means *more* than what it is. It is an object, a person, a situation, an action, or some other item that has a literal meaning in the story but suggests or represents other meanings as well. A very simple illustration is to be found in name-

[1] *Literary* symbols are to be distinguished from *arbitrary* symbols, like letters of the alphabet, numbers, and algebraic signs, which have no meaning in and of themselves but which mean only something *else,* not something *more* than what they are.

symbolism. Most names are simply labels. Seldom does a name tell anything about the person to whom it is attached, except possibly his nationality. In a story, however, the author may choose names for his characters that serve not only to label them but also to suggest something about them. In his fictional trilogy *The Forsyte Saga,* John Galsworthy chooses Forsyte as the family name of his principal characters to indicate their practical foresightedness. Does he follow a similar practice in "The Japanese Quince"? The name of Mr. Nilson might be analyzed as "Nil's son"—son of Nil or nothing. The name of his counterpart Mr. Tandram (it sounds like both "tandem" and "humdrum") is made up of "dram"—a very small measure—and "tan"—a substance for converting skin into leather. Whether Galsworthy consciously chose the names with these meanings in view or picked them because they "sounded right"—and whether or not the reader recognizes these suggestions—the names are *felt* to be not inappropriate. More obviously, in Conrad's "Youth" the name of Captain Beard was clearly chosen to support his age, and the name Mahon (pronounced Mann) is especially appropriate for the first mate on a voyage that seemed "ordered for the illustration of life, that might stand for a symbol of existence."

More important than name-symbolism is the symbolic use of objects and actions. In some stories these symbols will fit so naturally into the literal context that their symbolic value will not at first be apparent except to the most perceptive reader. In other stories—usually stories with a less realistic surface—they will be so central and so obvious that they will demand symbolical interpretation if the story is to yield significant meaning. In the first kind of story the symbols *reinforce* and *add* to the meaning. In the second kind of story they *carry* the meaning.

"The Kiss," by Chekhov, is a story that uses symbols to reinforce the meaning. For instance, when the officers return from the party at General von Rabbek's, they walk along the river bank and discover a nightingale:

> From beyond [the river] sighed a drowsy snipe, and beside them in a bush, heedless of the crowd, a nightingale chanted loudly. The officers gathered in a group, and swayed the bush, but the nightingale continued his song.
>
> "I like his cheek!" they echoed admiringly. "He doesn't care a *kopek!* The old rogue!"

Why does Chekhov include the nightingale? It serves, of course, like the drowsy snipe, to give body to the experience of the evening. It also fits in with the feeling of enchantment that the party has created. Yet these facts hardly justify the attention that Chekhov has given it; either it is something more than a background detail like the drowsy snipe or else the author has included an irrelevancy. Two facts about the nightingale are stressed. It is singing loudly; it is oblivious of the reality around it. Now, emotionally, this is exactly the condition of Riabovitch. His heart is singing like the nightingale, and, when he gets back to his quarters, he ignores the conversation of his roommates and fails to answer when Lobuitko invites him for a walk. "He was entirely absorbed in his new agreeable thoughts," we are told later on. The nightingale is a symbol, then, for the emotional condition of Riabovitch, and thus makes a distinct contribution to the story.

When Riabovitch makes his second trip to the general's home, his mood has changed.

> The river bank was as it had been in May; the bushes were the same; things differed only in that the nightingale no longer sang, that it smelt no longer of poplars and young grass.

Again the details symbolically suggest Riabovitch's condition: the difference is within as well as without.

After loitering for a while around the silent house, Riabovitch goes down to the river.

> In front rose the general's bathing box; and white towels hung on the rail of the bridge. He climbed on to the bridge and stood still; then, for no reason whatever, touched a towel. It was clammy and cold.

Then he looks down at the river.

> Near the left bank glowed the moon's ruddy reflection, overrun by ripples which stretched it, tore it in two, and, it seemed, would sweep it away as twigs and shavings are swept.

The touch of the cold, wet towel suggests the disillusioning effect of Riabovitch's return to reality. What is happening to the moon's reflection is like what is happening to Riabovitch's heart. Each of these aspects of the outside world is a symbol of something happening in Riabovitch's inner world.

Finally, *for Riabovitch,* the water of the river becomes a symbol.

> The water flew past him, whither and why no one knew. It had flown past in May; it had sped a stream into a great river; a river, into the sea; it had floated on high in mist and fallen again in rain; it might be, the water of May was again speeding past under Riabovitch's eyes. For what purpose? Why?

The endless cycle of the water here symbolizes for Riabovitch the futility and empty repetitiveness of a world without meaning.

The ability to recognize and identify symbols requires perception and tact. The great danger facing the student when he first becomes aware of symbolical values is a tendency to run wild—to find symbols everywhere and to read into the details of a story all sorts of fanciful meanings not legitimately supported by it. The beginning reader needs to remember that most stories operate almost wholly at the literal level and that, even in a story like "The Kiss," the majority of the details are purely literal. A story should not be made the excuse for an exercise in ingenuity. It is better, indeed, to miss the symbolical meanings of a story than to pervert its meaning by discovering symbols that are nonexistent. Better to miss the boat than to jump wildly for it and drown.

The ability to interpret symbols is nevertheless essential for a full understanding of literature. The beginning reader should be alert for symbolical meanings but should observe the following cautions:

1. The story itself must furnish a clue that a detail is to be taken symbolically. In "The Kiss," for instance, the nightingale is given an emphasis not given to the drowsy snipe. It is singled out for attention and is referred to again later in the story, and this attention cannot be explained by any function it has in the plot. Even greater emphasis is given to the flowering quince in the story by Galsworthy. Symbols nearly always signal their existence by emphasis, repetition, or position. In the absence of such signals, we should be reluctant to identify an idea as symbolical.

2. The meaning of a literary symbol must be established and supported by the entire context of the story. The symbol has its meaning *in* the story, not *outside* it. Our meaning for the nightingale, for instance, is supported by the behavior of Riabovitch, the story's protagonist. The strange effect of the kiss on him is central to the meaning of the story. In another work of literature, in another context, the nightingale might have an entirely different symbolical meaning or no symbolical meaning whatever. The nightingale in Keats's famous ode has a different meaning from that in "The Kiss."

3. To be called a symbol, an item must suggest a meaning different *in kind* from its literal meaning; a symbol is something more than the representative of a class or type. Riabovitch, for instance, is a shy, timid young man, and, in proportion as his story is successful, he comes to stand for shy, timid young men everywhere. The story acquaints us with a truth of human nature, not with just a biographical fact. But, to say this, is to say no more than that the story has a theme. Every interpretive story suggests a generalization about life, is more than a recounting of the specific fortunes of specific individuals. There is no point, therefore, in calling Riabovitch a *symbol* of a shy, timid young man. Riabovitch *is* a shy, timid young man. He is typical because he is like other shy, timid young men: a member of the class of shy, timid young men. We ought not to use the phrase *is a symbol of* when we can as easily use *is*, or *is an example of* or *is an evidence of*. The nightingale, the wet towel, and the moon's reflection are neither examples nor evidences of Riabovitch's emotional condition. The meanings they suggest are quite different from what they are.

4. A symbol may have more than one meaning. It may suggest a cluster of meanings. At its most effective a symbol is like a many-faceted jewel: it flashes different colors when turned in the light. This is not to say that it can mean anything we want it to: the area of possible meanings is always controlled by the context. Nevertheless, this possibility of complex meaning, plus concreteness and emotional power, gives the symbol its peculiar compressive value. The nightingale in "The Kiss" has an immediate emotional and imaginative force that an abstract statement of Riabovitch's condition would not have, and, though a relatively simple symbol, it suggests a variety of qualities—joyousness, self-absorption, instinctive and compelling emotion—that cannot be expressed in a single word. The Japanese quince in Galsworthy's story has a wider range of meaning—life, growth, beauty, freedom, joy—all qualities opposed to convention and habit and "foreign" to the proper and "respectable" English upper-middle-class environment it finds itself in. The meaning cannot be confined to any one of these qualities: it is all of them, and therein lies the symbol's value.

Irony is a term with a range of meanings, all of them involving some sort of discrepancy or incongruity. It is a contrast in which one term of the contrast in some way mocks the other term. It is not to be confused with sarcasm, however, which is simply language designed to cause pain. The story writer uses irony to suggest the complexity of experience, to furnish indirectly an evaluation of his material, and at the same time to achieve compression.

Three kinds of irony may be distinguished here. VERBAL IRONY, the simplest and, for the story writer, the least important kind, is a figure of speech in which the opposite is said from what is intended. The discrepancy is between what is said and what is meant. In "The Child by Tiger," when the narrator tells us that the man who fired the first shot into Dick Prosser was "telling the story of his own heroic accomplishments" and refers to him as "the hero," he is using the words "heroic" and "hero" ironically, for it is clear that he feels only contempt for both the man and his actions. In "Defender of the Faith," when Sergeant Marx says to Grossbart, "You're a regular Messiah, aren't you?" he is speaking ironically—and sarcastically—for he thinks Grossbart's motives are self-interested rather than Messianic. Another use of irony for sarcastic purposes is made by the girl in "Hills Like White Elephants." The man has been assuring her that, after the operation, they will be "just like" they were before, for her pregnancy has been the only thing making them unhappy:

> "And you think then we'll be all right and be happy."
>
> "I know we will. You don't have to be afraid. I've known lots of people that have done it."
>
> "So have I," said the girl. "And afterward they were all so happy."

Abortions, the girl implies, make couples anything but "all so happy" afterward.

In DRAMATIC IRONY the contrast is between what a character says and what the reader knows to be true. The value of this kind of irony lies in the comment it implies on the speaker or his expectations. Thus, in "Tears, Idle Tears," when we are told that Frederick's mother "seldom openly punished him, but often revenged herself on him in small ways" and that Frederick "could feel how just this was," we know that his mother's behavior is actually *un*just. But Frederick's implicit faith in his mother's rightness reveals to us how young and trusting he is, how unversed he is in the ways of adult hypocrisy, and how ashamed he is of his own behavior though he cannot help it. Another effective example occurs in "I'm a Fool" when the swipe blames his lie at the race track on the whisky he had drunk and the man in the Windsor tie. The reader sees, as the swipe does not, that these are simply additional symptoms of his plight, not its cause. But perhaps the most pregnant example of dramatic irony in these stories is in "That Evening Sun" when Father rebukes Nancy with "If you'd just leave white men alone." We know, of course, that the white man is the one who won't leave Nancy alone, and the discrepancy between this fact and Father's way of putting it tells us worlds about this whole society and the underlying causes of its paralysis of fear.

In IRONY OF SITUATION, usually the most important kind for the story writer, the discrepancy is between appearance and reality, or between expectation and fulfillment, or between what is and what would seem appropriate. In "The Most Dangerous Game," it is ironic that Rainsford, "the celebrated hunter," should become the hunted, for this is a reversal of his expected and appropriate role. In "The Destructors," it is ironic that Old Misery's horoscope should read, "Abstain from any dealings in first half of week. Danger of serious crash," for the horoscope is valid in a sense that is quite different from that which the words seem to indicate. In "The Silver Crown," it is ironic that Gans, by his angry outbreak against his father, should destroy any chance that might have existed of getting the beneficial result from the silver crown for which he had been hoping, and for which he had paid $986. This irony shows us how complex and contradictory the interworkings of love, hope, resentment, distrust, and self-love can be. In "The Kiss," it is ironic that a rather trivial accident should have such a disproportionate effect on Riabovitch's thoughts and feelings, and this disparity tells us something about Riabovitch and about human nature in general. It is also ironic that Riabovitch should finally neglect the invitation he had been so eagerly anticipating, and this irony underscores the extent of the change that has occurred in him. The story would have been complete without the second invitation, but the additional ironic twist gives the change in Riabovitch an emphasis it would not otherwise have had.

As a final example, the title of "Defender of the Faith" points to a complex irony, partly verbal, partly situational. The phrase "defender of the faith" ordinarily suggests a staunch religious champion and partisan, but, insofar as Sergeant Marx fills this role, he does so against his will, even against his intention, for his motivation is to give fair and equal treatment to all his men—he does not want to be partial to Jews. Unwillingly, he is trapped into being a "defender of the faith" by Private Grossbart.

> The next morning, while chatting with Captain Barrett, I recounted the incident of the previous evening. Somehow, in the telling, it must have seemed to the Captain that I was not so much explaining Grossbart's position as defending it.

At the end of the story, however, when Marx has Grossbart's orders changed to the Pacific, the irony is that he becomes most truly a defender of his faith when he seems to be turning against it. "You call this watching out for me—what you did?" asks Grossbart. "No," answers Marx. "For all of us." The cause of the whole Jewish faith is set back when Jews like Grossbart get special favors for themselves, for other peoples will mistakenly attribute Grossbart's objectionable qualities to the Jewish people as a whole. Thus Marx is unwillingly a "defender of the faith" when he helps his co-religionist, and becomes truly a defender of the faith when he turns against him. These ironies underscore the difficulties involved in being at the same time a good Jew and a good man in a world where Jews are so often the objects of prejudice and persecution.

In all these examples, irony enables the author to gain power with economy. Like symbolism, irony makes it possible to suggest meanings without stating them. Simply by juxtaposing two discordant facts in the right solution, the writer can start a current of meaning flowing between them, as between the two poles in an electric battery. We do not need to be *told* that Frederick has implicit faith in his mother; we see it. We do not need to be told that the race-track swipe is lacking in self-knowledge; we see it. We do not need to be told how difficult it is for a Jewish sergeant to balance justice and mercy in a position of command; we feel it. The ironic contrast generates meaning.

Shirley Jackson

THE LOTTERY

The morning of June 27th was clear and sunny, with the fresh warmth of a full-summer day; the flowers were blossoming profusely and the grass was richly green. The people of the village began to gather in the square, between the post office and the bank, around ten o'clock; in some towns there were so many people that the lottery took two days and had to be started on June 26th, but in this village, where there were only about three hundred people, the whole lottery took less than two hours, so it could begin at ten o'clock in the morning and still be through in time to allow the villagers to get home for noon dinner.

The children assembled first, of course. School was recently over for the summer, and the feeling of liberty sat uneasily on most of them; they tended to gather together quietly for a while before they broke into boisterous play, and their talk was still of the classroom and the teacher, of books and reprimands. Bobby Martin had already stuffed his pockets full of stones, and the other boys soon followed his example, selecting the smoothest and roundest stones; Bobby and Harry Jones and Dickie Delacroix—the villagers pronounced this name "Dellacroy"—eventually made a great pile of stones in one corner of the square and guarded it against the raids of the other boys. The girls stood aside, talking among themselves, looking over their shoulders at the boys, and the very small children rolled in the dust or clung to the hands of their older brothers or sisters.

Soon the men began to gather, surveying their own children, speaking of planting and rain, tractors and taxes. They stood together, away from the pile of stones in the corner, and their jokes were quiet and they smiled rather than laughed. The women, wearing faded house dresses and sweaters, came shortly after their menfolk. They greeted one another and exchanged bits of gossip as they went to join their husbands. Soon the women, standing by their husbands, began to call to their children, and the children came reluctantly, having to be called four or five times. Bobby Martin ducked under his mother's grasping hand and ran, laughing, back to the pile of stones. His father spoke up sharply, and Bobby came quickly and took his place between his father and his oldest brother.

The lottery was conducted—as were the square dances, the teen-age club, the Halloween program—by Mr. Summers, who had time and energy to devote to civic activities. He was a round-faced, jovial man and he ran the coal business, and people were sorry for him, because he had no children and his wife was a scold. When he arrived in the square, carrying the black wooden box, there was a murmur of conversation among the villagers, and he waved and called, "Little late today, folks." The postmaster, Mr. Graves, followed him, carrying a three-legged stool, and the stool was put in the center of the square and Mr. Summers set the black box down on it. The villagers kept their distance, leaving a space between themselves and the stool, and when Mr. Summers said, "Some of you fellows want to give me a hand?" there was a hesitation before two men, Mr. Martin and his oldest son, Baxter, came forward to hold the box steady on the stool while Mr. Summers stirred up the papers inside it.

The original paraphernalia for the lottery had been lost long ago, and the black box now resting on the stool had been put into use even before Old Man Warner, the oldest man in town, was born. Mr. Summers spoke frequently to the villagers about making a new box, but no one liked to upset even as much tradition as was represented by the black box. There was a story that the present box had been made with some pieces of the box that had preceded it, the one that had been constructed when the first people settled down to make a village here. Every year, after the lottery, Mr. Summers began talking again about a new box, but every year the subject was allowed to fade off without anything's being done. The black box grew shabbier each year; by now it was no longer completely black but splintered badly along one side to show the original wood color, and in some places faded or stained.

Mr. Martin and his oldest son, Baxter, held the black box securely on the stool until Mr. Summers had stirred the papers thoroughly with his hand. Because so much of the ritual had been forgotten or discarded, Mr. Summers had been successful in having slips of paper substituted for the chips of wood that had been used for generations. Chips of wood, Mr. Summers had argued, had been all very well when the village was tiny, but now that the population was more than three hundred and likely to keep on growing, it was necessary to use something that would fit more easily into the black box. The night before the lottery, Mr. Summers and Mr. Graves made up the slips of paper and put them in the box, and it was then taken to the safe of Mr. Summers' coal company and locked up until Mr. Summers was ready to take it to the square next morning. The rest of the year, the box was put away, sometimes one place, sometimes another; it had spent one year in Mr. Graves's barn and another year underfoot in the post office, and sometimes it was set on a shelf in the Martin grocery and left there.

There was a great deal of fussing to be done before Mr. Summers declared the lottery open. There were the lists to make up—of heads of families, heads of households in each family, members of each household in each family. There was the proper swearing-in of Mr. Summers by the postmaster, as the official of the lottery; at one time, some people remembered, there had been a recital of some sort, performed by the official of the lottery, a perfunctory, tuneless chant that had been rattled off duly each year; some people believed that the official of the lottery used to stand just so when he said or sang it, others believed that he was supposed to walk among the people, but years and years ago this part of the ritual had been allowed to lapse. There had been, also, a ritual salute, which the official of the lottery had had to use in addressing each person who came up to draw from the box, but this also had changed with time, until now it was felt necessary only for the official to speak to each person approaching. Mr. Summers was very good at all this; in his clean white shirt and blue jeans, with one hand resting carelessly on the black box, he seemed very proper and important as he talked interminably to Mr. Graves and the Martins.

Just as Mr. Summers finally left off talking and turned to the assembled villagers, Mrs. Hutchinson came hurriedly along the path to the square, her sweater thrown over her shoulders, and slid into place in the back of the crowd. "Clean forgot what day it was," she said to Mrs. Delacroix, who stood next to her, and they both laughed softly. "Thought my old man was out back stacking wood," Mrs. Hutchinson went on, "and then I looked out the window and the kids were gone, and then I remembered it was the twenty-seventh and came a-running." She dried her hands on her apron, and Mrs. Delacroix said, "You're in time, though. They're still talking away up there."

Mrs. Hutchinson craned her neck to see through the crowd and found her husband and children standing near the front. She tapped Mrs. Delacroix on the arm as a farewell and began to make her way through the crowd. The people separated good-humoredly to let her through; two or three people said, in voices just loud enough to be heard across the crowd, "Here comes your Missus, Hutchinson," and "Bill, she made it after all." Mrs. Hutchinson reached her husband, and Mr. Summers, who had been waiting, said cheerfully, "Thought we were going to have to get on without you, Tessie." Mrs. Hutchinson said, grinning, "Wouldn't have me leave m'dishes in the sink, now, would you, Joe?" and soft laughter ran through the crowd as the people stirred back into position after Mrs. Hutchinson's arrival.

"Well, now," Mr. Summers said soberly, "guess we better get started, get this over with, so's we can go back to work. Anybody ain't here?"

"Dunbar," several people said. "Dunbar, Dunbar."

Mr. Summers consulted his list. "Clyde Dunbar," he said. "That's right. He's broke his leg, hasn't he? Who's drawing for him?"

"Me, I guess," a woman said, and Mr. Summers turned to look at her. "Wife draws for her husband," Mr. Summers said. "Don't you have a grown boy to do it for you, Janey?" Although Mr. Summers and everyone else in the village knew the answer perfectly well, it was the business of the official of the lottery to ask such questions formally. Mr. Summers waited with an expression of polite interest while Mrs. Dunbar answered.

"Horace's not but sixteen yet," Mrs. Dunbar said regretfully. "Guess I gotta fill in for the old man this year."

"Right," Mr. Summers said. He made a note on the list he was holding. Then he asked, "Watson boy drawing this year?"

A tall boy in the crowd raised his hand. "Here," he said. "I'm drawing for m'mother and me." He blinked his eyes nervously and ducked his head as several voices in the crowd said things like "Good fellow, Jack," and "Glad to see your mother's got a man to do it."

"Well," Mr. Summers said, "guess that's everyone. Old Man Warner make it?"

"Here," a voice said, and Mr. Summers nodded.

A sudden hush fell on the crowd as Mr. Summers cleared his throat and looked at the list. "All ready?" he called. "Now, I'll read the names—heads of families first—and the men come up and take a paper out of the box. Keep the paper folded in your hand without looking at it until everyone has had a turn. Everything clear?"

The people had done it so many times that they only half listened to the directions; most of them were quiet, wetting their lips, not looking around. Then Mr. Summers raised one hand high and said, "Adams." A man disengaged himself from the crowd and came forward. "Hi, Steve," Mr. Summers said, and Mr. Adams said, "Hi, Joe." They grinned at one another humorlessly and nervously. Then Mr. Adams reached into the black box and took out a folded paper. He held it firmly by one corner as he turned and went hastily back to his place in the crowd, where he stood a little apart from his family, not looking down at his hand.

"Allen," Mr. Summers said. "Anderson . . . Bentham."

"Seems like there's no time at all between lotteries any more," Mrs. Delacroix said to Mrs. Graves in the back row. "Seems like we got through with the last one only last week."

"Time sure goes fast," Mrs. Graves said.

"Clark . . . Delacroix."

"There goes my old man," Mrs. Delacroix said. She held her breath while her husband went forward.

"Dunbar," Mr. Summers said, and Mrs. Dunbar went steadily to the box while one of the women said, "Go on, Janey," and another said, "There she goes."

"We're next," Mrs. Graves said. She watched while Mr. Graves came around from the side of the box, greeted Mr. Summers gravely, and selected a slip of paper from the box. By now, all through the crowd there were men holding the small folded papers in their large hands, turning them over and over nervously. Mrs. Dunbar and her two sons stood together, Mrs. Dunbar holding the slip of paper.

"Harburt . . . Hutchinson."

"Get up there, Bill," Mrs. Hutchinson said, and the people near her laughed.

"Jones."

"They do say," Mr. Adams said to Old Man Warner, who stood next to him, "that over in the north village they're talking of giving up the lottery."

Old Man Warner snorted. "Pack of crazy fools," he said. "Listening to the young folks, nothing's good enough for *them*. Next thing you know, they'll be wanting to go back to living in caves, nobody work any more, live *that* way for a while. Used to be a saying about 'Lottery in June, corn be heavy soon.' First thing you know, we'd all be eating stewed chickweed and acorns. There's *always* been a lottery," he added petulantly. "Bad enough to see young Joe Summers up there joking with everybody."

"Some places have already quit lotteries," Mrs. Adams said.

"Nothing but trouble in *that,*" Old Man Warner said stoutly. "Pack of young fools."

"Martin." And Bobby Martin watched his father go forward. "Overdyke . . . Percy."

"I wish they'd hurry," Mrs. Dunbar said to her older son. "I wish they'd hurry."

"They're almost through," her son said.

"You get ready to run tell Dad," Mrs. Dunbar said.

Mr. Summers called his own name and then stepped forward precisely and selected a slip from the box. Then he called, "Warner."

"Seventy-seventh year I been in the lottery," Old Man Warner said as he went through the crowd. "Seventy-seventh time."

"Watson." The tall boy came awkwardly through the crowd. Someone said, "Don't be nervous, Jack," and Mr. Summers said, "Take your time, son."

"Zanini."

After that, there was a long pause, a breathless pause, until Mr. Summers, holding his slip of paper in the air, said, "All right, fellows." For a minute, no one moved, and then all the slips of paper were opened. Suddenly, all the women began to speak at once, saying, "Who is it?" "Who's got it?" "Is it the Dunbars?" "Is it the Watsons?" Then the voices began to say, "It's Hutchinson. It's Bill," "Bill Hutchinson's got it."

"Go tell your father," Mrs. Dunbar said to her older son.

People began to look around to see the Hutchinsons. Bill Hutchinson was standing quiet, staring down at the paper in his hand. Suddenly, Tessie Hutchinson shouted to Mr. Summers, "You didn't give him time enough to take any paper he wanted. I saw you. It wasn't fair."

"Be a good sport, Tessie," Mrs. Delacroix called, and Mrs. Graves said, "All of us took the same chance."

"Shut up, Tessie," Bill Hutchinson said.

"Well, everyone," Mr. Summers said, "that was done pretty fast, and now we've got to be hurrying a little more to get done in time." He consulted his next list. "Bill," he said, "you draw for the Hutchinson family. You got any other households in the Hutchinsons?"

"There's Don and Eva," Mrs. Hutchinson yelled. "Make *them* take their chance!"

"Daughters draw with their husbands' families, Tessie," Mr. Summers said gently. "You know that as well as anyone else."

"It wasn't *fair*," Tessie said.

"I guess not, Joe," Bill Hutchinson said regretfully. "My daughter draws with her husband's family, that's only fair. And I've got no other family except the kids."

"Then, as far as drawing for families is concerned, it's you," Mr. Summers said in explanation, "and as far as drawing for households is concerned, that's you, too. Right?"

"Right," Bill Hutchinson said.

"How many kids, Bill?" Mr. Summers asked formally.

"Three," Bill Hutchinson said. "There's Bill, Jr., and Nancy, and little Dave. And Tessie and me."

"All right, then," Mr. Summers said. "Harry, you got their tickets back?"

Mr. Graves nodded and held up the slips of paper. "Put them in the box, then," Mr. Summers directed. "Take Bill's and put it in."

"I think we ought to start over," Mrs. Hutchinson said, as quietly as she could. "I tell you it wasn't *fair*. You didn't give him time enough to choose. *Every*body saw that."

Mr. Graves had selected the five slips and put them in the box, and he dropped all the papers but those onto the ground, where the breeze caught them and lifted them off.

"Listen, everybody," Mrs. Hutchinson was saying to the people around her.

"Ready, Bill?" Mr. Summers asked, and Bill Hutchinson, with one quick glance around at his wife and children, nodded.

"Remember," Mr. Summers said, "take the slips and keep them folded until each person has taken one. Harry, you help little Dave." Mr. Graves took the hand of the little boy, who came willingly with him up to the box. "Take a paper out of the box, Davy," Mr. Summers said. Davy put his hand into the box and laughed. "Take just *one* paper," Mr. Summers said. "Harry, you hold it for him." Mr. Graves took the child's hand and removed the folded paper from the tight fist and held it while little Dave stood next to him and looked up at him wonderingly.

"Nancy next," Mr. Summers said. Nancy was twelve, and her school friends breathed heavily as she went forward, switching her skirt, and took a slip daintily from the box. "Bill, Jr.," Mr. Summers said, and Billy, his face red and his feet over-large, nearly knocked the box over as he got a paper out. "Tessie," Mr. Summers said. She hesitated for a minute, looking around defiantly, and then set her lips and went up to the box. She snatched a paper out and held it behind her.

"Bill," Mr. Summers said, and Bill Hutchinson reached into the box and felt around, bringing his hand out at last with the slip of paper in it.

The crowd was quiet. A girl whispered, "I hope it's not Nancy," and the sound of the whisper reached the edges of the crowd.

"It's not the way it used to be," Old Man Warner said clearly. "People ain't the way they used to be."

"All right," Mr. Summers said. "Open the papers. Harry, you open little Dave's."

Mr. Graves opened the slip of paper and there was a general sigh through the crowd as he held it up and everyone could see that it was blank. Nancy and Bill, Jr., opened theirs at the same time, and both beamed and laughed, turning around to the crowd and holding their slips of paper above their heads.

"Tessie," Mr. Summers said. There was a pause, and then Mr. Summers looked at Bill Hutchinson, and Bill unfolded his paper and showed it. It was blank.

"It's Tessie," Mr. Summers said, and his voice was hushed. "Show us her paper, Bill."

Bill Hutchinson went over to his wife and forced the slip of paper out of her hand. It had a black spot on it, the black spot Mr. Summers had made the night before with the heavy pencil in the coal-company office. Bill Hutchinson held it up, and there was a stir in the crowd.

"All right, folks," Mr. Summers said. "Let's finish quickly."

Although the villagers had forgotten the ritual and lost the original black box, they still remembered to use stones. The pile of stones the boys had made earlier was ready; there were stones on the ground with the blowing scraps of paper that had come out of the box. Mrs. Delacroix selected a stone so large she had to pick it up with both hands and turned to Mrs. Dunbar. "Come on," she said. "Hurry up."

Mrs. Dunbar had small stones in both hands, and she said, gasping for breath, "I can't run at all. You'll have to go ahead and I'll catch up with you."

The children had stones already, and someone gave little Davy Hutchinson a few pebbles.

Tessie Hutchinson was in the center of a cleared space by now, and she held her hands out desperately as the villagers moved in on her. "It isn't fair," she said. A stone hit her on the side of the head.

Old Man Warner was saying, "Come on, come on, everyone." Steve Adams was in the front of the crowd of villagers, with Mrs. Graves beside him.

"It isn't fair, it isn't right," Mrs. Hutchinson screamed, and then they were upon her.

QUESTIONS

1. What is a scapegoat? Who is the scapegoat in this story? Look up other examples of scapegoats (Sir James Frazer's *The Golden Bough* is an excellent source).

2. What law of probability has the author suspended in writing this story? Granting this initial implausibility, does the story proceed naturally?

3. What is the fundamental irony of the story?

4. What is the significance of the fact that the original box has been lost and many parts of the ritual have been forgotten?

5. What different attitudes toward the ritual are represented by (a) Mr. Summers, (b) Old Man Warner, (c) Mr. and Mrs. Adams, (d) Mrs. Hutchinson, (e) the villagers in general? Which would you suppose most nearly represents the attitude of the author? Why?

6. By transporting a primitivistic ritual into a modern setting, the author is enabled to say something about human nature and human society. What?

7. "The Lottery" must obviously be interpreted symbolically or allegorically (as a pattern of symbols corresponding to some pattern in the outside world). How far is the meaning of its symbols fixed? how far open to various interpretations? What specific interpretations can you suggest?

Albert Camus

THE GUEST

The schoolmaster was watching the two men climb toward him. One was on horseback, the other on foot. They had not yet tackled the abrupt rise leading to the schoolhouse built on the hillside. They were toiling onward, making slow progress in the snow, among the stones, on the vast expanse of the high, deserted plateau. From time to time the horse stumbled. He could not be heard yet but the breath issuing from his nostrils could be seen. The schoolmaster calculated that it would take them a half hour to get onto the hill. It was cold; he went back into the school to get a sweater.

He crossed the empty, frigid classroom. On the blackboard the four rivers of France, drawn with four different colored chalks, had been flowing toward their estuaries for the past three days. Snow had suddenly fallen in mid-October after eight months of drought without the transition of rain, and the twenty pupils, more or less, who lived in the villages scattered over the plateau had stopped coming. With fair weather they would return. Daru now heated only the single room that was his lodging, adjoining the classroom. One of the windows faced, like the classroom windows, the south. On that side the school was a few kilometers from the point where the plateau began to slope toward the south. In clear weather the purple mass of the mountain range where the gap opened onto the desert could be seen.

Somewhat warmed, Daru returned to the window from which he had first noticed the two men. They were no longer visible. Hence they must have tackled the rise. The sky was not so dark, for the snow had stopped falling during the night. The morning had dawned with a dirty light which had scarcely become brighter as the ceiling of clouds lifted. At two in the afternoon it seemed as if the day were merely beginning. But still this was better than those three days when the thick snow was falling amidst unbroken darkness with little gusts of wind that rattled the double door of the classroom. Then Daru had spent long hours in his room, leaving it only to go to the shed and feed the chickens or get some coal. Fortunately the delivery truck from Tadjid, the nearest village to the north, had brought his supplies two days before the blizzard. It would return in forty-eight hours.

Besides, he had enough to resist a siege, for the little room was cluttered with bags of wheat that the administration had left as a supply to distribute to those of his pupils whose families had suffered from the drought. Actually they had all been victims because they were all poor. Every day Daru would distribute a ration to the children. They had missed it, he knew, during these bad days. Possibly one of the fathers or big brothers would come this afternoon and he could supply them with grain. It was just a matter of carrying them over to the next harvest. Now shiploads of wheat were arriving from France and the worst was over. But it would be hard to forget that poverty, that army of ragged ghosts wandering in the sunlight, the plateaus burned to a cinder month after month, the earth shriveled up little by little, literally scorched, every stone bursting into dust under one's foot. The sheep had died then by thousands, and even a few men, here and there, sometimes without anyone's knowing.

In contrast with such poverty, he who lived almost like a monk, in his remote schoolhouse, had felt like a lord with his whitewashed walls, his narrow couch, his unpainted shelves, his well, and his weekly provisioning with water and food. And suddenly this snow, without warning, without the foretaste of rain. This is the way the region was, cruel to live in, even without men, who didn't help matters either. But Daru had been born here. Everywhere else, he felt exiled.

He went out and stepped forward on the terrace in front of the schoolhouse. The two men were now halfway up the slope. He recognized the horseman to be Balducci, the old gendarme he had known for a long time. Balducci was holding at the end of a rope an Arab walking behind him with hands bound and head lowered. The gendarme waved a greeting to which Daru did not reply, lost as he was in contemplation of the Arab dressed in a faded blue *jellaba,* his feet in sandals but covered with socks of heavy raw wool, his head crowned with a narrow, short *chèche*. Balducci was holding back his horse in order not to hurt the Arab, and the group was advancing slowly.

Within earshot, Balducci shouted, "One hour to do the three kilometers from El Ameur!" Daru did not answer. Short and square in his thick sweater, he watched them climb. Not once had the Arab raised his head. "Hello," said Daru when they got up onto the terrace. "Come in and warm up." Balducci painfully got down from his horse without letting go of the rope. He smiled at the schoolmaster from under his bristling mustache. His little dark eyes, deepset under a tanned forehead, and his mouth surrounded with wrinkles made him look attentive and studious. Daru took the bridle, led the horse to the shed, and came back to the two men who were now waiting for him in the school. He led them into his room. "I am going to heat up the classroom," he said. "We'll be more comfortable there."

When he entered the room again, Balducci was on the couch. He had undone the rope tying him to the Arab, who had squatted near the stove. His hands still bound, the *chèche* pushed back on his head, the Arab was looking toward the window. At first Daru noticed only his huge lips, fat, smooth, almost Negroid; yet his nose was straight, his eyes dark and full of fever. The *chèche* uncovered an obstinate forehead and, under the weathered skin now rather discolored by the cold, the whole face had a restless and rebellious look. "Go into the other room," said the schoolmaster, "and I'll make you some mint tea." "Thanks," Balducci said. "What a chore! How I long for retirement." And addressing his prisoner in Arabic, he said, "Come on, you." The Arab got up and, slowly, holding his bound wrists in front of him, went into the classroom.

With the tea, Daru brought a chair. But Balducci was already sitting in state at the nearest pupil's desk, and the Arab had squatted against the teacher's platform facing the stove, which stood between the desk and the window. When he held out the glass of tea to the prisoner, Daru hesitated at the sight of his bound hands. "He might perhaps be untied." "Sure," said Balducci. "That was for the trip." He started to get to his feet. But Daru, setting the glass on the floor, had knelt beside the Arab. Without saying anything, the Arab watched him with his feverish eyes. Once his hands were free, he rubbed his swollen wrists against each other, took the glass of tea and sucked up the burning liquid in swift little sips.

"Good," said Daru. "And where are you headed?"

Balducci withdrew his mustache from the tea. "Here, son."

"Odd pupils! And you're spending the night?"

"No. I'm going back to El Ameur. And you will deliver this fellow to Tinguit. He is expected at police headquarters."

Balducci was looking at Daru with a friendly little smile.

"What's this story?" asked the schoolmaster. "Are you pulling my leg?"

"No, son. Those are the orders."

"The orders? I'm not . . ." Daru hesitated, not wanting to hurt the old Corsican. "I mean, that's not my job."

"What! What's the meaning of that? In wartime people do all kinds of jobs."

"Then I'll wait for the declaration of war!"

Balducci nodded. "O.K. But the orders exist and they concern you too. Things are bubbling, it appears. There is talk of a forthcoming revolt. We are mobilized, in a way."

Daru still had his obstinate look.

"Listen, son," Balducci said. "I like you and you've got to understand. There's only a dozen of us at El Ameur to patrol the whole territory of a small department and I must be back in a hurry. He couldn't be kept there. His village was beginning to stir; they wanted to take him back. You must take him to Tinguit tomorrow before the day is over. Twenty kilometers shouldn't faze a husky fellow like you. After that, all will be over. You'll come back to your pupils and your comfortable life."

Behind the wall the horse could be heard snorting and pawing the earth. Daru was looking out the window. Decidedly the weather was clearing and the light was increasing over the snowy plateau. When all the snow was melted, the sun would take over again and once more would burn the fields of stone. For days still, the unchanging sky would shed its dry light on the solitary expanse where nothing had any connection with man.

"After all," he said, turning around toward Balducci, "what did he do?" And, before the gendarme had opened his mouth, he asked, "Does he speak French?"

"No, not a word. We had been looking for him for a month, but they were hiding him. He killed his cousin."

"Is he against us?"

"I don't think so. But you can never be sure."

"Why did he kill?"

"A family squabble, I think. One owed grain to the other, it seems. It's not at all clear. In short, he killed his cousin with a billhook. You know, like a sheep, *kreezk!*"

Balducci made the gesture of drawing a blade across his throat, and the Arab, his attention attracted, watched him with a sort of anxiety. Daru felt a sudden wrath against the man, against all men with their rotten spite, their tireless hates, their blood lust.

But the kettle was singing on the stove. He served Balducci more tea, hesitated, then served the Arab again, who drank avidly a second time. His raised arms made the *jellaba* fall open, and the schoolmaster saw his thin, muscular chest.

"Thanks, son," Balducci said. "And now I'm off."

He got up and went toward the Arab, taking a small rope from his pocket.

"What are you doing?" Daru asked dryly.

Balducci, disconcerted, showed him the rope.

"Don't bother."

The old gendarme hesitated. "It's up to you. Of course, you are armed?"

"I have my shotgun."

"Where?"

"In the trunk."

"You ought to have it near your bed."

"Why? I have nothing to fear."

"You're crazy, son. If there's an uprising, no one is safe; we're all in the same boat."

"I'll defend myself. I'll have time to see them coming."

Balducci began to laugh, then suddenly the mustache covered the white teeth. "You'll have time? O.K. That's just what I was saying. You always have been a little cracked. That's why I like you; my son was like that."

At the same time he took out his revolver and put it on the desk. "Keep it; I don't need two weapons from here to El Ameur."

The revolver shone against the black paint of the table. When the gendarme turned toward him, the schoolmaster caught his smell of leather and horseflesh.

"Listen, Balducci," Daru said suddenly, "all this disgusts me, beginning with your fellow here. But I won't hand him over. Fight, yes, if I have to. But not that."

The old gendarme stood in front of him and looked at him severely.

"You're being a fool," he said slowly. "I don't like it either. You don't get used to putting a rope on a man even after years of it, and you're even ashamed—yes, ashamed. But you can't let them have their way."

"I won't hand him over," Daru said again.

"It's an order, son, and I repeat it."

"That's right. Repeat to them what I've said to you: I won't hand him over."

Balducci made a visible effort to reflect. He looked at the Arab and at Daru. At last he decided.

"No, I won't tell them anything. If you want to drop us, go ahead; I'll not denounce you. I have an order to deliver the prisoner and I'm doing so. And now you'll just sign this paper for me."

"There's no need. I'll not deny that you left him with me."

"Don't be mean with me. I know you'll tell the truth. You're from around these parts and you are a man. But you must sign; that's the rule."

Daru opened his drawer, took out a little square bottle of purple ink, the red wooden penholder with the "sergeant-major" pen he used for models of handwriting, and signed. The gendarme carefully folded the paper and put it into his wallet. Then he moved toward the door.

"I'll see you off," Daru said.

"No," said Balducci. "There's no use being polite. You insulted me."

He looked at the Arab, motionless in the same spot, sniffed peevishly, and turned away toward the door. "Good-by, son," he said. The door slammed behind him. His footsteps were muffled by the snow. The horse stirred on the other side of the wall and several chickens fluttered in fright. A moment later Balducci reappeared outside the window leading the horse by the bridle. He walked toward the little rise without turning around and disappeared from sight with the horse following him.

Daru walked back toward the prisoner, who, without stirring, never took his eyes off him. "Wait," the schoolmaster said in Arabic and went toward the bedroom. As he was going through the door, he had a second thought, went to the desk, took the revolver, and stuck it in his pocket. Then, without looking back, he went into his room.

For some time he lay on his couch watching the sky gradually close over, listening to the silence. It was this silence that had seemed painful to him during the first days here, after the war. He had requested a post in the little town at the base of the foothills separating the upper plateaus from the desert. There rocky walls, green and black to the north, pink and lavender to the south, marked the frontier of eternal summer. He had been named to a post farther north, on the plateau itself. In the beginning, the solitude and the silence had been hard for him on these wastelands peopled only by stones. Occasionally, furrows suggested cultivation, but they had been dug to uncover a certain kind of stone good for building. The only plowing here was to harvest rocks. Elsewhere a thin layer of soil accumulated in the hollows would be scraped out to enrich paltry village gardens. This is the way it was: bare rock covered three quarters of the region. Towns sprang up, flourished, then disappeared; men came by, loved one another or fought bitterly, then died. No one in this desert, neither he nor his guest, mattered. And yet, outside this desert neither of them, Daru knew, could have really lived.

When he got up, no noise came from the classroom. He was amazed at the unmixed joy he derived from the mere thought that the Arab might have fled and that he would be alone with no decision to make. But the prisoner was there. He had merely stretched out between the stove and the desk and he was staring at the ceiling. In that position, his thick lips were particularly noticeable, giving him a pouting look. "Come," said Daru. The Arab got up and followed him. In the bedroom the schoolmaster pointed to a chair near the table under the window. The Arab sat down without ceasing to watch Daru.

"Are you hungry?"

"Yes," the prisoner said.

Daru set the table for two. He took flour and oil, shaped a cake in a frying pan, and lighted the little stove that functioned on bottled gas. While the cake was cooking, he went out to the shed to get cheese, eggs, dates, and condensed milk. When the cake was done he set it on the window sill to cool, heated some condensed milk diluted with water, and beat up the eggs into an omelette. In one of his motions he bumped into the revolver stuck in his right pocket. He set the bowl down, went into the classroom, and put the revolver in his desk drawer. When he came back to the room, night was falling. He put on the light and served the Arab. "Eat," he said. The Arab took a piece of the cake, lifted it eagerly to his mouth, and stopped short.

"And you?" he asked.

"After you. I'll eat too."

The thick lips opened slightly. The Arab hesitated, then bit into the cake determinedly.

The meal over, the Arab looked at the schoolmaster. "Are you the judge?"

"No, I'm simply keeping you until tomorrow."

"Why do you eat with me?"

"I'm hungry."

The Arab fell silent. Daru got up and went out. He brought back a camp cot from the shed and set it up between the table and the stove, at right angles to his own bed. From a large suitcase which, upright in a corner, served as a shelf for papers, he took two blankets and arranged them on the cot. Then he stopped, felt useless, and sat down on his bed. There was nothing more to do or to get ready. He had to look at this man. He looked at him therefore, trying to imagine his face bursting with rage. He couldn't do so. He could see nothing but the dark yet shining eyes and the animal mouth.

"Why did you kill him?" he asked in a voice whose hostile tone surprised him.

The Arab looked away. "He ran away. I ran after him."

He raised his eyes to Daru again and they were full of a sort of woeful interrogation. "Now what will they do to me?"

"Are you afraid?"

The Arab stiffened, turning his eyes away.

"Are you sorry?"

The Arab stared at him openmouthed. Obviously he did not understand. Daru's annoyance was growing. At the same time he felt awkward and self-conscious with his big body wedged between the two beds.

"Lie down there," he said impatiently. "That's your bed."

The Arab didn't move. He cried out, "Tell me!"

The schoolmaster looked at him.

"Is the gendarme coming back tomorrow?"

"I don't know."

"Are you coming with us?"

"I don't know. Why?"

The prisoner got up and stretched out on top of the blankets, his feet toward the window. The light from the electric bulb shone straight into his eyes and he closed them at once.

"Why?" Daru repeated, standing beside the bed.

The Arab opened his eyes under the blinding light and looked at him, trying not to blink. "Come with us," he said.

In the middle of the night, Daru was still not asleep. He had gone to bed after undressing completely; he generally slept naked. But when he suddenly realized that he had nothing on, he wondered. He felt vulnerable and the temptation came to him to put his clothes back on. Then he shrugged his shoulders; after all, he wasn't a child and, if it came to that, he could break his adversary in two. From his bed, he could observe him lying on his back, still motionless, his eyes closed under the harsh light. When Daru turned out the light, the darkness seemed to congeal all of a sudden. Little by little, the night came back to life in the window where the starless sky was stirring gently. The schoolmaster soon made out the body lying at his feet. The Arab was still motionless but his eyes seemed open. A faint wind was prowling about the schoolhouse. Perhaps it would drive away the clouds and the sun would reappear.

During the night the wind increased. The hens fluttered a little and then were silent. The Arab turned over on his side with his back to Daru, who thought he heard him moan. Then he listened for his guest's breathing, which had become heavier and more regular. He listened to that breathing so close to him and mused without being able to go to sleep. In the room where he had been sleeping alone for a year, this presence bothered him. But it bothered him also because it imposed on him a sort of brotherhood he refused to accept in the present circumstances; yet he was familiar with it. Men who share the same rooms, soldiers or prisoners, develop a strange alliance as if, having cast off their armor with their clothing, they fraternized every evening, over and above their differences, in the ancient community of dream and fatigue. But Daru shook himself; he didn't like such musings, and it was essential for him to sleep.

A little later, however, when the Arab stirred slightly, the schoolmaster was still not asleep. When the prisoner made a second move, he stiffened, on the alert. The Arab was lifting himself slowly on his arms with almost the motion of a sleepwalker. Seated upright in bed, he waited motionless without turning his head toward Daru, as if he were listening attentively. Daru did not stir; it had just occurred to him that the revolver was still in the drawer of his desk. It was better to act at once. Yet he continued to observe the prisoner, who, with the same slithery motion, put his feet on the ground, waited again, then stood up slowly. Daru was about to call out to him when the Arab began to walk, in a quite natural but extraordinarily silent way. He was heading toward the door at the end of the room that opened into the shed. He lifted the latch with precaution and went out, pushing the door behind him but without shutting it.

Daru had not stirred. "He is running away," he merely thought. "Good riddance!" Yet he listened attentively. The hens were not fluttering; the guest must be on the plateau. A faint sound of water reached him, and he didn't know what it was until the Arab again stood framed in the doorway, closed the door carefully, and came back to bed without a sound. Then Daru turned his back on him and fell asleep. Still later he seemed, from the depths of his sleep, to hear furtive steps around the schoolhouse. "I'm dreaming! I'm dreaming!" he repeated to himself. And he went on sleeping.

When he awoke, the sky was clear; the loose window let in a cold, pure air. The Arab was asleep, hunched up under the blankets now, his mouth open, utterly relaxed. But when Daru shook him he started dreadfully, staring at Daru with wild eyes as if he had never seen him and with such a frightened expression that the schoolmaster stepped back. "Don't be afraid. It is I. You must eat." The Arab nodded his head and said yes. Calm had returned to his face, but his expression was vacant and listless.

The coffee was ready. They drank it seated together on the cot as they munched their pieces of the cake. Then Daru led the Arab under the shed and showed him the faucet where he washed. He went back into the room, folded the blankets on the cot, made his own bed, and put the room in order. Then he went through the classroom and out onto the terrace. The sun was already rising in the blue sky; a soft, bright light enveloped the deserted plateau. On the ridge the snow was melting in spots. The stones were about to reappear. Crouched on the edge of the plateau, the schoolmaster looked at the deserted expanse. He thought of Balducci. He had hurt him, for he had sent him off as though he didn't want to be associated with him. He could still hear the gendarme's farewell and, without knowing why, he felt strangely empty and vulnerable.

At that moment, from the other side of the schoolhouse, the prisoner coughed. Daru listened to him almost despite himself and then, furious, threw a pebble that whistled through the air before sinking into the snow. That man's stupid crime revolted him, but to hand him over was contrary to honor; just thinking of it made him boil with humiliation. He simultaneously cursed his own people who had sent him this Arab and the Arab who had dared to kill and not managed to get away. Daru got up, walked in a circle on the terrace, waited motionless, and then went back into the schoolhouse.

The Arab, leaning over the cement floor of the shed, was washing his teeth with two fingers. Daru looked at him and said, "Come." He went back into the room ahead of the prisoner. He slipped a hunting jacket on over his sweater and put on walking shoes. Standing, he waited until the Arab had put on his *chèche* and sandals. They went into the classroom, and the schoolmaster pointed to the exit saying, "Go ahead." The fellow didn't budge. "I'm coming," said Daru. The Arab went out. Daru went back into the room and made a package with pieces of rusk, dates, and sugar in it. In the classroom, before going out, he hesitated a second in front of his desk, then crossed the threshold and locked the door. "That's the way," he said. He started toward the east, followed by the prisoner. But a short distance from the schoolhouse he thought he heard a slight sound behind him. He retraced his steps and examined the surroundings of the house; there was no one there. The Arab watched him without seeming to understand. "Come on," said Daru.

They walked for an hour and rested beside a sharp needle of limestone. The snow was melting faster and faster and the sun was drinking up the puddles just as quickly, rapidly cleaning the plateau, which gradually dried and vibrated like the air itself. When they resumed walking, the ground rang under their feet. From time to time a bird rent the space in front of them with a joyful cry. Daru felt a sort of rapture before the vast familiar expanse, now almost entirely yellow under its dome of blue sky. They walked an hour more, descending toward the south. They reached a sort of flattened elevation made up of crumbly rocks. From there on, the plateau sloped down—eastward toward a low plain on which could be made out a few spindly trees, and to the south toward outcroppings of rock that gave the landscape a chaotic look.

Daru surveyed the two directions. Not a man could be seen. He turned toward the Arab, who was looking at him blankly. Daru offered the package to him. "Take it," he said. "There are dates, bread, and sugar. You can hold out for two days. Here are a thousand francs too."

The Arab took the package and the money but kept his full hands at chest level as if he didn't know what to do with what was being given him.

"Now look," the schoolmaster said as he pointed in the direction of the east, "there's the way to Tinguit. You have a two-hour walk. At Tinguit are the administration and the police. They are expecting you."

The Arab looked toward the east, still holding the package and the money against his chest. Daru took his elbow and turned him rather roughly toward the south. At the foot of the elevation on which they stood could be seen a faint path. "That's the trail across the plateau. In a day's walk from here you'll find pasturelands and the first nomads. They'll take you in and shelter you according to their law."

The Arab had now turned toward Daru, and a sort of panic was visible in his expression. "Listen," he said.

Daru shook his head. "No, be quiet. Now I'm leaving you." He turned his back on him, took two long steps in the direction of the school, looked hesitantly at the motionless Arab, and started off again. For a few minutes he heard nothing but his own step resounding on the cold ground, and he did not turn his head. A moment later, however, he turned around. The Arab was still there on the edge of the hill, his arms hanging now, and he was looking at the schoolmaster. Daru felt something rise in his throat. But he swore with impatience, waved vaguely, and started off again. He had already gone a distance when he again stopped and looked. There was no longer anyone on the hill.

Daru hesitated. The sun was now rather high in the sky and beginning to beat down on his head. The schoolmaster retraced his steps, at first somewhat uncertainly, then with decision. When he reached the little hill, he was bathed in sweat. He climbed it as fast as he could and stopped, out of breath, on the top. The rock fields to the south stood out sharply against the blue sky, but on the plain to the east a steamy heat was rising. And in that slight haze, Daru, with heavy heart, made out the Arab walking slowly on the road to prison.

A little later, standing before the window of the classroom, the schoolmaster was watching the clear light bathing the whole surface of the plateau.

Behind him on the blackboard, among the winding French rivers, sprawled the clumsily chalked up words he had just read: "You handed over our brother. You will pay for this." Daru looked at the sky, the plateau, and, beyond, the invisible lands stretching all the way to the sea. In this vast landscape he had loved so much, he was alone.

QUESTIONS

1. What is the central conflict of the story? Is it external or internal? Can it be defined in terms of a dilemma?

2. Compare and contrast the attitudes of Daru and Balducci toward the prisoner and the situation. What is their attitude toward each other? Is either a bad or a cruel man? How does the conflict between Daru and Balducci intensify the central conflict?

3. Why did Daru give the prisoner his freedom? What reasons were there for not giving him his freedom?

4. In what respect is the title ironical? What kind of irony is this? Why does "The Guest" make a better title than "The Prisoner"?

5. This story contains the materials of explosive action—a revolver, a murderer, a state of undeclared war, an incipient uprising, a revenge note—but no violence occurs in the story. In what aspect of the situation is Camus principally interested?

6. This story has as its background a specific political situation—the French Algerian crisis in the years following World War II. How does Daru reflect France's plight? Is the story's meaning limited to this situation? What does the story tell us about good and evil and the nature of moral choice? How does the story differ in its treatment of these things from the typical Western story or the patriotic editorial?

7. In what respect is the ending of the story ironical? What kind of irony is this? What does it contribute to the meaning of the story?

8. Besides the ironies of the title and the ending, there are other ironies in the story. Find and explain them. Daru uses verbal irony on page 228 when he exclaims, "Odd pupils!" Is verbal irony the same thing as sarcasm?

9. Comment on the following: (a) Daru's behavior toward firearms and how it helps reveal him; (b) Camus's reason for making the Arab a murderer; (c) the Arab's reason for taking the road to prison.

Flannery O'Connor

GREENLEAF

Mrs. May's bedroom window was low and faced on the east and the bull, silvered in the moonlight, stood under it, his head raised as if he listened —like some patient god come down to woo her—for a stir inside the room. The window was dark and the sound of her breathing too light to be carried outside. Clouds crossing the moon blackened him and in the dark he began to tear at the hedge. Presently they passed and he appeared again in the same spot, chewing steadily, with a hedge-wreath that he had ripped loose for himself caught in the tips of his horns. When the moon drifted into retirement again, there was nothing to mark his place but the sound of steady chewing. Then abruptly a pink glow filled the window. Bars of light slid across him as the venetian blind was slit. He took a step backward and lowered his head as if to show the wreath across his horns.

For almost a minute there was no sound from inside, then as he raised his crowned head again, a woman's voice, guttural as if addressed to a dog, said, "Get away from here, Sir!" and in a second muttered, "Some nigger's scrub bull."

The animal pawed the ground and Mrs. May, standing bent forward behind the blind, closed it quickly lest the light make him charge into the shrubbery. For a second she waited, still bent forward, her nightgown hanging loosely from her narrow shoulders. Green rubber curlers sprouted neatly over her forehead and her face beneath them was smooth as concrete with an egg-white paste that drew the wrinkles out while she slept.

She had been conscious in her sleep of a steady rhythmic chewing as if something were eating one wall of the house. She had been aware that whatever it was had been eating as long as she had had the place and had eaten everything from the beginning of her fence line up to the house and now was eating the house and calmly with the same steady rhythm would continue through the house, eating her and the boys, and then on, eating everything but the Greenleafs, on and on, eating everything until nothing was left but the Greenleafs on a little island all their own in the middle of what had been her place. When the munching reached her elbow, she jumped up and found herself, fully awake, standing in the middle of her room. She identified the sound at once: a cow was tearing at the shrubbery under her window. Mr. Greenleaf had left the lane gate open and she didn't doubt that the entire herd was on her lawn. She turned on the dim pink table lamp and then went to the window and slit the blind. The bull, gaunt and long-legged, was standing about four feet from her, chewing calmly like an uncouth country suitor.

For fifteen years, she thought as she squinted at him fiercely, she had been having shiftless people's hogs root up her oats, their mules wallow on her lawn, their scrub bulls breed her cows. If this one was not put up now, he would be over the fence, ruining her herd before morning—and Mr. Greenleaf was soundly sleeping a half mile down the road in the tenant house. There was no way to get him unless she dressed and got in her car and rode down there and woke him up. He would come but his expression, his whole figure, his every pause, would say: "Hit looks to me like one or both of them boys would not make their maw ride out in the middle of the night thisaway. If hit was my boys, they would have got thet bull up theirself."

The bull lowered his head and shook it and the wreath slipped down to the base of his horns where it looked like a menacing prickly crown. She had closed the blind then; in a few seconds she heard him move off heavily.

Mr. Greenleaf would say, "If hit was my boys they would never have allowed their maw to go after hired help in the middle of the night. They would have did it theirself."

Weighing it, she decided not to bother Mr. Greenleaf. She returned to bed thinking that if the Greenleaf boys had risen in the world it was because she had given their father employment when no one else would have him. She had had Mr. Greenleaf fifteen years but no one else would have had him five minutes. Just the way he approached an object was enough to tell anybody with eyes what kind of a worker he was. He walked with a high-shouldered creep and he never appeared to come directly forward. He walked on the perimeter of some invisible circle and if you wanted to look him in the face, you had to move and get in front of him. She had not fired him because she had always doubted she could do better. He was too shiftless to go out and look for another job; he didn't have the initiative to steal, and after she had told him three or four times to do a thing, he did it; but he never told her about a sick cow until it was too late to call the veterinarian and if her barn had caught on fire, he would have called his wife to see the flames before he began to put them out. And of the wife, she didn't even like to think. Beside the wife, Mr. Greenleaf was an aristocrat.

"If it had been my boys," he would have said, "they would have cut off their right arm before they would have allowed their maw to . . ."

"If your boys had any pride, Mr. Greenleaf," she would like to say to him some day, "there are many things that they would not *allow* their mother to do."

The next morning as soon as Mr. Greenleaf came to the back door, she told him there was a stray bull on the place and that she wanted him penned up at once.

"Done already been here three days," he said, addressing his right foot which he held forward, turned slightly as if he were trying to look at the sole. He was standing at the bottom of the three back steps while she leaned out the kitchen door, a small woman with pale near-sighted eyes and grey hair that rose on top like the crest of some disturbed bird.

"Three days!" she said in the restrained screech that had become habitual with her.

Mr. Greenleaf, looking into the distance over the near pasture, removed a package of cigarets from his shirt pocket and let one fall into his hand. He put the package back and stood for a while looking at the cigaret. "I put him in the bull pen but he torn out of there," he said presently. "I didn't see him none after that." He bent over the cigaret and lit it and then turned his head briefly in her direction. The upper part of his face sloped gradually into the lower which was long and narrow, shaped like a rough chalice. He had deep-set fox-colored eyes shadowed under a grey felt hat that he wore slanted forward following the line of his nose. His build was insignificant.

"Mr. Greenleaf," she said, "get that bull up this morning before you do anything else. You know he'll ruin the breeding schedule. Get him up and keep him up and the next time there's a stray bull on this place, tell me at once. Do you understand?"

"Where do you want him put at?" Mr. Greenleaf asked.

"I don't care where you put him," she said. "You are supposed to have some sense. Put him where he can't get out. Whose bull is he?"

For a moment Mr. Greenleaf seemed to hesitate between silence and speech. He studied the air to the left of him. "He must be somebody's bull," he said after a while.

"Yes, he must!" she said and shut the door with a precise little slam.

She went into the dining room where the two boys were eating breakfast and sat down on the edge of her chair at the head of the table. She never ate breakfast but she sat with them to see that they had what they wanted. "Honestly!" she said, and began to tell about the bull, aping Mr. Greenleaf saying, "It must be *somebody's* bull."

Wesley continued to read the newspaper folded beside his plate but Scofield interrupted his eating from time to time to look at her and laugh. The two boys never had the same reaction to anything. They were as different, she said, as night and day. The only thing they did have in common was that neither of them cared what happened on the place. Scofield was a business type and Wesley was an intellectual.

Wesley, the younger child, had had rheumatic fever when he was seven and Mrs. May thought that this was what had caused him to be an intellectual. Scofield, who had never had a day's sickness in his life, was an insurance salesman. She would not have minded his selling insurance if he had sold a nicer kind but he sold the kind that only negroes buy. He was what negroes call a "policy man." He said there was more money in nigger-insurance than any other kind, and before company, he was very loud about it. He would shout, "Mama don't like to hear me say it but I'm the best nigger-insurance salesman in this county!"

Scofield was thirty-six and he had a broad pleasant smiling face but he was not married. "Yes," Mrs. May would say, "and if you sold decent insurance, some *nice* girl would be willing to marry you. What nice girl wants to marry a nigger-insurance man? You'll wake up some day and it'll be too late."

And at this Scofield would yodel and say, "Why Mamma, I'm not going to marry until you're dead and gone and then I'm going to marry me some nice fat farm girl that can take over this place!" And once he had added, "—some nice lady like Mrs. Greenleaf." When he had said this, Mrs. May had risen from her chair, her back stiff as a rake handle, and had gone to her room. There she had sat down on the edge of her bed for some time with her small face drawn. Finally she had whispered, "I work and slave, I struggle and sweat to keep this place for them and as soon as I'm dead, they'll marry trash and bring it in here and ruin everything. They'll marry trash and ruin everything I've done," and she had made up her mind at that moment to change her will. The next day she had gone to her lawyer and had had the property entailed so that if they married, they could not leave it to their wives.

The idea that one of them might marry a woman even remotely like Mrs. Greenleaf was enough to make her ill. She had put up with Mr. Greenleaf for fifteen years, but the only way she had endured his wife had been by keeping entirely out of her sight. Mrs. Greenleaf was large and loose. The yard around her house looked like a dump and her five girls were always filthy; even the youngest one dipped snuff. Instead of making a garden or washing their clothes, her preoccupation was what she called "prayer healing."

Every day she cut all the morbid stories out of the newspaper—the accounts of women who had been raped and criminals who had escaped and children who had been burned and of train wrecks and plane crashes and the divorces of movie stars. She took these to the woods and dug a hole and buried them and then she fell on the ground over them and mumbled and groaned for an hour or so, moving her huge arms back and forth under her and out again and finally just lying down flat and, Mrs. May suspected, going to sleep in the dirt.

She had not found out about this until the Greenleafs had been with her a few months. One morning she had been out to inspect a field that she had wanted planted in rye but that had come up in clover because Mr. Greenleaf had used the wrong seeds in the grain drill. She was returning through a wooded path that separated two pastures, muttering to herself and hitting the ground methodically with a long stick she carried in case she saw a snake. "Mr. Greenleaf," she was saying in a low voice, "I cannot afford to pay for your mistakes. I am a poor woman and this place is all I have. I have two boys to educate. I cannot . . ."

Out of nowhere a guttural agonized voice groaned, "Jesus! Jesus!" In a second it came again with a terrible urgency. "Jesus! Jesus!"

Mrs. May stopped still, one hand lifted to her throat. The sound was so piercing that she felt as if some violent unleashed force had broken out of the ground and was charging toward her. Her second thought was more reasonable: somebody had been hurt on the place and would sue her for everything she had. She had no insurance. She rushed forward and turning a bend in the path, she saw Mrs. Greenleaf sprawled on her hands and knees off the side of the road, her head down.

"Mrs. Greenleaf!" she shrilled, "what's happened!"

Mrs. Greenleaf raised her head. Her face was a patchwork of dirt and tears and her small eyes, the color of two field peas, were red-rimmed and swollen, but her expression was as composed as a bulldog's. She swayed back and forth on her hands and knees and groaned, "Jesus, Jesus."

Mrs. May winced. She thought the word, Jesus, should be kept inside the church building like other words inside the bedroom. She was a good Christian woman with a large respect for religion, though she did not, of course, believe any of it was true. "What is the matter with you?" she asked sharply.

"You broken my healing," Mrs. Greenleaf said, waving her aside. "I can't talk to you until I finish."

Mrs. May stood, bent forward, her mouth open and her stick raised off the ground as if she were not sure what she wanted to strike with it.

"Oh Jesus, stab me in the heart!" Mrs. Greenleaf shrieked. "Jesus, stab me in the heart!" and she fell back flat in the dirt, a huge human mound, her legs and arms spread out as if she were trying to wrap them around the earth.

Mrs. May felt as furious and helpless as if she had been insulted by a child. "Jesus," she said, drawing herself back, "would be *ashamed* of you. He would tell you to get up from there this instant and go wash your children's clothes!" and she had turned and walked off as fast as she could.

Whenever she thought of how the Greenleaf boys had advanced in the world, she had only to think of Mrs. Greenleaf sprawled obscenely on the ground, and say to herself, "Well, no matter how far they go, they *came* from that."

She would like to have been able to put in her will that when she died, Wesley and Scofield were not to continue to employ Mr. Greenleaf. She was capable of handling Mr. Greenleaf; they were not. Mr. Greenleaf had pointed out to her once that her boys didn't know hay from silage. She had pointed out to him that they had other talents, that Scofield was a successful businessman and Wesley a successful intellectual. Mr. Greenleaf did not comment, but he never lost an opportunity of letting her see, by his expression or some simple gesture, that he held the two of them in infinite contempt. As scrub-human as the Greenleafs were, he never hesitated to let her know that in any like circumstance in which his own boys might have been involved, they—O. T. and E. T. Greenleaf—would have acted to better advantage.

The Greenleaf boys were two or three years younger than the May boys. They were twins and you never knew when you spoke to one of them whether you were speaking to O. T. or E. T., and they never had the politeness to enlighten you. They were long-legged and raw-boned and red-skinned, with bright grasping fox-colored eyes like their father's. Mr. Greenleaf's pride in them began with the fact that they were twins. He acted, Mrs. May said, as if this were something smart they had thought of themselves. They were energetic and hard-working and she would admit to anyone that they had come a long way—and that the Second World War was responsible for it.

They had both joined the service and, disguised in their uniforms, they could not be told from other people's children. You could tell, of course, when they opened their mouths but they did that seldom. The smartest thing they had done was to get sent overseas and there to marry French wives. They hadn't married French trash either. They had married nice girls who naturally couldn't tell that they murdered the king's English or that the Greenleafs were who they were.

Wesley's heart condition had not permitted him to serve his country but Scofield had been in the army for two years. He had not cared for it and at the end of his military service, he was only a Private First Class. The Greenleaf boys were both some kind of sergeants, and Mr. Greenleaf, in those days, had never lost an opportunity of referring to them by their rank. They had both managed to get wounded and now they both had pensions. Further, as soon as they were released from the army, they took advantage of all the benefits and went to the school of agriculture at the university—the taxpayers meanwhile supporting their French wives. The two of them were living now about two miles down the highway on a piece of land that the government had helped them to buy and in a brick duplex bungalow that the government had helped to build and pay for. If the war had made anyone, Mrs. May said, it had made the Greenleaf boys. They each had three little children apiece, who spoke Greenleaf English and French, and who, on account of their mothers' background, would be sent to the convent school and brought up with manners. "And in twenty years," Mrs. May asked Scofield and Wesley, "do you know what those people will be?

"Society," she said blackly.

She had spent fifteen years coping with Mr. Greenleaf and, by now, handling him had become second nature with her. His disposition on any particular day was as much a factor in what she could and couldn't do as the weather was, and she had learned to read his face the way real country people read the sunrise and sunset.

She was a country woman only by persuasion. The late Mr. May, a business man, had bought the place when land was down, and when he died it was all he had to leave her. The boys had not been happy to move to the country to a broken-down farm, but there was nothing else for her to do. She had the timber on the place cut and with the proceeds had set herself up in the dairy business after Mr. Greenleaf had answered her ad. "i seen yor add and i will come have 2 boys," was all his letter said, but he arrived the next day in a pieced-together truck, his wife and five daughters sitting on the floor in the back, himself and the two boys in the cab.

Over the years they had been on her place, Mr. and Mrs. Greenleaf had aged hardly at all. They had no worries, no responsibilities. They lived like the lilies of the field, off the fat that she struggled to put into the land. When she was dead and gone from overwork and worry, the Greenleafs healthy and thriving, would be just ready to begin draining Scofield and Wesley.

Wesley said the reason Mrs. Greenleaf had not aged was because she released all her emotions in prayer healing. "You ought to start praying, Sweetheart," he had said in the voice that, poor boy, he could not help making deliberately nasty.

Scofield only exasperated her beyond endurance but Wesley caused her real anxiety. He was thin and nervous and bald and being an intellectual was a terrible strain on his disposition. She doubted if he would marry until she died but she was certain that then the wrong woman would get him. Nice girls didn't like Scofield but Wesley didn't like nice girls. He didn't like anything. He drove twenty miles every day to the university where he taught and twenty miles back every night, but he said he hated the twenty-mile drive and he hated the second-rate university and he hated the morons who attended it. He hated the country and he hated the life he lived; he hated living with his mother and his idiot brother and he hated hearing about the damn dairy and the damn help and the damn broken machinery. But in spite of all he said, he never made any move to leave. He talked about Paris and Rome but he never went even to Atlanta.

"You'd go to those places and you'd get sick," Mrs. May would say. "Who in Paris is going to see that you get a salt-free diet? And do you think if you married one of those odd numbers you take out that *she* would cook a salt-free diet for you? No indeed, she would not!" When she took this line, Wesley would turn himself roughly around in his chair and ignore her. Once when she had kept it up too long, he had snarled, "Well, why don't you do something practical, Woman? Why don't you pray for me like Mrs. Greenleaf would?"

"I don't like to hear you boys make jokes about religion," she had said. "If you would go to church, you would meet some nice girls."

But it was impossible to tell them anything. When she looked at the two of them now, sitting on either side of the table, neither one caring the least if a stray bull ruined her herd—which was their herd, their future—when she looked at the two of them, one hunched over a paper and the other teetering back in his chair, grinning at her like an idiot, she wanted to jump up and beat her fist on the table and shout, "You'll find out one of these days, you'll find out what *Reality* is when it's too late!"

"Mamma," Scofield said, "don't you get excited now but I'll tell you whose bull that is." He was looking at her wickedly. He let his chair drop forward and he got up. Then with his shoulders bent and his hands held up to cover his head, he tiptoed to the door. He backed into the hall and pulled the door almost to so that it hid all of him but his face. "You want to know, Sugar-pie?" he asked.

Mrs. May sat looking at him coldly.

"That's O. T. and E. T.'s bull," he said. "I collected from their nigger yesterday and he told me they were missing it," and he showed her an exaggerated expanse of teeth and disappeared silently.

Wesley looked up and laughed.

Mrs. May turned her head forward again, her expression unaltered. "I am the only *adult* on this place," she said. She leaned across the table and pulled the paper from the side of his plate. "Do you see how it's going to be when I die and you boys have to handle him?" she began. "Do you see why he didn't know whose bull that was? Because it was theirs. Do you see what I have to put up with? Do you see that if I hadn't kept my foot on his neck all these years, you boys might be milking cows every morning at four o'clock?"

Wesley pulled the paper back toward his plate and staring at her full in the face, he murmured, "I wouldn't milk a cow to save your soul from hell."

"I know you wouldn't," she said in a brittle voice. She sat back and began rapidly turning her knife over at the side of her plate. "O. T. and E. T. are fine boys," she said. "They ought to have been my sons." The thought of this was so horrible that her vision of Wesley was blurred at once by a wall of tears. All she saw was his dark shape, rising quickly from the table. "And you two," she cried, "you two should have belonged to that woman!"

He was heading for the door.

"When I die," she said in a thin voice, "I don't know what's going to become of you."

"You're always yapping about when-you-die," he growled as he rushed out, "but you look pretty healthy to me."

For some time she sat where she was, looking straight ahead through the window across the room into a scene of indistinct greys and greens. She stretched her face and her neck muscles and drew in a long breath but the scene in front of her flowed together anyway into a watery grey mass. "They needn't think I'm going to die any time soon," she muttered, and some more defiant voice in her added: I'll die when I get good and ready.

She wiped her eyes with the table napkin and got up and went to the window and gazed at the scene in front of her. The cows were grazing on two pale green pastures across the road and behind them, fencing them in, was a black wall of trees with a sharp sawtooth edge that held off the indifferent sky. The pastures were enough to calm her. When she looked out any window in her house, she saw the reflection of her own character. Her city friends said she was the most remarkable woman they knew, to go, practically penniless and with no experience, out to a rundown farm and make a success of it. "Everything is against you," she would say, "the weather is against you and the dirt is against you and the help is against you. They're all in league against you. There's nothing for it but an iron hand!"

"Look at Mamma's iron hand!" Scofield would yell and grab her arm and hold it up so that her delicate blue-veined little hand would dangle from her wrist like the head of a broken lily. The company always laughed.

The sun, moving over the black and white grazing cows, was just a little brighter than the rest of the sky. Looking down, she saw a darker shape that might have been its shadow cast at an angle, moving among them. She uttered a sharp cry and turned and marched out of the house.

Mr. Greenleaf was in the trench silo, filling a wheelbarrow. She stood on the edge and looked down at him. "I told you to get up that bull. Now he's in with the milk herd."

"You can't do two thangs at oncet," Mr. Greenleaf remarked.

"I told you to do that first."

He wheeled the barrow out of the open end of the trench toward the barn and she followed close behind him. "And you needn't think, Mr. Greenleaf," she said, "that I don't know exactly whose bull that is or why you haven't been in any hurry to notify me he was here. I might as well feed O. T. and E. T.'s bull as long as I'm going to have him here ruining my herd."

Mr. Greenleaf paused with the wheelbarrow and looked behind him. "Is that them boys' bull?" he asked in an incredulous tone.

She did not say a word. She merely looked away with her mouth taut.

"They told me their bull was out but I never known that was him," he said.

"I want that bull put up now," she said, "and I'm going to drive over to O. T. and E. T.'s and tell them they'll have to come get him today. I ought to charge for the time he's been here—then it wouldn't happen again."

"They didn't pay but seventy-five dollars for him," Mr. Greenleaf offered.

"I wouldn't have had him as a gift," she said.

"They was just going to beef him," Mr. Greenleaf went on, "but he got loose and run his head into their pickup truck. He don't like cars and trucks. They had a time getting his horn out the fender and when they finally got him loose, he took off and they was too tired to run after him—but I never known that was him there."

"It wouldn't have paid you to know, Mr. Greenleaf," she said. "But you know now. Get a horse and get him."

In a half hour, from her front window she saw the bull, squirrel-colored, with jutting hips and long light horns, ambling down the dirt road that ran in front of the house. Mr. Greenleaf was behind him on the horse. "That's a Greenleaf bull if I ever saw one," she muttered. She went out on the porch and called, "Put him where he can't get out."

"He likes to bust loose," Mr. Greenleaf said, looking with approval at the bull's rump. "This gentleman is a sport."

"If those boys don't come for him, he's going to be a dead sport," she said. "I'm just warning you."

He heard her but he didn't answer.

"That's the awfullest looking bull I ever saw," she called but he was too far down the road to hear.

It was mid-morning when she turned into O. T. and E. T.'s driveway. The house, a new red-brick, low-to-the-ground building that looked like a warehouse with windows, was on top of a treeless hill. The sun was beating down directly on the white roof of it. It was the kind of house that everybody built now and nothing marked it as belonging to Greenleafs except three dogs, part hound and part spitz, that rushed out from behind it as soon as she stopped her car. She reminded herself that you could always tell the class of people by the class of dog, and honked her horn. While she sat waiting for someone to come, she continued to study the house. All the windows were down and she wondered if the government could have air-conditioned the thing. No one came and she honked again. Presently a door opened and several children appeared in it and stood looking at her, making no move to come forward. She recognized this as a true Greenleaf trait—they could hang in a door, looking at you for hours.

"Can't one of you children come here?" she called.

After a minute they all began to move forward, slowly. They had on overalls and were barefooted but they were not as dirty as she might have expected. There were two or three that looked distinctly like Greenleafs; the others not so much so. The smallest child was a girl with untidy black hair. They stopped about six feet from the automobile and stood looking at her.

"You're mighty pretty," Mrs. May said, addressing herself to the smallest girl.

There was no answer. They appeared to share one dispassionate expression between them.

"Where's your Mamma?" she asked.

There was no answer to this for some time. Then one of them said something in French. Mrs. May did not speak French.

"Where's your daddy?" she asked.

After a while, one of the boys said, "He ain't hyar neither."

"Ahhhh," Mrs. May said as if something had been proven. "Where's the colored man?"

She waited and decided no one was going to answer. "The cat has six little tongues," she said. "How would you like to come home with me and let me teach you how to talk?" She laughed and her laugh died on the silent air. She felt as if she were on trial for her life, facing a jury of Greenleafs. "I'll go down and see if I can find the colored man," she said.

"You can go if you want to," one of the boys said.

"Well, thank you," she murmured and drove off.

The barn was down the lane from the house. She had not seen it before but Mr. Greenleaf had described it in detail for it had been built according to the latest specifications. It was a milking parlor arrangement where the cows are milked from below. The milk ran in pipes from the machines to the milk house and was never carried in no bucket, Mr. Greenleaf said, by no human hand. "When you gonter get you one?" he had asked.

"Mr. Greenleaf," she had said, "I have to do for myself. I am not assisted hand and foot by the government. It would cost me $20,000 to install a milking parlor. I barely make ends meet as it is."

"My boys done it," Mr. Greenleaf had murmured and then—"but all boys ain't alike."

"No indeed!" she had said. "I thank God for that!"

"I thank Gawd for ever-thang," Mr. Greenleaf had drawled.

You might as well, she had thought in the fierce silence that followed; you've never done anything for yourself.

She stopped by the side of the barn and honked but no one appeared. For several minutes she sat in the car, observing the various machines parked around, wondering how many of them were paid for. They had a forage harvester and a rotary hay baler. She had those too. She decided that since no one was here, she would get out and have a look at the milking parlor and see if they kept it clean.

She opened the milking room door and stuck her head in and for the first second she felt as if she were going to lose her breath. The spotless white concrete room was filled with sunlight that came from a row of windows head-high along both walls. The metal stanchions gleamed ferociously and she had to squint to be able to look at all. She drew her head out the room quickly and closed the door and leaned against it, frowning. The light outside was not so bright but she was conscious that the sun was directly on top of her head, like a silver bullet ready to drop into her brain.

A negro carrying a yellow calf-feed bucket appeared from around the corner of the machine shed and came toward her. He was a light yellow boy dressed in the cast-off army clothes of the Greenleaf twins. He stopped at a respectable distance and set the bucket on the ground.

"Where's Mr. O. T. and Mr. E. T.?" she asked.

"Mist O. T. he in town, Mist E. T. he off yonder in the field," the negro said, pointing first to the left and then to the right as if he were naming the position of two planets.

"Can you remember a message?" she asked, looking as if she thought this doubtful.

"I'll remember it if I don't forget it," he said with a touch of sullenness.

"Well, I'll write it down then," she said. She got in her car and took a stub of pencil from her pocket book and began to write on the back of an empty envelope. The negro came and stood at the window. "I'm Mrs. May," she said as she wrote. "Their bull is on my place and I want him off *today*. You can tell them I'm furious about it."

"That bull lef here Sareday," the negro said, "and none of us ain't seen him since. We ain't knowed where he was."

"Well, you know now," she said, "and you can tell Mr. O. T. and Mr. E. T. that if they don't come get him today, I'm going to have their daddy shoot him the first thing in the morning. I can't have that bull ruining my herd." She handed him the note.

"If I knows Mist O. T. and Mist E. T.," he said, taking it, "they goin to say you go ahead on and shoot him. He done busted up one of our trucks already and we be glad to see the last of him."

She pulled her head back and gave him a look from slightly blared eyes. "Do they expect me to take my time and my worker to shoot their bull?" she asked. "They don't want him so they just let him loose and expect somebody else to kill him? He's eating my oats and ruining my herd and I'm expected to shoot him too?"

"I speck you is," he said softly. "He done busted up . . ."

She gave him a very sharp look and said, "Well, I'm not surprised. That's just the way some people are," and after a second she asked, "Which is boss, Mr. O. T. or Mr. E. T.?" She had always suspected that they fought between themselves secretly.

"They never quarls," the boy said. "They like one man in two skins."

"Hmp. I expect you just never heard them quarrel."

"Nor nobody else heard them neither," he said, looking away as if this insolence were addressed to someone else.

"Well," she said, "I haven't put up with their father for fifteen years not to know a few things about Greenleafs."

The negro looked at her suddenly with a gleam of recognition. "Is you my policy man's mother?" he asked.

"I don't know who your policy man is," she said sharply. "You give them that note and tell them if they don't come for that bull today, they'll be making their father shoot it tomorrow," and she drove off.

She stayed at home all afternoon waiting for the Greenleaf twins to come for the bull. They did not come. I might as well be working for them, she thought furiously. They are simply going to use me to the limit. At the supper table, she went over it again for the boys' benefit because she wanted them to see exactly what O. T. and E. T. would do. "They don't want that bull," she said, "—pass the butter—so they simply turn him loose and let somebody else worry about getting rid of him for them. How do you like that? I'm the victim. I've always been the victim."

"Pass the butter to the victim," Wesley said. He was in a worse humor than usual because he had had a flat tire on the way home from the university.

Scofield handed her the butter and said, "Why, Mamma, ain't you ashamed to shoot an old bull that ain't done nothing but give you a little scrub strain in your herd? I declare," he said, "with the Mamma I got it's a wonder I turned out to be such a nice boy!"

"You ain't her boy, Son," Wesley said.

She eased back in her chair, her fingertips on the edge of the table.

"All I know is," Scofield said, "I done mighty well to be as nice as I am seeing what I come from."

When they teased her they spoke Greenleaf English but Wesley made his own particular tone come through it like a knife edge. "Well lemme tell you one thang, Brother," he said, leaning over the table, "that if you had half a mind you would already know."

"What's that, Brother?" Scofield asked, his broad face grinning into the thin constricted one across from him.

"That is," Wesley said, "that neither you nor me is her boy . . . ," but he stopped abruptly as she gave a kind of hoarse wheeze like an old horse lashed unexpectedly. She reared up and ran from the room.

"Oh, for God's sake," Wesley growled, "what did you start her off for?"

"I never started her off," Scofield said. "You started her off."

"Hah."

"She's not as young as she used to be and she can't take it."

"She can only give it out," Wesley said. "I'm the one that takes it."

His brother's pleasant face had changed so that an ugly family resemblance showed between them. "Nobody feels sorry for a lousy bastard like you," he said and grabbed across the table for the other's shirtfront.

From her room she heard a crash of dishes and she rushed back through the kitchen into the dining room. The hall door was open and Scofield was going out of it. Wesley was lying like a large bug on his back with the edge of the over-turned table cutting him across the middle and broken dishes scattered on top of him. She pulled the table off him and caught his arm to help him rise but he scrambled up and pushed her off with a furious charge of energy and flung himself out the door after his brother.

She would have collapsed but a knock on the back door stiffened her and she swung around. Across the kitchen and back porch, she could see Mr. Greenleaf peering eagerly through the screenwire. All her resources returned in full strength as if she had only needed to be challenged by the devil himself to regain them. "I heard a thump," he called, "and I thought the plastering might have fell on you."

If he had been wanted someone would have had to go on a horse to find him. She crossed the kitchen and the porch and stood inside the screen and said, "No, nothing happened but the table turned over. One of the legs was weak," and without pausing, "the boys didn't come for the bull so tomorrow you'll have to shoot him."

The sky was crossed with thin red and purple bars and behind them the sun was moving down slowly as if it were descending a ladder. Mr. Greenleaf squatted down on the step, his back to her, the top of his hat on a level with her feet. "Tomorrow I'll drive him home for you," he said.

"Oh no, Mr. Greenleaf," she said in a mocking voice, "you drive him home tomorrow and next week he'll be back here. I know better than that." Then in a mournful tone, she said, "I'm surprised at O. T. and E. T. to treat me this way. I thought they'd have more gratitude. Those boys spent some mighty happy days on this place, didn't they, Mr. Greenleaf?"

Mr. Greenleaf didn't say anything.

"I think they did," she said. "I think they did. But they've forgotten all the nice little things I did for them now. If I recall, they wore my boys' old clothes and played with my boys' old toys and hunted with my boys' old guns. They swam in my pond and shot my birds and fished in my stream and I never forgot their birthday and Christmas seemed to roll around very often if I remember it right. And do they think of any of those things now?" she asked. "NOOOOO," she said.

For a few seconds she looked at the disappearing sun and Mr. Greenleaf examined the palms of his hands. Presently as if it had just occurred to her, she asked, "Do you know the real reason they didn't come for that bull?"

"Naw I don't," Mr. Greenleaf said in a surly voice.

"They didn't come because I'm a woman," she said. "You can get away with anything when you're dealing with a woman. If there were a man running this place . . ."

Quick as a snake striking Mr. Greenleaf said, "You got two boys. They know you got two men on the place."

The sun had disappeared behind the tree line. She looked down at the dark crafty face, upturned now, and at the wary eyes, bright under the shadow of the hatbrim. She waited long enough for him to see that she was hurt and then she said, "Some people learn gratitude too late, Mr. Greenleaf, and some never learn it at all," and she turned and left him sitting on the steps.

Half the night in her sleep she heard a sound as if some large stone were grinding a hole on the outside wall of her brain. She was walking on the inside, over a succession of beautiful rolling hills, planting her stick in front of each step. She became aware after a time that the noise was the sun trying to burn through the tree line and she stopped to watch, safe in the knowledge that it couldn't, that it had to sink the way it always did outside of her property. When she first stopped it was a swollen red ball, but as she stood watching it began to narrow and pale until it looked like a bullet. Then suddenly it burst through the tree line and raced down the hill toward her. She woke up with her hand over her mouth and the same noise, diminished but distinct, in her ear. It was the bull munching under her window. Mr. Greenleaf had let him out.

She got up and made her way to the window in the dark and looked out through the slit blind, but the bull had moved away from the hedge and at first she didn't see him. Then she saw a heavy form some distance away, paused as if observing her. This is the last night I am going to put up with this, she said, and watched until the iron shadow moved away in the darkness.

The next morning she waited until exactly eleven o'clock. Then she got in her car and drove to the barn. Mr. Greenleaf was cleaning milk cans. He had seven of them standing up outside the milk room to get the sun. She had been telling him to do this for two weeks. "All right, Mr. Greenleaf," she said, "go get your gun. We're going to shoot that bull."

"I thought you wanted theseyer cans . . ."

"Go get your gun, Mr. Greenleaf," she said. Her voice and face were expressionless.

"That gentleman torn out of there last night," he murmured in a tone of regret and bent again to the can he had his arm in.

"Go get your gun, Mr. Greenleaf," she said in the same triumphant toneless voice. "The bull is in the pasture with the dry cows. I saw him from my upstairs window. I'm going to drive you up to the field and you can run him into the empty pasture and shoot him there."

He detached himself from the can slowly. "Ain't nobody ever ast me to shoot my boys' own bull!" he said in a high rasping voice. He removed a rag from his back pocket and began to wipe his hands violently, then his nose.

She turned as if she had not heard this and said, "I'll wait for you in the car. Go get your gun."

She sat in the car and watched him stalk off toward the harness room where he kept a gun. After he had entered the room, there was a crash as if he had kicked something out of his way. Presently he emerged again with the gun, circled behind the car, opened the door violently and threw himself onto the seat beside her. He held the gun between his knees and looked straight ahead. He'd like to shoot me instead of the bull, she thought, and turned her face away so that he could not see her smile.

The morning was dry and clear. She drove through the woods for a quarter of a mile and then out into the open where there were fields on either side of the narrow road. The exhilaration of carrying her point had sharpened her senses. Birds were screaming everywhere, the grass was almost too bright to look at, the sky was an even piercing blue. "Spring is here!" she said gaily. Mr. Greenleaf lifted one muscle somewhere near his mouth as if he found this the most asinine remark ever made. When she stopped at the second pasture gate, he flung himself out of the car door and slammed it behind him. Then he opened the gate and she drove through. He closed it and flung himself back in, silently, and she drove around the rim of the pasture until she spotted the bull, almost in the center of it, grazing peacefully among the cows.

"The gentleman is waiting on you," she said and gave Mr. Greenleaf's furious profile a sly look. "Run him into that next pasture and when you get him in, I'll drive in behind you and shut the gate myself."

He flung himself out again, this time deliberately leaving the car door open so that she had to lean across the seat and close it. She sat smiling as she watched him make his way across the pasture toward the opposite gate. He seemed to throw himself forward at each step and then pull back as if he were calling on some power to witness that he was being forced. "Well," she said aloud as if he were still in the car, "it's your own boys who are making you do this, Mr. Greenleaf." O. T. and E. T. were probably splitting their sides laughing at him now. She could hear their identical nasal voices saying, "Made Daddy shoot our bull for us. Daddy don't know no better than to think that's a fine bull he's shooting. Gonna kill Daddy to shoot that bull!"

"If those boys cared a thing about you, Mr. Greenleaf," she said, "they would have come for that bull. I'm surprised at them."

He was circling around to open the gate first. The bull, dark among the spotted cows, had not moved. He kept his head down, eating constantly. Mr. Greenleaf opened the gate and then began circling back to approach him from the rear. When he was about ten feet behind him, he flapped his arms at his sides. The bull lifted his head indolently and then lowered it again and continued to eat. Mr. Greenleaf stooped again and picked up something and threw it at him with a vicious swing. She decided it was a sharp rock for the bull leapt and then began to gallop until he disappeared over the rim of the hill. Mr. Greenleaf followed at his leisure.

"You needn't think you're going to lose him!" she cried and started the car straight across the pasture. She had to drive slowly over the terraces and when she reached the gate, Mr. Greenleaf and the bull were nowhere in sight. This pasture was smaller than the last, a green arena, encircled almost entirely by woods. She got out and closed the gate and stood looking for some sign of Mr. Greenleaf but he had disappeared completely. She knew at once that his plan was to lose the bull in the woods. Eventually, she would see him emerge somewhere from the circle of trees and come limping toward her and when he finally reached her, he would say, "If you can find that gentleman in them woods, you're better than me."

She was going to say, "Mr. Greenleaf, if I have to walk into those woods with you and stay all afternoon, we are going to find that bull and shoot him. You are going to shoot him if I have to pull the trigger for you." When he saw she meant business, he would return and shoot the bull quickly himself.

She got back into the car and drove to the center of the pasture where he would not have so far to walk to reach her when he came out of the woods. At this moment she could picture him sitting on a stump, marking lines in the ground with a stick. She decided she would wait exactly ten minutes by her watch. Then she would begin to honk. She got out of the car and walked around a little and then sat down on the front bumper to wait and rest. She was very tired and she lay her head back against the hood and closed her eyes. She did not understand why she should be so tired when it was only mid-morning. Through her closed eyes, she could feel the sun, red-hot overhead. She opened her eyes slightly but the white light forced her to close them again.

For some time she lay back against the hood, wondering drowsily why she was so tired. With her eyes closed, she didn't think of time as divided into days and nights but into past and future. She decided she was tired because she had been working continuously for fifteen years. She decided she had every right to be tired, and to rest for a few minutes before she began working again. Before any kind of judgment seat, she would be able to say: I've worked, I have not wallowed. At this very instant while she was recalling a lifetime of work, Mr. Greenleaf was loitering in the woods and Mrs. Greenleaf was probably flat on the ground, asleep over her holeful of clippings. The woman had got worse over the years and Mrs. May believed that now she was actually demented. "I'm afraid your wife has let religion warp her," she said once tactfully to Mr. Greenleaf. "Everything in moderation, you know."

"She cured a man oncet that half his gut was eat out with worms," Mr. Greenleaf said, and she had turned away, half-sickened. Poor souls, she thought now, so simple. For a few seconds she dozed.

When she sat up and looked at her watch, more than ten minutes had passed. She had not heard any shot. A new thought occurred to her; suppose Mr. Greenleaf had aroused the bull chunking stones at him and the animal had turned on him and run him up against a tree and gored him? The irony of it deepened: O. T. and E. T. would then get a shyster lawyer and sue her. It would be the fitting end to her fifteen years with the Greenleafs. She thought of it almost with pleasure as if she had hit on the perfect ending for a story she was telling her friends. Then she dropped it, for Mr. Greenleaf had a gun with him and she had insurance.

She decided to honk. She got up and reached inside the car window and gave three sustained honks and two or three shorter ones to let him know she was getting impatient. Then she went back and sat down on the bumper again.

In a few minutes something emerged from the tree line, a black heavy shadow that tossed its head several times and then bounded forward. After a second she saw it was the bull. He was crossing the pasture toward her at a slow gallop, a gay almost rocking gait as if he were overjoyed to find her again. She looked beyond him to see if Mr. Greenleaf was coming out of the woods too but he was not. "Here he is, Mr. Greenleaf!" she called and looked on the other side of the pasture to see if he could be coming out there but he was not in sight. She looked back and saw that the bull, his head lowered, was racing toward her. She remained perfectly still, not in fright, but in a freezing unbelief. She stared at the violent black streak bounding toward her as if she had no sense of distance, as if she could not decide at once what his intention was, and the bull had buried his head in her lap, like a wild tormented lover, before her expression changed. One of his horns sank until it pierced her heart and the other curved around her side and held her in an unbreakable grip. She continued to stare straight ahead but the entire scene in front of her had changed—the tree line was a dark wound in a world that was nothing but sky—and she had the look of a person whose sight has been suddenly restored but who finds the light unbearable.

Mr. Greenleaf was running toward her from the side with his gun raised and she saw him coming though she was not looking in his direction. She saw him approaching on the outside of some invisible circle, the tree line gaping behind him and nothing under his feet. He shot the bull four times through the eye. She did not hear the shots but she felt the quake in the huge body as it sank, pulling her forward on its head, so that she seemed, when Mr. Greenleaf reached her, to be bent over whispering some last discovery into the animal's ear.

QUESTIONS

1. The characters and events of the story are all seen as reflected through Mrs. May's mind. How objective are her evaluations? How far are they reliable testimony and how far only an index of her own mind?

2. What is Mrs. May's mental image of herself? How does it compare with the image her sons have of her? How does it compare with the reader's image?

3. What is Mrs. May's dominant emotion? What is the consuming preoccupation of her mind? Are there any occasions on which she feels joy? What are they?

4. Describe the behavior of Mrs. May and Greenleaf toward each other. Why does Mrs. May keep Greenleaf on when she despises him so?

5. The two families—the Mays and the Greenleafs—are obviously contrasted. Describe this contrast as fully as possible, considering especially the following: (a) their social and economic status, past, present, and future, (b) their religious attitudes, (c) the attitudes of Mrs. May and Greenleaf respectively toward their children, (d) Wesley and Scofield versus O. T. and E. T. What are the reasons for Mrs. May's feelings toward the Greenleafs?

6. The turning-point of the story comes when Mrs. May commands Greenleaf to get his gun. What emotional reversal takes place at this point? What are Mrs. May's motivations in having the bull shot?

7. "Suppose [thinks Mrs. May on page 253] Mr. Greenleaf had aroused the bull chunking stones at him and the animal had turned on him and run him up against a tree and gored him? . . . She thought of it almost with pleasure as if she had hit on the perfect ending for a story she was telling her friends." From what points of view is the actual ending of the story a perfect ending? Is the ending of the story purely chance, or is there a sense in which Mrs. May has brought it on herself?

8. What symbolical implications, if any, have the following: (a) the name Greenleaf, (b) the bull, (c) the sun, (d) Mrs. May's two dreams (pages 237 and 249–50)? How important is symbolism to the final effect of the story?

9. What kinds of irony predominate in the story? Identify examples of each of the three kinds of irony. How important is irony to the final effect of the story?

CHAPTER SEVEN

Emotion and Humor

Interpretive fiction presents the reader with significant and therefore durable insights into life. But these insights represent something more than mere intellectual comprehension; otherwise, the story does nothing that cannot be done as well or better by psychology, history, or philosophy. Fiction derives its unique value from its power to give *felt* insights. Its truths take a deeper hold on our minds because they are conveyed through our feelings. Its effectiveness in awaking a sensuous and emotional apprehension of experience that enriches understanding is what distinguishes imaginative literature from other forms of discourse.

All successful stories arouse emotions in the reader. The adventure thriller causes fear, excitement, suspense, anxiety, exultation, surprise. Some stories make us laugh; some cause us to thrill with horror; some make us cry. We value all the arts precisely because they enrich and diversify our emotional life.

If a story is to be truly significant, however, it must pursue emotion indirectly, not directly. Emotion accompanying and producing insight, not emotion for itself, is the end of the interpretive writer. He writes in order to present a sample of experience truthfully; the emotions he arouses flow naturally from the experience presented.

Over a century ago, in a review of Hawthorne's *Tales,* Edgar Allan Poe made a famous but misleading pronouncement about the short story:

> A skilful literary artist has constructed a tale. If wise, he has not fashioned his thoughts to accommodate his incidents; but having con-

> ceived, with deliberate care, a certain unique or single *effect* to be brought out, he then invents such incidents—he then combines such events as may best aid him in establishing this preconceived effect. If his very initial sentence tend not to the outbringing of this effect, then he has failed in his first step. In the whole composition there should be no word written, of which the tendency, direct or indirect, is not to the one preestablished design.

Poe's formulation has been enormously influential, for both good and bad. Historically it is important as being one of the first discussions of the short story as a unique form. Critically it is important because Poe so clearly here enunciates the basic critical principle of all art—the principle of artistic unity, requiring all details and elements of a piece to contribute harmoniously to the total design. Its influence has been deleterious because of the emphasis Poe put on a "unique" and "preconceived" *effect*.

The serious writer is an interpreter, not an inventor. Like a good actor, he is an intermediary between a segment of experience and an audience. The actor must pay some consideration to his audience: he must be careful, for instance, to face *toward* it, not away from it. But the great actor is the one who is wrapped up in the thoughts and feelings of the role he is playing, not the one who is continually stealing glances at the audience to determine the effect of his last gesture or bit of business. The actor who begins taking his cues from the audience rather than from the script soon becomes a "ham": he exaggerates and falsifies for the sake of effects. The writer, too, though he must pay some consideration to his reader, must focus his attention primarily on his subject. If he begins to think primarily of the effect of his tale on his reader, he begins to manipulate his material, to heighten reality, to contrive and falsify for the sake of effects. The serious writer selects and arranges his material in order to convey most effectively the feeling or truth of a human situation. The less serious writer selects and arranges his material so as to stimulate a response in the reader.

The discriminating reader, then, will distinguish between contrived emotion and that which springs naturally from a human story truly told. He will mark a difference between the story that attempts to "play upon" his feelings directly, as if he were a piano, and that that draws emotion forth as naturally as a plucked string draws forth sympathetic vibrations from another instrument in a room. The difference between the two types of story is the difference between escape and interpretation. In interpretive fiction, emotion is the by-product, not the goal.

No doubt there is pleasure in having our emotions directly stimulated, and in some forms such pleasure is both delightful and innocent. We all enjoy the laugh that follows a good joke, and the story that attempts no more than to provoke laughter may be both pleasant and harmless. There is a difference, nevertheless, between the story written for humor's sake and that in which the humor springs from a way of viewing experience. Humor may be as idle as the wisecrack or as vicious as the practical joke; it becomes of significant value when it flows from a comic perception of life.

Most of us enjoy the gooseflesh and the tingle along the spine produced by the successful ghost story. There is something agreeable in letting our blood be chilled by bats in the moonlight, guttering candles, creaking doors, eerie shadows, piercing screams, inexplicable bloodstains, and weird noises. But the terror aroused by tricks and external "machinery" is a far cry from the terror evoked by some terrifying treatment of the human situation. The horror we experience in watching the Werewolf or Dracula or Frankenstein is far less significant than that we get from watching the bloody ambition of Macbeth or the jealousy of Othello. In the first, terror is the end-product; in the second, it is the natural accompaniment of a powerful revelation of life. In the first, we are always aware of a basic unreality; in the second, reality is terrifying.

The story designed merely to provoke laughter or to arouse terror may be an enjoyable and innocent pleasure. The story directed at stimulating tears belongs to a less innocent category. The difference is that the humor story and the terror story seldom ask to be taken for more than what they are: pleasant diversions to help us pass the time agreeably. We enjoy the custard pie in the face and the ghost in the moonlight without taking them seriously. The fiction that depends on such ingredients is pure escape. The tear-jerker, however, asks to be taken seriously. Like the street beggar who artfully disposes his rags, puts on dark glasses over perfectly good eyes, holds out a tin cup and wails about his seven starving children (there are really only two, and he doesn't know what has become of them), the tear-jerker cheats us. It is escape literature posing as its opposite; it is counterfeit interpretation. It cheats us by exaggerating and falsifying reality and by asking for compassion that is not deserved.

The quality in a story that aims at drawing forth unmerited tender feeling is known as SENTIMENTALITY. Sentimentality is not the same as genuine emotion. Sentimentality is contrived or excessive or faked emotion. A story contains genuine emotion when it treats life faithfully and perceptively. The sentimentalized story oversimplifies and sweetens life to get its feeling. It exaggerates, manipulates, and prettifies. It mixes tears with sugar.

Genuine emotion, like character, must be presented *indirectly*—must be *dramatized*. It cannot be produced by words that *describe* emotions, like *angry, sad, pathetic, heart-breaking,* or *passionate*. If a writer is to draw forth genuine emotion, he must produce a character in a situation that deserves our sympathy and must tell us enough about the character and the situation to make them real and convincing.

The sentimental writer is recognizable by a number of characteristics. First, he often tries to make words do what the situation faithfully presented by itself will not do. He *editorializes*—that is, comments on the story and, in a manner, instructs us how to feel. Or he overwrites and *poeticizes*—uses an immoderately heightened and distended language to accomplish his effect. Second, he makes an excessively selective use of detail. All artists, of course, must be selective in their use of detail, but the good writer uses representative details while the sentimentalist uses details that all point one way—toward producing emotion rather than conveying truth. The little child that dies will be shown as always uncomplaining and cheerful under adversity, never as naughty, querulous, or ungrateful. He will possibly be an orphan or the only child of a mother who loves him dearly; in addition, he may be lame, hungry, ragged, and possessed of one toy, from which he cannot be parted. The villain will be all-villain, with a cruel laugh and a sharp whip, though he may reform at the end, for the sentimentalist is a profound believer in the heart of gold beneath the rough exterior. In short, reality will be unduly heightened and drastically oversimplified. Third, the sentimentalist will rely heavily on the stock response—an emotion that has its source outside the facts established by the story. In some readers certain situations and objects—babies, mothers, grandmothers, young love, patriotism, worship—produce an almost automatic response, whether the immediate situation warrants it or not. The sentimental writer, to affect such readers, has only to draw out certain stops, as on an organ, to produce an easily anticipated effect. He depends on stock materials to produce a stock response. He thus need not go to the trouble of picturing the situation in realistic and convincing detail. Finally, the sentimental writer presents, nearly always, a fundamentally "sweet" picture of life. He relies not only on stock characters and situations but also on stock themes. For him every cloud has its silver lining, every bad event its good side, every storm its rainbow following. If the little child dies, he goes to heaven or makes some life better by his death. Virtue is characteristically triumphant: the villain is defeated, the ne'er-do-well redeemed. True love is rewarded in some fashion; it is love—never hate—that makes the world go round. In short, the sentimental writer specializes in the sad but sweet. The tears called for are warm tears, never bitter. There is always sugar at the bottom of the cup.

For the mature reader, emotion is a highly valued but not easily achieved component of a story. It is a by-product, not the end-product. It is gained by honestly portrayed characters in honestly drawn situations that reflect the complexity, the ambiguity, and the endless variety of life. It is produced by a carefully exercised restraint on the part of the writer rather than by his "pulling out all the stops." It is one of the chief rewards of art.

McKnight Malmar

THE STORM

She inserted her key in the lock and turned the knob. The March wind snatched the door out of her hand and slammed it against the wall. It took strength to close it against the pressure of the gale, and she had no sooner closed it than the rain came in a pounding downpour, beating noisily against the windows as if trying to follow her in. She could not hear the taxi as it started up and went back down the road.

She breathed a sigh of thankfulness at being home again and in time. In rain like this, the crossroads always were flooded. Half an hour later her cab could not have got through the rising water, and there was no alternative route.

There was no light anywhere in the house. Ben was not home, then. As she turned on the lamp by the sofa she had a sense of anticlimax. All the way home—she had been visiting her sister—she had seen herself going into a lighted house, to Ben, who would be sitting by the fire with his paper. She had taken delight in picturing his happy surprise at seeing her, home a week earlier than he had expected her. She had known just how his round face would light up, how his eyes would twinkle behind his glasses, how he would catch her by the shoulders and look down into her face to see the changes a month had made in her, and then kiss her resoundingly on both cheeks, like a French general bestowing a decoration. Then she would make coffee and find a piece of cake, and they would sit together by the fire and talk.

But Ben wasn't here. She looked at the clock on the mantel and saw it was nearly ten. Perhaps he had not planned to come home tonight, as he was not expecting her; even before she had left he frequently was in the city all night because business kept him too late to catch the last train. If he did not come soon, he would not be able to make it at all.

She did not like the thought. The storm was growing worse. She could hear the wild lash of the trees, the whistle of the wind around the corners of the little house. For the first time she regretted this move to the far suburbs. There had been neighbors at first, a quarter-mile down the road; but they moved away several months ago, and now their house stood empty.

She had thought nothing of the lonesomeness. It was perfect here—for two. She had taken such pleasure in fixing up her house—her very own house—and caring for it that she had not missed company other than Ben. But now, alone and with the storm trying to batter its way in, she found it frightening to be so far away from other people. There was no one this side of the crossroads; the road that passed the house wandered past farmland into nothingness in the thick woods a mile farther on.

She hung her hat and her coat in the closet and went to stand before the hall mirror to pin up the soft strands of hair that the wind had loosened. She did not really see the pale face with its blunt little nose, the slender, almost childish figure in its grown-up black dress, or the big brown eyes that looked back at her.

She fastened the last strands into the pompadour and turned away from the mirror. Her shoulders drooped a little. There was something childlike about her, like a small girl craving protection, something immature and yet appealing, in spite of her plainness. She was thirty-one and had been married for fifteen months. The fact that she had married at all still seemed a miracle to her.

Now she began to walk through the house, turning on lights as she went. Ben had left it in fairly good order. There was very little trace of an untidy masculine presence; but then, he was a tidy man. She began to realize that the house was cold. Of course, Ben would have lowered the thermostat. He was very careful about things like that. He would not tolerate waste.

No wonder it was cold; the thermostat was set at fifty-eight. She pushed the little needle up to seventy, and the motor in the cellar started so suddenly and noisily that it frightened her for a moment.

She went into the kitchen and made some coffee. While she waited for it to drip she began to prowl around the lower floor. She was curiously restless and could not relax. Yet it was good to be back again among her own things, in her own home. She studied the living-room with fresh eyes. Yes, it was a pleasant room even though it was small. The bright, flowered chintzes on the furniture and at the windows were cheerful and pretty, and the lowboy she had bought three months ago was just right for the middle of the long wall. But her plants, set so bravely along the window sill, had died. Ben had forgotten to water them, in spite of all her admonitions, and now they drooped, shrunken and pale, in whitened, powdery soil. The sight of them added to the depression that was beginning to blot out all the pleasure of homecoming.

She returned to the kitchen and poured herself a cup of coffee, wishing that Ben would come home to share it with her. She carried her cup into the living-room and set it on the small, round table beside Ben's special big chair. The furnace was still mumbling busily, sending up heat, but she was colder than ever. She shivered and got an old jacket of Ben's from the closet and wrapped it around her before she sat down.

The wind hammered at the door and the windows, and the air was full of the sound of water, racing in the gutters, pouring from the leaders, thudding on the roof. Listening, she wished for Ben almost feverishly. She never had felt so alone. And he was such a comfort. He had been so good about her going for this long visit, made because her sister was ill. He had seen to everything and had put her on the train with her arms loaded with books and candy and fruit. She knew those farewell gifts had meant a lot to him—he didn't spend money easily. To be quite honest, he was a little close.

But he was a good husband. She sighed unconsciously, not knowing it was because of youth and romance missed. She repeated it to herself, firmly, as she sipped her coffee. He was a good husband. Suppose he was ten years older than she, and a little set in his ways; a little—perhaps—dictatorial at times, and moody. He had given her what she thought she wanted, security and a home of her own; if security were not enough, she could not blame him for it.

Her eye caught a shred of white protruding under a magazine on the table beside her. She put out a hand toward it, yet her fingers were almost reluctant to grasp it. She pulled it out nevertheless and saw that it was, as she had known instinctively, another of the white envelopes. It was empty, and it bore, as usual, the neat, typewritten address: *Benj. T. Willsom, Esq., Wildwood Road, Fairport, Conn.* The postmark was *New York City*. It never varied.

She felt the familiar constriction about the heart as she held it in her hands. What these envelopes contained she never had known. What she did know was their effect on Ben. After receiving one—one came every month or two—he was irritable, at times almost ugly. Their peaceful life together fell apart. At first she had questioned him, had striven to soothe and comfort him; but she soon had learned that this only made him angry, and of late she had avoided any mention of them. For a week after one came they shared the same room and the same table like two strangers, in a silence that was morose on his part and a little frightened on hers.

This one was postmarked three days before. If Ben got home tonight he would probably be cross, and the storm would not help his mood. Just the same she wished he would come.

She tore the envelope into tiny pieces and tossed them into the fireplace. The wind shook the house in its giant grip, and a branch crashed on the roof. As she straightened, a movement at the window caught her eye.

She froze there, not breathing, still half-bent toward the cold fireplace, her hand still extended. The glimmer of white at the window behind the sheeting blur of rain had been—she was sure of it—a human face. There had been eyes. She was certain there had been eyes staring in at her.

The wind's shout took on a personal, threatening note. She was rigid for a long time, never taking her eyes from the window. But nothing moved there now except the water on the windowpane; beyond it there was blackness, and that was all. The only sounds were the thrashing of the trees, the roar of water, and the ominous howl of the wind.

She began to breathe again, at last found courage to turn out the light and go to the window. The darkness was a wall, impenetrable and secret, and the blackness within the house made the storm close in, as if it were a pack of wolves besieging the house. She hastened to put on the light again.

She must have imagined those staring eyes. Nobody could be out on a night like this. Nobody. Yet she found herself terribly shaken.

If only Ben would come home. If only she were not so alone.

She shivered and pulled Ben's coat tighter about her and told herself she was becoming a morbid fool. Nevertheless, she found the aloneness intolerable. Her ears strained to hear prowling footsteps outside the windows. She became convinced that she did hear them, slow and heavy.

Perhaps Ben could be reached at the hotel where he sometimes stayed. She no longer cared whether her homecoming was a surprise to him. She wanted to hear his voice. She went to the telephone and lifted the receiver.

The line was quite dead.

The wires were down, of course.

She fought panic. The face at the window had been an illusion, a trick of the light reflected on the sluicing pane; and the sound of footsteps was an illusion, too. Actual ones would be inaudible in the noise made by the wild storm. Nobody would be out tonight. Nothing threatened her, really. The storm was held at bay beyond these walls, and in the morning the sun would shine again.

The thing to do was to make herself as comfortable as possible and settle down with a book. There was no use going to bed—she couldn't possibly sleep. She would only lie there wide awake and think of that face at the window, hear those footsteps.

She would get some wood for a fire in the fireplace. She hesitated at the top of the cellar stairs. The light, as she switched it on, seemed insufficient; the concrete wall at the foot of the stairs was dank with moisture and somehow gruesome. And wind was chilling her ankles. Rain was beating in through the outside door to the cellar, because that door was standing open.

The inner bolt sometimes did not hold, she knew very well. If it had not been carefully closed, the wind could have loosened it. Yet the open door increased her panic. It seemed to argue the presence of something less impersonal than the gale. It took her a long minute to nerve herself to go down the steps and reach out into the darkness for the doorknob.

In just that instant she was soaked; but her darting eyes could find nothing outdoors but the black, wavering shapes of the maples at the side of the house. The wind helped her and slammed the door resoundingly. She jammed the bolt home with all her strength and then tested it to make sure it would hold. She almost sobbed with the relief of knowing it to be firm against any intruder.

She stood with her wet clothes clinging to her while the thought came that turned her bones to water. Suppose—suppose the face at the window had been real, after all. Suppose its owner had found shelter in the only shelter to be had within a quarter-mile—this cellar.

She almost flew up the stairs again, but then she took herself firmly in hand. She must not let herself go. There had been many storms before; just because she was alone in this one, she must not let morbid fancy run away with her. But she could not throw off the reasonless fear that oppressed her, although she forced it back a little. She began to hear again the tread of the prowler outside the house. Although she knew it to be imagination, it was fearfully real—the crunch of feet on gravel, slow, persistent, heavy, like the patrol of a sentinel.

She had only to get an armful of wood. Then she could have a fire, she would have light and warmth and comfort. She would forget these terrors.

The cellar smelled of dust and old moisture. The beams were fuzzed with cobwebs. There was only one light, a dim one in the corner. A little rivulet was running darkly down the wall and already had formed a foot-square pool on the floor.

The woodpile was in the far corner away from the light. She stopped and peered around. Nobody could hide here. The cellar was too open, the supporting stanchions too slender to hide a man.

The oil burner went off with a sharp click. Its mutter, she suddenly realized, had had something human and companionable about it. Nothing was down here with her now but the snarl of the storm.

She almost ran to the woodpile. Then something made her pause and turn before she bent to gather the logs.

What was it? Not a noise. Something she had seen as she hurried across that dusty floor. Something odd.

She searched with her eyes. It was a spark of light she had seen, where no spark should be.

An inexplicable dread clutched at her heart. Her eyes widened, round and dark as a frightened deer's. Her old trunk that stood against the wall was open just a crack; from the crack came this tiny pinpoint of reflected light to prick the cellar's gloom.

She went toward it like a woman hypnotized. It was only one more insignificant thing, like the envelope on the table, the vision of the face at the window, the open door. There was no reason for her to feel smothered in terror.

Yet she was sure she had not only closed, but clamped the lid on the trunk; she was sure because she kept two or three old coats in it, wrapped in newspapers and tightly shut away from moths.

Now the lid was raised perhaps an inch. And the twinkle of light was still there.

She threw back the lid.

For a long moment she stood looking down into the trunk, while each detail of its contents imprinted itself on her brain like an image on a film. Each tiny detail was indelibly clear and never to be forgotten.

She could not have stirred a muscle in that moment. Horror was a black cloak thrown around her, stopping her breath, hobbling her limbs.

Then her face dissolved into formlessness. She slammed down the lid and ran up the stairs like a mad thing. She was breathing again, in deep, sobbing breaths that tore at her lungs. She shut the door at the top of the stairs with a crash that shook the house; then she turned the key. Gasping, she clutched one of the sturdy maple chairs by the kitchen table and wedged it under the knob with hands she could barely control.

The wind took the house in its teeth and shook it as a dog shakes a rat.

Her first impulse was to get out of the house. But in the time it took her to get to the front door she remembered the face at the window.

Perhaps she had not imagined it. Perhaps it was the face of a murderer—a murderer waiting for her out there in the storm; ready to spring on her out of the dark.

She fell into the big chair, her huddled body shaken by great tremors. She could not stay here—not with that thing in her trunk. Yet she dared not leave. Her whole being cried out for Ben. He would know what to do. She closed her eyes, opened them again, rubbed them hard. The picture still burned into her brain as if it had been etched with acid. Her hair, loosened, fell in soft, straight wisps about her forehead, and her mouth was slack with terror.

Her old trunk had held the curled-up body of a woman.

She had not seen the face; the head had been tucked down into the hollow of the shoulder, and a shower of fair hair had fallen over it. The woman had worn a red dress. One hand had rested near the edge of the trunk, and on its third finger there had been a man's ring, a signet bearing the raised figure of a rampant lion with a small diamond between its paws. It had been the diamond that caught the light. The little bulb in the corner of the cellar had picked out this ring from the semidarkness and made it stand out like a beacon.

She never would be able to forget it. Never forget how the woman looked: the pale, luminous flesh of her arms; her doubled-up knees against the side of the trunk, with their silken covering shining softly in the gloom; the strands of hair that covered her face . . .

Shudders continued to shake her. She bit her tongue and pressed her hand against her jaw to stop the chattering of her teeth. The salty taste of blood in her mouth steadied her. She tried to force herself to be rational, to plan; yet all the time the knowledge that she was imprisoned with the body of a murdered woman kept beating at her nerves like a flail.

She drew the coat closer about her, trying to dispel the mortal cold that held her. Slowly something beyond the mere fact of murder, of death, began to penetrate her mind. Slowly she realized that beyond this fact there would be consequences. That body in the cellar was not an isolated phenomenon; some train of events had led to its being there and would follow its discovery there.

There would be policemen.

At first the thought of policemen was a comforting one; big, brawny men in blue, who would take the thing out of her cellar, take it away so she never need think of it again.

Then she realized it was *her* cellar—hers and Ben's; and policemen are suspicious and prying. Would they think *she* had killed the woman? Could they be made to believe she never had seen her before?

Or would they think Ben had done it? Would they take the letters in the white envelopes, and Ben's absences on business, and her own visit to her sister, about which Ben had been so helpful, and out of them build a double life for him? Would they insist that the woman had been a discarded mistress, who had hounded him with letters until out of desperation he had killed her? That was a fantastic theory, really; but the police might do that.

They might.

Now a sudden new panic invaded her. The dead woman must be taken out of the cellar, must be hidden. The police must never connect her with this house.

Yet the dead woman was bigger than she herself was; she could never move her.

Her craving for Ben became a frantic need. If only he would come home! Come home and take that body away, hide it somewhere so the police could not connect it with this house. He was strong enough to do it.

Even with the strength to move the body by herself she would not dare do it, because there was the prowler—real or imaginary—outside the house. Perhaps the cellar door had not been open by chance. Or perhaps it had been, and the murderer, seeing it so welcoming, had seized the opportunity to plant the evidence of his crime upon the Willsoms' innocent shoulders.

She crouched there, shaking. It was as if the jaws of a great trap had closed on her: on one side the storm and the silence of the telephone, on the other the presence of the prowler and of that still, cramped figure in her trunk. She was caught between them, helpless.

As if to accent her helplessness, the wind stepped up its shriek and a tree crashed thunderously out in the road. She heard glass shatter.

Her quivering body stiffened like a drawn bow. Was it the prowler attempting to get in? She forced herself to her feet and made a round of the windows on the first floor and the one above. All the glass was intact, staunchly resisting the pounding of the rain.

Nothing could have made her go into the cellar to see if anything had happened there.

The voice of the storm drowned out all other sounds, yet she could not rid herself of the fancy that she heard footsteps going round and round the house, that eyes sought an opening and spied upon her.

She pulled the shades down over the shiny black windows. It helped a little to make her feel more secure, more sheltered; but only a very little. She told herself sternly that the crash of glass had been nothing more than a branch blown through a cellar window.

The thought brought her no comfort—just the knowledge that it would not disturb that other woman. Nothing could comfort her now but Ben's plump shoulder and his arms around her and his neat, capable mind planning to remove the dead woman from this house.

A kind of numbness began to come over her, as if her capacity for fear were exhausted. She went back to the chair and curled up in it. She prayed mutely for Ben and for daylight.

The clock said half-past twelve.

She huddled there, not moving and not thinking, not even afraid, only numb, for another hour. Then the storm held its breath for a moment, and in the brief space of silence she heard footsteps on the walk—actual footsteps, firm and quick and loud. A key turned in the lock. The door opened and Ben came in.

He was dripping, dirty, and white with exhaustion. But it was Ben. Once she was sure of it she flung herself on him, babbling incoherently of what she had found.

He kissed her lightly on the cheek and took her arms down from around his neck. "Here, here, my dear. You'll get soaked. I'm drenched to the skin." He removed his glasses and handed them to her, and she began to dry them for him. His eyes squinted at the light. "I had to walk in from the crossroads. What a night!" He began to strip off rubbers and coat and shoes. "You'll never know what a difference it made, finding the place lighted. Lord, but it's good to be home."

She tried again to tell him of the past hours, but again he cut her short. "Now, wait a minute, my dear. I can see you're bothered about something. Just wait until I get into some dry things; then I'll come down and we'll straighten it out. Suppose you rustle up some coffee and toast. I'm done up—the whole trip out was a nightmare, and I didn't know if I'd ever make it from the crossing. I've been hours."

He did look tired, she thought with concern. Now that he was back, she could wait. The past hours had taken on the quality of a nightmare, horrifying but curiously unreal. With Ben here, so solid and commonplace and cheerful, she began to wonder if the hours *were* nightmare. She even began to doubt the reality of the woman in the trunk, although she could see her as vividly as ever. Perhaps only the storm was real.

She went to the kitchen and began to make fresh coffee. The chair, still wedged against the kitchen door, was a reminder of her terror. Now that Ben was home it seemed silly, and she put it back in its place by the table.

He came down very soon, before the coffee was ready. How good it was to see him in that old gray bathrobe of his, his hands thrust into its pockets. How normal and wholesome he looked with his round face rubbed pink by a rough towel and his hair standing up in damp little spikes around his bald spot. She was almost shamefaced when she told him of the face at the window, the open door, and finally of the body in the trunk. None of it, she saw quite clearly now, could possibly have happened.

Ben said so, without hesitation. But he came to put an arm around her. "You poor child. The storm scared you to death, and I don't wonder. It's given you the horrors."

She smiled dubiously. "Yes. I'm almost beginning to think so. Now that you're back, it seems so safe. But—but you will *look* in the trunk, Ben? I've got to *know*. I can see her so plainly. How could I imagine a thing like that?"

He said indulgently, "Of course I'll look, if it will make you feel better. I'll do it now. Then I can have my coffee in peace."

He went to the cellar door and opened it and snapped on the light. Her heart began to pound once more, a deafening roar in her ears. The opening of the cellar door opened, again, the whole vista of fear: the body, the police, the suspicions that would cluster about her and Ben. The need to hide this evidence of somebody's crime.

She could not have imagined it; it was incredible that she could have believed, for a minute, that her mind had played such tricks on her. In another moment Ben would know it, too.

She heard the thud as he threw back the lid of the trunk. She clutched at the back of a chair, waiting for his voice. It came in an instant.

She could not believe it. It was as cheerful and reassuring as before. He said, "There's nothing here but a couple of bundles. Come take a look."

Nothing!

Her knees were weak as she went down the stairs, down into the cellar again.

It was still musty and damp and draped with cobwebs. The rivulet was still running down the wall, but the pool was larger now. The light was still dim.

It was just as she remembered it except that the wind was whistling through a broken window and rain was splattering in on the bits of shattered glass on the floor. The branch lying across the sill had removed every scrap of glass from the frame and left not a single jagged edge.

Ben was standing by the open trunk, waiting for her. His stocky body was a bulwark. "See," he said, "there's nothing. Just some old clothes of yours, I guess."

She went to stand beside him. Was she losing her mind? Would she, now, see that crushed figure in there, see the red dress and the smooth, shining knees, when Ben could not? And the ring with the diamond between the lion's paws?

Her eyes looked, almost reluctantly, into the trunk. "It *is* empty!"

There were the neat, newspaper-wrapped packages she had put away so carefully, just as she had left them deep in the bottom of the trunk. And nothing else.

She must have imagined the body. She was light with the relief the knowledge brought her, and yet confused and frightened, too. If her mind could play such tricks, if she could imagine anything so gruesome in the complete detail with which she had seen the dead woman in the trunk, the thought of the future was terrifying. When might she not have another such hallucination?

The actual, physical danger did not exist, however, and never had existed. The threat of the law hanging over Ben had been based on a dream.

"I—dreamed it all. I must have," she admitted. "Yes it was so horribly clear and I wasn't asleep." Her voice broke. "I thought—oh, Ben, I thought—"

"What did you think, my dear?" His voice was odd, not like Ben's at all. It had a cold, cutting edge to it.

He stood looking down at her with an immobility that chilled her more than the cold wind that swept in through the broken window. She tried to read his face, but the light from the little bulb was too weak. It left his features shadowed in broad, dark planes that made him look like a stranger, and somehow sinister.

She said, "I—" and faltered.

He still did not move, but his voice hardened. "What was it you thought?"

She backed away from him.

He moved, then. It was only to take his hands from his pockets, to stretch his arms toward her; but she stood for an instant staring at the thing that left her stricken, with a voiceless scream forming in her throat.

She was never to know whether his arms had been outstretched to take her within their shelter or to clutch at her white neck. For she turned and fled, stumbling up the stairs in a mad panic of escape.

He shouted, "Janet! Janet!" His steps were heavy behind her. He tripped on the bottom step and fell on one knee and cursed.

Terror lent her strength and speed. She could not be mistaken. Although she had seen it only once, she knew that on the little finger of his left hand there had been the same, the unmistakable ring the dead woman had worn.

The blessed wind snatched the front door from her and flung it wide, and she was out in the safe, dark shelter of the storm.

QUESTIONS

1. By what means does this story create and build suspense? What uses does it make of mystery? At what points does it employ surprise?

2. Is the ending of the story determinate or indeterminate?

3. From what point of view is the story told? What advantages has this point of view for this story? Are there any places where the contents of Mrs. Willsom's consciousness are suppressed, at least temporarily? For what purpose?

4. Put together an account of Ben's activities that will explain as many as possible of the phenomena that Mrs. Willsom observes—or thinks she observes—during the course of the evening. Are any left unexplained? Is any motivation provided for the murder of the woman in the trunk? How?

5. What are the chief features of Ben's characterization? Why is he characterized as he is? Has the characterization been fashioned to serve the story or the story to serve the characterization?

6. To what extent does the story depend on coincidence?

7. What is the main purpose of the story? Does it have a theme? If so, what?

8. What do you find most effective in the story?

William Faulkner

THAT EVENING SUN

I

Monday is no different from any other weekday in Jefferson now. The streets are paved now, and the telephone and electric companies are cutting down more and more of the shade trees—the water oaks, the maples and locusts and elms—to make room for iron poles bearing clusters of bloated and ghostly and bloodless grapes, and we have a city laundry which makes the rounds on Monday morning, gathering the bundles of clothes into bright-colored, specially made motorcars: the soiled wearing of a whole week now flees apparitionlike behind alert and irritable electric horns, with a long diminishing noise of rubber and asphalt like tearing silk, and even the Negro women who still take in white people's washing after the old custom, fetch and deliver it in automobiles.

But fifteen years ago, on Monday morning the quiet, dusty, shady streets would be full of Negro women with, balanced on their steady, turbaned heads, bundles of clothes tied up in sheets, almost as large as cotton bales, carried so without touch of hand between the kitchen door of the white house and the blackened washpot beside a cabin door in Negro Hollow.

Nancy would set her bundle on the top of her head, then upon the bundle in turn she would set the black straw sailor hat which she wore winter and summer. She was tall, with a high, sad face sunken a little where her teeth were missing. Sometimes we would go a part of the way down the lane and across the pasture with her, to watch the balanced bundle and the hat that never bobbed nor wavered, even when she walked down into the ditch and up the other side and stooped through the fence. She would go down on her hands and knees and crawl through the gap, her head rigid, uptilted, the bundle steady as a rock or a balloon, and rise to her feet again and go on.

Sometimes the husbands of the washing women would fetch and deliver the clothes, but Jesus never did that for Nancy, even before Father told him to stay away from our house, even when Dilsey was sick and Nancy would come to cook for us.

And then about half the time we'd have to go down the lane to Nancy's cabin and tell her to come on and cook breakfast. We would stop at the ditch, because Father told us to not have anything to do with Jesus—he was a short black man, with a razor scar down his face—and we would throw rocks at Nancy's house until she came to the door, leaning her head around it without any clothes on.

"What yawl mean, chunking my house?" Nancy said. "What you little devils mean?"

"Father says for you to come on and get breakfast," Caddy said. "Father says it's over a half an hour now, and you've got to come this minute."

"I ain't studying no breakfast," Nancy said. "I going to get my sleep out."

"I bet you're drunk," Jason said. "Father says you're drunk. Are you drunk, Nancy?"

"Who says I is?" Nancy said. "I got to get my sleep out. I ain't studying no breakfast."

So after a while we quit chunking the cabin and went back home. When she finally came, it was too late for me to go to school. So we thought it was whiskey until that day they arrested her again and they were taking her to jail and they passed Mr. Stovall. He was the cashier in the bank and a deacon in the Baptist church, and Nancy began to say:

"When you going to pay me, white man? When you going to pay me, white man? It's been three times now since you paid me a cent—" Mr. Stovall knocked her down, but she kept on saying, "When you going to pay me, white man? It's been three times now since—" until Mr. Stovall kicked her in the mouth with his heel and the marshal caught Mr. Stovall back, and Nancy lying in the street, laughing. She turned her head and spat out some blood and teeth and said, "It's been three times now since he paid me a cent."

That was how she lost her teeth, and all that day they told about Nancy and Mr. Stovall, and all that night the ones that passed the jail could hear Nancy singing and yelling. They could see her hands holding to the window bars, and a lot of them stopped along the fence, listening to her and the jailer trying to make her stop. She didn't shut up until almost daylight, when the jailer began to hear a bumping and scraping upstairs and he went up there and found Nancy hanging from the window bar. He said that it was cocaine and not whiskey, because no nigger would try to commit suicide unless he wás full of cocaine, because a nigger full of cocaine wasn't a nigger any longer.

The jailer cut her down and revived her; then he beat her, whipped her. She had hung herself with her dress. She had fixed it all right, but when they arrested her she didn't have on anything except a dress and so she didn't have anything to tie her hands with and she couldn't make her hands let go of the window ledge. So the jailer heard the noise and ran up there and found Nancy hanging from the window, stark naked, her belly already swelling out a little, like a little balloon.

When Dilsey was sick in her cabin and Nancy was cooking for us, we could see her apron swelling out; that was before Father told Jesus to stay away from the house. Jesus was in the kitchen, sitting behind the stove, with his razor scar on his black face like a piece of dirty string. He said it was a watermelon that Nancy had under her dress.

"It never come off of your vine, though," Nancy said.

"Off of what vine?" Caddy said.

"I can cut down the vine it did come off of," Jesus said.

"What makes you want to talk like that before these chillen?" Nancy said. "Whyn't you go on to work? You done et. You want Mr. Jason to catch you hanging around his kitchen, talking that way before these chillen?"

"Talking what way?" Caddy said. "What vine?"

"I can't hang around white man's kitchen," Jesus said. "But white man can hang around mine. White man can come in my house, but I can't stop him. When white man want to come in my house, I ain't got no house. I can't stop him, but he can't kick me outen it. He can't do that."

Dilsey was still sick in her cabin. Father told Jesus to stay off our place. Dilsey was still sick. It was a long time. We were in the library after supper.

"Isn't Nancy through in the kitchen yet?" Mother said. "It seems to me that she has had plenty of time to have finished the dishes."

"Let Quentin go and see," Father said. "Go and see if Nancy is through, Quentin. Tell her she can go on home."

I went to the kitchen. Nancy was through. The dishes were put away and the fire was out. Nancy was sitting in a chair, close to the cold stove. She looked at me.

"Mother wants to know if you are through," I said.

"Yes," Nancy said. She looked at me. "I done finished." She looked at me.

"What is it?" I said. "What is it?"

"I ain't nothing but a nigger," Nancy said. "It ain't none of it my fault."

She looked at me, sitting in the chair before the cold stove, the sailor hat on her head. I went back to the library. It was the cold stove and all, when you think of a kitchen being warm and busy and cheerful. And with a cold stove and the dishes all put away, and nobody wanting to eat at that hour.

"Is she through?" Mother said.

"Yessum," I said.

"What is she doing?" Mother said.

"She's not doing anything. She's through."

"I'll go and see," Father said.

"Maybe she's waiting for Jesus to come and take her home," Caddy said.

"Jesus is gone," I said. Nancy told us how one morning she woke up and Jesus was gone.

"He quit me," Nancy said. "Done gone to Memphis, I reckon. Dodging them city *po*-lice for a while, I reckon."

"And a good riddance," Father said. "I hope he stays there."

"Nancy's scaired of the dark," Jason said.

"So are you," Caddy said.

"I'm not," Jason said.

"Scairy cat," Caddy said.

"I'm not," Jason said.

"You, Candace!" Mother said. Father came back.

"I am going to walk down the lane with Nancy," he said. "She says that Jesus is back."

"Has she seen him?" Mother said.

"No. Some Negro sent her word that he was back in town. I won't be long."

"You'll leave me alone, to take Nancy home?" Mother said. "Is her safety more precious to you than mine?"

"I won't be long," Father said.

"You'll leave these children unprotected, with that Negro about?"

"I'm going, too," Caddy said. "Let me go, Father."

"What would he do with them, if he were unfortunate enough to have them?" Father said.

"I want to go, too," Jason said.

"Jason!" Mother said. She was speaking to Father. You could tell that by the way she said the name. Like she believed that all day Father had been trying to think of doing the thing she wouldn't like the most, and that she knew all the time that after a while he would think of it. I stayed quiet, because Father and I both knew that Mother would want him to make me stay with her if she just thought of it in time. So Father didn't look at me. I was the oldest. I was nine and Caddy was seven and Jason was five.

"Nonsense," Father said. "We won't be long."

Nancy had her hat on. We came to the lane. "Jesus always been good to me," Nancy said. "Whenever he had two dollars, one of them was mine." We walked in the lane. "If I can just get through the lane," Nancy said, "I be all right then."

The lane was always dark. "This is where Jason got scaired on Halloween," Caddy said.

"I didn't," Jason said.

"Can't Aunt Rachel do anything with him?" Father said. Aunt Rachel was old. She lived in a cabin beyond Nancy's by herself. She had white hair and she smoked a pipe in the door, all day long; she didn't work any more. They said she was Jesus' mother. Sometimes she said she was and sometimes she said she wasn't any kin to Jesus.

"Yes you did," Caddy said. "You were scairder than Frony. You were scairder than T. P. even. Scairder than niggers."

"Can't nobody do nothing with him," Nancy said. "He say I done woke up the devil in him and ain't but one thing going to lay it down again."

"Well, he's gone now," Father said. "There's nothing for you to be afraid of now. And if you'd just let white men alone."

"Let what white men alone?" Caddy said. "How let them alone?"

"He ain't gone nowhere," Nancy said. "I can feel him. I can feel him now, in this lane. He hearing us talk, every word, hid somewhere, waiting. I ain't seen him, and I ain't going to see him again but once more, with that razor in his mouth. That razor on that string down his back, inside his shirt. And then I ain't going to be even surprised."

"I wasn't scaired," Jason said.

"If you'd behave yourself, you'd have kept out of this," Father said. "But it's all right now. He's probably in Saint Louis now. Probably got another wife by now and forgot all about you."

"If he has, I better not find out about it," Nancy said. "I'd stand there right over them, and every time he wropped her, I'd cut that arm off. I'd cut his head off and I'd slit her belly and I'd shove—"

"Hush," Father said.

"Slit whose belly, Nancy?" Caddy said.

"I wasn't scaired," Jason said. "I'd walk right down this lane by myself."

"Yah," Caddy said. "You wouldn't dare to put your foot down in it if we were not here too."

2

Dilsey was still sick, so we took Nancy home every night until Mother said, "How much longer is this going on? I to be left alone in this big house while you take home a frightened Negro?"

We fixed a pallet in the kitchen for Nancy. One night we waked up, hearing the sound. It was not singing and it was not crying, coming up the dark stairs. There was a light in Mother's room and we heard Father going down the hall, down the back stairs, and Caddy and I went into the hall. The floor was cold. Our toes curled away from it while we listened to the sound. It was like singing and it wasn't like singing, like the sound that Negroes make.

Then it stopped and we heard Father going down the back stairs, and we went to the head of the stairs. Then the sound began again, in the stairway, not loud, and we could see Nancy's eyes halfway up the stairs, against the wall. They looked like cat's eyes do, like a big cat against the wall, watching us. When we came down the steps to where she was, she quit making the sound again, and we stood there until Father came back up from the kitchen, with his pistol in his hand. He went back down with Nancy and they came back with Nancy's pallet.

We spread the pallet in our room. After the light in Mother's room went off, we could see Nancy's eyes again. "Nancy," Caddy whispered, "are you asleep, Nancy?"

Nancy whispered something. It was oh or no, I don't know which. Like nobody had made it, like it came from nowhere and went nowhere, until it was like Nancy was not there at all; that I had looked so hard at her eyes on the stairs that they had got printed on my eyeballs, like the sun does when you have closed your eyes and there is no sun. "Jesus," Nancy whispered. "Jesus."

"Was it Jesus?" Caddy said. "Did he try to come into the kitchen?"

"Jesus," Nancy said. Like this: Jeeeeeeeeeeeeesus, until the sound went out, like a match or a candle does.

"It's the other Jesus she means," I said.

"Can you see us, Nancy?" Caddy whispered. "Can you see our eyes too?"

"I ain't nothing but a nigger," Nancy said. "God knows. God knows."

"What did you see down there in the kitchen?" Caddy whispered. "What tried to get in?"

"God knows," Nancy said. We could see her eyes. "God knows."

Dilsey got well. She cooked dinner. "You'd better stay in bed a day or two longer," Father said.

"What for?" Dilsey said. "If I had been a day later, this place would be to rack and ruin. Get on out of here now, and let me get my kitchen straight again."

Dilsey cooked supper too. And that night, just before dark, Nancy came into the kitchen.

"How do you know he's back?" Dilsey said. "You ain't seen him."

"Jesus is a nigger," Jason said.

"I can feel him," Nancy said. "I can feel him laying yonder in the ditch."

"Tonight?" Dilsey said. "Is he there tonight?"

"Dilsey's a nigger too," Jason said.

"You try to eat something," Dilsey said.

"I don't want nothing," Nancy said.

"I ain't a nigger," Jason said.

"Drink some coffee," Dilsey said. She poured a cup of coffee for Nancy. "Do you know he's out there tonight? How come you know it's tonight?"

"I know," Nancy said. "He's there, waiting. I know. I done lived with him too long. I know what he is fixing to do fore he know it himself."

"Drink some coffee," Dilsey said. Nancy held the cup to her mouth and blew into the cup. Her mouth pursed out like a spreading adder's, like a rubber mouth, like she had blown all the color out of her lips with blowing the coffee.

"I ain't a nigger," Jason said. "Are you a nigger, Nancy?"

"I hellborn, child," Nancy said. "I won't be nothing soon. I going back where I come from soon."

3

She began to drink the coffee. While she was drinking, holding the cup in both hands, she began to make the sound again. She made the sound into the cup and the coffee sploshed out onto her hands and her dress. Her eyes looked at us and she sat there, her elbows on her knees, holding the cup in both hands, looking at us across the wet cup, making the sound.

"Look at Nancy," Jason said. "Nancy can't cook for us now. Dilsey's got well now."

"You hush up," Dilsey said. Nancy held the cup in both hands, looking at us, making the sound, like there were two of them: one looking at us and the other making the sound. "Whyn't you let Mr. Jason telefoam the marshal?" Dilsey said. Nancy stopped then, holding the cup in her long brown hands. She tried to drink some coffee again, but it sploshed out of the cup, onto her hands and her dress, and she put the cup down. Jason watched her.

"I can't swallow it," Nancy said. "I swallows but it won't go down me."

"You go down to the cabin," Dilsey said. "Frony will fix you a pallet and I'll be there soon."

"Won't no nigger stop him," Nancy said.

"I ain't a nigger," Jason said. "Am I, Dilsey?"

"I reckon not," Dilsey said. She looked at Nancy. "I don't reckon so. What you going to do, then?"

Nancy looked at us. Her eyes went fast, like she was afraid there wasn't time to look, without hardly moving at all. She looked at us, at all three of us at one time. "You member that night I stayed in yawls' room?" she said. She told about how we waked up early the next morning, and played. We had to play quiet, on her pallet, until Father woke up and it was time to get breakfast. "Go and ask your maw to let me stay here tonight," Nancy said. "I won't need no pallet. We can play some more."

Caddy asked Mother. Jason went too. "I can't have Negroes sleeping in the bedrooms," Mother said. Jason cried. He cried until Mother said he couldn't have any dessert for three days if he didn't stop. Then Jason said he would stop if Dilsey would make a chocolate cake. Father was there.

"Why don't you do something about it?" Mother said. "What do we have officers for?"

"Why is Nancy afraid of Jesus?" Caddy said. "Are you afraid of Father, Mother?"

"What could the officers do?" Father said. "If Nancy hasn't seen him, how could the officers find him?"

"Then why is she afraid?" Mother said.

"She says he is there. She says she knows he is there tonight."

"Yet we pay taxes," Mother said. "I must wait here alone in this big house while you take a Negro woman home."

"You know that I am not lying outside with a razor," Father said.

"I'll stop if Dilsey will make a chocolate cake," Jason said. Mother told us to go out and Father said he didn't know if Jason would get a chocolate cake or not, but he knew what Jason was going to get in about a minute. We went back to the kitchen and told Nancy.

"Father said for you to go home and lock the door, and you'll be all right," Caddy said. "All right from what, Nancy? Is Jesus mad at you?" Nancy was holding the coffee cup in her hands again, her elbows on her knees and her hands holding the cup between her knees. She was looking into the cup. "What have you done that made Jesus mad?" Caddy said. Nancy let the cup go. It didn't break on the floor, but the coffee spilled out, and Nancy sat there with her hands still making the shape of the cup. She began to make the sound again, not loud. Not singing and not unsinging. We watched her.

"Here," Dilsey said. "You quit that, now. You get aholt of yourself. You wait here. I going to get Versh to walk home with you." Dilsey went out.

We looked at Nancy. Her shoulders kept shaking, but she quit making the sound. We stood and watched her.

"What's Jesus going to do to you?" Caddy said. "He went away."

Nancy looked at us. "We had fun that night I stayed in yawls' room, didn't we?"

"I didn't," Jason said. "I didn't have any fun."

"You were asleep in Mother's room," Caddy said. "You were not there."

"Let's go down to my house and have some more fun," Nancy said.

"Mother won't let us," I said. "It's too late now."

"Don't bother her," Nancy said. "We can tell her in the morning. She won't mind."

"She wouldn't let us," I said.

"Don't ask her now," Nancy said. "Don't bother her now."

"She didn't say we couldn't go," Caddy said.

"We didn't ask," I said.

"If you go, I'll tell," Jason said.

"We'll have fun," Nancy said. "They won't mind, just to my house. I been working for yawl a long time. They won't mind."

"I'm not afraid to go," Caddy said. "Jason is the one that's afraid. He'll tell."

"I'm not," Jason said.

"Yes, you are," Caddy said. "You'll tell."

"I won't tell," Jason said. "I'm not afraid."

"Jason ain't afraid to go with me," Nancy said. "Is you, Jason?"

"Jason is going to tell," Caddy said. The lane was dark. We passed the pasture gate. "I bet if something was to jump out from behind that gate, Jason would holler."

"I wouldn't," Jason said. We walked down the lane. Nancy was talking loud.

"What are you talking so loud for, Nancy?" Caddy said.

"Who, me?" Nancy said. "Listen at Quentin and Caddy and Jason saying I'm talking loud."

"You talk like there was five of us here," Caddy said. "You talk like Father was here too."

"Who; me talking loud, Mr. Jason?" Nancy said.

"Nancy called Jason 'Mister,' " Caddy said.

"Listen how Caddy and Quentin and Jason talk," Nancy said.

"We're not talking loud," Caddy said. "You're the one that's talking like Father—"

"Hush," Nancy said; "hush, Mr. Jason."

"Nancy called Jason 'Mister' aguh—"

"Hush," Nancy said. She was talking loud when we crossed the ditch and stooped through the fence where she used to stoop through with the clothes on her head. Then we came to her house. We were going fast then. She opened the door. The smell of the house was like the lamp and the smell of Nancy was like the wick, like they were waiting for one another to begin to smell. She lit the lamp and closed the door and put the bar up. Then she quit talking loud, looking at us.

"What're we going to do?" Caddy said.

"What do yawl want to do?" Nancy said.

"You said we would have some fun," Caddy said.

There was something about Nancy's house; something you could smell besides Nancy and the house. Jason smelled it, even. "I don't want to stay here," he said. "I want to go home."

"Go home, then," Caddy said.

"I don't want to go by myself," Jason said.

"We're going to have some fun," Nancy said.

"How?" Caddy said.

Nancy stood by the door. She was looking at us, only it was like she had emptied her eyes, like she had quit using them. "What do you want to do?" she said.

"Tell us a story," Caddy said. "Can you tell a story?"

"Yes," Nancy said.

"Tell it," Caddy said. We looked at Nancy. "You don't know any stories."

"Yes," Nancy said. "Yes I do."

She came and sat in a chair before the hearth. There was a little fire there. Nancy built it up, when it was already hot inside. She built a good blaze. She told a story. She talked like her eyes looked, like her eyes watching us and her voice talking to us did not belong to her. Like she was living somewhere else, waiting somewhere else. She was outside the cabin. Her voice was inside and the shape of her, that Nancy that could stoop under a barbed wire fence with a bundle of clothes balanced on her head as though without weight, like a balloon, was there. But that was all. "And so this here queen come walking up to the ditch, where that bad man was hiding. She was walking up to the ditch, and she say, 'If I can just get past this here ditch,' was what she say . . ."

"What ditch?" Caddy said. "A ditch like that one out there? Why did a queen want to go into a ditch?"

"To get to her house," Nancy said. She looked at us. "She had to cross the ditch to get into her house quick and bar the door."

"Why did she want to go home and bar the door?" Caddy said.

4

Nancy looked at us. She quit talking. She looked at us. Jason's legs stuck straight out of his pants where he sat on Nancy's lap. "I don't think that's a good story," he said. "I want to go home."

"Maybe we had better," Caddy said. She got up from the floor. "I bet they are looking for us right now." She went toward the door.

"No," Nancy said. "Don't open it." She got up quick and passed Caddy. She didn't touch the door, the wooden bar.

"Why not?" Caddy said.

"Come back to the lamp," Nancy said. "We'll have fun. You don't have to go."

"We ought to go," Caddy said. "Unless we have a lot of fun." She and Nancy came back to the fire, the lamp.

"I want to go home," Jason said. "I'm going to tell."

"I know another story," Nancy said. She stood close to the lamp. She looked at Caddy, like when your eyes look up at a stick balanced on your nose. She had to look down to see Caddy, but her eyes looked like that, like when you are balancing a stick.

"I won't listen to it," Jason said. "I'll bang on the door."

"It's a good one," Nancy said. "It's better than the other one."

"What's it about?" Caddy said. Nancy was standing by the lamp. Her hand was on the lamp, against the light, long and brown.

"Your hand is on that hot globe," Caddy said. "Don't it feel hot to your hand?"

Nancy looked at her hand on the lamp chimney. She took her hand away, slow. She stood there, looking at Caddy, wringing her long hand as though it were tied to her wrist with a string.

"Let's do something else," Caddy said.

"I want to go home," Jason said.

"I got some popcorn," Nancy said. She looked at Caddy and then at Jason and then at me and then at Caddy again. "I got some popcorn."

"I don't like popcorn," Jason said. "I'd rather have candy."

Nancy looked at Jason. "You can hold the popper." She was still wringing her hand; it was long and limp and brown.

"All right," Jason said. "I'll stay a while if I can do that. Caddy can't hold it. I'll want to go home again if Caddy holds the popper."

Nancy built up the fire. "Look at Nancy putting her hands in the fire," Caddy said. "What's the matter with you, Nancy?"

"I got popcorn," Nancy said. "I got some." She took the popper from under the bed. It was broken. Jason began to cry.

"Now we can't have any popcorn," he said.

"We ought to go home anyway," Caddy said. "Come on, Quentin."

"Wait," Nancy said; "wait. I can fix it. Don't you want to help me fix it?"

"I don't think I want any," Caddy said. "It's too late now."

"You help me, Jason," Nancy said. "Don't you want to help me?"

"No," Jason said. "I want to go home."

"Hush," Nancy said; "hush. Watch. Watch me. I can fix it so Jason can hold it and pop the corn." She got a piece of wire and fixed the popper.

"It won't hold good," Caddy said.

"Yes it will," Nancy said. "Yawl watch. Yawl help me shell some corn."

The popcorn was under the bed too. We shelled it into the popper and Nancy helped Jason hold the popper over the fire.

"It's not popping," Jason said. "I want to go home."

"You wait," Nancy said. "It'll begin to pop. We'll have fun then."

She was sitting close to the fire. The lamp was turned up so high it was beginning to smoke. "Why don't you turn it down some?" I said.

"It's all right," Nancy said. "I'll clean it. Yawl wait. The popcorn will start in a minute."

"I don't believe it's going to start," Caddy said. "We ought to start home, anyway. They'll be worried."

"No," Nancy said. "It's going to pop. Dilsey will tell um yawl with me. I been working for yawl long time. They won't mind if yawl at my house. You wait, now. It'll start popping any minute now."

Then Jason got some smoke in his eyes and he began to cry. He dropped the popper into the fire. Nancy got a wet rag and wiped Jason's face, but he didn't stop crying.

"Hush," she said. "Hush." He didn't hush. Caddy took the popper out of the fire.

"It's burned up," she said. "You'll have to get some more popcorn, Nancy."

"Did you put all of it in?" Nancy said.

"Yes," Caddy said. Nancy looked at Caddy. Then she took the popper and opened it and poured the cinders into her apron and began to sort the grains, her hands long and brown, and we watched her.

"Haven't you got any more?" Caddy said.

"Yes," Nancy said; "yes. Look. This here ain't burnt. All we need to do is—"

"I want to go home," Jason said. "I'm going to tell."

"Hush," Caddy said. We all listened. Nancy's head was already turned toward the barred door, her eyes filled with red lamplight. "Somebody is coming," Caddy said.

Then Nancy began to make that sound again, not loud, sitting there above the fire, her long hands dangling between her knees; all of a sudden water began to come out on her face in big drops, running down her face, carrying in each one a little turning ball of firelight like a spark until it dropped off her chin. "She's not crying," I said.

"I ain't crying," Nancy said. Her eyes were closed. "I ain't crying. Who is it?"

"I don't know," Caddy said. She went to the door and looked out. "We've got to go now," she said. "Here comes Father."

"I'm going to tell," Jason said. "Yawl made me come."

The water still ran down Nancy's face. She turned in her chair. "Listen. Tell him. Tell him we going to have fun. Tell him I take good care of yawl until in the morning. Tell him to let me come home with yawl and sleep on the floor. Tell him I won't need no pallet. We'll have fun. You member last time how we had so much fun?"

"I didn't have fun," Jason said. "You hurt me. You put smoke in my eyes. I'm going to tell."

5

Father came in. He looked at us. Nancy did not get up.

"Tell him," she said.

"Caddy made us come down here," Jason said. "I didn't want to."

Father came to the fire. Nancy looked up at him. "Can't you go to Aunt Rachel's and stay?" he said. Nancy looked up at Father, her hands between her knees. "He's not here," Father said. "I would have seen him. There's not a soul in sight."

"He in the ditch," Nancy said. "He waiting in the ditch yonder."

"Nonsense," Father said. He looked at Nancy. "Do you know he's there?"

"I got the sign," Nancy said.

"What sign?"

"I got it. It was on the table when I came in. It was a hog-bone, with blood meat still on it, laying by the lamp. He's out there. When yawl walk out that door, I gone."

"Gone where, Nancy?" Caddy said.

"I'm not a tattletale," Jason said.

"Nonsense," Father said.

"He out there," Nancy said. "He looking through that window this minute, waiting for yawl to go. Then I gone."

"Nonsense," Father said. "Lock up your house and we'll take you on to Aunt Rachel's."

"'Twon't do no good," Nancy said. She didn't look at Father now, but he looked down at her, at her long, limp, moving hands. "Putting it off won't do no good."

"Then what do you want to do?" Father said.

"I don't know," Nancy said. "I can't do nothing. Just put it off. And that don't do no good. I reckon it belong to me. I reckon what I going to get ain't no more than mine."

"Get what?" Caddy said. "What's yours?"

"Nothing," Father said. "You all must get to bed."

"Caddy made me come," Jason said.

"Go on to Aunt Rachel's," Father said.

"It won't do no good," Nancy said. She sat before the fire, her elbows on her knees, her long hands between her knees. "When even your own kitchen wouldn't do no good. When even if I was sleeping on the floor in the room with your chillen, and the next morning there I am, and blood—"

"Hush," Father said. "Lock the door and put out the lamp and go to bed."

"I scaired of the dark," Nancy said. "I scaired for it to happen in the dark."

"You mean you're going to sit right here with the lamp lighted?" Father said. Then Nancy began to make the sound again, sitting before the fire, her long hands between her knees. "Ah, damnation," Father said. "Come along, chillen. It's past bedtime."

"When yawl go home, I gone," Nancy said. She talked quieter now, and her face looked quiet, like her hands. "Anyway, I got my coffin money saved up with Mr. Lovelady." Mr. Lovelady was a short, dirty man who collected the Negro insurance, coming around to the cabins or the kitchens every Saturday morning, to collect fifteen cents. He and his wife lived at the hotel. One morning his wife committed suicide. They had a child, a little girl. He and the child went away. After a week or two he came back alone. We would see him going along the lanes and the back streets on Saturday mornings.

"Nonsense," Father said. "You'll be the first thing I'll see in the kitchen tomorrow morning."

"You'll see what you'll see, I reckon," Nancy said. "But it will take the Lord to say what that will be."

6

We left her sitting before the fire.

"Come and put the bar up," Father said. But she didn't move. She didn't look at us again, sitting quietly there between the lamp and the fire. From some distance down the lane we could look back and see her through the open door.

"What, Father?" Caddy said. "What's going to happen?"

"Nothing," Father said. Jason was on Father's back, so Jason was the tallest of all of us. We went down into the ditch. I looked at it, quiet. I couldn't see much where the moonlight and the shadows tangled.

"If Jesus *is* hid here, he can see us, can't he?" Caddy said.

"He's not there," Father said. "He went away a long time ago."

"You made me come," Jason said, high; against the sky it looked like Father had two heads, a little one and a big one. "I didn't want to."

We went up out of the ditch. We could still see Nancy's house and the open door, but we couldn't see Nancy now, sitting before the fire with the door open, because she was tired. "I just done got tired," she said. "I just a nigger. It ain't no fault of mine."

But we could hear her, because she began just after we came up out of the ditch, the sound that was not singing and not unsinging. "Who will do our washing now, Father?" I said.

"I'm not a nigger," Jason said, high and close above Father's head.

"You're worse," Caddy said, "you are a tattletale. If something was to jump out, you'd be scairder than a nigger."

"I wouldn't," Jason said.

"You'd cry," Caddy said.

"Caddy," Father said.

"I wouldn't!" Jason said.

"Scairy cat," Caddy said.

"Candace!" Father said.

QUESTIONS

1. Who is the protagonist of this story? Characterize her fully. Is she a round or flat character? How does she differ from the typical protagonist of a commercial story?

2. The central conflict in this story is man versus man and is partly physical, the favorite kind of conflict of the writers of pulp fiction. But in this story the conflict is not resolved. The story ends without our knowing whether Jesus ever killed Nancy or not. Why? What is the real subject of the story?

3. Is Faulkner primarily interested in presenting Nancy's terror or in producing terror in the reader? Is he interested in terror for its own sake, or is he interested also in exploring the human causes of the terror?

4. Why is Jesus angry with Nancy? Is Jesus the villain of the story? Is Mr. Stovall? Explore the causes of the central situation, taking into account: (a) Jesus' speech about his house and the white man's house, (b) Nancy's attitude toward her sin, (c) Father's advice to Nancy and his

treatment of Jesus, (d) the jailer's treatment of Nancy, (e) Mother's attitude toward Negroes, (f) the attitudes of Caddy and Jason toward Negroes.

5. The story explores the relationships between two worlds—the black and the white—and also the relationships within each. In reference to the latter, describe the following relationships: (a) Jesus and Nancy, (b) Father and Mother, (c) Caddy and Jason. Does each of these involve a conflict? Is fright confined to the first?

6. How is Nancy's terror *dramatized*? How rational or irrational is it?

7. Explain the title.

8. This story is given an unusual twist because an adult problem is seen through the eyes of children. How much do the three children understand of what is going on? What advantages does this point of view have?

9. Compare this story with "The Storm" as a study in human terror. What are the most significant differences?

Eric Knight

FLURRY AT THE SHEEP DOG TRIAL

The wind came clear over the great flat part of the moor near Soderby. The gusts eddied, tearing away wisps of smell—the smell of men packed in knots, of sheep, of trampled heath grass. The size of the flatland made the noises small—the sharp barks of dogs, the voices of men speaking in deep dialect.

The men of the different sections stood in separate knots. Those from Polkingthorpe were ranged about Sam, their eyes on him trustingly, half fearfully, as if they were a little awed by what they had done, and the size of the bets they had made from village loyalty.

"Now, Sam," Gaffer Sitherthwick mumbled slowly, "tha's sure she can do it? For Ah've put up one pound again' two pound ten that she's the winner."

"Now hold up, Gaffer," Capper Wambley wavered. "Tha must remember she's never been really trained as a shepherd; but what Ah say is, the way Sam's trained her this past week she'll do owt he tells her best she can. And best ye can do is best, as any man'll agree."

"Thankee, Capper," Sam acknowledged. "Now, lads, if ye don't mind, Ah'd like to give her sort of secret instructions—and calm her down."

He led Flurry away from the knot of men, though she looked as though she needed no calming down. She was sedate and confident in her gait. At a distance, he knelt beside her and pretended to be brushing her coat.

"Now tha sees how it is, Flurry," he said. "There's t'four pens at each corner. In each is a sheep. Tha has to go to each one, take t'sheep out, and then put all four into t'middle pen . . . Now thee watch this one—this is t'Lancashire entry, and she was champion last year. And she's no slouch."

They watched the black sheep dog from Lancashire, sailing across the field at a gallop, neatly collecting the sheep.

"See how t'shepherd holds his crook like to make a door for t'middle pen, Flurry? Now that's all Ah can do to help. Ah can point or signal, but Ah can nobbut make a sort of angle to help wi' t'sheep at t'middle pen."

There was a burst of applause, which meant that the Lancashire dog had set the record time for the trial.

"Come on, then, Miss Smartie," Sam said. "It'll be us."

Sam heard his name being announced. He walked with Flurry to the ring. He knelt beside her.

"Now remember—no biting sheep or tha'll lose points."

She gave him a look that should have withered him.

"Go," said the judge.

Away Flurry sailed, her belly almost flat to the ground. She went from pen to pen, chivvying the sheep into a compact knot. She brought them to the center pen, driving at them adeptly so that before they could stand, sheep-wise and stubborn, and wonder where they were going, they were safe in the center pen. Then she sat at the gate, her tongue lolling out, and a burst of applause said she had made good time.

Sam hurried over to his mate. He rushed to Capper Wambley, who owned, without doubt, the finest watch in the village.

"How about it, Capper?"

The old man cleared his throat importantly and stared at his watch.

"Well. T'road Ah make it—wi' varry exact computations—is that there ain't a split-second difference between thee and Lancashire. But mind ye—that's unofficial, o' course."

So the chums rocked in impatience as the last tests were run off, and then they stood in the common hush as the judge took off his hat and advanced.

"First place," he announced, "is a tie between Joe Pettigill's Black Tad and Sam Small's Flurry, as far as time is concerned. But the judges unanimously award first place, on the basis o' calmer conduct in handling t'sheep, to Pettigill's Black Tad fro' Lancashire."

Of course, Sam and his friends were quite put out about it, and Gaffer Sitherthwick almost had apoplexy as he thought of his lost pound . . . Thus it might have been a black day in the history of Polkingthorpe Brig had not Pettigill decided to gloat a bit. He walked over past the chums and said triumphantly, "Why don't ye all coom over to Lancashire and learn reight how to handle a tyke?"

This was, of course, too, too much for any Yorkshireman to bear. So Sam came right back at him. "Oh, aye?" he said.

It wasn't a very good answer, but it was all he could think of at the moment.

"Oh, aye," echoed Pettigill . . .

"Ah admit tha's got a fine bitch there, Pettigill, but ma tyke ain't used to sheep. But if it came, now, to a test o' real intelligence—well, here's five pounds even fro' me and ma mates says we'll win at any contest tha says."

"Then thy good money goes after thy bad," the Lancashire lad said.

So it was arranged that an extra test would be held, with each man picking his own test to show the intelligence of his dog. Mr. Watcliffe, a well-to-do sheep dealer who was one of the judges, agreed to make the decision as to which dog was best.

The moor rang with excited chatter as the news spread, and everyone scurried around to lay bets. The Polkingthorpe men all got side bets down—except the Gaffer. He declined, morosely, to bet any more. So the contest got under way. Pettigill and Sam drew straws to see which dog should show off first.

Pettigill got the short straw and had to start. "Now, lass," he said to his dog, "over there Ah've put a stick, a stone, ma cap, and a handkerchief. Will some sporting gentleman call out which one Ah should bid her bring first?"

"T'stick!" a voice called.

"Tad. Fotch me yon stick," Pettigill ordered.

Away raced the dog and brought it. One by one, as requested, the champion brought back the correct articles, dropping them at its owner's feet. The men burst into applause, as it ended. Then up stepped Sam. He knelt beside Flurry and spoke so all could hear.

"Lying i' front o' Joe Pettigill," he announced, "is four articles. When Ah say 'Go!' ma tyke'll first take t'cap, go to the far sheep pen, and drop it inside there. Next she'll take t'stick, and drop it at the feet o' t'biggest lad on this moor. Third she'll take t'stone and drop it at t'feet o' t'second-best dog trainer on this moor. Finally, she'll take t'handkerchief—" and here Sam beamed floridly—"and drop it afore t'handsomest and knowingest man around these parts. Now ista ready?"

Sam looked at Flurry, who jumped to her feet and leaned forward as if held by an invisible leash. The crowd almost moaned in a sort of excitement, for they had never heard of a dog that could understand such a complicated set of commands.

"Go!" said Sam.

Away sailed Flurry, veering past Joe Pettigill's feet and snatching up the cap on the dead gallop without stopping. Going in the water-smooth racing stride of a collie, she went out to the far pen, dropped the cap, and streaked back. She snatched the stick and loped toward the crowd. The men parted to let her through. She quested about, until she saw Ian Cawper. She dropped it at his feet and the men moaned astonishment.

Back she went for the stone. She picked it up, and then stood, as if at a loss. The men drew in their breath.

But Flurry merely looked up at Joe Pettigill, walked forward one step and dropped the stone again.

The men roared in approval.

"That means Pettigill's second-best dog trainer," they said. "But now for Sam!"

Flurry now had the handkerchief. She was walking to Sam, who stood, waiting triumphantly. Flurry came nearer to his feet, and then began to circle round him.

"She's forgot," the men breathed. "She don't know what to do wi' it."

Sam looked down, with a sort of agony in his eyes, for Flurry was trotting away from him—going away with the handkerchief in a hesitating sort of way. She was looking about her. She was walking to the center.

And then everyone saw what it was.

Flurry was going up to Mr. Watcliffe, the judge. She dropped the handkerchief at his feet, walked back to Sam, and sat properly at heel.

This time there was no cheering, for in that entire crowd it seemed as if a ghost had passed and lightly touched the back of every man's head, touching low down toward the neck where the short hairs grow, a touch that left a tingling sensation.

All one could hear was the voice of Mr. Watcliffe. "Why, bless my soul," he was saying. "Bless my very body and soul. She's almost human. Bless my soul."

Then he seemed to waken to his responsibility.

"Ah judge that the test has been won by Sam Small's tyke. If he will step forward, Ah'll give him the wager money."

This broke the spell. Sam went forward to collect, and the Polkingthorpe men went round with a roar to garner in the side bets they had made in the crowd. Everyone was in pocket except Gaffer Sitherthwick, which was also something to make that day a memorable one in Polkingthorpe's history. Seldom, if ever, did the Gaffer come out on the wrong side of money matters.

Together the chums all started home. Joe Pettigill stopped them and spoke like a true sport.

"That's a champion tyke tha has there, lad," he said.

"Thankee," said Sam, with the customary modesty. "We nobbut won by luck."

"But how about ma cap up there?" the Lancashireman asked.

"Nay, Ah nobbut said she'd tak' it," Sam pointed out. "It'll cost thee another five pound to have her bring it back."

Pettigill frowned, then grinned in appreciation.

"Here, Tad," he said. "Go up and get ma cap." And away sailed his own fine dog.

Away, too, went Sam, with all the men slapping him on the back, applauding his wit, skill, acumen, and perspicacity. They streamed over the moor toward Polkingthorpe Brig to tell the story of their mighty triumph.

QUESTIONS

1. What elements of realism does the story contain? What is their purpose?

2. How do the geographic origins of the chief competitors contribute to their rivalry?

3. What distinguishes the tasks set for Flurry by Sam from those set for Black Tad by Joe Pettigill? Comment on the judge's remark that Flurry is "almost human."

4. What is the principal source of humor in this story? What are the subsidiary sources? To what extent does the humor illuminate human experience? To what extent does it exist for its own sake?

Frank O'Connor

THE DRUNKARD

It was a terrible blow to Father when Mr. Dooley on the terrace died. Mr. Dooley was a commercial traveller with two sons in the Dominicans and a car of his own, so socially he was miles ahead of us, but he had no false pride. Mr. Dooley was an intellectual, and, like all intellectuals the thing he loved best was conversation, and in his own limited way Father was a well-read man and could appreciate an intelligent talker. Mr. Dooley was remarkably intelligent. Between business acquaintances and clerical contacts, there was very little he didn't know about what went on in town, and evening after evening he crossed the road to our gate to explain to Father the news behind the news. He had a low, palavering voice and a knowing smile, and Father would listen in astonishment, giving him a conversational lead now and again, and then stump triumphantly in to Mother with his face aglow and ask: "Do you know what Mr. Dooley is after telling me?" Ever since, when somebody has given me some bit of information off the record I have found myself on the point of asking: "Was it Mr. Dooley told you that?"

THE DRUNKARD From *Traveller's Samples,* by Frank O'Connor. Originally appeared in *The New Yorker,* 1948.

Till I actually saw him laid out in his brown shroud with the rosary beads entwined between his waxy fingers I did not take the report of his death seriously. Even then I felt there must be a catch and that some summer evening Mr. Dooley must reappear at our gate to give us the lowdown on the next world. But Father was very upset, partly because Mr. Dooley was about one age with himself, a thing that always gives a distinctly personal turn to another man's demise; partly because now he would have no one to tell him what dirty work was behind the latest scene at the Corporation. You could count on your fingers the number of men in Blarney Lane who read the papers as Mr. Dooley did, and none of these would have overlooked the fact that Father was only a labouring man. Even Sullivan, the carpenter, a mere nobody, thought he was a cut above Father. It was certainly a solemn event.

"Half past two to the Curragh," Father said meditatively, putting down the paper.

"But you're not thinking of going to the funeral?" Mother asked in alarm.

" 'Twould be expected," Father said, scenting opposition. "I wouldn't give it to say to them."

"I think," said Mother with suppressed emotion, "it will be as much as anyone will expect if you go to the chapel with him."

("Going to the chapel," of course, was one thing, because the body was removed after work, but going to a funeral meant the loss of a half-day's pay.)

"The people hardly know us," she added.

"God between us and all harm," Father replied with dignity, "we'd be glad if it was our own turn."

To give Father his due, he was always ready to lose a half day for the sake of an old neighbour. It wasn't so much that he liked funerals as that he was a conscientious man who did as he would be done by, and nothing could have consoled him so much for the prospect of his own death as the assurance of a worthy funeral. And, to give Mother her due, it wasn't the half-day's pay she begrudged, badly as we could afford it.

Drink, you see, was Father's great weakness. He could keep steady for months, even for years, at a stretch, and while he did he was as good as gold. He was first up in the morning and brought the mother a cup of tea in bed, stayed at home in the evenings and read the paper; saved money and bought himself a new blue serge suit and bowler hat. He laughed at the folly of men who, week in, week out, left their hard-earned money with the publicans; and sometimes, to pass an idle hour, he took pencil and paper and calculated precisely how much he saved each week through being a teetotaller. Being a natural optimist he sometimes continued this calculation through the whole span of his prospective existence and the total was breathtaking. He would die worth hundreds.

If I had only known it, this was a bad sign; a sign he was becoming stuffed up with spiritual pride and imagining himself better than his neighbours. Sooner or later, the spiritual pride grew till it called for some form of celebration. Then he took a drink—not whisky, of course; nothing like that—just a glass of some harmless drink like lager beer. That was the end of Father. By the time he had taken the first he already realized that he had made a fool of himself, took a second to forget it and a third to forget that he couldn't forget, and at last came home reeling drunk. From this on it was "The Drunkard's Progress," as in the moral prints. Next day he stayed in from work with a sick head while Mother went off to make his excuses at the works, and inside a fortnight he was poor and savage and despondent again. Once he began he drank steadily through everything down to the kitchen clock. Mother and I knew all the phases and dreaded all the dangers. Funerals were one.

"I have to go to Dunphy's to do a half-day's work," said Mother in distress. "Who's to look after Larry?"

"I'll look after Larry," Father said graciously. "The little walk will do him good."

There was no more to be said, though we all knew I didn't need anyone to look after me, and that I could quite well have stayed at home and looked after Sonny, but I was being attached to the party to act as a brake on Father. As a brake I had never achieved anything, but Mother still had great faith in me.

Next day, when I got home from school, Father was there before me and made a cup of tea for both of us. He was very good at tea, but too heavy in the hand for anything else; the way he cut bread was shocking. Afterwards, we went down the hill to the church, Father wearing his best blue serge and a bowler cocked to one side of his head with the least suggestion of the masher. To his great joy he discovered Peter Crowley among the mourners. Peter was another danger signal, as I knew well from certain experiences after Mass on Sunday morning: a mean man, as Mother said, who only went to funerals for the free drinks he could get at them. It turned out that he hadn't even known Mr. Dooley! But Father had a sort of contemptuous regard for him as one of the foolish people who wasted their good money in public-houses when they could be saving it. Very little of his own money Peter Crowley wasted!

It was an excellent funeral from Father's point of view. He had it all well studied before we set off after the hearse in the afternoon sunlight.

"Five carriages!" he exclaimed. "Five carriages and sixteen covered cars! There's one alderman, two councillors and 'tis unknown how many priests. I didn't see a funeral like this from the road since Willie Mack, the publican, died."

"Ah, he was well liked," said Crowley in his husky voice.

"My goodness, don't I know that?" snapped Father. "Wasn't the man my best friend? Two nights before he died—only two nights—he was over telling me the goings-on about the housing contract. Them fellows in the Corporation are night and day robbers. But even I never imagined he was as well connected as that."

Father was stepping out like a boy, pleased with everything: the other mourners, and the fine houses along Sunday's Well. I knew the danger signals were there in full force: a sunny day, a fine funeral, and a distinguished company of clerics and public men were bringing out all the natural vanity and flightiness of Father's character. It was with something like genuine pleasure that he saw his old friend lowered into the grave; with the sense of having performed a duty and the pleasant awareness that however much he would miss poor Mr. Dooley in the long summer evenings, it was he and not poor Mr. Dooley who would do the missing.

"We'll be making tracks before they break up," he whispered to Crowley as the gravediggers tossed in the first shovelfuls of clay, and away he went, hopping like a goat from grassy hump to hump. The drivers, who were probably in the same state as himself, though without months of abstinence to put an edge on it, looked up hopefully.

"Are they nearly finished, Mick?" bawled one.

"All over now bar the last prayers," trumpeted Father in the tone of one who brings news of great rejoicing.

The carriages passed us in a lather of dust several hundred yards from the public-house, and Father, whose feet gave him trouble in hot weather, quickened his pace, looking nervously over his shoulder for any sign of the main body of mourners crossing the hill. In a crowd like that a man might be kept waiting.

When we did reach the pub the carriages were drawn up outside, and solemn men in black ties were cautiously bringing out consolation to mysterious females whose hands reached out modestly from behind the drawn blinds of the coaches. Inside the pub there were only the drivers and a couple of shawly women. I felt if I was to act as a brake at all, this was the time, so I pulled Father by the coattails.

"Dadda, can't we go home now?" I asked.

"Two minutes now," he said, beaming affectionately. "Just a bottle of lemonade and we'll go home."

This was a bribe, and I knew it, but I was always a child of weak character. Father ordered lemonade and two pints. I was thirsty and swallowed my drink at once. But that wasn't Father's way. He had long months of abstinence behind him and an eternity of pleasure before. He took out his pipe, blew through it, filled it, and then lit it with loud pops, his eyes bulging above it. After that he deliberately turned his back on the pint, leaned one elbow on the counter in the attitude of a man who did not know there was a pint behind him, and deliberately brushed the tobacco from his palms. He had settled down for the evening. He was steadily working through all the important funerals he had ever attended. The carriages departed and the minor mourners drifted in till the pub was half full.

"Dadda," I said, pulling his coat again, "can't we go home now?"

"Ah, your mother won't be in for a long time yet," he said benevolently enough. "Run out in the road and play, can't you?"

It struck me very cool, the way grown-ups assumed that you could play all by yourself on a strange road. I began to get bored as I had so often been bored before. I knew Father was quite capable of lingering there till nightfall. I knew I might have to bring him home, blind drunk, down Blarney Lane, with all the old women at their doors, saying: "Mick Delaney is on it again." I knew that my mother would be half crazy with anxiety; that next day Father wouldn't go out to work; and before the end of the week she would be running down to the pawn with the clock under her shawl. I could never get over the lonesomeness of the kitchen without a clock.

I was still thirsty. I found if I stood on tiptoe I could just reach Father's glass, and the idea occurred to me that it would be interesting to know what the contents were like. He had his back to it and wouldn't notice. I took down the glass and sipped cautiously. It was a terrible disappointment. I was astonished that he could even drink such stuff. It looked as if he had never tried lemonade.

I should have advised him about lemonade but he was holding forth himself in great style. I heard him say that bands were a great addition to a funeral. He put his arms in the position of someone holding a rifle in reverse and hummed a few bars of Chopin's Funeral March. Crowley nodded reverently. I took a longer drink and began to see that porter might have its advantages. I felt pleasantly elevated and philosophic. Father hummed a few bars of the Dead March in *Saul*. It was a nice pub and a very fine funeral, and I felt sure that poor Mr. Dooley in Heaven must be highly gratified. At the same time I thought they might have given him a band. As Father said, bands were a great addition.

But the wonderful thing about porter was the way it made you stand aside, or rather float aloft like a cherub rolling on a cloud, and watch yourself with your legs crossed, leaning against a bar counter, not worrying about trifles but thinking deep, serious, grown-up thoughts about life and death. Looking at yourself like that, you couldn't help thinking after a while how funny you looked, and suddenly you got embarrassed and wanted to giggle. But by the time I had finished the pint, that phase too had passed; I found it hard to put back the glass, the counter seemed to have grown so high. Melancholia was supervening again.

"Well," Father said reverently, reaching behind him for his drink, "God rest the poor man's soul, wherever he is!" He stopped, looked first at the glass, and then at the people round him. "Hello," he said in a fairly good-humoured tone, as if he were just prepared to consider it a joke, even if it was in bad taste, "who was at this?"

There was silence for a moment while the publican and the old women looked first at Father and then at his glass.

"There was no one at it, my good man," one of the women said with an offended air. "Is it robbers you think we are?"

"Ah, there's no one here would do a thing like that, Mick," said the publican in a shocked tone.

"Well, someone did it," said Father, his smile beginning to wear off.

"If they did, they were them that were nearer it," said the woman darkly, giving me a dirty look; and at the same moment the truth began to dawn on Father. I suppose I must have looked a bit starry-eyed. He bent and shook me.

"Are you all right, Larry?" he asked in alarm.

Peter Crowley looked down at me and grinned.

"Could you beat that?" he exclaimed in a husky voice.

I could, and without difficulty. I started to get sick. Father jumped back in holy terror that I might spoil his good suit, and hastily opened the back door.

"Run! run! run!" he shouted.

I saw the sunlit wall outside with the ivy overhanging it, and ran. The intention was good but the performance was exaggerated, because I lurched right into the wall, hurting it badly, as it seemed to me. Being always very polite, I said "Pardon" before the second bout came on me. Father, still concerned for his suit, came up behind and cautiously held me while I got sick.

"That's a good boy!" he said encouragingly. "You'll be grand when you get that up."

Begor, I was not grand! Grand was the last thing I was. I gave one unmerciful wail out of me as he steered me back to the pub and put me sitting on the bench near the shawlies. They drew themselves up with an offended air, still sore at the suggestion that they had drunk his pint.

"God help us!" moaned one, looking pityingly at me. "Isn't it the likes of them would be fathers?"

"Mick," said the publican in alarm, spraying sawdust on my tracks, "that child isn't supposed to be in here at all. You'd better take him home quick in case a bobby would see him."

"Merciful God!" whimpered Father, raising his eyes to heaven and clapping his hands silently as he only did when distraught. "What misfortune was on me? Or what will his mother say? . . . If women might stop at home and look after their children themselves!" he added in a snarl for the benefit of the shawlies. "Are them carriages all gone, Bill?"

"The carriages are finished long ago, Mick," replied the publican.

"I'll take him home," Father said despairingly . . . "I'll never bring you out again," he threatened me. "Here," he added, giving me the clean handkerchief from his breast pocket, "put that over your eye."

The blood on the handkerchief was the first indication I got that I was cut, and instantly my temple began to throb and I set up another howl.

"Whisht, whisht, whisht!" Father said testily, steering me out the door. "One'd think you were killed. That's nothing. We'll wash it when we get home."

"Steady now, old scout!" Crowley said, taking the other side of me. "You'll be all right in a minute."

I never met two men who knew less about the effects of drink. The first breath of fresh air and the warmth of the sun made me groggier than ever and I pitched and rolled between wind and tide till Father started to whimper again.

"God Almighty, and the whole road out! What misfortune was on me didn't stop at my work! Can't you walk straight?"

I couldn't. I saw plain enough that, coaxed by the sunlight, every woman old and young in Blarney Lane was leaning over her half-door or sitting on her doorstep. They all stopped gabbling to gape at the strange spectacle of two sober, middle-aged men bringing home a drunken small boy with a cut over his eye. Father, torn between the shamefast desire to get me home as quick as he could, and the neighbourly need to explain that it wasn't his fault, finally halted outside Mrs. Roche's. There was a gang of old women outside a door at the opposite side of the road. I didn't like the look of them from the first. They seemed altogether too interested in me. I leaned against the wall of Mrs. Roche's cottage with my hands in my trousers pockets, thinking mournfully of poor Mr. Dooley in his cold grave on the Curragh, who would never walk down the road again, and, with great feeling, I began to sing a favourite song of Father's.

> Though lost to Mononia and cold in the grave
> He returns to Kincora no more.

"Wisha, the poor child!" Mrs. Roche said. "Haven't he a lovely voice, God bless him!"

That was what I thought myself, so I was the more surprised when Father said "Whisht!" and raised a threatening finger at me. He didn't seem to realize the appropriateness of the song, so I sang louder than ever.

"Whisht, I tell you!" he snapped, and then tried to work up a smile for Mrs. Roche's benefit. "We're nearly home now. I'll carry you the rest of the way."

But, drunk and all as I was, I knew better than to be carried home ignominiously like that.

"Now," I said severely, "can't you leave me alone? I can walk all right. 'Tis only my head. All I want is a rest."

"But you can rest at home in bed," he said viciously, trying to pick me up, and I knew by the flush on his face that he was very vexed.

"Ah, Jasus," I said crossly, "what do I want to go home for? Why the hell can't you leave me alone?"

For some reason the gang of old women at the other side of the road thought this very funny. They nearly split their sides over it. A gassy fury began to expand in me at the thought that a fellow couldn't have a drop taken without the whole neighbourhood coming out to make game of him.

"Who are ye laughing at?" I shouted, clenching my fists at them. "I'll make ye laugh at the other side of yeer faces if ye don't let me pass."

They seemed to think this funnier still; I had never seen such ill-mannered people.

"Go away, ye bloody bitches!" I said.

"Whisht, whisht, whisht, I tell you!" snarled Father, abandoning all pretence of amusement and dragging me along behind him by the hand. I was maddened by the women's shrieks of laughter. I was maddened by Father's bullying. I tried to dig in my heels but he was too powerful for me, and I could only see the women by looking back over my shoulder.

"Take care or I'll come back and show ye!" I shouted. "I'll teach ye to let decent people pass. Fitter for ye to stop at home and wash yeer dirty faces."

" 'Twill be all over the road," whimpered Father. "Never again, never again, not if I lived to be a thousand!"

To this day I don't know whether he was forswearing me or the drink. By way of a song suitable to my heroic mood I bawled "The Boys of Wexford," as he dragged me in home. Crowley, knowing he was not safe, made off and Father undressed me and put me to bed. I couldn't sleep because of the whirling in my head. It was very unpleasant, and I got sick again. Father came in with a wet cloth and mopped up after me. I lay in a fever, listening to him chopping sticks to start a fire. After that I heard him lay the table.

Suddenly the front door banged open and Mother stormed in with Sonny in her arms, not her usual gentle, timid self, but a wild, raging woman. It was clear that she had heard it all from the neighbours.

"Mick Delaney," she cried hysterically, "what did you do to my son?"

"Whisht, woman, whisht, whisht!" he hissed, dancing from one foot to the other. "Do you want the whole road to hear?"

"Ah," she said with a horrifying laugh, "the road knows all about it by this time. The road knows the way you filled your unfortunate innocent child with drink to make sport for you and that other rotten, filthy brute."

"But I gave him no drink," he shouted, aghast at the horrifying interpretation the neighbours had chosen to give his misfortune. "He took it while my back was turned. What the hell do you think I am?"

"Ah," she replied bitterly, "everyone knows what you are now. God forgive you, wasting our hard-earned few ha'pence on drink, and bringing up your child to be a drunken corner-boy like yourself."

Then she swept into the bedroom and threw herself on her knees by the bed. She moaned when she saw the gash over my eye. In the kitchen Sonny set up a loud bawl on his own, and a moment later Father appeared in the bedroom door with his cap over his eyes, wearing an expression of the most intense self-pity.

"That's a nice way to talk to me after all I went through," he whined.

"That's a nice accusation, that I was drinking. Not one drop of drink crossed my lips the whole day. How could it when he drank it all? I'm the one that ought to be pitied, with my day ruined on me, and I after being made a show for the whole road."

But next morning, when he got up and went out quietly to work with his dinner-basket, Mother threw herself on me in the bed and kissed me. It seemed it was all my doing, and I was being given a holiday till my eye got better.

"My brave little man!" she said with her eyes shining. "It was God did it you were there. You were his guardian angel."

QUESTIONS

1. What are the sources of humor in this story? Does the humor arise from observation of life or from distortion of life? What elements of the story seem to you funniest?

2. Is this a purely humorous story, or are there undertones of pathos in it? If the latter, from what does the pathos arise?

3. List what seem to you the chief insights into life and character presented by the story.

4. Is the title seriously meant? To whom does it refer?

5. The boy's drunkenness is seen from four points of view. What are they, and how do they differ?

6. What is the principal irony in the story?

7. The story is told in retrospect by a man recalling an incident from his boyhood. What does this removal in time do to the treatment of the material?

8. *Did* Larry's father forswear liquor? Support your answer with evidence from the story.

Isaac Bashevis Singer

THE SPINOZA OF MARKET STREET

Dr. Nahum Fischelson paced back and forth in his garret room in Market Street, Warsaw. Dr. Fischelson was a short, hunched man with a grayish beard, and was quite bald except for a few wisps of hair remaining at the nape of the neck. His nose was as crooked as a beak and his eyes were large, dark, and fluttering like those of some huge bird. It was a hot summer

THE SPINOZA OF MARKET STREET Reprinted from *The Spinoza of Market Street* by Isaac Bashevis Singer and translated by Martha Glicklich and Cecil Hemley, by permission of Farrar, Straus & Giroux, Inc. First published in *Esquire* in 1961.

evening, but Dr. Fischelson wore a black coat which reached to his knees, and he had on a stiff collar and a bow tie. From the door he paced slowly to the dormer window set high in the slanting room and back again. One had to mount several steps to look out. A candle in a brass holder was burning on the table and a variety of insects buzzed around the flame. Now and again one of the creatures would fly too close to the fire and sear its wings, or one would ignite and glow on the wick for an instant. At such moments Dr. Fischelson grimaced. His wrinkled face would twitch and beneath his disheveled moustache he would bite his lips. Finally he took a handkerchief from his pocket and waved it at the insects.

"Away from there, fools and imbeciles," he scolded. "You won't get warm here; you'll only burn yourself."

The insects scattered but a second later returned and once more circled the trembling flame. Dr. Fischelson wiped the sweat from his wrinkled forehead and sighed, "Like men they desire nothing but the pleasure of the moment." On the table lay an open book written in Latin, and on its broad-margined pages were notes and comments printed in small letters by Dr. Fischelson. The book was Spinoza's *Ethics* and Dr. Fischelson had been studying it for the last thirty years. He knew every proposition, every proof, every corollary, every note by heart. When he wanted to find a particular passage, he generally opened to the place immediately without having to search for it. But, nevertheless, he continued to study the *Ethics* for hours every day with a magnifying glass in his bony hand, murmuring and nodding his head in agreement. The truth was that the more Dr. Fischelson studied, the more puzzling sentences, unclear passages, and cryptic remarks he found. Each sentence contained hints unfathomed by any of the students of Spinoza. Actually the philosopher had anticipated all of the criticisms of pure reason made by Kant and his followers. Dr. Fischelson was writing a commentary on the *Ethics*. He had drawers full of notes and drafts, but it didn't seem that he would ever be able to complete his work. The stomach ailment which had plagued him for years was growing worse from day to day. Now he would get pains in his stomach after only a few mouthfuls of oatmeal. "God in Heaven, it's difficult, very difficult," he would say to himself using the same intonation as had his father, the late Rabbi of Tishevitz. "It's very, very hard."

Dr. Fischelson was not afraid of dying. To begin with, he was no longer a young man. Secondly, it is stated in the fourth part of the *Ethics* that "a free man thinks of nothing less than of death and his wisdom is a meditation not of death, but of life." Thirdly, it is also said that "the human mind cannot be absolutely destroyed with the human body but there is some part of it that remains eternal." And yet Dr. Fischelson's ulcer (or perhaps it was a cancer) continued to bother him. His tongue was always coated. He belched frequently and emitted a different foul-smelling gas each time. He suffered from heartburn and cramps. At times he felt like vomiting and at other times he was hungry for garlic, onions, and fried foods. He had long ago discarded the medicines prescribed for him by the doctors and had sought his own remedies. He found it beneficial to take grated radish after meals and lie on his bed, belly down, with his head hanging over the side. But these home remedies offered only temporary relief. Some of the doctors he consulted insisted there was nothing the matter with him. "It's just nerves," they told him. "You could live to be a hundred."

But on this particular hot summer night, Dr. Fischelson felt his strength ebbing. His knees were shaky, his pulse weak. He sat down to read and his vision blurred. The letters on the page turned from green to gold. The lines became waved and jumped over each other, leaving white gaps as if the text had disappeared in some mysterious way. The heat was unbearable, flowing down directly from the tin roof; Dr. Fischelson felt he was inside of an oven. Several times he climbed the four steps to the window and thrust his head out into the cool of the evening breeze. He would remain in that position for so long his knees would become wobbly. "Oh it's a fine breeze," he would murmur, "really delightful," and he would recall that according to Spinoza, morality and happiness were identical, and that the most moral deed a man could perform was to indulge in some pleasure which was not contrary to reason.

2

Dr. Fischelson, standing on the top step at the window and looking out, could see into two worlds. Above him were the heavens, thickly strewn with stars. Dr. Fischelson had never seriously studied astronomy but he could differentiate between the planets, those bodies which like the earth, revolve around the sun, and the fixed stars, themselves distant suns, whose light reaches us a hundred or even a thousand years later. He recognized the constellations which mark the path of the earth in space and that nebulous sash, the Milky Way. Dr. Fischelson owned a small telescope he had bought in Switzerland where he had studied and he particularly enjoyed looking at the moon through it. He could clearly make out on the moon's surface the volcanoes bathed in sunlight and the dark, shadowy craters. He never wearied of gazing at these cracks and crevasses. To him they seemed both near and distant, both substantial and insubstantial. Now and then he would see a shooting star trace a wide arc across the sky and disappear, leaving a fiery trail behind it. Dr. Fischelson would know then that a meteorite had reached our atmosphere, and perhaps some unburned fragment of it had fallen into the ocean or had landed in the desert or perhaps even in some inhabited region. Slowly the stars which had appeared from behind Dr. Fischelson's roof rose until they were shining above the house across the street. Yes, when Dr. Fischelson looked up into the heavens, he became aware of that infinite extension which is, according to Spinoza, one of God's attributes. It comforted Dr. Fischelson to think that although he was only a weak, puny man, a changing mode of the absolutely infinite Substance, he was nevertheless a part of the cosmos, made of the same matter as the celestial bodies; to the extent that he was a part of the Godhead, he knew he could not be destroyed. In such moments, Dr. Fischelson experienced the *Amor Dei Intellectualis* which is, according to the philosopher of Amsterdam, the highest perfection of the mind. Dr. Fischelson breathed deeply, lifted his head as high as his stiff collar permitted and actually felt he was whirling in company with the earth, the sun, the stars of the Milky Way, and the infinite host of galaxies known only to infinite thought. His legs became light and weightless and he grasped the window frame with both hands as if afraid he would lose his footing and fly out into eternity.

When Dr. Fischelson tired of observing the sky, his glance dropped to Market Street below. He could see a long strip extending from Yanash's market to Iron Street with the gas lamps lining it merged into a string of fiery dots. Smoke was issuing from the chimneys on the black, tin roofs; the bakers were heating their ovens, and here and there sparks mingled with the black smoke. The street never looked so noisy and crowded as on a summer evening. Thieves, prostitutes, gamblers, and fences loafed in the square which looked from above like a pretzel covered with poppy seeds. The young men laughed coarsely and the girls shrieked. A peddler with a keg of lemonade on his back pierced the general din with his intermittent cries. A watermelon vendor shouted in a savage voice, and the long knife which he used for cutting the fruit dripped with the blood-like juice. Now and again the street became even more agitated. Fire engines, their heavy wheels clanging, sped by; they were drawn by sturdy black horses which had to be tightly curbed to prevent them from running wild. Next came an ambulance, its siren screaming. Then some thugs had a fight among themselves and the police had to be called. A passerby was robbed and ran about shouting for help. Some wagons loaded with firewood sought to get through into the courtyards where the bakeries were located but the horses could not lift the wheels over the steep curbs and the drivers berated the animals and lashed them with their whips. Sparks rose from the clanging hoofs. It was now long after seven, which was the prescribed closing time for stores, but actually business had only begun. Customers were led in stealthily through back doors. The Russian policemen on the street, having been paid off, noticed nothing of this. Merchants continued to hawk their wares, each seeking to outshout the others.

"Gold, gold, gold," a woman who dealt in rotten oranges shrieked.

"Sugar, sugar, sugar," croaked a dealer of overripe plums.

Amor Dei Intellectualis: intellectual love of God

"Heads, heads, heads," a boy who sold fishheads roared.

Through the window of a *Chassidic* study house across the way, Dr. Fischelson could see boys with long sidelocks swaying over holy volumes, grimacing and studying aloud in sing-song voices. Butchers, porters, and fruit dealers were drinking beer in the tavern below. Vapor drifted from the tavern's open door like steam from a bathhouse, and there was the sound of loud music. Outside of the tavern, streetwalkers snatched at drunken soldiers and at workers on their way home from the factories. Some of the men carried bundles of wood on their shoulders, reminding Dr. Fischelson of the wicked who are condemned to kindle their own fires in Hell. Husky record players poured out their raspings through open windows. The liturgy of the high holidays alternated with vulgar vaudeville songs.

Dr. Fischelson peered into the half-lit bedlam and cocked his ears. He knew that the behavior of this rabble was the very antithesis of reason. These people were immersed in the vainest of passions, were drunk with emotions, and, according to Spinoza, emotion was never good. Instead of the pleasure they ran after, all they succeeded in obtaining was disease and prison, shame and the suffering that resulted from ignorance. Even the cats which loitered on the roofs here seemed more savage and passionate than those in other parts of the town. They caterwauled with the voices of women in labor, and like demons scampered up walls and leaped onto eaves and balconies. One of the toms paused at Dr. Fischelson's window and let out a howl which made Dr. Fischelson shudder. The doctor stepped from the window and, picking up a broom, brandished it in front of the black beast's glowing, green eyes. "Scat, begone, you ignorant savage!"—and he rapped the broom handle against the roof until the tom ran off.

3

When Dr. Fischelson had returned to Warsaw from Zurich where he had studied philosophy, a great future had been predicted for him. His friends had known that he was writing an important book on Spinoza. A Jewish Polish journal had invited him to be a contributor; he had been a frequent guest at several wealthy households and he had been made head librarian at the Warsaw synagogue. Although even then he had been considered an old bachelor, the matchmakers had proposed several rich girls for him. But Dr. Fischelson had not taken advantage of these opportunities. He had wanted to be as independent as Spinoza himself. And he had been. But because of his heretical ideas he had come into conflict with the rabbi and had had to resign his post as librarian. For years after that, he had supported himself by giving private lessons in Hebrew and German. Then, when he had become sick, the Berlin Jewish community had voted a subsidy of five hundred marks a year. This had been made possible through the intervention of the famous Dr. Hildesheimer with whom he corresponded about philosophy. In order to get by on so small a pension, Dr. Fischelson had moved into the attic room and had begun cooking his own meals on a kerosene stove. He had a cupboard which had many drawers, and each drawer was labelled with the food it contained—buckwheat, rice, barley, onions, carrots, potatoes, mushrooms. Once a week Dr. Fischelson put on his widebrimmed black hat, took a basket in one hand and Spinoza's *Ethics* in the other, and went off to the market for his provisions. While he was waiting to be served, he would open the *Ethics*. The merchants knew him and would motion him to their stalls.

"A fine piece of cheese, Doctor—just melts in your mouth."

"Fresh mushrooms, Doctor, straight from the woods."

"Make way for the Doctor, ladies," the butcher would shout. "Please don't block the entrance."

During the early years of his sickness, Dr. Fischelson had still gone in the evening to a café which was frequented by Hebrew teachers and other intellectuals. It had been his habit to sit there and play chess while drinking a half a glass of black coffee. Sometimes he would stop at the bookstores on Holy Cross Street where all sorts of old books and magazines could be purchased cheap. On one occasion a former pupil of his had arranged to meet him at a restaurant one evening. When Dr. Fischelson arrived, he had been surprised to find a group of friends and admirers who forced him to sit at the head of the table while they made speeches about him. But these were things that had happened long ago. Now people were no longer interested in him. He had isolated himself completely and had become a forgotten man. The events of 1905 when the boys of Market Street had begun to organize strikes, throw bombs at police stations, and shoot strike breakers so that the stores were closed even on weekdays had greatly increased his isolation. He began to despise everything associated with the modern Jew—Zionism, socialism, anarchism. The young men in question seemed to him nothing but an ignorant rabble intent on destroying society, society without which no reasonable existence was possible. He still read a Hebrew magazine occasionally, but he felt contempt for modern Hebrew which had no roots in the Bible or the Mishnah. The spelling of Polish words had changed also. Dr. Fischelson concluded that even the so-called spiritual men had abandoned reason and were doing their utmost to pander to the mob. Now and again he still visited a library and browsed through some of the modern histories of philosophy, but he found that the professors did not understand Spinoza, quoted him incorrectly, attributed their own muddled ideas to the philosopher. Although Dr. Fischelson was well aware that anger was an emotion unworthy of those who walk the path of reason, he would become furious, and would quickly close the book and push it from him. "Idiots," he would mutter, "asses, upstarts." And he would vow never again to look at modern philosophy.

4

Every three months a special mailman who only delivered money orders brought Dr. Fischelson eighty rubles. He expected his quarterly allotment at the beginning of July but as day after day passed and the tall man with the blond moustache and the shiny buttons did not appear, the Doctor grew anxious. He had scarcely a groshen left. Who knows—possibly the Berlin Community had rescinded his subsidy; perhaps Dr. Hildesheimer had died, God forbid; the post office might have made a mistake. Every event has its cause, Dr. Fischelson knew. All was determined, all necessary, and a man of reason had no right to worry. Nevertheless, worry invaded his brain, and buzzed about like the flies. If the worst came to the worst, it occurred to him, he could commit suicide, but then he remembered that Spinoza did not approve of suicide and compared those who took their own lives to the insane.

One day when Dr. Fischelson went out to a store to purchase a composition book, he heard people talking about war. In Serbia somewhere, an Austrian Prince had been shot and the Austrians had delivered an ultimatum to the Serbs. The owner of the store, a young man with a yellow beard and shifty yellow eyes, announced, "We are about to have a small war," and he advised Dr. Fischelson to store up food because in the near future there was likely to be a shortage.

Everything happened so quickly. Dr. Fischelson had not even decided whether it was worthwhile to spend four groshen on a newspaper, and already posters had been hung up announcing mobilization. Men were to be seen walking on the street with round, metal tags on their lapels, a sign that they were being drafted. They were followed by their crying wives. One Monday when Dr. Fischelson descended to the street to buy some food with his last kopecks, he found the stores closed. The owners and their wives stood outside and explained that merchandise was unobtainable. But certain special customers were pulled to one side and let in through back doors. On the street all was confusion. Policemen with swords unsheathed could be seen riding on horseback. A large crowd had gathered around the tavern where, at the command of the Tsar, the tavern's stock of whiskey was being poured into the gutter.

Dr. Fischelson went to his old café. Perhaps he would find some acquaintances there who would advise him. But he did not come across a single person he knew. He decided, then, to visit the rabbi of the synagogue where he had once been librarian, but the sexton with the six-sided skull cap informed him that the rabbi and his family had gone off to the spas. Dr. Fischelson had other old friends in town but he found no one at home. His feet ached from so much walking; black and green spots appeared before his eyes and he felt faint. He stopped and waited for the giddiness to pass. The passers-by jostled him. A dark-eyed high school girl tried to give him a coin.

Although the war had just started, soldiers eight abreast were marching in full battle dress—the men were covered with dust and were sunburnt. Canteens were strapped to their sides and they wore rows of bullets across their chests. The bayonets on their rifles gleamed with a cold, green light. They sang with mournful voices. Along with the men came cannons, each pulled by eight horses; their blind muzzles breathed gloomy terror. Dr. Fischelson felt nauseous. His stomach ached; his intestines seemed about to turn themselves inside out. Cold sweat appeared on his face.

"I'm dying," he thought. "This is the end." Nevertheless, he did manage to drag himself home where he lay down on the iron cot and remained, panting and gasping. He must have dozed off because he imagined that he was in his home town, Tishvitz. He had a sore throat and his mother was busy wrapping a stocking stuffed with hot salt around his neck. He could hear talk going on in the house; something about a candle and about how a frog had bitten him. He wanted to go out into the street but they wouldn't let him because a Catholic procession was passing by. Men in long robes, holding double edged axes in their hands, were intoning in Latin as they sprinkled holy water. Crosses gleamed; sacred pictures waved in the air. There was an odor of incense and corpses. Suddenly the sky turned a burning red and the whole world started to burn. Bells were ringing; people rushed madly about. Flocks of birds flew overhead, screeching. Dr. Fischelson awoke with a start. His body was covered with sweat and his throat was now actually sore. He tried to meditate about his extraordinary dream, to find its rational connection with what was happening to him and to comprehend it *sub specie eternitatis,* but none of it made sense. "Alas, the brain is a receptacle for nonsense," Dr. Fischelson thought. "This earth belongs to the mad."

And he once more closed his eyes; once more he dozed; once more he dreamed.

5

The eternal laws, apparently, had not yet ordained Dr. Fischelson's end.

There was a door to the left of Dr. Fischelson's attic room which opened off a dark corridor, cluttered with boxes and baskets, in which the odor of fried onions and laundry soap was always present. Behind this door lived a spinster whom the neighbors called Black Dobbe. Dobbe was tall and lean, and as black as a baker's shovel. She had a broken nose and there was a mustache on her upper lip. She spoke with the hoarse voice of a man and she wore men's shoes. For years Black Dobbe had sold breads, rolls, and bagels which she had bought from the baker at the gate of the house. But

sub specie eternitatis: under the aspect of eternity

one day she and the baker had quarreled and she had moved her business to the market place and now she dealt in what were called "wrinklers" which was a synonym for cracked eggs. Black Dobbe had no luck with men. Twice she had been engaged to baker's apprentices but in both instances they had returned the engagement contract to her. Some time afterwards she had received an engagement contract from an old man, a glazier who claimed that he was divorced, but it had later come to light that he still had a wife. Black Dobbe had a cousin in America, a shoemaker, and repeatedly she boasted that this cousin was sending her passage, but she remained in Warsaw. She was constantly being teased by the women who would say, "There's no hope for you, Dobbe. You're fated to die an old maid." Dobbe always answered, "I don't intend to be a slave for any man. Let them all rot."

That afternoon Dobbe received a letter from America. Generally she would go to Leizer the Tailor and have him read it to her. However, that day Leizer was out and so Dobbe thought of Dr. Fischelson whom the other tenants considered a convert since he never went to prayer. She knocked on the door of the doctor's room but there was no answer. "The heretic is probably out," Dobbe thought but, nevertheless, she knocked once more, and this time the door moved slightly. She pushed her way in and stood there frightened. Dr. Fischelson lay fully clothed on his bed; his face was as yellow as wax; his Adam's apple stuck out prominently; his beard pointed upward. Dobbe screamed; she was certain that he was dead, but—no—his body moved. Dobbe picked up a glass which stood on the table, ran into the corridor, filled the glass with water from the faucet, hurried back, and threw the water into the face of the unconscious man. Dr. Fischelson shook his head and opened his eyes.

"What's wrong with you?" Dobbe asked. "Are you sick?"

"Thank you very much. No."

"Have you a family? I'll call them."

"No family," Dr. Fischelson said.

Dobbe wanted to fetch the barber from across the street but Dr. Fischelson signified that he didn't wish the barber's assistance. Since Dobbe was not going to the market that day, no "wrinklers" being available, she decided to do a good deed. She assisted the sick man to get off the bed and smoothed down the blanket. Then she undressed Dr. Fischelson and prepared some soup for him on the kerosene stove. The sun never entered Dobbe's room, but here squares of sunlight shimmered on the faded walls. The floor was painted red. Over the bed hung a picture of a man who was wearing a broad frill around his neck and had long hair. "Such an old fellow and yet he keeps his place so nice and clean," Dobbe thought approvingly. Dr. Fischelson asked for the *Ethics,* and she gave it to him disapprovingly. She was certain it was a gentile prayer book. Then she began bustling about, brought in a pail of water, swept the floor. Dr. Fischelson ate; after he had finished, he was much stronger and Dobbe asked him to read her the letter.

He read it slowly, the paper trembling in his hands. It came from New York, from Dobbe's cousin. Once more he wrote that he was about to send her a "really important letter" and a ticket to America. By now, Dobbe knew the story by heart and she helped the old man decipher her cousin's scrawl. "He's lying," Dobbe said. "He forgot about me a long time ago." In the evening, Dobbe came again. A candle in a brass holder was burning on the chair next to the bed. Reddish shadows trembled on the walls and ceiling. Dr. Fischelson sat propped up in bed, reading a book. The candle threw a golden light on his forehead which seemed as if cleft in two. A bird had flown in through the window and was perched on the table. For a moment Dobbe was frightened. This man made her think of witches, of black mirrors and corpses wandering around at night and terrifying women. Nevertheless, she took a few steps toward him and inquired, "How are you? Any better?"

"A little, thank you."

"Are you really a convert?" she asked although she wasn't quite sure what the word meant.

"Me, a convert? No, I'm a Jew like any other Jew," Dr. Fischelson answered.

The doctor's assurances made Dobbe feel more at home. She found the bottle of kerosene and lit the stove, and after that she fetched a glass of milk from her room and began cooking kasha. Dr. Fischelson continued to study the *Ethics,* but that evening he could make no sense of the theorems and proofs with their many references to axioms and definitions and other theorems. With trembling hand he raised the book to his eyes and read, "The idea of each modification of the human body does not involve adequate knowledge of the human body itself. . . . The idea of the idea of each modification of the human mind does not involve adequate knowledge of the human mind."

6

Dr. Fischelson was certain he would die any day now. He made out his will, leaving all of his books and manuscripts to the synagogue library. His clothing and furniture would go to Dobbe since she had taken care of him. But death did not come. Rather his health improved. Dobbe returned to her business in the market, but she visited the old man several times a day, prepared soup for him, left him a glass of tea, and told him news of the war. The Germans had occupied Kalish, Bendin, and Cestechow, and they were marching on Warsaw. People said that on a quiet morning one could hear the rumblings of the cannon. Dobbe reported that the casualties were heavy. "They're falling like flies," she said. "What a terrible misfortune for the women."

She couldn't explain why, but the old man's attic room attracted her.

She liked to remove the gold-rimmed books from the bookcase, dust them, and then air them on the window sill. She would climb the few steps to the window and look out through the telescope. She also enjoyed talking to Dr. Fischelson. He told her about Switzerland where he had studied, of the great cities he had passed through, of the high mountains that were covered with snow even in the summer. His father had been a rabbi, he said, and before he, Dr. Fischelson, had become a student, he had attended a yeshiva. She asked him how many languages he knew and it turned out that he could speak and write Hebrew, Russian, German, and French, in addition to Yiddish. He also knew Latin. Dobbe was astonished that such an educated man should live in an attic room on Market Street. But what amazed her most of all was that although he had the title "Doctor," he couldn't write prescriptions. "Why don't you become a real doctor?" she would ask him. "I am a doctor," he would answer. "I'm just not a physician." "What kind of a doctor?" "A doctor of philosophy." Although she had no idea of what this meant, she felt it must be very important. "Oh my blessed mother," she would say, "where did you get such a brain?"

Then one evening after Dobbe had given him his crackers and his glass of tea with milk, he began questioning her about where she came from, who her parents were, and why she had not married. Dobbe was surprised. No one had ever asked her such questions. She told him her story in a quiet voice and stayed until eleven o'clock. Her father had been a porter at the kosher butcher shops. Her mother had plucked chickens in the slaughterhouse. The family had lived in a cellar at No. 19 Market Street. When she had been ten, she had become a maid. The man she had worked for had been a fence who bought stolen goods from thieves on the square. Dobbe had had a brother who had gone into the Russian army and had never returned. Her sister had married a coachman in Praga and had died in childbirth. Dobbe told of the battles between the underworld and the revolutionaries in 1905, of blind Itche and his gang and how they collected protection money from the stores, of the thugs who attacked young boys and girls out on Saturday afternoon strolls if they were not paid money for security. She also spoke of the pimps who drove about in carriages and abducted women to be sold in Buenos Aires. Dobbe swore that some men had even sought to inveigle her into a brothel, but that she had run away. She complained of a thousand evils done to her. She had been robbed; her boy friend had been stolen; a competitor had once poured a pint of kerosene into her basket of bagels; her own cousin, the shoemaker, had cheated her out of a hundred rubles before he had left for America. Dr. Fischelson listened to her attentively. He asked her questions, shook his head, and grunted.

"Well, do you believe in God?" he finally asked her.

"I don't know," she answered. "Do you?"

"Yes, I believe."

"Then why don't you go to synagogue?" she asked.

"God is everywhere," he replied. "In the synagogue. In the market place. In this very room. We ourselves are parts of God."

"Don't say such things," Dobbe said. "You frighten me."

She left the room and Dr. Fischelson was certain she had gone to bed. But he wondered why she had not said "good night." "I probably drove her away with my philosophy," he thought. The very next moment he heard her footsteps. She came in carrying a pile of clothing like a peddler.

"I wanted to show you these," she said. "They're my trousseau." And she began to spread out, on the chair, dresses—woolen, silk, velvet. Taking each dress up in turn, she held it to her body. She gave him an account of every item in her trousseau—underwear, shoes, stockings.

"I'm not wasteful," she said. "I'm a saver. I have enough money to go to America."

Then she was silent and her face turned brick-red. She looked at Dr. Fischelson out of the corner of her eyes, timidly, inquisitively. Dr. Fischelson's body suddenly began to shake as if he had the chills. He said, "Very nice, beautiful things." His brow furrowed and he pulled at his beard with two fingers. A sad smile appeared on his toothless mouth and his large fluttering eyes, gazing into the distance through the attic window, also smiled sadly.

7

The day that Black Dobbe came to the rabbi's chambers and announced that she was to marry Dr. Fischelson, the rabbi's wife thought she had gone mad. But the news had already reached Leizer the Tailor, and had spread to the bakery, as well as to other shops. There were those who thought that the "old maid" was very lucky; the doctor, they said, had a vast hoard of money. But there were others who took the view that he was a run-down degenerate who would give her syphilis. Although Dr. Fischelson had insisted that the wedding be a small, quiet one, a host of guests assembled in the rabbi's rooms. The baker's apprentices who generally went about barefoot, and in their underwear, with paper bags on the tops of their heads, now put on light-colored suits, straw hats, yellow shoes, gaudy ties, and they brought with them huge cakes and pans filled with cookies. They had even managed to find a bottle of vodka although liquor was forbidden in wartime. When the bride and groom entered the rabbi's chamber, a murmur arose from the crowd. The women could not believe their eyes. The woman that they saw was not the one they had known. Dobbe wore a wide-brimmed hat which was amply adorned with cherries, grapes, and plumes, and the dress that she had on was of white silk and was equipped with a train; on her feet were high-heeled shoes, gold in color, and from her thin neck hung a string of imitation pearls. Nor was this all: her fingers sparkled with rings and glittering stones. Her face was veiled. She looked almost like one of those rich brides who were married in the Vienna Hall. The baker's apprentices whistled mockingly. As for Dr. Fischelson, he was wearing his black coat and broad-toed shoes. He was scarcely able to walk; he was leaning on Dobbe. When he saw the crowd from the doorway, he became frightened and began to retreat, but Dobbe's former employer approached him saying, "Come in, come in, bridegroom. Don't be bashful. We are all brethren now."

The ceremony proceeded according to the law. The rabbi, in a worn satin gabardine, wrote the marriage contract and then had the bride and groom touch his handkerchief as a token of agreement; the rabbi wiped the point of the pen on his skullcap. Several porters who had been called from the street to make up the quorum supported the canopy. Dr. Fischelson put on a white robe as a reminder of the day of his death and Dobbe walked around him seven times as custom required. The light from the braided candles flickered on the walls. The shadows wavered. Having poured wine into a goblet, the rabbi chanted the benedictions in a sad melody. Dobbe uttered only a single cry. As for the other women, they took out their lace handkerchiefs and stood with them in their hands, grimacing. When the baker's boys began to whisper wisecracks to each other, the rabbi put a finger to his lips and murmured, *"Eh nu oh,"* as a sign that talking was forbidden. The moment came to slip the wedding ring on the bride's finger, but the bridegroom's hand started to tremble and he had trouble locating Dobbe's index finger. The next thing, according to custom, was the smashing of the glass, but though Dr. Fischelson kicked the goblet several times, it remained unbroken. The girls lowered their heads, pinched each other gleefully, and giggled. Finally one of the apprentices struck the goblet with his heel and it shattered. Even the rabbi could not restrain a smile. After the ceremony the guests drank vodka and ate cookies. Dobbe's former employer came up to Dr. Fischelson and said, *"Mazel tov,* bridegroom. Your luck should be as good as your wife." "Thank you, thank you," Dr. Fischelson murmured, "but I don't look forward to any luck." He was anxious to return as quickly as possible to his attic room. He felt a pressure in his stomach and his chest ached. His face had become greenish. Dobbe had suddenly become angry. She pulled back her veil and called out to the crowd, "What are you laughing at? This isn't a show." And without picking up the cushion-cover in which the gifts were wrapped, she returned with her husband to their rooms on the fifth floor.

Dr. Fischelson lay down on the freshly made bed in his room and began reading the *Ethics*. Dobbe had gone back to her own room. The doctor had explained to her that he was an old man, that he was sick and without strength. He had promised her nothing. Nevertheless she returned wearing

Mazel tov: Good luck

a silk nightgown, slippers with pompoms, and with her hair hanging down over her shoulders. There was a smile on her face, and she was bashful and hesitant. Dr. Fischelson trembled and the *Ethics* dropped from his hands. The candle went out. Dobbe groped for Dr. Fischelson in the dark and kissed his mouth. "My dear husband," she whispered to him, "*Mazel tov.*"

What happened that night could be called a miracle. If Dr. Fischelson hadn't been convinced that every occurrence is in accordance with the laws of nature, he would have thought that Black Dobbe had bewitched him. Powers long dormant awakened in him. Although he had had only a sip of the benediction wine, he was as if intoxicated. He kissed Dobbe and spoke to her of love. Long forgotten quotations from Klopfstock, Lessing, Goethe, rose to his lips. The pressures and aches stopped. He embraced Dobbe, pressed her to himself, was again a man as in his youth. Dobbe was faint with delight; crying, she murmured things to him in a Warsaw slang which he did not understand. Later, Dr. Fischelson slipped off into the deep sleep young men know. He dreamed that he was in Switzerland and that he was climbing mountains—running, falling, flying. At dawn he opened his eyes; it seemed to him that someone had blown into his ears. Dobbe was snoring. Dr. Fischelson quietly got out of bed. In his long nightshirt he approached the window, walked up the steps and looked out in wonder. Market Street was asleep, breathing with a deep stillness. The gas lamps were flickering. The black shutters on the stores were fastened with iron bars. A cool breeze was blowing. Dr. Fischelson looked up at the sky. The black arch was thickly sown with stars—there were green, red, yellow, blue stars; there were large ones and small ones, winking and steady ones. There were those that were clustered in dense groups and those that were alone. In the higher sphere, apparently, little notice was taken of the fact that a certain Dr. Fischelson had in his declining days married someone called Black Dobbe. Seen from above even the Great War was nothing but a temporary play of the modes. The myriads of fixed stars continued to travel their destined courses in unbounded space. The comets, planets, satellites, asteroids kept circling these shining centers. Worlds were born and died in cosmic upheavals. In the chaos of nebulae, primeval matter was being formed. Now and again a star tore loose, and swept across the sky, leaving behind it a fiery streak. It was the month of August when there are showers of meteors. Yes, the divine substance was extended and had neither beginning nor end; it was absolute, indivisible, eternal, without duration, infinite in its attributes. Its waves and bubbles danced in the universal cauldron, seething with change, following the unbroken chain of causes and effects, and he, Dr. Fischelson, with his unavoidable fate, was part of this. The doctor closed his eyelids and allowed the breeze to cool the sweat on his forehead and stir the hair of his beard. He breathed deeply of the midnight air, supported his shaky hands on the window sill and murmured, "Divine Spinoza, forgive me. I have become a fool."

QUESTIONS

1. Characterize Dr. Fischelson. In what respects is he a person of true distinction? In what respects is he foolish or absurd? Is he a static or a developing character? Explain.

2. What idea does the story give of the general drift of Spinoza's philosophy? How successful is Dr. Fischelson in walking "the path of reason" with Spinoza? Are his failures a judgment on himself or on Spinoza's philosophy or both?

3. Though such knowledge is not required for an appreciation of the story, some familiarity with Spinoza's life and central ideas deepens one's enjoyment of it. To what extent does Dr. Fischelson model his life on Spinoza's? How many of Spinoza's central ideas does the story refer or allude to? How does Dr. Fischelson differ from Spinoza as a thinker?

4. In what year do the main events of the story take place? Does the historical background have any importance to the story?

5. Characterize Black Dobbe. In what ways are she and Dr. Fischelson opposites? In what ways are they alike?

6. In what ways is Dr. Fischelson's marriage ironic? In what ways is it appropriate?

7. Does this story have a happy ending? Evaluate Dr. Fischelson's final words.

Paul Gallico

THE ENCHANTED DOLL

Today is the anniversary of that afternoon in April a year ago that I first saw the strange and alluring doll in the window of Abe Sheftel's stationery, cigar, and toy shop on Third Avenue near Fifteenth Street, just around the corner from my office, where the white plate with the black lettering on my doors reads: SAMUEL AMONY, M.D.

And I feel impelled to try to set down on paper some record of the things that resulted from that meeting, though I am afraid it will be a crudely told story, for I am not a writer, but a doctor.

I remember just how it was that day: the first hint of spring wafted across the East River, mingling with the soft-coal smoke from the factories and the street smells of the poor neighborhood. The wagon of an itinerant flower seller at the curb was all gay with tulips, hyacinths, and boxes of pansies, and near by a hurdy-gurdy was playing "Some Enchanted Evening."

As I turned the corner and came abreast of Sheftel's, I was made once more aware of the poor collection of toys in the dusty window, and I remembered the approaching birthday of a small niece of mine in Cleveland, to whom I was in the habit of despatching modest gifts.

Therefore, I stopped and examined the window to see if there might be anything appropriate and browsed through the bewildering array of unappealing objects—a red toy fire engine, crudely made lead soldiers, cheap baseballs, gloves and bats, all a-jumble with boxes of withered cigars, cartons of cigarettes, bottles of ink, pens, pencils, gritty stationery, and garish cardboard cut-out advertisements for soft drinks.

And thus it was my eyes eventually came to rest upon the doll tucked away in one corner. She was overshadowed by the surrounding articles and barely visible through the grime of decades collected on Abe's window, but I could see that she was made all of rag, with a painted face, and represented a little girl with the strangest, tenderest, most alluring and winsome expression on her face.

I could not wholly make her out, due to the shadows and the film through which I was looking, but I was aware that a tremendous impression had been made upon me, that somehow a contact had been established between her and myself, almost as though she had called to me. It was exactly as though I had run into a person as one does sometimes with a stranger in a crowded room with whose personality one is indelibly impressed and which lingers on.

I went inside and replied to Abe's greeting of "Hello, Doc, what can I do for you? You out of tobacco again?" with: "Let me see that rag doll, the one in the corner by the roller skates. I've got to send something to a kid niece of mine. . . ."

Abe's eyebrows went up into his bald head and he came around the counter, the edges of his open vest flapping. "That doll?" he said. "That doll now could cost quite a bit of money, maybe more than you would want to pay. She's special made."

Nevertheless he took her from the window and placed her in my hands and here it was that I received my second shock, for she had the most amazing and wonderful quality. No more than a foot long, she was as supple and live to the touch as though there were flesh and bones beneath the clothes instead of rag stuffing.

It was indeed, as Abe had said, hand-made, and its creator had endowed it with such lifelike features and grace that it gave one the curious feeling of an alter presence. Yet there was even more than that to her. Could a doll be said to have sex appeal in the length and proportions of her legs, the shape of her head, the swirl of her skirt over her hips? Was it possible for an emotion to have been sewn into the seams marking the contours of the tiny figure? For though I am young, I have seen too much, both in peace and war, to be either sentimental or subject to hallucination. Yet to hold this doll was to feel a contact with something warm, mysterious, feminine, and wonderful. I felt that if I did not put her down I would become moved by her in some unbearable fashion.

I laid her on the counter. "What's the price, Abe?"

"Fifteen dollars."

It was my turn to look astonished. Abe said, "I told you, didn't I? I only make a dollar on it. I don't need to make no profit on you, Doc. You can have it for fourteen. Uptown in some a them big stores she gets as much as twenny and twenny-fi dollars for 'em."

"Who is 'she'?"

"Some woman over on Thirteenth Street who makes 'em. She been there about a couple of years. She buys her cigarettes and papers here. That's how I come to get one once in a while. They sell quick."

"What is she like? What is her name?"

Abe replied, "I dunno, exactly—something like 'Calamity.' She's a big, flashy, red-haired dame, but hard. Wears a lot of furs. Not your type, Doc."

I couldn't understand it, or make the connection between the woman Abe described and the exquisite little creature that lay on the counter. "I'll take her," I said. It was more than I could afford, for my practice is among the poor, where one goes really to learn medicine. Yet I could not leave her lying there on the counter amidst the boxes of chewing gum, matches, punchboards, and magazines, for she was a creation, and something, some part of a human soul, had gone into the making of her. I counted out $14 and felt like a fool.

I felt even more of one when I had got her home and was repacking her to send her off to Cleveland. Again I felt that powerful impact of the tiny figure and realized that I had the greatest reluctance to part with her. She filled the small bedroom I had behind my consulting room with her presence and brought an indescribable longing to my throat and a sadness to my heart. For the first time since I had come out of the Army and had taken up practice I realized that I was lonely and that sometimes the satisfaction to be derived through helping the sick is not enough.

I said to myself, "Okay, Sam, boy. That's all you need now, is to start playing with dolls. The guys with the butterfly net will be along any moment."

When I came back from posting it to my niece, I thought that would be the end of it, but it wasn't. I couldn't get it out of my head. I thought about it often and tried to reconcile the emotion it had aroused with what Abe had told me of the flashy red-haired woman who had created the object, but I could not. Once I was even tempted to pursue the matter, find out who she was and perhaps see her. But just at that time Virus X hit in our neighborhood and drove everything else out of my head.

It was three months or so later that my telephone rang and a woman's voice said, "Dr. Amony?"

"Yes?"

"I passed by your place once and saw your sign. Are you expensive? Do you cost a lot for a visit?"

I was repelled by the quality of the voice and the calculation in it. Nevertheless I replied, "I charge a dollar. If you are really ill and cannot afford to pay, I charge nothing."

"Okay, I could pay a dollar. But no more. You can come over. Callamit is the name. Rose Callamit, 937 East Thirteenth Street, second floor."

I did not make the connection at the time.

When I pushed the button under the name plate at that address, the buzzer sounded, the latch gave way, and I mounted two narrow, musty flights of stairs, dimly lighted and creaking. A door was opened an inch or so and I felt I was being subjected to scrutiny. Then the unpleasant voice said, "Dr. Amony? You can come in. I'm Rose Callamit."

I was startled by her. She was almost six feet tall, with brick, henna-dyed hair and an overpowering smell of cheap perfume. She had dark eyes, almond-shaped and slanted slightly in an Oriental fashion, and her mouth was full, thick-lipped, and heavily made up. There was a horrible vitality and flashy beauty about her. I placed her age at somewhere between forty-five and fifty.

The deepest shock, however, I sustained when I entered the room, which was one of those front parlor-bedrooms of the old-fashioned brownstone houses, furnished femininely, but with utter vulgarity by means of cheap prints, cheap satin cushions, and cheap glass perfume bottles. But hanging from the wall, lying about on the bed, or tossed carelessly onto the top of an old trunk were a dozen or so rag dolls, all of them different, yet, even at first glance, filled with the same indescribable appeal and charm as that of the similar little creature that had made such a profound impression upon me. I realized that I was in the presence of the creator of those astonishing puppets.

Rose Callamit said, "Tall, dark, and handsome, eh? Ain't you kind of young to be around doctoring people?"

I answered her sharply, for I was angry, uncomfortable, and irritated. The rediscovery of these beautiful and touching creatures in this cheap, disgusting atmosphere and in connection with this horrible woman had upset me. "I'm older than you think, and my looks are none of your business. If you don't want me to treat you I'd just as soon go."

"Now now, Doctor. Can't you take a compliment?"

"I'm not interested in compliments. Are you the patient?"

"No. It's my cousin. She's sick in the back room. I'll take you to her."

Before we went in, I had to know. I asked. "Do you make these dolls?"

"Yup. Why?"

I was filled with a sense of desolation. I mumbled, "I bought one once, for a niece . . ."

She laughed. "Bet you paid plenty for it. They're the rage. Okay, come on."

She led me through a connecting bath and washroom into the smaller room at the back and opened the door partly, shouting, "Essie, it's the doctor!" Then, before she pushed it wide to admit me, she cried loudly and brutally, "Don't be surprised, Doctor, she's a cripple!"

The pale girl, clad in a flannel peignoir, in the chair over by the window had a look of utter despair on her countenance. I was disgusted and angry again. The way the woman had said it was in itself crippling. She was not alone telling me that Essie was a cripple; she was reminding Essie.

I tried to observe as much and as quickly as possible, for the doctor who comes into the sickroom must hear and feel and see with his skin as well as his eyes and ears.

She could not have been more than twenty-four or twenty-five. She seemed to be nothing but a pair of huge and misery-stricken eyes and what was shocking was how low the lamp of life appeared to be burning in them. She was very ill. From that first visit I remembered the underlying sweetness of her presence, the lovely brow and shapely head, now too big for her wasted frame, the translucent, blue-veined hands, flaxen hair but limp and lusterless. She had a mouth shaped to incredible pathos, soft, pale coral, and ready to tremble.

But I saw something else that astounded me and gave my heart a great lift. She was surrounded by small tables. On one of them were paints and brushes, on others, rag material, linen, stuffing threads and needles, the paraphernalia needed for the making of dolls.

Her present illness and her deformity were two separate things, yet it was the latter that caught my attention immediately even from the door, something about the way she sat, and made me wonder. The technical name for her condition would be unintelligible to you, but if it was what it looked to me at first glance, it was curable.

I asked, "Can you walk, Essie?"

She nodded listlessly.

"Please walk to me."

"Oh don't," Essie said. "Don't make me."

The pleading in her voice touched me, but I had to be sure. I said, "I'm sorry, Essie. Please do as I ask."

She rose unsteadily from her chair and limped toward me, dragging her left leg. I was certain I was right. "That's good," I said to her, smiled encouragingly, and held out my hands to her. Something strange happened. For a moment we seemed to be caught up in one another's eyes. I felt she was being swept away and drowning in the dark pool of her misery and despair while the air all about me was shaken with the force of her silent cry to me for help. Her hands lifted toward mine for an instant in imitation of my gesture, then fell back to her side. The spell was broken.

I asked, "How long have you been this way, Essie?"

Rose Callamit said, "Oh, Essie's been a cripple for years. I didn't call you for that. She's sick. I want to know what's the matter with her."

Oh yes, she was sick. Sick unto death perhaps. I had felt that as soon as I came into the room. With my glance I invited the big, vulgar woman to leave, but she only laughed. "Not on your life, Doc. I'm staying right here. You find out what's the matter with Essie and then you can tell me."

When I had finished my examination I accompanied Rose into the front room. "Well?" she said.

I asked, "Did you know that her deformity could be cured? That with the proper treatment she could be walking normally in—"

"Shut up, you!" Her cry of rage struck like a blow against my ears. "Don't you ever dare mention that to her. I've had her looked at by people who know. I won't have any young idiot raising false hopes. If you ever do, you're through here. I want to know what's ailing her. She don't eat or sleep or work good any more. What did you find out?"

"Nothing," I replied. "I don't know. There is nothing wrong organically. But there is something terribly wrong somewhere. I want to see her again. In the meantime I'm prescribing a tonic and a stimulant. I'd like to look in again after a few days."

"You'll keep your big mouth shut about curing her cripple, you understand? Otherwise I'll get another doctor."

"All right," I said. I had to be able to return to visit Essie again. Later, we would see . . .

When I picked up my hat and bag to leave I said, "I thought you told me it was you who made those dolls."

She looked startled for a moment as though she had never expected the subject to come up again. "I do," she snapped. "I design 'em. I let the kid work at 'em sometimes to help take her mind off she's a cripple and won't ever have a man."

But when I walked out into the bright, hot July day with the kids playing hopscotch on the sidewalk and handball against the old brewery wall and traffic grinding by, my heart told me that Rose Callamit had lied and that I had found the sweet spirit behind the enchanted doll. But the cold, clammy messenger of doctor's instinct warned me also that unless I could determine the cause of her decline, that spirit would not be long for this earth.

Her name, I found out later, was Nolan, Essie Nolan, and she was slowly dying from no determinable cause. I was sure that Rose Callamit had something to do with it. Not that Rose was killing her consciously. The red-haired woman was actually frightened. She wanted Essie alive, not dead, for Essie was her source of revenue and meal ticket.

After I had made a number of visits, Rose did not even bother to keep up the pretense that it was she herself who made the dolls, and I was able to piece together something of the picture.

When Essie was fifteen, her parents had been killed in an accident which also resulted in her injury. A court had awarded her in guardianship to her only relative, the cousin, Rose Callamit. When Essie's inheritance proved meager, Rose vented her spite by harping on her deformity. Through the years of their association, the older woman had made her deeply sensitive to and ashamed of her lameness. Her theme was always, "You are a hopeless cripple. No man will ever look at you. You will never be married or have children."

When Essie came of age, her spirit apparently was broken and she was completely subjugated to the will of her cousin, for she continued to remain with her and under her sway, living a lonely and hopeless existence. It was about this time that Essie first began to make the rag dolls, and Rose, for all of her vulgarity, greed, and indolence, had the shrewdness to recognize their unique quality and irresistible appeal. After she had sold the first ones she kept Essie at it from morning until night. Some weeks she was able to clear as much as $300 or $400. None of this, as far as I was able to determine, went to Essie.

Essie was completely under the domination of Rose and was afraid of her, but it was not that which was killing her. It was something else, and I could not find out what. Nor was I ever allowed to see her alone. Rose was always present. Never had I been so conscious of the difference between good and evil as in that room with the girl, whose poor suppressed nature fluttered so feebly in her wasted body, and that gross, thick-lipped woman with the greedy eyes and patchouli smell who exhaled the odor of wickedness.

I did not mention my belief in the possibility of cure for Essie's lameness. It was more important to discover immediately what it was that was killing her. Rose would not let her be moved to a hospital. She would not spare the money.

For ten days I thought I had arrested the process that was destroying Essie before my eyes. I stopped her work on the dolls. I brought her some books to read, some sweets, and a bottle of sherry. When I returned for my next visit, she smiled at me for the first time, and the tremulousness, longing, hunger, the womanliness and despair of the smile would have broken a heart of stone.

"That's better," I said. "Another ten days of no work. Rest, sleep, read. Then we'll see."

But Rose Callamit glowered and there was an unpleasant expression about her mouth. Her huge, overpowering bulk seemed to fill the room with hatred.

The next time I came to call she was waiting for me in her own room. She had seven one dollar bills in her hand. She said, "Okay, Doc. That's all. We don't need you any more."

"But Essie—"

"Essie's okay. Fit as a fiddle. So long, Doc . . ."

My eyes wandered to the old trunk in the corner. There were three new dolls lying on top of it. Was it only my imagination, or was there yet a new quality to these mute, bewitched figurines? Was each in its way a birth and a death in one, a greeting to the beauties, desires, and pleasures of life and at the same time a farewell?

I had the most powerful impulse to push the monstrous woman aside and crash through the doors to see my patient. But the habits of medical ethics are too hard to break. When a physician is dismissed, it is his duty to go unless he has reason to suspect that his patient is meeting with foul play. I had no such reason. I had failed to determine the cause of Essie's illness; Rose was undoubtedly calling in another doctor, for she needed Essie's work for an easy living and would unquestionably try to protect such a meal ticket.

Thus, with great heaviness of heart, I departed. But I thought about Essie night and day.

It was shortly after this that I became ill myself. Imperceptibly at first, then finally noticeably: loss of appetite, loss of weight, lethargy, irritability, at night a half a degree to a degree of temperature, moments of weakness when I felt as though somehow I could not go on with my work. I let Dr. Saul up at the hospital go over me. He thumped and pounded and listened, the obvious routine, and reported, "Nothing wrong with you, Sam. Take it a little easier. You've probably been overworking. Nature's protest."

But I knew it wasn't that.

I began to look shocking; my skin was losing its tone, my cheekbones were beginning to show, and I was hollow-eyed from loss of sleep. I did not like the look in my eyes, or the expression about my mouth. Sometimes my nights and my dreams were filled with fever and in them I saw Essie struggling to reach me while Rose Callamit held her imprisoned in her ugly, shapeless arms. I had never been free from worry over failure to diagnose Essie's case.

My whole faith in myself as a doctor was badly shaken. A desperately stricken human being had called upon me for help and I had failed. I could not even help myself. What right had I to call myself a doctor? All through one awful night of remorse and reproach the phrase burned through my brain as though written in fire:

"Physician, heal thyself!"

Yes, heal myself before I was fit to heal others. But heal myself from what? If anything, my symptoms resembled those of Essie Nolan. Essie! Essie! Essie! Always Essie!

Was Essie my sickness? Had she always been from the first moment that I had encountered that extension of her enchanted spirit embodied in the rag doll in Abe Sheftel's shop?

And as morning grayed my back-yard window and the elevated train thundered by in increasing tempo, I knew my disease. I was in love with Essie Nolan. When I could couple the words "love" and "Essie," when I could look up and cry "I love Essie Nolan! I want her! I need her person and her soul, forever at my side!" it was as though I could feel the fire of healing medicine glowing through my veins.

It had always been Essie, the warmth and yearning need, the tenderness that she expressed with her presence, and the odd, offbeat beauty of her, too, a beauty that would only reach its full flower when I had cured and restored her in every way.

For now, as the scales fell from my eyes and my powers were released again through the acknowledging and freeing inside of me of the hunger, love, and compassion I had for her, I knew the sickness of Essie Nolan in full, to its last pitiful detail, and what I must do and why I must see her alone if only for a few minutes if she were not to be lost to me and to the world forever.

That morning I telephoned Abe Sheftel and said, "This is Dr. Amony, Abe. Will you do something for me?"

"Are you kiddin'? After what you done for my boy—you name it."

"Look here! You remember Rose Callamit? The doll woman? Yes. The next time she comes into the store, find some means of telephoning me. Then hold her there, somehow. Talk, or do something, anything to make her stay there a little. I need twenty minutes. Okay? Got it? I'll bless you the rest of my life."

I was in a sweat for fear it would happen while I was on an outside call, and each time I returned to the office that day I stopped by the store, but Abe would merely shake his head. Then, at five o'clock in the afternoon the phone rang. It was Abe. He said merely, "It could be now," and hung up.

It took me no more than a minute or two to run the few blocks to the brownstone house where Essie lived and press the buzzer under another name plate. When the door clicked open I went upstairs, two steps at a time. If the door was locked I would have to get the landlady. But I was in luck. Rose had expected to be gone only a few moments, apparently, and it was open. I hurried through the connecting bath and, entering the back room, found Essie.

There was so little of her left.

She was sitting up in bed, but now the absolute pallor had been replaced with two red fever spots that burned in the middle of her cheeks, a danger sign more deadly than the wastage of her hands and body. She was still surrounded by the paints and bits of colored cloth and threads, as though she did not wish to die before she had put together one more image, one more dream, one last reflection of the sweet self that life had apparently so cruelly doomed to wither.

She looked up when I came in, startled out of her lethargy. She had expected it to be Rose. Her hand went to her breast and she said my name. Not "Dr. Amony," but my given one—"Samuel!"

I cried, "Essie! Thank God I'm in time. I came to help you. I know what it is that has been . . . making you ill . . ."

She was in that state where nothing escaped her. She felt my hesitation and knew I had avoided saying ". . . that is killing you," for she whispered, "Does it matter now?"

I said, "There's still time, Essie. I know your secret. I know how to make you well. But you must listen to me while I tell you. Your life depends on it."

A change came over her. She closed her eyes for an instant and murmured, "No. Don't, please. Let me go. I don't want to know. It will be over soon."

I had not thought that she might be unwilling or unable to face it. And yet I had to go on now. I sat down and took her hand.

"Essie. Please listen. Give me your mind. When a body is undernourished we give it food; when it is anemic, we supply blood; when it lacks iron or hormones we give it tonic. But you have had a different kind of leakage. You have been drained dry of something else without which the soul and body cannot be held together."

Her eyes opened and I saw that they were filled with horror and a glazing fear. She seemed about to lose consciousness as she begged, "No! Don't say it!"

I thought perhaps she might die then and there. But the only hope for her, for us both, was to go on.

"Essie! My brave, dear girl. It is nothing so terrible. You need not be afraid. It is only that you have been drained of love. Look at me, Essie!"

My eyes caught and held her. I willed her to remain alive, to stay with me, to hear me out. "See, Essie, a person has just so great a reservoir of love to expend. It is drawn upon through life and must ever be replenished with tenderness, affection, warmth, and hope. Thus the supply is always renewed. But yours has been emptied until there was nothing left."

I could not be sure that she still heard me. "It was Rose Callamit," I continued. "She took away your every hope of life, love, and fulfillment. But what she did later to you was a much blacker crime. For she took away *your children*!"

There, it was out! Had I killed her? Had it been I who loved her beyond words who had administered the death blow? And yet I thought I saw a flicker of life in those poor, stricken eyes, and even perhaps the faintest reflection of relief.

"Oh yes, they were your children, Essie, those enchanted creatures you created. When you were convinced that you had lost your chance to be a woman, you compensated for it by embodying your hopes, your dreams, and, like every creator, whether mother or artist, a piece of your heart went into each of the dolls you made. You created them with love; you loved them like your own children and then each one was taken from you at birth by that money-hungry monster and nothing was given to you to replace them. And so you continued to take them from your heart, your tissue, and your blood until your life was being drained away from you. Persons can die from lack of love."

Essie stirred. Her head beneath the flaxen hair moved ever so slightly. The glaze passed from her eyes. I thought I felt the response of faint pressure from the cold hand in mine.

I cried, "But you won't, Essie, because I am here to tell you that I love you, to refill you to overflowing with all that has been taken from you. Do you hear me, Essie? I am not your doctor. I am a man telling you that I love you and cannot live without you."

I caught her incredulous whisper. "Love me? But I am a cripple."

"If you were a thousand times a cripple, I would only love you a thousand times more. But it isn't true. Rose Callamit lied to you. You can be cured. In a year I will have you walking like any other girl."

For the first time since I had known her I saw tears in her eyes and a tinge of color to her lovely brow. Then she lifted her arms to me with an utter and loving simplicity.

I picked her up out of the bed, with the blanket wrapped around her. She had no weight at all: she was like a bird. And she clung to me with a kind of sweet desperation, so that I wondered where the strength in her arms came from and the glow of her cheek against mine; she who but a moment ago had seemed so close to death.

A door slammed. Another crashed open. Rose Callamit stormed into the room. I felt Essie shudder with the old fear and bury her face in my shoulder.

But Rose was too late. It was all over. There was nothing she could do any more, and she knew it. There was not even a word spoken as I walked past her then and there carrying my burden held closely to me and went out the door and down into the street.

August had come to New York. Heat was shimmering from the melting pavements; no air stirred; water from the hydrants was flushing the streets and kids were bathing in the flow, screaming and shouting, as I carried Essie home.

That was three years ago and I am writing this on an anniversary. Essie is busy with our son and is preparing to welcome our second-to-be-born. She does not make dolls now. There is no need.

We have many kinds of anniversaries, but this is the one I celebrate privately and give humble thanks for—the day when I first saw and fell in love with the message from Essie's soul imprisoned in the enchanted doll that cried out to me from the grimy window of Abe Sheftel's shop on Third Avenue.

QUESTIONS

1. In what ways does the opening setting (paragraphs 3, 5, 6) set the tone for the story? Describe its tone.

2. Though the title suggests a fairy tale, nothing supernatural happens in the story. Is the story a fairy tale or is it realistic? Consider both events and characters in your answer.

3. Characterize Samuel, Rose, and Essie. Are they round or flat characters?

4. Comment on the protagonist's declaration, "I have seen too much, both in peace and war, to be either sentimental or subject to hallucination." Are his actions and responses in the story those of a war veteran?

5. What function is served by Abe Sheftel's inaccurate memory of Rose Callamit's name?

6. Does the story contain any coincidences?

7. In both this story and "The Spinoza of Market Street" boy meets girl and marries her. In both, at the time of their meeting, one of the lovers is apparently near death, and a kind of "miracle" is accomplished. In both, the action is set in a large city. Find other comparisons between the two stories; then explore their differences. Which says more about human nature and the human condition? Which says what it says more convincingly? Which story is sentimental?

CHAPTER EIGHT

Fantasy

Truth in fiction is not the same as fidelity to fact. Fiction after all, is the opposite of fact. It is a game of make-believe—though, at its best, a serious game—in which the author conceives characters and situations in his mind and sets them down on paper. And yet these characters and situations, if deeply imagined, may embody truths of human life and behavior more fully and significantly than any number of the miscellaneous facts reported on the front pages of our morning papers. The purpose of the interpretive artist is to communicate truths by means of imagined facts.

The story writer begins, then, by saying "Let's suppose. . . ." "Let's suppose," for instance, "that a shy, timid, but romantically imaginative young man is invited to a party at which he receives an eager kiss in the dark from an unknown young lady who has mistaken him for her lover." From this initial supposition the author goes on to write a story ("The Kiss") which, though entirely imaginary in the sense that it never happened, nevertheless reveals convincingly to us some truths of human behavior.

But now, what if the author goes a step further and supposes not just something that might very well have happened though it didn't but something highly improbable—something that could happen, say, only as the result of a very surprising coincidence? What if he begins, "Let's suppose that a woman-hater and a charming female siren find themselves alone on a desert island"? This initial supposition causes us to stretch our imaginations a bit further, but is not this situation just as capable of revealing human truths as the former? The psychologist puts a rat in a maze (certainly an improbable situation for a rat), observes his reactions to the maze, and discovers some truth of rat-nature. The author may put his imagined characters on an imagined desert island, imaginatively study their reactions, and reveal some truth of human nature. The improbable initial situation may yield as much truth as the probable one.

From the improbable it is but one step further to the impossible (as we know it in this life). Why should not our author begin "Let's suppose that a miser and his termagant wife find themselves in hell" or "Let's suppose that a timid but ambitious man discovers how to make himself invisible" or "Let's suppose that a primitive scapegoat ritual still survives in contemporary America." Could not these situations also be used to exhibit human truth?

The nonrealistic story, or **FANTASY**, is one that transcends the bounds of known reality. Commonly, it conjures up a strange and marvelous world, which one enters by falling down a rabbit-hole or climbing up a beanstalk or getting shipwrecked in an unfamiliar ocean or dreaming a dream; or else it introduces strange powers and occult forces into the world of ordinary reality, allowing one to foretell the future or communicate with the dead or separate his mind from his body or turn himself into a monster. It introduces human beings into a world where the ordinary laws of nature are suspended or superseded and where the landscape and its creatures are unfamiliar, or it introduces ghosts or fairies or dragons or werewolves or talking animals or invaders from Mars or miraculous occurrences into the normal world of human beings. Fables, ghost stories, science fiction—all are types of fantasy.

Fantasy may be escapist or interpretive, true or false. The space ship on its way to a distant planet may be filled with stock characters or with human beings. The author may be interested chiefly in exhibiting its mechanical marvels or providing thrills and adventures, or he may use it as a means of creating exacting circumstances in which human behavior may be sharply observed and studied. Fantasy, like other elements of fiction, may be employed sheerly for its own sake or as a means of communicating an important insight. The appeal may be to our taste for the strange or to our need for the true. The important point to remember is that truth in fiction is not to be identified with realism in method. Stories that never depart from the three dimensions of actuality may distort and falsify life. Stories that fly on the wings of fantasy may be vehicles for truth. Fantasy may convey truth through symbolism or allegory or simply by providing an unusual setting for the observation of human beings. Some of the world's greatest works of literature have been partly or wholly fantasy: *The Odyssey, The Book of Job, The Divine Comedy, The Tempest, Pilgrim's Progress, Gulliver's Travels,*

Faust, Alice in Wonderland. All these have had important things to say about the human condition.

We must not judge a story, then, by whether or not it stays within the limits of the possible. Rather, we begin by granting every story a "Let's suppose"—an initial assumption. The initial assumption may be plausible or implausible. The writer may begin with an ordinary, everyday situation or with a far-fetched, improbable coincidence. Or he may be allowed to suspend a law of nature or to create a marvelous being or machine or place. But once we have granted him his impossibility, we have a right to demand probability in his treatment of it. The realm of fantasy is not a realm in which *all* laws of logic are suspended. We need to ask, too, for what reason the story employs the element of fantasy. Is it used simply for its own strangeness or for thrills or surprises or laughs? Or is it used to illumine the more normal world of our experience? What is the purpose of the author's invention? Is it, like a roller coaster, simply a machine for producing thrills? Or does it, like an observation balloon, provide a vantage point from which we may view the world?

D. H. Lawrence

THE ROCKING-HORSE WINNER

There was a woman who was beautiful, who started with all the advantages, yet she had no luck. She married for love, and the love turned to dust. She had bonny children, yet she felt they had been thrust upon her, and she could not love them. They looked at her coldly, as if they were finding fault with her. And hurriedly she felt she must cover up some fault in herself. Yet what it was that she must cover up she never knew. Nevertheless, when her children were present, she always felt the centre of her heart go hard. This troubled her, and in her manner she was all the more gentle and anxious for her children, as if she loved them very much. Only she herself knew that at the centre of her heart was a hard little place that could not feel love, no, not for anybody. Everybody else said of her: "She is such a good mother. She adores her children." Only she herself, and her children themselves, knew it was not so. They read it in each other's eyes.

There were a boy and two little girls. They lived in a pleasant house, with a garden, and they had discreet servants, and felt themselves superior to anyone in the neighbourhood.

Although they lived in style, they felt always an anxiety in the house. There was never enough money. The mother had a small income, and the father had a small income, but not nearly enough for the social position which they had to keep up. The father went into town to some office. But though he had good prospects, these prospects never materialized. There was always the grinding sense of the shortage of money, though the style was always kept up.

At last the mother said: "I will see if I can't make something." But she did not know where to begin. She racked her brains, and tried this thing and the other, but could not find anything successful. The failure made deep lines come into her face. Her children were growing up, they would have to go to school. There must be more money, there must be more money. The father, who was always very handsome and expensive in his tastes, seemed as if he never would be able to do anything worth doing. And the mother, who had a great belief in herself, did not succeed any better, and her tastes were just as expensive.

And so the house came to be haunted by the unspoken phrase: There must be more money! There must be more money! The children could hear it all the time, though nobody said it aloud. They heard it at Christmas, when the expensive and splendid toys filled the nursery. Behind the shining modern rocking horse, behind the smart doll's-house, a voice would start whispering: "There must be more money! There must be more money!" And the children would stop playing, to listen for a moment. They would look into each other's eyes, to see if they had all heard. And each one saw in the eyes of the other two that they too had heard. "There must be more money! There must be more money!"

It came whispering from the springs of the still-swaying rocking horse, and even the horse, bending his wooden, champing head, heard it. The big doll, sitting so pink and smirking in her new pram, could hear it quite plainly, and seemed to be smirking all the more self-consciously because of it. The foolish puppy, too, that took the place of the Teddy bear, he was looking so extraordinarily foolish for no other reason but that he heard the secret whisper all over the house: "There must be more money!"

Yet nobody ever said it aloud. The whisper was everywhere, and therefore no one spoke it. Just as no one ever says: "We are breathing!" in spite of the fact that breath is coming and going all the time.

"Mother," said the boy Paul one day, "why don't we keep a car of our own? Why do we always use uncle's, or else a taxi?"

"Because we're the poor members of the family," said the mother.

"But why are we, mother?"

"Well—I suppose," she said slowly and bitterly, "it's because your father has no luck."

The boy was silent for some time.

"Is luck money, mother?" he asked, rather timidly.

"No, Paul. Not quite. It's what causes you to have money."

"Oh!" said Paul vaguely. "I thought when Uncle Oscar said filthy lucker, it meant money."

"Filthy lucre does mean money," said the mother. "But it's lucre, not luck."

"Oh!" said the boy. "Then what is luck, mother?"

"It's what causes you to have money. If you're lucky you have money. That's why it's better to be born lucky than rich. If you're rich, you may lose your money. But if you're lucky, you will always get more money."

"Oh! Will you? And is father not lucky?"

"Very unlucky, I should say," she said bitterly.

The boy watched her with unsure eyes.

"Why?" he asked.

"I don't know. Nobody ever knows why one person is lucky and another unlucky."

"Don't they? Nobody at all? Does nobody know?"

"Perhaps God. But He never tells."

"He ought to, then. And aren't you lucky either, mother?"

"I can't be, if I married an unlucky husband."

"But by yourself, aren't you?"

"I used to think I was, before I married. Now I think I am very unlucky indeed."

"Why?"

"Well—never mind! Perhaps I'm not really," she said.

The child looked at her, to see if she meant it. But he saw, by the lines of her mouth, that she was only trying to hide something from him.

"Well, anyhow," he said stoutly, "I'm a lucky person."

"Why?" said his mother, with a sudden laugh.

He stared at her. He didn't even know why he had said it.

"God told me," he asserted, brazening it out.

"I hope He did, dear!" she said, again with a laugh, but rather bitter.

"He did, mother!"

"Excellent!" said the mother, using one of her husband's exclamations.

The boy saw she did not believe him; or, rather, that she paid no attention to his assertion. This angered him somewhat, and made him want to compel her attention.

He went off by himself, vaguely, in a childish way, seeking for the clue to "luck." Absorbed, taking no heed of other people, he went about with a sort of stealth, seeking inwardly for luck. He wanted luck, he wanted it, he wanted it. When the two girls were playing dolls in the nursery, he would sit on his big rocking horse, charging madly into space, with a frenzy that made the little girls peer at him uneasily. Wildly the horse careered, the waving dark hair of the boy tossed, his eyes had a strange glare in them. The little girls dared not speak to him.

When he had ridden to the end of his mad little journey, he climbed down and stood in front of his rocking horse, staring fixedly into its lowered face. Its red mouth was slightly open, its big eye was wide and glassy-bright.

"Now!" he would silently command the snorting steed. "Now, take me to where there is luck! Now take me!"

And he would slash the horse on the neck with the little whip he had asked Uncle Oscar for. He knew the horse could take him to where there was luck, if only he forced it. So he would mount again, and start on his furious ride, hoping at last to get there. He knew he could get there.

"You'll break your horse, Paul!" said the nurse.

"He's always riding like that! I wish he'd leave off!" said his elder sister Joan.

But he only glared down on them in silence. Nurse gave him up. She could make nothing of him. Anyhow he was growing beyond her.

One day his mother and his Uncle Oscar came in when he was on one of his furious rides. He did not speak to them.

"Hallo, you young jockey! Riding a winner?" said his uncle.

"Aren't you growing too big for a rocking horse? You're not a very little boy any longer, you know," said his mother.

But Paul only gave a blue glare from his big, rather close-set eyes. He would speak to nobody when he was in full tilt. His mother watched him with an anxious expression on her face.

At last he suddenly stopped forcing his horse into the mechanical gallop, and slid down.

"Well, I got there!" he announced fiercely, his blue eyes still flaring, and his sturdy long legs straddling apart.

"Where did you get to?" asked his mother.

"Where I wanted to go," he flared back at her.

"That's right, son!" said Uncle Oscar. "Don't you stop till you get there. What's the horse's name?"

"He doesn't have a name," said the boy.

"Gets on without all right?" asked the uncle.

"Well, he has different names. He was called Sansovino last week."

"Sansovino, eh? Won the Ascot. How did you know his name?"

"He always talks about horse races with Bassett," said Joan.

The uncle was delighted to find that his small nephew was posted with all the racing news. Bassett, the young gardener, who had been wounded in the left foot in the war and had got his present job through Oscar Cresswell, whose batman he had been, was a perfect blade of the "turf." He lived in the racing events, and the small boy lived with him.

Oscar Cresswell got it all from Bassett.

"Master Paul comes and asks me, so I can't do more than tell him, sir," said Bassett, his face terribly serious, as if he were speaking of religious matters.

"And does he ever put anything on a horse he fancies?"

"Well—I don't want to give him away—he's a young sport, a fine sport, sir. Would you mind asking him yourself? He sort of takes a pleasure in it, and perhaps he'd feel I was giving him away, sir, if you don't mind."

Bassett was serious as a church.

The uncle went back to his nephew, and took him off for a ride in the car.

"Say, Paul, old man, do you ever put anything on a horse?" the uncle asked.

The boy watched the handsome man closely.

"Why, do you think I oughtn't to?" he parried.

"Not a bit of it! I thought perhaps you might give me a tip for the Lincoln."

The car sped on into the country, going down to Uncle Oscar's place in Hampshire.

"Honour bright?" said the nephew.

"Honour bright, son!" said the uncle.

"Well, then, Daffodil."

"Daffodil! I doubt it, sonny. What about Mirza?"

"I only know the winner," said the boy. "That's Daffodil."

"Daffodil, eh?"

There was a pause. Daffodil was an obscure horse comparatively.

"Uncle!"

"Yes, son?"

"You won't let it go any further, will you? I promised Bassett."

"Bassett be damned, old man! What's he got to do with it?"

"We're partners. We've been partners from the first. Uncle, he lent me my first five shillings, which I lost. I promised him, honour bright, it was only between me and him; only you gave me that ten-shilling note I started winning with, so I thought you were lucky. You won't let it go any further, will you?"

The boy gazed at his uncle from those big, hot, blue eyes, set rather close together. The uncle stirred and laughed uneasily.

"Right you are, son! I'll keep your tip private. Daffodil, eh? How much are you putting on him?"

"All except twenty pounds," said the boy. "I keep that in reserve."

The uncle thought it a good joke.

"You keep twenty pounds in reserve, do you, you young romancer? What are you betting, then?"

"I'm betting three hundred," said the boy gravely. "But it's between you and me, Uncle Oscar! Honour bright?"

The uncle burst into a roar of laughter.

"It's between you and me all right, you young Nat Gould," he said, laughing. "But where's your three hundred?"

"Bassett keeps it for me. We're partners."

"You are, are you! And what is Bassett putting on Daffodil?"

"He won't go quite as high as I do, I expect. Perhaps he'll go a hundred and fifty."

"What, pennies?" laughed the uncle.

"Pounds," said the child, with a surprised look at his uncle. "Bassett keeps a bigger reserve than I do."

Between wonder and amusement Uncle Oscar was silent. He pursued the matter no further, but he determined to take his nephew with him to the Lincoln races.

"Now, son," he said, "I'm putting twenty on Mirza, and I'll put five for you on any horse you fancy. What's your pick?"

"Daffodil, uncle."

"No, not the fiver on Daffodil!"

"I should if it was my own fiver," said the child.

"Good! Good! Right you are! A fiver for me and a fiver for you on Daffodil."

The child had never been to a race meeting before, and his eyes were blue fire. He pursed his mouth tight, and watched. A Frenchman just in front had put his money on Lancelot. Wild with excitement, he flayed his arms up and down, yelling "Lancelot! Lancelot!" in his French accent.

Daffodil came in first, Lancelot second, Mirza third. The child, flushed and with eyes blazing, was curiously serene. His uncle brought him four five-pound notes, four to one.

"What am I to do with these?" he cried, waving them before the boy's eyes.

"I suppose we'll talk to Bassett," said the boy. "I expect I have fifteen hundred now; and twenty in reserve; and this twenty."

His uncle studied him for some moments.

"Look here, son!" he said. "You're not serious about Bassett and that fifteen hundred, are you?"

"Yes, I am. But it's between you and me, uncle. Honour bright!"

"Honour bright all right, son! But I must talk to Bassett."

"If you'd like to be a partner, uncle, with Bassett and me, we could all be partners. Only, you'd have to promise, honour bright, uncle, not to let it go beyond us three. Bassett and I are lucky, and you must be lucky, because it was your ten shillings I started winning with . . ."

Uncle Oscar took both Bassett and Paul into Richmond Park for an afternoon, and there they talked.

"It's like this, you see, sir," Bassett said. "Master Paul would get me talking about racing events, spinning yarns, you know, sir. And he was always keen on knowing if I'd made or if I'd lost. It's about a year since, now, that I put five shillings on Blush of Dawn for him—and we lost. Then the luck turned, with that ten shillings he had from you, that we put on Singhalese. And since that time, it's been pretty steady, all things considering. What do you say, Master Paul?"

"We're all right when we're sure," said Paul. "It's when we're not quite sure that we go down."

"Oh, but we're careful then," said Bassett.

"But when are you sure?" smiled Uncle Oscar.

"It's Master Paul, sir," said Bassett, in a secret, religious voice. "It's as if he had it from heaven. Like Daffodil, now, for the Lincoln. That was as sure as eggs."

"Did you put anything on Daffodil?" asked Oscar Cresswell.

"Yes, sir, I made my bit."

"And my nephew?"

Bassett was obstinately silent, looking at Paul.

"I made twelve hundred, didn't I, Bassett? I told uncle I was putting three hundred on Daffodil."

"That's right," said Bassett, nodding.

"But where's the money?" asked the uncle.

"I keep it safe locked up, sir. Master Paul he can have it any minute he likes to ask for it."

"What, fifteen hundred pounds?"

"And twenty! and forty, that is, with the twenty he made on the course."

"It's amazing!" said the uncle.

"If Master Paul offers you to be partners, sir, I would, if I were you; if you'll excuse me," said Bassett.

Oscar Cresswell thought about it.

"I'll see the money," he said.

They drove home again, and sure enough, Bassett came round to the garden-house with fifteen hundred pounds in notes. The twenty pounds reserve was left with Joe Glee, in the Turf Commission deposit.

"You see, it's all right, uncle, when I'm sure! Then we go strong, for all we're worth. Don't we, Bassett?"

"We do that, Master Paul."

"And when are you sure?" said the uncle, laughing.

"Oh, well, sometimes I'm absolutely sure, like about Daffodil," said the boy; "and sometimes I have an idea; and sometimes I haven't even an idea, have I, Bassett? Then we're careful, because we mostly go down."

"You do, do you! And when you're sure, like about Daffodil, what makes you sure, sonny?"

"Oh, well, I don't know," said the boy uneasily. "I'm sure, you know, uncle; that's all."

"It's as if he had it from heaven, sir," Bassett reiterated.

"I should say so!" said the uncle.

But he became a partner. And when the Leger was coming on, Paul was "sure" about Lively Spark, which was a quite inconsiderable horse. The boy insisted on putting a thousand on the horse, Bassett went for five hundred, and Oscar Cresswell two hundred. Lively Spark came in first, and the betting had been ten to one against him. Paul had made ten thousand.

"You see," he said, "I was absolutely sure of him."

Even Oscar Cresswell had cleared two thousand.

"Look here, son," he said, "this sort of thing makes me nervous."

"It needn't, uncle! Perhaps I shan't be sure again for a long time."

"But what are you going to do with your money?" asked the uncle.

"Of course," said the boy, "I started it for mother. She said she had no luck, because father is unlucky, so I thought if I was lucky, it might stop whispering."

"What might stop whispering?"

"Our house. I hate our house for whispering."

"What does it whisper?"

"Why—why"—the boy fidgeted—"why, I don't know. But it's always short of money, you know, uncle."

"I know it, son, I know it."

"You know people send mother writs, don't you, uncle?"

"I'm afraid I do," said the uncle.

"And then the house whispers, like people laughing at you behind your back. It's awful, that is! I thought if I was lucky . . ."

"You might stop it," added the uncle.

The boy watched him with big blue eyes that had an uncanny cold fire in them, and he said never a word.

"Well, then!" said the uncle. "What are we doing?"

"I shouldn't like mother to know I was lucky," said the boy.

"Why not, son?"

"She'd stop me."

"I don't think she would."

"Oh!"—and the boy writhed in an odd way—"I don't want her to know, uncle."

"All right, son! We'll manage it without her knowing."

They managed it very easily. Paul, at the other's suggestion, handed over five thousand pounds to his uncle, who deposited it with the family lawyer, who was then to inform Paul's mother that a relative had put five thousand pounds into his hands, which sum was to be paid out a thousand pounds at a time, on the mother's birthday, for the next five years.

"So she'll have a birthday present of a thousand pounds for five successive years," said Uncle Oscar. "I hope it won't make it all the harder for her later."

Paul's mother had her birthday in November. The house had been "whispering" worse than ever lately, and, even in spite of his luck, Paul could not bear up against it. He was very anxious to see the effect of the birthday letter, telling his mother about the thousand pounds.

When there were no visitors, Paul now took his meals with his parents, as he was beyond the nursery control. His mother went into town nearly every day. She had discovered that she had an odd knack of sketching furs and dress materials, so she worked secretly in the studio of a friend who was the chief "artist" for the leading drapers. She drew the figures of ladies in furs and ladies in silk and sequins for the newspaper advertisements. This young woman artist earned several thousand pounds a year, but Paul's mother only made several hundreds, and she was again dissatisfied. She so wanted to be first in something, and she did not succeed, even in making sketches for drapery advertisements.

She was down to breakfast on the morning of her birthday. Paul watched her face as she read her letters. He knew the lawyer's letter. As his mother read it, her face hardened and became more expressionless. Then a cold, determined look came on her mouth. She hid the letter under the pile of others, and said not a word about it.

"Didn't you have anything nice in the post for your birthday, mother?" said Paul.

"Quite moderately nice," she said, her voice cold and absent.

She went away to town without saying more.

But in the afternoon Uncle Oscar appeared. He said Paul's mother had had a long interview with the lawyer, asking if the whole five thousand could be advanced at once, as she was in debt.

"What do you think, uncle?" said the boy.

"I leave it to you, son."

"Oh, let her have it, then! We can get some more with the other," said the boy.

"A bird in the hand is worth two in the bush, laddie!" said Uncle Oscar.

"But I'm sure to know for the Grand National; or the Lincolnshire; or else the Derby. I'm sure to know for one of them," said Paul.

So Uncle Oscar signed the agreement, and Paul's mother touched the whole five thousand. Then something very curious happened. The voices in the house suddenly went mad, like a chorus of frogs on a spring evening. There were certain new furnishings, and Paul had a tutor. He was really going to Eton, his father's school, in the following autumn. There were flowers in the winter, and a blossoming of the luxury Paul's mother had been used to. And yet the voices in the house, behind the sprays of mimosa and almond blossom, and from under the piles of iridescent cushions, simply trilled and screamed in a sort of ecstasy: "There must be more money! Oh-h-h, there must be more money. Oh, now, now-w! Now-w-w—there must be more money—more than ever! More than ever!"

It frightened Paul terribly. He studied away at his Latin and Greek with his tutors. But his intense hours were spent with Bassett. The Grand National had gone by: he had not "known," and had lost a hundred pounds. Summer was at hand. He was in agony for the Lincoln. But even for the Lincoln he didn't "know" and he lost fifty pounds. He became wild-eyed and strange, as if something were going to explode in him.

"Let it alone, son! Don't you bother about it!" urged Uncle Oscar. But it was as if the boy couldn't really hear what his uncle was saying.

"I've got to know for the Derby! I've got to know for the Derby!" the child reiterated, his big blue eyes blazing with a sort of madness.

His mother noticed how overwrought he was.

"You'd better go to the seaside. Wouldn't you like to go now to the seaside, instead of waiting? I think you'd better," she said, looking down at him anxiously, her heart curiously heavy because of him.

But the child lifted his uncanny blue eyes.

"I couldn't possibly go before the Derby, mother!" he said. "I couldn't possibly!"

"Why not?" she said, her voice becoming heavy when she was opposed. "Why not? You can still go from the seaside to see the Derby with your Uncle Oscar, if that's what you wish. No need for you to wait here. Besides, I think you care too much about these races. It's a bad sign. My family has been a gambling family, and you won't know till you grow up how much damage it has done. But it has done damage. I shall have to send Bassett away, and ask Uncle Oscar not to talk racing to you, unless you promise to be reasonable about it; go away to the seaside and forget it. You're all nerves!"

"I'll do what you like, mother, so long as you don't send me away till after the Derby," the boy said.

"Send you away from where? Just from this house?"

"Yes," he said, gazing at her.

"Why, you curious child, what makes you care about this house so much, suddenly? I never knew you loved it."

He gazed at her without speaking. He had a secret within a secret, something he had not divulged, even to Bassett or to his Uncle Oscar.

But his mother, after standing undecided and a little bit sullen for some moments, said:

"Very well, then! Don't go to the seaside till after the Derby, if you don't wish it. But promise me you won't let your nerves go to pieces. Promise you won't think so much about horse racing and events, as you call them!"

"Oh, no," said the boy casually. "I won't think much about them, mother. You needn't worry. I wouldn't worry, mother, if I were you."

"If you were me and I were you," said his mother, "I wonder what we should do!"

"But you know you needn't worry, mother, don't you?" the boy repeated.

"I should be awfully glad to know it," she said wearily.

"Oh, well, you can, you know. I mean, you ought to know you needn't worry," he insisted.

"Ought I? Then I'll see about it," she said.

Paul's secret of secrets was his wooden horse, that which had no name. Since he was emancipated from a nurse and a nursery-governess, he had had his rocking horse removed to his own bedroom at the top of the house.

"Surely, you're too big for a rocking horse!" his mother had remonstrated.

"Well, you see, mother, till I can have a real horse, I like to have some sort of animal about," had been his quaint answer.

"Do you feel he keeps you company?" she laughed.

"Oh, yes! He's very good, he always keeps me company, when I'm there," said Paul.

So the horse, rather shabby, stood in an arrested prance in the boy's bedroom.

The Derby was drawing near, and the boy grew more and more tense. He hardly heard what was spoken to him, he was very frail, and his eyes were really uncanny. His mother had sudden seizures of uneasiness about him. Sometimes, for half-an-hour, she would feel a sudden anxiety about him that was almost anguish. She wanted to rush to him at once, and know he was safe.

Two nights before the Derby, she was at a big party in town, when one of her rushes of anxiety about her boy, her first-born, gripped her heart till she could hardly speak. She fought with the feeling, might and main, for she believed in common sense. But it was too strong. She had to leave the dance and go downstairs to telephone to the country. The children's nursery-governess was terribly surprised and startled at being rung up in the night.

"Are the children all right, Miss Wilmot?"

"Oh, yes, they are quite all right."

"Master Paul? Is he all right?"

"He went to bed as right as a trivet. Shall I run up and look at him?"

"No," said Paul's mother reluctantly. "No! Don't trouble. It's all right. Don't sit up. We shall be home fairly soon." She did not want her son's privacy intruded upon.

"Very good," said the governess.

It was about one o'clock when Paul's mother and father drove up to their house. All was still. Paul's mother went to her room and slipped off her white fur coat. She had told her maid not to wait up for her. She heard her husband downstairs, mixing a whisky-and-soda.

And then, because of the strange anxiety at her heart, she stole upstairs to her son's room. Noiselessly she went along the upper corridor. Was there a faint noise? What was it?

She stood, with arrested muscles, outside his door, listening. There was a strange, heavy, and yet not loud noise. Her heart stood still. It was a soundless noise, yet rushing and powerful. Something huge, in violent, hushed motion. What was it? What in God's name was it? She ought to know. She felt that she knew the noise. She knew what it was.

Yet she could not place it. She couldn't say what it was. And on and on it went, like a madness.

Softly, frozen with anxiety and fear, she turned the door handle.

The room was dark. Yet in the space near the window, she heard and saw something plunging to and fro. She gazed in fear and amazement.

Then suddenly she switched on the light, and saw her son, in his green pyjamas, madly surging on the rocking horse. The blaze of light suddenly lit him up, as he urged the wooden horse, and lit her up, as she stood, blonde, in her dress of pale green and crystal, in the doorway.

"Paul!" she cried. "Whatever are you doing?"

"It's Malabar!" he screamed, in a powerful, strange voice. "It's Malabar."

His eyes blazed at her for one strange and senseless second, as he ceased urging his wooden horse. Then he fell with a crash to the ground, and she, all her tormented motherhood flooding upon her, rushed to gather him up.

But he was unconscious, and unconscious he remained, with some brain-fever. He talked and tossed, and his mother sat stonily by his side.

"Malabar! It's Malabar! Bassett, Bassett, I know it! It's Malabar!"

So the child cried, trying to get up and urge the rocking horse that gave him his inspiration.

"What does he mean by Malabar?" asked the heart-frozen mother.

"I don't know," said the father stonily.

"What does he mean by Malabar?" she asked her brother Oscar.

"It's one of the horses running for the Derby," was the answer.

And, in spite of himself, Oscar Cresswell spoke to Bassett, and himself put a thousand on Malabar: at fourteen to one.

The third day of the illness was critical: they were waiting for a change. The boy, with his rather long, curly hair, was tossing ceaselessly on the pillow. He neither slept nor regained consciousness, and his eyes were like blue stones. His mother sat, feeling her heart had gone, turned actually into a stone.

In the evening, Oscar Cresswell did not come, but Bassett sent a message, saying could he come up for one moment, just one moment? Paul's mother was very angry at the intrusion, but on second thought she agreed. The boy was the same. Perhaps Bassett might bring him to consciousness.

The gardener, a shortish fellow with a little brown moustache, and sharp little brown eyes, tiptoed into the room, touched his imaginary cap to Paul's mother, and stole to the bedside, staring with glittering, smallish eyes, at the tossing, dying child.

"Master Paul!" he whispered. "Master Paul! Malabar come in first all right, a clean win. I did as you told me. You've made over seventy thousand pounds, you have; you've got over eighty thousand. Malabar came in all right, Master Paul."

"Malabar! Malabar! Did I say Malabar, mother? Did I say Malabar? Do you think I'm lucky, mother? I knew Malabar, didn't I? Over eighty thousand pounds! I call that lucky, don't you, mother? Over eighty thousand pounds! I knew, didn't I know I knew? Malabar came in all right. If I ride my horse till I'm sure, then I tell you, Bassett, you can go as high as you like. Did you go for all you were worth, Bassett?"

"I went a thousand on it, Master Paul."

"I never told you, mother, that if I can ride my horse, and get there, then I'm absolutely sure—oh, absolutely! Mother, did I ever tell you? I'm lucky."

"No, you never did," said the mother.

But the boy died in the night.

And even as he lay dead, his mother heard her brother's voice saying to her: "My God, Hester, you're eighty-odd thousand to the good and a poor devil of a son to the bad. But, poor devil, poor devil, he's best gone out of a life where he rides his rocking horse to find a winner."

QUESTIONS

1. In the phraseology of its beginning ("There was a woman . . ."), its simple style, its direct characterization, and its use of the wish motif—especially that of the wish that is granted only on conditions that nullify its desirability (compare the story of King Midas)—this story has the qualities of a fairy tale. Its differences, however—in characterization, setting, and ending—are especially significant. What do they tell us about the purpose of the story?

2. Characterize the mother fully. How does she differ from the stepmothers in fairy tales like "Cinderella" and "Hansel and Gretel"? How does the boy's mistake about *filthy lucker* clarify her thinking and her motivations? Why had her love for her husband turned to dust? Why is she "unlucky"?

3. What kind of a child is Paul? What are his motivations?

4. The initial assumptions of the story are that (a) a boy might get divinatory powers by riding a rocking horse, (b) a house can whisper. Could the second of these be accepted as little more than a metaphor? Once we have granted these initial assumptions, does the story develop plausibly?

5. It is ironical that the boy's attempt to stop the whispers should only increase them. Is this a plausible irony? Why? What does it tell us about the theme of the story? Why is it ironical that the whispers should be especially audible at Christmas time? What irony is contained in the boy's last speech?

6. In what way is the boy's furious riding on the rocking horse an appropriate symbol for materialistic pursuits?

7. How might a sentimental writer have ended the story?

8. How many persons in the story are affected (or infected) by materialism?

9. What is the theme of the story?

I. L. Peretz

BONTSHA THE SILENT

Here on earth the death of Bontsha the Silent made no impression at all. Ask anyone: Who was Bontsha, how did he live, and how did he die? Did his strength slowly fade, did his heart slowly give out—or did the very marrow of his bones melt under the weight of his burdens? Who knows? Perhaps he just died from not eating—starvation, it's called.

If a horse, dragging a cart through the streets, should fall, people would run from blocks around to stare, newspapers would write about this fascinating event, a monument would be put up to mark the very spot where the horse had fallen. Had the horse belonged to a race as numerous as that of human beings, he wouldn't have been paid this honor. How many horses are there, after all? But human beings—there must be a thousand million of them!

Bontsha was a human being; he lived unknown, in silence, and in silence he died. He passed through our world like a shadow. When Bontsha was born no one took a drink of wine; there was no sound of glasses clinking. When he was confirmed he made no speech of celebration. He existed like a grain of sand at the rim of a vast ocean, amid millions of other grains of sand exactly similar, and when the wind at last lifted him up and carried him across to the other shore of that ocean, no one noticed, no one at all.

During his lifetime his feet left no mark upon the dust of the streets; after his death the wind blew away the board that marked his grave. The wife of the gravedigger came upon that bit of wood, lying far off from the grave, and she picked it up and used it to make a fire under the potatoes she was cooking; it was just right. Three days after Bontsha's death no one knew where he lay, neither the gravedigger nor anyone else. If Bontsha had had a headstone, someone, even after a hundred years, might have come across it, might still have been able to read the carved words, and his name, Bontsha the Silent, might not have vanished from this earth.

His likeness remained in no one's memory, in no one's heart. A shadow! Nothing! Finished!

In loneliness he lived, and in loneliness he died. Had it not been for the infernal human racket someone or other might have heard the sound of Bontsha's bones cracking under the weight of his burdens; someone might have glanced around and seen that Bontsha was also a human being, that he had two frightened eyes and a silent trembling mouth; someone might have noticed how, even when he bore no actual load upon his back, he still walked with his head bowed down to earth, as though while living he was already searching for his grave.

When Bontsha was brought to the hospital ten people were waiting for him to die and leave them his narrow little cot; when he was brought from the hospital to the morgue twenty were waiting to occupy his pall; when he was taken out of the morgue forty were waiting to lie where he would lie forever. Who knows how many are now waiting to snatch from him that bit of earth?

In silence he was born, in silence he lived, in silence he died—and in an even vaster silence he was put into the ground.

Ah, but in the other world it was not so! No! In Paradise the death of Bontsha was an overwhelming event. The great trumpet of the Messiah announced through the seven heavens: Bontsha the Silent is dead! The most exalted angels, with the most imposing wings, hurried, flew, to tell one another, "Do you know who has died? Bontsha! Bontsha the Silent!"

And the new, the young little angels with brilliant eyes, with golden wings and silver shoes, ran to greet Bontsha, laughing in their joy. The sound of their wings, the sound of their silver shoes, as they ran to meet him, and the bubbling of their laughter, filled all Paradise with jubilation, and God Himself knew that Bontsha the Silent was at last here.

In the great gateway to heaven Abraham, our father, stretched out his arms in welcome and benediction. "Peace be with you!" And on his old face a deep sweet smile appeared.

What, exactly, was going on up there in Paradise?

There, in Paradise, two angels came bearing a golden throne for Bontsha to sit upon, and for his head a golden crown with glittering jewels.

"But why the throne, the crown, already?" two important saints asked. "He hasn't even been tried before the heavenly court of justice to which each new arrival must submit." Their voices were touched with envy. "What's going on here, anyway?"

And the angels answered the two important saints that, yes, Bontsha's trial hadn't started yet, but it would only be a formality, even the prosecutor wouldn't dare open his mouth. Why, the whole thing wouldn't take five minutes!

"What's the matter with you?" the angels asked. "Don't you know whom you're dealing with? You're dealing with Bontsha, Bontsha the Silent!"

When the young, the singing angels encircled Bontsha in love, when Abraham, our father, embraced him again and again, as a very old friend, when Bontsha heard that a throne waited for him, and for his head a crown, and that when he would stand trial in the court of heaven no one would say a word against him—when he heard all this, Bontsha, exactly as in the other world, was silent. He was silent with fear. His heart shook, in his veins ran ice, and he knew this must all be a dream or simply a mistake.

He was used to both, to dreams and mistakes. How often, in that other world, had he not dreamed that he was wildly shoveling up money from the street, that whole fortunes lay there on the street beneath his hands—and then he would wake and find himself a beggar again, more miserable than before the dream.

How often in that other world had someone smiled at him, said a pleasant word—and then, passing and turning back for another look, had seen his mistake and spat at Bontsha.

Wouldn't that be just my luck, he thought now, and he was afraid to lift his eyes, lest the dream end, lest he awake and find himself again on earth, lying somewhere in a pit of snakes and loathesome vipers, and he was afraid to make the smallest sound, to move so much as an eyelash; he trembled and he could not hear the paeans of the angels; he could not see them as they danced in stately celebration about him; he could not answer the loving greeting of Abraham, our father, "Peace be with you!" And when at last he was led into the great court of justice in Paradise he couldn't even say "Good morning." He was paralyzed with fear.

And when his shrinking eyes beheld the floor of the courtroom of justice, his fear, if possible, increased. The floor was of purest alabaster, embedded with glittering diamonds. On such a floor stand my feet, thought Bontsha. My feet! He was beside himself with fear. Who knows, he thought, for what very rich man, or great learned rabbi, or even saint, this whole thing's meant? The rich man will arrive, and then it will all be over. He lowered his eyes; he closed them.

In his fear he did not hear when his name was called out in the pure angelic voice: "Bontsha the Silent!" Through the ringing in his ears he could make out no words, only the sound of that voice like the sound of music, of a violin.

Yet did he, perhaps, after all, catch the sound of his own name, "Bontsha the Silent?" And then the voice added, "To him that name is as becoming as a frock coat to a rich man."

What's that? What's he saying? Bontsha wondered, and then he heard an impatient voice interrupting the speech of his defending angel. "Rich man! Frock coat! No metaphors, please! And no sarcasm!"

"He never," began the defending angel again, "complained, not against God, not against man; his eye never grew red with hatred, he never raised a protest against heaven."

Bontsha couldn't understand a word, and the harsh voice of the prosecuting angel broke in once more. "Never mind the rhetoric, please!"

"His sufferings were unspeakable. Here, look upon a man who was more tormented than Job!"

Who? Bontsha wondered. Who is this man?

"Facts! Facts! Never mind the flowery business and stick to the facts, please!" the judge called out.

"When he was eight days old he was circumcised—"

"Such realistic details are unnecessary—"

"The knife slipped, and he did not even try to staunch the flow of blood—"

"—are distasteful. Simply give us the important facts."

"Even then, an infant, he was silent, he did not cry out his pain," Bontsha's defender continued. "He kept his silence, even when his mother died, and he was handed over, a boy of thirteen, to a snake, a viper—a stepmother!"

Hm, Bontsha thought, could they mean me?

"She begrudged him every bite of food, even the moldy rotten bread and the gristle of meat that she threw at him, while she herself drank coffee with cream."

"Irrelevant and immaterial," said the judge.

"For all that, she didn't begrudge him her pointed nails in his flesh—flesh that showed black and blue through the rags he wore. In winter, in the bitterest cold, she made him chop wood in the yard, barefoot! More than once were his feet frozen, and his hands, that were too young, too tender, to lift the heavy logs and chop them. But he was always silent, he never complained, not even to his father—"

"Complain! To that drunkard!" The voice of the prosecuting angel rose derisively, and Bontsha's body grew cold with the memory of fear.

"He never complained," the defender continued, "and he was always lonely. He never had a friend, never was sent to school, never was given a new suit of clothes, never knew one moment of freedom."

"Objection! Objection!" the prosecutor cried out angrily. "He's only trying to appeal to the emotions with these flights of rhetoric!"

"He was silent even when his father, raving drunk, dragged him out of the house by the hair and flung him into the winter night, into the snowy, frozen night. He picked himself up quietly from the snow and wandered into the distance where his eyes led him.

"During his wanderings he was always silent; during his agony of hunger he begged only with his eyes. And at last, on a damp spring night, he drifted to a great city, drifted there like a leaf before the wind, and on his very first night, scarcely seen, scarcely heard, he was thrown into jail. He remained silent, he never protested, he never asked, Why, what for? The doors of the jail were opened again, and, free, he looked for the most lowly filthy work, and still he remained silent.

"More terrible even than the work itself was the search for work. Tormented and ground down by pain, by the cramp of pain in an empty stomach, he never protested, he always kept silent.

"Soiled by the filth of a strange city, spat upon by unknown mouths, driven from the streets, into the roadways, where, a human beast of burden, he pursued his work, a porter, carrying the heaviest loads upon his back, scurrying between carriages, carts, and horses, staring death in the eyes every moment, he still kept silent.

"He never reckoned up how many pounds he must haul to earn a penny; how many times, with each step, he stumbled and fell for that penny. He never reckoned up how many times he almost vomited out his very soul, begging for his earnings. He never reckoned up his bad luck, the other's good luck. No, never. He remained silent. He never even demanded his own earnings; like a beggar, he waited at the door for what was rightfully his, and only in the depths of his eyes was there an unspoken longing. 'Come back later!' they'd order him; and, like a shadow, he would vanish, and then, like a shadow, would return and stand waiting, his eyes begging, imploring, for what was his. He remained silent even when they cheated him, keeping back, with one excuse or another, most of his earnings, or giving him bad money. Yes, he never protested, he always remained silent.

"Once," the defending angel went on, "Bontsha crossed the roadway to the fountain for drink, and in that moment his whole life was miraculously changed. What miracle happened to change his whole life? A splendid coach, with tires of rubber, plunged past, dragged by runaway horses; the coachman, fallen, lay in the street, his head split open. From the mouths of the frightened horses spilled foam, and in their wild eyes sparks struck like fire in a dark night, and inside the carriage sat a man, half alive, half dead, and Bontsha caught at the reins and held the horses. The man who sat inside and whose life was saved, a Jew, a philanthropist, never forgot what Bontsha had done for him. He handed him the whip of the dead driver, and Bontsha, then and there, became a coachman—no longer a common porter! And what's more, his great benefactor married him off, and what's still more, this great philanthropist himself provided a child for Bontsha to look after.

"And still Bontsha never said a word, never protested."

They mean me, I really do believe they mean me, Bontsha encouraged himself, but still he didn't have the gall to open his eyes, to look up at his judge.

"He never protested. He remained silent even when that great philanthropist shortly thereafter went into bankruptcy without even having paid Bontsha one cent of his wages.

"He was silent even when his wife ran off and left him with her helpless infant. He was silent when, fifteen years later, that same helpless infant had grown up and become strong enough to throw Bontsha out of the house."

They mean me, Bontsha rejoiced, they really mean me.

"He even remained silent," continued the defending angel, "when that same benefactor and philanthropist went out of bankruptcy, as suddenly as he'd gone into it, and still didn't pay Bontsha one cent of what he owed him. No, more than that. This person, as befits a fine gentleman who has gone through bankruptcy, again went driving the great coach with the tires of rubber, and now, now he had a new coachman, and Bontsha, again a porter in the roadway, was run over by coachman, carriage, horses. And still, in his agony, Bontsha did not cry out; he remained silent. He did not even tell the police who had done this to him. Even in the hospital, where everyone is allowed to scream, he remained silent. He lay in utter loneliness on his cot, abandoned by the doctor, by the nurse; he had not the few pennies to pay them—and he made no murmur. He was silent in that awful moment just before he was about to die, and he was silent in that very moment when he did die. And never one murmur of protest against man, never one murmur of protest against God!"

Now Bontsha begins to tremble again. He senses that after his defender has finished, his prosecutor will rise to state the case against him. Who knows of what he will be accused? Bontsha, in that other world on earth, forgot each present moment as it slipped behind him to become the past. Now the defending angel has brought everything back to his mind again—but who knows what forgotten sins the prosecutor will bring to mind?

The prosecutor rises. "Gentlemen!" he begins in a harsh and bitter voice, and then he stops. "Gentlemen—" he begins again, and now his voice is less harsh, and again he stops. And finally, in a very soft voice, the same prosecutor says, "Gentlemen, he was always silent—and now I too will be silent."

The great court of justice grows very still, and at last from the judge's chair a new voice rises, loving, tender. "Bontsha my child, Bontsha"—the voice swells like a great harp—"my heart's child . . ."

Within Bontsha his very soul begins to weep. He would like to open his eyes, to raise them, but they are darkened with tears. It is so sweet to cry. Never until now has it been sweet to cry.

"My child, my Bontsha . . ."

Not since his mother died has he heard such words, and spoken in such a voice.

"My child," the judge begins again, "you have always suffered, and you have always kept silent. There isn't one secret place in your body without its bleeding wound; there isn't one secret place in your soul without its wound and blood. And you never protested. You always were silent.

"There, in that other world, no one understood you. You never understood yourself. You never understood that you need not have been silent, that you could have cried out and that your outcries would have brought down the world itself and ended it. You never understood your sleeping strength. There in that other world, that world of lies, your silence was never rewarded, but here in Paradise is the world of truth, here in Paradise you will be rewarded. You, the judge can neither condemn nor pass sentence upon. For you there is not only one little portion of Paradise, one little share. No, for you there is everything! Whatever you want! Everything is yours!"

Now for the first time Bontsha lifts his eyes. He is blinded by light. The splendor of light lies everywhere, upon the walls, upon the vast ceiling, the angels blaze with light, the judge. He drops his weary eyes.

"Really?" he asks, doubtful, and a little embarrassed.

"Really!" the judge answers. "Really! I tell you, everything is yours. Everything in Paradise is yours. Choose! Take! Whatever you want! You will only take what is yours!"

"Really?" Bontsha asks again, and now his voice is stronger, more assured.

And the judge and all the heavenly host answer, "Really! Really! Really!"

"Well then"—and Bontsha smiles for the first time—"well then, what I would like, Your Excellency, is to have, every morning for breakfast, a hot roll with fresh butter."

A silence falls upon the great hall, and it is more terrible than Bontsha's has ever been, and slowly the judge and the angels bend their heads in shame at this unending meekness they have created on earth.

Then the silence is shattered. The prosecutor laughs aloud, a bitter laugh.

QUESTIONS

1. What were the reasons for Bontsha's silence on earth? Was his silence a virtue? Why is he so well received in heaven?

2. Why does Bontsha rejoice when he decides that the angels are really talking about him?

3. What is meant by the assertion that, if Bontsha could have cried out, his outcries "would have brought down the earth and ended it"?

4. In what respect does the story have a surprise ending? Is the ending fairly achieved? Does it exist for its own sake or does it provide revelation?

5. What different kinds of irony are employed in the story? For what purposes? Point out examples.

6. What elements of humor has the author's treatment of heaven? Is there humor also in the treatment of Bontsha's life on earth? What are its sources?

7. What is the theme of the story? To what extent does acceptance of this theme depend on a belief in angels, heaven, or immortality?

CHAPTER NINE

The Scale of Value

Our purpose in the preceding chapters has been to develop not literary critics but proficient readers—readers who choose wisely and read well. Yet good reading involves criticism, for choice necessitates judgment. Though we need not, to read well, be able to settle the relative claims of Conrad and Lawrence or of Hemingway and Faulkner, we do need to discriminate between the genuine and the spurious, the consequential and the trivial, the significant and the merely entertaining. Our first object, naturally, is enjoyment; but full development as human beings requires that we enjoy most what is most worth enjoying.

There are no easy rules for literary judgment. Such judgment depends ultimately on our perceptivity, intelligence, and experience; it is a product of how much and how alertly we have lived and how much and how well we have read. Yet at least two basic principles may be set up. *First, every story is to be initially judged by how fully it achieves its central purpose.* Each element in the story is to be judged by the effectiveness of its contribution to the central purpose. In a good story every element works with every other element for the accomplishment of this central purpose. It follows that no element in the story may be judged in isolation.

Perhaps the most frequent mistakes made by poor readers when called upon for a judgment is to judge the elements of the story in isolation, independently of each other. For example, a student once wrote of "I'm a Fool" that it is not a very good story "because it is not written in good English." And certainly the style of the story, if judged by itself, is very poor indeed: the language is slangy and ungrammatical; the sentences are often disjointed and broken-backed; the narrator constantly digresses and is at times so incapable of expressing himself that he can only say "etc., etc., you know." But no high level of discrimination is needed to see that just such a style is essential to the purpose of the story. The uneducated race-track swipe, whose failure in school life has made him feel both scornful and envious of boys who "go to high schools and college," can hardly speak otherwise than as he does here; the digressions, moreover, are not truly digressions, for each of them supplies additional insight into the character of the swipe, which is the true subject of the story. In "The Enchanted Doll," on the other hand, which is also told from the first-person point of view, the style fails to support the intelligence and sensitivity of the narrator. Here the protagonist is represented as an educated man more than ordinarily perceptive and open to fresh experience. He responds to a doll in a window as though the doll had actually called to him, and he tells us that "the doctor who comes into the sickroom must hear and see with his skin as well as his eyes and ears." Yet this discriminating narrator (who, like Sergeant Marx in "Defender of the Faith," is a war veteran) continually uses sentimental clichés in telling his story. The felt presence of the doll in his room, he says, "brought an indescribable longing to my throat and a sadness to my heart." When he visits Essie, "Something strange happened. For a moment we seemed to be caught up in one another's eyes." Unless he can determine the cause of her sickness, "that spirit would not be long for this earth." Departing "with great heaviness of heart," he thinks about her "night and day." Then, "the scales" fall from his eyes, and he cries out, "I love Essie Nolan! . . . I need her person and her soul forever at my side." And so on. The other characters—Rose Callamit and Abe Sheftel—also speak in clichés, but we expect it of them. We do not expect it of the doctor.

The principle of judgment just applied to style may be applied to every other element in a story. We cannot say that "The Japanese Quince" is a poor story because it does not have an exciting, fast-moving plot: plot can be judged only in relation to the other elements in the story and to its central purpose, and in this relationship the plot of "The Japanese Quince" is a good one. We cannot say that "The Lottery" is a poor story because it contains no such complex characterization as is to be found in "I'm a Fool." The purpose of "The Lottery" is to make a generalization about the persistence of dark communal impulses in human life and for this purpose its characterization is adequate: a more complete characterization might obscure this central purpose. Similarly, we cannot call "The Enchanted Doll" a good story just because it has a true and deeply significant theme. A theme is successful insofar as it is supported and justified by the other elements in the story, and in this story the characterizations are so flat, the contrasts between good and evil so exaggerated, the plot so obviously derived from formula, and the appeals to stock response so blatant (flower-sellers, hurdy-gurdies, children playing hopscotch, young lovers fond of children, an idealistic doctor living in poverty and ministering to the poor, innocence oppressed, a quotation from Jesus, and, finally, motherhood) that the theme (itself designed to appeal to stock response) is robbed of reality and significance.

Every first-rate story is an organic whole. All its parts are related, and all are necessary to the central purpose. In "The Storm" we are presented with an experience of mounting terror in a woman who (1) returns to an empty, lonely house during the outbreak of a storm and who (2) discovers that her husband is a murderer. There is, of course, no logical connection between the storm and the fact that her husband is a murderer or her discovery of that fact: the co-incidence of the storm and the discovery is simply that—a coincidence. The presence of this coincidence and the author's manipulation of point of view (his temporary suppression of Mrs. Willsom's consciousness, in order to prolong suspense, when she sees the body in the trunk and when she recognizes the ring on her husband's finger) are partial clues that the author's purpose is not really to provide insight into human terror so much as to produce terror in the reader. In the light of this purpose, the storm and the discovery of the murder are both justified in the story, for both help to produce terror in the reader. At the same time, their co-presence largely prevents the story from being more meaningful, for what might have been either (1) a study of irrational terror in a woman left alone in an isolated house during a storm or (2) a study of rational terror in a woman who discovers that her husband is a murderer is prevented from being either. Thus "The Storm" is a skillfully written suspense story rather than a story of human insight.

Once a story has been judged successful in achieving its central purpose, we may apply a second principle of judgment. *A story, if successful, may be judged by the significance of its purpose.* If every story is to be judged by how successfully it integrates its materials into an organic unity, it is also to be judged by the extent and the range and the value of the materials integrated. This principle returns us to our distinction between escape and interpretation. If a story's only aim is to entertain, whether by mystifying, surprising, thrilling, provoking to laughter or tears, or furnishing a substitute dream life, we may judge it of less value than a story whose aim is to *reveal.* "The Drunkard," "Flurry at the Sheep Dog Trial," "That Evening Sun," and "The Storm" are all successful stories if we judge them by the degree to which they fulfill their central purpose. But "The Drunkard" has a more significant purpose than "Flurry at the Sheep Dog Trial," and "That Evening Sun" a more significant one than "The Storm." When a story does provide some revelation—does make some serious statement about life—we may measure it by the breadth and depth of that revelation. "The Drunkard" and "That Evening Sun" are both fine stories, but "That Evening Sun" attempts a deeper probing than does "The Drunkard." The situation with which it is concerned is more crucial, cuts deeper. The story reveals a more significant range and depth of life.

Some stories, then, like "The Storm" and "Flurry at the Sheep Dog Trial," provide good fun and innocent merriment. Others, like "The Drunkard" and "That Evening Sun," afford the good reader a deeper enjoyment through the insights they give into life. A third type, like many of the soap operas of television and radio, offer a cheaper and less innocent pleasure by providing escape under the guise of interpretation. Such stories, while professing to present real life situations and everyday people and happenings, actually, by their shallowness of characterization, their falsifications of plot, their use of stock themes and stock emotions, present us with dangerous oversimplifications and distortions. They seriously misrepresent life and are harmful to the extent that they keep us from a more sensitive, more discriminating response to experience.

The above types of stories do not fall into sharp, distinct categories. There are no fortified barriers running between them to inform us when we are passing from one realm into another. There are no appointed officials to whom we can apply for certain information. Our only passports are our own good judgments, based on our accumulated experience both with literature and life. Nevertheless, certain questions, if asked wisely and with consideration for the two principles developed in this chapter, may help us both to understand the stories we read and to place them with rough accuracy on a scale of value that rises through many gradations from "poor" to "good" to "great." These questions, most of them explored in the previous chapters of this book, are, for convenience, summarized here.

GENERAL QUESTIONS FOR ANALYSIS AND EVALUATION

Plot

1. Who is the protagonist of the story? What are the conflicts? Are they physical, intellectual, moral, or emotional? Is the main conflict between sharply differentiated good and evil, or is it more subtle and complex?

2. Does the plot have unity? Are all the episodes relevant to the total meaning or effect of the story? Does each incident grow logically out of the preceding incident and lead naturally to the next? Is the ending happy, unhappy, or indeterminate? Is it fairly achieved?

3. What use does the story make of chance and coincidence? Are these occurrences used to initiate, to complicate, or to resolve the story? How improbable are they?

4. How is suspense created in the story? Is the interest confined to "What happens next?" or are larger concerns involved? Can you find examples of mystery? of dilemma?

5. What use does the story make of surprise? Are the surprises achieved fairly? Do they serve a significant purpose? Do they divert the reader's attention from weaknesses in the story?

6. To what extent is this a "formula" story?

Characters

7. What means does the author use to reveal character? Are the characters sufficiently dramatized? What use is made of character contrasts?

8. Are the characters consistent in their actions? adequately motivated? plausible? Does the author successfully avoid stock characters?

9. Is each character fully enough developed to justify his role in the story? Are the main characters round or flat?

10. Is any of the characters a developing character? If so, is his change a large or a small one? Is it a plausible change for him? Is it sufficiently motivated? Is it given sufficient time?

Theme

11. Does the story have a theme? What is it? Is it implicit or explicit?

12. Does the theme reinforce or oppose popular notions of life? Does it furnish a new insight or refresh or deepen an old one?

Point of View

13. What point of view does the story use? Is it consistent in its use of this point of view? If shifts are made, are they justified?

14. What advantages has the chosen point of view? Does it furnish any clues as to the purpose of the story?

15. If the point of view is that of one of the characters, does this character have any limitations that affect his interpretation of events or persons?

16. Does the author use point of view primarily to reveal or conceal? Does he ever unfairly withhold important information known to the focal character?

Symbol and Irony

17. Does the story make use of symbols? If so, do the symbols carry or merely reinforce the meaning of the story?
18. Does the story anywhere utilize irony of situation? dramatic irony? verbal irony? What functions do the ironies serve?

Emotion and Humor

19. Does the story aim directly at an emotional *effect,* or is emotion merely its natural by-product?
20. Is the emotion sufficiently dramatized? Is the author anywhere guilty of sentimentality?

Fantasy

21. Does the story employ fantasy? If so, what is the initial assumption? Does the story operate logically from this assumption?
22. Is the fantasy employed for its own sake or to express some human truth? If the latter, what truth?

General

23. Is the primary interest of the story in plot, character, theme, or some other element?
24. What contribution to the story is made by its setting? Is the particular setting essential, or could the story have happened anywhere?
25. What are the characteristics of the author's style? Are they appropriate to the nature of his story?
26. What light is thrown on the story by its title?
27. Do all elements of the story work together to support a central purpose? Is any part irrelevant or inappropriate?
28. What do you conceive to be the story's central purpose? How fully has it achieved that purpose?
29. Does the story offer chiefly escape or interpretation? How significant is the story's purpose?
30. Does the story gain or lose on a second reading?

EXERCISE

The two stories that follow have a number of plot features in common; in purpose, however, they are quite different. One attempts to reveal certain truths about aspects of human life and succeeds in doing so. The other attempts to do little more than entertain the reader, and, in achieving this end, it falsifies human life. Which story is which? Support your decision by making a thorough analysis of both.

O. Henry

A MUNICIPAL REPORT

The cities are full of pride,
Challenging each to each—
This from her mountainside,
That from her burthened beach.
R. KIPLING

Fancy a novel about Chicago or Buffalo, let us say, or Nashville, Tennessee! There are just three big cities in the United States that are "story cities" —New York, of course, New Orleans, and, best of the lot, San Francisco.— Frank Norris.

East is east, and west is San Francisco, according to Californians. Californians are a race of people; they are not merely inhabitants of a State. They are the Southerners of the West. Now, Chicagoans are no less loyal to their city; but when you ask them why, they stammer and speak of lake fish and the new Odd Fellows Building. But Californians go into detail.

Of course they have, in the climate, an argument that is good for half an hour while you are thinking of your coal bills and heavy underwear. But as soon as they come to mistake your silence for conviction, madness comes upon them, and they picture the city of the Golden Gate as the Bagdad of the New World. So far, as a matter of opinion, no refutation is necessary. But dear cousins all (from Adam and Eve descended), it is a rash one who will lay his finger on the map and say "In this town there can be no romance—what could happen here?" Yes, it is a bold and a rash deed to challenge in one sentence history, romance, and Rand and McNally.

Nashville.—A city, port of delivery, and the capital of the State of Tennessee, is on the Cumberland River and on the N.C. & St. L. and the L. & N. railroads. This city is regarded as the most important educational centre in the South.

A MUNICIPAL REPORT First published in 1909.

I stepped off the train at 8 P.M. Having searched thesaurus in vain for adjectives, I must, as a substitution, hie me to comparison in the form of a recipe.

Take of London fog 30 parts; malaria 10 parts; gas leaks 20 parts; dew-drops gathered in a brick yard at sunrise, 25 parts; odor of honeysuckle 15 parts. Mix.

The mixture will give you an approximate conception of a Nashville drizzle. It is not so fragrant as a moth-ball nor as thick as peasoup; but 'tis enough—'twill serve.

I went to a hotel in a tumbril. It required strong self-suppression for me to keep from climbing to the top of it and giving an imitation of Sidney Carton. The vehicle was drawn by beasts of a bygone era and driven by something dark and emancipated.

I was sleepy and tired, so when I got to the hotel I hurriedly paid it the fifty cents it demanded (with approximate lagniappe, I assure you). I knew its habits; and I did not want to hear it prate about its old "marster" or anything that happened "befo' de wah."

The hotel was one of the kind described as "renovated." That means $20,000 worth of new marble pillars, tiling, electric lights and brass cuspidors in the lobby, and a new L. & N. time table and a lithograph of Lookout Mountain in each one of the great rooms above. The management was without reproach, the attention full of exquisite Southern courtesy, the service as slow as the progress of a snail and as good-humored as Rip Van Winkle. The food was worth traveling a thousand miles for. There is no other hotel in the world where you can get such chicken livers *en brochette*.

At dinner I asked a Negro waiter if there was anything doing in town. He pondered gravely for a minute, and then replied: "Well, boss, I don't really reckon there's anything at all doin' after sundown."

Sundown had been accomplished: it had been drowned in the drizzle long before. So that spectacle was denied me. But I went forth upon the streets in the drizzle to see what might be there.

It is built on undulating grounds; and the streets are lighted by electricity at a cost of $32,470 per annum.

As I left the hotel there was a race riot. Down upon me charged a company of freedmen, or Arabs, or Zulus, armed with—no, I saw with relief that they were not rifles, but whips. And I saw dimly a caravan of black, clumsy vehicles; and at the reassuring shouts, "Kyar you anywhere in the town, boss, fuh fifty cents," I reasoned that I was merely a "fare" instead of a victim.

I walked through long streets, all leading uphill. I wondered how those streets ever came down again. Perhaps they didn't until they were "graded." On a few of the "main streets" I saw lights in stores here and there; saw street cars go by conveying worthy burghers hither and yon; saw people pass engaged in the art of conversation, and heard a burst of semi-lively laughter issuing from a soda-water and ice-cream parlor. The streets other than "main" seemed to have enticed upon their borders houses consecrated to peace and domesticity. In many of them lights shone behind discreetly drawn window shades, in a few pianos tinkled orderly and irreproachable music. There was indeed, little "doing." I wished I had come before sundown. So I returned to my hotel.

In November, 1864, the Confederate General Hood advanced against Nashville, where he shut up a National force under General Thomas. The latter then sallied forth and defeated the Confederates in a terrible conflict.

All my life I have heard of, admired, and witnessed the fine marksmanship of the South in its peaceful conflicts in the tobacco-chewing regions. But in my hotel a surprise awaited me. There were twelve bright, new, imposing, capacious brass cuspidors in the great lobby, tall enough to be called urns and so wide-mouthed that the crack pitcher of a lady baseball team should have been able to throw a ball into one of them at five paces distant. But, although a terrible battle had raged and was still raging, the enemy had not suffered. Bright, new, imposing, capacious, untouched, they stood. But, shades of Jefferson Brick! the tile floor—the beautiful tile floor! I could not avoid thinking of the battle of Nashville, and trying to draw, as is my foolish habit, some deductions about hereditary marksmanship.

Here I first saw Major (by misplaced courtesy) Wentworth Caswell. I knew him for a type the moment my eyes suffered from the sight of him. A rat has no geographical habitat. My old friend, A. Tennyson, said, as he so well said almost everything:

Prophet, curse me the blabbing lip,
And curse me the British vermin, the rat.

Let us regard the word "British" as interchangeable *ad lib.* A rat is a rat.

This man was hunting about the hotel lobby like a starved dog that had forgotten where he had buried a bone. He had a face of great acreage, red, pulpy, and with a kind of sleepy massiveness like that of Buddha. He possessed one single virtue—he was very smoothly shaven. The mark of the beast is not indelible upon a man until he goes about with a stubble. I think that if he had not used his razor that day I would have repulsed his advances, and the criminal calendar of the world would have been spared the addition of one murder.

I happened to be standing within five feet of a cuspidor when Major Caswell opened fire upon it. I had been observant enough to perceive that the attacking force was using Gatlings instead of squirrel rifles, so I sidestepped so promptly that the major seized the opportunity to apologize to a noncombatant. He had the blabbing lip. In four minutes he had become my friend and had dragged me to the bar.

I desire to interpolate here that I am a Southerner. But I am not one by profession or trade. I eschew the string tie, the slouch hat, the Prince Albert, the number of bales of cotton destroyed by Sherman, and plug chewing. When the orchestra plays "Dixie" I do not cheer. I slide a little lower on the leather-cornered seat and, well, order another Würzburger and wish that Longstreet had—but what's the use?

Major Caswell banged the bar with his fist, and the first gun at Fort Sumter re-echoed. When he fired the last one at Appomattox I began to hope. But then he began on family trees, and demonstrated that Adam was only a third cousin of a collateral branch of the Caswell family. Genealogy disposed of, he took up, to my distaste, his private family matters. He spoke of his wife, traced her descent back to Eve, and profanely denied any possible rumor that she may have had relations in the land of Nod.

By this time I began to suspect that he was trying to obscure by noise the fact that he had ordered the drinks, on the chance that I would be bewildered into paying for them. But when they were down he crashed a silver dollar loudly upon the bar. Then, of course, another serving was obligatory. And when I had paid for that I took leave of him brusquely; for I wanted no more of him. But before I had obtained my release he had prated loudly of an income that his wife received, and showed a handful of silver money.

When I got my key at the desk the clerk said to me courteously: "If that man Caswell has annoyed you, and if you would like to make a complaint, we will have him ejected. He is a nuisance, a loafer, and without any known means of support, although he seems to have some money most the time. But we don't seem to be able to hit upon any means of throwing him out legally."

"Why, no," said I, after some reflection; "I don't see my way clear to making a complaint. But I would like to place myself on record as asserting that I do not care for his company. Your town," I continued, "seems to be a quiet one. What manner of entertainment, adventure, or excitement, have you to offer to the stranger within your gates?"

"Well, sir," said the clerk, "there will be a show here next Thursday. It is—I'll look it up and have the announcement sent up to your room with the ice water. Good-night."

After I went up to my room I looked out the window. It was only about ten o'clock, but I looked upon a silent town. The drizzle continued, spangled with dim lights, as far apart as currants in a cake sold at the Ladies' Exchange.

"A quiet place," I said to myself, as my first shoe struck the ceiling of the occupant of the room beneath mine. "Nothing of the life here that gives color and good variety to the cities in the East and West. Just a good, ordinary, hum-drum, business town."

Nashville occupies a foremost place among the manufacturing centres of the country. It is the fifth boot and shoe market in the United States, the largest candy and cracker manufacturing city in the South, and does an enormous wholesale drygoods, grocery, and drug business.

I must tell you how I came to be in Nashville, and I assure you the digression brings as much tedium to me as it does to you. I was traveling elsewhere on my own business, but I had a commission from a Northern literary magazine to stop over there and establish a personal connection between the publication and one of its contributors, Azalea Adair.

Adair (there was no clue to the personality except the handwriting) had sent in some essays (lost art!) and poems that had made the editors swear approvingly over their one o'clock luncheon. So they had commissioned me to round up said Adair and corner by contract his or her output at two cents a word before some other publisher offered her ten or twenty.

At nine o'clock the next morning, after my chicken livers *en brochette* (try them if you can find that hotel), I strayed out into the drizzle, which was still on for an unlimited run. At the first corner I came upon Uncle Caesar. He was a stalwart Negro, older than the pyramids, with gray wool and a face that reminded me of Brutus, and a second afterwards of the late King Cettiwayo. He wore the most remarkable coat that I ever had seen or expect to see. It reached to his ankles and had once been a Confederate gray in colors. But rain and sun and age had so variegated it that Joseph's coat, beside it, would have faded to a pale monochrome. I must linger with that coat, for it has to do with the story—the story that is so long in coming, because you can hardly expect anything to happen in Nashville.

Once it must have been the military coat of an officer. The cape of it had vanished, but all adown its front it had been frogged and tasseled magnificently. But now the frogs and tassels were gone. In their stead had been patiently stitched (I surmised by some surviving "black mammy") new frogs made of cunningly twisted common hempen twine. This twine was frayed and disheveled. It must have been added to the coat as a substitute for vanished splendors, with tasteless but painstaking devotion, for it followed faithfully the curves of the long-missing frogs. And, to complete the comedy and pathos of the garment, all its buttons were gone save one. The second button from the top alone remained. The coat was fastened by other twine strings tied through the buttonholes and other holes rudely pierced in the opposite side. There was never such a weird garment so fantastically bedecked and of so many mottled hues. The lone button was the size of a half-dollar, made of yellow horn and sewed on with coarse twine.

This Negro stood by a carriage so old that Ham himself might have started a hack line with it after he left the ark with the two animals hitched to it. As I approached he threw open the door, drew out a feather duster, waved it without using it, and said in deep, rumbling tones:

"Step right in, suh; ain't a speck of dust in it—jus' got back from a funeral, suh."

I inferred that on such gala occasions carriages were given an extra cleaning. I looked up and down the street and perceived that there was little choice among the vehicles for hire that lined the curb. I looked in my memorandum book for the address of Azalea Adair.

"I want to go to 861 Jessamine Street," I said, and was about to step into the hack. But for an instant the thick, long, gorilla-like arm of the Negro barred me. On his massive and saturnine face a look of sudden suspicion and enmity flashed for a moment. Then, with quickly returning conviction, he asked, blandishingly: "What are you gwine there for, boss?"

"What is that to you?" I asked, a little sharply.

"Nothin', suh, jus' nothin'. Only it's a lonesome kind of part of town and few folks ever has business out there. Step right in. The seats is clean—jes' got back from a funeral, suh."

A mile and a half it must have been to our journey's end. I could hear nothing but the fearful rattle of the ancient hack over the uneven brick paving; I could smell nothing but the drizzle, now further flavored with coal smoke and something like a mixture of tar and oleander blossoms. All I could see through the streaming windows were two rows of dim houses.

The city has an area of 10 square miles; 181 miles of streets, of which 137 miles are paved; a system of waterworks that cost $2,000,000, with 77 miles of mains.

Eighty-sixty-one Jessamine Street was a decayed mansion. Thirty yards back from the street it stood, outmerged in a splendid grove of trees and untrimmed shrubbery. A row of box bushes overflowed and almost hid the paling fence from sight; the gate was kept closed by a rope noose that encircled the gate post and the first paling of the gate. But when you got inside you saw that 861 was a shell, a shadow, a ghost of former grandeur and excellence. But in the story, I have not yet got inside.

When the hack had ceased from rattling and the weary quadrupeds came to a rest I handed my jehu his fifty cents with an additional quarter, feeling a glow of conscious generosity as I did so. He refused it.

"It's two dollars, suh," he said.

"How's that?" I asked. "I plainly heard you call out at the hotel. 'Fifty cents to any part of the town.' "

"It's two dollars, suh," he repeated obstinately. "It's a long ways from the hotel."

"It is within the city limits and well within them," I argued. "Don't think that you have picked up a greenhorn Yankee. Do you see those hills over there?" I went on, pointing toward the east (I could not see them, myself, for the drizzle); "well, I was born and raised on their other side. You old fool nigger, can't you tell people from other people when you see 'em?"

The grim face of King Cettiwayo softened. "Is you from the South, suh? I reckon it was them shoes of yourn' fooled me. They is somethin' sharp in the toes for a Southern gen'l'man to wear."

"Then the charge is fifty cents, I suppose?" said I, inexorably.

His former expression, a mingling of cupidity and hostility, returned, remained ten seconds, and vanished.

"Boss," he said, "fifty cents is right; but I *needs* two dollars, suh; I'm *obleeged* to have two dollars. I ain't *demandin'* it now, suh; after I knows whar you's from; I'm jus sayin' that I *has* to have two dollars to-night and business is mighty po'."

Peace and confidence settled upon his heavy features. He had been luckier than he had hoped. Instead of having picked up a greenhorn, ignorant of rates, he had come upon an inheritance.

"You confounded old rascal," I said, reaching down to my pocket, "you ought to be turned over to the police."

For the first time I saw him smile. He knew; *he knew;* HE KNEW.

I gave him two one-dollar bills. As I handed them over I noticed that one of them had seen parlous times. Its upper right-hand corner was missing, and it had been torn through in the middle, but joined again. A strip of blue tissue paper, pasted over the split, preserved its negotiability.

Enough of the African bandit for the present: I left him happy, lifted the rope, and opened the creaky gate.

The house, as I said, was a shell. A paint brush had not touched it in twenty years. I could not see why a strong wind should not have bowled it over like a house of cards until I looked again at the trees that hugged it close—the trees that saw the battle of Nashville and still drew their protecting branches around it against storm and enemy and cold.

Azalea Adair, fifty years old, white-haired, a descendant of the cavaliers, as thin and frail as the house she lived in, robed in the cheapest and cleanest dress I ever saw, with an air as simple as a queen's, received me.

The reception room seemed a mile square, because there was nothing in it except some rows of books, on unpainted white-pine bookshelves, a cracked marble-topped table, a rag rug, a hairless horsehair sofa, and two or three chairs. Yes, there was a picture on the wall, a colored crayon drawing of a cluster of pansies. I looked around for the portrait of Andrew Jackson and the pine-cone hanging basket but they were not there.

Azalea Adair and I had conversation, a little of which will be repeated to you. She was a product of the old South, gently nurtured in the sheltered life. Her learning was not broad, but was deep and of splendid originality in its somewhat narrow scope. She had been educated at home, and her knowledge of the world was derived from inference and by inspiration. Of such is the precious, small group of essayists made. While she talked to me I kept brushing my fingers, trying, unconsciously, to rid them guiltily of the absent dust from the half-calf backs of Lamb, Chaucer, Hazlitt, Marcus Aurelius, Montaigne, and Hood. She was exquisite, she was a valuable discovery. Nearly everybody nowadays knows too much—oh, so much too much—of real life.

I could perceive clearly that Azalea Adair was very poor. A house and a dress she had, not much else, I fancied. So, divided between my duty to the magazine and my loyalty to the poets and essayists who fought Thomas in the valley of the Cumberland, I listened to her voice which was like a harpsichord's, and found that I could not speak of contracts. In the presence of the nine Muses and the three Graces one hesitated to lower the topic to two cents. There would have to be another colloquy after I had regained my commercialism. But I spoke of my mission, and three o'clock of the next afternoon was set for the discussion of the business proposition.

"Your town," I said, as I began to make ready to depart (which is the time for smooth generalities) "seems to be a quiet, sedate place. A home town, I should say, where few things out of the ordinary ever happen."

It carries on an extensive trade in stoves and hollow ware with the West and South, and its flouring mills have a daily capacity of more than 2,000 barrels.

Azalea Adair seemed to reflect.

"I have never thought of it that way," she said, with a kind of sincere intensity that seemed to belong to her. "Isn't it in the still, quiet places that things do happen? I fancy that when God began to create the earth on the first Monday morning one could have leaned out one's window and heard the drops of mud splashing from His trowel as He built up the everlasting hills. What did the noisiest project in the world—I mean the building of the tower of Babel—result in finally? A page and a half of Esperanto in the *North American Review*."

"Of course," said I, platitudinously, "human nature is the same everywhere; but there is more color—er—more drama and movement and—er—romance in some cities than in others."

"On the surface," said Azalea Adair. "I have traveled many times around the world in a golden airship wafted on two wings—print and dreams. I have seen (on one of my imaginary tours) the Sultan of Turkey bowstring with his own hands one of his wives who had uncovered her face in public. I have seen a man in Nashville tear up his theatre tickets because his wife was going out with her face covered—with rice powder. In San Francisco's Chinatown I saw the slave girl Sing Yee dipped slowly, inch by inch, in boiling almond oil to make her swear she would never see her American lover again. She gave in when the boiling oil had reached three inches above her knee. At a euchre party in East Nashville the other night I saw Kitty Morgan cut dead by seven of her schoolmates and lifelong friends because she had married a house painter. The boiling oil was sizzling as high as her heart; but I wish you could have seen the fine little smile that she carried from table to table. Oh, yes, it is a hum-drum town. Just a few miles of red brick houses and mud and stores and lumber yards."

Some one had knocked hollowly at the back of the house. Azalea Adair breathed a soft apology and went to investigate the sound. She came back in three minutes with brightened eyes, a faint flush on her cheeks, and ten years lifted from her shoulders.

"You must have a cup of tea before you go," she said, "and a sugar cake."

She reached and shook a little iron bell. In shuffled a small Negro girl about twelve, barefoot, not very tidy, glowering at me with thumb in mouth and bulging eyes.

Azalea Adair opened a tiny, worn purse and drew out a dollar bill, a dollar bill with the upper right-hand corner missing, torn in two pieces and pasted together again with a strip of blue tissue paper. It was one of those bills I had given the piratical Negro—there was no doubt of it.

"Go up to Mr. Baker's store on the corner, Impy," she said, handing the girl the dollar bill, "and get a quarter of a pound of tea—the kind he always sends me—and ten cents' worth of sugar cakes. Now, hurry. The supply of tea in the house happens to be exhausted," she explained to me.

Impy left by the back way. Before the scrape of her hard, bare feet had died away on the back porch, a wild shriek—I was sure it was hers—filled the hollow house. Then the deep, gruff tones of an angry man's voice mingled with the girl's further squeals and unintelligible words.

Azalea Adair rose without surprise or emotion and disappeared. For two minutes I heard the hoarse rumble of the man's voice; then something like an oath and a slight scuffle, and she returned calmly to her chair.

"This a roomy house," she said, "and I have a tenant for part of it. I am sorry to have to rescind my invitation to tea. It is impossible to get the kind I always use at the store. Perhaps to-morrow Mr. Baker will be able to supply me."

I was sure that Impy had not had time to leave the house. I inquired concerning street-car lines and took my leave. After I was well on my way I remembered that I had not learned Azalea Adair's name. But tomorrow would do.

The same day I started in on the course of iniquity that this uneventful city forced upon me. I was in the town only two days, but in that time I managed to lie shamelessly by telegraph, and to be an accomplice—after the fact, if that is the correct legal term—to a murder.

As I rounded the corner nearest my hotel the Afrite coachman of the polychromatic, nonpareil coat seized me, swung open the dungeony door of his peripatetic sarcophagus, flirted his feather duster and began his ritual:

"Step right in, boss. Carriage is clean—jus' got back from a funeral. Fifty cents to any——"

And then he knew me and grinned broadly. " 'Scuse me, boss; you is de gen'l'man what rid out with me dis mawnin'. Thank you kindly, suh."

"I am going out to 861 again to-morrow afternoon at three," said I, "and if you will be here, I'll let you drive me. So you know Miss Adair?" I concluded, thinking of my dollar bill.

"I belonged to her father, Judge Adair, suh," he replied.

"I judge that she is pretty poor," I said, "She hasn't much money to speak of, has she?"

For an instant I looked again at the fierce countenance of King Cettiwayo, and then he changed back to an extortionate old Negro hack driver.

"She ain't gwine to starve, suh," he said, slowly. "She has reso'ces, suh; she has reso'ces."

"I shall pay you fifty cents for the trip," said I.

"Dat is puffeckly correct, suh," he answered, humbly. "I jus' *had* to have dat two dollars dis mawnin' boss."

I went to the hotel and lied by electricity. I wired the magazine: "A. Adair holds out for eight cents a word."

The answer that came back was: "Give it to her quick, you duffer."

Just before dinner "Major" Wentworth Caswell bore down upon me with the greetings of a long-lost friend. I have seen few men whom I have so instantaneously hated, and of whom it was so difficult to be rid. I was standing at the bar when he invaded me; therefore I could not wave the white ribbon in his face. I would have paid gladly for the drinks, hoping thereby, to escape another; but he was one of those despicable, roaring, advertising bibbers who must have brass bands and fireworks attend upon every cent that they waste in their follies.

With an air of producing millions he drew two one-dollar bills from a pocket and dashed one of them upon the bar. I looked once more at the dollar bill with the upper right-hand corner missing, torn through the middle, and patched with a strip of blue tissue paper. It was my dollar again. It could have been no other.

I went up to my room. The drizzle and the monotony of a dreary, eventless Southern town had made me tired and listless. I remember that just before I went to bed I mentally disposed of the mysterious dollar bill (which might have formed the clue to a tremendously fine detective story of San Francisco) by saying to myself sleepily: "Seems as if a lot of people here own stock in the Hack-Drivers' Trust. Pays dividends promptly, too. Wonder if——" Then I fell asleep.

King Cettiwayo was at his post the next day, and rattled my bones over the stones out to 861. He was to wait and rattle me back again when I was ready.

Azalea Adair looked paler and cleaner and frailer than she had looked on the day before. After she had signed the contract at eight cents per word she grew still paler and began to slip out of her chair. Without much trouble I managed to get her up on the antediluvian horsehair sofa and then I ran out to the sidewalk and yelled to the coffee-colored Pirate to bring a doctor. With a wisdom that I had not suspected in him, he abandoned his team and struck off up the street afoot, realizing the value of speed. In ten minutes he returned with a grave, gray-haired, and capable man of medicine. In a few words (worth much less than eight cents each) I explained to him my presence in the hollow house of mystery. He bowed with stately understanding, and turned to the old Negro.

"Uncle Caesar," he said, calmly, "run up to my house and ask Miss Lucy to give you a cream pitcher full of fresh milk and half a tumbler of port wine. And hurry back. Don't drive—run. I want you to get back sometime this week."

It occurred to me that Dr. Merriman also felt a distrust as to the speeding powers of the land-pirate's steeds. After Uncle Caesar was gone, lumberingly, but swiftly, up the street, the doctor looked me over with great politeness and as much careful calculation until he had decided that I might do.

"It is only a case of insufficient nutrition," he said. "In other words, the result of poverty, pride, and starvation. Mrs. Caswell has many devoted friends who would be glad to aid her, but she will accept nothing except from that old Negro, Uncle Caesar, who was once owned by her family."

"Mrs. Caswell!" said I, in surprise. And then I looked at the contract and saw that she had signed it "Azalea Adair Caswell."

"I thought she was Miss Adair," I said.

"Married to a drunken, worthless loafer, sir," said the doctor. "It is said that he robs her even of the small sums that her old servant contributes toward her support."

When the milk and wine had been brought the doctor soon revived Azalea Adair. She sat up and talked of the beauty of the autumn leaves that were then in season and their height of color. She referred lightly to her fainting seizure as the outcome of an old palpitation of the heart. Impy fanned her as she lay on the sofa. The doctor was due elsewhere, and I followed him to the door. I told him that it was within my power and intentions to make a reasonable advance of money to Azalea Adair on future contributions to the magazine, and he seemed pleased.

"By the way," he said, "perhaps you would like to know that you have had royalty for a coachman. Old Caesar's grandfather was a king in Congo. Caesar himself has royal ways, as you may have observed."

As the doctor was moving off I heard Uncle Caesar's voice inside: "Did he git bofe of dem two dollars from you, Mis' Zalea?"

"Yes, Caesar," I heard Azalea Adair answer, weakly. And then I went in and concluded business negotiations with our contributor. I assumed the responsibility of advancing fifty dollars, putting it as a necessary formality in binding our bargain. And then Uncle Caesar drove me back to the hotel.

Here ends all of the story as far as I can testify as a witness. The rest must be only bare statements of facts.

At about six o'clock I went out for a stroll. Uncle Caesar was at his corner. He threw open the door of his carriage, flourished his duster, and began his depressing formula: "Step right in, suh. Fifty cents to anywhere in the city—hack's pufficklу clean, suh—jus' got back from a funeral——"

And then he recognized me. I think his eyesight was getting bad. His coat had taken on a few more faded shades of color, the twine strings were more frayed and ragged, the last remaining button—the button of yellow horn—was gone. A motley descendant of kings was Uncle Caesar!

About two hours later I saw an excited crowd besieging the front of the drug store. In a desert where nothing happens this was manna; so I wedged my way inside. On an extemporized couch of empty boxes and chairs was stretched the mortal corporeality of Major Wentworth Caswell. A doctor was testing him for the mortal ingredient. His decision was that it was conpicuous by its absence.

The erstwhile Major had been found dead on a dark street and brought by curious and ennuied citizens to the drug store. The late human being had been engaged in terrific battle—the details showed that. Loafer and reprobate though he had been, he had been also a warrior. But he had lost. His hands were yet clinched so tightly that his fingers could not be opened. The gentle citizens who had known him stood about and searched their vocabularies to find some good words, if it were possible, to speak of him. One kind-looking man said, after much thought: "When 'Cas' was about fo'teen he was one of the best spellers in the school."

While I stood there the fingers of the right hand of "the man that was," which hung down the side of a white pine box, relaxed, and dropped something at my feet. I covered it with one foot quietly, and a little later on I picked it up and pocketed it. I reasoned that in his last struggle his hand must have seized that object unwittingly and held it in a death grip.

At the hotel that night the main topic of conversation, with the possible exceptions of politics and prohibition, was the demise of Major Caswell. I heard one man say to a group of listeners:

"In my opinion, gentlemen, Caswell was murdered by some of these no-account niggers for his money. He had fifty dollars this afternoon which he showed to several gentlemen in the hotel. When he was found the money was not on his person."

I left the city the next morning at nine, and as the train was crossing the bridge over the Cumberland River I took out of my pocket a yellow horn overcoat button the size of a fifty-cent piece, with frayed ends of coarse twine hanging from it, and cast it out of the window into the slow, muddy waters below.

I wonder what's doing in Buffalo!

Susan Glaspell

A JURY OF HER PEERS

When Martha Hale opened the storm-door and got a cut of the north wind, she ran back for her big woolen scarf. As she hurriedly wound that round her head her eye made a scandalized sweep of her kitchen. It was no ordinary thing that called her away—it was probably farther from ordinary than anything that had ever happened in Dickson County. But what her eye took in was that her kitchen was in no shape for leaving: her bread all ready for mixing, half the flour sifted and half unsifted.

She hated to see things half done; but she had been at that when the team from town stopped to get Mr. Hale, and then the sheriff came running in to say his wife wished Mrs. Hale would come too—adding, with a grin, that he guessed she was getting scarey and wanted another woman along. So she had dropped everything right where it was.

"Martha!" now came her husband's impatient voice. "Don't keep folks waiting out here in the cold."

She again opened the storm-door, and this time joined the three men and the one woman waiting for her in the big two-seated buggy.

After she had the robes tucked around her she took another look at the woman who sat beside her on the back seat. She had met Mrs. Peters the year before at the county fair, and the thing she remembered about her was that she didn't seem like a sheriff's wife. She was small and thin and didn't have a strong voice. Mrs. Gorman, sheriff's wife before Gorman went out and Peters came in, had a voice that somehow seemed to be backing up the law with every word. But if Mrs. Peters didn't look like a sheriff's wife, Peters made it up in looking like a sheriff. He was to a dot the kind of man who could get himself elected sheriff—a heavy man with a big voice, who was particularly genial with the law-abiding, as if to make it plain that he knew the difference between criminals and non-criminals. And right there it came into Mrs. Hale's mind, with a stab, that this man who was so pleasant and lively with all of them was going to the Wrights' now as a sheriff.

"The country's not very pleasant this time of year," Mrs. Peters at last ventured, as if she felt they ought to be talking as well as the men.

Mrs. Hale scarcely finished her reply, for they had gone up a little hill and could see the Wright place now, and seeing it did not make her feel like talking. It looked very lonesome this cold March morning. It had always been a lonesome-looking place. It was down in a hollow, and the poplar trees around it were lonesome-looking trees. The men were looking at it and talk-

A JURY OF HER PEERS Reprinted by permission of Mr. S. C. Cook. First published in 1917.

ing about what had happened. The county attorney was bending to one side of the buggy, and kept looking steadily at the place as they drew up to it.

"I'm glad you came with me," Mrs. Peters said nervously, as the two women were about to follow the men in through the kitchen door.

Even after she had her foot on the door-step, her hand on the knob, Martha Hale had a moment of feeling she could not cross that threshold. And the reason it seemed she couldn't cross it now was simply because she hadn't crossed it before. Time and time again it had been in her mind, "I ought to go over and see Minnie Foster"—she still thought of her as Minnie Foster, though for twenty years she had been Mrs. Wright. And then there was always something to do and Minnie Foster would go from her mind. But *now* she could come.

The men went over to the stove. The women stood close together by the door. Young Henderson, the county attorney, turned around and said, "Come up to the fire, ladies."

Mrs. Peters took a step forward, then stopped. "I'm not—cold," she said.

And so the two women stood by the door, at first not even so much as looking around the kitchen.

The men talked for a minute about what a good thing it was the sheriff had sent his deputy out that morning to make a fire for them, and then Sheriff Peters stepped back from the stove, unbuttoned his outer coat, and leaned his hands on the kitchen table in a way that seemed to mark the beginning of official business. "Now, Mr. Hale," he said in a sort of semi-official voice, "before we move things about, you tell Mr. Henderson just what it was you saw when you came here yesterday morning."

The county attorney was looking around the kitchen.

"By the way," he said, "has anything been moved?" He turned to the sheriff. "Are things just as you left them yesterday?"

Peters looked from cupboard to sink; from that to a small worn rocker a little to one side of the kitchen table.

"It's just the same."

"Somebody should have been left here yesterday," said the county attorney.

"Oh—yesterday," returned the sheriff, with a little gesture as of yesterday having been more than he could bear to think of. "When I had to send Frank to Morris Center for that man who went crazy—let me tell you, I had my hands full *yesterday*. I knew you could get back from Omaha by to-day, George, and as long as I went over everything here myself—"

"Well, Mr. Hale," said the county attorney, in a way of letting what was past and gone go, "tell just what happened when you came here yesterday morning."

Mrs. Hale, still leaning against the door, had that sinking feeling of the mother whose child is about to speak a piece. Lewis often wandered along and got things mixed up in a story. She hoped he would tell this straight and plain, and not say unnecessary things that would just make things harder for Minnie Foster. He didn't begin at once, and she noticed that he looked queer —as if standing in that kitchen and having to tell what he had seen there yesterday morning made him almost sick.

"Yes, Mr. Hale?" the county attorney reminded.

"Harry and I had started to town with a load of potatoes," Mrs. Hale's husband began.

Harry was Mrs. Hale's oldest boy. He wasn't with them now, for the very good reason that those potatoes never got to town yesterday and he was taking them this morning, so he hadn't been home when the sheriff stopped to say he wanted Mr. Hale to come over to the Wright place and tell the county attorney his story there, where he could point it all out. With all Mrs. Hale's other emotions came the fear now that maybe Harry wasn't dressed warm enough—they hadn't any of them realized how that north wind did bite.

"We come along this road," Hale was going on, with a motion of his hand to the road over which they had just come, "and as we got in sight of the house I says to Harry, 'I'm goin' to see if I can't get John Wright to take a telephone.' You see," he explained to Henderson, "unless I can get somebody to go in with me they won't come out this branch road except for a price *I* can't pay. I'd spoke to Wright about it once before; but he put me off, saying folks talked too much anyway, and all he asked was peace and quiet—guess you know about how much he talked himself. But I thought maybe if I went to the house and talked about it before his wife, and said all the women-folks liked the telephones, and that in this lonesome stretch of road it would be a good thing—well, I said to Harry that that was what I was going to say—though I said at the same time that I didn't know as what his wife wanted made much difference to John—"

Now, there he was!—saying things he didn't need to say. Mrs. Hale tried to catch her husband's eye, but fortunately the county attorney interrupted with:

"Let's talk about that a little later, Mr. Hale. I do want to talk about that, but I'm anxious now to get along to just what happened when you got here."

When he began this time, it was very deliberately and carefully:

"I didn't see or hear anything. I knocked at the door. And still it was all quiet inside. I knew they must be up—it was past eight o'clock. So I knocked again, louder, and I thought I heard somebody say, 'Come in.' I wasn't sure—I'm not sure yet. But I opened the door—this door," jerking a hand toward the door by which the two women stood, "and there, in that rocker"—pointing to it—"sat Mrs. Wright."

Every one in the kitchen looked at the rocker. It came into Mrs. Hale's mind that that rocker didn't look in the least like Minnie Foster—the Minnie Foster of twenty years before. It was a dingy red, with wooden rungs up the back, and the middle rung was gone, and the chair sagged to one side.

"How did she—look?" the county attorney was inquiring.

"Well," said Hale, "she looked—queer."

"How do you mean—queer?"

As he asked it he took out a note-book and pencil. Mrs. Hale did not like the sight of that pencil. She kept her eye fixed on her husband, as if to keep him from saying unnecessary things that would go into that note-book and make trouble.

Hale did speak guardedly, as if the pencil had affected him too.

"Well, as if she didn't know what she was going to do next. And kind of —done up."

"How did she seem to feel about your coming?"

"Why, I don't think she minded—one way or other. She didn't pay much attention. I said, 'Ho' do, Mrs. Wright? It's cold, ain't it?' And she said, 'Is it?'—and went on pleatin' at her apron.

"Well, I was surprised. She didn't ask me to come up to the stove, or to sit down, but just set there, not even lookin' at me. And so I said: 'I want to see John.'

"And then she—laughed. I guess you would call it a laugh.

"I thought of Harry and the team outside, so I said, a little sharp, 'Can I see John?' 'No,' says she—kind of dull like. 'Ain't he home?' says I. Then she looked at me. 'Yes,' says she, 'he's home.' 'Then why can't I see him?' I asked her, out of patience with her now. ' 'Cause he's dead,' says she, just as quiet and dull—and fell to pleatin' her apron. 'Dead?' says I, like you do when you can't take in what you've heard.

"She just nodded her head, not getting a bit excited, but rockin' back and forth.

" 'Why—where is he?' says I, not knowing *what* to say.

"She just pointed upstairs—like this"—pointing to the room above.

"I got up, with the idea of going up there myself. By this time I—didn't know what to do. I walked from there to here; then I says: 'Why, what did he die of?'

" 'He died of a rope round his neck,' says she; and just went on pleatin' at her apron."

Hale stopped speaking, and stood staring at the rocker, as if he were still seeing the woman who had sat there the morning before. Nobody spoke; it was as if every one were seeing the woman who had sat there the morning before.

"And what did you do then?" the county attorney at last broke the silence.

"I went out and called Harry. I thought I might—need help. I got Harry in, and we went upstairs." His voice fell almost to a whisper. "There he was —lying over the—"

"I think I'd rather have you go into that upstairs," the county attorney interrupted, "where you can point it all out. Just go on now with the rest of the story."

"Well, my first thought was to get that rope off. It looked—"

He stopped, his face twitching.

"But Harry, he went up to him, and he said, 'No, he's dead all right, and we'd better not touch anything.' So we went downstairs.

"She was still sitting that same way. 'Has anybody been notified?' I asked. 'No,' says she, unconcerned.

" 'Who did this, Mrs. Wright?' said Harry. He said it business-like, and she stopped pleatin' at her apron. 'I don't know,' she says. 'You don't *know*?' says Harry. 'Weren't you sleepin' in the bed with him?' 'Yes,' says she, 'but I was on the inside.' 'Somebody slipped a rope round his neck and strangled him, and you didn't wake up?' says Harry. 'I didn't wake up,' she said after him.

"We may have looked as if we didn't see how that could be, for after a minute she said, 'I sleep sound.'

"Harry was going to ask her more questions, but I said maybe that weren't our business; maybe we ought to let her tell her story first to the coroner or the sheriff. So Harry went fast as he could over to High Road—the Rivers' place, where there's a telephone."

"And what did she do when she knew you had gone for the coroner?" The attorney got his pencil in his hand all ready for writing.

"She moved from that chair to this one over here"—Hale pointed to a small chair in the corner—"and just sat there with her hands held together and looking down. I got a feeling that I ought to make some conversation, so I said I had come in to see if John wanted to put in a telephone; and at that she started to laugh, and then she stopped and looked at me—scared."

At the sound of a moving pencil the man who was telling the story looked up.

"I dunno—maybe it wasn't scared," he hastened; "I wouldn't like to say it was. Soon Harry got back, and then Dr. Lloyd came, and you, Mr. Peters, and so I guess that's all I know that you don't."

He said that last with relief, and moved a little, as if relaxing. Every one moved a little. The county attorney walked toward the stair door.

"I guess we'll go upstairs first—then out to the barn and around there."

He paused and looked around the kitchen.

"You're convinced there was nothing important here?" he asked the sheriff. "Nothing that would—point to any motive?"

The sheriff too looked all around, as if to re-convince himself.

"Nothing here but kitchen things," he said, with a little laugh for the insignificance of kitchen things.

The county attorney was looking at the cupboard—a peculiar, ungainly structure, half closet and half cupboard, the upper part of it being built in the wall, and the lower part just the old-fashioned kitchen cupboard. As if its queerness attracted him, he got a chair and opened the upper part and looked in. After a moment he drew his hand away sticky.

"Here's a nice mess," he said resentfully.

The two women had drawn nearer, and now the sheriff's wife spoke.

"Oh—her fruit," she said, looking to Mrs. Hale for sympathetic understanding. She turned back to the county attorney and explained: "She worried about that when it turned so cold last night. She said the fire would go out and her jars might burst."

Mrs. Peters' husband broke into a laugh.

"Well, can you beat the women! Held for murder, and worrying about her preserves!"

The young attorney set his lips.

"I guess before we're through with her she may have something more serious than preserves to worry about."

"Oh, well," said Mrs. Hale's husband, with good-natured superiority, "women are used to worrying over trifles."

The two women moved a little closer together. Neither of them spoke. The county attorney seemed suddenly to remember his manners—and think of his future.

"And yet," said he, with the gallantry of a young politician, "for all their worries, what would we do without the ladies?"

The women did not speak, did not unbend. He went to the sink and began washing his hands. He turned to wipe them on the roller towel—whirled it for a cleaner place.

"Dirty towels! Not much of a housekeeper, would you say, ladies?"

He kicked his foot against some dirty pans under the sink.

"There's a great deal of work to be done on a farm" said Mrs. Hale stiffly.

"To be sure. And yet"—with a little bow to her—"I know there are some Dickson County farm-houses that do not have such roller towels." He gave it a pull to expose its full length again.

"Those towels get dirty awful quick. Men's hands aren't always as clean as they might be."

"Ah, loyal to your sex, I see," he laughed He stopped and gave her a keen look. "But you and Mrs. Wright were neighbors. I suppose you were friends, too."

Martha Hale shook her head.

"I've seen little enough of her of late years. I've not been in this house—it's more than a year."

"And why was that? You didn't like her?"

"I liked her well enough," she replied with spirit. "Farmers' wives have their hands full, Mr. Henderson. And then"—She looked around the kitchen.

"Yes?" he encouraged.

"It never seemed a very cheerful place," said she, more to herself than to him.

"No," he agreed; "I don't think any one would call it cheerful. I shouldn't say she had the home-making instinct."

"Well, I don't know as Wright had, either," she muttered.

"You mean they didn't get on very well?" he was quick to ask.

"No; I don't mean anything," she answered, with decision. As she turned a little away from him, she added: "But I don't think a place would be any the cheerfuler for John Wright's bein' in it."

"I'd like to talk to you about that a little later, Mrs. Hale," he said. "I'm anxious to get the lay of things upstairs now."

He moved toward the stair door, followed by the two men.

"I suppose anything Mrs. Peters does'll be all right?" the sheriff inquired. "She was to take in some clothes for her, you know—and a few little things. We left in such a hurry yesterday."

The county attorney looked at the two women whom they were leaving alone there among the kitchen things.

"Yes—Mrs. Peters," he said, his glance resting on the woman who was not Mrs. Peters, the big farmer woman who stood behind the sheriff's wife. "Of course Mrs. Peters is one of us," he said, in a manner of entrusting responsibility. "And keep your eye out, Mrs. Peters, for anything that might be of use. No telling; you women might come upon a clue to the motive—and that's the thing we need."

Mr. Hale rubbed his face after the fashion of a show man getting ready for a pleasantry.

"But would the women know a clue if they did come upon it?" he said; and, having delivered himself of this, he followed the others through the stair door.

The women stood motionless and silent, listening to the footsteps, first upon the stairs, then in the room above them.

Then, as if releasing herself from something strange, Mrs. Hale began to arrange the dirty pans under the sink, which the county attorney's disdainful push of the foot had deranged.

"I'd hate to have men comin' into my kitchen," she said testily—"snoopin' round and criticizin'."

"Of course it's no more than their duty," said the sheriff's wife, in her manner of timid acquiescence.

"Duty's all right," replied Mrs. Hale bluffly; "but I guess that deputy sheriff that come out to make the fire might have got a little of this on." She gave the roller towel a pull. "Wish I'd thought of that sooner! Seems mean to talk about her for not having things slicked up, when she had to come away in such a hurry."

She looked around the kitchen. Certainly it was not "slicked up." Her eye was held by a bucket of sugar on a low shelf. The cover was off the wooden bucket, and beside it was a paper bag—half full.

Mrs. Hale moved toward it.

"She was putting this in there," she said to herself—slowly.

She thought of the flour in her kitchen at home—half sifted, half not sifted. She had been interrupted, and had left things half done. What had interrupted Minnie Foster? Why had that work been left half done? She made a move as if to finish it,—unfinished things always bothered her,—and then she glanced around and saw that Mrs. Peters was watching her—and she didn't want Mrs. Peters to get that feeling she had got of work begun and then—for some reason—not finished.

"It's a shame about her fruit," she said, and walked toward the cupboard that the county attorney had opened, and got on the chair, murmuring: "I wonder if it's all gone."

It was a sorry enough looking sight, but "Here's one that's all right," she said at last. She held it toward the light. "This is cherries, too." She looked again. "I declare I believe that's the only one."

With a sigh, she got down from the chair, went to the sink, and wiped off the bottle.

"She'll feel awful bad, after all her hard work in the hot weather. I remember the afternoon I put up my cherries last summer."

She set the bottle on the table, and, with another sigh, started to sit down in the rocker. But she did not sit down. Something kept her from sitting down in that chair. She straightened—stepped back, and, half turned away, stood looking at it, seeing the woman who had sat there "pleatin' at her apron."

The thin voice of the sheriff's wife broke in upon her: "I must be getting those things from the front room closet." She opened the door into the other room, started in, stepped back. "You coming with me, Mrs. Hale?" she asked nervously. "You—you could help me get them."

They were soon back—the stark coldness of that shut-up room was not a thing to linger in.

"My!" said Mrs. Peters, dropping the things on the table and hurrying to the stove.

Mrs. Hale stood examining the clothes the woman who was being detained in town had said she wanted.

"Wright was close!" she exclaimed, holding up a shabby black skirt that bore the marks of much making over. "I think maybe that's why she kept so much to herself. I s'pose she felt she couldn't do her part; and then, you don't enjoy things when you feel shabby. She used to wear pretty clothes and be lively—when she was Minnie Foster, one of the town girls, singing in the choir. But that—oh, that was twenty years ago."

With a carefulness in which there was something tender, she folded the shabby clothes and piled them at one corner of the table. She looked up at

Mrs. Peters, and there was something in the other woman's look that irritated her.

"She don't care," she said to herself. "Much difference it makes to her whether Minnie Foster had pretty clothes when she was a girl."

Then she looked again, and she wasn't so sure; in fact, she hadn't at any time been perfectly sure about Mrs. Peters. She had that shrinking manner, and yet her eyes looked as if they could see a long way into things.

"This all you was to take in?" asked Mrs. Hale.

"No," said the sheriff's wife; "she said she wanted an apron. Funny thing to want," she ventured in her nervous little way, "for there's not much to get you dirty in jail, goodness knows. But I suppose just to make her feel more natural. If you're used to wearing an apron—. She said they were in the bottom drawer of this cupboard. Yes—here they are. And then her little shawl that always hung on the stair door."

She took the small gray shawl from behind the door leading upstairs, and stood a minute looking at it.

Suddenly Mrs. Hale took a quick step toward the other woman.

"Mrs. Peters!"

"Yes, Mrs. Hale?"

"Do you think she—did it?"

A frightened look blurred the other thing in Mrs. Peters' eyes.

"Oh, I don't know," she said, in a voice that seemed to shrink away from the subject.

"Well, I don't think she did," affirmed Mrs. Hale stoutly. "Asking for an apron, and her little shawl. Worryin' about her fruit."

"Mr. Peters says—." Footsteps were heard in the room above; she stopped, looked up, then went on in a lowered voice: "Mr. Peters says—it looks bad for her. Mr. Henderson is awful sarcastic in a speech, and he's going to make fun of her saying she didn't—wake up."

For a moment Mrs. Hale had no answer. Then, "Well, I guess John Wright didn't wake up—when they was slippin' that rope under his neck," she muttered.

"No, it's *strange*," breathed Mrs. Peters. "They think it was such a—funny way to kill a man."

She began to laugh; at sound of the laugh, abruptly stopped.

"That's just what Mr. Hale said," said Mrs. Hale, in a resolutely natural voice. "There was a gun in the house. He says that's what he can't understand."

"Mr. Henderson said, coming out, that what was needed for the case was a motive. Something to show anger—or sudden feeling."

"Well, I don't see any signs of anger around here," said Mrs. Hale. "I don't—"

She stopped. It was as if her mind tripped on something. Her eye was caught by a dish-towel in the middle of the kitchen table. Slowly she moved toward the table. One half of it was wiped clean, the other half messy. Her eyes made a slow, almost unwilling turn to the bucket of sugar and the half empty bag beside it. Things begun—and not finished.

After a moment she stepped back, and said, in that manner of releasing herself:

"Wonder how they're finding things upstairs? I hope she had it a little more red up up there. You know,"—she paused, and feeling gathered,—"it seems kind of *sneaking*: locking her up in town and coming out here to get her own house to turn against her!"

"But, Mrs. Hale," said the sheriff's wife, "the law is the law."

"I s'pose 'tis," answered Mrs. Hale shortly.

She turned to the stove, saying something about that fire not being much to brag of. She worked with it a minute, and when she straightened up she said aggressively:

"The law is the law—and a bad stove is a bad stove. How'd you like to cook on this?"—pointing with the poker to the broken lining. She opened the oven door and started to express her opinion of the oven; but she was swept into her own thoughts, thinking of what it would mean, year after year, to have that stove to wrestle with. The thought of Minnie Foster trying to bake in that oven—and the thought of her never going over to see Minnie Foster—.

She was startled by hearing Mrs. Peters say: "A person gets discouraged—and loses heart."

The sheriff's wife had looked from the stove to the sink—to the pail of water which had been carried in from outside. The two women stood there silent, above them the footsteps of the men who were looking for evidence against the woman who had worked in that kitchen. That look of seeing into things, of seeing through a thing to something else, was in the eyes of the sheriff's wife now. When Mrs. Hale next spoke to her, it was gently:

"Better loosen up your things, Mrs. Peters. We'll not feel them when we go out."

Mrs. Peters went to the back of the room to hang up the fur tippet she was wearing. A moment later she exclaimed, "Why, she was piecing a quilt," and held up a large sewing basket piled high with quilt pieces.

Mrs. Hale spread some of the blocks out on the table.

"It's log-cabin pattern," she said, putting several of them together. "Pretty, isn't it?"

They were so engaged with the quilt that they did not hear the footsteps on the stairs. Just as the stair door opened Mrs. Hale was saying:

"Do you suppose she was going to quilt it or just knot it?"

The sheriff threw up his hands.

"They wonder whether she was going to quilt it or just knot it!"

There was a laugh for the ways of women, a warming of hands over the stove, and then the county attorney said briskly:

"Well, let's go right out to the barn and get that cleared up."

"I don't see as there's anything so strange," Mrs. Hale said resentfully, after the outside door had closed on the three men—"our taking up our time with little things while we're waiting for them to get the evidence. I don't see as it's anything to laugh about."

"Of course they've got awful important things on their minds," said the sheriff's wife apologetically.

They returned to an inspection of the block for the quilt. Mrs. Hale was looking at the fine, even sewing, and preoccupied with thoughts of the woman who had done that sewing, when she heard the sheriff's wife say, in a queer tone:

"Why, look at this one."

She turned to take the block held out to her.

"The sewing," said Mrs. Peters, in a troubled way. "All the rest of them have been so nice and even—but—this one. Why, it looks as if she didn't know what she was about!"

Their eyes met—something flashed to life, passed between them; then, as if with an effort, they seemed to pull away from each other. A moment Mrs. Hale sat there, her hands folded over that sewing which was so unlike all the rest of the sewing. Then she had pulled a knot and drawn the threads.

"Oh, what are you doing, Mrs. Hale?" asked the sheriff's wife, startled.

"Just pulling out a stitch or two that's not sewed very good," said Mrs. Hale mildly.

"I don't think we ought to touch things," Mrs. Peters said, a little helplessly.

"I'll just finish up this end," answered Mrs. Hale, still in that mild, matter-of-fact fashion.

She threaded a needle and started to replace bad sewing with good. For a little while she sewed in silence. Then, in that thin, timid voice, she heard:

"Mrs. Hale!"

"Yes, Mrs. Peters?"

"What do you suppose she was so—nervous about?"

"Oh, *I* don't know," said Mrs. Hale, as if dismissing a thing not important enough to spend much time on. "I don't know as she was—nervous. I sew awful queer sometimes when I'm just tired."

She cut a thread, and out of the corner of her eye looked up at Mrs. Peters. The small, lean face of the sheriff's wife seemed to have tightened up. Her eyes had that look of peering into something. But next moment she moved, and said in her thin, indecisive way:

"Well, I must get those clothes wrapped. They may be through sooner than we think. I wonder where I could find a piece of paper—and string."

"In that cupboard, maybe," suggested Mrs. Hale, after a glance around.

One piece of the crazy sewing remained unripped. Mrs. Peters' back turned, Martha Hale now scrutinized that piece, compared it with the dainty, accurate sewing of the other blocks. The difference was startling. Holding this block made her feel queer, as if the distracted thoughts of the woman who had perhaps turned to it to try and quiet herself were communicating themselves to her.

Mrs. Peters' voice roused her.

"Here's a bird-cage," she said. "Did she have a bird, Mrs. Hale?"

"Why, I don't know whether she did or not." She turned to look at the cage Mrs. Peters was holding up. "I've not been here in so long." She sighed. "There was a man round last year selling canaries cheap—but I don't know as she took one. Maybe she did. She used to sing real pretty herself."

Mrs. Peters looked around the kitchen.

"Seems kind of funny to think of a bird here." She half laughed—an attempt to put up a barrier. "But she must have had one—or why would she have a cage? I wonder what happened to it."

"I suppose maybe the cat got it," suggested Mrs. Hale, resuming her sewing.

"No; she didn't have a cat. She's got that feeling some people have about cats—being afraid of them. When they brought her to our house yesterday, my cat got in the room, and she was real upset and asked me to take it out."

"My sister Bessie was like that," laughed Mrs. Hale.

The sheriff's wife did not reply. The silence made Mrs. Hale turn round. Mrs. Peters was examining the bird-cage.

"Look at this door," she said slowly. "It's broke. One hinge has been pulled apart."

Mrs. Hale came nearer.

"Looks as if some one must have been—rough with it."

Again their eyes met—startled, questioning, apprehensive. For a moment neither spoke nor stirred. Then Mrs. Hale, turning away, said brusquely:

"If they're going to find any evidence, I wish they'd be about it. I don't like this place."

"But I'm awful glad you came with me, Mrs. Hale." Mrs. Peters put the bird-cage on the table and sat down. "It would be lonesome for me—sitting here alone."

"Yes, it would, wouldn't it?" agreed Mrs. Hale, a certain determined naturalness in her voice. She had picked up the sewing, but now it dropped in her lap, and she murmured in a different voice: "But I tell you what I *do* wish, Mrs. Peters. I wish I had come over sometimes when she was here. I wish—I had."

"But of course you were awful busy, Mrs. Hale. Your house—and your children."

"I could've come," retorted Mrs. Hale shortly. "I stayed away because it weren't cheerful—and that's why I ought to have come. I"—she looked around—"I've never liked this place. Maybe because it's down in a hollow and you don't see the road. I don't know what it is, but it's a lonesome place, and always was. I wish I had come over to see Minnie Foster sometimes. I can see now—" She did not put it into words.

"Well, you mustn't reproach yourself," counseled Mrs. Peters. "Somehow, we just don't see how it is with other folks till—something comes up."

"Not having children makes less work," mused Mrs. Hale, after a silence, "but it makes a quiet house—and Wright out to work all day—and no company when he did come in. Did you know John Wright, Mrs. Peters?"

"Not to know him. I've seen him in town. They say he was a good man."

"Yes—good," conceded John Wright's neighbor grimly. "He didn't drink, and kept his word as well as most, I guess, and paid his debts. But he was a hard man, Mrs. Peters. Just to pass the time of day with him—." She stopped, shivered a little. "Like a raw wind that gets to the bone." Her eye fell upon the cage on the table before her, and she added, almost bitterly: "I should think she would've wanted a bird!"

Suddenly she leaned forward, looking intently at the cage. "But what do you s'pose went wrong with it?"

"I don't know," returned Mrs. Peters; "unless it got sick and died."

But after she said it she reached over and swung the broken door. Both women watched it as if somehow held by it.

"You didn't know—her?" Mrs. Hale asked, a gentler note in her voice.

"Not till they brought her yesterday," said the sheriff's wife.

"She—come to think of it, she was kind of like a bird herself. Real sweet and pretty, but kind of timid and—fluttery. How—she—did—change."

That held her for a long time. Finally, as if struck with a happy thought and relieved to get back to everyday things, she exclaimed:

"Tell you what, Mrs. Peters, why don't you take the quilt in with you? It might take up her mind."

"Why, I think that's a real nice idea, Mrs. Hale," agreed the sheriff's wife, as if she too were glad to come into the atmosphere of a simple kindness. "There couldn't possibly be any objection to that, could there? Now, just what will I take? I wonder if her patches are in here—and her things."

They turned to the sewing basket.

"Here's some red," said Mrs. Hale, bringing out a roll of cloth. Underneath that was a box. "Here, maybe her scissors are in here—and her things." She held it up. "What a pretty box! I'll warrant that was something she had a long time ago—when she was a girl."

She held it in her hand a moment; then, with a little sigh, opened it.

Instantly her hand went to her nose.

"Why—!"

Mrs. Peters drew nearer—then turned away.

"There's something wrapped up in this piece of silk," faltered Mrs. Hale.

"This isn't her scissors," said Mrs. Peters, in a shrinking voice.

Her hand not steady, Mrs. Hale raised the piece of silk. "Oh, Mrs. Peters!" she cried. "It's—"

Mrs. Peters bent closer.

"It's the bird," she whispered.

"But, Mrs. Peters!" cried Mrs. Hale. "*Look* at it! Its neck—look at its neck! It's all—other side *to.*"

She held the box away from her.

The sheriff's wife again bent closer.

"Somebody wrung its neck," said she, in a voice that was slow and deep.

And then again the eyes of the two women met—this time clung together in a look of dawning comprehension, of growing horror. Mrs. Peters looked from the dead bird to the broken door of the cage. Again their eyes met. And just then there was a sound at the outside door.

Mrs. Hale slipped the box under the quilt pieces in the basket, and sank into the chair before it. Mrs. Peters stood holding to the table. The county attorney and the sheriff came in from outside.

"Well, ladies," said the county attorney, as one turning from serious things to little pleasantries, "have you decided whether she was going to quilt it or knot it?"

"We think," began the sheriff's wife in a flurried voice, "that she was going to—knot it."

He was too preoccupied to notice the change that came in her voice on that last.

"Well, that's very interesting, I'm sure," he said tolerantly. He caught sight of the bird-cage. "Has the bird flown?"

"We think the cat got it," said Mrs. Hale in a voice curiously even.

He was walking up and down, as if thinking something out.

"Is there a cat?" he asked absently.

Mrs. Hale shot a look up at the sheriff's wife.

"Well, not *now,*" said Mrs. Peters. "They're superstitious, you know; they leave."

She sank into her chair.

The county attorney did not heed her. "No sign at all of any one having come in from the outside," he said to Peters, in the manner of continuing an interrupted conversation. "Their own rope. Now let's go upstairs again and go over it, piece by piece. It would have to have been some one who knew just the—"

The stair door closed behind them and their voices were lost.

The two women sat motionless, not looking at each other, but as if peering into something and at the same time holding back. When they spoke now it was as if they were afraid of what they were saying, but as if they could not help saying it.

"She liked the bird," said Martha Hale, low and slowly. "She was going to bury it in that pretty box."

"When I was a girl," said Mrs. Peters, under her breath, "my kitten—there was a boy took a hatchet, and before my eyes—before I could get there—" She covered her face an instant. "If they hadn't held me back I would have"—she caught herself, looked upstairs where footsteps were heard, and finished weakly—"hurt him."

Then they sat without speaking or moving.

"I wonder how it would seem," Mrs. Hale at last began, as if feeling her way over strange ground—"never to have had any children around?" Her eyes made a slow sweep of the kitchen, as if seeing what that kitchen had meant through all the years. "No, Wright wouldn't like the bird," she said after that—"a thing that sang. She used to sing. He killed that too." Her voice tightened.

Mrs. Peters moved uneasily.

"Of course we don't know who killed the bird."

"I knew John Wright," was Mrs. Hale's answer.

"It was an awful thing was done in this house that night, Mrs. Hale," said the sheriff's wife. "Killing a man while he slept—slipping a thing round his neck that choked the life out of him."

Mrs. Hale's hand went out to the bird-cage.

"His neck. Choked the life out of him."

"We don't *know* who killed him," whispered Mrs. Peters wildly. "We don't *know*."

Mrs. Hale had not moved. "If there had been years and years of—nothing, then a bird to sing to you, it would be awful—still—after the bird was still."

It was as if something within her not herself had spoken, and it found in Mrs. Peters something she did not know as herself.

"I know what stillness is," she said, in a queer, monotonous voice. "When we homesteaded in Dakota, and my first baby died—after he was two years old—and me with no other then—"

Mrs. Hale stirred.

"How soon do you suppose they'll be through looking for the evidence?"

"I know what stillness is," repeated Mrs. Peters, in just that same way. Then she too pulled back. "The law has got to punish crime, Mrs. Hale," she said in her tight little way.

"I wish you'd seen Minnie Foster," was the answer, "when she wore a white dress with blue ribbons, and stood up there in the choir and sang."

The picture of that girl, the fact that she had lived neighbor to that girl for twenty years, and had let her die for lack of life, was suddenly more than she could bear.

"Oh, I *wish* I'd come over here once in a while!" she cried. "That was a crime! That was a crime! Who's going to punish that?"

"We mustn't take on," said Mrs. Peters, with a frightened look toward the stairs.

"I might 'a' *known* she needed help! I tell you, it's *queer*, Mrs. Peters. We live close together, and we live far apart. We all go through the same things—it's all just a different kind of the same thing! If it weren't—why do you and I *understand*? Why do we *know*—what we know this minute?"

She dashed her hand across her eyes. Then, seeing the jar of fruit on the table, she reached for it and choked out:

"If I was you I wouldn't *tell* her her fruit was gone! Tell her it *ain't*. Tell her it's all right—all of it. Here—take this in to prove it to her! She—she may never know whether it was broke or not."

She turned away.

Mrs. Peters reached out for the bottle of fruit as if she were glad to take it—as if touching a familiar thing, having something to do, could keep her from something else. She got up, looked about for something to wrap the fruit in, took a petticoat from the pile of clothes she had brought from the front room, and nervously started winding that round the bottle.

"My!" she began, in a high, false voice, "it's a good thing the men couldn't hear us! Getting all stirred up over a little thing like a—dead canary." She hurried over that. "As if that could have anything to do with—with—My, wouldn't they *laugh?*"

Footsteps were heard on the stairs.

"Maybe they would," muttered Mrs. Hale—"maybe they wouldn't."

"No, Peters," said the county attorney incisively; "it's all perfectly clear, except the reason for doing it. But you know juries when it comes to women. If there was some definite thing—something to show. Something to make a story about. A thing that would connect up with this clumsy way of doing it."

In a covert way Mrs. Hale looked at Mrs. Peters. Mrs. Peters was looking at her. Quickly they looked away from each other. The outer door opened and Mr. Hale came in.

"I've got the team round now," he said. "Pretty cold out there."

"I'm going to stay here awhile by myself," the county attorney suddenly announced. "You can send Frank out for me, can't you?" he asked the sheriff. "I want to go over everything. I'm not satisfied we can't do better."

Again, for one brief moment, the two women's eyes found one another.

The sheriff came up to the table.

"Did you want to see what Mrs. Peters was going to take in?"

The county attorney picked up the apron. He laughed.

"Oh, I guess they're not very dangerous things the ladies have picked out."

Mrs. Hale's hand was on the sewing basket in which the box was concealed. She felt that she ought to take her hand off the basket. She did not seem able to. He picked up one of the quilt blocks which she had piled on to cover the box. Her eyes felt like fire. She had a feeling that if he took up the basket she would snatch it from him.

But he did not take it up. With another little laugh, he turned away, saying:

"No; Mrs. Peters doesn't need supervising. For that matter, a sheriff's wife is married to the law. Ever think of it that way, Mrs. Peters?"

Mrs. Peters was standing beside the table. Mrs. Hale shot a look up at her; but she could not see her face. Mrs. Peters had turned away. When she spoke, her voice was muffled.

"Not—just that way," she said.

"Married to the law!" chuckled Mrs. Peters' husband. He moved toward the door into the front room, and said to the county attorney:

"I just want you to come in here a minute, George. We ought to take a look at these windows."

"Oh—windows," said the county attorney scoffingly.

"We'll be right out, Mr. Hale," said the sheriff to the farmer, who was still waiting by the door.

Hale went to look after the horses. The sheriff followed the county attorney into the other room. Again—for one final moment—the two women were alone in that kitchen.

Martha Hale sprang up, her hands tight together, looking at that other woman, with whom it rested. At first she could not see her eyes, for the sheriff's wife had not turned back since she turned away at that suggestion of being married to the law. But now Mrs. Hale made her turn back. Her eyes made her turn back. Slowly, unwillingly, Mrs. Peters turned her head until her eyes met the eyes of the other woman. There was a moment when they held each other in a steady, burning look in which there was no evasion nor flinching. Then Martha Hale's eyes pointed the way to the basket in which was hidden the thing that would make certain the conviction of the other woman—that woman who was not there and yet who had been there with them all through that hour.

For a moment Mrs. Peters did not move. And then she did it. With a rush forward, she threw back the quilt pieces, got the box, tried to put it in her handbag. It was too big. Desperately she opened it, started to take the bird out. But there she broke—she could not touch the bird. She stood there helpless, foolish.

There was the sound of a knob turning in the inner door. Martha Hale snatched the box from the sheriff's wife, and got it in the pocket of her big coat just as the sheriff and the county attorney came back into the kitchen.

"Well, Henry," said the county attorney facetiously, "at least we found out that she was not going to quilt it. She was going to—what is it you call it, ladies?"

Mrs. Hale's hand was against the pocket of her coat.

"We call it—knot it, Mr. Henderson."

EXERCISE

The two stories by Thomas Mann and Franz Kafka that follow are both interpretive stories of unquestioned merit. Most qualified judges, however, would place one of the stories higher on the scale of literary value than the other. Which story, in your estimation, deserves the higher ranking? Support your decision with a reasoned and thorough analysis, using the study questions for what help they may provide.

Thomas Mann

THE INFANT PRODIGY

The infant prodigy entered. The hall became quiet.

It became quiet and then the audience began to clap, because somewhere at the side a leader of mobs, a born organizer, clapped first. The audience had heard nothing yet, but they applauded; for a mighty publicity organization had heralded the prodigy and people were already hypnotized, whether they knew it or not.

The prodigy came from behind a splendid screen embroidered with Empire garlands and great conventionalized flowers, and climbed nimbly up the steps to the platform, diving into the applause as into a bath; a little chilly and shivering, but yet as though into a friendly element. He advanced to the edge of the platform and smiled as though he were about to be photographed; he made a shy, charming gesture of greeting, like a little girl.

He was dressed entirely in white silk, which the audience found enchanting. The little white jacket was fancifully cut, with a sash underneath it, and even his shoes were made of white silk. But against the white socks his bare little legs stood out quite brown; for he was a Greek boy.

He was called Bibi Saccellaphylaccas. And such indeed was his name. No one knew what Bibi was the pet name for, nobody but the impresario, and he regarded it as a trade secret. Bibi had smooth black hair reaching to his shoulders; it was parted on the side and fastened back from the narrow domed forehead by a little silk bow. His was the most harmless childish countenance in the world, with an unfinished nose and guileless mouth. The area beneath his pitch-black mouselike eyes was already a little tired and visibly lined. He looked as though he were nine years old but was really eight and given out for seven. It was hard to tell whether to believe this or not. Probably everybody knew better and still believed it, as happens about so many things. The average man thinks that a little falseness goes with beauty. Where should we get any excitement out of our daily life if we were not willing to pretend a bit? And the average man is quite right, in his average brains!

The prodigy kept on bowing until the applause died down, then he went up to the grand piano, and the audience cast a last look at its programmes. First came a *Marche solonnelle,* then a *Rêverie,* and then *Le Hibou et les moineaux*—all by Bibi Saccellaphylaccas. The whole programme was by him, they were all his compositions. He could not score them, of course, but he had them all in his extraordinary little head and they possessed real artistic significance, or so it said, seriously and objectively, in the programme. The programme sounded as though the impresario had wrested these concessions from his critical nature after a hard struggle.

The prodigy sat down upon the revolving stool and felt with his feet for the pedals, which were raised by means of a clever device so that Bibi could reach them. It was Bibi's own piano, he took it everywhere with him. It rested upon wooden trestles and its polish was somewhat marred by the constant transportation—but all that only made things more interesting.

Bibi put his silk-shod feet on the pedals; then he made an artful little face, looked straight ahead of him, and lifted his right hand. It was a brown, childish little hand; but the wrist was strong and unlike a child's, with well-developed bones.

Bibi made his face for the audience because he was aware that he had to entertain them a little. But he had his own private enjoyment in the thing too, an enjoyment which he could never convey to anybody. It was that prickling delight, that secret shudder of bliss, which ran through him every time he sat at an open piano—it would always be with him. And here was the keyboard again, these seven black and white octaves, among which he had so often lost himself in abysmal and thrilling adventures—and yet it always looked as clean and untouched as a newly washed blackboard. This was the realm of music that lay before him. It lay spread out like an inviting ocean, where he might plunge in and blissfully swim, where he might let himself be borne and carried away, where he might go under in night and storm, yet keep the mastery: control, ordain—he held his right hand poised in the air.

A breathless stillness reigned in the room—the tense moment before the first note came . . . How would it begin? It began so. And Bibi, with his index finger, fetched the first note out of the piano, a quite unexpectedly powerful first note in the middle register, like a trumpet blast. Others followed, an introduction developed—the audience relaxed.

The concert was held in the palatial hall of a fashionable first-class hotel. The walls were covered with mirrors framed in gilded arabesques, between frescoes of the rosy and fleshly school. Ornamental columns supported a ceiling that displayed a whole universe of electric bulbs, in clusters darting a brilliance far brighter than day and filling the whole space with thin, vibrating golden light. Not a seat was unoccupied, people were standing in the side aisles and at the back. The front seats cost twelve marks; for the impresario believed that anything worth having was worth paying for. And they were occupied by the best society, for it was in the upper classes, of course, that the greatest enthusiasm was felt. There were even some children, with their legs hanging down demurely from their chairs and their shining eyes staring at their gifted little white-clad contemporary.

Down in front on the left side sat the prodigy's mother, an extremely obese woman with a powdered double chin and a feather on her head. Beside her was the impresario, a man of oriental appearance with large gold buttons on his conspicuous cuffs. The princess was in the middle of the front row—a wrinkled, shrivelled little old princess but still a patron of the arts, especially everything full of sensibility. She sat in a deep, velvet-upholstered arm chair, and a Persian carpet was spread before her feet. She held her hands folded over her grey striped-silk breast, put her head on one side, and presented a picture of elegant composure as she sat looking up at the performing prodigy. Next to her sat her lady-in-waiting, in a green striped silk gown. Being only a lady-in-waiting she had to sit up very straight in her chair.

Bibi ended in a grand climax. With what power this wee manikin belaboured the keyboard! The audience could scarcely trust its ears. The march theme, an infectious, swinging tune, broke out once more, fully harmonized, bold and showy; with every note Bibi flung himself back from the waist as though he were marching in a triumphal procession. He ended *fortissimo,* bent over, slipped sideways off the stool, and stood with a smile awaiting the applause.

And the applause burst forth, unanimously, enthusiastically; the child made his demure little maidenly curtsy and people in the front seat thought: "Look what slim little hips he has! Clap, clap! Hurrah, bravo, little chap, Saccophylax or whatever your name is! Wait, let me take off my gloves—what a little devil of a chap he is!"

Bibi had to come out three times from behind the screen before they would stop. Some latecomers entered the hall and moved about looking for seats. Then the concert continued. Bibi's *Rêverie* murmured its numbers, consisting almost entirely of arpeggios, above which a bar of melody rose now and then, weak-winged. Then came *Le Hibou et les moineaux.* This piece was brilliantly successful, it made a strong impression; it was an effective childhood fantasy, remarkably well envisaged. The bass represented the owl, sitting morosely rolling his filmy eyes; while in the treble the impudent, half-frightened sparrows chirped. Bibi received an ovation when he finished, he was called out four times. A hotel page with shiny buttons carried up three great laurel wreaths onto the stage and proffered them from one side while Bibi nodded and expressed his thanks. Even the princess shared in the applause, daintily and noiselessly pressing her palms together.

Ah, the knowing little creature understood how to make people clap! He stopped behind the screen, they had to wait for him; lingered a little on the steps of the platform, admired the long streamers on the wreaths—although actually such things bored him stiff by now. He bowed with the utmost charm, he gave the audience plenty of time to rave itself out, because applause is valuable and must not be cut short. "*Le Hibou* is my drawing card," he thought—this expression he had learned from the impresario. "Now I will play the fantasy, it is a lot better than *Le Hibou,* of course, especially the C-sharp passage. But you idiots dote on the *Hibou,* though it is the first and the silliest thing I wrote." He continued to bow and smile.

Next came a *Méditation* and then an *Étude*—the programme was quite comprehensive. The *Méditation* was very like the *Rêverie*—which was nothing against it—and the *Étude* displayed all of Bibi's virtuosity, which naturally fell a little short of his inventiveness. And then the *Fantaisie.* This was his favourite; he varied it a little each time, giving himself free rein and sometimes surprising even himself, on good evenings, by his own inventiveness.

He sat and played, so little, so white and shining, against the great black grand piano, elect and alone, above that confused sea of faces, above the heavy, insensitive mass soul, upon which he was labouring to work with his individual, differentiated soul. His lock of soft black hair with the white silk bow had fallen over his forehead, his trained and bony little wrists pounded away, the muscles stood out visibly on his brown childish cheeks.

Sitting there he sometimes had moments of oblivion and solitude, when the gaze of his strange little mouselike eyes with the big rings beneath them would lose itself and stare through the painted stage into space that was peopled with strange vague life. Then out of the corner of his eye he would give a quick look back into the hall and be once more with his audience.

"Joy and pain, the heights and the depths—that is my *Fantaisie,*" he thought lovingly. "Listen, here is the C-sharp passage." He lingered over the approach, wondering if they would notice anything. But no, of course not, how should they? And he cast his eyes up prettily at the ceiling so that at least they might have something to look at.

All these people sat there in their regular rows, looking at the prodigy and thinking all sorts of things in their regular brains. An old gentleman with a white beard, a seal ring on his finger and a bulbous swelling on his bald spot, a growth if you like, was thinking to himself: "Really, one ought to be ashamed." He had never got any further than "Ah, thou dearest Augustin" on the piano, and here he sat now, a grey old man, looking on while this little hop-o'-my-thumb performed miracles. Yes, yes, it is a gift of God, we must remember that. God grants His gifts, or He withholds them, and there is no shame in being an ordinary man. Like with the Christ Child.—Before a child one may kneel without feeling ashamed. Strange that thoughts like these should be so satisfying—he would even say so sweet, if it was not too silly for a tough old man like him to use the word. That was how he felt, anyhow.

Art . . . the business man with the parrot-nose was thinking. "Yes, it adds something cheerful to life, a little good white silk and a little tumty-ti-ti-tum. Really he does not play so badly. Fully fifty seats, twelve marks apiece, that makes six hundred marks—and everything else besides. Take off the rent of the hall, the lighting and the programmes, you must have fully a thousand marks profit. That is worth while."

That was Chopin he was just playing, thought the piano teacher, a lady with a pointed nose; she was of an age when the understanding sharpens as the hopes decay. "But not very original—I will say that afterwards, it sounds well. And his hand position is entirely amateur. One must be able to lay a coin on the back of the hand—I would use a ruler on him."

Then there was a young girl, at that self-conscious and chlorotic time of life when the most ineffable ideas come into the mind. She was thinking to herself: "What is it he is playing? It is expressive of passion, yet he is a child. If he kissed me it would be as though my little brother kissed me—no kiss at all. Is there such a thing as passion all by itself, without any earthly object, a sort of child's-play of passion? What nonsense! If I were to say such things aloud they would just be at me with some more cod-liver oil. Such is life."

An officer was leaning against a column. He looked on at Bibi's success and thought: "Yes, you are something and I am something, each in his own way." So he clapped his heels together and paid to the prodigy the respect which he felt to be due to all the powers that be.

Then there was a critic, an elderly man in a shiny black coat and turned-up trousers splashed with mud. He sat in his free seat and thought: "Look at him, this young beggar of a Bibi. As an individual he has still to develop, but as a type he is already quite complete, the artist *par excellence*. He has in himself all the artist's exaltation and his utter worthlessness, his charlatanry and his sacred fire, his burning contempt and his secret raptures. Of course I can't write all that, it is too good. Of course, I should have been an artist myself if I had not seen through the whole business so clearly."

Then the prodigy stopped playing and a perfect storm arose in the hall. He had to come out again and again from behind his screen. The man with the shiny buttons carried up more wreaths: four laurel wreaths, a lyre made of violets, a bouquet of roses. He had not arms enough to convey all these tributes, the impresario himself mounted the stage to help him. He hung a laurel wreath round Bibi's neck, he tenderly stroked the black hair—and suddenly as though overcome he bent down and gave the prodigy a kiss, a resounding kiss, square on the mouth. And then the storm became a hurricane. That kiss ran through the room like an electric shock, it went direct to people's marrow and made them shiver down their backs. They were carried away by a helpless compulsion of sheer noise. Loud shouts mingled with the hysterical clapping of hands. Some of Bibi's commonplace little friends down there waved their handkerchiefs. But the critic thought: "Of course that kiss had to come—it's a good old gag. Yes, good Lord, if only one did not see through everything quite so clearly—"

And so the concert drew to a close. It began at half past seven and finished at half past eight. The platform was laden with wreaths and two little pots of flowers stood on the lamp stands of the piano. Bibi played as his last number his *Rhapsodie grecque,* which turned into the Greek national hymn at the end. His fellow-countrymen in the audience would gladly have sung it with him if the company had not been so august. They made up for it with a powerful noise and hullabaloo, a hot-blooded national demonstration. And the aging critic was thinking: "Yes, the hymn had to come too. They have to exploit every vein—publicity cannot afford to neglect any means to its end. I think I'll criticize that as inartistic. But perhaps I am wrong, perhaps that is the most artistic thing of all. What is the artist? A jack-in-the-box. Criticism is on a higher plane. But I can't say that." And away he went in his muddy trousers.

After being called out nine or ten times the prodigy did not come any more from behind the screen but went to his mother and the impresario down in the hall. The audience stood about among the chairs and applauded and pressed forward to see Bibi close at hand. Some of them wanted to see the princess too. Two dense circles formed, one round the prodigy, the other round the princess, and you could actually not tell which of them was receiving more homage. But the court lady was commanded to go over to Bibi; she smoothed down his silk jacket a bit to make it look suitable for a court function, led him by the arm to the princess, and solemnly indicated to him that he was to kiss the royal hand. "How do you do it, child?" asked the princess. "Does it come into your head of itself when you sit down?" "*Oui, madame,*" answered Bibi. To himself he thought: "Oh, what a stupid old princess!" Then he turned round shyly and uncourtierlike and went back to his family.

Outside in the cloak room there was a crowd. People held up their numbers and received with open arms furs, shawls, and galoshes. Somewhere among her acquaintances the piano teacher stood making her critique. "He is not very original," she said audibly and looked about her.

In front of one of the great mirrors an elegant young lady was being arrayed in her evening cloak and fur shoes by her brothers, two lieutenants. She was exquisitely beautiful, with her steel-blue eyes and her clean-cut, well-bred face. A really noble dame. When she was ready she stood waiting for her brothers. "Don't stand so long in front of the glass, Adolf," she said softly to one of them, who could not tear himself away from the sight of his simple, good-looking young features. But Lieutenant Adolf thinks: What cheek! He would button his overcoat in front of the glass, just the same. Then they went out on the street where the arc lights gleamed cloudily through the white mist. Lieutenant Adolf struck up a little nigger dance on the frozen snow to keep warm, with his hands in his slanting overcoat pockets and his collar turned up.

A girl with untidy hair and swinging arms, accompanied by a gloomy-faced youth, came out just behind them. A child! she thought. A charming child. But in there he was an awe-inspiring . . . and aloud in a toneless voice she said: "We are all infant prodigies, we artists."

"Well, bless my soul!" thought the old gentleman who had never got further than Augustin on the piano, and whose boil was now concealed by a top hat. "What does all that mean? She sounds very oracular." But the gloomy youth understood. He nodded his head slowly.

Then they were silent and the untidy-haired girl gazed after the brothers and sister. She rather despised them, but she looked after them until they had turned the corner.

QUESTIONS

1. How pure an artist is the infant prodigy? What are his attitudes toward music, toward his audience, toward the performance? How much of his performance is genuine, how much contrived?

2. What is the attitude of the impresario toward the performance? How great is his musical understanding? What are his motivations?

3. What various attitudes toward the prodigy and his performance are displayed by the audience? Analyze the reactions of the old gentleman with the boil on his bald spot, of the businessman, of the piano teacher, of the self-conscious young girl, of the officer, of the critic. How discerning or appropriate is each of their responses? What is the role in the story of the elegant young lady and her lieutenant brothers? of the gloomy-faced youth and the girl with untidy hair? What does the latter mean by her remark, "We are all infant prodigies, we artists"?

4. What contributions to the story are made by: the man who starts the applause, the description of the prodigy's suit, the description of the hall, the account of the seating arrangements, the presence of the princess?

5. What are the major ironies of the story?

6. What is the theme of the story? What is Mann saying about musical performances by infant prodigies and about artistic performances in general —the motivations behind them and the responses to them?

Franz Kafka

A HUNGER ARTIST

During these last decades the interest in professional fasting has markedly diminished. It used to pay very well to stage such great performances under one's own management, but today that is quite impossible. We live in a different world now. At one time the whole town took a lively interest in the hunger artist; from day to day of his fast the excitement mounted; everybody wanted to see him at least once a day; there were people who bought season tickets for the last few days and sat from morning till night in front of his small barred cage; even in the nighttime there were visiting hours, when the whole effect was heightened by torch flares; on fine days the cage was set out in the open air, and then it was the children's special treat to see the hunger artist; for their elders he was often just a joke that happened to be in fashion, but the children stood open-mouthed, holding each other's hands for greater security, marveling at him as he sat there pallid in black tights, with his ribs sticking out so prominently, not even on a seat but down among straw on the ground, sometimes giving a courteous nod, answering questions with a constrained smile, or perhaps stretching an arm through the bars so that one might feel how thin it was, and then again withdrawing deep into himself, paying no attention to anyone or anything, not even to the all-important striking of the clock that was the only piece of furniture in his cage, but merely staring into vacancy with half-shut eyes, now and then taking a sip from a tiny glass of water to moisten his lips.

Besides casual onlookers there were also relays of permanent watchers selected by the public, usually butchers, strangely enough, and it was their task to watch the hunger artist day and night, three of them at a time, in case he should have some secret recourse to nourishment. This was nothing but a formality, instituted to reassure the masses, for the initiates knew well enough that during his fast the artist would never in any circumstances, not even under forcible compulsion, swallow the smallest morsel of food; the honor of his profession forbade it. Not every watcher, of course, was capable of understanding this, there were often groups of night watchers who were very lax in carrying out their duties and deliberately huddled together in a retired corner to play cards with great absorption, obviously intending to give the hunger artist the chance of a little refreshment, which they supposed he could draw from some private hoard. Nothing annoyed the artist more than such watchers; they made him miserable; they made his fast seem unendurable; sometimes he mastered his feebleness sufficiently to sing during

A HUNGER ARTIST Translated by Edwin and Willa Muir. Reprinted by permission of Schocken Books Inc., from *The Penal Colony* by Franz Kafka. Copyright © 1948 by Schocken Books Inc. First published in 1924.

their watch for as long as he could keep going, to show them how unjust their suspicions were. But that was of little use; they only wondered at his cleverness in being able to fill his mouth even while singing. Much more to his taste were the watchers who sat close up to the bars, who were not content with the dim night lighting of the hall but focused him in the full glare of the electric pocket torch given them by the impresario. The harsh light did not trouble him at all, in any case he could never sleep properly, and he could always drowse a little, whatever the light, at any hour, even when the hall was thronged with noisy onlookers. He was quite happy at the prospect of spending a sleepless night with such watchers; he was ready to exchange jokes with them, to tell them stories out of his nomadic life, anything at all to keep them awake and demonstrate to them again that he had no eatables in his cage and that he was fasting as not one of them could fast. But his happiest moment was when the morning came and an enormous breakfast was brought them, at his expense, on which they flung themselves with the keen appetite of healthy men after a weary night of wakefulness. Of course there were people who argued that this breakfast was an unfair attempt to bribe the watchers, but that was going rather too far, and when they were invited to take on a night's vigil without a breakfast, merely for the sake of the cause, they made themselves scarce, although they stuck stubbornly to their suspicions.

Such suspicions, anyhow, were a necessary accompaniment to the profession of fasting. No one could possibly watch the hunger artist continuously, day and night, and so no one could produce first-hand evidence that the fast had really been rigorous and continuous; only the artist himself could know that, he was therefore bound to be the sole completely satisfied spectator of his own fast. Yet for other reasons he was never satisfied; it was not perhaps mere fasting that had brought him to such skeleton thinness that many people had regretfully to keep away from his exhibitions, because the sight of him was too much for them, perhaps it was dissatisfaction with himself that had worn him down. For he alone knew, what no other initiate knew, how easy it was to fast. It was the easiest thing in the world. He made no secret of this, yet people did not believe him, at the best they set him down as modest, most of them, however, thought he was out for publicity or else was some kind of cheat who found it easy to fast because he had discovered a way of making it easy, and then had the impudence to admit the fact, more or less. He had to put up with all that, and in the course of time had got used to it, but his inner dissatisfaction always rankled, and never yet, after any term of fasting—this must be granted to his credit—had he left the cage of his own free will. The longest period of fasting was fixed by his impresario at forty days, beyond that term he was not allowed to go, not even in great cities, and there was good reason for it, too. Experience had proved that for about forty days the interest of the public could be stimulated by a steadily increasing pressure of advertisement, but after that the town began to lose interest, sympathetic support began notably to fall off; there were of course local variations as between one town and another or one country and another, but as a general rule forty days marked the limit. So on the fortieth day the flower-bedecked cage was opened, enthusiastic spectators filled the hall, a military band played, two doctors entered the cage to measure the results of the fast, which were announced through a megaphone, and finally two young ladies appeared, blissful at having been selected for the honor, to help the hunger artist down the few steps leading to a small table on which was spread a carefully chosen invalid repast. And at this very moment the artist always turned stubborn. True, he would entrust his bony arms to the outstretched helping hands of the ladies bending over him, but stand up he would not. Why stop fasting at this particular moment, after forty days of it? He had held out for a long time, an illimitably long time; why stop now, when he was in his best fasting form, or rather, not yet quite in his best fasting form? Why should he be cheated of the fame he would get for fasting longer, for being not only the record hunger artist of all time, which presumably he was already, but for beating his own record by a performance beyond human imagination, since he felt that there were no limits to his capacity for fasting? His public pretended to admire him so much, why should it have so little patience with him; if he could endure fasting longer, why shouldn't the public endure it? Besides, he was tired, he was comfortable sitting in the straw, and now he was supposed to lift himself to his full height and go down to a meal the very thought of which gave him a nausea that only the presence of the ladies kept him from betraying, and even that with an effort. And he looked up into the eyes of the ladies who were apparently so friendly and in reality so cruel, and shook his head, which felt too heavy on its strengthless neck. But then there happened yet again what always happened. The impresario came forward, without a word—for the band made speech impossible—lifted his arms in the air above the artist, as if inviting Heaven to look down upon its creature here in the straw, this suffering martyr, which indeed he was, although in quite another sense; grasped him round the emaciated waist, with exaggerated caution, so that the frail condition he was in might be appreciated; and committed him to the care of the blenching ladies, not without secretly giving him a shaking so that his legs and body tottered and swayed. The artist now submitted completely; his head lolled on his breast as if it had landed there by chance; his body was hollowed out; his legs in a spasm of self-preservation clung close to each other at the knees, yet scraped on the ground as if it were not really solid ground, as if they were only trying to find solid ground; and the whole weight of his body, a featherweight after all, relapsed onto one of the ladies, who, looking round for help and panting a little—this post of honor was not at all what she had expected it to be—first stretched her neck as far as she could to keep her face at least free from contact with the artist, when finding this impossible, and her more fortunate companion not coming to her aid but merely holding extended on her own trembling hand the little bunch of knucklebones that was the artist's, to the great delight of the spectators burst into tears and had to be replaced by an attendant who had long been stationed in readiness. Then came the food, a little of which the impresario managed to get between the artist's lips, while he sat in a kind of half-fainting trance, to the accompaniment of cheerful patter designed to distract the public's attention from the artist's condition; after that, a toast was drunk to the public, supposedly prompted by a whisper from the artist in the impresario's ear; the band confirmed it with a mighty flourish, the spectators melted away, and no one had any cause to be dissatisfied with the proceedings, no one except the hunger artist himself, he only, as always.

So he lived for many years, with small regular intervals of recuperation, in visible glory, honored by the world, yet in spite of that troubled in spirit, and all the more troubled because no one would take his trouble seriously. What comfort could he possibly need? What more could he possibly wish for? And if some good-natured person, feeling sorry for him, tried to console him by pointing out that his melancholy was probably caused by fasting, it could happen, especially when he had been fasting for some time, that he reacted with an outburst of fury and to the general alarm began to shake the bars of his cage like a wild animal. Yet the impresario had a way of punishing these outbreaks which he rather enjoyed putting into operation. He would apologize publicly for the artist's behavior, which was only to be excused, he admitted, because of the irritability caused by fasting; a condition hardly to be understood by well-fed people; then by natural transition he went on to mention the artist's equally incomprehensible boast that he could fast for much longer than he was doing; he praised the high ambition, the good will, the great self-denial undoubtedly implicit in such a statement; and then quite simply countered it by bringing out photographs, which were also on sale to the public, showing the artist on the fortieth day of a fast lying in bed almost dead from exhaustion. This perversion of the truth, familiar to the artist though it was, always unnerved him afresh and proved too much for him. What was a consequence of the premature ending of his fast was here presented as the cause of it! To fight against this lack of understanding, against a whole world of non-understanding, was impossible. Time and again in good faith he stood by the bars listening to the impresario, but as soon as the photographs appeared he always let go and sank with a groan back on to his straw, and the reassured public could once more come close and gaze at him.

A few years later when the witnesses of such scenes called them to mind, they often failed to understand themselves at all. For meanwhile the aforementioned change in public interest had set in; it seemed to happen almost overnight; there may have been profound causes for it, but who was going to bother about that; at any rate the pampered hunger artist suddenly found himself deserted one fine day by the amusement seekers, who went streaming past him to other more favored attractions. For the last time the impresario hurried him over half Europe to discover whether the old interest might still survive here and there; all in vain; everywhere, as if by secret agreement, a positive revulsion from professional fasting was in evidence. Of course it could not really have sprung up so suddenly as all that, and many premonitory symptoms which had not been sufficiently remarked or suppressed during the rush and glitter of success now came retrospectively to mind, but it was now too late to take any countermeasures. Fasting would surely come into fashion again at some future date, yet that was no comfort for those living in the present. What, then, was the hunger artist to do? He had been applauded by thousands in his time and could hardly come down to showing himself in a street booth at village fairs, and as for adopting another profession, he was not only too old for that but too fanatically devoted to fasting. So he took leave of the impresario, his partner in an unparalleled career, and hired himself to a large circus; in order to spare his own feelings he avoided reading the conditions of his contract.

A large circus with its enormous traffic in replacing and recruiting men, animals and apparatus can always find a use for people at any time, even for a hunger artist, provided of course that he does not ask too much, and in this particular case anyhow it was not only the artist who was taken on but his famous and long-known name as well, indeed considering the peculiar nature of his performance, which was not impaired by advancing age, it could not be objected that here was an artist past his prime, no longer at the height of his professional skill, seeking a refuge in some quiet corner of a circus; on the contrary, the hunger artist averred that he could fast as well as ever, which was entirely credible, he even alleged that if he were allowed to fast as he liked, and this was at once promised him without more ado, he could astound the world by establishing a record never yet achieved, a statement which certainly provoked a smile among the other professionals, since it left out of account the change in public opinion, which the hunger artist in his zeal conveniently forgot.

He had not, however, actually lost his sense of the real situation and took it as a matter of course that he and his cage should be stationed, not in the middle of the ring as a main attraction, but outside, near the animal cages, on a site that was after all easily accessible. Large and gaily painted placards made a frame for the cage and announced what was to be seen inside it. When the public came thronging out in the intervals to see the animals, they could hardly avoid passing the hunger artist's cage and stopping there for a moment, perhaps they might even have stayed longer had not those pressing behind them in the narrow gangway, who did not understand why they should be held up on their way toward the excitements of the menagerie, made it impossible for anyone to stand gazing quietly for any length of time. And that was the reason why the hunger artist, who had of course been looking forward to these visiting hours as the main achievement of his life, began instead to shrink from them. At first he could hardly wait for the intervals; it was exhilarating to watch the crowds come streaming his way, until only too soon—not even the most obstinate self-deception, clung to almost consciously, could hold out against the fact—the conviction was borne in upon him that these people, most of them, to judge from their actions, again and again, without exception, were all on their way to the menagerie. And the first sight of them from the distance remained the best. For when they reached his cage he was at once deafened by the storm of shouting and abuse that arose from the two contending factions, which renewed themselves continuously, of those who wanted to stop and stare at him—he soon began to dislike them more than the others—not out of real interest but only out of obstinate self-assertiveness, and those who wanted to go straight on to the animals. When the first great rush was past, the stragglers came along, and these, whom nothing could have prevented from stopping to look at him as long as they had breath, raced past with long strides, hardly even glancing at him, in their haste to get to the menagerie in time. And all too rarely did it happen that he had a stroke of luck, when some father of a family fetched up before him with his children, pointed a finger at the hunger artist and explained at length what the phenomenon meant, telling stories of earlier years when he himself had watched similar but much more thrilling performances, and the children, still rather uncomprehending, since neither inside nor outside school had they been sufficiently prepared for this lesson—what did they care about fasting?—yet showed by the brightness of their intent eyes that new and better times might be coming. Perhaps, said the hunger artist to himself many a time, things would be a little better if his cage were set not quite so near the menagerie. That made it too easy for people to make their choice, to say nothing of what he suffered from the stench of the menagerie, the animals' restlessness by night, the carrying past of raw lumps of flesh for the beasts of prey, the roaring at feeding times, which depressed him continually. But he did not dare to lodge a complaint with the management; after all, he had the animals to thank for the troops of people who passed his cage, among whom there might always be one here and there to take an interest in him, and who could tell where they might seclude him if he called attention to his existence and thereby to the fact that, strictly speaking, he was only an impediment on the way to the menagerie.

A small impediment, to be sure, one that grew steadily less. People grew familiar with the strange idea that they could be expected, in times like these, to take an interest in a hunger artist, and with this familiarity the verdict went out against him. He might fast as much as he could, and he did so; but nothing could save him now, people passed him by. Just try to explain to anyone the art of fasting! Anyone who has no feeling for it cannot be made to understand it. The fine placards grew dirty and illegible, they were torn down; the little notice board telling the number of fast days achieved, which at first was changed carefully every day, had long stayed at the same figure, for after the first few weeks even this small task seemed pointless to the staff; and so the artist simply fasted on and on, as he had once dreamed of doing, and it was no trouble to him, just as he had always foretold, but no one counted the days, no one, not even the artist himself, knew what records he was already breaking, and his heart grew heavy. And when once in a time some leisurely passer-by stopped, made merry over the old figure on the board and spoke of swindling, that was in its way the stupidest lie ever invented by indifference and inborn malice, since it was not the hunger artist who was cheating; he was working honestly, but the world was cheating him of his reward.

Many more days went by, however, and that too came to an end. An overseer's eye fell on the cage one day and he asked the attendants why this perfectly good cage should be left standing there unused with dirty straw inside it; nobody knew, until one man, helped out by the notice board, remembered about the hunger artist. They poked into the straw with sticks and found him in it. "Are you still fasting?" asked the overseer. "When on earth do you mean to stop?" "Forgive me, everybody," whispered the hunger artist; only the overseer, who had his ear to the bars, understood him. "Of course," said the overseer, and tapped his forehead with a finger to let the attendants know what state the man was in, "we forgive you." "I always wanted you to admire my fasting," said the hunger artist. "We do admire it," said the overseer, affably. "But you shouldn't admire it," said the hunger artist. "Well, then we don't admire it," said the overseer, "but why shouldn't we admire it?" "Because I have to fast, I can't help it," said the hunger artist. "What a fellow you are," said the overseer, "and why can't you help it?" "Because," said the hunger artist, lifting his head a little and speaking, with his lips pursed, as if for a kiss, right into the overseer's ear, so that no syllable might be lost, "because I couldn't find the food I liked. If I had found it, believe me, I should have made no fuss and stuffed myself like you or anyone else." These were his last words, but in his dimming eyes remained the firm though no longer proud persuasion that he was still continuing to fast.

"Well, clear this out now!" said the overseer, and they buried the hunger artist, straw and all. Into the cage they put a young panther. Even the most insensitive felt it refreshing to see this wild creature leaping around the cage that had so long been dreary. The panther was all right. The food he liked was brought him without hesitation by the attendants; he seemed not even to miss his freedom; his noble body, furnished almost to the bursting point with all that it needed, seemed to carry freedom around with it too; somewhere in his jaws it seemed to lurk; and the joy of life streamed with such ardent passion from his throat that for the onlookers it was not easy to stand the shock of it. But they braced themselves, crowded round the cage, and did not want ever to move away.

QUESTIONS

1. Explain the attitudes of the hunger artist toward his art, toward "the permanent watchers," toward the impresario, toward his audience.

2. What is the principal motivation of the impresario? How does it differ from the hunger artist's?

3. What are the motivations of the audience? What attitudes do they display toward the hunger artist and his performance?

4. Both Mann's story and Kafka's say something about the relations of the ideal and the actual in this life. Phrase a thematic statement that will fit both stories. Express it first in general terms, then in a more specific statement concerning the relationships between artists, artistic performances, and audiences.

5. The hunger artist in this story has been interpreted as a symbol for (a) the artist in the modern world—poet, painter, or musician, (b) the religious mystic, priest, or holy man, (c) spirit—the spiritual element in man. What details in the story support each of these interpretations? Of what significance is the shift in popular taste, on which the story pivots, in terms of historical perspective? Of what significance, according to each interpretation, are the incomprehension of the audiences, the attitudes of children, the cage, the artist's final disclaimer that he fasts because he can't help it, the panther? Must the reader choose between the above interpretations, or are all three possible?

Stories for Further Reading

Nathaniel Hawthorne

YOUNG GOODMAN BROWN

Young Goodman Brown came forth at sunset, into the street of Salem village, but put his head back, after crossing the threshold, to exchange a parting kiss with his young wife. And Faith, as the wife was aptly named, thrust her own pretty head into the street, letting the wind play with the pink ribbons of her cap, while she called to Goodman Brown.

"Dearest heart," whispered she, softly and rather sadly, when her lips were close to his ear, "prithee, put off your journey until sunrise, and sleep in your own bed to-night. A lone woman is troubled with such dreams and such thoughts, that she's afeard of herself, sometimes. Pray, tarry with me this night, dear husband, of all nights in the year!"

"My love and my Faith," replied young Goodman Brown, "of all nights in the year, this one night must I tarry away from thee. My journey, as thou callest it, forth and back again, must needs be done 'twixt now and sunrise. What, my sweet, pretty wife, dost thou doubt me already, and we but three months married!"

"Then God bless you!" said Faith with the pink ribbons, "and may you find all well, when you come back."

"Amen!" cried Goodman Brown. "Say thy prayers, dear Faith, and go to bed at dusk, and no harm will come to thee."

So they parted; and the young man pursued his way, until, being about to turn the corner by the meeting-house, he looked back and saw the head of Faith still peeping after him, with a melancholy air, in spite of her pink ribbons.

"Poor little Faith!" thought he, for his heart smote him. "What a wretch am I, to leave her on such an errand! She talks of dreams, too. Methought, as she spoke, there was trouble in her face, as if a dream had warned her what work is to be done to-night. But no, no! 't would kill her to think it. Well; she's a blessed angel on earth; and after this one night, I'll cling to her skirts and follow her to Heaven."

With this excellent resolve for the future, Goodman Brown felt himself justified in making more haste on his present evil purpose. He had taken a dreary road, darkened by all the gloomiest trees of the forest, which barely stood aside to let the narrow path creep through, and closed immediately behind. It was all as lonely as could be; and there is this peculiarity in such a solitude, that the traveller knows not who may be concealed by the in-

YOUNG GOODMAN BROWN First published in 1846.

numerable trunks and the thick boughs overhead; so that, with lonely footsteps, he may yet be passing through an unseen multitude.

"There may be a devilish Indian behind every tree," said Goodman Brown to himself; and he glanced fearfully behind him, as he added, "What if the devil himself should be at my very elbow!"

His head being turned back, he passed a crook of the road, and looking forward again, beheld the figure of a man, in grave and decent attire, seated at the foot of an old tree. He arose at Goodman Brown's approach, and walked onward, side by side with him.

"You are late, Goodman Brown," said he. "The clock of the Old South was striking, as I came through Boston; and that is full fifteen minutes agone."

"Faith kept me back awhile," replied the young man, with a tremor in his voice, caused by the sudden appearance of his companion, though not wholly unexpected.

It was now deep dusk in the forest, and deepest in that part of it where these two were journeying. As nearly as could be discerned, the second traveller was about fifty years old, apparently in the same rank of life as Goodman Brown, and bearing a considerable resemblance to him, though perhaps more in expression than features. Still, they might have been taken for father and son. And yet, though the elder person was as simply clad as the younger, and as simple in manner too, he had an indescribable air of one who knew the world, and would not have felt abashed at the governor's dinner-table, or in King William's court, were it possible that his affairs should call him thither. But the only thing about him that could be fixed upon as remarkable, was his staff, which bore the likeness of a great black snake, so curiously wrought, that it might almost be seen to twist and wriggle itself like a living serpent. This, of course, must have been an ocular deception, assisted by the uncertain light.

"Come, Goodman Brown!" cried his fellow-traveller, "this is a dull pace for the beginning of a journey. Take my staff, if you are so soon weary."

"Friend," said the other, exchanging his slow pace for a full stop, "having kept covenant by meeting thee here, it is my purpose now to return whence I came. I have scruples, touching the matter thou wot'st of."

"Sayest thou so?" replied he of the serpent, smiling apart. "Let us walk on, nevertheless, reasoning as we go, and if I convince thee not, thou shalt turn back. We are but a little way in the forest, yet."

"Too far, too far!" exclaimed the goodman, unconsciously resuming his walk. "My father never went into the woods on such an errand, nor his father before him. We have been a race of honest men and good Christians, since the days of the martyrs. And shall I be the first of the name of Brown that ever took this path and kept—"

"Such company, thou wouldst say," observed the elder person, interrupting his pause. "Well said, Goodman Brown! I have been as well acquainted with your family as with ever a one among the Puritans; and that's no trifle to say. I helped your grandfather, the constable, when he lashed the Quaker woman so smartly through the streets of Salem. And it was I that brought your father a pitch-pine knot, kindled at my own hearth, to set fire to an Indian village, in King Philip's war. They were my good friends, both; and many a pleasant walk have we had along this path, and returned merrily after midnight. I would fain be friends with you, for their sake."

"If it be as thou sayest," replied Goodman Brown, "I marvel they never spoke of these matters. Or, verily, I marvel not, seeing that the least rumor of the sort would have driven them from New England. We are a people of prayer, and good works to boot, and abide no such wickedness."

"Wickedness or not," said the traveller with twisted staff, "I have a very general acquaintance here in New England. The deacons of many a church have drunk the communion wine with me; the selectmen, of divers towns, make me their chairman; and a majority of the Great and General Court are firm supporters of my interest. The governor and I, too—but these are state secrets."

"Can this be so!" cried Goodman Brown, with a stare of amazement at his undisturbed companion. "Howbeit, I have nothing to do with the governor and council; they have their own ways, and are no rule for a simple husbandman like me. But, were I to go on with thee, how should I meet the eye of that good old man, our minister, at Salem village? Oh, his voice would make me tremble, both Sabbath-day and lecture-day!"

Thus far, the elder traveller had listened with due gravity, but now burst into a fit of irrepressible mirth, shaking himself so violently, that his snakelike staff actually seemed to wriggle in sympathy.

"Ha! ha! ha!" shouted he, again and again; then composing himself, "Well, go on, Goodman Brown, go on; but, prithee, don't kill me with laughing!"

"Well, then, to end the matter at once," said Goodman Brown, considerably nettled, "there is my wife, Faith. It would break her dear little heart; and I'd rather break my own!"

"Nay, if that be the case," answered the other, "e'en go thy ways, Goodman Brown. I would not, for twenty old women like the one hobbling before us, that Faith should come to any harm."

As he spoke, he pointed his staff at a female figure on the path, in whom Goodman Brown recognized a very pious and exemplary dame, who had taught him his catechism in youth, and was still his moral and spiritual adviser, jointly with the minister and Deacon Gookin.

"A marvel, truly, that Goody Cloyse should be so far in the wilderness, at nightfall!" said he. "But, with your leave, friend, I shall take a cut through the woods, until we have left this Christian woman behind. Being a stranger to you, she might ask whom I was consorting with, and whither I was going."

"Be it so," said his fellow-traveller. "Betake you to the woods, and let me keep the path."

Accordingly, the young man turned aside, but took care to watch his companion, who advanced softly along the road, until he had come within a staff's length of the old dame. She, meanwhile, was making the best of her way, with singular speed for so aged a woman, and mumbling some indistinct words, a prayer, doubtless, as she went. The traveller put forth his staff, and touched her withered neck with what seemed the serpent's tail.

"The devil!" screamed the pious old lady.

"Then Goody Cloyse knows her old friend?" observed the traveller, confronting her, and leaning on his writhing stick.

"Ah, forsooth, and is it your worship, indeed?" cried the good dame. "Yea, truly is it, and in the very image of my old gossip, Goodman Brown, the grandfather of the silly fellow that now is. But, would your worship believe it? my broomstick hath strangely disappeared, stolen, as I suspect, by that unhanged witch, Goody Cory, and that, too, when I was all anointed with the juice of smallage and cinque-foil and wolf's-bane—"

"Mingled with fine wheat and the fat of a new-born babe," said the shape of old Goodman Brown.

"Ah, your worship knows the recipe," cried the old lady, cackling aloud. "So, as I was saying, being all ready for the meeting, and no horse to ride on, I made up my mind to foot it; for they tell me there is a nice young man to be taken into communion to-night. But now your good worship will lend me your arm, and we shall be there in a twinkling."

"That can hardly be," answered her friend. "I may not spare you my arm, Goody Cloyse, but here is my staff, if you will."

So saying, he threw it down at her feet, where, perhaps, it assumed life, being one of the rods which its owner had formerly lent to the Egyptian Magi. Of this fact, however, Goodman Brown could not take cognizance. He had cast up his eyes in astonishment, and looking down again, beheld neither Goody Cloyse nor the serpentine staff, but his fellow-traveller alone, who waited for him as calmly as if nothing had happened.

"That old woman taught me my catechism!" said the young man; and there was a world of meaning in this simple comment.

They continued to walk onward, while the elder traveller exhorted his companion to make good speed and persevere in the path, discoursing so aptly, that his arguments seemed rather to spring up in the bosom of his auditor, than to be suggested by himself. As they went he plucked a branch of maple, to serve for a walking-stick, and began to strip it of the twigs and little boughs, which were wet with evening dew. The moment his fingers touched them, they became strangely withered and dried up, as with a week's sunshine. Thus the pair proceeded, at a good free pace, until suddenly, in a gloomy hollow of the road, Goodman Brown sat himself down on the stump of a tree, and refused to go any farther.

"Friend," said he, stubbornly, "my mind is made up. Not another step will I budge on this errand. What if a wretched old woman do choose to go to the devil, when I thought she was going to Heaven! Is that any reason why I should quit my dear Faith, and go after her?"

"You will think better of this by and by," said his acquaintance, composedly. "Sit here and rest yourself awhile; and when you feel like moving again, there is my staff to help you along."

Without more words, he threw his companion the maple stick, and was as speedily out of sight as if he had vanished into the deepening gloom. The young man sat a few moments by the roadside, applauding himself greatly, and thinking with how clear a conscience he should meet the minister, in his morning walk, nor shrink from the eye of good old Deacon Gookin. And what calm sleep would be his, that very night, which was to have been spent so wickedly, but purely and sweetly now, in the arms of Faith! Amidst these pleasant and praiseworthy meditations, Goodman Brown heard the tramp of horses along the road, and deemed it advisable to conceal himself within the verge of the forest, conscious of the guilty purpose that had brought him thither, though now so happily turned from it.

On came the hoof-tramps and the voices of the riders, two grave old voices, conversing soberly as they drew near. These mingled sounds appeared to pass along the road, within a few yards of the young man's hiding-place; but owing, doubtless, to the depth of the gloom, at that particular spot, neither the travellers nor their steeds were visible. Though their figures brushed the small boughs by the wayside, it could not be seen that they intercepted, even for a moment, the faint gleam from the strip of bright sky, athwart which they must have passed. Goodman Brown alternately crouched and stood on tiptoe, pulling aside the branches, and thrusting forth his head as far as he durst, without discerning so much as a shadow. It vexed him the more, because he could have sworn, were such a thing possible, that he recognized the voices of the minister and Deacon Gookin, jogging along quietly, as they were wont to do, when bound to some ordination or ecclesiastical council. While yet within hearing, one of the riders stopped to pluck a switch.

"Of the two, reverend Sir," said the voice like the deacon's, "I had rather miss an ordination dinner than to-night's meeting. They tell me that some of our community are to be here from Falmouth and beyond, and others from Connecticut and Rhode Island; besides several of the Indian powwows, who, after their fashion, know almost as much deviltry as the best of us. Moreover, there is a goodly young woman to be taken into communion."

"Mighty well, Deacon Gookin!" replied the solemn old tones of the minister. "Spur up, or we shall be late. Nothing can be done, you know, until I get on the ground."

The hoofs clattered again, and the voices, talking so strangely in the empty air, passed on through the forest, where no church had ever been gathered, nor solitary Christian prayed. Whither, then, could these holy men be journeying, so deep into the heathen wilderness? Young Goodman Brown caught hold of a tree, for support, being ready to sink down on the ground, faint and over-burthened with the heavy sickness of his heart. He looked up to the sky, doubting whether there really was a Heaven above him. Yet, there was the blue arch, and the stars brightening in it.

"With Heaven above, and Faith below, I will yet stand firm against the devil!" cried Goodman Brown.

While he still gazed upward, into the deep arch of the firmament, and had lifted his hands to pray, a cloud, though no wind was stirring, hurried across the zenith, and hid the brightening stars. The blue sky was still visible, except directly overhead, where this black mass of cloud was sweeping swiftly northward. Aloft in the air, as if from the depths of the cloud, came a confused and doubtful sound of voices. Once, the listener fancied that he could distinguish the accents of town's-people of his own, men and women, both pious and ungodly, many of whom he had met at the communion-table, and had seen others rioting at the tavern. The next moment, so indistinct were the sounds, he doubted whether he had heard aught but the murmur of the old forest, whispering without a wind. Then came a stronger swell of those familiar tones, heard daily in the sunshine, at Salem village, but never, until now, from a cloud at night. There was one voice, of a young woman, uttering lamentations, yet with an uncertain sorrow, and entreating for some favor, which, perhaps, it would grieve her to obtain. And all the unseen multitude, both saints and sinners, seemed to encourage her onward.

"Faith!" shouted Goodman Brown, in a voice of agony and desperation; and the echoes of the forest mocked him, crying—"Faith! Faith!" as if bewildered wretches were seeking her, all through the wilderness.

The cry of grief, rage, and terror was yet piercing the night, when the unhappy husband held his breath for a response. There was a scream, drowned immediately in a louder murmur of voices fading into far-off laughter, as the dark cloud swept away, leaving the clear and silent sky above Goodman Brown. But something fluttered lightly down through the air, and caught on the branch of a tree. The young man seized it and beheld a pink ribbon.

"My Faith is gone!" cried he, after one stupefied moment. "There is no good on earth, and sin is but a name. Come, devil! for to thee is this world given."

And maddened with despair, so that he laughed loud and long, did Goodman Brown grasp his staff and set forth again, at such a rate, that he seemed to fly along the forest path, rather than to walk or run. The road grew wilder and drearier, and more faintly traced, and vanished at length, leaving him in the heart of the dark wilderness, still rushing onward, with the instinct that guides mortal man to evil. The whole forest was peopled with frightful sounds; the creaking of the trees, the howling of wild beasts, and the yell of Indians; while, sometimes, the wind tolled like a distant church bell, and sometimes gave a broad roar around the traveller, as if all Nature were laughing him to scorn. But he was himself the chief horror of the scene, and shrank not from its other horrors.

"Ha! ha! ha!" roared Goodman Brown, when the wind laughed at him. "Let us hear which will laugh loudest! Think not to frighten me with your deviltry! Come witch, come wizard, come Indian powwow, come devil himself! and here comes Goodman Brown. You may as well fear him as he fear you!"

In truth, all through the haunted forest, there could be nothing more frightful than the figure of Goodman Brown. On he flew, among the black pines, brandishing his staff with frenzied gestures, now giving vent to an inspiration of horrid blasphemy, and now shouting forth such laughter, as set all the echoes of the forest laughing like demons around him. The fiend in his own shape is less hideous, than when he rages in the breast of man. Thus sped the demoniac on his course, until, quivering among the trees, he saw a red light before him, as when the felled trunks and branches of a clearing have been set on fire, and throw up their lurid blaze against the sky, at the hour of midnight. He paused, in a lull of the tempest that had driven him onward, and heard the swell of what seemed a hymn, rolling solemnly from a distance, with the weight of many voices. He knew the tune. It was a familiar one in the choir of the village meeting-house. The verse died heavily away, and was lengthened by a chorus, not of human voices, but of all the sounds of the benighted wilderness, pealing in awful harmony together. Goodman Brown cried out; and his cry was lost to his own ear, by its unison with the cry of the desert.

In the interval of silence, he stole forward, until the light glared full upon his eyes. At one extremity of an open space, hemmed in by the dark wall of the forest, arose a rock, bearing some rude, natural resemblance either to an altar or a pulpit, and surrounded by four blazing pines, their tops aflame, their stems untouched, like candles at an evening meeting. The mass of foliage, that had overgrown the summit of the rock, was all on fire, blazing high into the night, and fitfully illuminating the whole field. Each pendent twig and leafy festoon was in a blaze. As the red light arose and fell, a numerous congregation alternately shone forth, then disappeared in shadow, and again grew, as it were, out of the darkness, peopling the heart of the solitary woods at once.

"A grave and dark-clad company!" quoth Goodman Brown.

In truth, they were such. Among them, quivering to-and-fro, between gloom and splendor, appeared faces that would be seen, next day, at the council-board of the province, and others which, Sabbath after Sabbath, looked devoutly heavenward, and benignantly over the crowded pews, from the holiest pulpits in the land. Some affirm that the lady of the governor was there. At least, there were high dames well known to her, and wives of honored husbands, and widows a great multitude, and ancient maidens, all of excellent repute, and fair young girls, who trembled lest their mothers should espy them. Either the sudden gleams of light, flashing over the obscure field, bedazzled Goodman Brown, or he recognized a score of the church members of Salem village, famous for their especial sanctity. Good old Deacon Gookin had arrived, and waited at the skirts of that venerable saint, his reverend pastor. But, irreverently consorting with these grave, reputable, and pious people, these elders of the church, these chaste dames and dewy virgins, there were men of dissolute lives and women of spotted fame, wretches given over to all mean and filthy vice, and suspected even of horrid crimes. It was strange to see, that the good shrank not from the wicked, nor were the sinners abashed by the saints. Scattered, also, among their pale-faced enemies, were the Indian priests, or powwows, who had often scared their native forest with more hideous incantations than any known to English witchcraft.

"But, where is Faith?" thought Goodman Brown; and, as hope came into his heart, he trembled.

Another verse of the hymn arose, a slow and mournful strain, such as the pious love, but joined to words which expressed all that our nature can conceive of sin, and darkly hinted at far more. Unfathomable to mere mortals is the lore of fiends. Verse after verse was sung, and still the chorus of the desert swelled between, like the deepest tone of a mighty organ. And, with the final peal of that dreadful anthem, there came a sound, as if the roaring wind, the rushing streams, the howling beasts, and every other voice of the unconverted wilderness were mingling and according with the voice of guilty man, in homage to the prince of all. The four blazing pines threw up a loftier flame, and obscurely discovered shapes and visages of horror on the smoke-wreaths, above the impious assembly. At the same moment, the fire on the rock shot redly forth, and formed a glowing arch above its base, where now appeared a figure. With reverence be it spoken, the apparition bore no slight similitude, both in garb and manner, to some grave divine of the New England churches.

"Bring forth the converts!" cried a voice, that echoed through the field and rolled into the forest.

At the word, Goodman Brown stepped forth from the shadow of the trees, and approached the congregation, with whom he felt a loathful brotherhood, by the sympathy of all that was wicked in his heart. He could have well-nigh sworn, that the shape of his own dead father beckoned him to advance, looking downward from a smoke-wreath, while a woman, with dim features of despair, threw out her hand to warn him back. Was it his mother? But he had no power to retreat one step, nor to resist, even in thought, when the minister and good old Deacon Gookin seized his arms, and led him to the blazing rock. Thither came also the slender form of a veiled female, led between Goody Cloyse, that pious teacher of the catechism, and Martha Carrier, who had received the devil's promise to be queen of hell. A rampant hag was she! And there stood the proselytes, beneath the canopy of fire.

"Welcome, my children," said the dark figure, "to the communion of your race! Ye have found, thus young, your nature and your destiny. My children, look behind you!"

They turned; and flashing forth, as it were, in a sheet of flame, the fiend-worshippers were seen; the smile of welcome gleamed darkly on every visage.

"There," resumed the sable form, "are all whom ye have reverenced from youth. Ye deemed them holier than yourselves, and shrank from your own sin, contrasting it with their lives of righteousness and prayerful aspirations heavenward. Yet, here are they all, in my worshipping assembly! This night it shall be granted you to know their secret deeds; how hoary-bearded elders of the church have whispered wanton words to the young maids of their households; how many a woman, eager for widow's weeds, has given her husband a drink at bedtime, and let him sleep his last sleep in her bosom; how beardless youths have made haste to inherit their father's wealth; and how fair damsels—blush not, sweet ones!—have dug little graves in the garden, and bidden me, the sole guest, to an infant's funeral. By the sympathy of your human hearts for sin, ye shall scent out all the places—whether in church, bed-chamber, street, field, or forest—where crime has been committed, and shall exult to behold the whole earth one stain of guilt, one mighty blood-spot. Far more than this! It shall be yours to penetrate, in every bosom, the deep mystery of sin, the fountain of all wicked arts, and which inexhaustibly supplies more evil impulses than human power—than my power, at its utmost!—can make manifest in deeds. And now, my children, look upon each other."

They did so; and, by the blaze of the hell-kindled torches, the wretched man beheld his Faith, and the wife her husband, trembling before that unhallowed altar.

"Lo! there ye stand, my children," said the figure, in a deep and solemn tone, almost sad, with its despairing awfulness, as if his once angelic nature could yet mourn for our miserable race. "Depending upon one another's hearts, ye had still hoped that virtue were not all a dream! Now are ye undeceived!—Evil is the nature of mankind. Evil must be your only happiness. Welcome, again, my children, to the communion of your race!"

"Welcome!" repeated the fiend-worshippers, in one cry of despair and triumph.

And there they stood, the only pair, as it seemed, who were yet hesitating on the verge of wickedness, in this dark world. A basin was hollowed, naturally, in the rock. Did it contain water, reddened by the lurid light? or was it blood? or, perchance, a liquid flame? Herein did the Shape of Evil dip his hand, and prepare to lay the mark of baptism upon their foreheads, that they might be partakers of the mystery of sin, more conscious of the secret guilt of others, both in deed and thought, than they could now be of their own. The husband cast one look at his pale wife, and Faith at him. What polluted wretches would the next glance show them to each other, shuddering alike at what they disclosed and what they saw!

"Faith! Faith!" cried the husband. "Look up to Heaven, and resist the Wicked One!"

Whether Faith obeyed, he knew not. Hardly had he spoken, when he found himself amid calm night and solitude, listening to a roar of the wind, which died heavily away through the forest. He staggered against the rock, and felt it chill and damp, while a hanging twig, that had been all on fire, besprinkled his cheek with the coldest dew.

The next morning, young Goodman Brown came slowly into the street of Salem village staring around him like a bewildered man. The good old minister was taking a walk along the grave-yard, to get an appetite for breakfast and meditate his sermon, and bestowed a blessing, as he passed, on Goodman Brown. He shrank from the venerable saint, as if to avoid an anathema. Old Deacon Gookin was at domestic worship, and the holy words of his prayer were heard through the open window. "What God doth the wizard pray to?" quoth Goodman Brown. Goody Cloyse, that excellent old Christian, stood in the early sunshine, at her own lattice, catechising a little girl, who had brought her a pint of morning's milk. Goodman Brown snatched away the child, as from the grasp of the fiend himself. Turning the corner by the meetinghouse, he spied the head of Faith, with the pink ribbons, gazing anxiously forth, and bursting into such joy at sight of him that she skipt along the street, and almost kissed her husband before the whole village. But Goodman Brown looked sternly and sadly into her face, and passed on without a greeting.

Had Goodman Brown fallen asleep in the forest, and only dreamed a wild dream of a witch-meeting?

Be it so, if you will. But, alas! it was a dream of evil omen for young Goodman Brown. A stern, a sad, a darkly meditative, a distrustful, if not a desperate man did he become, from the night of that fearful dream. On the Sabbath day, when the congregation were singing a holy psalm, he could not listen, because an anthem of sin rushed loudly upon his ear, and drowned all the blessed strain. When the minister spoke from the pulpit, with power and fervid eloquence, and with his hand on the open Bible, of the sacred truths of our religion, and of saint-like lives and triumphant deaths, and of future bliss or misery unutterable, then did Goodman Brown turn pale, dreading lest the roof should thunder down upon the gray blasphemer and his hearers. Often, awaking suddenly at midnight, he shrank from the bosom of Faith, and at morning or eventide, when the family knelt down at prayer, he scowled, and muttered to himself, and gazed sternly at his wife, and turned away. And when he had lived long, and was borne to his grave, a hoary corpse, followed by Faith, an aged woman, and children and grandchildren, a goodly procession, besides neighbors not a few, they carved no hopeful verse upon his tombstone; for his dying hour was gloom.

Guy de Maupassant

TWO LITTLE SOLDIERS

Every Sunday, the moment they were dismissed, the two little soldiers made off. Once outside the barracks, they struck out to the right through Courbevoie, walking with long rapid strides, as though they were on a march.

When they were beyond the last of the houses, they slackened pace along the bare, dusty roadway which goes toward Bézons.

They were both small and thin, and looked quite lost in their coats, which were too big and too long. Their sleeves hung down over their hands, and they found their enormous red breeches, which compelled them to waddle, very much in the way. Under their stiff, high helmets their faces had little character—two poor, sallow Breton faces, simple with an almost animal simplicity, and with gentle and quiet blue eyes.

They never conversed during these walks, but went straight on, each with the same thought in his head. This thought atoned for the lack of conversation; it was this, that just inside the little wood near Les Champioux they had found a place which reminded them of their own country, where they could feel happy again.

When they arrived under the trees where the roads from Colombes and from Chatou cross, they would take off their heavy helmets and wipe their foreheads. They always halted on the Bézons bridge to look at the Seine, and would remain there two or three minutes, bent double, leaning on the parapet.

Sometimes they would gaze out over the great basin of Argenteuil, where the skiffs might be seen scudding, with their white, careening sails, recalling perhaps the look of the Breton waters, the harbor of Vanne, near which they lived, and the fishing-boats standing out across the Morbihan to the open sea.

Just beyond the Seine they bought their provisions from a sausage merchant, a baker, and a wine-seller. A piece of blood-pudding, four sous' worth of bread, and a liter of "petit bleu" constituted the provisions, which they

TWO LITTLE SOLDIERS First published in 1884.

carried off in their handkerchiefs. After they had left Bézons they traveled slowly and began to talk.

In front of them a barren plain studded with clumps of trees led to the wood, to the little wood which had seemed to them to resemble the one at Kermarivan. Grainfields and hayfields bordered the narrow path, which lost itself in the young greenness of the crops, and Jean Kerderen would always say to Luc le Ganidec:

"It looks like it does near Plounivon."

"Yes; exactly."

Side by side they strolled, their souls filled with vague memories of their own country, with awakened images as naive as the pictures on the colored broadsheets which you buy for a penny. They kept on recognizing, as it were, now a corner of a field, a hedge, a bit of moorland, now a crossroad, now a granite cross. Then, too, they would always stop beside a certain landmark, a great stone, because it looked something like the cromlech at Locneuven.

Every Sunday on arriving at the first clump of trees Luc le Ganidec would cut a switch, a hazel switch, and begin gently to peel off the bark, thinking meanwhile of the folk at home. Jean Kerderen carried the provisions.

From time to time Luc would mention a name, or recall some deed of their childhood in a few brief words, which caused long thoughts. And their own country, their dear, distant country, recaptured them little by little, seizing on their imaginations, and sending to them from afar her shapes, her sounds, her well-known prospects, her odors—odors of the green lands where the salt sea-air was blowing.

No longer conscious of the exhalations of the Parisian stables, on which the earth of the *banlieue* fattens, they scented the perfume of the flowering broom, which the salt breeze of the open sea plucks and bears away. And the sails of the boats from the river banks seemed like the white wings of the coasting vessels seen beyond the great plain which extended from their homes to the very margin of the sea.

They walked with short steps, Luc le Ganidec and Jean Kerderen, content and sad, haunted by a sweet melancholy, by the lingering, ever-present sorrow of a caged animal who remembers his liberty.

By the time that Luc had stripped the slender wand of its bark they reached the corner of the wood where every Sunday they took breakfast. They found the two bricks which they kept hidden in the thicket, and kindled a little fire of twigs, over which to roast the blood-pudding at the end of a bayonet.

When they had breakfasted, eaten their bread to the last crumb, and drunk their wine to the last drop, they remained seated side by side upon the

banlieue: suburbs or outskirts of a town

grass, saying nothing, their eyes on the distance, their eyelids drooping, their fingers crossed as at mass, their red legs stretched out beside the poppies of the field. And the leather of their helmets and the brass of their buttons glittered in the ardent sun, making the larks, which sang and hovered above their heads, cease in mid-song.

Toward noon they began to turn their eyes from time to time in the direction of the village of Bézons, because the girl with the cow was coming. She passed by them every Sunday on her way to milk and change the pasture of her cow—the only cow in this district which ever went out of the stable to grass. It was pastured in a narrow field along the edge of the wood a little farther on.

They soon perceived the girl, the only human being within vision, and were gladdened by the brilliant reflections thrown off by the tin milk-pail under the rays of the sun. They never talked about her. They were simply glad to see her, without understanding why.

She was a big strong wench with red hair, burned by the heat of sunny days, a sturdy product of the environs of Paris.

Once, finding them seated in the same place, she said:

"Good morning. You two are always here, aren't you?"

Luc le Ganidec, the bolder, stammered:

"Yes, we come to rest."

That was all. But the next Sunday she laughed on seeing them, laughed with a protecting benevolence and a feminine keenness which knew well enough that they were bashful. And she asked:

"What are you doing there? Are you trying to see the grass grow?"

Luc was cheered up by this, and smiled likewise: "Maybe we are."

"That's pretty slow work," said she.

He answered, still laughing: "Well, yes, it is."

She went on. But coming back with a milk-pail full of milk, she stopped again before them, and said:

"Would you like a little? It will taste like home."

With the instinctive feeling that they were of the same peasant race as she, being herself perhaps also far away from home, she had divined and touched the spot.

They were both touched. Then with some difficulty, she managed to make a little milk run into the neck of the glass bottle in which they carried their wine. And Luc drank first, with little swallows, stopping every minute to see whether he had drunk more than his half. Then he handed the bottle to Jean.

She stood upright before them, her hands on her hips, her pail on the ground at her feet, glad at the pleasure which she had given.

Then she departed, shouting: "*Allons,* adieu! Till next Sunday!"

Allons, adieu!: Let's say goodbye!

And as long as they could see her at all, they followed with their eyes her tall silhouette, which faded, growing smaller and smaller, seeming to sink into the verdure of the fields.

When they were leaving the barracks the week after, Jean said to Luc:

"Oughtn't we to buy her something good?"

They were in great embarrassment before the problem of the choice of a delicacy for the girl with the cow. Luc was of the opinion that a little tripe would be the best, but Jean preferred some *berlingots* because he was fond of sweets. His choice fairly made him enthusiastic, and they bought at a grocer's two sous' worth of white and red candies.

They ate their breakfast more rapidly than usual, being nervous with expectation.

Jean saw her first. "There she is!" he cried. Luc added: "Yes, there she is."

While yet some distance off she laughed at seeing them. Then she cried:

"Is everything going as you like it?"

And in unison they asked:

"Are you getting on all right?"

Then she conversed, talked to them of simple things in which they felt an interest—of the weather, of the crops, and of her master.

They were afraid to offer her the candies, which were slowly melting away in Jean's pocket.

At last Luc grew bold, and murmured.

"We have brought you something."

She demanded, "What is it? Tell me!"

Then Jean, blushing up to his ears, managed to get at the little paper cornucopia, and held it out.

She began to eat the little bonbons, rolling them from one cheek to the other where they made little round lumps. The two soldiers, seated before her, gazed at her with emotion and delight.

Then she went to milk her cow, and once more gave them some milk on coming back.

They thought of her all the week; several times they even spoke of her. The next Sunday she sat down with them for a little longer talk; and all three, seated side by side, their eyes lost in the distance, clasping their knees with their hands, told the small doings, the minute details of life in the villages where they had been born, while over there the cow, seeing that the milkmaid had stopped on her way, stretched out toward her its heavy head with its dripping nostrils, and gave a long low to call her.

Soon the girl consented to eat a bit of bread with them and drink a mouthful of wine. She often brought them plums in her pocket, for the

berlingots: sweetmeats made with caramel

season of plums had come. Her presence sharpened the wits of the two little Breton soldiers, and they chattered like two birds.

But, one Tuesday, Luc le Ganidec asked for leave—a thing which had never happened before—and he did not return until ten o'clock at night. Jean racked his brains uneasily for a reason for his comrade's going out in this way.

The next Thursday Luc, having borrowed ten sous from his bedfellow, again asked and obtained permission to leave the barracks for several hours. When he set off with Jean on their Sunday walk his manner was very queer, quite restless, and quite changed. Kerderen did not understand, but he vaguely suspected something without divining what it could be.

They did not say a word to one another until they reached their usual halting-place, where, from their constant sitting in the same spot the grass was quite worn away. They ate their breakfast slowly. Neither of them felt hungry.

Before long the girl appeared. As on every Sunday, they watched her coming. When she was quite near, Luc rose and made two steps forward. She put her milk-pail on the ground and kissed him. She kissed him passionately, throwing her arms about his neck, without noticing Jean, without remembering that he was there, without even seeing him.

And he sat there desperate, poor Jean, so desperate that he did not understand, his soul quite overwhelmed, but heart bursting, but not yet understanding himself. Then the girl seated herself beside Luc, and they began to chatter.

Jean did not look at them. He now divined why his comrade had gone out twice during the week, and he felt within him a burning grief, a kind of wound, that sense of rending which is caused by treason.

Luc and the girl went off together to change the position of the cow. Jean followed them with his eyes. He saw them departing side by side. The red breeches of his comrade made a bright spot on the road. It was Luc who picked up the mallet and hammered down the stake to which they tied the beast.

The girl stooped to milk her, while he stroked the cow's sharp spine with a careless hand. Then they left the milk-pail on the grass, and went deep into the wood.

Jean saw nothing but the wall of leaves where they had entered; and he felt himself so troubled that if he had tried to rise he would certainly have fallen. He sat motionless, stupefied by astonishment and suffering, with an agony which was simple but deep. He wanted to cry, to run away, to hide himself, never to see anybody any more.

Soon he saw them issuing from the thicket. They returned slowly, holding each other's hands as in the villages do those who are promised. It was Luc who carried the pail.

They kissed one another again before they separated, and the girl went off after having thrown Jean a friendly "Good evening" and a smile which was full of meaning. Today she no longer thought of offering him any milk.

The two little soldiers sat side by side, motionless as usual, silent and calm, their placid faces betraying nothing of all which troubled their hearts. The sun fell on them. Sometimes the cow lowed, looking at them from afar.

At their usual hour they rose to go back. Luc cut a switch. Jean carried the empty bottle to return it to the wine-seller at Bézons. Then they sallied out upon the bridge, and, as they did every Sunday, stopped several minutes in the middle to watch the water flowing.

Jean leaned, leaned more and more, over the iron railing, as though he saw in the current something which attracted him. Luc said: "Are you trying to drink?" Just as he uttered the last word Jean's head overbalanced his body, his legs described a circle in the air, and the little blue and red soldier fell in a heap, struck the water, and disappeared.

Luc, his tongue paralyzed with anguish, tried in vain to shout. Farther down he saw something stir; then the head of his comrade rose to the surface of the river and sank immediately. Farther still he again perceived a hand, a single hand, which issued from the stream and then disappeared. That was all.

The bargemen who dragged the river did not find the body that day.

Luc set out alone for the barracks, going at a run, his soul filled with despair. He told of the accident, with tears in his eyes, and a husky voice, blowing his nose again and again: "He leaned over—he—he leaned over—so far—so far that his head turned a somersault; and—and—so he fell—he fell—"

Choked with emotion, he could say no more. If he had only known!

Stephen Crane

THE BRIDE COMES TO YELLOW SKY

I

The great Pullman was whirling onward with such dignity of motion that a glance from the window seemed simply to prove that the plains of Texas were pouring eastward. Vast flats of green grass, dull-hued spaces of mesquite and cactus, little groups of frame houses, woods of light and tender trees, all were sweeping into the east, sweeping over the horizon, a precipice.

A newly married pair had boarded this coach at San Antonio. The man's face was reddened from many days in the wind and sun, and a direct result of his new black clothes was that his brick-colored hands were constantly performing in a most conscious fashion. From time to time he looked down

THE BRIDE COMES TO YELLOW SKY First published in 1898.

respectfully at his attire. He sat with a hand on each knee, like a man waiting in a barber's shop. The glances he devoted to other passengers were furtive and shy.

The bride was not pretty, nor was she very young. She wore a dress of blue cashmere, with small reservations of velvet here and there, and with steel buttons abounding. She continually twisted her head to regard her puff sleeves, very stiff, straight, and high. They embarrassed her. It was quite apparent that she had cooked, and that she expected to cook, dutifully. The blushes caused by the careless scrutiny of some passengers as she had entered the car were strange to see upon this plain, underclass countenance, which was drawn in placid, almost emotionless lines.

They were evidently very happy. "Ever been in a parlor car before?" he asked, smiling with delight.

"No," she answered, "I never was. It's fine, ain't it?"

"Great! And then after a while we'll go forward to the diner, and get a big lay-out. Finest meal in the world. Charge a dollar."

"Oh, do they?" cried the bride. "Charge a dollar? Why, that's too much —for us—ain't it, Jack?"

"Not this trip, anyhow," he answered bravely. "We're going to go the whole thing."

Later he explained to her about the trains. "You see, it's a thousand miles from one end of Texas to the other; and this train runs right across it, and never stops but four times." He had the pride of an owner. He pointed out to her the dazzling fittings of the coach; and in truth her eyes opened wider as she contemplated the sea-green figured velvet, the shining brass, silver, and glass, the wood that gleamed as darkly brilliant as the surface of a pool of oil. At one end a bronze figure sturdily held a support for a separated chamber, and at convenient places on the ceiling were frescos in olive and silver.

To the minds of the pair, their surroundings reflected the glory of their marriage that morning in San Antonio; this was the environment of their new estate; and the man's face in particular beamed with an elation that made him appear ridiculous to the Negro porter. This individual at times surveyed them from afar with an amused and superior grin. On other occasions he bullied them with skill in ways that did not make it exactly plain to them that they were being bullied. He subtly used all the manners of the most unconquerable kind of snobbery. He oppressed them; but of this oppression they had small knowledge, and they speedily forgot that infrequently a number of travelers covered them with stares of derisive enjoyment. Historically there was supposed to be something infinitely humorous in their situation.

"We are due in Yellow Sky at 3:42," he said, looking tenderly into her eyes.

"Oh, are we?" she said, as if she had not been aware of it. To evince surprise at her husband's statement was part of her wifely amiability. She took from a pocket a little silver watch; and as she held it before her, and stared at it with a frown of attention, the new husband's face shone.

"I bought it in San Anton' from a friend of mine," he told her gleefully.

"It's seventeen minutes past twelve," she said, looking up at him with a kind of shy and clumsy coquetry. A passenger, noting this play, grew excessively sardonic, and winked at himself in one of the numerous mirrors.

At last they went to the dining car. Two rows of Negro waiters, in glowing white suits, surveyed their entrance with the interest, and also the equanimity, of men who had been forewarned. The pair fell to the lot of a waiter who happened to feel pleasure in steering them through their meal. He viewed them with the manner of a fatherly pilot, his countenance radiant with benevolence. The patronage, entwined with the ordinary deference, was not plain to them. And yet, as they returned to their coach, they showed in their faces a sense of escape.

To the left, miles down a long purple slope, was a little ribbon of mist where moved the keening Rio Grande. The train was approaching it at an angle, and the apex was Yellow Sky. Presently it was apparent that, as the distance from Yellow Sky grew shorter, the husband became commensurately restless. His brick-red hands were more insistent in their prominence. Occasionally he was even rather absent-minded and faraway when the bride leaned forward and addressed him.

As a matter of truth, Jack Potter was beginning to find the shadow of a deed weigh upon him like a leaden slab. He, the town marshal of Yellow Sky, a man known, liked, and feared in his corner, a prominent person, had gone to San Antonio to meet a girl he believed he loved, and there, after the usual prayers, had actually induced her to marry him, without consulting Yellow Sky for any part of the transaction. He was now bringing his bride before an innocent and unsuspecting community.

Of course people in Yellow Sky married as it pleased them, in accordance with a general custom; but such was Potter's thought of his duty to his friends, or of their idea of his duty, or of an unspoken form which does not control men in these matters, that he felt he was heinous. He had committed an extraordinary crime. Face to face with this girl in San Antonio, and spurred by his sharp impulse, he had gone headlong over all the social hedges. At San Antonio he was like a man hidden in the dark. A knife to sever any friendly duty, any form, was easy to his hand in that remote city. But the hour of Yellow Sky—the hour of daylight—was approaching.

He knew full well that his marriage was an important thing to his town. It could only be exceeded by the burning of the new hotel. His friends could not forgive him. Frequently he had reflected on the advisability of telling them by telegraph, but a new cowardice had been upon him. He feared to do it. And now the train was hurrying him toward a scene of amazement, glee, and reproach. He glanced out of the window at the line of haze swinging slowly in toward the train.

Yellow Sky had a kind of brass band, which played painfully, to the delight of the populace. He laughed without heart as he thought of it. If the citizens could dream of his prospective arrival with his bride, they would parade the band at the station and escort them, amid cheers and laughing congratulations, to his adobe home.

He resolved that he would use all the devices of speed and plains-craft in making the journey from the station to his house. Once within that safe citadel, he could issue some sort of vocal bulletin, and then not go among the citizens until they had time to wear off a little of their enthusiasm.

The bride looked anxiously at him. "What's worrying you, Jack?"

He laughed again. "I'm not worrying, girl; I'm only thinking of Yellow Sky."

She flushed in comprehension.

A sense of mutual guilt invaded their minds and developed a finer tenderness. They looked at each other with eyes softly aglow. But Potter often laughed the same nervous laugh; the flush upon the bride's face seemed quite permanent.

The traitor to the feelings of Yellow Sky narrowly watched the speeding landscape. "We're nearly there," he said.

Presently the porter came and announced the proximity of Potter's home. He held a brush in his hand, and, with all his airy superiority gone, he brushed Potter's new clothes as the latter slowly turned this way and that way. Potter fumbled out a coin and gave it to the porter, as he had seen others do. It was a heavy and muscle-bound business, as that of a man shoeing his first horse.

The porter took their bag, and as the train began to slow they moved forward to the hooded platform of the car. Presently the two engines and their long string of coaches rushed into the station of Yellow Sky.

"They have to take water here," said Potter, from a constricted throat and in mournful cadence, as one announcing death. Before the train stopped, his eye had swept the length of the platform, and he was glad and astonished to see there was none upon it but the station agent, who, with a slightly hurried and anxious air, was walking toward the water tanks. When the train had halted, the porter alighted first, and placed in position a little temporary step.

"Come on, girl," said Potter, hoarsely. As he helped her down they each laughed on a false note. He took the bag from the Negro, and bade his wife cling to his arm. As they slunk rapidly away, his hangdog glance perceived that they were unloading the two trunks, and also that the station agent, far ahead near the baggage car, had turned and was running toward him, making gestures. He laughed, and groaned as he laughed, when he noted the first effect of his marital bliss upon Yellow Sky. He gripped his wife's arm firmly to his side, and they fled. Behind them the porter stood, chuckling fatuously.

2

The California express on the Southern Railway was due at Yellow Sky in twenty-one minutes. There were six men at the bar of the Weary Gentleman saloon. One was a drummer who talked a great deal and rapidly; three were Texans who did not care to talk at that time; and two were Mexican sheep-herders, who did not talk as a general practice in the Weary Gentleman saloon. The barkeeper's dog lay on the boardwalk that crossed in front of the door. His head was on his paws, and he glanced drowsily here and there with the constant vigilance of a dog that is kicked on occasion. Across the sandy street were some vivid green grass-plots, so wonderful in appearance, amid the sands that burned near them in a blazing sun, that they caused a doubt in the mind. They exactly resembled the grass mats used to represent lawns on the stage. At the cooler end of the railway station, a man without a coat sat in a tilted chair and smoked his pipe. The fresh-cut bank of the Rio Grande circled near the town, and there could be seen beyond it a great plum-colored plain of mesquite.

Save for the busy drummer and his companions in the saloon, Yellow Sky was dozing. The newcomer leaned gracefully upon the bar, and recited many tales with the confidence of a bard who has come upon a new field.

"—and at the moment that the old man fell downstairs with the bureau in his arms, the old woman was coming up with two scuttles of coal, and of course—"

The drummer's tale was interrupted by a young man who suddenly appeared in the open door. He cried: "Scratchy Wilson's drunk, and has turned loose with both hands." The two Mexicans at once set down their glasses and faded out of the rear entrance of the saloon.

The drummer, innocent and jocular, answered: "All right, old man. S'pose he has? Come in and have a drink, anyhow."

But the information had made such an obvious cleft in every skull in the room that the drummer was obliged to see its importance. All had become instantly solemn. "Say," said he, mystified, "what is this?" His three companions made the introductory gesture of eloquent speech; but the young man at the door forestalled them.

"It means, my friend," he answered, as he came into the saloon, "that for the next two hours this town won't be a health resort."

The barkeeper went to the door, and locked and barred it; reaching out of the window, he pulled in heavy wooden shutters, and barred them. Immediately a solemn, chapel-like gloom was upon the place. The drummer was looking from one to another.

"But say," he cried, "what is this, anyhow? You don't mean there is going to be a gun fight?"

"Don't know whether there'll be a fight or not," answered one man, grimly, "but there'll be some shootin'—some good shootin'."

The young man who had warned them waved his hand. "Oh, there'll be a fight fast enough, if any one wants it. Anybody can get a fight out there in the street. There's a fight just waiting."

The drummer seemed to be swayed between the interest of a foreigner and a perception of personal danger.

"What did you say his name was?" he asked.

"Scratchy Wilson," they answered in chorus.

"And will he kill anybody? What are you going to do? Does this happen often? Does he rampage around like this once a week or so? Can he break in that door?"

"No, he can't break down that door," replied the barkeeper. "He's tried it three times. But when he comes you'd better lay down on the floor, stranger. He's dead sure to shoot at it, and a bullet may come through."

Thereafter the drummer kept a strict eye upon the door. The time had not yet been called for him to hug the floor, but, as a minor precaution, he sidled near to the wall. "Will he kill anybody?" he said again.

The men laughed low and scornfully at the question.

"He's out to shoot, and he's out for trouble. Don't see any good in experimentin' with him."

"But what do you do in a case like this? What do you do?"

A man responded: "Why, he and Jack Potter—"

"But," in chorus the other men interrupted, "Jack Potter's in San Anton'."

"Well, who is he? What's he got to do with it?"

"Oh, he's the town marshal. He goes out and fights Scratchy when he gets on one of these tears."

"Wow!" said the drummer, mopping his brow. "Nice job he's got."

The voices had toned away to mere whisperings. The drummer wished to ask further questions, which were born of an increasing anxiety and bewilderment; but when he attempted them, the men merely looked at him in irritation and motioned him to remain silent. A tense waiting hush was upon them. In the deep shadows of the room their eyes shone as they listened for sounds from the street. One man made three gestures at the barkeeper; and the latter, moving like a ghost, handed him a glass and a bottle. The man poured a full glass of whisky, and set down the bottle noiselessly. He gulped the whisky in a swallow, and turned again toward the door in immovable silence. The drummer saw that the barkeeper, without a sound, had taken a Winchester from beneath the bar. Later he saw this individual beckoning to him, so he tip-toed across the room.

"You better come with me back of the bar."

"No, thanks," said the drummer, perspiring; "I'd rather be where I can make a break for the back door."

Whereupon the man of bottles made a kindly but peremptory gesture. The drummer obeyed it, and, finding himself seated on a box with his head below the level of the bar, balm was laid upon his soul at sight of various zinc and copper fittings that bore a resemblance to armor plate. The barkeeper took a seat comfortably upon an adjacent box.

"You see," he whispered, "this here Scratchy Wilson is a wonder with a gun—a perfect wonder; and when he goes on the war-trail, we hunt our holes—naturally. He's about the last one of the old gang that used to hang out along the river here. He's a terror when he's drunk. When he's sober he's all right—kind of simple—wouldn't hurt a fly—nicest fellow in town. But when he's drunk—whoo!"

There were periods of stillness. "I wish Jack Potter was back from San Anton'," said the barkeeper. "He shot Wilson up once—in the leg—and he would sail in and pull out the kinks in this thing."

Presently they heard from a distance the sound of a shot, followed by three wild yowls. It instantly removed a bond from the men in the darkened saloon. There was a shuffling of feet. They looked at each other. "Here he comes," they said.

3

A man in a maroon-colored flannel shirt, which had been purchased for purposes of decoration, and made principally by some Jewish women on the East Side of New York, rounded a corner and walked into the middle of the main street of Yellow Sky. In either hand the man held a long, heavy, blue-black revolver. Often he yelled, and these cries rang through a semblance of a deserted village, shrilly flying over the roofs in a volume that seemed to have no relation to the ordinary vocal strength of a man. It was as if the surrounding stillness formed the arch of a tomb over him. These cries of ferocious challenge rang against walls of silence. And his boots had red tops with gilded imprints, of the kind beloved in winter by little sledding boys on the hillsides of New England.

The man's face flamed in a rage begot of whisky. His eyes, rolling, and yet keen for ambush, hunted the still doorways and windows. He walked with the creeping movement of the midnight cat. As it occurred to him, he roared menacing information. The long revolvers in his hands were as easy as straws; they were moved with an electric swiftness. The little fingers of each hand played sometimes in a musician's way. Plain from the low collar of the shirt, the cords of his neck straightened and sank, straightened and sank, as passion moved him. The only sounds were his terrible invitations. The calm adobes preserved their demeanor at the passing of this small thing in the middle of the street.

There was no offer of fight—no offer of fight. The man called to the sky. There were no attractions. He bellowed and fumed and swayed his revolvers here and everywhere.

The dog of the barkeeper of the Weary Gentleman saloon had not appreciated the advance of events. He yet lay dozing in front of his master's door. At sight of the dog, the man paused and raised his revolver humorously. At sight of the man, the dog sprang up and walked diagonally away, with a sullen head, and growling. The man yelled, and the dog broke into a gallop. As it was about to enter an alley, there was a loud noise, a whistling, and something spat the ground directly before it. The dog screamed, and, wheeling in terror, galloped headlong in a new direction. Again there was a noise, a whistling, and sand was kicked viciously before it. Fear-stricken, the dog turned and flurried like an animal in a pen. The man stood laughing, his weapons at his hips.

Ultimately the man was attracted by the closed door of the Weary Gentleman saloon. He went to it and, hammering with a revolver, demanded drink.

The door remaining imperturbable, he picked a bit of paper from the walk, and nailed it to the framework with a knife. He then turned his back contemptuously upon this popular resort and, walking to the opposite side of the street and spinning there on his heel quickly and lithely, fired at the bit of paper. He missed it by a half-inch. He swore at himself, and went away. Later he comfortably fusilladed the windows of his most intimate friend. The man was playing with this town; it was a toy for him.

But still there was no offer of fight. The name of Jack Potter, his ancient antagonist, entered his mind, and he concluded that it would be a glad thing if he should go to Potter's house, and by bombardment induce him to come out and fight. He moved in the direction of his desire, chanting Apache scalp-music.

When he arrived at it, Potter's house presented the same still front as had the other adobes. Taking up a strategic position, the man howled a challenge. But this house regarded him as might a great stone god. It gave no sign. After a decent wait, the man howled further challenges, mingling with them wonderful epithets.

Presently there came the spectacle of a man churning himself into deepest rage over the immobility of a house. He fumed at it as the winter wind attacks a prairie cabin in the North. To the distance there should have gone the sound of a tumult like the fighting of two hundred Mexicans. As necessity bade him, he paused for breath or to reload his revolvers.

4

Potter and his bride walked sheepishly and with speed. Sometimes they laughed together shamefacedly and low.

"Next corner, dear," he said finally.

They put forth the efforts of a pair walking bowed against a strong wind. Potter was about to raise a finger to point the first appearance of the new home when, as they circled the corner, they came face to face with a man in a maroon-colored shirt, who was feverishly pushing cartridges into a large revolver. Upon the instant the man dropped his revolver to the ground and, like lightning, whipped another from its holster. The second weapon was aimed at the bridegroom's chest.

There was a silence. Potter's mouth seemed to be merely a grave for his tongue. He exhibited an instinct to at once loosen his arm from the woman's grip, and he dropped the bag to the sand. As for the bride, her face had gone as yellow as old cloth. She was a slave to hideous rites, gazing at the apparitional snake.

The two men faced each other at a distance of three paces. He of the revolver smiled with a new and quiet ferocity.

"Tried to sneak up on me," he said. "Tried to sneak up on me!" His eyes grew more baleful. As Potter made a slight movement, the man thrust his revolver venomously forward. "No, don't you do it, Jack Potter. Don't you move a finger toward a gun just yet. Don't you move an eyelash. The time has come for me to settle with you, and I'm goin' to do it my own way, and loaf along with no interferin'. So if you don't want a gun bent on you, just mind what I tell you."

Potter looked at his enemy. "I ain't got a gun on me, Scratchy," he said. "Honest, I ain't." He was stiffening and steadying, but yet somewhere at the back of his mind a vision of the Pullman floated: the sea-green figured velvet, the shining brass, silver, and glass, the wood that gleamed as darkly brilliant as the surface of a pool of oil—all the glory of the marriage, the environment of the new estate. "You know I fight when it comes to fighting, Scratchy Wilson; but I ain't got a gun on me. You'll have to do all the shootin' yourself."

His enemy's face went livid. He stepped forward and lashed his weapon to and fro before Potter's chest. "Don't you tell me you ain't got no gun on you, you whelp. Don't tell me no lie like that. There ain't a man in Texas ever seen you without no gun. Don't take me for no kid." His eyes blazed with light, and his throat worked like a pump.

"I ain't takin' you for no kid," answered Potter. His heels had not moved an inch backward. "I'm takin' you for a damn fool. I tell you I ain't got a gun, and I ain't. If you're goin' to shoot me up, you better begin now; you'll never get a chance like this again."

So much enforced reasoning had told on Wilson's rage; he was calmer. "If you ain't got a gun, why ain't you got a gun?" he sneered. "Been to Sunday school?"

"I ain't got a gun because I've just come from San Anton' with my wife. I'm married," said Potter. "And if I'd thought there was going to be any galoots like you prowling around when I brought my wife home, I'd had a gun, and don't you forget it."

"Married!" said Scratchy, not at all comprehending.

"Yes, married. I'm married," said Potter, distinctly.

"Married?" said Scratchy. Seemingly for the first time, he saw the drooping, drowning woman at the other man's side. "No!" he said. He was like a creature allowed a glimpse of another world. He moved a pace backward, and his arm, with the revolver, dropped to his side. "Is this the lady?" he asked.

"Yes, this is the lady," answered Potter.

There was another period of silence.

"Well," said Wilson at last, slowly, "I s'pose it's all off now."

"It's all off if you say so, Scratchy. You know I didn't make the trouble." Potter lifted his valise.

"Well, I 'low it's off, Jack," said Wilson. He was looking at the ground. "Married!" He was not a student of chivalry; it was merely that in the presence of this foreign condition he was a simple child of the earlier plains. He picked up his starboard revolver, and, placing both weapons in their holsters, he went away. His feet made funnel-shaped tracks in the heavy sand.

James Joyce

CLAY

The matron had given her leave to go out as soon as the women's tea was over and Maria looked forward to her evening out. The kitchen was spick and span: the cook said you could see yourself in the big copper boilers. The fire was nice and bright and on one of the side-tables were four very big barmbracks. These barmbracks seemed uncut; but if you went closer you would see that they had been cut into long thick even slices and were ready to be handed round at tea. Maria had cut them herself.

Maria was a very, very small person indeed but she had a very long nose and a very long chin. She talked a little through her nose, always soothingly: *Yes, my dear,* and *No, my dear*. She was always sent for when the women quarrelled over their tubs and always succeeded in making peace. One day the matron had said to her:

—Maria, you are a veritable peace-maker!

And the sub-matron and two of the Board ladies had heard the compliment. And Ginger Mooney was always saying what she wouldn't do to the dummy who had charge of the irons if it wasn't for Maria. Everyone was so fond of Maria.

The women would have their tea at six o'clock and she would be able to get away before seven. From Ballsbridge to the Pillar, twenty minutes; from the Pillar to Drumcondra, twenty minutes; and twenty minutes to buy the things. She would be there before eight. She took out her purse with the silver clasps and read again the word *A Present from Belfast*. She was very fond of that purse because Joe had brought it to her five years before when he and Alphy had gone to Belfast on a Whit-Monday trip. In the purse were two half-crowns and some coppers. She would have five shillings clear after paying tram fare. What a nice evening they would have, all the children singing! Only she hoped that Joe wouldn't come in drunk. He was so different when he took any drink.

Often he had wanted her to go and live with them; but she would have felt herself in the way (though Joe's wife was ever so nice with her) and she had become accustomed to the life of the laundry. Joe was a good fellow. She had nursed him and Alphy too; and Joe used often say:

—Mamma is mamma but Maria is my proper mother.

After the break-up at home the boys had got her that position in the *Dublin by Lamplight* laundry, and she liked it. She used to have such a bad opinion of Protestants but now she thought they were very nice people, a little quiet and serious, but still very nice people to live with. Then she had her plants in the conservatory and she liked looking after them. She had lovely ferns and wax-plants and, whenever anyone came to visit her, she always gave the visitor one or two slips from her conservatory. There was one thing she didn't like and that was the tracts on the walls; but the matron was such a nice person to deal with, so genteel.

When the cook told her everything was ready she went into the women's room and began to pull the big bell. In a few minutes the women began to come in by twos and threes, wiping their steaming hands in their petticoats and pulling down the sleeves of their blouses over their red steaming arms. They settled down before their huge mugs which the cook and the dummy filled up with hot tea, already mixed with milk and sugar in huge tin cans. Maria superintended the distribution of the barmbrack and saw that every woman got her four slices. There was a great deal of laughing and joking during the meal. Lizzie Fleming said Maria was sure to get the ring and, though Fleming had said that for so many Hallow Eves, Maria had to laugh and say she didn't want any ring or man either; and when she laughed her grey-green eyes sparkled with disappointed shyness and the tip of her nose nearly met the tip of her chin. Then Ginger Mooney lifted up her mug of tea and proposed Maria's health while all the other women clattered with their mugs on the table, and said she was sorry she hadn't a sup of porter to drink it in. And Maria laughed again till the tip of her nose nearly met the tip of her chin and till her minute body nearly shook itself asunder because she knew that Mooney meant well though, of course, she had the notions of a common woman.

But wasn't Maria glad when the women had finished their tea and the cook and the dummy had begun to clear away the tea-things! She went into her little bedroom and, remembering that the next morning was a mass morning, changed the hand of the alarm from seven to six. Then she took off her working skirt and her house-boots and laid her best skirt out on the bed and her tiny dress-boots beside the foot of the bed. She changed her blouse too and, as she stood before the mirror, she thought of how she used to dress for mass on Sunday morning when she was a young girl; and she looked with quaint affection at the diminutive body which she had so often adorned. In spite of its years she found it a nice tidy little body.

When she got outside the streets were shining with rain and she was glad of her old brown raincloak. The tram was full and she had to sit on the little stool at the end of the car, facing all the people, with her toes barely touching the floor. She arranged in her mind all she was going to do and thought how much better it was to be independent and to have your own money in your pocket. She hoped they would have a nice evening. She was sure they would but she could not help thinking what a pity it was Alphy and Joe were not speaking. They were always falling out now but when they were boys together they used to be the best of friends: but such was life.

She got out of her tram at the Pillar and ferreted her way quickly among the crowds. She went into Downes's cakeshop but the shop was so full of people that it was a long time before she could get herself attended to. She bought a dozen of mixed penny cakes, and at last came out of the shop laden with a big bag. Then she thought what else would she buy: she wanted to buy something really nice. They would be sure to have plenty of apples and nuts. It was hard to know what to buy and all she could think of was cake. She decided to buy some plumcake but Downes's plumcake had not enough almond icing on top of it so she went over to a shop in Henry Street. Here she was a long time in suiting herself and the stylish young lady behind the counter, who was evidently a little annoyed by her, asked her was it wedding-cake she wanted to buy. That made Maria blush and smile at the young lady; but the young lady took it all very seriously and finally cut a thick slice of plumcake, parcelled it up and said:

—Two-and-four, please.

She thought she would have to stand in the Drumcondra tram because none of the young men seemed to notice her but an elderly gentleman made room for her. He was a stout gentleman and he wore a brown hard hat; he had a square red face and a greyish moustache. Maria thought he was a colonel-looking gentleman and she reflected how much more polite he was than the young men who simply stared straight before them. The gentleman began to chat with her about Hallow Eve and the rainy weather. He supposed the bag was full of good things for the little ones and said it was only right that the youngsters should enjoy themselves while they were young. Maria agreed with him and favoured him with demure nods and hems. He was very nice with her, and when she was getting out at the Canal Bridge she thanked him and bowed, and he bowed to her and raised his hat and smiled agreeably; and while she was going up along the terrace, bending her tiny head under the rain, she thought how easy it was to know a gentleman even when he has a drop taken.

Everybody said: *O, here's Maria!* when she came to Joe's house. Joe was there, having come home from business, and all the children had their Sunday dresses on. There were two big girls in from next door and games were going on. Maria gave the bag of cakes to the eldest boy, Alphy, to divide and Mrs. Donnelly said it was too good of her to bring such a big bag of cakes and made all the children say:

—Thanks, Maria.

But Maria said she had brought something special for papa and mamma, something they would be sure to like, and she began to look for her plumcake. She tried in Downes's bag and then in the pockets of her raincloak and then on the hall-stand but nowhere could she find it. Then she asked all the children had any of them eaten it—by mistake, of course—but the children all said no and looked as if they did not like to eat cakes if they were to be accused of stealing. Everybody had a solution for the mystery and Mrs. Donnelly said it was plain that Maria had left it behind her in the tram. Maria, remembering how confused the gentleman with the greyish moustache had made her, coloured with shame and vexation and disappointment. At the thought of the failure of her little surprise and of the two and fourpence she had thrown away for nothing she nearly cried outright.

But Joe said it didn't matter and made her sit down by the fire. He was very nice with her. He told her all that went on in his office, repeating for her a smart answer which he had made to the manager. Maria did not understand why Joe laughed so much over the answer he had made but she said that the manager must have been a very overbearing person to deal with. Joe said he wasn't so bad when you knew how to take him, that he was a decent sort so long as you didn't rub him the wrong way. Mrs. Donnelly played the piano for the children and they danced and sang. Then the two next-door girls handed round the nuts. Nobody could find the nutcrackers and Joe was nearly getting cross over it and asked how did they expect Maria to crack nuts without a nutcracker. But Maria said she didn't like nuts and that they weren't to bother about her. Then Joe asked would she take a bottle of stout and Mrs. Donnelly said there was port wine too in the house if she would prefer that. Maria said she would rather they didn't ask her to take anything: but Joe insisted.

So Maria let him have his way and they sat by the fire talking over old times and Maria thought she would put in a good word for Alphy. But Joe cried that God might strike him stone dead if ever he spoke a word to his brother again and Maria said she was sorry she had mentioned the matter. Mrs. Donnelly told her husband it was a great shame for him to speak that way of his own flesh and blood but Joe said that Alphy was no brother of his and there was nearly being a row on the head of it. But Joe said he would not lose his temper on account of the night it was and asked his wife to open some more stout. The two next-door girls had arranged some Hallow Eve games and soon everything was merry again. Maria was delighted to see the children so merry and Joe and his wife in such good spirits. The next-door girls put some saucers on the table and then led the children up to the table, blindfold. One got the prayer-book and the other three got the water; and when one of the next-door girls got the ring Mrs. Donnelly shook her finger at the blushing girl as much as to say: *O, I know all about it!* They insisted then on blindfolding Maria and leading her up to the table to see what she would get; and, while they were putting on the bandage, Maria laughed and laughed again till the tip of her nose nearly met the tip of her chin.

They led her up to the table amid laughing and poking and she put her hand out in the air as she was told to do. She moved her hand about here and there in the air and descended on one of the saucers. She felt a soft wet substance with her fingers and was surprised that nobody spoke or took off her bandage. There was a pause for a few seconds; and then a great deal of scuffling and whispering. Somebody said something about the garden, and at last Mrs. Donnelly said something very cross to one of the next-door girls and told her to throw it out at once: that was no play. Maria understood that it was wrong that time and so she had to do it over again: and this time she got the prayer-book.

After that Mrs. Donnelly played Miss McCloud's Reel for the children and Joe made Maria take a glass of wine. Soon they were all quite merry again and Mrs. Donnelly said Maria would enter a convent before the year was out because she had got the prayer-book. Maria had never seen Joe so nice to her as he was that night, so full of pleasant talk and reminiscences. She said they were all very good to her.

At last the children grew tired and sleepy and Joe asked Maria would she not sing some little song before she went, one of the old songs. Mrs. Donnelly said *Do, please, Maria!* and so Maria had to get up and stand beside the piano. Mrs. Donnelly bade the children be quiet and listen to Maria's song. Then she played the prelude and said *Now, Maria!* and Maria, blushing very much, began to sing in a tiny quavering voice. She sang *I Dreamt that I Dwelt,* and when she came to the second verse she sang again:

I dreamt that I dwelt in marble halls
With vassals and serfs at my side
And of all who assembled within those walls
That I was the hope and the pride.

I had riches too great to count, could boast
Of a high ancestral name,
But I also dreamt, which pleased me most,
That you loved me still the same.

But no one tried to show her her mistake; and when she had ended her song Joe was very much moved. He said that there was no time like the long ago and no music for him like poor old Balfe, whatever other people might say; and his eyes filled up so much with tears that he could not find what he was looking for and in the end he had to ask his wife to tell him where the corkscrew was.

Eudora Welty

DEATH OF A TRAVELLING SALESMAN

R. J. Bowman, who for fourteen years had travelled for a shoe company through Mississippi, drove his Ford along a rutted dirt path. It was a long day! The time did not seem to clear the noon hurdle and settle into soft afternoon. The sun, keeping its strength here even in winter, stayed at the top of the sky, and every time Bowman stuck his head out of the dusty car to stare up the road, it seemed to reach a long arm down and push against the top of his head, right through his hat—like the practical joke of an old drummer, long on the road. It made him feel all the more angry and helpless. He was feverish, and he was not quite sure of the way.

This was his first day back on the road after a long siege of influenza. He had had very high fever, and dreams, and had become weakened and pale, enough to tell the difference in the mirror, and he could not think clearly . . . All afternoon, in the midst of his anger, and for no reason, he had thought of his dead grandmother. She had been a comfortable soul. Once more Bowman wished he could fall into the big feather bed that had been in her room . . . Then he forgot her again.

This desolate hill country! And he seemed to be going the wrong way—it was as if he were going back, far back. There was not a house in sight. . . . There was no use wishing he were back in bed, though. By paying the hotel doctor his bill he had proved his recovery. He had not even been sorry when the pretty trained nurse said good-bye. He did not like illness, he distrusted it, as he distrusted the road without signposts. It angered him. He had given the nurse a really expensive bracelet, just because she was packing up her bag and leaving.

But now—what if in fourteen years on the road he had never been ill before and never had an accident? His record was broken, and he had even begun almost to question it . . . He had gradually put up at better hotels, in the bigger towns, but weren't they all, eternally, stuffy in summer and draughty in winter? Women? He could only remember little rooms within little rooms, like a nest of Chinese paper boxes, and if he thought of one woman he saw the worn loneliness that the furniture of that room seemed built of. And he himself—he was a man who always wore rather wide-brimmed black hats, and in the wavy hotel mirrors had looked something like a bull-fighter, as he paused for that inevitable instant on the landing, walking downstairs to supper . . . He leaned out of the car again, and once more the sun pushed at his head.

Bowman had wanted to reach Beulah by dark, to go to bed and sleep off his fatigue. As he remembered, Beulah was fifty miles away from the last town, on a gravelled road. This was only a cow trail. How had he ever come to such a place? One hand wiped the sweat from his face, and he drove on.

He had made the Beulah trip before. But he had never seen this hill or this petering-out path before—or that cloud, he thought shyly, looking up and then down quickly—any more than he had seen this day before. Why did he not admit he was simply lost and had been for miles? . . . He was not in the habit of asking the way of strangers, and these people never knew where the very roads they lived on went to; but then he had not even been close enough to anyone to call out. People standing in the fields now and then, or on top of the haystacks, had been too far away, looking like leaning sticks or weeds, turning a little at the solitary rattle of his car across their countryside, watching the pale sobered winter dust where it chunked out behind like big squashes down the road. The stares of these distant people had followed him solidly like a wall, impenetrable, behind which they turned back after he had passed.

The cloud floated there to one side like the bolster on his grandmother's bed. It went over a cabin on the edge of a hill, where two bare chinaberry trees clutched at the sky. He drove through a heap of dead oak leaves, his wheels stirring their weightless sides to make a silvery melancholy whistle as the car passed through their bed. No car had been along this way ahead of him. Then he saw that he was on the edge of a ravine that fell away, a red erosion, and that this was indeed the road's end.

He pulled the brake. But it did not hold, though he put all his strength into it. The car, tipped toward the edge, rolled a little. Without doubt, it was going over the bank.

He got out quietly, as though some mischief had been done him and he had his dignity to remember. He lifted his bag and sample case out, set them down, and stood back and watched the car roll over the edge. He heard something—not the crash he was listening for, but a slow un-uproarious crackle. Rather distastefully he went to look over, and he saw that his car had fallen into a tangle of immense grape vines as thick as his arm, which caught it and held it, rocked it like a grotesque child in a dark cradle, and then, as he watched, concerned somehow that he was not still inside it, released it gently to the ground.

He sighed.

Where am I? he wondered with a shock. Why didn't I do something? All his anger seemed to have drifted away from him. There was the house, back on the hill. He took a bag in each hand and with almost childlike willingness went toward it. But his breathing came with difficulty, and he had to stop to rest.

It was a shotgun house, two rooms and an open passage between, perched on the hill. The whole cabin slanted a little under the heavy heaped-up vine that covered the roof, light and green, as though forgotten from summer. A woman stood in the passage.

He stopped still. Then all of a sudden his heart began to behave strangely. Like a rocket set off, it began to leap and expand into uneven patterns of beats which showered into his brain, and he could not think. But in scattering and falling it made no noise. It shot up with great power, almost elation, and fell gently, like acrobats into nets. It began to pound profoundly, then waited irresponsibly, hitting in some sort of inward mockery first at his ribs, then against his eyes, then under his shoulder blades, and against the roof of his mouth when he tried to say, "Good afternoon, madam." But he could not hear his heart—it was as quiet as ashes falling. This was rather comforting; still, it was shocking to Bowman to feel his heart beating at all.

Stockstill in his confusion, he dropped his bags, which seemed to drift in slow bulks gracefully through the air and to cushion themselves on the grey prostrate grass near the doorstep.

As for the woman standing there, he saw at once that she was old. Since she could not possibly hear his heart, he ignored the pounding and now looked at her carefully, and yet in his distraction dreamily, with his mouth open.

She had been cleaning the lamp, and held it, half blackened, half clear, in front of her. He saw her with the dark passage behind her. She was a big woman with a weather-beaten but unwrinkled face; her lips were held tightly together, and her eyes looked with a curious dulled brightness into his. He looked at her shoes, which were like bundles. If it were summer she would be barefoot . . . Bowman, who automatically judged a woman's age on sight, set her age at fifty. She wore a formless garment of some grey coarse material, rough-dried from a washing, from which her arms appeared pink and unexpectedly round. When she never said a word, and sustained her quiet pose of holding the lamp, he was convinced of the strength in her body.

"Good afternoon, madam," he said.

She stared on, whether at him or at the air around him he could not tell, but after a moment she lowered her eyes to show that she would listen to whatever he had to say.

"I wonder if you would be interested—" He tried once more. "An accident—my car . . ."

Her voice emerged low and remote, like a sound across a lake. "Sonny he ain't here."

"Sonny?"

"Sonny ain't here now."

Her son—a fellow able to bring my car up, he decided in blurred relief. He pointed down the hill. "My car's in the bottom of the ditch. I'll need help."

"Sonny ain't here, but he'll be here."

She was becoming clearer to him and her voice stronger, and Bowman saw that she was stupid.

He was hardly surprised at the deepening postponement and tedium of his journey. He took a breath, and heard his voice speaking over the silent blows of his heart. "I was sick. I am not strong yet . . . May I come in?"

He stooped and laid his big black hat over the handle on his bag. It was a humble motion, almost a bow, that instantly struck him as absurd and betraying of all his weakness. He looked up at the woman, the wind blowing his hair. He might have continued for a long time in this unfamiliar attitude; he had never been a patient man, but when he was sick he had learned to sink submissively into the pillows, to wait for his medicine. He waited on the woman.

Then she, looking at him with blue eyes, turned and held open the door, and after a moment Bowman, as if convinced in his action, stood erect and followed her in.

Inside, the darkness of the house touched him like a professional hand, the doctor's. The woman set the half-cleaned lamp on a table in the centre of the room and pointed, also like a professional person, a guide, to a chair with a yellow cowhide seat. She herself crouched on the hearth, drawing her knees up under the shapeless dress.

At first he felt hopefully secure. His heart was quieter. The room was enclosed in the gloom of yellow pine boards. He could see the other room, with the foot of an iron bed showing, across the passage. The bed had been made up with a red-and-yellow pieced quilt that looked like a map or a picture, a little like his grandmother's girlhood painting of Rome burning.

He had ached for coolness, but in this room it was cold. He stared at the hearth with dead coals lying on it and iron pots in the corners. The hearth and smoked chimney were of the stone he had seen ribbing the hills, mostly slate. Why is there no fire? he wondered.

And it was so still. The silence of the fields seemed to enter and move familiarly through the house. The wind used the open hall. He felt that he was in a mysterious, quiet, cool danger. It was necessary to do what? . . . To talk.

"I have a nice line of women's low-priced shoes . . ." he said.

But the woman answered, "Sonny'll be here. He's strong. Sonny'll move your car."

"Where is he now?"

"Farms for Mr. Redmond."

Mr. Redmond. Mr. Redmond. That was someone he would never have to encounter, and he was glad. Somehow the name did not appeal to him . . . In a flare of touchiness and anxiety, Bowman wished to avoid even mention of unknown men and their unknown farms.

"Do you two live here alone?" He was surprised to hear his old voice, chatty, confidential, inflected for selling shoes, asking a question like that—a thing he did not even want to know.

"Yes. We are alone."

He was surprised at the way she answered. She had taken a long time to say that. She had nodded her head in a deep way too. Had she wished to affect him with some sort of premonition? he wondered unhappily. Or was it only that she would not help him, after all, by talking with him? For he was not strong enough to receive the impact of unfamiliar things without a little talk to break their fall. He had lived a month in which nothing had happened except in his head and his body—an almost inaudible life of heartbeats and dreams that came back, a life of fever and privacy, a delicate life which had left him weak to the point of—what? Of begging. The pulse in his palm leapt like a trout in a brook.

He wondered over and over why the woman did not go ahead with cleaning the lamp. What prompted her to stay there across the room, silently bestowing her presence upon him? He saw that with her it was not a time for doing little tasks. Her face was grave; she was feeling how right she was. Perhaps it was only politeness. In docility he held his eyes stiffly wide; they fixed themselves on the woman's clasped hands as though she held the cord they were strung on.

Then, "Sonny's coming," she said.

He himself had not heard anything, but there came a man passing the window and then plunging in at the door, with two hounds beside him. Sonny was a big enough man, with his belt slung low about his hips. He looked at least thirty. He had a hot, red face that was yet full of silence. He wore muddy blue pants and an old military coat stained and patched. World War? Bowman wondered. Great God, it was a Confederate coat. On the back of his light hair he had a wide filthy black hat which seemed to insult Bowman's own. He pushed down the dogs from his chest. He was strong with dignity and heaviness in his way of moving . . . There was the resemblance to his mother.

They stood side by side . . . He must account again for his presence here.

"Sonny, this man, he had his car to run off over the prec'pice an' wants to know if you will git it out for him," the woman said after a few minutes.

Bowman could not even state his case.

Sonny's eyes lay upon him.

He knew he should offer explanations and show money—at least appear either penitent or authoritative. But all he could do was to shrug slightly.

Sonny brushed by him going to the window, followed by the eager dogs, and looked out. There was effort even in the way he was looking, as if he could throw his sight out like a rope. Without turning Bowman felt that his own eyes could have seen nothing: it was too far.

"Got me a mule out there an' got me a block an' tackle," said Sonny meaningfully. "I *could* catch me my mule an' git me my ropes, an' before long I'd git your car out the ravine."

He looked completely round the room, as if in meditation, his eyes roving in their own distance. Then he pressed his lips firmly and yet shyly together, and with the dogs ahead of him this time, he lowered his head and strode out. The hard earth sounded, cupping to his powerful way of walking —almost a stagger.

Mischievously, at the suggestion of those sounds, Bowman's heart leapt again. It seemed to walk about inside him.

"Sonny's goin' to do it," the woman said. She said it again, singing it almost, like a song. She was sitting in her place by the hearth.

Without looking out, he heard some shouts and the dogs barking and the pounding of hoofs in short runs on the hill. In a few minutes Sonny passed under the window with a rope, and there was a brown mule with quivering, shining, purple-looking ears. The mule actually looked in the window. Under his eyelashes it turned target-like eyes into his. Bowman averted his head and saw the woman looking serenely back at the mule, with only satisfaction in her face.

She sang a little more, under her breath. It occurred to him, and it seemed quite marvellous, that she was not really talking to him, but rather following the thing that came about with words that were unconscious and part of her looking.

So he said nothing, and this time when he did not reply he felt a curious and strong emotion, not fear, rise up in him.

This time, when his heart leapt, something—his soul—seemed to leap too, like a little colt invited out of a pen. He stared at the woman while the frantic nimbleness of his feeling made his head sway. He could not move; there was nothing he could do, unless perhaps he might embrace this woman who sat there growing old and shapeless before him.

But he wanted to leap up, to say to her, I have been sick and I found out then, only then, how lonely I am. Is it too late? My heart puts up a struggle inside me, and you may have heard it, protesting against emptiness . . . It should be full, he would rush on to tell her, thinking of his heart now as a deep lake, it should be holding love like other hearts. It should be flooded with love. There would be a warm spring day . . . Come and stand in my heart, whoever you are, and a whole river would cover your feet and rise higher and take your knees in whirlpools, and draw you down to itself, your whole body, your heart too.

But he moved a trembling hand across his eyes, and looked at the placid crouching woman across the room. She was still as a statue. He felt ashamed and exhausted by the thought that he might, in one more moment, have tried by simple words and embraces to communicate some strange thing—something which seemed always to have just escaped him . . .

Sunlight touched the farthest pot on the hearth. It was late afternoon. This time to-morrow he would be somewhere on a good gravelled road, driving his car past things that happened to people, quicker than their happening. Seeing ahead to the next day, he was glad, and knew that this was no time to embrace an old woman. He could feel in his pounding temples the readying of his blood for motion and for hurrying away.

"Sonny's hitched up your car by now," said the woman. "He'll git it out the ravine right shortly."

"Fine!" he cried with his customary enthusiasm.

Yet it seemed a long time that they waited. It began to get dark. Bowman was cramped in his chair. Any man should know enough to get up and walk around while he waited. There was something like guilt in such stillness and silence.

But instead of getting up, he listened . . . His breathing restrained, his eyes powerless in the growing dark, he listened uneasily for a warning sound, forgetting in wariness what it would be. Before long he heard something—soft, continuous, insinuating.

"What's the noise?" he asked, his voice jumping into the dark. Then wildly he was afraid it would be his heart beating so plainly in the quiet room, and she would tell him so.

"You might hear the stream," she said grudgingly.

Her voice was closer. She was standing by the table. He wondered why she did not light the lamp. She stood there in the dark and did not light it.

Bowman would never speak to her now, for the time was past. I'll sleep in the dark, he thought, in his bewilderment pitying himself.

Heavily she moved on to the window. Her arm, vaguely white, rose straight from her full side and she pointed out into the darkness.

"That white speck's Sonny," she said, talking to herself.

He turned unwillingly and peered over her shoulder; he hesitated to rise and stand beside her. His eyes searched the dusky air. The white speck floated smoothly toward her finger, like a leaf on a river, growing whiter in the dark. It was as if she had shown him something secret, part of her life, but had offered no explanation. He looked away. He was moved almost to tears, feeling for no reason that she had made a silent declaration equivalent to his own. His hand waited upon his chest.

Then a step shook the house, and Sonny was in the room. Bowman felt how the woman left him there and went to the other man's side.

"I done got your car out, mister," said Sonny's voice in the dark. "She's settin' a-waitin' in the road, turned to go back where she come from."

"Fine!" said Bowman, projecting his own voice to loudness. "I'm surely much obliged—I could never have done it myself—I was sick . . ."

"I could do it easy," said Sonny.

Bowman could feel them both waiting in the dark, and he could hear the dogs panting out in the yard, waiting to bark when he should go. He felt strangely helpless and resentful. Now that he could go, he longed to stay. From what was he being deprived? His chest was rudely shaken by the violence of his heart. These people cherished something here that he could not see, they withheld some ancient promise of food and warmth and light. Between them they had a conspiracy. He thought of the way she had moved away from him and gone to Sonny, she had flowed toward him. He was shaking with cold, he was tired, and it was not fair. Humbly and yet angrily he stuck his hand into his pocket.

"Of course I'm going to pay you for everything—"

"We don't take money for such," said Sonny's voice belligerently.

"I want to pay. But do something more . . . Let me stay—to-night . . ." He took another step toward them. If only they could see him, they would know his sincerity, his real need! His voice went on, "I'm not very strong yet, I'm not able to walk far, even back to my car, maybe, I don't know—I don't know exactly where I am—"

He stopped. He felt as if he might burst into tears. What would they think of him!

Sonny came over and put his hands on him. Bowman felt them pass (they were professional too) across his chest, over his hips. He could feel Sonny's eyes upon him in the dark.

"You ain't no revenuer come sneakin' here, mister, ain't got no gun?"

To this end of nowhere! And yet *he* had come. He made a grave answer. "No."

"You can stay."

"Sonny," said the woman, "you'll have to borry some fire."

"I'll go git it from Redmond's," said Sonny.

"What?" Bowman strained to hear their words to each other.

"Our fire, it's out, and Sonny's got to borry some, because it's dark an' cold," she said.

"But matches—I have matches—"

"We don't have no need for 'em," she said proudly. "Sonny's goin' after his own fire."

"I'm goin' to Redmond's," said Sonny with an air of importance, and he went out.

After they had waited a while, Bowman looked out the window and saw a light moving over the hill. It spread itself out like a little fan. It zigzagged along the field, darting and swift, not like Sonny at all . . . Soon enough, Sonny staggered in, holding a burning stick behind him in tongs, fire flowing in his wake, blazing light into the corners of the room.

"We'll make a fire now," the woman said, taking the brand.

When that was done she lit the lamp. It showed its dark and light. The whole room turned golden-yellow like some sort of flower, and the walls smelled of it and seemed to tremble with the quiet rushing of the fire and the waving of the burning lampwick in its funnel of light.

The woman moved among the iron pots. With the tongs she dropped hot coals on top of the iron lids. They made a set of soft vibrations, like the sound of a bell far away.

She looked up and over at Bowman, but he could not answer. He was trembling . . .

"Have a drink, mister?" Sonny asked. He had brought in a chair from the other room and sat astride it with his folded arms across the back. Now we are all visible, to one another, Bowman thought, and cried, "Yes sir, you bet, thanks!"

"Come after me and do just what I do," said Sonny.

It was another excursion into the dark. They went through the hall, out to the back of the house, past a shed and a hooded well. They came to a wilderness of thicket.

"Down on your knees," said Sonny.

"What?" Sweat broke out on his forehead.

He understood when Sonny began to crawl through a sort of tunnel that the bushes made over the ground. He followed, startled in spite of himself when a twig or a thorn touched him gently without making a sound, clinging to him and finally letting him go.

Sonny stopped crawling and, crouched on his knees, began to dig with both his hands into the dirt. Bowman shyly struck matches and made a light. In a few minutes Sonny pulled up a jug. He poured out some of the whisky into a bottle from his coat pocket, and buried the jug again. "You never know who's liable to knock at your door," he said, and laughed. "Start back," he said, almost formally. "Ain't no need for us to drink outdoors, like hogs."

At the table by the fire, sitting opposite each other in their chairs, Sonny and Bowman took drinks out of the bottle, passing it across. The dogs slept; one of them was having a dream.

"This is good," said Bowman. "That is what I needed." It was just as though he were drinking the fire off the hearth.

"He makes it," said the woman with quiet pride.

She was pushing the coals off the pots, and the smells of corn bread and coffee circled the room. She set everything on the table before the men, with a bone-handled knife stuck into one of the potatoes, splitting out its golden fiber. Then she stood for a minute looking at them, tall and full above them where they sat. She leaned a little toward them.

"You-all can eat now," she said, and suddenly smiled.

Bowman had just happened to be looking at her. He set his cup back on the table in unbelieving protest. A pain pressed at his eyes. He saw that she was not an old woman. She was young, still young. He could think of no number of years for her. She was the same age as Sonny, and she belonged to him. She stood with the deep dark corner of the room behind her, the shifting yellow light scattering over her head and her grey formless dress, trembling over her tall body when it bent over them in its sudden communication. She was young. Her teeth were shining and her eyes glowed. She turned and walked slowly and heavily out of the room, and he heard her sit down on the cot and then lie down. The pattern on the quilt moved.

"She goin' to have a baby," said Sonny, popping a bite into his mouth.

Bowman could not speak. He was shocked with knowing what was really in this house. A marriage, a fruitful marriage. That simple thing. Anyone could have had that.

Somehow he felt unable to be indignant or protest, although some sort of joke had certainly been played upon him. There was nothing remote or mysterious here—only something private. The only secret was the ancient communication between two people. But the memory of the woman's waiting silently by the cold hearth, of the man's stubborn journey a mile away to get fire, and how they finally brought out their food and drink and filled the room proudly with all they had to show, was suddenly too clear and too enormous within him for response . . .

"You ain't as hungry as you look," said Sonny.

The woman came out of the bedroom as soon as the men had finished, and ate her supper while her husband stared peacefully into the fire.

Then they put the dogs out, with the food that was left.

"I think I'd better sleep here by the fire, on the floor," said Bowman.

He felt that he had been cheated, and that he could afford now to be generous. Ill though he was, he was not going to ask them for their bed. He was through with asking favors in this house, now that he understood what was there.

"Sure, mister."

But he had not known yet how slowly he understood. They had not meant to give him their bed. After a little interval they both rose and looking at him gravely went into the other room.

He lay stretched by the fire until it grew low and dying. He watched every tongue of blaze lick out and vanish. "There will be special reduced prices on all footwear during the month of January," he found himself repeating quietly, and then he lay with his lips tight shut.

How many noises the night had! He heard the stream running, the fire dying, and he was sure now that he heard his heart beating, too, the sound it made under his ribs. He heard breathing, round and deep, of the man and his wife in the room across the passage. And that was all. But emotion swelled patiently within him, and he wished that the child were his.

He must get back to where he had been before. He stood weakly before the red coals, and put on his overcoat. It felt too heavy on his shoulders. As he started out he looked and saw that the woman had never got through with cleaning the lamp. On some impulse he put all the money from his billfold under its fluted glass base, almost ostentatiously.

Ashamed, shrugging a little, and then shivering, he took his bags and went out. The cold of the air seemed to lift him bodily. The moon was in the sky.

On the slope he began to run, he could not help it. Just as he reached the road, where his car seemed to sit in the moonlight like a boat, his heart began to give off tremendous explosions like a rifle, bang bang bang.

He sank in fright on to the road, his bags falling about him. He felt as if all this had happened before. He covered his heart with both hands to keep anyone from hearing the noise it made.

But nobody heard it.

John Cheever

CLEMENTINA

She was born and brought up in Nascosta, in the time of the wonders—the miracle of the jewels and the winter of the wolves. She was ten years old when thieves broke into the shrine of the Holy Virgin after the last Mass on San Giovanni and stole the jewels that had been given to the Madonna by a princess who was cured there of a malady of the liver. On the next day, when Uncle Serafino was walking up from the fields, he saw, in the mouth of the cave where the Etruscans had buried their dead, a youth of great radiance, who beckoned to him, but he was afraid and ran away. Then Serafino was stricken with a fever, and he called for the priest and told him what he had seen, and the priest went to the cave and found the jewels of the Madonna there in the dead leaves where the angel had been standing. That same year, on the road below the farm, her Cousin Maria saw the

Devil, with horns, a pointed tail, and a tight red suit, just as in the pictures. She was fourteen at the time of the big snow, and she went that night after dark to the fountain and, turning back toward the tower where they then lived, she saw the wolves. It was a pack of six or seven, trotting up the stairs of the Via Cavour in the snow. She dropped her pitcher and ran into the tower, and her tongue was swollen with terror, but she looked out the cracks in the door and saw them, more churlish than dogs, more ragged, their ribs showing in their mangy coats and the blood of the sheep they had murdered falling from their mouths. She was terrified and she was rapt, as if the sight of the wolves moving over the snow was the spirits of the dead or some other part of the mystery that she knew to lie close to the heart of life, and when they had passed she would not have believed she had seen them if they had not left their tracks in the snow. She was seventeen when she went to work as a donna di servizio for the baron of little importance who had a villa on the hill, and it was the same summer that Antonio, in the dark field, called her his dewy rose and made her head swim. She confessed to the priest and did her penance and was absolved, but when this had happened six times the priest said they should become engaged, and so Antonio became her fidanzato. The mother of Antonio was not sympathetic, and after three years Clementina was still his rose and he was still her fidanzato and whenever the marriage was mentioned the mother of Antonio would hold her head and scream. In the autumn, the baron asked her to come to Rome as a donna and how could she say no when she had dreamed all the nights of her life of seeing the Pope with her own eyes and walking on streets that were lighted after dark with electricity?

In Rome she slept on straw and washed in a bucket, but the streets were a spectacle, although she had to work such hours that she was not often able to walk in the city. The baron promised to pay her twelve thousand lire a month, but he paid her nothing at the end of the first month and nothing at the end of the second, and the cook said that he often brought girls in from the country and paid them nothing. Opening the door for him one evening, she asked with great courtesy for her wages, and he said he had given her a room, a change of air, and a visit to Rome and that she was badly educated to ask for more. She had no coat to wear in the street, and there were holes in her shoes, and all she was given to eat was the leftovers from the baron's table. She saw that she would have to find another post, because she didn't have the money to go back to Nascosta. That next week, the cousin of the cook found her a place where she was both seamstress and donna, and here she worked even harder, but when the month was over there were no wages. Then she refused to finish a dress the signora had asked her to make for a reception. She said she would not finish the dress

donna di servizio: serving-girl
fidanzato: fiancé

until she had her wages. The signora angered herself and tore her hair, but she paid the wages. Then that night the cousin of the cook said that some Americans needed a donna. She put all the dirty dishes in the oven to give a false appearance of cleanliness, said her prayers in San Marcello, and flew across Rome to where the Americans lived, feeling that every girl on the street that night was looking for the same post. The Americans were a family with two boys—well-educated people, although she could see that they were sad and foolish. They offered her twenty thousand lire in wages and showed her a very commodious room where she would live and said they hoped she would not be uncomfortable, and in the morning she moved her things to the Americans'.

She had heard much about Americans, about how they were generous and ignorant, and some of this was true, for they were very generous and treated her like a guest in the house, always asking her if she had time to do this and that and urging her to take a passage in the streets on Thursdays and Sundays. The signore was meager and tall and worked in the Embassy. His hair was cropped close like a German or a prisoner or someone recovering from an operation of the brain. His hair was black and strong, and if he had let it go and waved it with frissone the girls in the street would have admired him, but he went each week to the barber and had himself disfigured. He was very modest in other things and wore at the beach a concealing bathing costume, but he walked through the streets of Rome with the shape of his head naked for everyone to see. The signora was fine, with a skin like marble and many clothes, and it was a commodious and diverting life, and Clementina prayed at San Marcello's that it would never end. They left all the lights burning as if electricity cost nothing, and they burned wood in the fireplace only to take off the evening chill, and they drank iced gin and vermouth before dinner. They smelled different. It was a pale smell, she thought—a weak smell—and it might have had something to do with the blood of northerners, or it might be because they took so many hot baths. They took so many hot baths that she could not understand why they were not neurasthenics. They ate Italian food and drank wine, and she hoped that if they ate enough pasta and oil they would have a strong and wholesome smell. Sometimes when she waited on table, she smelled them, but it was always a very weak smell and sometimes nothing. They spoiled their children, and sometimes the children spoke sharply or in an ill temper to their genitori, for which they should have been whipped, but they never whipped their children, these strangers, or even raised their voices in anger, or did anything else that would explain to the children the importance of their genitori, and once when the smallest boy was very badly disposed and should have been whipped, his mother took him instead to a toy store and bought him a sailboat. And sometimes when they were dressing to go out in

genitori: parents

the evening the signore would fasten his wife's clothes or her pearls, like a cafone, instead of ringing for Clementina. And once when there was no water in the flat and she had gone down the stairs to the fountain to get some, he came after her to help, and when she said that it was not possible for him to carry water, he said that it was not possible for him to sit by his fire while a young woman carried a heavy demijohn up and down the stairs. Then he took the demijohn out of her hands and went down to the fountain, where he could be seen getting water by the porter and all the other servants in the palace, and she watched this from the kitchen window and was so angry and ashamed that she had to take some wine for her stomach, for everyone would say that she was lazy and that she worked for a vulgar and badly educated family. And they did not believe in the dead. Once, walking down the sala in the dusk, she saw the spirit of a dead man before her so clearly that at first she thought it was the signore, until she saw him standing in the door. Then she screamed and dropped the tray with the glasses and bottles on it, and when the signore asked her why she had screamed and she said it was because she had seen a ghost he was not sympathetic. And once, in the back hall, she saw another ghost, the ghost of a bishop with a mitre, and when she screamed and told the signore what she had seen he was not sympathetic.

But the children were sympathetic, and in the evening, when they were in bed, she told them the stories of Nascosta. The story they liked best was of the young farmer in Nascosta who was married to a beautiful woman named Assunta. When they had been married a year, they had a fine son with dark curls and a golden skin, but from the first he was sickly, and he cried, and they thought there was a spell on him, and they took him to the doctor in Conciliano, riding all the way there on an asino, and the doctor said the baby was dying of starvation. But how could this be, they asked, for the breasts of Assunta were so full of milk they stained her blouse. But the doctor said to watch at night, and they went home by asino and ate their supper, and Assunta fell asleep, but the husband stayed awake to watch, and then at midnight he saw in the moonlight a great viper come over the threshold of the farmhouse and come into the bed and suck the milk from the breasts of the woman, but the husband could not move, for if he moved, the viper would have put his fangs into her breast and killed her, and when the serpent had sucked her breasts dry he went back across the floor and over the threshold in the moonlight, and then the farmer gave the alarm, and all the farmers from around came, and they found against the wall of the farm a nest of eight great serpents, fat with milk, who were so poisonous that even their breath was mortal, and they beat them to death

cafone: boor
sala: hall
asino: donkey

with clubs, and this was a true story, because she had passed the farm where it happened a hundred times. And the story they preferred after this was of the lady in Conciliano who became the lover of a handsome stranger from America. But one night she noticed on his back a small mark like a leaf and remembered that the son who had been taken away from her many years ago was so marked, and knew then that this lover was her son. She ran then to the church to ask forgiveness in the confessional, but the priest—he was a fat and a haughty man—said there was no forgiveness for her sin and, subito, there was in the confessional a loud clatter of bones. Then the people came and opened the confessional and saw that where there had been a proud and a haughty priest there was nothing but bones. And she also told the children about the miracle of the jewels of the Madonna, and the tempo infame when she had seen the wolves coming up the Via Cavour, and the time her Cousin Maria had seen the Devil in his red suit.

She went with this American family to the mountains in July, and in August to Venice and, coming back to Rome in the fall, she understood them to say that they were leaving Italy, and they had the trunks brought up from the cellar, and she helped the signora with the packing. Now she had five pairs of shoes and eight dresses and money in the bank, but the thought of looking for another post with a Roman signora who might spit in her eye whenever she felt like it was discouraging, and one day when she was repairing a dress for the signora she became so discouraged that she cried. Then she explained to the signora how hard the life of a donna was working for Romans, and the signora said they would take her to the new world if she liked. They would take her for six months on an impermanent visa; it would be diverting for her and a help to them. Then all the arrangements were made, and she went to Nascosta, and the Mamma cried and asked her not to go, and everyone in the village said she should not go, but this was jealousy, because they had never had a chance to go anywhere—not even Conciliano. And for once the world where she had lived and been so happy seemed to her truly to be an old world where the customs and the walls were older than the people, and she felt that she would be happier in a world where the walls were all new, even if the people were savage.

When the time came to go, they drove to Naples, stopping whenever the signore felt like it to have a little coffee and cognac, traveling very commodiously like millionaires and staying in a di-lusso hotel in Naples, where she had a room to herself. But on the morning when they sailed she felt a great sadness, for who can live out a good life but in his own country? Then she told herself that it was only a voyage—she would come home in

subito: directly
tempo infame: terrible time
di-lusso: deluxe

six months—and what had the good God made the world so strange and various for if it was not to be seen? She had her passport stamped and went aboard the ship feeling very emotional. It was an American ship, as cold as winter, and at lunch there was ice water on the table, and what was not cold was flavorless and badly cooked, and she came back to her deep feeling that, while these people were kind and generous, they were ignorant and the men fastened their wives' pearls and, with all their money, they did not know any better than to eat platefuls of raw steak washed down with coffee that tasted like medicine. They were not beautiful or elegant and they had pale eyes, but what disgusted her most on the ship were the old women, who in her country would be wearing black in memory of their numerous dead and, as suited their time of life, would move slowly and inspire dignity. But here the old ladies spoke in shrill voices and wore bright clothes and as much jewelry, all of it false, as you would find on the Madonna of Nascosta, and painted their faces and tinted their hair. But who was deceived, for you could see how haggard under the paint were their cheeks, and that their necks were rucked and seamed like the necks of turtles, and although they smelled like the campagna in spring they were as withered and dry as the flowers on a tomb. They were like straw, and this must be a savage country where the old had no wisdom or taste and did not deserve or receive the respect of their children and their grandchildren and had forgotten their dead.

But it would be beautiful, she thought, because she had seen in magazines and newspapers photographs of the towers of the city of New York, towers of gold and silver, against the blue sky, in a city that had never once been touched by the damage of war. But it was raining when they came up the Narrows, and when she looked for the towers they were not to be seen, and when she asked for the towers she was told they were lost in the rain. She was disappointed, for what she could see of this new world seemed ugly, and all the people who dreamed of it were deceived. It was like Naples in the time of the war, and she wished she had not come. The customs man who went through her bags was badly educated. They took a taxi and a train to Washington, the capital of the new world, and then another taxi, and she could see out of the window that all the buildings were copies of the buildings of Imperial Rome, and they looked ghostly to her in the night lights, as if the Forum had risen again from the dust. They drove into the country where the houses were all of wood and all new and where the washbasins and bathtubs were very commodious, and in the morning her signora showed her the machines and how to work them.

At first she was suspicious of the washing machine, for it used a fortune in soap and hot water and did not clean the clothes, and it reminded her of how happy she had been at the fountain in Nascosta, talking with her friends and making everything as clean as new. But little by little the machine seemed to her more carina, for it was after all only a machine, and it filled itself and emptied itself and turned around and around, and it seemed marvelous to her that a machine could remember so much and was always there, ready and waiting to do its work. And then there was the machine for washing the dishes, and you could wash the dishes in a costume for the evening without getting a drop of water on your gloves. When the signora was away and the boys were at school, first she would put some dirty clothes in the washing machine and start that, and then she would put some dirty dishes in the other machine and start that, and then she would put a nice saltimbocca alla romana in the electric frying pan and start that, and then she would sit in the salone in front of the TV and listen to all the machines around her doing the work, and it delighted her and made her feel powerful. Then there was the frigidario in the kitchen, making ice and keeping the butter as hard as stone, and there was the deep freeze full of lamb and beef as fresh as the day when they had been killed, and there was an electric egg beater, and a machine for squeezing the oranges, and a machine for breathing in the dust, and she would have them all going at once, and a machine for making the toast—all bright silver—where you put in the plain bread and turned your back and allora, there were two pieces of toast just the color you had asked for, and all done by the machine.

During the day, her signore was away at the office, but her signora, who in Rome had lived like a princess, seemed in the new world to be a secretary, and she thought perhaps that they were poor and the signora must work. She was always talking on the telephone and making computations and writing letters like a secretary. She was always hurried during the day and tired at night, like a secretary. Because they were both tired at night, the house was not as peaceful as it had been in Rome. Finally she asked the signora to explain what she was a secretary for, and the signora said that she was not a secretary but that she was kept busy raising money for the poor and the sick and the mad. This seemed to Clementina very strange. The climate also seemed to her strange and humid, bad for the lungs and the liver, but the trees at that season were very colorful—she had never seen this before; they were gold and red and yellow, and their leaves fell through the air as in some great hall in Rome or Venice where the paint is flaking from the pictures on the ceiling.

There was a paisano, an old man they called Joe, from bas-Italia, who delivered the milk. He had sixty years or more and was bent with carrying milk bottles, but she went with him to the movies, where he could explain the story to her in Italian and where he pinched her and asked her to marry

carina: appealing
saltimbocca alla romana: a dish of ham and veal
allora: at that moment
paisano: countryman
bas-Italia: southern Italy

him. This was a joke, as far as Clementina was concerned. There were strange festas in the new world—one with a turkey and no saints—and then there was the festa of the Natale, and she herself had never seen anything so discourteous to the Holy Virgin and the sainted baby. First they bought a green tree and then they put it up in the salone and hung it with shining necklaces, as if it were a holy saint with the power of curing evil and hearing prayers. Mamma mia. A tree! She was confessed by a priest who gave her the tail of the Devil for not coming to church every Sunday of her life and who was very rigid. When she went to Mass, they took the collection three times. She thought that when she returned to Rome she would write an article for the paper about the church in this new world where there was not even the wristbone of a saint to kiss and where they made offerings to a green tree and forgot the travail of the Holy Virgin and took the collection three times. And then there was the snow, but it was more carina than the snow in Nascosta—there were no wolves, and the signori skied in the mountains, and the children played in the snow and the house was always warm.

She still went with Joe every Sunday to the movies, where he told her the story, asked her to marry him, and pinched her. Once, before the movies, he stopped at a fine house all made of wood and neatly painted, and he unlocked the door and took her upstairs to a nice apartment with paper on the walls, the floor shining with varnish, and five rooms in all, with a modern bathroom, and he said that if she would marry him it would all be hers. He would buy her a machine for washing the dishes and a machine for beating the eggs and a frying pan like the signora had that knew when to turn off the saltimbocca alla romana. When she asked him where he would find all the money to do this, he said that he had saved seventeen thousand dollars, and he took a book out of his pocket, a bankbook, and there was stamped in it seventeen thousand two hundred and thirty dollars and seventeen cents. It would all be hers if she would come and be his wife. She said no, but after the movies, when she was in bed, it made her sad to think of all the machinery and she wished that she had never come to the new world. Nothing would ever be the same again. When she went back to Nascosta and told them that a man—not a beautiful man, but one who was honest and gentle—had offered her seventeen thousand dollars and a place with five rooms, they would never believe her. They would think she was crazy, and how could she lie again on straw in a cold room and be contented? Her impermanent visa expired in April and she would have to go home then, but the signore said that he could apply for an extension if she liked, and she begged him to do this. In the kitchen one night, she heard them speaking in low voices and she guessed they were speaking about her affairs, but he did not speak to her until much later when the others had gone up and she came into the room to say good night.

"I'm very sorry, Clementina," he said, "but they won't give me an extension."

"It doesn't matter," she said. "If I am not wanted in this country, I will go home."

"It isn't that, Clementina, it's the law. I'm very sorry. Your visa expires on the twelfth. I'll get your passage on a boat before then."

"Thank you, Signore," she said. "Good night."

She would go back, she thought. She would take the boat, she would debark at Naples, she would catch a train at the Mergellina and in Rome a *pullman*, and go out the Tiburtina with the curtains of the bus swaying and the purple clouds of exhaust rolling out behind them when they climbed the hill at Tivoli. Her eyes filled with tears when she thought of kissing Mamma and giving her the silver-framed photograph of Dana Andrews that she had bought at Woolworth's for her present. Then she would sit on the piazza with such a ring of people around her as would form for an accident, speaking in her own tongue and drinking the wine they had made and talking about the new world where there were frying pans with brains and where even the powder for cleaning the gabinetti smelled of roses. She saw the scene distinctly, the fountain spray blowing on the wind, but then she saw gathering in the imagined faces of her townsmen a look of disbelief. Who would believe her tales? Who would listen? They would have admired her if she had seen the Devil, like Cousin Maria, but she had seen a sort of paradise and no one cared. In leaving one world and coming to another she had lost both.

Then she opened and reread a package of letters written from Nascosta by her Uncle Sebastiano. That night, his letters all seemed dolorous. The autumn had come on quickly, he wrote, and it was cold, even in September, and many of the olives and the grapes were lost, and la bomba atomica had ruined the seasons of Italy. Now the shadow of the town fell over the valley earlier, and she remembered herself the beginnings of winter—the sudden hoarfrost lying on the grapes and wild flowers, and the contadini coming in at dark on their asini, loaded down with roots and other scraps of wood, for wood was hard to find in that country and one would ride ten kilometri for a bundle of green olive cuttings, and she could remember the cold in her bones and see the asini against the yellow light of evening and hear the lonely noise of stones falling down the steep path, falling away from their hoofs. And in December Sebastiano wrote that it was again the time of the wolves. The tempo infame had come again to Nascosta, and wolves had killed six of the padrone's sheep, and there was no abbacchio, and no eggs, either, for pasta, and the piazza was buried in snow up to the edge of the fountain, and they knew hunger and cold, and she could remember both.

The room where she read these letters was warm. The lights were pink.

gabinetti: lavatories
contadini: peasants
padrone: master
abbacchio: lamb

She had a silver ashtray like a signora, and, if she had wanted, in her private bathroom she could have drawn a hot bath up to her neck. Did the Holy Virgin mean for her to live in a wilderness and die of starvation? Was it wrong to take the comforts that were held out to her? The faces of her people appeared to her again, and how dark were their skin, their hair, and their eyes, she thought, as if through living with fair people she had taken on the dispositions and the prejudices of the fair. The faces seemed to regard her with reproach, with earthen patience, with a sweet, dignified, and despairing regard, but why should she be compelled to return and drink sour wine in the darkness of the hills? In this new world they had found the secret of youth, and would the saints in Heaven have refused a life of youthfulness if it had been God's will? She remembered how in Nascosta even the most beautiful fell quickly under the darkness of time, like flowers without care; how even the most beautiful became bent and toothless, their dark clothes smelling, as the Mamma's did, of smoke and manure. But in this country she could have forever white teeth and color in her hair. Until the day she died she would have shoes with heels and rings on her fingers, and the attention of men, for in this new world one lived ten lifetimes and never felt the pinch of age; no, never. She would marry Joe. She would stay here and live ten lives, with a skin like marble and always the teeth with which to bite the meat.

On the next night, her signore told her when the boats were leaving, and when he had finished she said, "I am not going back."

"I don't understand."

"I will marry Joe."

"But Joe's a great deal older than you, Clementina."

"Joe is sixty-three."

"And you?"

"I am twenty-four."

"Do you love Joe?"

"Oh no, Signore. How could I love him, with his big paunch like a sackful of apples and so many wrinkles at the back of his neck you could tell your fortune there? It is not possible."

"Clementina, I admire Joe," the signore said. "He's an honest man. If you marry him, you must care for him."

"Oh, I'll care for him, Signore. I'll make his bed and cook his supper, but I will never let him touch me."

He deliberated, looked down at the floor, and finally said, "I will not let you marry Joe, Clementina."

"But why?"

"I won't let you marry him unless you'll be his wife. You must love him."

"But, Signore, in Nascosta there would be no sense in marrying a man whose land did not adjoin yours, and does that mean then that your heart will fly out to him?"

"This is not Nascosta."

"But all marriages are like this, Signore. If people married for love, the world would not be a place in which to live, it would be a hospital for the mad. Did not the Signora marry you because of the money and the conveniences you bring her?" He did not answer, but she saw his face flush dark with blood. "Oh Signore, my Signore," she said, "you talk like a boy with stars in your eyes, a thin boy at the fountain, his head full of the poesia. I am only trying to unfold to you that I am only marrying Joe so that I can stay in this country, and you are talking like a boy."

"I am not talking like a boy," he said. Then he rose from the chair. "I am not talking like a boy. Who do you think you are? When you came to us in Rome you didn't have shoes or a coat."

"Signore, you do not understand me. Perhaps I will love him, but I am only trying to unfold to you that I am not marrying for love."

"And that's what I'm trying to explain to you. I won't stand for it."

"I will leave your house, Signore."

"I'm responsible for you."

"No, Signore. Joe is responsible for me now."

"Then get out of my house."

She went upstairs to her room and cried and cried, in anger and pity for this grown fool, but she packed her things. In the morning she cooked the breakfast, but she stayed in the kitchen until the signore had gone to work, and then the signora came down and cried, and the children cried, and at noon Joe came to get her in his car and took her to the Pelluchis', who were paisani and with whom she would stay until she and Joe were married. Maria Pelluchi explained to her that in the new world one was married like a princess, and this was so. For three weeks she was in and out of the stores with Maria—first to buy the wedding dress for herself, all white and the latest mode, with a tail of satin to drag along the ground, but economical, too, because the tail could be adjusted, making the dress like a costume for the grand evening. Then there were the costumes for Maria and her sister, who would be the attendants, and these were yellow and lavender and could be used later as costumes for the evening. Then there were the shoes and the flowers and the clothes for traveling and the suitcase, and nothing was rented. And when the day of the wedding arrived she was so tired that she had milk in the knees and walked through it all like a dream, of which she could remember very little. There were many paisani at the reception and much wine, food, and music, and then she took with Joe a train to New York, where the buildings were so tall they made her feel homesick and of little importance. In New York, they spent the night in a hotel, and the next day they took a di-lusso train, only for signori who were going to Atlantic City, with a special chair for each passenger and a waiter to bring things to eat and drink. She hung behind her chair the mink stole that Joe had given her for a present, and everyone saw it and admired it and judged her to be a rich signora. Joe called the waiter over and told him to bring some whiskey and seltz, but the waiter pretended not to understand what Joe was saying and to be so busy waiting on other people that they would have to be the last, and she felt again that shame and anger at discovering that because they could not speak elegantly the language of this new country they would be treated with great discourtesy, as if they were pigs. And that is the way they were treated on the passage, for the waiter did not come near them again, as if their money was not as good as the money of the others. They went first through a great, dark galleria and then out into a country that was ugly and potent with fire exploding from many chimneys, and there were trees and rivers and places for boating. She looked out of the window at the country that streamed by as swiftly and gently as water, to see if it was as fair as Italy, but what she saw was that it was not her country, her earth. Near the cities they passed those places where the poor lived and where washing was hung on lines, and she thought that this was the same—that washing on lines must be the same all over the world. And the houses of the poor were the same, too, the way they leaned against one another and had gardens that were not commodious but that were cultivated, you could see, with gentleness and love. It was in the middle of the day or later when they left, and, as they sped through the country and the afternoon, she saw that the schools were closing and that on the streets there were many children carrying books and riding bicycles and playing games, and many of them waved to the train as it rolled along and she waved back to them. She waved to some children who were walking through the high grass in a field, and she waved to two boys on a bridge, and she waved to an old man, and they all waved back to her, and she waved to three girls, and she waved to a lady who was pushing a baby carriage, and she waved to a little boy who was wearing a yellow coat and carrying a valise, and he waved back. They all waved back. Then she could see that they were coming close to the ocean, for there was a bareness in the air and not so many trees and many pictures of hotels painted on wood saying how many hundreds of rooms they had and how many different kinds of places for drinking cocktails, and she was happy to see the name of their hotel on one of these signs and to be sure that it was di lusso. Then the train stopped and it was the end of the passage and she felt shy and timid, but Joe said andiamo, and the waiter who had been so discourteous to them took their bags away and reached for her mink stole, but she said, "No, thank you," and got it away from him, the pig. And then there was the largest black car she had ever seen in her life, with a sign on it saying the name of their hotel, and they got into this with some other people, but they did not speak to one another on the passage, because she did

galleria: tunnel
andiamo: let's go

not want the others to know that she could not speak the language of this country.

The hotel was very di lusso, and they ascended in an elevator, and walked down a hall that was covered with thick carpet, into a fine room, also with thick carpet everywhere, and a toilet—only with no bidet—and when the waiter had gone Joe got a bottle of whiskey out of his valise and had a drink and asked her to come and sit in his lap, and she said a little later, later, for it was unlucky in the daylight, and it would be better to wait for the moon to rise, and she would like to go down and see the dining rooms and lounges. She wondered if the salt air would be bad for the mink, and Joe had another drink, and out of the window she could see the ocean and the lines of white waves coming in, and because the windows were closed and she could not hear the sound the waves made when they broke it seemed like something she was dreaming. They went down again, not speaking, because she had distinctly come to feel that it was better not to speak the bella lingua in such a luxurious place, and they looked in the bars and dining rooms, which were grand, and then went out onto a broad walk beside the sea and there was salt in the air, like Venice, and it smelled like Venice, and there was also a smell of frying food in the air, which reminded her of the feast of San Giuseppe in Rome. On one side of them was the green, cold sea, which she had crossed to come to this new world, and on the other side of them there were many diverting things. They walked along until they came to the gypsies, where there was in the window a drawing of the human hand and where one's fortune could be told, and when she asked if they could speak Italian they said, "Si, si, si, non c'è dubbio!" and Joe gave her a dollar, and she went behind a curtain with the gypsy, who looked at her hand and began to tell her fortune, but it was not Italian she was speaking, it was a bastard language of a little Spanish and a little something that Clementina had never heard before, and she could only understand a word here and there, like "the sea" and "the voyage," but she could not tell if this was a voyage she would make or a voyage she had made, and she became impatient with the gypsy, who had made a lie in saying that she spoke in Italian, and she asked for her money back, but the gypsy said that if the money was given back there would be a curse on it. And, knowing what strong curses the gypsies make, she did not create a further disturbance, and went out where Joe was waiting for her on the wooden walk, and walked along again between the green sea and the diversions of frying food, where people called to them to come in and spend their money, smiling and beckoning wickedly like the angels of Hell. And then there was the tramonto, and the lights went on gloriously like pearls, and, looking back, she could see the pink windows of the hotel where they were known, where they

bella lingua: beautiful language
Si, si, si, non c'è dubbio: Yes, yes, yes, there is no doubt
tramonto: sunset

had a room of their own they could return to when they pleased, and the noise of the sea sounded like distant blasting in the mountains.

She was a good wife to him, and in the morning he was so grateful that he bought her a silver dish for the butter and a cover for the ironing board and a pair of red pants, laced with gold. The mother would give her the tail of the Devil, she knew, for wearing pants, and in Rome she herself would spit in the eye of a woman who was so badly educated as to wear pants, but this was a new world and it was no sin, and in the afternoon she wore the mink stole and the red pants and went with Joe up and down the wooden walk above the sea. On Saturday they went home, and on Monday they bought the furniture, and on Tuesday it was delivered, and on Friday she put on the red pants and went to the supermarket with Maria Pelluchi, who explained the labels on the boxes to her, and she looked so much like an American that people were surprised when she could not speak the language.

But if she could not speak the language she could do everything else, and she even learned to drink whiskey without coughing and spitting. In the morning, she would turn on all the machines and watch the TV, learning the words of the songs, and in the afternoons Maria Pelluchi came to her house and they watched the TV together, and in the evening she watched it with Joe. She tried to write the mother about the things she had bought—much finer things than the Pope possessed—but she realized that the letter would only bewilder the mother, and in the end she sent her nothing but postcards. No one could describe how diverting and commodious her life had become. In the summer, in the evenings, Joe took her to the races in Baltimore, and she had never seen anything so carina—the little horses and the lights and the flowers and the red coat of the marshal with his bugle. That summer, they went to the races every Friday and sometimes oftener, and it was one night there, when she was wearing her red pants and drinking whiskey, that she saw her signore for the first time since they had quarreled.

She asked him how he was, and how was his family, and he said, "We are not together. We are divorced." Looking into his face then, she saw not the end of his marriage but the end of his happiness. The advantage was hers, because hadn't she explained to him that he was like a boy with stars in his eyes, but some part of his loss seemed to be hers as well. Then he went away, and, although the race was beginning, she saw instead the white snow and the wolves of Nascosta, the pack coming up the Via Cavour and crossing the piazza as if they were bent on some errand of that darkness that she knew to lie at the heart of life, and, remembering the cold on her skin and the whiteness of the snow and the stealth of the wolves, she wondered why the good God had opened up so many choices and made life so strange and diverse.

Katherine Mansfield

MISS BRILL

Although it was so brilliantly fine—the blue sky powdered with gold and great spots of light like white wine splashed over the Jardins Publiques—Miss Brill was glad that she had decided on her fur. The air was motionless, but when you opened your mouth there was just a faint chill, like a chill from a glass of iced water before you sip, and now and again a leaf came drifting—from nowhere, from the sky. Miss Brill put up her hand and touched her fur. Dear little thing! It was nice to feel it again. She had taken it out of its box that afternoon, shaken out the moth powder, given it a good brush, and rubbed the life back into the dim little eyes. "What has been happening to me?" said the sad little eyes. Oh, how sweet it was to see them snap at her again from the red eiderdown! . . . But the nose, which was of some black composition, wasn't at all firm. It must have had a knock, somehow. Never mind—a little dab of black sealing-wax when the time came—when it was absolutely necessary . . . Little rogue! Yes, she really felt like that about it. Little rogue biting its tail just by her left ear. She could have taken it off and laid it on her lap and stroked it. She felt a tingling in her hands and arms, but that came from walking, she supposed. And when she breathed, something light and sad—no, not sad, exactly—something gentle seemed to move in her bosom.

There were a number of people out this afternoon, far more than last Sunday. And the band sounded louder and gayer. That was because the Season had begun. For although the band played all the year round on Sundays, out of season it was never the same. It was like some one playing with only the family to listen; it didn't care how it played if there weren't any strangers present. Wasn't the conductor wearing a new coat, too? She was sure it was new. He scraped with his foot and flapped his arms like a rooster about to crow, and the bandsmen sitting in the green rotunda blew out their cheeks and glared at the music. Now there came a little "flutey" bit—very pretty!—a little chain of bright drops. She was sure it would be repeated. It was; she lifted her head and smiled.

Only two people shared her "special" seat: a fine old man in a velvet coat, his hands clasped over a huge carved walking-stick, and a big old woman, sitting upright, with a roll of knitting on her embroidered apron. They did not speak. This was disappointing, for Miss Brill always looked forward to the conversation. She had become really quite expert, she thought, at listening as though she didn't listen, at sitting in other people's lives just for a minute while they talked round her.

She glanced, sideways, at the old couple. Perhaps they would go soon. Last Sunday, too, hadn't been as interesting as usual. An Englishman and his wife, he wearing a dreadful Panama hat and she button boots. And she'd gone on the whole time about how she ought to wear spectacles; she knew she needed them; but that it was no good getting any; they'd be sure to break and they'd never keep on. And he'd been so patient. He'd suggested everything—gold rims, the kind that curved round your ears, little pads inside the bridge. No, nothing would please her. "They'll always be sliding down my nose!" Miss Brill had wanted to shake her.

The old people sat on the bench, still as statues. Never mind, there was always the crowd to watch. To and fro, in front of the flower beds and the band rotunda, the couples and groups paraded, stopped to talk, to greet, to buy a handful of flowers from the old beggar who had his tray fixed to the railings. Little children ran among them, swooping and laughing; little boys with big white silk bows under their chins, little girls, little French dolls, dressed up in velvet and lace. And sometimes a tiny staggerer came suddenly rocking into the open from under the trees, stopped, stared, as suddenly sat down "flop," until its small high-stepping mother, like a young hen, rushed scolding to its rescue. Other people sat on the benches and green chairs, but they were nearly always the same, Sunday after Sunday, and—Miss Brill had often noticed—there was something funny about nearly all of them. They were odd, silent, nearly all old, and from the way they stared they looked as though they'd just come from dark little rooms or even—even cupboards!

Behind the rotunda the slender trees with yellow leaves down drooping, and through them just a line of sea, and beyond the blue sky with gold-veined clouds.

Tum-tum-tum tiddle-um! tiddle-um! tum tiddley-um tum ta! blew the band.

Two young girls in red came by and two young soldiers in blue met them, and they laughed and paired and went off arm-in-arm. Two peasant women with funny straw hats passed, gravely, leading beautiful smoke-colored donkeys. A cold, pale nun hurried by. A beautiful woman came along and dropped her bunch of violets, and a little boy ran after to hand them to her, and she took them and threw them away as if they'd been poisoned. Dear me! Miss Brill didn't know whether to admire that or not! And now an ermine toque and a gentleman in gray met just in front of her. He was tall, stiff, dignified, and she was wearing the ermine toque she'd bought when her hair was yellow. Now everything, her hair, her face, even her eyes, was the same color as the shabby ermine, and her hand, in its cleaned glove, lifted to dab her lips, was a tiny yellowish paw. Oh, she was so pleased to see him—delighted! She rather thought they were going to meet that afternoon.

She described where she'd been—everywhere, here, there, along by the sea. The day was so charming—didn't he agree? And wouldn't he, perhaps? . . . But he shook his head, lighted a cigarette, slowly breathed a great deep puff into her face, and, even while she was still talking and laughing, flicked the match away and walked on. The ermine toque was alone; she smiled more brightly than ever. But even the band seemed to know what she was feeling and played more softly, played tenderly, and the drum beat, "The Brute! The Brute!" over and over. What would she do? What was going to happen now? But as Miss Brill wondered, the ermine toque turned, raised her hand as though she'd seen some one else, much nicer, just over there, and pattered away. And the band changed again and played more quickly, more gayly than ever, and the old couple on Miss Brill's seat got up and marched away, and such a funny old man with long whiskers hobbled along in time to the music and was nearly knocked over by four girls walking abreast.

Oh, how fascinating it was! How she enjoyed it! How she loved sitting here, watching it all! It was like a play. It was exactly like a play. Who could believe the sky at the back wasn't painted? But it wasn't till a little brown dog trotted on solemn and then slowly trotted off, like a little "theater" dog, a little dog that had been drugged, that Miss Brill discovered what it was that made it so exciting. They were all on the stage. They weren't only the audience, not only looking on; they were acting. Even she had a part and came every Sunday. No doubt somebody would have noticed if she hadn't been there; she was part of the performance after all. How strange she'd never thought of it like that before! And yet it explained why she made such a point of starting from home at just the same time each week—so as not to be late for the performance—and it also explained why she had quite a queer, shy feeling at telling her English pupils how she spent her Sunday afternoons. No wonder! Miss Brill nearly laughed out loud. She was on the stage. She thought of the old invalid gentleman to whom she read the newspaper four afternoons a week while he slept in the garden. She had got quite used to the frail head on the cotton pillow, the hollowed eyes, the open mouth and the high pinched nose. If he'd been dead she mightn't have noticed for weeks; she wouldn't have minded. But suddenly he knew he was having the paper read to him by an actress! "An actress!" The old head lifted; two points of light quivered in the old eyes. "An actress—are ye?" And Miss Brill smoothed the newspaper as though it were the manuscript of her part and said gently: "Yes, I have been an actress for a long time."

The band had been having a rest. Now they started again. And what they played was warm, sunny, yet there was just a faint chill—a something, what was it?—not sadness—no, not sadness—a something that made you want to sing. The tune lifted, lifted, the light shone; and it seemed to Miss Brill that in another moment all of them, all the whole company, would begin singing. The young ones, the laughing ones who were moving together, they would begin, and the men's voices, very resolute and brave, would join them. And then she too, she too, and the others on the benches—

they would come in with a kind of accompaniment—something low, that scarcely rose or fell, something so beautiful—moving . . . And Miss Brill's eyes filled with tears and she looked smiling at all the other members of the company. Yes, we understand, we understand, she thought—though what they understood she didn't know.

Just at that moment a boy and a girl came and sat down where the old couple had been. They were beautifully dressed; they were in love. The hero and heroine, of course, just arrived from his father's yacht. And still soundlessly singing, still with that trembling smile, Miss Brill prepared to listen.

"No, not now," said the girl. "Not here, I can't."

"But why? Because of that stupid old thing at the end there?" asked the boy. "Why does she come here at all—who wants her? Why doesn't she keep her silly old mug at home?"

"It's her fu-fur which is so funny," giggled the girl. "It's exactly like a fried whiting."

"Ah, be off with you!" said the boy in an angry whisper. Then: "Tell me, ma petite chère—"

"No, not here," said the girl. "Not *yet*."

On her way home she usually bought a slice of honeycake at the baker's. It was her Sunday treat. Sometimes there was an almond in her slice, sometimes not. It made a great difference. If there was an almond it was like carrying home a tiny present—a surprise—something that might very well not have been there. She hurried on the almond Sundays and struck the match for the kettle in quite a dashing way.

But today she passed the baker's by, climbed the stairs, went into the little dark room—her room like a cupboard—and sat down on the red eiderdown. She sat there for a long time. The box that the fur came out of was on the bed. She unclasped the necklet quickly; quickly, without looking, laid it inside. But when she put the lid on she thought she heard something crying.

Katherine Anne Porter

ROPE

On the third day after they moved to the country he came walking back from the village carrying a basket of groceries and a twenty-four-yard coil of rope. She came out to meet him, wiping her hands on her green smock. Her hair was tumbled, her nose was scarlet with sunburn; he told her that already she looked like a born country woman. His gray flannel shirt stuck to him, his heavy shoes were dusty. She assured him he looked like a rural character in a play.

Had he brought the coffee? She had been waiting all day long for coffee. They had forgot it when they ordered at the store the first day.

Gosh, no, he hadn't. Lord, now he'd have to go back. Yes, he would if it killed him. He thought, though, he had everything else. She reminded him it was only because he didn't drink coffee himself. If he did he would remember it quick enough. Suppose they ran out of cigarettes? Then she saw the rope. What was that for? Well, he thought it might do to hang clothes on, or something. Naturally she asked him if he thought they were going to run a laundry? They already had a fifty-foot line hanging right before his eyes? Why, hadn't he noticed it, really? It was a blot on the landscape to her.

He thought there were a lot of things a rope might come in handy for. She wanted to know what, for instance. He thought a few seconds, but nothing occurred. They could wait and see, couldn't they? You need all sorts of strange odds and ends around a place in the country. She said, yes, that was so; but she thought just at that time when every penny counted, it seemed funny to buy more rope. That was all. She hadn't meant anything else. She hadn't just seen, not at first, why he felt it was necessary.

Well, thunder, he had bought it because he wanted to, and that was all there was to it. She thought that was reason enough, and couldn't understand why he hadn't said so, at first. Undoubtedly it would be useful, twenty-four yards of rope, there were hundreds of things, she couldn't think of any at the moment, but it would come in. Of course. As he had said, things always did in the country.

But she was a little disappointed about the coffee, and oh, look, look, look at the eggs! Oh, my, they're all running! What had he put on top of them? Hadn't he known eggs mustn't be squeezed? Squeezed, who had squeezed them, he wanted to know. What a silly thing to say. He had simply brought them along in the basket with the other things. If they got broke it was the grocer's fault. He should know better than to put heavy things on top of eggs.

She believed it was the rope. That was the heaviest thing in the pack, she saw him plainly when he came in from the road, the rope was a big package on top of everything. He desired the whole wide world to witness that this was not a fact. He had carried the rope in one hand and the basket in the other, and what was the use of her having eyes if that was the best they could do for her?

Well, anyhow, she could see one thing plain: no eggs for breakfast. They'd have to scramble them now, for supper. It was too damned bad. She had planned to have steak for supper. No ice, meat wouldn't keep. He wanted to know why she couldn't finish breaking the eggs in a bowl and set them in a cool place.

Cool place! if he could find one for her, she'd be glad to set them there.

Well, then, it seemed to him they might very well cook the meat at the same time they cooked the eggs and then warm up the meat for tomorrow. The idea simply choked her. Warmed-over meat, when they might as well have had it fresh. Second best and scraps and makeshifts, even to the meat! He rubbed her shoulder a little. It doesn't really matter so much, does it, darling? Sometimes when they were playful, he would rub her shoulder and she would arch and purr. This time she hissed and almost clawed. He was getting ready to say that they could surely manage somehow when she turned on him and said, if he told her they could manage somehow she would certainly slap his face.

He swallowed the words red hot, his face burned. He picked up the rope and started to put it on the top shelf. She would not have it on the top shelf, the jars and tins belonged there; positively she would not have the top shelf cluttered up with a lot of rope. She had borne all the clutter she meant to bear in the flat in town, there was space here at least and she meant to keep things in order.

Well, in that case, he wanted to know what the hammer and nails were doing up there? And why had she put them there when she knew very well he needed that hammer and those nails upstairs to fix the window sashes? She simply slowed down everything and made double work on the place with her insane habit of changing things around and hiding them.

She was sure she begged his pardon, and if she had had any reason to believe he was going to fix the sashes this summer she would have left the hammer and nails right where he put them; in the middle of the bedroom floor where they could step on them in the dark. And now if he didn't clear the whole mess out of there she would throw them down the well.

Oh, all right, all right—could he put them in the closet? Naturally not, there were brooms and mops and dustpans in the closet, and why couldn't he find a place for his rope outside her kitchen? Had he stopped to consider there were seven God-forsaken rooms in the house, and only one kitchen?

He wanted to know what of it? And did she realize she was making a complete fool of herself? And what did she take him for, a three-year-old idiot? The whole trouble with her was she needed something weaker than she was to heckle and tyrannize over. He wished to God now they had a couple of children she could take it out on. Maybe he'd get some rest.

Her face changed at this, she reminded him he had forgot the coffee and had bought a worthless piece of rope. And when she thought of all the things they actually needed to make the place even decently fit to live in, well, she could cry, that was all. She looked so forlorn, so lost and despairing he couldn't believe it was only a piece of rope that was causing all the racket. What *was* the matter, for God's sake?

Oh, would he please hush and go away, and *stay* away, if he could, for five minutes? By all means, yes, he would. He'd stay away indefinitely if she wished. Lord, yes, there was nothing he'd like better than to clear out and never come back. She couldn't for the life of her see what was holding him, then. It was a swell time. Here she was, stuck, miles from a railroad, with a half-empty house on her hands, and not a penny in her pocket, and everything on earth to do; it seemed the God-sent moment for him to get out from under. She was surprised he hadn't stayed in town as it was until she had come out and done the work and got things straightened out. It was his usual trick.

It appeared to him that this was going a little far. Just a touch out of bounds, if she didn't mind his saying so. Why the hell had he stayed in town the summer before? To do a half-dozen extra jobs to get the money he had sent her. That was it. She knew perfectly well they couldn't have done it otherwise. She had agreed with him at the time. And that was the only time so help him he had ever left her to do anything by herself.

Oh, he could tell that to his great-grandmother. She had her notion of what had kept him in town. Considerably more than a notion, if he wanted to know. So, she was going to bring all that up again, was she? Well, she could just think what she pleased. He was tired of explaining. It may have looked funny but he had simply got hooked in, and what could he do? It was impossible to believe that she was going to take it seriously. Yes, yes, she knew how it was with a man: if he was left by himself a minute, some woman was certain to kidnap him. And naturally he couldn't hurt her feelings by refusing!

Well, what was she raving about? Did she forget she had told him those two weeks alone in the country were the happiest she had known for four years? And how long had they been married when she said that? All right, shut up! If she thought that hadn't stuck in his craw.

She hadn't meant she was happy because she was away from him. She meant she was happy getting the devilish house nice and ready for him. That was what she had meant, and now look! Bringing up something she had said a year ago simply to justify himself for forgetting her coffee and breaking the eggs and buying a wretched piece of rope they couldn't afford. She really thought it was time to drop the subject, and now she wanted only two things in the world. She wanted him to get that rope from underfoot, and go back to the village and get her coffee, and if he could remember it, he might bring a metal mitt for the skillets, and two more curtain rods, and if there were any rubber gloves in the village, her hands were simply raw, and a bottle of milk of magnesia from the drugstore.

He looked out at the dark blue afternoon sweltering on the slopes, and mopped his forehead and sighed heavily and said, if only she could wait a minute for *anything,* he was going back. He had said so, hadn't he, the very instant they found he had overlooked it?

Oh, yes, well . . . run along. She was going to wash windows. The country was so beautiful! She doubted they'd have a moment to enjoy it. He meant to go, but he could not until he had said that if she wasn't such a hopeless melancholiac she might see that this was only for a few days. Couldn't she remember anything pleasant about the other summers? Hadn't they ever had any fun? She hadn't time to talk about it, and now would he please not leave that rope lying around for her to trip on? He picked it up, somehow it had toppled off the table, and walked out with it under his arm.

Was he going this minute? He certainly was. She thought so. Sometimes it seemed to her he had second sight about the precisely perfect moment to leave her ditched. She had meant to put the mattresses out to sun, if they put them out this minute they would get at least three hours, he must have heard her say that morning she meant to put them out. So of course he would walk off and leave her to it. She supposed he thought the exercise would do her good.

Well, he was merely going to get her coffee. A four-mile walk for two pounds of coffee was ridiculous, but he was perfectly willing to do it. The habit was making a wreck of her, but if she wanted to wreck herself there was nothing he could do about it. If he thought it was coffee that was making a wreck of her, she congratulated him: he must have a damned easy conscience.

Conscience or no conscience, he didn't see why the mattresses couldn't very well wait until tomorrow. And anyhow, for God's sake, were they living *in* the house, or were they going to let the house ride them to death? She paled at this, her face grew livid about the mouth, she looked quite dangerous, and reminded him that housekeeping was no more her work than it was his: she had other work to do as well, and when did he think she was going to find time to do it at this rate?

Was she going to start on that again? She knew as well as he did that his work brought in the regular money, hers was only occasional, if they depended on what *she* made—and she might as well get straight on this question once for all!

That was positively not the point. The question was, when both of them were working on their own time, was there going to be a division of the housework, or wasn't there? She merely wanted to know, she had to make her plans. Why, he thought that was all arranged. It was understood that he was to help. Hadn't he always, in summers?

Hadn't he, though? Oh, just hadn't he? And when, and where, and doing what? Lord, what an uproarious joke!

It was such a very uproarious joke that her face turned slightly purple, and she screamed with laughter. She laughed so hard she had to sit down, and finally a rush of tears spurted from her eyes and poured down into the lifted corners of her mouth. He dashed towards her and dragged her up to her feet and tried to pour water on her head. The dipper hung by a string on a nail and he broke it loose. Then he tried to pump water with one hand while she struggled in the other. So he gave it up and shook her instead.

She wrenched away, crying out for him to take his rope and go to hell, she had simply given him up: and ran. He heard her high-heeled bedroom slippers clattering and stumbling on the stairs.

He went out around the house and into the lane; he suddenly realized he had a blister on his heel and his shirt felt as if it were on fire. Things broke so suddenly you didn't know where you were. She could work herself into a fury about simply nothing. She was terrible, damn it: not an ounce of reason. You might as well talk to a sieve as that woman when she got going. Damned if he'd spend his life humoring her! Well, what to do now? He would take back the rope and exchange it for something else. Things accumulated, things were mountainous, you couldn't move them or sort them out or get rid of them. They just lay and rotted around. He'd take it back. Hell, why should he? He wanted it. What was it anyhow? A piece of rope. Imagine anybody caring more about a piece of rope than about a man's feelings. What earthly right had she to say a word about it? He remembered all the useless, meaningless things she bought for herself: Why? because I wanted it, that's why! He stopped and selected a large stone by the road. He would put the rope behind it. He would put it in the tool-box when he got back. He'd heard enough about it to last him a life-time.

When he came back she was leaning against the post box beside the road waiting. It was pretty late, the smell of broiled steak floated nose high in the cooling air. Her face was young and smooth and fresh-looking. Her unmanageable funny black hair was all on end. She waved to him from a distance, and he speeded up. She called out that supper was ready and waiting, was he starved?

You bet he was starved. Here was the coffee. He waved it at her. She looked at his other hand. What was that he had there?

Well, it was the rope again. He stopped short. He had meant to exchange it but forgot. She wanted to know why he should exchange it, if it was something he really wanted. Wasn't the air sweet now, and wasn't it fine to be here?

She walked beside him with one hand hooked into his leather belt. She pulled and jostled him a little as he walked, and leaned against him. He put his arm clear around her and patted her stomach. They exchanged wary smiles. Coffee, coffee for the Ootsum-Wootsums! He felt as if he were bringing her a beautiful present.

He was a love, she firmly believed, and if she had had her coffee in the morning, she wouldn't have behaved so funny . . . There was a whippoorwill still coming back, imagine, clear out of season, sitting in the crab-apple tree calling all by himself. Maybe his girl stood him up. Maybe she did. She hoped to hear him once more, she loved whippoorwills . . . He knew how she was, didn't he?

Sure, he knew how she was.

Ernest J. Gaines

THE SKY IS GRAY

I

Go'n be coming in a few minutes. Coming round that bend down there full speed. And I'm go'n get out my handkerchief and wave it down, and we go'n get on it and go.

I keep on looking for it, but Mama don't look that way no more. She's looking down the road where we just come from. It's a long old road, and far 's you can see you don't see nothing but gravel. You got dry weeds on both sides, and you got trees on both sides, and fences on both sides, too. And you got cows in the pastures and they standing close together. And when we was coming out here to catch the bus I seen the smoke coming out of the cows's noses.

I look at my mama and I know what she's thinking. I been with Mama so much, just me and her, I know what she's thinking all the time. Right now it's home—Auntie and them. She's thinking if they got enough wood—if she left enough there to keep them warm till we get back. She's thinking if it go'n rain and if any of them go'n have to go out in the rain. She's thinking 'bout the hog—if he go'n get out, and if Ty and Val be able to get him back in. She always worry like that when she leaves the house. She don't worry too much if she leave me there with the smaller ones, 'cause she know I'm go'n look after them and look after Auntie and everything else. I'm the oldest and she say I'm the man.

I look at my mama and I love my mama. She's wearing that black coat and that black hat and she's looking sad. I love my mama and I want put my arm round her and tell her. But I'm not supposed to do that. She say that's weakness and that's crybaby stuff, and she don't want no crybaby round her. She don't want you to be scared, either. 'Cause Ty's scared of ghosts and she's always whipping him. I'm scared of the dark, too, but I make 'tend I ain't. I make 'tend I ain't 'cause I'm the oldest, and I got to set a good sample for the rest. I can't ever be scared and I can't ever cry. And that's why I never said nothing 'bout my teeth. It's been hurting me and hurting me close to a month now, but I never said it. I didn't say it 'cause I didn't want act like a crybaby, and 'cause I know we didn't have enough money to go have it pulled. But, Lord, it been hurting me. And look like it wouldn't start till at night when you was trying to get yourself little sleep. Then soon 's you shut your eyes—ummm-ummm, Lord, look like it go right down to your heartstring.

"Hurting, hanh?" Ty'd say.

I'd shake my head, but I wouldn't open my mouth for nothing. You open your mouth and let that wind in, and it almost kill you.

I'd just lay there and listen to them snore. Ty there, right 'side me, and Auntie and Val over by the fireplace. Val younger than me and Ty, and he sleeps with Auntie. Mama sleeps round the other side with Louis and Walker.

I'd just lay there and listen to them, and listen to that wind out there, and listen to that fire in the fireplace. Sometimes it'd stop long enough to let me get little rest. Sometimes it just hurt, hurt, hurt. Lord, have mercy.

2

Auntie knowed it was hurting me. I didn't tell nobody but Ty, 'cause we buddies and he ain't go'n tell nobody. But some kind of way Auntie found out. When she asked me, I told her no, nothing was wrong. But she knowed it all the time. She told me to mash up a piece of aspirin and wrap it in some cotton and jugg it down in that hole. I did it, but it didn't do no good. It stopped for a little while, and started right back again. Auntie wanted to tell Mama, but I told her, "Uh-uh." 'Cause I knowed we didn't have any money, and it just was go'n make her mad again. So Auntie told Monsieur Bayonne, and Monsieur Bayonne came over to the house and told me to kneel down 'side him on the fireplace. He put his finger in his mouth and made the Sign of the Cross on my jaw. The tip of Monsieur Bayonne's finger is some hard, 'cause he's always playing on that guitar. If we sit outside at night we can always hear Monsieur Bayonne playing on his guitar. Sometimes we leave him out there playing on the guitar.

Monsieur Bayonne made the Sign of the Cross over and over on my jaw, but that didn't do no good. Even when he prayed and told me to pray some, too, that tooth still hurt me.

"How you feeling?" he say.

"Same," I say.

He kept on praying and making the Sign of the Cross and I kept on praying, too.

"Still hurting?" he say.

"Yes, sir."

Monsieur Bayonne mashed harder and harder on my jaw. He mashed so hard he almost pushed me over on Ty. But then he stopped.

"What kind of prayers you praying, boy?" he say.

"Baptist," I say.

"Well, I'll be—no wonder that tooth still killing him. I'm going one way and he pulling the other. Boy, don't you know any Catholic prayers?"

"I know 'Hail Mary,' " I say.

"Then you better start saying it."

"Yes, sir."

He started mashing on my jaw again, and I could hear him praying at the same time. And, sure enough, after while it stopped hurting me.

Me and Ty went outside where Monsieur Bayonne's two hounds was and we started playing with them. "Let's go hunting," Ty say. "All right," I say; and we went on back in the pasture. Soon the hounds got on a trail, and me and Ty followed them all 'cross the pasture and then back in the woods, too. And then they cornered this little old rabbit and killed him, and me and Ty made them get back, and we picked up the rabbit and started on back home. But my tooth had started hurting me again. It was hurting me plenty now, but I wouldn't tell Monsieur Bayonne. That night I didn't sleep a bit, and first thing in the morning Auntie told me to go back and let Monsieur Bayonne pray over me some more. Monsieur Bayonne was in his kitchen making coffee when I got there. Soon 's he seen me he knowed what was wrong.

"All right, kneel down there 'side that stove," he say. "And this time make sure you pray Catholic. I don't know nothing 'bout that Baptist, and I don't want know nothing 'bout him."

3

Last night Mama say, "Tomorrow we going to town."

"It ain't hurting me no more," I say. "I can eat anything on it."

"Tomorrow we going to town," she say.

And after she finished eating, she got up and went to bed. She always go to bed early now. 'Fore Daddy went in the Army, she used to stay up late. All of us sitting out on the gallery or round the fire. But now, look like soon 's she finish eating she go to bed.

This morning when I woke up, her and Auntie was standing 'fore the fireplace. She say: "Enough to get there and get back. Dollar and a half to have it pulled. Twenty-five for me to go, twenty-five for him. Twenty-five for me to come back, twenty-five for him. Fifty cents left. Guess I get little piece of salt meat with that."

"Sure can use it," Auntie say. "White beans and no salt meat ain't white beans."

"I do the best I can," Mama say.

They was quiet after that, and I made 'tend I was still asleep.

"James, hit the floor," Auntie say.

I still made 'tend I was asleep. I didn't want them to know I was listening.

"All right," Auntie say, shaking me by the shoulder. "Come on. Today's the day."

I pushed the cover down to get out, and Ty grabbed it and pulled it back.

"You, too, Ty," Auntie say.

"I ain't getting no teef pulled," Ty say.

"Don't mean it ain't time to get up," Auntie say. "Hit it, Ty."

Ty got up grumbling.

"James, you hurry up and get in your clothes and eat your food," Auntie say. "What time y'all coming back?" she said to Mama.

"That 'leven o'clock bus," Mama say. "Got to get back in that field this evening."

"Get a move on you, James," Auntie say.

I went in the kitchen and washed my face, then I ate my breakfast. I was having bread and syrup. The bread was warm and hard and tasted good. And I tried to make it last a long time.

Ty came back there grumbling and mad at me.

"Got to get up," he say. "I ain't having no teefes pulled. What I got to be getting up for?"

Ty poured some syrup in his pan and got a piece of bread. He didn't wash his hands, neither his face, and I could see that white stuff in his eyes.

"You the one getting your teef pulled," he say. "What I got to get up for. I bet if I was getting a teef pulled, you wouldn't be getting up. Shucks; syrup again. I'm getting tired of this old syrup. Syrup, syrup, syrup. I'm go'n take with the sugar diabetes. I want me some bacon sometime."

"Go out in the field and work and you can have your bacon," Auntie say. She stood in the middle door looking at Ty. "You better be glad you got syrup. Some people ain't got that—hard 's time is."

"Shucks," Ty say. "How can I be strong."

"I don't know too much 'bout your strength," Auntie say; "but I know where you go'n be hot at, you keep that grumbling up. James, get a move on you; your mama waiting."

I ate my last piece of bread and went in the front room. Mama was standing 'fore the fireplace warming her hands. I put on my coat and my cap, and we left the house.

4

I look down there again, but it still ain't coming. I almost say, "It ain't coming yet," but I keep my mouth shut. 'Cause that's something else she don't like. She don't like for you to say something just for nothing. She can see it ain't coming, I can see it ain't coming, so why say it ain't coming. I don't say it, I turn and look at the river that's back of us. It's so cold the smoke's just raising up from the water. I see a bunch of pool-doos not too far out—just on the other side the lilies. I'm wondering if you can eat pool-doos. I ain't too sure, 'cause I ain't never ate none. But I done ate owls and black-birds, and I done ate redbirds, too. I didn't want kill the redbirds, but she made me kill them. They had two of them back there. One in my trap, one in Ty's trap. Me and Ty was go'n play with them and let them go, but she made me kill them 'cause we needed the food.

"I can't," I say. "I can't."

"Here," she say. "Take it."

"I can't," I say. "I can't. I can't kill him, Mama, please."

"Here," she say. "Take this fork, James."

"Please, Mama, I can't kill him," I say.

I could tell she was go'n hit me. I jerked back, but I didn't jerk back soon enough.

"Take it," she say.

I took it and reached in for him, but he kept on hopping to the back.

"I can't, Mama," I say. The water just kept on running down my face. "I can't," I say.

"Get him out of there," she say.

I reached in for him and he kept on hopping to the back. Then I reached in farther, and he pecked me on the hand.

"I can't, Mama," I say.

She slapped me again.

I reached in again, but he kept on hopping out my way. Then he hopped to one side and I reached there. The fork got him on the leg and I heard his leg pop. I pulled my hand out 'cause I had hurt him.

"Give it here," she say, and jerked the fork out my hand.

She reached in and got the little bird right in the neck. I heard the fork go in his neck, and I heard it go in the ground. She brought him out and helt him right in front of me.

"That's one," she say. She shook him off and gived me the fork. "Get the other one."

"I can't, Mama," I say. "I'll do anything, but don't make me do that."

She went to the corner of the fence and broke the biggest switch over there she could find. I knelt 'side the trap, crying.

"Get him out of there," she say.

"I can't, Mama."

She started hitting me 'cross the back. I went down on the ground, crying.

"Get him," she say.

"Octavia?" Auntie say.

'Cause she had come out of the house and she was standing by the tree looking at us.

"Get him out of there," Mama say.

"Octavia," Auntie say, "explain to him. Explain to him. Just don't beat him. Explain to him."

But she hit me and hit me and hit me.

I'm still young—I ain't no more than eight; but I know now; I know why I had to do it. (They was so little, though. They was so little. I 'member how I picked the feathers off them and cleaned them and helt them over the fire. Then we all ate them. Ain't had but a little bitty piece each, but we all had a little bitty piece, and everybody just looked at me 'cause they was so proud.) Suppose she had to go away? That's why I had to do it. Suppose she had to go away like Daddy went away? Then who was go'n look after us? They had to be somebody left to carry on. I didn't know it then, but I know it now. Auntie and Monsieur Bayonne talked to me and made me see.

5

Time I see it I get out my handkerchief and start waving. It's still 'way down there, but I keep waving anyhow. Then it come up and stop and me and Mama get on. Mama tell me go sit in the back while she pay. I do like she say, and the people look at me. When I pass the little sign that say "White" and "Colored," I start looking for a seat. I just see one of them back there, but I don't take it, 'cause I want my mama to sit down herself. She comes in the back and sit down, and I lean on the seat. They got seats in the front, but I know I can't sit there, 'cause I have to sit back of the sign. Anyhow, I don't want sit there if my mama go'n sit back here.

They got a lady sitting 'side my mama and she looks at me and smiles little bit. I smile back, but I don't open my mouth, 'cause the wind'll get in and make that tooth ache. The lady take out a pack of gum and reach me a slice, but I shake my head. The lady just can't understand why a little boy'll turn down gum, and she reach me a slice again. This time I point to my jaw. The lady understands and smiles little bit, and I smile little bit, but I don't open my mouth, though.

They got a girl sitting 'cross from me. She got on a red overcoat and her hair's plaited in one big plait. First, I make 'tend I don't see her over there, but then I start looking at her little bit. She make 'tend she don't see me, either, but I catch her looking that way. She got a cold, and every now and then she h'ist that little handkerchief to her nose. She ought to blow it, but she don't. Must think she's too much a lady or something.

Every time she h'ist that little handkerchief, the lady 'side her say something in her ear. She shakes her head and lays her hands in her lap again. Then I catch her kind of looking where I'm at. I smile at her little bit. But think she'll smile back? Uh-uh. She just turn up her little old nose and turn her head. Well, I show her both of us can turn us head. I turn mine too and look out at the river.

The river is gray. The sky is gray. They have pool-doos on the water. The water is wavy, and the pool-doos go up and down. The bus go round a turn, and you got plenty trees hiding the river. Then the bus go round another turn, and I can see the river again.

I look toward the front where all the white people sitting. Then I look at that little old gal again. I don't look right at her, 'cause I don't want all them people to know I love her. I just look at her little bit, like I'm looking out that window over there. But she knows I'm looking that way, and she kind of look at me, too. The lady sitting 'side her catch her this time, and she leans over and says something in her ear.

"I don't love him nothing," that little old gal says out loud.

Everybody back there hear her mouth, and all of them look at us and laugh.

"I don't love you, either," I say. "So you don't have to turn up your nose, Miss."

"You the one looking," she say.

"I wasn't looking at you," I say. "I was looking out that window, there."

"Out that window, my foot," she say. "I seen you. Everytime I turned round you was looking at me."

"You must of been looking yourself if you seen me all them times," I say.

"Shucks," she say, "I got me all kind of boyfriends."

"I got girlfriends, too," I say.

"Well, I just don't want you getting your hopes up," she say.

I don't say no more to that little old gal 'cause I don't want have to bust her in the mouth. I lean on the seat where Mama sitting, and I don't even look that way no more. When we get to Bayonne, she jugg her little old tongue out at me. I make 'tend I'm go'n hit her, and she duck down 'side her mama. And all the people laugh at us again.

6

Me and Mama get off and start walking in town. Bayonne is a little bitty town. Baton Rouge is a hundred times bigger than Bayonne. I went to Baton Rouge once—me, Ty, Mama, and Daddy. But that was 'way back yonder, 'fore Daddy went in the Army. I wonder when we go'n see him again. I wonder when. Look like he ain't ever coming back home. . . . Even the pavement all cracked in Bayonne. Got grass shooting right out the sidewalk. Got weeds in the ditch, too; just like they got at home.

It's some cold in Bayonne. Look like it's colder than it is home. The wind blows in my face, and I feel that stuff running down my nose. I sniff. Mama says use that handkerchief. I blow my nose and put it back.

We pass a school and I see them white children playing in the yard. Big old red school, and them children just running and playing. Then we pass a café, and I see a bunch of people in there eating. I wish I was in there 'cause I'm cold. Mama tells me keep my eyes in front where they belong.

We pass stores that's got dummies, and we pass another café, and then we pass a shoe shop, and that bald-head man in there fixing on a shoe. I look at him and I butt into that white lady, and Mama jerks me in front and tells me stay there.

We come up to the courthouse, and I see the flag waving there. This flag ain't like the one we got at school. This one here ain't got but a handful of stars. One at school got a big pile of stars—one for every state. We pass it and we turn and there it is—the dentist office. Me and Mama go in, and they got people sitting everywhere you look. They even got a little boy in there younger than me.

Me and Mama sit on that bench, and a white lady come in there and ask me what my name is. Mama tells her and the white lady goes on back. Then I hear somebody hollering in there. Soon 's that little boy hear him hollering, he starts hollering, too. His mama pats him and pats him, trying to make him hush up, but he ain't thinking 'bout his mama.

The man that was hollering in there comes out holding his jaw. He is a big old man and he's wearing overalls and a jumper.

"Got it, hanh?" another man asks him.

The man shakes his head—don't want open his mouth.

"Man, I thought they was killing you in there," the other man says. "Hollering like a pig under a gate."

The man don't say nothing. He just heads for the door, and the other man follows him.

"John Lee," the white lady says. "John Lee Williams."

The little boy juggs his head down in his mama's lap and holler more now. His mama tells him go with the nurse, but he ain't thinking 'bout his mama. His mama tells him again, but he don't even hear her. His mama picks him up and takes him in there, and even when the white lady shuts the door I can still hear little old John Lee.

"I often wonder why the Lord let a child like that suffer," a lady says to my mama. The lady's sitting right in front of us on another bench. She's got on a white dress and a black sweater. She must be a nurse or something herself, I reckon.

"Not us to question," a man says.

"Sometimes I don't know if we shouldn't," the lady says.

"I know definitely we shouldn't," the man says. The man looks like a preacher. He's big and fat and he's got on a black suit. He's got a gold chain, too.

"Why?" the lady says.

"Why anything?" the preacher says.

"Yes," the lady says. "Why anything?"

"Not us to question," the preacher says.

The lady looks at the preacher a little while and looks at Mama again.

"And look like it's the poor who suffers the most," she says. "I don't understand it."

"Best not to even try," the preacher says. "He works in mysterious ways—wonders to perform."

Right then little John Lee bust out hollering, and everybody turn they head to listen.

"He's not a good dentist," the lady says. "Dr. Robillard is much better. But more expensive. That's why most of the colored people come here. The white people go to Dr. Robillard. Y'all from Bayonne?"

"Down the river," my mama says. And that's all she go'n say, 'cause she don't talk much. But the lady keeps on looking at her, and so she says, "Near Morgan."

"I see," the lady says.

7

"That's the trouble with the black people in this country today," somebody else says. This one here's sitting on the same side me and Mama's sitting, and he is kind of sitting in front of that preacher. He looks like a teacher or somebody that goes to college. He's got on a suit, and he's got a book that he's been reading. "We don't question is exactly our problem," he says. "We should question and question and question—question everything."

The preacher just looks at him a long time. He done put a toothpick or something in his mouth, and he just keeps on turning it and turning it. You can see he don't like that boy with that book.

"Maybe you can explain what you mean," he says.

"I said what I meant," the boy says. "Question everything. Every stripe, every star, every word spoken. Everything."

"It 'pears to me that this young lady and I was talking 'bout God, young man," the preacher says.

"Question Him, too," the boy says.

"Wait," the preacher says. "Wait now."

"You heard me right," the boy says. "His existence as well as everything else. Everything."

The preacher just looks across the room at the boy. You can see he's getting madder and madder. But mad or no mad, the boy ain't thinking 'bout him. He looks at that preacher just 's hard 's the preacher looks at him.

"Is this what they coming to?" the preacher says. "Is this what we educating them for?"

"You're not educating me," the boy says. "I wash dishes at night so that I can go to school in the day. So even the words you spoke need questioning."

The preacher just looks at him and shakes his head.

"When I come in this room and seen you there with your book, I said to myself, 'There's an intelligent man.' How wrong a person can be."

"Show me one reason to believe in the existence of a God," the boy says.

"My heart tells me," the preacher says.

" 'My heart tells me,' " the boy says. " 'My heart tells me.' Sure, 'My heart tells me.' And as long as you listen to what your heart tells you, you will have only what the white man gives you and nothing more. Me, I don't listen to my heart. The purpose of the heart is to pump blood throughout the body, and nothing else."

"Who's your paw, boy?" the preacher says.

"Why?"

"Who is he?"

"He's dead."

"And your mom?"

"She's in Charity Hospital with pneumonia. Half killed herself, working for nothing."

"And 'cause he's dead and she's sick, you mad at the world?"

"I'm not mad at the world. I'm questioning the world. I'm questioning it with cold logic, sir. What do words like Freedom, Liberty, God, White, Colored mean? I want to know. That's why *you* are sending us to school, to read and to ask questions. And because we ask these questions, you call us mad. No sir, it is not us who are mad."

"You keep saying 'us'?"

" 'Us.' Yes—us. I'm not alone."

The preacher just shakes his head. Then he looks at everybody in the room—everybody. Some of the people look down at the floor, keep from looking at him. I kind of look 'way myself, but soon 's I know he done turn his head, I look that way again.

"I'm sorry for you," he says to the boy.

"Why?" the boy says. "Why not be sorry for yourself? Why are you so much better off than I am? Why aren't you sorry for these other people in here? Why not be sorry for the lady who had to drag her child into the dentist office? Why not be sorry for the lady sitting on that bench over there? Be sorry for them. Not for me. Some way or the other I'm going to make it."

"No, I'm sorry for you," the preacher says.

"Of course, of course," the boy says, nodding his head. "You're sorry for me because I rock that pillar you're leaning on."

"You can't ever rock the pillar I'm leaning on, young man. It's stronger than anything man can ever do."

"You believe in God because a man told you to believe in God," the boy says. "A white man told you to believe in God. And why? To keep you ignorant so he can keep his feet on your neck."

"So now we the ignorant?" the preacher says.

"Yes," the boy says. "Yes." And he opens his book again.

The preacher just looks at him sitting there. The boy done forgot all about him. Everybody else make 'tend they done forgot the squabble, too.

Then I see that preacher getting up real slow. Preacher's a great big old man and he got to brace himself to get up. He comes over where the boy is sitting. He just stands there a little while looking down at him, but the boy don't raise his head.

"Get up, boy," preacher says.

The boy looks up at him, then he shuts his book real slow and stands up. Preacher just hauls back and hit him in the face. The boy falls back 'gainst the wall, but he straightens himself up and looks right back at that preacher.

"You forgot the other cheek," he says.

The preacher hauls back and hit him again on the other side. But this time the boy braces himself and don't fall.

"That hasn't changed a thing," he says.

The preacher just looks at the boy. The preacher's breathing real hard like he just run up a big hill. The boy sits down and opens his book again.

"I feel sorry for you," the preacher says. "I never felt so sorry for a man before."

The boy makes 'tend he don't even hear that preacher. He keeps on reading his book. The preacher goes back and gets his hat off the chair.

"Excuse me," he says to us. "I'll come back some other time. Y'all, please excuse me."

And he looks at the boy and goes out the room. The boy h'ist his hand up to his mouth one time to wipe 'way some blood. All the rest of the time he keeps on reading. And nobody else in there say a word.

8

Little John Lee and his mama come out the dentist office, and the nurse calls somebody else in. Then little bit later they come out, and the nurse calls another name. But fast 's she calls somebody in there, somebody else comes in the place where we sitting, and the room stays full.

The people coming in now, all of them wearing big coats. One of them says something 'bout sleeting, another one says he hope not. Another one says he think it ain't nothing but rain. 'Cause, he says, rain can get awful cold this time of year.

All round the room they talking. Some of them talking to people right by them, some of them talking to people clear 'cross the room, some of them talking to anybody'll listen. It's a little bitty room, no bigger than us kitchen, and I can see everybody in there. The little old room's full of smoke, 'cause you got two old men smoking pipes over by that side door. I think I feel my tooth thumping me some, and I hold my breath and wait. I wait and wait, but it don't thump me no more. Thank God for that.

I feel like going to sleep, and I lean back 'gainst the wall. But I'm scared to go to sleep. Scared 'cause the nurse might call my name and I won't hear her. And Mama might go to sleep, too, and she'll be mad if neither one of us heard the nurse.

I look up at Mama. I love my mama. I love my mama. And when cotton come I'm go'n get her a new coat. And I ain't go'n get a black one, either. I think I'm go'n get her a red one.

"They got some books over there," I say. "Want read one of them?"

Mama looks at the books, but she don't answer me.

"You got yourself a little man there," the lady says.

Mama don't say nothing to the lady, but she must've smiled, 'cause I seen the lady smiling back. The lady looks at me a little while, like she's feeling sorry for me.

"You sure got that preacher out here in a hurry," she says to that boy.

The boy looks up at her and looks in his book again. When I grow up I want be just like him. I want clothes like that and I want keep a book with me, too.

"You really don't believe in God?" the lady says.

"No," he says.

"But why?" the lady says.

"Because the wind is pink," he says.

"What?" the lady says.

The boy don't answer her no more. He just reads in his book.

"Talking 'bout the wind is pink," that old lady says. She's sitting on the same bench with the boy and she's trying to look in his face. The boy makes 'tend the old lady ain't even there. He just keeps on reading. "Wind is pink," she says again. "Eh, Lord, what children go'n be saying next?"

The lady 'cross from us bust out laughing.

"That's a good one," she says. "The wind is pink. Yes sir, that's a good one."

"Don't you believe the wind is pink?" the boy says. He keeps his head down in the book.

"Course I believe it, honey," the lady says. "Course I do." She looks at us and winks her eye. "And what color is grass, honey?"

"Grass? Grass is black."

She bust out laughing again. The boy looks at her.

"Don't you believe grass is black?" he says.

The lady quits her laughing and looks at him. Everybody else looking at him, too. The place quiet, quiet.

"Grass is green, honey," the lady says. "It was green yesterday, it's green today, and it's go'n be green tomorrow."

"How do you know it's green?"

"I know because I know."

"You don't know it's green," the boy says. "You believe it's green because someone told you it was green. If someone had told you it was black you'd believe it was black."

"It's green," the lady says. "I know green when I see green."

"Prove it's green," the boy says.

"Sure, now," the lady says. "Don't tell me it's coming to that."

"It's coming to just that," the boy says. "Words mean nothing. One means no more than the other."

"That's what it all coming to?" that old lady says. That old lady got on a turban and she got on two sweaters. She got a green sweater under a black sweater. I can see the green sweater 'cause some of the buttons on the other sweater's missing.

"Yes ma'am," the boy says. "Words mean nothing. Action is the only thing. Doing. That's the only thing."

"Other words, you want the Lord to come down here and show Hisself to you?" she says.

"Exactly, ma'am," he says.

"You don't mean that, I'm sure?" she says.

"I do, ma'am," he says.

"Done, Jesus," the old lady says, shaking her head.

"I didn't go 'long with that preacher at first," the other lady says; "but now—I don't know. When a person say the grass is black, he's either a lunatic or something's wrong."

"Prove to me that it's green," the boy says.

"It's green because the people say it's green."

"Those same people say we're citizens of these United States," the boy says.

"I think I'm a citizen," the lady says.

"Citizens have certain rights," the boy says. "Name me one right that you have. One right, granted by the Constitution, that you can exercise in Bayonne."

The lady don't answer him. She just looks at him like she don't know what he's talking 'bout. I know I don't.

"Things changing," she says.

"Things are changing because some black men have begun to think with their brains and not their hearts," the boy says.

"You trying to say these people don't believe in God?"

"I'm sure some of them do. Maybe most of them do. But they don't believe that God is going to touch these white people's hearts and change things tomorrow. Things change through action. By no other way."

Everybody sit quiet and look at the boy. Nobody says a thing. Then the lady 'cross the room from me and Mama just shakes her head.

"Let's hope that not all your generation feel the same way you do," she says.

"Think what you please, it doesn't matter," the boy says. "But it will be men who listen to their heads and not their hearts who will see that your children have a better chance than you had."

"Let's hope they ain't all like you, though," the old lady says. "Done forgot the heart absolutely."

"Yes ma'am, I hope they aren't all like me," the boy says. "Unfortunately, I was born too late to believe in your God. Let's hope that the ones who come after will have your faith—if not in your God, then in something else, something definitely that they can lean on. I haven't anything. For me, the wind is pink, the grass is black."

9

The nurse comes in the room where we all sitting and waiting and says the doctor won't take no more patients till one o'clock this evening. My mama jumps up off the bench and goes up to the white lady.

"Nurse, I have to go back in the field this evening," she says.

"The doctor is treating his last patient now," the nurse says. "One o'clock this evening."

"Can I at least speak to the doctor?" my mama asks.

"I'm his nurse," the lady says.

"My little boy's sick," my mama says. "Right now his tooth almost killing him."

The nurse looks at me. She's trying to make up her mind if to let me come in. I look at her real pitiful. The tooth ain't hurting me at all, but Mama say it is, so I make 'tend for her sake.

"This evening," the nurse says, and goes on back in the office.

"Don't feel 'jected, honey," the lady says to Mama. "I been round them a long time—they take you when they want to. If you was white, that's something else; but we the wrong color."

Mama don't say nothing to the lady, and me and her go outside and stand 'gainst the wall. It's cold out there. I can feel that wind going through my coat. Some of the other people come out of the room and go up the street. Me and Mama stand there a little while and we start walking. I don't know where we going. When we come to the other street we just stand there.

"You don't have to make water, do you?" Mama says.

"No, ma'am," I say.

We go on up the street. Walking real slow. I can tell Mama don't know where she's going. When we come to a store we stand there and look at the dummies. I look at a little boy wearing a brown overcoat. He's got on brown shoes, too. I look at my old shoes and look at his'n again. You wait till summer, I say.

Me and Mama walk away. We come up to another store and we stop and look at them dummies, too. Then we go on again. We pass a café where the white people in there eating. Mama tells me keep my eyes in front where they belong, but I can't help from seeing them people eat. My stomach starts to growling 'cause I'm hungry. When I see people eating, I get hungry; when I see a coat, I get cold.

A man whistles at my mama when we go by a filling station. She makes 'tend she don't even see him. I look back and I feel like hitting him in the mouth. If I was bigger, I say; if I was bigger, you'd see.

We keep on going. I'm getting colder and colder, but I don't say nothing. I feel that stuff running down my nose and I sniff.

"That rag," Mama says.

I get it out and wipe my nose. I'm getting cold all over now—my face, my hands, my feet, everything. We pass another little café, but this'n for white people, too, and we can't go in there, either. So we just walk. I'm so cold now I'm 'bout ready to say it. If I knowed where we was going I wouldn't be so cold, but I don't know where we going. We go, we go, we go. We walk clean out of Bayonne. Then we cross the street and we come back. Same thing I seen when I got off the bus this morning. Same old trees, same old walk, same old weeds, same old cracked pave—same old everything.

I sniff again.

"That rag," Mama says.

I wipe my nose real fast and jugg that handkerchief back in my pocket 'fore my hand gets too cold. I raise my head and I can see David's hardware store. When we come up to it, we go in. I don't know why, but I'm glad.

It's warm in there. It's so warm in there you don't ever want to leave. I look for the heater, and I see it over by them barrels. Three white men standing round the heater talking in Creole. One of them comes over to see what my mama want.

"Got any axe handles?" she says.

Me, Mama and the white man start to the back, but Mama stops me when we come up to the heater. She and the white man go on. I hold my hands over the heater and look at them. They go all the way to the back, and I see the white man pointing to the axe handles 'gainst the wall. Mama takes one of them and shakes it like she's trying to figure how much it weighs. Then she rubs her hand over it from one end to the other end. She turns it over and looks at the other side, then she shakes it again, and shakes her head and puts it back. She gets another one and she does it just like she did the first one, then she shakes her head. Then she gets a brown one and do it that, too. But she don't like this one, either. Then she gets another one, but 'fore she shakes it or anything, she looks at me. Look like she's trying to say something to me, but I don't know what it is. All I know is I done got warm now and I'm feeling right smart better. Mama shakes this axe handle just like she did the others, and shakes her head and says something to the white man. The white man just looks at his pile of axe handles, and when Mama pass him to come to the front, the white man just scratch his head and follows her. She tells me come on and we go on out and start walking again.

We walk and walk, and no time at all I'm cold again. Look like I'm colder now 'cause I can still remember how good it was back there. My stomach growls and I suck it in to keep Mama from hearing it. She's walking right 'side me, and it growls so loud you can hear it a mile. But Mama don't say a word.

10

When we come up to the courthouse, I look at the clock. It's got quarter to twelve. Mean we got another hour and a quarter to be out here in the cold. We go and stand 'side a building. Something hits my cap and I look up at the sky. Sleet's falling.

I look at Mama standing there. I want stand close 'side her, but she don't like that. She say that's crybaby stuff. She say you got to stand for yourself, by yourself.

"Let's go back to that office," she says.

We cross the street. When we get to the dentist office I try to open the door, but I can't. I twist and twist, but I can't. Mama pushes me to the side and she twist the knob, but she can't open the door, either. She turns 'way from the door. I look at her, but I don't move and I don't say nothing. I done seen her like this before and I'm scared of her.

"You hungry?" she says. She says it like she's mad at me, like I'm the cause of everything.

"No, ma'am," I say.

"You want eat and walk back, or you rather don't eat and ride?"

"I ain't hungry," I say.

I ain't just hungry, but I'm cold, too. I'm so hungry and cold I want to cry. And look like I'm getting colder and colder. My feet done got numb. I try to work my toes, but I don't even feel them. Look like I'm go'n die. Look like I'm go'n stand right here and freeze to death. I think 'bout home. I think 'bout Val and Auntie and Ty and Louis and Walker. It's 'bout twelve o'clock and I know they eating dinner now. I can hear Ty making jokes. He done forgot 'bout getting up early this morning and right now he's probably making jokes. Always trying to make somebody laugh. I wish I was right there listening to him. Give anything in the world if I was home round the fire.

"Come on," Mama says.

We start walking again. My feet so numb I can't hardly feel them. We turn the corner and go on back up the street. The clock on the courthouse starts hitting for twelve.

The sleet's coming down plenty now. They hit the pave and bounce like rice. Oh, Lord; oh, Lord, I pray. Don't let me die, don't let me die, don't let me die, Lord.

11

Now I know where we going. We going back of town where the colored people eat. I don't care if I don't eat. I been hungry before. I can stand it. But I can't stand the cold.

I can see we go'n have a long walk. It's 'bout a mile down there. But I don't mind. I know when I get there I'm go'n warm myself. I think I can hold out. My hands numb in my pockets and my feet numb, too, but if I keep moving I can hold out. Just don't stop no more, that's all.

The sky's gray. The sleet keeps on falling. Falling like rain now—plenty, plenty. You can hear it hitting the pave. You can see it bouncing. Sometimes it bounces two times 'fore it settles.

We keep on going. We don't say nothing. We just keep on going, keep on going.

I wonder what Mama's thinking. I hope she ain't mad at me. When summer come I'm go'n pick plenty cotton and get her a coat. I'm go'n get her a red one.

I hope they'd make it summer all the time. I'd be glad if it was summer all the time—but it ain't. We got to have winter, too. Lord, I hate the winter. I guess everybody hate the winter.

I don't sniff this time. I get out my handkerchief and wipe my nose. My hands's so cold I can hardly hold the handkerchief.

I think we getting close, but we ain't there yet. I wonder where everybody is. Can't see a soul but us. Look like we the only two people moving round today. Must be too cold for the rest of the people to move round in.

I can hear my teeth. I hope they don't knock together too hard and make that bad one hurt. Lord, that's all I need, for that bad one to start off.

I hear a church bell somewhere. But today ain't Sunday. They must be ringing for a funeral or something.

I wonder what they doing at home. They must be eating. Monsieur Bayonne might be there with his guitar. One day Ty played with Monsieur Bayonne's guitar and broke one of the strings. Monsieur Bayonne was some mad with Ty. He say Ty wasn't go'n ever 'mount to nothing. Ty can go just like Monsieur Bayonne when he ain't there. Ty can make everybody laugh when he starts to mocking Monsieur Bayonne.

I used to like to be with Mama and Daddy. We used to be happy. But they took him in the Army. Now, nobody happy no more. . . . I be glad when Daddy comes home.

Monsieur Bayonne say it wasn't fair for them to take Daddy and give Mama nothing and give us nothing. Auntie say, "Shhh, Etienne. Don't let them hear you talk like that." Monsieur Bayonne say, "It's God truth. What they giving his children? They have to walk three and a half miles to school hot or cold. That's anything to give for a paw? She's got to work in the field rain or shine just to make ends meet. That's anything to give for a husband?" Auntie say, "Shhh, Etienne, shhh." "Yes, you right," Monsieur Bayonne say. "Best don't say it in front of them now. But one day they go'n find out. One day." "Yes, I suppose so," Auntie say. "Then what, Rose Mary?" Monsieur Bayonne say. "I don't know, Etienne," Auntie say. "All we can do is us job, and leave everything else in His hand . . ."

We getting closer, now. We getting closer. I can even see the railroad tracks.

We cross the tracks, and now I see the café. Just to get in there, I say. Just to get in there. Already I'm starting to feel little better.

12

We go in. Ahh, it's good. I look for the heater; there 'gainst the wall. One of them little brown ones. I just stand there and hold my hands over it. I can't open my hands too wide 'cause they almost froze.

Mama's standing right 'side me. She done unbuttoned her coat. Smoke rises out of the coat, and the coat smells like a wet dog.

I move to the side so Mama can have more room. She opens out her hands and rubs them together. I rub mine together, too, 'cause this keep them from hurting. If you let them warm too fast, they hurt you sure. But if you let them warm just little bit at a time, and you keep rubbing them, they be all right every time.

They got just two more people in the café. A lady back of the counter, and a man on this side the counter. They been watching us ever since we come in.

Mama gets out the handkerchief and count up the money. Both of us know how much money she's got there. Three dollars. No, she ain't got three dollars, 'cause she had to pay us way up here. She ain't got but two dollars and a half left. Dollar and a half to get my tooth pulled, and fifty cents for us to go back on, and fifty cents worth of salt meat.

She stirs the money round with her finger. Most of the money is change 'cause I can hear it rubbing together. She stirs it and stirs it. Then she looks at the door. It's still sleeting. I can hear it hitting 'gainst the wall like rice.

"I ain't hungry, Mama," I say.

"Got to pay them something for they heat," she says.

She takes a quarter out the handkerchief and ties the handkerchief up again. She looks over her shoulder at the people, but she still don't move. I hope she don't spend the money. I don't want her spending it on me. I'm hungry, I'm almost starving I'm so hungry, but I don't want her spending the money on me.

She flips the quarter over like she's thinking. She's must be thinking 'bout us walking back home. Lord, I sure don't want walk home. If I thought it'd do any good to say something, I'd say it. But Mama makes up her own mind 'bout things.

She turns 'way from the heater right fast, like she better hurry up and spend the quarter 'fore she change her mind. I watch her go toward the counter. The man and the lady look at her, too. She tells the lady something and the lady walks away. The man keeps on looking at her. Her back's turned to the man, and she don't even know he's standing there.

The lady puts some cakes and a glass of milk on the counter. Then she pours up a cup of coffee and sets it 'side the other stuff. Mama pays her for the things and comes on back where I'm standing. She tells me sit down at the table 'gainst the wall.

The milk and the cakes's for me; the coffee's for Mama. I eat slow and I look at her. She's looking outside at the sleet. She's looking real sad. I say to myself, I'm go'n make all this up one day. You see, one day, I'm go'n make all this up. I want say it now; I want tell her how I feel right now; but Mama don't like for us to talk like that.

"I can't eat all this," I say.

They ain't got but just three little old cakes there. I'm so hungry right now, the Lord knows I can eat a hundred times three, but I want my mama to have one.

Mama don't even look my way. She knows I'm hungry, she knows I want it. I let it stay there a little while, then I get it and eat it. I eat just on my front teeth, though 'cause if cake touch that back tooth I know what'll happen. Thank God it ain't hurt me at all today.

After I finish eating I see the man go to the juke box. He drops a nickel in it, then he just stand there a little while looking at the record. Mama tells me keep my eyes in front where they belong. I turn my head like she say, but then I hear the man coming toward us.

"Dance, pretty?" he says.

Mama gets up to dance with him. But 'fore you know it, she done grabbed the little man in the collar and done heaved him 'side the wall. He hit the wall so hard he stop the juke box from playing.

"Some pimp," the lady back of the counter says. "Some pimp."

The little man jumps up off the floor and starts toward my mama. 'Fore you know it, Mama done sprung open her knife and she's waiting for him.

"Come on," she says. "Come on. I'll gut you from your neighbo to your throat. Come on."

I go up to the little man to hit him, but Mama makes me come and stand 'side her. The little man looks at me and Mama and goes on back to the counter.

"Some pimp," the lady back of the counter says. "Some pimp." She starts laughing and pointing at the little man. "Yes sir, you a pimp, all right. Yes sir-ree."

13

"Fasten that coat, let's go," Mama says.

"You don't have to leave," the lady says.

Mama don't answer the lady, and we right out in the cold again. I'm warm right now—my hands, my ears, my feet—but I know this ain't go'n last too long. It done sleet so much now you got ice everywhere you look.

We cross the railroad tracks, and soon's we do, I get cold. That wind goes through this little old coat like it ain't even there. I got on a shirt and a sweater under the coat, but that wind don't pay them no mind. I look up and I can see we got a long way to go. I wonder if we go'n make it 'fore I get too cold.

We cross over to walk on the sidewalk. They got just one sidewalk back here, and it's over there.

After we go just a little piece, I smell bread cooking. I look, then I see a baker shop. When we get closer, I can smell it more better, I shut my eyes and make 'tend I'm eating. But I keep them shut too long and I butt up 'gainst a telephone post. Mama grabs me and see if I'm hurt. I ain't bleeding or nothing and she turns me loose.

I can feel I'm getting colder and colder, and I look up to see how far we still got to go. Uptown is 'way up yonder. A half mile more, I reckon. I try to think of something. They say think and you won't get cold. I think of that poem, "Annabel Lee." I ain't been to school in so long—this bad weather—I reckon they done passed "Annabel Lee" by now. But passed it or not, I'm sure Miss Walker go'n make me recite it when I get there. That woman don't never forget nothing. I ain't never seen nobody like that in my life.

I'm still getting cold. "Annabel Lee" or no "Annabel Lee," I'm still getting cold. But I can see we getting closer. We getting there gradually.

Soon 's we turn the corner, I see a little old white lady up in front of us. She's the only lady on the street. She's all in black and she's got a long black rag over her head.

"Stop," she says.

Me and Mama stop and look at her. She must be crazy to be out in all this bad weather. Ain't got but a few other people out there, and all of them's men.

"Y'all done ate?" she says.

"Just finish," Mama says.

"Y'all must be cold then?" she says.

"We headed for the dentist," Mama says. "We'll warm up when we get there."

"What dentist?" the old lady says. "Mr. Bassett?"

"Yes, ma'am," Mama says.

"Come on in," the old lady says. "I'll telephone him and tell him y'all coming."

Me and Mama follow the old lady in the store. It's a little bitty store, and it don't have much in there. The old lady takes off her head rag and folds it up.

"Helena?" somebody calls from the back.

"Yes, Alnest?" the old lady says.

"Did you see them?"

"They're here. Standing beside me."

"Good. Now you can stay inside."

The old lady looks at Mama. Mama's waiting to hear what she brought us in here for. I'm waiting for that, too.

"I saw y'all each time you went by," she says. "I came out to catch you, but you were gone."

"We went back of town," Mama says.

"Did you eat?"

"Yes, ma'am."

The old lady looks at Mama a long time, like she's thinking Mama might be just saying that. Mama looks right back at her. The old lady looks at me to see what I have to say. I don't say nothing. I sure ain't going 'gainst my mama.

"There's food in the kitchen," she says to Mama. "I've been keeping it warm."

Mama turns right around and starts for the door.

"Just a minute," the old lady says. Mama stops. "The boy'll have to work for it. It isn't free."

"We don't take no handout," Mama says.

"I'm not handing out anything," the old lady says. "I need my garbage moved to the front. Ernest has a bad cold and can't go out there."

"James'll move it for you," Mama says.

"Not unless you eat," the old lady says. "I'm old, but I have my pride, too, you know."

Mama can see she ain't go'n beat this old lady down, so she just shakes her head.

"All right," the old lady says. "Come into the kitchen."

She leads the way with that rag in her hand. The kitchen is a little bitty little old thing, too. The table and the stove just 'bout fill it up. They got a little room to the side. Somebody in there laying 'cross the bed—'cause I can see one of his feet. Must be the person she was talking to: Ernest or Alnest —something like that.

"Sit down," the old lady says to Mama. "Not you," she says to me. "You have to move the cans."

"Helena?" the man says in the other room.

"Yes, Alnest?" the old lady says.

"Are you going out there again?"

"I must show the boy where the garbage is, Alnest," the old lady says.

"Keep that shawl over your head," the old man says.

"You don't have to remind me, Alnest. Come, boy," the old lady says.

We go out in the yard. Little old back yard ain't no bigger than the store or the kitchen. But it can sleet here just like it can sleet in any big back yard. And 'fore you know it, I'm trembling.

"There," the old lady says, pointing to the cans. I pick up one of the cans and set it right back down. The can's so light, I'm go'n see what's inside of it.

"Here," the old lady says. "Leave that can alone."

I look back at her standing there in the door. She's got that black rag wrapped around her shoulders, and she's pointing one of her little old fingers at me.

"Pick it up and carry it to the front," she says. I go by her with the can, and she's looking at me all the time. I'm sure the can's empty. I'm sure she could've carried it herself—maybe both of them at the same time. "Set it on the sidewalk by the door and come back for the other one," she says.

I go and come back, and Mama looks at me when I pass her. I get the other can and take it to the front. It don't feel a bit heavier than that first one. I tell myself I ain't go'n be nobody's fool, and I'm go'n look inside this can to see just what I been hauling. First, I look up the street, then down the street. Nobody coming. Then I look over my shoulder toward the door. That little old lady done slipped up there quiet 's mouse, watching me again. Look like she knowed what I was go'n do.

"Ehh, Lord," she says. "Children, children. Come in here, boy, and go wash your hands."

I follow her in the kitchen. She points toward the bathroom, and I go in there and wash up. Little bitty old bathroom, but it's clean, clean. I don't use any of her towels; I wipe my hands on my pants legs.

When I come back in the kitchen, the old lady done dished up the food. Rice, gravy, meat—and she even got some lettuce and tomato in a saucer. She even got a glass of milk and a piece of cake there, too. It looks so good, I almost start eating 'fore I say my blessing.

"Helena?" the old man says.

"Yes, Alnest?"

"Are they eating?"

"Yes," she says.

"Good," he says. "Now you'll stay inside."

The old lady goes in there where he is and I can hear them talking. I look at Mama. She's eating slow like she's thinking. I wonder what's the matter now. I reckon she's thinking 'bout home.

The old lady comes back in the kitchen.

"I talked to Dr. Bassett's nurse," she says. "Dr. Bassett will take you as soon as you get there."

"Thank you, ma'am," Mama says.

"Perfectly all right," the old lady says. "Which one is it?"

Mama nods toward me. The old lady looks at me real sad. I look sad, too.

"You're not afraid, are you?" she says.

"No, ma'am," I say.

"That's a good boy," the old lady says. "Nothing to be afraid of. Dr. Bassett will not hurt you."

When me and Mama get through eating, we thank the old lady again.

"Helena, are they leaving?" the old man says.

"Yes, Alnest."

"Tell them I say good-bye."

"They can hear you, Alnest."

"Good-bye both mother and son," the old man says. "And may God be with you."

Me and Mama tell the old man good-bye, and we follow the old lady in the front room. Mama opens the door to go out, but she stops and comes back in the store.

"You sell salt meat?" she says.

"Yes."

"Give me two bits worth."

"That isn't very much salt meat," the old lady says.

"That's all I have," Mama says.

The old lady goes back of the counter and cuts a big piece off the chunk. Then she wraps it up and puts it in a paper bag.

"Two bits," she says.

"That looks like awful lot of meat for a quarter," Mama says.

"Two bits," the old lady says. "I've been selling salt meat behind this counter twenty-five years. I think I know what I'm doing."

"You got a scale there," Mama says.

"What?" the old lady says.

"Weigh it," Mama says.

"What?" the old lady says. "Are you telling me how to run my business?"

"Thanks very much for the food," Mama says.

"Just a minute," the old lady says.

"James," Mama says to me. I move toward the door.

"Just one minute, I said," the old lady says.

Me and Mama stop again and look at her. The old lady takes the meat out of the bag and unwraps it and cuts 'bout half of it off. Then she wraps it up again and juggs it back in the bag and gives the bag to Mama. Mama lays the quarter on the counter.

"Your kindness will never be forgotten," she says. "James," she says to me.

We go out, and the old lady comes to the door to look at us. After we go a little piece I look back, and she's still there watching us.

The sleet's coming down heavy, heavy now, and I turn up my coat collar to keep my neck warm. My mama tells me turn it right back down.

"You not a bum," she says. "You a man."

Prudencio de Pereda

CONQUISTADOR

I thought, when I was young, that you worked according to your nationality. We were Spanish, and my father, grandfather, and uncles were all in the cigar business. There was a definite rule about this, I believed—a *law*. I thought so particularly during those times when I listened to my father and the other men of our family talk business, and heard them complain bitterly about the cigar business and about what a dishonorable trade it was, and how they were cursed the moment they took it up.

This used to surprise me—especially in regard to my father, because on the rare visits to his store it had seemed like a wonderful place. It had a broad, rich-looking, nickel-plated counter, neatly stacked with bright-colored boxes of cigars, and with shining hookahs and lighters along its top. The floor was white tile, and the inside wall of the store was a great mirror. The customers I'd seen had been well-dressed men with booming voices, rich gold chains around their full stomachs, and canes and gloves in their hands. There had been an air of wealth and strength in that store as I remembered it.

Still, my father was one of the most vehement in his denunciations of the cigar business. "Let them raise the blood to my face in shame," he once said, in his correct, intense Spanish, "if I permit any of my sons to go into this business. Yes. Let them do that!" I admired my father for his feelings, but felt that he was just talking, that my three brothers and I were all fated for the cigar business, just as my father and uncles had been. Indeed, even at this time, my older brother, who was only ten but figured himself a wise American, had already begun to do some special errands for my father. He would not only deliver boxes of cigars to the hotels in the neighborhood of my father's store in the Borough Hall section of Brooklyn, but would even take the elevated and go over the river and into the city to make deliveries.

When I begged him to tell me about this, he acted very casual and unafraid, and when, out of my genuine concern for him, I asked, "Aren't you going to be an aviator any more?" he said, "Sure! What's the matter with you? What d'you think I'm saving my money for?" I pitied him all the more, and worried myself inside for him. He was doomed—just as my father and uncles had been doomed. He would never be an aviator; nor would I ever be a bullfighter—and poor Justo would never have his big shoeshine parlor, or have his twin, Bifanio, as a sweeper. Bifanio hadn't made up his mind, yet, as to what he wanted to be, but the twins always did things together.

My older brother would never take me with him when he went on his errands. I was too young—though I was only two years younger than he.

After we came home from school, he would put on his Sunday suit and new shoes and go down to my father's store on the trolley. I often wept as I pleaded with him to take me—just once, just this once! I didn't want to get into the cigar business, and was afraid of the city, but I would have risked anything to be allowed to ride on an elevated train.

My brother never relented, and my first experience in the cigar business came through an accident and without his help. It was something bigger than he'd ever done, and I should have felt boastful; instead, it filled me with terror and shame, and, at once, I understood the feelings of my father and the other men of our family.

How it happened was natural enough. Mother was making another try to have a girl, "a little sister," as she explained formally to us, and we three younger boys were farmed out. My older brother, Joe, stayed at home because he could do errands, make phone calls, and generally help around the house, and besides, as he explained to me, he was old enough to understand things. I didn't feel too bad, because I was going to Grandmother's and not to an aunt's, as the twins had. Going to Grandmother's had some responsibility, for there were always errands to be done and I would often have to act as translator. My grandmother spoke only about ten words of English, and my grandfather just a few more.

On the third day of my stay there—it was the Fourth of July—Grandfather had announced early that he wouldn't "go out" today. "Going out" meant going to work. My grandfather was in the most stigmatized form of the cigar business—he was a *teveriano* or "junk dealer," one of those itinerant salesmen who were scorned by the rest of the trade because they dealt completely in lies: in false labels, false representation, and false merchandise—very cheap cigars for which they secured exorbitant prices—and so brought still more disgrace to the Spaniards who had enough as it was by merely being in the legitimate cigar business.

I had heard all this at home—listening eagerly because the *teveriano* was certainly the most interesting of all the cigar men—but I'd never been able to connect the fabulous stories of *teverianos* with my mild, sad grandfather. For one thing, he was always very poor.

Grandmother didn't turn to look at him as she answered: "Do you observe American holidays now?" She had a great dislike for everything American. She had been a great lady in Spain.

"One has to dance to the song they play," Grandfather said, shrugging his shoulders.

"And one has to pay the rent they ask!" Grandmother said this very sharply. I knew I should have left the room then, but I felt too sorry for my grandfather. He was growing very red. "We're at the fourth, now," Grandmother said. "That's five days late."

"I know that."

"Well?" Grandmother said, turning.

"I know that. I'm in accord with you. But not in front of the boy, please! Not in front of the boy, woman!"

"The boy knows it!"

"But not from me!" Grandfather stood up suddenly and came over to me. His hands were trembling. He took my arm and led me into the front parlor. He stood me by the window and sat down in the big chair. "Watch the celebrations!" he said. "Watch the celebrations!" I stared fixedly out the open window, knowing there weren't going to be any celebrations around here, but not wanting to tell my grandfather.

We stayed there only a short time, because the bell rang in a few moments—I couldn't see who it was—and quick, happy steps came up the stairs and we heard Agapito's voice greeting my grandmother. He called her "Dona," the most respectful title in Spanish, but he was laughing and warm as he talked.

Just as Grandfather was not, Agapito was the perfect example of the *teveriano*. He was still a very young man and had only been in America a short time, but he was easily the most famous—as well as the most criticized—of the salesmen. He was dressed that day as I imagined a *teveriano* would dress: a fine white linen suit, brown patent-leather shoes with button tops, a bright polka-dot bow tie, and a Panama straw with a multicolored band. When he came smiling into the front room, I thought he looked like the perfect man of the world, and he seemed to fill the room with brightness. He was very respectful to my grandfather, as he'd been to Grandmother, and when he suggested that they go out for a little bit, he said it in a quiet, serious voice. "We'll take the boy with us, yes?" he said, patting my shoulder and smiling at me. Agapito had neat white teeth and a small black mustache. He had a dark Spanish skin, and I thought he was very handsome. I'd always liked him, in spite of the stories I'd heard about him.

Grandfather answered Agapito's suggestion to go out by quietly shrugging his shoulders, but when Agapito suggested that they take me, his face took on the dark, stubborn look again.

"Yes, take the boy!" my grandmother called from the kitchen. "He hasn't been out. He may see some things. Holiday things." My grandfather shrugged his shoulders again.

We took a trolley—an open summer trolley—and we stayed on till the end of the line, and I saw that we'd come to the dock section. We could see the colored stacks of the big liners tied up at the piers. The big street was empty and quiet and that made the wonderful ships seem more intimate in the sun. Agapito kept pointing out things to me, but Grandfather walked along very quietly. He was dressed in his best black suit, with a black derby hat, and his face looked very worried. His black, drooping mustache made his face look very sad.

When we'd gone a few blocks, we turned into a side street and went into a small cigar store. I saw that this was Miguelin's. I knew Miguelin from seeing him at home and at the Spanish dances. He was a little, gray old man, and his store was dusty and old. He wrapped up seven new boxes of cigars for us, not wrapping them in brown paper but just with a heavy string so that you could see it was cigars and all the beautiful labels showed. Agapito gave him fourteen dollars. I counted them—and figured out that meant two dollars per box. Grandfather wanted to pay, but Agapito stopped him and made him put his wallet away. Agapito seemed to have charge of everything—he'd paid our fares on the trolley, too—and he would bend over and talk to Grandfather in a low voice while he patted him on the shoulder. I felt happy about this. I wanted my grandfather to lose his worry.

When we left Miguelin's, we turned to the big street again, and walked back the way we'd come. We walked very slowly, and Agapito kept talking to Grandfather and looking into each saloon that we passed. The saloons were the only places that were open today and there weren't many men in any of them. We were coming to a big one on the opposite corner, when Agapito said to my grandfather: "This one! This one seems good." The saloon had a big, bright shiny front and had a big hotel upstairs. I read the name "Monaghan" on the big sign over the swinging doors. As we crossed, Agapito took my hand firmly, and as we went in, I saw that the saloon was big and shiny and clean. It reminded me of my father's store. There was a big counter on one side with a great mirror on the wall and another counter on the other side with trays of food filling it all along. The tile floor was very clean and had no sawdust on it, and there was a big back room with tables that had white tablecloths.

Agapito stood inside the doorway, smiling and looking around as if he liked the place. Then, he led us over to the big counter with the mirror. We found a place easily because there were only a few men standing there, and Agapito placed the cigar boxes on the counter and nodded and smiled to the man behind the counter. He pointed to my grandfather and then to himself and said "Whiskey!" very plainly. He pronounced it "vhiskey." He patted me on the head, and smiled at the man again, and said, "Ginger ale!" He pronounced this well, except that he said "al" instead of "ale."

There was another man behind the counter, standing farther back. He had his jacket off and his sleeves rolled up, but he didn't have an apron on. He was a big man with a red face and he was smoking a big cigar. He had a gold chain across his vest and two big rings on his right hand, and he looked like one of my father's rich customers. When I stared at him, he winked at me and laughed. He'd been watching Agapito and my grandfather who were leaning on the big counter with their feet on the brass rail. Agapito had been talking in Spanish and laughing as he and my grandfather drank their whiskey.

The big man walked up to them slowly and patted the cigar boxes.

Agapito turned his head up suddenly, in surprise, and then smiled at the big man and bowed to him.

"Havanas?" the big man said. He had a strong deep voice.

Agapito nodded quickly. "Yes! I am from Havana. I am from Havana."

"I mean the cigars," the big man said, laughing. He had brown teeth, but a nice face.

"Oh! Also, also!" Agapito said. He laughed and kept nodding his head. "From Havana, also. For my friend! I bring them." He pointed outside. "The ship! You understand? From Havana to Spain. I bring them to friend here. I stop off." He spoke in short spurts, but he pronounced very clearly. He stopped smiling and became very serious as he pulled one of the boxes out of the bundle, opened it with his little gold knife and picked out two cigars carefully. He handed them over to the big man and nodded vigorously when the big man seemed to hesitate.

"For Fourth of July!" Agapito said. He smiled again. "Happy Fourth of July!" He nodded and pressed the cigars into the man's hand.

The big man smelled the cigars and nodded to him. "Good flavor," he said. He turned and said something to the man in the apron and this man took the bottle and poured more whiskey into Agapito's and my grandfather's glasses. Agapito raised his glass to him, and then my grandfather did.

The big man kept smelling the cigars and then he patted the boxes again. "What would they cost?—How much?" he said, when Agapito looked puzzled. Agapito spread his hands. "For a friend," he said. "You understand. No. . . ." He made the motion with his hands again.

"Customs?" the big man said.

"Customs!" Agapito nodded quickly and smiled. He rubbed his hands. "No customs! Customs."

"Well, how much? How much, anyway?" The big man patted the boxes.

Agapito held a finger up, and turned to my grandfather. "This one seems to have money," he said in Spanish. "This one can pay."

"Take care, hombre," my grandfather said.

"No, don't disquiet yourself, Don Jose. I know what I'm doing." Agapito patted Grandfather's arm, turned to the big man and smiled. "My friend, here. He remember. He remember everything." He ran his finger up and down the boxes. "All the boxes. Seven! Sixty dollars. Cost for my friend."

Sixty dollars! This was a shock to me—if a man buys seven boxes of cigars for fourteen dollars, two dollars per box, and sells them for—sixty dollars! I understood why the big man made such a face and then laughed. I hadn't minded all the lies that Agapito had told because I knew that *teverianos* worked like that, but when he asked this high, high figure, I got shocked and embarrassed—and then, very frightened for us. The glass felt heavy in my hand, and I held my head down because I knew that I was blushing.

I'd heard that *teverianos* asked robber prices, but I never thought that Agapito would take the chance today, when he had my grandfather and me with him. He was going to get us into trouble. He was making us take a chance—because he wanted to. And we were all going to get into trouble.

The big man said something to Agapito and Agapito said, "Well—you know, sir, Havanas!"

I didn't hear the big man answer but then Agapito said very brightly, "You interested? You interested in cigars?" I hated his accent, now. His lying.

"I was looking for ten boxes. I could use ten boxes," the big man said slowly.

Agapito was talking in Spanish, then. He must have been talking to my grandfather. "You stay here," he said, still speaking respectfully. "I will run to Miguelin's and get three more boxes. I will run fast. You stay here. This is a good thing."

"Yes, hombre, it is," I heard my grandfather say. "Let him take these seven boxes and let us be through here. Let it stay a good thing."

"There is no danger," Agapito said quickly.

"If there is, entrust it to me," my grandfather said sternly and I looked up suddenly to see that his face had taken on the stubborn look again. "I wasn't thinking of that. I was thinking that we have a good thing. Let us take it, and be gone."

"I don't work like that," Agapito said. "You know that, Don Jose," he said more softly.

"Then, as you wish."

"You will stay?"

"As you wish!"

I watched, in rage but fascinated, as Agapito turned back to smile at the big man who was leaning on the counter with his old cigar in his mouth. Agapito brought his hands together. "We fix it," he said, and nodded. "Three more boxes, I will bring from the boat. For ten boxes"—he ran his fingers up and down the seven on the counter and held up three fingers—"ten boxes—for eighty dollars—for you!" He pointed at the big man.

The big man stared at Agapito for a moment, and then nodded and said, "Okay. Eighty dollars." What a fool this one is, too, I thought. His face looked stupid to me, now.

"You give me fifty dollars, now," Agapito said. He smiled. "I give money to guard—small money. You understand? My friend wait here, I come back. With three more."

Did Grandfather understand that? Did Grandfather know what Agapito was saying? I stared at his face, but couldn't see anything. I was weak with fright and fear, but I didn't dare say a word. The big man had taken out his wallet without hesitation and given Agapito five new bills—tens they must have been. Agapito smiled and nodded as he put them in his wallet quickly.

He patted Grandfather on the arm, saying, "Don't worry yourself. I'll be back immediately," and then patted me on the head—I couldn't duck fast enough—and went out into the street.

I stared at the floor. I wouldn't look at my grandfather. I'd finished the ginger ale, but I wouldn't go over to put the glass on the counter. I heard the big man say something to Grandfather that Grandfather didn't answer. "No speak English, eh?" the big man said, and laughed. He took up the bundle of cigars and moved down to the end of the counter—where I could see him by just lifting my eyes a little—and he began to open every box.

I had to look at my grandfather, then. Did he see what danger we were in? He was staring at the mirror. His hands were steady, but he was sweating. I glared at him, at first, but then wanted to cry. I went up and put the glass by his side and he looked down at me and then turned to stare up at the big man as he was opening each box. Then, he turned back, finished his drink in one slug and turned to me. His back was to the big man and he put his hand on my shoulder. I could smell the whiskey on his breath as he bent down. "Get thee out of here," he said. "Act as if thou art going out calmly." My grandfather always used the familiar "thee" with us, and his voice was calm and easy now but I could see that he was sweating badly. His hand felt very tight on my shoulder. "Get thyself to the trolley station. Stand by the trees there and wait for me. No matter how long, I will come. Do nothing but wait for me. I will escape this in some way. I will get out, and get to thee. I will escape this and get to thee. In whatever way, I will.

"Without crying, thee!" he said. "Without crying!" I hadn't started to cry yet, but my lip had begun to tremble. I bit my lip and started to shake my head even before he'd finished. "And think well of me," he was saying. "Think well of me. I did not want this situation for thee. Thou wilt not? Thou wilt not do it?"

"No. I stay. I stay here with you." His face had the stubborn look again and he pushed my shoulder but held his grip tightly on it. He glared at me, but I kept shaking my head. "Stay, then!" he said. "Stay!" He dropped his hand from my shoulder but reached to take my hand and then turned to lean on the bar again, holding my hand. A moment later, when he poured more whiskey into his glass, he did it with his left hand, but poured it very neatly. He lifted the glass in his left hand, and began to sip the whiskey slowly.

Grandfather had been a waiter in Spain. He was very proud of that. He'd been a waiter at the best hotel in Tangier just before he'd come to the United States, and a prince, a duke, and two princesses had been among his patrons. My mother was born in Tangier, and, though she couldn't remember anything of her part in the life there, she told us many stories about it. The three years spent in Tangier had been the happiest time in the life of her family.

My grandmother's brother had come to the United States some years before and made an immediate success as a *teveriano*. He wrote glowing letters to my grandmother, telling her of the wonderful opportunities in the trade and urging her to make Jose, my grandfather, see reason and come to America. Does he want to be a waiter all his life? the brother would ask. He'd felt very bad when she'd married a waiter. He was her only brother and they were very close.

Grandfather was content. He didn't want to leave. The letters got more boastful, and then pleading. Finally, my granduncle sent enough money to pay first-class passage for all three and the pressure was too much for my grandfather. He consented, and he came to the United States with his family—to a tenement district in Hoboken, New Jersey. They moved to Brooklyn shortly after, when my aunt was born, but to a tenement district again, and they had never lived better than that. Grandfather—as Mother would say, in ending these stories—was just not a good salesman.

I was thinking these things as I gripped Grandfather's hand and stared up at him, and the anger that I'd felt before turned to pity. I love you, I thought. Once, I pulled his arm and said, "We could go to the bathroom—first me, then you—sneak out that way." He glared down at me with a stubborn look. "No. In no such manner. When we go, we go through the front door. We are men." He turned to stare at the mirror, but then turned quickly back to me. "Dost thou have to go to the toilet? Truly?"

I shook my head.

"Good!" he said, and turned to the mirror.

I thought we stood like that for a long time—it seemed like a long, long time to me—but Agapito said later that he'd only been gone sixteen minutes, that he'd counted them. Agapito's face was sweating when he came back, and his Panama was pushed back on his head, but he was smiling and looked very happy, and his clothes were still very neat. "I run! I run!" he said to the big man. "To ship. To ship and back!" He'd put the new boxes on the counter and was opening each one with his penknife and holding the open box up to the big man. The boxes looked very new and I thought that one of the labels looked wet. Surely, the big man would see, now. He would see the truth, now, I thought. And it would serve Agapito right. He'd be in it, now. Grandfather and I could run. We'd get away. Agapito was the one they'd hold.

The big man smelled every box and even touched the wet wrapper, but he nodded seriously and then stupidly took out his wallet and gave Agapito three more ten dollar bills. The man with the apron had filled Agapito's glass again and Agapito held out one of the bills to him, but he shook his head. Then, Agapito put the bills in his wallet and picked out a one-dollar bill that he folded and handed to the man in the apron. "For you," he said. "For you." He smiled and nodded. Then, he held up the whiskey, smiled and nodded again, and drank it in one gulp.

I had been tugging at Grandfather's hand, wanting to start, wanting us to go, but Grandfather held his tight grip and waited until Agapito had shaken hands with both men, and then he himself nodded to them, and we all turned towards the door.

We walked very slowly as we went outside and crossed the street. Grandfather wanted to walk fast, but Agapito was holding his arm and walking very slowly. "Don't worry yourself," he said, after a moment. "We'll turn down the first street. For now, we walk slowly—very slowly, and with dignity."

We turned down the first street, walked down that block, and then turned in the direction of the trolleys. As soon as we'd made this last turn, Agapito stopped and took out his wallet. He handed Grandfather three ten-dollar bills. Grandfather pushed them back. "Hombre!" he said, "don't embarrass me."

"Please!" Agapito said. "This is your share."

"It's too much."

"It's half. We were equally involved." Agapito pressed the bills into Grandfather's hand. "Equally!" he said, letting go.

Grandfather put the bills in his little black purse. "I'm very appreciative. Very!" he said.

"For nothing!" Agapito said. "For nothing!" As we walked, now, he was smiling and happy again. He took off his hat and rubbed his face with a big silk handkerchief. "One has to see these things, Don Jose. One has to see them. To believe them, one has to see them. Havanas!" he shook his head and laughed. "And you mustn't feel that we cheat them!" he said, when Grandfather didn't answer. "This one buys them as Havanas. He gives them out as Havanas—probably at some festival—and those who take them, take them as Havanas, and smoke them. No matter how bad the cigars, for them they are Havanas. Yes, Don Jose. We sell Havanas—they buy Havanas!"

On the trolley, after he'd paid our fares, Agapito slipped a half dollar into the conductor's pocket. "For Fourth of July!" he said. The conductor blushed, and nodded. Later, Agapito stood up and took off his hat. "Life for the United States of America!" he called out. "Happy Fourth of July to everybody!" The two people who were sitting up at the front end of the trolley smiled and shook their heads. They thought he was drunk.

Agapito left, soon after we got home. Then, Grandmother went out. "I'll get some ham," she said. "We'll eat well, tonight." Grandfather and I were in the front room, and she'd come to the door. "The delicatessen has good ham."

Grandfather nodded. "We're most fortunate," he said, without looking up. "Most fortunate."

Grandmother turned back and stared at him with a cold face. She was dressed in her black skirt and black silk waist, and she looked like the pictures of the Queen Mother in the Spanish magazines we had, except that Grandmother was much more beautiful. "Yes," she said, in a calm voice.

"Most fortunate. You, in particular! You needn't go out for some days, now. Perhaps grow a beard, here."

Grandfather got very red, but didn't look up. He shrugged his shoulders as Grandmother turned and went out. After a moment, he reached over to me and pulled me to the side of the chair. He kept his arm around me and patted my head. "Thou!" he said. He looked straight at me. "Thou must forget what thou heardst today, what thou sawst. All of it! Forget especially what thy grandmother said. She is a fine woman. Nothing of today was like her. It is I who am weak. The fault is mine. Thou wilt understand this some day. Thou wilt, yes. What thou must remember is this"—he pressed my shoulder—"that thou must be strong. Remember that! Let no woman—whether she be thy mother who is my own flesh, or the woman thou wilt marry—let none of them press thee or influence thee in choosing thy profession. Thou, thou alone, must move through the world to make thy money, thou alone must suffer—so thou must choose. And hold to that!

"Thou art the bullfighter, no?"

"Or one who guides an elevated train," I said. "One of those."

"Good. Thou might change, but whatever thou shouldst choose—hold to it. Grip it well."

I nodded.

"Dost thou know what she referred to in that of the beard?" he said, in a softer voice.

"No, Grandfather," I lied.

"Well, it was this: I had a fine beard when I was a waiter in Tangier. It was a full, well-cut beard and I was a fine figure with it. One afternoon, the major-domo—he who was chief of all our waiters—the major-domo, Don Felix, came to me and said, 'Jose, you must shave that beard. Too many patrons are coming in and talking to you and treating you as the major-domo. I regret this, but you must shave it, because there is only one major-domo here, and it is me. No one else can look like a major-domo. No one else will.'

"I went home to thy grandmother and told her this, and she said, 'Yes. The man has reason. You must shave your beard.' I had thought that she would have objections, that she would show anger. I had thought that she loved the beard as I did—it was a fine beard. But she did not—or, if she did, she would not let it stand before Don Felix's objection.

"So, I cut it off!" my grandfather said. He brushed his hand under his chin. "That was a mistake. I should have held to my first thought. I should have defended myself. I should have left my place and sought another job in Tangier—or Gibraltar or La Linea where there are fine hotels. *I* was doing the waiting, and *I* should have thought of *myself*." He stopped and stared at me. "Thou seest?" he said. "Stop thou at the first mistake. Stop there."

I nodded, and he pressed my shoulder again and then reached over and lifted me on to his lap. He cradled my head on his shoulder and rocked slowly back and forth. "We must gladden ourselves," he said, "before she comes. We must gladden ourselves and be smiling. This is difficult for her, too. Difficult. We must gladden ourselves, now. Yes! We must gladden ourselves for her."

I was nodding my head to say, Yes, when my forehead felt something wet, and I looked up and saw that the tears were falling down his cheeks.

Isaac Babel

MY FIRST GOOSE

Savitsky, Commander of the VI Division, rose when he saw me, and I wondered at the beauty of his giant's body. He rose, the purple of his riding breeches and the crimson of his little tilted cap and the decorations stuck on his chest cleaving the hut as a standard cleaves the sky. A smell of scent and the sickly sweet freshness of soap emanated from him. His long legs were like girls sheathed to the neck in shining riding boots.

He smiled at me, struck his riding whip on the table, and drew toward him an order that the Chief of Staff had just finished dictating. It was an order for Ivan Chesnokov to advance on Chugunov-Dobryvodka with the regiment entrusted to him, to make contact with the enemy and destroy the same.

"For which destruction," the Commander began to write, smearing the whole sheet, "I make this same Chesnokov entirely responsible, up to and including the supreme penalty, and will if necessary strike him down on the spot; which you, Chesnokov, who have been working with me at the front for some months now, cannot doubt."

The Commander signed the order with a flourish, tossed it to his orderlies and turned upon me gray eyes that danced with merriment.

I handed him a paper with my appointment to the Staff of the Division.

"Put it down in the Order of the Day," said the Commander. "Put him down for every satisfaction save the front one. Can you read and write?"

"Yes, I can read and write," I replied, envying the flower and iron of that youthfulness. "I graduated in law from St. Petersburg University."

"Oh, are you one of those grinds?" he laughed. "Specs on your nose, too! What a nasty little object! They've sent you along without making any enquiries; and this is a hot place for specs. Think you'll get on with us?"

"I'll get on all right," I answered, and went off to the village with the quartermaster to find a billet for the night.

The quartermaster carried my trunk on his shoulder. Before us stretched the village street. The dying sun, round and yellow as a pumpkin, was giving up its roseate ghost to the skies.

We went up to a hut painted over with garlands. The quartermaster stopped, and said suddenly, with a guilty smile:

"Nuisance with specs. Can't do anything to stop it, either. Not a life for the brainy type here. But you go and mess up a lady, and a good lady too, and you'll have the boys patting you on the back."

He hesitated, my little trunk on his shoulder; then he came quite close to me, only to dart away again despairingly and run to the nearest yard. Cossacks were sitting there, shaving one another.

"Here, you soldiers," said the quartermaster, setting my little trunk down on the ground. "Comrade Savitsky's orders are that you're to take this chap in your billets, so no nonsense about it, because the chap's been through a lot in the learning line."

The quartermaster, purple in the face, left us without looking back. I raised my hand to my cap and saluted the Cossacks. A lad with long straight flaxen hair and the handsome face of the Ryazan Cossacks went over to my little trunk and tossed it out at the gate. Then he turned his back on me and with remarkable skill emitted a series of shameful noises.

"To your guns—number double-zero!" an older Cossack shouted at him, and burst out laughing. "Running fire!"

His guileless art exhausted, the lad made off. Then, crawling over the ground, I began to gather together the manuscript and tattered garments that had fallen out of the trunk. I gathered them up and carried them to the other end of the yard. Near the hut, on a brick stove, stood a cauldron in which pork was cooking. The steam that rose from it was like the far-off smoke of home in the village, and it mingled hunger with desperate loneliness in my head. Then I covered my little broken trunk with hay, turning it into a pillow, and lay down on the ground to read in *Pravda* Lenin's speech at the Second Congress of the Comintern. The sun fell upon me from behind the toothed hillocks, the Cossacks trod on my feet, the lad made fun of me untiringly, the beloved lines came toward me along a thorny path and could not reach me. Then I put aside the paper and went out to the landlady, who was spinning on the porch.

"Landlady," I said, "I've got to eat."

The old woman raised to me the diffused whites of her purblind eyes and lowered them again.

"Comrade," she said, after a pause, "what with all this going on, I want to go and hang myself."

"Christ!" I muttered, and pushed the old woman in the chest with my fist. "You don't suppose I'm going to go into explanations with you, do you?"

And turning around I saw somebody's sword lying within reach. A severe-looking goose was waddling about the yard, inoffensively preening its feathers. I overtook it and pressed it to the ground. Its head cracked beneath my boot, cracked and emptied itself. The white neck lay stretched out in the dung, the wings twitched.

"Christ!" I said, digging into the goose with my sword. "Go and cook it for me, landlady."

Her blind eyes and glasses glistening, the old woman picked up the slaughtered bird, wrapped it in her apron, and started to bear it off toward the kitchen.

"Comrade," she said to me, after a while, "I want to go and hang myself." And she closed the door behind her.

The Cossacks in the yard were already sitting around their cauldron. They sat motionless, stiff as heathen priests at a sacrifice, and had not looked at the goose.

"The lad's all right," one of them said, winking and scooping up the cabbage soup with his spoon.

The Cossacks commenced their supper with all the elegance and restraint of peasants who respect one another. And I wiped the sword with sand, went out at the gate, and came in again, depressed. Already the moon hung above the yard like a cheap earring.

"Hey, you," suddenly said Surovkov, an older Cossack. "Sit down and feed with us till your goose is done."

He produced a spare spoon from his boot and handed it to me. We supped up the cabbage soup they had made, and ate the pork.

"What's in the newspaper?" asked the flaxen-haired lad, making room for me.

"Lenin writes in the paper," I said, pulling out *Pravda*. "Lenin writes that there's a shortage of everything."

And loudly, like a triumphant man hard of hearing, I read Lenin's speech out to the Cossacks.

Evening wrapped about me the quickening moisture of its twilight sheets; evening laid a mother's hand upon my burning forehead. I read on and rejoiced, spying out exultingly the secret curve of Lenin's straight line.

"Truth tickles everyone's nostrils," said Surovkov, when I had come to the end. "The question is, how's it to be pulled from the heap. But he goes and strikes at it straight off like a hen pecking at a grain!"

This remark about Lenin was made by Surovkov, platoon commander of the Staff Squadron; after which we lay down to sleep in the hayloft. We slept, all six of us, beneath a wooden roof that let in the stars, warming one another, our legs intermingled. I dreamed: and in my dreams saw women. But my heart, stained with bloodshed, grated and brimmed over.

Heinrich Böll

LIKE A BAD DREAM

That evening we had invited the Zumpens over for dinner, nice people; it was through my father-in-law that we had got to know them: ever since we have been married he has helped me to meet people who can be useful to me in business, and Zumpen can be useful: he is chairman of a committee which places contracts for large housing projects, and I have married into the excavating business.

I was tense that evening, but Bertha, my wife, reassured me. "The fact," she said, "that he's coming at all is promising. Just try and get the conversation round to the contract. You know it's tomorrow they're going to be awarded."

I stood looking through the net curtains of the glass front door, waiting for Zumpen. I smoked, ground the cigarette butts under my foot, and shoved them under the mat. Next I took up a position at the bathroom window and stood there wondering why Zumpen had accepted the invitation; he couldn't be that interested in having dinner with us, and the fact that the big contract I was involved in was going to be awarded tomorrow must have made the whole thing as embarrassing to him as it was to me.

I thought about the contract too: it was a big one, I would make 20,000 marks on the deal, and I wanted the money.

Bertha had decided what I was to wear: a dark jacket, trousers a shade lighter and a conservative tie. That's the kind of thing she learned at home, and at boarding school from the nuns. Also what to offer guests: when to pass the cognac, and when the vermouth, how to arrange dessert. It is comforting to have a wife who knows all about such things.

But Bertha was tense too: as she put her hands on my shoulders, they touched my neck, and I felt her thumbs damp and cold against it.

"It's going to be all right," she said, "You'll get the contract."

"Christ," I said, "it means 20,000 marks to me, and you know how we need the money."

"One should never," she said gently, "mention Christ's name in connection with money!"

A dark car drew up in front of our house, a make I didn't recognize, but it looked Italian. "Take it easy," Bertha whispered, "wait till they've rung, let them stand there for a couple of seconds, then walk slowly to the door and open it."

I watched Mr. and Mrs. Zumpen come up the steps: he is slender and tall, with graying temples, the kind of man who fifty years ago would have been known as a "ladies' man"; Mrs. Zumpen is one of those thin dark women who always make me think of lemons. I could tell from Zumpen's face that it was a frightful bore for him to have dinner with us.

Then the doorbell rang, and I waited one second, two seconds, walked slowly to the door and opened it.

"Well," I said, "how nice of you to come!"

Cognac glasses in hand, we went from room to room in our apartment, which the Zumpens wanted to see. Bertha stayed in the kitchen to squeeze some mayonnaise out of a tube onto the appetizers; she does this very nicely: hearts, loops, little houses. The Zumpens complimented us on our apartment; they exchanged smiles when they saw the big desk in my study, at that moment it seemed a bit too big even to me.

Zumpen admired a small rococo cabinet, a wedding present from my grandmother, and a baroque Madonna in our bedroom.

By the time we got back to the dining room, Bertha had dinner on the table; she had done this very nicely too, it was all so attractive yet so natural, and dinner was pleasant and relaxed. We talked about movies and books, about the recent elections, and Zumpen praised the assortment of cheeses, and Mrs. Zumpen praised the coffee and the pastries. Then we showed the Zumpens our honeymoon pictures: photographs of the Breton coast, Spanish donkeys, and street scenes from Casablanca.

After that we had some more cognac, and when I stood up to get the box with the photos of the time when we were engaged, Bertha gave me a sign, and I didn't get the box. For two minutes there was absolute silence, because we had nothing more to talk about, and we all thought about the contract; I thought of the 20,000 marks, and it struck me that I could deduct the bottle of cognac from my income tax. Zumpen looked at his watch and said: "Too bad, it's ten o'clock; we have to go. It's been such a pleasant evening!" And Mrs. Zumpen said: "It was really delightful, and I hope you'll come to us one evening."

"We would love to," Bertha said, and we stood around for another half-minute, all thinking again about the contract, and I felt Zumpen was waiting for me to take him aside and bring up the subject. But I didn't. Zumpen kissed Bertha's hand, and I went ahead, opened the doors, and held the car door open for Mrs. Zumpen down below.

"Why," said Bertha gently, "didn't you mention the contract to him? You know it's going to be awarded tomorrow."

"Well," I said, "I didn't know how to bring the conversation round to it."

"Now look," she said in a quiet voice, "you could have used any excuse to ask him into your study, that's where you should have talked to him. You must have noticed how interested he is in art. You ought to have said: I have an eighteenth-century crucifix in there you might like to have a look at, and then . . ."

I said nothing, and she sighed and tied on her apron. I followed her into the kitchen; we put the rest of the appetizers back in the refrigerator, and I crawled about on the floor looking for the top of the mayonnaise tube. I put away the remains of the cognac, counted the cigars: Zumpen had smoked only one. I emptied the ashtrays, ate another pastry, and looked to see if there was any coffee left in the pot. When I went back to the kitchen, Bertha was standing there with the car key in her hand.

"What's up?" I asked.

"We have to go over there, of course," she said.

"Over where?"

"To the Zumpens," she said, "where do you think?"

"It's nearly half past ten."

"I don't care if it's midnight," Bertha said, "all I know is, there's 20,000 marks involved. Don't imagine they're squeamish."

She went into the bathroom to get ready, and I stood behind her watching her wipe her mouth and draw in new outlines, and for the first time I noticed how wide and primitive that mouth is. When she tightened the knot of my tie I could have kissed her, the way I always used to when she fixed my tie, but I didn't.

Downtown the cafés and restaurants were brightly lit. People were sitting outside on the terraces, and the light from the street lamps was caught in the silver ice-cream dishes and ice buckets. Bertha gave me an encouraging look; but she stayed in the car when we stopped in front of the Zumpens' house, and I pressed the bell at once and was surprised how quickly the door was opened. Mrs. Zumpen did not seem surprised to see me; she had on some black lounging pajamas with loose full trousers embroidered with yellow flowers, and this made me think more than ever of lemons.

"I beg your pardon," I said, "I would like to speak to your husband."

"He's gone out again," she said, "he'll be back in half an hour."

In the hall I saw a lot of Madonnas, gothic and baroque, even rococo Madonnas, if there is such a thing.

"I see," I said, "well then, if you don't mind, I'll come back in half an hour."

Bertha had bought an evening paper; she was reading it and smoking, and when I sat down beside her she said: "I think you could have talked about it to her too."

"But how do you know he wasn't there?"

"Because I know he is at the Gaffel Club playing chess, as he does every Wednesday evening at this time."

"You might have told me that earlier."

"Please try and understand," said Bertha, folding the newspaper. "I am trying to help you, I want you to find out for yourself how to deal with such things. All we had to do was call up Father and he would have settled the whole thing for you with one phone call, but I want you to get the contract on your own."

"All right," I said, "then what'll we do: wait here half an hour, or go up right away and have a talk with her?"

"We'd better go up right away," said Bertha.

We got out of the car and went up the elevator together. "Life," said Bertha, "consists of making compromises and concessions."

Mrs. Zumpen was no more surprised now than she had been earlier, when I had come alone. She greeted us, and we followed her into her husband's study. Mrs. Zumpen brought some cognac, poured it out, and before I could say anything about the contract she pushed a yellow folder toward me: "Housing Project Fir Tree Haven," I read, and looked up in alarm at Mrs. Zumpen, at Bertha, but they both smiled, and Mrs. Zumpen said: "Open the folder," and I opened it; inside was another one, pink, and on this I read: "Housing Project Fir Tree Haven—Excavation Work." I opened this too, saw my estimate lying there on top of the pile; along the upper edge someone had written in red: "Lowest bid."

I could feel myself flushing with pleasure, my heart thumping, and I thought of the 20,000 marks.

"Christ," I said softly, and closed the file, and this time Bertha forgot to rebuke me.

"Prost," said Mrs. Zumpen with a smile, "let's drink to it then."

We drank, and I stood up and said: "It may seem rude of me, but perhaps you'll understand that I would like to go home now."

"I understand perfectly," said Mrs. Zumpen, "there's just one small item to be taken care of." She took the file, leafed through it, and said: "Your price per square meter is thirty pfennigs below that of the next-lowest bidder. I suggest you raise your price by fifteen pfennigs: that way you'll still be the lowest and you'll have made an extra four thousand five hundred marks. Come on, do it now!" Bertha took her pen out of her purse and offered it to me, but I was in too much of a turmoil to write; I gave the file to Bertha and watched her alter the price with a steady hand, re-write the total, and hand the file back to Mrs. Zumpen.

"And now," said Mrs. Zumpen, "just one more little thing. Get out your check book and write a check for three thousand marks; it must be a cash check and endorsed by you."

She had said this to me, but it was Bertha who pulled our check book out of her purse and made out the check.

"It won't be covered," I said in a low voice.

"When the contract is awarded, there will be an advance, and then it will be covered," said Mrs. Zumpen.

Perhaps I failed to grasp what was happening at the time. As we went down in the elevator, Bertha said she was happy, but I said nothing.

Bertha chose a different way home, we drove through quiet residential districts, I saw lights in open windows, people sitting on balconies drinking wine; it was a clear, warm night.

"I suppose the check was for Zumpen?" was all I said, softly, and Bertha replied, just as softly: "Of course."

I looked at Bertha's small, brown hands on the steering wheel, so confident and quiet. Hands, I thought, that sign checks and squeeze mayonnaise tubes, and I looked higher—at her mouth, and still felt no desire to kiss it.

That evening I did not help Bertha put the car away in the garage, nor did I help her with the dishes. I poured myself a large cognac, went up to my study, and sat down at my desk, which was much too big for me. I was wondering about something. I got up, went into the bedroom and looked at the baroque Madonna, but even there I couldn't put my finger on the thing I was wondering about.

The ringing of the phone interrupted my thoughts; I lifted the receiver and was not surprised to hear Zumpen's voice.

"Your wife," he said, "made a slight mistake. She raised the price by twenty-five pfennigs instead of fifteen."

I thought for a moment and then said: "That wasn't a mistake, she did it with my consent."

He was silent for a second or two, then said with a laugh: "So you had already discussed the various possibilities?"

"Yes," I said.

"All right, then make out another check for a thousand."

"Five hundred," I said, and I thought: It's like a bad dream—that's what it's like.

"Eight hundred," he said, and I said with a laugh: "Six hundred," and I knew, although I had no experience to go on, that he would now say seven hundred and fifty, and when he did I said "Yes" and hung up.

It was not yet midnight when I went downstairs and over to the car to give Zumpen the check; he was alone and laughed as I reached in to hand him the folded check. When I walked slowly back into the house, there was no sign of Bertha; she didn't appear when I went back into my study; she didn't appear when I went downstairs again for a glass of milk from the refrigerator, and I knew what she was thinking; she was thinking: he has to get over it, and I have to leave him alone; this is something he has to understand.

But I never did understand. It is beyond understanding.

Donald Barthelme

SOME OF US HAD BEEN THREATENING OUR FRIEND COLBY

Some of us had been threatening our friend Colby for a long time, because of the way he had been behaving. And now he'd gone too far, so we decided to hang him. Colby argued that just because he had gone too far (he did not deny that he had gone too far) did not mean that he should be subjected to hanging. Going too far, he said, was something everybody did sometimes. We didn't pay much attention to this argument. We asked him what sort of music he would like played at the hanging. He said he'd think about it but it would take him a while to decide. I pointed out that we'd have to know soon, because Howard, who is a conductor, would have to hire and rehearse the musicians and he couldn't begin until he knew what the music was going to be. Colby said he'd always been fond of Ives' Fourth Symphony. Howard said that this was a "delaying tactic" and that everybody knew that the Ives was almost impossible to perform and would involve weeks of rehearsal, and that the size of the orchestra and chorus would put us way over the music budget. "Be reasonable," he said to Colby. Colby said he'd try to think of something a little less exacting.

Hugh was worried about the wording of the invitations. What if one of them fell into the hands of the authorities? Hanging Colby was doubtless against the law, and if the authorities learned in advance what the plan was they would very likely come in and try to mess everything up. I said that although hanging Colby was almost certainly against the law, we had a perfect *moral* right to do so because he was *our* friend, *belonged* to us in various important senses, and he had after all gone too far. We agreed that the invitations would be worded in such a way that the person invited could not know for sure what he was being invited to. We decided to refer to the event as "An Event Involving Mr. Colby Williams." A handsome script was selected from a catalogue and we picked a cream-colored paper. Magnus said he'd see to having the invitations printed, and wondered whether we should serve drinks. Colby said he thought drinks would be nice but was worried about the expense. We told him kindly that the expense didn't matter, that we were after all his dear friends and if a group of his dear friends couldn't get together and do the thing with a little bit of *éclat,* why, what was the world coming to? Colby asked if he would be able to have drinks, too, before the event. We said, "Certainly."

The next item of business was the gibbet. None of us knew too much about gibbet design, but Tomás, who is an architect, said he'd look it up in old books and draw the plans. The important thing, as far as he recollected, was that the trapdoor function perfectly. He said that just roughly, counting labor and materials, it shouldn't run us more than four hundred dollars. "Good God!" Howard said. He said what was Tomás figuring on, rosewood? No, just a good grade of pine, Tomás said. Victor asked if unpainted pine wouldn't look kind of "raw," and Tomás replied that he thought it could be stained a dark walnut without too much trouble.

I said that although I thought the whole thing ought to be done really well, and all, I also thought four hundred dollars for a gibbet, on top of the expense for the drinks, invitations, musicians and everything, was a bit steep, and why didn't we just use a tree—a nice-looking oak, or something? I pointed out that since it was going to be a June hanging the trees would be in glorious leaf and that not only would a tree add a kind of "natural" feeling but it was also strictly traditional, especially in the West. Tomás, who had been sketching gibbets on the backs of envelopes, reminded us that an outdoor hanging always had to contend with the threat of rain. Victor said he liked the idea of doing it outdoors, possibly on the bank of a river, but noted that we would have to hold it some distance from the city, which presented the problem of getting the guests, musicians, etc., to the site and then back to town.

At this point everybody looked at Harry, who runs a car-and-truck-rental business. Harry said he thought he could round up enough limousines to take care of that end but that the drivers would have to be paid. The drivers, he pointed out, wouldn't be friends of Colby's and couldn't be expected to donate their services, any more than the bartender or the musicians. He said that he had about ten limousines, which he used mostly for funerals, and that he could probably obtain another dozen by calling around to friends of his in the trade. He said also that if we did it outside, in the open air, we'd better figure on a tent or awning of some kind to cover at least the principals and the orchestra, because if the hanging was being rained on he thought it would look kind of dismal. As between gibbet and tree, he said, he had no particular preferences, and he really thought that the choice ought to be left up to Colby, since it was his hanging. Colby said that everybody went too far, sometimes, and weren't we being a little Draconian. Howard said rather sharply that all that had already been discussed, and which did he want, gibbet or tree? Colby asked if he could have a firing squad. No, Howard said, he could not. Howard said a firing squad would just be an ego trip for Colby, the blindfold and last-cigarette bit, and that Colby was in enough hot water already without trying to "upstage" everyone with unnecessary theatrics. Colby said he was sorry, he hadn't meant it that way, he'd take the tree. Tomás crumpled up the gibbet sketches he'd been making, in disgust.

Then the question of the hangman came up. Paul said did we really need a hangman? Because if we used a tree, the noose could be adjusted to the appropriate level and Colby could just jump off something—a chair or stool or something. Besides, Paul said, he very much doubted if there were any free-lance hangmen wandering around the country, now that capital punishment has been done away with absolutely, temporarily, and that we'd probably have to fly one in from England or Spain or one of the South American countries, and even if we did that how could we know in advance that the man was a professional, a real hangman, and not just some money-hungry amateur who might bungle the job and shame us all, in front of everybody? We all agreed then that Colby should just jump off something and that a chair was not what he should jump off of, because that would look, we felt, extremely tacky—some old kitchen chair sitting out there under our beautiful tree. Tomás, who is quite modern in outlook and not afraid of innovation, proposed that Colby be standing on a large round rubber ball ten feet in diameter. This, he said, would afford a sufficient "drop" and would also roll out of the way if Colby suddenly changed his mind after jumping off. He reminded us that by not using a regular hangman we were placing an awful lot of the responsibility for the success of the affair on Colby himself, and that although he was sure Colby would perform creditably and not disgrace his friends at the last minute, still, men have been known to get a little irresolute at times like that, and the ten-foot-round rubber ball, which could probably be fabricated rather cheaply, would insure a "bang-up" production right down to the wire.

At the mention of "wire," Hank, who had been silent all this time, suddenly spoke up and said he wondered if it wouldn't be better if we used wire instead of rope—more efficient and in the end kinder to Colby, he suggested. Colby began looking a little green, and I didn't blame him, because there is something extremely distasteful in thinking about being hanged with wire instead of rope—it gives you sort of a revulsion, when you think about it. I thought it was really quite unpleasant of Hank to be sitting there talking about wire, just when we had solved the problem of what Colby was going to jump off of so neatly, with Tomás's idea about the rubber ball, so I hastily said that wire was out of the question, because it would injure the tree—cut into the branch it was tied to when Colby's full weight hit it—and that in these days of increased respect for environment, we didn't want that, did we? Colby gave me a grateful look, and the meeting broke up.

Everything went off very smoothly on the day of the event (the music Colby finally picked was standard stuff, Elgar, and it was played very well by Howard and his boys). It didn't rain, the event was well attended, and we didn't run out of Scotch, or anything. The ten-foot rubber ball had been painted a deep green and blended in well with the bucolic setting. The two things I remember best about the whole episode are the grateful look Colby gave me when I said what I said about the wire, and the fact that nobody has ever gone too far again.

Jorge Luis Borges

THE IMMORTALS

And see, no longer blinded by our eyes.
Rupert Brooke

Whoever could have foreseen, way back in that innocent summer of 1923, that the novelette *The Chosen One* by Camilo N. Huergo, presented to me by the author with his personal inscription on the flyleaf (which I had the decorum to tear out before offering the volume for sale to successive men of the book trade), hid under the thin varnish of fiction a prophetic truth. Huergo's photograph, in an oval frame, adorns the cover. Each time I look at it, I have the impression that the snapshot is about to cough, a victim of that lung disease which nipped in the bud a promising career. Tuberculosis, in short, denied him the happiness of acknowledging the letter I wrote him in one of my characteristic outbursts of generosity.

The epigraph prefixed to this thoughtful essay has been taken from the aforementioned novelette; I requested Dr. Montenegro, of the Academy, to render it into Spanish, but the results were negative. To give the unprepared reader the gist of the matter, I shall now sketch, in condensed form, an outline of Huergo's narrative, as follows:

The storyteller pays a visit, far to the south in Chubut, to the English rancher don Guillermo Blake, who devotes his energies not only to the breeding of sheep but also to the ramblings of the world-famous Plato and to the latest and more freakish experiments in the field of surgical medicine. On the basis of his reading, don Guillermo concludes that the five senses obstruct or deform the apprehension of reality and that, could we free ourselves of them, we would see the world as it is—endless and timeless. He comes to think that the eternal models of things lie in the depths of the soul and that the organs of perception with which the Creator has endowed us are, *grosso modo,* hindrances. They are no better than dark spectacles that blind us to what exists outside, diverting our attention at the same time from the splendor we carry within us.

Blake begets a son by one of the farm girls so that the boy may one day become acquainted with reality. To anesthetize him for life, to make him blind and deaf and dumb, to emancipate him from the senses of smell and taste, were the father's first concerns. He took, in the same way, all possible measures to make the chosen one unaware of his own body. As to the rest, this was arranged with contrivances designed to take over respiration, circulation, nourishment, digestion, and elimination. It was a pity that the boy, fully liberated, was cut off from all human contact.

Owing to the press of practical matters, the narrator goes away. After ten years, he returns. Don Guillermo has died; his son goes on living after his fashion, with natural breathing, heart regular, in a dusty shack cluttered with mechanical devices. The narrator, about to leave for good, drops a cigarette butt that sets fire to the shack and he never quite knows whether this act was done on purpose or by pure chance. So ends Huergo's story, strange enough for its time but now, of course, more than outstripped by the rockets and astronauts of our men of science.

Having dashed off this disinterested compendium of the tale of a now dead and forgotten author—from whom I have nothing to gain—I steer back to the heart of the matter. Memory restores to me a Saturday morning in 1964 when I had an appointment with the eminent gerontologist Dr. Raúl Narbondo. The sad truth is that we young bloods of yesteryear are getting on; the thick mop begins to thin, one or another ear stops up, the wrinkles collect grime, molars grow hollow, a cough takes root, the backbone hunches up, the foot trips on a pebble, and, to put it plainly, the paterfamilias falters and withers. There was no doubt about it, the moment had come to see Dr. Narbondo for a general checkup, particularly considering the fact that he specialized in the replacement of malfunctioning organs.

Sick at heart because that afternoon the Palermo Juniors and the Spanish Sports were playing a return match and maybe I could not occupy my place in the front row to bolster my team, I betook myself to the clinic on Corrientes Avenue near Pasteur. The clinic, as its fame betrays, occupies the fifteenth floor of the Adamant Building. I went up by elevator (manufactured by the Electra Company). Eye to eye with Narbondo's brass shingle, I pressed the bell, and at long last, taking my courage in both hands, I slipped through the partly open door and entered into the waiting room proper. There, alone with the latest issues of the *Ladies' Companion* and *Jumbo,* I whiled away the passing hours until a cuckoo clock struck twelve and sent me leaping from my armchair. At once, I asked myself, What happened? Planning my every move now like a sleuth, I took a step or two toward the next room, peeped in, ready, admittedly, to fly the coop at the slightest sound. From the streets far below came the noise of horns and traffic, the cry of a newspaper hawker, the squeal of brakes sparing some pedestrian, but, all around me, a reign of silence. I crossed a kind of laboratory, or pharmaceutical back room, furnished with instruments and flasks of all sorts. Stimulated by the aim of reaching the men's room, I pushed open a door at the far end of the lab.

Inside, I saw something that my eyes did not understand. The small enclosure was circular, painted white, with a low ceiling and neon lighting, and without a single window to relieve the sense of claustrophobia. The room was inhabited by four personages, or pieces of furniture. Their color was the same as the walls, their material wood, their form cubic. On each cube was another small cube with a latticed opening and below it a slot as in a mailbox. Carefully scrutinizing the grilled opening, you noted with alarm that from the interior you were being watched by something like eyes. The slots emitted, from time to time, a chorus of sighs or whisperings that the good Lord himself could not have made head or tail of. The placement of these cubes was such that they faced each other in the form of a square, composing a kind of conclave. I don't know how many minutes lapsed. At this point, the doctor came in and said to me, "My pardon, Bustos, for having kept you waiting. I was just out getting myself an advance ticket for today's match between the Palermo Juniors and the Spanish Sports." He went on, indicating the cubes, "Let me introduce you to Santiago Silberman, to retired clerk-of-court Ludueña, to Aquiles Molinari, and to Miss Bugard."

Out of the furniture came faint rumbling sounds. I quickly reached out a hand and, without the pleasure of shaking theirs, withdrew in good order, a frozen smile on my lips. Reaching the vestibule as best I could, I managed to stammer, "A drink. A stiff drink."

Narbondo came out of the lab with a graduated beaker filled with water and dissolved some effervescent drops into it. Blessed concoction—the wretched taste brought me to my senses. Then, the door to the small room closed and locked tight, came the explanation:

"I'm glad to see, my dear Bustos, that my immortals have made quite an impact on you. Whoever would have thought that *Homo sapiens,* Darwin's barely human ape, could achieve such perfection? This, my house, I assure you, is the only one in all Indo-America where Dr. Eric Stapledon's methodology has been fully applied. You recall, no doubt, the consternation that the death of the late lamented doctor, which took place in New Zealand, occasioned in scientific circles. I flatter myself, furthermore, for having implemented his precursory labors with a few Argentinean touches. In itself, the thesis—Newton's apple all over again—is fairly simple. The death of the body is a result, always, of the failure of some organ or other, call it the kidney, lungs, heart, or what you like. With the replacement of the organism's various components, in themselves perishable, with other corresponding stainless or polyethylene parts, there is no earthly reason whatever why the soul, why you yourself—Bustos Domecq—should not be immortal. None of your philosophical niceties here; the body can be vulcanized and from time to time recaulked, and so the mind keeps going. Surgery brings immortality to mankind. Life's essential aim has been attained—the mind lives on without fear of cessation. Each of our immortals is comforted by the certainty, backed by our firm's guarantee, of being a witness *in aeternum.* The brain, refreshed night and day by a system of electrical charges, is the last organic bulwark in which ball bearings and cells collaborate. The rest is Formica, steel, plastics. Respiration, alimentation, generation, mobility—elimination itself!—belong to the past. Our immortal is real estate. One or two minor touches are still missing, it's true. Oral articulation, dialogue, may still be improved. As for the costs, you need not worry yourself. By means of a procedure that circumvents legal red tape, the candidate transfers his property to us, and the Narbondo Company, Inc.—I, my son, his descendants—guarantees your upkeep, *in statu quo,* to the end of time. And, I might add, a money-back guarantee."

It was then that he laid a friendly hand on my shoulder. I felt his will taking power over me. "Ha-ha! I see I've whetted your appetite, I've tempted you, dear Bustos. You'll need a couple of months or so to get your affairs in order and to have your stock portfolio signed over to us. As far as the operation goes, naturally, as a friend, I want to save you a little something. Instead of our usual fee of ten thousand dollars, for you, ninety-five hundred—in cash, of course. The rest is yours. It goes to pay your lodging, care, and service. The medical procedure in itself is painless. No more than a question of amputation and replacement. Nothing to worry about. On the eve, just keep yourself calm, untroubled. Avoid heavy meals, tobacco, and alcohol, apart from your accustomed and imported, I hope, Scotch or two. Above all, refrain from impatience."

"Why two months?" I asked him. "One's enough, and then some. I come out of the anesthesia and I'm one more of your cubes. You have my address and phone number. We'll keep in touch. I'll be back next Friday at the latest."

At the escape hatch he handed me the card of Nemirovski, Nemirovski, & Nemirovski, Counsellors at Law, who would put themselves at my disposal for all the details of drawing up the will. With perfect composure I walked to the subway entrance, then took the stairs at a run. I lost no time. That same night, without leaving the slightest trace behind, I moved to the New Impartial, in whose register I figure under the assumed name of Aquiles Silberman. Here, in my bedroom at the far rear of this modest hotel, wearing a false beard and dark spectacles, I am setting down this account of the facts.

Leo Tolstoy

THE DEATH OF IVAN ILYCH

I

During an interval in the Melvinski trial in the large building of the Law Courts, the members and public prosecutor met in Ivan Egorovich Shebek's private room, where the conversation turned on the celebrated Krasovski case. Fëdor Vasilievich warmly maintained that it was not subject to their jurisdiction, Ivan Egorovich maintained the contrary, while Peter Ivanovich, not having entered into the discussion at the start, took no part in it but looked through the *Gazette* which had just been handed in.

"Gentlemen," he said, "Ivan Ilych has died!"

"You don't say so!"

"Here, read it yourself," replied Peter Ivanovich, handing Fëdor Vasilievich the paper still damp from the press. Surrounded by a black border were the words: "Praskovya Fëdorovna Golovina, with profound sorrow, informs relatives and friends of the demise of her beloved husband Ivan Ilych Golovin, Member of the Court of Justice, which occurred on February the 4th of this year 1882. The funeral will take place on Friday at one o'clock in the afternoon."

Ivan Ilych had been a colleague of the gentlemen present and was liked by them all. He had been ill for some weeks with an illness said to be incurable. His post had been kept open for him, but there had been conjectures that in case of his death Alexeev might receive his appointment, and that either Vinnikov or Shtabel would succeed Alexeev. So on receiving the news of Ivan Ilych's death the first thought of each of the gentlemen in that private room was of the changes and promotions it might occasion among themselves or their acquaintances.

"I shall be sure to get Shtabel's place or Vinnikov's," thought Fëdor Vasilievich. "I was promised that long ago, and the promotion means an extra eight hundred rubles a year for me beside the allowance."

"Now I must apply for my brother-in-law's transfer from Kaluga," thought Peter Ivanovich. "My wife will be very glad, and then she won't be able to say that I never do anything for her relations."

"I thought he would never leave his bed again," said Peter Ivanovich aloud. "It's very sad."

"But what really was the matter with him?"

"The doctors couldn't say—at least they could, but each of them said

THE DEATH OF IVAN ILYCH From *The Death of Ivan Ilych and Other Stories* by Leo Tolstoy, translated by Louise and Aylmer Maude and published by Oxford University Press. Written in 1886.

something different. When last I saw him I thought he was getting better."

"And I haven't been to see him since the holidays. I always meant to go."

"Had he any property?"

"I think his wife had a little—but something quite trifling."

"We shall have to go to see her, but they live so terribly far away."

"Far away from you, you mean. Everything's far away from your place."

"You see, he never can forgive my living on the other side of the river," said Peter Ivanovich, smiling at Shebek. Then, still talking of the distances between different parts of the city, they returned to the Court.

Besides considerations as to the possible transfers and promotions likely to result from Ivan Ilych's death, the mere fact of the death of a near acquaintance aroused, as usual, in all who heard of it the complacent feeling that, "it is he who is dead and not I."

Each one thought or felt, "Well, he's dead but I'm alive!" But the more intimate of Ivan Ilych's acquaintances, his so-called friends, could not help thinking also that they would now have to fulfil the very tiresome demands of propriety by attending the funeral service and paying a visit of condolence to the widow.

Fëdor Vasilievich and Peter Ivanovich had been his nearest acquaintances. Peter Ivanovich had studied law with Ivan Ilych and had considered himself to be under obligations to him.

Having told his wife at dinner-time of Ivan Ilych's death and of his conjecture that it might be possible to get her brother transferred to their circuit, Peter Ivanovich sacrificed his usual nap, put on his evening clothes, and drove to Ivan Ilych's house.

At the entrance stood a carriage and two cabs. Leaning against the wall in the hall downstairs near the cloak-stand was a coffin-lid covered with cloth of gold, ornamented with gold cord and tassels, that had been polished up with metal powder. Two ladies in black were taking off their fur cloaks. Peter Ivanovich recognized one of them as Ivan Ilych's sister, but the other was a stranger to him. His colleague Schwartz was just coming downstairs, but on seeing Peter Ivanovich enter he stopped and winked at him, as if to say: "Ivan Ilych has made a mess of things—not like you and me."

Schwartz's face with his Piccadilly whiskers and his slim figure in evening dress, had as usual an air of elegant solemnity which contrasted with the playfulness of his character and had a special piquancy here, or so it seemed to Peter Ivanovich.

Peter Ivanovich allowed the ladies to precede him and slowly followed them upstairs. Schwartz did not come down but remained where he was, and Peter Ivanovich understood that he wanted to arrange where they should play bridge that evening. The ladies went upstairs to the widow's room, and Schwartz with seriously compressed lips but a playful look in his eyes, indicated by a twist of his eyebrows the room to the right where the body lay.

Peter Ivanovich, like everyone else on such occasions, entered feeling uncertain what he would have to do. All he knew was that at such times it is always safe to cross oneself. But he was not quite sure whether one should make obeisances while doing so. He therefore adopted a middle course. On entering the room he began crossing himself and made a slight movement resembling a bow. At the same time, as far as the motion of his head and arm allowed, he surveyed the room. Two young men—apparently nephews, one of whom was a high-school pupil—were leaving the room, crossing themselves as they did so. An old woman was standing motionless, and a lady with strangely arched eyebrows was saying something to her in a whisper. A vigorous, resolute Church Reader, in a frock-coat, was reading something in a loud voice with an expression that precluded any contradiction. The butler's assistant, Gerasim, stepping lightly in front of Peter Ivanovich, was strewing something on the floor. Noticing this, Peter Ivanovich was immediately aware of a faint odour of a decomposing body.

The last time he had called on Ivan Ilych, Peter Ivanovich had seen Gerasim in the study. Ivan Ilych had been particularly fond of him and he was performing the duty of a sick nurse.

Peter Ivanovich continued to make the sign of the cross slightly inclining his head in an intermediate direction between the coffin, the Reader, and the icons on the table in a corner of the room. Afterwards, when it seemed to him that this movement of his arm in crossing himself had gone on too long, he stopped and began to look at the corpse.

The dead man lay, as dead men always lie, in a specially heavy way, his rigid limbs sunk in the soft cushions of the coffin, with the head forever bowed on the pillow. His yellow waxen brow with bald patches over his sunken temples was thrust up in the way peculiar to the dead, the protruding nose seeming to press on the upper lip. He was much changed and had grown even thinner since Peter Ivanovich had last seen him, but, as is always the case with the dead, his face was handsomer and above all more dignified than when he was alive. The expression on the face said that what was necessary had been accomplished, and accomplished rightly. Besides this there was in that expression a reproach and a warning to the living. This warning seemed to Peter Ivanovich out of place, or at least not applicable to him. He felt a certain discomfort and so he hurriedly crossed himself once more and turned and went out of the door—too hurriedly and too regardless of propriety, as he himself was aware.

Schwartz was waiting for him in the adjoining room with legs spread wide apart and both hands toying with his top-hat behind his back. The mere sight of that playful, well-groomed, and elegant figure refreshed Peter Ivanovich. He felt that Schwartz was above all these happenings and would not surrender to any depressing influences. His very look said that this incident of a church service for Ivan Ilych could not be a sufficient reason for infringing the order of the session—in other words, that it would certainly not prevent his unwrapping a new pack of cards and shuffling them that evening while a footman placed four fresh candles on the table: in fact, that there was no reason for supposing that this incident would hinder their spending the evening agreeably. Indeed he said this in a whisper as Peter Ivanovich passed him, proposing that they should meet for a game at Fëdor Vasilievich's. But apparently Peter Ivanovich was not destined to play bridge that evening. Praskovya Fëdorovna (a short, fat woman who despite all efforts to the contrary had continued to broaden steadily from her shoulders downwards and who had the same extraordinarily arched eyebrows as the lady who had been standing by the coffin), dressed all in black, her head covered with lace, came out of her own room with some other ladies, conducted them to the room where the dead body lay, and said: "The service will begin immediately. Please go in."

Schwartz, making an indefinite bow, stood still, evidently neither accepting nor declining this invitation. Praskovya Fëdorovna, recognizing Peter Ivanovich, sighed, went close to him, took his hand, and said: "I know you were a true friend to Ivan Ilych . . ." and looked at him awaiting some suitable response. And Peter Ivanovich knew that, just as it had been the right thing to cross himself in that room, so what he had to do here was to press her hand, sigh, and say, "Believe me. . . ." So he did all this and as he did it felt that the desired result had been achieved: that both he and she were touched.

"Come with me. I want to speak to you before it begins," said the widow. "Give me your arm."

Peter Ivanovich gave her his arm and they went to the inner rooms, passing Schwartz, who winked at Peter Ivanovich compassionately.

"That does for our bridge! Don't object if we find another player. Perhaps you can cut in when you do escape," said his playful look.

Peter Ivanovich sighed still more deeply and despondently, and Praskovya Fëdorovna pressed his arm gratefully. When they reached the drawing-room, upholstered in pink cretonne and lighted by a dim lamp, they sat down at the table—she on a sofa and Peter Ivanovich on a low pouffe, the springs of which yielded spasmodically under his weight. Praskovya Fëdorovna had been on the point of warning him to take another seat, but felt that such a warning was out of keeping with her present condition and so changed her mind. As he sat down on the pouffe Peter Ivanovich recalled how Ivan Ilych had arranged this room and had consulted him regarding this pink cretonne with green leaves. The whole room was full of furniture and knick-knacks, and on her way to the sofa the lace of the widow's black shawl caught on the carved edge of the table. Peter Ivanovich rose to detach it, and the springs of the pouffe, relieved of his weight, rose also and gave him a push. The widow began detaching her shawl herself, and Peter Ivanovich again sat down, suppressing the rebellious springs of the pouffe under him. But the widow had not quite freed herself and Peter Ivanovich got up again, and again the pouffe rebelled and even creaked. When this was all over she took out a clean cambric handkerchief and began to weep. The episode with the shawl and the struggle with the pouffe had cooled Peter Ivanovich's emotions and he sat there with a sullen look on his face. This awkward situation was interrupted by Sokolov, Ivan Ilych's butler, who came to report that the plot in the cemetery that Praskovya Fëdorovna had chosen would cost two hundred rubles. She stopped weeping and, looking at Peter Ivanovich with the air of a victim, remarked in French that it was very hard for her. Peter Ivanovich made a silent gesture signifying his full conviction that it must indeed be so.

"Please smoke," she said in a magnanimous yet crushed voice, and turned to discuss with Sokolov the price of the plot for the grave.

Peter Ivanovich while lighting his cigarette heard her inquiring very circumstantially into the prices of different plots in the cemetery and finally decide which she would take. When that was done she gave instructions about engaging the choir. Sokolov then left the room.

"I look after everything myself," she told Peter Ivanovich, shifting the albums that lay on the table; and noticing that the table was endangered by his cigarette-ash, she immediately passed him an ash-tray, saying as she did so: "I consider it an affectation to say that my grief prevents my attending to practical affairs. On the contrary, if anything can—I won't say console me, but—distract me, it is seeing to everything concerning him." She again took out her handkerchief as if preparing to cry, but suddenly, as if mastering her feeling, she shook herself and began to speak calmly. "But there is something I want to talk to you about."

Peter Ivanovich bowed, keeping control of the springs of the pouffe, which immediately began quivering under him.

"He suffered terribly the last few days."

"Did he?" said Peter Ivanovich.

"Oh, terribly! He screamed unceasingly, not for minutes but for hours. For the last three days he screamed incessantly. It was unendurable. I cannot understand how I bore it; you could hear him three rooms off. Oh, what I have suffered!"

"Is it possible that he was conscious all that time?" asked Peter Ivanovich.

"Yes," she whispered. "To the last moment. He took leave of us a quarter of an hour before he died, and asked us to take Volodya away."

The thought of the sufferings of this man he had known so intimately, first as a merry little boy, then as a school-mate, and later as a grown-up colleague, suddenly struck Peter Ivanovich with horror, despite an unpleasant consciousness of his own and this woman's dissimulation. He again saw that brow, and that nose pressing down on the lip, and felt afraid for himself.

"Three days of frightful suffering and then death! Why, that might suddenly, at any time, happen to me," he thought, and for a moment felt terrified. But—he did not himself know how—the customary reflection at once occurred to him that this had happened to Ivan Ilych and not to him, and that it should not and could not happen to him, and to think that it could would be yielding to depression which he ought not to do, as Schwartz's expression plainly showed. After which reflection Peter Ivanovich felt reassured, and began to ask with interest about the details of Ivan Ilych's death, as though death was an accident natural to Ivan Ilych but certainly not to himself.

After many details of the really dreadful physical sufferings Ivan Ilych had endured (which details he learnt only from the effect those sufferings had produced on Praskovya Fëdorovna's nerves) the widow apparently found it necessary to get to business.

"Oh, Peter Ivanovich, how hard it is! How terribly, terribly hard!" and she again began to weep.

Peter Ivanovich sighed and waited for her to finish blowing her nose. When she had done so he said, "Believe me . . ." and she again began talking and brought out what was evidently her chief concern with him—namely, to question him as to how she could obtain a grant of money from the government on the occasion of her husband's death. She made it appear that she was asking Peter Ivanovich's advice about her pension, but he soon saw that she already knew about that to the minutest detail, more even than he did himself. She knew how much could be got out of the government in consequence of her husband's death, but wanted to find out whether she could not possibly extract something more. Peter Ivanovich tried to think of some means of doing so, but after reflecting for a while and, out of propriety, condemning the government for its niggardliness, he said he thought that nothing more could be got. Then she sighed and evidently began to devise means of getting rid of her visitor. Noticing this, he put out his cigarette, rose, pressed her hand, and went out into the anteroom.

In the dining-room where the clock stood that Ivan Ilych had liked so much and had bought at an antique shop, Peter Ivanovich met a priest and a few acquaintances who had come to attend the service, and he recognized Ivan Ilych's daughter, a handsome young woman. She was in black and her slim figure appeared slimmer than ever. She had a gloomy, determined, almost angry expression, and bowed to Peter Ivanovich as though he were in some way to blame. Behind her, with the same offended look, stood a wealthy young man, an examining magistrate, whom Peter Ivanovich also knew and who was her fiancé, as he had heard. He bowed mournfully to them and was about to pass into the death-chamber, when from under the stairs appeared the figure of Ivan Ilych's schoolboy son, who was extremely like his father. He seemed a little Ivan Ilych, such as Peter Ivanovich remembered when they studied law together. His tear-stained eyes had in them the look that is seen in the eyes of boys of thirteen or fourteen who are not pure-minded. When he saw Peter Ivanovich he scowled morosely and shamefacedly. Peter Ivanovich nodded to him and entered the death-chamber. The service began: candles, groans, incense, tears, and sobs. Peter

Ivanovich stood looking gloomily down at his feet. He did not look once at the dead man, did not yield to any depressing influence, and was one of the first to leave the room. There was no one in the anteroom, but Gerasim darted out of the dead man's room, rummaged with his strong hands among the fur coats to find Peter Ivanovich's and helped him on with it.

"Well, friend Gerasim," said Peter Ivanovich, so as to say something. "It's a sad affair, isn't it?"

"It's God's will. We shall all come to it some day," said Gerasim, displaying his teeth—the even, white teeth of a healthy peasant—and, like a man in the thick of urgent work, he briskly opened the front door, called the coachman, helped Peter Ivanovich into the sledge, and sprang back to the porch as if in readiness for what he had to do next.

Peter Ivanovich found the fresh air particularly pleasant after the smell of incense, the dead body, and carbolic acid.

"Where to, sir?" asked the coachman.

"It's not too late even now. . . . I'll call round on Fëdor Vasilievich."

He accordingly drove there and found them just finishing the first rubber, so that it was quite convenient for him to cut in.

2

Ivan Ilych's life had been most simple and most ordinary and therefore most terrible.

He had been a member of the Court of Justice, and died at the age of forty-five. His father had been an official who after serving in various ministries and departments in Petersburg had made the sort of career which brings men to positions from which by reason of their long service they cannot be dismissed, though they are obviously unfit to hold any responsible position, and for whom therefore posts are especially created, which though fictitious carry salaries of from six to ten thousand rubles that are not fictitious, and in receipt of which they live on to a great age.

Such was the Privy Councillor and superfluous member of various superfluous institutions, Ilya Epimovich Golovin.

He had three sons, of whom Ivan Ilych was the second. The eldest son was following in his father's footsteps only in another department, and was already approaching that stage in the service at which a similar sinecure would be reached. The third son was a failure. He had ruined his prospects in a number of positions and was now serving in the railway department. His father and brothers, and still more their wives, not merely disliked meeting him, but avoided remembering his existence unless compelled to do so. His sister had married Baron Greff, a Petersburg official of her father's type. Ivan Ilych was *le phénix de la famille* as people said. He was neither as cold and formal as his elder brother nor as wild as the younger, but was a happy mean between them—an intelligent, polished, lively and agreeable man. He had studied with his younger brother at the School of Law, but the latter had failed to complete the course and was expelled when he was in the fifth class. Ivan Ilych finished the course well. Even when he was at the School of Law he was just what he remained for the rest of his life: a capable, cheerful, good-natured, and sociable man, though strict in the fulfilment of what he considered to be his duty: and he considered his duty to be what was so considered by those in authority. Neither as a boy nor as a man was he a toady, but from early youth was by nature attracted to people of high station as a fly is drawn to the light, assimilating their ways and views of life and establishing friendly relations with them. All the enthusiasms of childhood and youth passed without leaving much trace on him; he succumbed to sensuality, to vanity, and latterly among the highest classes to liberalism, but always within limits which his instinct unfailingly indicated to him as correct.

At school he had done things which had formerly seemed to him very horrid and made him feel disgusted with himself when he did them; but when later on he saw that such actions were done by people of good position and that they did not regard them as wrong, he was able not exactly to regard them as right, but to forget about them entirely or not be at all troubled at remembering them.

Having graduated from the School of Law and qualified for the tenth rank of the civil service, and having received money from his father for his equipment, Ivan Ilych ordered himself clothes at Scharmer's, the fashionable tailor, hung a medallion inscribed *respice finem* on his watch-chain, took leave of his professor and the prince who was patron of the school, had a farewell dinner with his comrades at Donon's first-class restaurant, and with his new and fashionable portmanteau, linen, clothes, shaving and other toilet appliances, and a travelling rug, all purchased at the best shops, he set off for one of the provinces where, through his father's influence, he had been attached to the Governor as an official for special service.

In the province Ivan Ilych soon arranged as easy and agreeable a position for himself as he had had at the School of Law. He performed his official tasks, made his career, and at the same time amused himself pleasantly and decorously. Occasionally he paid official visits to country districts, where he behaved with dignity both to his superiors and inferiors, and performed the duties entrusted to him, which related chiefly to the sectarians, with an exactness and incorruptible honesty of which he could not but feel proud.

In official matters, despite his youth and taste for frivolous gaiety, he was exceedingly reserved, punctilious, and even severe; but in society he was often amusing and witty, and always good-natured, correct in his manner, and *bon enfant,* as the governor and his wife—with whom he was like one of the family—used to say of him.

respice finem: look to the end
bon enfant: a good child

In the province he had an affair with a lady who made advances to the elegant young lawyer, and there was also a milliner; and there were carousals with aides-de-camp who visited the district, and after-supper visits to a certain outlying street of doubtful reputation; and there was too some obsequiousness to his chief and even to his chief's wife, but all this was done with such a tone of good breeding that no hard names could be applied to it. It all came under the heading of the French saying: *"Il faut que jeunesse se passe."* It was all done with clean hands, in clean linen, with French phrases, and above all among people of the best society and consequently with the approval of people of rank.

So Ivan Ilych served for five years and then came a change in his official life. The new and reformed judicial institutions were introduced, and new men were needed. Ivan Ilych became such a new man. He was offered the post of examining magistrate, and he accepted it though the post was in another province and obliged him to give up the connexions he had formed and to make new ones. His friends met to give him a send-off; they had a group-photograph taken and presented him with a silver cigarette-case, and he set off to his new post.

As examining magistrate Ivan Ilych was just as *comme il faut* and decorous a man, inspiring general respect and capable of separating his official duties from his private life, as he had been when acting as an official on special service. His duties now as examining magistrate were far more interesting and attractive than before. In his former position it had been pleasant to wear an undress uniform made by Scharmer, and to pass through the crowd of petitioners and officials who were timorously awaiting an audience with the governor, and who envied him as with free and easy gait he went straight into his chief's private room to have a cup of tea and a cigarette with him. But not many people had then been directly dependent on him—only police officials and the sectarians when he went on special missions—and he liked to treat them politely, almost as comrades, as if he were letting them feel that he who had the power to crush them was treating them in this simple, friendly way. There were then but few such people. But now, as an examining magistrate, Ivan Ilych felt that everyone without exception, even the most important and self-satisfied, was in his power, and that he need only write a few words on a sheet of paper with a certain heading, and this or that important, self-satisfied person would be brought before him in the role of an accused person or a witness, and if he did not choose to allow him to sit down, would have to stand before him and answer his questions. Ivan Ilych never abused his power; he tried on the contrary to soften its expression, but the consciousness of it and of the possibility of softening its effect, supplied the chief interest and attraction of his office. In his work itself, especially in his examinations, he very soon acquired a method of eliminating all considerations irrelevant to the legal aspect of the case, and reducing even

Il faut . . . passe: You're only young once

the most complicated case to a form in which it would be presented on paper only in its externals, completely excluding his personal opinion of the matter, while above all observing every prescribed formality. The work was new and Ivan Ilych was one of the first men to apply the new Code of 1864.

On taking up the post of examining magistrate in a new town, he made new acquaintances and connexions, placed himself on a new footing, and assumed a somewhat different tone. He took up an attitude of rather dignified aloofness towards the provincial authorities, but picked out the best circle of legal gentlemen and wealthy gentry living in the town and assumed a tone of slight dissatisfaction with the government, of moderate liberalism, and of enlightened citizenship. At the same time, without at all altering the elegance of his toilet, he ceased shaving his chin and allowed his beard to grow as it pleased.

Ivan Ilych settled down very pleasantly in this new town. The society there, which inclined towards opposition to the Governor, was friendly, his salary was larger, and he began to play *vint*, which he found added not a little to the pleasure of life, for he had a capacity for cards, played good-humouredly, and calculated rapidly and astutely, so that he usually won.

After living there for two years he met his future wife, Praskovya Fëdorovna Mikhel, who was the most attractive, clever, and brilliant girl of the set in which he moved, and among other amusements and relaxations from his labours as examining magistrate, Ivan Ilych established light and playful relations with her.

While he had been an official on special service he had been accustomed to dance, but now as an examining magistrate it was exceptional for him to do so. If he danced now, he did it as if to show that though he served under the reformed order of things, and had reached the fifth official rank, yet when it came to dancing he could do it better than most people. So at the end of an evening he sometimes danced with Praskovya Fëdorovna, and it was chiefly during these dances that he captivated her. She fell in love with him. Ivan Ilych had at first no definite intention of marrying, but when the girl fell in love with him he said to himself: "Really, why shouldn't I marry?"

Praskovya Fëdorovna came of a good family, was not bad looking, and had some little property. Ivan Ilych might have aspired to a more brilliant match, but even this was good. He had his salary, and she, he hoped, would have an equal income. She was well connected, and was a sweet, pretty, and thoroughly correct young woman. To say that Ivan Ilych married because he fell in love with Praskovya Fëdorovna and found that she sympathized with his views of life would be as incorrect as to say that he married because his social circle approved of the match. He was swayed by both these considerations: the marriage gave him personal satisfaction, and at the same time it was considered the right thing by the most highly placed of his associates.

So Ivan Ilych got married.

The preparations for marriage and the beginning of married life, with its conjugal caresses, the new furniture, new crockery, and new linen, were very pleasant until his wife became pregnant—so that Ivan Ilych had begun to think that marriage would not impair the easy, agreeable gay and always decorous character of his life, approved of by society and regarded by himself as natural, but would even improve it. But from the first months of his wife's pregnancy, something new, unpleasant, depressing, and unseemly, and from which there was no way of escape, unexpectedly showed itself.

His wife, without any reason—*de gaieté de coeur* as Ivan Ilych expressed it to himself—began to disturb the pleasure and propriety of their life. She began to be jealous without any cause, expected him to devote his whole attention to her, found fault with everything, and made coarse and ill-mannered scenes.

At first Ivan Ilych hoped to escape from the unpleasantness of this state of affairs by the same easy and decorous relation to life that had served him heretofore: he tried to ignore his wife's disagreeable moods, continued to live in his usual easy and pleasant way, invited friends to his house for a game of cards, and also tried going out to his club or spending his evenings with friends. But one day his wife began upbraiding him so vigorously, using such coarse words, and continued to abuse him every time he did not fulfil her demands, so resolutely and with such evident determination not to give way till he submitted—that is, till he stayed at home and was bored just as she was—that he became alarmed. He now realized that matrimony—at any rate with Praskovya Fëdorovna—was not always conducive to the pleasures and amenities of life, but on the contrary often infringed both comfort and propriety, and that he must therefore entrench himself against such infringement. And Ivan Ilych began to seek for means of doing so. His official duties were the one thing that imposed upon Praskovya Fëdorovna, and by means of his official work and the duties attached to it he began struggling with his wife to secure his own independence.

With the birth of their child, the attempts to feed it and the various failures in doing so, and with the real and imaginary illnesses of mother and child, in which Ivan Ilych's sympathy was demanded but about which he understood nothing, the need of securing for himself an existence outside his family life became still more imperative.

As his wife grew more irritable and exacting and Ivan Ilych transferred the centre of gravity of his life more and more to his official work, so did he grow to like his work better and became more ambitious than before.

Very soon, within a year of his wedding, Ivan Ilych had realized that marriage, though it may add some comforts to life, is in fact a very intricate and difficult affair towards which in order to perform one's duty, that is, to

de gaieté de coeur: out of sheer wantonness

lead a decorous life approved of by society, one must adopt a definite attitude just as towards one's official duties.

And Ivan Ilych evolved such an attitude towards married life. He only required of it those conveniences—dinner at home, housewife, and bed—which it could give him, and above all that propriety of external forms required by public opinion. For the rest he looked for light-hearted pleasure and propriety, and was very thankful when he found them, but if he met with antagonism and querulousness he at once retired into his separate fenced-off world of official duties, where he found satisfaction.

Ivan Ilych was esteemed a good official, and after three years was made Assistant Public Prosecutor. His new duties, their importance, the possibility of indicting and imprisoning anyone he chose, the publicity his speeches received, and the success he had in all these things, made his work still more attractive.

More children came. His wife become more and more querulous and ill-tempered, but the attitude Ivan Ilych had adopted towards his home life rendered him almost impervious to her grumbling.

After seven years' service in that town he was transferred to another province as Public Prosecutor. They moved, but were short of money and his wife did not like the place they moved to. Though the salary was higher the cost of living was greater, besides which two of their children died and family life became still more unpleasant for him.

Praskovya Fëdorovna blamed her husband for every inconvenience they encountered in their new home. Most of the conversations between husband and wife, especially as to the children's education, led to topics which recalled former disputes, and those disputes were apt to flare up again at any moment. There remained only those rare periods of amorousness which still came to them at times but did not last long. These were islets at which they anchored for a while and then again set out upon that ocean of veiled hostility which showed itself in their aloofness from one another. This aloofness might have grieved Ivan Ilych had he considered that it ought not to exist, but he now regarded the position as normal, and even made it the goal at which he aimed in family life. His aim was to free himself more and more from those unpleasantnesses and to give them a semblance of harmlessness and propriety. He attained this by spending less and less time with his family, and when obliged to be at home he tried to safeguard his position by the presence of outsiders. The chief thing however was that he had his official duties. The whole interest of his life now centred in the official world and that interest absorbed him. The consciousness of his power, being able to ruin anybody he wished to ruin, the importance, even the external dignity of his entry into court, or meetings with his subordinates, his success with superiors and inferiors, and above all his masterly handling of cases, of which he was conscious—all this gave him pleasure and filled his life, together with chats with his colleagues, dinners, and bridge. So that on the whole Ivan Ilych's life continued to flow as he considered it should do—pleasantly and properly.

So things continued for another seven years. His eldest daughter was already sixteen, another child had died, and only one son was left, a schoolboy and a subject of dissension. Ivan Ilych wanted to put him in the School of Law, but to spite him Praskovya Fëdorovna entered him at the High School. The daughter had been educated at home and had turned out well: the boy did not learn badly either.

3

So Ivan Ilych lived for seventeen years after his marriage. He was already a Public Prosecutor of long standing, and had declined several proposed transfers while awaiting a more desirable post, when an unanticipated and unpleasant occurrence quite upset the peaceful course of his life. He was expecting to be offered the post of presiding judge in a University town, but Happe somehow came to the front and obtained the appointment instead. Ivan Ilych became irritable, reproached Happe, and quarrelled both with him and with his immediate superiors—who became colder to him and again passed him over when other appointments were made.

This was in 1880, the hardest year of Ivan Ilych's life. It was then that it became evident on the one hand that his salary was insufficient for them to live on, and on the other that he had been forgotten, and not only this, but that what was for him the greatest and most cruel injustice appeared to others a quite ordinary occurrence. Even his father did not consider it his duty to help him. Ivan Ilych felt himself abandoned by everyone, and that they regarded his position with a salary of 3,500 rubles as quite normal and even fortunate. He alone knew that with the consciousness of the injustices done him, with his wife's incessant nagging, and with the debts he had contracted by living beyond his means, his position was far from normal.

In order to save money that summer he obtained leave of absence and went with his wife to live in the country at her brother's place.

In the country, without his work, he experienced *ennui* for the first time in his life, and not only *ennui* but intolerable depression, and he decided that it was impossible to go on living like that, and that it was necessary to take energetic measures.

Having passed a sleepless night pacing up and down the veranda, he decided to go to Petersburg and bestir himself, in order to punish those who had failed to appreciate him and to get transferred to another ministry.

Next day, despite many protests from his wife and her brother, he started for Petersburg with the sole object of obtaining a post with a salary of five thousand rubles a year. He was no longer bent on any particular department, or tendency, or kind of activity. All he now wanted was an appointment to another post with a salary of five thousand rubles, either in the administration, in the banks, with the railways, in one of the Empress Marya's Institutions, or even in the customs—but it had to carry with it a salary of five thousand rubles and be in a ministry other than that in which they had failed to appreciate him.

And this quest of Ivan Ilych's was crowned with remarkable and unexpected success. At Kursk an acquaintance of his, F. I. Ilyin, got into the first-class carriage, sat down beside Ivan Ilych, and told him of a telegram just received by the Governor of Kursk announcing that a change was about to take place in the ministry: Peter Ivanovich was to be superseded by Ivan Semënovich.

The proposed change, apart from its significance for Russia, had a special significance for Ivan Ilych, because by bringing forward a new man, Peter Petrovich, and consequently his friend Zachar Ivanovich, it was highly favourable for Ivan Ilych, since Zachar Ivanovich was a friend and colleague of his.

In Moscow this news was confirmed, and on reaching Petersburg Ivan Ilych found Zachar Ivanovich and received a definite promise of an appointment in his former department of Justice.

A week later he telegraphed to his wife: "Zachar in Miller's place. I shall receive appointment on presentation of report."

Thanks to this change of personnel, Ivan Ilych had unexpectedly obtained an appointment in his former ministry which placed him two stages above his former colleagues besides giving him five thousand rubles salary and three thousand five hundred rubles for expenses connected with his removal. All his ill humour towards his former enemies and the whole department vanished, and Ivan Ilych was completely happy.

He returned to the country more cheerful and contented than he had been for a long time. Praskovya Fëdorovna also cheered up and a truce was arranged between them. Ivan Ilych told of how he had been fêted by everybody in Petersburg, how all those who had been his enemies were put to shame and now fawned on him, how envious they were of his appointment, and how much everybody in Petersburg had liked him.

Praskovya Fëdorovna listened to all this and appeared to believe it. She did not contradict anything, but only made plans for their life in the town to which they were going. Ivan Ilych saw with delight that these plans were his plans, that he and his wife agreed, and that, after a stumble, his life was regaining its due and natural character of pleasant lightheartedness and decorum.

Ivan Ilych had come back for a short time only, for he had to take up his new duties on the 10th of September. Moreover, he needed time to settle into the new place, to move all his belongings from the province, and to buy and order many additional things: in a word, to make such arrangements as he had resolved on, which were almost exactly what Praskovya Fëdorovna too had decided on.

Now that everything had happened so fortunately, and that he and his wife were at one in their aims and moreover saw so little of one another, they got on together better than they had done since the first years of marriage. Ivan Ilych had thought of taking his family away with him at once, but the insistence of his wife's brother and her sister-in-law, who had suddenly become particularly amiable and friendly to him and his family, induced him to depart alone.

So he departed, and the cheerful state of mind induced by his success and by the harmony between his wife and himself, the one intensifying the other, did not leave him. He found a delightful house, just the thing both he and his wife had dreamt of. Spacious, lofty reception rooms in the old style, a convenient and dignified study, rooms for his wife and daughter, a study for his son—it might have been specially built for them. Ivan Ilych himself superintended the arrangements, chose the wallpapers, supplemented the furniture (preferably with antiques which he considered particularly *comme il faut*), and supervised the upholstering. Everything progressed and progressed and approached the ideal he had set himself: even when things were only half completed they exceeded his expectations. He saw what a refined and elegant character, free from vulgarity, it would all have when it was ready. On falling asleep he pictured to himself how the reception-room would look. Looking at the yet unfinished drawing-room he could see the fireplace, the screen, the what-not, the little chairs dotted here and there, the dishes and plates on the walls, and the bronzes, as they would be when everything was in place. He was pleased by the thought of how his wife and daughter, who shared his taste in this matter, would be impressed by it. They were certainly not expecting as much. He had been particularly successful in finding, and buying cheaply, antiques which gave a particularly aristocratic character to the whole place. But in his letters he intentionally understated everything in order to be able to surprise them. All this so absorbed him that his new duties—though he liked his official work—interested him less than he had expected. Sometimes he even had moments of absent-mindedness during the Court Sessions, and would consider whether he should have straight or curved cornices for his curtains. He was so interested in it all that he often did things himself, rearranging the furniture, or rehanging the curtains. Once when mounting a step-ladder to show the upholsterer, who did not understand, how he wanted the hangings draped, he made a false step and slipped, but being a strong and agile man he clung on and only knocked his side against the knob of the window frame. The bruised place was painful but the pain soon passed, and he felt particularly bright and well just then. He wrote: "I feel fifteen years younger." He thought he would have everything ready by September, but it dragged on till mid-October. But the result was charming not only in his eyes but to everyone who saw it.

In reality it was just what is usually seen in the houses of people of moderate means who want to appear rich, and therefore succeed only in resembling others like themselves: there were damasks, dark wood, plants, rugs, and dull and polished bronzes—all the things people of a certain class have in order to resemble other people of that class. His house was so like the others that it would never have been noticed, but to him it all seemed to be quite exceptional. He was very happy when he met his family at the station and brought them to the newly furnished house all lit up, where a footman in a white tie opened the door into the hall decorated with plants, and when they went on into the drawing-room and the study uttering exclamations of delight. He conducted them everywhere, drank in their praises eagerly, and beamed with pleasure. At tea that evening, when Praskovya Fëdorovna among other things asked him about his fall, he laughed and showed them how he had gone flying and had frightened the upholsterer.

"It's a good thing I'm a bit of an athlete. Another man might have been killed, but I merely knocked myself, just here; it hurts when it's touched, but it's passing off already—it's only a bruise."

So they began living in their new home—in which, as always happens, when they got thoroughly settled in they found they were just one room short—and with the increased income, which as always was just a little (some five hundred rubles) too little, but it was all very nice.

Things went particularly well at first, before everything was finally arranged and while something had still to be done: this thing bought, that thing ordered, another thing moved, and something else adjusted. Though there were some disputes between husband and wife, they were both so well satisfied and had so much to do that it all passed off without any serious quarrels. When nothing was left to arrange it became rather dull and something seemed to be lacking, but they were then making acquaintances, forming habits, and life was growing fuller.

Ivan Ilych spent his mornings at the law court and came home to dinner, and at first he was generally in a good humour, though he occasionally became irritable just on account of his house. (Every spot on the tablecloth or the upholstery, and every broken window-blind string, irritated him. He had devoted so much trouble to arranging it all that every disturbance of it distressed him.) But on the whole his life ran its course as he believed life should do: easily, pleasantly, and decorously.

He got up at nine, drank his coffee, read the paper, and then put on his undress uniform and went to the law courts. There the harness in which he worked had already been stretched to fit him and he donned it without a hitch: petitioners, inquiries at the chancery, the chancery itself, and the sittings public and administrative. In all this the thing was to exclude everything fresh and vital, which always disturbs the regular course of official business, and to admit only official relations with people, and then only on official grounds. A man would come, for instance, wanting some information. Ivan Ilych, as one in whose sphere the matter did not lie, would have nothing to do with him: but if the man had some business with him in his official capacity, something that could be expressed on officially stamped paper, he would do everything, positively everything he could within the limits of such relations, and in doing so would maintain the semblance of friendly human relations, that is, would observe the courtesies of life. As soon as the official relations ended, so did everything else. Ivan Ilych possessed this capacity to separate his real life from the official side of affairs and not mix the two, in the highest degree, and by long practice and natural aptitude had brought it to such a pitch that sometimes, in the manner of a virtuoso, he would even allow himself to let the human and official relations mingle. He let himself do this just because he felt that he could at any time he chose resume the strictly official attitude again and drop the human relation. And he did it all easily, pleasantly, correctly, and even artistically. In the intervals between the sessions he smoked, drank tea, chatted a little about politics, a little about general topics, a little about cards, but most of all about official appointments. Tired, but with the feelings of a virtuoso—one of the first violins who has played his part in an orchestra with precision—he would return home to find that his wife and daughter had been out paying calls, or had a visitor, and that his son had been to school, had done his homework with his tutor, and was duly learning what is taught at High Schools. Everything was as it should be. After dinner, if they had no visitors, Ivan Ilych sometimes read a book that was being much discussed at the time, and in the evening settled down to work, that is, read official papers, compared the depositions of witnesses, and noted paragraphs of the Code applying to them. This was neither dull nor amusing. It was dull when he might have been playing bridge, but if no bridge was available it was at any rate better than doing nothing or sitting with his wife. Ivan Ilych's chief pleasure was giving little dinners to which he invited men and women of good social position, and just as his drawing-room resembled all other drawing-rooms so did his enjoyable little parties resemble all other such parties.

Once they even gave a dance. Ivan Ilych enjoyed it and everything went off well, except that it led to a violent quarrel with his wife about the cakes and sweets. Praskovya Fëdorovna had made her own plans, but Ivan Ilych insisted on getting everything from an expensive confectioner and ordered too many cakes, and the quarrel occurred because some of those cakes were left over and the confectioner's bill came to forty-five rubles. It was a great and disagreeable quarrel. Praskovya Fëdorovna called him "a fool and an imbecile," and he clutched at his head and made angry allusions to divorce.

But the dance itself had been enjoyable. The best people were there, and Ivan Ilych had danced with Princess Trufonova, a sister of the distinguished founder of the Society "Bear my Burden."

The pleasures connected with his work were pleasures of ambition; his social pleasures were those of vanity; but Ivan Ilych's greatest pleasure was playing bridge. He acknowledged that whatever disagreeable incident happened in his life, the pleasure that beamed like a ray of light above everything else was to sit down to bridge with good players, not noisy partners, and of course to four-handed bridge (with five players it was annoying to have to stand out, though one pretended not to mind), to play a clever and serious game (when the cards allowed it) and then to have supper and drink a glass of wine. After a game of bridge, especially if he had won a little (to win a large sum was unpleasant), Ivan Ilych went to bed in specially good humour.

So they lived. They formed a circle of acquaintances among the best people and were visited by people of importance and by young folk. In their views as to their acquaintances, husband, wife and daughter were entirely agreed, and tacitly and unanimously kept at arm's length and shook off the shabby friends and relations who, with much show of affection, gushed into the drawing-room with its Japanese plates on the walls. Soon these shabby friends ceased to obtrude themselves and only the best people remained in the Golovins' set.

Young men made up to Lisa, and Petrishchev, an examining magistrate and Dmitri Ivanovich Petrishchev's son and sole heir, began to be so attentive to her that Ivan Ilych had already spoken to Praskovya Fëdorovna about it, and considered whether they should not arrange a party for them, or get up some private theatricals.

So they lived, and all went well, without change, and life flowed pleasantly.

4

They were all in good health. It could not be called ill health if Ivan Ilych sometimes said that he had a queer taste in his mouth and felt some discomfort in his left side.

But this discomfort increased and, though not exactly painful, grew into a sense of pressure in his side accompanied by ill humour. And his irritability became worse and worse and began to mar the agreeable, easy, and correct life that had established itself in the Golovin family. Quarrels between husband and wife became more and more frequent, and soon the ease and amenity disappeared and even the decorum was barely maintained. Scenes again became frequent, and very few of those islets remained on which husband and wife could meet without an explosion. Praskovya Fëdorovna now had good reason to say that her husband's temper was trying. With characteristic exaggeration she said he had always had a dreadful temper, and that it had needed all her good nature to put up with it for twenty years. It was true that now the quarrels were started by him. His bursts of temper always came just before dinner, often just as he began to eat his soup. Sometimes he noticed that a plate or dish was chipped, or the food was not right, or his son put his elbow on the table, or his daughter's hair was not done as he liked it, and for all this he blamed Praskovya Fëdorovna. At first she retorted and said disagreeable things to him, but once or twice he fell into such a rage at the beginning of dinner that she realized it was due to some physical derangement brought on by taking food, and so she restrained herself and did not answer, but only hurried to get the dinner over. She regarded this self-restraint as highly praiseworthy. Having come to the conclusion that her husband had a dreadful temper and made her life miserable, she began to feel sorry for herself, and the more she pitied herself the more she hated her husband. She began to wish he would die; yet she did not want him to die because then his salary would cease. And this irritated her against him still more. She considered herself dreadfully unhappy just because not even his death could save her, and though she concealed her exasperation, that hidden exasperation of hers increased his irritation also.

After one scene in which Ivan Ilych had been particularly unfair and after which he had said in explanation that he certainly was irritable but that it was due to his not being well, she said that if he was ill it should be attended to, and insisted on his going to see a celebrated doctor.

He went. Everything took place as he had expected and as it always does. There was the usual waiting and the important air assumed by the doctor, with which he was so familiar (resembling that which he himself assumed in court), and the sounding and listening, and the questions which called for answers that were foregone conclusions and were evidently unnecessary, and the look of importance which implied that "if only you put yourself in our hands we will arrange everything—we know indubitably how it has to be done, always in the same way for everybody alike." It was all just as it was in the law courts. The doctor put on just the same air towards him as he himself put on towards an accused person.

The doctor said that so-and-so indicated that there was so-and-so inside the patient, but if the investigation of so-and-so did not confirm this, then he must assume that and that. If he assumed that and that, then . . . and so on. To Ivan Ilych only one question was important: was his case serious or not? But the doctor ignored that inappropriate question. From his point of view it was not the one under consideration, the real question was to decide between a floating kidney, chronic catarrh, or appendicitis. It was not a question of Ivan Ilych's life or death, but one between a floating kidney and appendicitis. And that question the doctor solved brilliantly, as it seemed to Ivan Ilych, in favour of the appendix, with the reservation that should an examination of the urine give fresh indications the matter would be reconsidered. All this was just what Ivan Ilych had himself brilliantly accomplished a thousand times in dealing with men on trial. The doctor summed up just as brilliantly, looking over his spectacles triumphantly and even gaily at the accused. From the doctor's summing up Ivan Ilych concluded that things were bad, but that for the doctor, and perhaps for everybody else, it was a matter of indifference, though for him it was bad. And this conclusion struck him painfully, arousing in him a great feeling of pity for himself and of bitterness towards the doctor's indifference to a matter of such importance.

He said nothing of this, but rose, placed the doctor's fee on the table, and remarked with a sigh: "We sick people probably often put inappropriate questions. But tell me, in general, is this complaint dangerous, or not? . . ."

The doctor looked at him sternly over his spectacles with one eye, as if to say: "Prisoner, if you will not keep to the questions put to you, I shall be obliged to have you removed from the court."

"I have already told you what I consider necessary and proper. The analysis may show something more." And the doctor bowed.

Ivan Ilych went out slowly, seated himself disconsolately in his sledge, and drove home. All the way home he was going over what the doctor had said, trying to translate those complicated, obscure, scientific phrases into plain language and find in them an answer to the question: "Is my condition bad? Is it very bad? Or is there as yet nothing much wrong?" And it seemed to him that the meaning of what the doctor had said was that it was very bad. Everything in the streets seemed depressing. The cabmen, the houses, the passers-by, and the shops, were dismal. His ache, this dull gnawing ache that never ceased for a moment, seemed to have acquired a new and more serious significance from the doctor's dubious remarks. Ivan Ilych now watched it with a new and oppressive feeling.

He reached home and began to tell his wife about it. She listened, but in the middle of his account his daughter came in with her hat on, ready to go out with her mother. She sat down reluctantly to listen to this tedious story, but could not stand it long, and her mother too did not hear him to the end.

"Well, I am very glad," she said. "Mind now to take your medicine regularly. Give me the prescription and I'll send Gerasim to the chemist's." And she went to get ready to go out.

While she was in the room Ivan Ilych had hardly taken time to breathe, but he sighed deeply when she left it.

"Well," he thought, "perhaps it isn't so bad after all."

He began taking his medicine and following the doctor's directions, which had been altered after the examination of the urine. But then it happened that there was a contradiction between the indications drawn from the examination of the urine and the symptoms that showed themselves. It turned out that what was happening differed from what the doctor had told him, and that he had either forgotten, or blundered, or hidden something from him. He could not, however, be blamed for that, and Ivan Ilych still obeyed his orders implicitly and at first derived some comfort from doing so.

From the time of his visit to the doctor, Ivan Ilych's chief occupation was the exact fulfilment of the doctor's instructions regarding hygiene and the taking of medicine, and the observation of his pain and his excretions. His chief interests came to be people's ailments and people's health. When sickness, deaths, or recoveries were mentioned in his presence, especially when the illness resembled his own, he listened with agitation which he tried to hide, asked questions, and applied what he heard to his own case.

The pain did not grow less, but Ivan Ilych made efforts to force himself to think that he was better. And he could do this so long as nothing agitated him. But as soon as he had any unpleasantness with his wife, or a lack of success in his official work, or held bad cards at bridge, he was at once acutely sensible of his disease. He had formerly borne such mischances, hoping soon to adjust what was wrong, to master it and attain success, or make a grand slam. But now every mischance upset him and plunged him into despair. He would say to himself: "There now, just as I was beginning to get better and the medicine had begun to take effect, comes this accursed misfortune, or unpleasantness . . ." And he was furious with the mishap, or with the people who were causing the unpleasantness and killing him, for he felt that this fury was killing him but could not restrain it. One would have thought that it should have been clear to him that this exasperation with circumstances and people aggravated his illness, and that he ought therefore to ignore unpleasant occurrences. But he drew the very opposite conclusion: he said that he needed peace, and he watched for everything that might disturb it and became irritable at the slightest infringement of it. His condition was rendered worse by the fact that he read medical books and consulted doctors. The progress of his disease was so gradual that he could deceive himself when comparing one day with another—the difference was so slight. But when he consulted the doctors it seemed to him that he was getting worse, and even very rapidly. Yet despite this he was continually consulting them.

That month he went to see another celebrity, who told him almost the same as the first had done but put his questions rather differently, and the interview with this celebrity only increased Ivan Ilych's doubts and fears. A friend of a friend of his, a very good doctor, diagnosed his illness again quite differently from the others, and though he predicted recovery, his questions and suppositions bewildered Ivan Ilych still more and increased his doubts. A homoeopathist diagnosed the disease in yet another way, and prescribed medicine which Ivan Ilych took secretly for a week. But after a week, not feeling any improvement and having lost confidence both in the former doctor's treatment and in this one's, he became still more despondent. One day a lady acquaintance mentioned a cure effected by a wonder-working icon. Ivan Ilych caught himself listening attentively and beginning to believe that it had occurred. This incident alarmed him. "Has my mind really weakened to such an extent?" he asked himself. "Nonsense! It's all rubbish. I mustn't give way to nervous fears but having chosen a doctor must keep strictly to his treatment. That is what I will do. Now it's all settled. I won't think about it, but will follow the treatment seriously till summer, and then we shall see. From now there must be no more of this wavering!" This was easy to say but impossible to carry out. The pain in his side oppressed him and seemed to grow worse and more incessant, while the taste in his mouth grew stranger and stranger. It seemed to him that his breath had a disgusting smell, and he was conscious of a loss of appetite and strength. There was no deceiving himself: something terrible, new, and more important than anything before in his life, was taking place within him of which he alone was aware. Those about him did not understand or would not understand it, but thought everything in the world was going on as usual. That tormented Ivan Ilych more than anything. He saw that his household, especially his wife and daughter who were in a perfect whirl of visiting, did not understand anything of it and were annoyed that he was so depressed and so exacting, as if he were to blame for it. Though they tried to disguise it he saw that he was an obstacle in their path, and that his wife had adopted a definite line in regard to his illness and kept to it regardless of anything he said or did. Her attitude was this: "You know," she would say to her friends, "Ivan Ilych can't do as other people do, and keep to the treatment prescribed for him. One day he'll take his drops and keep strictly to his diet and go to bed in good time, but the next day unless I watch him he'll suddenly forget his medicine, eat sturgeon—which is forbidden—and sit up playing cards till one o'clock in the morning."

"Oh, come, when was that?" Ivan Ilych would ask in vexation. "Only once at Peter Ivanovich's."

"And yesterday with Shebek."

"Well, even if I hadn't stayed up, this pain would have kept me awake."

"Be that as it may you'll never get well like that, but will always make us wretched."

Praskovya Fëdorovna's attitude to Ivan Ilych's illness, as she expressed it both to others and to him, was that it was his own fault and was another of the annoyances he caused her. Ivan Ilych felt that this opinion escaped her involuntarily—but that did not make it easier for him.

At the law courts too, Ivan Ilych noticed, or thought he noticed, a strange attitude towards himself. It sometimes seemed to him that people were watching him inquisitively as a man whose place might soon be vacant. Then again, his friends would suddenly begin to chaff him in a friendly way about his low spirits, as if the awful, horrible, and unheard-of thing that was going on within him, incessantly gnawing at him and irresistibly drawing him away, was a very agreeable subject for jests. Schwartz in particular irritated him by his jocularity, vivacity, and *savoir-faire,* which reminded him of what he himself had been ten years ago.

Friends came to make up a set and they sat down to cards. They dealt, bending the new cards to soften them, and he sorted the diamonds in his hand and found he had seven. His partner said "No trumps" and supported him with two diamonds. What more could be wished for? It ought to be jolly and lively. They would make a grand slam. But suddenly Ivan Ilych was conscious of that gnawing pain, that taste in his mouth, and it seemed ridiculous that in such circumstances he should be pleased to make a grand slam.

He looked at his partner, Mikhail Mikhaylovich, who rapped the table with his strong hand and instead of snatching up the tricks pushed the cards courteously and indulgently towards Ivan Ilych that he might have the pleasure of gathering them up without the trouble of stretching out his hand for them. "Does he think I am too weak to stretch out my arm?" thought Ivan Ilych, and forgetting what he was doing he over-trumped his partner, missing the grand slam by three tricks. And what was most awful of all was that he saw how upset Mikhail Mikhaylovich was about it but did not himself care. And it was dreadful to realize why he did not care.

They all saw that he was suffering, and said: "We can stop if you are tired. Take a rest." Lie down? No, he was not at all tired, and he finished the rubber. All were gloomy and silent. Ivan Ilych felt that he had diffused this gloom over them and could not dispel it. They had supper and went away, and Ivan Ilych was left alone with the consciousness that his life was poisoned and was poisoning the lives of others, and that this poison did not weaken but penetrated more and more deeply into his whole being.

With this consciousness, and with physical pain besides that terror, he must go to bed, often to lie awake the greater part of the night. Next morning he had to get up again, dress, go to the law courts, speak, and write; or if he did not go out, spend at home those twenty-four hours a day each of which was a torture. And he had to live thus all alone on the brink of an abyss, with no one who understood or pitied him.

5

So one month passed and then another. Just before the New Year his brother-in-law came to town and stayed at their house. Ivan Ilych was at the law courts and Praskovya Fëdorovna had gone shopping. When Ivan Ilych came home and entered his study he found his brother-in-law there—a healthy, florid man—unpacking his portmanteau himself. He raised his head on hearing Ivan Ilych's footsteps and looked up at him for a moment without a word. That stare told Ivan Ilych everything. His brother-in-law opened his mouth to utter an exclamation of surprise but checked himself, and that action confirmed it all.

"I have changed, eh?"

"Yes, there is a change."

And after that, try as he would to get his brother-in-law to return to the subject of his looks, the latter would say nothing about it. Praskovya Fëdorovna came home and her brother went out to her. Ivan Ilych locked the door and began to examine himself in the glass, first full face, then in profile. He took up a portrait of himself taken with his wife, and compared it with what he saw in the glass. The change in him was immense. Then he bared his arms to the elbow, looked at them, drew the sleeves down again, sat down on an ottoman, and grew blacker than night.

"No, no, this won't do!" he said to himself, and jumped up, went to the table, took up some law papers and began to read them, but could not continue. He unlocked the door and went into the reception-room. The door leading to the drawing-room was shut. He approached it on tiptoe and listened.

"No, you are exaggerating!" Praskovya Fëdorovna was saying.

"Exaggerating! Don't you see it? Why, he's a dead man! Look at his eyes—there's no light in them. But what is it that is wrong with him?"

"No one knows. Nikolaevich [that was another doctor] said something, but I don't know what. And Leshchetitsky [this was the celebrated specialist] said quite the contrary . . ."

Ivan Ilych walked away, went to his own room, lay down, and began musing: "The kidney, a floating kidney." He recalled all the doctors had told him of how it detached itself and swayed about. And by an effort of imagination he tried to catch that kidney and arrest it and support it. So little was needed for this, it seemed to him. "No, I'll go to see Peter Ivanovich again." [That was the friend whose friend was a doctor.] He rang, ordered the carriage, and got ready to go.

"Where are you going, Jean?" asked his wife, with a specially sad and exceptionally kind look.

This exceptionally kind look irritated him. He looked morosely at her.

"I must go to see Peter Ivanovich."

He went to see Peter Ivanovich, and together they went to see his friend, the doctor. He was in, and Ivan Ilych had a long talk with him.

Reviewing the anatomical and physiological details of what in the doctor's opinion was going on inside him, he understood it all.

There was something, a small thing, in the vermiform appendix. It might all come right. Only stimulate the energy of one organ and check the activity of another, then absorption would take place and everything would come right. He got home rather late for dinner, ate his dinner, conversed cheerfully, but could not for a long time bring himself to go back to work in his room. At last, however, he went to his study and did what was necessary, but the consciousness that he had put something aside—an important, intimate matter which he would revert to when his work was done—never left him. When he had finished his work he remembered that this intimate matter was the thought of his vermiform appendix. But he did not give himself up to it, and went to the drawing-room for tea. There were callers there, including the examining magistrate who was a desirable match for his daughter, and they were conversing, playing the piano, and singing. Ivan Ilych, as Praskovya Fëdorovna remarked, spent that evening more cheerfully than usual, but he never for a moment forgot that he had postponed the important matter of the appendix. At eleven o'clock he said good-night and went to his bedroom. Since his illness he had slept alone in a small room next to his study. He undressed and took up a novel by Zola, but instead of reading it fell into thought, and in his imagination that desired improvement in the vermiform appendix occurred. There was the absorption and evacuation and the re-establishment of normal activity. "Yes, that's it!" he said to himself. "One need only assist nature, that's all." He remembered his medicine, rose, took it, and lay down on his back watching for the beneficent action of the medicine and for it to lessen the pain. "I need only take it regularly and avoid all injurious influences. I am already feeling better, much better." He began touching his side: it was not painful to the touch. "There, I really don't feel it. It's much better already." He put out the light and turned on his side . . . "The appendix is getting better, absorption is occurring." Suddenly he felt the old, familiar, dull, gnawing pain, stubborn and serious. There was the same familiar loathsome taste in his mouth. His heart sank and he felt dazed. "My God! My God!" he muttered. "Again, again! and it will never cease." And suddenly the matter presented itself in a quite different aspect. "Vermiform appendix! Kidney!" he said to himself. "It's not a question of appendix or kidney, but of life and . . . death. Yes, life was there and now it is going, going and I cannot stop it. Yes. Why deceive myself? Isn't it obvious to everyone but me that I'm dying, and that it's only a question of weeks, days . . . it may happen this moment. There was light and now there is darkness. I was here and now I'm going there! Where?" A chill came over him, his breathing ceased, and he felt only the throbbing of his heart.

"When I am not, what will there be? There will be nothing. Then where shall I be when I am no more? Can this be dying? No, I don't want to!" He jumped up and tried to light the candle, felt for it with trembling hands, dropped candle and candlestick on the floor, and fell back on his pillow.

"What's the use? It makes no difference," he said to himself, staring with wide-open eyes into the darkness. "Death. Yes, death. And none of them know or wish to know it, and they have no pity for me. Now they are playing." (He heard through the door the distant sound of a song and its accompaniment.) "It's all the same to them, but they will die too! Fools! I first, and they later, but it will be the same for them. And now they are merry . . . the beasts!"

Anger choked him and he was agonizingly, unbearably, miserable. "It is impossible that all men have been doomed to suffer this awful horror!" He raised himself.

"Something must be wrong. I must calm myself—must think it all over from the beginning." And he again began thinking. "Yes, the beginning of my illness: I knocked my side, but I was quite well that day and the next. It hurt a little, then rather more. I saw the doctor, then followed despondency and anguish, more doctors, and I drew nearer to the abyss. My strength grew less and I kept coming nearer and nearer, and now I have wasted away and there is no light in my eyes. I think of the appendix—but this is death! I think of mending the appendix, and all the while here is death! Can it really be death?" Again terror seized him and he gasped for breath. He leant down and began feeling for the matches, pressing with his elbow on the stand beside the bed. It was in the way and hurt him, he grew furious with it, pressed on it still harder, and upset it. Breathless and in despair he fell on his back, expecting death to come immediately.

Meanwhile the visitors were leaving. Praskovya Fëdorovna was seeing them off. She heard something fall and came in.

"What has happened?"

"Nothing. I knocked it over accidentally."

She went out and returned with a candle. He lay there panting heavily, like a man who has run a thousand yards, and stared upwards at her with a fixed look.

"What is it, Jean?"

"No . . . o . . . thing. I upset it." ("Why speak of it? She won't understand," he thought.)

And in truth she did not understand. She picked up the stand, lit his candle, and hurried away to see another visitor off. When she came back he still lay on his back, looking upwards.

"What is it? Do you feel worse?"

"Yes."

She shook her head and sat down.

"Do you know, Jean, I think we must ask Leshchetitsky to come and see you here."

This meant calling in the famous specialist, regardless of expense. He smiled malignantly and said "No." She remained a little longer and then went up to him and kissed his forehead.

While she was kissing him he hated her from the bottom of his soul and with difficulty refrained from pushing her away.

"Good-night. Please God you'll sleep."

"Yes."

6

Ivan Ilych saw that he was dying, and he was in continual despair.

In the depth of his heart he knew he was dying, but not only was he not accustomed to the thought, he simply did not and could not grasp it.

The syllogism he had learnt from Kiezewetter's Logic: "Caius is a man, men are mortal, therefore Caius is mortal," had always seemed to him correct as applied to Caius, but certainly not as applied to himself. That Caius—man in the abstract—was mortal, was perfectly correct, but he was not Caius, not an abstract man, but a creature quite, quite separate from all others. He had been little Vanya, with a mamma and a papa, with Mitya and Volodya, with the toys, a coachman and a nurse, afterwards with Katenka and with all the joys, griefs, and delights of childhood, boyhood, and youth. What did

Caius know of the smell of that striped leather ball Vanya had been so fond of? Had Caius kissed his mother's hand like that, and did the silk of her dress rustle so for Caius? Had he rioted like that at school when the pastry was bad? Had Caius been in love like that? Could Caius preside at a session as he did? "Caius really was mortal, and it was right for him to die; but for me, little Vanya, Ivan Ilych, with all my thoughts and emotions, it's altogether a different matter. It cannot be that I ought to die. That would be too terrible."

Such was his feeling.

"If I had to die like Caius, I should have known it was so. An inner voice would have told me so, but there was nothing of the sort in me and I and all my friends felt that our case was quite different from that of Caius. And now here it is!" he said to himself. "It can't be. It's impossible! But here it is. How is this? How is one to understand it?"

He could not understand it, and tried to drive this false, incorrect, morbid thought away and to replace it by other proper and healthy thoughts. But that thought, and not the thought only but the reality itself, seemed to come and confront him.

And to replace that thought he called up a succession of others, hoping to find in them some support. He tried to get back into the former current of thoughts that had once screened the thought of death from him. But strange to say, all that had formerly shut off, hidden, and destroyed, his consciousness of death, no longer had that effect. Ivan Ilych now spent most of his time in attempting to re-establish that old current. He would say to himself: "I will take up my duties again—after all I used to live by them." And banishing all doubts he would go to the law courts, enter into conversation with his colleagues, and sit carelessly as was his wont, scanning the crowd with a thoughtful look and leaning both his emaciated arms on the arms of his oak chair; bending over as usual to a colleague and drawing his papers nearer he would interchange whispers with him, and then suddenly raising his eyes and sitting erect would pronounce certain words and open the proceedings. But suddenly in the midst of those proceedings the pain in his side, regardless of the stage the proceedings had reached, would begin its own gnawing work. Ivan Ilych would turn his attention to it and try to drive the thought of it away, but without success. *It* would come and stand before him and look at him, and he would be petrified and the light would die out of his eyes, and he would again begin asking himself whether *It* alone was true. And his colleagues and subordinates would see with surprise and distress that he, the brilliant and subtle judge, was becoming confused and making mistakes. He would shake himself, try to pull himself together, manage somehow to bring the sitting to a close, and return home with the sorrowful consciousness that his judicial labours could not as formerly hide from him what he wanted them to hide, and could not deliver him from *It*. And what was worst of all was that *It* drew his attention to itself not in order to make him take some action but only that he should look at *It,* look it straight in the face: look at it and without doing anything, suffer inexpressibly.

And to save himself from this condition Ivan Ilych looked for consolations—new screens—and new screens were found and for a while seemed to save him, but then they immediately fell to pieces or rather became transparent, as if *It* penetrated them and nothing could veil *It.*

In these latter days he would go into the drawing-room he had arranged—that drawing-room where he had fallen and for the sake of which (how bitterly ridiculous it seemed) he had sacrificed his life—for he knew that his illness originated with that knock. He would enter and see that something had scratched the polished table. He would look for the cause of this and find that it was the bronze ornamentation of an album, that had got bent. He would take up the expensive album which he had lovingly arranged, and feel vexed with his daughter and her friends for their untidiness—for the album was torn here and there and some of the photographs turned upside down. He would put it carefully in order and bend the ornamentation back into position. Then it would occur to him to place all those things in another corner of the room, near the plants. He would call the footman, but his daughter or wife would come to help him. They would not agree, and his wife would contradict him, and he would dispute and grow angry. But that was all right, for then he did not think about *It. It* was invisible.

But then, when he was moving something himself, his wife would say: "Let the servants do it. You will hurt yourself again." And suddenly *It* would flash through the screen and he would see it. It was just a flash, and he hoped it would disappear, but he would involuntarily pay attention to his side. "It sits there as before, gnawing just the same!" And he could no longer forget *It,* but could distinctly see it looking at him from behind the flowers. "What is it all for?"

"It really is so! I lost my life over the curtain as I might have done when storming a fort. Is that possible? How terrible and how stupid. It can't be true! It can't, but it is."

He would go to his study, lie down, and again be alone with *It:* face to face with *It.* And nothing could be done with *It* except to look at it and shudder.

7

How it happened it is impossible to say because it came about step by step, unnoticed, but in the third month of Ivan Ilych's illness, his wife, his daughter, his son, his acquaintances, the doctors, the servants, and above all he himself, were aware that the whole interest he had for other people was whether he would soon vacate his place, and at last release the living from the discomfort caused by his presence and be himself released from his sufferings.

He slept less and less. He was given opium and hypodermic injections of morphine, but this did not relieve him. The dull depression he experienced in a somnolent condition at first gave him a little relief, but only as something new, afterwards it became as distressing as the pain itself or even more so.

Special foods were prepared for him by the doctors' orders, but all those foods became increasingly distasteful and disgusting to him.

For his excretions also special arrangements had to be made, and this was a torment to him every time—a torment from the uncleanliness, the unseemliness, and the smell, and from knowing that another person had to take part in it.

But just through this most unpleasant matter, Ivan Ilych obtained comfort. Gerasim, the butler's young assistant, always came in to carry the things out. Gerasim was a clean, fresh peasant lad, grown stout on town food and always cheerful and bright. At first the sight of him, in his clean Russian peasant costume, engaged in that disgusting task embarrassed Ivan Ilych.

Once when he got up from the commode too weak to draw up his trousers, he dropped into a soft armchair and looked with horror at his bare, enfeebled thighs with the muscles so sharply marked on them.

Gerasim with a firm light tread, his heavy boots emitting a pleasant smell of tar and fresh winter air, came in wearing a clean Hessian apron, the sleeves of his print shirt tucked up over his strong bare young arms; and refraining from looking at his sick master out of consideration for his feelings, and restraining the joy of life that beamed from his face, he went up to the commode.

"Gerasim!" said Ivan Ilych in a weak voice.

Gerasim started, evidently afraid he might have committed some blunder, and with a rapid movement turned his fresh, kind, simple young face which just showed the first downy signs of a beard.

"Yes, sir?"

"That must be very unpleasant for you. You must forgive me. I am helpless."

"Oh, why, sir," and Gerasim's eyes beamed and he showed his glistening white teeth, "what's a little trouble? It's a case of illness with you, sir."

And his deft strong hands did their accustomed task, and he went out of the room stepping lightly. Five minutes later he as lightly returned.

Ivan Ilych was still sitting in the same position in the armchair.

"Gerasim," he said when the latter had replaced the freshly-washed utensil. "Please come here and help me." Gerasim went up to him. "Lift me up. It is hard for me to get up, and I have sent Dmitri away."

Gerasim went up to him, grasped his master with his strong arms deftly but gently, in the same way that he stepped—lifted him, supported him with one hand, and with the other drew up his trousers and would have set him down again, but Ivan Ilych asked to be led to the sofa. Gerasim, without an effort and without apparent pressure, led him, almost lifting him, to the sofa and placed him on it.

"Thank you. How easily and well you do it all!"

Gerasim smiled again and turned to leave the room. But Ivan Ilych felt his presence such a comfort that he did not want to let him go.

"One thing more, please move up that chair. No, the other one—under my feet. It is easier for me when my feet are raised."

Gerasim brought the chair, set it down gently in place, and raised Ivan Ilych's legs on to it. It seemed to Ivan Ilych that he felt better while Gerasim was holding up his legs.

"It's better when my legs are higher," he said. "Place that cushion under them."

Gerasim did so. He again lifted the legs and placed them, and again Ivan Ilych felt better while Gerasim held his legs. When he set them down Ivan Ilych fancied he felt worse.

"Gerasim," he said. "Are you busy now?"

"Not at all, sir," said Gerasim, who had learnt from the townfolk how to speak to gentlefolk.

"What have you still to do?"

"What have I to do? I've done everything except chopping the logs for tomorrow."

"Then hold my legs up a bit higher, can you?"

"Of course I can. Why not?" And Gerasim raised his master's legs higher and Ivan Ilych thought that in that position he did not feel any pain at all.

"And how about the logs?"

"Don't trouble about that, sir. There's plenty of time."

Ivan Ilych told Gerasim to sit down and hold his legs, and began to talk to him. And strange to say it seemed to him that he felt better while Gerasim held his legs up.

After that Ivan Ilych would sometimes call Gerasim and get him to hold his legs on his shoulders, and he liked talking to him. Gerasim did it all easily, willingly, simply, and with a good nature that touched Ivan Ilych. Health, strength, and vitality in other people were offensive to him, but Gerasim's strength and vitality did not mortify but soothed him.

What tormented Ivan Ilych most was the deception, the lie, which for some reason they all accepted, that he was not dying but was simply ill, and that he only need keep quiet and undergo a treatment and then something very good would result. He however knew that do what they would nothing would come of it, only still more agonizing suffering and death. This deception tortured him—their not wishing to admit what they all knew and what he knew, but wanting to lie to him concerning his terrible condition, and wishing and forcing him to participate in that lie. Those lies—lies enacted over him on the eve of his death and destined to degrade this awful, solemn act to the level of their visitings, their curtains, their sturgeon for dinner—were a terrible agony for Ivan Ilych. And strangely enough, many times when they were going through their antics over him he had been within a hairbreadth of calling out to them: "Stop lying! You know and I know that I am dying. Then at least stop lying about it!" But he had never had the spirit to do it. The awful, terrible act of his dying was, he could see, reduced by those about him to the level of a casual, unpleasant, and almost indecorous incident (as if someone entered a drawing-room diffusing an unpleasant odour) and this was done by that very decorum which he had served all his life long. He saw that no one felt for him, because no one even wished to grasp his position. Only Gerasim recognized it and pitied him. And so Ivan Ilych felt at ease only with him. He felt comforted when Gerasim supported his legs (sometimes all night long) and refused to go to bed, saying: "Don't you worry, Ivan Ilych. I'll get sleep enough later on," or when he suddenly became familiar and exclaimed: "If you weren't sick it would be another matter, but as it is, why should I grudge a little trouble?" Gerasim alone did not lie; everything showed that he alone understood the facts of the case and did not consider it necessary to disguise them, but simply felt sorry for his emaciated and enfeebled master. Once when Ivan Ilych was sending him away he even said straight out: "We shall all of us die, so why should I grudge a little trouble?"—expressing the fact that he did not think his work burdensome, because he was doing it for a dying man and hoped someone would do the same for him when his time came.

Apart from this lying, or because of it, what most tormented Ivan Ilych was that no one pitied him as he wished to be pitied. At certain moments after prolonged suffering he wished most of all (though he would have been ashamed to confess it) for someone to pity him as a sick child is pitied. He longed to be petted and comforted. He knew he was an important functionary, that he had a beard turning grey, and that therefore what he longed for was impossible, but still he longed for it. And in Gerasim's attitude towards him there was something akin to what he wished for, and so that attitude comforted him. Ivan Ilych wanted to weep, wanted to be petted and cried over, and then his colleague Shebek would come, and instead of weeping and being petted, Ivan Ilych would assume a serious, severe, and profound air, and by force of habit would express his opinion on a decision of the Court of Cassation and would stubbornly insist on that view. This falsity around him and within him did more than anything else to poison his last days.

8

It was morning. He knew it was morning because Gerasim had gone, and Peter the footman had come and put out the candles, drawn back one of the curtains, and begun quietly to tidy up. Whether it was morning or evening, Friday or Sunday, made no difference, it was all just the same: the gnawing, unmitigated, agonizing pain, never ceasing for an instant, the consciousness of life inexorably waning but not yet extinguished, the approach of that ever dreaded and hateful Death which was the only reality, and always the same falsity. What were days, weeks, hours, in such a case?

"Will you have some tea, sir?"

"He wants things to be regular, and wishes the gentlefolk to drink tea in the morning," thought Ivan Ilych, and only said "No."

"Wouldn't you like to move onto the sofa, sir?"

"He wants to tidy up the room, and I'm in the way. I am uncleanliness and disorder," he thought, and said only:

"No, leave me alone."

The man went on bustling about. Ivan Ilych stretched out his hand. Peter came up, ready to help.

"What is it, sir?"

"My watch."

Peter took the watch which was close at hand and gave it to his master.

"Half-past eight. Are they up?"

"No, sir, except Vladimir Ivanich" (the son) "who has gone to school. Praskovya Fëdorovna ordered me to wake her if you asked for her. Shall I do so?"

"No, there's no need to." "Perhaps I'd better have some tea," he thought, and added aloud: "Yes, bring me some tea."

Peter went to the door, but Ivan Ilych dreaded being left alone. "How can I keep him here? Oh yes, my medicine." "Peter, give me my medicine." "Why not? Perhaps it may still do me some good." He took a spoonful and swallowed it. "No, it won't help. It's all tomfoolery, all deception," he decided as soon as he became aware of the familiar, sickly, hopeless taste. "No, I can't believe in it any longer. But the pain, why this pain? If it would only cease just for a moment!" And he moaned. Peter turned towards him. "It's all right. Go and fetch me some tea."

Peter went out. Left alone Ivan Ilych groaned not so much with pain, terrible though that was, as from mental anguish. Always and for ever the same, always these endless days and nights. If only it would come quicker! If only *what* would come quicker? Death, darkness? . . . No, no! Anything rather than death!

When Peter returned with the tea on a tray, Ivan Ilych stared at him for a time in perplexity, not realizing who and what he was. Peter was disconcerted by that look and his embarrassment brought Ivan Ilych to himself.

"Oh, tea! All right, put it down. Only help me to wash and put on a clean shirt."

And Ivan Ilych began to wash. With pauses for rest, he washed his hands and then his face, cleaned his teeth, brushed his hair, and looked in the glass.

He was terrified by what he saw, especially by the limp way in which his hair clung to his pallid forehead.

While his shirt was being changed he knew that he would be still more frightened at the sight of his body, so he avoided looking at it. Finally he was ready. He drew on a dressing-gown, wrapped himself in a plaid, and sat down in the armchair to take his tea. For a moment he felt refreshed, but as soon as he began to drink the tea he was again aware of the same taste, and the pain also returned. He finished it with an effort, and then lay down stretching out his legs, and dismissed Peter.

Always the same. Now a spark of hope flashes up, then a sea of despair rages, and always pain; always pain, always despair, and always the same. When alone he had a dreadful and distressing desire to call someone, but he knew beforehand that with others present it would be still worse. "Another dose of morphine—to lose consciousness. I will tell him, the doctor, that he must think of something else. It's impossible, impossible, to go on like this."

An hour and another pass like that. But now there is a ring at the door bell. Perhaps it's the doctor? It is. He comes in fresh, hearty, plump, and cheerful, with that look on his face that seems to say: "There now, you're in a panic about something, but we'll arrange it all for you directly!" The doctor knows this expression is out of place here, but he has put it on once for all and can't take it off—like a man who has put on a frock-coat in the morning to pay a round of calls.

The doctor rubs his hands vigorously and reassuringly.

"Brr! How cold it is! There's such a sharp frost; just let me warm myself!" he says, as if it were only a matter of waiting till he was warm, and then he would put everything right.

"Well now, how are you?"

Ivan Ilych feels that the doctor would like to say: "Well, how are your affairs?" but that even he feels that this would not do, and says instead: "What sort of a night have you had?"

Ivan Ilych looks at him as much as to say: "Are you really never ashamed of lying?" But the doctor does not wish to understand this question, and Ivan Ilych says: "Just as terrible as ever. The pain never leaves me and never subsides. If only something . . ."

"Yes, you sick people are always like that . . . There, now I think I am warm enough. Even Praskovya Fëdorovna, who is so particular, could find no fault with my temperature. Well, now I can say good-morning," and the doctor presses his patient's hand.

Then, dropping his former playfulness, he begins with a most serious face to examine the patient, feeling his pulse and taking his temperature, and then begins the sounding and auscultation.

Ivan Ilych knows quite well and definitely that all this is nonsense and pure deception, but when the doctor, getting down on his knee, leans over him, putting the ear first higher than lower, and performs various gymnastic movements over him with a significant expression on his face, Ivan Ilych submits to it all as he used to submit to the speeches of the lawyers, though he knew very well that they were all lying and why they were lying.

The doctor, kneeling on the sofa, is still sounding him when Praskovya Fëdorovna's silk dress rustles at the door and she is heard scolding Peter for not having let her know of the doctor's arrival.

She comes in, kisses her husband, and at once proceeds to prove that she has been up a long time already, and only owing to a misunderstanding failed to be there when the doctor arrived.

Ivan Ilych looks at her, scans her all over, sets against her the whiteness and plumpness and cleanness of her hands and neck, the gloss of her hair, and the sparkle of her vivacious eyes. He hates her with his whole soul. And the thrill of hatred he feels for her makes him suffer from her touch.

Her attitude towards him and his disease is still the same. Just as the doctor had adopted a certain relation to his patient which he could not abandon, so had she formed one towards him—that he was not doing something he ought to do and was himself to blame, and that she reproached him lovingly for this—and she could not now change that attitude.

"You see he doesn't listen to me and doesn't take his medicine at the proper time. And above all he lies in a position that is no doubt bad for him—with his legs up."

She described how he made Gerasim hold his legs up.

The doctor smiled with a contemptuous affability that said: "What's to be done? These sick people do have foolish fancies of that kind, but we must forgive them."

When the examination was over the doctor looked at his watch, and then Praskovya Fëdorovna announced to Ivan Ilych that it was of course as he pleased, but she had sent today for a celebrated specialist who would examine him and have a consultation with Michael Danilovich (their regular doctor).

"Please don't raise any objections. I am doing this for my own sake," she said ironically, letting it be felt that she was doing it all for his sake and only said this to leave him no right to refuse. He remained silent, knitting his brows. He felt that he was so surrounded and involved in a mesh of falsity that it was hard to unravel anything.

Everything she did for him was entirely for her own sake, and she told him she was doing for herself what she actually was doing for herself, as if that was so incredible that he must understand the opposite.

At half-past eleven the celebrated specialist arrived. Again the sounding began and the significant conversations in his presence and in another room, about the kidneys and the appendix, and the questions and answers, with such an air of importance that again, instead of the real question of life and death which now alone confronted him, the question arose of the kidney and appendix which were not behaving as they ought to and would now be attacked by Michael Danilovich and the specialist and forced to mend their ways.

The celebrated specialist took leave of him with a serious though not hopeless look, and in reply to the timid question Ivan Ilych, with eyes glistening with fear and hope, put to him as to whether there was a chance of recovery, said that he could not vouch for it but there was a possibility. The look of hope with which Ivan Ilych watched the doctor out was so pathetic that Praskovya Fëdorovna, seeing it, even wept as she left the room to hand the doctor his fee.

The gleam of hope kindled by the doctor's encouragement did not last long. The same room, the same pictures, curtains, wall-paper, medicine bottles, were all there, and the same aching suffering body, and Ivan Ilych began to moan. They gave him a subcutaneous injection and he sank into oblivion.

It was twilight when he came to. They brought him his dinner and he swallowed some beef tea with difficulty, and then everything was the same again and night was coming on.

After dinner, at seven o'clock, Praskovya Fëdorovna came into the room in evening dress, her full bosom pushed up by her corset, and with traces of powder on her face. She had reminded him in the morning that they were going to the theatre. Sarah Bernhardt was visiting the town and they had a box, which he had insisted on their taking. Now he had forgotten about it and her toilet offended him, but he concealed his vexation when he remembered that he had himself insisted on their securing a box and going because it would be an instructive and aesthetic pleasure for the children.

Praskovya Fëdorovna came in, self-satisfied but yet with a rather guilty air. She sat down and asked how he was, but, as he saw, only for the sake of asking and not in order to learn about it, knowing that there was nothing to learn—and then went on to what she really wanted to say: that she would not on any account have gone but that the box had been taken and Helen and their daughter were going, as well as Petrishchev (the examining magistrate, their daughter's fiancé) and that it was out of the question to let them go alone; but that she would have much preferred to sit with him for a while; and he must be sure to follow the doctor's orders while she was away.

"Oh, and Fëdor Petrovich" (the fiancé) "would like to come in. May he? And Lisa?"

"All right."

Their daughter came in in full evening dress, her fresh young flesh exposed (making a show of that very flesh which in his own case caused so much suffering), strong, healthy, evidently in love, and impatient with illness, suffering, and death, because they interfered with her happiness.

Fëdor Petrovich came in too, in evening dress, his hair curled *à la Capoul,* a tight stiff collar round his long sinewy neck, an enormous white shirt-front and narrow black trousers tightly stretched over his strong thighs. He had one white glove tightly drawn on, and was holding his opera hat in his hand.

Following him the schoolboy crept in unnoticed, in a new uniform, poor little fellow, and wearing gloves. Terribly dark shadows showed under his eyes, the meaning of which Ivan Ilych knew well.

His son had always seemed pathetic to him, and now it was dreadful to see the boy's frightened look of pity. It seemed to Ivan Ilych that Vasya was the only one besides Gerasim who understood and pitied him.

They all sat down and again asked how he was. A silence followed. Lisa asked her mother about the opera-glasses, and there was an altercation between mother and daughter as to who had taken them and where they had been put. This occasioned some unpleasantness.

Fëdor Petrovich inquired of Ivan Ilych whether he had ever seen Sarah Bernhardt. Ivan Ilych did not at first catch the question, but then replied: "No, have you seen her before?"

"Yes, in *Adrienne Lecouvreur*."

Praskovya Fëdorovna mentioned some rôles in which Sarah Bernhardt was particularly good. Her daughter disagreed. Conversation sprang up as to the elegance and realism of her acting—the sort of conversation that is always repeated and is always the same.

In the midst of the conversation Fëdor Petrovich glanced at Ivan Ilych and became silent. Ivan Ilych was staring with glittering eyes straight before him, evidently indignant with them. This had to be rectified, but it was impossible to do so. The silence had to be broken, but for a time no one dared to break it and they all became afraid that the conventional deception would suddenly become obvious and the truth become plain to all. Lisa was the first to pluck up courage and break that silence, but by trying to hide what everybody was feeling, she betrayed it.

"Well, if we are going it's time to start," she said, looking at her watch, a present from her father, and with a faint and significant smile at Fëdor Petrovich relating to something known only to them. She got up with a rustle of her dress.

They all rose, said good-night, and went away.

When they had gone it seemed to Ivan Ilych that he felt better; the falsity had gone with them. But the pain remained—that same pain and that same fear that made everything monotonously alike, nothing harder and nothing easier. Everything was worse.

Again minute followed minute and hour followed hour. Everything remained the same and there was no cessation. And the inevitable end of it all became more and more terrible.

"Yes, send Gerasim here," he replied to a question Peter asked.

9

His wife returned late at night. She came in on tiptoe, but he heard her, opened his eyes, and made haste to close them again. She wished to send Gerasim away and to sit with him herself, but he opened his eyes and said: "No, go away."

"Are you in great pain?"

"Always the same."

"Take some opium."

He agreed and took some. She went away.

Till about three in the morning he was in a state of stupefied misery. It seemed to him that he and his pain were being thrust into a narrow, deep black sack, but though they were pushed further and further in they could not be pushed to the bottom. And this, terrible enough in itself, was accompanied by suffering. He struggled but yet cooperated. And suddenly he broke through, fell, and regained consciousness. Gerasim was sitting at the foot of the bed dozing quietly, while he himself lay with his emaciated stockinged legs resting on Gerasim's shoulders; the same shaded candle was there and the same unceasing pain.

"Go away, Gerasim," he whispered.

"It's all right, sir. I'll stay a while."

"No. Go away."

He removed his legs from Gerasim's shoulders, turned sideways onto his arm, and felt sorry for himself. He only waited till Gerasim had gone into the next room and then restrained himself no longer but wept like a child. He wept on account of his helplessness, his terrible loneliness, the cruelty of man, the cruelty of God, and the absence of God.

"Why hast Thou done all this? Why hast Thou brought me here? Why, why dost Thou torment me so terribly?"

He did not expect an answer and yet wept because there was no answer and could be none. The pain again grew more acute, but he did not stir and did not call. He said to himself: "Go on! Strike me! But what is it for? What have I done to Thee? What is it for?"

Then he grew quiet and not only ceased weeping but even held his breath and became all attention. It was as though he were listening not to an audible voice but to the voice of his soul, to the current of thoughts arising within him.

"What is it you want?" was the first clear conception capable of expression in words, that he heard.

"What do you want? What do you want?" he repeated to himself.

"What do I want? To live and not to suffer," he answered.

And again he listened with such concentrated attention that even his pain did not distract him.

"To live? How?" asked his inner voice.

"Why, to live as I used to—well and pleasantly."

"As you lived before, well and pleasantly?" the voice repeated.

And in imagination he began to recall the best moments of his pleasant life. But strange to say none of those best moments of his pleasant life now seemed at all what they had then seemed—none of them except the first recollections of childhood. There, in childhood, there had been something really pleasant with which it would be possible to live if it could return. But the child who had experienced that happiness existed no longer, it was like a reminiscence of somebody else.

As soon as the period began which had produced the present Ivan Ilych, all that had then seemed joys now melted before his sight and turned into something trivial and often nasty.

And the further he departed from childhood and the nearer he came to the present the more worthless and doubtful were the joys. This began with the School of Law. A little that was really good was still found there—there was light-heartedness, friendship, and hope. But in the upper classes there had already been fewer of such good moments. Then during the first years of his official career, when he was in the service of the Governor, some pleasant moments again occurred: they were the memories of love for a woman. Then all became confused and there was still less of what was good; later on again there was still less that was good, and the further he went the less there was. His marriage, a mere accident, then the disenchantment that followed it, his wife's bad breath and the sensuality and hypocrisy: then that deadly official life and those preoccupations about money, a year of it, and two, and ten, and twenty, and always the same thing. And the longer it lasted the more deadly it became. "It is as if I had been going downhill while I imagined I was going up. And that is really what it was. I was going up in public opinion, but to the same extent life was ebbing away from me. And now it is all done and there is only death."

"Then what does it mean? Why? It can't be that life is so senseless and horrible. But if it really has been so horrible and senseless, why must I die and die in agony? There is something wrong!"

"Maybe I did not live as I ought to have done," it suddenly occurred to him. "But how could that be, when I did everything properly?" he replied, and immediately dismissed from his mind this, the sole solution of all the riddles of life and death, as something quite impossible.

"Then what do you want now? To live? Live how? Live as you lived in the law courts when the usher proclaimed 'The judge is coming!' The judge is coming, the judge!" he repeated to himself. "Here he is, the judge. But I am not guilty!" he exclaimed angrily. "What is it for?" And he ceased crying, but turning his face to the wall continued to ponder on the same question: Why, and for what purpose, is there all this horror? But however much he pondered he found no answer. And whenever the thought occurred to him, as it often did, that it all resulted from his not having lived as he ought to have done, he at once recalled the correctness of his whole life and dismissed so strange an idea.

10

Another fortnight passed. Ivan Ilych now no longer left his sofa. He would not lie in bed but lay on the sofa, facing the wall nearly all the time. He suffered ever the same unceasing agonies and in his loneliness pondered always on the same insoluble question: "What is this? Can it be that it is Death?" And the inner voice answered: "Yes, it is Death."

"Why these sufferings?" And the voice answered, "For no reason—they just are so." Beyond and besides this there was nothing.

From the very beginning of his illness, ever since he had first been to see the doctor, Ivan Ilych's life had been divided between two contrary and alternating moods: now it was despair and the expectation of this uncomprehended and terrible death, and now hope and an intently interested observation of the functioning of his organs. Now before his eyes there was only a kidney or an intestine that temporarily evaded its duty, and now only that incomprehensible and dreadful death from which it was impossible to escape.

These two states of mind had alternated from the very beginning of his illness, but the further it progressed the more doubtful and fantastic became the conception of the kidney, and the more real the sense of impending death.

He had but to call to mind what he had been three months before and what he was now, to call to mind with what regularity he had been going downhill, for every possibility of hope to be shattered.

Latterly during that loneliness in which he found himself as he lay facing the back of the sofa, a loneliness in the midst of a populous town and surrounded by numerous acquaintances and relations but that yet could not have been more complete anywhere—either at the bottom of the sea or under the earth—during that terrible loneliness Ivan Ilych had lived only in memories of the past. Pictures of his past rose before him one after another. They always began with what was nearest in time and then went back to what was the most remote—to his childhood—and rested there. If he thought of the stewed prunes that had been offered him that day, his mind went back to the raw shrivelled French plums of his childhood, their peculiar flavour and the flow of saliva when he sucked their stones, and along with the memory of that taste came a whole series of memories of those days: his nurse, his brother, and their toys. "No, I mustn't think of that . . . It is too painful," Ivan Ilych said to himself, and brought himself back to the present—to the button on the back of the sofa and the creases in its morocco. "Morocco is expensive, but it does not wear well: there had been a quarrel about it. It was a different kind of quarrel and a different kind of morocco that time when we tore father's portfolio and were punished, and Mamma brought us some tarts . . ." And again his thoughts dwelt on his childhood, and again it was painful and he tried to banish them and fix his mind on something else.

Then again together with that chain of memories another series passed through his mind—of how his illness had progressed and grown worse. There also the further back he looked the more life there had been. There had been more of what was good in life and more of life itself. The two merged together. "Just as the pain went on getting worse and worse, so my life grew worse and worse," he thought. "There is one bright spot there at the back, at the beginning of life, and afterwards all becomes blacker and blacker and proceeds more and more rapidly—in inverse ratio to the square of the distance from death," thought Ivan Ilych. And the example of a stone falling downwards with increasing velocity entered his mind. Life, a series of increasing sufferings, flies further and further towards its end—the most terrible suffering. "I am flying . . ." He shuddered, shifted himself, and tried to resist, but was already aware that resistance was impossible, and again with eyes weary of gazing but unable to cease seeing what was before them, he stared at the back of the sofa and waited—awaiting that dreadful fall and shock and destruction.

"Resistance is impossible!" he said to himself. "If I could only understand what it is all for! But that too is impossible. An explanation would be possible if it could be said that I have not lived as I ought to. But it is impossible to say that," and he remembered all the legality, correctitude, and propriety of his life. "That at any rate can certainly not be admitted," he thought, and his lips smiled ironically as if someone could see that smile and be taken in by it. "There is no explanation! Agony, death . . . What for?"

11

Another two weeks went by in this way and during that fortnight an event occurred that Ivan Ilych and his wife had desired. Petrishchev formally proposed. It happened in the evening. The next day Praskovya Fëdorovna came into her husband's room considering how best to inform him of it, but that very night there had been a fresh change for the worse in his condition. She found him still lying on the sofa but in a different position. He lay on his back, groaning and staring fixedly in front of him.

She began to remind him of his medicines, but he turned his eyes towards her with such a look that she did not finish what she was saying; so great an animosity, to her in particular, did that look express.

"For Christ's sake let me die in peace!" he said.

She would have gone away, but just then their daughter came in and went up to say good morning. He looked at her as he had done at his wife, and in reply to her inquiry about his health said dryly that he would soon free them all of himself. They were both silent and after sitting with him for a while went away.

"Is it our fault?" Lisa said to her mother. "It's as if we were to blame! I am sorry for papa, but why should we be tortured?"

The doctor came at his usual time. Ivan Ilych answered "Yes" and "No," never taking his angry eyes from him, and at last said: "You know you can do nothing for me, so leave me alone."

"We can ease your sufferings."

"You can't even do that. Let me be."

The doctor went into the drawing-room and told Praskovya Fëdorovna that the case was very serious and that the only resource left was opium to allay her husband's sufferings, which must be terrible.

It was true, as the doctor said, that Ivan Ilych's physical sufferings were terrible, but worse than the physical sufferings were his mental sufferings, which were his chief torture.

His mental sufferings were due to the fact that that night, as he looked at Gerasim's sleepy, good-natured face with its prominent cheek-bones, the question suddenly occurred to him: "What if my whole life has really been wrong?"

It occurred to him that what had appeared perfectly impossible before, namely that he had not spent his life as he should have done, might after all be true. It occurred to him that his scarcely perceptible attempts to struggle against what was considered good by the most highly placed people, those scarcely noticeable impulses which he had immediately suppressed, might have been the real thing, and all the rest false. And his professional duties and the whole arrangement of his life and of his family, and all his social and official interests, might all have been false. He tried to defend all those things to himself and suddenly felt the weakness of what he was defending. There was nothing to defend.

"But if that is so," he said to himself, "and I am leaving this life with the consciousness that I have lost all that was given me and it is impossible to rectify it—what then?"

He lay on his back and began to pass his life in review in quite a new way. In the morning when he saw first his footman, then his wife, then his daughter, and then the doctor, their every word and movement confirmed to him the awful truth that had been revealed to him during the night. In them he saw himself—all that for which he had lived—and saw clearly that it was not real at all, but a terrible and huge deception which had hidden both life and death. This consciousness intensified his physical suffering tenfold. He groaned and tossed about, and pulled at his clothing which choked and stifled him. And he hated them on that account.

He was given a large dose of opium and became unconscious, but at noon his sufferings began again. He drove everybody away and tossed from side to side.

His wife came to him and said:

"Jean, my dear, do this for me. It can't do any harm and often helps. Healthy people often do it."

He opened his eyes wide.

"What? Take communion? Why? It's unnecessary! However . . ."

She began to cry.

"Yes, do, my dear. I'll send for our priest. He is such a nice man."

"All right. Very well," he muttered.

When the priest came and heard his confession, Ivan Ilych was softened and seemed to feel a relief from his doubts and consequently from his sufferings, and for a moment there came a ray of hope. He again began to think of the vermiform appendix and the possibility of correcting it. He received the sacrament with tears in his eyes.

When they laid him down again afterwards he felt a moment's ease, and the hope that he might live awoke in him again. He began to think of the operation that had been suggested to him. "To live! I want to live!" he said to himself.

His wife came to congratulate him after his communion, and when uttering the usual conventional words she added:

"You feel better, don't you?"

Without looking at her he said "Yes."

Her dress, her figure, the expression of her face, the tone of her voice, all revealed the same thing. "This is wrong, it is not as it should be. All you have lived for and still live for is falsehood and deception, hiding life and death from you." And as soon as he admitted that thought, his hatred and his agonizing physical suffering again sprang up, and with that suffering a consciousness of the unavoidable, approaching end. And to this was added a new sensation of grinding shooting pain and a feeling of suffocation.

The expression of his face when he uttered that "yes" was dreadful. Having uttered it, he looked her straight in the eyes, turned on his face with a rapidity extraordinary in his weak state and shouted:

"Go away! Go away and leave me alone!"

12

From that moment the screaming began that continued for three days, and was so terrible that one could not hear it through two closed doors without horror. At the moment he answered his wife he realized that he was lost, that there was no return, that the end had come, the very end, and his doubts were still unsolved and remained doubts.

"Oh! Oh! Oh!" he cried in various intonations. He had begun by screaming "I won't!" and continued screaming on the letter *O*.

For three whole days, during which time did not exist for him, he struggled in that black sack into which he was being thrust by an invisible, resistless force. He struggled as a man condemned to death struggles in the hands of the executioner, knowing that he cannot save himself. And every moment he felt that despite all his efforts he was drawing nearer and nearer to what terrified him. He felt that his agony was due to his being thrust into that black hole and still more to his not being able to get right into it. He was hindered from getting into it by his conviction that his life had been a good one. That very justification of his life held him fast and prevented his moving forward, and it caused him most torment of all.

Suddenly some force struck him in the chest and side, making it still harder to breathe, and he fell through the hole and there at the bottom was a light. What had happened to him was like the sensation one sometimes experiences in a railway carriage when one thinks one is going backwards while one is really going forwards and suddenly becomes aware of the real direction.

"Yes, it was all not the right thing," he said to himself, "but that's no matter. It can be done. But what *is* the right thing?" he asked himself, and suddenly grew quiet.

This occurred at the end of the third day, two hours before his death. Just then his schoolboy son had crept softly in and gone up to the bedside. The dying man was still screaming and waving his arms. His hand fell on the boy's head, and the boy caught it, pressed it to his lips, and began to cry.

At that very moment Ivan Ilych fell through and caught sight of the light, and it was revealed to him that though his life had not been what it should have been, this could still be rectified. He asked himself, "What *is* the right thing?" and grew still, listening. Then he felt that someone was kissing his hand. He opened his eyes, looked at his son, and felt sorry for him. His wife came up to him and he glanced at her. She was gazing at him open-mouthed, with undried tears on her nose and cheek and a despairing look on her face. He felt sorry for her too.

"Yes, I am making them wretched," he thought. "They are sorry, but it will be better for them when I die." He wished to say this but had not the strength to utter it. "Besides, why speak? I must act," he thought. With a look at his wife he indicated his son and said: "Take him away . . . sorry for him . . . sorry for you too . . ." He tried to add, "forgive me," but said "forgo" and waved his hand, knowing that He whose understanding mattered would understand.

And suddenly it grew clear to him that what had been oppressing him and would not leave him was dropping away at once from two sides, from ten sides, and from all sides. He was sorry for them, he must act so as not to hurt them and free himself from these sufferings. "How good and how simple!" he thought. "And the pain?" he asked himself. "What has become of it? Where are you, pain?"

He turned his attention to it.

"Yes, here it is. Well, what of it? Let the pain be."

"And death . . . where is it?"

He sought his former accustomed fear of death and did not find it. "Where is it? What death?" There was no fear because there was no death.

In place of death there was light.

"So that's what it is!" he suddenly exclaimed aloud. "What joy!"

To him all this happened in a single instant, and the meaning of that instant did not change. For those present his agony continued for another two hours. Something rattled in his throat, his emaciated body twitched, then the gasping and rattle became less and less frequent.

"It is finished!" said someone near him.

He heard these words and repeated them in his soul.

"Death is finished," he said to himself. "It is no more!"

He drew in a breath, stopped in the midst of a sigh, stretched out, and died.

POETRY

The Elements of Poetry

CHAPTER ONE

What Is Poetry?

Poetry is as universal as language and almost as ancient. The most primitive peoples have used it, and the most civilized have cultivated it. In all ages, and in all countries, poetry has been written—and eagerly read or listened to—by all kinds and conditions of people, by soldiers, statesmen, lawyers, farmers, doctors, scientists, clergymen, philosophers, kings, and queens. In all ages it has been especially the concern of the educated, the intelligent, and the sensitive, and it has appealed, in its simpler forms, to the uneducated and to children. Why? First, because it has given pleasure. People have read it or listened to it or recited it because they liked it, because it gave them enjoyment. But this is not the whole answer. Poetry in all ages has been regarded as important, not simply as one of several alternative forms of amusement, as one man might choose bowling, another chess, and another poetry. Rather, it has been regarded as something central to each man's existence, something having unique value to the fully realized life, something that he is better off for having and spiritually impoverished without. To understand the reasons for this, we need to have at least a provisional understanding of what poetry is—provisional, because man has always been more successful at appreciating poetry than at defining it.

Initially, poetry might be defined as a kind of language that says *more* and says it *more intensely* than does ordinary language. In order to understand this fully, we need to understand what it is that poetry "says." For language is employed on different occasions to say quite different kinds of things; in other words, language has different uses.

Perhaps the commonest use of language is to communicate *information.* We say that it is nine o'clock, that there is a good movie downtown, that George Washington was the first president of the United States, that bromine and iodine are members of the halogen group of chemical elements. This we might call the *practical* use of language; it helps us with the ordinary business of living.

But it is not primarily to communicate information that novels and short stories and plays and poems are written. These exist to bring us a sense and a perception of life, to widen and sharpen our contacts with existence. Their concern is with *experience.* We all have an inner need to live more deeply and fully and with greater awareness, to know the experience of others and to know better our own experience. The poet, from his own store of felt, observed, or imagined experiences, selects, combines, and reorganizes. He creates significant new experiences for the reader—significant because focused and formed—in which the reader can participate and that he may use to give him a greater awareness and understanding of his world. Literature, in other words, can be used as a gear for stepping up the intensity and increasing the range of our experience and as a glass for clarifying it. This is the *literary* use of language, for literature is not only an aid to living but a means of living.*

Suppose, for instance, that we are interested in eagles. If we want simply to acquire information about eagles, we may turn to an encyclopedia or a book of natural history. There we find that the family Falconidae, to which eagles belong, is characterized by imperforate nostrils, legs of medium length, a hooked bill, the hind toe inserted on a level with the three front ones, and the claws roundly curved and sharp; that land eagles are feathered to the toes and sea-fishing eagles halfway to the toes; that their length is about three feet, the extent of wing seven feet; that the nest is usually placed on some inaccessible cliff; that

* A third use of language is as an instrument of persuasion. This is the use we find in advertisements, propaganda bulletins, sermons, and political speeches. These three uses of language—the practical, the literary, and the hortatory—are not sharply divided. They may be thought of as three points of a triangle; most actual specimens of written language fall somewhere within the triangle. Most poetry conveys some information, and some poetry has a design on the reader. But language becomes *literature* when the desire to communicate experience predominates.

the eggs are spotted and do not exceed three; and perhaps that the eagle's "great power of vision, the vast height to which it soars in the sky, the wild grandeur of its abode, have . . . commended it to the poets of all nations."*

But unless we are interested in this information only for practical purposes, we are likely to feel a little disappointed, as though we had grasped the feathers of the eagle but not its soul. True, we have learned many facts about the eagle, but we have missed somehow its lonely majesty, its power, and the "wild grandeur" of its surroundings that would make the eagle something living rather than a mere museum specimen. For the living eagle we must turn to literature.

THE EAGLE

He clasps the crag with crooked hands;
Close to the sun in lonely lands,
Ringed with the azure world, he stands.

The wrinkled sea beneath him crawls;
He watches from his mountain walls,
And like a thunderbolt he falls.

Alfred, Lord Tennyson (1809–1892)

QUESTIONS

1. What is peculiarly effective about the expressions "crooked hands," "close to the sun," "ringed with the azure world," "wrinkled," "crawls," and "like a thunderbolt"?

2. Notice the formal pattern of the poem, particularly the contrast of "he stands" in the first stanza and "he falls" in the second. Is there any other contrast between the two stanzas?

If the preceding poem has been read well, the reader will feel that he has enjoyed a significant experience and understands eagles better, though in a different way, than he did from the encyclopedia article alone. For if the article *analyzes* man's experience with eagles, the poem in some sense *synthesizes* such an experience. Indeed, the two approaches to experience—the scientific and the literary—may be said to complement each other. And it may be contended that the kind of understanding one

* *Encyclopedia Americana,* IX, 473–74.

gets from the second is at least as valuable as the kind he gets from the first.

Literature, then, exists to communicate significant experience—significant because concentrated and organized. Its function is not to tell us *about* experience but to allow us imaginatively to *participate* in it. It is a means of allowing us, through the imagination, to live more fully, more deeply, more richly, and with greater awareness. It can do this in two ways: by *broadening* our experience—that is, by making us acquainted with a range of experience with which, in the ordinary course of events, we might have no contact—or by *deepening* our experience—that is, by making us feel more poignantly and more understandingly the everyday experiences all of us have.

Two false approaches often taken to poetry can be avoided if we keep this conception of literature firmly in mind. The first approach always looks for a lesson or a bit of moral instruction. The second expects to find poetry always beautiful. Let us consider a song from Shakespeare:

WINTER

When icicles hang by the wall,
    And Dick the shepherd blows his nail,
And Tom bears logs into the hall,
    And milk comes frozen home in pail,
When blood is nipped and ways be foul,
Then nightly sings the staring owl,
        "Tu-whit, tu-who!"
A merry note,
While greasy Joan doth keel° the pot.   skim

When all aloud the wind doth blow,
    And coughing drowns the parson's saw,
And birds sit brooding in the snow,
    And Marian's nose looks red and raw,
When roasted crabs° hiss in the bowl,   crab apples
Then nightly sings the staring owl,
        "Tu-whit, tu-who!"

A merry note,
While greasy Joan doth keel the pot.

William Shakespeare (1564–1616)

QUESTIONS

1. What are the meanings of *nail* (2) and *saw* (11)?
2. Is the owl's cry really a *merry* note? How are this adjective and the verb *sings* employed?
3. In what way does the owl's cry contrast with the other details of the poem?

In the poem "Winter" Shakespeare is attempting to communicate the quality of winter life around a sixteenth-century English country house. But instead of telling us flatly that winter in such surroundings is cold and in many respects unpleasant, though with some pleasant features too (the adjectives *cold, unpleasant,* and *pleasant* are not even used in the poem), he gives us a series of concrete homely details that suggest these qualities and enable us, imaginatively, to experience this winter life ourselves. The shepherd lad blows on his fingernails to warm his hands; the milk freezes in the pail between the cowshed and the kitchen; the roads are muddy; the folk listening to the parson have colds; the birds "sit brooding in the snow"; and the servant girl's nose is raw from cold. But pleasant things are in prospect. Logs are being brought in for a fire, hot cider or ale is being prepared, and the kitchen maid is making a hot soup or stew. In contrast to all these homely, familiar details of country life comes in the mournful, haunting, and eerie note of the owl.

Obviously the poem contains no moral. Readers who always look in poetry for some lesson, message, or noble truth about life are bound to be disappointed. Moral-hunters see poetry as a kind of sugar-coated pill—a wholesome truth or lesson made palatable by being put into pretty words. What they are really after is a sermon—not a poem, but something inspirational. Yet "Winter," which has appealed to readers now for nearly four centuries, is not inspirational and contains no moral preachment.

Neither is the poem "Winter" beautiful. Though it is appealing in its way and contains elements of beauty, there is little that is really beautiful in red raw noses, coughing in chapel, nipped blood, foul roads, and greasy kitchen maids. Yet some readers think that poetry deals exclusively with beauty—with sunsets, flowers, butterflies, love, God—and that the one appropriate response to any poem is, after a moment of awed silence, "Isn't that beautiful!" For such readers poetry is a precious affair, the enjoyment only of delicate souls, removed from the heat and sweat of ordinary life. But theirs is too narrow an approach to poetry. The function of poetry is sometimes to be ugly rather than beautiful. And poetry may deal with common colds and greasy kitchen maids as legitimately as with sunsets and flowers. Consider another example:

DULCE ET DECORUM EST

Bent double, like old beggars under sacks,
Knock-kneed, coughing like hags, we cursed through sludge,
Till on the haunting flares we turned our backs,
And towards our distant rest began to trudge.
Men marched asleep. Many had lost their boots,
But limped on, blood-shod. All went lame, all blind;
Drunk with fatigue; deaf even to the hoots
Of gas-shells dropping softly behind.

Gas! GAS! Quick, boys!—An ecstasy of fumbling,
Fitting the clumsy helmets just in time,
But someone still was yelling out and stumbling
And flound'ring like a man in fire or lime.—
Dim through the misty panes and thick green light,
As under a green sea, I saw him drowning.

In all my dreams before my helpless sight
He plunges at me, guttering, choking, drowning.

If in some smothering dreams, you too could pace
Behind the wagon that we flung him in,
And watch the white eyes writhing in his face,
His hanging face, like a devil's sick of sin,
If you could hear, at every jolt, the blood
Come gargling from the froth-corrupted lungs
Bitter as the cud
Of vile, incurable sores on innocent tongues,—
My friend, you would not tell with such high zest
To children ardent for some desperate glory,
The old lie: *Dulce et decorum est*
Pro patria mori.

Wilfred Owen (1893–1918)

QUESTIONS

1. The Latin quotation, from the Roman poet Horace, means "It is sweet and becoming to die for one's country." (Wilfred Owen died fighting for England in World War I, a week before the armistice.) What is the poem's comment on this statement?

2. List the elements of the poem that to you seem not beautiful and therefore unpoetic. Are there any elements of beauty in the poem?

3. How do the comparisons in lines 1, 14, 20, and 23–24 contribute to the effectiveness of the poem?

Poetry takes all life as its province. Its primary concern is not with beauty, not with philosophical truth, not with persuasion, but with experience. Beauty and philosophical truth are aspects of experience, and the poet is often engaged with them. But poetry as a whole is concerned with all kinds of experience—beautiful or ugly, strange or common, noble or ignoble, actual or imaginary. One of the paradoxes of human existence is that all experience—even painful experience—when transmitted through the medium of art is, for the good reader, enjoyable. In real life, death and pain and suffering are not pleasurable, but in poetry they may be. In real life, getting soaked in a rainstorm is not pleasurable, but in poetry it can be. In actual life, if we cry, usually we are unhappy; but if we cry in a movie, we are manifestly enjoying it. We do not ordinarily like to be terrified in real life, but we sometimes seek movies or books that will terrify us. We find some value in all intense living. To be intensely alive is the opposite of being dead. To be dull, to be bored, to be imperceptive is in one sense to be dead. Poetry comes to us bringing life and therefore pleasure. Moreover, art focuses and so organizes experience as to give us a better understanding of it. And to understand life is partly to be master of it.

Between poetry and other forms of imaginative literature there is no sharp distinction. You may have been taught to believe that poetry can be recognized by the arrangement of its lines on the page or by its use of rime and meter. Such superficial tests are almost worthless. The Book of Job in the Bible and Melville's *Moby Dick* are highly poetical, but the familiar verse that begins: "Thirty days hath September, / April, June, and November . . ." is not. The difference between poetry and other literature is one only of degree. Poetry is the most condensed and concentrated form of literature, saying most in the fewest number of words.

It is language whose individual lines, either because of their own brilliance or because they focus so powerfully what has gone before, have a higher voltage than most language has. It is language that grows frequently incandescent, giving off both light and heat.

Ultimately, therefore, poetry can be recognized only by the response made to it by a good reader. But there is a catch here. We are not all good readers. If we were, there would be no purpose for this book. And if you are a poor reader, much of what has been said about poetry so far must have seemed nonsensical. "How," you may ask, "can poetry be described as moving or exciting, when I have found it dull and boring? Poetry is just a fancy way of writing something that could be said more simply." So might a color-blind man deny that there is such a thing as color.

The act of communication involved in reading poetry is like the act of communication involved in receiving a message by radio. Two factors are involved: a transmitting station and a receiving set. The completeness of the communication depends on both the power and clarity of the transmitter and the sensitivity and tuning of the receiver. When a person reads a poem and no experience is transmitted, either the poem is not a good poem or the reader is a poor reader or not properly tuned. With new poetry, we cannot always be sure which is at fault. With older poetry, if it has acquired critical acceptance—has been enjoyed by generations of good readers—we may assume that the receiving set is at fault. Fortunately, the fault is not irremediable. Though we cannot all become expert readers, we can become good enough to find both pleasure and value in much good poetry, or we can increase the amount of pleasure we already find in poetry and the number of kinds of poetry we find it in. To help you increase your sensitivity and range as a receiving set is the purpose of this book.

Poetry, finally, is a kind of multidimensional language. Ordinary language—the kind that we use to communicate information—is one-dimensional. It is directed at only part of the listener, his understanding. Its one dimension is intellectual. Poetry, which is language used to communicate experience, has at least four dimensions. If it is to communicate experience, it must be directed at the *whole* man, not just at his understanding. It must involve not only his intelligence but also his senses, emotions, and imagination. Poetry, to the intellectual dimension, adds a sensuous dimension, an emotional dimension, and an imaginative dimension.

Poetry achieves its extra dimensions—its greater pressure per word and its greater tension per poem—by drawing more fully and more consistently than does ordinary language on a number of language resources, none of which is peculiar to poetry. These various resources form the subjects of a number of the following chapters. Among them are connotation, imagery, metaphor, symbol, paradox, irony, allusion, sound repetition, rhythm, and pattern. Using these resources and the materials of life, the poet shapes and makes his poem. Successful poetry is never effusive language. If it is to come alive it must be as cunningly put together and as efficiently organized as a tree. It must be an organism whose every part serves a useful purpose and cooperates with every other part to preserve and express the life that is within it.

SPRING

When daisies pied and violets blue,
    And lady-smocks all silver-white,
And cuckoo-buds of yellow hue
    Do paint the meadows with delight,
The cuckoo then, on every tree,
Mocks married men; for thus sings he,
                    "Cuckoo!
Cuckoo, cuckoo!" O word of fear,
Unpleasing to a married ear!

When shepherds pipe on oaten straws,
    And merry larks are ploughmen's clocks,
When turtles tread, and rooks, and daws,
    And maidens bleach their summer smocks,
The cuckoo then, on every tree,
Mocks married men; for thus sings he,
                    "Cuckoo!
Cuckoo, cuckoo!" O word of fear,
Unpleasing to a married ear!

William Shakespeare (1564–1616)

QUESTIONS

1. Vocabulary: *pied* (1), *lady-smocks* (2), *oaten straws* (10), *turtles* (12), *tread* (12), *daws* (12).

2. This song is a companion piece to "Winter." In what respects are the two poems similar? How do they contrast? What details show that this poem, like "Winter," was written by a realist, not simply by a man carried away with the beauty of spring?

3. The word *cuckoo* is "unpleasing to a married ear" because it sounds like *cuckold*. Cuckolds were a frequent butt of humor in earlier English literature. If you do not know the meaning of the word, look it up.

4. Is the tone of this poem solemn or light and semihumorous?

THE TWA CORBIES

As I was walking all alane,° — alone
I heard twa corbies° making a mane;° — two ravens; moan
The tane° unto the tither did say, — one
"Where sall we gang° and dine the day?" — shall we go

"In behint yon auld fail dyke,° — old turf wall
I wot° there lies a new-slain knight; — know
And naebody kens° that he lies there, — knows
But his hawk, his hound, and his lady fair.

"His hound is to the hunting gane,
His hawk to fetch the wild-fowl hame,
His lady's ta'en anither mate,
So we may mak our dinner sweet.

"Ye'll sit on his white hause-bane,° — neck-bone
And I'll pike° out his bony blue een;° — pick; eyes
Wi' ae° lock o' his gowden° hair — With one; golden
We'll theek° our nest when it grows bare. — thatch

"Mony a one for him maks mane,° — moan
But nane sall ken whar he is gane;
O'er his white banes, when they are bare,
The wind sall blaw for evermair."

Anonymous

QUESTIONS

1. Here is an implied story of false love, murder, and disloyalty. What

purpose is served by having the story told from the point of view of the "twa corbies"? How do they emphasize the atmosphere of the poem?

2. Although we do not know exactly what happened to the knight, much is suggested. What is implied by the fact that "mony a one for him maks mane" but no one knows what has become of him except his hawk, his hound, and his lady? What is implied by the fact that he is "new-slain" but his lady has already taken another mate? Does the poem lose or gain in effect by not being entirely clear?

3. The language of the old English and Scottish folk ballads, of which this is one, presents a considerable initial obstacle, but if you accept it you will probably find that it contributes a unique flavor. An English critic has written of this poem: "Modernize the spelling [of the last stanza], and you have destroyed . . . the key of the poem: the thin high music of the lament, the endlessly subtle variations on the *a* sound, the strange feeling that all things have been unified with the shrillness of the wind through the heather."* Does this seem to you a valid comment?

4. How would you describe the experience created by the poem?

THE GRIESLY WIFE

"Lie still, my newly married wife,
    Lie easy as you can.
You're young and ill accustomed yet
    To sleeping with a man."

The snow lay thick, the moon was full
    And shone across the floor.
The young wife went with never a word
    Barefooted to the door.

He up and followed sure and fast,
    The moon shone clear and white.
But before his coat was on his back
    His wife was out of sight.

He trod the trail wherever it turned
    By many a mound and scree,° — stony slope
And still the barefoot track led on,
    And an angry man was he.

He followed fast, he followed slow,
    And still he called her name,

* T. R. Henn, *The Apple and the Spectroscope* (London: Methuen, 1951), p. 11.

But only the dingoes° of the hills   wild dogs
Yowled back at him again.

His hair stood up along his neck,
His angry mind was gone,
For the track of the two bare feet gave out
And a four-foot track went on.

Her nightgown lay upon the snow
As it might upon the sheet,
But the track that led from where it lay
Was never of human feet.

His heart turned over in his chest,
He looked from side to side,
And he thought more of his gumwood fire
Than he did of his griesly° bride.   uncanny

And first he started walking back
And then began to run,
And his quarry wheeled at the end of her track
And hunted him in turn.

Oh, long the fire may burn for him
And open stand the door,
And long the bed may wait empty:
He'll not be back any more.

John Manifold (b. 1915)

QUESTION

This modern imitation of an old ballad is by an Australian poet, as the references to "dingoes" (19) and "gumwood" (31) indicate. What kind of animal did "the griesly wife" turn into? Why does the poet not tell us?

"MORE LIGHT! MORE LIGHT!"

Composed in the Tower before his execution
These moving verses, and being brought at that time
Painfully to the stake, submitted, declaring thus:
"I implore my God to witness that I have made no crime."

Nor was he forsaken of courage, but the death was horrible,
The sack of gunpowder failing to ignite.

His legs were blistered sticks on which the black sap
Bubbled and burst as he howled for the Kindly Light.

And that was but one, and by no means one of the worst;
Permitted at least his pitiful dignity;
And such as were by made prayers in the name of Christ,
That shall judge all men, for his soul's tranquility.

We move now to outside a German wood.
Three men are there commanded to dig a hole
In which the two Jews are ordered to lie down
And be buried alive by the third, who is a Pole.

Not light from the shrine at Weimar beyond the hill
Nor light from heaven appeared. But he did refuse.
A Lüger settled back deeply in its glove.
He was ordered to change places with the Jews.

Much casual death had drained away their souls.
The thick dirt mounted toward the quivering chin.
When only the head was exposed the order came
To dig him out again and to get back in.

No light, no light in the blue Polish eye.
When he finished a riding boot packed down the earth.
The Lüger hovered lightly in its glove.
He was shot in the belly and in three hours bled to death.

No prayers or incense rose up in those hours
Which grew to be years, and every day came mute
Ghosts from the ovens, sifting through crisp air,
And settled upon his eyes in a black soot.

Anthony Hecht (b. 1923)

QUESTIONS

1. *The Tower of London* (1) was, for centuries, a place of imprisonment and execution for high-ranking offenders against the English Crown. The account in stanzas 1–3 is composite, though based largely on the death of Bishop Nicholas Ridley, burned at Oxford in 1553. Why does Hecht not tell us whose execution it is? Why does he not use even a pronoun at the beginning of the poem?

2. Stanzas 4–8 give an accurate account of an incident that occurred at Buchenwald in 1944. In what respects do these deaths compare with that

described in stanzas 1–3? In what important respects do they differ? What are the "ovens" (31)? Comment on the effectiveness of the metaphor "mute /ghosts" (30–31).

3. "Lead, Kindly Light" (8) are the opening words of a famous hymn ("The Pillar of Cloud") by Cardinal Newman (1801–1890). "More light! More light!" were the last words uttered by Goethe (1749–1832), the German poet and scientist, before his death. Perhaps Germany's greatest literary genius, he died at Weimar (17) where, for most of his adult life, he had been the center of a brilliant intellectual circle. Trace all references to light or lack of light in the poem. In what different ways is the word used? What different meanings does it suggest?

4. Why does Hecht write in this poem about two separate incidents instead of just one? What thematic statement does the poem suggest?

TERENCE, THIS IS STUPID STUFF

"Terence, this is stupid stuff:
You eat your victuals fast enough;
There can't be much amiss, 'tis clear,
To see the rate you drink your beer.
But oh, good Lord, the verse you make,
It gives a chap the belly-ache.
The cow, the old cow, she is dead;
It sleeps well, the horned head:
We poor lads, 'tis our turn now
To hear such tunes as killed the cow.
Pretty friendship 'tis to rhyme
Your friends to death before their time
Moping melancholy mad:
Come, pipe a tune to dance to, lad."

Why, if 'tis dancing you would be,
There's brisker pipes than poetry.
Say, for what were hop-yards meant,
Or why was Burton built on Trent?
Oh many a peer of England brews
Livelier liquor than the Muse,
And malt does more than Milton can
To justify God's ways to man.
Ale, man, ale's the stuff to drink
For fellows whom it hurts to think:
Look into the pewter pot

To see the world as the world's not.
And faith, 'tis pleasant till 'tis past:
The mischief is that 'twill not last.
Oh I have been to Ludlow fair
And left my necktie God knows where,
And carried half-way home, or near,
Pints and quarts of Ludlow beer:
Then the world seemed none so bad,
And I myself a sterling lad;
And down in lovely muck I've lain,
Happy till I woke again.
Then I saw the morning sky:
Heigho, the tale was all a lie;
The world, it was the old world yet,
I was I, my things were wet,
And nothing now remained to do
But begin the game anew.

Therefore, since the world has still
Much good, but much less good than ill,
And while the sun and moon endure
Luck's a chance, but trouble's sure,
I'd face it as a wise man would,
And train for ill and not for good.
'Tis true, the stuff I bring for sale
Is not so brisk a brew as ale:
Out of a stem that scored the hand
I wrung it in a weary land.
But take it: if the smack is sour,
The better for the embittered hour;
It should do good to heart and head
When your soul is in my soul's stead;
And I will friend you, if I may,
In the dark and cloudy day.

There was a king reigned in the East:
There, when kings will sit to feast,
They get their fill before they think
With poisoned meat and poisoned drink.
He gathered all that springs to birth
From the many-venomed earth;

First a little, thence to more,
He sampled all her killing store;
And easy, smiling, seasoned sound,
Sate the king when healths went round.
They put arsenic in his meat
And stared aghast to watch him eat;
They poured strychnine in his cup
And shook to see him drink it up:
They shook, they stared as white's their shirt:
Them it was their poison hurt.
—I tell the tale that I heard told.
Mithridates, he died old.

A. E. Housman (1859–1936)

QUESTIONS

1. *Terence* (1) is Housman's poetic name for himself. Housman's poetry is largely pessimistic or sad; and this poem, placed near the end of his volume *A Shropshire Lad,* is his defense of the kind of poetry he wrote. Who is the speaker in the first fourteen lines? Who is the speaker in the rest of the poem? What is "the stuff I bring for sale" (49)?

2. *Hops* (17) and *malt* (21) are principal ingredients of beer and ale. *Burton-upon-Trent* (18) is an English city famous for its breweries. *Milton* (21), in the invocation of his epic poem *Paradise Lost,* declares that his purpose is to "justify the ways of God to men." What, in Housman's eyes, is the efficacy of liquor in helping one live a difficult life?

3. What six lines of the poem most explicitly sum up the poet's philosophy? Most people like reading material that is cheerful and optimistic (on the argument that "there's enough suffering and unhappiness in the world already"). What for Housman is the value of pessimistic and tragic literature?

4. *Mithridates* (76) was a king of Pontus and a contemporary of Julius Caesar; his "tale" is told in Pliny's *Natural History*. What is the connection of this last verse paragraph with the rest of the poem?

Reading the Poem

The primary purpose of this book is to develop your ability to understand and appreciate poetry. Here are some preliminary suggestions:

1. Read a poem more than once. A good poem will no more yield its full meaning on a single reading than will a Beethoven symphony on a single hearing. Two readings may be necessary simply to let you get your bearings. And if the poem is a work of art, it will repay repeated and prolonged examination. One does not listen to a good piece of music once and forget it; one does not look at a good painting once and throw it away. A poem is not like a newspaper, to be hastily read and cast into the wastebasket. It is to be hung on the wall of one's mind.

2. Keep a dictionary by you and use it. It is futile to try to understand poetry without troubling to learn the meanings of the words of which it is composed. One might as well attempt to play tennis without a ball. One of your primary purposes while in college should be to build a good vocabulary, and the study of poetry gives you an excellent opportunity. A few other reference books will also be invaluable. Particularly desirable are a good book on mythology (your instructor can recommend one) and a Bible.

3. Read so as to hear the sounds of the words in your mind. Poetry is written to be heard: its meanings are conveyed through sound as well as through print. Every word is therefore important. The best way to read a poem is just the opposite of the best way to read a newspaper. One reads a newspaper as rapidly as he can; one should read a poem as slowly

as he can. When you cannot read a poem aloud, lip-read it: form the words with your tongue and mouth though you do not utter them. With ordinary reading material, lip reading is a bad habit; with poetry it is a good habit.

4. Always pay careful attention to what the poem is saying. Though one should be conscious of the sounds of the poem, he should never be so exclusively conscious of them that he pays no attention to what the poem means. For some readers reading a poem is like getting on board a rhythmical roller coaster. The car starts, and off they go, up and down, paying no attention to the landscape flashing past them, arriving at the end of the poem breathless, with no idea of what it has been about.* This is the wrong way to read a poem. One should make the utmost effort to follow the thought continuously and to grasp the full implications and suggestions. Because a poem says so much, several readings may be necessary, but on the very first reading one should determine which noun goes with which verb.

5. Practice reading poems aloud. When you find one you especially like, make your roommate or a friend listen to it. Try to read it to him in such a way that he will like it too. (a) Read it affectionately, but not affectedly. The two extremes oral readers often fall into are equally deadly. One is to read as if one were reading a tax report or a railroad timetable, unexpressively, in a monotone. The other is to elocute, with artificial flourishes and vocal histrionics. It is not necessary to put emotion into reading a poem. The emotion is already there. It only wants a fair chance to get out. It will express *itself* if the poem is read naturally and sensitively. (b) Of the two extremes, reading too fast offers greater danger than reading too slow. Read slowly enough that each word is clear and distinct and that the meaning has time to sink in. Remember that your roommate does not have the advantage, as you do, of having the text before him. Your ordinary rate of reading will probably be too fast. (c) Read the poem so that the rhythmical pattern is felt but not exaggerated. Remember that poetry is written in sentences, just as prose is, and that punctuation is a signal as to how it should be read. Give all grammatical pauses their full due. Do not distort the natural pronunciation of words or a normal accentuation of the sentence to fit into what

* Some poems encourage this type of reading. When this is so, usually the poet has not made the best use of his rhythm to support his sense.

you have decided is its metrical pattern. One of the worst ways to read a poem is to read it ta-*dum* ta-*dum* ta-*dum* with an exaggerated emphasis on every other syllable. On the other hand, it should not be read as if it were prose. An important test of your reading will be how you handle the end of a line when there is no punctuation there. A frequent mistake of the beginning reader is to treat each line as if it were a complete thought, whether grammatically complete or not, and to drop his voice at the end of it. A frequent mistake of the sophisticated reader is to take a running start upon approaching the end of a line and fly over it as if it were not there. The line is a rhythmical unit, and its end should be observed whether there is punctuation or not. If there is no punctuation, one observes it ordinarily by the slightest of pauses or by holding onto the last word in the line just a little longer than usual. One should not drop his voice. In line 12 of the following poem, one should hold onto the word *although* longer than if it occurred elsewhere in the line. But one should not lower his voice on it: it is part of the clause that follows in the next stanza.

THE MAN HE KILLED

Had he and I but met
By some old ancient inn,
We should have sat us down to wet
Right many a nipperkin!° half-pint cup

But ranged as infantry,
And staring face to face,
I shot at him as he at me,
And killed him in his place.

I shot him dead because—
Because he was my foe,
Just so: my foe of course he was;
That's clear enough; although

He thought he'd 'list, perhaps,
Off-hand-like—just as I—
Was out of work—had sold his traps—
No other reason why.

Yes; quaint and curious war is!
You shoot a fellow down
You'd treat, if met where any bar is,
Or help to half-a-crown.

Thomas Hardy (1840–1928)

QUESTIONS

1. Vocabulary: *traps* (15).

2. In informational prose the repetition of a word like *because* (9–10) would be an error. What purpose does the repetition serve here? Why does the speaker repeat to himself his "clear" reason for killing a man (10–11)? The word *although* (12) gets more emphasis than it ordinarily would because it comes not only at the end of a line but at the end of a stanza. What purpose does this emphasis serve? Can the redundancy of "old ancient" (2) be poetically justified?

3. Someone has defined poetry as "the expression of elevated thought in elevated language." Comment on the adequacy of this definition in the light of Hardy's poem.

To aid us in the understanding of a poem, we may ask ourselves a number of questions about it. One of the most important is: *Who is the speaker and what is the occasion?* A cardinal error of beginning readers is to assume always that the speaker is the poet himself. A far safer course is to assume always that the speaker is someone other than the poet himself. For even when the poet does speak directly and express his own thoughts and emotions, he does so ordinarily as a representative human being rather than as an individual who lives at a particular address, dislikes dill pickles, and favors blue neckties. We must always be cautious about identifying anything in a poem with the biography of the poet. Like the novelist and the playwright, he is fully justified in changing actual details of his own experience to make the experience of the poem more universal. We may well think of every poem, therefore, as being to some degree *dramatic,* that is, the utterance of a fictional character rather than of the poet himself. Many poems are expressly dramatic.

In "The Man He Killed" the speaker is a soldier; the occasion is his having been in battle and killed a man—obviously for the first time in his life. We can tell a good deal about him. He is not a career soldier:

he enlisted only because he was out of work. He is a workingman: he speaks a simple and colloquial language (*nipperkin, 'list, off-hand-like, traps*), and he has sold the tools of his trade—he may have been a tinker or plumber. He is a friendly, kindly sort who enjoys a neighborly drink of ale in a bar and will gladly lend a friend a half crown when he has it. He has known what it is to be poor. In any other circumstances he would have been horrified at taking a human life. He has been given pause as it is. He is trying to figure it out. But he is not a deep thinker and thinks he has supplied a reason when he has only supplied a name: "I killed the man . . . because he was my foe." The critical question, of course, is *Why was the man his "foe"?* Even the speaker is left unsatisfied by his answer, though he is not analytical enough to know what is wrong with it. Obviously this poem is expressly dramatic. We need know nothing about Thomas Hardy's life (he was never a soldier and never killed a man) to realize that the poem is dramatic. The internal evidence of the poem tells us so.

A second important question that we should ask ourselves upon reading any poem is *What is the central purpose of the poem?** The purpose may be to tell a story, to reveal human character, to impart a vivid impression of a scene, to express a mood or an emotion, or to convey to us vividly some idea or attitude. Whatever the purpose is, we must determine it for ourselves and define it mentally as precisely as possible. Only then can we fully understand the function and meaning of the various details in the poem, by relating them to this central purpose. Only then can we begin to assess the value of the poem and determine whether it is a good one or a poor one. In "The Man He Killed" the central purpose is quite clear: it is to make us realize more keenly the irrationality of war. The puzzlement of the speaker may be our puzzlement. But even if we are able to give a more sophisticated answer than his as to why men kill each other, we ought still to have a greater awareness, after reading the poem, of the fundamental irrationality in war

* Our only reliable evidence of the poem's purpose, of course, is the poem itself. External evidence, when it exists, though often helpful, may also be misleading. Some critics have objected to the use of such terms as "purpose" and "intention" altogether; we cannot know, they maintain, what was *attempted* in the poem; we can know only what was *done*. Philosophically this position is impeccable. Yet it is possible to make inferences about what was attempted, and such inferences furnish a convenient and helpful way of talking about poetry.

that makes men kill who have no grudge against each other and who might under different circumstances show each other considerable kindness.

IS MY TEAM PLOUGHING

"Is my team ploughing,
That I was used to drive
And hear the harness jingle
When I was man alive?"

Aye, the horses trample,
The harness jingles now;
No change though you lie under
The land you used to plough.

"Is football playing
Along the river shore,
With lads to chase the leather,
Now I stand up no more?"

Aye, the ball is flying,
The lads play heart and soul;
The goal stands up, the keeper
Stands up to keep the goal.

"Is my girl happy,
That I thought hard to leave,
And has she tired of weeping
As she lies down at eve?"

Aye, she lies down lightly,
She lies not down to weep:
Your girl is well contented.
Be still, my lad, and sleep.

"Is my friend hearty,
Now I am thin and pine;
And has he found to sleep in
A better bed than mine?"

Yes, lad, I lie easy,
I lie as lads would choose;

I cheer a dead man's sweetheart,
Never ask me whose.

A. E. Housman (1859–1936)

QUESTIONS

1. What is meant by *whose* in line 32?
2. Is Housman cynical in his observation of human nature and human life?
3. The word *sleep* in the concluding stanzas suggests three different meanings. What are they? How many meanings are suggested by the word *bed*?

Once we have answered the question *What is the central purpose of the poem?* we can consider another question, equally important to full understanding: *By what means is that purpose achieved?* It is important to distinguish means from ends. A student on an examination once used the poem "Is My Team Ploughing" as evidence that A. E. Housman believed in immortality, because in it a man speaks from the grave. This is as naive as to say that Thomas Hardy in "The Man He Killed" joined the army because he was out of work. The purpose of Housman's poem is to communicate poignantly a certain truth about human life: life goes on after our deaths pretty much as it did before—our dying does not disturb the universe. This purpose is achieved by means of a fanciful dramatic framework in which a dead man converses with his still-living friend. The framework tells us nothing about whether Housman believed in immortality (as a matter of fact, he did not). It is simply an effective means by which we *can* learn how Housman felt a man's death affected the life he left behind. The question *By what means is the purpose of the poem achieved?* is partially answered by describing the poem's dramatic framework, if it has any. The complete answer requires an accounting of various resources of communication that it will take us the rest of this book to discuss.

The most important preliminary advice we can give for reading poetry is to maintain always, while reading it, the utmost mental alertness. The most harmful idea one can get about poetry is that its purpose is to soothe and relax and that the best place to read it is lying in a hammock with a cool drink beside one and low music in the background. One *can* read poetry lying in a hammock but only if he refuses to put his mind in the same attitude as his body. Its purpose is not to soothe and relax but to arouse and awake, to shock one into life, to make one more alive. Poetry is not a substitute for a sedative.

An analogy can be drawn between reading poetry and playing tennis. Both offer great enjoyment if the game is played hard. A good tennis player must be constantly on the tip of his toes, concentrating on his opponent's every move. He must be ready for a drive to the right or a drive to the left, a lob overhead or a drop shot barely over the net. He must be ready for top spin or underspin, a ball that bounces crazily to the left or crazily to the right. He must jump for the high ones and run for the far ones. He will enjoy the game almost exactly in proportion to the effort he puts into it. The same is true of poetry. Great enjoyment is there, but this enjoyment demands a mental effort equivalent to the physical effort one puts into tennis.

The reader of poetry has one advantage over the tennis player. The poet is not trying to win a match. He may expect the reader to stretch for his shots, but he *wants* the reader to return them.

EXERCISE

Most of the poems in this book are accompanied by study questions that are by no means exhaustive. Following is a list of questions that you may apply to any poem or that your instructor may wish to use, in whole or in part, to supplement the questions to any particular poem. You will not be able to answer many of them until you have read further into the book.

1. Who is the speaker? What kind of person is he?
2. To whom is he speaking? What kind of person is he?
3. What is the occasion?
4. What is the setting in time (time of day, season, century, etc.)?
5. What is the setting in place (indoors or out, city or country, nation, etc.)?
6. What is the central purpose of the poem?
7. State the central idea or theme of the poem in a sentence.
8. Discuss the tone of the poem. How is it achieved?
9. a. Outline the poem so as to show its structure and development, or
   b. Summarize the events of the poem.
10. Paraphrase the poem.
11. Discuss the diction of the poem. Point out words that are particularly well chosen and explain why.

12. Discuss the imagery of the poem. What kinds of imagery are used?
13. Point out examples of metaphor, simile, personification, and metonymy and explain their appropriateness.
14. Point out and explain any symbols. If the poem is allegorical, explain the allegory.
15. Point out and explain examples of paradox, overstatement, understatement, and irony. What is their function?
16. Point out and explain any allusions. What is their function?
17. Point out significant examples of sound repetition and explain their function.
18. a. What is the meter of the poem?
    b. Copy the poem and mark its scansion.
19. Discuss the adaptation of sound to sense.
20. Describe the form or pattern of the poem.
21. Criticize and evaluate the poem.

IT IS NOT GROWING LIKE A TREE

It is not growing like a tree
In bulk, doth make man better be;
Or standing long an oak, three hundred year,
To fall a log at last, dry, bald, and sere:
A lily of a day
Is fairer far in May
Although it fall and die that night;
It was the plant and flower of light.
In small proportions we just beauties see;
And in short measures, life may perfect be.

Ben Jonson (1573?–1637)

QUESTIONS

1. Your instructor may occasionally ask you, as a test of your understanding of a poem at its lowest level, or as a means of clearing up misunderstanding, to paraphrase its content. To PARAPHRASE a poem means to restate it in different language, so as to make its prose sense as plain as possible. The paraphrase may be longer or shorter than the poem, but it should contain as far as possible all the ideas in the poem in such a way as to make them clear to a puzzled reader. Figurative language should be reduced when pos-

sible to literal language; metaphors should be turned into similes. Though it is neither necessary nor possible to avoid using some words occurring in the original, you should in general use your own language.

The central idea of the above poem, which is actually one stanza from a longer poem, "To the Immortal Memory and Friendship of that Noble Pair, Sir Lucius Cary and Sir H. Morison," is approximately this: life is to be measured by its excellence, not by its length. The poem may be paraphrased as follows:

> A man does not become more excellent by simply growing in size, as a tree grows, nor by merely living for a very long time, as an oak does, only to die at length, old, bald, and wizened. A lily that lives only for one day in the spring is far more estimable than the long-lived tree, even though it dies at nightfall, for while it lives it is the essence and crown of beauty and excellence. Thus we may see perfect beauty in small things. Thus human life, too, may be most excellent though very brief.

2. A paraphrase is useful only if you understand that it is the barest, most inadequate approximation of what the poem really says and is no more equivalent to the poem than a corpse is equivalent to a man. Once having made a paraphrase, you should endeavor to see how far short of the poem it falls and why. In what respects does the above poem say more, and say it more memorably, than the paraphrase?

3. Does *bald* (4) apply only to the man or also to the log? May line 8 be interpreted in a way other than the way the paraphrase interprets it? What is the meaning of *just* (9)? Could *measures* (10) mean anything in addition to "amounts"? Comment on the effectiveness of the comparisons to tree and lily.

BEDTIME STORY

Long long ago when the world was a wild place
Planted with bushes and peopled by apes, our
Mission Brigade was at work in the jungle.
    Hard by the Congo

Once, when a foraging detail was active
Scouting for green-fly, it came on a grey man, the
Last living man, in the branch of a baobab
    Stalking a monkey.

Earlier men had disposed of, for pleasure,
Creatures whose names we scarcely remember—

Zebra, rhinoceros, elephants, wart-hog,
    Lion, rats, deer. But

After the wars had extinguished the cities
Only the wild ones were left, half-naked
Near the Equator: and here was the last one,
    Starved for a monkey.

By then the Mission Brigade had encountered
Hundreds of such men: and their procedure,
History tells us, was only to feed them:
    Find them and feed them;

Those were the orders. And this was the last one.
Nobody knew that he was, but he was. Mud
Caked on his flat grey flanks. He was crouched, half-
    Armed with a shaved spear

Glinting beneath broad leaves. When their jaws cut
Swathes through the bark and he saw fine teeth shine,
Round eyes roll round and forked arms waver
    Huge as the rough trunks

Over his head, he was frightened. Our workers
Marched through the Congo before he was born, but
This was the first time perhaps that he'd seen one.
    Staring in hot still

Silence, he crouched there: then jumped. With a long swing
Down from his branch, he had angled his spear too
Quickly, before they could hold him, and hurled it
    Hard at the soldier

Leading the detail. How could he know Queen's
Orders were only to help him? The soldier
Winced when the tipped spear pricked him. Unsheathing his
    Sting was a reflex.

Later the Queen was informed. There were no more
Men. An impetuous soldier had killed off,
Purely by chance, the penultimate primate.
    When she was certain,

Squadrons of workers were fanned through the Congo
Detailed to bring back the man's picked bones to be

Sealed in the archives in amber. I'm quite sure
    Nobody found them

After the most industrious search, though.
Where had the bones gone? Over the earth, dear,
Ground by the teeth of the termites, blown by the
    Wind, like the dodo's.

George MacBeth (b. 1932)

QUESTIONS

1. Vocabulary: *green-fly* (6), *penultimate* (43), *primate* (43), *amber* (47).

2. Who is speaking? Describe him. To whom is he speaking? When?

3. What comments does the poem suggest about the nature, history, and destiny of the human species? Are contrasts implied between the human species and the speaker's species?

4. What is the force of the final comparison to the dodo (52)?

5. How would you read the first two stanzas aloud? The last three?

DEVIL, MAGGOT AND SON*

Three things seek my death,
    Hard at my heels they run—
Hang them, sweet Christ, all three,—
    Devil, maggot and son.

So much does each of them crave
    The morsel that falls to his share,
He cares not a thrauneen° what — straw
    Falls to the other pair.

If the devil, that crafty one,
    Can capture my soul in sin
He'll leave my flesh to the worm,
    My money to my kin.

My sons think more of the money
    That will come to them when I die
Than a soul that they could not spend,
    A body that none would buy.

* Translated from the Irish.

And how would the maggots fare
    On a soul too thin to eat
And money too tough to chew?
    The maggots must have meat.

Christ, speared by the blind man,
    Christ, nailed to a naked tree,
The three that are seeking my end
    Hang them, sweet Christ, all three!

Frank O'Connor (1903–1966)

QUESTIONS

1. Who and what kind of person is the speaker?

2. According to medieval Christian belief, the Roman soldier Longinus, who thrust a spear into Christ's side at the crucifixion, was blind (21). What element in this poem most underscores its horror?

WHEN IN ROME

Marrie dear
the box is full . . .
take
whatever you like
to eat . . .

        (an egg
        or soup
        . . . there ain't no meat.)

there's endive there
and
cottage cheese . . .
        (whew! if I had some
        black-eyed peas . . .)

there's sardines
on the shelves
and such . . .
but
don't
get my anchovies . . .

they cost
too much!

(me get the
anchovies indeed!
what she think, she got—
a bird to feed?)

there's plenty in there
to fill you up . . .

(yes'm. just the
sight's
enough!

Hope I lives till I get
home
I'm tired of eatin'
what they eats in Rome . . .)

Mari Evans

QUESTIONS

1. Who are the two speakers? What is the situation? Why are the second speaker's words enclosed in parentheses?
2. What are the attitudes of the two speakers toward one another?
3. What implications have the title and the last two lines?

MIRROR

I am silver and exact. I have no preconceptions.
Whatever I see I swallow immediately
Just as it is, unmisted by love or dislike.
I am not cruel, only truthful—
The eye of a little god, four-cornered.
Most of the time I meditate on the opposite wall.
It is pink, with speckles. I have looked at it so long
I think it is a part of my heart. But it flickers.
Faces and darkness separate us over and over.

Now I am a lake. A woman bends over me,
Searching my reaches for what she really is.
Then she turns to those liars, the candles or the moon.

I see her back, and reflect it faithfully.
She rewards me with tears and an agitation of hands.
I am important to her. She comes and goes.
Each morning it is her face that replaces the darkness.
In me she has drowned a young girl, and in me an old woman
Rises toward her day after day, like a terrible fish.

Sylvia Plath (1932–1963)

QUESTIONS

1. Who is the speaker? Distinguish means from ends.

2. In what ways is the mirror like and unlike a person (stanza 1)? In what ways is it like a lake (stanza 2)?

3. What is the meaning of the last two lines?

TO A YOUNG GIRL

My dear, my dear, I know
More than another
What makes your heart beat so;
Not even your own mother
Can know it as I know,
Who broke my heart for her
When the wild thought,
That she denies
And has forgot,
Set all her blood astir
And glittered in her eyes.

William Butler Yeats (1865–1939)

QUESTIONS

1. To whom do the pronouns *who* (6), *her* (6), *she* (8), and *her* (10, 11) respectively refer?

2. What is it that the speaker knows better than the young girl's mother? What is the "wild thought" (7) that "she" (8) "has forgot," and why does "she" deny it?

3. Reconstruct the present and past relationships of the three persons in the poem.

A STUDY OF READING HABITS

When getting my nose in a book
Cured most things short of school,
It was worth ruining my eyes
To know I could still keep cool,
And deal out the old right hook
To dirty dogs twice my size.

Later, with inch-thick specs,
Evil was just my lark:
Me and my cloak and fangs
Had ripping times in the dark.
The women I clubbed with sex!
I broke them up like meringues.

Don't read much now: the dude
Who lets the girl down before
The hero arrives, the chap
Who's yellow and keeps the store,
Seem far too familiar. Get stewed:
Books are a load of crap.

Philip Larkin (b. 1922)

QUESTIONS

1. The three stanzas delineate three stages in the speaker's life. Describe each.

2. What kind of person is the speaker? What kind of books does he read? May he be identified with the poet?

3. Contrast the advice given by the speaker in stanza 3 with the advice given by Terence in "Terence, This Is Stupid Stuff" (page 566). Are A. E. Housman and Philip Larkin at odds in their attitudes toward drinking and reading? Discuss.

EPITAPH ON AN INFANT EIGHT MONTHS OLD

Since I have been so quickly done for,
I wonder what I was begun for.

Anonymous

Denotation and Connotation

A primary distinction between the practical use of language and the literary use is that in literature, especially in poetry, a *fuller* use is made of individual words. To understand this, we need to examine the composition of a word.

The average word has three component parts: sound, denotation, and connotation. It begins as a combination of tones and noises, uttered by the lips, tongue, and throat, for which the written word is a notation. But it differs from a musical tone or a noise in that it has a meaning attached to it. The basic part of this meaning is its DENOTATION or denotations: that is, the dictionary meaning or meanings of the word. Beyond its denotations, a word may also have connotations. The CONNOTATIONS are what it suggests beyond what it expresses: its overtones of meaning. It acquires these connotations by its past history and associations, by the way and the circumstances in which it has been used. The word *home,* for instance, by denotation means only a place where one lives, but by connotation it suggests security, love, comfort, and family. The words *childlike* and *childish* both mean "characteristic of a child," but *childlike* suggests meekness, innocence, and wide-eyed wonder, while *childish* suggests pettiness, willfulness, and temper tantrums. If we name over a series of coins: *nickel, peso, lira, shilling, sen, doubloon,* the word *doubloon,* to four out of five readers, will immediately suggest pirates, though one will find nothing about pirates in looking up its meaning in the dictionary. Pirates are part of its connotation.

Connotation is very important to the poet, for it is one of the means by which he can concentrate or enrich his meaning—say more in fewer words. Consider, for instance, the following short poem:

THERE IS NO FRIGATE LIKE A BOOK

There is no frigate like a book
    To take us lands away,
Nor any coursers like a page
    Of prancing poetry:
This traverse may the poorest take
    Without oppress of toll;
How frugal is the chariot
    That bears the human soul!

Emily Dickinson (1830–1886)

In this poem Emily Dickinson is considering the power of a book or of poetry to carry us away, to let us escape from our immediate surroundings into a world of the imagination. To do this she has compared literature to various means of transportation: a boat, a team of horses, a wheeled land vehicle. But she has been careful to choose kinds of transportation and names for them that have romantic connotations. *Frigate* suggests exploration and adventure; *coursers,* beauty, spirit, and speed; *chariot,* speed and the ability to go through the air as well as on land. (Compare "Swing Low, Sweet Chariot" and the myth of Phaethon, who tried to drive the chariot of Apollo, and the famous painting of Aurora with her horses, once hung in almost every school.) How much of the meaning of the poem comes from this selection of vehicles and words is apparent if we try to substitute for them, say, *steamship, horses,* and *streetcar.*

QUESTIONS

1. What is lost if *miles* is substituted for *lands* (2) or *cheap* for *frugal* (7)?

2. How is *prancing* (4) peculiarly appropriate to poetry as well as to coursers? Could the poet have without loss compared a book to coursers and poetry to a frigate?

3. Is this account appropriate to all kinds of poetry or just to certain kinds? That is, was the poet thinking of poems like Wilfred Owen's "Dulce et Decorum Est" (page 558) or of poems like Coleridge's "Kubla Khan" (page 840) and Walter de la Mare's "The Listeners" (page 841)?

Just as a word has a variety of connotations, so also it may have more than one denotation. If we look up the word *spring* in the dictionary, for instance, we will find that it has between twenty-five and thirty distinguishable meanings: It may mean (1) a pounce or leap, (2) a season of the year, (3) a natural source of water, (4) a coiled elastic wire, etc. This variety of denotation, complicated by additional tones of connotation, makes language confusing and difficult to use. Any person using words must be careful to define by context precisely the meanings that he wishes. But the difference between the writer using language to communicate information and the poet is this: the practical writer will always attempt to confine his words to one meaning at a time; the poet will often take advantage of the fact that the word has more than one meaning by using it to mean more than one thing at the same time. Thus when Edith Sitwell in one of her poems writes, "This is the time of the wild spring and the mating of tigers," she uses the word *spring* to denote both a season of the year and a sudden leap, and she uses *tigers* rather than *lambs* or *birds* because it has a connotation of fierceness and wildness that the other two lack.

WHEN MY LOVE SWEARS THAT SHE IS MADE OF TRUTH

When my love swears that she is made of truth,
I do believe her, though I know she lies,
That she might think me some untutored youth,
Unlearnèd in the world's false subtleties.
Thus vainly thinking that she thinks me young,
Although she knows my days are past the best,
Simply I credit her false-speaking tongue;
On both sides thus is simple truth suppress.
But wherefore says she not she is unjust?° unfaithful
And wherefore say not I that I am old?
Oh, love's best habit is in seeming trust,
And age in love loves not to have years told:

Therefore I lie with her and she with me,
And in our faults by lies we flattered be.

William Shakespeare (1564–1616)

QUESTIONS

1. How old is the speaker in the poem? How old is his beloved? What is the nature of their relationship?

2. How is the contradiction in line 2 to be resolved? How is the one in lines 5–6 to be resolved? Who is lying to whom?

3. How do *simply* (7) and *simple* (8) differ in meaning? What meanings have the two words *vainly* (5), *habit* (11), *told* (12), and *lie* (13)?

4. What is the tone of the poem—i.e. the attitude of the speaker toward his situation? Should line 11 be taken as an expression of (a) wisdom, (b) conscious rationalization, or (c) unconscious self-deception? In answering these questions, consider both the situation and the connotations of all the important words beginning with *swears* (1) and ending with *flattered* (14).

A frequent misconception of poetic language is that the poet seeks always the most beautiful or noble-sounding words. What he really seeks are the most *meaningful* words, and these vary from one context to another. Language has many levels and varieties, and the poet may choose from them all. His words may be grandiose or humble, fanciful or matter of fact, romantic or realistic, archaic or modern, technical or everyday, monosyllabic or polysyllabic. Usually his poem will be pitched pretty much in one key. The words in Emily Dickinson's "There is no frigate like a book" and those in Thomas Hardy's "The Man He Killed" (page 571) are chosen from quite different areas of language, but each poet has chosen the words most meaningful for his own poetic context. Sometimes a poet may import a word from one level or area of language into a poem composed mostly of words from a different level or area. If he does this clumsily, the result will be incongruous and sloppy. If he does it skillfully, the result will be a shock of surprise and an increment of meaning for the reader. In fact, the many varieties of language open to the poet provide his richest resource. His task is one of constant exploration and discovery. He searches always for the secret affinities of words that allow them to be brought together with soft explosions of meaning.

THE NAKED AND THE NUDE

For me, the naked and the nude
(By lexicographers construed
As synonyms that should express
The same deficiency of dress
Or shelter) stand as wide apart
As love from lies, or truth from art.

Lovers without reproach will gaze
On bodies naked and ablaze;
The hippocratic eye will see
In nakedness, anatomy;
And naked shines the Goddess when
She mounts her lion among men.

The nude are bold, the nude are sly
To hold each treasonable eye.
While draping by a showman's trick
Their dishabille in rhetoric,
They grin a mock-religious grin
Of scorn at those of naked skin.

The naked, therefore, who compete
Against the nude may know defeat;
Yet when they both together tread
The briary pastures of the dead,
By Gorgons with long whips pursued,
How naked go the sometime nude!

Robert Graves (b. 1895)

QUESTIONS

1. Vocabulary: *lexicographers* (2), *construed* (2), *hippocratic* (9), *dishabille* (16), *Gorgons* (23).
2. What kind of language is used in lines 2–5? Why? (For example, why is *deficiency* used in preference to *lack*? Purely because of meter?)
3. What is meant by *rhetoric* (16)? Why is the word *dishabille* used in this line instead of some less fancy word?

4. Explain why the poet chose his wording instead of the following alternatives: *brave* for *bold* (13), *clever* for *sly* (13), *clothing* for *draping* (15), *smile* for *grin* (17).

5. What, for the poet, is the difference in connotation between *naked* and *nude*? Try to explain reasons for the difference. If your own sense of the two words differs from that of Graves, state the difference and give reasons to support your sense of them.

6. Explain the reversal in the last line.

The person using language to convey information is largely indifferent to the sound of his words and is hampered by their connotations and multiple denotations. He tries to confine each word to a single exact meaning. He uses, one might say, a fraction of the word and throws the rest away. The poet, on the other hand, tries to use as much of the word as he can. He is interested in sound and uses it to reinforce meaning (see chapter 13). He is interested in connotation and uses it to enrich and convey meaning. And he may use more than one denotation.

The purest form of practical language is scientific language. The scientist needs a precise language for conveying information precisely. The fact that words have multiple denotations and various overtones of meaning is a hindrance to him in accomplishing his purpose. His ideal language would be a language with a one-to-one correspondence between word and meaning; that is, every word would have one meaning only, and for every meaning there would be only one word. Since ordinary language does not fulfill these conditions, he has invented one that does. A statement in his language looks something like this:

$$SO_2 + H_2O = H_2SO_3$$

In such a statement the symbols are entirely unambiguous; they have been stripped of all connotation and of all denotations but one. The word *sulfurous,* if it occurred in poetry, might have all kinds of connotations: fire, smoke, brimstone, hell, damnation. But H_2SO_3 means one thing and one thing only: sulfurous acid.

The ambiguity and multiplicity of meanings that words have, then, are an obstacle to the scientist but a resource to the poet. Where the scientist wants singleness of meaning, the poet wants richness of meaning. Where the scientist requires and has invented a strictly one-dimensional language, in which every word is confined to one denotation, the poet needs a multidimensional language, and he creates it partly by using a multidimensional vocabulary, in which to the dimension of denotation he adds the dimensions of connotation and sound.

The poet, we may say, plays on a many-stringed instrument. And he sounds more than one note at a time.

The first problem in reading poetry, therefore, or in reading any kind of literature, is to develop a sense of language, a feeling for words. One needs to become acquainted with their shape, their color, and their flavor. There are two ways of doing this: extensive use of the dictionary and extensive reading.

EXERCISES

1. Robert Frost has said that "Poetry is what evaporates from all translations." On the basis of this chapter, can you explain why this statement is true? How much of a word can be translated?

2. Which of the following words have the most "romantic" connotations?
   a. horse ( ) steed ( ) equine quadruped ( )
   b. China ( ) Cathay ( )
   Which of the following is the most emotionally connotative?
   c. mother ( ) female parent ( ) dam ( )
   Which of the following have the more favorable connotations?
   d. average ( ) mediocre ( )
   e. secret agent ( ) spy ( )
   f. adventurer ( ) adventuress ( )

3. Fill each blank with the word richest in meaning in the given context. Explain.

   a. I still had hopes, my latest hours to crown,
   Amidst these humble bowers to lay me down;
   To husband out life's ______________ at the close, — ***candle, taper***
   And keep the flame from wasting by repose.
   Goldsmith

   b. She was a ______________ of delight — ***ghost, phantom, spectre, spook***
   When first she gleamed upon my sight.
   Wordsworth

   c. His sumptuous watch-case, though concealed it lies,
   Like a good conscience, ______________ joy supplies. — ***perfect, solid thorough***
   Edward Young

d. Charmed magic ________ opening on the foam — ***casements, windows***
Of ____________ seas, in faery lands forlorn. — ***dangerous, perilous***
Keats

e. Thou __________ unravished bride of quietness. — ***still, yet***
Keats

f. I'll __________ the guts into the neighbor room. — ***bear, carry, convey, lug***
Shakespeare

g. The iron tongue of midnight hath ____________ — ***said, struck, told***
twelve.
Shakespeare

h. In poetry each word reverberates like the note of
a well-tuned ____________ and always leaves — ***banjo, guitar, lyre***
behind it a multitude of vibrations. *Joubert*

i. I think that with this __________ new alliance — ***holy, sacred***
I may ensure the public, and defy
All other magazines of art or science. *Byron*

j. Care on thy maiden brow shall put
A wreath of wrinkles, and thy foot
Be shod with pain: not silken dress
But toil shall ____________ thy loveliness. — ***clothe, tire, weary***
C. Day Lewis

4. Ezra Pound has defined great literature as being "simply language charged with meaning to the utmost possible degree." Would this be a good definition of poetry? The word *charged* is roughly equivalent to *filled*. Why is *charged* a better word in Pound's definition? What do its associations with storage batteries, guns, and dynamite suggest about poetry?

RICHARD CORY

Whenever Richard Cory went down town,
We people on the pavement looked at him:
He was a gentleman from sole to crown,
Clean favored, and imperially slim.

And he was always quietly arrayed,
And he was always human when he talked;
But still he fluttered pulses when he said,
"Good-morning," and he glittered when he walked.

And he was rich—yes, richer than a king—
And admirably schooled in every grace:
In fine, we thought that he was everything
To make us wish that we were in his place.

So on we worked, and waited for the light,
And went without the meat, and cursed the bread;
And Richard Cory, one calm summer night,
Went home and put a bullet through his head.

Edwin Arlington Robinson (1869–1935)

QUESTIONS

1. In how many senses is Richard Cory a gentleman?

2. The word *crown* (3), meaning the top of the head, is familiar to you from "Jack and Jill," but why does Robinson use the unusual phrase "from sole to crown" instead of the common "from head to foot" or "from top to toe"?

3. List the words in the poem that express or suggest the idea of aristocracy or royalty.

4. Try to explain why the poet chose his wording rather than the following alternatives: *sidewalk* for *pavement* (2), *good-looking* for *clean favored* (4), *thin* for *slim* (4), *dressed* for *arrayed* (5), *courteous* for *human* (6), *wonderfully* for *admirably* (10), *trained* for *schooled* (10), *manners* for *every grace* (10), *in short* for *in fine* (11). What other examples of effective diction do you find in the poem?

5. Why is "Richard Cory" a good name for the character in this poem?

6. This poem is a good example of how ironic contrast (see chapter 7) generates meaning. The poem makes no direct statement about life; it simply relates an incident. What larger meanings about life does it suggest?

7. A leading American critic has said of this poem: "In 'Richard Cory' . . . we have a superficially neat portrait of the elegant man of mystery; the poem builds up deliberately to a very cheap surprise ending; but all surprise endings are cheap in poetry, if not, indeed, elsewhere, for poetry is written to be read not once but many times."* Do you agree with this evaluation of the poem? Discuss.

THE RICH MAN

The rich man has his motor-car,
    His country and his town estate.

* Yvor Winters, *Edwin Arlington Robinson* (Norfolk, Conn., New Directions, 1946), p. 52.

He smokes a fifty-cent cigar
And jeers at Fate.

He frivols through the livelong day,
He knows not Poverty her pinch.
His lot seems light, his heart seems gay,
He has a cinch.

Yet though my lamp burns low and dim,
Though I must slave for livelihood—
Think you that I would change with him?
You bet I would!

Franklin P. Adams (1881–1960)

QUESTIONS

1. What meanings has *lot* (7)?

2. Bearing in mind the criticism cited of Robinson's "Richard Cory," state whether you think that poem or this has more poetic value. Which poem is merely clever? Which is something more?

NAMING OF PARTS

To-day we have naming of parts. Yesterday,
We had daily cleaning. And to-morrow morning,
We shall have what to do after firing. But to-day,
To-day we have naming of parts. Japonica
Glistens like coral in all of the neighboring gardens,
And to-day we have naming of parts.

This is the lower sling swivel. And this
Is the upper sling swivel, whose use you will see,
When you are given your slings. And this is the piling swivel,
Which in your case you have not got. The branches
Hold in the gardens their silent, eloquent gestures,
Which in our case we have not got.

This is the safety-catch, which is always released
With an easy flick of the thumb. And please do not let me
See anyone using his finger. You can do it quite easy
If you have any strength in your thumb. The blossoms
Are fragile and motionless, never letting anyone see
Any of them using their finger.

And this you can see is the bolt. The purpose of this
Is to open the breech, as you see. We can slide it
Rapidly backwards and forwards: we call this
Easing the spring. And rapidly backwards and forwards
The early bees are assaulting and fumbling the flowers:
They call it easing the Spring.

They call it easing the Spring: it is perfectly easy
If you have any strength in your thumb: like the bolt,
And the breech, and the cocking-piece, and the point of balance,
Which in our case we have not got; and the almond-blossom
Silent in all of the gardens and the bees going backwards and forwards,
For to-day we have naming of parts.

Henry Reed (b. 1914)

QUESTIONS

1. Who is the speaker (or speakers) in the poem, and what is the situation?

2. What basic contrasts are represented by the trainees and by the gardens?

3. What is it that the trainees "have not got" (28)? How many meanings have the phrases "easing the Spring" (22) and "point of balance" (27)?

4. What differences in language and rhythm do you find between the lines concerning "naming of parts" and those describing the gardens?

5. Does the repetition of certain phrases throughout the poem have any special function or is it done only to create a kind of refrain?

6. What statement does the poem make about war as it affects men and their lives?

JUDGING DISTANCES

Not only how far away, but the way that you say it
Is very important. Perhaps you may never get
The knack of judging a distance, but at least you know
How to report on a landscape: the central sector,
The right of arc and that, which we had last Tuesday,
And at least you know

That maps are of time, not place, so far as the army
Happens to be concerned—the reason being,

Is one which need not delay us. Again, you know
There are three kinds of tree, three only, the fir and the poplar,
And those which have bushy tops to; and lastly
    That things only seem to be things.

A barn is not called a barn, to put it more plainly,
Or a field in the distance, where sheep may be safely grazing.
You must never be over-sure. You must say, when reporting:
At five o'clock in the central sector is a dozen
Of what appear to be animals; whatever you do,
    Don't call the bleeders *sheep*.

I am sure that's quite clear; and suppose, for the sake of example,
The one at the end, asleep, endeavors to tell us
What he sees over there to the west, and how far away,
After first having come to attention. There to the west,
On the fields of summer the sun and the shadows bestow
    Vestments of purple and gold.

The still white dwellings are like a mirage in the heat,
And under the swaying elms a man and a woman
Lie gently together. Which is, perhaps, only to say
That there is a row of houses to the left of arc,
And that under some poplars a pair of what appear to be humans
    Appear to be loving.

Well that, for an answer, is what we might rightly call
Moderately satisfactory only, the reason being,
Is that two things have been omitted, and those are important.
The human beings, now: in what direction are they,
And how far away, would you say? And do not forget
    There may be dead ground in between.

There may be dead ground in between; and I may not have got
The knack of judging a distance; I will only venture
A guess that perhaps between me and the apparent lovers,
(Who, incidentally, appear by now to have finished,)
At seven o'clock from the houses, is roughly a distance
    Of about one year and a half.

Henry Reed (b. 1914)

QUESTIONS

1. In what respect are maps "of time, not place" (7) in the army?

2. Though they may be construed as belonging to the same speaker, there are two speaking voices in this poem. Identify each and put quotation marks around the lines spoken by the second voice.

3. Two kinds of language are used in this poem—army "officialese" and the language of human experience. What are the characteristics of each? What is the purpose of each? Which is more precise?

4. The word *bleeders* (18)—i.e., "bloody creatures"—is British profanity. To which of the two kinds of language does it belong? Or is it perhaps a third kind of language?

5. As in "Naming of Parts" (these two poems are part of a series of three with the general title "Lessons of War") the two kinds of language used might possibly be called "unpoetic" and "poetic." Is the "unpoetic" language *really* unpoetic? In other words, is its use inappropriate in these two poems? Explain.

6. The phrase "dead ground" (36) takes on symbolic meaning in the last stanza. What is its literal meaning? What is its symbolic meaning? What does the second speaker mean by saying that the distance between himself and the lovers is "about one year and a half" (42)? In what respect is the contrast between the recruits and the lovers similar to that between the recruits and the gardens in "Naming of Parts"? What meanings are generated by the former contrast?

CROSS

My old man's a white old man
And my old mother's black.
If ever I cursed my white old man
I take my curses back.

If ever I cursed my black old mother
And wished she were in hell,
I'm sorry for that evil wish
And now I wish her well.

My old man died in a fine big house.
My ma died in a shack.
I wonder where I'm gonna die,
Being neither white nor black?

Langston Hughes (1902–1967)

QUESTIONS

1. What different denotations does the title have? Explain.

2. The language in this poem, such as *old man* (1, 3, 9), *ma* (10), and *gonna* (11), is plain, and even colloquial. Is it appropriate to the subject? Why?

BASE DETAILS

If I were fierce, and bald, and short of breath,
  I'd live with scarlet Majors at the Base,
And speed glum heroes up the line to death.
  You'd see me with my puffy petulant face,
Guzzling and gulping in the best hotel,
  Reading the Roll of Honor. "Poor young chap,"
I'd say—"I used to know his father well;
  Yes, we've lost heavily in this last scrap."
And when the war is done and youth stone dead,
I'd toddle safely home and die—in bed.

Siegfried Sassoon (1886–1967)

QUESTIONS

1. Vocabulary: *petulant* (4).

2. In what two ways may the title be interpreted? (Both words have two pertinent meanings.) What applications has *scarlet* (2)? What is the force of *fierce* (1)? Try to explain why the poet chose his wording rather than the following alternatives: *fleshy* for *puffy* (4), *eating and drinking* for *guzzling and gulping* (5), *battle* for *scrap* (8), *totter* for *toddle* (10).

3. Who evidently is the speaker? (The poet, a British captain in World War I, was decorated for bravery on the battlefield.) Does he mean what he says? What is the purpose of the poem?

KISSING AND BUSSING

Kissing and bussing differ both in this:
We buss our wantons, but our wives we kiss.

Robert Herrick (1591–1674)

CHAPTER FOUR

Imagery

Experience comes to us largely through the senses. My experience of a spring day, for instance, may consist partly of certain emotions I feel and partly of certain thoughts I think, but most of it will be a cluster of sense impressions. It will consist of *seeing* blue sky and white clouds, budding leaves and daffodils; of *hearing* robins and bluebirds singing in the early morning; of *smelling* damp earth and blossoming hyacinths; and of *feeling* a fresh wind against my cheek. The poet seeking to express his experience of a spring day must therefore provide a selection of the sense impressions he has. Like Shakespeare (page 561), he must give the reader "daisies pied" and "lady-smocks all silver-white" and "merry larks" and the song of the cuckoo and maidens bleaching their summer smocks. Without doing so he will probably fail to evoke the emotions that accompanied his sensations. His language, therefore, must be more *sensuous* than ordinary language. It must be more full of imagery.

IMAGERY may be defined as the representation through language of sense experience. Poetry appeals directly to our senses, of course, through its music and rhythm, which we actually hear when it is read aloud. But indirectly it appeals to our senses through imagery, the representation to the imagination of sense experience. The word *image* perhaps most often suggests a mental picture, something seen in the mind's eye—and *visual* imagery is the most frequently occurring kind of imagery in poetry. But an image may also represent a sound; a smell; a taste; a tactile experience, such as hardness, wetness, or cold; an internal sensation, such as hunger, thirst, or nausea; or movement or tension in the muscles or joints. If we wished to be scientific, we could extend this list further, for psychologists no longer confine themselves to five or even six senses, but for purposes of discussing poetry the above classification should ordinarily be sufficient.

MEETING AT NIGHT

The gray sea and the long black land;
And the yellow half-moon large and low;
And the startled little waves that leap
In fiery ringlets from their sleep,
As I gain the cove with pushing prow,
And quench its speed i' the slushy sand.

Then a mile of warm sea-scented beach;
Three fields to cross till a farm appears;
A tap at the pane, the quick sharp scratch
And blue spurt of a lighted match,
And a voice less loud, through its joys and fears,
Than the two hearts beating each to each!

Robert Browning (1812–1889)

"Meeting at Night" is a poem about love. It makes, one might say, a number of statements about love: being in love is a sweet and exciting experience; when one is in love everything seems beautiful to him, and the most trivial things become significant; when one is in love his sweetheart seems the most important object in the world. But the poet actually *tells* us none of these things directly. He does not even use the word *love* in his poem. His business is to communicate experience, not information. He does this largely in two ways. First, he presents us with a specific situation, in which a lover goes to meet his sweetheart. Second, he describes the lover's journey so vividly in terms of sense impressions that the reader not only sees and hears what the lover saw and heard but also shares his anticipation and excitement.

Every line in the poem contains some image, some appeal to the senses: the gray sea, the long black land, the yellow half-moon, the startled little waves with their fiery ringlets, the blue spurt of the lighted match—all appeal to our sense of sight and convey not only shape but also color and motion. The warm sea-scented beach appeals to the senses of both smell and touch. The pushing prow of the boat on the slushy sand, the tap at the pane, the quick sharp scratch of the match, the low speech of the lovers, and the sound of their two hearts beating—all appeal to the sense of hearing.

PARTING AT MORNING

Round the cape of a sudden came the sea,
And the sun looked over the mountain's rim:
And straight was a path of gold for him,
And the need of a world of men for me.

Robert Browning (1812–1889)

QUESTIONS

1. This poem is a sequel to "Meeting at Night." *Him* (3) refers to the sun. Does the last line mean that the lover needs the world of men or that the world of men needs the lover? Or both?

2. Does the sea *actually* come suddenly around the cape or *appear* to? Why does Browning mention the *effect* before its *cause* (the sun looking over the mountain's rim)?

3. Do these two poems, taken together, suggest any larger truths about love? Browning, in answer to a question, said that the second part is the man's confession of "how fleeting is the belief (implied in the first part) that such raptures are self-sufficient and enduring—as for the time they appear."

The sharpness and vividness of any image will ordinarily depend on how specific it is and on the poet's use of effective detail. The word *hummingbird,* for instance, conveys a more definite image than does *bird,* and *ruby-throated hummingbird* is sharper and more specific still. It is not necessary, however, that for a vivid representation something be completely described. One or two especially sharp and representative details will ordinarily serve the alert reader, allowing his imagination to fill in the rest. Tennyson in "The Eagle" (page 555) gives only one detail about the eagle itself—that he clasps the crag with "crooked hands"—but this detail is an effective and memorable one. Robinson tells us that Richard Cory (page 592) was "clean favored," "slim," and "quietly arrayed," but the detail that really brings Cory before us is that he "glittered when he walked." Browning, in "Meeting at Night," calls up a whole scene with "A tap at the pane, the quick sharp scratch/And blue spurt of a lighted match."

Since imagery is a peculiarly effective way of evoking vivid experience, and since it may be used by the poet to convey emotion and suggest ideas as well as to cause a mental reproduction of sensations, it is an invaluable resource of the poet. In general, he will seek concrete or image-bearing words in preference to abstract or non-image-bearing words. We cannot evaluate a poem, however, by the amount or quality of its imagery alone. Sense impression is only one of the elements of experience. A poet may attain his ends by other means. We must never judge any single element of a poem except in reference to the total intention of that poem.

A LATE AUBADE

You could be sitting now in a carrel
Turning some liver-spotted page,
Or rising in an elevator-cage
Toward Ladies' Apparel.

You could be planting a raucous bed
Of salvia, in rubber gloves,
Or lunching through a screed of someone's loves
With pitying head,

Or making some unhappy setter
Heel, or listening to a bleak
Lecture on Schoenberg's serial technique.
Isn't this better?

Think of all the time you are not
Wasting, and would not care to waste,
Such things, thank God, not being to your taste.
Think what a lot

Of time, by woman's reckoning,
You've saved, and so may spend on this,
You who had rather lie in bed and kiss
Than anything.

It's almost noon, you say? If so,
Time flies, and I need not rehearse

The rosebuds-theme of centuries of verse.
If you *must* go,

Wait for a while, then slip downstairs
And bring us up some chilled white wine,
And some blue cheese, and crackers, and some fine
Ruddy-skinned pears.

Richard Wilbur (b. 1921)

QUESTIONS

1. Vocabulary: *Aubade* (title), *carrel* (1), *screed* (7), *Schoenberg* (11).
2. Who is the speaker? What is the situation? What plea is the speaker making?
3. As lines 22–23 suggest, this poem treats an age-old theme of poetry. What is it? In what respects is this an original treatment of it? Though line 23 is general in reference, it alludes specifically to a famous poem by Robert Herrick (page 635). In what respects are these two poems similar? In what respects are they different?
4. What clues are there in the poem as to the characters and personalities of the two people involved?
5. How does the last stanza provide a fitting conclusion to the poem?

ON MOONLIT HEATH AND LONESOME BANK

On moonlit heath and lonesome bank
The sheep beside me graze;
And yon the gallows used to clank
Fast by the four cross ways.

A careless shepherd once would keep
The flocks by moonlight there,
And high amongst the glimmering sheep
The dead man stood on air.

They hang us now in Shrewsbury jail:
The whistles blow forlorn,
And trains all night groan on the rail
To men that die at morn.

There sleeps in Shrewsbury jail to-night,
Or wakes, as may betide,

A better lad, if things went right,
Than most that sleep outside.

And naked to the hangman's noose
The morning clocks will ring
A neck God made for other use
Than strangling in a string.

And sharp the link of life will snap,
And dead on air will stand
Heels that held up as straight a chap
As treads upon the land.

So here I'll watch the night and wait
To see the morning shine,
When he will hear the stroke of eight
And not the stroke of nine;

And wish my friend as sound a sleep
As lads' I did not know,
That shepherded the moonlit sheep
A hundred years ago.

A. E. Housman (1859–1936)

QUESTIONS

1. Vocabulary: *heath* (1).
2. Housman explains in a note to lines 5–6 that "Hanging in chains was called keeping sheep by moonlight." Where is this idea repeated?
3. What is the speaker's attitude toward his friend? Toward other young men who have died by hanging? What is the purpose of the reference to the young men hanged "a hundred years ago"?
4. Discuss the kinds of imagery present in the poem and their role in the development of the dramatic situation.
5. Discuss the use of language in stanza 5.

SPRING

Nothing is so beautiful as spring—
When weeds, in wheels, shoot long and lovely and lush;
Thrush's eggs look little low heavens, and thrush
Through the echoing timber does so rinse and wring

The ear, it strikes like lightnings to hear him sing;
    The glassy peartree leaves and blooms, they brush
    The descending blue; that is all in a rush
With richness; the racing lambs too have fair their fling.

What is all this juice and all this joy?
    A strain of the earth's sweet being in the beginning
In Eden garden.—Have, get, before it cloy,

    Before it cloud, Christ, lord, and sour with sinning,
Innocent mind and Mayday in girl and boy,
    Most, O maid's child, thy choice and worthy the winning.

Gerard Manley Hopkins (1844–1889)

QUESTIONS

1. The first line makes an abstract statement. How is this statement brought to carry conviction?

2. The sky is described as being "all in a rush/With richness" (7–8). In what other respects is the poem "rich"?

3. The author was a Catholic priest as well as a poet. To what two things does he compare the spring in lines 9–14? In what ways are the comparisons appropriate?

A DESCRIPTION OF THE MORNING

Now hardly here and there a hackney-coach
Appearing, showed the ruddy morn's approach.
Now Betty from her master's bed had flown,
And softy stole to discompose her own.
The slip-shod 'prentice from his master's door
Had pared the dirt, and sprinkled round the floor.
Now Moll had whirled her mop with dextrous airs,
Prepared to scrub the entry and the stairs.
The youth with broomy stumps began to trace
The kennel's edge, where wheels had worn the place.
The small-coal man was heard with cadence deep,
Till drowned in shriller notes of chimney-sweep.
Duns at his lordship's gate began to meet;
And Brickdust Moll had screamed through half the street.
The turnkey now his flock returning sees,

Duly let out a-nights to steal for fees.
The watchful bailiffs take their silent stands;
And schoolboys lag with satchels in their hands.

Jonathan Swift (1667–1745)

QUESTIONS

1. Vocabulary: *hardly* (1), *hackney-coach* (1), *kennel* (10), *duns* (13), *turnkey* (15), *bailiffs* (17).

2. The images in this poem differ sharply from those in the previous poem. Do they differ also from the expectations set up by the title? What is the poem's purpose?

3. The poem gives a good brief picture of London street life in the eighteenth century. List the various types of people mentioned and explain what each is doing. (The "youth with broomy stumps" in line 9 is apparently searching for salvage.)

THE FORGE

All I know is a door into the dark.
Outside, old axles and iron hoops rusting;
Inside, the hammered anvil's short-pitched ring,
The unpredictable fantail of sparks
Or hiss when a new shoe toughens in water.
The anvil must be somewhere in the centre,
Horned as a unicorn, at one end square,
Set there immovable: an altar
Where he expends himself in shape and music.
Sometimes, leather-aproned, hairs in his nose,
He leans out on the jamb, recalls a clatter
Of hoofs where traffic is flashing in rows;
Then grunts and goes in, with a slam and flick
To beat real iron out, to work the bellows.

Seamus Heaney (b. 1939)

QUESTIONS

1. What does the speaker mean when he says that "all" he knows is "a door into the dark"? How does he make it evident that he really knows more?

2. Who is "He" (11)? What is his attitude toward his work and toward the changing times?

3. On what contrasts does the poem rest?

TO AUTUMN

Season of mists and mellow fruitfulness,
    Close bosom-friend of the maturing sun;
Conspiring with him how to load and bless
    With fruit the vines that round the thatch-eves run;
To bend with apples the mossed cottage-trees,
    And fill all fruit with ripeness to the core;
        To swell the gourd, and plump the hazel shells
With a sweet kernel; to set budding more,
    And still more, later flowers for the bees,
    Until they think warm days will never cease,
        For Summer has o'er-brimmed their clammy cells.

Who hath not seen thee oft amid thy store?
    Sometimes whoever seeks abroad may find
Thee sitting careless on a granary floor,
    Thy hair soft-lifted by the winnowing wind;
Or on a half-reaped furrow sound asleep,
    Drowsed with the fume of poppies, while thy hook
        Spares the next swath and all its twinèd flowers:
And sometimes like a gleaner thou dost keep
    Steady thy laden head across a brook;
    Or by a cider-press, with patient look,
        Thou watchest the last oozings hours by hours.

Where are the songs of Spring? Ay, where are they?
    Think not of them, thou hast thy music too,—
While barred clouds bloom the soft-dying day,
    And touch the stubble-plains with rosy hue;
Then in a wailful choir the small gnats mourn
    Among the river sallows, borne aloft
        Or sinking as the light wind lives or dies;
And full-grown lambs loud bleat from hilly bourn;
    Hedge-crickets sing; and now with treble soft
    The red-breast whistles from a garden-croft;
        And gathering swallows twitter in the skies.

John Keats (1795–1821)

QUESTIONS

1. Vocabulary: *hook* (17), *barred* (25), *sallows* (28), *bourn* (30), *croft* (32).

2. How many kinds of imagery do you find in the poem? Give examples of each.

3. Are the images arranged haphazardly or are they carefully organized? In answering this question, consider: (a) With what aspect of autumn is each stanza particularly concerned? (b) What kind of imagery is dominant in each stanza? (c) What time of the season is presented in each stanza? (d) Is there any progression in time of day?

4. What is Autumn personified as in stanza 2? Is there any suggestion of personification in the other two stanzas?

5. Although the poem is primarily descriptive, what attitude toward transience and passing beauty is implicit in it?

TO SATCH

Sometimes I feel like I will *never* stop
Just go on forever
Till one fine mornin'
I'm gonna reach up and grab me a handfulla stars
Throw out my long lean leg
And whip three hot strikes burnin' down the heavens
And look over at God and say
How about that!

Samuel Allen (b. 1917)

QUESTION

"Satch" or "Satchelfoot" Paige, one of the great baseball pitchers of all time, had an extraordinarily prolonged career. After more than two brilliant decades of pitching in organized Negro baseball, he played in the major leagues after their integration. As late as 1953, when he was over 47 years old, he participated in over 57 games as a relief pitcher. Who is the speaker in this poem? How does the poem capture his spirit?

Figurative Language 1

Metaphor, Personification, Metonymy

> *Poetry provides the one permissible way of saying one thing and meaning another.* ROBERT FROST

Let us assume that your roommate has just come in out of a rainstorm and you say to him, "Well, you're a pretty sight! Got slightly wet, didn't you?" And he replies, "Wet? I'm drowned! It's raining cats and dogs outside, and my raincoat's just like a sieve!"

It is likely that you and your roommate understand each other well enough, and yet if you examine this conversation literally, that is to say unimaginatively, you will find that you have been speaking nonsense. Actually you have been speaking figuratively. You have been saying less than what you mean, or more than what you mean, or the opposite of what you mean, or something else than what you mean. You did not mean that your roommate was a pretty sight but that he was a wretched sight. You did not mean that he got slightly wet but that he got very wet. Your roommate did not mean that he got drowned but that he got drenched. It was not raining cats and dogs; it was raining water. And your roommate's raincoat is so unlike a sieve that not even a baby would confuse them.

If you are familiar with Molière's play *Le Bourgeois Gentilhomme,* you will remember how delighted M. Jourdain was to discover that he had been speaking prose all his life. You may be equally surprised to discover that you have been speaking a kind of subpoetry all your life. The difference between your figures of speech and the poet's is that yours are worn and trite, his fresh and original.

On first examination, it might seem absurd to say one thing and mean another. But we all do it and with good reason. We do it because we can say what we want to say more vividly and forcefully by figures than we can by saying it directly. And we can say more by figurative statement than we can by literal statement. Figures of speech are another way of adding extra dimensions to language. We shall examine their usefulness more particularly later in this chapter.

Broadly defined, a FIGURE OF SPEECH is any way of saying something other than the ordinary way, and some rhetoricians have classified as many as 250 separate figures. For our purposes, however, a figure of speech is more narrowly definable as a way of saying one thing and meaning another, and we need be concerned with no more than a dozen. FIGURATIVE LANGUAGE—language using figures of speech—is language that cannot be taken literally.

METAPHOR and SIMILE are both used as a means of comparing things that are essentially unlike. The only distinction between them is that in simile the comparison is *expressed* by the use of some word or phrase, such as *like, as, than, similar to, resembles,* or *seems;* in metaphor the comparison is *implied*—that is the figurative term is *substituted for* or *identified with* the literal term.

THE GUITARIST TUNES UP

With what attentive courtesy he bent
Over his instrument;
Not as a lordly conquerer who could
Command both wire and wood,
But as a man with a loved woman might,
Inquiring with delight
What slight essential things she had to say
Before they started, he and she, to play.

Frances Cornford (1886–1960)

QUESTION

Explore the comparison. Does it principally illuminate the guitarist or the lovers or both? What one word brings its two terms together?

THE HOUND

Life the hound
Equivocal
Comes at a bound
Either to rend me
Or to befriend me.
I cannot tell
The hound's intent
Till he has sprung
At my bare hand
With teeth or tongue.
Meanwhile I stand
And wait the event.

Robert Francis (b. 1901)

QUESTION

What does *equivocal* mean? Show how this is the key word in the poem. What is the effect of placing it on a line by itself?

Metaphors may take one of four forms. In the first form, as in simile, both the literal and the figurative terms are *named.* In Francis's poem, for example, the literal term is *life* and the figurative one is *hound.* In the second, the literal term is *named* and the figurative term is *implied.*

TO DIANEME

Give me one kiss,
    And no more;
If so be, this
    Makes you poor,
To enrich you
    I'll restore

For that one, two
Thousand score.

Robert Herrick (1591–1674)

QUESTION

To what are kisses being compared? What words imply this comparison?

In the third form of metaphor, the literal term is *implied* and the figurative term is *named.*

WHY DO THE GRACES

Why do the Graces now desert the Muse?
They hate bright ribbons tying wooden shoes.

Walter Savage Landor (1775–1864)

QUESTIONS

1. What charge is Landor making against the poetry of his time? What is lost in attempting to name the literal terms of the two metaphors in line 2?
2. Why is *Graces* capitalized?

In the fourth form of metaphor, a comparatively rare one, neither the literal nor the figurative terms are named: *both* are *implied.* We see an example of this in Emily Dickinson's "I like to see it lap the miles" (page 764).

Personification consists in giving the attributes of a human being to an animal, an object, or an idea. It is really a subtype of metaphor, an implied comparison in which the figurative term of the comparison is always a human being. When Sylvia Plath makes a mirror speak and think (page 582), she is personifying an object. When Keats describes autumn as a harvester "sitting careless on a granary floor" or "on a half-reaped furrow sound asleep" (page 607), he is personifying a concept. Personifications differ in the degree to which they ask the reader actually to visualize the literal term in human form. In Keats's comparison we are asked to make a complete identification of autumn with a human being. In "The

Twa Corbies" (page 562), we are asked to think of the two ravens as speaking, thinking, and feeling like human beings, but not as having human form; similarly, in Sylvia Plath's poem, we continue to visualize the mirror as a mirror. In Browning's reference to "the startled little waves" (page 600), a personification is barely suggested; we would make a mistake if we tried to visualize the waves in human form or even, really, to think of them as having human emotions.*

Closely related to personification is APOSTROPHE, which consists in addressing someone absent or something nonhuman as if it were alive and present and could reply to what is being said. When the speaker in James Joyce's poem (page 726) cries out, "My love, my love, my love, why have you left me alone?" he is apostrophizing his departed sweetheart. The speaker in Shakespeare's "Fear no more the heat o' the sun" (page 879) is apostrophizing the body of a dead boy. William Blake apostrophizes the tiger throughout his famous poem (page 836) but does not otherwise personify it. Keats apostrophizes as well as personifies autumn (page 607). Personification and apostrophe are both ways of giving life and immediacy to one's language, but since neither requires great imaginative power on the part of the poet—apostrophe especially does not—they may degenerate into mere mannerisms and are to be found as often in bad and mediocre poetry as in good. We need to distinguish between their effective use and their merely conventional use.

DR. SIGMUND FREUD DISCOVERS THE SEA SHELL

Science, that simple saint, cannot be bothered
Figuring what anything is for:

* The various figures of speech blend into each other, and it is sometimes difficult to classify a specific example as definitely metaphor or symbol, symbolism or allegory, understatement or irony, irony or paradox. Often a given example may exemplify two or more figures at once. When Hardy writes of the "weakening eye of day (page 851), the metaphorical substitution of *eye* for *sun* has the secondary effect of personifying *day*. In the poem "A White Rose" (page 629), beginning "The red rose whispers of passion," the red rose is personified by the verb *whispers* but is at the same time a symbol. The important consideration in reading poetry is not that we classify figures definitively but that we construe them correctly.

Enough for her devotions that things are
And can be contemplated soon as gathered.

She knows how every living thing was fathered,
She calculates the climate of each star,
She counts the fish at sea, but cannot care
Why any one of them exists, fish, fire or feathered.

Why should she? Her religion is to tell
By rote her rosary of perfect answers.
Metaphysics she can leave to man:
She never wakes at night in heaven or hell

Staring at darkness. In her holy cell
There is no darkness ever: the pure candle
Burns, the beads drop briskly from her hand.

Who dares to offer Her the curled sea shell!
She will not touch it!—knows the world she sees
Is all the world there is! Her faith is perfect!

And still he offers the sea shell . . .
                                        What surf
Of what far sea upon what unknown ground
Troubles forever with that asking sound?
What surge is this whose question never ceases?

Archibald MacLeish (b. 1892)

QUESTIONS

1. Vocabulary: *metaphysics* (11).

2. This poem employs an extended personification. List the ways in which science is appropriately compared to a saint. In what way is its faith *perfect* (18)?

3. Who is *he* in line 19?

4. Who was Sigmund Freud, and what discoveries did he make about human nature?

5. What does the sea shell represent?

THE SEA-GULL

Hark to the whimper of the sea-gull;
He weeps because he's not an ea-gull.
Suppose you were, you silly sea-gull,
Could you explain it to your she-gull?

Ogden Nash (1902–1971)

QUESTION

What is lost in effectiveness, and why, if the last two lines are rewritten thus:

> But if it were, how could the sea-gull
> Explain the matter to its she-gull?

SYNECDOCHE (the use of the part for the whole) and METONYMY (the use of something closely related for the thing actually meant) are alike in that both substitute some significant detail or aspect of an experience for the experience itself. Thus, Shakespeare uses synecdoche when he says that the cuckoo's song is unpleasing to a "married ear" (page 561), for he means a married *man*. Robert Graves uses synecdoche in "The Naked and the Nude" (page 589) when he refers to a doctor as a "hippocratic eye," and T. S. Eliot uses it in "The Love Song of J. Alfred Prufrock" when he refers to a crab or lobster as "a pair of ragged claws" (page 817). Shakespeare uses metonymy when he says that the yellow cuckoo-buds "paint the meadows with delight" (page 561), for he means with bright color, which produces delight. Robert Frost uses metonymy in "Out, Out—" (page 676) when he describes an injured boy holding up his cut hand "as if to keep/The life from spilling," for literally he means to keep the blood from spilling. In each case, however, there is a gain in vividness and meaning. Eliot, by substituting for the crab that part which seizes its prey, tells us something important about the crab and makes us see it more vividly. Shakespeare, by referring to bright color as "delight" evokes not only the visual effect but the emotional response it arouses. Frost tells us both that the boy's hand is bleeding and that his life is in danger.

Many synecdoches and metonymies, of course, like many metaphors, have become so much a part of the language that they no longer strike us as figurative; such is the case with *redskin* for Indian, *paleface* for white man, and *salt* and *tar* for sailor. Such figures are referred to as dead metaphors or dead figures. Synecdoche and metonymy are so much alike that it is hardly worth while to distinguish between them, and the latter term is increasingly coming to be used for both. In this book metonymy will be used for both figures—that is, for any figure in which a part or something closely related is substituted for the thing literally meant.

LINES ON A PAID MILITIA*

The country rings around with loud alarms,
And raw in fields the rude militia swarms;
Mouths without hands; maintained at vast expense,
In peace a charge, in war a weak defense:
Stout once a month they march, a blustering band,
And ever, but in times of need, at hand.
This was the morn when, issuing on the guard,
Drawn up in rank and file they stood prepared
Of seeming arms to make a short essay,
Then hasten to be drunk, the business of the day.

John Dryden (1631–1700)

QUESTIONS

1. Vocabulary: *essay* (9).
2. Comment on the meanings or force of *charge* (4), *business* (10).
3. The art of this passage depends on effective juxtapositions. Point out and comment on the most effective.
4. Explain the meaning of "mouths without hands" (3). Although this book proposes that the single term *metonymy* be used for the figures once distinguished as metonymy and synecdoche, it may be instructive to make the distinction here. Which is *mouths*? Which is *hands*? Why?

We said at the beginning of this chapter that figurative language often provides a more effective means of saying what we mean than does direct statement. What are some of the reasons for that effectiveness?

First, figurative language affords us imaginative pleasure. Imagination might be described in one sense as that faculty or ability of the mind that proceeds by sudden leaps from one point to another, that goes up a stair by leaping in one jump from the bottom to the top rather than by climbing up one step at a time.† The mind takes delight in these sudden leaps, in seeing likenesses between unlike things. We have probably all taken pleasure in staring into a fire and seeing castles and cities

* From *Cymon and Iphigenia.*

† It is also the faculty of mind that is able to "picture" or "image" absent objects as if they were present. It was with imagination in this sense that we were concerned in the chapter on imagery.

and armies in it, or in looking into the clouds and shaping them into animals or faces, or in seeing a man in the moon. We name our plants and flowers after fancied resemblances: jack-in-the-pulpit, babies'-breath, Queen Anne's lace. Figures of speech are therefore satisfying in themselves, providing us with a source of pleasure in the exercise of the imagination.

Second, figures of speech are a way of bringing additional imagery into verse, of making the abstract concrete, of making poetry more sensuous. When MacLeish personifies science (page 613), he gives body and form to what had previously been only a concept. When Emily Dickinson compares poetry to "prancing coursers" (page 586), she objectifies imaginative and rhythmical qualities by presenting them in visual terms. When Robert Browning compares the crisping waves to "fiery ringlets" (page 600), he starts with one image and transforms it into three. Figurative language is a way of multiplying the sense appeal of poetry.

Third, figures of speech are a way of adding emotional intensity to otherwise merely informative statements and of conveying attitudes along with information. If we say, "So-and-so is a rat" or "My feet are killing me," our meaning is as much emotional as informative. When Thomas Hardy compares "tangled bine-stems" to "strings of broken lyres" (page 851), he not only draws an exact visual comparison but also conjures up a feeling of despondency through the suggestion of discarded instruments no longer capable of making music. When Wilfred Owen compares a soldier caught in a gas attack to a man drowning under a green sea (page 558), he conveys a feeling of despair and suffocation as well as a visual image.

Fourth, figures of speech are a means of concentration, a way of saying much in brief compass. Like words, they may be multidimensional. Consider, for instance, the merits of comparing life to a candle, as Shakespeare does in a passage from *Macbeth* (page 678). Life is like a candle in that it begins and ends in darkness; in that while it burns, it gives off light and energy, is active and colorful; in that it gradually consumes itself, gets shorter and shorter; in that it can be snuffed out at any moment; in that it is brief at best, burns only for a short duration. Possibly your imagination can suggest other similarities. But at any rate, Macbeth's compact metaphorical description of life as a "brief candle" suggests certain truths about life that would require dozens of words to state in literal language. At the same time it makes the abstract concrete, provides imaginative pleasure, and adds a degree of emotional intensity.

Obviously one of the necessary abilities for reading poetry is the ability to interpret figurative language. Every use of figurative language involves a risk of misinterpretation, though the risk is well worth taking. For the person who can translate the figure, the dividends are immense. Fortunately all people have imagination to some degree, and imagination can be cultivated. By practice one's ability to interpret figures of speech can be increased.

EXERCISE

1. Identify each of the following quotations as literal or figurative. If figurative, explain what is being compared to what and explain the appropriateness of the comparison. EXAMPLE: "Talent is a cistern; genius is a fountain." ANSWER: A metaphor. Talent = cistern; genius = fountain. Talent exists in finite supply; it can be used up. Genius is inexhaustible, ever renewing.

   a. O tenderly the haughty day
   Fills his blue urn with fire. *Emerson*

   b. It is with words as with sunbeams—the more they are condensed, the deeper they burn. *Robert Southey*

   c. Joy and Temperance and Repose
   Slam the door on the doctor's nose. *Anonymous*

   d. The pen is mightier than the sword. *Edward Bulwer-Lytton*

   e. The strongest oaths are straw
   To the fire i' the blood. *Shakespeare*

   f. The Cambridge ladies . . . live in furnished souls. *e. e. cummings*

   g. The green lizard and the golden snake,
   Like unimprisoned flames, out of their trance awake. *Shelley*

   h. Dorothy's eyes, with their long brown lashes, looked very much like her mother's. *Laetitia Johnson*

   i. Is this the face that launched a thousand ships? *Marlowe*

   j. What should such fellows as I do crawling between earth and heaven? *Shakespeare*

k. Love's feeling is more soft and sensible
Than are the tender horns of cockled snails. *Shakespeare*

l. The tawny-hided desert crouches watching her. *Francis Thompson*

m. . . . Let us sit upon the ground
And tell sad stories of the death of kings. *Shakespeare*

n. See, from his [Christ's, on the cross] head, his hands, his side
Sorrow and love flow mingled down. *Isaac Watts*

o. Now half [of the departing guests] to the setting moon are gone,
And half to the rising day. *Tennyson*

p. I do not know whether my present poems are better than the earlier ones. But this is certain: they are much sadder and sweeter, like pain dipped in honey. *Heinrich Heine*

q. . . . clouds. . . . Shepherded by the slow, unwilling wind. *Shelley*

r. Let us eat and drink, for tomorrow we shall die. *Isaiah 22:13*

s. Let us eat and drink, for tomorrow we may die.
Common misquotation of the above

THE SILKEN TENT

She is as in a field a silken tent
At midday when a sunny summer breeze
Has dried the dew and all its ropes relent,
So that in guys it gently sways at ease,
And its supporting central cedar pole,
That is its pinnacle to heavenward
And signifies the sureness of the soul,
Seems to owe naught to any single cord,
But strictly held by none, is loosely bound
By countless silken ties of love and thought
To everything on earth the compass round,
And only by one's going slightly taut
In the capriciousness of summer air
Is of the slightest bondage made aware.

Robert Frost (1874–1963)

QUESTIONS

1. A poet may use a variety of metaphors and similes in developing his subject or may, as Frost does here, develop a single figure at length (this poem is an excellent example of EXTENDED or SUSTAINED SIMILE). What are the advantages of each type of development?

2. Explore the similarities between the two things compared.

METAPHORS

I'm a riddle in nine syllables,
An elephant, a ponderous house,
A melon strolling on two tendrils.
O red fruit, ivory, fine timbers!
This loaf's big with its yeasty rising.
Money's new-minted in this fat purse.
I'm a means, a stage, a cow in calf.
I've eaten a bag of green apples,
Boarded the train there's no getting off.

Sylvia Plath (1932–1963)

QUESTIONS

1. Like its first metaphor, this poem is a riddle to be solved by identifying the literal terms of its metaphors. After you have identified the speaker (*riddle, elephant, house, melon, stage, cow*), identify the literal meanings of the related metaphors (*syllables, tendrils, fruit, ivory, timbers, loaf, yeasty rising, money, purse, train*). How is line 8 to be interpreted?

2. How does the form of the poem relate to its content?

IT SIFTS FROM LEADEN SIEVES

It sifts from leaden sieves,
It powders all the wood.
It fills with alabaster wool
The wrinkles of the road.

It makes an even face
Of mountain and of plain—
Unbroken forehead from the east
Unto the east again.

It reaches to the fence,
It wraps it rail by rail

Till it is lost in fleeces;
It deals celestial veil

To stump and stack and stem—
A summer's empty room—
Acres of joints where harvests were,
Recordless, but for them.

It ruffles wrists of posts
As ankles of a queen,
Then stills its artisans like ghosts,
Denying they have been.

Emily Dickinson (1830–1886)

THE SNOW THAT NEVER DRIFTS

The snow that never drifts—
The transient, fragrant snow
That comes a single time a year—
Is softly driving now;

So thorough in the tree
At night below the star
That it was February's self
Experience would swear;

Like winter as a face
We stern and former knew
Repaired of all but loneliness
By nature's alibi.

Were every snow so spice
The value could not be;
We buy with contrast—pang is good
As near as memory.

Emily Dickinson (1830–1886)

QUESTIONS

1. Compare or contrast the two foregoing poems as to subject and technique. Are they essentially different or alike?

2. The first poem, in its first and last stanzas, contains two metaphors of the fourth form—that is, metaphors in which neither the literal nor the figurative term is named. Identify and interpret each.

A VALEDICTION: FORBIDDING MOURNING

As virtuous men pass mildly away,
    And whisper to their souls to go,
While some of their sad friends do say,
    The breath goes now, and some say, no:

So let us melt, and make no noise,
    No tear-floods, nor sigh-tempests move,
'Twere profanation of our joys
    To tell the laity our love.

Moving of th' earth brings harms and fears,
    Men reckon what it did and meant,
But trepidation of the spheres,
    Though greater far, is innocent.

Dull sublunary lovers' love
    (Whose soul is sense) cannot admit
Absence, because it doth remove
    Those things which elemented it.

But we by a love so much refined,
    That ourselves know not what it is,
Inter-assurèd of the mind,
    Care less, eyes, lips, and hands to miss.

Our two souls therefore, which are one,
    Though I must go, endure not yet
A breach, but an expansion,
    Like gold to airy thinness beat.

If they be two, they are two so
    As stiff twin compasses are two,
Thy soul the fixed foot, makes no show
    To move, but doth, if th' other do.

And though it in the center sit,
    Yet when the other far doth roam,
It leans, and hearkens after it,
    And grows erect, as that comes home.

Such wilt thou be to me, who must
    Like th' other foot, obliquely run;

Thy firmness makes my circle just,
And makes me end, where I begun.

John Donne (1572–1631)

QUESTIONS

1. Vocabulary: *valediction* (title), *profanation* (7), *laity* (8), *trepidation* (11), *innocent* (12), *sublunary* (13), *elemented* (16). Line 11 is a reference to the spheres of the Ptolemaic cosmology, whose movement caused no such disturbance as does a movement of the earth—that is, an earthquake.

2. Is the speaker in the poem about to die? Or about to leave on a journey?

3. The poem is organized around a contrast of two kinds of lovers: the *laity* (8) and, as their opposite, the priesthood. What two major contrasts are drawn between these two kinds of lovers?

4. Find and explain three similes and one metaphor used to describe the parting of true lovers. The figure in the last three stanzas is one of the most famous in English literature. Demonstrate its appropriateness by obtaining a drawing compass or by using two pencils to imitate the two legs.

5. What kind of language is used in the poem? Is the language consonant with the figures of speech?

TO HIS COY MISTRESS

Had we but world enough, and time,
This coyness, lady, were no crime.
We would sit down, and think which way
To walk, and pass our long love's day.
Thou by the Indian Ganges' side
Shouldst rubies find; I by the tide
Of Humber would complain. I would
Love you ten years before the Flood,
And you should, if you please, refuse
Till the conversion of the Jews.
My vegetable love should grow
Vaster than empires, and more slow;
An hundred years should go to praise
Thine eyes, and on thy forehead gaze;
Two hundred to adore each breast,
But thirty thousand to the rest;
An age at least to every part,

And the last age should show your heart.
For, lady, you deserve this state,
Nor would I love at lower rate.
    But at my back I always hear
Time's wingèd chariot hurrying near;
And yonder all before us lie
Deserts of vast eternity.
Thy beauty shall no more be found,
Nor, in thy marble vault, shall sound
My echoing song; then worms shall try
That long-preserved virginity,
And your quaint honor turn to dust,
And into ashes all my lust:
The grave's a fine and private place,
But none, I think, do there embrace.
    Now therefore, while the youthful hue
Sits on thy skin like morning dew,
And while thy willing soul transpires
At every pore with instant fires,
Now let us sport us while we may,
And now, like amorous birds of prey,
Rather at once our time devour
Than languish in his slow-chapped power.
Let us roll all our strength and all
Our sweetness up into one ball,
And tear our pleasures with rough strife
Thorough° the iron gates of life. through
Thus, though we cannot make our sun
Stand still, yet we will make him run.

Andrew Marvell (1621–1678)

QUESTIONS

1. Vocabulary: *mistress* (title), *Humber* (7), *transpires* (35), *chapped* (40).

2. Outline the speaker's argument in three sentences, beginning with *If, But,* and *Therefore.* Is the speaker urging his mistress to marry him?

3. Explain the appropriateness of "vegetable love" (11). What simile in the third section contrasts with it and how? What image in the third section contrasts with the distance between the Ganges and the Humber in section one?

4. Explain the figures in lines 22, 24, and 40 and their implications.

5. Explain the last two lines. For what is *sun* a metonymy?

6. Is this poem principally about love or about time? If the latter, what might making love represent? What philosophy is the poet advancing here?

THE FOLLY OF BEING COMFORTED

One that is ever kind said yesterday:
"Your well-belovèd's hair has threads of grey,
And little shadows come about her eyes;
Time can but make it easier to be wise
Though now it seems impossible, and so
All that you need is patience."
Heart cries, "No,
I have not a crumb of comfort, not a grain.
Time can but make her beauty over again:
Because of that great nobleness of hers
The fire that stirs about her, when she stirs,
Burns but more clearly. O she had not these ways
When all the wild summer was in her gaze."

O heart! O heart! if she'd but turn her head,
You'd know the folly of being comforted.

William Butler Yeats (1865–1939)

QUESTIONS

1. For some thirty years Yeats suffered an unrequited love for a famous Irish beauty who was working in the cause of Irish freedom. What comfort is here held out to him? On what grounds does he reject it? What is the meaning of the last two lines?

2. Find two personifications, one apostrophe, and five metaphors in the poem, and comment on their effectiveness.

DREAM DEFERRED

What happens to a dream deferred?

Does it dry up
like a raisin in the sun?

Or fester like a sore—
And then run?

Does it stink like rotten meat?
Or crust and sugar over—
like a syrupy sweet?

Maybe it just sags
like a heavy load.

Or does it explode?

Langston Hughes (1902–1967)

QUESTIONS

1. Of the six images, five are similes. Which is a metaphor? Comment on its position and its effectiveness.

2. Since the dream could be any dream, the poem is general in its implication. What happens to your understanding of it on learning that its author was an American Negro?

ENTICER

A married man who begs his friend,
A bachelor, to wed and end
    His lonesome, sorry state,
Is like a bather in the sea,
Goose-pimpled, blue from neck to knee,
    Who cries, "The water's great!"

Richard Armour (b. 1906)

ON A CLERGYMAN'S HORSE BITING HIM

The steed bit his master;
    How came this to pass?
He heard the good pastor
    Cry, "All flesh is grass."

Anonymous

Figurative Language 2

Symbol, Allegory

THE ROAD NOT TAKEN

Two roads diverged in a yellow wood,
And sorry I could not travel both
And be one traveler, long I stood
And looked down one as far as I could
To where it bent in the undergrowth;

Then took the other, as just as fair,
And having perhaps the better claim,
Because it was grassy and wanted wear;
Though as for that the passing there
Had worn them really about the same,

And both that morning equally lay
In leaves no step had trodden black.
Oh, I kept the first for another day!
Yet knowing how way leads on to way,
I doubted if I should ever come back.

I shall be telling this with a sigh
Somewhere ages and ages hence:
Two roads diverged in a wood, and I—
I took the one less traveled by,
And that has made all the difference.

Robert Frost (1874–1963)

QUESTIONS

1. Does the speaker feel that he made the wrong choice in taking the road "less traveled by"? If not, why does he sigh? What does he regret?
2. Why does the choice between two roads that seem very much alike make such a big difference many years later?

A SYMBOL may be roughly defined as something that means *more* than what it is. "The Road Not Taken," for instance, concerns a choice made between two roads by a person out walking in the woods. He would like to explore both roads. He tells himself that he will explore one and then come back and explore the other, but he knows that he shall probably be unable to do so. By the last stanza, however, we realize that the poet is talking about something more than the choice of paths in a wood, for such a choice would be relatively unimportant, while this choice is one that will make a great difference in the speaker's life and that he will remember with a sigh "ages and ages hence." We must interpret his choice of a road as a symbol for any choice in life between alternatives that appear almost equally attractive but will result through the years in a large difference in the kind of experience one knows.

Image, metaphor, and symbol shade into each other and are sometimes difficult to distinguish. In general, however, an image means only what it is; a metaphor means something other than what it is; and a symbol means what it is and something more too.* If I say that a shaggy brown dog was rubbing its back against a white picket fence, I am talking about nothing but a dog (and a picket fence) and am therefore presenting an image. If I say, "Some dirty dog stole my wallet at the party," I am not talking about a dog at all and am therefore using a metaphor. But if I say, "You can't teach an old dog new tricks," I am talking not only about dogs but about living creatures of any species and am therefore speaking symbolically. Images, of course, do not cease to be images when they become incorporated in metaphors or symbols. If we are discussing the sensuous qualities of "The Road Not Taken" we should refer to the two leaf-strewn roads in the yellow wood as an

* This account does not hold for nonliterary symbols such as the letters of the alphabet and algebraic signs (the symbol ∞ for infinity or $=$ for equals). Here, the symbol is meaningless except as it stands for something else, and the connection between the sign and what it stands for is purely arbitrary.

image; if we are discussing the significance of the poem, we talk about them as symbols.

Symbols vary in the degree of identification and definition that their authors give them. Frost in this poem forces us to interpret the choice of roads symbolically by the degree of importance he gives it in the last stanza. Sometimes poets are much more specific in identifying their symbols. Sometimes they do not identify them at all. Consider, for instance, the following poems.

A WHITE ROSE

The red rose whispers of passion,
    And the white rose breathes of love;
Oh, the red rose is a falcon,
    And the white rose is a dove.

But I send you a cream-white rosebud,
    With a flush on its petal tips;
For the love that is purest and sweetest
    Has a kiss of desire on the lips.

John Boyle O'Reilly (1844–1890)

QUESTIONS

1. Could the poet have made the white rose a symbol of passion and the red rose a symbol of love? Why not?

2. In the second stanza, why does the speaker send a rosebud rather than a rose?

MY STAR

All that I know
    Of a certain star
Is, it can throw
    (Like the angled spar)
Now a dart of red,
    Now a dart of blue;
Till my friends have said
    They would fain see, too,
My star that dartles the red and the blue!

Then it stops like a bird; like a flower, hangs furled:
They must solace themselves with the Saturn above it.
What matter to me if their star is a world?
Mine has opened its soul to me; therefore I love it.

Robert Browning (1812–1889)

In his first two lines O'Reilly indicates so clearly that his red rose is a symbol of physical desire and his white rose a symbol of spiritual attachment that when we get to the metaphor in the third line we unconsciously substitute passion for the red rose in our minds, knowing without thinking that what O'Reilly is really likening is falcons and passion, not falcons and roses. Similarly in the second stanza, the symbolism of the white rosebud with pink tips is specifically indicated in the last two lines, although, as a matter of fact, it would have been clear from the first stanza. In Browning's poem, on the other hand, there is nothing specific to tell us that Browning is talking about anything other than just a star, and it is only the star's importance to him that makes us suspect that he is talking about something more.

The symbol is the richest and at the same time the most difficult of the poetical figures. Both its richness and its difficulty result from its imprecision. Although the poet may pin down the meaning of his symbol to something fairly definite and precise, as O'Reilly does in "A White Rose," more often the symbol is so general in its meaning that it is able to suggest a great variety of more specific meanings. It is like an opal that flashes out different colors when slowly turned in the light. The choice in "The Road Not Taken," for instance, concerns some choice in life, but what choice? Was it a choice of profession? (Frost took the road "less traveled by" in deciding to become a poet.) A choice of hobby? A choice of wife? It might be any or all or none of these. We cannot determine what particular choice the poet had in mind, if any, and it is not important that we do so. The general meaning of the poem is clear enough. It is an expression of regret that the possibilities of life-experience are so sharply limited. One must live with one wife, have one native country, follow one profession. The speaker in the poem would have liked to explore both roads, but he could explore only one. The person with a craving for life, however satisfied with his own choice, will always long for the realms of experience that had to be passed by. Because the symbol is a rich one, the poem suggests other meanings too. It affirms a belief in the possibility of choice and says something of the nature of choice—how each choice limits the range of possible future choices, so that we make our lives as we go, both freely choosing and being determined by past choices. Though not primarily a philosophical poem, it obliquely comments on the issue of free will versus determinism and indicates the poet's own position. It is able to do all these things, concretely and compactly, by its use of an effective symbol.

"My Star," if we interpret it symbolically, likewise suggests a variety of meanings. It has been most often interpreted as a tribute to Browning's wife, Elizabeth Barrett Browning. As one critic writes, "She shone upon his life like a star of various colors; but the moment the world attempted to pry into the secret of her genius, she shut off the light altogether."* The poem has also been taken to refer to Browning's own peculiar genius, "his gift for seeing in events and things a significance hidden from other men."† A third suggestion is that Browning was thinking of his own peculiar poetic style. He loved harsh, jagged sounds and rhythms and grotesque images; most people of his time found beauty only in the smoother-flowing, melodic rhythms and more conventionally poetic images of his contemporary Tennyson's style, which could be symbolized by Saturn in the poem. The point is not that any one of these interpretations is right or necessarily wrong. We cannot say what the poet had specifically in mind. Literally, the poem is an expression of affection for a particular star in the sky that has a unique beauty and fascination for the poet but in which no one else can see the qualities that the poet sees. If we interpret the poem symbolically, the star is a symbol for anything in life that has unique meanings and value for an individual, which other people cannot see. Beyond this, the meaning is "open." And because the meaning is open, the reader is justified in bringing his own experience to its interpretation. Browning's cherished star might remind him of, for instance, an old rag doll he particularly loved as a child, though its button eyes were off and its stuffing coming

* William Lyon Phelps, *Robert Browning: How to Know Him* (Indianapolis: Bobbs-Merrill, 1932), p. 165.

† Quoted from William Clyde DeVane, *A Browning Handbook* (New York: Crofts, 1935), p. 202.

out and it had none of the crisp bright beauty of waxen dolls with real hair admired by other children.

Between the extremes represented by "The White Rose" and "My Star" a poem may exercise all degrees of control over the range and meaning of its symbolism. Consider another example.

YOU, ANDREW MARVELL

And here face down beneath the sun
And here upon earth's noonward height
To feel the always coming on
The always rising of the night:

To feel creep up the curving east
The earthly chill of dusk and slow
Upon those under lands the vast
And ever-climbing shadow grow

And strange at Ecbatan the trees
Take leaf by leaf the evening strange
The flooding dark about their knees
The mountains over Persia change

And now at Kermanshah the gate
Dark empty and the withered grass
And through the twilight now the late
Few travelers in the westward pass

And Baghdad darken and the bridge
Across the silent river gone
And through Arabia the edge
Of evening widen and steal on

And deepen on Palmyra's street
The wheel rut in the ruined stone
And Lebanon fade out and Crete
High through the clouds and overblown

And over Sicily the air
Still flashing with the landward gulls
And loom and slowly disappear
The sails above the shadowy hulls

Once we are aware of this larger concern of the poem, two symbolical levels of interpretation open to us. Marvell's poem is primarily concerned with the swift passing of man's life; and the word *night,* we know, if we have had any experience with other literature, is a natural and traditional metaphor or symbol for death. The poet, then, is thinking not only about the passing of a day but about the passing of his life. He is at present "upon earth's noonward height"—in the full flush of manhood—but he is acutely conscious of the declining years ahead and of "how swift how secretly" his death comes on.

If we are to account fully for all the data of the poem, however, a third level of interpretation is necessary. What has dictated the poet's choice of geographical references? The places named, of course, progress from east to west; but they have a further linking characteristic. Ecbatan, Kermanshah, Baghdad, and Palmyra are all ancient or ruined cities, the relics of past empires and crumbled civilizations. Lebanon, Crete, Sicily, Spain, and North Africa are places where civilization once flourished more vigorously than it does at present. On a third level, then, the poet is concerned, not with the passage of a day nor with the passage of a lifetime, but with the passage of historical epochs. The poet's own country—the United States—now shines "upon earth's noonward height" as a favored nation in the sun of history, but its civilization, too, will pass.

Meanings ray out from a symbol, like the corona around the sun or like connotations around a richly suggestive word. But the very fact that a symbol may be so rich in its meanings makes it necessary that we use the greatest tact in its interpretation. Though Browning's "My Star" might, if memory and reason be stretched, make us think of a rag doll, still we should not go around telling people that in this poem Browning uses the star to symbolize a rag doll, for this interpretation is private, idiosyncratic, and narrow. The poem allows it but does not itself suggest it. Moreover, we should never assume that because the meaning of a symbol is more or less open, we may make it mean anything we choose. We would be wrong, for instance, in interpreting the choice in "The Road Not Taken" as some choice between good and evil, for the poem tells us that the two roads are much alike and that both lie "in leaves no step had trodden black." Whatever the choice is, it is a choice between two goods. Whatever our interpretation of a symbolical poem, it must be tied firmly to the facts of the poem. We must not let loose of the string and let our imaginations go ballooning up among the clouds. Because the symbol is capable of adding so many dimensions to a poem, it is a peculiarly effective resource of the poet, but it is also peculiarly susceptible of misinterpretation by the untrained or incautious reader.

Accurate interpretation of the symbol requires delicacy, tact, and good sense. The reader must keep his balance while walking a tightrope between too little and too much—between underinterpretation and overinterpretation. If he falls off, however, it is much more desirable that he fall off on the side of too little. The reader who reads "The Road Not Taken" as being only about a choice between two roads in a wood has at least gotten part of the experience that the poem communicates, but the reader who reads into it anything he chooses might as well discard the poem and simply daydream.

Above all, we should avoid the disease of seeing symbols everywhere, like a man with hallucinations, whether there are symbols there or not. It is better to miss a symbol now and then than to walk constantly among shadows and mirages.

TO THE VIRGINS, TO MAKE MUCH OF TIME

Gather ye rosebuds while ye may,
 Old Time is still a-flying;
And this same flower that smiles today
 Tomorrow will be dying.

The glorious lamp of heaven, the Sun,
 The higher he's a-getting,
The sooner will his race be run,
 And nearer he's to setting.

That age is best which is the first,
 When youth and blood are warmer;
But being spent, the worse, and worst
 Times still succeed the former.

Then be not coy, but use your time;
 And while ye may, go marry;
For having lost but once your prime,
 You may forever tarry.

Robert Herrick (1591–1674)

QUESTIONS

1. The first two stanzas might be interpreted literally if the third and fourth stanzas did not force us to interpret them symbolically. What do the rosebuds symbolize (stanza 1)? What does the course of a day symbolize (stanza 2)? Does the poet fix the meaning of the rosebud symbol in the last stanza or merely name *one* of its specific meanings?

2. How does the title help us interpret the meaning of the symbol? Why did Herrick use *virgins* instead of *maidens?*

3. Why is such haste necessary in gathering the rosebuds? True, the blossoms die quickly, but they are replaced by others. Who *really* is dying?

4. What are the "worse, and worst" times (11)? Why?

5. Why did the poet use his wording rather than the following alternative: *blooms* for *smiles* (3), *course* for *race* (7), *used* for *spent* (11), *spend* for *use* (13)?

ALLEGORY is a narrative or description that has a second meaning beneath the surface one. Although the surface story or description may have its own interest, the author's major interest is in the ulterior meaning. When Pharaoh in the Bible, for instance, has a dream in which seven fat kine are devoured by seven lean kine, the story does not really become significant until Joseph interprets its allegorical meaning: that Egypt is to enjoy seven years of fruitfulness and prosperity followed by seven years of famine. Allegory has been defined sometimes as an extended metaphor and sometimes as a series of related symbols. But it is usually distinguishable from both of these. It is unlike extended metaphor in that it involves a *system* of related comparisons rather than one comparison drawn out. It differs from symbolism in that it puts less emphasis on the images for their own sake and more on their ulterior meanings. Also, these meanings are more fixed. In allegory usually there is a one-to-one correspondence between the details and a single set of ulterior meanings. In complex allegories the details may have more than one meaning, but these meanings tend to be definite. Meanings do not ray out from allegory as they do from a symbol.

Allegory is less popular in modern literature than it was in medieval and Renaissance writing, and it is much less often found in short poems than in long works such as *The Faerie Queene, Everyman,* and *Pilgrim's Progress.* It has sometimes, especially with political allegory, been used to conceal meaning rather than reveal it (or, rather, to conceal it from some people while revealing it to others). Though less rich than the symbol, allegory is an effective way of making the abstract concrete and has occasionally been used effectively even in fairly short poems.

THE PILGRIMAGE

I traveled on, seeing the hill, where lay
My expectation.
A long it was and weary way.
The gloomy cave of Desperation
I left on the one, and on the other side
The rock of Pride.

And so I came to Fancy's meadow strowed
With many a flower:
Fain would I here have made abode,
But I was quickened by my hour.
So to Care's copse I came, and there got through
With much ado.

That led me to the wild of Passion, which
Some call the wold;
A wasted place, but sometimes rich.
Here I was robbed of all my gold,
Save one good Angel, which a friend had tied
Close to my side.

At length I got unto the gladsome hill,
Where lay my hope,
Where lay my heart; and climbing still,
When I had gained the brow and top,
A lake of brackish waters on the ground
Was all I found.

With that abashed and struck with many a sting
Of swarming fears,
I fell, and cried, Alas my King!
Can both the way and end be tears?
Yet taking heart I rose, and then perceived
I was deceived:

My hill was further; so I flung away,
Yet heard a cry
Just as I went, *None goes that way*
And lives. If that be all, said I,
After so foul a journey death is fair,
And but a chair.

George Herbert (1593–1633)

QUESTIONS

1. Vocabulary: *fain* (9), *copse* (11), *wold* (14). What two meanings has *Angel* (17)? In Herbert's day, *chair* (36) meant not only a seat but a chariot. How do both meanings contribute to the meaning of the poem?

2. As is often done in allegories, life is here compared to a journey. (This poem was written half a century before *Pilgrim's Progress*.) Draw a map of the journey and then describe, in literal language, what is happening to the speaker at each place indicated on it. What is the point of his being deceived by the first hill? What is the second hill? Why is the journey called a "pilgrimage"?

EXERCISE

Determine whether *sleep*, in the following poems, is literal, metaphorical, symbolical, or other. In each case explain and justify your answer.

1. "On moonlit heath and lonesome bank," page 603, line 13.
2. Same poem, line 29.
3. "Stopping by Woods on a Snowy Evening," page 691.
4. "The Chimney Sweeper," page 655.
5. "Is my team ploughing," page 574.
6. "Ulysses," page 639, line 5.
7. "The Toys," page 803.
8. "The Love Song of J. Alfred Prufrock," page 815, line 22.
9. "Reveille," page 693.
10. "I will go back to the great sweet mother," page 721.
11. "Ode to a Nightingale," page 861, line 80.
12. "Judging Distances," page 595, line 20.

STARS, I HAVE SEEN THEM FALL

Stars, I have seen them fall,
But when they drop and die

No star is lost at all
From all the star-sown sky.
The toil of all that be
Helps not the primal fault;
It rains into the sea,
And still the sea is salt.

A. E. Housman (1859–1936)

QUESTION

Relate the symbols employed to the meaning of the poem.

ULYSSES

It little profits that an idle king,
By this still hearth, among these barren crags,
Matched with an agèd wife, I mete and dole
Unequal laws unto a savage race,
That hoard, and sleep, and feed, and know not me.
I cannot rest from travel; I will drink
Life to the lees. All times I have enjoyed
Greatly, have suffered greatly, both with those
That loved me, and alone; on shore, and when
Through scudding drifts the rainy Hyades
Vext the dim sea. I am become a name;
For always roaming with a hungry heart
Much have I seen and known,—cities of men
And manners, climates, councils, governments,
Myself not least, but honored of them all;
And drunk delight of battle with my peers,
Far on the ringing plains of windy Troy.
I am a part of all that I have met;
Yet all experience is an arch wherethrough
Gleams that untraveled world, whose margin fades
For ever and for ever when I move.
How dull it is to pause, to make an end,
To rust unburnished, not to shine in use!
As though to breathe were life! Life piled on life
Were all too little, and of one to me
Little remains; but every hour is saved
From that eternal silence, something more,
A bringer of new things; and vile it were

For some three suns to store and hoard myself,
And this grey spirit yearning in desire
To follow knowledge like a sinking star,
Beyond the utmost bound of human thought.

This is my son, mine own Telemachus,
To whom I leave the scepter and the isle—
Well-loved of me, discerning to fulfil
This labor, by slow prudence to make mild
A rugged people, and through soft degrees
Subdue them to the useful and the good.
Most blameless is he, centered in the sphere
Of common duties, decent not to fail
In offices of tenderness, and pay
Meet adoration to my household gods,
When I am gone. He works his work, I mine.

There lies the port; the vessel puffs her sail:
There gloom the dark, broad seas. My mariners,
Souls that have toiled, and wrought, and thought with me—
That ever with a frolic welcome took
The thunder and the sunshine, and opposed
Free hearts, free foreheads—you and I are old;
Old age hath yet his honor and his toil.
Death closes all; but something ere the end,
Some work of noble note, may yet be done,
Not unbecoming men that strove with Gods.
The lights begin to twinkle from the rocks;
The long day wanes; the slow moon climbs; the deep
Moans round with many voices. Come, my friends,
'Tis not too late to seek a newer world.
Push off, and sitting well in order smite
The sounding furrows; for my purpose holds
To sail beyond the sunset, and the baths
Of all the western stars, until I die.
It may be that the gulfs will wash us down;
It may be we shall touch the Happy Isles,
And see the great Achilles, whom we knew.
Though much is taken, much abides; and though
We are not now that strength which in old days
Moved earth and heaven, that which we are, we are:

One equal temper of heroic hearts,
Made weak by time and fate, but strong in will
To strive, to seek, to find, and not to yield.

Alfred, Lord Tennyson (1809–1892)

QUESTIONS

1. Vocabulary: *Hyades* (10), *meet* (42).

2. Ulysses, king of Ithaca, is a legendary Greek hero, a major figure in Homer's *Iliad,* the hero of Homer's *Odyssey,* and a minor figure in Dante's *Divine Comedy.* After ten years at the siege of Troy, Ulysses set sail for home but, having incurred the wrath of the god of the sea, he was subjected to storms and vicissitudes and was forced to wander for another ten years, having many adventures and seeing most of the Mediterranean world before again reaching Ithaca, his wife, and his son. Once back home, according to Dante, he still wished to travel and "to follow virtue and knowledge." In Tennyson's poem, Ulysses is represented as about to set sail on a final voyage from which he will not return. Where is Ulysses standing during his speech? Whom is he addressing? Locate Ithaca on a map. Where exactly, in geographical terms, does Ulysses intend to sail (59–64)? (The Happy Isles were the Elysian fields, or Greek paradise; Achilles was another Greek prince, the hero of the *Iliad,* who was killed at the siege of Troy.)

3. Characterize Ulysses. What kind of person is he as Tennyson represents him?

4. What does Ulysses symbolize? What way of life is being recommended?

5. Find as many evidences as you can that Ulysses' desire for travel represents something more than mere wanderlust and wish for adventure.

6. Give two reasons why Tennyson might have Ulysses travel westward.

7. Interpret lines 18–21 and 26–29. What is symbolized by "the thunder and the sunshine" (48)? What do the two metonymies in line 49 stand for? What metaphor is implied in line 23?

CURIOSITY

may have killed the cat; more likely
the cat was just unlucky, or else curious
to see what death was like, having no cause
to go on licking paws, or fathering
litter on litter of kittens, predictably.

Nevertheless, to be curious
is dangerous enough. To distrust

what is always said, what seems,
to ask old questions, interfere in dreams,
leave home, smell rats, have hunches
do not endear cats to those doggy circles
where well-smelt baskets, suitable wives, good lunches
are the order of things, and where prevails
much wagging of incurious heads and tails.

Face it. Curiosity
will not cause us to die—
only lack of it will.
Never to want to see
the other side of the hill
or that improbable country
where living is an idyll
(although a probable hell)
would kill us all.
Only the curious
have, if they live, a tale
worth telling at all.

Dogs say cats love too much, are irresponsible,
are changeable, marry too many wives,
desert their children, chill all dinner tables
with tales of their nine lives.
Well, they are lucky. Let them be
nine-lived and contradictory,
curious enough to change, prepared to pay
the cat price, which is to die
and die again and again,
each time with no less pain.
A cat minority of one
is all that can be counted on
to tell the truth. And what cats have to tell
on each return from hell
is this: that dying is what the living do,
that dying is what the loving do,
and that dead dogs are those who do not know
that dying is what, to live, each has to do.

Alastair Reid (b. 1926)

QUESTIONS

1. On the surface this poem is a dissertation on cats. What deeper comments does it make? Of what are cats and dogs, in this poem, symbols?

2. In what different senses are the words *death, die,* and *dying* here used?

3. Compare and contrast this poem in meaning and manner with "Ulysses."

HYMN TO GOD MY GOD, IN MY SICKNESS

Since I am coming to that holy room
  Where, with thy choir of saints for evermore,
I shall be made thy music, as I come
  I tune the instrument here at the door,
  And what I must do then, think here before.

Whilst my physicians by their love are grown
  Cosmographers, and I their map, who lie
Flat on this bed, that by them may be shown
  That this is my southwest discovery,
  Per fretum febris,° by these straits to die, — through the raging of fever

I joy that in these straits I see my west;
  For though their currents yield return to none,
What shall my west hurt me? As west and east
  In all flat maps (and I am one) are one,
  So death doth touch the resurrection.

Is the Pacific Sea my home? Or are
  The eastern riches? Is Jerusalem?
Anyan,° and Magellan, and Gibralter, — Bering Strait
  All straits, and none but straits, are ways to them,
 Whether where Japhet dwelt, or Cham, or Sem.

We think that Paradise and Calvary,
  Christ's cross and Adam's tree, stood in one place;
Look Lord, and find both Adams met in me;
  As the first Adam's sweat surrounds my face,
  May the last Adam's blood my soul embrace.

So, in his purple wrapped receive me Lord,
  By these his thorns give me his other crown;
And as to others' souls I preached thy word,

Be this my text, my sermon to mine own:
Therefore, that he may raise, the Lord throws down.

John Donne (1572–1631)

QUESTIONS

1. Vocabulary: *cosmographers* (7).

2. For the last ten years of his life John Donne was Dean of St. Paul's Cathedral in London, and he is famous for his sermons (lines 28–30) as well as his poems. According to his earliest biographer, this poem was written eight days before his death. What are "that holy room" (1) and "the instrument" (4)? What is Donne engaged in doing in stanza 1?

3. During Donne's lifetime such explorers as Henry Hudson and Martin Frobisher sought for a northwest passage to the East Indies. Why does Donne speak instead of a "southwest discovery" (9)? In what ways is his raging fever like a strait? What different meanings of the word *straits* (10) are operative here? What do the straits symbolize?

4. In what ways does Donne's body resemble a map?

5. Though the map is metaphorical, its parts are symbolical. What does the west symbolize? the east? the fact that west and east are one?

6. What meanings has the word *return* (12)? (Compare line 17.)

7. Japhet, Cham, and Sem (20), the sons of Noah, are in Christian legend the ancestors of three races of man, roughly identifiable with the populations of Europe, Africa, and Asia. What must one go through, according to Donne, to reach any place important? In what ways are the Pacific Ocean, the East Indies, and Jerusalem (16–17) each a fitting symbol for Donne's own destination?

8. The locations of Eden and Calvary (21) were identical according to early Christian scholars. How does this tie in with Donne's geographical symbolism? What connection is there between Adam's "sweat" (24) and Christ's "blood" (25)? Because Adam is said in the Bible to prefigure Christ (Romans 5:12–21), Christ is sometimes called the second Adam. How do the two Adams meet in Donne? What do sweat and blood (together and separately) symbolize?

9. For what are "eastern riches" (17), "his purple" (26), and "his thorns" (27) respectively metonymies? What do "purple" and "thorns" symbolize? What is Christ's "other crown" (27)?

10. With what earlier paradoxes in the poem does the paradox in the final line tie in? What, according to Donne, is the explanation and meaning of human suffering?

LOVE SONG: I AND THOU

Nothing is plumb, level or square:
    the studs are bowed, the joists
are shaky by nature, no piece fits
    any other piece without a gap
or pinch, and bent nails
    dance all over the surfacing
like maggots. By Christ
    I am no carpenter. I built
the roof for myself, the walls
    for myself, the floors
for myself, and got
    hung up in it myself. I
danced with a purple thumb
    at this house-warming, drunk
with my prime whiskey: rage.
    Oh I spat rage's nails
into the frame-up of my work:
    it held. It settled plumb,
level, solid, square and true
    for that one moment. Then
it screamed and went on through
    skewing as wrong the other way.
God damned it. This is hell,
    but I planned it, I sawed it,
I nailed it, and I
    will live in it until it kills me.
I can nail my left palm
    to the left-hand cross-piece but
I can't do everything myself.
    I need a hand to nail the right,
a help, a love, a you, a wife.

Alan Dugan (b. 1923)

QUESTIONS

1. What clues are there that this house is not literal? What does it stand for?
2. Why does the speaker swear "By Christ" rather than "By God" (7)?

Where else in the poem is Christ alluded to? What parallels and differences does the speaker see between himself and Christ?

3. "God damned it" (23) at first sounds like another curse, but the past tense makes its meaning more precise. What are the implications of lines 24–26? What implications are added in the phrase "by nature" (3)? What meanings has "prime" (15)?

4. What is the meaning of the last three lines?

5. Allegory, symbol, and extended metaphor are often difficult to tell apart, and perhaps have no fixed boundaries. (Some writers have defined allegory as extended metaphor.) Classification is unimportant so long as meanings are perceived. Nevertheless, how would you classify this?

SOUTHERN MANSION

Poplars are standing there still as death
And ghosts of dead men
Meet their ladies walking
Two by two beneath the shade
And standing on the marble steps.

There is a sound of music echoing
Through the open door
And in the field there is
Another sound tinkling in the cotton:
Chains of bondmen dragging on the ground.

The years go back with an iron clank,
A hand is on the gate,
A dry leaf trembles on the wall.
Ghosts are walking.
They have broken roses down
And poplars stand there still as death.

Arna Bontemps (b. 1902)

QUESTIONS

1. In what condition is the mansion? In addition to the actual ghosts, what details of imagery give the poem a "ghostly" atmosphere? What words suggest death?

2. Comment on the effectiveness of the metaphor in line 11. Whose hand is on the gate in line 12?

3. In the last stanza, the ghosts are said to have "broken roses down," something which ghosts, being immaterial, do not ordinarily do. What is

symbolically suggested by the mansion? the ghosts? the roses? What cause-and-effect relationship is implied by the poem?

EXERCISE

In what respects are the following poems alike? In what respects are they essentially different?

DUST OF SNOW

The way a crow
Shook down on me
The dust of snow
From a hemlock tree

Has given my heart
A change of mood
And saved some part
Of a day I had rued.

Robert Frost (1874–1963)

SOFT SNOW

I walked abroad in a snowy day;
I asked the soft snow with me to play;
She played and she melted in all her prime,
And the winter called it a dreadful crime.

William Blake (1757–1827)

EXERCISE

Which of the following poems are symbolical? Which are not?

THE TUFT OF KELP

All dripping in tangles green,
    Cast up by a lonely sea,
If purer for that, O Weed,
    Bitterer, too, are ye?

Herman Melville (1819–1891)

FOG

The fog comes
on little cat feet.

It sits looking
over harbor and city
on silent haunches
and then moves on.

Carl Sandburg (1878–1967)

EPIGRAM

Oh, God of dust and rainbows, help us see
That without dust the rainbow would not be.

Langston Hughes (1902–1967)

WIND AND SILVER

Greatly shining,
The Autumn moon floats in the thin sky;
And the fish-ponds shake their backs and flash their dragon scales
As she passes over them.

Amy Lowell (1874–1925)

I MAY, I MIGHT, I MUST

If you will tell me why the fen
appears impassable, I then
Will tell you why I think that I
can get across it if I try.

Marianne Moore (1887–1972)

AN EVERYWHERE OF SILVER

An everywhere of silver
With ropes of sand
To keep it from effacing
The track called land.

Emily Dickinson (1830–1886)

CHAPTER SEVEN

Figurative Language 3

Paradox, Overstatement, Understatement, Irony

Aesop tells the tale of a traveler who sought refuge with a Satyr on a bitter winter night. On entering the Satyr's lodging, he blew on his fingers, and was asked by the Satyr what he did it for. "To warm them up," he explained. Later, on being served with a piping hot bowl of porridge, he blew also on it, and again was asked what he did it for. "To cool it off," he explained. The Satyr thereupon thrust him out of doors, for he would have nothing to do with a man who could blow hot and cold with the same breath.

A PARADOX is an apparent contradiction that is nevertheless somehow true. It may be either a situation or a statement. Aesop's tale of the traveler illustrates a paradoxical situation. As a figure of speech, paradox is a statement. When Alexander Pope wrote that a literary critic of his time would "damn with faint praise," he was using a verbal paradox, for how can a man damn by praising?

When we understand all the conditions and circumstances involved in a paradox, we find that what at first seemed impossible is actually entirely plausible and not strange at all. The paradox of the cold hands and hot porridge is not strange to a man who knows that a stream of air directed upon an object of different temperature will tend to bring that object closer to its own temperature. And Pope's paradox is not strange when we realize that *damn* is being used figuratively, and that Pope means only that a too reserved praise may damage an author with the public almost as much as adverse criticism. In a paradoxical statement the contradiction usually stems from one of the words being used figuratively or in more than one sense.

The value of paradox is its shock value. Its seeming impossibility startles the reader into attention and, thus, by the fact of its apparent absurdity, it underscores the truth of what is being said.

TO LUCASTA, GOING TO THE WARS

Tell me not, Sweet, I am unkind,
    That from the nunnery
Of thy chaste breast and quiet mind
    To war and arms I fly.

True, a new mistress now I chase,
    The first foe in the field;
And with a stronger faith embrace
    A sword, a horse, a shield.

Yet this inconstancy is such
    As you too shall adore
I could not love thee, Dear, so much,
    Loved I not honor more.

Richard Lovelace (1618–1658)

QUESTIONS

1. State the basic paradox of the poem in a sentence. How is the paradox to be resolved?
2. Do you find any words in the poem used in more than one meaning?

Overstatement, understatement, and verbal irony form a continuous series, for they consist, respectively, of saying more, saying less, and saying the opposite of what one really means.

Overstatement, or *hyperbole,* is simply exaggeration but exaggeration in the service of truth. It is not the same as a fish story. If you say, "I'm starved!" or "You could have knocked me over with a feather!" or "I'll die if I don't pass this course!" you do not expect to be believed; you are merely adding emphasis to what you really mean. (And if you say,

"There were literally millions of people at the dance!" you are merely piling one overstatement on top of another, for you really mean that "There were figuratively millions of people at the dance," or, literally, "The dance hall was very crowded.") Like all figures of speech, overstatement may be used with a variety of effects. It may be humorous or grave, fanciful or restrained, convincing or unconvincing. When Tennyson says of his eagle (page 555) that it is "*Close* to the sun in lonely lands," he says what appears to be literally true, though we know from our study of astronomy that it is not. When Wordsworth reports of his daffodils in "I wandered lonely as a cloud" that they "stretched *in never-ending line*" along the margin of a bay, he too reports faithfully a visual appearance. When Frost says, at the conclusion of "The Road Not Taken" (page 627),

> I shall be saying this with a sigh
> Somewhere *ages and ages hence,*

we are scarcely aware of the overstatement, so quietly is the assertion made. Unskillfully used, however, overstatement may seem strained and ridiculous, leading us to react as Gertrude does to the player-queen's speeches in *Hamlet:* "The lady doth protest too much."

It is paradoxical that one can emphasize a truth either by overstating it or by understating it. UNDERSTATEMENT, or saying less than one means, may exist in what one says or merely in how one says it. If, for instance, upon sitting down to a loaded dinner plate, you say, "This looks like a good bite," you are actually stating less than the truth; but if you say, with Artemus Ward, that a man who holds his hand for half an hour in a lighted fire will experience "a sensation of excessive and disagreeable warmth," you are stating what is literally true but with a good deal less force than the situation might seem to warrant.

A RED, RED ROSE

O my luve is like a red, red rose,
    That's newly sprung in June.
O my luve is like the melodie
    That's sweetly played in tune.

As fair art thou, my bonnie lass,
    So deep in luve am I,

And I will luve thee still, my dear,
    Till a'° the seas gang° dry. all; go

Till a' the seas gang dry, my dear,
    And the rocks melt wi' the sun!
And I will love thee still, my dear,
    While the sands o' life shall run.

And fare thee wel, my only luve,
    And fare thee wel awhile!
And I will come again, my luve,
    Though it were ten thousand mile!

Robert Burns (1759–1796)

THE ROSE FAMILY

The rose is a rose,
And was always a rose.
But the theory now goes
That the apple's a rose,
And the pear is, and so's
The plum, I suppose.
The dear only knows
What will next prove a rose.
You, of course, are a rose—
But were always a rose.

Robert Frost (1874–1963)

QUESTION

Burns and Frost use the same metaphor in paying tribute to their loved ones; otherwise their methods are opposed. Burns begins with a couple of conventionally poetic similes and proceeds to a series of overstatements. Frost begins with literal and scientific fact (the apple, pear, plum, and rose all belong to the same botanical family, the Rosaceae), and then slips in his metaphor so casually and quietly that the assertion has the effect of understatement. What is the function of *of course* and *but* in the last two lines?

Like paradox, *irony* has meanings that extend beyond its use merely as a figure of speech.

VERBAL IRONY, saying the opposite of what one means, is often confused with sarcasm and with satire, and for that reason it may be well to look at the meanings of all three terms. SARCASM and SATIRE both imply ridicule, one on the colloquial level, the other on the literary level. Sarcasm is simply bitter or cutting speech, intended to wound the feelings (it comes from a Greek word meaning to tear flesh). Satire is a more formal term, usually applied to written literature rather than to speech and ordinarily implying a higher motive: it is ridicule (either bitter or gentle) of human folly or vice, with the purpose of bringing about reform or at least of keeping other people from falling into similar folly or vice. Irony, on the other hand, is a literary device or figure that may be used in the service of sarcasm or ridicule or may not. It is popularly confused with sarcasm and satire because it is so often used as their tool: but irony may be used without either sarcastic or satirical intent, and sarcasm and satire may exist (though they do not usually) without irony. If, for instance, one of the members of your class raises his hand on the discussion of this point and says, "I don't understand," and your instructor replies, with a tone of heavy disgust in his voice, "Well, I wouldn't expect *you* to," he is being sarcastic but not ironical; he means exactly what he says. But if, after you have done particularly well on an examination, your instructor brings your test papers into the classroom saying, "Here's some *bad* news for you: you all got A's and B's!" he is being ironical but not sarcastic. Sarcasm, we may say, is cruel, as a bully is cruel: it intends to give hurt. Satire is both cruel and kind, as a surgeon is cruel and kind: it gives hurt in the interest of the patient or of society. Irony is neither cruel nor kind: it is simply a device, like a surgeon's scalpel, for performing any operation more skillfully.

Though verbal irony always implies the opposite of what is said, it has many gradations, and only in its simplest forms does it mean *only* the opposite of what is said. In more complex forms it means both what is said and the opposite of what is said, at once, though in different ways and with different degrees of emphasis. When Terence's critic, in "Terence, this is stupid stuff" (page 566) says, "*Pretty* friendship 'tis to rhyme / Your friends to death before their time" (11–12), we may substitute the literal "sorry" for "pretty" with little or no loss of meaning. However, when Dryden writes of the paid militia (page 616) that they "hasten to be drunk, the *business* of the day," we cannot substitute

Oh, what an impure
Irreligious man is he!

The term *irony* always implies some sort of discrepancy or incongruity. In verbal irony the discrepancy is between what is said and what is meant. In other forms the discrepancy may be between appearance and reality or between expectation and fulfillment. These other forms of irony are, on the whole, more important resources for the poet than is verbal irony. Two types, especially, are important for the beginning student to know.

In DRAMATIC IRONY* the discrepancy is not between what the speaker says and what he means but between what the speaker says and what the author means. The speaker's words may be perfectly straightforward, but the author, by putting these words in a particular speaker's mouth, may be indicating to the reader ideas or attitudes quite opposed to those the speaker is voicing. This form of irony is more complex than verbal irony and demands a more complex response from the reader. It may be used not only to convey attitudes but also to illuminate character, for the author who uses it is indirectly commenting not only upon the value of the ideas uttered but also upon the nature of the person who utters them. Such comment may be harsh, gently mocking, or sympathetic.

THE CHIMNEY SWEEPER

When my mother died I was very young,
And my father sold me while yet my tongue

* The term *dramatic irony,* which stems from Greek tragedy, often connotes something more specific and perhaps a little different from what I am developing here. It is used of a speech or an action in a story which has much greater significance to the audience than to the character who speaks or performs it, because of possession by the audience of knowledge the character does not have, as when the enemies of Ulysses, in the *Odyssey,* wish good luck and success to a man who the reader knows is Ulysses himself in disguise, or as when Oedipus, in the play by Sophocles, bends every effort to discover the murderer of Laius so that he may avenge the death, not knowing, as the audience does, that Laius is the man whom he himself once slew. I have appropriated the term for a perhaps slightly different situation, because no other suitable term exists. Both uses have the common characteristic—that the author conveys to the reader something different, or at least something more, than the character himself intends.

Could scarcely cry " 'weep! 'weep! 'weep! 'weep!"
So your chimneys I sweep, and in soot I sleep.

There's little Tom Dacre, who cried when his head,
That curled like a lamb's back, was shaved; so I said,
"Hush, Tom! never mind it, for, when your head's bare,
You know that the soot cannot spoil your white hair."

And so he was quiet, and that very night,
As Tom was asleeping, he had such a sight!
That thousands of sweepers, Dick, Joe, Ned, and Jack,
Were all of them locked up in coffins of black.

And by came an Angel who had a bright key,
And he opened the coffins and set them all free;
Then down a green plain leaping, laughing, they run,
And wash in a river, and shine in the sun.

Then naked and white, all their bags left behind,
They rise upon clouds and sport in the wind;
And the Angel told Tom, if he'd be a good boy,
He'd have God for his father, and never want joy.

And so Tom awoke, and we rose in the dark,
And got with our bags and our brushes to work.
Though the morning was cold, Tom was happy and warm;
So if all do their duty they need not fear harm.

William Blake (1757–1827)

QUESTIONS

1. In the eighteenth century small boys, sometimes no more than four or five years old, were employed to climb up the narrow chimney flues and clean them, collecting the soot in bags. Such boys, sometimes sold to the master sweepers by their parents, were miserably treated by their masters and often suffered disease and physical deformity. Characterize the boy who speaks in this poem. How do his and the poet's attitudes toward his lot in life differ? How, especially, are the meanings of the poet and the speaker different in lines 3, 7–8, and 24?

2. The dream in lines 11–20, besides being a happy dream, is capable of symbolic interpretations. Point out possible significances of the sweepers' being "locked up in coffins of black" and the Angel's releasing them with a bright key to play upon green plains.

A third type of irony is IRONY OF SITUATION. This occurs when there is a discrepancy between the actual circumstances and those that would seem appropriate or between what one anticipates and what actually comes to pass. If a man and his second wife, on the first night of their honeymoon, are accidentally seated at the theater next to the man's first wife, we should call the situation ironical. When, in O. Henry's famous short story "The Gift of the Magi" a poor young husband pawns his most prized possession, a gold watch, in order to buy his wife a set of combs for her hair for Christmas, and his wife sells her most prized possession, her long brown hair, in order to buy a fob for her husband's watch, we call the situation ironical. When King Midas, in the famous fable, is granted his fondest wish, that anything he touch turn to gold, and then finds that he cannot eat because even his food turns to gold, we call the situation ironical. When Coleridge's Ancient Mariner finds himself in the middle of the ocean with "Water, water, everywhere" but not a "drop to drink," we call the situation ironical. In each case the circumstances are not what would seem appropriate or what we would expect.

Dramatic irony and irony of situation are powerful devices for the poet, for, like symbol, they enable him to suggest meanings without stating them—to communicate a great deal more than he says. We have seen one effective use of irony of situation in "Richard Cory" (page 592). Another is in "Ozymandias," which follows.

Irony and paradox may be trivial or powerful devices, depending on their use. At their worst they may degenerate into mere mannerism and mental habit. At their best they may greatly extend the dimensions of meaning in a work of literature. Because irony and paradox are devices that demand an exercise of critical intelligence, they are particularly valuable as safeguards against sentimentality.

OZYMANDIAS

I met a traveller from an antique land
Who said: Two vast and trunkless legs of stone
Stand in the desert . . . Near them, on the sand,
Half sunk, a shattered visage lies, whose frown,
And wrinkled lip, and sneer of cold command,
Tell that its sculptor well those passions read

Which yet survive, stamped on these lifeless things,
The hand that mocked them, and the heart that fed:
And on the pedestal these words appear:
"My name is Ozymandias, king of kings:
Look on my works, ye Mighty, and despair!"
Nothing beside remains. Round the decay
Of that colossal wreck, boundless and bare
The lone and level sands stretch far away.

Percy Bysshe Shelley (1792–1822)

QUESTIONS

1. *Survive* (7) is a transitive verb with *hand* and *heart* as direct objects. Whose hand? Whose heart? What figure of speech is exemplified in *hand* and *heart*?
2. Characterize Ozymandias.
3. Ozymandias was an an ancient Egyptian tyrant. This poem was first published in 1817. Of what is Ozymandias a *symbol*? What contemporary reference might the poem have had in Shelley's time?
4. What is the theme of the poem and how is it "stated"?

EXERCISE

Identify each of the following quotations as literal or figurative. If figurative, identify the figure as paradox, overstatement, understatement, or irony and explain the use to which it is put (emotional emphasis, humor, satire, etc.).

1. Poetry is a language that tells us, through a more or less emotional reaction, something that cannot be said. *Edwin Arlington Robinson*
2. Have not the Indians been kindly and justly treated? Have not the temporal things, the vain baubles and filthy lucre of this world, which were too apt to engage their worldly and selfish thoughts, been benevolently taken from them? And have they not instead thereof, been taught to set their affections on things above? *Washington Irving*
3. A man who could make so vile a pun would not scruple to pick a pocket. *John Dennis*
4. Last week I saw a woman flayed, and you will hardly believe how much it altered her person for the worse. *Swift*
5. . . . Where ignorance is bliss,
'Tis folly to be wise. *Thomas Gray*
6. All night I made my bed to swim; with my tears I dissolved my couch. *Psalms 6:6*

7. Believe him, he has known the world too long,
And seen the death of much immortal song. *Pope*

8. Give me my Romeo: and, when he shall die,
Take him and cut him out in little stars,
And he will make the face of heaven so fine
That all the world will be in love with night,
And pay no worship to the garish sun. *Juliet, in Shakespeare*

9. Immortality will come to such as are fit for it; and he who would be a great soul in the future must be a great soul now. *Emerson*

10. Whoe'er their crimes for interest only quit,
Sin on in virtue, and good deeds *commit.* *Edward Young*

THE HABIT OF PERFECTION

Elected Silence, sing to me
And beat upon my whorlèd ear,
Pipe me to pastures still and be
The music that I care to hear.

Shape nothing, lips; be lovely-dumb:
It is the shut, the curfew sent
From there where all surrenders come
Which only makes you eloquent.

Be shellèd, eyes, with double dark
And find the uncreated light:
This ruck and reel which you remark
Coils, keeps, and teases simple sight.

Palate, the hutch of tasty lust,
Desire not to be rinsed with wine:
The can must be so sweet, the crust
So fresh that come in fasts divine!

Nostrils, your careless breath that spend
Upon the stir and keep of pride,
What relish shall the censers send
Along the sanctuary side!

O feel-of-primrose hands, O feet
That want the yield of plushy sward,

But you shall walk the golden street
And you unhouse and house the Lord.

And, Poverty, be thou the bride
And now the marriage feast begun,
And lily-colored clothes provide
Your spouse not labored-at nor spun.

Gerard Manley Hopkins (1844–1889)

QUESTIONS

1. Vocabulary: *ruck* (11), *remark* (11), *coils* (12), *hutch* (13), *stir* (18), *keep* (18), *censers* (19).

2. Gerard Manley Hopkins, in the year he wrote this poem, was converted to Roman Catholicism; he later became a Jesuit priest. In this poem he writes about the monastic, ascetic life of the priest, who traditionally takes vows of poverty (25). Line 24 refers to taking the Host from the tabernacle of the altar in a Catholic mass. What central paradox underlies the poem? How is this paradox developed in each of the separate stanzas?

3. Lines 27–28 are an allusion to Matthew 6:28–29. How does it contribute to the meaning of the poem?

4. What meanings have *Habit* (title)? *simple* (12)? *want* (22)?

THE KISS

"I saw you take his kiss!" " 'Tis true."
"O modesty!" " 'Twas strictly kept:
He thought me asleep—at least, I knew
He thought I thought he thought I slept."

Coventry Patmore (1823–1896)

QUESTIONS

1. Which speech exhibits verbal irony?
2. Evaluate the second speaker's defense of her modesty.

MARY HINES

(After the Irish of Raftery)

That Sunday, on my oath, the rain was a heavy overcoat
On a poor poet, and when the rain began

In fleeces of water to buckleap like a goat
I was only a walking penance reaching Kiltartan;
And there, so suddenly that my cold spine
Broke out on the arch of my back in a rainbow,
This woman surged out of the day with so much sunlight
I was nailed there like a scarecrow,

But I found my tongue and the breath to balance it
And I said: "If I bow to you with this hump of rain
I'll fall on my collarbone, but look, I'll chance it,
And after falling, bow again."
She laughed, ah, she was gracious, and softly said to me,
"For all your lovely talking I go marketing with an ass,
I'm no hill-queen, alas, or Ireland, that grass widow,
So hurry on, sweet Raftery, or you'll keep me late for Mass!"

The parish priest has blamed me for missing second Mass
And the bell talking on the rope of the steeple,
But the tonsure of the poet is the bright crash
Of love that blinds the irons on his belfry;
Were I making an Aisling I'd tell the tale of her hair,
But now I've grown careful of my listeners
So I pass over one long day and the rainy air
Where we sheltered in whispers.

When we left the dark evening at last outside her door,
She lighted a lamp though a gaming company
Could have sighted each trump by the light of her unshawled poll,
And indeed she welcomed me
With a big quart bottle and I mooned there over glasses
Till she took that bird, the phoenix, from the spit;
And "Raftery," says she, "a feast is no bad dowry,
Sit down now and taste it!"

If I praised Ballylea before it was only for the mountains
Where I broke horses and ran wild,
And not for its seven crooked smoky houses
Where seven crones are tied
All day to the listening top of a half door,
And nothing to be heard or seen

But the drowsy dropping of water
And a gander on the green.

But, Boys! I was blind as a kitten till last Sunday.
This town is earth's very navel!
Seven palaces are thatched there of a Monday,
And O the seven queens whose pale
Proud faces with their seven glimmering sisters,
The Pleiads, light the evening where they stroll,
And one can find the well by their wet footprints,
And make one's soul;

For Mary Hynes, rising, gathers up there
Her ripening body from all the love stories;
And, rinsing herself at morning, shakes her hair
And stirs the old gay books in libraries;
And what shall I do with sweet Boccaccio?
And shall I send Ovid back to school again
With a new headline for his copy book,
And a new pain?

Like a nun she will play you a sweet tune on a spinet,
And from such grasshopper music leap
Like Herod's hussy who fancied a saint's head
For grace after meat;
Yet she'll peg out a line of clothes on a windy morning
And by noonday put them ironed in the chest,
And you'll swear by her white fingers she does nothing
But take her fill of rest.

And I'll wager now that my song is ended,
Loughrea, that old dead city where the weavers
Have pined at the mouldering looms since Helen broke the thread,
Will be piled again with silver fleeces:
O the new coats and big horses! The raving and the ribbons!
And Ballylea in hubbub and uproar!
And may Raftery be dead if he's not there to ruffle it
On his own mare, Shank's mare, that never needs a spur!

But ah, Sweet Light, though your face coins
My heart's very metals, isn't it folly without a pardon
For Raftery to sing so that men, east and west, come
Spying on your vegetable garden?

We could be so quiet in your chimney corner—
Yet how could a poet hold you any more than the sun,
Burning in the big bright hazy heart of harvest,
Could be tied in a henrun?

Bless your poet then and let him go!
He'll never stack a haggard with his breath:
His thatch of words will not keep rain or snow
Out of the house, or keep back death.
But Raftery, rising, curses as he sees you
Stir the fire and wash delph,
That he was bred a poet whose selfish trade it is
To keep no beauty to himself.

Padraic Fallon (b. 1906)

QUESTIONS

1. Vocabulary: *tonsure* (19), *poll* (27), *phoenix* (30), *Pleiads* (46). *Crash* (19) has several meanings: a heavy linen fabric; a brilliant reddish-yellow color; a loud noise: which ones are relevant here? What two relevant meanings has *tell the tale* (20–21), and why must Raftery be "careful" of his listeners (22)? *Aisling* (21) is a vision of a maiden, usually Ireland personified. *Shank's mare* (72) is shanks' mare, i.e., one's own legs. *Haggard* (82) is an enclosure of stacked grain. *Delph* (86) is china.

2. Raftery (1784?–1835) was a famous itinerant Irish bardic poet, and Mary Hynes was the peasant girl whom he made famous in his verse. The present poem, while not a translation of any Raftery poem, does depend on a sense of Raftery as a folk figure, as well as on a mixture of Irish and classical mythology. What kind of person is Raftery? Whom is he addressing? Where? When?

3. Examine and comment on the figures of speech used by Raftery. What kind of bird, literally, does Mary Hynes cook for Raftery? What is the essential quality of his language and of his praise of Mary Hynes?

4. *Ballylea* (33) is in the barony of *Kiltartan* (4) in County Galway, Ireland; *Loughrea* (66) is a nearby town. *Boccaccio* (53) was a fourteenth-century storyteller and poet whose *Decameron* revolves about the enticing figure of Fiametta. *Ovid* (54) was a first-century B.C. Roman poet, famous for his *Art of Love*. *Herod's hussy* (59) is Salome, the famous dancing wench of the Bible (Matthew 14:1–11). *Helen* (67) is Helen of Troy. What does Raftery's use of literary, Biblical, and classical allusions tell us about him?

5. For what qualities does Raftery praise Mary Hynes? Enumerate her accomplishments. What is the main difference between her and Raftery?

Does she acquire any symbolic values in the course of the poem?

6. Why, in Raftery's thinking, will Loughrea revive, and Ballylea again become a busy center of commerce (65–70)? What will be the ultimate result of Raftery's praise?

7. Explain the paradox with which the poem ends. State the theme of the poem, in a paragraph if necessary.

NO LONGER MOURN FOR ME

No longer mourn for me when I am dead
Than you shall hear the surly sullen bell
Give warning to the world that I am fled
From this vile world, with vilest worms to dwell.
Nay, if you read this line, remember not
The hand that writ it, for I love you so,
That I in your sweet thoughts would be forgot,
If thinking on me then should make you woe.
O, if, I say, you look upon this verse
When I perhaps compounded am with clay,
Do not so much as my poor name rehearse,
But let your love even with my life decay,
    Lest the wise world should look into your moan
    And mock you with me after I am gone.

William Shakespeare (1564–1616)

QUESTIONS

1. What paradoxical idea informs the first twelve lines of the poem, and how is it resolved?

2. What word in the concluding couplet is ironical?

THE CONSTANT LOVER

Out upon it! I have loved
    Three whole days together;
And am like to love three more,
    If it prove fair weather.

Time shall moult away his wings,
    Ere he shall discover
In the whole wide world again
    Such a constant lover.

But the spite on 't is, no praise
Is due at all to me:
Love with me had made no stays
Had it any been but she.

Had it any been but she,
And that very face,
There had been at least ere this
A dozen dozen in her place.

Sir John Suckling (1609–1642)

QUESTIONS

1. What figures of speech are used in stanzas 2 and 4?

2. Traditionally, lovers vow to be faithful forever to their sweethearts. Burns, in "A Red, Red Rose" (page 651), declares he will love his sweetheart "till a' the seas gang dry." Suckling's lover, on the other hand, *complains* that he has been faithful for three whole days and may be so for three more. The discrepancy between our expectation (aroused by the title) and this fulfillment constitutes a form of irony. Is this irony employed ultimately for the purpose of making a cynical observation about love or of paying an exaggerated compliment to the lady in question? In what respect does the speaker pay his sweetheart a greater compliment than does the lover who vows to be faithful forever?

3. Does the lover's complaint in the first stanza support his assertion in the third that no praise is due at all to him for this constancy?

FIRE AND ICE

Some say the world will end in fire,
Some say in ice.
From what I've tasted of desire
I hold with those who favor fire.
But if it had to perish twice,
I think I know enough of hate
To say that for destruction ice
Is also great
And would suffice.

Robert Frost (1874–1963)

QUESTIONS

1. Who are "Some"? To what two theories do lines 1–2 refer?
2. Discuss the poem in terms of symbolism and understatement. What are the different meanings of *the world* (1)?

INCIDENT

Once riding in old Baltimore
    Heart-filled, head-filled with glee,
I saw a Baltimorean
    Keep looking straight at me.

Now I was eight and very small,
    And he was no whit bigger,
And so I smiled, but he poked out
    His tongue, and called me, "Nigger."

I saw the whole of Baltimore
    From May until December;
Of all the things that happened there
    That's all that I remember.

Countee Cullen (1903–1946)

QUESTION

What accounts for the effectiveness of the last stanza? Comment on the title. Is it in key with the meaning of the poem?

FORMAL APPLICATION

"The poets apparently want to rejoin the human race." Time

I shall begin by learning to throw
the knife, first at trees, until it sticks
in the trunk and quivers every time;

next from a chair, using only wrist
and fingers, at a thing on the ground,
a fresh ant hill or a fallen leaf;

then at a moving object, perhaps
a pieplate swinging on twine, until
I pot it at least twice in three tries.

Meanwhile, I shall be teaching the birds
that the skinny fellow in sneakers
is a source of suet and bread crumbs,

first putting them on a shingle nailed
to a pine tree, next scattering them
on the needles, closer and closer

to my seat, until the proper bird,
a towhee, I think, in black and rust
and gray, takes tossed crumbs six feet away.

Finally, I shall coordinate
conditioned reflex and functional
form and qualify as Modern Man.

You see the splash of blood and feathers
and the blade pinning it to the tree?
It's called an "Audubon Crucifix."

The phrase has pleasing (even pious)
connotations, like *Arbeit Macht Frei,*
"Molotov Cocktail," and *Enola Gay.*

Donald W. Baker (b. 1923)

QUESTIONS

1. *Arbeit Macht Frei* (26) ("Labor liberates") was the slogan of the German Nazi Party. "Molotov Cocktail" (27), a homemade hand grenade named after Stalin's foreign minister, was widely used during the Spanish Civil War and World War II. *Enola Gay* (27) was the American plane that dropped the first atom bomb on Hiroshima. In what ways are the connotations of these phrases—and of "Audubon Crucifix" (24)—"pleasing"?
2. What different kinds of irony operate in this poem? Discuss.
3. What meanings has the title?

ADVICE TO YOUNG LADIES

A.U.C. 334: about this date
For a sexual misdemeanour, which she denied,
The vestal virgin Postumia was tried.
Livy records it among affairs of state.

They let her off: it seems she was perfectly pure;
The charge arose because some thought her talk
Too witty for a young girl, her eyes, her walk
Too lively, her clothes too smart to be demure.

The Pontifex Maximus, summing up the case,
Warned her in future to abstain from jokes,
To wear less modish and more pious frocks.
She left the court reprieved, but in disgrace.

What then? With her the annalist is less
Concerned than what the men achieved that year:
Plots, quarrels, crimes, with oratory to spare!
I see Postumia with her dowdy dress,

Stiff mouth and listless step; I see her strive
To give dull answers. She had to knuckle down.
A vestal virgin who scandalized that town
Had fair trial, then they buried her alive.

Alive, bricked up in suffocating dark,
A ration of bread, a pitcher if she was dry,
Preserved the body they did not wish to die
Until her mind was quenched to the last spark.

How many the black maw has swallowed in its time!
Spirited girls who would not know their place;
Talented girls who found that the disgrace
Of being a woman made genius a crime;

How many others, who would not kiss the rod
Domestic bullying broke or public shame?
Pagan or Christian, it was much the same:
Husbands, St. Paul declared, rank next to God.

Livy and Paul, it may be, never knew
That Rome was doomed; each spoke of her with pride.
Tacitus, writing after both had died,
Showed that whole fabric rotten through and through.

Historians spend their lives and lavish ink
Explaining how great commonwealths collapse
From great defects of policy—perhaps
The cause is sometimes simpler than they think.

It may not seem so grave an act to break
Postumia's spirit as Galileo's, to gag
Hypatia as crush Socrates, or drag
Joan as Giordano Bruno to the stake.

Can we be sure? Have more states perished, then,
For having shackled the enquiring mind,
Than those who, in their folly not less blind,
Trusted the servile womb to breed free men?

A. D. Hope (b. 1907)

QUESTIONS

1. *A.U.C.* (1) Stands for *Ab Urbe Condita* which means "from the founding of the city." *A.U.C.* 334 is the same as 420 B.C. Is this poem about the past or the present?

2. The vestal virgins were maidens under the supervision of the high priest or *Pontifex Maximus* (9) appointed to keep the sacred fire in ancient Rome burning. When found guilty of breaking the vows of chastity they were buried alive, as described in stanza 6. Is the "black maw" (25) literal, metaphorical, or symbolical?

3. *Livy* (4) (59 B.C.–17 A.D.) and *Tacitus* (35) (55?–117?) were Roman historians. For St. Paul's teaching on wives (32), see Ephesians 5:22–24. What were the fates of Galileo, Hypatia, Socrates, Joan of Arc, and Giordano Bruno (42–44)?

4. What advice does the poem give to young ladies? How are we to interpret the title?

MR. Z

Taught early that his mother's skin was the sign of error,
He dressed and spoke the perfect part of honor;
Won scholarships, attended the best schools,
Disclaimed kinship with jazz and spirituals;
Chose prudent, raceless views for each situation,
Or when he could not cleanly skirt dissension,
Faced up to the dilemma, firmly seized
Whatever ground was Anglo-Saxonized.

In diet, too, his practice was exemplary:
Of pork in its profane forms he was wary;

Expert in vintage wines, sauces and salads,
His palate shank from cornbread, yams and collards.

He was as careful whom he chose to kiss:
His bride had somewhere lost her Jewishness,
But kept her blue eyes; an Episcopalian
Prelate proclaimed them matched chameleon.
Choosing the right addresses, here, abroad,
They shunned those places where they might be barred;
Even less anxious to be asked to dine
Where hosts catered to kosher accent or exotic skin.

And so he climbed, unclogged by ethnic weights,
An airborne plant, flourishing without roots.
Not one false note was struck—until he died:
His subtly grieving widow could have flayed
The obit writers, ringing crude changes on a clumsy phrase:
"One of the most distinguished members of his race."

M. Carl Holman (b. 1919)

QUESTIONS

1. Vocabulary: *profane* (10), *kosher* (20), *exotic* (20), *ethnic* (21), *obit* (25).

2. Explain Mr. Z's motivation and the strategies he used to achieve his goal.

3. What is the author's attitude toward Mr. Z? Is he satirizing him or the society that produced him? Why does he not give Mr. Z a name?

4. What judgments on Mr. Z are implied by the metaphors in lines 16 and 22? Explain them.

5. What kind of irony is operating in the last line? As you reread the poem, where else do you detect ironic overtones?

6. What is Mr. Z's color?

THE UNKNOWN CITIZEN

(To JS/07/M/378 This Marble Monument Is Erected by the State)

He was found by the Bureau of Statistics to be
One against whom there was no official complaint,
And all the reports on his conduct agree
That, in the modern sense of an old-fashioned word, he was a saint,
For in everything he did he served the Greater Community.
Except for the War till the day he retired
He worked in a factory and never got fired,

But satisfied his employers, Fudge Motors Inc.
Yet he wasn't a scab or odd in his views,
For his Union reports that he paid his dues,
(Our report on his Union shows it was sound)
And our Social Psychology workers found
That he was popular with his mates and liked a drink.
The Press are convinced that he bought a paper every day
And that his reactions to advertisements were normal in every way.
Policies taken out in his name prove that he was fully insured,
And his Health-card shows he was once in hospital but left it cured.
Both Producers Research and High-Grade Living declare
He was fully sensible to the advantages of the Installment Plan
And had everything necessary to the Modern Man,
A phonograph, a radio, a car and a frigidaire.
Our researchers into Public Opinion are content
That he held the proper opinions for the time of year;
When there was peace, he was for peace; when there was war, he went.
He was married and added five children to the population,
Which our Eugenist says was the right number for a parent of his
    generation,
And our teachers report that he never interfered with their education,
Was he free? Was he happy? The question is absurd:
Had anything been wrong, we should certainly have heard.

W. H. Auden (1907–1973)

QUESTIONS

1. Vocabulary: *scab* (9), *Eugenist* (26).

2. Explain the allusion and the irony in the title. Why was the citizen *unknown?*

3. This obituary of an unknown state "hero" was apparently prepared by a functionary of the state. Give an account of the citizen's life and character from Auden's own point of view.

4. What trends in modern life and social organization does the poem satirize?

MY LAST DUCHESS

Ferrara

That's my last Duchess painted on the wall,
Looking as if she were alive. I call
That piece a wonder, now; Fra Pandolf's hands

Worked busily a day, and there she stands.
Will 't please you sit and look at her? I said
"Fra Pandolf" by design, for never read
Strangers like you that pictured countenance,
The depth and passion of its earnest glance,
But to myself they turned (since none puts by
The curtain I have drawn for you, but I)
And seemed as they would ask me, if they durst,
How such a glance came there; so, not the first
Are you to turn and ask thus. Sir, 'twas not
Her husband's presence only, called that spot
Of joy into the Duchess' cheek; perhaps
Fra Pandolf chanced to say, "Her mantle laps
Over my lady's wrist too much," or, "Paint
Must never hope to reproduce the faint
Half-flush that dies along her throat." Such stuff
Was courtesy, she thought, and cause enough
For calling up that spot of joy. She had
A heart—how shall I say?—too soon made glad,
Too easily impressed; she liked whate'er
She looked on, and her looks went everywhere.
Sir, 'twas all one! My favor at her breast,
The dropping of the daylight in the West,
The bough of cherries some officious fool
Broke in the orchard for her, the white mule
She rode with round the terrace—all and each
Would draw from her alike the approving speech,
Or blush, at least. She thanked men—good! but thanked
Somehow—I know not how—as if she ranked
My gift of a nine-hundred-years-old name
With anybody's gift. Who'd stoop to blame
This sort of trifling? Even had you skill
In speech—which I have not—to make your will
Quite clear to such an one, and say, "Just this
Or that in you disgusts me; here you miss,
Or there exceed the mark"—and if she let
Herself be lessoned so, nor plainly set
Her wits to yours, forsooth, and made excuse—
E'en then would be some stooping; and I choose
Never to stoop. Oh, sir, she smiled, no doubt,

Whene'er I passed her; but who passed without
Much the same smile? This grew; I gave commands;
Then all smiles stopped together. There she stands
As if alive. Will 't please you rise? We'll meet
The company below, then. I repeat,
The Count your master's known munificence
Is ample warrant that no just pretense
Of mine for dowry will be disallowed;
Though his fair daughter's self, as I avowed
At starting, is my object. Nay, we'll go
Together down, sir. Notice Neptune, though,
Taming a sea-horse, thought a rarity,
Which Claus of Innsbruck cast in bronze for me!

Robert Browning (1812–1889)

QUESTIONS

1. Vocabulary: *officious* (27), *munificence* (49).
2. Ferrara is in Italy. The time is during the Renaissance, probably the sixteenth century. To whom is the Duke speaking? What is the occasion? Are the Duke's remarks about his last Duchess a digression, or do they have some relation to the business at hand?
3. Characterize the Duke as fully as you can. How does your characterization differ from the Duke's opinion of himself? What kind of irony is this?
4. Why was the Duke dissatisfied with his last Duchess? Was it sexual jealousy? What opinion do you get of the Duchess's personality, and how does it differ from the Duke's opinion?
5. What characteristics of the Italian Renaissance appear in the poem (marriage customs, social classes, art)? What is the Duke's attitude toward art? Is it insincere?
6. What happened to the Duchess? Should we have been told?

EPIGRAM

As Thomas was cudgeled one day by his wife,
He took to the street, and fled for his life.
Tom's three dearest friends came by in the squabble,
And saved him at once from the shrew and the rabble,
Then ventured to give him some sober advice.
But Tom is a person of honor so nice,

Too wise to take counsel, too proud to take warning,
That he sent to all three a challenge next morning.
Three duels he fought, thrice ventured his life,
Went home, and was cudgeled again by his wife.

Jonathan Swift (1667–1745)

QUESTIONS

1. Vocabulary: nice (6).
2. What two lines of the poem contain verbal irony? Explain.
3. The poem pivots on two situational ironies. What are they?

EARTH

"A planet doesn't explode of itself," said drily
The Martian astronomer, gazing off into the air—
"That they were able to do it is proof that highly
Intelligent beings must have been living there."

John Hall Wheelock (b. 1886)

LINES FOR A CHRISTMAS CARD

May all my enemies go to hell,
Noel, Noel, Noel, Noel.

Hilaire Belloc (1870–1953)

CHAPTER EIGHT

Allusion

The famous English diplomat and letter writer Lord Chesterfield was once invited to a great dinner given by the Spanish ambassador. At the conclusion of the meal the host rose and proposed a toast to his master, the king of Spain, whom he compared to the sun. The French ambassador followed with a health to the king of France, whom he likened to the moon. It was then Lord Chesterfield's turn. "Your excellencies have taken from me," he said, "all the greatest luminaries of heaven, and the stars are too small for me to make a comparison of my royal master; I therefore beg leave to give your excellencies—Joshua!"*

For a reader familiar with the Bible—that is, for one who recognizes the Biblical allusion—Lord Chesterfield's story will come as a stunning revelation of his wit. For an ALLUSION—a reference to something in history or previous literature—is, like a richly connotative word or a symbol, a means of suggesting far more than it says. The one word "Joshua," in the context of Chesterfield's toast, calls up in the reader's mind the whole Biblical story of how the Israelite captain stopped the sun and the moon in order that the Israelites might finish a battle and conquer their enemies before nightfall.† The force of the toast lies in its extreme economy; it says so much in so little, and it exercises the mind of the reader to make the connection for himself.

The effect of Chesterfield's allusion is chiefly humorous or witty, but allusions may also have a powerful emotional effect. The essayist William Hazlitt writes of addressing a fashionable audience about the lexicog-

* Samuel Shellabarger, *Lord Chesterfield and His World* (Boston: Little, Brown, 1951), p. 132.

† Joshua 10:12–14.

rapher Samuel Johnson. Speaking of Johnson's great heart and of his charity to the unfortunate, Hazlitt recounted how, finding a drunken prostitute lying in Fleet Street late at night, Johnson carried her on his broad back to the address she managed to give him. The audience, unable to face the picture of the famous dictionary-maker doing such a thing, broke out in titters and expostulations. Whereupon Hazlitt simply said: "I remind you, ladies and gentlemen, of the parable of the Good Samaritan." The audience was promptly silenced.*

Allusions are a means of reinforcing the emotion or the ideas of one's own work with the emotion or ideas of another work or occasion. Because they are capable of saying so much in so little, they are extremely useful to the poet.

"OUT, OUT—"

The buzz-saw snarled and rattled in the yard
And made dust and dropped stove-length sticks of wood,
Sweet-scented stuff when the breeze drew across it.
And from there those that lifted eyes could count
Five mountain ranges one behind the other
Under the sunset far into Vermont.
And the saw snarled and rattled, snarled and rattled,
As it ran light, or had to bear a load.
And nothing happened: day was all but done.
Call it a day, I wish they might have said
To please the boy by giving him the half hour
That a boy counts so much when saved from work.
His sister stood beside them in her apron
To tell them "Supper." At the word, the saw,
As if to prove saws knew what supper meant,
Leaped out at the boy's hand, or seemed to leap—
He must have given the hand. However it was,
Neither refused the meeting. But the hand!
The boy's first outcry was a rueful laugh,
As he swung toward them holding up the hand
Half in appeal, but half as if to keep
The life from spilling. Then the boy saw all—
Since he was old enough to know, big boy

* Jacques Barzun, *Teacher in America* (Boston: Little, Brown, 1945), p. 160.

Doing a man's work, though a child at heart—
He saw all spoiled. "Don't let him cut my hand off—
The doctor, when he comes. Don't let him, sister!"
So. But the hand was gone already.
The doctor put him in the dark of ether.
He lay and puffed his lips out with his breath.
And then—the watcher at his pulse took fright.
No one believed. They listened at his heart.
Little—less—nothing!—and that ended it.
No more to build on there. And they, since they
Were not the one dead, turned to their affairs.

Robert Frost (1874–1963)

QUESTIONS

1. How does this poem differ from a newspaper account that might have dealt with the same incident?

2. To whom does *they* (33) refer? The boy's family? The doctor and hospital attendants? Casual onlookers? Need we assume that all these people—whoever they are—turned immediately "to their affairs"? Does the ending of this poem seem to you callous or merely realistic? Would a more tearful and sentimental ending have made the poem better or worse?

3. What figure of speech is used in lines 21–22?

Allusions vary widely in the amount of reliance that the poet puts on them to convey his meaning. Lord Chesterfield risked his whole meaning on his hearers' recognizing his allusion. Robert Frost in "Out, Out—" makes his meaning entirely clear even for the reader who does not recognize the allusion contained in his title. His theme is the uncertainty and unpredictability of life, which may be accidentally ended at any moment, and the tragic waste of human potentiality which takes place when such premature deaths occur. A boy who is already "doing a man's work" and gives every promise of having a useful life ahead of him is suddenly wiped out. There seems no rational explanation for either the accident or the death. The only comment to be made is, "No more to build on there."

Frost's title, however, is an allusion to one of the most famous passages in all English literature, and it offers a good illustration of how a poet may use allusion not only to reinforce emotion but also to help define his theme. The passage is that in *Macbeth* in which Macbeth has just been informed of his wife's death. A good many readers will recall the key phrase, "Out, out, brief candle!" with its underscoring of the tragic brevity and uncertainty of life that can be snuffed out at any moment. For some readers, however, the allusion will summon up the whole passage in act V, scene 5, in which this phrase occurs. Macbeth's words are:

> She should have died hereafter;
> There would have been a time for such a word.
> To-morrow, and to-morrow, and to-morrow
> Creeps in this petty pace from day to day
> To the last syllable of recorded time;
> And all our yesterdays have lighted fools
> The way to dusty death. Out, out, brief candle!
> Life's but a walking shadow, a poor player,
> That struts and frets his hour upon the stage
> And then is heard no more. It is a tale
> Told by an idiot, full of sound and fury,
> Signifying nothing.

Macbeth's first words underscore the theme of premature death. The boy also "should have died hereafter." The rest of the passage, with its marvelous evocation of the vanity and meaninglessness of life, expresses neither Shakespeare's philosophy nor, ultimately, Frost's, but it is Macbeth's philosophy at the time of his bereavement, and it is likely to express the feelings of us all when such tragic accidents occur. Life does indeed seem cruel and meaningless, a tale told by an idiot, signifying nothing, when human life and potentiality are thus without explanation so suddenly ended.

Allusions vary widely in the number of readers to whom they will be familiar. The poet, in using an allusion as in using a figure of speech, is always in danger of not being understood. In appealing powerfully to one reader, he may lose another reader altogether. But the poet must assume a certain fund of common experience with his readers. He could not even write about the ocean unless he could assume that his reader had seen the ocean or pictures of it. In the same way he will assume a certain common fund of literary experience. He is often justified in expecting a rather wide range of literary experience in his readers, for the people who read poetry for pleasure are generally people of good minds and good education who have read widely. But, obviously, beginning readers will not have this range, just as they will not know the meanings of as many words as will maturer readers. The student ought therefore to be prepared to look up certain allusions, just as he should be eager to look up in his dictionary the meanings of unfamiliar words. He will find that every increase in knowledge will broaden his base for understanding both literature and life.

IN HEAVENLY REALMS OF HELLAS

in heavenly realms of hellas dwelt
two very different sons of zeus:
one, handsome strong and born to dare
—a fighter to his eyelashes—
the other, cunning ugly lame;
but as you'll shortly comprehend
a marvellous artificer

now Ugly was the husband of
(as happens every now and then
upon a merely human plane)
someone completely beautiful;
and Beautiful, who (truth to sing)
could never quite tell right from wrong,
took brother Fearless by the eyes
and did the deed of joy with him

then Cunning forged a web so subtle
air is comparatively crude;
an indestructible occult
supersnare of resistless metal:
and (stealing toward the blissful pair)
skilfully wafted over themselves this implacable unthing

next, our illustrious scientist
petitions the celestial host
to scrutinize his handiwork:

they (summoned by that savage yell
from shining realms of regions dark)
laugh long at Beautiful and Brave
—wildly who rage, vainly who strive;
and being finally released
flee one another like the pest

thus did immortal jealousy
quell divine generosity,
thus reason vanquished instinct and
matter became the slave of mind;
thus virtue triumphed over vice
and beauty bowed to ugliness
and logic thwarted life: and thus—
but look around you, friends and foes

my tragic tale concludes herewith:
soldier, beware of mrs smith

e. e. cummings (1894–1962)

QUESTIONS

1. In Book VIII of the *Odyssey,* Homer recounts how Hephaestus, god of the underworld and the forge, by means of a cunningly devised invisible snare, traps his wife, Aphrodite, in adultery with Ares, and then summons the other gods from Olympus to witness their shame. How does Cummings apply this ancient myth to modern times?

2. List the qualities associated with Hephaestus and those associated with Ares and Aphrodite. With which qualities is the poet more sympathetic? Can you justify the positions of "virtue" and "vice" on this list?

3. The poem concludes with a "moral." Exactly what is that moral and how are we to take it? Does it or does it not sum up the meaning of the poem?

4. What does the use of puns, refurbished clichés, polysyllabic adjectives, coinages, and metrical variations contribute to the poem?

ON HIS BLINDNESS

When I consider how my light is spent
    Ere half my days in this dark world and wide,
    And that one talent which is death to hide
    Lodged with me useless, though my soul more bent

To serve therewith my Maker, and present
My true account, lest he returning chide,
"Doth God exact day-labor, light denied?"
I fondly ask. But Patience, to prevent
That murmur, soon replies, "God doth not need
Either man's work or his own gifts. Who best
Bear his mild yoke, they serve him best. His state
Is kingly: thousands at his bidding speed,
And post o'er land and ocean without rest;
They also serve who only stand and wait."

John Milton (1608–1674)

QUESTIONS

1. Vocabulary: *spent* (1), *fondly* (8), *prevent* (8), *post* (13).
2. What two meanings has *talent* (3)? What is Milton's "one talent"?
3. The poem is unified and expanded in its dimensions by a Biblical allusion that Milton's original readers would have recognized immediately. What is it? If you do not know, look up Matthew 25:14–30. In what ways is the situation in the poem similar to that in the parable? In what ways is it different?
4. What is the point of the poem?

LEDA AND THE SWAN

A sudden blow: the great wings beating still
Above the staggering girl, her thighs caressed
By the dark webs, her nape caught in his bill,
He holds her helpless breast upon his breast.

How can those terrified vague fingers push
The feathered glory from her loosening thighs?
And how can body, laid in that white rush,
But feel the strange heart beating where it lies?

A shudder in the loins engenders there
The broken wall, the burning roof and tower
And Agamemnon dead.
Being so caught up,
So mastered by the brute blood of the air,
Did she put on his knowledge with his power
Before the indifferent beak could let her drop?

William Butler Yeats (1865–1939)

QUESTIONS

1. What is the connection between Leda and "the broken wall, the burning roof and tower / And Agamemnon dead"? If you do not know, look up the myth of Leda, and, if necessary, the story of Agamemnon.

2. What is the significance of the question asked in the last two lines?

FRAGMENT

Locke sank into a swoon;
The Garden died;
God took the spinning-jenny
Out of his side.

William Butler Yeats (1865–1939)

QUESTIONS

1. Yeats here combines historical and Biblical allusions to produce a critique of modern history. What faculty of the mind does Locke symbolize? What historical phenomenon does he see as a product of that faculty?

2. In what senses may "The Garden died" be taken? What are the implications of substituting "Locke" and "the spinning-jenny" for Adam and Eve? What are Yeats's attitudes toward reason and industrial progress?

THE SHIELD OF ACHILLES

She looked over his shoulder
    For vines and olive trees,
Marble well-governed cities,
    And ships upon untamed seas,
But there on the shining metal
    His hands had put instead
An artificial wilderness
    And a sky like lead.

A plain without a feature, bare and brown,
    No blade of grass, no sign of neighborhood,
Nothing to eat and nowhere to sit down,
    Yet, congregated on its blankness, stood
    An unintelligible multitude.
A million eyes, a million boots in line,
Without expression, waiting for a sign.

Out of the air a voice without a face
    Proved by statistics that some cause was just
In tones as dry and level as the place:
    No one was cheered and nothing was discussed;
    Column by column in a cloud of dust
They marched away enduring a belief
Whose logic brought them, somewhere else, to grief.

She looked over his shoulder
    For ritual pieties,
White flower-garlanded heifers,
    Libation and sacrifice,
But there on the shining metal
    Where the altar should have been,
She saw by his flickering forge-light
    Quite another scene.

Barbed wire enclosed an arbitrary spot
    Where bored officials lounged (one cracked a joke)
And sentries sweated, for the day was hot:
    A crowd of ordinary decent folk
    Watched from without and neither moved nor spoke
As three pale figures were led forth and bound
To three posts driven upright in the ground.

The mass and majesty of this world, all
    That carries weight and always weighs the same,
Lay in the hands of others; they were small
    And could not hope for help and no help came:
    What their foes like to do was done, their shame
Was all the worst could wish; they lost their pride
And died as men before their bodies died.

She looked over his shoulder
    For athletes at their games,
Men and women in a dance
    Moving their sweet limbs
Quick, quick, to music,
    But there on the shining shield
His hands had set no dancing-floor
    But a weed-choked field.

A ragged urchin, aimless and alone,
    Loitered about that vacancy; a bird
Flew up to safety from his well-aimed stone:
    That girls are raped, that two boys knife a third,
    Were axioms to him, who'd never heard
Of any world where promises were kept
Or one could weep because another wept.

The thin-lipped armorer,
    Hephaestos, hobbled away;
Thetis of the shining breasts
    Cried out in dismay
At what the god had wrought
    To please her son, the strong
Iron-hearted man-slaying Achilles
    Who would not live long.

W. H. Auden (1907–1973)

QUESTIONS

1. Vocabulary: *libation* (26).

2. The description of Achilles' shield, made for him at the request of his mother Thetis by Hephaestos, god of the forge, is one of the most famous passages in the *Iliad* (Book XVIII). On the shield Hephaestos depicted scenes from the Hellenic world. From what world do the three scenes in the poem come? Comment specifically on each and on the contrast between each and the expectation of Thetis preceding it.

3. What possible allusion is made in lines 36–37, and what is its purpose?

4. What figure of speech occurs in line 14? What meanings has *arbitrary* (31)?

THE CARPENTER'S SON

"Here the hangman stops his cart:
Now the best of friends must part.
Fare you well, for ill fare I:
Live, lads, and I will die.

"Oh, at home had I but stayed
'Prenticed to my father's trade,
Had I stuck to plane and adze,
I had not been lost, my lads.

"Then I might have built perhaps
Gallow-trees for other chaps,
Never dangled on my own,
Had I but left ill alone.

"Now, you see, they hang me high,
And the people passing by
Stop to shake their fists and curse;
So 'tis come from ill to worse.

"Here hang I, and right and left
Two poor fellows hang for theft:
All the same's the luck we prove,
Though the midmost hangs for love.

"Comrades all, that stand and gaze,
Walk henceforth in other ways;
See my neck and save your own:
Comrades all, leave ill alone.

"Make some day a decent end,
Shrewder fellows than your friend.
Fare you well, for ill fare I:
Live, lads, and I will die."

A. E. Housman (1859–1936)

QUESTIONS

1. With whom is the speaker being implicitly compared and contrasted? How do you know?

2. In what sense is the speaker being hanged "for love"? In what sense was his prototype?

3. What is the import of "Live, lad, and I will die" in the mouth of the speaker as contrasted with its traditional import in the story of his prototype?

4. What meaning has the speaker's advice to "leave ill alone" when transferred to the story of his prototype? What general meanings are implicit in the poem?

SIX POETS IN SEARCH OF A LAWYER

Finesse be first, whose elegance deplores
All things save beauty, and the swinging doors;
Whose cleverness in writing verse is just
Exceeded by his lack of taste and lust;
Who lives off lady lovers of his verse
And thanks them by departing with their purse;
Who writes his verse in order to amaze,
To win the Pulitzer, or *Time*'s sweet praise;
Who will endure a moment, and then pass,
As hopeless as an olive in his glass.

Dullard be second, as he always will,
From lack of brains as well as lack of skill.
Expert in some, and dilettante in all
The ways of making poems gasp and fall,
He teaches at a junior college where
He's recognized as Homer's son and heir.
Respectable, brown-suited, it is he
Who represents on forums poetry,
And argues to protect the libeled Muse,
Who'd tear his flimsy tongue out, could she choose.

His opposite is anarchistic *Bomb,*
Who writes a manifesto with aplomb.
Revolt! Revolt! No matter why or when,
It's novelty, old novelty again.
Yet *Bomb* if read intently may reveal
A talent not to murder but to steal;
First from old *Gone,* whose fragmentary style
Disguised his sawdust Keats a little while;
And now from one who writes at very best
What ne'er was thought and much the less expressed.

Lucre be next, who takes to poetry
The businessman he swore he would not be.
Anthologies and lecture tours and grants
Create a solvency which disenchants.
He writes his poems now to suit his purse,
Short-lined and windy, and reserves his curse
For all the little magazines so fine

That offer only fifty cents a line.
He makes his money, certainly, to write,
But writes for money. Such is appetite.

Of *Mucker* will I tell, who tries to show
He is a kind of poet men don't know.
To shadow box at literary teas
And every girl at Bennington to seize,
To talk of baseball rather than of Yeats,
To drink straight whisky while the bard creates—
This is his pose, and so his poems seem
Incongruous in proving life a dream.
Some say, with Freud, that *Mucker* has a reason
For acting virile in and out of season.

Scoundrel be last. Be deaf, be dumb, be blind,
Who writes satiric verses on his kind.

Donald Hall (b. 1928)

QUESTIONS

1. Vocabulary: *dilettante* (13).

2. The title conceals a literary allusion. What is it, and what are its implications? Why are the six poets in search of a lawyer?

3. Does the author include himself in the satire? Where?

4. Why does the author's curse on *Scoundrel* take the form of "Be deaf, be dumb, be blind"? What allusion is made here?

5. Explain the allusions in lines 30 and 49–50. Are there other allusions in the poem?

6. Discuss the figures of speech used in lines 10, 14, 20, 24, 26, 28, 30, and 32. Are *Finesse, Dullard, Bomb,* and the rest examples of personification or of metonymy?

ECHO'S LAMENT OF NARCISSUS

Slow, slow, fresh fount, keep time with my salt tears;
    Yet slower yet, oh faintly, gentle springs;
List to the heavy part the music bears
    Woe weeps out her division when she sings.
        Droop herbs and flowers,
        Fall grief in showers;
        Our beauties are not ours;
        Oh, I could still,

Like melting snow upon some craggy hill,
Drop, drop, drop, drop,
Since nature's pride is now a withered daffodil.

Ben Jonson (1573?–1637)

QUESTION

A *division* (4) is a counterpointed melody. By looking up the myth of Echo and Narcissus, reconstruct the dramatic situation in this lyric.

IN THE GARDEN

In the garden there strayed
A beautiful maid
As fair as the flowers of the morn;
The first hour of her life
She was made a man's wife,
And was buried before she was born.

Anonymous

QUESTION

Resolve the paradox by identifying the allusion.

QUATRAIN

Jack, eating rotten cheese, did say,
Like Samson I my thousands slay;
I vow, quoth Roger, so you do.
And with the self-same weapon too.

***Benjamin Franklin** (1706–1790)*

"The Eagle" (page 555) is primarily descriptive; "A Red, Red Rose" (page 651) is an expression of emotion; "My Last Duchess" (page 671) is an account of human character. None of these poems is directly concerned with ideas. The message-hunter will be baffled and disappointed by poetry of this kind, for he will not find what he is looking for, and he may attempt to read some idea into the poem that is really not there. Yet ideas are also part of human experience, and therefore many poems are concerned at least partially, with presenting ideas. But with these poems message-hunting is an even more dangerous activity. For the message-hunter is likely to think that the whole object of reading the poem is to find the message—that the idea is really the only important thing in it. Like Little Jack Horner, he will reach in and pluck it out and say, "What a good boy am I!" as if the pie existed for the plum.

The idea in a poem is only part of the total experience it communicates. The value and worth of the poem are determined by the value of the total experience, not by the truth or the nobility of the idea itself. This is not to say that the truth of the idea is unimportant, or that its validity should not be examined and appraised. But a good idea will not make a good poem, nor need an idea with which the reader does not agree ruin one. The good reader of poetry will be a reader receptive to all kinds of experience. He will be able to make that "willing suspension of disbelief" that Coleridge characterized as constituting poetic faith. When one attends a performance of *Hamlet* he is willing to forget for the time being that such a person as Hamlet never existed and that the events on the stage are fictions. The reader of poetry should also be willing to enter imaginatively, for the time being, into ideas he objectively regards as untrue. It is one way of understanding these ideas better and of enlarging his own experience. The Christian should be able to enjoy a good poem expressing atheistic ideas, and the atheist a good poem in praise of God. The optimist by temperament should be able to find pleasure in pessimistic poetry, and the pessimist in optimistic poetry. The teetotaler should be able to enjoy "The Rubáiyát of Omar Khayyám," and the winebibber a good poem in praise of austerity. The primary value of a poem depends not so much on the truth of the idea presented as on the power with which it is communicated and on its being made a convincing part of a meaningful total experience. We must feel that the idea has been truly and deeply *felt* by the poet and that he is doing something more than merely moralizing. The plum must be made part of a pie. If the plum is properly combined with other ingredients and if the pie is well cooked, it should be enjoyable even for persons who do not care for the brand of plums it is made of. Let us consider, for instance, the following two poems.

BARTER

Life has loveliness to sell,
    All beautiful and splendid things,
Blue waves whitened on a cliff,
    Soaring fire that sways and sings,
And children's faces looking up,
Holding wonder like a cup.

Life has loveliness to sell,
    Music like a curve of gold,
Scent of pine trees in the rain,
    Eyes that love you, arms that hold,
And for your spirit's still delight,
Holy thoughts that star the night.

Spend all you have for loveliness,
    Buy it and never count the cost;
For one white singing hour of peace
    Count many a year of strife well lost,
And for a breath of ecstasy
Give all you have been, or could be.

Sara Teasdale (1884–1933)

STOPPING BY WOODS ON A SNOWY EVENING

Whose woods these are I think I know.
His house is in the village though;
He will not see me stopping here
To watch his woods fill up with snow.

My little horse must think it queer
To stop without a farmhouse near
Between the woods and frozen lake
The darkest evening of the year.

He gives his harness bells a shake
To ask if there is some mistake.
The only other sound's the sweep
Of easy wind and downy flake.

The woods are lovely, dark and deep,
But I have promises to keep,
And miles to go before I sleep,
And miles to go before I sleep.

Robert Frost (1874–1963)

QUESTIONS

1. How do these two poems differ in idea?
2. What contrasts are suggested between the speaker in the second poem and (a) his horse and (b) the owner of the woods?

Both of these poems present ideas, the first more or less explicitly, the second symbolically. Perhaps the best way to get at the idea of the second poem is to ask two questions. First, why does the speaker stop? Second, why does he go on? He stops, we answer, to watch the woods fill up with snow—to observe a scene of natural beauty. He goes on, we answer, because he has "promises" to keep, that is, he has obligations to fulfill. He is momentarily torn between his love of beauty and these other various and complex claims that life has upon him. The small conflict in the poem is symbolical of a larger conflict in life. One part of the sensitive thinking man would like to give up his life to the enjoyment of beauty and art. But another part is aware of larger duties and responsibilities—responsibilities owed, at least in part, to other human beings. The speaker in the poem would like to satisfy both impulses. But when the two come into conflict, he seems to suggest, the "promises" must be given precedence.

The first poem also presents a philosophy but an opposed one. For this poet, beauty is of such supreme value that any conflicting demand should be sacrificed to it. "Spend all you have for loveliness, / Buy it and never count the cost . . . And for a breath of ecstasy / Give all you have been, or could be." The reader, if he is a thinking person, will have to choose between these two philosophies—to commit himself to one or the other. But if he is a good reader of poetry, this commitment should not destroy for him his enjoyment of either poem. If it does, he is reading for plums and not for pies.

Nothing so far said in this chapter should be construed as meaning that the truth or falsity of the idea in a poem is a matter of no importance. *Other things being equal*, the good reader naturally will, and properly should, value more highly the poem whose idea he feels to be maturer and nearer to the heart of human experience. There may be some ideas, moreover, that he feels to be so vicious or so foolish or so beyond the pale of normal human decency as to discredit *by themselves* the poems in which he finds them. A rotten plum may spoil a pie. But a good reader will always be a person of considerable intellectual flexibility and tolerance, able to entertain sympathetically ideas other than his own. He will often like a poem whose idea he disagrees with better than one with an idea he accepts. And, above all, he will not confuse the prose meaning of any poem with its total meaning. He will not mistake plums for pies.

REVEILLE

Wake: the silver dusk returning
  Up the beach of darkness brims,
And the ship of sunrise burning
  Strands upon the eastern rims.

Wake: the vaulted shadow shatters,
  Trampled to the floor it spanned,
And the tent of night in tatters
  Straws the sky-pavilioned land.

Up, lad, up, 'tis late for lying:
  Hear the drums of morning play;
Hark, the empty highways crying
  "Who'll beyond the hills away?"

Towns and countries woo together,
  Forelands beacon, belfries call;

Never lad that trod on leather
    Lived to feast his heart with all.

Up, lad: thews that lie and cumber
    Sunlit pallets never thrive;
Morns abed and daylight slumber
    Were not meant for man alive.

Clay lies still, but blood's a rover;
    Breath's a ware that will not keep.
Up, lad: when the journey's over
    There'll be time enough to sleep.

A. E. Housman (1859–1936)

QUESTIONS

1. Explain the figures of speech in lines 1–4, 5–8, 10, 15, and 21.
2. What symbolic meanings have *journey* (23) and *sleep* (24)?

WHEN SMOKE STOOD UP FROM LUDLOW

When smoke stood up from Ludlow,
    And mist blew off from Teme,
And blithe afield to ploughing
    Against the morning beam
    I strode beside my team,

The blackbird in the coppice
    Looked out to see me stride,
And hearkened as I whistled
    The trampling team beside,
    And fluted and replied:

"Lie down, lie down, young yeoman;
    What use to rise and rise?
Rise man a thousand mornings
    Yet down at last he lies,
    And then the man is wise."

I heard the tune he sang me,
    And spied his yellow bill;
I picked a stone and aimed it
    And threw it with a will:
    Then the bird was still.

Then my soul within me
Took up the blackbird's strain,
And still beside the horses
Along the dewy lane
It sang the song again:

"Lie down, lie down, young yeoman;
The sun moves always west;
The road one treads to labor
Will lead one home to rest,
And that will be the best."

A. E. Housman (1859–1936)

QUESTION

Compare and contrast this poem with the foregoing one as to its use of symbols, its attitude toward life, and its counsel for existence. How do you account for its having been written by the same poet? Is either poem superior to the other?

TO A WATERFOWL

Whither, midst falling dew,
While glow the heavens with the last steps of day,
Far, through their rosy depths, dost thou pursue
Thy solitary way?

Vainly the fowler's eye
Might mark thy distant flight to do thee wrong,
As, darkly seen against the crimson sky,
Thy figure floats along.

Seek'st thou the plashy brink
Of weedy lake, or marge of river wide,
Or where the rocking billows rise and sink
On the chafed ocean side?

There is a Power whose care
Teaches thy way along that pathless coast—
The desert and illimitable air—
Lone wandering, but not lost.

All day thy wings have fanned,
At that far height, the cold, thin atmosphere,

Yet stoop not, weary, to the welcome land,
Though the dark night is near.

And soon that toil shall end;
Soon shalt thou find a summer home, and rest,
And scream among thy fellows; reeds shall bend,
Soon, o'er thy sheltered nest.

Thou'rt gone, the abyss of heaven
Hath swallowed up thy form; yet, on my heart
Deeply has sunk the lesson thou hast given,
And shall not soon depart.

He who, from zone to zone,
Guides through the boundless sky thy certain flight,
In the long way that I must tread alone,
Will lead my steps aright.

William Cullen Bryant (1794–1878)

DESIGN

I found a dimpled spider, fat and white,
On a white heal-all, holding up a moth
Like a white piece of rigid satin cloth—
Assorted characters of death and blight
Mixed ready to begin the morning right,
Like the ingredients of a witches' broth—
A snow-drop spider, a flower like a froth,
And dead wings carried like a paper kite.

What had that flower to do with being white,
The wayside blue and innocent heal-all?
What brought the kindred spider to that height,
Then steered the white moth thither in the night?
What but design of darkness to appall?—
If design govern in a thing so small.

Robert Frost (1874–1963)

QUESTIONS

1. Vocabulary: *characters* (4).

2. The heal-all is a wildflower, usually blue or violet but occasionally white, found blooming along roadsides in the summer. It was once supposed to have healing qualities, hence its name. Of what significance, scientific and

poetic, is the fact that the spider, the heal-all, and the moth are all white? Of what poetic significance is the fact that the spider is "dimpled" and "fat" and like a "snow-drop," and that the flower is "innocent" and named "heal-all"?

3. The "argument from design," as it was called, was a favorite eighteenth-century argument for the existence of God. What twist does Frost give the argument? What questions does the poem pose?

4. Contrast Frost's poem in content with "To a Waterfowl." Is it possible to admire both?

FAREWELL, LOVE

Farewell, love, and all thy laws for ever,
Thy baited hooks shall tangle me no more;
Senec and Plato call me from thy lore
To perfect wealth, my wit for to endeavor,° — to exert my mind
In blind error when I did persever,
Thy sharp repulse that pricketh aye so sore
Hath taught me to set in trifles no store,
And scape forth, since liberty is lever.° — preferable
Therefore, farewell! Go trouble younger hearts,
And in me claim no more authority;
With idle youth go use thy property,
And thereon spend thy many brittle darts.
For hitherto though I have lost my time,
Me lusteth° no longer rotten boughs to climb. — I desire

Sir Thomas Wyatt (1503?–1542)

QUESTION

Senec (3) is Seneca, the Roman Stoic philosopher, who taught that man's felicity lies in liberating oneself from bondage to the passions and appetites; Plato (3) likewise believed that man's highest good is to be found in the mind rather than in sensual satisfactions. What evaluation of love is made by Wyatt, both through his metaphors and in literal statement?

THE SPUR

You think it horrible that lust and rage
Should dance attention upon my old age;
They were not such a plague when I was young;
What else have I to spur me into song?

William Butler Yeats (1865–1939)

QUESTIONS

1. How do Yeats's metaphors for "lust and rage" resemble, and differ from, Wyatt's metaphors for love? How does his evaluation of sensuality and passion differ from Wyatt's? His view of youth and age?

2. Wyatt turns to philosophy; Yeats wishes to continue with poetry (4). Does this difference help to explain their different attitudes toward sensuality and love? Why?

WHAT IF A MUCH OF A WHICH OF A WIND

what if a much of a which of a wind
gives the truth to summer's lie;
bloodies with dizzying leaves the sun
and yanks immortal stars awry?
Blow king to beggar and queen to seem
(blow friend to fiend: blow space to time)
—when skies are hanged and oceans drowned,
the single secret will still be man

what if a keen of a lean wind flays
screaming hills with sleet and snow:
strangles valleys by ropes of thing
and stifles forests in white ago?
Blow hope to terror; blow seeing to blind
(blow pity to envy and soul to mind)
—whose hearts are mountains, roots are trees,
it's they shall cry hello to the spring

what if a dawn of a doom of a dream
bites this universe in two,
peels forever out of his grave
and sprinkles nowhere with me and you?
Blow soon to never and never to twice
(blow life to isn't:blow death to was)
—all nothing's only our hugest home;
the most who die, the more we live

e. e. cummings (1894–1962)

QUESTIONS

1. What unconventional uses does cummings make of grammar and diction? Can you justify them?

2. What kind of storm is described? What does it signify?

3. What assertions does the poet make about man in each of the three stanzas?

WHEN SERPENTS BARGAIN FOR THE RIGHT TO SQUIRM

when serpents bargain for the right to squirm
and the sun strikes to gain a living wage—
when thorns regard their roses with alarm
and rainbows are insured against old age

when every thrush may sing no new moon in
if all screech-owls have not okayed his voice
—and any wave signs on the dotted line
or else an ocean is compelled to close

when the oak begs permission of the birch
to make an acorn—valleys accuse their
mountains of having altitude—and march
denounces april as a saboteur

then we'll believe in that incredible
unanimal mankind (and not until)

e. e. cummings (1894–1962)

QUESTIONS

1. What characteristics do the various activities not engaged in by nature have in common? What qualities of thought and feeling or kinds of behavior ought to replace these activities, in the poet's view?

2. What does the poet imply by calling man an *unanimal* (14)? What is the precise force here of *incredible* (13)?

3. How does the view of man implied in this poem differ from that implied in the preceding poem? Which of the two poems is *satirical* (see page 103)?

TO NIGHT

Mysterious Night! when our first parent knew
Thee from report divine, and heard thy name,
Did he not tremble for this lovely frame,
This glorious canopy of light and blue?
Yet 'neath the curtain of translucent dew,
Bathed in the rays of the great setting flame,

Hesperus with the host of heaven came,
And lo! creation widened on man's view.
Who could have thought such darkness lay concealed
Within thy beams, O Sun! or who could find,
While fly, and leaf, and insect stood revealed,
That to such countless orbs thou mad'st us blind!
    Why do we, then, shun Death with anxious strife?—
    If Light can thus deceive, wherefore not Life?

Joseph Blanco White (1775–1841)

QUESTIONS

1. Vocabulary: *canopy* (4), *translucent* (5), *Hesperus* (7).

2. Explain "our first parent" (1), "this lovely frame" (3), "the great setting flame" (6), "the host of heaven" (7), and "thou" (12).

3. State the argument of the poem in one sentence.

SEA-SHELL MURMURS

The hollow sea-shell which for years hath stood
    On dusty shelves, when held against the ear
    Proclaims its stormy parent; and we hear
The faint far murmur of the breaking flood.
We hear the sea. The sea? It is the blood
    In our own veins, impetuous and near,
    And pulses keeping pace with hope and fear
And with our feelings' every shifting mood.
Lo, in my heart I hear, as in a shell,
    The murmur of a world beyond the grave,
Distinct, distinct, though faint and far it be.
Thou fool; this echo is a cheat as well,—
    The hum of earthly instincts; and we crave
A world unreal as the shell-heard sea.

Eugene Lee-Hamilton (1845–1907)

QUESTIONS

1. Explain "its stormy parent" (3), and "thou fool" (12).

2. State the argument in one sentence.

3. Compare this sonnet with the preceding one. Is either argument better than the other? Is either poem better than the other?

ARS POETICA

A poem should be palpable and mute
As a globed fruit,

Dumb
As old medallions to the thumb,

Silent as the sleeve-worn stone
Of casement ledges where the moss has grown—

A poem should be wordless
As the flight of birds.

*

A poem should be motionless in time
As the moon climbs,

Leaving, as the moon releases
Twig by twig the night-entangled trees,

Leaving, as the moon behind the winter leaves,
Memory by memory the mind—

A poem should be motionless in time
As the moon climbs.

*

A poem should be equal to:
Not true.

For all the history of grief
An empty doorway and a maple leaf.

For love
The leaning grasses and two lights above the sea—

A poem should not mean
But be.

Archibald MacLeish (b. 1892)

QUESTIONS

1. How can a poem be "wordless" (7)? How can it be "motionless in time" (15)?

2. The Latin title, literally translatable as "The Art of Poetry," is a traditional title for works on the philosophy of poetry. What is *this* poet's philosophy of poetry? What does he mean by saying that a poem should not *mean* and should not be *true*?

CHAPTER TEN

Tone

Tone, in literature, may be defined as the writer's or speaker's attitude toward his subject, his audience, or himself. It is the emotional coloring, or the emotional meaning, of the work and is an extremely important part of the full meaning. In spoken language it is indicated by the inflections of the speaker's voice. If, for instance, a friend tells you, "I'm going to get married today," the facts of his statement are entirely clear. But the emotional meaning of his statement may vary widely according to the tone of voice with which he utters it. He may be ecstatic ("Hooray! I'm going to get married today!"); he may be incredulous ("I can't believe it! I'm going to get married today"); he may be resigned ("Might as well face it. I'm going to get married today"); he may be in despair ("Horrors! I'm going to get married today!"). Obviously, a correct interpretation of his tone will be an important part of understanding his full meaning. It may even have rather important consequences. If someone calls you a fool, your interpretation of his tone may determine whether you roll up your sleeves for a fight or walk off with your arm around his shoulder. If a girl says "No" to your proposal of marriage, your interpretation of her tone may determine whether you ask her again and win her or start going with someone else.

In poetry tone is likewise important. We have not really understood a poem unless we have accurately sensed whether the attitude it manifests is playful or solemn, mocking or reverent, calm or excited. But the correct determination of tone in literature is a much more delicate matter than it is with spoken language, for we do not have the speaker's voice to guide us. We must learn to recognize tone by other means. Almost all the elements of poetry go into indicating its tone: connotation, imagery, and metaphor; irony and understatement; rhythm, sentence construction, and formal pattern. There is therefore no simple formula for recognizing tone. It is an end product of all the elements in a poem. The best we can do is illustrate.

Robert Frost's "Stopping by Woods on a Snowy Evening" (page 691) seems a simple poem, but it has always afforded trouble to beginning readers. A very good student, asked to interpret it, once wrote this: "The poem means that we are forever passing up pleasures to go onward to what we wrongly consider our obligations. We would like to watch the snow fall on the peaceful countryside, but we always have to rush home to supper and other engagements. Mr. Frost feels that the average man considers life too short to stop and take time to appreciate true pleasures." This student did a good job in recognizing the central conflict of the poem. He went astray in recognizing its tone. Let's examine why.

In the first place, the fact that the speaker in the poem *does* stop to watch the snow fall in the woods immediately establishes him as a human being with more sensitivity and feeling for beauty than most. He is not one of the people of Wordsworth's sonnet who, "getting and spending," have laid waste their powers and lost the capacity to be stirred by nature. Frost's speaker is contrasted with his horse, who, as a creature of habit and an animal without esthetic perception, cannot understand the speaker's reason for stopping. There is also a suggestion of contrast with the "owner" of the woods, who, if he saw the speaker stopping, might be as puzzled as the horse. (Who most truly "profits" from the woods—its absentee owner or the person who can enjoy its beauty?) The speaker goes on because he has "promises to keep." But the word *promises*, though it may here have a wry ironic undertone of regret, has a favorable connotation: people almost universally agree that promises ought to be kept. If the poet had used a different term, say, "things to do," or "business to attend to," or "financial affairs to take care of," or "money to make," the connotations would have been quite different. As it is, the tone of the poem tells us that the poet is sympathetic to the speaker, is endorsing rather than censuring his action. Perhaps we may go even further. In the concluding two lines, because of their climactic position, because they are repeated, and because "sleep" in poetry is often used figuratively to refer to death, there is a suggestion of symbolic interpretation: "and many years to live before I die." If we accept this interpretation, it poses a parallel between giving oneself up to contemplation of the woods and dying. The poet's total implication would seem to be that beauty is a distinctively human value that deserves its place in a full life but that to devote one's life to its pursuit, at the expense of other obligations and duties, is tantamount to one's death as a responsible being. The poet therefore accepts the choice the speaker makes, though not without a touch of regret.

Differences in tone, and their importance, can perhaps be studied best in poems with similar content. Consider, for instance, the following pair.

THE VILLAIN

While joy gave clouds the light of stars,
    That beamed where'er they looked;
And calves and lambs had tottering knees,
    Excited, while they sucked;
While every bird enjoyed his song,
Without one thought of harm or wrong—
I turned my head and saw the wind,
    Not far from where I stood,
Dragging the corn by her golden hair,
    Into a dark and lonely wood.

W. H. Davies (1871–1940)

QUESTIONS

1. Vocabulary: *corn* (9).

2. From what realm of experience is the image in the title and the last two lines taken? What implications does your answer have for the way this image should be taken—that is, for its relation to reality?

APPARENTLY WITH NO SURPRISE

Apparently with no surprise
To any happy flower,
The frost beheads it at its play
In accidental power.

The blond assassin passes on,
The sun proceeds unmoved
To measure off another day
For an approving God.

Emily Dickinson (1830–1886)

QUESTIONS

1. What is the "blond assassin"?
2. What ironies are involved in this poem?

Both of these poems are concerned with nature; both use contrast as their basic organizing principle—a contrast between innocence and evil, joy and tragedy. But in tone the two poems are sharply different. The first is light and fanciful; its tone is one of delight or delighted surprise. The second, though superficially fanciful, is basically grim, almost savage; its tone is one of horror. Let's examine the difference.

In "The Villain" the images of the first six lines all suggest joy and innocence. The last four introduce the sinister. The poet, on turning his head, sees a villain dragging a beautiful maiden toward a dark wood to commit there some unmentionable deed, or so his metaphor tells us. But our response is one not of horror but of delight, for we realize that the poet does not mean us to take his metaphor seriously. He has actually seen only the wind blowing through the wheat and bending its golden tops gracefully toward a shady wood. The beauty of the scene has delighted him, and he has been further delighted by the fanciful metaphor which he has found to express it. The reader shares his delight both in the scene and in the metaphor.

The second poem makes the same contrast of joyful innocence (the "happy flower . . . at its play") with the sinister ("the blond assassin"). The chief difference would seem to be that the villain is this time the frost rather than the wind. But this time the poet, though her metaphor is no less fanciful, is earnest in what she is saying. For the frost actually *does* kill the flower. What makes the horror of the killing even worse is that nothing else in nature is disturbed over it or seems even to notice it. The sun "proceeds unmoved / To measure off another day." Nothing in nature stops or pauses. The flower itself is not surprised. And even God—the God who we have all been told is benevolent and concerned over the least sparrow's fall—seems to approve of what has happened, for he shows no displeasure, and it was he who created the frost as well as the flower. Further irony lies in the fact that the "assassin" (the word's connotations are of terror and violence) is not dark but "blond," or white (the connotations here are of innocence and beauty). The destructive agent, in other words, is among the most exquisite creations of God's handiwork. The poet, then, is shocked at what has happened, and is even more shocked that nothing else in nature is shocked. What has happened seems inconsistent with a rule of benevolence in the universe. In her ironic reference to an "approving God," therefore, the poet is raising a dreadful question: are the forces that created and govern the universe actually benevolent? And if we think that the poet is unduly disturbed over the death of a flower, we may consider that what is true for the flower is true throughout nature. Death—even early or accidental death, in terrible juxtaposition with beauty—is its constant condition; the fate that befalls the flower befalls us all.

These two poems, then, though superficially similar, are basically as different as night and day. And the difference is primarily one of tone.

Accurate determination of tone, therefore, is extremely important, whether in the reading of poetry or the interpretation of a woman's "No." For the good reader it will be instinctive and automatic. For the beginning reader it will require study. But beyond the general suggestions for reading that have already been made, no specific instructions can be given. Recognition of tone requires an increasing familiarity with the meanings and connotations of words, alertness to the presence of irony and other figures, and, above all, careful reading. Poetry cannot be read as one would skim a newspaper or a mystery novel, looking merely for facts.

EXERCISES

1. Marvell's "To His Coy Mistress" (page 623) and Herrick's "To the Virgins, to Make Much of Time" (page 635) both treat a traditional poetic theme known as the *carpe diem* ("seize the day") theme. They differ, however, in tone. Characterize the tone of each, and point out the differences in poetic management that account for the difference in tone.
2. Describe and account for the differences in tone between the poems in each of the following pairs: (a) "Spring," by Shakespeare (page 561) and "Spring," by Hopkins (page 604); (b) "When my love swears that she is

made of truth" (page 587) and "Let me not to the marriage of true minds" (page 880); (c) "Ulysses" (page 631) and "Curiosity" (page 641).

THE COMING OF WISDOM WITH TIME

Though leaves are many, the root is one;
Through all the lying days of my youth
I swayed my leaves and flowers in the sun;
Now I may wither into the truth.

William Butler Yeats (1865–1939)

QUESTION

Is the poet exulting over a gain or lamenting over a loss?

SINCE THERE'S NO HELP

Since there's no help, come let us kiss and part;
Nay, I have done, you get no more of me,
And I am glad, yea, glad with all my heart
That thus so cleanly I myself can free;
Shake hands forever, cancel all our vows,
And when we meet at any time again,
Be it not seen in either of our brows
That we one jot of former love retain.
Now at the last gasp of Love's latest breath,
When, his pulse failing, Passion speechless lies,
When Faith is kneeling by his bed of death,
And Innocence is closing up his eyes,
Now, if thou wouldst, when all have given him over,
From death to life thou mightst him yet recover.

Michael Drayton (1563–1631)

QUESTIONS

1. What difference in tone do you find between the first eight lines and the last six? What differences in rhythm and the kind of language used help to establish this difference in tone?

2. How many figures are there in the allegorical scene in lines 9–12? Why is "Love" dying?

3. Define the dramatic situation as precisely as possible, taking into consideration both the man's attitude and the woman's.

GOD, THAT MADEST ALL THINGS

God, that madest all things of nought
And with thy precious blood us bought,
    Mercy, help, and grace.
As thou art very god and man,
And of thy side thy blood ran,
    Forgive us our trespass.
The world, our flesh, the fiend our foe
Maketh us mis-think, mis-speak, mis-do—
    All thus we fall in blame.
Of all our sins, less and more,
Sweet Jesu, us rueth sore.
    Mercy, for thine holy name.

Anonymous (15th century)

MY GHOSTLY FATHER, I ME CONFESS

My ghostly father, I me confess,
    First to God and then to you,
    That at a window (wot° ye how) — know
I stole a kiss of great sweetness,
Which done was out° advisedness, — without
    But it is done, not undone, now,
My ghostly father, I me confess,
    First to God and then to you.
But I restore it shall doubtless
    Again, if so be that I mow,° — may
    And that, God, I make a vow,
And else I ask forgiveness—
My ghostly father, I me confess,
    First to God and then to you.

Charles d'Orleans (1391–1465)

QUESTIONS

1. Who is "My ghostly father"? What is the situation?

2. How is this poem like and how is it unlike the preceding one? Which is greater, the similarity or the difference?

ELEGY FOR ALFRED HUBBARD

Hubbard is dead, the old plumber;
who will mend our burst pipes now,
the tap that has dripped all the summer,
testing the sink's overflow?

No other like him. Young men with knowledge
of new techniques, theories from books,
may better his work straight from college,
but who will challenge his squint-eyed looks

in kitchen, bathroom, under floorboards,
rules of thumb which were often wrong;
seek as erringly stopcocks in cupboards,
or make a job last half as long?

He was a man who knew the ginnels,
alleyways, streets—the whole district,
family secrets, minor annals,
time-honored fictions fused to fact.

Seventy years of gossip muttered
under his cap, his tufty thatch,
so that his talk was slow and clotted,
hard to follow, and too much.

As though nothing fell, none vanished,
and time were the maze of Cheetham Hill,
in which the dead—with jobs unfinished—
waited to hear him ring the bell.

For much he never got round to doing,
but meant to, when weather bucked up,
or worsened, or when his pipe was drawing,
or when he'd finished this cup.

I thought time, he forgot so often,
had forgotten him, but here's Death's pomp
over his house, and by the coffin
the son who will inherit his blowlamp,

tools, workshop, cart, and cornet
(pride of Cheetham Prize Brass Band),
and there's his mourning widow, Janet,
stood at the gate he'd promised to mend.

ELEGY FOR ALFRED HUBBARD. 13. *ginnels:* tunnels that punctuate rows of houses, giving access to the "backs."

Soon he will make his final journey;
shaved and silent, strangely trim,
with never a pause to talk to anybody: how arrow-like, for him!

In St. Mark's church, whose dismal tower
he pointed and painted when a lad,
they will sing his praises amidst flowers
while, somewhere, a cellar starts to flood,

and the housewife banging his front-door knocker
is not surprised to find him gone,
and runs for Thwaite, who's a better worker,
and sticks at a job until it's done.

Tony Connor (b. 1930)

QUESTIONS

1. Characterize Hubbard. How does this *elegy* differ from the *eulogy* that will be said for him in St. Mark's Church (41–43)? Compose his eulogy.
2. What is the poet's attitude toward his subject?

JOHN ANDERSON

John Anderson, a scholarly gentleman
advancing with his company in the attack
received some bullets through him as he ran.

So his creative brain whirled, and he fell back
in the bloody dust (it was a fine day there
and warm). Blood turned his tunic black

while past his desperate final stare
the other simple soldiers run
and leave the hero unaware.

Apt epitaph or pun
he could not hit upon, to grace
a scholar's death; he only eyed the sun.

But I think, the last moment of his gaze
beheld the father of gods and men,
Zeus, leaning from heaven as he dies,

whom in his swoon he hears again
summon Apollo in the Homeric tongue:
Descend Phoebus and cleanse the stain

of dark blood from the body of John Anderson.
Give him to Death and Sleep,
who'll bear him as they can

out of the range of darts to the broad vale
of Lycia; there lay him in a deep
solemn content on some bright dale.

And the brothers, Sleep and Death
lift up John Anderson at his last breath.

Keith Douglas (1920–1944)

QUESTIONS

1. Vocabulary: *tunic* (6), *simple* (8). *Lycia* (23) was in ancient times a region of southwest Asia Minor bordering on the Mediterranean; Apollo was supposed to have had his winter palace there.

2. What kind of person is John Anderson? Why is Phoebus Apollo the god summoned by Zeus to descend to him? Why is Zeus—not Jehovah—the god he "sees"? (The author, an English poet, wrote this poem at Oxford in 1940. He was himself later killed in the invasion of Normandy.)

3. "Elegy for Alfred Hubbard" implied a contrast between the real Alfred Hubbard and the character he would be given in the funeral eulogy. Is any contrast implied in this poem? What is the precise force of the word *hero* (9)? At whose expense is any irony possibly latent in the word?

4. Why does the poet (or Zeus) consign John Anderson to both Sleep and Death, not Death alone?

5. The poem is based on an allusion to the death of Sarpedon in the *Iliad* (Book XVI). How do the similarities and contrasts with Homer's account enrich the meanings of the poem?

6. What is the poet's attitude toward John Anderson? Compare or contrast the tone of this poem with that of "Elegy for Alfred Hubbard."

A SONNET OF THE MOON

Look how the pale Queen of the silent night
Doth cause the ocean to attend upon her,
And he, as long as she is in his sight,
With his full tide is ready her to honor;

But when the silver waggon of the Moon
Is mounted up so high he cannot follow,
The sea calls home his crystal waves to moan,
And with low ebb doth manifest his sorrow.

So you, that are the sovereign of my heart,
Have all my joys attending on your will,
My joys low-ebbing when you do depart,
When you return, their tide my heart doth fill.
So as you come and as you do depart,
Joys ebb and flow within my tender heart.

Charles Best (poem written c. 1608)

QUESTION

The relationship of the speaker with his beloved is compared, by simile and metaphor, to two other types of relationships—one scientific, the other social. Supply the paired terms for each of these three relationships, and discuss the development of each comparison.

TARGET

The moon holds nothing in her arms;
  She is as empty as a drum.
She is a cipher, though she charms;
  She is delectable but dumb.
She has no factories or farms,
Or men to sound the fire-alarms
  When the marauding missiles come.

We have no cause to spare that face
  Suspended fatly in the sky.
She does not help the human race.
  Surely, she shines when bats flit by
And burglars seek their burgling-place
And lovers in a soft embrace
  Among the whispering bushes lie—

But that is all. Dogs still will bark
  When cottage doors are lightly knocked,
And poachers crawl about the park
  Cursing the glint on guns halfcocked;

None of the creatures of the dark
Will, in their self-absorption, mark
    That visage growing slightly pocked.

R. P. Lister (b. 1914)

QUESTIONS

1. The primary subject of Charles Best's poem is love; that of Lister is the moon (or shooting missiles at the moon). However, Best talks also about the moon, and Lister about love. By an analysis of the tone of each, determine whether their attitudes toward love and toward the moon are similar or different.

2. Comment on the rimes employed in the last stanza of each poem.

YES; I WRITE VERSES

Yes; I write verses now and then,
But blunt and flaccid is my pen,
No longer talked of by young men
    As rather clever;
In the last quarter are my eyes,
You see it by their form and size;
Is it not time then to be wise?
    Or now or never.

Fairest that ever sprang from Eve!
While Time allows the short reprieve,
Just look at me! would you believe
    'Twas once a lover?
I cannot clear the five-bar gate,
But, trying first its timbers' state,
Climb stiffly up, take breath, and wait
    To trundle over.

Through gallopade I cannot swing
The entangling blooms of Beauty's spring;
I cannot say the tender thing,
    Be't true or false,
And am beginning to opine
Those girls are only half-divine
Whose waists yon wicked boys entwine
    In giddy waltz.

I fear that arm above that shoulder,
I wish them wiser, graver, older,
Sedater, and no harm if colder,
    And panting less.
Ah! people were not half so wild
In former days, when, starchly mild,
Upon her high-heeled Essex smiled
    The brave Queen Bess.

Walter Savage Landor (1775–1864)

QUESTIONS

1. Vocabulary: *flaccid* (2), *trundle* (16), *gallopade* (17).

2. Identify and explain the figures of speech in lines 2, 5, 9, and 18 and the allusion in lines 31–32.

TO AGE

Welcome, old friend! These many years
    Have we lived door by door;
The Fates have laid aside their shears
    Perhaps for some few more.

I was indocile at an age
    When better boys were taught,
But thou at length hast made me sage,
    If I am sage in aught.

Little I know from other men,
    Too little they from me,
But thou hast pointed well the pen
    That writes these lines to thee.

Thanks for expelling Fear and Hope,
    One vile, the other vain;
One's scourge, the other's telescope,
    I shall not see again.

Rather what lies before my feet
    My notice shall engage—
He who hath braved Youth's dizzy heat
    Dreads not the frost of Age.

Walter Savage Landor (1775–1864)

QUESTIONS

1. Vocabulary: *indocile* (5), *scourge* (15).

2. Identify and explain the figures of speech in lines 1–2, 11, 13–16, and 19–20 and the allusion in lines 3–4.

3. Define the poet's attitude toward himself and advancing old age in this poem and in the preceding one. (He was 71 when "Yes; I Write Verses" was published, 78 when "To Age" was published.) What are the apparent differences? Try to account for them.

4. Describe the difference in tone between the two poems.

A MAD ANSWER OF A MADMAN

One asked a madman if a wife he had.
"A wife?" quoth he. "I never was so mad."

Robert Hayman (b. 1628?)

QUESTION

Considering its title, in how many ways might this epigram be interpreted? Considering its tone, which interpretation is uppermost?

LOVE

There's the wonderful love of a beautiful maid,
    And the love of a staunch true man,
And the love of a baby that's unafraid—
    All have existed since time began.
But the most wonderful love, the Love of all loves,
    Even greater than the love for Mother,
Is the infinite, tenderest, passionate love
    Of one dead drunk for another.

Anonymous

QUESTION

The radical shift in tone makes "Love" come off. If such a shift were unintentional in a poem, what would our view be?

CHAPTER ELEVEN

Musical Devices

It is obvious to the most uninitiated reader that poetry makes a greater use of the "music" of language than does language that is not poetry. The poet, unlike the man who uses language to convey only information, chooses his words for sound as well as for meaning, and he uses the sound as a means of reinforcing his meaning. So prominent is this musical quality of poetry that some writers have made it the distinguishing term in their definitions of poetry. Edgar Allan Poe, for instance, describes poetry as "music . . . combined with a pleasurable idea." Whether or not it deserves this much importance, verbal music, like connotation, imagery, and figurative language, is one of the important resources that enable the poet to do something more than communicate mere information. The poet may indeed sometimes pursue verbal music for its own sake; more often, at least in first-rate poetry, it is an adjunct to the total meaning or communication of the poem.

There are two broad ways by which the poet achieves his musical quality: by his choice and arrangement of sounds and by his arrangement of accents. In this chapter we will consider one aspect of the first of these.

An essential element in all music is repetition. In fact, we might say that all art consists of giving structure to two elements: repetition and variation. All things we enjoy greatly and lastingly have these two elements. We enjoy the sea endlessly because it is always the same yet always different. We enjoy a baseball game because it contains the same complex combination of pattern and variation. Our love of art, then, is rooted in human psychology. We like the familiar, we like variety, but we like them combined. If we get too much sameness, the result is monotony and tedium; if we get too much variety, the result is bewilderment and confusion. The composer of music, therefore, repeats certain musical tones; he repeats them in certain combinations, or chords; and he repeats them in certain patterns, or melodies. The poet likewise repeats certain sounds in certain combinations and arrangements, and thus gives organization and structure to his verse. Consider the following short example.

THE TURTLE

The turtle lives 'twixt plated decks
Which practically conceal its sex.
I think it clever of the turtle
In such a fix to be so fertile.

Ogden Nash (1902–1971)

Here is a little joke, a paradox of animal life to which the author has cleverly drawn our attention. An experiment will show us, however, that much of its appeal lies not so much in what it says as in the manner in which it says it. If, for instance, we recast the verse as prose: "The turtle lives in a shell which almost conceals its sex. It is ingenious of the turtle, in such a situation, to be so prolific," the joke falls flat. Some of its appeal must lie in its metrical form. So now we cast it in unrimed verse:

Because he lives between two decks,
It's hard to tell a turtle's gender.
The turtle is a clever beast
In such a plight to be so fertile.

Here, perhaps, is *some* improvement, but still the piquancy of the original is missing. Much of that appeal must have consisted in the use of rime—the repetition of sound in *decks* and *sex, turtle* and *fertile.* So we try once more:

The turtle lives 'twixt plated decks
Which practically conceal its sex.

I think it clever of the turtle
In such a plight to be so fertile.

But for the perceptive reader there is still something missing—he does not at first see what—but some little touch that makes the difference between a good piece of verse and a little masterpiece in its kind. And then he sees it: *plight* has been substituted for *fix*.

But why should *fix* make such a difference? Its meaning is little different from that of *plight*; its only important difference is in sound. But there we are. The final *x* in *fix* catches up the concluding consonant sound in *sex*, and its initial *f* is repeated in the initial consonant sound of *fertile*. Not only do these sound recurrences provide a subtle gratification to the ear, but they also give the verse structure; they emphasize and draw together the key words of the piece: *sex*, *fix*, and *fertile*.

The poet may repeat any unit of sound from the smallest to the largest. He may repeat individual vowel and consonant sounds, whole syllables, words, phrases, lines, or groups of lines. In each instance, in a good poem, the repetition will serve several purposes: it will please the ear, it will emphasize the words in which the repetition occurs, and it will give structure to the poem. The popularity and initial impressiveness of such repetitions is evidenced by their becoming in many instances embedded in the language as clichés like "wild and woolly," "first and foremost," "footloose and fancy-free," "penny-wise, pound-foolish," "dead as a doornail," "might and main," "sink or swim," "do or die," "pell-mell," "helter-skelter," "harum-scarum," "hocus-pocus." Some of these kinds of repetition have names, as we will see.

A syllable consists of a vowel sound that may be preceded or followed by consonant sounds. Any of these sounds may be repeated. The repetition of initial consonant sounds, as in "tried and true," "safe and sound," "fish or fowl," "rime or reason," is ALLITERATION. The repetition of vowel sounds, as in "mad as a hatter," "time out of mind," "free and easy," "slapdash," is ASSONANCE. The repetition of final consonant sounds, as in "first and last," "odds and ends," "short and sweet," "a stroke of luck," or Shakespeare's "struts and frets" (page 678) is CONSONANCE.*

* There is no established terminology for these various repetitions. *Alliteration* is used by some writers to mean any repetition of consonant sounds. *Assonance* has been used to mean the similarity as well as the identity of vowel sounds, or even the similarity of any sounds whatever. *Consonance* has often been reserved

Repetitions may be used alone or in combination. Alliteration and assonance are combined in such phrases as "time and tide," "thick and thin," "kith and kin," "alas and alack," "fit as a fiddle," and Edgar Allan Poe's famous line, "The viol, the violet, and the vine." Alliteration and consonance are combined in such phrases as "crisscross," "last but not least," "lone and lorn," "good as gold," Housman's "strangling in a string" (page 604) and "fleet foot" (page 857), and e. e. cummings's "blow friend to fiend" and "a doom of a dream" (page 698). The combination of assonance and consonance is rime.

RIME is the repetition of the accented vowel sound and all succeeding sounds. It is called MASCULINE when the rime sounds involve only one syllable, as in *decks* and *sex* or *support* and *retort*. It is FEMININE when the rime sounds involve two or more syllables, as in *turtle* and *fertile* or *spitefully* and *delightfully*. It is referred to as INTERNAL RIME when one or both riming words are within the line and as END RIME when both riming words are at the *ends* of lines. End rime is probably the most frequently used and most consciously sought-after sound repetition in English poetry. Because it comes at the end of the line, it receives emphasis as a musical effect and perhaps contributes more than any other musical resource except rhythm and meter to give poetry its musical effect as well as its structure. There exists, however, a large body of poetry that does not employ rime and for which rime would not be appropriate. Also, there has always been a tendency, especially noticeable in modern poetry, to substitute approximate rimes for perfect rimes at the ends of lines. APPROXIMATE RIMES include words with any kind of sound similarity, from close to fairly remote. Under approximate rime we include alliteration, assonance, and consonance or their combinations when used at the end of the line; half-rime (feminine rimes in which only half of the word rimes—the accented half, as in *lightly* and *frightful*, or the unaccented half, as in *yellow* and *willow*); and other similarities too elusive to name. "The Forge" (page 606), "Dr. Sigmund Freud Discovers

---

for words in which both the initial *and* final consonant sounds correspond, as in *green* and *groan, moon* and *mine*. *Rime* (or rhyme) has been used to mean any sound repetition, including alliteration, assonance, and consonance. In the absence of clear agreement on the meanings of these terms, the terminology chosen here has appeared most useful, with support in usage. Labels are useful in analysis. The student should, however, learn to recognize the devices and, more important, to see their function, without worrying too much over nomenclature.

the Sea Shell" (page 613), "It sifts from leaden sieves" and "The snow that never drifts" (pages 620–21), "Mr. Z" (page 669), "what if a much of a which of a wind" and "when serpents bargain for the right to squirm" (pages 698–99), "Wind" (page 765), and "Poem in October" (page 781), among others, employ various kinds of approximate rime.

THAT NIGHT WHEN JOY BEGAN

That night when joy began
Our narrowest veins to flush,
We waited for the flash
Of morning's levelled gun.

But morning let us pass,
And day by day relief
Outgrew his nervous laugh,
Grows credulous of peace.

As mile by mile is seen
No trespasser's reproach,
And love's best glasses reach
No fields but are his own.

W. H. Auden (1907–1973)

QUESTIONS

1. What has been the past experience with love of the two people in the poem? What is their present experience? What precisely is the tone of the poem?

2. What basic metaphor underlies the poem? Work it out stanza by stanza. What is "the flash of morning's levelled gun"? Does line 10 mean that no trespasser reproaches the lovers or that no one reproaches the lovers for being trespassers? Does *glasses* (11) refer to spectacles, tumblers, or field glasses? Point out three personfications.

3. The rime pattern in this poem is intricate and exact. Work it out, considering alliteration, assonance, and consonance.

In addition to the repetition of individual sounds and syllables, the poet may repeat whole words, phrases, lines, or groups of lines. When such repetition is done according to some fixed pattern, it is called a REFRAIN. The refrain is especially common in songlike poetry. Examples are to be found in Shakespeare's "Winter" (page 556) and "Spring" (page 561).

It is not to be thought that we have exhausted the possibilities of sound repetition by giving names to a few of the more prominent kinds. The complete study of possible kinds of sound repetition in poetry would be so complex that it would break down under its own machinery. Some of the subtlest and loveliest effects escape our net of names. In as short a phrase as this from the prose of John Ruskin—"ivy as light and lovely as the vine"—we notice alliteration in *light* and *lovely*, assonance in *ivy*, *light*, and *vine*, and consonance in *ivy* and *lovely*, but we have no name to connect the *v* in *vine* with the *v*'s in *ivy* and *lovely*, or the second *l* in *lovely* with the first *l*, or the final syllables of *ivy* and *lovely* with each other; but these are all an effective part of the music of the line. Also contributing to the music of poetry is the use of related rather than identical sounds, such as *m* and *n* or *p* and *b* or the vowel sound's in *boat*, *boot*, and *book*.

These various musical repetitions, for a trained reader, will ordinarily make an almost subconscious contribution to his reading of the poem: the reader will feel their effect without necessarily being aware of what has caused it. There is value, however, in occasionally analyzing a poem for these devices in order to increase awareness of them. A few words of caution are necessary. First, the repetitions are entirely a matter of sound; spelling is irrelevant. *Bear* and *pair* are rimes, but *through* and *rough* are not. *Cell* and *sin*, *folly* and *philosophy* alliterate, but *sin* and *sugar*, *gun* and *gem* do not. Second, alliteration, assonance, consonance, and masculine rime are matters that ordinarily involve only stressed or accented syllables; for only such syllables ordinarily make enough impression on the ear to be significant in the sound pattern of the poem. We should hardly consider *which* and *its* in the second line of "The Turtle," for instance, as an example of assonance, for neither word is stressed enough in the reading to make it significant as a sound. Third, the words involved in these repetitions must be close enough together that the ear retains the sound, consciously or subconsciously, from its first occurrence to its second. This distance varies according to circumstances, but for alliteration, assonance, and consonance the words ordinarily have to be in the same line or adjacent lines. End rime bridges a longer gap.

I WILL GO BACK TO THE GREAT SWEET MOTHER

I will go back to the great sweet mother,
    Mother and lover of men, the sea.

I will go down to her, I and none other,
    Close with her, kiss her and mix her with me;
Cling to her, strive with her, hold her fast:
O fair white mother, in days long past
Born without sister, born without brother,
    Set free my soul as thy soul is free.

O fair green-girdled mother of mine,
    Sea, that art clothed with the sun and the rain,
Thy sweet hard kisses are strong like wine,
    Thy large embraces are keen like pain.
Save me and hide me with all thy waves,
Find me one grave of thy thousand graves,
Those pure cold populous graves of thine
    Wrought without hand in a world without stain.

I shall sleep, and move with the moving ships,
    Change as the winds change, veer in the tide;
My lips will feast on the foam of thy lips,
    I shall rise with thy rising, with thee subside;
Sleep, and not know if she be, if she were,
Filled full with life to the eyes and hair,
As a rose is fulfilled to the roseleaf tips
    With splendid summer and perfume and pride.

This woven raiment of nights and days,
    Were it once cast off and unwound from me,
Naked and glad would I walk in thy ways,
    Alive and aware of thy ways and thee;
Clear of the whole world, hidden at home,
Clothed with the green and crowned with the foam,
A pulse of the life of thy straits and bays,
    A vein in the heart of the streams of the sea.

Fair mother, fed with the lives of men,
    Thou art subtle and cruel of heart, men say,
Thou hast taken, and shalt not render again;
    Thou art full of they dead, and cold as they.
But death is the worst that comes of thee;
Thou art fed with our dead, O mother, O sea,
But when hast thou fed on our hearts? or when,
    Having given us love, hast thou taken away?

O tender-hearted, O perfect lover,
    Thy lips are bitter, and sweet thine heart.
The hopes that hurt and the dreams that hover,
    Shall they not vanish away and apart?
But thou, thou art sure, thou art older than earth;
Thou art strong for death and fruitful of birth;
Thy depths conceal and thy gulfs discover;
    From the first thou wert; in the end thou art.

Algernon Charles Swinburne (1837–1909)

QUESTIONS

1. These six stanzas are excerpted from a longer poem, "The Triumph of Time," which expresses the poet's grief over a disappointment in love. Why, for the poet, is the sea the "perfect lover" (41)? In what sense are the "lips" of the sea "bitter" (42)? Why is the sea a "mother" (1)? Who is "she" (21)? Why does dying at sea seem more appealing to the poet than any other kind of death?

2. Copy whichever of the stanzas seems to you most musical (double-space if you type) and, using different-colored pencils, encircle and tie together all examples of alliteration, assonance, consonance, internal rime, and word repetition. Do these represent all of the kinds of musical repetition used in the poem? Indicate any other noteworthy effects.

3. One criticism of Swinburne's works has been that the "music" of many of his poems detracts from rather than contributes to their meaning. Do you think the criticism applicable to this poem?

We should not leave the impression that the use of these musical devices is necessarily or always valuable. Like the other resources of poetry, they can be judged only in the light of the poem's total intention. Many of the greatest works of English poetry—for instance, *Hamlet* and *King Lear* and *Paradise Lost*—do not employ end rime. Both alliteration and rime, especially feminine rime, if used excessively or unskillfully, become humorous or silly. If the intention is humorous, the result is delightful; if not, fatal. Shakespeare, who knew how to use all these devices to the utmost advantage, parodied their unskillful use in lines like "The preyful princess pierced and pricked a pretty pleasing prickett" in *Love's Labor's Lost* and

Whereat with blade, with bloody, blameful blade,
He bravely broached his boiling bloody breast

in *Midsummer Night's Dream.* Swinburne parodied his own highly alliterative style in "Nephelidia" with lines like "Life is the lust of a lamp for the light that is dark till the dawn of the day when we die." Used skillfully and judiciously, however, musical devices provide a palpable and delicate pleasure to the ear and, even more important, add dimension to meaning.

EXERCISE

Discuss the various ways in which the following poems make use of REFRAIN:

1. "Winter," page 556.
2. "Spring," page 561.
3. "The Shield of Achilles," page 682.
4. "what if a much of a which of a wind," page 698.
5. "My ghostly father, I me confess," page 708.
6. "The New Mistress," page 745.
7. "The Barrel-Organ," page 746.
8. "The Bench of Boors," page 769.
9. "May-Fly," page 784.
10. "Edward," page 786.
11. "Cha Till Maccruimein," page 804.
12. "Morning Song from 'Senlin'," page 829.
13. "The Lamb," page 836.
14. "Fear no more the heat o' the sun," page 879.
15. "Do not go gentle into that good night," page 890.

GOD'S GRANDEUR

The world is charged with the grandeur of God.
    It will flame out, like shining from shook foil;
    It gathers to a greatness, like the ooze of oil
Crushed. Why do men then now not reck his rod?
Generations have trod, have trod, have trod;
    And all is seared with trade; bleared, smeared with toil;
    And wears man's smudge and shares man's smell: the soil
Is bare now, nor can foot feel, being shod.
And for all this, nature is never spent;
    There lives the dearest freshness deep down things;

And though the last lights off the black West went
Oh, morning, at the brown brink eastward, springs—
Because the Holy Ghost over the bent
World broods with warm breast and with ah! bright wings.

Gerald Manley Hopkins (1844–1889)

QUESTIONS

1. What is the theme of this sonnet?
2. The image in lines 3–4 refers probably to olive oil being collected in great vats from crushed olives. Explain the simile in line 2 and the symbols in lines 7–8 and 11–12.
3. Explain "reck his rod" (4), "spent" (9), "bent" (13).
4. Using different-colored pencils, encircle and connect examples of alliteration, assonance, consonance, and internal rime. Do these help to carry the meaning?

WE REAL COOL

The Pool Players.
Seven at the Golden Shovel.

We real cool. We
Left school. We

Lurk late. We
Strike straight. We

Sing sin. We
Thin gin. We

Jazz June. We
Die soon.

Gwendolyn Brooks (b. 1917)

QUESTIONS

1. In addition to end rime, what other musical devices does this poem employ?
2. Try reading this poem with the pronouns at the beginning of the lines instead of at the end. What is lost?
3. English teachers in a certain urban school were criticized recently for having their students read this poem: it was said to be immoral. Was the criticism justified? Why or why not?

I HEAR AN ARMY

I hear an army charging upon the land,
    And the thunder of horses plunging, foam about their knees:
Arrogant, in black armor, behind them stand,
    Disdaining the reins, with fluttering whips, the charioteers.

They cry unto the night their battle-name:
    I moan in sleep when I hear afar their whirling laughter.
They cleave the gloom of dreams, a blinding flame,
    Clanging, clanging upon the heart as upon an anvil.

They come shaking in triumph their long, green hair:
    They come out of the sea and run shouting by the shore.
My heart, have you no wisdom thus to despair?
    My love, my love, my love, why have you left me alone?

James Joyce (1882–1941)

QUESTIONS

1. What is the rime scheme of the poem? What kinds of rime does it employ?

2. Find examples of assonance, consonance, and alliteration in the poem: circle similar sounds and connect them. Do any of these sound correspondences seem to you to contribute to the meaning? Are there any other types of sound repetition in the poem?

3. What is the situation in the poem? (Who is the speaker? Where is he? Why is he in despair? What are the army and the charioteers?)

4. What different kinds of imagery are used in the poem? What figures of speech? How do they contribute to the meaning of the poem?

PARTING, WITHOUT A SEQUEL

She has finished and sealed the letter
At last, which he so richly has deserved,
With characters venomous and hatefully curved,
And nothing could be better.

But even as she gave it
Saying to the blue-capped functioner of doom,
"Into his hands," she hoped the leering groom
Might somewhere lose and leave it.

Then all the blood
Forsook the face. She was too pale for tears,

Observing the ruin of her younger years.
She went and stood

Under her father's vaunting oak
Who kept his peace in wind and sun and glistened
Stoical in the rain; to whom she listened
If he spoke.

And now the agitation of the rain
Rasped his sere leaves, and he talked low and gentle
Reproaching the wan daughter by the lintel;
Ceasing and beginning again.

Away went the messenger's bicycle,
Her serpent's track went up the hill forever,
And all the time she stood there hot as fever
And cold as an icicle.

John Crowe Ransom (b. 1888)

QUESTIONS

1. Identify the figures of speech in lines 3 and 22 and discuss their effectiveness. Are there traces of dramatic irony in the poem? Where?

2. Is the oak literal or figurative? Neither? Both? Discuss the meanings of *vaunting* (13), *stoical* (15), *sere* (18), and *lintel* (19).

3. Do you find any trite language in the poem? Where? What does it tell us about the girl's action?

4. W. H. Auden has defined poetry as "the clear expression of mixed feelings." Discuss the applicability of the definition to this poem. Try it out on other poems.

5. A feminine rime that involves two syllables is known also as a DOUBLE RIME. Find examples in the poem of both perfect and approximate double rimes. A feminine rime that involves three syllables is a TRIPLE RIME. Find one example of a triple rime. Which lines employ masculine or SINGLE RIMES, either perfect or approximate?

WINTER OCEAN

Many-maned scud-thumper, tub
of male whales, maker of worn wood, shrub-
ruster, sky-mocker, rave!
portly pusher of waves, wind-slave.

John Updike (b. 1932)

QUESTIONS

1. The fun of this poem lies chiefly in two features: in its invention of elaborate epithets (descriptive names) for something familiar (in Old English poetry, partially imitated here, these descriptive names were called *kennings*), and in its equally elaborate sound correspondences. How apt are the names? List or chart the sound correspondences. Are they also appropriate?

2. What figure of speech is most central to the poem?

THE HUNT

The dog fox rolls on his lolling tongue
The frosty grape of the morning.
He points his nose to the scent of day,
He slits his eyes to the yellow sun,
He feels in his haunch a rising thunder
And his lifted ear takes warning:
    The horn blows true,
    The hounds break through,
    The hunter spreads,
    The huntsman rides,
And the red-tailed fox goes under.

The dog fox breaks to a hidden hole
And deep in the fern goes under.
He stiffens haunch and poises pads,
He gulps his spittle and drops his tail,
He downs his ears to the gathering thunder,
Crouching as they go over:
    Blowing horn,
    Baying hound,
    Shuddering hoof
    Shaking ground,
And the red-tailed fox goes under.

Heavy the huntsman will fall to bed
And heavily snore till morning.
The hunter will drowse and shake the stall
With a heavy hoof and hang his head.
The hound will whimper, and done with yawning,
Sleep as the moon goes under,
    And deep in the shade
    Of night will creep

The fox to his feast
On the feathered roost
And dine till the sun is dawning.

Louis Kent (b. 1910)

QUESTIONS

1. How do the three stanzas organize the poem? What are huntsman, hunter, hounds, and fox doing in each?

2. In each stanza the four short lines have a different syntactical pattern. Describe each.

3. Pick out the most prominent examples of alliteration, assonance, consonance, masculine rime, feminine rime, internal rime, approximate rime. Analyze the four short lines in each stanza for sound. What elements of refrain does the poem have? How much rime pattern does it have? Beyond their purely musical appeal, how do these sound repetitions contribute to the effectiveness of the poem?

THE CHANGELING

Toll no bell for me, dear Father, dear Mother,
Waste no sighs;
There are my sisters, there is my little brother
Who plays in the place called Paradise,
Your children all, your children for ever;
But I, so wild,
Your disgrace, with the queer brown face, was never,
Never, I know, but half your child!

In the garden at play, all day, last summer,
Far and away I heard
The sweet "tweet-tweet" of a strange new-comer,
The dearest, clearest call of a bird.
It lived down there in the deep green hollow,
My own old home, and the fairies say
The word of a bird is a thing to follow,
So I was away a night and a day.

One evening, too, by the nursery fire,
We snuggled close and sat round so still,
When suddenly as the wind blew higher,

Something scratched on the window-sill.
A pinched brown face peered in—I shivered;
No one listened or seemed to see;
The arms of it waved and the wings of it quivered,
Whoo—I knew it had come for me;
Some are as bad as bad can be!
All night long they danced in the rain,
Round and round in a dripping chain,
Threw their caps at the window-pane,
Tried to make me scream and shout
And fling the bedclothes all about:
I meant to stay in bed that night,
And if only you had left a light
They would never have got me out!

Sometimes I wouldn't speak, you see,
Or answer when you spoke to me,
Because in the long, still dusks of Spring
You can hear the whole world whispering:
The shy green grasses making love,
The feathers grow on the dear, grey dove,
The tiny heart of the redstart beat,
The patter of the squirrel's feet,
The pebbles pushing in the silver streams,
The rushes talking in their dreams,
The swish-swish of the bat's black wings,
The wild-wood bluebell's sweet ting-tings,
Humming and hammering at your ear,
Everything there is to hear
In the heart of hidden things,
But not in the midst of the nursery riot.
That's why I wanted to be quiet,
Couldn't do my sums, or sing,
Or settle down to anything.
And when, for that, I was sent upstairs
I *did* kneel down to say my prayers;
But the King who sits on your high church steeple
Has nothing to do with us fairy people!

'Times I pleased you, dear Father, dear Mother,
Learned all my lessons and liked to play,

And dearly I loved the little pale brother
Whom some other bird must have called away.
Why did They bring me here to make me
Not quite bad and not quite good,
Why, unless They're wicked, do They want in spite, to take me
Back to their wet, wild wood?
Now, every night I shall see the windows shining,
The gold lamp's glow, and the fire's red gleam,
While the best of us are twining twigs and the rest of us are whining
In the hollow by the stream.
Black and chill are Their nights on the wold;
And They live so long and They feel no pain:
I shall grow up, but never grow old,
I shall always, always be very cold,
I shall never come back again!

Charlotte Mew (1869–1928)

QUESTIONS

1. Vocabulary: *redstart* (40), *wold* (69).

2. In fairy lore a changeling is a fairy child, usually defective in some way, that has been left in place of a stolen human baby. What kind of child is the speaker? What characteristics denote him as a changeling?

3. Two kinds of world are juxtaposed in the poem: the human world and the fairy world. What kind of world is each? Does the contrast of the two, even though the fairy world is imaginary, help to illuminate the quality of the human world?

4. How does the speaker feel toward his family, the human world, and the fairy world? Which world does he prefer?

5. Take any ten or twelve lines of the poem and analyze them for internal rime, alliteration, assonance, consonance, masculine end rime, and feminine end rime. How is the effect of these devices different from their effect in the preceding poem?

THREE GREY GEESE

Three grey geese in a green field grazing,
Grey were the geese and green was the grazing.

Anonymous

CHAPTER TWELVE

Rhythm and Meter

Our love of rhythm and meter is rooted even deeper in us than our love for musical repetition. It is related to the beat of our hearts, the pulse of our blood, the intake and outflow of air from our lungs. Everything that we do naturally and gracefully we do rhythmically. There is rhythm in the way we walk, the way we swim, the way we ride a horse, the way we swing a golf club or a baseball bat. So native is rhythm to us that we read it, when we can, into the mechanical world around us. Our clocks go tick-tick-tick-tick, but we hear them go tick-tock, tick-tock in an endless trochaic. The click of the railway wheels beneath us patterns itself into a tune in our heads. There is a strong appeal for us in language that is rhythmical.

The term RHYTHM refers to any wavelike recurrence of motion or sound. In speech it is the natural rise and fall of language. All language is to some degree rhythmical, for all language involves some kind of alternation between accented and unaccented syllables. Language varies considerably, however, in the degree to which it exhibits rhythm. In some forms of speech the rhythm is so unobtrusive or so unpatterned that we are scarcely, if at all, aware of it. In other forms of speech the rhythm is so pronounced that we may be tempted to tap our foot to it.

METER is the kind of rhythm we can tap our foot to. In language that is metrical the accents are so arranged as to occur at apparently equal intervals of time, and it is this interval we mark off with the tap of our foot. Metrical language is called VERSE. Nonmetrical language is PROSE. Not all poetry is metrical, nor is all metrical language poetry.

Verse and *poetry* are not synonymous terms, nor is a *versifier* necessarily a *poet.*

The study of meter is a fascinating but highly complex subject. It is by no means an absolute prerequisite to an enjoyment, even a rich enjoyment, of poetry. But a knowledge of its fundamentals does have certain values. It can make the beginning reader more aware of the rhythmical effects of poetry and of how poetry should be read. It can enable the more advanced reader to analyze how certain effects are achieved, to see how rhythm is adapted to thought, and to explain what makes one poem (in this respect) better than another. The beginning student ought to have at least an elementary knowledge of the subject. It is not so difficult as its terminology might suggest.

In every word of more than one syllable, one syllable is *accented* or *stressed*, that is, given more prominence in pronunciation than the rest.* We say to*day*, to*mor*row, *yes*terday, *dai*ly, inter*vene*. If words of even one syllable are arranged into a sentence, we give certain words, or syllables, more prominence in pronunciation than the rest. We say: "He *went* to the *store*," or "*Jack* is *driving* his *car*." There is nothing mysterious about this; it is the normal process of language. The only difference between prose and verse is that in prose these accents occur more-or-less haphazardly; in verse the poet has arranged them to occur at regular intervals.

The word *meter* comes from a word meaning "measure." To measure something we must have a unit of measurement. For measuring length we use the inch, the foot, and the yard; for measuring time we use the second, the minute, and the hour. For measuring verse we use the foot, the line, and (sometimes) the stanza.

The basic metrical unit, the FOOT, consists normally of one accented syllable plus one or two unaccented syllables, though occasionally there may be no unaccented syllables, and very rarely there may be three. For diagramming verse, various systems of visual symbols have been invented. In this book we shall use a short curved line to indicate an unaccented

* Though the words *accent* and *stress* are generally used interchangeably, as here, a distinction is sometimes made between them in technical discussions. *Accent,* the relative prominence given a syllable in relation to its neighbors, is then said to result from one or more of four causes: *stress,* or force of utterance, producing loudness; *duration; pitch;* and *juncture,* the manner of transition between successive sounds. Of these, *stress,* in English verse, is most important.

syllable, a short horizontal line to indicate an accented syllable, and a vertical bar to indicate the division between feet. The basic kinds of feet are thus as follows:

Example	*Name of foot*	*Name of meter**	
◡ — to-*day*	Iamb	Iambic	Duple meters
— ◡ *dai*-ly	Trochee	Trochaic	Duple meters
◡ ◡ — in-ter-*vene*	Anapest	Anapestic	Triple meters
— ◡ ◡ *yes*-ter-day	Dactyl	Dactylic	Triple meters
— — *day*-*break*	Spondee	(Spondaic)	
— *day*	Monosyllabic foot		

The secondary unit of measurement, the LINE, is measured by naming the number of feet in it. The following names are used:

Monometer	one foot	Pentameter	five feet
Dimeter	two feet	Hexameter	six feet
Trimeter	three feet	Heptameter	seven feet
Tetrameter	four feet	Octameter	eight feet

The third unit, the STANZA, consists of a group of lines whose metrical pattern is repeated throughout the poem. Since not all verse is written in stanzas, we shall save our discussion of this unit till a later chapter.

The process of measuring verse is referred to as SCANSION. To *scan* any specimen of verse, we do three things: (1) we identify the prevailing foot, (2) we name the number of feet in a line—if this length follows any regular pattern, and (3) we describe the stanza pattern—if there is one. Suppose we try out our skill on the poem "To Lucasta, Going to the Wars" (page 650).

* In the spondee the accent is thought of as being distributed equally or almost equally over the two syllables and is sometimes referred to as a hovering accent. No whole poems are written in spondees or monosyllabic feet; hence there are only four basic meters: iambic, trochaic, anapestic, and dactylic. Iambic and trochaic are DUPLE METERS because they employ two-syllable feet; anapestic and dactylic are TRIPLE METERS because they employ three-syllable feet.

The first step in scanning a poem is to read it normally, listening to where the accents fall, and perhaps keeping time with your hand. In "To Lucasta" we immediately run into difficulty, for the first line is highly irregular and may leave us uncertain as to just where the accents fall. Let us pass over it, then, and look for easier lines. Though the second stanza, we discover, is more regular than the first, the third stanza is the most regular of the three. So let us begin with it. Lines 9, 11, and 12 go regularly, and we mark them as follows:

> Yet this | in-con- | stan-cy | is such |
> As you too shall a-dore;
> I could | not love | thee, Dear, | so much, |
> Loved I | not hon- | or more. |

Line 10 might also be marked regularly, but if we listen carefully we shall probably detect a slightly stronger stress on *too,* though it comes in an unstressed position, than on either of the adjacent syllables. So we'll mark it thus:

> As you | too shall | a-dore. |

We now see that this stanza is written in lines of alternating iambic tetrameter and iambic trimeter. Knowing this, we return to the first and second stanzas, expecting them, since they look similar, to conform to a similar pattern.

In the second stanza, lines 7 and 8 are perfectly regular, so we mark them confidently, but lines 5 and 6 offer some variation. Here is what we hear:

> True, a new mis-tress now I chase,
> The first foe in the field;
> And with | a strong- | er faith | em-brace |
> A sword, | a horse, | a shield. |

Since we are expecting lines 5 and 6 to conform to the established pattern, we shall assume that they are respectively a tetrameter and a trimeter line, and we shall mark the divisions between the feet in such a way as to yield the maximum number of iambs. The result is as follows:

True, a new mis-tress now I chase,
The first foe in the field.

We are now ready for the difficult first stanza. Following the same process of first marking the accents where we hear them and then dividing the feet so as to yield tetrameter and trimeter lines with the maximum possible number of iambic feet, we get something like the following:

Tell me not, Sweet, I am un-kind,
That from the nun-ner-y
Of thy chaste breast and qui-et mind
To war and arms I fly.

We are now ready to make a few generalizations about scansion.

1. A good reader will not ordinarily stop to scan a poem he is reading, and he certainly will not read a poem with the exaggerated emphasis on accented syllables that we sometimes give them in order to make the scansion more apparent. However, occasional scansion of a poem does have value. We hope to make this more apparent in the next chapter.

2. Scansion is at best a gross way of describing the rhythmical quality of a poem. It depends on classifying all syllables into either accented or unaccented categories and on ignoring the sometimes considerable difference between degrees of accent. Actually "accented" and "unaccented" are relative terms. and seldom will two syllables have exactly the same degree of accent. Whether we call a syllable accented or unaccented depends, moreover, on its degree of accent relative to the syllables on either side of it. In line 7 of "To Lucasta," for instance, the accent on *with* is not nearly so great as the accent on *strong,* and in line 2 the accent on the final *y* in *nunnery* is *lighter* than that on the *un*accented *thee* in line 11. Scansion therefore is incapable of dealing with the subtlest rhythmical effects in poetry. It is nevertheless a useful device, and probably any device more sensitive would be so complicated as to be no longer useful.

3. Scansion is not an altogether exact science. Within certain limits we may say that a certain scansion is right or wrong, but beyond these limits there is legitimate room for personal interpretation and disagreement between qualified readers. Lines 11 and 12 of "To Lucasta," for

instance, have been scanned above as perfectly regular. But a different reader might read line 11 thus:

I could not love thee, Dear, so much,

or line 12 thus:

Loved I not hon-or more.

The divisions between feet, moreover, are highly arbitrary and have little meaning except to help us name the meter of the poem. They correspond to no real divisions in the reading of the line, coming often, as they do, in the middle of a word. They are placed where they are usually only for the purpose of yielding the most possible of a single kind of foot. Accordingly, line 6 has been marked:

The first foe in the field,

though it might more plausibly have been marked:

The first foe in the field.

4. Finally—and this is the most important generalization of all—perfect regularity of meter is no criterion of merit. Beginning students sometimes get the notion that it is. If the meter is smooth and perfectly regular, they feel that the poet has handled his meter successfully and deserves all credit for it. Actually there is nothing easier than for any moderately talented versifier to make language go ta-*dum* ta-*dum* ta-*dum*. But there are two reasons why this is not generally desirable. The first is that, as we have said, all art consists essentially of repetition and variation. If a meter alternates too regularly between light and heavy beats, the result is to banish variation; the meter becomes mechanical and, for any sensitive reader, monotonous. The second is that, once a basic meter has been established, any deviations from it become highly significant and are the means by which the poet can use meter to reinforce meaning. If a meter is too perfectly regular, the probability is that the poet, instead of adapting rhythm to meaning, has simply forced his meaning into a metrical straitjacket.

Actually what gives the skillful use of meter its greatest effectiveness is that it consists, not of one rhythm, but of two. One of these is the *expected* rhythm. The other is the *heard* rhythm. Once we have determined the basic meter of a poem, say, iambic tetrameter, we have an expectation that this rhythm will continue. Thus a silent drumbeat is set up in our minds, and this drumbeat constitutes the expected rhythm. But the actual rhythm of the words—the heard rhythm—will sometimes confirm this expected rhythm and sometimes not. Thus the two rhythms are counterpointed against each other, and the appeal of the verse is magnified just as when two melodies are counterpointed against each other in music or as when we see two swallows flying together and around each other, following the same general course but with individual variations and making a much more eye-catching pattern than one swallow flying alone. If the heard rhythm conforms too closely to the expected rhythm, the meter becomes dull and uninteresting. If it departs too far from the expected rhythm, there ceases to be an expected rhythm. If the irregularity is too great, meter disappears, and the result is prose rhythm or free verse.

There are several ways by which variation can be introduced into the poet's use of meter. The most obvious way is by the substitution of different kinds of feet for regular feet. In our scansion of "To Lucasta," for instance, we noted one spondaic and two trochaic substitutions in the very first line. A less obvious but equally important means of variation is through simple phrasing and variation of degrees of accent. Lines 2, 4, 8, and 12 of "To Lucasta" have all been marked as regular, but actually there is considerable difference between them. Line 4 is quite regular, for the phrasing corresponds with the metrical pattern, and the line can be read ta-*dum* ta-*dum* ta-*dum*. Line 8 is even more regular, for the unaccented syllables are all *very* light, the accented syllables are all *very* strong, and the divisions between the feet are marked off by grammatical pauses indicated in the punctuation. This line goes ta-*dumm!* ta-*dumm!* ta-*dumm!* Line 12, on the other hand, is less regular, because the word *honor* cuts across the division between two feet. We should read it ta-*dum* ta-*dump*ty *dum*. And line 2 is even less regular because not only does *nunnery* cut across the division between two feet, but its final syllable is so lightly stressed as hardly to be accented at all. We should read this line something like ta-*dum* ta-*dump*teree. Finally, variation can be introduced by grammatical and rhetorical pauses. Line 11 of "To Lucasta," though scanned as regular, actually introduces variation because of the pause indicated by the commas around *Dear*.

The uses of rhythm and meter are several. Like the musical repetitions of sound, the musical repetitions of accent can be pleasing for their own sake. In addition, rhythm works as an emotional stimulus and serves, when used skillfully, to heighten our attention and awareness to what is going on in a poem. Finally, by his choice of meter, and by his skillful use of variation within the metrical framework, the poet can adapt the sound of his verse to its content and thus make meter a powerful reinforcement of meaning. We should avoid, however, the notion that there is any mystical correspondence between certain meters and certain emotions. There are no "happy" meters and no "melancholy" ones. The poet's choice of meter is probably less important than how he handles it after he has chosen it. However, some meters are swifter than others, some slower; some are more lilting than others, some more dignified. The poet can choose a meter that is appropriate or one that is inappropriate to his content, and by his handling of it can increase the appropriateness or inappropriateness. If he chooses a swift, lilting meter for a serious and grave subject, the meter will probably act to keep the reader from feeling any really deep emotion. But if he chooses a more dignified meter, it will intensify the emotion. In all great poetry, meter works intimately with the other elements of the poem to produce the appropriate total effect.

We must not forget, of course, that poetry need not be metrical at all. Like alliteration and rime, like metaphor and irony, like even imagery, meter is simply one resource the poet may or may not use. His job is to employ his resources to the best advantage for the object he has in mind—the kind of experience he wishes to express. And on no other basis can we judge him.

EXERCISES

1. Two additional terms that every student should be familiar with and should be careful to discriminate between are *blank verse* and *free verse*. BLANK VERSE is a very specific meter: *iambic pentameter, unrimed*. It has a special name because it is the principal English meter, that is, the meter that has been used for a large proportion of the greatest English poetry, including the tragedies of Shakespeare and the epics of Milton. Iambic pentameter in English seems especially suitable for the serious treatment of serious themes. The natural movement of the English language tends to be iambic. Lines shorter than pentameter tend to be songlike, not suited

to sustained treatment of serious material. Lines longer than pentameter tend to break up into shorter units, the hexameter line being read as two three-foot units, the heptameter line as a four-foot and a three-foot unit, and so on. Rime, while highly appropriate to most short poems, often proves a handicap for a long and lofty work. (The word *blank* implies that the end of the line is "blank," that is, bare of rime.) The above generalizations of course represent tendencies, not laws.

FREE VERSE, by our definition, is not verse at all; that is, it is not metrical. It may be rimed or unrimed. The word *free* means that it is free of metrical restrictions. The only difference between free verse and rhythmical prose is that free verse introduces one additional rhythmical unit, the line. The arrangement into lines divides the material into rhythmical units or cadences. Beyond its line arrangement there are no necessary differences between it and rhythmical prose.

Of the following poems, some are in free verse (*F*), some in blank verse (*B*), and some in other (*O*) meters. Determine into which category each belongs and indicate by putting an *F, B,* or *O* after it.

a. "Dulce et Decorum Est," page 558.
b. "It is not growing like a tree," page 577.
c. "To Satch," page 608.
d. "Ulysses," page 639.
e. "Out, Out—," page 676.
f. "A Christmas Tree," page 789.
g. "City Life," page 864.
h. "Portrait d'une Femme," page 873.
i. "There Was a Child Went Forth," page 891.
j. "A Blessing," page 900.

2. Another useful distinction is that between end-stopped lines and run-on lines. An END-STOPPED LINE is one in which the end of the line corresponds with a natural speech pause; a RUN-ON LINE is one in which the sense of the line hurries on into the next line. (There are, of course, all degrees of end-stop and run-on. A line ending with a period or semicolon is heavily end-stopped. A line without punctuation at the end but representing a slight pause between phrases or sense units would be lightly end-stopped.) The use of run-on lines is one way the poet can make use of grammatical or rhetorical pauses to vary his basic meter. Examine, for instance, Swift's "A Description of the Morning" (page 605) and Browning's "My Last Duchess" (page 671). Both of these poems are written in the same meter: iambic pentameter, rimed in couplets. Is their general rhythmical effect quite similar or markedly different? What accounts for the difference? Does this contrast support our statement that the poet's choice of meter is probably less important than the way he handles it?

VIRTUE

Sweet day, so cool, so calm, so bright,
    The bridal of the earth and sky;
The dew shall weep thy fall to night,
        For thou must die.

Sweet rose, whose hue, angry and brave,
    Bids the rash gazer wipe his eye;
Thy root is ever in its grave,
        And thou must die.

Sweet spring, full of sweet days and roses,
    A box where sweets compacted lie;
My music shows ye have your closes,
        And all must die.

Only a sweet and virtuous soul,
    Like seasoned timber, never gives;
But though the whole world turn to coal,
        Then chiefly lives.

George Herbert (1593–1633)

QUESTIONS

1. Vocabulary: *brave* (5), *closes* (11).

2. How are the four stanzas interconnected? How do they build to a climax? How does the fourth contrast with the first three?

3. Scan the poem, identify its meter, and point out the principal variations from the expected rhythm.

THE OAK

Live thy Life,
    Young and old,
Like yon oak,
Bright in spring,
    Living gold;

Summer-rich
    Then; and then
Autumn-changed,

Soberer-hued
    Gold again.

All his leaves
    Fall'n at length,
Look, he stands,
Trunk and bough,
    Naked strength.

Alfred, Lord Tennyson (1809–1892)

QUESTIONS

1. Scan the poem without putting in the bar divisions. Should this poem be regarded as iambic or trochaic? Could it be either? Some metrists have discarded the traditional distinction between iambic and trochaic and between anapestic and dactylic as being artificial. The only real distinction, they feel, is between duple and triple meters. Does this poem support their claim?

2. With the above question in mind, turn to Donne's "Song: Go and catch a falling star" (page 847) and scan it. How would you classify it?

THE "JE NE SAIS QUOI"

Yes, I'm in love, I feel it now,
    And Celia has undone me;
And yet I'll swear I can't tell how
    The pleasing plague stole on me.

'Tis not her face that love creates,
    For there no Graces revel;
'Tis not her shape, for there the Fates
    Have rather been uncivil.

'Tis not her air, for sure in that,
    There's nothing more than common;
And all her sense is only chat,
    Like any other woman.

Her voice, her touch, might give the alarm—
    'Tis both perhaps, or neither;
In short, 'tis that provoking charm
    Of Celia altogether.

William Whitehead (1715–1785)

QUESTIONS

1. *Je ne sais quoi* is a French expression meaning "I do not know what"—an indefinable something. Does the use of approximate rimes rather than perfect rimes in the even lines of this poem help to establish the quality of uncertainty which is the subject of the poem?

2. Find examples of OXYMORON (a compact paradox in which two successive words seemingly contradict each other) in the first and last stanzas. What broad paradox underlies the whole poem?

3. What is the reason for the capitalization and pluralization of *grace* and *fate* in the second stanza? What is the image here conveyed? Is *love* (5) the subject or object of the verb?

4. Because of the feminine rimes of the even-numbered lines, you will find, on scanning the poem, that there is an extra unaccented syllable left over in these lines. For instance, the first two lines may be scanned as follows:

> ◡ — | ◡ — | ◡ — | ◡ — |
> Yes, I'm in love, I feel it now,
> ◡ — | ◡ — | ◡ — | ◡
> And Cel-ia has un-done me.

It will often happen that one or two unaccented syllables are left over—at the end of the line with iambic and anapestic meter, at the beginning of the line with trochaic and dactylic meter. Although we ignore these unaccented extras in naming the meter (the above poem is written in alternating iambic tetrameter and iambic trimeter), they make considerable difference in the rhythmical effect. They are another way the poet can vary his basic meter.

5. All the lines of Tennyson's "The Oak" begin and end with accented syllables (the rimes are masculine); half of the lines of "The 'Je Ne Sais Quoi' " begin and end with unaccented syllables (and have feminine rimes). Do you see any correlation between this metrical difference of the two poems and their difference of subject? Could the subject matter of either poem be treated as successfully in the meter of the other?

IF EVERYTHING HAPPENS THAT CAN'T BE DONE

if everything happens that can't be done
(and anything's righter
than books
could plan)
the stupidest teacher will almost guess
(with a run
skip
around we go yes)
there's nothing as something as one

one hasn't a why or because or although
(and buds know better
than books
don't grow)
one's anything old being everything new
(with a what
which
around we come who)
one's everyanything so

so world is a leaf so tree is a bough
(and birds sing sweeter
than books
tell how)
so here is away and so your is a my
(with a down
up
around again fly)
forever was never till now

now i love you and you love me
(and books are shuter
than books
can be)
and deep in the high that does nothing but fall
(with a shout
each
around we go all)
there's somebody calling who's we

we're anything brighter than even the sun
(we're everything greater
than books
might mean)
we're everyanything more than believe
(with a spin
leap
alive we're alive)
we're wonderful one times one

e. e. cummings (1894–1962)

QUESTIONS

1. Explain the last line. Of what very familiar idea is this poem a fresh treatment?

2. The poem is based on a contrast between heart and mind, or love and learning. Which does the poet prefer? What symbols does he use for each?

3. What is the tone of the poem?

4. Which lines of each stanza regularly rime with each other (either perfect or approximate rime)? How does the poet link the stanzas together?

5. What is the basic metrical scheme of the poem? What does the meter contribute to the tone? What line (in the fifth stanza) most clearly states the subject and occasion of the poem? How does meter underline its significance?

6. Can you suggest any reason why the poet wrote lines 2–4 and 6–8 of each stanza as three lines rather than one? What metrical variations does the poet use in lines 6–8 of each stanza and with what effect?

THE NEW MISTRESS

"Oh, sick I am to see you, will you never let me be?
You may be good for something but you are not good for me.
Oh, go where you are wanted, for you are not wanted here.
And that was all the farewell when I parted from my dear.

"I will go where I am wanted, to a lady born and bred
Who will dress me free for nothing in a uniform of red;
She will not be sick to see me if I only keep it clean:
I will go where I am wanted for a soldier of the Queen.

"I will go where I am wanted, for the sergeant does not mind;
He may be sick to see me but he treats me very kind:
He gives me beer and breakfast and a ribbon for my cap,
And I never knew a sweetheart spend her money on a chap.

"I will go where I am wanted, where there's room for one or two,
And the men are none too many for the work there is to do;
Where the standing line wears thinner and the dropping dead lie
thick;
And the enemies of England they shall see me and be sick."

A. E. Housman (1859–1936)

QUESTIONS

1. Show how the sweetheart's words in the first three lines are echoed throughout the poem. What psychological mechanisms are at work? What are the implications of line 5?

2. To what famous poem in chapter 7 does the title allude? What function does the allusion serve? How do this poem and the earlier one differ in tone?

3. Point out an understatement in stanza 4. Is there an allusion in line 15?

4. This poem represents a kind of meter that we have not yet discussed. It *may* be scanned as iambic heptameter:

Oh, sick | I am | to see | you, will | you ne- | ver let | me be?

But you will probably find yourself reading it as a four-beat line:

Oh, sick | I am to see | you, will you ne- | ver let me be?

Although the meter is duple, insofar as there is an alternation between unaccented and accented syllables, there is also an alternation in the degree of stress on the accented syllables: the first, third, fifth, and seventh stresses are heavier than the second, fourth, and sixth; the result is that the two-syllable feet tend to group themselves into larger units. We may scan it as follows, using a short line for a light accent, a longer one for a heavy accent:

I will go | where I am want- | ed, for the ser- | geant does not mind; |
He may | be sick to see | me but he treats | me ve-ry kind: |
He gives | me beer and break- | fast and a rib- | bon for my cap, |
And I ne- | ver knew a sweet- | heart spend her mon- | ey on a chap. |

This kind of meter, in which there is an alternation between heavy and light stresses, is known as DIPODIC (two-footed) VERSE. (For another example of dipodic verse, see "America for Me" (page 808). The alternation may not be perfect throughout, but it will be frequent enough to establish a pattern in the reader's mind. Now, scan the last stanza.

THE BARREL-ORGAN

There's a barrel-organ carolling across a golden street
    In the City as the sun sinks low,
With a silvery cry of linnets in its dull mechanic beat,
    As it dies into the sunset glow;
And it pulses through the pleasures of the City and the pain
    That surround the singing organ like a large eternal light;
And they've given it a glory and a part to play again
    In the Symphony that rules the day and night.

And now it's marching onward through the realms of old romance,
    And trolling out a fond familiar tune,
And now it's roaring cannon down to fight the King of France,

And now it's prattling softly to the moon,
And all around the organ there's a sea without a shore
Of human joys and wonders and regrets,
To remember and to recompense the music evermore
For what the cold machinery forgets . . .

Yes; as the music changes,
Like a prismatic glass,
It takes the light and ranges
Through all the moods that pass;
Dissects the common carnival
Of passions and regrets,
And gives the world a glimpse of all
The colors it forgets.

And there *La Traviata* sighs
Another sadder song;
And there *Il Trovatore* cries
A tale of deeper wrong;
And bolder knights to battle go
With sword and shield and lance,
Than ever here on earth below
Have whirled into—*a dance!*—

Go down to Kew in lilac-time, in lilac-time, in lilac-time;
Go down to Kew in lilac-time (it isn't far from London!)
And you shall wander hand in hand with love in summer's wonderland;
Go down to Kew in lilac-time (it isn't far from London!)

The cherry-trees are seas of bloom and soft perfume and sweet perfume,
The cherry-trees are seas of bloom (and oh, so near to London!)
And there they say, when dawn is high and all the world's a blaze of sky
The cuckoo, though he's very shy, will sing a song for London.

The Dorian nightingale is rare and yet they say you'll hear him there
At Kew, at Kew in lilac-time (and oh, so near to London!)
The linnet and the throstle, too, and after dark the long halloo
And golden-eyed *tu-whit, tu-whoo* of owls that ogle London.

For Noah hardly knew a bird of any kind that isn't heard
At Kew, at Kew in lilac-time (and oh, so near to London!)
And when the rose begins to pout and all the chestnut spires are out
You'll hear the rest without a doubt, all chorusing for London:—

Come down to Kew in lilac-time, in lilac-time, in lilac-time;
    Come down to Kew in lilac-time (it isn't far from London!)
And you shall wander hand in hand with love in summer's wonderland;
    Come down to Kew in lilac-time (it isn't far from London!)

And then the troubadour begins to thrill the golden street,
    In the City as the sun sinks low;
And in all the gaudy busses there are scores of weary feet
Marking time, sweet time, with a dull mechanic beat,
And a thousand hearts are plunging to a love they'll never meet,
Through the meadows of the sunset, through the poppies and the wheat,
    In the land where the dead dreams go.

. . . .

So it's Jeremiah, Jeremiah,
    What have you to say
When you meet the garland girls
    Tripping on their way?

All around my gala hat
    I wear a wreath of roses
(A long and lonely year it is
    I've waited for the May!)
If any one should ask you,
    The reason why I wear it is—
My own love, my true love
    Is coming home to-day.

And it's buy a bunch of violets for the lady
    (It's lilac-time in London; it's lilac-time in London!)
Buy a bunch of violets for the lady
    While the sky burns blue above:

On the other side the street you'll find it shady
    (It's lilac-time in London; it's lilac-time in London!)
But buy a bunch of violets for the lady,
    And tell her she's your own true love.

There's a barrel-organ carolling across a golden street
    In the City as the sun sinks glittering and slow;
And the music's not immortal; but the world has made it sweet
And enriched it with the harmonies that make a song complete

In the deeper heavens of music where the night and morning meet,
    As it dies into the sunset-glow;
And it pulses through the pleasures of the City and the pain
    That surround the singing organ like a large eternal light,
And they've given it a glory and a part to play again
    In the Symphony that rules the day and night.

And there, as the music changes,
    The song runs round again.
Once more it turns and ranges
    Through all its joy and pain,
Dissects the common carnival
    Of passions and regrets;
And the wheeling world remembers all
    The wheeling song forgets.

Once more *La Traviata* sighs
    Another sadder song:
Once more *Il Trovatore* cries
    A tale of deeper wrong;
Once more the knights to battle go
    With sword and shield and lance
Till once, once more, the shattered foe
    Has whirled into—*a dance!*

Come down to Kew in lilac-time, in lilac-time, in lilac-time;
    Come down to Kew in lilac-time (it isn't far from London!)
And you shall wander hand in hand with love in summer's wonderland;
    Come down to Kew in lilac-time (it isn't far from London!)

Alfred Noyes (1880–1958)

QUESTIONS

1. A barrel-organ is a mechanical hand organ played by turning a crank. The City is the business section of London. Kew, a suburb of London, is famous for its large public gardens. *La Traviata* and *Il Trovatore* are popular operas by Verdi. What precisely is the hour of the day in the poem?

2. The poem describes the music of the barrel-organ and its effect on the people on the street. Lines 17–52, 60–79, and 90–109 represent melodies played by the organ. How many different melodies are metrically indicated? What effect does the music have on the people? Do the people have any effect on the music?

3. The four-line refrain with which the poem ends is about as appealing

for pure melodiousness as anything in poetry. Analyze the musical devices which it makes use of and try to account for its effectiveness.

4. The narrative stanzas and two of the songs are in dipodic verse* and illustrate additional varieties of dipodic feet. Notice that a dipodic foot (like a spondee in duple meter) *may* have no unaccented syllables at all:

> There's a bar-rel-or-gan car-ol-ling a-cross a gold-en street
> In the Cit-y as the sun sinks low.

An additional variation is the metrical pause or rest. Unlike grammatical and rhetorical pauses, the metrical pause affects the scansion. If you beat out the rhythm of lines 72–75 with your hand, you will find that some of the beats fall *between* syllables. The METRICAL PAUSE, then, is a pause that replaces an accented syllable. It is usually found in verse that has a pronounced lilt or swing. We have represented it in the scansion with an *x*:

> And it's buy a bunch of vi-o-lets for the la-dy
> *(It's li-lac-time in Lon-don; it's li-lac-time in Lon-don!)*
> Buy a bunch of vi-o-lets for the la-dy
> While the sky burns blue a-bove.

Scan the rest of the song, and also the song before it, looking out for metrical pauses.

DOWN BY THE SALLEY GARDENS

Down by the salley gardens my love and I did meet;
She passed the salley gardens with little snow-white feet.
She bid me take love easy, as the leaves grow on the tree;
But I, being young and foolish, with her would not agree.
In a field by the river my love and I did stand,
And on my leaning shoulder she laid her snow-white hand.
She bid me take life easy, as the grass grows on the weirs;
But I was young and foolish, and now am full of tears.

William Butler Yeats (1865–1939)

QUESTIONS

1. Vocabulary: *salley* (1), *weirs* (8).
2. Metrical pauses are integral to the pattern of this poem. Demonstrate this by scanning it.

*See question 4 to "The New Mistress" (page 746) for a definition of dipodic.

ARIEL'S SONG

Where the bee sucks, there suck I;
In a cowslip's bell I lie;
There I couch when owls do cry;
On the bat's back I do fly
After summer merrily:
Merrily, merrily, shall I live now
Under the blossom that hangs on the bough.

William Shakespeare (1564–1616)

QUESTIONS

1. Ariel, in *The Tempest,* is a spirit of the air. How are the content and the meter of this song appropriate to its speaker?

2. How does the meter of the first five lines differ from that of the last two? What else changes? Is *merrily* in line 5 scanned the same as it is in line 6? Why or why not? Can this poem be described as iambic, trochaic, anapestic, or dactylic?

HAD I THE CHOICE

Had I the choice to tally greatest bards,
To limn their portraits, stately, beautiful, and emulate at will,
Homer with all his wars and warriors—Hector, Achilles, Ajax,
Or Shakespeare's woe-entangled Hamlet, Lear, Othello—Tennyson's fair ladies,
Meter or wit the best, or choice conceit to wield in perfect rhyme, delight of singers;
These, these, O sea, all these I'd gladly barter,
Would you the undulation of one wave, its trick to me transfer,
Or breathe one breath of yours upon my verse,
And leave its odor there.

Walt Whitman (1819–1892)

QUESTIONS

1. Vocabulary: *tally* (1), *limn* (2), *conceit* (5).

2. What poetic qualities does Whitman propose to barter in exchange for what? What qualities do the sea and its waves symbolize?

3. What kind of "verse" is this? Why does Whitman prefer it to "meter" and "perfect rhyme"?

THE AIM WAS SONG

Before man came to blow it right
    The wind once blew itself untaught,
And did its loudest day and night
    In any rough place where it caught.

Man came to tell it what was wrong:
    It hadn't found the place to blow;
It blew too hard—the aim was song.
    And listen—how it ought to go!

He took a little in his mouth,
    And held it long enough for north
To be converted into south,
    And then by measure blew it forth.

By measure. It was word and note,
    The wind the wind had meant to be—
A little through the lips and throat.
    The aim was song—the wind could see.

Robert Frost (1874–1963)

QUESTIONS

1. In this poem, Frost invents a myth about the origin of poetry. What implications does the myth suggest about the relation of man to nature and about poetry to nature?

2. Compare and contrast the thought and form of this poem with that of Whitman's.

3. Scan the poem and identify its meter. How does the poet give variety to a regular metrical pattern?

Sound and Meaning

Rhythm and sound cooperate to produce what we call the music of poetry. This music, as we have pointed out, may serve two general functions: it may be enjoyable in itself; it may be used to reinforce meaning and intensify the communication.

Pure pleasure in sound and rhythm exists from a very early age in the human being—probably from the age the baby first starts cooing in its cradle, certainly from the age that children begin chanting nursery rimes and skipping rope. The appeal of the following verse, for instance, depends almost entirely on its "music":

> Pease por-ridge hot,
>   Pease por-ridge cold,
> Pease por-ridge in the pot
>   Nine days old.

There is very little sense here; the attraction comes from the emphatic rhythm, the emphatic rimes (with a strong contrast between the short vowel and short final consonant of *hot-pot* and the long vowel and long final consonant combination of *cold-old*), and the heavy alliteration (exactly half the words begin with *p*). From nonsense rimes such as this, many of us graduate into a love of more meaningful poems whose appeal resides largely in the sound they make. Much of the pleasure that we find in Swinburne's "I will go back to the great sweet mother" (page 721) lies in its musical quality. Other famous examples are Vachel

Lindsay's "The Congo," Edgar Allan Poe's "The Bells," and Alfred Noyes's "The Barrel-Organ" (page 746).

The peculiar function of poetry as distinguished from music, however, is to convey not sounds but meaning or experience *through* sounds. In third and fourth-rate poetry sound and rhythm sometimes distract attention from sense. In first-rate poetry the sound exists, not for its own sake, not for mere decoration, but as a medium of meaning. Its function is to support the leading player, not to steal the scene.

There are numerous ways in which the poet may reinforce meaning through sound. Without claiming to exhaust them, perhaps we can include most of the chief means under four general headings.

First, the poet can choose words whose sound in some degree suggests their meaning. In its narrowest sense this is called onomatopoeia. ONOMATOPOEIA, strictly defined, means the use of words which, at least supposedly, sound like what they mean, such as *hiss*, *snap*, and *bang*.

SONG: HARK, HARK!

Hark, hark!
    Bow-wow.
The watch-dogs bark!
    Bow-wow.
Hark, hark! I hear
The strain of strutting chanticleer
Cry, "Cock-a-doodle-doo!"

William Shakespeare (1564–1616)

In this lyric, *bark*, *bow-wow*, and *cock-a-doodle-doo* are onomatopoetic words. In addition Shakespeare has reinforced the onomatopoetic effect with the repeated use of *hark*, which sounds like *bark*. The usefulness of onomatopoeia, of course, is strictly limited, because it can be used only where the poet is describing sound, and most poems do not describe sound. And the use of pure onomatopoeia, as in the above example, is likely to be fairly trivial except as it forms an incidental part of a more complex poem. But by combining onomatopoeia with other devices that help convey meaning, the poet can achieve subtle and beautiful effects whose recognition is one of the keenest pleasures in reading poetry.

In addition to onomatopoetic words there is another group of words, sometimes called PHONETIC INTENSIVES, whose sound, by a process as yet obscure, to some degree suggests their meaning. An initial *fl-* sound, for instance, is often associated with the idea of moving light, as in *flame, flare, flash, flicker, flimmer*. An initial *gl-* also frequently accompanies the idea of light, usually unmoving, as in *glare, gleam, glint, glow, glisten*. An initial *sl-* often introduces words meaning "smoothly wet," as in *slippery, slick, slide, slime, slop, slosh, slobber, slushy*. Short *-i-* often goes with the idea of smallness, as in *inch, imp, thin, slim, little, bit, chip, sliver, chink, slit, sip, whit, tittle, snip, wink, glint, glimmer, flicker, pigmy, midge, chick, kid, kitten, minikin, miniature*. Long *-o-* or *-oo-* may suggest melancholy or sorrow, as in *moan, groan, woe, mourn, forlorn, toll, doom, gloom, moody*. Medial and final *-are* sometimes goes with the idea of a big light or noise, as *flare, glare, stare, blare*. Medial *-att-* suggests some kind of particled movement, as in *spatter, scatter, shatter, chatter, rattle, prattle, clatter, batter*. Final *-er* and *-le* indicate repetition, as in *glitter, flutter, shimmer, whisper, jabber, chatter, clatter, sputter, flicker, twitter, mutter,* and *ripple, bubble, twinkle, sparkle, rattle, rumble, jingle*. None of these various sounds is invariably associated with the idea that it seems to suggest, and, in fact, a short *-i-* is found in *thick* as well as *thin*, in *big* as well as *little*. Language is a complex phenomenon. But there is enough association between these sounds and ideas to suggest some sort of intrinsic if obscure relationship, and a word like *flicker*, though not onomatopoetic, for it does not refer to sound, would seem somehow to suggest its sense, the *fl-* suggesting moving light, the *-i-* suggesting smallness, the *-ck-* suggesting sudden cessation of movement (as in *crack, peck, pick, hack,* and *flick*), and the *-er* suggesting repetition. The above list of sound-idea correspondences is only a very partial one. A complete list, though it would involve only a small proportion of words in the language, would probably be a longer list than that of the more strictly onomatopoetic words, to which they are related.

SPLINTER

The voice of the last cricket
across the first frost
is one kind of good-by.
It is so thin a splinter of singing.

Carl Sandburg (1878–1967)

QUESTIONS

1. Why is "so thin a splinter" a better choice of metaphor than "so small an atom" or "so meager a morsel"?

2. How does the poet intensify the effect of the two phonetic intensives in line 4?

Second, the poet can choose sounds and group them so that the effect is smooth and pleasant sounding (*euphonious*) or rough and harsh sounding (*cacophonous*). The vowels are in general more pleasing than the consonants, for the vowels are musical tones, whereas the consonants are merely noises. A line with a high percentage of vowel sounds in proportion to consonant sounds will therefore tend to be more melodious than one in which the proportion is low. The vowels and consonants themselves differ considerably in quality. The "long" vowels, such as those in *fate, reed, rime, coat, food,* and *dune* are fuller and more resonant than the "short" vowels, as in *fat, red, rim, cot, foot,* and *dun.* Of the consonants, some are fairly mellifluous, such as the "liquids," *l, m, n,* and *r;* the soft *v* and *f* sounds; the semi-vowels *w* and *y;* and such combinations as *th* and *wh.* Others, such as the "explosives," *b, d, g, k, p,* and *t,* are harsher and sharper in their effect. These differences in sound are the poet's materials. However, he will not necessarily seek out the sounds that are pleasing and attempt to combine them in melodious combinations. Rather, he will use euphonious and cacophonous combinations as they are appropriate to his content. Consider, for instance, the following poem.

UPON JULIA'S VOICE

So smooth, so sweet, so silv'ry is thy voice,
As, could they hear, the Damned would make no noise,
But listen to thee (walking in thy chamber)
Melting melodious words to Lutes of Amber.

Robert Herrick (1591–1674)

QUESTION

Literally, an amber lute is as nonsensical as a silver voice. What connotations do *Amber* and *silv'ry* have that contribute to the meaning of this poem?

There are no strictly onomatopoetic words in this poem, and yet the sound seems marvelously adapted to the sense. Especially remarkable are the first and last lines, those most directly concerned with Julia's voice. In the first line the sounds that most strike the ear are the unvoiced *s*'s and the soft *v*'s, supported by *th:* "So smooth, so sweet, so silv'ry is thy voice." In the fourth line the predominating sounds are the liquid consonants *m, l,* and *r,* supported by a *w:* "Melting melodious words to Lutes of Amber." The least euphonious line in the poem, on the other hand, is the second, where the subject is the tormented in hell, not Julia's voice. Here the prominent sounds are the *d*'s, supported by a voiced *s* (a voiced *s* buzzes, unlike the unvoiced *s*'s in line 1), and two *k* sounds: "As, could they hear, the damned would make no noise." Throughout the poem there is a remarkable correspondence between the pleasant-sounding and the pleasant in idea, the unpleasant-sounding and the unpleasant in idea.

A third way in which a poet can reinforce meaning through sound is by controlling the speed and movement of his lines by his choice and use of meter, by his choice and arrangement of vowel and consonant sounds, and by his disposition of pauses. In meter the unaccented syllables go faster than the accented syllables; hence the triple meters are swifter than the duple. But the poet can vary the tempo of any meter by the use of substitute feet. Whenever two or more unaccented syllables come together, the effect will be to speed up the pace of the line; when two or more accented syllables come together, the effect will be to slow it down. This pace will also be affected by the vowel lengths and by whether the sounds are easily run together. The long vowels take longer to pronounce than the short ones. Some words are easily run together, while others demand that the position of the mouth be re-formed before the next word is uttered. It takes much longer, for instance, to say, "Watch dogs catch much meat" than to say, "My aunt is away," though the number of syllables is the same. And finally the poet can slow down the speed of a line through the introduction of grammatical and rhetorical pauses. Consider lines 54–56 from Tennyson's "Ulysses" (page 640):

The lights be-gin to twin-kle from the rocks;
The long day wanes; the slow moon climbs; the deep
Moans round with man-y voi-ces . . .

In these lines Tennyson wished the movement to be slow, in accordance with the slow waning of the long day and the slow climbing of the moon. His meter is iambic pentameter. This is not a swift meter, but in lines 55–56 he slows it down, (1) by introducing three spondaic feet, thus bringing three accented syllables together in three separate places; (2) by choosing for his accented syllables words that have long vowel sounds or diphthongs that the voice hangs on to: *long, day, wanes, slow, moon, climbs, deep, moans, round*; (3) by choosing words that are not easily run together (except for *day* and *slow*, each of these words begins and ends with consonant sounds that demand varying degrees of readjustment of the mouth before pronunciation is continued); (4) by introducing two grammatical pauses, after *wanes* and *climbs*, and a rhetorical pause after *deep*. The result is an extremely effective use of the movement of the verse to accord with the movement suggested by the words.*

A fourth way for a poet to fit sound to sense is to control both sound and meter in such a way as to put emphasis on words that are important in meaning. He can do this by marking out such words by alliteration, assonance, consonance, or rime; by placing them before a pause; or by skillfully placing or displacing them in the metrical pattern. Look again at Shakespeare's "Spring" (page 561):

When dai-sies pied | and vi-o-lets blue |
  And la-dy-smocks | all sil-ver-white |
And cuck-oo-buds | of yel-low hue |
  Do paint | the mea-dows | with de-light, |
The cuck-oo then, | on ev-ery tree, |
Mocks mar-ried men; | for thus | sings he, |
  "Cuckoo!
Cuckoo, cuckoo!" O, word of fear,
Unpleasing to a married ear!

The scansion is regular until the beginning of the sixth line: there we find a spondaic substitution in the first foot. In addition, the first three

* In addition, Tennyson uses one onomatopoetic word (*moans*) and one phonetic intensive (*twinkle*).

words in this line are heavily alliterated, all beginning with *m*. And further, each of these words ends in a consonant, thus preventing their being run together. The result is to throw heavy emphasis on these three words: to give them, one might almost say, a tone of solemnity, or mock-solemnity. Whether or not the solemnity is in the sound, the emphasis on these three words is appropriate, for it serves to signal the shift in tone that takes place at this point. The first five lines have contained nothing but delightful images; the concluding four introduce the note of irony.

Just as Shakespeare uses metrical irregularity, plus alliteration, to give emphasis to important words, Tennyson, in the concluding line of "Ulysses," uses marked regularity, plus skillful use of grammatical pause, to achieve the same effect:

> Though much is ta-ken, much a-bides; and though
> We are not now that strength which in old days
> Moved earth and heav-en, that which we are, we are:
> One e-qual tem-per of he-ro-ic hearts,
> Made weak by time and fate, but strong in will
> To strive, to seek, to find, and not to yield.

The blank verse rhythm throughout "Ulysses" is remarkably subtle and varied, but the last line is not only regular in its scansion but heavily regular, for a number of reasons. First, all the words are monosyllables: no words cross over the divisions between feet. Second, the unaccented syllables are all very small and unimportant words—four *to*'s and one *and*, whereas the accented syllables consist of four important verbs and a very important *not*. Third, each of the verbs is followed by a grammatical pause pointed off by a mark of punctuation. The result is to cause a pronounced alternation between light and heavy syllables that brings the accent down on the four verbs and the *not* with sledgehammer blows. The line rings out like a challenge, which it is.

THE SPAN OF LIFE

> The old dog barks backward without getting up.
> I can remember when he was a pup.

Robert Frost (1874–1963)

QUESTIONS

1. Is the dog a dog only or also a symbol?

2. The first line presents a visual and auditory image; the second line makes a comment. But does the second line *call up images?* Does it suggest more than it says? Would the poem have been more or less effective if the second line had been, "He was frisky and lively when he was a pup"?

We may well conclude our discussion of the adaptation of sound to sense by analyzing this very brief poem. It consists of one riming anapestic tetrameter couplet. Its content is a contrast between the decrepitude of an old dog and his friskiness as a pup. The scansion is as follows:

> ⏑ — | — — — | ⏑ ⏑ — | ⏑ ⏑ — |
> The old dog barks back-ward with-out get-ting up.
> — | ⏑ ⏑ — | ⏑ ⏑ — | ⏑ ⏑ — |
> I can re-mem-ber when he was a pup.

How is sound fitted to sense? In the first place, the triple meter chosen by the poet is a swift meter, but in the first line he has jammed it up in a remarkable way by substituting a kind of foot so rare that we do not even have a name for it. It might be called a triple spondee: at any rate it is a foot in which the accent is distributed over three syllables. This foot, following the accented syllable in the first foot, creates a situation where four accented syllables are pushed up together. In addition, each of these accented syllables begins and ends with a strong consonant sound or cluster of consonant sounds, so that they cannot be run together in pronunciation: the mouth must be re-formed between each syllable: "The o*ld dog barks back*ward." The result is to slow down the line drastically, to almost destroy its rhythmical quality, and to make it difficult to utter. Indeed, the line is as decrepit as the old dog who turns his head but does not get up. When we get to the second line, however, the contrast is startling. The rhythm is swift and regular, the syllables end in vowels or liquid consonants and are easily run together, the whole line ripples fluently off the tongue. In addition, where the first line has a high proportion of explosive and cacophonous consonants—"The ol*d* *dog barks back*ward withou*t* *get*ting u*p*"—the second line contains predominantly consonants which are smoother and more graceful—"I ca*n* *remem*ber *when he was* a pup." Thus the motion and the sound of the lines are remarkably in accord with the visual images they suggest. In addition, in the first line the poet has supported the onomatopoetic word *barks* with a near echo *back*, so that the sound reinforces the auditory image. If the poem does a great deal in just two lines, this skillful adaptation of sound to sense is one very important reason.

In analyzing verse for correspondence between sound and sense, we need to be very cautious not to make exaggerated claims. A great deal of nonsense has been written about the moods of certain meters and the effects of certain sounds, and it is easy to suggest correspondences that exist really only in our imaginations. Nevertheless, the first-rate poet has nearly always an instinctive tact about handling his sound so that it in some degree supports his meaning; the inferior poet is usually obtuse to these correspondences. One of the few absolute rules that can be applied to the judgment of poetry is that the form should be adequate to the content. This rule does not mean that there must always be a close and easily demonstrable correspondence. It does mean that there will be no glaring discrepancies. Poor poets, and even good poets in their third-rate work, sometimes go horribly wrong.

The two selections we introduced this chapter with illustrate, first, the use of sound in verse almost purely for its own sake ("Pease porridge hot"), and second, the use of sound in verse almost purely to *imitate* meaning ("Hark, hark! Bow-wow"), and they are, as significant poetry, perhaps the most trivial pieces in the whole book. But in between these extremes there is an abundant range of poetic possibilities where sound is pleasurable for itself without violating meaning and where sound to varying degrees corresponds with and corroborates meaning; and in this rich middle range, for the reader who can learn to perceive them, lie many of the greatest pleasures of reading poetry.

EXERCISE

In which of the following pairs of quotations is sound more successfully adapted to sense? As precisely as possible, explain why. (The poet whose name is given is in each case the author of the superior version.)

1. a. Go forth—and Virtue, ever in your sight,
Shall be your guide by day, your guard by night.

b. Go forth—and Virtue, ever in your sight,
Shall point your way by day, and keep you safe at night.

Charles Churchill

2. a. How charming is divine philosophy!
Not harsh and rough as foolish men suppose
But musical as is the lute of Phoebus.

b. How charming is divine philosophy!
Not harsh and crabbed as dull fools suppose
But musical as is Apollo's lute.

Milton

3. a. All day the fleeing crows croak hoarsely over the snow.

b. All day the out-cast crows croak hoarsely across the whiteness.

Elizabeth Coatsworth

4. a. Your talk attests how bells of singing gold
Would sound at evening over silent water.

b. Your low voice tells how bells of singing gold
Would sound at twilight over silent water.

Edwin Arlington Robinson

5. a. A thousand streamlets flowing through the lawn,
The moan of doves in gnarled ancient oaks,
And quiet murmuring of countless bees.

b. Myriads of rivulets hurrying through the lawn,
The moan of doves in immemorial elms,
And murmuring of innumerable bees.

Tennyson

6. a. It is the lark that sings so out of tune,
Straining harsh discords and unpleasing sharps.

b. It is the lark that warbles out of tune
With harsh discordant voice and hateful flats.

Shakespeare

7. a. "Artillery" and "armaments" and "implements of war"
Are phrases too severe to please the gentle Muse.

b. Bombs, drums, guns, bastions, batteries, bayonets, bullets,—
Hard words, which stick in the soft Muses' gullets.

Byron

8. a. The hands of the sisters Death and Night incessantly softly wash again, and ever again, this soiled world.

b. The hands of the soft twins Death and Night repeatedly wash again, and ever again, this dirty world.

Whitman

9. a. The curfew sounds the knell of parting day,
The lowing cattle slowly cross the lea,
The plowman goes wearily plodding his homeward way,
Leaving the world to the darkening night and me.

b. The curfew tolls the knell of parting day,
The lowing herd wind slowly o'er the lea,
The plowman homeward plods his weary way,
And leaves the world to darkness and to me.

Thomas Gray

10. a. Let me chastise this odious, gilded bug,
This painted son of dirt, that smells and bites.

b. Yet let me flap this bug with gilded wings,
This painted child of dirt, that stinks and stings.

Pope

SOUND AND SENSE

True ease in writing comes from art, not chance,
As those move easiest who have learned to dance.
'Tis not enough no harshness gives offense,
The sound must seem an echo to the sense:
Soft is the strain when Zephyr gently blows,
And the smooth stream in smoother numbers flows;
But when loud surges lash the sounding shore,
The hoarse, rough verse should like the torrent roar;
When Ajax strives some rock's vast weight to throw,
The line too labors, and the words move slow;
Not so, when swift Camilla scours the plain,
Flies o'er the unbending corn, and skims along the main.
Hear how Timotheus' varied lays surprise,
And bid alternate passions fall and rise!

Alexander Pope (1688–1744)

QUESTIONS

1. Vocabulary: *numbers* (6), *lays* (13).

2. This excerpt is from a long poem (called *An Essay on Criticism*) on the arts of writing and judging poetry. Which line is the topic sentence of the passage?

3. There are four classical allusions: *Zephyr* (5) was god of the west

wind; *Ajax* (9), a Greek warrior noted for his strength; *Camilla* (11), a legendary queen reputedly so fleet of foot that she could run over a field of corn without bending the blades or over the sea without wetting her feet; *Timotheus* (13), a famous Greek rhapsodic poet. Does the use of these allusions enable Pope to achieve greater economy?

4. Copy the passage and scan it. Then, considering both meter and sounds, show how Pope practices what he preaches. (Incidentally, on which syllable should *alternate* in line 14 be accented?)

I LIKE TO SEE IT LAP THE MILES

I like to see it lap the miles,
And lick the valleys up,
And stop to feed itself at tanks;
And then, prodigious, step

Around a pile of mountains,
And, supercilious, peer
In shanties by the sides of roads;
And then a quarry pare

To fit its ribs,
And crawl between,
Complaining all the while
In horrid, hooting stanza;
Then chase itself down hill

And neigh like Boanerges;
Then, punctual as a star,
Stop—docile and omnipotent—
At its own stable door.

Emily Dickinson (1830–1886)

QUESTIONS

1. Vocabulary: *prodigious* (4), *supercilious* (6), *Boanerges* (14).

2. What basic metaphor underlies the poem? Identify the literal and the metaphorical terms and explain how you were able to make both identifications.

3. What additional figures of speech do you find in lines 8, 12, 15, 16, and 17? Explain their appropriateness.

4. Point out examples of alliteration, assonance, and consonance. Does this poem have a rime scheme?

5. Considering such things as sounds and sound repetitions, grammatical pauses, run-on lines, monosyllabic and polysyllabic words, onomatopoeia, and meter, explain in detail how sound is fitted to sense in this poem.

WIND

This house has been far out at sea all night,
The woods crashing through darkness, the booming hills,
Winds stampeding the fields under the window
Floundering black astride and blinding wet

Till day rose; then under an orange sky
The hills had new places, and wind wielded
Blade-like, luminous black and emerald,
Flexing like the lens of a mad eye.

At noon I scaled along the house-side as far as
The coal-house door. I dared once to look up—
Through the brunt wind that dented the balls of my eyes
The tent of the hills drummed and strained its guyrope,

The fields quivering, the skyline a grimace,
At any second to bang and vanish with a flap:
The wind flung a magpie away and a black-
Back gull bent like an iron bar slowly. The house

Rang like some fine green goblet in the note
That any second would shatter it. Now deep
In chairs, in front of the great fire, we grip
Our hearts and cannot entertain book, thought,

Or each other. We watch the fire blazing,
And feel the roots of the house move, but sit on,
Seeing the window tremble to come in,
Hearing the stones cry out under the horizons.

Ted Hughes (b. 1930)

QUESTIONS

1. Explain the images, or metaphors, in lines 1, 3, 6, 7–8, 12–14, 15–16, and 22. What kind of weather is the poem describing?
2. Discuss the adaptation of sound to sense.

HEAVEN-HAVEN

A Nun Takes the Veil

I have desired to go
    Where springs not fail,
To fields where flies no sharp and sided hail
    And a few lilies blow.

And I have asked to be
    Where no storms come,
Where the green swell is in the havens dumb,
    And out of the swing of the sea.

Gerard Manley Hopkins (1844–1889)

QUESTIONS

1. Who is the speaker and what is the situation? Explain the metaphors that form the substance of the poem. What things are being compared?

2. Comment on the meaning of *springs* (2) and on the effectiveness of the poet's choice of *lilies* (4).

3. How do the sound repetitions of the title reinforce the meaning? Are there other instances in the poem where sound reinforces meaning?

4. Scan the poem. (The meter is basically iambic, but there is a great deal of variation.) How does the meter reinforce meaning, especially in the last line? What purpose is served by the displacement of *not* (2) from its normal order?

ANTHEM FOR DOOMED YOUTH

What passing-bells for these who die as cattle?
Only the monstrous anger of the guns.
Only the stuttering rifles' rapid rattle
Can patter out their hasty orisons.
No mockeries now for them; no prayers nor bells,
Nor any voice of mourning save the choirs,—
The shrill, demented choirs of wailing shells;
And bugles calling for them from sad shires.

What candles may be held to speed them all?
Not in the hands of boys, but in their eyes
Shall shine the holy glimmers of good-byes.
The pallor of girls' brows shall be their pall;

Their flowers the tenderness of patient minds,
And each slow dusk a drawing-down of blinds.

Wilfred Owen (1893–1918)

QUESTIONS

1. Vocabulary: *passing-bells* (1), *orisons* (4), *shires* (8), *pall* (12).

2. How do the octave and the sestet of this sonnet differ in (a) geographical setting, (b) subject matter, (c) kind of imagery used, and (d) tone? Who are the "boys" (10) and "girls" (12) referred to in the sestet? —It was the custom during World War I to draw down the blinds in homes where a son had been lost (14).

3. What central metaphorical image runs throughout the poem? What secondary metaphors build up the central one?

4. Why are the "doomed youth" said to die "as cattle"? Why would prayers, bells, etc., be "mockeries" for them (5)?

5. Show how sound is adapted to sense throughout the poem.

IN MEMORIAM, VII

Dark house, by which once more I stand
    Here in the long unlovely street,
    Doors, where my heart was used to beat
So quickly, waiting for a hand,

A hand that can be clasped no more—
    Behold me, for I cannot sleep,
    And like a guilty thing I creep
At earliest morning to the door.

He is not here; but far away
    The noise of life begins again
    And ghastly through the drizzling rain
On the bald street breaks the blank day.

Alfred, Lord Tennyson (1809–1892)

QUESTIONS

1. *In Memoriam* is a sequence of poems composed after the death at the age of twenty-two of the poet's closest friend. Whose is the "dark house" (1)? What is the situation?

2. What function is served by the imagery of the last two lines?

3. Demonstrate how the poet uses sound and meter to reinforce his meaning.

IN MEMORIAM, XXVIII

The time draws near the birth of Christ:
    The moon is hid; the night is still;
    The Christmas bells from hill to hill
Answer each other in the mist.

Four voices of four hamlets round,
    From far and near, on mead and moor,
    Swell out and fail, as if a door
Were shut between me and the sound:

Each voice four changes on the wind,
    That now dilate, and now decrease,
    Peace and goodwill, goodwill and peace,
Peace and goodwill, to all mankind.

This year I slept and woke with pain,
    I almost wished no more to wake,
    And that my hold on life would break
Before I heard those bells again:

But they my troubled spirit rule,
    For they controlled me when a boy;
    They bring me sorrow touched with joy,
The merry merry bells of Yule.

Alfred, Lord Tennyson (1809–1892)

QUESTIONS

1. How does the mood of this section differ from that of VII? Why?
2. How does Tennyson, without using onomatopoeia, nevertheless give something of a bell-like sound to this section?
3. How does this section, though written in the same meter as VII, differ in rhythmical effect? How does this difference contribute to the difference in mood? Study especially the placement of grammatical pauses.
4. Contrast the last lines of VII and XXVIII.

ALL DAY I HEAR

All day I hear the noise of waters
        Making moan,
Sad as the sea-bird is, when going
        Forth alone,

He hears the winds cry to the waters'
Monotone.

The grey winds, the cold winds are blowing
Where I go.
I hear the noise of many waters
Far below.
All day, all night, I hear them flowing
To and fro.

James Joyce (1882–1941)

QUESTIONS

1. What is the central purpose of the poem? Is it primarily descriptive?
2. What kinds of imagery does the poem contain?
3. Discuss the adaptation of sound to meaning, commenting on the use of onomatopoeia, phonetic intensives, alliteration, consonance, rime, vowel quality, stanzaic structure, the counterpointing of the rhythmically varied long lines with the rhythmically regular short lines.

THE BENCH OF BOORS

In bed I muse on Teniers' boors,
Embrowned and beery losels all:
A wakeful brain
Elaborates pain:
Within low doors the slugs of boors
Laze and yawn and doze again.

In dreams they doze, the drowsy boors,
Their hazy hovel warm and small:
Thought's ampler bound
But chill is found:
Within low doors the basking boors
Snugly hug the ember-mound.

Sleepless, I see the slumberous boors
Their blurred eyes blink, their eyelids fall:
Thought's eager sight
Aches—overbright!
Within low doors the boozy boors
Cat-naps take in pipe-bowl light.

Herman Melville (1819–1891)

QUESTIONS

1. Vocabulary: *boors* (title), *losels* (2), *slugs* (5).

2. David Teniers, the Younger, a seventeenth-century Flemish painter, was famous for his genre paintings of peasant life. What was the essential characteristic of this life according to the poem? What symbolism do you find in the fifth line of each stanza?

3. What is the relation of the third and fourth lines of each stanza to the speaker? To the boors? How does the form of the stanza emphasize the contrast in thought?

4. Comment on other correspondences between sound and meaning.

THE DANCE

In Breughel's great picture, The Kermess,
the dancers go round, they go round and
around, the squeal and the blare and the
tweedle of bagpipes, a bugle and fiddles
tipping their bellies (round as the thick-
sided glasses whose wash they impound)
their hips and their bellies off balance
to turn them. Kicking and rolling about
the Fair Grounds, swinging their butts, those
shanks must be sound to bear up under such
rollicking measures, prance as they dance
in Breughel's great picture, The Kermess.

William Carlos Williams (1883–1963)

QUESTIONS

1. Peter Breughel, the Elder, was a sixteenth-century Flemish painter of peasant life. A *kermess* is an annual outdoor festival or fair. How do the form, the meter, and the sounds of this poem reinforce its content?

2. Explore the similarities and differences between this poem and the preceding one as to both form and content.

TO FOOL, OR KNAVE

Thy praise or dispraise is to me alike:
One doth not stroke me, nor the other strike.

Ben Jonson (1573?–1637)

CHAPTER FOURTEEN

Pattern

Art, ultimately, is organization. It is a searching after order, after form. The primal artistic act was God's creation of the universe out of chaos, shaping the formless into form; and every artist since, on a lesser scale, has sought to imitate Him—by selection and arrangement to reduce the chaotic in experience to a meaningful and pleasing order. For this reason we evaluate a poem partially by the same criteria that an English instructor uses to evaluate a theme—by its unity, its coherence, and its proper placing of emphasis. In a well-constructed poem there is neither too little nor too much; every part of the poem belongs where it is and could be placed nowhere else; any interchanging of two stanzas, two lines, two words, or even two accents, would to some extent damage the poem and make it less effective. We come to feel, with a truly first-rate poem, that the choice and placement of every word is inevitable, that it could not be otherwise.

In addition to the internal ordering of materials, images, ideas, and sounds, the poet may also impose some external pattern on his poem, may give it not only an inside logical order but an outside symmetry. In doing so, he appeals to the human instinct for design, the instinct that makes primitive men tattoo and paint their bodies, later men to decorate their swords and shields with beautiful and complex designs, and modern men to choose patterned ties, carpets, curtains, and wallpapers. The poet appeals to our love of the shapely.

In general, there are three broad kinds of form into which the poet may cast his work: continuous form, stanzaic form, and fixed form.

In CONTINUOUS FORM, as illustrated by "Had I the Choice" (page 751), "Dover Beach" (page 833), "Ulysses" (page 639), and "My Last

Duchess" (page 671), the element of formal design is slight. The lines follow each other without formal grouping, the only breaks being dictated by units of meaning, as paragraph breaks are in prose. Even here there are degrees of formal pattern. The free verse "Had I the Choice" has neither regular meter nor rime. "Dover Beach," on the other hand, is metrical; it has no regularity in length of line, but the meter is prevailingly iambic. "Ulysses" is regular in both meter and length of line; it is unrimed iambic pentameter, or blank verse. And to these regularities "My Last Duchess" adds regularity of rime, for it is written in riming iambic pentameter couplets. Thus, in increasing degrees, the authors of "Dover Beach," "Ulysses," and "My Last Duchess" have chosen a predetermined pattern in which to cast their work.

In STANZAIC FORM the poet writes in a series of STANZAS, that is, repeated units having the same number of lines, the same metrical pattern, and often an identical rime scheme. The poet may choose some traditional stanza pattern (for poetry, like colleges, is rich in tradition) or invent his own. The traditional stanza patterns (for example, terza rima, ballad meter, rime royal, Spenserian stanza) are many, and the student specializing in literature will wish to familiarize himself with some of them; the general student should know that they exist. Often the use of one of these traditional stanza forms constitutes a kind of literary allusion. The reader who is conscious of its traditional use or of its use by a previous great poet will be aware of subtleties in the communication that a less well-read reader may miss.

As with continuous form, there are degrees of formal pattern in stanzaic form. In "Poem in October" (page 781), for instance, the stanzas are alike in length of line but are without a regular pattern of rime. In "To Lucasta" (page 650), a rime pattern is added to a metrical pattern. In Shakespeare's "Winter" (page 556) and "Spring" (page 561), a refrain is employed in addition to the patterns of meter and rime. The following poem illustrates additional elements of design:

THE GREEDY THE PEOPLE

the greedy the people
(as if as can yes)
they sell and they buy

and they die for because
though the bell in the steeple
says Why

the chary the wary
(as all as can each)
they don't and they do
and they turn to a which
though the moon in her glory
says Who

the busy the millions
(as you're as can i'm)
they flock and they flee
through a thunder of seem
though the stars in their silence
say Be

the cunning the craven
(as think as can feel)
they when and they how
and they live for until
though the sun in his heaven
says Now

the timid the tender
(as doubt as can trust)
they work and they pray
and they bow to a must
though the earth in her splendor
says May

e. e. cummings (1894–1962)

QUESTIONS

1. This poem is a constellation of interlocking patterns. To appreciate them fully, read it first in the normal fashion, one line after another; then read all the first lines of the stanzas, followed by the second lines, the third lines, and so on. Having done this, describe (a) the rime scheme; (b) the metrical design; (c) the sound pattern (How are the two main words in each of the first lines related?); (d) the syntactical pattern. Prepare a model of the poem in which the recurring words are written out, blanks are left for varying words, and recurring parts of speech are indicated in parentheses.

The model for the third lines would be: *they [verb] and they [verb]*. Describe the pattern of meaning. How do the first four lines of each stanza relate to the last two? What blanks in your model are to be filled in by words related in meaning?

2. A trademark of e. e. cummings as a poet is his imaginative freedom with parts of speech. For instance, in line 21 he uses conjunctions as verbs. What different parts of speech does he use as nouns in the fourth line of each stanza? Can you see meanings for these unusual nouns? Explain the contrast between the last words in the fourth and sixth lines of each stanza. What two meanings has the final word of the poem?

3. Sum up briefly the meaning of the poem.

A stanza form may be described by designating four things: the rime scheme (if there is one), the position of the refrain (if there is one), the prevailing metrical foot, and the number of feet in each line. Rime scheme is traditionally designated by using letters of the alphabet to indicate the riming lines, and *x* for unrimed lines. Refrain lines may be indicated by a capital letter, and the number of feet in the line by a numerical exponent after the letter. Thus the stanza pattern of Browning's "Meeting at Night" (page 600) is iambic tetrameter *abccba* (or iambic $abccba^4$); that of cummings's "if everything happens that can't be done" (page 743) is anapestic $a^4x^2x^1a^1b^4x^1x^1b^2a^3$; that of Shakespeare's "Spring" (page 561) is iambic $ababcc^4X^1DD^4$.

A FIXED FORM is a traditional pattern that applies to a whole poem. In French poetry many fixed forms have been widely used: rondeaus, roundels, villanelles, triolets, sestinas, ballades, double ballades, and others. In English poetry, though most of the fixed forms have been experimented with, perhaps only two—the limerick and the sonnet—have really taken hold.

The LIMERICK, though really a subliterary form, will serve to illustrate the fixed form in general. Its pattern is anapestic $aa^3bb^2a^3$:

There was a young la-dy of Ni-ger
Who smiled as she rode on a ti-ger;
They re-turned from the ride
With the la-dy in-side,
And the smile on the face of the ti-ger.

Anonymous

The limerick form is used exclusively for humorous and nonsense verse, for which, with its swift catchy meter, short lines, and emphatic rimes, it is particularly suitable. By trying to recast these little jokes and bits of nonsense in a different meter and pattern or into prose, we may discover how much of their effect they owe particularly to the limerick form. There is, of course, no magical or mysterious identity between certain forms and certain types of content, but there may be more or less correspondence. A form may be appropriate or inappropriate. The limerick form is apparently inappropriate for the serious treatment of serious material.

The SONNET is less rigidly prescribed than the limerick. It must be fourteen lines in length, and it almost always is iambic pentameter, but in structure and rime scheme there may be considerable leeway. Most sonnets, however, conform more or less closely to one of two general models or types, the Italian and the English.

The ITALIAN or *Petrarchan* SONNET (so called because the Italian poet Petrarch practiced it so extensively) is divided usually between eight lines called the octave, using two rimes arranged *abbaabba,* and six lines called the sestet, using any arrangement of either two or three rimes: *cdcdcd* and *cdecde* are common patterns. Usually in the Italian sonnet, corresponding to the division between octave and sestet indicated by the rime scheme (and sometimes marked off in printing by a space), there is a division in thought. The octave presents a situation and the sestet a comment, or the octave an idea and the sestet an example, or the octave a question and the sestet an answer.

ON FIRST LOOKING INTO CHAPMAN'S HOMER

Much have I travelled in the realms of gold,
    And many goodly states and kingdoms seen;
    Round many western islands have I been
Which bards in fealty to Apollo hold.
    Oft of one wide expanse had I been told
    That deep-browed Homer ruled as his demesne;
Yet did I never breathe its pure serene
Till I heard Chapman speak out loud and bold:
Then felt I like some watcher of the skies
    When a new planet swims into his ken;

Or like stout Cortez when with eagle eyes
He stared at the Pacific—and all his men
Looked at each other with a wild surmise—
Silent, upon a peak in Darien.

John Keats (1795–1821)

QUESTIONS

1. Vocabulary: *fealty* (4), *Apollo* (4), *demesne* (6), *ken* (10), *Darien* (14).

2. John Keats, at twenty-one, could not read Greek, and was probably acquainted with Homer's *Iliad* and *Odyssey* only through the translations of Alexander Pope, which to him would have seemed prosy and stilted. Then one day he and a friend found a vigorous poetic translation by the Elizabethan poet George Chapman. Keats and his friend, enthralled, sat up late at night excitedly reading aloud to each other from Chapman's book. Toward morning Keats walked home and, before going to bed, wrote the above sonnet and sent it to his friend. What common ideas underlie the three major figures of speech in the poem?

3. What is the rime scheme? What division of thought corresponds to the division between octave and sestet?

4. Balboa, not Cortez, discovered the Pacific. Does this mistake seriously detract from the value of the poem? Why or why not?

The ENGLISH or *Shakespearean* SONNET (invented by the English poet Surrey and made famous by Shakespeare) is composed of three quatrains and a concluding couplet, riming *abab cdcd efef gg*. Again, there is usually a correspondence between the units marked off by the rimes and the development of the thought. The three quatrains, for instance, may present three examples and the couplet a conclusion or (as in the following example) three metaphorical statements of one idea plus an application.

THAT TIME OF YEAR

That time of year thou mayst in me behold
When yellow leaves, or none, or few, do hang
Upon those boughs which shake against the cold,
Bare ruined choirs where late the sweet birds sang.
In me thou see'st the twilight of such day

As after sunset fadeth in the west,
Which by and by black night doth take away,
Death's second self, that seals up all in rest.
In me thou see'st the glowing of such fire,
That on the ashes of his youth doth lie
As the deathbed whereon it must expire,
Consumed with that which it was nourished by.
  This thou perceivest, which makes thy love more strong,
  To love that well which thou must leave ere long.

William Shakespeare (1564–1616)

QUESTIONS

1. What are the three major images introduced by the three quatrains? What do they have in common? Can you see any reason for presenting them in this particular order, or might they be rearranged without loss?
2. Each of the images is to some degree complicated rather than simple. For instance, what additional image is introduced by "bare ruined choirs"(4)? Explain its appropriateness.
3. What additional comparisons are introduced in the second and third quatrains?
4. Explain line 12.

At first glance it may seem absurd that a poet should choose to confine himself in an arbitrary fourteen-line mold with prescribed meter and rime scheme. He does so partly from the desire to carry on a tradition, as all of us carry out certain traditions for their own sake, else why should we bring a tree indoors at Christmas time? But, in addition, the tradition of the sonnet has proved a useful one for, like the limerick, it seems effective for certain types of subject matter and treatment. Though this area cannot be as narrowly limited or as rigidly described as for the limerick, the sonnet is usually most effective when used for the serious treatment of love but has also been used for the discussion of death, religion, political situations, and related subjects. Again, there is no magical affinity between form and subject, or treatment, and excellent sonnets have been written outside these traditional areas. The sonnet tradition has also proved useful because it has provided a challenge to the poet. The inferior poet, of course, is often defeated by that challenge: he will use unnecessary words to fill out his meter or inappropriate words for the sake of his rime. The good poet is inspired by the challenge: it will call forth ideas and images that might not otherwise have come. He will subdue his form rather than be subdued by it; he will make it do his will. There is no doubt that the presence of a net makes good tennis players more precise in their shots than they otherwise would be. And finally, there is in all form the pleasure of form itself.

EXERCISES

1. "The Griesly Wife" (page 563) and "The Wife of Usher's Well" (page 831) are both written in *ballad stanza,* so called because so many medieval folk ballads were written in this form. After examining these two poems, define *ballad stanza.* Then, show how "On moonlit heath and lonesome bank" (page 603), "Edward" (page 786), and "Cha Till Maccruimein" (page 804) complicate the form.
2. "The Waking" (page 878) and "Do not go gentle into that good night" (page 890) are both examples of the French fixed form known as the *villanelle.* After reading the poems, define the *villanelle.*
3. Most of "John Anderson" (page 710) is written in the stanzaic form known as *terza rima* (most famous for its use by Dante in *The Divine Comedy*). Read the poem and give a description of *terza rima.*
4. How many sonnets can you find in this book? List them by page number, designate whether they are English or Italian, and note any irregularities of form. Can you make any generalizations from the examples you found about the nature or subject matter of the sonnet?

A HANDFUL OF LIMERICKS*

I sat next the Duchess at tea.
It was just as I feared it would be:
    Her rumblings abdominal
    Were simply abominable,
And everyone thought it was me.

There was a young lady of Lynn
Who was so uncommonly thin

* Most limericks are anonymous. If not written anonymously, they soon become so, unfortunately for the glory of their authors, because of repeated oral transmission and reprinting without accreditation.

That when she essayed
To drink lemonade
She slipped through the straw and fell in.

A tutor who tooted the flute
Tried to tutor two tooters to toot.
Said the two to the tutor,
"Is it harder to toot or
To tutor two tooters to toot?"

There was a young maid who said, "Why
Can't I look in my ear with my eye?
If I put my mind to it,
I'm sure I can do it.
You never can tell till you try."

There was an old man of Peru
Who dreamt he was eating his shoe.
He awoke in the night
In a terrible fright,
And found it was perfectly true!

A decrepit old gas man named Peter,
While hunting around for the meter,
Touched a leak with his light.
He arose out of sight,
And, as anyone can see by reading this, he
also destroyed the meter.

Well, it's partly the shape of the thing
That gives the old limerick wing;
These accordion pleats
Full of airy conceits
Take it up like a kite on a string.

HUNTING SONG

The fox came lolloping, lolloping,
Lolloping. His tongue hung out
And his ears were high.
He was like death at the end of a string

When he came to the hollow
Log. Ran in one side
And out of the other. O
He was sly.

The hounds came tumbling, tumbling,
Tumbling. Their heads were low
And their eyes were red.
The sound of their breath was louder than death
When they came to the hollow
Log. They held at one end
But a bitch found the scent. O
They were mad.

The hunter came galloping, galloping,
Galloping. All damp was his mare
From her hooves to her mane.
His coat and his mouth were redder than death
When he came to the hollow
Log. He took in the rein
And over he went. O
He was fine.

The log, he just lay there, alone in
The clearing. No fox nor hound
Nor mounted man
Saw his black round eyes in their perfect disguise
(As the ends of a hollow
Log). He watched death go through him,
Around him and over him. O
He was wise.

Donald Finkel (b. 1929)

QUESTIONS

1. Delight in pattern is clearly a major attraction of this poem. Point out all the elements of pattern, including stanza organization, meter, rime, repeated words, and grammatical structures.

2. Chart the elements that are constant throughout the four stanzas of the poem, then those that are alike in three stanzas but not in all four. Can you find justification or compensation for the variations?

POEM IN OCTOBER

It was my thirtieth year to heaven
Woke to my hearing from harbor and neighbor wood
And the mussel pooled and the heron
Priested shore
The morning beckon
With water praying and call of seagull and rook
And the knock of sailing boats on the net webbed wall
Myself to set foot
That second
In the still sleeping town and set forth.

My birthday began with the water-
Birds and the birds of the winged trees flying my name
Above the farms and the white horses
And I rose
In rainy autumn
And walked abroad in a shower of all my days.
High tide and the heron dived when I took the road
Over the border
And the gates
Of the town closed as the town awoke.

A springful of larks in a rolling
Cloud and the roadside bushes brimming with whistling
Blackbirds and the sun of October
Summery
On the hill's shoulder,
Here were fond climates and sweet singers suddenly
Come in the morning where I wandered and listened
To the rain wringing
Wind blow cold
In the woods faraway under me.

Pale rain over the dwindling harbor
And over the sea wet church the size of a snail
With its horns through mist and the castle
Brown as owls
But all the gardens
Of spring and summer were blooming in the tall tales
Beyond the border and under the lark full cloud.

There could I marvel
My birthday
Away but the weather turned around.

It turned away from the blithe country
And down the other air and the blue altered sky
Streamed again a wonder of summer
With apples
Pears and red currants
And I saw in the turning so clearly a child's
Forgotten mornings when he walked with his mother
Through the parables
Of sun light
And the legends of the green chapels

And the twice told fields of infancy
That his tears burned my cheeks and his heart moved in mine.
These were the woods the river and sea
Where a boy
In the listening
Summertime of the dead whispered the truth of his joy
To the trees and the stones and the fish in the tide.
And the mystery
Sang alive
Still in the water and singingbirds.

And there could I marvel my birthday
Away but the weather turned around. And the true
Joy of the long dead child sang burning
In the sun.
It was my thirtieth
Year to heaven stood there then in the summer noon
Though the town below lay leaved with October blood.
O may my heart's truth
Still be sung
On this high hill in a year's turning.

Dylan Thomas (1914–1953)

QUESTIONS

1. The setting is a small fishing village on the coast of Wales. The poet's first name in Welsh means "water" (12). Trace the poet's walk in relation to the village, the weather, and the time of day.

2. "The weather turned around" is an expression indicating a change in the weather or the direction of the wind. In what psychological sense does the weather turn around during the poet's walk? Who is "the long dead child" (63), and what kind of child was he? With what wish does the poem close?

3. Explain "thirtieth year to heaven" (1), "horns" (33), "tall tales" (36), "green chapels" (50), "October blood" (67).

4. The elaborate stanza pattern in this poem is based not on the meter (which is very free) but on a syllable count. How many syllables are there in each line of the stanza? (In line 1 *thirtieth* is counted as only two syllables.) Notice that the stanzas 1 and 3 consist of exactly one sentence each.

5. The poem makes a considerable use of approximate rime, though not according to a regular pattern. Point out examples.

THE SONNET

A Sonnet is a moment's monument—
Memorial from the Soul's eternity
To one dead deathless hour. Look that it be,
Whether for lustral rite or dire portent,
Of its own arduous fullness reverent:
Carve it in ivory or in ebony,
As Day or Night may rule; and let Time see
Its flowering crest impearled and orient.

A Sonnet is a coin; its face reveals
The Soul—its converse, to what Power 'tis due:—
Whether for tribute to the august appeals
Of Life, or dower in Love's high retinue,
It serve; or, 'mid the dark wharf's cavernous breath,
In Charon's palm it pay the toll to Death.

Dante Gabriel Rossetti (1828–1882)

QUESTIONS

1. Vocabulary: *lustral* (4), *portent* (4), *arduous* (5), *orient* (8), *retinue* (12), *Charon* (14). The Greeks buried their dead with coins over their eyes or in their mouths to pay for their passage to the underworld.

2. Rossetti "defines" the sonnet and gives advice about writing it. What characteristics of the Italian sonnet does Rossetti bring out?

3. What is Rossetti's advice for writing the sonnet? Keats once advised poets to "rift every vein with ore." Is Rossetti's advice similar or different?

4. This sonnet consists essentially of two extended metaphors, one in the octave and one in the sestet. Trace the development and implications of each. Which is the more consistently and remarkably worked out?

FROM ROMEO AND JULIET

ROMEO If I profane with my unworthiest hand
This holy shrine, the gentle sin is this;
My lips, two blushing pilgrims, ready stand
To smooth that rough touch with a tender kiss.
JULIET Good pilgrim, you do wrong your hand too much,
Which mannerly devotion shows in this;
For saints have hands that pilgrims' hands do touch,
And palm to palm is holy palmers' kiss.
ROMEO Have not saints lips, and holy palmers too?
JULIET Ay, pilgrim, lips that they must use in prayer.
ROMEO O! then, dear saint, let lips do what hands do;
They pray, Grant thou, lest faith turn to despair.
JULIET Saints do not move,° though grant for prayers' sake. propose, instigate
ROMEO Then move not, while my prayers' effect I take.

William Shakespeare (1564–1616)

QUESTIONS

1. These fourteen lines have been lifted out of Act I, scene 5, of Shakespeare's play. They are the first words exchanged between Romeo and Juliet, who are meeting, for the first time, at a masquerade ball given by her father. Romeo is dressed as a pilgrim. Struck by Juliet's beauty, he has come up to greet her. What stage action accompanies this passage?

2. What is the basic metaphor employed? How does it affect the tone of the relationship between Romeo and Juliet?

3. What play on words do you find in lines 8 and 13–14? What two meanings has line 11?

4. By meter and rime scheme, these lines form a sonnet. Do you think this was coincidental or intentional on Shakespeare's part? Discuss.

MAY-FLY

Under the willow whose roots are shallow
The dismissed lover laid his head down,
And down, and down:

May-fly, May-fly, living a day,
It was good while it lasted—even gay?

Under the oak which storm-winds broke
The defeated general laid his head down,
And down, and down:
May-fly, May-fly, dead in an hour,
What then is glory, what precisely is power?

Under the elm, the treacherous elm,
Whose boughs can break, the ruined businessman,
For his country's sake, laid his head down,
And down, and down:
May-fly, May-fly, grub in a stream
Eating dirt, for years eating filth—for a dream.

Under the fire of the sweet-briar
The fading beauty laid her head down,
And down, and down:
Bridal May-flies thick in the haze—
Once and once only! Praise! Praise!

Under crossed boughs the unfrocked priest
Laid his head down—"I have been a beast!"—
And down, and down:
Finished May-flies falling to death—
God is spirit, spirit is breath.

Under the laurel in continual quarrel
The obscure poet laid his head down,
And down, and down:
Dead May-flies on the waters strewn,
And dead words are drifted on.

John Heath-Stubbs (b. 1918)

QUESTIONS

1. Chart the pattern of repetition including meter, end rime, internal rime, and repetitions of words, phrases, lines, or grammatical structure. What purpose, beyond their own appeal, do these repetitions serve? Can you explain any notable departures from the pattern?

2. What connection, if any, is there between the subject of each stanza

and the kind of tree referred to in it? Between the subject of each stanza and its last line?

3. What is the theme of the poem?

EDWARD

"Why dois° your brand° sae drap wi bluid, — does; sword
Edward, Edward,
Why dois your brand sae drap wi bluid,
And why sae sad gang° yee O?" — go
"O I hae killed my hauke sae guid,
Mither, mither,
O I hae killed my hauke sae guid,
And I had nae mair bot hee O."

"Your haukis bluid was nevir sae reid,
Edward, Edward,
Your haukis bluid was nevir sae reid,
My deir son I tell thee O."
"O I hae killed my reid-roan steid,
Mither, mither,
O I hae killed my reid-roan steid,
That erst° was sae fair and frie° O." — formerly; spirited

"Your steid was auld, and ye hae got mair,
Edward, Edward,
Your steid was auld, and ye hae got mair,
Sum other dule° ye drie° O." — grief; suffer
"O I hae killed my fadir deir,
Mither, mither,
O I hae killed my fadir deir,
Alas, and wae is mee O!"

"And whatten penance wul ye drie for that,
Edward, Edward,
And whatten penance wul ye drie for that?
My deir son, now tell me O."
"Ile set my feit in yonder boat,
Mither, mither,
Ile set my feit in yonder boat,
And Ile fare ovir the sea O."

"And what wul ye doe wi your towirs and your ha,° hall
Edward, Edward,
And what wul ye doe wi your towirs and your ha,
That were sae fair to see O?"
"Ile let thame stand tul they doun fa,° fall
Mither, mither,
Ile let thame stand tul they doun fa,
For here nevir mair maun° I bee O." must

"And what wul ye leive to your bairns° and your wife, children
Edward, Edward,
And what wul ye leive to your bairns and your wife,
Whan ye gang ovir the sea O?"
"The warldis° room, late them beg thrae° life, world's; through
Mither, mither,
The warldis room, late them beg thrae life,
For thame nevir mair wul I see O."

And what wul ye leive to your ain mither deir,
Edward, Edward?
And what wul ye leive to your ain mither deir?
My deir son, now tell me O."
"The curse of hell frae me sall ye beir,
Mither, mither,
The curse of hell frae me sall ye beir,
Sic° counseils ye gave to me O." Such

Anonymous

QUESTIONS

1. What has Edward done and why? Where do the two climaxes of the poem come?

2. Tell as much as you can about Edward and his feelings toward what he has done. From what class of society is he? Why does he at first give false answers to his mother's questions? What reversal of feelings and loyalties has he undergone? Do his answers about his hawk and steed perhaps indicate his present feelings toward his father? How do you explain his behavior to his wife and children? What are his present feelings toward his mother?

3. Tell as much as you can about Edward's mother. Why does she ask what Edward has done—doesn't she already know? Is there any clue as to the motivation of her deed? How skillful is she in her questioning? What do we learn about her from her dismissal of Edward's steed as "auld" and only one of many (17)? From her asking Edward what penance *he* will do for

his act (25)? From her reference to herself as Edward's "ain mither deir" (49)?

4. Structure and pattern are both important in this poem. Could any of the stanzas be interchanged without loss, or do they build up steadily to the two climaxes? What effect has the constant repetition of the two short refrains, "Edward, Edward" and "Mither, mither"? What is the effect of the final "O" at the end of each speech? Does the repetition of each question and answer simply waste words or does it add to the suspense and emotional intensity? (Try reading the poem omitting the third and seventh lines of each stanza. Is it improved or weakened?)

5. Much of what happened is implied, much is omitted. Does the poem gain anything in power from what is *not* told?

SPECTRUM

Brown from the sun's mid-afternoon caress,
And where not brown, white as a bridal dress,
And where not white, pink as an opened plum.

And where not pink, darkly mysterious,
And when observed, openly furious,
And then obscured, while the red blushes come.

William Dickey (b. 1928)

QUESTIONS

1. The situation described is not explicitly identified. What do the adjectives modify? Would the poem be better if it were clearer?

2. Describe the elements of pattern. What kind of rime is used in lines 4–5?

3. What applications has the title?

TWO JAPANESE HAIKU

The lightning flashes!
And slashing through the darkness,
A night-heron's screech.

A lightning gleam:
into darkness travels
a night heron's scream.

Matsuo Bashō (1644–1694)

The falling flower
I saw drift back to the branch
Was a butterfly.

Fallen flowers rise
back to the branch—I watch:
oh . . . butterflies!

Moritake (1452–1540)

QUESTION

The haiku, a Japanese form, consists of three lines with five, seven, and five syllables respectively. The translators of the left-hand versions above (Earl Miner and Babette Deutsch respectively) preserve this syllable count; the translator of the right-hand versions (Harold G. Henderson) seeks to preserve the sense of formal structure by making the first and last lines rime. Moritake's haiku, as Miss Deutsch points out, "refers to the Buddhist proverb that the fallen flower never returns to the branch; the broken mirror never again reflects." From these two examples, what would you say are the characteristics of effective haiku?

SKIPPING STONES

One sure hand,
  a deliberate wrist;
Seven times,
   seven times it dared
     to kiss, the stone,
       and tease the waiting grave—
         leapsplash: the abandoned dance—
           then disappear
             behind a rippling trail.

Allan D. Farber (b. 19—)

A CHRISTMAS TREE

Star,
If you are
A love compassionate,
You will walk with us this year.
We face a glacial distance, who are here
Huddld
At your feet.

William Burford (b. 1927)

QUESTION

Why do you think the author misspelled "huddled" in line 6?

CHAPTER FIFTEEN

Bad Poetry and Good

The attempt to evaluate a poem should never be made before the poem is understood; and, unless you have developed the capacity to feel some poetry deeply, any judgments you make will be worthless. A person who likes no wines can hardly be a judge of them. The ability to make judgments, to discriminate between good and bad, great and good, good and half-good, is surely a primary object of all liberal education, and one's appreciation of poetry is incomplete unless it includes discrimination. Of the mass of verse that appears each year in print, as of all literature, most is "flat, stale, and unprofitable"; a very, very little is of any enduring value.

In judging a poem, as in judging any work of art, we need to ask three basic questions: (1) *What is its central purpose?* (2) *How fully has this purpose been accomplished?* (3) *How important is this purpose?* The first question we need to answer in order to understand the poem. The last two questions are those by which we evaluate it. The first of these measures the poem on a scale of perfection. The second measures it on a scale of significance. And, just as the area of a rectangle is determined by multiplying its measurements on two scales, breadth and height, so the greatness of a poem is determined by multiplying its measurements on two scales, perfection and significance. If the poem measures well on the first of these scales, we call it a good poem, at least of its kind. If it measures well on both scales, we call it a great poem.*

* As indicated in the footnote on page 573, some objection has been made to the use of the term "purpose" in literary criticism. For the two criteria suggested

The measurement of a poem is a much more complex process, of course, than is the measurement of a rectangle. It cannot be done as exactly. Agreement on the measurements will never be complete. Yet over a period of time the judgments of qualified readers* tend to coalesce: there comes to be more agreement than disagreement. There is almost universal agreement, for instance, that Shakespeare is the greatest of English poets. Although there might be sharp disagreements among qualified readers as to whether Donne or Keats is the superior poet, or Wordsworth or Chaucer, or Shelley or Pope, there is almost universal agreement among them that each of these is superior to Kipling or Longfellow. And there is almost universal agreement that Kipling and Longfellow are superior to James Whitcomb Riley and Edgar Guest.

But your problem is to be able to discriminate, not between already established reputations, but between poems—poems you have not seen before and of which, perhaps, you do not even know the author. Here, of course, you will not always be right—even the most qualified readers occasionally go badly astray—but you should, we hope, be able to make broad distinctions with a higher average of success than you could when you began this book. And, unless you allow yourself to petrify, your ability to do this should improve throughout your college years and beyond.

For answering the first of our evaluative questions, *How fully has the poem's purpose been accomplished?* there are no easy yardsticks that we can apply. We cannot ask, Is the poem melodious? Does it have smooth meter? Does it use good grammar? Does it contain figures of speech? Are the rimes perfect? Excellent poems exist without any of

---

above may be substituted these two: (1) How thoroughly are the materials of the poem integrated or unified? (2) How many and how diverse are the materials that it integrates? Thus a poem becomes successful in proportion to the tightness of its organization—that is, according to the degree to which all its elements work together and require each other to produce the total effect—and it becomes great in proportion to its scope—that is, according to the amount and diversity of the material it amalgamates into unity.

* Throughout this discussion the term "qualified reader" is of utmost importance. By a qualified reader we mean briefly a person with considerable experience of literature and considerable experience of life: a person of intelligence, sensitivity, and knowledge. Without these qualities a person is no more qualified to judge literature than would be a color-blind man to judge painting, or a tone-deaf man to judge music, or a man who had never seen a horse before to judge a horse.

these attributes. We can judge any element in a poem only as it contributes or fails to contribute to the achievement of the central purpose; and we can judge the total poem only as these elements work together to form an integrated whole. But we can at least attempt a few generalizations. In a perfect poem there are no excess words, no words that do not bear their full weight in contributing to the total meaning, and no words just to fill out the meter. Each word is the best word for expressing the total meaning: there are no inexact words forced by the rime scheme or the metrical pattern. The word order is the best order for expressing the author's total meaning; distortions or departures from normal order are for emphasis or some other meaningful purpose. The diction, the images, and the figures of speech are fresh, not trite (except, of course, when the poet uses trite language deliberately for purposes of irony). There are no clashes between the sound of the poem and its sense, or its form and its content; and in general the poet uses both sound and pattern in such a way as to support his meaning. The organization of the poem is the best possible organization: images and ideas are so effectively arranged that any rearrangement would be harmful to the poem. We will always remember, however, that a good poem may have flaws. We should never damn a poem for its flaws if these flaws are amply compensated for by positive excellence.

If a poem is to have true excellence, it must be in some sense a "new" poem; it must exact a fresh response from the qualified reader—make him respond in a new way. It will not be merely imitative of previous literature nor appeal to stock, preestablished ways of thinking and feeling that in some readers are automatically stimulated by words like *mother, baby, home, country, faith,* or *God,* as a coin put into a slot always gets an expected reaction.

And here, perhaps, may be discussed the kinds of poems that most frequently "fool" poor readers (and occasionally a few good ones) and achieve sometimes a tremendous popularity without winning the respect of most good readers. These poems are found pasted in great numbers in the scrapbooks of sweet old ladies and appear in anthologies entitled *Poems of Inspiration, Poems of Courage,* or *Heart-Throbs.* The people who write such poems and the people who like them are often the best of people, but they are not poets or lovers of poetry in any genuine sense. They are lovers of conventional ideas or sentiments or feelings, which they like to see expressed with the adornment of rime and meter, and which, when so expressed, they respond to in predictable ways.

Of the several varieties of inferior poetry, we shall concern ourselves with three: the sentimental, the rhetorical, and the purely didactic. All three are perhaps unduly dignified by the name of poetry. They might more aptly be described as verse.

SENTIMENTALITY is indulgence in emotion for its own sake, or expression of more emotion than an occasion warrants. A sentimental *person* is gushy, stirred to tears by trivial or inappropriate causes; he weeps at all weddings and all funerals; he is made ecstatic by manifestations of young love; he clips locks of hair, gilds baby shoes, and talks baby talk; he grows compassionate over hardened criminals when he hears of their being punished. His opposite is the callous or unfeeling person. The ideal is the person who responds sensitively on appropriate occasions and feels deeply on occasions that deserve deep feeling, but who has nevertheless a certain amount of emotional reserve, a certain command over his feelings. Sentimental *literature* is "*tear-jerking*" literature. It aims primarily at stimulating the emotions directly rather than at communicating experience truly and freshly; it depends on trite and well-tried formulas for exciting emotion; it revels in old oaken buckets, rocking chairs, mother love, and the pitter-patter of little feet; it oversimplifies; it is unfaithful to the full complexity of human experience. In our book the best example of sentimental verse is the first seven lines of the anonymous "Love" (page 715). If this verse had ended as it began, it would have been pure sentimentalism. The eighth line redeems it by making us realize that the writer is not serious and thus transfers the piece from the classification of sentimental verse to that of humorous verse. In fact, the writer is poking fun at sentimentality by showing that in its most maudlin form it is characteristic of drunks.

RHETORICAL poetry uses a language more glittering and high flown than its substance warrants. It offers a spurious vehemence of language—language without a corresponding reality of emotion or thought underneath. It is oratorical, overelegant, artificially eloquent. It is superficial and, again, often basically trite. It loves rolling phrases like "from the rocky coast of Maine to the sun-washed shores of California" and "our heroic dead" and "Old Glory." It deals in generalities. At its worst it is bombast. In this book an example is offered by the two lines quoted from the play-within-a-play in Shakespeare's *A Midsummer Night's Dream:*

> Whereat with blade, with bloody, blameful blade,
> He bravely broached his boiling bloody breast.

Another example may be found in the player's recitation in *Hamlet* (in Act II, scene 2):

> Out, out, thou strumpet Fortune! All you gods,
> In general synod take away her power,
> Break all the spokes and fellies from her wheel,
> And bowl the round nave down the hill of heaven
> As low as to the fiends!

Didactic poetry has as a primary purpose to teach or preach. It is probable that all the very greatest poetry teaches in subtle ways, without being expressly didactic; and much expressly didactic poetry ranks high in poetic excellence: that is, it accomplishes its teaching without ceasing to be poetry. But when the didactic purpose supersedes the poetic purpose, when the poem communicates information or moral instruction only, then it ceases to be didactic poetry and becomes didactic verse. Such verse appeals to people who go to poetry primarily for noble thoughts or inspiring lessons and like them prettily expressed. It is recognizable often by the flatness of its diction, the poverty of its imagery and figurative language, its emphasis on moral platitudes, its lack of poetic freshness. It is either very trite or has little to distinguish it from informational prose except rime or meter. Tennyson's "The Oak" (page 741) is an excellent example of didactic *poetry*. The familiar couplet

> Early to bed and early to rise,
> Makes a man healthy, wealthy, and wise

is more aptly characterized as didactic *verse*.

Undoubtedly, so far in this chapter, we have spoken too categorically, have made our distinctions too sharp and definite. All poetic excellence is a matter of degree. There are no absolute lines between sentimentality and true emotion, artificial and genuine eloquence, didactic verse and didactic poetry. Though the difference between extreme examples is easy to recognize, subtler discriminations are harder to make. But a primary distinction between the educated man and the ignorant man is the ability to make value judgments.

A final caution to students. In making judgments on literature, always be honest. Do not pretend to like what you really do not like. Do not be afraid to admit a liking for what you do like. A genuine enthusiasm for the second-rate is much better than false enthusiasm or no enthusiasm at all. Be neither hasty nor timorous in making your judgments. When you have attentively read a poem and thoroughly considered it, decide what you think. Do not hedge, equivocate, or try to find out others' opinions before forming your own. Having formed an opinion and expressed it, do not allow it to petrify. Compare your opinion *then* with the opinions of others; allow yourself to change it when convinced of its error: in this way you learn. Honesty, courage, and humility are the necessary moral foundations for all genuine literary judgment.

In the poems for comparison in this chapter, the distinction to be made is not always between black and white; it may be between varying degrees of poetic merit.

EXERCISE

Poetry is not so much a thing as a quality; it exists in varying degrees in different specimens of language. Though we cannot always say definitely, "This is poetry; that is not," we can often say, "This is more poetical than that." Rank the following passages from most poetical to least poetical or not poetical at all.

1. Why should we be in such desperate haste to succeed and in such desperate enterprises? If a man does not keep pace with his companions, perhaps it is because he hears a different drummer. Let him step to the music which he hears, however measured or far away.
2. $(x - 12)(x - 2) = x^2 - 14x + 24$.
3. Thirty days hath September,
April, June, and November.
All the rest have thirty-one,
Except February alone,
To which we twenty-eight assign,
Till leap year makes it twenty-nine.
4. "Meeting at Night" (page 600).
5. Thus, through the serene tranquilities of the tropical sea, among waves whose handclappings were suspended by exceeding rapture, Moby Dick moved on, still withholding from sight the full terrors of his submerged trunk, entirely hiding the wrenched hideousness of his jaw.

But soon the fore part of him slowly rose from the water; for an instant his whole marbleized body formed a high arch, like Virginia's Natural Bridge, and warningly waving his bannered flukes in the air, the grand god revealed himself, sounded, and went out of sight. Hoveringly halting, and dipping on the wing, the white sea fowls longingly lingered over the agitated pool that he left.

6. Nature in the abstract is the aggregate of the powers and properties of all things. Nature means the sum of all phenomena, together with the causes which produce them; including not only all that happens, but all that is capable of happening; the unused capabilities of causes being as much a part of the idea of Nature, as those which take effect.

LOITERING WITH A VACANT EYE

Loitering with a vacant eye
Along the Grecian gallery,
And brooding on my heavy ill,
I met a statue standing still.
Still in marble stone stood he,
And steadfastly he looked at me.
"Well met," I thought the look would say,
"We both were fashioned far away;
We neither knew, when we were young,
These Londoners we live among."

Still he stood and eyed me hard,
An earnest and a grave regard:
"What, lad, drooping with your lot?
I too would be where I am not.
I too survey that endless line
Of men whose thoughts are not as mine.
Years, ere you stood up from rest,
On my neck the collar prest;
Years, when you lay down your ill,
I shall stand and bear it still.
Courage, lad, 'tis not for long:
Stand, quit you like stone, be strong."
So I thought his look would say;
And light on me my trouble lay,
And I stept out in flesh and bone
Manful like the man of stone.

BE STRONG

Be strong!
We are not here to play,—to dream, to drift.
We have hard work to do and loads to lift.
Shun not the struggle,—face it: 'tis God's gift.

Be strong!
Say not the days are evil. Who's to blame?
And fold the hands and acquiesce,—O shame!
Stand up, speak out, and bravely, in God's name.

Be strong!
It matters not how deep intrenched the wrong,
How hard the battle goes, the day how long;
Faint not,—fight on! Tomorrow comes the song.

QUESTIONS

1. The "Grecian gallery" (2), in the first poem of this pair, is a room in the British Museum in London. Who is the speaker? Who is the speaker in the second poem?

2. Which is the superior poem? Discuss.

A PRAYER IN SPRING

Oh, give us pleasure in the flowers today;
And give us not to think so far away
As the uncertain harvest; keep us here
All simply in the springing of the year.

Oh, give us pleasure in the orchard white,
Like nothing else by day, like ghosts by night;
And make us happy in the happy bees,
The swarm dilating round the perfect trees.

And make us happy in the darting bird
That suddenly above the bees is heard,
The meteor that thrusts in with needle bill,
And off a blossom in mid air stands still.

For this is love and nothing else is love,
The which it is reserved for God above
To sanctify to what far ends He will,
But which it only needs that we fulfill.

PRAY IN MAY

Today the birds are singing and
The grass and leaves are green,
And all the gentle earth presents
A bright and sunny scene.
It is the merry month of May
When flowers bloom once more,
And there are hopes and happy dreams
And promises in store.
What time could be more wisely spent
Than this the first of May
To say that we are thankful for
Our blessings every day?
To give our gratitude to God
In humbleness and prayer
And offer deeds of charity
As incense in the air?
Then let us love our neighbor and
Our rich and fruitful sod,
And let us go to church today
And thank almighty God.

QUESTION

Which poem treats its subject with greater truth, freshness, and technical skill?

THE SIN OF OMISSION

It isn't the thing you do;
    It's the thing you leave undone,
Which gives you a bit of heartache
    At the setting of the sun.

The tender word forgotten,
    The letter you did not write,
The flower you might have sent,
    Are your haunting ghosts tonight.

The stone you might have lifted
    Out of a brother's way,

The bit of heartsome counsel
You were hurried too much to say.

The loving touch of the hand,
The gentle and winsome tone,
That you had no time or thought for
With troubles enough of your own.

The little acts of kindness,
So easily out of mind;
Those chances to be helpful
Which everyone may find—

No, it's not the thing you do,
It's the thing you leave undone,
Which gives you the bit of heartache
At the setting of the sun.

PORTRAIT OF THE ARTIST AS A PREMATURELY OLD MAN

It is common knowledge to every schoolboy and even every Bachelor of Arts,
That all sin is divided into two parts.
One kind of sin is called a sin of commission, and that is very important,
And it is what you are doing when you are doing something you ortant,
And the other kind of sin is just the opposite and is called a sin of omission and is equally bad in the eyes of all right-thinking people, from Billy Sunday to Buddha,
And it consists of not having done something you shuddha.
I might as well give you my opinion of these two kinds of sin as long as, in a way, against each other we are pitting them,
And that is, don't bother your head about sins of commission because however sinful, they must at least be fun or else you wouldn't be committing them.
It is the sin of omission, the second kind of sin,
That lays eggs under your skin.
The way you get really painfully bitten
Is by the insurance you haven't taken out and the checks you haven't added up the stubs of and the appointments you haven't kept and the bills you haven't paid and the letters you haven't written.
Also, about sins of omission there is one particularly painful lack of beauty,
Namely, it isn't as though it had been a riotous red-letter day or night every time you neglected to do your duty;

You didn't get a wicked forbidden thrill
Every time you let a policy lapse or forgot to pay a bill;
You didn't slap the lads in the tavern on the back and loudly cry
    Whee,
Let's all fail to write just one more letter before we go home, and this round
    of unwritten letters is on me.
No, you never get any fun
Out of the things you haven't done,
But they are the things that I do not like to be amid,
Because the suitable things you didn't do give you a lot more trouble than
    the unsuitable things you did.
The moral is that it is probably better not to sin at all, but if some kind of
    sin you must be pursuing,
Well, remember to do it by doing rather than by not doing.

QUESTION

Which poem shows greater originality and imagination? Explain.

TO MY SON

Do you know that your soul is of my soul such part
That you seem to be fibre and cord of my heart?
None other can pain me as you, dear, can do;
None other can please me or praise me as you.

Remember the world will be quick with its blame
If shadow or stain ever darken your name;
"Like mother like son" is a saying so true,
The world will judge largely of "Mother" by you.

Be yours then the task, if task it shall be,
To force the proud world to do homage to me;
Be sure it will say when its verdict you've won,
"She reaped as she sowed. Lo! this is her son."

ON THE BEACH AT FONTANA

Wind whines and whines the shingle,
The crazy pierstakes groan;
A senile sea numbers each single
Slimesilvered stone.

From whining wind and colder
Grey sea I wrap him warm
And touch his trembling fineboned shoulder
And boyish arm.

Around us fear, descending
Darkness of fear above
And in my heart how deep unending
Ache of love!

QUESTIONS

1. Vocabulary: *shingle* (1).

2. The first poem was written by a woman, the second by a man. Who is the speaker in each? Which is the better poem? Why?

ON A DEAD CHILD

Man proposes, God in His time disposes,
And so I wandered up to where you lay,
A little rose among the little roses,
And no more dead than they.

It seemed your childish feet were tired of straying,
You did not greet me from your flower-strewn bed,
Yet still I knew that you were only playing—
Playing at being dead.

I might have thought that you were really sleeping,
So quiet lay your eyelids to the sky,
So still your hair, but surely you were peeping;
And so I did not cry.

God knows, and in His proper time disposes,
And so I smiled and gently called your name,
Added my rose to your sweet heap of roses,
And left you to your game.

BELLS FOR JOHN WHITESIDE'S DAUGHTER

There was such speed in her little body,
And such lightness in her footfall,
It is no wonder her brown study
Astonishes us all.

Her wars were bruited in our high window.
We looked among orchard trees and beyond
Where she took arms against her shadow,
Or harried unto the pond

The lazy geese, like a snow cloud
Dripping their snow on the green grass,
Tricking and stopping, sleepy and proud,
Who cried in goose, Alas,

For the tireless heart within the little
Lady with rod that made them rise
From their noon apple-dreams and scuttle
Goose-fashion under the skies!

But now go the bells, and we are ready,
In one house we are sternly stopped
To say we are vexed at her brown study,
Lying so primly propped.

QUESTION

Which is the sentimental poem? Which is the honest one? Explain.

LITTLE BOY BLUE

The little toy dog is covered with dust,
    But sturdy and staunch he stands;
And the little toy soldier is red with rust,
    And his musket moulds in his hands.
Time was when the little toy dog was new,
    And the soldier was passing fair;
And that was the time when our Little Boy Blue
    Kissed them and put them there.

"Now, don't you go till I come," he said,
    "And don't you make any noise!"
So, toddling off to his trundle-bed,
    He dreamt of the pretty toys;
And, as he was dreaming, an angel song
    Awakened our Little Boy Blue—
Oh! the years are many, the years are long,
    But the little toy friends are True!

Ay, faithful to Little Boy Blue they stand,
    Each in the same old place—
Awaiting the touch of a little hand,
    The smile of a little face;
And they wonder, as waiting the long years through
    In the dust of that little chair,
What has become of our Little Boy Blue,
    Since he kissed them and put them there.

THE TOYS

My little Son, who looked from thoughtful eyes
And moved and spoke in quiet grown-up wise,
Having my law the seventh time disobeyed,
I struck him, and dismissed
With hard words and unkissed,
His Mother, who was patient, being dead.
Then, fearing lest his grief should hinder sleep,
I visited his bed,
But found him slumbering deep,
With darkened eyelids, and their lashes yet
From his late sobbing wet.
And I, with moan,
Kissing away his tears, left others of my own;
For, on a table drawn beside his head,
He had put, within his reach,
A box of counters and a red-veined stone,
A piece of glass abraded by the beach,
And six or seven shells,
A bottle with bluebells,
And two French copper coins, ranged there with careful art,
To comfort his sad heart.
So when that night I prayed
To God, I wept, and said:
Ah, when at last we lie with trancèd breath,
Not vexing Thee in death,
And thou rememberest of what toys
We made our joys,
How weakly understood
Thy great commanded good,

Then, fatherly not less
Than I whom Thou hast moulded from the clay,
Thou'lt leave Thy wrath, and say,
"I will be sorry for their childishness."

QUESTION

One of these poems has an obvious appeal for the beginning reader. The other is likely to have more meaning for the mature reader. Try to explain in terms of sentimentality and honesty.

THE SEND-OFF

Down the close, darkening lanes they sang their way
To the siding-shed,
And lined the train with faces grimly gay.

Their breasts were stuck all white with wreath and spray
As men's are, dead.

Dull porters watched them, and a casual tramp
Stood staring hard,
Sorry to miss them from the upland camp.
Then, unmoved, signals nodded, and a lamp
Winked to the guard.

So secretly, like wrongs hushed-up, they went.
They were not ours:
We never heard to which front these were sent.

Nor there if they yet mock what women meant
Who gave them flowers.

Shall they return to beatings of great bells
In wild train-loads?
A few, a few, too few for drums and yells,
May creep back, silent, to village wells
Up half-known roads.

CHA TILL MACCRUIMEIN

The pipes in the street were playing bravely,
The marching lads went by,

With merry hearts and voices singing
    My friends marched out to die;
But I was hearing a lonely pibroch
    Out of an older war,
"Farewell, farewell, farewell, MacCrimmon,
    MacCrimmon comes no more."

And every lad in his heart was dreaming
    Of honor and wealth to come,
And honor and noble pride were calling
    To the tune of the pipes and drum;
But I was hearing a woman singing
    On dark Dunvegan shore,
"In battle or peace, with wealth or honor,
    MacCrimmon comes no more."

And there in front of the men were marching,
    With feet that made no mark,
The grey old ghosts of the ancient fighters
    Come back again from the dark;
And in front of them all MacCrimmon piping
    A weary tune and sore,
"On the gathering day, for ever and ever,
    MacCrimmon comes no more."

QUESTIONS

1. Vocabulary: *pibroch* (5).

2. The first poem was written by an English poet, the second by a Scottish one; both poets were killed in World War I. "Cha Till Maccruimein" is Gaelic and means "MacCrimmon comes no more." The MacCrimmons were a famous race of hereditary pipers from the Isle of Skye. One of them, when his clan was about to leave on a dangerous expedition, composed a lament in which he accurately prophesied his own death in the coming fight. According to Sir Walter Scott, emigrants from the West Highlands and Western Isles usually left their native shore to the accompaniment of this strain. Compare these two poems as to subject and purpose. Taking into account their rhythm, imagery, freshness, and emotional content, decide which is the superior poem.*

* For this pairing I am indebted to Denys Thompson, *Reading and Discrimination,* rev. ed. (London: Chatto & Windus, 1954).

THE LONG VOYAGE

Not that the pines were darker there,
nor mid-May dogwood brighter there,
nor swifts more swift in summer air;
it was my own country,

having its thunderclap of spring,
its long midsummer ripening,
its corn hoar-stiff at harvesting,
almost like any country,

yet being mine; its face, its speech,
its hills bent low within my reach,
its river birch and upland beech
were mine, of my own country.

Now the dark waters at the bow
fold back, like earth against the plow;
foam brightens like the dogwood now
at home, in my own country.

BREATHES THERE THE MAN

Breathes there the man, with soul so dead,
Who never to himself hath said,
This is my own, my native land!
Whose heart hath ne'er within him burned,
As home his footsteps he hath turned,
From wandering on a foreign strand?
If such there breathe, go, mark him well;
For him no minstrel raptures swell;
High though his titles, proud his name,
Boundless his wealth as wish can claim—
Despite those titles, power, and pelf,
The wretch, concentered all in self,
Living, shall forfeit fair renown,
And, doubly dying, shall go down
To the vile dust from whence he sprung,
Unwept, unhonored, and unsung.

QUESTIONS

1. Which poem communicates the more genuine poetic emotion? Which is more rhetorical? Justify your answer.

2. Compare the first poem with "America for Me" (page 808). Which exhibits the greater maturity of attitude?

BOY-MAN

England's lads are miniature men
To start with, grammar in their shiny hats,
And serious: in America who knows when
Manhood begins? Presidents dance and hug
And while the kind King waves and gravely chats
America wets on England's old green rug.

The boy-man roars. Worry alone will give
This one the verisimilitude of age.
Those white teeth are his own, for he must live
Longer, grow taller than the Texas race.
Fresh are his eyes, his darkening skin the gauge
Of bloods that freely mix beneath his face.

He knows the application of the book
But not who wrote it; shuts it like a shot.
Rather than read he thinks that he will look,
Rather than look he thinks that he will talk,
Rather than talk he thinks that he will not
Bother at all; would rather ride than walk.

His means of conversation is the joke,
Humor his language underneath which lies
The undecoded dialect of the folk.
Abroad he scorns the foreigner: what's old
Is worn, what's different bad, what's odd unwise.
He gives off heat and is enraged by cold.

Charming, becoming to the suits he wears,
The boy-man, younger than his eldest son,
Inherits the state; upon his silver hairs
Time like a panama hat sits at a tilt
And smiles. To him the world has just begun
And every city waiting to be built.

Mister, remove your shoulder from the wheel
And say this prayer, "Increase my vitamins,
Make my decisions of the finest steel,

Pour motor oil upon my troubled spawn,
Forgive the Europeans for their sins,
Establish them, that values may go on."

QUESTIONS

1. Vocabulary: *verisimilitude* (8), *spawn* (34).
2. What is the subject of the poem?
3. What is the tone—admiration? Mockery? Both?
4. Explain fully the figures of speech in lines 2, 6, 26, 28–29 and their appropriateness. What kind of irony appears in the last stanza?

AMERICA FOR ME

'Tis fine to see the Old World, and travel up and down
Among the famous palaces and cities of renown,
To admire the crumbly castles and the statues of the kings—
But now I think I've had enough of antiquated things.

So it's home again, and home again, America for me!
My heart is turning home again, and there I long to be,
In the land of youth and freedom beyond the ocean bars,
Where the air is full of sunlight and the flag is full of stars.

Oh, London is a man's town, there's power in the air;
And Paris is a woman's town, with flowers in her hair;
And it's sweet to dream in Venice, and it's great to study Rome;
But when it comes to living there is no place like home.

I like the German fir-woods, in green battalions drilled;
I like the gardens of Versailles with flashing fountains filled;
But, oh, to take your hand, my dear, and ramble for a day
In the friendly western woodlands where Nature has her way!

I know that Europe's wonderful, yet something seems to lack:
The Past is too much with her, and the people looking back.
But the glory of the Present is to make the Future free—
We love our land for what she is and what she is to be.

Oh, it's home again, and home again, America for me!
I want a ship that's westward bound to plow the rolling sea,
To the blessèd Land of Room Enough beyond the ocean bars,
Where the air is full of sunlight and the flag is full of stars.

QUESTIONS

1. In what respects do the attitudes expressed in this poem fit the characterization made in "Boy-Man"?

2. "America for Me" and "Boy-Man" were both written by Americans. Which is more worthy of prolonged consideration? Why?

TODAY!

With every rising of the sun
Think of your life as just begun.
The Past has cancelled and buried deep
All yesterdays. There let them sleep.
Concern yourself with but Today.
Grasp it, and teach it to obey
Your will and plan. Since time began
Today has been the friend of man.
You and Today! A soul sublime
And the great heritage of time.
With God himself to bind the twain,
Go forth, brave heart! Attain! attain!

DAYS

Daughters of Time, the hypocritic Days,
Muffled and dumb like barefoot dervishes,
And marching single in an endless file,
Bring diadems and faggots in their hands.
To each they offer gifts after his will,
Bread, kingdoms, stars, and sky that holds them all.
I, in my pleached garden, watched the pomp,
Forgot my morning wishes, hastily
Took a few herbs and apples, and the Day
Turned and departed silent. I, too late,
Under her solemn fillet saw the scorn.

QUESTION

Which poem has the greater poetic merit? Why?

CHAPTER SIXTEEN

Good Poetry and Great

If a poem has successfully met the test in the question, *How fully has it accomplished its purpose?* we are ready to subject it to our second question, *How important is its purpose?*

Great poetry must, of course, be good poetry. Noble intent alone cannot redeem a work that does not measure high on the scale of accomplishment; otherwise the sentimental and purely didactic verse of much of the last chapter would stand with the world's masterpieces. But once a work has been judged as successful on the scale of execution, its final standing will depend on its significance of purpose.

Suppose, for instance, we consider three poems in our text: the limerick "There was a young lady of Niger" (page 774), Emily Dickinson's poem "It sifts from leaden sieves" (page 620), and Shakespeare's sonnet "That time of year" (page 776). Each of these would probably be judged by competent critics as highly successful in accomplishing what it sets out to do. The limerick tells its little story without an unnecessary word, with no "wrong" word, with no distortion of normal sentence order forced by exigencies of meter or rime; the limerick form is ideally suited to the author's humorous purpose; and the manner in which the story is told, with its understatement, its neat shift in position of the lady and her smile, is economical and delicious. Yet we should hardly call this poetry at all: it does not really communicate experience, nor does it attempt to. It attempts merely to relate a brief anecdote humorously and effectively. On the other hand, Emily Dickinson's poem *is* poetry, and very good poetry. It appeals richly to our senses and to our imaginations, and it succeeds excellently in its purpose: to convey the appearance and the quality of falling and newly fallen snow as well as a sense of the magic and the mystery of nature. Yet, when we compare this excellent poem with Shakespeare's, we again see important differences. Although the first poem engages the senses and the imagination and may affect us with wonder and cause us to meditate on nature, it does not deeply engage the emotions or the intellect. It does not come as close to the core of human living and suffering as does Shakespeare's sonnet. In fact, it is concerned primarily with that staple of small talk, the weather. On the other hand, Shakespeare's sonnet is concerned with the universal human tragedy of growing old, with approaching death, and with love. Of these three selections, then, Shakespeare's is the greatest. It "says" more than Emily Dickinson's poem or the limerick; it communicates a richer experience; it successfully accomplishes a more significant purpose. The discriminating reader will get from it a deeper enjoyment, because he has been nourished as well as delighted.

Great poetry engages the whole man in his response—senses, imagination, emotion, intellect; it does not touch him merely on one or two sides of his nature. Great poetry seeks not merely to entertain the reader but to bring him, along with pure pleasure, fresh insights, or renewed insights, and important insights, into the nature of human experience. Great poetry, we might say, gives its reader a broader and deeper understanding of life, of his fellow men, and of himself, always with the qualification, of course, that the kind of insight literature gives is not necessarily the kind that can be summed up in a simple "lesson" or "moral." It is *knowledge—felt* knowledge, *new* knowledge—of the complexities of human nature and of the tragedies and sufferings, the excitements and joys, that characterize human experience.

Is Shakespeare's sonnet a *great* poem? It is, at least, a great *sonnet*. Greatness, like goodness, is relative. If we compare any of Shakespeare's sonnets with his greatest plays—*Macbeth, Othello, Hamlet, King Lear*—another big difference appears. What is undertaken and accomplished in these tragedies is enormously greater, more difficult, and more complex than could ever be undertaken or accomplished in a single sonnet. Greatness in literature, in fact, cannot be entirely dissociated from size. In literature, as in basketball and football, a good big man is better than a good little man. The greatness of a poem is in proportion to the range and depth and intensity of experience that it brings to us: its amount of life. Shakespeare's plays offer us a multiplicity of life and a depth of living that could never be compressed into the fourteen lines of a sonnet. They organize a greater complexity of life and experience into unity.

Yet, after all, we have provided no easy yardsticks or rule-of-thumb measures for literary judgment. There are no mechanical tests. The final measuring rod can be only the responsiveness, the maturity, the taste and discernment of the cultivated reader. Such taste and discernment are partly a native endowment, partly the product of maturity and experience, partly the achievement of conscious study, training, and intellectual effort. They cannot be achieved suddenly or quickly; they can never be achieved in perfection. The pull is a long and a hard one. But success, even relative success, brings enormous rewards in enrichment and command of life.

WEST-RUNNING BROOK

"Fred, where is north?"

"North? North is there, my love.
The brook runs west."

"West-running Brook then call it."
(West-running Brook men call it to this day.)
"What does it think it's doing running west
When all the other country brooks flow east
To reach the ocean? It must be the brook
Can trust itself to go by contraries
The way I can with you—and you with me—
Because we're—we're—I don't know what we are.
What are we?"

"Young or new?"

"We must be something.
We've said we two. Let's change that to we three.
As you and I are married to each other,
We'll both be married to the brook. We'll build
Our bridge across it, and the bridge shall be

Our arm thrown over it asleep beside it.
Look, look, it's waving to us with a wave
To let us know it hears me."

"Why, my dear,
That wave's been standing off this jut of shore—"
(The black stream, catching on a sunken rock,
Flung backward on itself in one white wave,
And the white water rode the black forever,
Not gaining but not losing, like a bird
White feathers from the struggle of whose breast
Flecked the dark stream and flecked the darker pool
Below the point, and were at last driven wrinkled
In a white scarf against the far shore alders.)
"That wave's been standing off this jut of shore
Ever since rivers, I was going to say,
Were made in heaven. It wasn't waved to us."

"It wasn't, yet it was. If not to you
It was to me—in an annunciation."

"Oh, if you take it off to lady-land,
As't were the country of the Amazons
We men must see you to the confines of
And leave you there, ourselves forbid to enter,—
It is your brook! I have no more to say."

"Yes, you have, too. Go on. You thought of something."

"Speaking of contraries, see how the brook
In that white wave runs counter to itself.
It is from that in water we were from
Long, long before we were from any creature.
Here we, in our impatience of the steps,
Get back to the beginning of beginnings,
The stream of everything that runs away.
Some say existence like a Pirouot
And Pirouette, forever in one place,
Stands still and dances, but it runs away,
It seriously, sadly, runs away
To fill the abyss' void with emptiness.
It flows beside us in this water brook,
But it flows over us. It flows between us.

To separate us for a panic moment.
It flows between us, over us, and *with* us.
And it is time, strength, tone, light, life, and love—
And even substance lapsing unsubstantial;
The universal cataract of death
That spends to nothingness—and unresisted,
Save by some strange resistance in itself,
Not just a swerving, but a throwing back,
As if regret were in it and were sacred.
It has this throwing backward on itself
So that the fall of most of it is always
Raising a little, sending up a little.
Our life runs down in sending up the clock.
The brook runs down in sending up our life.
The sun runs down in sending up the brook.
And there is something sending up the sun.
It is this backward motion toward the source,
Against the stream, that most we see ourselves in,
The tribute of the current to the source.
It is from this in nature we are from.
It is most us."

"Today will be the day
You said so."

"No, today will be the day
You said the brook was called West-running Brook."

"Today will be the day of what we both said."

Robert Frost (1874–1963)

QUESTIONS

1. Vocabulary: *annunciation* (31), *Amazons* (33). In *Pirouot* and *Pirouette* (45–46) Frost is punning on *Pierrot* and *Pierette,* traditional pantomime characters, and *pirouette,* a spin on one foot in ballet. How does the pun serve the meaning?

2. In what section of the country is this poem set? How is the setting important to the meaning?

3. Characterize the man and his wife. How are they alike? How different? What "contraries" do they exhibit in their conversation? How are these harmonized?

4. According to the second law of thermodynamics, we live in a universe that is running down, in which usable energy is being exhausted. What symbol does Frost (or the husband) use for this notion? What countersymbol does he set against it? In what does he find a source of meaning and value in existence?

5. Point out all the "contraries" in the poem. What function do they serve?

6. Using the criteria for literary greatness developed in this chapter, how would you rate this poem as compared with Alfred Noyes's "The Barrel-Organ" (page 746)? Why?

THE LOVE SONG OF J. ALFRED PRUFROCK

S'io credesse che mia risposta fosse
A persona che mai tornasse al mondo,
Questa fiamma staria senza piu scosse.
Ma perciocche giammai di questo fondo
Non torno vivo alcun, s'i'odo il vero,
Senza tema d'infamia ti rispondo.

Let us go then, you and I,
When the evening is spread out against the sky
Like a patient etherized upon a table;
Let us go, through certain half-deserted streets,
The muttering retreats
Of restless nights in one-night cheap hotels
And sawdust restaurants with oyster-shells:
Streets that follow like a tedious argument
Of insidious intent
To lead you to an overwhelming question . . .
Oh, do not ask, "What is it?"
Let us go and make our visit.

In the room the women come and go
Talking of Michelangelo.

The yellow fog that rubs its back upon the window-panes,
The yellow smoke that rubs its muzzle on the window-panes
Licked its tongue into the corners of the evening,
Lingered upon the pools that stand in drains,
Let fall upon its back the soot that falls from chimneys,
Slipped by the terrace, made a sudden leap,

And seeing that it was a soft October night,
Curled once about the house, and fell asleep.

And indeed there will be time
For the yellow smoke that slides along the street,
Rubbing its back upon the window-panes;
There will be time, there will be time
To prepare a face to meet the faces that you meet;
There will be time to murder and create,
And time for all the works and days of hands
That lift and drop a question on your plate;
Time for you and time for me,
And time yet for a hundred indecisions,
And for a hundred visions and revisions,
Before the taking of a toast and tea.

In the room the women come and go
Talking of Michelangelo.

And indeed there will be time
To wonder, "Do I dare?" and, "Do I dare?"
Time to turn back and descend the stair,
With a bald spot in the middle of my hair—
[They will say: "How his hair is growing thin!"]
My morning coat, my collar mounting firmly to the chin,
My necktie rich and modest, but asserted by a simple pin—
[They will say: "But how his arms and legs are thin!"]
Do I dare
Disturb the universe?
In a minute there is time
For decisions and revisions which a minute will reverse.

For I have known them all already, known them all:—
Have known the evenings, mornings, afternoons,
I have measured out my life with coffee spoons;
I know the voices dying with a dying fall
Beneath the music from a farther room.
So how should I presume?

And I have known the eyes already, known them all—
The eyes that fix you in a formulated phrase,
And when I am formulated, sprawling on a pin,
When I am pinned and wriggling on the wall,

Then how should I begin
To spit out all the butt-ends of my days and ways
    And how should I presume?

    And I have known the arms already, known them all—
Arms that are braceleted and white and bare
[But in the lamplight, downed with light brown hair!]
Is it perfume from a dress
That makes me so digress?
Arms that lie along a table, or wrap about a shawl.
    And should I then presume?
    And how should I begin?

. . . . .

Shall I say, I have gone at dusk through narrow streets
And watched the smoke that rises from the pipes
Of lonely men in shirt-sleeves, leaning out of windows? . . .

    I should have been a pair of ragged claws
Scuttling across the floors of silent seas.

. . . . .

And the afternoon, the evening, sleeps so peacefully!
Smoothed by long fingers,
Asleep . . . tired . . . or it malingers,
Stretched on the floor, here beside you and me.
Should I, after tea and cakes and ices,
Have the strength to force the moment to its crisis?
But though I have wept and fasted, wept and prayed,
Though I have seen my head [grown slightly bald] brought in
        upon a platter,
I am no prophet—and here's no great matter;
I have seen the moment of my greatness flicker,
And I have seen the eternal Footman hold my coat, and snicker,
And in short, I was afraid.

    And would it have been worth it, after all,
After the cups, the marmalade, the tea,
Among the porcelain, among some talk of you and me,
Would it have been worth while,
To have bitten off the matter with a smile,
To have squeezed the universe into a ball

To roll it toward some overwhelming question,
To say: "I am Lazarus, come from the dead,
Come back to tell you all, I shall tell you all"—
If one, settling a pillow by her head,
    Should say: "That is not what I meant at all.
    That is not it, at all."

    And would it have been worth it, after all,
Would it have been worth while,
After the sunsets and the dooryards and the sprinkled streets,
After the novels, after the teacups, after the skirts that trail
        along the floor—
And this, and so much more?—
It is impossible to say just what I mean!
But as if a magic lantern threw the nerves in patterns on a screen:
Would it have been worth while
If one, settling a pillow or throwing off a shawl,
And turning toward the window, should say:
    "That is not it at all,
    That it not what I meant, at all."

. . . . .

No! I am not Prince Hamlet, nor was meant to be;
Am an attendant lord, one that will do
To swell a progress, start a scene or two,
Advise the prince; no doubt, an easy tool,
Deferential, glad to be of use,
Politic, cautious, and meticulous:
Full of high sentence, but a bit obtuse;
At times, indeed, almost ridiculous—
Almost, at times, the Fool.

    I grow old . . . I grow old . . .
I shall wear the bottoms of my trousers rolled.° cuffed

    Shall I part my hair behind? Do I dare to eat a peach?
I shall wear white flannel trousers, and walk upon the beach.
I have heard the mermaids singing, each to each.

    I do not think that they will sing to me.

    I have seen them riding seaward on the waves
Combing the white hair of the waves blown back

When the wind blows the water white and black.

We have lingered in the chambers of the sea
By sea-girls wreathed with seaweed red and brown
Till human voices wake us, and we drown.

T. S. Eliot (1888–1965)

QUESTIONS

1. Vocabulary: *insidious* (9), *Michelangelo* (14), *muzzle* (16), *malingers* (77), *progress* (113), *deferential* (115), *politic* (116), *meticulous* (116), *sentence* (117).

2. This poem may be for you the most difficult in the book, because it uses a "stream of consciousness" technique (that is, presents the apparently random thoughts going through a person's head within a certain time interval), in which the transitional links are psychological rather than logical, and also because it uses allusions you may be unfamiliar with. Even though you do not at first understand the poem in detail, you should be able to get from it a quite accurate picture of Prufrock's character and personality. What kind of person is he? (Answer this as fully as possible.) From what class of society is he? What one line especially well sums up the nature of his past life? A brief initial orientation may be helpful: Prufrock is apparently on his way, at the beginning of the poem, to a late afternoon tea, at which he wishes (or does he?) to make a declaration of love to some lady who will be present. The "you and I" of the first line are divided parts of Prufrock's own nature, for he is undergoing internal conflict. Does he make the declaration? Why not? Where does the climax of the poem come? If the first half of the poem (up to the climax) is devoted to Prufrock's effort to prepare himself psychologically to make the declaration (or to postpone such effort), what is the latter half (after the climax) devoted to?

3. There are a number of striking or unusual figures of speech in the poem. Most of them in some way reflect Prufrock's own nature or his desires or fears. From this point of view discuss lines 2–3; 15–22 and 75–78; 57–58; 73–74; and 124–31. What figure of speech is lines 73–74? In what respect is the title ironical?

4. The poem makes an extensive use of literary allusion. The Italian epigraph is a passage from Dante's *Inferno* in which a man in Hell tells a visitor that he would never tell his story if there were a chance that it would get back to living ears. In line 29 the phrase "works and days" is the title of a long poem—a description of agricultural life and a call to toil—by the early Greek poet Hesiod. Line 52 echoes the opening speech of Shakespeare's *Twelfth Night*. The prophet of lines 81–83 is John the Baptist, whose head was delivered to Salome by Herod as a reward for her dancing (Matthew 14:1–11, and Oscar Wilde's play *Salome*). Line 92 echoes the closing six

lines of Marvell's "To His Coy Mistress" (page 623). Lazarus (94–95) may be either the beggar Lazarus (of Luke 16) who was not permitted to return from the dead to warn the brothers of a rich man about Hell or the Lazarus (of John 11) whom Christ raised from death or both. Lines 111–19 allude to a number of characters from Shakespeare's *Hamlet:* Hamlet himself, the chamberlain Polonius, and various minor characters including probably Rosencrantz, Guildenstern, and Osric. "Full of high sentence" (117) echoes Chaucer's description of the Clerk of Oxford in the Prologue to *The Canterbury Tales.* Relate as many of these allusions as you can to the character of Prufrock. How is Prufrock particularly like Hamlet, and how is he unlike him? Contrast Prufrock with the speaker in "To His Coy Mistress."

5. This poem and "West-running Brook" are dramatic in structure. One is a dialogue between two characters who speak in their own voices; the other is a highly allusive soliloquy or interior monologue. In what ways do their dramatic structures facilitate what they have to say?

6. This poem and Charlotte Mew's "The Changeling" (page 729) both focus on a conflict between two worlds—one real, the other unreal. Using the criteria for literary greatness developed in this chapter, how would you rate the two poems as compared to each other? Why?

AMONG SCHOOL CHILDREN

I

I walk through the long schoolroom questioning;
A kind old nun in a white hood replies;
The children learn to cipher and to sing,
To study reading-books and history,
To cut and sew, be neat in everything
In the best modern way—the children's eyes
In momentary wonder stare upon
A sixty-year-old smiling public man.

II

I dream of a Ledaean body, bent
Above a sinking fire, a tale that she
Told of a harsh reproof, or trivial event
That changed some childish day to tragedy—
Told, and it seemed that our two natures blent
Into a sphere from youthful sympathy,
Or else, to alter Plato's parable,
Into the yolk and white of the one shell.

III

And thinking of that fit of grief or rage
I look upon one child or t'other there
And wonder if she stood so at that age—
For even daughters of the swan can share
Something of every paddler's heritage—
And had that color upon cheek or hair,
And thereupon my heart is driven wild:
She stands before me as a living child.

IV

Her present image floats into the mind—
Did Quattrocento finger fashion it
Hollow of cheek as though it drank the wind
And took a mess of shadows for its meat?
And I though never of Ledaean kind
Had pretty plumage once—enough of that,
Better to smile on all that smile, and show
There is a comfortable kind of old scarecrow.

V

What youthful mother, a shape upon her lap
Honey of generation had betrayed,
And that must sleep, shriek, struggle to escape
As recollection or the drug decide,
Would think her son, did she but see that shape
With sixty or more winters on its head,
A compensation for the pang of his birth,
Or the uncertainty of his setting forth?

VI

Plato thought nature but a spume that plays
Upon a ghostly paradigm of things;
Solider Aristotle played the taws
Upon the bottom of a king of kings;
World-famous golden-thighed Pythagoras
Fingered upon a fiddle-stick or strings
What a star sang and careless Muses heard:
Old clothes upon old sticks to scare a bird.

VII

Both nuns and mothers worship images,
But those the candles light are not as those

That animate a mother's reveries,
But keep a marble or a bronze repose.
And yet they too break hearts—O Presences
That passion, piety or affection knows,
And that all heavenly glory symbolize—
O self-born mockers of man's enterprise;

VIII

Labor is blossoming or dancing where
The body is not bruised to pleasure soul,
Nor beauty born out of its own despair,
Nor blear-eyed wisdom out of midnight oil.
O chestnut-tree, great-rooted blossomer,
Are you the leaf, the blossom or the bole?
O body swayed to music, O brightening glance,
How can we know the dancer from the dance?

William Butler Yeats (1865–1939)

QUESTIONS

1. Vocabulary: *Quattrocento* (26), *mess* (28), *spume* (41), *paradigm* (42), *bole* (62).

2. William Butler Yeats was a senator of the Irish Free State from 1922 to 1928. This poem, written in 1926, arises out of a visit of inspection to an Irish school, probably Catholic since Ireland is primarily a Catholic country. In stanza II Yeats is thinking of the talented Maud Gonne, to whom he paid court so long and unsuccessfully (see "The Folly of Being Comforted," page 625). Plato (15), discussing love in the *Symposium,* represents male and female as having resulted from the division of an originally single being, round in shape, into two halves which are forever seeking to regain their original unity. What is "a Ledaean body" (9)? See line 20 and "Leda and the Swan" (page 681). What additional fairy-tale allusion is there in lines 20–21? What are the literal and symbolical implications of "bent" (9) and of "a sinking fire" (10)? What is the "present image" of Maud Gonne (25–28)? What figure of speech is "Quattrocento finger" (26), and what historical persons might it refer to?

3. What is the meaning of lines 33–34—especially, why is the child "betrayed"? "Shape" (33) and "winters" (38) are both metonymies; what is their contribution? Why does Yeats use "winters" instead of, say, "springs"?

4. Plato (41) thought the visible world simply a pale reflection or copy of a divine and more real world of "forms" or "ideas." Aristotle (43), a more realistic philosopher, was tutor to the youthful Alexander the Great,

whom he may have occasionally whipped with "taws" (a whip made of leather thongs). Pythagoras (45), a philosopher and mathematician, discovered the laws of vibrating strings upon which harmony is based, thus demonstrating a correspondence between music and mathematics; conceiving of the universe as mathematically ordered and therefore harmonious, he supposed that the planets in their courses must give off varying musical tones—"the music of the spheres." According to ancient legend, he had a golden hip or thigh. What do these philosophers have in common in Yeats's mind, and how does this stanza relate to stanzas IV or V?

5. What "images" are worshipped by nuns (49), and why are nuns mentioned here? What other kinds of "images" have been mentioned in the poem? What are the "Presences" of lines 53–54? Why do they mock "man's enterprise"?

6. What main contrasts have been made in the poem? How does stanza VIII bring together and comment on these contrasts? What two meanings has "Labor" (57)? What is Yeats's conclusion about the relationship of body and mind or body and soul, of the real and the ideal? What is symbolized by the blossoming chestnut tree and the dancing dancer? Why does Yeats use two symbols rather than just one?

7. Using the criteria for literary greatness developed in this chapter, how would you rate "Among School Children" as compared with Swinburne's "I will go back to the great sweet mother" (page 721)?

EXERCISES

In the following exercises, use both scales of poetic measurement—perfection and significance of accomplishment.

1. Which of the poems "Richard Cory" (page 592) and "The Rich Man" (page 593) is finer and why?

2. Considering such matters as economy and richness of poetic communication, inevitability of organization, and the complexity and maturity of the attitude or philosophy expressed, decide whether "Barter" (page 691) or "Stopping by Woods on a Snowy Evening" (page 691) is the superior poem.

3. Which of the ballads "The Twa Corbies" (page 562) and "Edward" (page 786) is superior as judged by the power and complexity of its poetic achievement and the human significance of its result?

4. Rank the following short poems and explain the reasons for your ranking:
   a. "Why do the Graces" (page 612), "The Span of Life" (page 759).
   b. "Fog" (page 648), "In the Garden" (page 688), "The Death of the Ball Turret Gunner" (page 858).

c. "The Coming of Wisdom with Time" (page 707), "The Turtle" (page 717), "Splinter" (page 755).
d. "The Sea-Gull" (page 614), "I May, I Might, I Must" (page 648), "Quatrain" (page 688).
e. "There is no frigate like a book" (page 586), "Stars, I have seen them fall" (page 638), "Song: Hark, hark!" (page 754).
f. "The Tuft of Kelp" (page 647), "Wind and Silver" (page 648).

5. "The Eagle" (page 555), "The Twa Corbies" (page 562), and "The Sea-Gull" (page 614) all deal with birds. Rank them on a scale of poetic worth.

6. The following poems are all on seasons of the year. Rank them on a scale of poetic accomplishment: "Winter" (page 555), "To Autumn" (page 607), "Spring" (page 561).

7. "The Man He Killed" (page 571) and "Naming of Parts" (page 594) both treat of the subject of war. Which is the superior poem?

8. "A Valediction: Forbidding Mourning" (page 622), "To Lucasta, Going to the Wars" (page 650), and "The 'Je Ne Sais Quoi' " (page 742) all in one way or another treat of the subject of love. Evaluate and rank them.

9. Rank the following poems by Robert Browning in order of their excellence and defend your ranking: "Meeting at Night" and "Parting at Morning" (considered as one poem) (pages 600–01), "My Star" (page 629), "My Last Duchess" (page 671).

10. Rank the following poems by Alfred, Lord Tennyson and defend your ranking: "The Eagle" (page 555), "Ulysses" (page 639), "The Oak" (page 741).

11. Bryant's "To a Waterfowl" and Frost's "Design" (pages 695–96) have a similar subject. Which is the greater poem? Why?

12. Herrick's "To the Virgins, to Make Much of Time" (page 635) and Marvell's "To His Coy Mistress" (page 623) are both *carpe diem* poems of acknowledged excellence. Which achieves the more complex unity?

13. Each of the following pairs is written by a single author. Pick the poem of each pair that you think represents the higher poetic accomplishment and explain why:
a. "The Silken Tent" (page 619), "The Rose Family," (page 652).
b. "On moonlit heath and lonesome bank" (page 603), "The New Mistress" (page 745).
c. "Stopping by Woods on a Snowy Evening" (page 691), "The Aim Was Song" (page 752).

d. "To Autumn" (page 607), "Ode on a Grecian Urn" (page 859).
e. "You, Andrew Marvell" (page 632), "Ars Poetica" (page 701).
f. "There is no frigate like a book" (page 586), "Apparently with no surprise" (page 704).
g. "I like to see it lap the miles" (page 764), "Because I could not stop for Death" (page 844).
h. "Winter" (page 555), "Spring" (page 561).
i. "Yes; I Write Verses" (page 713), "To Age" (page 714).
j. "The Lamb" (page 836), "The Tiger" (page 836).
k. "Had I the Choice" (page 751), "A Noiseless Patient Spider" (page 891).
l. "The Folly of Being Comforted" (page 625), "Sailing to Byzantium" (page 905).
m. "A Valediction: Forbidding Mourning" (page 622), "Song" (page 881).
n. "Spring" (page 561), "God's Grandeur" (page 724).
o. "Wind" (page 765), "View of a Pig" (page 857).
p. "A Late Aubade" (page 602), "A Baroque Wall-Fountain in the Villa Sciarra" (page 893).

Poems for Further Reading

MORNING SONG FROM "SENLIN"

It is morning, Senlin says, and in the morning
When the light drips through the shutters like the dew,
I arise, I face the sunrise,
And do the things my fathers learned to do.
Stars in the purple dusk above the rooftops
Pale in a saffron mist and seem to die,
And I myself on a swiftly tilting planet
Stand before a glass and tie my tie.

Vine leaves tap my window,
Dew-drops sing to the garden stones,
The robin chirps in the chinaberry tree
Repeating three clear tones.

It is morning. I stand by the mirror
And tie my tie once more.
While waves far off in a pale rose twilight
Crash on a coral shore.
I stand by a mirror and comb my hair:
How small and white my face!—
The green earth tilts through a sphere of air
And bathes in a flame of space.

There are houses hanging above the stars
And stars hung under a sea.
And a sun far off in a shell of silence
Dapples my walls for me.

It is morning, Senlin says, and in the morning
Should I not pause in the light to remember god?
Upright and firm I stand on a star unstable,
He is immense and lonely as a cloud.
I will dedicate this moment before my mirror
To him alone, for him I will comb my hair.
Accept these humble offerings, cloud of silence!
I will think of you as I descend the stair.

Vine leaves tap my window,
The snail-track shines on the stones,
Dew-drops flash from the chinaberry tree
Repeating two clear tones.

It is morning, I awake from a bed of silence,
Shining I rise from the starless waters of sleep.
The walls are about me still as in the evening,
I am the same, and the same name still I keep.
The earth revolves with me, yet makes no motion,
The stars pale silently in a coral sky.
In a whistling void I stand before my mirror,
Unconcerned, and tie my tie.

There are horses neighing on far-off hills
Tossing their long white manes,
And mountains flash in the rose-white dusk,
Their shoulders black with rains.
It is morning. I stand by the mirror
And surprise my soul once more;
The blue air rushes above my ceiling,
There are suns beneath my floor.

. . . It is morning, Senlin says, I ascend from darkness
And depart on the winds of space for I know not where,
My watch is wound, a key is in my pocket,
And the sky is darkened as I descend the stair.
There are shadows across the windows, clouds in heaven,
And a god among the stars; and I will go
Thinking of him as I might think of daybreak
And humming a tune I know.

Vine leaves tap at the window,
Dew-drops sing to the garden stones,
The robin chirps in the chinaberry tree
Repeating three clear tones.

Conrad Aiken (1889–1973)

A BOOKSHOP IDYLL

Between the *gardening* and the *cookery*
    Comes the brief *Poetry* shelf;
By the Nonesuch Donne, a thin anthology
    Offers itself.

Critical, and with nothing else to do,
    I scan the Contents page,

Relieved to find the names are mostly new;
    No one my age.

Like all strangers, they divide by sex:
    Landscape near Parma
Interests a man, so does *The Double Vortex,*
    So does *Rilke and Buddha.*

"I travel, you see," "I think" and "I can read"
    These titles seem to say;
But *I Remember You, Love is my Creed,*
    Poem for J.,

The ladies' choice, discountenance my patter
    For several seconds;
From somewhere in this (as in any) matter
    A moral beckons.

Should poets bicycle-pump the human heart
    Or squash it flat?
Man's love is of man's life a thing apart;
    Girls aren't like that.

We men have got love well weighed up; our stuff
    Can get by without it.
Women don't seem to think that's good enough;
    They write about it.

And the awful way their poems lay them open
    Just doesn't strike them.
Women are really much nicer than men:
    No wonder we like them.

Deciding this, we can forget those times
    We sat up half the night
Chock-full of love, crammed with bright thoughts, names, rhymes,
    And couldn't write.

Kingsley Amis (b. 1922)

THE WIFE OF USHER'S WELL

There lived a wife at Usher's Well,
    And a wealthy wife was she;

She had three stout and stalwart sons,
    And sent them o'er the sea.

They hadna been a week from her,
    A week but barely ane,
When word came to the carline° wife   peasant
    That her three sons were gane.

They hadna been a week from her,
    A week but barely three,
Whan word came to the carline wife
    That her sons she'd never see.

"I wish the wind may never cease,
    Nor flashes° in the flood,   troubles
Till my three sons come hame to me
    In earthly flesh and blood."

It fell about the Martinmass
    When nights are lang and mirk,
The carline wife's three sons came hame,
    And their hats were o the birk.°   birch

It neither grew in syke° nor ditch,   trench
    Nor yet in ony sheugh;°   furrow
But at the gates o Paradise
    That birk grew fair eneugh.

"Blow up the fire, my maidens,
    Bring water from the well;
For a' my house shall feast this night
    Since my three sons are well."

And she has made to them a bed,
    She's made it large and wide,
And she's ta'en her mantle her about,
    Sat down at the bed-side.

Up then crew the red, red cock,
    And up and crew the gray;
The eldest to the youngest said,
    " 'Tis time we were away."

The cock he hadna crawd but once
    And clappd his wings at a',

When the youngest to the eldest said,
"Brother, we must awa.

"The cock doth craw, the day doth daw,
The channerin° worm doth chide; devouring
Gin° we be mist out o our place, if
A sair pain we maun bide.

"Fare ye weel, my mother dear!
Fareweel to barn and byre!° cattle-shed
And fare ye weel, the bonny lass
That kindles my mother's fire!"

Anonymous

DOVER BEACH

The sea is calm tonight,
The tide is full, the moon lies fair
Upon the straits;—on the French coast the light
Gleams and is gone; the cliffs of England stand,
Glimmering and vast, out in the tranquil bay.
Come to the window, sweet is the night-air!
Only, from the long line of spray
Where the sea meets the moon-blanched land,
Listen! you hear the grating roar
Of pebbles which the waves draw back, and fling,
At their return, up the high strand,
Begin, and cease, and then again begin,
With tremulous cadence slow, and bring
The eternal note of sadness in.

Sophocles long ago
Heard it on the Aegean, and it brought
Into his mind the turbid ebb and flow
Of human misery; we
Find also in the sound a thought,
Hearing it by this distant northern sea.

The Sea of Faith
Was once, too, at the full, and round earth's shore
Lay like the folds of a bright girdle furled.
But now I only hear

Its melancholy, long, withdrawing roar,
Retreating, to the breath
Of the night-wind, down the vast edges drear
And naked shingles° of the world. pebbled beaches

Ah, love, let us be true
To one another! for the world, which seems
To lie before us like a land of dreams,
So various, so beautiful, so new,
Hath really neither joy, nor love, nor light,
Nor certitude, nor peace, nor help for pain;
And we are here as on a darkling plain
Swept with confused alarms of struggle and flight,
Where ignorant armies clash by night.

Matthew Arnold (1822–1888)

ON READING POEMS TO A SENIOR CLASS AT SOUTH HIGH

Before
I opened my mouth
I noticed them sitting there
as orderly as frozen fish
in a package.

Slowly water began to fill the room
though I did not notice it
till it reached
my ears

and then I heard the sounds
of fish in an aquarium

and I knew that though I had
tried to drown them
with my words
that they had only opened up
like gills for them
and let me in.

Together we swam around the room
like thirty tails whacking words

till the bell rang
puncturing
a hole in the door

where we all leaked out

They went to another class
I suppose and I home

where Queen Elizabeth
my cat met me
and licked my fins
till they were hands again.

D. C. Berry (b. 1947)

THE BALL POEM

What is the boy now, who has lost his ball,
What, what is he to do? I saw it go
Merrily bouncing, down the street, and then
Merrily over—there it is in the water!
No use to say 'O there are other balls':
An ultimate shaking grief fixes the boy
As he stands rigid, trembling, staring down
All his young days into the harbour where
His ball went. I would not intrude on him,
A dime, another ball, is worthless. Now
He senses first responsibility
In a world of possessions. People will take balls,
Balls will be lost always, little boy,
And no one buys a ball back. Money is external.
He is learning, well behind his desperate eyes,
The epistemology of loss, how to stand up
Knowing what every man must one day know
And most know many days, how to stand up
And gradually light returns to the street,
A whistle blows, the ball is out of sight,
Soon part of me will explore the deep and dark
Floor of the harbour . . . I am everywhere,
I suffer and move, my mind and my heart move

With all that move me, under the water
Or whistling, I am not a little boy.

John Berryman (1914–1972)

THE LAMB

Little Lamb, who made thee?
Dost thou know who made thee?
Gave thee life and bid thee feed,
By the stream and o'er the mead;
Gave thee clothing of delight,
Softest clothing wooly bright;
Gave thee such a tender voice,
Making all the vales rejoice!
Little Lamb, who made thee?
Dost thou know who made thee?

Little Lamb, I'll tell thee,
Little Lamb, I'll tell thee!
He is callèd by thy name,
For he calls himself a Lamb;
He is meek and he is mild,
He became a little child;
I a child and thou a lamb,
We are callèd by his name.
Little Lamb, God bless thee.
Little Lamb, God bless thee.

William Blake (1757–1827)

THE TIGER

Tiger! Tiger! burning bright
In the forests of the night,
What immortal hand or eye
Could frame thy fearful symmetry?

In what distant deeps or skies
Burnt the fire of thine eyes?
On what wings dare he aspire?
What the hand dare seize the fire?

And what shoulder, and what art,
Could twist the sinews of thy heart?
And when thy heart began to beat,
What dread hand forged thy dread feet?

What the hammer? what the chain?
In what furnace was thy brain?
What the anvil? what dread grasp
Dare its deadly terrors clasp?

When the stars threw down their spears,
And watered heaven with their tears,
Did he smile his work to see?
Did he who made the Lamb make thee?

Tiger! Tiger! burning bright
In the forests of the night,
What immortal hand or eye,
Dare frame thy fearful symmetry?

William Blake (1757–1827)

THE SCIENTIST

"There's nothing mysterious about the skull."
He may have been suspicious of my request,
That being mainly a poet, I mainly guessed
There might be an esoteric chance to cull

Some succulent, unfamiliar word; that being
Mainly a woman, I now for his sake embraced
An object I held in fact in some distaste.
But he complied, his slender fingers freeing

(There must be a surgeon somewhere with stubby hands)
The latch that held a coil across "The suture
Between the parietals and occipital feature."
And gently, his flesh on the bone disturbed the bands

Which illustrated the way that "The mandible
Articulates with the temple next to the ear.
The nasal bone gives onto the maxilla here."
He laughed, "It's a bore, but it's not expendable;

"The features depend, if not for their shape, on the narrow
Cranium, formed of the commonest elements;
Weighing nine ounces, worth about fourteen cents;
Not even room for what you would call a marrow."

In words resembling these, he judged them dull;
The specimen, his detail, and my suggestion.
"The skin and the brain, of course, are another question,"
He said again, "but there's nothing to the skull."

And that must be so. The quick mind most demands a
Miracle in the covering or the core.
What lies between is shallow and functional fare:
My hand between this thought and the posturing stanza.

But his face belied us both. As he spoke his own
Eyes rhymed depth from the sockets of that example;
His jawline articulated with the temple
Over the words, and his fingers along the bone

Revealed his god in the praying of their plying.
So that, wonderfully, I justify his doubt:
Am moved, as woman to love, as poet to write,
By the mystery and the function of his denying.

Janet Burroway (b. 1936)

SO WE'LL GO NO MORE A-ROVING

So we'll go no more a-roving
  So late into the night,
Though the heart be still as loving,
  And the moon be still as bright.

For the sword outwears its sheath,
  And the soul wears out the breast,
And the heart must pause to breathe,
  And Love itself have rest.

Though the night was made for loving,
  And the day returns too soon,
Yet we'll go no more a-roving
  By the light of the moon.

George Gordon, Lord Byron (1788–1824)

MOUSE'S NEST

I found a ball of grass among the hay
And progged it as I passed and went away; prodded
And when I looked I fancied something stirred,
And turned again and hoped to catch the bird—
When out an old mouse bolted in the wheats
With all her young ones hanging at her teats;
She looked so odd and so grotesque to me,
I ran and wondered what the thing could be,
And pushed the knapweed bunches where I stood;
Then the mouse hurried from the craking brood.
The young ones squeaked, and as I went away
She found her nest again among the hay.
The water o'er the pebbles scarce could run
And broad old cesspools glittered in the sun.

John Clare (1793–1864)

THE LATEST DECALOGUE

Thou shalt have one God only; who
Would be at the expense of two?
No graven images may be
Worshipped, except the currency.
Swear not at all; for, for thy curse
Thine enemy is none the worse.
At church on Sunday to attend
Will serve to keep the world thy friend.
Honor thy parents; that is, all
From whom advancement may befall.
Thou shalt not kill; but need'st not strive
Officiously to keep alive.
Do not adultery commit;
Advantage rarely comes of it.
Thou shalt not steal: an empty feat,
When it's so lucrative to cheat.
Bear not false witness; let the lie
Have time on its own wings to fly.

Thou shalt not covet, but tradition
Approves all forms of competition.

Arthur Hugh Clough (1819–1861)

KUBLA KHAN

In Xanadu did Kubla Khan
A stately pleasure-dome decree:
Where Alph, the sacred river, ran
Through caverns measureless to man
    Down to a sunless sea.
So twice five miles of fertile ground
With walls and towers were girdled round:
And here were gardens bright with sinuous rills,
Where blossomed many an incense-bearing tree;
And here were forests ancient as the hills,
Enfolding sunny spots of greenery.

But oh! that deep romantic chasm which slanted
Down the green hill athwart a cedarn cover!
A savage place! as holy and enchanted
As e'er beneath a waning moon was haunted
By woman wailing for her demon-lover!
And from this chasm, with ceaseless turmoil seething,
As if this earth in fast thick pants were breathing,
A mighty fountain momently was forced:
Amid whose swift half-intermitted burst
Huge fragments vaulted like rebounding hail,
Or chaffy grain beneath the thresher's flail:
And 'mid these dancing rocks at once and ever
It flung up momently the sacred river.
Five miles meandering with a mazy motion
Through wood and dale the sacred river ran,
Then reached the caverns measureless to man,
And sank in tumult to a lifeless ocean:
And 'mid this tumult Kubla heard from far
Ancestral voices prophesying war!
    The shadow of the dome of pleasure
    Floated midway on the waves;
    Where was heard the mingled measure

From the fountain and the caves.
It was a miracle of rare device,
A sunny pleasure-dome with caves of ice!

A damsel with a dulcimer
In a vision once I saw:
It was an Abyssinian maid,
And on her dulcimer she played,
Singing of Mount Abora.
Could I revive within me
Her symphony and song,
To such a deep delight, 'twould win me,
That with music loud and long,
I would build that dome in air,
That sunny dome! those caves of ice!
And all who heard should see them there,
And all should cry, Beware! Beware!
His flashing eyes, his floating hair!
Weave a circle round him thrice,
And close your eyes with holy dread,
For he on honey-dew hath fed,
And drunk the milk of Paradise.

Samuel Taylor Coleridge (1772–1834)

THE LISTENERS

"Is there anybody there?" said the traveler,
Knocking on the moonlit door;
And his horse in the silence champed the grasses
Of the forest's ferny floor:
And a bird flew up out of the turret,
Above the Traveller's head:
And he smote upon the door again a second time;
"Is there anybody there?" he said.
But no one descended to the Traveller;
No head from the leaf-fringed sill
Leaned over and looked into his grey eyes,
Where he stood perplexed and still.
But only a host of phantom listeners
That dwelt in the lone house then

Stood listening in the quiet of the moonlight
    To that voice from the world of men:
Stood thronging the faint moonbeams on the dark stair,
    That goes down to the empty hall,
Hearkening in an air stirred and shaken
    By the lonely Traveller's call.
And he felt in his heart their strangeness,
    Their stillness answering his cry,
While his horse moved, cropping the dark turf,
    'Neath the starred and leafy sky;
For he suddenly smote on the door, even
    Louder, and lifted his head:—
"Tell them I came, and no one answered,
    That I kept my word," he said.
Never the least stir made the listeners,
    Though every word he spake
Fell echoing through the shadowiness of the still house
    From the one man left awake:
Ay, they heard his foot upon the stirrup,
    And the sound of iron on stone,
And how the silence surged softly backward,
    When the plunging hoofs were gone.

Walter de la Mare (1873–1956)

THE BEE

To the football coaches of Clemson College, 1942

One dot
Grainily shifting   we at roadside and
The smallest wings coming   along the rail fence out
Of the woods   one dot   of all that green. It now
Becomes flesh-crawling   then the quite still
Of stinging. I must live faster for my terrified
Small son   it is on him. Has come. Clings.

Old wingback, come
To life. If your knee action is high
Enough, the fat may fall in time   God damn
You, Dickey, *dig*   this is your last time to cut
And run   but you must give it everything you have

Left, for screaming near your screaming child is the sheer
Murder of California traffic: some bee hangs driving

Your child
Blindly onto the highway. Get there however
Is still possible. Long live what I badly did
At Clemson   and all of my clumsiest drives
For the ball   all of my trying to turn
The corner downfield   and my spindling explosions
Through the five-hole over tackle. O backfield

Coach Shag Norton,
Tell me as you never yet have told me
To get the lead out   scream whatever will get
The slow-motion of middle age off me   I cannot
Make it this way   I will have to leave
My feet   they are gone   I have him where
He lives   and down we go singing with screams into

The dirt,
Son-screams of fathers   screams of dead coaches turning
To approval   and from between us the bee rises screaming
With flight   grainily shifting   riding the rail fence
Back into the woods   traffic blasting past us
Unchanged, nothing heard through the air-
conditioning glass   we lying at roadside full

Of the forearm prints
Of roadrocks   strawberries on our elbows as from
Scrimmage with the varsity   now we can get
Up   stand   turn away from the highway   look straight
Into trees. See, there is nothing coming out   no
Smallest wing   no shift of a flight-grain   nothing
Nothing. Let us go in, son, and listen

For some tobacco-
mumbling voice in the branches   to say "That's
a little better,"   to our lives still hanging
By a hair. There is nothing to stop us   we can go
Deep   deeper   into elms, and listen to traffic die
Roaring, like a football crowd from which we have
Vanished. Dead coaches live in the air, son   live

In the ear
Like fathers, and *urge*   and *urge*. They want you better
Than you are. When needed, they rise and curse you   they scream
When something must be saved. Here, under this tree,
We can sit down. You can sleep, and I can try
To give back what I have earned by keeping us
Alive, and safe from bees: the smile of some kind

Of savior—
Of touchdowns, of fumbles, battles,
Lives. Let me sit here with you, son
As on the bench, while the first string takes back
Over, far away   and say with my silentest tongue, with the man-
creating bruises of my arms   with a live leaf a quick
Dead hand on my shoulder, "Coach Norton, I am your boy."

James Dickey (b. 1923)

BECAUSE I COULD NOT STOP FOR DEATH

Because I could not stop for Death,
He kindly stopped for me;
The carriage held but just ourselves
And Immortality.

We slowly drove; he knew no haste,
And I had put away
My labor and my leisure too,
For his civility.

We passed the school, where children strove,
At recess, in the ring,
We passed the fields of gazing grain,
We passed the setting sun.

Or rather, he passed us;
The dews drew quivering and chill;
For only gossamer, my gown;
My tippet, only tulle.

We paused before a house that seemed
A swelling of the ground;

The roof was scarcely visible.
The cornice, in the ground.

Since then, 'tis centuries, and yet
Feels shorter than the day
I first surmised the horses' heads
Were toward eternity.

Emily Dickinson (1830–1886)

MY LIFE HAD STOOD, A LOADED GUN

My life had stood, a loaded gun,
In corners, till a day
The owner passed, identified,
And carried me away.

And now we roam in sovereign woods,
And now we hunt the doe,
And every time I speak for him,
The mountains straight reply.

And do I smile, such cordial light
Upon the valley glow,
It is as a Vesuvian face
Had let its pleasure through.

And when at night, our good day done,
I guard my master's head,
'Tis better than the eider-duck's
Deep pillow, to have shared.

To foe of his I'm deadly foe:
None stir the second time
On whom I lay a yellow eye
Or an emphatic thumb.

Though I than he may longer live,
He longer must than I,
For I have but the power to kill.
Without the power to die.

Emily Dickinson (1830–1886)

THE GOOD-MORROW

I wonder, by my troth, what thou and I
Did till we loved? were we not weaned till then,
But sucked on country pleasures childishly?
Or snorted we in the seven sleepers' den?
'Twas so; but this, all pleasures fancies be.
If ever any beauty I did see,
Which I desired, and got, 'twas but a dream of thee.

And now good-morrow to our waking souls,
Which watch not one another out of fear;
For love all love of other sights controls,
And makes one little room an everywhere.
Let sea-discoverers to new worlds have gone;
Let maps to other,° worlds on worlds have shown   others
Let us possess one world; each hath one, and is one.

My face in thine eye, thine in mine appears,
And true plain hearts do in the faces rest;
Where can we find two better hemispheres
Without sharp north, without declining west?
Whatever dies was not mixed equally;
If our two loves be one, or thou and I
Love so alike that none can slacken, none can die.

John Donne (1572–1631)

THE SUN RISING

Busy old fool, unruly Sun,
Why dost thou thus
Through windows and through curtains call on us?
Must to thy motions lovers' seasons run?
Saucy pedantic wretch, go chide
Late schoolboys and sour prentices,
Go tell court-huntsmen that the king will ride,
Call country ants to harvest offices;
Love, all alike, no season knows, nor clime,
Nor hours, days, months, which are the rags of time.

THE GOOD MORROW. 4. *seven sleepers' den:* a cave where, according to Christian legend, seven youths escaped persecution and slept for two centuries.

Thy beams so reverend and strong
Why shouldst thou think?
I could eclipse and cloud them with a wink,
But that I would not lose her sight so long;
If her eyes have not blinded thine,
Look, and tomorrow late tell me,
Whether both th' Indias of spice and mine
Be where thou left'st them, or lie here with me.
Ask for those kings whom thou saw'st yesterday,
And thou shalt hear, "All here in one bed lay."
She's all states, and all princes I;
Nothing else is.

Princes do but play us; compared to this,
All honor's mimic, all wealth alchemy.
Thou, Sun, art half as happy as we,
In that the world's contracted thus;
Thine age asks ease, and since thy duties be
To warm the world, that's done in warming us.
Shine here to us, and thou art everywhere;
This bed thy center is, these walls thy sphere.

John Donne (1572–1631)

SONG: GO AND CATCH A FALLING STAR

Go and catch a falling star,
Get with child a mandrake root,
Tell me where all past years are,
Or who cleft the devil's foot,
Teach me to hear mermaids singing,
Or to keep off envy's stinging,
And find
What wind
Serves to advance an honest mind.

If thou be'st born to strange sights,
Things invisible to see,
Ride ten thousand days and nights,
Till age snow white hairs on thee,

SONG. 2. *mandrake:* supposed to resemble a human being because of its forked root.

Thou, when thou return'st, wilt tell me
All strange wonders that befell thee,
And swear
No where
Lives a woman true and fair.

If thou find'st one, let me know;
Such a pilgrimage were sweet.
Yet do not; I would not go,
Though at next door we might meet.
Though she were true when you met her,
And last till you write your letter,
Yet she
Will be
False, ere I come, to two or three.

John Donne (1572–1631)

VERGISSMEINICHT

Three weeks gone and the combatants gone,
returning over the nightmare ground
we found the place again, and found
the soldiers sprawling in the sun.

The frowning barrel of his gun
overshadowing. As we came on
that day, he hit my tank with one
like the entry of a demon.

Look. Here in the gunpit spoil
the dishonored picture of his girl
who has put: *Steffi.*° *Vergissmeinicht* — ° a girl's name
in a copybook gothic script.

We see him almost with content
abased, and seeming to have paid
and mocked at by his own equipment
that's hard and good when he's decayed.

VERGISSMEINICHT. The German title means "Forget me not." The author, an English poet, fought with a tank battalion in World War II and was killed in the invasion of Normandy.

But she would weep to see to-day
how on his skin the swart flies move;
the dust upon the paper eye
and the burst stomach like a cave.

For here the lover and killer are mingled
who had one body and one heart.
And death who had the soldier singled
has done the lover mortal hurt.

Keith Douglas (1920–1944)

CONSTANTLY RISKING ABSURDITY

Constantly risking absurdity
and death
whenever he performs
above the heads
of his audience
the poet like an acrobat
climbs on rime
to a high wire of his own making
and balancing on eyebeams
above a sea of faces
paces his way
to the other side of day
performing entrechats
and slight-of-foot tricks
and other high theatrics
and all without mistaking
any thing
for what it may not be
For he's the super realist
who must perforce perceive
taut truth
before the taking of each stance or step
in his supposed advance
toward that still higher perch
where Beauty stands and waits
with gravity
to start her death-defying leap

And he
a little charleychaplin man
who may or may not catch
her fair eternal form
spreadeagled in the empty air
of existence

Lawrence Ferlinghetti (b. 1919)

THE TROLL'S NOSEGAY

A simple nosegay! was that much to ask?
(Winter still nagged, with scarce a bud yet showing.)
He loved her ill, if he resigned the task.
"Somewhere," she cried, "there *must* be blossom blowing."
It seems my lady wept and the troll swore
By Heaven he hated tears: he'd cure her spleen—
Where she had begged one flower he'd shower fourscore,
A bunch fit to amaze a China Queen.

Cold fog-drawn Lily, pale mist-magic Rose
He conjured, and in a glassy cauldron set
With elvish unsubstantial Mignonette
And such vague bloom as wandering dreams enclose.
But she?
Awed,
Charmed to tears,
Distracted,
Yet—
Even yet, perhaps, a trifle piqued—who knows?

Robert Graves (b. 1895)

AFTERWARDS

When the Present has latched its postern behind my tremulous stay,
And the May month flaps its glad green leaves like wings,
Delicate-filmed as new-spun silk, will the neighbors say,
"He was a man who used to notice such things"?

If it be in the dusk when, like an eyelid's soundless blink,
The dewfall-hawk comes crossing the shades to alight
Upon the wind-warped upland thorn, a gazer may think,
"To him this must have been a familiar sight."

If I pass during some nocturnal blackness, mothy and warm,
When the hedgehog travels furtively over the lawn,
One may say, "He strove that such innocent creatures should come to no harm,
But he could do little for them; and now he is gone."

If, when hearing that I have been stilled at last, they stand at the door,
Watching the full-starred heavens that winter sees,
Will this thought rise on those who will meet my face no more,
"He was one who had an eye for such mysteries"?

And will any say when my bell of quittance is heard in the gloom,
And a crossing breeze cuts a pause in its outrollings,
Till they rise again, as they were a new bell's boom,
"He hears it not now, but used to notice such things"?

Thomas Hardy (1840–1928)

THE DARKLING THRUSH

I leant upon a coppice gate
When Frost was specter-gray,
And Winter's dregs made desolate
The weakening eye of day.
The tangled bine-stems scored the sky
Like strings of broken lyres,
And all mankind that haunted nigh
Had sought their household fires.

The land's sharp features seemed to be
The Century's corpse outleant,
His crypt the cloudy canopy,
The wind his death-lament.
The ancient pulse of germ and birth
Was shrunken hard and dry,
And every spirit upon earth
Seemed fervorless as I.

At once a voice arose among
The bleak twigs overhead

In a full-hearted evensong
Of joy illimited;
An aged thrush, frail, gaunt, and small,
In blast-beruffled plume,
Had chosen thus to fling his soul
Upon the growing gloom.

So little cause for carolings
Of such ecstatic sound
Was written on terrestrial things
Afar or nigh around,
That I could think there trembled through
His happy good-night air
Some blessed Hope, whereof he knew
And I was unaware.

December 1900.

Thomas Hardy (1840–1928)

REDEMPTION

Having been tenant long to a rich Lord,
Not thriving, I resolvèd to be bold,
And make a suit unto him, to afford
A new small-rented lease and cancel the old.
In heaven at his manor I him sought:
They told me there that he was lately gone
About some land which he had dearly bought
Long since on earth, to take possession.
I straight returned, and knowing his great birth,
Sought him accordingly in great resorts;
In cities, theaters, gardens, parks, and courts:
At length I heard a ragged noise and mirth
Of thieves and murderers; there I him espied,
Who straight, "Your suit is granted," said, and died.

George Herbert (1593–1633)

EVE

Eve, with her basket, was
Deep in the bells and grass
Wading in bells and grass
Up to her knees,

Picking a dish of sweet
Berries and plums to eat,
Down in the bells and grass
Under the trees.

Mute as a mouse in a
Corner the cobra lay,
Curled round a bough of the
Cinnamon tall . . .
Now to get even and
Humble proud heaven and
Now was the moment or
Never at all.

"Eva!" Each syllable
Light as a flower fell,
"Eva!" he whispered the
Wondering maid,
Soft as a bubble sung
Out of a linnet's lung,
Soft and most silverly
"Eva!" he said.

Picture that orchard sprite,
Eve, with her body white,
Supple and smooth to her
Slim finger tips,
Wondering, listening,
Listening, wondering,
Eve with a berry
Half-way to her lips.

Oh had our simple Eve
Seen through the make-believe!
Had she but known the
Pretender he was!
Out of the boughs he came,
Whispering still her name,
Tumbling in twenty rings
Into the grass.

Here was the strangest pair
In the world anywhere,

Eve in the bells and grass
Kneeling, and he
Telling his story low . . .
Singing birds saw them go
Down the dark path to
The Blasphemous Tree.

Oh, what a clatter when
Titmouse and Jenny Wren
Saw him successful and
Taking his leave!
How the birds rated him,
How they all hated him!
How they all pitied
Poor motherless Eve!

Picture her crying
Outside in the lane,
Eve, with no dish of sweet
Berries and plums to eat,
Haunting the gate of the
Orchard in vain . . .
Picture the lewd delight
Under the hill tonight—
"Eva!" the toast goes round,
"Eva!" again.

Ralph Hodgson (1872–1962)

AN OLD PHOTO IN AN OLD LIFE

A squad of soldiers lies beside a river.
They're in China—see the brimmed gables piled
On the pagoda. The rows of trees are lopped
And the Chinese soldiers have been stopped
In their tracks. Their bodies lie
In bodily postures of the dead,

Arms bound, legs akimbo and askew,
But look how independently their heads
Lie thereabouts, some upright, some of the heads
Tipped on their sides or standing on their heads.

Mostly, the eyes are open
And their mouths twisted in a sort of smile.

Some seem to be saying or just to have said
Some message in Chinese just as the blade
Nicked the sunlight and the head dropped
Like a sliced canteloupe to the ground, the cropped
Body twisting from the execution block.
And see, there kneels the executioner

Wiping his scimitar upon a torso's ripped
Sash. At ease, the victors smoke. A gash
Of throats darkens the riverbed. 1900. The Boxer
Rebellion. Everyone there is dead now.
What was it those unbodied mouths were saying?
A million arteries stain the Yellow River.

Daniel Hoffman (b. 1923)

AGONY COLUMN

Sir George and Lady Cepheus of Upper Slaughter
Desire to announce to family and friends
That the death has been arranged of their only daughter
Andromeda, aged twenty—Sir George intends

To avoid undesirable pomp and ostentation:
A simple ceremony, a quiet funeral feast
And the usual speeches; a train will leave the station
For the Virgin's Rock at four. No flowers by Request!

Owing to the informal nature of the occasion
Guests are requested to wear ordinary dress.
It is hoped that, in view of Sir George's official station
The event will be treated discreetly by the press.

In accord with religious custom and public duty,
The populace is expected to maintain order and quiet;
But, because of her daughter's quite exceptional beauty
And numerous suitors, to discourage scandal or riot,

Lady Cepheus wishes it to be distinctly stated
That any attempt at rescue has been banned;

Offenders will be summarily emasculated;
Heroes are warned: the police have the matter in hand.

As the victim is to be chained wearing only her skin,
The volunteer armorers will be blinded at once.
On the following morning her lovers and next-of-kin
May assist in gathering any remaining bones.

A. D. Hope (b. 1907)

THE CAGED SKYLARK

As a dare-gale skylark scanted in a dull cage
  Man's mounting spirit in his bone-house, mean house, dwells—
  That bird beyond the remembering his free fells;
This in drudgery, day-laboring-out life's age.

Though aloft on turf or perch or poor low stage,
  Both sing sometimes the sweetest, sweetest spells,
  Yet both droop deadly sometimes in their cells
Or wring their barriers in bursts of fear or rage.

Not that the sweet-fowl, song-fowl, needs no rest—
Why, hear him, hear him babble and drop down to his nest,
  But his own nest, wild nest, no prison.

Man's spirit will be flesh-bound when found at best,
But uncumbered: meadow-down is not distressed
  For a rainbow footing it nor he for his bones risen.

Gerard Manley Hopkins (1844–1889)

TO AN ATHLETE DYING YOUNG

The time you won your town the race
We chaired you through the market-place;
Man and boy stood cheering by,
And home we brought you shoulder-high.

To-day, the road all runners come,
Shoulder-high we bring you home,
And set you at your threshold down,
Townsman of a stiller town.

Smart lad, to slip betimes away
From fields where glory does not stay
And early though the laurel grows
It withers quicker than the rose.

Eyes the shady night has shut
Cannot see the record cut,
And silence sounds no worse than cheers
After earth has stopped the ears:

Now you will not swell the rout
Of lads that wore their honors out,
Runners whom renown outran
And the name died before the man.

So set, before its echoes fade,
The fleet foot on the sill of shade,
And hold to the low lintel up
The still-defended challenge-cup.

And round that early-laurelled head
Will flock to gaze the strengthless dead,
And find unwithered on its curls
The garland briefer than a girl's.

A. E. Housman (1859–1936)

VIEW OF A PIG

The pig lay on a barrow dead.
It weighed, they said, as much as three men.
Its eyes closed, pink white eyelashes.
Its trotters stuck straight out.

Such weight and thick pink bulk
Set in death seemed not just dead.
It was less than lifeless, further off.
It was like a sack of wheat.

I thumped it without feeling remorse.
One feels guilty insulting the dead,
Walking on graves. But this pig
Did not seem able to accuse.

It was too dead. Just so much
A poundage of lard and pork.
Its last dignity had entirely gone.
It was not a figure of fun.

Too dead now to pity.
To remember its life, din, stronghold
Of earthly pleasure as it had been,
Seemed a false effort, and off the point.

Too deadly factual. Its weight
Oppressed me—how could it be moved?
And the trouble of cutting it up!
The gash in its throat was shocking, but not pathetic.

Once I ran at a fair in the noise
To catch a greased piglet
That was faster and nimbler than a cat,
Its squeal was the rending of metal.

Pigs must have hot blood, they feel like ovens.
Their bite is worse than a horse's—
They chop a half-moon clean out.
They eat cinders, dead cats.

Distinctions and admirations such
As this one was long finished with.
I stared at it a long time. They were going to scald it,
Scald it and scour it like a doorstep.

Ted Hughes (b. 1930)

THE DEATH OF THE BALL TURRET GUNNER

From my mother's sleep I fell into the State,
And I hunched in its belly till my wet fur froze.
Six miles from earth, loosed from its dream of life,
I woke to black flak and the nightmare fighters.
When I died they washed me out of the turret with a hose.

Randall Jarrell (1914–1965)

ODE ON A GRECIAN URN

Thou still unravished bride of quietness,
Thou foster-child of silence and slow time,
Sylvan historian, who canst thus express
A flowery tale more sweetly than our rhyme:
What leaf-fringed legend haunts about thy shape
Of deities or mortals, or of both,
In Tempe or the dales of Arcady?
What men or gods are these? What maidens loth?
What mad pursuit? What struggle to escape?
What pipes and timbrels? What wild ecstasy?

Heard melodies are sweet, but those unheard
Are sweeter; therefore, ye soft pipes, play on;
Not to the sensual ear, but, more endeared,
Pipe to the spirit ditties of no tone:
Fair youth, beneath the trees, thou canst not leave
Thy song, nor ever can those trees be bare;
Bold Lover, never, never canst thou kiss,
Though winning near the goal—yet, do not grieve;
She cannot fade, though thou hast not thy bliss,
For ever wilt thou love, and she be fair!

Ah, happy, happy boughs! that cannot shed
Your leaves, nor ever bid the Spring adieu;
And, happy melodist, unwearied,
For ever piping songs for ever new;
More happy love! more happy, happy love!
For ever warm and still to be enjoyed,
For ever panting and for ever young;
All breathing human passion far above,
That leaves a heart high-sorrowful and cloyed,
A burning forehead, and a parching tongue.

Who are these coming to the sacrifice?
To what green altar, O mysterious priest,

ODE ON A GRECIAN URN. 49–50. In the 1820 edition of Keats's poems the words "Beauty is truth, truth beauty" were enclosed in quotation marks. Critics have disagreed as to whether only this statement is uttered by the Urn, with the remainder of the poem spoken *to* the Urn (or the figures on the Urn) by the speaker of the poem; or whether the entire last two lines are spoken by the Urn.

Lead'st thou that heifer lowing at the skies,
And all her silken flanks with garlands drest?
What little town by river or sea shore,
Or mountain-built with peaceful citadel,
Is emptied of its folks, this pious morn?
And, little town, thy streets for evermore
Will silent be; and not a soul to tell
Why thou art desolate, can e'er return.

O Attic shape! Fair attitude! with brede
Of marble men and maidens overwrought,
With forest branches and the trodden weed;
Thou, silent form, dost tease us out of thought
As doth eternity: Cold Pastoral!
When old age shall this generation waste,
Thou shalt remain, in midst of other woe
Than ours, a friend to man, to whom thou say'st,
Beauty is truth, truth beauty,—that is all
Ye know on earth, and all ye need to know.

John Keats (1795–1821)

ODE TO A NIGHTINGALE

I

My heart aches, and a drowsy numbness pains
My sense, as though of hemlock° I had drunk, a poisonous drink
Or emptied some dull opiate to the drains
One minute past, and Lethe-wards had sunk:
'Tis not through envy of thy happy lot,
But being too happy in thine happiness,—
That thou, light-wingèd Dryad° of the trees, a wood nymph
In some melodious plot
Of beechen green, and shadows numberless,
Singest of summer in full-throated ease.

2

O, for a draught of vintage! that hath been
Cooled a long age in the deep-delvèd earth,

ODE TO A NIGHTINGALE. 4. *Lethe:* river of forgetfulness in the Greek underworld. 14. *Provençal:* Provence, a wine-growing region in southern France famous, in the Middle Ages, for troubadours. 16. *Hippocrene:* fountain of the Muses on Mt. Helicon in Greece. 32. *Bacchus . . . pards:* Bacchus, god of wine, had a chariot drawn by leopards. 66. *Ruth:* see Bible, Ruth 2.

Tasting of Flora° and the country green, — goddess of flowers
Dance, and Provençal song, and sunburnt mirth!
O for a beaker full of the warm South,
Full of the true, the blushful Hippocrene,
With beaded bubbles winking at the brim,
And purple-stainèd mouth;
That I might drink, and leave the world unseen,
And with thee fade away into the forest dim:

3

Fade far away, dissolve, and quite forget
What thou among the leaves hast never known,
The weariness, the fever, and the fret
Here, where men sit and hear each other groan;
Where palsy shakes a few, sad, last gray hairs,
Where youth grows pale, and specter-thin, and dies;
Where but to think is to be full of sorrow
And leaden-eyed despairs,
Where Beauty cannot keep her lustrous eyes,
Or new Love pine at them beyond to-morrow.

4

Away! away! for I will fly to thee,
Not charioted by Bacchus and his pards,
But on the viewless° wings of Poesy, — invisible
Though the dull brain perplexes and retards:
Already with thee! tender is the night,
And haply the Queen-Moon is on her throne,
Clustered around by all her starry Fays;
But here there is no light,
Save what from heaven is with the breezes blown
Through verdurous glooms and winding mossy ways.

5

I cannot see what flowers are at my feet,
Nor what soft incense hangs upon the boughs,
But, in embalmèd° darkness, guess each sweet — perfumed
Wherewith the seasonable month endows

The grass, the thicket, and the fruit-tree wild;
White hawthorn, and the pastoral eglantine;
Fast fading violets covered up in leaves;
And mid-May's eldest child,
The coming musk-rose, full of dewy wine,
The murmurous haunt of flies on summer eves.

6

Darkling° I listen; and, for many a time — in darkness
I have been half in love with easeful Death,
Called him soft names in many a musèd rhyme,
To take into the air my quiet breath;
Now more than ever seems it rich to die,
To cease upon the midnight with no pain,
While thou art pouring forth thy soul abroad
In such an ecstasy!
Still wouldst thou sing, and I have ears in vain—
To thy high requiem become a sod.

7

Thou wast not born for death, immortal Bird!
No hungry generations tread thee down;
The voice I hear this passing night was heard
In ancient days by emperor and clown:
Perhaps the self-same song that found a path
Through the sad heart of Ruth, when, sick for home,
She stood in tears amid the alien corn;
The same that oft-times hath
Charmed magic casements, opening on the foam
Of perilous seas, in faery lands forlorn.

8

Forlorn! the very word is like a bell
To toll me back from thee to my sole self!
Adieu! the fancy cannot cheat so well
As she is fained to do, deceiving elf.
Adieu! adieu! thy plaintive anthem fades
Past the near meadows, over the still stream,

Up the hill-side; and now 'tis buried deep
In the next valley-glades:
Was it a vision, or a waking dream?
Fled is that music:—Do I wake or sleep?

John Keats (1795–1821)

CHURCH GOING

Once I am sure there's nothing going on
I step inside, letting the door thud shut.
Another church: matting, seats, and stone,
And little books; sprawlings of flowers, cut
For Sunday, brownish now; some brass and stuff
Up at the holy end; the small neat organ;
And a tense, musty, unignorable silence,
Brewed God knows how long. Hatless, I take off
My cycle-clips in awkward reverence,

Move forward, run my hand around the font.
From where I stand, the roof looks almost new—
Cleaned, or restored? Someone would know: I don't.
Mounting the lectern, I peruse a few
Hectoring large-scale verses, and pronounce
"Here endeth" much more loudly than I'd meant.
The echoes snigger briefly. Back at the door
I sign the book, donate an Irish sixpence,
Reflect the place was not worth stopping for.

Yet stop I did: in fact I often do,
And always end much at a loss like this,
Wondering what to look for; wondering, too,
When churches fall completely out of use
What we shall turn them into, if we shall keep
A few cathedrals chronically on show,
Their parchment, plate and pyx in locked cases,
And let the rest rent-free to rain and sheep.
Shall we avoid them as unlucky places?

Or, after dark, will dubious women come
To make their children touch a particular stone;
Pick simples for a cancer; or on some
Advised night see walking a dead one?

Power of some sort or other will go on
In games, in riddles, seemingly at random;
But superstition, like belief, must die,
And what remains when disbelief has gone?
Grass, weedy pavement, brambles, buttress, sky,

A shape less recognizable each week,
A purpose more obscure. I wonder who
Will be the last, the very last, to seek
This place for what it was; one of the crew
That tap and jot and know what rood-lofts were?
Some ruin-bibber, randy° for antique, wild, lustful
Or Christmas-addict, counting on a whiff
Of gowns-and-bands and organ-pipes and myrrh?
Or will he be my representative,

Bored, uninformed, knowing the ghostly silt
Dispersed, yet tending to this cross of ground
Through suburb scrub because it held unspilt
So long and equably what since is found
Only in separation—marriage, and birth,
And death, and thoughts of these—for which was built
This special shell? For though I've no idea
What this accoutred frowsty barn is worth,
It pleases me to stand in silence here;

A serious house on serious earth it is,
In whose blent air all our compulsions meet,
Are recognized, and robed as destinies.
And that much never can be obsolete,
Since someone will forever be surprising
A hunger in himself to be more serious,
And gravitating with it to this ground,
Which, he once heard, was proper to grow wise in,
If only that so many dead lie round.

Philip Larkin (b. 1922)

CITY LIFE

When I am in a great city, I know that I despair.
I know there is no hope for us, death waits, it is useless to care.

For oh the poor people, that are flesh of my flesh,
I, that am flesh of their flesh,
when I see the iron hooked into their faces
their poor, their fearful faces
I scream in my soul, for I know I cannot
take the iron hooks out of their faces, that make them so drawn,
nor cut the invisible wires of steel that pull them
back and forth, to work,
back and forth to work,
like fearful and corpse-like fishes hooked and being played
by some malignant fisherman on an unseen shore
where he does not choose to land them yet, hooked fishes of
the factory world.

D. H. Lawrence (1885–1930)

LOSING TRACK

Long after you have swung back
away from me
I think you are still with me:

you come in close to the shore
on the tide
and nudge me awake the way

a boat adrift nudges the pier:
am I a pier
half-in half-out of the water?

and in the pleasure of that communion
I lose track,
the moon I watch goes down, the

tide swings you away before
I know I'm
alone again long since,

mud sucking at gray and black
timbers of me,
a light growth of green dreams drying.

Denise Levertov (b. 1923)

SHEEPDOG TRIALS IN HYDE PARK

A shepherd stands at one end of the arena.
Five sheep are unpenned at the other. His dog runs out
In a curve to behind them, fetches them straight to the shepherd,
Then drives the flock round a triangular course
Through a couple of gates and back to his master; two
Must be sorted there from the flock, then all five penned.
Gathering, driving away, shedding and penning
Are the plain words for a miraculous game.

An abstract game. What can the sheepdog make of such
Simplified terrain?—no hills, dales, bogs, walls, tracks,
Only a quarter-mile plain of grass, dumb crowds
Like crowds on hoardings around it, and behind them
Traffic or mounds of lovers and children playing.
Well, the dog is no landscape-fancier; his whole concern
Is with his master's whistle, and of course
With the flock—sheep are sheep anywhere for him.

The sheep are the chanciest element. Why, for instance,
Go through this gate when there's on either side of it
No wall or hedge but huge and viable space?
Why not eat the grass instead of being pushed around it?
Like blobs of quicksilver on a tilting board
The flock erratically runs, dithers, breaks up,
Is reassembled: their ruling idea is the dog;
And behind the dog, though they know it not yet, is a shepherd.

The shepherd knows that time is of the essence
But haste calamitous. Between dog and sheep
There is always an ideal distance, a perfect angle;
But these are constantly varying, so the man
Should anticipate each move through the dog, his medium.
The shepherd is the brain behind the dog's brain,
But his control of dog, like dog's of sheep,
Is never absolute—that's the beauty of it

For beautiful it is. The guided missiles,
The black-and-white angels follow each quirk and jink of
The evasive sheep, play grandmother's steps behind them,
Freeze to the ground, or leap to head off a straggler
Almost before it knows that it wants to stray,
As if radar-controlled. But they are not machines—

SHEEPDOG TRIALS IN HYDE PARK. This poem may be compared or contrasted with the story by Eric Knight, "Flurry at the Sheep Dog Trial," page 285.

You can feel them feeling mastery, doubt, chagrin:
Machines don't frolic when their job is done.

What's needfully done in the solitude of sheep-runs—
Those tough, real tasks—become this stylized game,
A demonstration of intuitive wit
Kept natural by the saving grace of error.
To lift, to fetch, to drive, to shed, to pen
Are acts I recognize, with all they mean
Of shepherding the unruly, for a kind of
Controlled woolgathering is my work too.

C. Day Lewis (1904–1972)

ON THE LATE MASSACRE IN PIEMONT

Avenge, O Lord, thy slaughtered saints, whose bones
  Lie scattered on the Alpine mountains cold,
  Even them who kept thy truth so pure of old
  When all our fathers worshiped stocks and stones,
Forget not; in thy book record their groans
  Who were thy sheep, and in their ancient fold
  Slain by the bloody Piemontese that rolled
  Mother with infant down the rocks. Their moans
The vales redoubled to the hills, and they
  To heaven. Their martyred blood and ashes sow
  O'er all the Italian fields, where still doth sway
The triple tyrant, that from these may grow
  A hundredfold, who, having learnt thy way,
  Early may fly the Babylonian woe.

John Milton (1608–1674)

ON THE LATE MASSACRE IN PIEMONT. This poem has for its background the bitter religious struggles between Protestants and Roman Catholics during the late Reformation. When, in 1655, the soldiers of an Italian Catholic duke massacred a group of Waldensian Protestants in Piedmont (in Northern Italy), Milton, a Puritan poet, wrote this sonnet. 4. *stocks and stones:* wooden and stone images in English churches before England turned Protestant. 12. *triple tyrant:* the pope, who wore a triple crown. 14. *Babylonian:* Babylon in the Bible is associated with idolatry, pagan luxury, and abuse of power.

A CARRIAGE FROM SWEDEN

They say there is a sweeter air
    where it was made, than we have here;
    a Hamlet's castle atmosphere.
At all events there is in Brooklyn
something that makes me feel at home.

No one may see this put-away
    museum-piece, this country cart
    that inner happiness made art;
and yet, in this city of freckled
integrity it is a vein

of resined straightness from north-wind
    hardened Sweden's once-opposed-to-
    compromise archipelago
of rocks. Washington and Gustavus
Adolphus, forgive our decay.

Seats, dashboard and sides of smooth gourd-
    rind texture, a flowered step, swan-
    dart brake, and swirling crustacean-
tailed equine amphibious creatures
that garnish the axle-tree! What

a fine thing! What unannoying
    romance! And how beautiful, she
    with the natural stoop of the
snowy egret, gray-eyed and straight-haired,
for whom it should come to the door—

of whom it reminds me. The split
    pine fair hair, steady gannet-clear
    eyes and the pine-needled-path deer-
swift step; that is Sweden, land of the
free and the soil for a spruce-tree—

A CARRIAGE FROM SWEDEN. 14–15. *Gustavus Adolphus:* Swedish king and military hero (1594–1632). 35. *Denmark's sanctuaried Jews:* Many Jewish refugees fled to Sweden after the German invasion of Denmark in World War II. 52. *Dalen light-house:* Gustaf Dalén, Swedish scientist, won a Nobel Prize in 1912 chiefly for his invention of an automatic regulator, responsive to the sun's rays, for turning on and off the gas lights used in marine buoys and beacons and in railway signals.

vertical though a seedling—all
needles: from a green trunk, green shelf
on shelf fanning out by itself.
The deft white-stockinged dance in thick-soled
shoes! Denmark's sanctuaried Jews!

The puzzle-jugs and hand-spun rugs,
the root-legged kracken° shaped like dogs, wooden
the hanging buttons and the frogs stools
that edge the Sunday jackets! Sweden,
you have a runner called the Deer, who

when he's won a race, likes to run
more; you have the sun-right gable-
ends due east and west, the table
spread as for a banquet; and the put-
in twin vest-pleats with a fish-fin

effect when you need none. Sweden,
what makes the people dress that way
and those who see you wish to stay?
The runner, not too tired to run more
at the end of the race? And that

cart, dolphin-graceful? A Dalen
lighthouse, self-lit?—responsive and
responsible. I understand;
it's not pine-needle-paths that give spring
when they're run on, it's a Sweden

of moated white castles—the bed
of white flowers densely grown in an S
meaning Sweden and stalwartness,
skill, and a surface that says
Made in Sweden: carts are my trade.

Marianne Moore (1887–1972)

THE HORSES

Barely a twelvemonth after
The seven days war that put the world to sleep,
Late in the evening the strange horses came.

By then we had made our covenant with silence,
But in the first few days it was so still
We listened to our breathing and were afraid.
On the second day
The radios failed; we turned the knobs; no answer.
On the third day a warship passed us, heading north,
Dead bodies piled on the deck. On the sixth day
A plane plunged over us into the sea. Thereafter
Nothing. The radios dumb;
And still they stand in corners of our kitchens,
And stand, perhaps, turned on, in a million rooms
All over the world. But now if they should speak,
If on a sudden they should speak again,
If on the stroke of noon a voice should speak,
We would not listen, we would not let it bring
That old bad world that swallowed its children quick
At one great gulp. We would not have it again.
Sometimes we think of the nations lying asleep,
Curled blindly in impenetrable sorrow,
And then the thought confounds us with its strangeness.

The tractors lie about our fields; at evening
They look like dank sea-monsters couched and waiting.
We leave them where they are and let them rust:
"They'll moulder away and be like other loam."
We make our oxen drag our rusty ploughs,
Long laid aside. We have gone back
Far past our fathers' land.

And then, that evening
Late in the summer the strange horses came.
We heard a distant tapping on the road,
A deepening drumming; it stopped, went on again
And at the corner changed to hollow thunder.
We saw the heads
Like a wild wave charging and were afraid.
We had sold our horses in our fathers' time
To buy new tractors. Now they were strange to us
As fabulous steeds set on an ancient shield
Or illustrations in a book of knights.

We did not dare go near them. Yet they waited,
Stubborn and shy, as if they had been sent
By an old command to find our whereabouts
And that long-lost archaic companionship.
In the first moment we had never a thought
That they were creatures to be owned and used.
Among them were some half-a-dozen colts
Dropped in some wilderness of the broken world,
Yet new as if they had come from their own Eden.
Since then they have pulled our ploughs and borne our loads,
But that free servitude still can pierce our hearts.
Our life is changed; their coming our beginning.

Edwin Muir (1887–1959)

LOVE POEM

My clumsiest dear, whose hands shipwreck vases,
At whose quick touch all glasses chip and ring,
Whose palms are bulls in china, burs in linen,
And have no cunning with any soft thing

Except all ill-at-ease fidgeting people:
The refugee uncertain at the door
You make at home; deftly you steady
The drunk clambering on his undulant floor.

Unpredictable dear, the taxi drivers' terror,
Shrinking from far headlights pale as a dime
Yet leaping before red apoplectic streetcars—
Misfit in any space. And never on time.

A wrench in clocks and the solar system. Only
With words and people and love you move at ease.
In traffic of wit expertly manoeuvre
And keep us, all devotion, at your knees.

Forgetting your coffee spreading on our flannel,
Your lipstick grinning on our coat,
So gayly in love's unbreakable heaven
Our souls on glory of spilt bourbon float.

Be with me, darling, early and late. Smash glasses—
I will study wry music for your sake.
For should your hands drop white and empty
All the toys of the world would break.

John Frederick Nims (b. 1914)

EPISTLE TO A YOUNG LADY, ON HER LEAVING THE TOWN AFTER THE CORONATION

As some fond virgin, whom her mother's care
Drags from the town to wholesome country air,
Just when she learns to roll a melting eye,
And hear a spark,° yet think no danger nigh— beau
From the dear man unwilling she must sever,
Yet takes one kiss before she parts forever—
Thus from the world fair Zephalinda flew,
Saw others happy, and with sighs withdrew;
Not that their pleasures caused her discontent:
She sighed not that they stayed, but that she went.
She went—to plain-work and to purling brooks,
Old-fashioned halls, dull aunts, and croaking rooks;
She went from opera, park, assembly, play,
To morning walks, and prayers three hours a day;
To part her time 'twixt reading and bohea,° black tea
To muse, and spill her solitary tea;
Or o'er cold coffee trifle with the spoon,
Count the slow clock, and dine exact at noon;
Divert her eyes with pictures in the fire,
Hum half a tune, tell stories to the squire;
Up to her godly garret after seven,
There starve and pray, for that's the way to heaven.

EPISTLE TO A YOUNG LADY. The young lady, whom Pope here calls *Zephalinda* (7), was in actuality his good friend Teresa Blount, and *Parthenia* (46) was his even better friend, her younger sister, Martha. *Your slave* (41) is Pope himself, and *Gay* (47) is the poet John Gay, also a good friend of Pope's. The coronation was that of George I in 1714.

Some squire, perhaps, you take delight to rack,
Whose game is "whisk,"° whose treat a toast in sack; whist
Who visits with a gun, presents you birds,
Then gives a smacking buss, and cries, "No words!"
Or with his hound comes hollowing from the stable,
Makes love with nods, and knees beneath a table;
Whose laughs are hearty, though his jests are coarse,
And loves you best of all things—but his horse.
In some fair evening, on your elbow laid,
You dream of triumphs in the rural shade;
In pensive thought recall the fancied scene,
See coronations rise on every green:
Before you pass the imaginary sights
Of Lords, and Earls, and Dukes, and gartered Knights,
While the spread fan o'ershades your closing eyes,
Then gives one flirt, and all the vision flies.
Thus vanish sceptres, coronets, and balls,
And leave you in lone woods, or empty walls!
So when your slave, at some dear idle time
(Not plagued with headaches, or the want of rhyme)
Stands in the streets, abstracted from the crew,
And while he seems to study, thinks of you;
Just when his fancy paints your sprightly eyes,
Or sees the blush of soft Parthenia rise,
Gay pats my shoulder, and you vanish quite,
Streets, chairs,° and coxcombs rush upon my sight. sedan chairs
Vexed to be still in town, I knit my brow,
Look sour, and hum a tune—as you may now.

Alexander Pope (1688–1744)

PORTRAIT D'UNE FEMME

Your mind and you are our Sargasso Sea,
London has swept about you this score years
And bright ships left you this or that in fee:
Ideas, old gossip, oddments of all things,
Strange spars of knowledge and dimmed wares of price.
Great minds have sought you—lacking someone else.
You have been second always. Tragical?

No. You preferred it to the usual thing:
One dull man, dulling and uxorious,
One average mind—with one thought less, each year.
Oh, you are patient. I have seen you sit
Hours, where something might have floated up.
And now you pay one. Yes, you richly pay.
You are a person of some interest, one comes to you
And takes strange gain away:
Trophies fished up; some curious suggestion;
Fact that leads nowhere; and a tale or two,
Pregnant with mandrakes, or with something else
That might prove useful and yet never proves,
That never fits a corner or shows use,
Or finds its hour upon the loom of days:
The tarnished, gaudy, wonderful old work;
Idols, and ambergris and rare inlays.
These are your riches, your great store; and yet
For all this sea-hoard of deciduous things,
Strange woods half sodden, and new brighter stuff:
In the slow float of differing light and deep,
No! there is nothing! In the whole and all,
Nothing that's quite your own.
Yet this is you.

Ezra Pound (1885–1972)

THE MILL

The miller's wife had waited long,
The tea was cold, the fire was dead;
And there might yet be nothing wrong
In how he went and what he said:
"There are no millers any more,"
Was all that she had heard him say;
And he had lingered at the door
So long that it seemed yesterday.
Sick with a fear that had no form
She knew that she was there at last;
And in the mill there was a warm
And mealy fragrance of the past.

What else there was would only seem
To say again what he had meant;
And what was hanging from a beam
Would not have heeded where she went.

And if she thought it followed her,
She may have reasoned in the dark
That one way of the few there were
Would hide her and would leave no mark:
Black water, smooth above the weir
Like starry velvet in the night,
Though ruffled once, would soon appear
The same as ever to the sight.

Edwin Arlington Robinson (1869–1935)

MR. FLOOD'S PARTY

Old Eben Flood, climbing alone one night
Over the hill between the town below
And the forsaken upland hermitage
That held as much as he should ever know
On earth again of home, paused warily.
The road was his with not a native near;
And Eben, having leisure, said aloud,
For no man else in Tilbury Town to hear:

"Well, Mr. Flood, we have the harvest moon
Again, and we may not have many more;
The bird is on the wing, the poet says,
And you and I have said it here before.
Drink to the bird." He raised up to the light
The jug that he had gone so far to fill,
And answered huskily: "Well, Mr. Flood,
Since you propose it, I believe I will."

MR. FLOOD'S PARTY. 11. *bird:* Mr. Flood is quoting from *The Rubáiyát of Omar Khayyám,* "The bird of Time . . . is on the wing." 20. *Roland:* hero of the French epic poem *The Song of Roland*. He died fighting a rearguard action for Charlemagne against the Moors in Spain; before his death he sounded a call for help on his famous horn, but the king's army arrived too late.

Alone, as if enduring to the end
A valiant armor of scarred hopes outworn,
He stood there in the middle of the road
Like Roland's ghost winding a silent horn.
Below him, in the town among the trees,
Where friends of other days had honored him,
A phantom salutation of the dead
Rang thinly till old Eben's eyes were dim.

Then, as a mother lays her sleeping child
Down tenderly, fearing it may awake,
He set the jug down slowly at his feet
With trembling care, knowing that most things break;
And only when assured that on firm earth
It stood, as the uncertain lives of men
Assuredly did not, he paced away,
And with his hand extended paused again:

"Well, Mr. Flood, we have not met like this
In a long time; and many a change has come
To both of us, I fear, since last it was
We had a drop together. Welcome home!"
Convivially returning with himself,
Again he raised the jug up to the light;
And with an acquiescent quaver said:
"Well, Mr. Flood, if you insist, I might.

"Only a very little, Mr. Flood—
For auld lang syne. No more, sir; that will do."
So, for the time, apparently it did,
And Eben evidently thought so too;
For soon amid the silver loneliness
Of night he lifted up his voice and sang,
Secure, with only two moons listening,
Until the whole harmonious landscape rang—

"For auld lang syne." The weary throat gave out,
The last word wavered, and the song was done.
He raised again the jug regretfully
And shook his head, and was again alone.
There was not much that was ahead of him,

And there was nothing in the town below—
Where strangers would have shut the many doors
That many friends had opened long ago.

Edwin Arlington Robinson (1869–1935)

I KNEW A WOMAN

I knew a woman, lovely in her bones,
When small birds sighed, she would sigh back at them;
Ah, when she moved, she moved more ways than one:
The shapes a bright container can contain!
Of her choice virtues only gods should speak,
Or English poets who grew up on Greek
(I'd have them sing in chorus, cheek to cheek).

How well her wishes went! She stroked my chin,
She taught me Turn, and Counter-turn, and Stand;
She taught me Touch, that undulant white skin;
I nibbled meekly from her proffered hand;
She was the sickle; I, poor I, the rake,
Coming behind her for her pretty sake
(But what prodigious mowing we did make).

Love likes a gander, and adores a goose:
Her full lips pursed, the errant note to seize;
She played it quick, she played it light and loose;
My eyes, they dazzled at her flowing knees;
Her several parts could keep a pure repose,
Or one hip quiver with a mobile nose
(She moved in circles, and those circles moved).

Let seed be grass, and grass turn into hay:
I'm martyr to a motion not my own;
What's freedom for? To know eternity.
I swear she cast a shadow white as stone.
But who would count eternity in days?
These old bones live to learn her wanton ways:
(I measure time by how a body sways).

Theodore Roethke (1908–1963)

THE WAKING

I wake to sleep, and take my waking slow.
I feel my fate in what I cannot fear.
I learn by going where I have to go.

We think by feeling. What is there to know?
I hear my being dance from ear to ear.
I wake to sleep, and take my waking slow.

Of those so close beside me, which are you?
God bless the Ground! I shall walk softly there,
And learn by going where I have to go.

Light takes the Tree; but who can tell us how?
The lowly worm climbs up a winding stair;
I wake to sleep, and take my waking slow.

Great Nature has another thing to do
To you and me; so take the lively air,
And, lovely, learn by going where to go.

This shaking keeps me steady. I should know.
What falls away is always. And is near.
I wake to sleep, and take my waking slow.
I learn by going where I have to go.

Theodore Roethke (1908–1963)

UNDERWATER

Underwater, this is the cathedral
sea. Diving, our bubbles rise
as prayers are said to do, and burst
into our natural atmosphere—
occupying, from this perspective,
the position of a heaven.

The ceiling is silver, and the air
deep green translucency. The worshippers
pray quietly, wave their fins.
You can see the color of their prayer
deep within their throats: scarlet, some,
and some, fine scaled vermilion; others

pass tight-lipped with moustaches
trailing and long paunches, though
they are almost wafer-thin seen sideways,
or unseen except for whiskers.
Further down, timorous sea-spiders slam
their doors, shy fish disappear

into their tenement of holes, and eels
warn that they have serpent tails.
Deep is wild, with beasts one meets
usually in dreams. Here the giant octopus
drags in its arms. We meet it.
We are hungry in the upper air, and you

have the sea-spear that shoots deep;
you fire accurately, raising a conflagration
of black ink. The animal grabs stone
in slow motion, pulls far under a ledge
and piles the loose rock there as if
to hide might be enough. It holds tight,

builds sanctuary, and I think cries
"sanctuary!"—it dies at your second shot.
We come aboveboard then, with our eight-armed
dinner and no hunger left, pursued by the bland
eyes of fish who couldn't care, by black
water and the death we made there.

Michael Schmidt (b. 1947)

FEAR NO MORE

Fear no more the heat o' the sun,
    Nor the furious winter's rages;
Thou thy worldly task hast done,
    Home art gone, and ta'en thy wages.
Golden lads and girls all must,
As chimney-sweepers, come to dust.

Fear no more the frown o' the great;
    Thou art past the tyrant's stroke;
Care no more to clothe and eat;
    To thee the reed is as the oak.

The scepter, learning, physic,° must   art of healing
All follow this, and come to dust.

Fear no more the lightning-flash,
  Nor the all-dreaded thunder-stone;°   thunderbolt
Fear not slander, censure rash;
  Thou hast finished joy and moan.
All lovers young, all lovers must
Consign to thee,° and come to dust.   yield to your condition

William Shakespeare (1564–1616)

LET ME NOT TO THE MARRIAGE OF TRUE MINDS

Let me not to the marriage of true minds
Admit impediments. Love is not love
Which alters when it alteration finds,
Or bends with the remover to remove.
O no! it is an ever-fixèd mark
That looks on tempests and is never shaken;
It is the star to every wandering bark,
Whose worth's unknown, although his height be taken.
Love's not Time's fool, though rosy lips and cheeks
Within his bending sickle's compass come;
Love alters not with his brief hours and weeks,
But bears it out even to the edge of doom.
  If this be error and upon me proved,
  I never writ, nor no man ever loved.

William Shakespeare (1564–1616)

MY MISTRESS' EYES ARE NOTHING LIKE THE SUN

My mistress' eyes are nothing like the sun;
Coral is far more red than her lips' red:
If snow be white, why then her breasts are dun;
If hairs be wires, black wires grow on her head.
I have seen roses damasked,° red and white,   of different colors
But no such roses see I in her cheeks;
And in some perfumes is there more delight
Than in the breath that from my mistress reeks.
I love to hear her speak, yet well I know

That music hath a far more pleasing sound:
I grant I never saw a goddess go,—
My mistress, when she walks, treads on the ground.
And yet, by heaven, I think my love as rare
As any she belied with false compare.

William Shakespeare (1564–1616)

THE GLORIES OF OUR BLOOD AND STATE

The glories of our blood and state
Are shadows, not substantial things;
There is no armor against fate;
Death lays his icy hand on kings:
Scepter and crown
Must tumble down,
And in the dust be equal made
With the poor crooked scythe and spade.

Some men with swords may reap the field,
And plant fresh laurels where they kill;
But their strong nerves at last must yield;
They tame but one another still:
Early or late,
They stoop to fate,
And must give up their murmuring breath,
When they, pale captives, creep to death.

The garlands wither on your brow,
Then boast no more your mighty deeds;
Upon death's purple altar now,
See where the victor-victim bleeds:
Your heads must come
To the cold tomb;
Only the actions of the just
Smell sweet and blossom in their dust.

James Shirley (1596–1666)

SONG

Sweet beast, I have gone prowling,
a proud rejected man

who lived along the edges
    catch as catch can;
in darkness and in hedges
    I sang my sour tone
and all my love was howling
    conspicuously alone.

I curled and slept all day
    or nursed my bloodless wounds
until the squares were silent
    where I could make tunes
singular and violent.
    Then, sure as hearers came
I crept and flinched away.
    And, girl, you've done the same.

A stray from my own type,
    led along by blindness,
my love was near to spoiled
    and curdled all my kindness.
I find no kin, no child;
    only the weasel's ilk.
Sweet beast, cat of my own stripe,
    come and take my milk.

W. D. Snodgrass (b. 1926)

TELEPHONE CONVERSATION

The price seemed reasonable, location
Indifferent. The landlady swore she lived
Off premises. Nothing remained
But self-confession. "Madam," I warned,
"I hate a wasted journey—I am African."
Silence. Silenced transmission of
Pressurized good-breeding. Voice, when it came,
Lipstick-coated, long gold-rolled
Cigarette-holder tipped. Caught I was, foully.
"HOW DARK?" . . . I had not misheard . . . "ARE YOU LIGHT
OR VERY DARK?" Button B. Button A. Stench
Of rancid breath of public hide-and-speak.
Red booth. Red pillar box. Red double-tiered
Omnibus squelching tar. It *was* real! Shamed

By ill-mannered silence, surrender
Pushed dumbfounded to beg simplification.
Considerate she was, varying the emphasis—
"ARE YOU DARK? OR VERY LIGHT?" Revelation came.
"You mean—like plain or milk chocolate?"
Her assent was clinical, crushing in its light
Impersonality. Rapidly, wave-length adjusted,
I chose. "West African sepia"—and as afterthought,
"Down in my passport." Silence for spectroscopic
Flight of fancy, till truthfulness clanged her accent
Hard on the mouthpiece. "WHAT'S THAT?" conceding
"DON'T KNOW WHAT THAT IS." "Like brunette."
"THAT'S DARK, ISN'T IT?" "Not altogether.
Facially, I am brunette, but madam, you should see
The rest of me. Palm of my hand, soles of my feet
Are a peroxide blonde. Friction, caused—
Foolishly madam—by sitting down, has turned
My bottom raven black—One moment, madam!—sensing
Her receiver rearing on the thunderclap
About my ears—"Madam," I pleaded, "wouldn't you rather
See for yourself?"

Wole Soyinka (b. 1935)

RETURN AGAIN

Return again, my forces late dismayed,
Unto the siege by you abandoned quite.
Great shame it is to leave, like one afraid,
So fair a piece for one repulse so light.
'Gainst such strong castles needeth greater might
Than those small forts which ye were wont belay:
Such haughty minds, inured to hardy fight,
Disdain to yield unto the first assay.
Bring therefore all the forces that ye may,
And lay incessant battery to her heart;
Plaints, prayers, vows, ruth, sorrow, and dismay:
Those engines can the proudest love convert.
And if those fail, fall down and die before her;
So dying live, and living do adore her.

Edmund Spenser (1552?–1599)

AT THE UN–NATIONAL MONUMENT ALONG THE CANADIAN BORDER

This is the field where the battle did not happen,
where the unknown soldier did not die.
This is the field where grass joined hands,
where no monument stands,
and the only heroic thing is the sky.

Birds fly here without any sound,
unfolding their wings across the open.
No people killed—or were killed—on this ground
hallowed by neglect and an air so tame
that people celebrate it by forgetting its name.

William Stafford (b. 1914)

A GLASS OF BEER

The lanky hank of a she in the inn over there
Nearly killed me for asking the loan of a glass of beer;
May the devil grip the whey-faced slut by the hair,
And beat bad manners out of her skin for a year.

That parboiled ape, with the toughest jaw you will see
On virtue's path, and a voice that would rasp the dead,
Came roaring and raging the minute she looked at me,
And threw me out of the house on the back of my head!

If I asked her master he'd give me a cask a day;
But she, with the beer at hand, not a gill would arrange!
May she marry a ghost and bear him a kitten, and may
The High King of Glory permit her to get the mange.

James Stephens (1882–1950)

A HIGH-TONED OLD CHRISTIAN WOMAN

Poetry is the supreme fiction, madame.
Take the moral law and make a nave of it
And from the nave build haunted heaven. Thus,
The conscience is converted into palms,
Like windy citherns hankering for hymns.
We agree in principle. That's clear. But take

The opposing law and make a peristyle,
And from the peristyle project a masque
Beyond the planets. Thus, our bawdiness,
Unpurged by epitaph, indulged at last,
Is equally converted into palms,
Squiggling like saxophones. And palm for palm,
Madame, we are where we began. Allow,
Therefore, that in the planetary scene
Your disaffected flagellants, well-stuffed,
Smacking their muzzy bellies in parade,
Proud of such novelties of the sublime,
Such tink and tank and tunk-a-tunk-tunk,
May, merely may, madame, whip from themselves
A jovial hullabaloo among the spheres.
This will make widows wince. But fictive things
Wink as they will. Wink most when widows wince.

Wallace Stevens (1879–1955)

PETER QUINCE AT THE CLAVIER

I

Just as my fingers on these keys
Make music, so the self-same sounds
On my spirit make a music, too.

Music is feeling, then, not sound;
And thus it is that what I feel,
Here in this room, desiring you,

Thinking of your blue-shadowed silk,
Is music. It is like the strain
Waked in the elders by Susanna:

Of a green evening, clear and warm,
She bathed in her still garden, while
The red-eyed elders, watching, felt

PETER QUINCE AT THE CLAVIER. The story of Susanna and the Elders is to be found in the *Apocrypha* and in the *Douay Bible* (Daniel, 13). The name Peter Quince comes from Shakespeare's *Midsummer Night's Dream*.

The bases of their beings throb
In witching chords, and their thin blood
Pulse pizzicati of Hosanna.

II

In the green water, clear and warm,
Susanna lay.
She searched
The touch of springs,
And found
Concealed imaginings.
She sighed,
For so much melody.

Upon the bank, she stood
In the cool
Of spent emotions,
She felt, among the leaves,
The dew
Of old devotions.

She walked upon the grass,
Still quavering.
The winds were like her maids
On timid feet,
Fetching her woven scarves,
Yet wavering.

A breath upon her hand
Muted the night.
She turned—
A cymbal crashed,
And roaring horns.

III

Soon, with a noise like tambourines,
Came her attendant Byzantines.

They wondered why Susanna cried
Against the elders by her side;

And as they whispered, the refrain
Was like a willow swept by rain.

Anon, their lamps' uplifted flame
Revealed Susanna and her shame.

And then, the simpering Byzantines
Fled with a noise like tambourines.

IV

Beauty is momentary in the mind—
The fitful tracing of a portal;
But in the flesh it is immortal.

The body dies; the body's beauty lives.
So evenings die, in their green going,
A wave, interminably flowing.
So gardens die, their meek breath scenting
The cowl of Winter, done repenting.
So maidens die, to the auroral
Celebration of a maiden's choral.

Susanna's music touched the bawdy strings
Of those white elders; but, escaping,
Left only Death's ironic scraping.
Now, in its immortality, it plays
On the clear viol of her memory,
And makes a constant sacrament of praise.

Wallace Stevens (1879–1955)

FEEL LIKE A BIRD

feel like A Bird
understand
he has no hand

instead A Wing
close-lapped
mysterious thing

in sleeveless coat
he halves The Air

skipping there
like water-licked boat

lands on star-toes
finger-beak in
feather-pocket
finds no coin
in neat head like
seeds in A Quartered
Apple eyes join
sniping at opposites
stereoscope The Scene
Before

close to floor giddy
no arms to fling
A Third Sail
spreads for calm
his tail

hand better
than A Wing?
to gather A Heap
to count
to clasp A Mate?

or leap
lone-free and mount
on muffled shoulders
to span A Fate?

May Swenson (b. 1919)

HOME THEY BROUGHT HER WARRIOR DEAD

Home they brought her warrior dead,
She nor swooned nor uttered cry.
All her maidens, watching, said,
"She must weep or she will die."

Then they praised him, soft and low,

Called him worthy to be loved,
Truest friend and noblest foe;
Yet she neither spoke nor moved.

Stole a maiden from her place,
Lightly to the warrior stepped,
Took the face-cloth from the face;
Yet she neither moved nor wept.

Rose a nurse of ninety years,
Set his child upon her knee—
Like summer tempest came her tears—
"Sweet my child, I live for thee."

Alfred, Lord Tennyson (1809–1892)

TEARS, IDLE TEARS

Tears, idle tears, I know not what they mean,
Tears from the depth of some divine despair
Rise in the heart, and gather to the eyes,
In looking on the happy autumn-fields,
And thinking of the days that are no more.

Fresh as the first beam glittering on a sail,
That brings our friends up from the underworld,
Sad as the last which reddens over one
That sinks with all we love below the verge;
So sad, so fresh, the days that are no more.

Ah, sad and strange as in dark summer dawns
The earliest pipe of half-awakened birds
To dying ears, when unto dying eyes
The casement slowly grows a glimmering square;
So sad, so strange, the days that are no more.

Dear as remembered kisses after death,
And sweet as those by hopeless fancy feigned
On lips that are for others; deep as love,
Deep as first love, and wild with all regret;
O Death in Life, the days that are no more!

Alfred, Lord Tennyson (1809–1892)

DO NOT GO GENTLE INTO THAT GOOD NIGHT

Do not go gentle into that good night,
Old age should burn and rave at close of day;
Rage, rage against the dying of the light.

Though wise men at their end know dark is right,
Because their words had forked no lightning they
Do not go gentle into that good night.

Good men, the last wave by, crying how bright
Their frail deeds might have danced in a green bay,
Rage, rage against the dying of the light.

Wild men who caught and sang the sun in flight,
And learn, too late, they grieved it on its way,
Do not go gentle into that good night.

Grave men, near death, who see with blinding sight
Blind eyes could blaze like meteors and be gay,
Rage, rage against the dying of the light.

And you, my father, there on the sad height,
Curse, bless, me now with your fierce tears, I pray.
Do not go gentle into that good night.
Rage, rage against the dying of the light.

Dylan Thomas (1914–1953)

ON A GIRDLE

That which her slender waist confined
Shall now my joyful temples bind;
No monarch but would give his crown
His arms might do what this has done.

It was my heaven's extremest sphere,
The pale which held that lovely deer.
My joy, my grief, my hope, my love,
Did all within this circle move!

A narrow compass, and yet there
Dwelt all that's good and all that's fair;

Give me but what this riband bound,
Take all the rest the sun goes round.

Edmund Waller (1606–1687)

A NOISELESS PATIENT SPIDER

A noiseless patient spider,
I marked where on a little promontory it stood isolated,
Marked how to explore the vacant vast surrounding,
It launched forth filament, filament, filament, out of itself,
Ever unreeling them, ever tirelessly speeding them.

And you O my soul where you stand,
Surrounded, detached, in measureless oceans of space,
Ceaselessly musing, venturing, throwing, seeking the spheres to connect them,
Till the bridge you will need be formed, till the ductile anchor hold,
Till the gossamer thread you fling catch somewhere, O my soul.

Walt Whitman (1819–1892)

THERE WAS A CHILD WENT FORTH

There was a child went forth every day,
And the first object he looked upon, that object he became,
And that object became part of him for the day or a certain part of the day,
Or for many years or stretching cycles of years.
The early lilacs became part of this child,
And grass and white and red morning-glories, and white and red clover, and the song of the phoebe-bird,
And the Third-month lambs and the sow's pink-faint litter, and the mare's foal and the cow's calf,
And the noisy brood of the barnyard or by the mire of the pond-side,
And the fish suspending themselves so curiously below there, and the beautiful curious liquid,
And the water-plants with their graceful flat heads, all became part of him.

The field-sprouts of Fourth-month and Fifth-month became part of him,
Winter-grain sprouts and those of the light-yellow corn, and the esculent roots of the garden,
And the apple-trees covered with blossoms and the fruit afterward, and wood-berries, and the commonest weeds by the road,

And the old drunkard staggering home from the outhouse of the tavern whence he had lately risen,
And the schoolmistress that passed on her way to the school,
And the friendly boys that passed, and the quarrelsome boys,
And the tidy and fresh-cheeked girls, and the barefoot negro boy and girl,
And all the changes of city and country wherever he went.

His own parents, he that had fathered him and she that had conceived him in her womb and birthed him,
They gave this child more of themselves than that,
They gave him afterward every day, they became part of him.

The mother at home quietly placing the dishes on the supper-table,
The mother with mild words, clean her cap and gown, a wholesome odor falling off her person and clothes as she walks by,
The father, strong, self-sufficient, manly, mean, angered, unjust,
The blow, the quick loud word, the tight bargain, the crafty lure,
The family usages, the language, the company, the furniture, the yearning and swelling heart,
Affection that will not be gainsayed, the sense of what is real, the thought if after all it should prove unreal,
The doubts of day-time and the doubts of night-time, the curious whether and how,
Whether that which appears so is so, or is it all flashes and specks?
Men and women crowding fast in the streets, if they are not flashes and specks what are they?

The streets themselves and the façades of houses, and goods in the windows,
Vehicles, teams, the heavy-planked wharves, the huge crossing at the ferries,
The village on the highland seen from afar at sunset, the river between,
Shadows, aureola and mist, the light falling on roofs and gables of white or brown two miles off,
The schooner near by sleepily dropping down the tide, the little boat slack-towed astern,
The hurrying tumbling waves, quick-broken crests, slapping,
The strata of colored clouds, the long bar of maroon-tint away solitary by itself, the spread of purity it lies motionless in,
The horizon's edge, the flying sea-crow, the fragrance of salt marsh and shore mud,
These became part of that child who went forth every day, and who now goes, and will always go forth every day.

Walt Whitman (1819–1892)

A BAROQUE WALL-FOUNTAIN IN THE VILLA SCIARRA

Under the bronze crown
Too big for the head of the stone cherub whose feet
A serpent has begun to eat,
Sweet water brims a cockle and braids down

Past spattered mosses, breaks
On the tipped edge of a second shell, and fills
The massive third below. It spills
In threads then from the scalloped rim, and makes

A scrim or summery tent
For a faun-ménage and their familiar goose.
Happy in all that ragged, loose
Collapse of water, its effortless descent

And flatteries of spray,
The stocky god upholds the shell with ease,
Watching, about his shaggy knees,
The goatish innocence of his babes at play;

His fauness all the while
Leans forward, slightly, into a clambering mesh
Of water-lights, her sparkling flesh
In a saecular ecstasy, her blinded smile

Bent on the sand floor
Of the trefoil pool, where ripple-shadows come
And go in swift reticulum,
More addling to the eye than wine, and more

Interminable to thought
Than pleasure's calculus. Yet since this all
Is pleasure, flash, and waterfall,
Must it not be too simple? Are we not

More intricately expressed
In the plain fountains that Maderna set

A BAROQUE WALL-FOUNTAIN IN THE VILLA SCIARRA. The Villa Sciarra is in Rome, as is St. Peter's Cathedral (31). 20. *saecular:* a variant spelling of *secular* that here gathers in the sense of *saeculum,* a period of long duration, an age. 30. *Maderna:* Italian architect (1556–1629). 43. *areté*: a Greek word meaning roughly "virtue" (Wilbur's note). 52. *Francis:* St. Francis of Assisi.

Before St. Peter's—the main jet
Struggling aloft until it seems at rest

In the act of rising, until
The very wish of water is reversed,
That heaviness borne up to burst
In a clear, high, cavorting head, to fill

With blaze, and then in gauze
Delays, in a gnatlike shimmering, in a fine
Illumined version of itself, decline,
And patter on the stones in its own applause?

If that is what men are
Or should be, if those water-saints display
The pattern of our areté,
What of these showered fauns in their bizarre,

Spangled, and plunging house?
They are at rest in fulness of desire
For what is given, they do not tire
Of the smart of the sun, the pleasant water-douse

And riddled pool below,
Reproving our disgust and our ennui
With humble insatiety.
Francis, perhaps, who lay in sister snow

Before the wealthy gate
Freezing and praising, might have seen in this
No trifle, but a shade of bliss—
That land of tolerable flowers, that state

As near and far as grass
Where eyes become the sunlight, and the hand
Is worthy of water: the dreamt land
Toward which all hungers leap, all pleasures pass.

Richard Wilbur (b. 1921)

THIS IS JUST TO SAY

I have eaten
the plums

that were in
the icebox

and which
you were probably
saving
for breakfast

Forgive me
they were delicious
so sweet
and so cold

William Carlos Williams (1883–1963)

RESOLUTION AND INDEPENDENCE

There was a roaring in the wind all night;
The rain came heavily and fell in floods;
But now the sun is rising calm and bright;
The birds are singing in the distant woods;
Over his own sweet voice the Stock-dove broods;
The Jay makes answer as the Magpie chatters;
And all the air is filled with pleasant noise of waters.

All things that love the sun are out of doors;
The sky rejoices in the morning's birth;
The grass is bright with rain-drops;—on the moors
The hare is running races in her mirth;
And with her feet she from the plashy earth
Raises a mist; that, glittering in the sun,
Runs with her all the way, wherever she doth run.

I was a Traveller then upon the moor;
I saw the hare that raced about with joy;
I heard the woods and distant waters roar;
Or heard them not, as happy as a boy:
The pleasant season did my heart employ:

RESOLUTION AND INDEPENDENCE. 43. *Chatterton:* A promising young English poet (1752–1770) who, reduced to despair by poverty, poisoned himself at the age of 17. 45. *Him who walked . . . :* Robert Burns, the peasant poet (1759–1796), died in want at the age of 37.

My old remembrances went from me wholly:
And all the ways of men, so vain and melancholy.

But, as it sometimes chanceth, from the might
Of joy in minds that can no further go,
As high as we have mounted in delight
In our dejection do we sink as low;
To me that morning did it happen so;
And fears and fancies thick upon me came;
Dim sadness—and blind thoughts, I knew not, nor could name.

I heard the skylark warbling in the sky;
And I bethought me of the playful hare:
Even such a happy child of earth am I;
Even as these blissful creatures do I fare;
Far from the world I walk, and from all care;
But there may come another day to me—
Solitude, pain of heart, distress, and poverty.

My whole life I have lived in pleasant thought,
As if life's business were a summer mood;
As if all needful things would come unsought
To genial faith, still rich in genial good;
But how can He expect that others should
Build for him, sow for him, and at his call
Love him, who for himself will take no heed at all?

I thought of Chatterton, the marvellous Boy,
The sleepless Soul that perished in his pride;
Of Him who walked in glory and in joy
Following his plough, along the mountainside:
By our own spirits are we deified:
We Poets in our youth begin in gladness;
But thereof come in the end despondency and madness.

Now, whether it were by peculiar grace,
A leading from above, a something given,
Yet it befell that, in this lonely place,
When I with these untoward thoughts had striven,
Beside a pool bare to the eye of heaven
I saw a Man before me unawares:
The oldest man he seemed that ever wore grey hairs.

As a huge stone is sometimes seen to lie
Couched on the bald top of an eminence;
Wonder to all who do the same espy,
By what means it could thither come, and whence;
So that it seems a thing endued with sense:
Like a sea-beast crawled forth, that on a shelf
Of rock or sand reposeth, there to sun itself;

Such seemed this Man, not all alive nor dead,
Such seemed this Man, not all alive nor dear,
Nor all asleep—in his extreme old age:
His body was bent double, feet and head
Coming together in life's pilgrimage;
As if some dire constraint of pain, or rage
Of sickness felt by him in times long past,
A more than human weight upon his frame had cast.

Himself he propped, limbs, body, and pale face,
Upon a long grey staff of shaven wood:
And, still as I drew near with gentle pace,
Upon the margin of that moorish flood
Motionless as a cloud the old Man stood,
That heareth not the loud winds when they call;
And moveth all together, if it move at all.

At length, himself unsettling, he the pond
Stirred with his staff, and fixedly did look
Upon the muddy water, which he conned,
As if he had been reading in a book:
And now a stranger's privilege I took;
And, drawing to his side, to him did say,
"This morning gives us promise of a glorious day."

A gentle answer did the old Man make,
In courteous speech which forth he slowly drew:
And him with further words I thus bespake,
"What occupation do you there pursue?
This is a lonesome place for one like you."
Ere he replied, a flash of mild surprise
Broke from the sable orbs of his yet-vivid eyes.

His words came feebly, from a feeble chest,
But each in solemn order followed each,
With something of a lofty utterance drest—

Choice word and measured phrase, above the reach
Of ordinary men; a stately speech;
Such as grave Livers do in Scotland use,
Religious men, who give to God and man their dues.

He told, that to these waters he had come
To gather leeches, being old and poor:
Employment hazardous and wearisome!
And he had many hardships to endure:
From pond to pond he roamed, from moor to moor;
Housing, with God's help, by choice or chance;
And in this way he gained an honest maintenance.

The old Man still stood talking by my side;
But now *his* voice to me was like a stream
Scarce heard; nor word from word could I divide;
And the whole body of the Man did seem
Like one whom I had met with in a dream;
Or like a man from some far region sent,
To give me human strength, by apt admonishment.

My former thoughts returned: the fear that kills;
And hope that is unwilling to be fed;
Cold, pain, and labour, and all fleshly ills;
And mighty Poets in their misery dead.
—Perplexed, and longing to be comforted
My question eagerly did I renew,
"How is it that you live, and what is it you do?"

He with a smile did then his words repeat;
And said that, gathering leeches, far and wide
He travelled; stirring thus about his feet
The waters of the pools where they abide.
"Once I could meet with them on every side;
But they have dwindled long by slow decay;
Yet still I persevere, and find them where I may."

While he was talking thus, the lonely place,
The old Man's shape, and speech—all troubled me:
In my mind's eye I seemed to see him pace
About the weary moors continually,
Wandering about alone and silently.

While I these thoughts within my self pursued,
He, having made a pause, the same discourse renewed.

And soon with this he other matter blended,
Cheerfully uttered, with demeanour kind,
But stately in the main; and, when he ended,
I could have laughed myself to scorn to find
In that decrepit Man so firm a mind.
"God," said I, "be my help and stay secure;
I'll think of the Leech-gatherer on the lonely moor!"

William Wordsworth (1770–1850)

THE SOLITARY REAPER

Behold her, single in the field,
Yon solitary Highland lass!
Reaping and singing by herself;
Stop here, or gently pass!
Alone she cuts and binds the grain,
And sings a melancholy strain;
O listen! for the vale profound
Is overflowing with the sound.

No nightingale did ever chaunt
More welcome notes to weary bands
Of travellers in some shady haunt
Among Arabian sands.
A voice so thrilling ne'er was heard
In springtime from the cuckoo-bird,
Breaking the silence of the seas
Among the farthest Hebrides.

Will no one tell me what she sings?—
Perhaps the plaintive numbers° flow — measures
For old, unhappy, far-off things,
And battles long ago.
Or is it some more humble lay,° — song
Familiar matter of today?

THE SOLITARY REAPER. 2. *Highland:* Scottish upland. The girl is singing in the Highland language, a form of Gaelic, quite different from English. 16. *Hebrides:* islands off the northwest tip of Scotland.

Some natural sorrow, loss, or pain,
That has been, and may be again?

Whate'er the theme, the maiden sang
As if her song could have no ending;
I saw her singing at her work,
And o'er the sickle bending—
I listened, motionless and still;
And, as I mounted up the hill,
The music in my heart I bore
Long after it was heard no more.

William Wordsworth (1770–1850)

STRANGE FITS OF PASSION

Strange fits° of passion have I known: whims
And I will dare to tell,
But in the lover's ear alone,
What once to me befell.

When she I love looked every day
Fresh as a rose in June,
I to her cottage bent my way,
Beneath an evening-moon.

Upon the moon I fixed my eye,
All over the wide lea;
With quickening pace my horse drew nigh
Those paths so dear to me.

And now we reached the orchard-plot;
And, as we climbed the hill,
The sinking moon to Lucy's cot° cottage
Came near, and nearer still.

In one of those sweet dreams I slept,
Kind Nature's gentlest boon!
And all the while my eyes I kept
On the descending moon.

My horse moved on; hoof after hoof
He raised, and never stopped:
When down behind the cottage roof,
At once, the bright moon dropped.

What fond° and wayward thoughts will slide — foolish
Into a Lover's head!
"O mercy!" to myself I cried,
"If Lucy should be dead!"

William Wordsworth (1770–1850)

A BLESSING

Just off the highway to Rochester, Minnesota,
Twilight bounds softly forth on the grass.
And the eyes of those two Indian ponies
Darken with kindness.
They have come gladly out of the willows
To welcome my friend and me.
We step over the barbed wire into the pasture
Where they have been grazing all day, alone.
They ripple tensely, they can hardly contain their happiness
That we have come.
They bow shyly as wet swans. They love each other.
There is no loneliness like theirs.
At home once more,
They begin munching the young tufts of spring in the darkness.
I would like to hold the slenderer one in my arms,
For she has walked over to me
And nuzzled my left hand.
She is black and white,
Her mane falls wild on her forehead,
And the light breeze moves me to caress her long ear
That is delicate as the skin over a girl's wrist.
Suddenly I realize
That if I stepped out of my body I would break
Into blossom.

James Wright (b. 1927)

THEY FLEE FROM ME

They flee from me that sometime did me seek,
With naked foot stalking in my chamber.
I have seen them gentle, tame, and meek,

THEY FLEE FROM ME. 20. *kindëly:* kindly. In addition to its modern meaning, it means *typically,* according to her type or kind.

That now are wild, and do not remember
That sometime they put themselves in danger
To take bread at my hand; and now they range,
Busily seeking with a continual change.

Thanked be fortune, it hath been otherwise
Twenty times better; but once, in special,
In thin array, after a pleasant guise,
When her loose gown from her shoulders did fall,
And she me caught in her arms long and small.
Therewith all sweetly did me kiss,
And softly said, "Dear heart, how like you this?"

It was no dream: I lay broad waking.
But all is turned, thorough° my gentleness, through
Into a strange fashion of forsaking;
And I have leave to go of° her goodness, because of
And she also to use newfangleness.
But since that I so kindëly am served,
I would fain know what she hath deserved.

Sir Thomas Wyatt (1503?–1542)

A PRAYER FOR MY DAUGHTER

Once more the storm is howling, and half hid
Under this cradle-hood and coverlid
My child sleeps on. There is no obstacle
But Gregory's wood and one bare hill
Whereby the haystack- and roof-levelling wind,
Bred on the Atlantic, can be stayed;
And for an hour I have walked and prayed
Because of the great gloom that is in my mind.

A PRAYER FOR MY DAUGHTER. 10, 14. *tower, future years:* When Yeats wrote this poem he lived in an old tower near the west coast of Ireland. It was a time of civil strife, and Yeats foresaw worse times coming. 25–26. Helen of Troy found life dull as the wife of Menelaus, was later given trouble by Paris, who abducted her to Troy, precipitating the Trojan War. 27. *great Queen:* Aphrodite, goddess of beauty, born full-grown out of the ocean, chose for her husband the lame and ill-favored Hephaestos, god of the forge. 32. *Horn of Plenty:* the cornucopia, which poured out to its recipient anything he desired. 59–64: *loveliest woman born:* Maud Gonne, whom Yeats wooed unsuccessfully (see "The Folly of Being Comforted," question 1, page 625, and "Among School Children," question 2, page 822), became a speaker for political and nationalistic causes.

I have walked and prayed for this young child an hour
And heard the sea-wind scream upon the tower,
And under the arches of the bridge, and scream
In the elms above the flooded stream;
Imagining in excited reverie
That the future years had come,
Dancing to a frenzied drum,
Out of the murderous innocence of the sea.

May she be granted beauty and yet not
Beauty to make a stranger's eye distraught,
Or hers before a looking-glass, for such,
Being made beautiful overmuch,
Consider beauty a sufficient end,
Lose natural kindness and maybe
The heart-revealing intimacy
That chooses right, and never find a friend.

Helen being chosen found life flat and dull
And later had much trouble from a fool,
While that great Queen, that rose out of the spray,
Being fatherless could have her way
Yet chose a bandy-leggèd smith for man.
It's certain that fine women eat
A crazy salad with their meat
Whereby the Horn of Plenty is undone.

In courtesy I'd have her chiefly learned;
Hearts are not had as a gift but hearts are earned
By those that are not entirely beautiful;
Yet many, that have played the fool
For beauty's very self, has charm made wise,
And many a poor man that has roved,
Loved and thought himself beloved,
From a glad kindness cannot take his eyes.

May she become a flourishing hidden tree
That all her thoughts may like the linnet be,
And have no business but dispensing round
Their magnanimities of sound,
Nor but in merriment begin a chase,

Nor but in merriment a quarrel.
O may she live like some green laurel
Rooted in one dear perpetual place.

My mind, because the minds that I have loved,
The sort of beauty that I have approved,
Prosper but little, has dried up of late,
Yet knows that to be choked with hate
May well be of all evil chances chief.
If there's no hatred in a mind
Assault and battery of the wind
Can never tear the linnet from the leaf.

An intellectual hatred is the worst,
So let her think opinions are accursed.
Have I not seen the loveliest woman born
Out of the mouth of Plenty's horn,
Because of her opinionated mind
Barter that horn and every good
By quiet natures understood
For an old bellows full of angry wind?

Considering that, all hatred driven hence,
The soul recovers radical innocence
And learns at last that it is self-delighting,
Self-appeasing, self-affrighting,
And that its own sweet will is Heaven's will;
She can, though every face should scowl
And every windy quarter howl
Or every bellows burst, be happy still.

And may her bridegroom bring her to a house
Where all's accustomed, ceremonious;
For arrogance and hatred are the wares
Peddled in the thoroughfares.
How but in custom and in ceremony
Are innocence and beauty born?
Ceremony's a name for the rich horn,
And custom for the spreading laurel tree.

William Butler Yeats (1865–1939)

SAILING TO BYZANTIUM

I

That is no country for old men. The young
In one another's arms, birds in the trees
—Those dying generations—at their song,
The salmon-falls, the mackerel-crowded seas,
Fish, flesh, or fowl, commend all summer long
Whatever is begotten, born, and dies.
Caught in that sensual music all neglect
Monuments of unageing intellect.

II

An aged man is but a paltry thing,
A tattered coat upon a stick, unless
Soul clap its hands and sing, and louder sing
For every tatter in its mortal dress,
Nor is there singing school but studying
Monuments of its own magnificence;
And therefore I have sailed the seas and come
To the holy city of Byzantium.

III

O sages standing in God's holy fire
As in the gold mosaic of a wall,
Come from the holy fire, perne in a gyre,° (spin in spiralling or cone-shaped flight)
And be the singing-masters of my soul.
Consume my heart away; sick with desire
And fastened to a dying animal
It knows not what it is; and gather me
Into the artifice of eternity.

SAILING TO BYZANTIUM. *Byzantium:* Ancient eastern capital of the Holy Roman Empire; here symbolically a holy city of the imagination. 1. *That:* Ireland, or the ordinary sensual world. 27–31. *such . . . Byzantium:* The Byzantine Emperor Theophilus had made for himself mechanical golden birds which sang upon the branches of a golden tree.

IV

Once out of nature I shall never take
My bodily form from any natural thing,
But such a form as Grecian goldsmiths make
Of hammered gold and gold enamelling
To keep a drowsy Emperor awake;
Or set upon a golden bough to sing
To lords and ladies of Byzantium
Of what is past, or passing, or to come.

William Butler Yeats (1865–1939)

FROM SATIRE ON WOMEN

Atheists are few; most nymphs° a godhead own,° — maidens; acknowledge
And nothing but his attributes dethrone.
From atheists far, they steadfastly believe
God is, and is almighty—to forgive.
His other excellence they'll not dispute;
But mercy, sure, is his chief attribute.
Shall pleasures of a short duration chain
A lady's soul in everlasting pain?
Will the great author us poor worms destroy
For now and then a sip of transient joy?
No, he's forever in a smiling mood,
He's like themselves; or how could he be good?
And they blaspheme who blacker schemes suppose.
Devoutly, thus, Jehovah they depose,
The pure! the just! and set up in his stead
A Deity, that's perfectly well bred.

Edward Young (1683–1765)

DRAMA

The Elements of Drama

CHAPTER ONE

The Nature of Drama

Drama, like prose fiction, utilizes plot and characters, develops a theme, arouses emotion or appeals to humor, and may be either escapist or interpretive in its dealings with life. Like poetry, it may draw upon all the resources of language, including verse. Much drama *is* poetry. But drama has one characteristic peculiar to itself. It is written primarily to be *performed,* not read. It normally presents its action (1) *through* actors, (2) *on* a stage, and (3) *before* an audience. Each of these circumstances has important consequences for the nature of drama. Each presents the playwright with a potentially enormous source of power, and each imposes limitations on the directions his work may take.

Because a play presents its action *through* actors, its impact is direct, immediate, and heightened by the actor's skills. Instead of responding to words on a printed page, the spectator sees what is done and hears what is said. The experience of the play is registered directly upon his senses. It may therefore be fuller and more compact. Where the work of prose fiction may tell us what a character looks like in one paragraph, how he moves or speaks in a second, what he says in a third, and how his auditors respond in a fourth, the acted play presents this material all at once. Simultaneous impressions are not temporally separated. Moreover, this experience is interpreted by actors who may be highly skilled in rendering nuances of meaning and strong emotion. Through facial expression, gesture, speech rhythm, and intonation, they may be able to make a speaker's words more expressive than can the reader's unaided imagination. Thus, the performance of a play by skilled actors expertly directed gives the playwright[1] a tremendous source of power.

But the playwright pays a price for this increased power. Of the four major points of view open to the fiction writer, the dramatist is practically limited to one—the *objective,* or *dramatic.* He cannot directly comment on the action or the characters. He cannot enter the minds of his characters and tell us what is going on there. Although there are ways around these limitations, each has its own limitations. Authorial commentary may be placed in the mouth of a character, but only at the risk of distorting characterization and of leaving the character's reliability uncertain. (Does the character speak for the author or only for himself?) Entry can be made into a character's mind through the conventions of the soliloquy and the aside. In the *soliloquy,* a character is presented as speaking to himself—that is, he is made to think out loud. In the *aside,* a character turns from the person with whom he is conversing to speak directly to the audience, thus letting the audience know what he is really thinking or feeling as opposed to what he pretends to be thinking or feeling. Both of these devices can be used very effectively in the theater, but they interrupt the action and must therefore be used sparingly. Also, they are inappropriate if the playwright is working in a strictly realistic mode.

Because a play presents its action *on* a stage, it is able powerfully to focus the spectator's attention. The stage is lighted; the theater is dark; extraneous noises are shut out; the spectator is almost literally pinned to his seat; there is nowhere he can go; there is nothing else to look at; there is nothing to distract. The playwright has extraordinary means by which to command the undivided attention of his audience. He is not, like the fiction writer or the poet, dependent on the power of his words alone.

But the necessity to confine his action to a stage, rather than to the imagination's vast arena, limits the playwright in the kind of materials he can easily and effectively present. For the most part, he must present human beings in spoken interaction with each other. He cannot easily use materials in which the main interest is in unspoken thoughts and reflections. He cannot present complex actions that involve nonhuman creatures such as dogs or charging bulls. He finds it more difficult to shift scenes rapidly than the writer of prose fiction does. The latter may whisk his reader from heaven to earth and back again in the twinkling of an eye, but the playwright must usually stick to one setting for an

[1] The word *wright*—as in *playwright, shipwright, wheelwright, cartwright,* and the common surname *Wright*—comes from an Anglo-Saxon word meaning a workman or craftsman. It is related to the verb *wrought* (a past-tense form of *work*) and has nothing whatever to do with the verb *write.*

extended period of time, and may feel constrained to do so for the whole play.[2] Moreover, the events he depicts must be of a magnitude appropriate to the stage. He cannot present the movements of armies and warfare on the vast scale that Tolstoi uses in *War and Peace*. He cannot easily present adventures at sea or action on a ski slope. Conversely, he cannot depict a fly crawling around the rim of a saucer or falling into a cup of milk. At best he can present a general on a hilltop reporting the movements of a battle or two persons bending over a cup of milk reacting to a fly that the members of the audience cannot see.

Because a play presents its action *before* an audience, the experience it creates is a communal experience, and its impact is intensified. Reading a short story or a novel is a private transaction between the reader and a book, but the performance of a play is public. The spectator's response is affected by the presence of other spectators. A comedy becomes funnier when one hears others laughing, a tragedy more moving when others are present to carry the current of feeling. A dramatic experience, in fact, becomes more intense almost exactly to the extent that it is shared and the individual spectator becomes aware that others are having the same experience. This intensification is partly dependent on the size of the audience, but more on their sense of community with each other. A play will be more successful performed before a small audience in a packed auditorium than before a larger audience in a half-filled one.

But, again, the advantage given the playwright by the fact of theatrical performance is paid for by limitations on the material he can present. His play must be able to hold the attention of a group audience. A higher premium than in prose fiction is placed on a well-defined plot,

[2] The ease, and therefore the rapidity, with which a playwright can change from one scene to another depends, first, on the elaborateness of the stage setting and, second, on the means by which one scene is separated from another. In ancient plays and in many modern ones, stage settings have been extremely simple, depending only on a few easily moved properties or even entirely on the actors' words and the spectators' imaginations. In such cases, change of scenes is made fairly easily, especially if the actors themselves are allowed to carry on and off any properties that may be needed. Various means have been used to separate scenes from each other. In Greek plays, dancing and chanting by a chorus served as a scene-divider. More recently, the closing and opening or dropping and raising of a curtain has been the means used. In contemporary theater, with its command of electrical technology, increased reliance has been placed on darkening and illuminating the stage or on darkening one part of it while lighting up another. But even where there is no stage scenery and where the shift of scene is made only by a change in lighting, the playwright can hardly change his setting as rapidly as the writer of prose fiction. On the stage, too frequent shifts of scene make a play seem jerky. A reader's imagination, on the other hand, can change from one setting to another without even shifting gears.

swift exposition, strong conflict, dramatic confrontations. Unless the play is very brief, it must usually be divided into parts separated by an intermission or intermissions, and each part must work up to its own climax or point of suspense. It must be written so that its central meanings may be grasped in a single hearing. The spectator at a play cannot back up and rerun a passage whose import he has missed; he cannot, in one night, sit through the whole performance a second time. In addition, the playwright must avoid extensive use of materials that are purely narrative or lyrical. Long narrative passages must be interrupted. Descriptive passages must be short, or eliminated altogether. Primarily, human beings must be presented in spoken interaction with each other. Clearly, many of the world's literary masterpieces—stories and poems that enthrall the reader of a book—would not hold the attention of a group audience in a theater.

Drama, then, imposes sharp limitations on its writer but holds out the opportunity for extraordinary power. The successful playwright combines the power of words, the power of fiction, and the power of dramatic technique to make possible the achievement of that extraordinary power.

EXERCISES AND DISCUSSION TOPICS

1. Movie production is in many ways more flexible than stage production, and movies are more easily brought to a mass audience. What limitations of stage performance discussed in this chapter can be minimized or circumvented in a movie production? In view of the greater flexibility of moving pictures as a medium, why is there still an eager audience for plays? What advantages do stage performances have over moving pictures?
2. If plays are written to be *performed,* what justification is there for reading them?
3. Works written as short stories or novels have sometimes been dramatized for stage production. In light of the advantages and limitations discussed in this chapter, however, some works of fiction are clearly more easily adapted for the stage than others. Of the following works, which could be most easily and effectively dramatized? Which would be possible but more difficult? Which would be impossible? Why? "Tears, Idle Tears" (page 95), "Youth" (page 109), "Hills Like White Elephants" (page 206), "The Lottery" (page 218), "The Guest" (page 226), "Flurry at the Sheep Dog Trial" (page 285), "West-Running Brook" (page 812), "The Love Song of J. Alfred Prufrock" (page 815).
4. Write a stage adaptation of "The Grasshopper and the Cricket" (page 175). What are the difficulties involved? How effective would such a presentation be?

August Strindberg

THE STRONGER

CHARACTERS

Mrs. X., *an actress, married*
Miss Y., *an actress, unmarried*
A Waitress

Scene. *The corner of a ladies' cafe. Two little iron tables, a red velvet sofa, several chairs. Enter* Mrs. X., *dressed in winter clothes, carrying a Japanese basket on her arm.*

Miss Y. *sits with a half-empty beer bottle before her, reading an illustrated paper, which she changes later for another.*

Mrs. X. Good afternoon, Amelia. You're sitting here alone on Christmas eve like a poor bachelor!

Miss Y. (*Looks up, nods, and resumes her reading.*)

Mrs. X. Do you know it really hurts me to see you like this, alone, in a café, and on Christmas eve, too. It makes me feel as I did one time when I saw a bridal party in a Paris restaurant, and the bride sat reading a comic paper, while the groom played billiards with the witnesses. Huh, thought I, with such a beginning, what will follow, and what will be the end? He played billiards on his wedding eve! (Miss Y. *starts to speak*) And she read a comic paper, you mean? Well, they are not altogether the same thing.

(A Waitress *enters, places a cup of chocolate before* Mrs. X. *and goes out.*)

Mrs. X. You know what, Amelia! I believe you would have done better to have kept him! Do you remember, I was the first to say "Forgive him?" Do you remember that? You would be married now and have a home. Remember that Christmas when you went out to visit your fiancé's parents in the country? How you gloried in the happiness of home life and really longed to quit the theatre forever? Yes, Amelia dear, home is the best of all—next to the theatre—and as for children—well, you don't understand that.

Miss Y. (*Looks up scornfully.*)

(Mrs. X. *sips a few spoonfuls out of the cup, then opens her basket and shows Christmas presents.*)

Mrs. X. Now you shall see what I bought for my piggywigs. [*Takes*

THE STRONGER. First performed in 1889.

up a doll] Look at this! This is for Lisa, ha! Do you see how she can roll her eyes and turn her head, eh? And here is Maja's popgun.

(*Loads it and shoots at* Miss Y.)

Miss Y. (*Makes a startled gesture.*)

Mrs. X. Did I frighten you? Do you think I would like to shoot you, eh? On my soul, if I don't think you did! If you wanted to shoot *me* it wouldn't be so surprising, because I stood in your way—and I know you can never forget that—although I was absolutely innocent. You still believe I intrigued and got you out of the Stora theatre, but I didn't. I didn't do that, although you think so. Well, it doesn't make any difference what I say to you. You still believe I did it. (*Takes up a pair of embroidered slippers*) And these are for my better half. I embroidered them myself—I can't bear tulips, but he wants tulips on everything.

Miss Y. (*Looks up ironically and curiously.*)

Mrs. X. (*putting a hand in each slipper*) See what little feet Bob has! What? And you should see what a splendid stride he has! You've never seen him in slippers! (Miss Y. *laughs aloud.*) Look! (*She makes the slippers walk on the table.* Miss Y. *laughs loudly.*) And when he is grumpy he stamps like this with his foot. "What! damn those servants who can never learn to make coffee. Oh, now those creatures haven't trimmed the lamp wick properly!" And then there are draughts on the floor and his feet are cold. "Ugh, how cold it is; the stupid idiots can never keep the fire going." (*She rubs the slippers together, one sole over the other.*)

Miss Y. (*Shrieks with laughter.*)

Mrs. X. And then he comes home and has to hunt for his slippers which Marie has stuck under the chiffonier—oh, but it's sinful to sit here and make fun of one's husband this way when he is kind and a good little man. You ought to have had such a husband, Amelia. What are you laughing at? What? What? And you see he's true to me. Yes, I'm sure of that, because he told me himself—what are you laughing at?—that when I was touring in Norway that brazen Frederika came and wanted to seduce him! Can you fancy anything so infamous? (*pause*) I'd have torn her eyes out if she had come to see him when I was at home. (*pause*) It was lucky that Bob told me about it himself and that it didn't reach me through gossip. (*pause*) But would you believe it, Frederika wasn't the only one! I don't know why, but the women are crazy about my husband. They must think he has influence about getting them theatrical engagements, because he is connected with the government. Perhaps you were after him yourself. I didn't use to trust you any too much. But now I know hė never bothered his head about you, and you always seemed to have a grudge against him someway.

(*Pause. They look at each other in a puzzled way.*)

Mrs. X. Come and see us this evening, Amelia, and show us that you're not put out with us—not put out with me at any rate. I don't know, but I think it would be uncomfortable to have you for an enemy. Perhaps it's because I stood in your way (*more slowly*) or—I really—don't know why—in particular.

(*Pause.* Miss Y. *stares at* Mrs. X *curiously.*)

Mrs. X (*thoughtfully*) Our acquaintance has been so queer. When I saw you for the first time I was afraid of you, so afraid that I didn't dare let you out of my sight; no matter when or where, I always found myself near you—I didn't dare have you for an enemy, so I became your friend. But there was always discord when you came to our house, because I saw that my husband couldn't endure you, and the whole thing seemed as awry to me as an ill-fitting gown—and I did all I could to make him friendly toward you, but with no success until you became engaged. Then came a violent friendship between you, so that it looked all at once as though you both dared show your real feelings only when you were secure—and then—how was it later? I didn't get jealous—strange to say! And I remember at the christening, when you acted as godmother, I made him kiss you—he did so, and you became so confused—as it were; I didn't notice it then—didn't think about it later, either—have never thought about it until—now! (*Rises suddenly.*) Why are you silent? You haven't said a word this whole time, but you have let me go on talking! You have sat there, and your eyes have reeled out of me all these thoughts which lay like raw silk in its cocoon—thoughts—suspicious thoughts, perhaps. Let me see—why did you break your engagement? Why do you never come to our house any more? Why won't you come to see us tonight?

(Miss Y. *appears as if about to speak.*)

Mrs. X. Hush, you needn't speak—I understand it all! It was because —and because— and because! Yes, yes! Now all the accounts balance. That's it. Fie, I won't sit at the same table with you. (*Moves her things to another table.*)That's the reason I had to embroider tulips—which I hate—on his slippers, because you are fond of tulips; that's why (*throws slippers on the floor*) we go to Lake Mälarn in the summer, because you don't like salt water; that's why my boy is named Eskil—because it's your father's name; that's why I wear your colors, read your authors, eat your favorite dishes, drink your drinks—chocolate, for instance; that's why—oh—my God—it's terrible, when I think about it; it's terrible. Everything, everything came from you to me, even your passions. Your soul crept into mine, like a worm into an apple, ate and ate, bored and bored, until nothing was left but the rind and a little black dust within. I wanted to get away from you, but I couldn't; you lay like a snake and charmed me with your black eyes; I felt that when I lifted my wings they only dragged me down; I lay in the water with bound feet, and the stronger I strove to keep up the deeper I worked myself down, down, until I sank to the bottom, where you lay like a giant crab to clutch me in your claws—and there I am lying now.

I hate you, hate you, hate you! And you only sit there silent—silent and indifferent; indifferent whether it's new moon or waning moon, Christmas or New Year's, whether others are happy or unhappy; without power to hate or to love; as quiet as a stork by a rat hole—you couldn't scent your prey and capture it, but you could lie in wait for it! You sit here in your corner of the café—did you know it's called "The Rat Trap" for you?—and read the papers to see if misfortune hasn't befallen someone, to see if someone hasn't been given notice at the theatre, perhaps; you sit here and calculate about your next victim and reckon on your chances of recompense like a pilot in a shipwreck. Poor Amelia, I pity you, nevertheless, because I know you are unhappy, unhappy like one who has been wounded, and angry because you are wounded. I can't be angry with you, no matter how much I want to be—because you come out the weaker one. Yes, all that with Bob doesn't trouble me. What is that to me, after all? And what difference does it make whether I learned to drink chocolate from you or some one else. (*Sips a spoonful from her cup*) Besides, chocolate is very healthful. And if you taught me how to dress—tant mieux!—that has only made me more attractive to my husband; so you lost and I won there. Well, judging by certain signs, I believe you have already lost him; and you certainly intended that I should leave him—do as you did with your fiancé and regret as you now regret; but, you see, I don't do that—we mustn't be too exacting. And why should I take only what no one else wants?

Perhaps, take it all in all, I am at this moment the stronger one. You received nothing from me, but you gave me much. And now I seem like a thief since you have awakened and find I possess what is your loss. How could it be otherwise when everything is worthless and sterile in your hands? You can never keep a man's love with your tulips and your passions—but I can keep it. You can't learn how to live from your authors, as I have learned. You have no little Eskil to cherish, even if your father's name was Eskil. And why are you always silent, silent, silent? I thought that was strength, but perhaps it is because you have nothing to say! Because you never think about anything! (*Rises and picks up slippers.*) Now I'm going home—and take the tulips with me—*your* tulips! You are unable to learn from another; you can't bend—therefore, you broke like a dry stalk. But I won't break! Thank you, Amelia, for all your good lessons. Thanks for teaching my husband how to love. Now I'm going home to love him. (*Goes.*)

QUESTIONS

1. Much of the action of this play lies in the past, but to reconstruct that action we must separate what is true from what is untrue and from what may

or may not be true in Mrs. X's account of it. Point out places where Mrs. X (a) is probably lying, (b) is clearly rationalizing, (c) has very likely or has certainly been deceived, (d) is clearly giving an accurate account. In each case, explain your reason for your opinion. To what extent can we be certain of what has happened in the past?

2. Now put together as reliable an account as possible of the past relationships of Mrs. X, her husband, and Miss Y. How did the friendship between the two women start? How did it proceed? How and why did it terminate? In what two ways have the two women consciously or unconsciously been rivals? In what ways and by what means has Miss Y influenced Mrs. X's behavior and her life?

3. In a sense the play has two plots, one in the past and one in the present, though the plot in the present is really only the culminating phase of that in the past. At what point does Mrs. X discover something about the past that she had not known before? What is it she discovers? How does she react to the discovery? Why can this discovery be called the turning point of the play?

4. Trace the successive attitudes expressed by Mrs. X toward Miss Y, together with the real attitudes underlying the expressed attitudes. At what points do the expressed attitudes and the real attitudes coincide? At what points do they clearly differ?

5. What kind of person is Mrs. X? Characterize her.

6. Although Miss Y says nothing during the course of the play, we can infer a good deal about her from her reactions to Mrs. X, from her past actions, and from what Mrs. X says about her (cautiously interpreted). What kind of person is she? How, especially, does she differ from Mrs. X? What is the nature of her present life? Would this role be easy or difficult to act?

7. Although Mr. X never appears, he also is an important character in the play. What kind of man is he?

8. To which character does the title refer? Consider carefully before answering, and support your answer with a reasoned argument, including a definition of what is meant by "stronger."

Anton Chekhov

THE BRUTE

A Joke in One Act

English Version *by ERIC BENTLEY*

CHARACTERS

Mrs. Popov, *widow and landowner, small, with dimpled cheeks.*
Mr. Grigory S. Smirnov, *gentleman farmer, middle-aged.*
Luka, *Mrs. Popov's footman, an old man.*
Gardener
Coachman
Hired Men

The drawing room of a country house. Mrs. Popov, *in deep mourning, it staring hard at a photograph.* Luka *is with her.*

Luka. It's not right, ma'am, you're killing yourself. The cook has gone off with the maid to pick berries. The cat's having a high old time in the yard catching birds. Every living thing is happy. But you stay moping here in the house like it was a convent, taking no pleasure in nothing. I mean it, ma'am! It must be a full year since you set foot out of doors.

Mrs. Popov. I must never set foot out of doors again, Luka. Never! I have nothing to set foot out of doors *for*. My life is done. *He* is in his grave. I have buried myself alive in this house. We are *both* in our graves.

Luka. You're off again, ma'am. I just won't listen to you no more. Mr. Popov is dead, but what can we do about that? It's God's doing. God's will be done. You've cried over him, you've done your share of mourning, haven't you? There's a limit to everything. You can't go on weeping and wailing forever. My old lady died, for that matter, and I wept and wailed over her a whole month long. Well, that was it. I couldn't weep and wail all my life, she just wasn't worth it. (*He sighs.*) As for the neighbours, you've forgotten all about them, ma'am. You don't visit them and you don't let them visit you. You and I are like a pair of spiders—excuse the expression, ma'am—here we are in this house like a pair of spiders, we never see the light of day. And it isn't like there was no nice people around either. The whole county's swarming with 'em. There's a regiment quartered at Riblov, and the officers are so good-looking! The girls can't take their eyes off them—There's a ball at the camp every Friday—The military band plays most every day of the week—What do you say, ma'am? You're young, you're pretty, you could enjoy yourself! Ten years from now you may want to strut and show your feathers to the officers, and it'll be too late.

MRS. POPOV (*firmly*). You must never bring this subject up again, Luka. Since Popov died, life has been an empty dream to me, you know that. *You* may think I am alive. Poor ignorant Luka! You are wrong. I am dead. I'm in my grave. Never more shall I see the light of day, never strip from my body this . . . raiment of death! Are you listening, Luka? Let his ghost learn how I love him! Yes, *I* know, and *you* know, he was often unfair to me, he was cruel to me, and he was unfaithful to me. What of it? *I* shall be faithful to *him,* that's all. I will show him how *I* can love. Hereafter, in a better world than this, he will welcome me back, the same loyal girl I always was—

LUKA. Instead of carrying on this way, ma'am, you should go out in the garden and take a bit of a walk, ma'am. Or why not harness Toby and take a drive? Call on a couple of the neighbours, ma'am?

MRS. POPOV (*breaking down*). Oh, Luka!

LUKA. Yes, ma'am? What have I said, ma'am? Oh dear!

MRS. POPOV. Toby! You said Toby! He adored that horse. When he drove me out to the Korchagins and the Vlasovs, it was always with Toby! He was a wonderful driver, do you remember, Luka? So graceful! So strong! I can see him now, pulling at those reins with all his might and main! Toby! Luka, tell them to give Toby an extra portion of oats today.

LUKA. Yes, ma'am.

(*A bell rings.*)

MRS. POPOV. Who is that? Tell them I'm not at home.

LUKA. Very good, ma'am. (*Exit.*)

MRS. POPOV (*gazing again at the photograph*). You shall see, my Popov, how a wife can love and forgive. Till death do us part. Longer than that. Till death re-unite us forever! (*Suddenly a titter breaks through her tears.*) Aren't you ashamed of yourself, Popov? Here's your little wife, being good, being faithful, so faithful she's locked up here waiting for her own funeral, while you—doesn't it make you ashamed, you naughty boy? You were terrible, you know. You were unfaithful, and you made those awful scenes about it, you stormed out and left me alone for weeks—

(*Enter* Luka.)

LUKA (*upset*). There's someone asking for you, ma'am. Says he must—

MRS. POPOV. I suppose you told him that since my husband's death I see no one?

LUKA. Yes, ma'am. I did, ma'am. But he wouldn't listen, ma'am. He says it's urgent.

MRS. POPOV (*shrilly*). I see no one!!

LUKA. He won't take no for an answer, ma'am. He just curses and swears and comes in anyway. He's a perfect monster, ma'am. He's in the dining room right now.

MRS. POPOV. In the dining room, is he? I'll give him his come uppance. Bring him in here this minute.

(*Exit* LUKA.)

(*Suddenly sad again.*) Why do they do this to me? Why? Insulting my grief, intruding on my solitude? (*She sighs.*) I'm afraid I'll have to enter a convent. I will, I *must* enter a convent!

(*Enter* MR. SMIRNOV and LUKA.)

SMIRNOV (*to* LUKA). Dolt! Idiot! You talk too much! (*Seeing* MRS. POPOV. *With dignity.*) May I have the honour of introducing myself, madam? Gregory S. Smirnov, landowner and lieutenant of artillery, retired. Forgive me, madam, if I disturb your peace and quiet, but my business is both urgent and weighty.

MRS. POPOV (*declining to offer him her hand*). What is it you wish, sir?

SMIRNOV. At the time of his death, your late husband—with whom I had the honour to be acquainted, ma'am—was in my debt to the tune of twelve hundred rubles. I have two notes to prove it. Tomorrow, ma'am, I must pay the interest on a bank loan. I have therefore no alternative, ma'am, but to ask you to pay me the money today.

MRS. POPOV. Twelve hundred rubles? But what did my husband owe it to you for?

SMIRNOV. He used to buy his oats from me, madam.

MRS. POPOV (*to* LUKA, *with a sigh*). Remember what I said, Luka: tell them to give Toby an extra portion of oats today!

(*Exit* LUKA.)

My dear Mr.—what was the name again?

SMIRNOV. Smirnov, ma'am.

MRS. POPOV. My dear Mr. Smirnov, if Mr. Popov owed you money, you shall be paid—to the last ruble, to the last kopeck. But today—you must excuse me, Mr.—what was it?

SMIRNOV. Smirnov, ma'am.

MRS. POPOV. Today, Mr. Smirnov, I have no ready cash in the house.

(SMIRNOV *starts to speak.*)

Tomorrow, Mr. Smirnov, no, the day after tomorrow, all will be well. My steward will be back from town. I shall see that he pays what is owing. Today, no. In any case, today is exactly seven months from Mr. Popov's death. On such a day you will understand that I am in no mood to think of money.

SMIRNOV. Madam, if you don't pay up now, you can carry me out feet foremost. They'll seize my estate.

MRS. POPOV. You can have your money.

(*He starts to thank her.*)

Tomorrow.

(*He again starts to speak.*)

That is: the day after tomorrow.

SMIRNOV. I don't need the money the day after tomorrow. I need it today.

MRS. POPOV. I'm sorry, Mr.—

SMIRNOV (*shouting*). Smirnov!

MRS. POPOV (*sweetly*). Yes, of course. But you can't have it today.

SMIRNOV. But I can't wait for it any longer!

MRS. POPOV. Be sensible, Mr. Smirnov. How can I pay you if I don't have it?

SMIRNOV. You don't have it?

MRS. POPOV. I don't have it.

SMIRNOV. Sure?

MRS. POPOV. Positive.

SMIRNOV. Very well. I'll make a note to that effect. (*Shrugging.*) And then they want me to keep cool. I meet the tax commissioner on the street, and he says, 'Why are you always in such a bad humour, Smirnov?' Bad humour! How can I help it, in God's name? I need money, I need it desperately. Take yesterday: I leave home at the crack of dawn, I call on all my debtors. Not a one of them pays up. Footsore and weary, I creep at midnight into some little dive, and try to snatch a few winks of sleep on the floor by the vodka barrel. Then today, I come here, fifty miles from home, saying to myself, 'At last, at last, I can be sure of something,' and you're not in the mood! You give me a mood! Christ, how can I help getting all worked up?

MRS. POPOV. I thought I'd made it clear, Mr. Smirnov, that you'll get your money the minute my steward is back from town?

SMIRNOV. What the hell do I care about your steward? Pardon the expression, ma'am. But it was you I came to see.

MRS. POPOV. What language! What a tone to take to a lady! I refuse to hear another word. (*Quickly, exit.*)

SMIRNOV. Not in the mood, huh? 'Exactly seven month since Popov's death,' huh? How about me? (*Shouting after her.*) Is there this interest to pay, or isn't there? I'm asking you a question: is there this interest to pay, or isn't there? So your husband died, and you're not in the mood, and your steward's gone off some place, and so forth and so on, but what *I* can do about all that, huh? What do *you* think I should do? Take a running jump and shove my head through the wall? Take off in a balloon? You don't know my *other* debtors. I call on Gruzdeff. Not at home. I look for Yaroshevitch. He's hiding out. I find Kooritsin. He kicks up a row, and I have to throw him through the window. I work my way right down the list. Not a kopeck. Then I come to you, and God damn it to hell, if you'll pardon the expression, you're not in the mood! (*Quietly, as he realizes he's talking to air.*) I've spoiled them all, that's what, I've let them play me for a sucker. Well, I'll show them. I'll show this one. I'll stay right here till she pays up. Ugh! (*He shudders with rage.*) I'm in a rage! I'm in a positively towering rage! Every nerve in my body is trembling at forty to the dozen! I can't breathe, I feel ill, I think I'm going to faint, hey, you there!

(*Enter* LUKA.)

LUKA. Yes, sir? Is there anything you wish, sir?

SMIRNOV. Water! Water! ! No, make it vodka.

(*Exit* LUKA.)

Consider the logic of it. A fellow creature is desperately in need of cash, so desperately in need that he has to seriously contemplate hanging himself, and this woman, this mere chit of a girl, won't pay up, and why not? Because, forsooth, she isn't in the mood! Oh, the logic of women! Come to that, I never have liked them, I could do without the whole sex. Talk to a woman? I'd rather sit on a barrel of dynamite, the very thought gives me gooseflesh. Women! Creatures of poetry and romance! Just to see one in the distance gets me mad. My legs start twitching with rage. I feel like yelling for help.

(*Enter* LUKA, *handing* SMIRNOV *a glass of water.*)

LUKA. Mrs. Popov is indisposed, sir. She is seeing no one.

SMIRNOV. Get out.

(*Exit* LUKA.)

Indisposed, is she? Seeing no one, huh? Well, she can see me or not, but I'll be here, I'll be right here till she pays up. If you're sick for a week, I'll be here for a week. If you're sick for a year, I'll be here for a year. You won't get around *me* with your widow's weeds and your schoolgirl dimples. I know all about dimples. (*Shouting through the window.*) Semyon, let the horses out of those shafts, we're not leaving, we're staying, and tell them to give the horses some oats, yes, oats, you fool, what do you think? (*Walking away from the window.*) What a mess, what an unholy mess! I didn't sleep last night, the heat is terrific today, not a damn one of 'em has paid up, and here's this—this skirt in mourning that's not in the mood! My head aches, where's that— (*He drinks from the glass.*) Water, ugh! You there!

(*Enter* LUKA.)

LUKA. Yes, sir. You wish for something, sir?

SMIRNOV. Where's that confounded vodka I asked for?

(*Exit* LUKA.)

(SMIRNOV *sits and looks himself over.*) Oof! A fine figure of a man *I* am! Unwashed, uncombed, unshaven, straw on my vest, dust all over me. The little woman must've taken me for a highwayman. (*Yawns.*) I suppose it wouldn't be considered polite to barge into a drawing room in this state, but who cares? I'm not a visitor, I'm a creditor—most unwelcome of guests, second only to Death.

(*Enter* LUKA.)

LUKA *(handing him the vodka)*. If I may say so, sir, you take too many liberties, sir.

SMIRNOV. What?!

LUKA. Oh, nothing, sir, nothing.

SMIRNOV. Who in hell do you think you're talking to? Shut your mouth!

LUKA (*aside*). There's an evil spirit abroad. The Devil must have sent him. Oh! (*Exit* LUKA.)

SMIRNOV. What a rage I'm in! I'll grind the whole world to powder. Oh, I feel ill again. You there!

(*Enter* MRS. POPOV.)

MRS. POPOV (*looking at the floor*). In the solitude of my rural retreat, Mr. Smirnov, I've long since grown unaccustomed to the sound of the human voice. Above all, I cannot bear shouting. I must beg you not to break the silence.

SMIRNOV. Very well. Pay me my money and I'll go.

MRS. POPOV. I told you before, and I tell you again, Mr. Smirnov. I have no cash, you'll have to wait till the day after tomorrow. Can I express myself more plainly?

SMIRNOV. And *I* told *you* before, and *I* tell *you* again, that I need the money today, that the day after tomorrow is too late, and that if you don't pay, and pay now, I'll have to hang myself in the morning!

MRS. POPOV. But I have no cash. This is quite a puzzle.

SMIRNOV. You won't pay, huh?

MRS. POPOV. I *can't* pay, Mr. Smirnov.

SMIRNOV. In that case, I'm going to sit here and wait. (*Sits down.*) You'll pay up the day after tomorrow? Very good. Till the day after tomorrow, here I sit. (*Pause. He jumps up.*) Now look, do I have to pay that interest tomorrow, or don't I? Or do you think I'm joking?

MRS. POPOV. I must ask you not to raise your voice, Mr. Smirnov. This is not a stable.

SMIRNOV. Who said it was? Do I have to pay the interest tomorrow or not?

MRS. POPOV. Mr. Smirnov, do you know how to behave in he presence of a lady?

SMIRNOV. No, madam, I do not know how to behave in the presence of a lady.

MRS. POPOV. Just what I thought. I look at you, and I say: ugh! I hear you talk, and I say to myself: 'That man doesn't know how to talk to a lady.'

SMIRNOV. You'd like me to come simpering to you in French, I suppose.

'Enchanté, madame! Merci beaucoup for not paying zee money, *madame! Pardonnez-moi* if I 'ave disturbed you, *madame!* How *charmante* you look in mourning, *madame!'*

Mrs. Popov. Now you're being silly, Mr. Smirnov.

Smirnov (*mimicking*). 'Now you're being silly, Mr. Smirnov.' 'You don't know how to talk to a lady, Mr. Smirnov.' Look here, Mrs. Popov, I've known more women than you've known pussy cats. I've fought three duels on their account. I've jilted twelve, and been jilted by nine others. Oh, yes, Mrs. Popov, I've played the fool in my time, whispered sweet nothings, bowed and scraped and endeavoured to please. Don't tell me I don't know what it is to love, to pine away with longing, to have the blues, to melt like butter, to be weak as water. I was full of tender emotion. I was carried away with passion. I squandered half my fortune on the sex. I chattered about women's emancipation. But there's an end to everything, dear madam. Burning eyes, dark eyelashes, ripe, red lips, dimpled cheeks, heaving bosoms, soft whisperings, the moon above, the lake below—I don't give a rap for that sort of nonsense any more, Mrs. Popov. I've found out about women. Present company excepted, they're liars. Their behaviour is mere play acting; their conversation is sheer gossip. Yes, dear lady, women, young or old, are false, petty, vain, cruel, malicious, unreasonable. As for intelligence, any sparrow could give them points. Appearances, I admit, can be deceptive. In appearance, a woman may be all poetry and romance, goddess and angel, muslin and fluff. To look at her exterior is to be transported to heaven. But I have looked at her interior, Mrs. Popov, and what did I find there—in her very soul? A crocodile. (*He has gripped the back of the chair so firmly that it snaps.*) And, what is more revolting, a crocodile with an illusion, a crocodile that imagines tender sentiments are its own special province, a crocodile that thinks itself queen of the realm of love! Whereas, in sober fact, dear madam, if a woman can love anything except a lapdog you can hang me by the feet on that nail. For a man, love is suffering, love is sacrifice. A woman just swishes her train around and tightens her grip on your nose. Now, you're a woman, aren't you, Mrs. Popov? You must be an expert on some of this. Tell me, quite frankly, did you ever know a woman to be—faithful, for instance? Or even sincere? Only old hags, huh? Though some women are old hags from birth. But as for the others? You're right: a faithful woman is a freak of nature—like a cat with horns.

Mrs. Popov. Who *is* faithful, then? Who *have* you cast for the faithful lover? Not man?

Smirnov. Right first time, Mrs. Popov: man.

Mrs. Popov (*going off into a peal of bitter laughter*). Man! Man is faithful! that's a new one! (*Fiercely.*) What right do you have to say this, Mrs. Smirnov? Men faithful? Let me tell you something. Of all the men I have ever known my late husband Popov was the best. I loved him, and there are women who know how to love, Mr. Smirnov. I gave him my youth, my happiness, my life, my fortune. I worshipped the ground he trod on—and what happened? The best of men was unfaithful to me, Mr. Smirnov. Not once in a while. All the time. After he died, I found his desk drawer full of love letters. While he was alive, he was always going away for the week-end. He squandered my money. He made love to other women before my very eyes. But, in spite of all, Mr. Smirnov, *I* was faithful. Unto death. And beyond. I am *still* faithful, Mr. Smirnov! Buried alive in this house, I shall wear mourning till the day I, too, am called to my eternal rest.

SMIRNOV (*laughing scornfully*). Expect me to believe that? As if I couldn't see through all this hocus-pocus. Buried alive! Till you're called to your eternal rest! Till when? Till some little poet—or some little subaltern with his first moustache—comes riding by and asks: 'Can that be the house of the mysterious Tamara who for love of her late husband has buried herself alive, vowing to see no man?' Ha!

MRS. POPOV (*flaring up*). How dare you? How dare you insinuate—?

SMIRNOV. You may have buried yourself alive, Mrs. Popov, but you haven't forgotten to powder your nose.

MRS. POPOV (*incoherent*). How dare you? How—?

SMIRNOV. Who's raising his voice now? Just because I call a spade a spade. Because I shoot straight from the shoulder. Well, don't shout at me, I'm not your steward.

MRS. POPOV. I'm not shouting, you're shouting! Oh, leave me alone!

SMIRNOV. Pay me the money, and I will.

MRS. POPOV. You'll get no money out of me!

SMIRNOV. Oh, so that's it!

MRS. POPOV. Not a ruble, not a kopeck. Get out! Leave me alone!

SMIRNOV. Not being your husband, I must ask you not to make scenes with me. (*He sits.*) I don't like scenes.

MRS. POPOV (*choking with rage*). You're sitting down?

SMIRNOV. Correct, I'm sitting down.

MRS. POPOV. I asked you to leave!

SMIRNOV. Then give me the money. (*Aside.*) Oh, what a rage I'm in, what a rage!

MRS. POPOV. The impudence of the man! I won't talk to you a moment longer. Get out. (*Pause.*) Are you going?

SMIRNOV. No.

MRS. POPOV. No?!

SMIRNOV. No.

MRS. POPOV. On your head be it. Luka!

(*Enter* LUKA.)

Show the gentleman out, Luka.

LUKA (*approaching*). I'm afraid, sir, I'll have to ask you, um, to leave, sir, now, um—

SMIRNOV (*jumping up*). Shut your mouth, you old idiot! Who do you think you're talking to? I'll make mincemeat of you.

LUKA (*clutching his heart*). Mercy on us! Holy saints above! (*He falls into an armchair.*) I'm taken sick! I can't breathe!!

MRS. POPOV. Then where's Dasha? Dasha! Dasha! Come here at once! (*She rings.*)

LUKA. They gone picking berries, ma'am, I'm alone here—Water, water, I'm taken sick!

MRS. POPOV (*to* SMIRNOV). Get out, you!

SMIRNOV. Can't you even be polite with me, Mrs. Popov?

MRS. POPOV (*clenching her fists and stamping her feet*). With you? You're a wild animal, you were never house-broken!

SMIRNOV. What? What did you say?

MRS. POPOV. I said you were a wild animal, you were never house-broken.

SMIRNOV (*advancing upon her*). And what right do you have to talk to me like that?

MRS. POPOV. Like what?

SMIRNOV. You have insulted me, madam.

MRS. POPOV. What of it? Do you think I'm scared of you?

SMIRNOV. So you think you can get away with it because you're a woman. A creature of poetry and romance, huh? Well, it doesn't go down with me. I hereby challenge you to a duel.

LUKA. Mercy on us! Holy saints alive! Water!

SMIRNOV. I propose we shoot it out.

MRS. POPOV. Trying to scare me again? Just because you have big fists and a voice like a bull? You're a brute.

SMIRNOV. No one insults Grigory S. Smirnov with impunity! And I don't care if you *are* a female.

MRS. POPOV (*trying to outshout him*). Brute, brute, brute!

SMIRNOV. The sexes are equal, are they? Fine: then it's just prejudice to expect men alone to pay for insults. I hereby challenge—

MRS. POPOV (*screaming*). All right! You want to shoot it out? All right! Let's shoot it out!

SMIRNOV. And let it be here and now!

MRS. POPOV. Here and now! All right! I'll have Popov's pistols here in one minute! (*Walks away, then turns.*) Putting one of Popov's bullets through your silly head will be a pleasure! Au revoir. (*Exit.*)

SMIRNOV. I'll bring her down like a duck, a sitting duck. I'm not one of your little poets, I'm no little subaltern with his first moustache. No, sir, there's no weaker sex where I'm concerned!

LUKA. Sir! Master! (*He goes down on his knees.*) Take pity on a poor old man, and do me a favour: go away. It was bad enough before, you nearly scared me to death. But a duel—!

SMIRNOV (*ignoring him*). A duel! That's equality of the sexes for you!

That's women's emancipation! Just as a matter of principle I'll bring her down like a duck. But what a woman! 'Putting one of Popov's bullets through your silly head . . .' Her cheeks were flushed, her eyes were gleaming! And, by God, she's accepted the challenge! I never knew a woman like this before!

LUKA. Sir! Master! Please go away! I'll always pray for you!

SMIRNOV (*again ignoring him*). What a woman! Phew!! *She's* no sour puss, *she's* no cry baby. She's fire and brimstone. She's a human cannon ball. What a shame I have to kill her!

LUKA (*weeping*). Please, kind sir, please, go away!

SMIRNOV (*as before*). I like her, isn't that funny? With those dimples and all? I like her. I'm even prepared to consider letting her off that debt. And where's my rage? It's gone. I never knew a woman like this before.

(*Enter* MRS. POPOV *with pistols.*)

MRS. POPOV (*boldly*). Pistols, Mr. Smirnov! (*Matter of fact.*) But before we start, you'd better show me how it's done, I'm not too familiar with these things. In fact I never gave a pistol a second look.

LUKA. Lord, have mercy on us, I must go hunt up the gardener and the coachman. Why has this catastrophe fallen upon us, O Lord? (*Exit.*)

SMIRNOV (*examining the pistols*). Well, it's like this. There are several makes: one is the Mortimer, with capsules, especially constructed for duelling. What you have here are Smith and Wesson triple-action revolvers, with extractor, first-rate job, worth ninety rubles at the very least. You hold it this way. (*Aside.*) My God, what eyes she has! They're setting me on fire.

MRS. POPOV. This way?

SMIRNOV. Yes, that's right. You cock the trigger, take aim like this, head up, arm out like this. Then you just press with this finger here, and it's all over. The main thing is, keep cool, take slow aim, and don't let your arm jump.

MRS. POPOV. I see. And if it's inconvenient to do the job here, we can go out in the garden.

SMIRNOV. Very good. Of course, I should warn you: I'll be firing in the air.

MRS. POPOV. What? This is the end. Why?

SMIRNOV. Oh, well—because—for private reasons.

MRS. POPOV. Scared, huh? (*She laughs heartily.*) Now don't you try to get out of it, Mr. Smirnov. My blood is up. I won't be happy till I've drilled a hole through that skull of yours. Follow me. What's the matter? Scared?

SMIRNOV. That's right. I'm scared.

MRS. POPOV. Oh, come on, what's the matter with you?

SMIRNOV. Well, um, Mrs. Popov, I, um, I like you.

MRS. POPOV (*laughing bitterly*). Good God! He likes me, does he? The gall of the man. (*Showing him the door.*) You may leave, Mr. Smirnov.

SMIRNOV (*quietly puts the gun down, takes his hat, and walks to the door. Then he stops and the pair look at each other without a word. Then, approaching gingerly*). Listen, Mrs. Popov. Are you still mad at me? I'm in the devil of a temper myself, of course. But then, you see—what I mean is—it's this way—the fact is— (*Roaring.*) Well, is it my fault, damn it, if I like you? (*Clutches the back of a chair. It breaks.*) Christ, what fragile furniture you have here. I like you. Know what I mean? I could fall in love with you.

MRS. POPOV. I hate you. Get out!

SMIRNOV. What a woman! I never saw anything like it. Oh, I'm lost, I'm done for, I'm a mouse in a trap.

MRS. POPOV. Leave this house, or I shoot!

SMIRNOV. Shoot away! What bliss to die of a shot that was fired by that little velvet hand! To die gazing into those enchanting eyes. I'm out of my mind. I know: you must decide at once. Think for one second, then decide. Because if I leave now, I'll never be back. Decide! I'm a pretty decent chap. Landed gentleman, I should say. Ten thousand a year. Good stable. Throw a kopeck up in the air, and I'll put a bullet through it. Will you marry me?

MRS. POPOV (*indignant, brandishing the gun*). We'll shoot it out! Get going! Take your pistol!

SMIRNOV. I'm out of my mind. I don't understand anything any more. (*Shouting.*) You there! That vodka!

MRS. POPOV. No excuses! No delays! We'll shoot it out!

SMIRNOV. I'm out of my mind. I'm falling in love. I *have* fallen in love. (*He takes her hand vigorously; she squeals.*) I love you. (*He goes down on his knees.*) I love you as I've never loved before. I jilted twelve, and was jilted by nine others. But I didn't love a one of them as I love you. I'm full of tender emotion. I'm melting like butter. I'm weak as water. I'm on my knees like a fool, and I offer you my hand. It's a shame, it's a disgrace. I haven't been in love in five years. I took a vow against it. And now, all of a sudden, to be swept off my feet, it's a scandal. I offer you my hand, dear lady. Will you or won't you? You won't? Then don't! (*He rises and walks toward the door.*)

MRS. POPOV. I didn't say anything.

SMIRNOV (*stopping*). What?

MRS. POPOV. Oh, nothing, you can go. Well, no, just a minute. No, you can go. Go! I detest you! But, just a moment. Oh, if you knew how furious I feel! (*Throws the gun on the table.*) My fingers have gone to sleep holding that horrid thing. (*She is tearing her handkerchief to shreds.*) And what are you standing around for? Get out of here!

SMIRNOV. Goodbye.

MRS. POPOV. Go, go, go! (*Shouting.*) Where are you going? Wait a minute! No, no, it's all right, just go. I'm fighting mad. Don't come near me, don't come near me!

SMIRNOV (*who is coming near her*). I'm pretty disgusted with myself—falling in love like a kid, going down on my knees like some moongazing whippersnapper, the very thought gives me gooseflesh. (*Rudely.*) I love you. But it doesn't make sense. Tomorrow, I have to pay that interest, and we've already started mowing. (*He puts his arm about her waist.*) I shall never forgive myself for this.

MRS. POPOV. Take your hands off me, I hate you! Let's shoot it out!

(*A long kiss. Enter* LUKA *with an axe, the* GARDENER *with a rake, the* COACHMAN *with a pitchfork,* HIRED MEN *with sticks.*)

LUKA (*seeing the kiss*). Mercy on us! Holy saints above!

MRS. POPOV (*dropping her eyes*). Luka, tell them in the stable that Toby is *not* to have any oats today.

QUESTIONS

1. In what way are Mrs. Popov and Smirnov alike? In what ways, respectively, do both transgress the norms of reason? Who in the play serves as the voice of reason?

2. What are the sources of Mrs. Popov's fidelity to the memory of her late husband? Is there a name for her attitude?

3. In what respect do Mrs. Popov and Smirnov undergo a reversal of roles—that is, how is Mrs. Popov in the latter part of the play like Smirnov in the earlier part, and Smirnov in the latter part like Mrs. Popov in the earlier part?

4. At what point does the turning point in the play come? What causes it?

5. Is the sudden change in Mrs. Popov's feelings believable? What explanations can be given for it?

6. Does either character undergo a change in character?

7. What is the significance of Mrs. Popov's final speech?

8. Unlike "The Stronger," this play has a number of soliloquies and three asides. What is their effect? Why do they "work" here when they would be out of place in "The Stronger"?

9. How do you visualize the stage action when Smirnov shows Mrs. Popov how to hold the revolver?

Anonymous

EVERYMAN

CHARACTERS

MESSENGER
GOD
DEATH
EVERYMAN
FELLOWSHIP
COUSIN
KINDRED
GOODS
GOOD DEEDS
KNOWLEDGE
CONFESSION
BEAUTY
STRENGTH
DISCRETION
FIVE WITS
ANGEL
DOCTOR

Here beginneth a treatise how the High Father of Heaven sendeth Death to summon every creature to come and give account of their lives in this world, and is in manner of a moral play.

Enter MESSENGER *as Prologue.*

MESSENGER. I pray you all give your audience,
And hear this matter with reverence,
By figure a moral play—
The *Summoning of Everyman* called it is,
That of our lives and ending shows
How transitory we be all day.
This matter is wondrous precious,
But the intent of it is more gracious,
And sweet to bear away.
The story saith: Man, in the beginning,
Look well, and take good heed to the ending,
Be you never so gay!
Ye think sin in the beginning full sweet,
Which in the end causeth the soul to weep,
When the body lieth in clay.
Here shall you see how Fellowship and Jollity,
Both Strength, Pleasure, and Beauty,
Will fade from thee as flower in May.
For ye shall hear how our Heaven King
Calleth Everyman to a general reckoning.

EVERYMAN. The author and date of this play are unknown. The earliest existing printed versions date from the early 1500s.

Give audience, and hear what he doth say. (*Exit.*)

(God *speaks from above.*)

God. I perceive, here in my majesty,
How that all creatures be to me unkind,
Living without dread in worldly prosperity.
Of ghostly° sight the people be so blind,
Drowned in sin, they know me not for their God.
In worldly riches is all their mind,
They fear not my rightwiseness, the sharp rod;
My love that I showed when I for them died
They forget clean, and shedding of my blood red;
I hanged between two, it cannot be denied;
To get them life I suffered to be dead;
I healed their feet, with thorns hurt was my head.
I could do no more than I did, truly;
And now I see the people do clean forsake me.
They use the seven deadly sins damnable,
As pride, covetise,° wrath, and lechery,
Now in the world be made commendable;
And thus they leave of angels the heavenly company.
Every man liveth so after his own pleasure,
And yet of their life they be nothing sure.
I see the more that I them forbear
The worse they be from year to year;
All that liveth appaireth° fast.
Therefore I will, in all the haste,
Have a reckoning of every man's person;
For, and° I leave the people thus alone
In their life and wicked tempests,
Verily they will become much worse than beasts;
For now one would by envy another up eat;
Charity they all do clean forget.
I hoped well that every man
In my glory should make his mansion,
And thereto I had them all elect,°
But now I see, like traitors deject,°
They thank me not for the pleasure that I to them meant,
Nor yet for their being that I them have lent.

25. ghostly: spiritual. **37. covetise:** covetousness. **44. appaireth:** becomes worse. **47. and:** if; so used frequently throughout the play. **54. elect:** numbered among the redeemed. **55. deject:** abject.

I proffered the people great multitude of mercy,
And few there be that asketh it heartily;
They be so cumbered with worldly riches,
That needs on them I must do justice,
On every man living without fear.
Where art thou, Death, thou mighty messenger?

(*Enter* DEATH.)

DEATH. Almighty God, I am here at your will,
Your commandment to fulfil.
GOD. Go thou to Everyman,
And show him, in my name,
A pilgrimage he must on him take,
Which he in no wise may escape;
And that he bring with him a sure reckoning
Without delay or any tarrying. (*Exit* GOD.)
DEATH. Lord, I will in the world go run over all,
And cruelly out search both great and small.
Every man will I beset that liveth beastly
Out of God's laws, and dreadeth not folly.
He that loveth riches I will strike with my dart,
His sight to blind, and from heaven to depart,
Except that alms be his good friend,
In hell for to dwell, world without end.

(EVERYMAN *enters, at a distance.*)

Lo, yonder I see Everyman walking;
Full little he thinketh on my coming.
His mind is on fleshly lusts and his treasure,
And great pain it shall cause him to endure
Before the Lord, Heaven King.
Everyman, stand still! Whither art thou going
Thus gaily? Hast thou thy Maker forgot?
EVERYMAN. Why askest thou?
Wouldst thou wete?°
DEATH. Yea, sir, I will show you:
In great haste I am sent to thee
From God out of his Majesty.
EVERYMAN. What, sent to me?
DEATH. Yea, certainly.
Though thou have forgot him here,

88. wete: know.

He thinketh on thee in the heavenly sphere,
As, ere we depart, thou shalt know.
EVERYMAN. What desireth God of me?
DEATH. That shall I show thee:
A reckoning he will needs have
Without any longer respite.
EVERYMAN. To give a reckoning, longer leisure I crave.
This blind matter troubleth my wit.
DEATH. On thee thou must take a long journey;
Therefore thy book of count° with thee thou bring;
For turn again thou can not by no way.
And look thou be sure of thy reckoning,
For before God thou shalt answer and show
Thy many bad deeds, and good but a few,
How thou hast spent thy life, and in what wise,
Before the Chief Lord of paradise.
Have ado that we were in that way,°
For, wete thou well, thou shalt make none attourney.°
EVERYMAN. Full unready I am such reckoning to give.
I know thee not. What messenger art thou?
DEATH. I am Death, that no man dreadeth.°
For every man I 'rest,° and no man spareth;
For it is God's commandment
That all to me should be obedient.
EVERYMAN. O Death! thou comest when I had thee least in mind!
In thy power it lieth me to save.
Yet of my goods will I give thee, if thou will be kind;
Yea, a thousand pound shalt thou have,
If thou defer this matter till another day.
DEATH. Everyman, it may not be, by no way!
I set not by° gold, silver, nor riches,
Nor by pope, emperor, king, duke, nor princes.
For, and I would receive gifts great,
All the world I might get;
But my custom is clean contrary.
I give thee no respite. Come hence, and not tarry.
EVERYMAN. Alas! shall I have no longer respite?
I may say Death giveth no warning.
To think on thee, it maketh my heart sick,

104. count: accounts. **111. Have ado . . . way:** get busy so that we may be on the way. **112. thou shalt . . . attourney:** you shall have no attorney to plead for you. **115. no man dreadeth:** fears no man. **116. 'rest:** arrest. **125. set not by:** care nothing for.

For all unready is my book of reckoning.
But twelve year and I might have abiding,
My counting-book I would make so clear,
That my reckoning I should not need to fear.
Wherefore, Death, I pray thee, for God's mercy,
Spare me till I be provided of remedy.
    DEATH. Thee availeth not to cry, weep, and pray;
But haste thee lightly that thou were gone that journey,
And prove thy friends if thou can.
For wete thou well the tide abideth no man;
And in the world each living creature
For Adam's sin must die of nature.
    EVERYMAN. Death, if I should this pilgrimage take,
And my reckoning surely make,
Show me, for saint charity,
Should I not come again shortly?
    DEATH. No, Everyman; and thou be once there,
Thou mayest never more come here,
Trust me verily.
    EVERYMAN. O gracious God, in the high seat celestial,
Have mercy on me in this most need!
Shall I have no company from this vale terrestrial
Of mine acquaintance that way me to lead?
    DEATH. Yea, if any be so hardy,
That would go with thee and bear thee company.
Hie thee that thou were gone to God's magnificence,
Thy reckoning to give before his presence.
What! weenest° thou thy life is given thee,
And thy worldly goods also?
    EVERYMAN. I had weened so, verily.
    DEATH. Nay, nay; it was but lent thee;
For, as soon as thou art gone,
Another a while shall have it, and then go therefrom
Even as thou hast done.
Everyman, thou art mad! Thou hast thy wits five,
And here on earth will not amend thy life;
For suddenly I do come.
    EVERYMAN. O wretched caitiff! whither shall I flee,
That I might 'scape endless sorrow?
Now, gentle Death, spare me till tomorrow,
That I may amend me

161. weenest: think.

With good advisement.°
DEATH. Nay, thereto I will not consent,
Nor no man will I respite,
But to the heart suddenly I shall smite
Without any advisement.
And now out of thy sight I will me hie;
See thou make thee ready shortly,
For thou mayst say this is the day
That no man living may 'scape away. (*Exit* DEATH.)
EVERYMAN. Alas! I may well weep with sighs deep.
Now have I no manner of company
To help me in my journey and me to keep;
And also my writing is full unready.
How shall I do now for to excuse me?
I would to God I had never been get!
To my soul a full great profit it had be,
For now I fear pains huge and great.
The time passeth; Lord, help, that all wrought.
For though I mourn it availeth naught.
The day passeth, and is almost a-go;
I wot° not well what for to do.
To whom were I best my complaint to make?
What if I to Fellowship thereof spake,
And showed him of this sudden chance?
For in him is all mine affiance,°
We have in the world so many a day
Been good friends in sport and play.
I see him yonder, certainly;
I trust that he will bear me company;
Therefore to him will I speak to ease my sorrow.

(*Enter* FELLOWSHIP.)

Well met, good Fellowship, and good morrow!
FELLOWSHIP. Everyman, good morrow, by this day!
Sir, why lookest thou so piteously?
If any thing be amiss, I pray thee me say,
That I may help to remedy.
EVERYMAN. Yea, good Fellowship, yea,
I am in great jeopardy.
FELLOWSHIP. My true friend, show to me your mind.
I will not forsake thee to my life's end

175. advisement: warning. **195. wot:** know. **199. affiance:** trust.

In the way of good company.
    EVERYMAN. That was well spoken, and lovingly.
    FELLOWSHIP. Sir, I must needs know your heaviness;
I have pity to see you in any distress;
If any have you wronged, ye shall revenged be,
Though I on the ground be slain for thee,
Though that I know before that I should die.
    EVERYMAN. Verily, Fellowship, gramercy.°
    FELLOWSHIP. Tush! by thy thanks I set not a straw!
Show me your grief, and say no more.
    EVERYMAN. If I my heart should to you break,°
And then you to turn your mind from me,
And would not me comfort when you hear me speak.
Then should I ten times sorrier be.
    FELLOWSHIP. Sir, I say as I will do, indeed.
    EVERYMAN. Then be you a good friend at need;
I have found you true here before.
    FELLOWSHIP. And so ye shall evermore;
For, in faith, and thou go to hell,
I will not forsake thee by the way!
    EVERYMAN. Ye speak like a good friend. I believe you well;
I shall deserve it, and I may.
    FELLOWSHIP. I speak of no deserving, by this day!
For he that will say and nothing do
Is not worthy with good company to go;
Therefore show me the grief of your mind,
As to your friend most loving and kind.
    EVERYMAN. I shall show you how it is:
Commanded I am to go a journey,
A long way, hard and dangerous,
And give a strait° count without delay
Before the high judge, Adonai.°
Wherefore, I pray you, bear me company,
As ye have promised, in this journey.
    FELLOWSHIP. That is matter indeed! Promise is duty;
But, and I should take such a voyage on me,
I know it well, it should be to my pain.
Also it maketh me afeared, certain.
But let us take counsel here as well as we can,
For your words would fear° a strong man.

221. gramercy: thanks. **224. break:** reveal. **244. strait:** strict. **245. Adonai:** an Old Testament name for God. **253. fear:** frighten.

EVERYMAN. Why, ye said if I had need,
Ye would me never forsake, quick° nor dead,
Though it were to hell, truly.
FELLOWSHIP. So I said, certainly,
But such pleasures be set aside, the sooth to say.
And also, if we took such a journey,
When should we come again?
EVERYMAN. Nay, never again till the day of doom.
FELLOWSHIP. In faith, then will not I come there!
Who hath you these tidings brought?
EVERYMAN. Indeed, Death was with me here.
FELLOWSHIP. Now, by God that all hath bought,
If Death were the messenger,
For no man that is living today
I will not go that loath° journey—
Not for the father that begat me!
EVERYMAN. Ye promised otherwise, pardie.°
FELLOWSHIP. I wot well I said so, truly;
And yet if thou wilt eat, and drink, and make good cheer,
Or haunt to women the lusty company,
I would not forsake you while the day is clear,
Trust me verily!
EVERYMAN. Yea, thereto you would be ready.
To go to mirth, solace, and play,
Your mind will sooner apply
Than to bear me company in my long journey.
FELLOWSHIP. Now, in good faith, I will not that way.
But and thou wilt murder, or any man kill,
In that I will help thee with a good will!
EVERYMAN. O, that is a simple advice indeed!
Gentle fellow, help me in my necessity;
We have loved long, and now I need,
And now, gentle Fellowship, remember me!
FELLOWSHIP. Whether ye have loved me or no,
By Saint John, I will not with thee go.
EVERYMAN. Yet, I pray thee, take the labor, and do so much for me
To bring me forward, for saint charity,
And comfort me till I come without the town.
FELLOWSHIP. Nay, and thou would give me a new gown,
I will not a foot with thee go;

255. quick: living. **268. loath:** loathsome. **270. pardie:** by God.

But, and thou had tarried, I would not have left thee so.
And as now God speed thee in thy journey,
For from thee I will depart as fast as I may.

EVERYMAN. Whither away, Fellowship? Will you forsake me?

FELLOWSHIP. Yea, by my fay,° to God I betake° thee.

EVERYMAN. Farewell, good Fellowship! For thee my heart is sore;
Adieu for ever! I shall see thee no more.

FELLOWSHIP. In faith, Everyman, farewell now at the end!
For you I will remember that parting is mourning.

(*Exit* FELLOWSHIP.)

EVERYMAN. Alack! shall we thus depart indeed
(Ah, Lady, help), without any more comfort?
Lo, Fellowship forsaketh me in my most need.
For help in this world whither shall I resort?
Fellowship here before with me would merry make,
And now little sorrow for me doth he take.
It is said, "In prosperity men friends may find,
Which in adversity be full unkind."
Now whither for succor shall I flee,
Sith° that Fellowship hath forsaken me?
To my kinsmen I will, truly,
Praying them to help me in my necessity;
I believe that they will do so,
For "kind° will creep where it may not go.°"
I will go say,° for yonder I see them go.
Where be ye now, my friends and kinsmen?

(*Enter* KINDRED *and* COUSIN.)

KINDRED. Here be we now, at your commandment.
Cousin, I pray you show us your intent
In any wise, and do not spare.

COUSIN. Yea, Everyman, and to us declare
If ye be disposed to go any whither,
For, wete you well, we will live and die together.

KINDRED. In wealth° and woe we will with you hold,
For over his kin a man may be bold.

EVERYMAN. Gramercy, my friends and kinsmen kind.
Now shall I show you the grief of my mind.
I was commanded by a messenger

298. fay: faith. **betake:** commend. **312. Sith:** since. **316. kind:** kinship. **go:** walk. **317. say:** assay, try. **325. wealth:** weal, happiness.

That is a high king's chief officer;
He bade me go a pilgrimage, to my pain,
And I know well I shall never come again;
Also I must give a reckoning straight,
For I have a great enemy that hath me in wait,°
Which intended me for to hinder.

KINDRED. What account is that which ye must render?
That would I know.

EVERYMAN. Of all my works I must show
How I have lived, and my days spent;
Also of ill deeds that I have used
In my time, sith life was me lent;
And of all virtues that I have refused.
Therefore I pray you go thither with me,
To help to make mine account, for saint charity.

COUSIN. What, to go thither? Is that the matter?
Nay, Everyman, I had liefer fast bread and water
All this five year and more.

EVERYMAN. Alas, that ever I was bore!
For now shall I never be merry
If that you forsake me.

KINDRED. Ah, sir, what! Ye be a merry man!
Take good heart to you, and make no moan.
But one thing I warn you, by Saint Anne,
As for me, ye shall go alone.

EVERYMAN. My Cousin, will you not with me go?

COUSIN. No, by our Lady! I have the cramp in my toe.
Trust not to me, for, so God me speed,°
I will deceive you in your most need.

KINDRED. It availeth not us to tice.°
Ye shall have my maid with all my heart;
She loveth to go to feasts, there to be nice,°
And to dance, and abroad to start;
I will give her leave to help you in that journey,
If that you and she may agree.

EVERYMAN. Now show me the very effect of your mind.
Will you go with me, or abide behind?

KINDRED. Abide behind? Yea, that will I, and I may!
Therefore, farewell till another day. (*Exit* KINDRED.)

EVERYMAN. How should I be merry or glad?

334. **hath me in wait:** lies in wait for me. 357. **speed:** prosper. 359. **tice:** entice. 361. **nice:** wanton, gay.

For fair promises men to me make,
But when I have most need, they me forsake.
I am deceived; that maketh me said.

Cousin. Cousin Everyman, farewell now,
For verily I will not go with you;
Also of mine own life an unready reckoning
I have to account; therefore I make tarrying.
Now, God keep thee, for now I go. (*Exit* Cousin.)

Everyman. Ah, Jesus! is all come hereto?
Lo, fair words maketh fools fain;°
They promise and nothing will do, certain.
My kinsmen promised me faithfully
For to abide with me steadfastly,
And now fast away do they flee.
Even so Fellowship promised me.
What friend were best me of to provide?
I lose my time here longer to abide.
Yet in my mind a thing there is:
All my life I have loved riches;
If that my good now help me might,
He would make my heart full light.
I will speak to him in this distress.
Where art thou, my Goods and riches?

(Goods *speaks from within.*)

Goods. Who calleth me? Everyman? What, hast thou haste?
I lie here in corners, trussed and piled so high,
And in chests I am locked so fast,
Also sacked in bags—thou mayest see with thine eye—
I cannot stir; in packs low I lie.
What would ye have? Lightly me say.°

Everyman. Come hither, Goods, in all the haste thou may.
For of counsel I must desire thee.

(*Enter* Goods.)

Goods. Sir, and ye in the world have sorrow or adversity,
That can I help you to remedy shortly.

Everyman. It is another disease that grieveth me;
In this world it is not, I tell thee so.
I am sent for another way to go,
To give a strict count general
Before the highest Jupiter of all;

379. fain: joyful. **398. Lightly me say:** tell me quickly.

And all my life I have had joy and pleasure in thee,
Therefore I pray thee go with me,
For, peradventure, thou mayst before God Almighty
My reckoning help to clean and purify;
For it is said ever among,
That "money maketh all right that is wrong."
GOODS. Nay, Everyman; I sing another song,
I follow no man in such voyages;
For, and I went with thee,
Thou shouldst fare much the worse for me;
For because on me thou did set thy mind,
Thy reckoning I have made blotted and blind,
That thine account thou cannot make truly;
And that hast thou for the love of me.
EVERYMAN. That would grieve me full sore,
When I should come to that fearful answer.
Up, let us go thither together.
GOODS. Nay, not so! I am too brittle, I may not endure;
I will follow no man one foot, be ye sure.
EVERYMAN. Alas! I have thee loved, and had great pleasure
All my life-days on goods and treasure.
GOODS. That is to thy damnation, without lesing!°
For my love is contrary to the love everlasting.
But if thou had me loved moderately during,°
As to the poor to give part of me,
Then shouldst thou not in this dolor be,
Nor in this great sorrow and care.
EVERYMAN. Lo, now was I deceived ere I was ware,
And all I may wyte° my spending of time.
GOODS. What, weenest thou that I am thine?
EVERYMAN. I had weened so.
GOODS. Nay, Everyman, I say no;
As for a while I was lent thee,
A season thou hast had me in prosperity.
My condition is man's soul to kill;
If I save one, a thousand I do spill;°
Weenest thou that I will follow thee
From this world? Nay, verily.
EVERYMAN. I had weened otherwise.
GOODS. Therefore to thy soul Goods is a thief;

429. lesing: lying. **431. during:** while living. **436. wyte:** blame on. **443. spill:** destroy.

For when thou art dead, this is my guise,°
Another to deceive in the same wise
As I have done thee, and all to his soul's reprief.°
EVERYMAN. O false Goods, curséd may thou be!
Thou traitor to God, that hast deceived me
And caught me in thy snare.
GOODS. Marry!° thou brought thyself in care,°
Whereof I am right glad.
I must needs laugh, I cannot be sad.
EVERYMAN. Ah, Goods, thou hast has long my heartly love;
I gave thee that which should be the Lord's above.
But wilt thou not go with me indeed?
I pray thee truth to say.
GOODS. No, so God me speed!
Therefore farewell, and have good day. (*Exit* GOODS.)
EVERYMAN. O, to whom shall I make my moan
For to go with me in that heavy journey?
First Fellowship said he would with me gone;
His words were very pleasant and gay,
But afterward he left me alone.
Then spake I to my kinsmen, all in despair,
And also they gave me words fair,
They lacked no fair speaking,
But all forsook me in the ending.
Then want I to my Goods, that I loved best,
In hope to have comfort, but there had I least;
For my Goods sharply did me tell
That he bringeth many into hell.
Then of myself I was ashamed,
And so I am worthy to be blamed;
Thus may I well myself hate.
Of whom shall I now counsel take?
I think that I shall never speed
Till that I go to my Good Deeds.
But alas! she is so weak
That she can neither go nor speak.
Yet will I venture on her now.
My Good Deeds, where be you?

(GOOD DEEDS *speaks from the ground.*)

GOOD DEEDS. Here I lie, cold in the ground.

448. guise: custom. **450. reprief:** reproach. **454. Marry:** "by Mary," a mild oath. **care:** trouble.

Thy sins hath me sore bound,
That I cannot stir.

EVERYMAN. O Good Deeds, I stand in fear!
I must you pray of counsel,
For help now should come right well.

GOOD DEEDS. Everyman, I have understanding
That ye be summoned account to make
Before Messias, of Jerusalem King;
And you do by me,° that journey with you will I take.

EVERYMAN. Therefore I come to you my moan to make;
I pray you that ye will go with me.

GOOD DEEDS. I would full fain, but I cannot stand, verily.

EVERYMAN. Why, is there anything on you fall?

GOOD DEEDS. Yea, sir, I may thank you of all;°
If ye had perfectly cheered° me,
Your book of count full ready had be.
Look, the books of your works and deeds eke.°
Behold how they lie under the feet,
To your soul's heaviness.

EVERYMAN. Our Lord Jesus help me!
For one letter here I can not see.°

GOOD DEEDS. There is a blind reckoning in time of distress!°

EVERYMAN. Good Deeds, I pray you, help me in this need,
Or else I am for ever damned indeed.
Therefore help me to make my reckoning.
Before the Redeemer of all thing,
That King is, and was, and ever shall.

GOOD DEEDS. Everyman, I am sorry of your fall,
And fain would I help you, and I were able.

EVERYMAN. Good Deeds, your counsel I pray you give me.

GOOD DEEDS. That shall I do verily;
Though that on my feet I may not go,
I have a sister that shall with you also,
Called Knowledge,° which shall with you abide,
To help you to make that dreadful reckoning.

(*Enter* KNOWLEDGE.)

KNOWLEDGE. Everyman, I will go with thee, and be thy guide,
In thy most need to go by thy side.

495. do by me: follow my advice. **500. of all:** for everything. **501. cheered:** cherished. **503. eke:** also. **507. one . . . see:** I cannot make out a single letter. **508. There . . . distress:** the account is hard to read in time of trouble. **520. Knowledge:** i.e., knowledge of sin.

EVERYMAN. In good condition I am now in every thing,
And am wholly content with this good thing;
Thanked be God my Creator.

GOOD DEEDS. And when he hath brougth thee there,
Where thou shalt heal thee of thy smart,
Then go you with your reckoning and your Good Deeds together
For to make you joyful at heart
Before the blesséd Trinity.

EVERYMAN. My Good Deeds, gramercy!
I am well content, certainly,
With your words sweet.

KNOWLEDGE. Now go we together lovingly
To Confession, that cleansing river.

EVERYMAN. For Joy I weep; I would we were there!
But, I pray you, give me cognition°
Where dwelleth that holy man, Confession.

KNOWLEDGE. In the house of salvation,
We shall find him in that place,
That shall us comfort, by God's grace.

(*Enter* CONFESSION.)

Lo, this is Confession. Kneel down and ask mercy,
For he is in good conceit° with God almighty.

EVERYMAN. O glorious fountain, that all uncleanness doth clarify,
Wash from me the spots of vice unclean,
That on me no sin may be seen.
I come, with Knowledge, for my redemption,
Redempt with hearty and full contrition;
For I am commanded a pilgrimage to take,
And great accounts before God to make.
Now, I pray you, Shrift,° mother of salvation,
Help my Good Deeds for my piteous exclamation.

CONFESSION. I know your sorrow well, Everyman.
Because with Knowledge ye come to me,
I will you comfort as well as I can,
And a precious jewel I will give thee,
Called penance, voider of adversity.
Therewith shall your body chastised be
With abstinence and perseverance in God's service.
Here shall you receive that scourge of me

(*Gives* EVERYMAN *a scourge.*)

538. cognition: understanding. **544. conceit:** favor. **552. Shrift:** absolution.

Which is penance strong that ye must endure
To remember thy Savior was scourged for thee
With sharp scourges and suffered it patiently.
So must thou ere thou 'scape° that painful pilgrimage.
Knowledge, keep him in this voyage,
And by that time Good Deeds will be with thee.
But in any wise be sure of mercy,
For your time draweth fast, and ye will saved be;
Ask God mercy, and He will grant truly;
When with the scourge of penance man doth him bind,
The oil of forgiveness then shall he find. (*Exit* CONFESSION.)

EVERYMAN. Thanked be God for his gracious work!
For now I will my penance begin;
This hath rejoiced and lighted my heart,
Though the knots be painful and hard within.

KNOWLEDGE. Everyman, look your penance that ye fulfil,
What pain that ever it to you be,
And Knowledge shall give you counsel at will
How your account ye shall make clearly.

(EVERYMAN *kneels.*)

EVERYMAN. O eternal God! O heavenly figure!
O way of rightwiseness! O goodly vision!
Which descended down in a virgin pure
Because he would Everyman redeem,
Which Adam forfeited by his disobedience.
O blesséd Godhead! elect and high divine,
Forgive me my grievous offence;
Here I cry thee mercy in this presence.
O ghostly treasure! O ransomer and redeemer!
Of all the world hope and conductor,
Mirror of joy, and founder of mercy,
Which illumineth heaven and earth thereby,
Hear my clamorous complaint, though it late be.
Receive my prayers; unworthy in this heavy life.
Though I be a sinner most abominable,
Yet let my name be written in Moses' table.°
O Mary! pray to the Maker of all thing,
Me for to help at my ending,
And save me from the power of my enemy,

565. 'scape: finish. **596. table:** tablets, i.e., among the saved.

For Death assaileth me strongly.
And, Lady, that I may by means of thy prayer
Of your Son's glory to be partner,
By the means of his passion I it crave.
I beseech you, help my soul to save. (*He rises.*)
Knowledge, give me the scourge of penance.
My flesh therewith shall give you a quittance.°
I will now begin, if God give me grace.
KNOWLEDGE. Everyman, God give you time and space.
Thus I bequeath you in the hands of our Savior,
Now may you make your reckoning sure.
EVERYMAN. In the name of the Holy Trinity,
My body sore punished shall be. (*Scourges himself.*)
Take this, body, for the sin of the flesh.
Also thou delightest to go gay and fresh,
And in the way of damnation thou did me bring;
Therefore suffer now strokes of punishing.
Now of penance I will wade the water clear,
To save me from purgatory, that sharp fire.

(GOOD DEEDS *rises.*)

GOOD DEEDS. I thank God, now I can walk and go,
And am delivered of my sickness and woe.
Therefore with Everyman I will go, and not spare;
His good works I will help him to declare.
KNOWLEDGE. Now, Everyman, be merry and glad!
Your Good Deeds cometh now, ye may not be sad.
Now is your Good Deeds whole and sound,
Going upright upon the ground.
EVERYMAN. My heart is light, and shall be evermore.
Now will I smite faster than I did before.
GOOD DEEDS. Everyman, pilgrim, my special friend,
Blesséd be thou without end.
For thee is prepared the eternal glory.
Ye have me made whole and sound,
Therefore I will bide by thee in every stound.°
EVERYMAN. Welcome, my Good Deeds; now I hear thy voice,
I weep for very sweetness of love.
KNOWLEDGE. Be no more sad, but ever rejoice;
God seeth thy living in his throne above.

606. a quittance: full payment. **633. stound:** trial.

Put on this garment to thy behoof,°
Which is wet with your tears,
Or else before God you may it miss,
When you to your journey's end come shall.
EVERYMAN. Gentle Knowledge, what do ye it call?
KNOWLEDGE. It is the garment of sorrow;
From pain it will you borrow,°
Contrition it is
That getteth forgiveness;
It pleaseth God passing well.
GOOD DEEDS. Everyman, will you wear it for your heal?

(EVERYMAN *puts on garment of contrition.*)

EVERYMAN. Now blesséd be Jesu, Mary's Son,
For now have I on true contrition.
And let us go now without tarrying;
Good Deeds, have we clear our reckoning?
GOOD DEEDS. Yea, indeed I have it here.
EVERYMAN. Then I trust we need not fear.
Now, friends, let us not part in twain.
KNOWLEDGE. Nay, Everyman, that will we not, certain.
GOOD DEEDS. Yet must thou lead with thee
Three persons of great might.
EVERYMAN. Who should they be?
GOOD DEEDS. Discretion and Strength they hight,°
And thy Beauty may not abide behind.
KNOWLEDGE. Also ye must call to mind
Your Five Wits° as for your counselors.
GOOD DEEDS. You must have them ready at all hours.
EVERYMAN. How shall I get them hither?
KNOWLEDGE. You must call them all together,
And they will hear you incontinent.°
EVERYMAN. My friends, come hither and be present,
Discretion, Strength, my Five Wits, and Beauty.

(*Enter* DISCRETION, STRENGTH, FIVE WITS, *and* BEAUTY.)

BEAUTY. Here at your will we be all ready.
What will ye that we should do?
GOOD DEEDS. That ye would with Everyman go,
And help him in his pilgrimage.
Advise you, will ye with him or not in that voyage?

638. behoof: benefit. **644. borrow:** redeem. **660. hight:** are called. **663. Five Wits:** five senses. **667. incontinent:** at once.

Strength. We will bring him all thither,
To his help and comfort, ye may believe me.
Discretion. So will we go with him all together.
Everyman. Almighty God, lovéd may thou be!
I give thee laud° that I have hither brought
Strength, Discretion, Beauty, and Five Wits. Lack I naught.
And my Good Deeds, with Knowledge clear,
All be in company at my will here.
I desire no more to my business.
Strength. And I, Strength, will by you stand in distress,
Though thou would in battle fight on the ground.
Five Wits. And though it were through the world round,
We will not depart for sweet nor sour.
Beauty. No more will I, unto death's hour,
Whatsoever thereof befall.
Discretion. Everyman, advise you first of all,
Go with a good advisement and deliberation.
We all give you virtuous monition
That all shall be well.
Everyman. My friends, hearken what I will tell:
I pray God reward you in his heavenly sphere.
Now hearken, all that be here,
For I will make my testament
Here before you all present:
In alms half my goods I will give my hands twain
In the way of charity, with good intent,
And the other half still shall remain,
I it bequeath to be returned there it ought to be.
This I do in despite of the fiend of hell,
To go quite out of his peril
Ever after and this day.
Knowledge. Everyman, hearken what I say;
Go to Priesthood, I you advise,
And receive of him in any wise
The holy sacrament and ointment together,°
Then shortly see ye turn again hither;
We will all abide you here.
Five Wits. Yea, Everyman, hie you that ye ready were.
There is no emperor, king, duke, nor baron,
That of God hath commission
As hath the least priest in the world being;
For of the blesséd sacraments pure and benign

679. laud: praise. **709. The . . . together:** Communion and extreme unction.

He beareth the keys, and thereof hath the cure
For man's redemption—it is ever sure—
Which God for our soul's medicine
Gave us out of his heart with great pain,
Here in this transitory life, for thee and me.
The blesséd sacraments seven there be:
Baptism, confirmation, with priesthood good,
And the sacrament of God's precious flesh and blood,
Marriage, the holy extreme unction, and penance.
These seven be good to have in remembrance,
Gracious sacraments of high divinity.
EVERYMAN. Fain would I receive that holy body
And meekly to my ghostly father I will go.
FIVE WITS. Everyman, that is the best that ye can do.
God will you to salvation bring,
For priesthood exceedeth all other thing;
To us Holy Scripture they do teach,
And converteth man from sin, heaven to reach;
God hath to them more power given,
Than to any angel that is in heaven.
With five words he may consecrate
God's body in flesh and blood to make,
And handleth his Maker between his hands.
The priest bindeth and unbindeth all bands,
Both in earth and in heaven.
Thou, ministers all the sacraments seven,
Though we kissed thy feet, thou wert worthy;
Thou art the surgeon that cureth sin deadly:
No remedy we find under God
But all only priesthood.
Everyman, God gave priests that dignity,
And setteth them in his stead among us to be;
Thus be they above angels, in degree.

(EVERYMAN *goes out to receive the last rites of the church.*)

KNOWLEDGE. If priests be good, it is so, surely.
But when Jesus hanged on the cross with great smart,
There he gave out of his blesséd heart
The same sacrament in great torment.
He sold them not to us, that Lord omnipotent.
Therefore Saint Peter the Apostle doth say
That Jesus' curse hath all they
Which God their Savior do buy or sell,

Or they for any money do take or tell.°
Sinful priests giveth the sinners example bad;
Their children sitteth by other men's fires, I have heard;
And some haunteth women's company
With unclean life, as lusts of lechery.
These be with sin made blind.
FIVE WITS. I trust to God no such way we find.
Therefore let us priesthood honor,
And follow their doctrine for our souls' succour.
We be their sheep, and they shepherds be
By whom we all be kept in surety.
Peace! for yonder I see Everyman come,
Which hath made true satisfaction.
GOOD DEEDS. Methinketh it is he indeed.

(*Re-enter* EVERYMAN.)

EVERYMAN. Now Jesu be your alder speed.°
I have received the sacrament for my redemption,
And then mine extreme unction.
Blesséd be all they that counseled me to take it!
And now, friends, let us go without longer respite.
I thank God that ye have tarried so long.
Now set each of you on this rood° your hand,
And shortly follow me.
I go before, there I would be. God be our guide.
STRENGTH. Everyman, we will not from you go,
Till ye have done this voyage long.
DISCRETION. I, Discretion, will bide by you also.
KNOWLEDGE. And though this pilgrimage be never so strong,°
I will never part you fro.°
Everyman, I will be as sure by thee
As ever I did by Judas Maccabee.

(*They go to a grave.*)

EVERYMAN. Alas! I am so faint I may not stand,
My limbs under me do fold.
Friends, let us not turn again to this land,
Not for all the world's gold;
For into this cave must I creep
And turn to earth, and there to sleep.
BEAUTY. What, into this grave? Alas!

758. tell: count. **772. your alder speed:** the help of you all. **778. rood:** cross. **784. strong:** hard. **785. fro:** from.

EVERYMAN. Yea, there shall you consume, more and less.
BEAUTY. And what, should I smother here?
EVERYMAN. Yea, by my faith, and never more appear.
In this world live no more we shall,
But in heaven before the highest Lord of all.
BEAUTY. I cross out all this; adieu; by Saint John!
I take my cap in my lap and am gone.
EVERYMAN. What, Beauty, whither will ye?
BEAUTY. Peace! I am deaf. I look not behind me,
Not and thou would give me all the gold in thy chest.

(*Exit* BEAUTY.)

EVERYMAN. Alas, whereto may I trust?
Beauty goeth fast away from me;
She promised with me to live and die.
STRENGTH. Everyman, I will thee also forsake and deny.
Thy game liketh me not at all.
EVERYMAN. Why, then ye will forsake me all?
Sweet Strength, tarry a little space.
STRENGTH. Nay, sir, by the rood of grace,
I will hie me from thee fast,
Though thou weep till thy heart to-brast.°
EVERYMAN. Ye would ever bide by me, ye said.
STRENGTH. Yea, I have you far enough conveyed.
Ye be old enough, I understand,
Your pilgrimage to take on hand.
I repent me that I hither came.
EVERYMAN. Strength, you to displease I am to blame;
Yet promise is debt, this ye well wot.
STRENGTH. In faith, I care not!
Thou art but a fool to complain.
You spend your speech and waste your brain.
Go, thrust thee into the ground. (*Exit* STRENGTH.)
EVERYMAN. I had weened surer I should you have found.
He that trusteth in his Strength
She him deceiveth at the length.
Both Strength and Beauty forsaketh me,
Yet they promised me fair and lovingly.
DISCRETION. Everyman, I will after Strength be gone;
As for me I will leave you alone.
EVERYMAN. Why, Discretion, will ye forsake me?
DISCRETION. Yea, in faith, I will go from thee;

814. to-brast: burst.

For when Strength goeth before
I follow after evermore.
EVERYMAN. Yet, I pray thee, for the love of the Trinity,
Look in my grave once piteously.
DISCRETION. Nay, so nigh will I not come.
Farewell, every one! (*Exit* DISCRETION.)
EVERYMAN. O all thing faileth, save God alone,
Beauty, Strength, and Discretion;
For when Death bloweth his blast,
They all run from me full fast.
FIVE WITS. Everyman, my leave now of thee I take;
I will follow the other, for here I thee forsake.
EVERYMAN. Alas! then may I wail and weep,
For I took you for my best friend.
FIVE WITS. I will no longer thee keep;
Now farewell, and there an end. (*Exit* FIVE WITS.)
EVERYMAN. O Jesu, help! All hath forsaken me!
GOOD DEEDS. Nay, Everyman; I will bide with thee,
I will not forsake thee indeed;
Thou shalt find me a good friend at need.
EVERYMAN. Gramercy, Good Deeds! Now may I true friends see.
They have forsaken me, every one;
I loved them better than my Good Deeds alone.
Knowledge, will ye forsake me also?
KNOWLEDGE. Yea, Everyman, when ye to death shall go;
But not yet, for no manner of danger.
EVERYMAN. Gramercy, Knowledge, with all my heart.
KNOWLEDGE. Nay, yet I will not from hence depart
Till I see where ye shall be come.
EVERYMAN. Methink, alas, that I must be gone
To make my reckoning and my debts pay,
For I see my time is nigh spent away.
Take example, all ye that this do hear or see,
How they that I loved best do forsake me,
Except my Good Deeds that bideth truly.
GOOD DEEDS. All earthly things is but vanity.
Beauty, Strength, and Discretion do man forsake,
Foolish friends and kinsmen, that fair spake,
All fleeth save Good Deeds, and that am I.
EVERYMAN. Have mercy on me, God most mighty;
And stand by me, thou Mother and Maid, holy Mary!
GOOD DEEDS. Fear not, I will speak for thee.
EVERYMAN. Here I cry God mercy!

GOOD DEEDS. Short° our end, and 'minish° our pain.
Let us go and never come again.
EVERYMAN. Into thy hands, Lord, my soul I commend.
Receive it, Lord, that it be not lost.
As thou me boughtest, so me defend.
And save me from the fiend's boast,
That I may appear with that blesséd host.
That shall be saved at the day of doom.
In manus tuas—of might's most
For ever—*commendo spiritum meum.*°

(EVERYMAN *and* GOOD DEEDS *go into the grave.*)

KNOWLEDGE. Now hath he suffered that we all shall endure;
The Good Deeds shall make all sure.
Now hath he made ending.
Methinketh that I hear angels sing
And make great joy and melody
Where Everyman's soul received shall be.
ANGEL. Come, excellent elect spouse to Jesu!
Here above thou shalt go
Because of thy singular virtue.
Now the soul is taken the body fro,
Thy reckoning is crystal clear.
Now shalt thou into the heavenly sphere,
Unto the which all ye shall come
That liveth well before the day of doom. (*Exit* KNOWLEDGE.)

(*Enter* DOCTOR *as Epilogue.*)

DOCTOR.° This moral men may have in mind;
Ye hearers, take it of worth, old and young,
And forsake Pride, for he deceiveth you in the end,
And remember Beauty, Five Wits, Strength, and Discretion,
They all at the last do Everyman forsake,
Save his Good Deeds there doth he take.
But beware, and they be small
Before God he hath no help at all.
None excuse may be there for Everyman.
Alas, how shall he do then?
For, after death, amends may no man make,
For then mercy and pity doth him forsake.

878. Short: shorten. **'minish:** diminish. **886–87. In manus . . . meum:** "Into thy hands I commend my spirit." **902. Doctor:** teacher.

If his reckoning be not clear when he doth come,
God will say, "*Ite, maledicti, in ignem aeternum.*" °
And he that hath his account whole and sound,
High in heaven he shall be crowned.
Unto which place God bring us all thither,
That we may live body and soul together.
Thereto help the Trinity!
Amen, say ye, for saint charity.

Thus endeth this moral play of Everyman.

QUESTIONS

1. Composed by an unknown author probably before 1500, *Everyman* is a characteristically medieval play, yet it has been produced in recent years on radio and stage with notable success. What qualities continue to make it effective and moving?

2. *Everyman* belongs to a class of medieval plays known as moralities. Briefly, a morality is a moral allegory in dramatic form. What characteristics of this play make it an allegory? On what central metaphor is the allegory based?

3. Unlike most plays, this play is frankly didactic (intended to teach). List its didactic devices. Does this didacticism weaken the force or appeal of the play? Why or why not? What are the central lessons of the play? Draw up a brief account of the religious doctrines it embodies.

4. Of what relative importance are plot, character, and theme in the play? Discuss the importance of each.

5. At what points in the play does Everyman undergo a change of mood or attitude? Chart the rising and falling of his morale. What causes each change?

6. Everyman has four soliloquies during the first half of the play, none during the second half. Can you relate this fact to the action and meaning of the play? What effect do the soliloquies have?

7. Discuss the characterization of (a) God, (b) Death, (c) Everyman. How is each conceived? How might they have been conceived differently?

8. What sort of stage setting would you design for this play? Would it be effective if performed on the steps of a cathedral? How would you present God? How old an actor would you choose for Everyman? What parts would you assign to female actors? How would you costume the various characters?

9. Contrast the play with *The Stronger* and *The Brute*. What qualities does it lack that they have? What qualities does it have that they lack?

915. Ite maledicti, in ignem aeternum: "Go, ye accursed, into everlasting fire."

CHAPTER TWO

Realistic and Nonrealistic Drama

As in fiction and poetry, so in drama, literary truth is not the same as fidelity to fact. Fantasy is as much the property of the theater as of poetry or the prose tale. Shakespeare in *A Midsummer Night's Dream* and *The Tempest* uses fairies and goblins and monsters as characters, and in *Hamlet* and *Macbeth* he introduces ghosts and witches. These supernatural characters, nevertheless, serve as a vehicle for truth. When Bottom, in *A Midsummer Night's Dream,* is given an ass's head, the enchantment is a visual metaphor. The witches in *Macbeth* truthfully prefigure a tragic destiny.

Because it is written to be performed, however, drama adds still another dimension of possible unreality. It may be realistic or unrealistic in mode of production as well as in content. Staging, make-up, costuming, and acting may all be handled in such a way as to emphasize the realistic or the fanciful.

It must be recognized, however, that all stage production, no matter how realistic, involves a certain necessary artificiality. If an indoor scene is presented on a picture-frame stage, the spectator is asked to imagine that a room with only three walls is actually a room with four walls. In an arena-type theater, he must imagine all four walls. Both types of presentation, moreover, require adjustments in the acting. In a traditional theater, the actors most of the time must be facing the missing fourth wall. In an arena-type theater, they must not turn their backs too long on any "wall." Both types of presentation, in the interests of effective presentation, require the actors to depart from an absolute realism.

From this point on, the departure from the appearance of reality may be little or great. In many late nineteenth- and early twentieth-century productions, an effort was made to make stage sets as realistic as possible. If the play called for a setting in a study, there had to be real book shelves on the wall and real books on the shelves. If the room contained a wash basin, real water had to flow from the taps. More recently, however, plays have been performed on a stage furnished only with drapes and platforms. In between these two extremes, all degrees of realism are possible. The scenery may consist of painted flats, with painted bookshelves and painted books and painted pictures on the wall. Or, instead of scenery, a play may use only a few movable properties to suggest the required setting. Thornton Wilder's famous play *Our Town* (1938) utilized a bare stage, without curtain, with exposed ropes and backstage equipment, and with a few chairs, two ladders, and a couple of trellises as the only properties. For a scene at a soda fountain, a plank was laid across the backs of two chairs. In fact, provision of elaborately realistic stage sets has been the exception rather than the rule in the long history of the theater. Neither in Greek nor in Shakespearean theater was setting much more than suggested.

But the choice of realistic or unrealistic stage sets, costuming, and make-up may lie with the producer rather than the playwright. When we move to the realm of language and the management of dialogue, the choice is entirely the playwright's. Here again all degrees of realism and nonrealism are possible. In the realistic theater of the early twentieth century, playwrights often made an elaborate effort to reproduce the flat quality of ordinary speech, with all its stumblings and inarticulateness. In real life, of course, few lovers speak with the eloquence of Romeo and Juliet, and many people, in daily conversation, have difficulty getting through a grammatically correct sentence of any length or complexity. They break off, they begin again, they end lamely with an apology, a grammatical blunder, a "you know." Such broken-backed and inadequate speech, skillfully used by the playwright, may faithfully render the quality of human life at some levels, yet its limitations for expressing the heights and depths of human experience are obvious. Most dramatic dialogue, even when most realistic, is more coherent and expressive than speech in actual life. Art is always a heightening or an intensification of reality; else it would have no value. The heightening may be little or great. It is greatest in poetic drama. The love exchanges of Romeo and Juliet, spoken in rhymed iambic pentameter and at one point taking the form of a perfectly regular sonnet, are absurdly unrealistic if judged as an imitation of actual speech, but they vividly express the emotional truth of passionate, idealistic young love. It is no criticism of Shakespearean tragedy, therefore, to say that in real life people do not speak in blank verse. The deepest purpose of the playwright is not to imitate actual human speech but to give accurate and powerful expression to human thought and emotion.

All drama asks us to accept certain departures from reality—certain dramatic *conventions*. That a room with three walls or fewer may represent one with four walls, that the actors speak in the language of the audience whatever the nationality of the persons they play, that the actors stand or sit so as to face the audience most of the time—these are all necessary conventions. Other conventions are optional—for example, that the characters may reveal their inner thoughts through soliloquies and asides or may speak in the heightened language of poetry. The playwright working in a strictly realistic mode will avoid the optional conventions, for they conflict with the realistic method that he has chosen to achieve his purpose. The playwright working in a freer mode will feel free to use any or all of them, for they make possible the revelation of dimensions of reality unreachable by a strictly realistic method. Hamlet's famous soliloquy that begins "To be or not to be," in which he debates in blank verse the merits of continued life and suicide, is unrealistic on two counts, but it enables Shakespeare to present Hamlet's introspective mind more powerfully than he otherwise could have done. The characteristic device of Greek drama, a chorus—a group of actors speaking in unison, often in a chant, while going through the steps of an elaborate formalized dance—is another unrealistic device but a useful one for conveying communal or group emotion. It has been revived, in different forms, in many modern plays. The use of a narrator, as in *Our Town* and Tennessee Williams' *Glass Menagerie,* is a related unrealistic device that has served playwrights as a vehicle for dramatic truth.

In most plays, however unreal the world into which we are taken, this world is treated as self-contained, and we are asked to regard it temporarily as a real world. Thus Shakespeare's world of fairies in *A Midsummer Night's Dream* is real to us while we watch the play. Because of Shakespeare's magic, we quite willingly make that "temporary suspension of disbelief" that, according to Coleridge, "constitutes poetic faith." And the step from crediting Bottom as real, though we know in fact he is only a dressed-up actor, to regarding Bottom with an ass's head as real is relatively a small one. But some playwrights abandon even this much attempt to give their work an illusion of reality. They deliberately violate the self-containment of the fictional world and keep

Henrik Ibsen

AN ENEMY OF THE PEOPLE

CHARACTERS

DR. THOMAS STOCKMANN, *Medical Officer of the Municipal Baths*
MRS. STOCKMANN, *his wife*
PETRA, *their daughter, a teacher*
EJLIF } *their sons, aged 13 and 10 respectively*
MORTEN }
PETER STOCKMANN, *the Doctor's elder brother; Mayor of the Town and Chief Constable, Chairman of the Baths' Committee, etc., etc.*
MORTEN KIIL, *a tanner* (MRS. STOCKMANN'S *adoptive father*)
HOVSTAD, *editor of the* People's Messenger
BILLING, *subeditor*
CAPTAIN HORSTER
ASLAKSEN, *a printer*
MEN, *of various conditions and occupations, some few women, and a troop of schoolboys—the audience at a public meeting.*

The action takes place in a coast town in southern Norway.

ACT I

SCENE. DR. STOCKMANN'S *sitting-room. It is evening. The room is plainly but neatly appointed and furnished. In the right-hand wall are two doors; the farther leads out to the hall, the nearer to the doctor's study. In the left-hand wall, opposite the door leading to the hall, is a door leading to the other rooms occupied by the family. In the middle of the same wall stands the stove, and, further forward, a couch with a looking-glass hanging over it and an oval table in front of it. On the table, a lighted lamp, with a lamp-shade. At the back of the room, an open door leads to the dining-room.* BILLING *is seen sitting at the dining table, on which a lamp is burning. He has a napkin tucked under his chin, and* MRS. STOCKMANN *is standing by the table handing him a large plate-full of roast beef. The other places at the table are empty, and the table somewhat in disorder, a meal having evidently recently been finished.*

MRS. STOCKMANN. You see, if you come an hour late, Mr. Billing, you have to put up with cold meat.

AN ENEMY OF THE PEOPLE. First performed in 1882.

Billing (*as he eats*). It is uncommonly good, thank you—remarkably good.

Mrs. Stockmann. My husband makes such a point of having his meals punctually, you know—

Billing. That doesn't affect me a bit. Indeed, I almost think I enjoy a meal all the better when I can sit down and eat all by myself and undisturbed.

Mrs. Stockmann. Oh well, as long as you are enjoying it—. (*Turns to the hall door, listening*) I expect that is Mr. Hovstad coming too.

Billing. Very likely.

(Peter Stockmann *comes in. He wears an overcoat and his official hat, and carries a stick.*)

Peter Stockmann. Good evening, Katherine.

Mrs. Stockmann (*coming forward into the sitting-room*). Ah, good evening—is it you? How good of you to come up and see us!

Peter Stockmann. I happened to be passing, and so— (*Looks into the dining-room*) But you have company with you, I see.

Mrs. Stockmann (*a little embarrassed*). Oh, no—it was quite by chance he came in. (*Hurriedly*) Won't you come in and have something, too?

Peter Stockmann. I! No, thank you. Good gracious—hot meat at night! Not with my digestion.

Mrs. Stockmann. Oh, but just once in a way—

Peter Stockmann. No, no, my dear lady; I stick to my tea and bread and butter. It is much more wholesome in the long run—and a little more economical, too.

Mrs. Stockmann (*smiling*). Now you mustn't think that Thomas and I are spendthrifts.

Peter Stockmann. Not you, my dear; I would never think that of you. (*Points to the Doctor's study*) Is he not at home?

Mrs. Stockmann. No, he went out for a little turn after supper—he and the boys.

Peter Stockmann. I doubt if that is a wise thing to do. (*Listens.*) I fancy I hear him coming now.

Mrs. Stockmann. No, I don't think it is he. (*A knock is heard at the door.*) Come in! (Hovstad *comes in from the hall.*) Oh, it is you, Mr. Hovstad!

Hovstad. Yes, I hope you will forgive me, but I was delayed at the printer's. Good evening, Mr. Mayor.

Peter Stockmann (*bowing a little distantly*). Good evening. You have come on business, no doubt.

Hovstad. Partly. It's about an article for the paper.

PETER STOCKMANN. So I imagined. I hear my brother has become a prolific contributor to the "People's Messenger."

HOVSTAD. Yes, he is good enough to write in the "People's Messenger" when he has any home truths to tell.

MRS. STOCKMANN (*to* HOVSTAD). But won't you—? (*Points to the dining-room.*)

PETER STOCKMANN. Quite so, quite so. I don't blame him in the least, as a writer, for addressing himself to the quarters where he will find the readiest sympathy. And, besides that, I personally have no reason to bear any ill will to your paper, Mr. Hovstad.

HOVSTAD. I quite agree with you.

PETER STOCKMANN. Taking one thing with another, there is an excellent spirit of toleration in the town—an admirable municipal spirit. And it all springs from the fact of our having a great common interest to unite us—an interest that is in an equally high degree the concern of every right-minded citizen—

HOVSTAD. The Baths, yes.

PETER STOCKMANN. Exactly—our fine, new, handsome Baths. Mark my words, Mr. Hovstad—the Baths will become the focus of our municipal life! Not a doubt of it!

MRS. STOCKMANN. That is just what Thomas says.

PETER STOCKMANN. Think how extraordinarily the place has developed within the last year or two! Money has been flowing in, and there is some life and some business doing in the town. Houses and landed property are rising in value every day.

HOVSTAD. And unemployment is diminishing.

PETER STOCKMANN. Yes, that is another thing. The burden of the poor rates has been lightened, to the great relief of the propertied classes; and that relief will be even greater if only we get a really good summer this year, and lots of visitors—plenty of invalids, who will make the Baths talked about.

HOVSTAD. And there is a good prospect of that, I hear.

PETER STOCKMANN. It looks very promising. Enquiries about apartments and that sort of thing are reaching us every day.

HOVSTAD. Well, the doctor's article will come in very suitably.

PETER STOCKMANN. Has he been writing something just lately?

HOVSTAD. This is something he wrote in the winter; a recommendation of the Baths—an account of the excellent sanitary conditions here. But I held the article over, temporarily.

PETER STOCKMANN. Ah,—some little difficulty about it, I suppose?

HOVSTAD. No, not at all; I thought it would be better to wait till the spring, because it is just at this time that people begin to think seriously about their summer quarters.

PETER STOCKMANN. Quite right; you were perfectly right, Mr. Hovstad.

HOVSTAD. Yes, Thomas is really indefatigable when it is a question of the Baths.

PETER STOCKMANN. Well—remember, he is the Medical Officer to the Baths.

HOVSTAD. Yes, and what is more, they owe their existence to him.

PETER STOCKMANN. To him? Indeed! It is true I have heard from time to time that some people are of that opinion. At the same time I must say I imagined that I look a modest part in the enterprise.

MRS. STOCKMANN. Yes, that is what Thomas is always saying.

HOVSTAD. But who denies it, Mr. Stockmann? You set the thing going and made a practical concern of it; we all know that. I only meant that the idea of it came first from the doctor.

PETER STOCKMANN. Oh, ideas—yes! My brother has had plenty of them in his time—unfortunately. But when it is a question of putting an idea into practical shape, you have to apply to a man of different mettle, Mr. Hovstad. And I certainly should have thought that in this house at least—

MRS. STOCKMANN. My dear Peter—

HOVSTAD. How can you think that—?

MRS. STOCKMANN. Won't you go in and have something, Mr. Hovstad? My husband is sure to be back directly.

HOVSTAD. Thank you, perhaps just a morsel. (*Goes into the dining-room.*)

PETER STOCKMANN (*lowering his voice a little*). It is a curious thing that these farmers' sons never seem to lose their want of tact.

MRS. STOCKMANN. Surely it is not worth bothering about! Cannot you and Thomas share the credit as brothers?

PETER STOCKMANN. I should have thought so; but apparently some people are not satisfied with a share.

MRS. STOCKMANN. What nonsense! You and Thomas get on so capitally together. (*Listens*) There he is at last, I think. (*Goes out and opens the door leading to the hall.*)

DR. STOCKMANN (*laughing and talking outside*). Look here—here is another guest for you, Katherine. Isn't that jolly! Come in, Captain Horster; hang your coat up on this peg. Ah, you don't wear an overcoat. Just think, Katherine; I met him in the street and could hardly persuade him to come up! (CAPTAIN HORSTER *comes into the room and greets* MRS. STOCKMANN. *He is followed by* DR. STOCKMANN.) Come along in, boys. They are ravenously hungry again, you know. Come along, Captain Horster; you must have a slice of beef. (*Pushes* HORSTER *into the dining-room.* EJLIF *and* MORTEN *go in after them.*)

MRS. STOCKMANN. But, Thomas, don't you see—?

DR. STOCKMANN (*turning in the doorway*). Oh, is it you, Peter? (*Shakes hands with him.*) Now that is very delightful.

PETER STOCKMANN. Unfortunately I must go in a moment—

Dr. Stockmann. Rubbish! There is some toddy just coming in. You haven't forgotten the toddy, Katherine?

Mrs. Stockmann. Of course not; the water is boiling now. (*Goes into the dining-room.*)

Peter Stockmann. Toddy too!

Dr. Stockmann. Yes, sit down and we will have it comfortably.

Peter Stockmann. Thanks, I never care about an evening's drinking.

Dr. Stockmann. But this isn't an evening's drinking.

Peter Stockmann. It seems to me—. (*Looks towards the dining-room*) It is extraordinary how they can put away all that food.

Dr. Stockmann (*rubbing his hands*). Yes, isn't it splendid to see young people eat? They have always got an appetite, you know! That's as it should be. Lots of food—to build up their strength! They are the people who are going to stir up the fermenting forces of the future, Peter.

Peter Stockmann. May I ask what they will find here to "stir up," as you put it?

Dr. Stockmann. Ah, you must ask the young people that—when the time comes. We shan't be able to see it, of course. That stands to reason—two old fogies, like us—

Peter Stockmann. Really, really! I must say that is an extremely odd expression to—

Dr. Stockmann. Oh, you mustn't take me too literally, Peter. I am so heartily happy and contented, you know. I think it is such an extraordinary piece of good fortune to be in the middle of all this growing, germinating life. It is a splendid time to live in! It is as if a whole new world were being created around one.

Peter Stockmann. Do you really think so?

Dr. Stockmann. Ah, naturally you can't appreciate it as keenly as I. You have lived all your life in these surroundings, and your impressions have got blunted. But I, who have been buried all these years in my little corner up north, almost without ever seeing a stranger who might bring new ideas with him—well, in my case it has just the same effect as if I had been transported into the middle of a crowded city.

Peter Stockmann. Oh, a city—!

Dr. Stockmann. I know, I know; it is all cramped enough here, compared with many other places. But there is life here—there is promise—there are innumerable things to work for and fight for; and that is the main thing. (*Calls*) Katherine, hasn't the postman been here?

Mrs. Stockmann (*from the dining-room*). No.

Dr. Stockmann. And then to be comfortably off, Peter! That is something one learns to value, when one has been on the brink of starvation, as we have.

Peter Stockmann. Oh, surely—

Dr. Stockmann. Indeed I can assure you we have often been very hard put to it, up there. And now to be able to live like a lord! To-day, for instance, we had roast beef for dinner—and, what is more, for supper too. Won't you come and have a little bit? Or let me show it you, at any rate? Come here—

PETER STOCKMANN. No, no—not for worlds!

DR. STOCKMANN. Well, but just come here then. Do you see, we have got a table-cover?

PETER STOCKMANN. Yes, I noticed it.

DR. STOCKMANN. And we have got a lamp-shade too. Do you see? All out of Katherine's savings! It makes the room so cosy. Don't you think so? Just stand here for a moment—no, no, not there—just here, that's it! Look now, when you get the light on it altogether—I really think it looks very nice, doesn't it?

PETER STOCKMANN. Oh, if you can afford luxuries of this kind—

DR. STOCKMANN. Yes, I can afford it now. Katherine tells me I earn almost as much as we spend.

PETER STOCKMANN. Almost—yes!

DR. STOCKMANN. But a scientific man must live in a little bit of style. I am quite sure an ordinary civil servant spends more in a year than I do.

PETER STOCKMANN. I daresay. A civil servant—a man in a well-paid position—

DR. STOCKMANN. Well, any ordinary merchant, then! A man in that position spends two or three times as much as—

PETER STOCKMANN. It just depends on circumstances.

DR. STOCKMANN. At all events I assure you I don't waste money unprofitably. But I can't find it in my heart to deny myself the pleasure of entertaining my friends. I need that sort of thing, you know. I have lived for so long shut out of it all, that it is a necessity of life to me to mix with young, eager, ambitious men, men of liberal and active minds; and that describes every one of those fellows who are enjoying their supper in there. I wish you knew more of Hovstad—

PETER STOCKMANN. By the way, Hovstad was telling me he was going to print another article of yours.

DR. STOCKMANN. An article of mine?

PETER STOCKMANN. Yes, about the Baths. An article you wrote in the winter.

DR. STOCKMANN. Oh, that one! No, I don't intend that to appear just for the present.

PETER STOCKMANN. Why not? It seems to me that this would be the most opportune moment.

DR. STOCKMANN. Yes, very likely—under normal conditions. (*Crosses the room.*)

PETER STOCKMANN (*following him with his eyes*). Is there anything abnormal about the present conditions?

Dr. Stockmann (*standing still*). To tell you the truth, Peter, I can't say just at this moment—at all events not to-night. There may be much that is very abnormal about the present conditions—and it is possible there may be nothing abnormal about them at all. It is quite possible it may be merely my imagination.

Peter Stockmann. I must say it all sounds most mysterious. Is there something going on that I am to be kept in ignorance of? I should have imagined that I, as Chairman of the governing body of the Baths—

Dr. Stockmann. And I should have imagined that I—. Oh, come, don't let us fly out at one another, Peter.

Peter Stockmann. Heaven forbid! I am not in the habit of flying out at people, as you call it. But I am entitled to request most emphatically that all arrangements shall be made in a business-like manner, through the proper channels, and shall be dealt with by the legally constituted authorities. I can allow no going behind our backs by any roundabout means.

Dr. Stockmann. Have I ever at any time tried to go behind your backs!

Peter Stockmann. You have an ingrained tendency to take your own way, at all events; and that is almost equally inadmissible in a well-ordered community. The individual ought undoubtedly to acquiesce in subordinating himself to the community—or, to speak more accurately, to the authorities who have the care of the community's welfare.

Dr. Stockmann. Very likely. But what the deuce has all this got to do with me?

Peter Stockmann. That is exactly what you never appear to be willing to learn, my dear Thomas. But, mark my words, some day you will have to suffer for it—sooner or later. Now I have told you. Good-bye.

Dr. Stockmann. Have you taken leave of your senses? You are on the wrong scent altogether.

Peter Stockmann. I am not usually that. You must excuse me now if I—(*calls into the dining-room*) Good night, Katherine. Good night, gentlemen. (*Goes out.*)

Mrs. Stockmann (*coming from the dining-room*). Has he gone?

Dr. Stockmann. Yes, and in such a bad temper.

Mrs. Stockmann. But, dear Thomas, what have you been doing to him again?

Dr. Stockmann. Nothing at all. And, anyhow, he can't oblige me to make my report before the proper time.

Mrs. Stockmann. What have you got to make a report to him about?

Dr. Stockmann. Hm! Leave that to me, Katherine.—It is an extraordinary thing that the postman doesn't come.

(Hovstad, Billings *and* Horster *have got up from the table and come into the sitting-room.* Ejlif *and* Morten *come in after them.*)

Billing (*stretching himself*). Ah—one feels a new man after a meal like that.

Hovstad. The mayor wasn't in a very sweet temper tonight, then.

Dr. Stockmann. It is his stomach; he has a wretched digestion.

Hovstad. I rather think it was us two of the "People's Messenger" that he couldn't digest.

Mrs. Stockmann. I thought you came out of it pretty well with him.

Hovstad. Oh yes; but it isn't anything more than a sort of truce.

Billing. That is just what it is! That word sums up the situation.

Dr. Stockmann. We must remember that Peter is a lonely man, poor chap. He has no home comforts of any kind; nothing but everlasting business. And all that infernal weak tea wash that he pours into himself! Now then, my boys, bring chairs up to the table. Aren't we going to have that toddy, Katherine?

Mrs. Stockmann (*going into the dining-room*). I am just getting it.

Dr. Stockmann. Sit down here on the couch beside me, Captain Horster. We so seldom see you—. Please sit down, my friends.

(*They sit down at the table.* Mrs. Stockmann *brings a tray, with a spirit-lamp, glasses, bottles, etc., upon it.*)

Mrs. Stockmann. There you are! This is arrack, and this is rum, and this one is the brandy. Now every one must help himself.

Dr. Stockmann (*taking a glass*). We will. (*They all mix themselves some toddy.*) And let us have the cigars. Ejlif, you know where the box is. And you, Morten, can fetch my pipe. (*The two boys go into the room on the right.*) I have a suspicion that Ejlif pockets a cigar now and then!—but I take no notice of it. (*Calls out*) And my smoking-cap too, Morten. Katherine, you can tell him where I left it. Ah, he has got it. (*The boys bring the various things.*) Now, my friends. I stick to my pipe, you know. This one has seen plenty of bad weather with me up north. (*Touches glasses with them*) Your good health! Ah! it is good to be sitting snug and warm here.

Mrs. Stockmann (*who sits knitting*). Do you sail soon, Captain Horster?

Horster. I expect to be ready to sail next week.

Mrs. Stockmann. I suppose you are going to America?

Horster. Yes, that is the plan.

Mrs. Stockmann. Then you won't be able to take part in the coming election.

Horster. Is there going to be an election?

Billing. Didn't you know?

Horster. No, I don't mix myself up with those things.

Billing. But do you not take an interest in public affairs?

Horster. No, I don't know anything about politics.

Billing. All the same, one ought to vote, at any rate.

HORSTER. Even if one doesn't know anything about what is going on?

BILLING. Doesn't know! What do you mean by that? A community is like a ship; every one ought to be prepared to take the helm.

HORSTER. Maybe that is all very well on shore; but on board ship it wouldn't work.

HOVSTAD. It is astonishing how little most sailors care about what goes on on shore.

BILLING. Very extraordinary.

DR. STOCKMANN. Sailors are like birds of passage; they feel equally at home in any latitude. And that is only an additional reason for our being all the more keen, Hovstad. Is there to be anything of public interest in to-morrow's "Messenger"?

HOVSTAD. Nothing about municipal affairs. But the day after to-morrow I was thinking of printing your article—

DR. STOCKMANN. Ah, devil take it—my article! Look here, that must wait a bit.

HOVSTAD. Really? We had just got convenient space for it, and I thought it was just the opportune moment—

DR. STOCKMANN. Yes, yes, very likely you are right; but it must wait all the same. I will explain to you later.

(PETRA *comes in from the hall, in hat and cloak and with a bundle of exercise books under her arm.*)

PETRA. Good evening.

DR. STOCKMANN. Good evening, Petra; come along.

(*Mutual greetings;* PETRA *takes off her things and puts them down on a chair by the door.*)

PETRA. And you have all been sitting here enjoying yourselves, while I have been out slaving!

DR. STOCKMANN. Well, come and enjoy yourself too!

BILLING. May I mix a glass for you?

PETRA (*coming to the table*). Thanks, I would rather do it; you always mix it too strong. But I forgot, father—I have a letter for you. (*Goes to the chair where she had laid her things.*)

DR. STOCKMAN. A letter? From whom?

PETRA (*looking in her coat pocket*). The postman gave it to me just as I was going out—

DR. STOCKMANN (*getting up and going to her*). And you only give to me now!

PETRA. I really had not time to run up again. There it is!

DR. STOCKMANN (*seizing the letter*). Let's see, let's see, child! (*Looks at the address*) Yes, that's all right!

Mrs. Stockmann. Is it the one you have been expecting so anxiously, Thomas?

Dr. Stockmann. Yes, it is. I must go to my room now and—. Where shall I get a light, Katherine? Is there no lamp in my room again?

Mrs. Stockmann. Yes, your lamp is all ready lit on your desk.

Dr. Stockmann. Good, good. Excuse me for a moment—. (*Goes into his study.*)

Petra. What do you suppose it is, mother?

Mrs. Stockmann. I don't know; for the last day or two he has always been asking if the postman has not been.

Billing. Probably some country patient.

Petra. Poor old dad!—he will overwork himself soon. (*Mixes a glass for herself*) There, that will taste good!

Hovstad. Have you been teaching in the evening school again to-day?

Petra (*sipping from her glass*). Two hours.

Billing. And four hours of school in the morning—

Petra. Five hours.

Mrs. Stockmann. And you have still got exercises to correct, I see.

Petra. A whole heap, yes.

Horster. You are pretty full up with work too, it seems to me.

Petra. Yes—but that is good. One is so delightfully tired after it.

Billing. Do you like that?

Petra. Yes, because one sleeps so well then.

Morten. You must be dreadfully wicked, Petra.

Petra. Wicked?

Morten. Yes, because you work so much. Mr. Rörlund says work is a punishment for our sins.

Ejlif. Pooh, what a duffer you are, to believe a thing like that!

Mrs. Stockmann. Come, come, Ejlif!

Billing (*laughing*). That's capital!

Hovstad. Don't you want to work as hard as that, Morten?

Morten. No, indeed I don't.

Hovstad. What do you want to be, then?

Morten. I should like best to be a Viking.

Ejlif. You would have to be a pagan then.

Morten. Well, I could become a pagan, couldn't I?

Billing. I agree with you, Morten! My sentiments, exactly.

Mrs. Stockmann (*signalling to him*). I am sure that is not true, Mr. Billing.

Billing. Yes, I swear it is! I am a pagan, and I am proud of it. Believe me, before long we shall all be pagans.

Morten. And then we shall be allowed to do anything we like?

Billing. Well, you see, Morten—.

MRS. STOCKMANN. You must go to your room now, boys; I am sure you have some lessons to learn for to-morrow.

EJLIF. I should like so much to stay a little longer—

MRS. STOCKMANN. No, no; away you go, both of you.

(*The boys say good-night and go into the room on the left.*)

HOVSTAD. Do you really think it can do the boys any harm to hear such things?

MRS. STOCKMANN. I don't know; but I don't like it.

PETRA. But you know, mother, I think you really are wrong about it.

MRS. STOCKMANN. Maybe, but I don't like it—not in our own home.

PETRA. There is so much falsehood both at home and at school. At home one must not speak, and at school we have to stand and tell lies to the children.

HORSTER. Tell lies?

PETRA. Yes, don't you suppose we have to teach them all sorts of things that we don't believe?

BILLING. That is perfectly true.

PETRA. If only I had the means I would start a school of my own, and it would be conducted on very different lines.

BILLING. Oh, bother the means—!

HORSTER. Well if you are thinking of that, Miss Stockmann, I shall be delighted to provide you with a schoolroom. The great big old house my father left me is standing almost empty; there is an immense dining-room downstairs—

PETRA (*laughing*). Thank you very much; but I am afraid nothing will come of it.

HOVSTAD. No, Miss Petra is much more likely to take to journalism, I expect. By the way, have you had time to do anything with that English story you promised to translate for us?

PETRA. No, not yet; but you shall have it in good time.

(DR. STOCKMANN *comes in from his room with an open letter in his hand.*)

DR. STOCKMANN (*waving the letter*). Well, now the town will have something new to talk about, I can tell you!

BILLING. Something new?

MRS. STOCKMANN. What is this?

DR. STOCKMANN. A great discovery, Katherine.

HOVSTAD. Really?

MRS. STOCKMANN. A discovery of yours?

DR. STOCKMANN. A discovery of mine. (*Walks up and down.*) Just let them come saying, as usual, that it is all fancy and a crazy man's imagination! But they will be careful what they say this time, I can tell you!

PETRA. But, father, tell us what it is.

DR. STOCKMANN. Yes, yes—only give me time, and you shall know all about it. If only I had Peter here now! It just shows how we men can go about forming our judgments, when in reality we are as blind as any moles—

HOVSTAD. What are you driving at, Doctor?

DR. STOCKMANN (*standing still by the table*). Isn't it the universal opinion that our town is a healthy spot?

HOVSTAD. Certainly.

DR. STOCKMANN. Quite an unusually healthy spot, in fact—a place that deserves to be recommended in the warmest possible manner either for invalids or for people who are well—

MRS. STOCKMANN. Yes, but my dear Thomas—

DR. STOCKMANN. And we have been recommending it and praising it—I have written and written, both in the "Messenger" and in pamphlets—

HOVSTAD. Well, what then?

DR. STOCKMANN. And the Baths—we have called them the "main artery of the town's life-blood," the "nerve-centre of our town," and the devil knows what else—

BILLING. "The town's pulsating heart" was the expression I once used on an important occasion—

DR. STOCKMANN. Quite so. Well, do you know what they really are, these great, splendid, much praised Baths that have cost so much money—do you know what they are?

HOVSTAD. No, what are they?

MRS. STOCKMANN. Yes, what are they?

DR. STOCKMANN. The whole place is a pesthouse!

PETRA. The Baths, father?

MRS. STOCKMANN (*at the same time*). Our Baths!

HOVSTAD. But, Doctor—

BILLING. Absolutely incredible!

DR. STOCKMANN. The whole Bath establishment is a whited, poisoned sepulchre, I tell you—the gravest possible danger to the public health! All the nastiness up at Mölledal, all that stinking filth, is infecting the water in the conduit-pipes leading to the reservoir; and the same cursed, filthy poison oozes out on the shore too—

HORSTER. Where the bathing-place is?

DR. STOCKMANN. Just there.

HOVSTAD. How do you come to be so certain of all this, Doctor?

DR. STOCKMANN. I have investigated the matter most conscientiously. For a long time past I have suspected something of the kind. Last year we had some very strange cases of illness among the visitors—typhoid cases, and cases of gastric fever—

MRS. STOCKMANN. Yes, that is quite true.

DR. STOCKMANN. At the time, we supposed the visitors had been infected before they came; but later on, in the winter, I began to have a different opinion; and so I set myself to examine the water, as well as I could.

MRS. STOCKMANN. Then that is what you have been so busy with?

DR. STOCKMANN. Indeed I have been busy, Katherine. But here I had none of the necessary scientific apparatus; so I sent samples, both of the drinking-water and of the sea-water, up to the University, to have an accurate analysis made by a chemist.

HOVSTAD. And have you got that?

DR. STOCKMANN (*showing him the letter*). Here it is! It proves the presence of decomposing organic matter in the water—it is full of infusoria. The water is absolutely dangerous to use, either internally or externally.

MRS. STOCKMANN. What a mercy you discovered it in time.

DR. STOCKMANN. You may well say so.

HOVSTAD. And what do you propose to do now, Doctor?

DR. STOCKMANN. To see the matter put right—naturally.

HOVSTAD. Can that be done?

DR. STOCKMANN. It must be done. Otherwise the Baths will be absolutely useless and wasted. But we need not anticipate that; I have a very clear idea what we shall have to do.

MRS. STOCKMANN. But why have you kept this all so secret, dear?

DR. STOCKMANN. Do you suppose I was going to run about the town gossiping about it, before I had absolute proof? No, thank you. I am not such a fool.

PETRA. Still, you might have told us—

DR. STOCKMANN. Not a living soul. But to-morrow you may run round to the old Badger—

MRS. STOCKMANN. Oh, Thomas! Thomas!

DR. STOCKMANN. Well, to your grandfather, then. The old boy will have something to be astonished at! I know he thinks I am cracked—and there are lots of other people think so too, I have noticed. But now these good folks shall see—they shall just see—! (*Walks about, rubbing his hands.*) There will be a nice upset in the town, Katherine; you can't imagine what it will be. All the conduit-pipes will have to be relaid.

HOVSTAD (*getting up*). All the conduit-pipes—?

DR. STOCKMANN. Yes, of course. The intake is too low down; it will have to be lifted to a position much higher up.

PETRA. Then you were right after all.

DR. STOCKMANN. Ah, you remember, Petra—I wrote opposing the plans before the work was begun. But at that time no one would listen to me. Well, I am going to let them have it, now! Of course I have prepared a report for the Baths Committee; I have had it ready for a week, and was only waiting for this to come. (*Shows the letter.*) Now it shall go off at once. (*Goes into his room and comes back with some papers.*) Look at that! Four closely written sheets!—and the letter shall go with them. Give me a bit of paper, Katherine—something to wrap them up in. That will do! Now give it to—to—(*stamps his foot*)—what the deuce is her name?—give it to the maid, and tell her to take it at once to the Mayor.

(MRS. STOCKMANN *takes the packet and goes out through the dining-room.*)

PETRA. What do you think uncle Peter will say, father?

DR. STOCKMANN. What is there for him to say? I should think he would be very glad that such an important truth has been brought to light.

HOVSTAD. Will you let me print a short note about your discovery in the "Messenger"?

DR. STOCKMANN. I shall be very much obliged if you will.

HOVSTAD. It is very desirable that the public should be informed of it without delay.

DR. STOCKMANN. Certainly.

MRS. STOCKMANN (*coming back*). She has just gone with it.

BILLING. Upon my soul, Doctor, you are going to be the foremost man in the town!

DR. STOCKMANN (*walking about happily*). Nonsense! As a matter of fact I have done nothing more than my duty. I have only made a lucky find—that's all. Still, all the same—

BILLING. Hovstad, don't you think the town ought to give Dr. Stockmann some sort of testimonial?

HOVSTAD. I will suggest it, anyway.

BILLING. And I will speak to Aslaksen about it.

DR. STOCKMANN. No, my good friends, don't let us have any of that nonsense. I won't hear of anything of the kind. And if the Baths Committee should think of voting me an increase of salary, I will not accept it. Do you hear, Katherine—I won't accept it.

MRS. STOCKMANN. You are quite right, Thomas.

PETRA (*lifting her glass*). Your health, father!

HOVSTAD *and* BILLING. Your health, Doctor! Good health!

HORSTER (*touches glasses with* DR. STOCKMANN). I hope it will bring you nothing but good luck.

DR. STOCKMANN. Thank you, thank you, my dear fellows! I feel tremendously happy! It is a splendid thing for a man to be able to feel that he has done a service to his native town and to his fellow-citizens. Hurrah, Katherine!

(*He puts his arms round her and whirls her round and round, while she protests with laughing cries. They all laugh, clap their hands and cheer the* DOCTOR. *The boys put their heads in at the door to see what is going on.*)

ACT II

SCENE. *The same. The door into the dining-room is shut. It is morning.* MRS. STOCKMANN, *with a sealed letter in her hand, comes in from the dining-room, goes to the door of the* DOCTOR'S *study and peeps in.*

MRS. STOCKMANN. Are you in, Thomas?

DR. STOCKMANN (*from within his room*). Yes, I have just come in. (*Comes into the room*) What is it?

MRS. STOCKMANN. A letter from your brother.

DR. STOCKMANN. Aha, let us see! (*Opens the letter and reads*) "I return herewith the manuscript you sent me"—(*reads on in a low murmer*) Hm!—

MRS. STOCKMANN. What does he say?

DR. STOCKMANN (*putting the papers in his pocket*). Oh, he only writes that he will come up here himself about midday.

MRS. STOCKMANN. Well, try and remember to be at home this time.

DR. STOCKMANN. That will be all right; I have got through all my morning visits.

MRS. STOCKMANN. I am extremely curious to know how he takes it.

DR. STOCKMANN. You will see he won't like it's having been I, and not he, that made the discovery.

MRS. STOCKMANN. Aren't you a little nervous about that?

DR. STOCKMANN. Oh, he really will be pleased enough, you know. But, at the same time, Peter is so confoundedly afraid of anyone's doing any service to the town except himself.

MRS. STOCKMANN. I will tell you what, Thomas—you should be good-natured, and share the credit of this with him. Couldn't you make out that it was he who set you on the scent of this discovery?

DR. STOCKMANN. I am quite willing. If only I can get the thing set right. I—

(MORTEN KIIL *puts his head in through the door leading from the hall, looks around in an inquiring manner and chuckles.*)

MORTEN KIIL (*slyly*). Is it—is it true?

MRS. STOCKMANN (*going to the door*). Father!—is it you?

DR. STOCKMANN. Ah, Mr. Kiil—good morning, good morning!

MRS. STOCKMANN. But come along in.

MORTEN KIIL. If it is true, I will; if not, I am off.

DR. STOCKMANN. If what is true?

MORTEN KIIL. This tale about the water-supply. Is it true?

DR. STOCKMANN. Certainly it is true. But how did you come to hear it?

MORTEN KIIL (*coming in*). Petra ran in on her way to the school—

DR. STOCKMANN. Did she?

Morten Kiil. Yes; and she declares that—. I thought she was only making a fool of me, but it isn't like Petra to do that.

Dr. Stockmann. Of course not. How could you imagine such a thing!

Morten Kiil. Oh well, it is better never to trust anybody; you may find you have been made a fool of before you know where you are. But it is really true, all the same?

Dr. Stockmann. You can depend upon it that it is true. Won't you sit down? (*Settles him on the couch.*) Isn't it a real bit of luck for the town—

Morten Kiil (*suppressing his laughter*). A bit of luck for the town?

Dr. Stockmann. Yes, that I made the discovery in good time.

Morten Kiil (*as before*). Yes, yes, yes!—But I should never have thought you the sort of man to pull your own brother's leg like this!

Dr. Stockmann. Pull his leg!

Mrs. Stockmann. Really, father dear—

Morten Kiil (*resting his hands and his chin in the handle of his stick and winking slyly at the* Doctor). Let me see, what was the story? Some kind of beast that had got into the water-pipes, wasn't it?

Dr. Stockmann. Infusoria—yes.

Morten Kiil. And a lot of these beasts had got in, according to Petra—a tremendous lot.

Dr. Stockmann. Certainly; hundreds of thousands of them, probably.

Morten Kiil. But no one can see them—isn't that so?

Dr. Stockmann. Yes; you can't see them.

Morten Kiil (*with a quiet chuckle*). Damme—it's the finest story I have ever heard!

Dr. Stockmann. What do you mean?

Morten Kiil. But you will never get the Mayor to believe a thing like that.

Dr. Stockmann. We shall see.

Morten Kiil. Do you think he will be fool enough to—?

Dr. Stockmann. I hope the whole town will be fools enough.

Morten Kiil. The whole town! Well, it wouldn't be a bad thing. It would just serve them right and teach them a lesson. They think themselves so much cleverer than we old fellows. They hounded me out of the council; they did, I tell you—they hounded me out. Now they shall pay for it. You pull their legs too, Thomas!

Dr. Stockmann. Really, I—

Morten Kiil. You pull their legs! (*Gets up.*) If you can work it so that the Mayor and his friends all swallow the same bait, I will give ten pounds to a charity—like a shot!

Dr. Stockmann. That is very kind of you.

Morten Kiil. Yes, I haven't got much money to throw away, I can tell you; but if you can work this, I will give five pounds to a charity at Christmas.

(HOVSTAD *comes in by the hall door.*)

HOVSTAD. Good morning! (*Stops.*) Oh, I beg your pardon—

DR. STOCKMANN. Not at all; come in.

MORTEN KIIL (*with another chuckle*). Oho!—is he in this too?

HOVSTAD. What do you mean?

DR. STOCKMANN. Certainly he is.

MORTEN KIIL. I might have known it! It must get into the papers. You know how to do it, Thomas! Set your wits to work. Now I must go.

DR. STOCKMANN. Won't you stay a little while?

MORTEN KIIL. No, I must be off now. You keep up this game for all it is worth; you won't repent it, I'm damned if you will!

(*He goes out;* MRS. STOCKMANN *follows him into the hall.*)

DR. STOCKMANN (*laughing*). Just imagine—the old chap doesn't believe a word of all this about the water-supply.

HOVSTAD. Oh that was it, then?

DR. STOCKMANN. Yes, that was what we were talking about. Perhaps it is the same thing that brings you here?

HOVSTAD. Yes, it is. Can you spare me a few minutes, Doctor?

DR. STOCKMANN. As long as you like, my dear fellow.

HOVSTAD. Have you heard from the Mayor yet?

DR. STOCKMANN. Not yet. He is coming here later.

HOVSTAD. I have given the matter a great deal of thought since last night.

DR. STOCKMANN. Well?

HOVSTAD. From your point of view, as a doctor and a man of science, this affair of the water-supply is an isolated matter. I mean, you do not realise that it involves a great many other things.

DR. STOCKMANN. How, do you mean—let us sit down, my dear fellow. No, sit here on the couch. (HOVSTAD *sits down on the couch,* DR. STOCKMANN *on a chair on the other side of the table.*) Now then. You mean that—?

HOVSTAD. You said yesterday that the pollution of the water was due to impurities in the soil.

DR. STOCKMANN. Yes, unquestionably it is due to that poisonous morass up at Mölledal.

HOVSTAD. Begging your pardon, doctor, I fancy it is due to quite another morass altogether.

DR. STOCKMANN. What morass?

HOVSTAD. The morass that the whole life of our town is built on and is rotting in.

DR. STOCKMANN. What the deuce are you driving at, Hovstad?

Hovstad. The whole of the town's interests have, little by little, got into the hands of a pack of officials.

Dr. Stockmann. Oh, come!—they are not all officials.

Hovstad. No, but those that are not officials are at any rate the officials' friends and adherents; it is the wealthy folk, the old families in the town, that have got us entirely in their hands.

Dr. Stockmann. Yes, but after all they are men of ability and knowledge.

Hovstad. Did they show any ability or knowledge when they laid the conduit-pipes where they are now?

Dr. Stockmann. No, of course that was a great piece of stupidity on their part. But that is going to be set right now.

Hovstad. Do you think that will be all such plain sailing?

Dr. Stockmann. Plain sailing or no, it has got to be done, anyway.

Hovstad. Yes, provided the press takes up the question.

Dr. Stockmann. I don't think that will be necessary, my dear fellow, I am certain my brother—

Hovstad. Excuse me, doctor; I feel bound to tell you I am inclined to take the matter up.

Dr. Stockmann. In the paper?

Hovstad. Yes. When I took over the "People's Messenger" my idea was to break up this ring of self-opinionated old fossils who had got hold of all the influence.

Dr. Stockmann. But you know you told me yourself what the result had been; you nearly ruined your paper.

Hovstad. Yes, at the time we were obliged to climb down a peg or two, it is quite true; because there was a danger of the whole project of the Baths coming to nothing if they failed us. But now the scheme has been carried through, and we can dispense with these grand gentlemen.

Dr. Stockmann. Dispense with them, yes; but we owe them a great debt of gratitude.

Hovstad. That shall be recognised ungrudgingly. But a journalist of my democratic tendencies cannot let such an opportunity as this slip. The bubble of official infallibility must be pricked. This superstition must be destroyed, like any other.

Dr. Stockmann. I am whole-heartedly with you in that, Mr. Hovstad; if it is a superstition, away with it!

Hovstad. I should be very reluctant to bring the Mayor into it, because he is your brother. But I am sure you will agree with me that truth should be the first consideration.

Dr. Stockmann. That goes without saying. (*With sudden emphasis*) Yes, but—but—

Hovstad. You must not misjudge me. I am neither more self-interested nor more ambitious than most men.

Dr. Stockmann. My dear fellow—who suggests anything of the kind?

Hovstad. I am of humble origin, as you know; and that has given me opportunities of knowing what is the most crying need in the humbler ranks of life. It is that they should be allowed some part in the direction of public affairs, Doctor. That is what will develop their faculties and intelligence and self-respect—

Dr. Stockmann. I quite appreciate that.

Hovstad. Yes—and in my opinion a journalist incurs a heavy responsibility if he neglects a favourable opportunity of emancipating the masses—the humble and oppressed. I know well enough that in exalted circles I shall be called an agitator, and all that sort of thing; but they may call what they like. If only my conscience doesn't reproach me, then—

Dr. Stockmann. Quite right! Quite right, Mr. Hovstad. But all the same—devil take it! (*A knock is heard at the door.*) Come in!

(Aslaksen *appears at the door. He is poorly but decently dressed, in black, with a slightly crumpled white neckcloth; he wears gloves and has a felt hat in his hand.*)

Aslaksen (*bowing*). Excuse my taking the liberty, Doctor—

Dr. Stockmann (*getting up*). Ah, it is you, Aslaksen!

Aslaksen. Yes, Doctor.

Hovstad (*standing up*). Is it me you want, Aslaksen?

Aslaksen. No; I didn't know I should find you here. No, it was the Doctor I—

Dr. Stockmann. I am quite at your service. What is it?

Aslaksen. Is what I heard from Mr. Billing true, sir—that you mean to improve our water-supply?

Dr. Stockmann. Yes, for the Baths.

Aslaksen. Quite so, I understand. Well, I have come to say that I will back that up by every means in my power.

Hovstad (*to the Doctor*). You see!

Dr. Stockmann. I shall be very grateful to you, but—

Aslaksen. Because it may be no bad thing to have us small tradesmen at your back. We form, as it were, a compact majority in the town—if we choose. And it is always a good thing to have the majority with you, Doctor.

Dr. Stockmann. That is undeniably true; but I confess I don't see why such unusual precautions should be necessary in this case. It seems to me that such a plain, straight-forward thing—

Aslaksen. Oh, it may be very desirable, all the same. I know our local authorities so well; officials are not generally very ready to act on proposals that come from other people. That is why I think it would not be at all amiss if we made a little demonstration.

Hovstad. That's right.

Dr. Stockmann. Demonstration, did you say? What on earth are you going to make a demonstration about?

Aslaksen. We shall proceed with the greatest moderation, Doctor. Moderation is always my aim; it is the greatest virtue in a citizen—at least, I think so.

Dr. Stockmann. It is well known to be a characteristic of yours, Mr. Aslaksen.

Aslaksen. Yes, I think I may pride myself on that. And this matter of the water-supply is of the greatest importance to us small tradesmen. The Baths promise to be a regular gold-mine for the town. We shall all make our living out of them, especially those of us who are householders. That is why we will back up the project as strongly as possible. And as I am at present Chairman of the Householders' Association—

Dr. Stockmann. Yes—?

Aslaksen. And, what is more, local secretary of the Temperance Society—you know sir, I suppose, that I am a worker in the temperance cause?

Dr. Stockmann. Of course, of course.

Aslaksen. Well, you can understand that I come into contact with a great many people. And as I have the reputation of a temperate and law-abiding citizen—like yourself, Doctor—I have a certain influence in the town, a little bit of power, if I may be allowed to say so.

Dr. Stockmann. I know that quite well, Mr. Aslaksen.

Aslaksen. So you see it would be an easy matter for me to set on foot some testimonial, if necessary.

Dr. Stockmann. A testimonial?

Aslaksen. Yes, some kind of an address of thanks from the townsmen for your share in a matter of such importance to the community. I need scarcely say that it would have to be drawn up with the greatest regard to moderation, so as not to offend the authorities—who, after all, have the reins in their hands. If we pay strict attention to that, no one can take it amiss, I should think!

Hovstad. Well, and even supposing they didn't like it—

Aslaksen. No, no, no; there must be no discourtesy to the authorities, Mr. Hovstad. It is no use falling foul of those upon whom our welfare so closely depends. I have done that in my time, and no good ever comes of it. But no one can take exception to a reasonable and frank expression of a citizen's views.

Dr. Stockmann (*shaking him by the hand*). I can't tell you, dear Mr. Aslaksen, how extremely pleased I am to find such hearty support among my fellow-citizens. I am delighted—delighted! Now, you will take a small glass of sherry, eh?

Aslaksen. No, thank you; I never drink alcohol of that kind.

Dr. Stockmann. Well, what do you say to a glass of beer, then?

Aslaksen. Nor that either, thank you, Doctor. I never drink anything as early as this. I am going into town now to talk this over with one or two householders, and prepare the ground.

Dr. Stockmann. It is tremendously kind of you, Mr. Aslaksen; but I really cannot understand the necessity for all these precautions. It seems to me that the thing should go of itself.

Aslaksen. The authorities are somewhat slow to move, Doctor. Far be it from me to seem to blame them—

Hovstad. We are going to stir them up in the paper tomorrow, Aslaksen.

Aslaksen. But not violently, I trust, Mr. Hovstad. Proceed with moderation, or you will do nothing with them. You may take my advice; I have gathered my experience in the school of life. Well, I must say good-bye, Doctor. You know now that we small tradesmen are at your back at all events, like a solid wall. You have the compact majority on your side, Doctor.

Dr. Stockmann. I am very much obliged, dear Mr. Aslaksen. (*Shakes hands with him*) Good-bye, good-bye.

Aslaksen. Are you going my way, towards the printing-office, Mr. Hovstad?

Hovstad. I will come later; I have something to settle up first.

Aslaksen. Very well.

(*Bows and goes out;* Stockmann *follows him into the hall.*)

Hovstad (*as* Stockmann *comes in again*). Well, what do you think of that, Doctor? Don't you think it is high time we stirred a little life into all this slackness and vacillation and cowardice?

Dr. Stockmann. Are you referring to Aslaksen?

Hovstad. Yes, I am. He is one of those who are floundering in a bog—decent enough fellow though he may be, otherwise. And most of the people here are in just the same case—see-sawing and edging first to one side and then to the other, so overcome with caution and scruple that they never dare to take any decided step.

Dr. Stockmann. Yes, but Aslaksen seemed to me so thoroughly well-intentioned.

Hovstad. There is one thing I esteem higher than that; and that is for a man to be self-reliant and sure of himself.

Dr. Stockmann. I think you are perfectly right there.

Hovstad. That is why I want to seize this opportunity, and try if I cannot manage to put a little virility into these well-intentioned people for once. The idol of Authority must be shattered in this town. This gross and inexcusable blunder about the water-supply must be brought home to the mind of every municipal voter.

Dr. Stockmann. Very well; if you are of opinion that it is for the good of the community, so be it. But not until I have had a talk with my brother.

HOVSTAD. Anyway, I will get a leading article ready; and if the Mayor refuses to take the matter up—

DR. STOCKMANN. How can you suppose such a thing possible?

HOVSTAD. It is conceivable. And in that case—

DR. STOCKMANN. In that case I promise you—. Look here, in that case you may print my report—every word of it.

HOVSTAD. May I? Have I your word for it?

DR. STOCKMANN (*giving him the MS.*). Here it is; take it with you. It can do no harm for you to read it through, and you can give it me back later on.

HOVSTAD. Good, good! That is what I will do. And now good-bye, Doctor.

DR. STOCKMANN. Good-bye, good-bye. You will see everything will run quite smoothly, Mr. Hovstad—quite smoothly.

HOVSTAD. Hm!—we shall see. (*Bows and goes out.*)

DR. STOCKMANN (*opens the dining-room door and looks in*). Katherine! Oh, you are back, Petra?

PETRA (*coming in*). Yes, I have just come from the school.

MRS. STOCKMANN (*coming in*). Has he not been here yet?

DR. STOCKMANN. Peter? No. But I have had a long talk with Hovstad. He is quite excited about my discovery. I find it has a much wider bearing than I at first imagined. And he has put his paper at my disposal if necessity should arise.

MRS. STOCKMANN. Do you think it will?

DR. STOCKMANN. Not for a moment. But at all events it makes me feel proud to know that I have the liberal-minded independent press on my side. Yes, and—just imagine—I have had a visit from the Chairman of the Householders' Association!

MRS. STOCKMANN. Oh! What did he want?

DR. STOCKMANN. To offer me his support too. They will support me in a body if it should be necessary. Katherine—do you know what I have got behind me?

MRS. STOCKMANN. Behind you? No, what have you got behind you?

DR. STOCKMANN. The compact majority.

MRS. STOCKMANN. Really? Is that a good thing for you, Thomas?

DR. STOCKMANN. I should think it was a good thing. (*Walks up and down rubbing his hands.*) By Jove, it's a fine thing to feel this bond of brotherhood between oneself and one's fellow-citizens!

PETRA. And to be able to do so much that is good and useful, father!

DR. STOCKMANN. And for one's own native town into the bargain, my child!

MRS. STOCKMANN. That was a ring at the bell.

DR. STOCKMANN. It must be he, then. (*A knock is heard at the door.*) Come in!

PETER STOCKMANN (*comes in from the hall*). Good morning.

DR. STOCKMANN. Glad to see you, Peter!

MRS. STOCKMANN. Good morning, Peter. How are you?

PETER STOCKMANN. So so, thank you. (*To* DR. STOCKMANN) I received from you yesterday, after office-hours, a report dealing with the condition of the water at the Baths.

DR. STOCKMANN. Yes. Have you read it?

PETER STOCKMANN. Yes, I have.

DR. STOCKMANN. And what have you to say to it?

PETER STOCKMANN (*with a sidelong glance*). Hm!—

MRS. STOCKMANN. Come along, Petra.

(*She and* PETRA *go into the room on the left.*)

PETER STOCKMANN (*after a pause*). Was it necessary to make all these investigations behind my back?

DR. STOCKMANN. Yes, because until I was absolutely certain about it—

PETER STOCKMANN. Then you mean that you are absolutely certain now?

DR. STOCKMANN. Surely you are convinced of that.

PETER STOCKMANN. Is it your intention to bring this document before the Baths Committee as a sort of official communication?

DR. STOCKMANN. Certainly. Something must be done in the matter—and that quickly.

PETER STOCKMANN. As usual, you employ violent expressions in your report. You say, amongst other things, that what we offer visitors in our Baths is a permanent supply of poison.

DR. STOCKMANN. Well, can you describe it any other way, Peter? Just think—water that is poisonous, whether you drink it or bathe in it! And this we offer to the poor sick folk who come to us trustfully and pay us at an exorbitant rate to be made well again!

PETER STOCKMANN. And your reasoning leads you to this conclusion, that we must build a sewer to draw off the alleged impurities from Mölledal and must relay the water-conduits.

DR. STOCKMANN. Yes. Do you see any other way out of it? I don't.

PETER STOCKMANN. I made a pretext this morning to go and see the town engineer, and, as if only half seriously, broached the subject of these proposals as a thing we might perhaps have to take under consideration some time later on.

DR. STOCKMANN. Some time later on!

PETER STOCKMANN. He smiled at what he considered to be my extravagance, naturally. Have you taken the trouble to consider what your proposed alterations would cost? According to the information I obtained, the expenses would probably mount up to fifteen or twenty thousand pounds.

DR. STOCKMANN. Would it cost so much?

PETER STOCKMANN. Yes; and the worst part of it would be that the work would take at least two years.

DR. STOCKMANN. Two years? Two whole years?

PETER STOCKMANN. At least. And what are we to do with the Baths in the meantime? Close them? Indeed we should be obliged to. And do you suppose any one would come near the place after it had got about that the water was dangerous?

DR. STOCKMANN. Yes, but, Peter, that is what it is.

PETER STOCKMANN. And all this at this juncture—just as the Baths are beginning to be known. There are other towns in the neighbourhood with qualifications to attract visitors for bathing purposes. Don't you suppose they would immediately strain every nerve to divert the entire stream of strangers to themselves? Unquestionably they would; and then where should we be? We should probably have to abandon the whole thing, which has cost us so much money—and then you would have ruined your native town.

DR. STOCKMANN. I—should have ruined—!

PETER STOCKMANN. It is simply and solely through the Baths that the town has before it any future worth mentioning. You know that just as well as I.

DR. STOCKMANN. But what do you think ought to be done, then?

PETER STOCKMANN. Your report has not convinced me that the condition of the water at the Baths is as bad as you represent it to be.

DR. STOCKMANN. I tell you it is even worse!—or at all events it will be in summer, when the warm weather comes.

PETER STOCKMANN. As I said, I believe you exaggerate the matter considerably. A capable physician ought to know what measures to take—he ought to be capable of preventing injurious influences or of remedying them if they become obviously persistent.

DR. STOCKMANN. Well? What more?

PETER STOCKMANN. The water-supply for the Baths is now an established fact, and in consequence must be treated as such. But probably the Committee, at its discretion, will not be disinclined to consider the question of how far it might be possible to introduce certain improvements consistently with a reasonable expenditure.

DR. STOCKMANN. And do you suppose that I will have anything to do with such a piece of trickery as that?

PETER STOCKMANN. Trickery!!

DR. STOCKMANN. Yes, it would be a trick—a fraud, a lie, a downright crime towards the public, towards the whole community!

PETER STOCKMANN. I have not, as I remarked before, been able to convince myself that there is actually any imminent danger.

DR. STOCKMANN. You have! It is impossible that you should not be convinced. I know I have represented the facts absolutely truthfully and fairly. And you know it very well, Peter, only you won't acknowledge it. It was owing to your action that both the Baths and the water-conduits were built where they are; and that is what you won't acknowledge—that damnable blunder of yours. Pooh!—do you suppose I don't see through you?

PETER STOCKMANN. And even if that were true? If I perhaps guard my reputation somewhat anxiously, it is in the interests of the town. Without moral authority I am powerless to direct public affairs as seems, to my judgment, to be best for the common good. And on that account—and for various other reasons, too—it appears to me to be a matter of importance that your report should not be delivered to the Committee. In the interests of the public, you must withhold it. Then, later on, I will raise the question and we will do our best, privately; but nothing of this unfortunate affair—not a single word of it—must come to the ears of the public.

DR. STOCKMANN. I am afraid you will not be able to prevent that now, my dear Peter.

PETER STOCKMANN. It must and shall be prevented.

DR. STOCKMANN. It is no use, I tell you. There are too many people that know about it.

PETER STOCKMANN. That know about it? Who? Surely you don't mean those fellows on the "People's Messenger"?

DR. STOCKMANN. Yes, they know. The liberal-minded independent press is going to see that you do your duty.

PETER STOCKMANN (*after a short pause*). You are an extraordinarily independent man, Thomas. Have you given no thought to the consequences this may have for yourself?

DR. STOCKMANN. Consequences?—for me?

PETER STOCKMANN. For you and yours, yes.

DR. STOCKMANN. What the deuce do you mean?

PETER STOCKMANN. I believe I have always behaved in a brotherly way to you—have always been ready to oblige or to help you?

DR. STOCKMANN. Yes, you have, and I am grateful to you for it.

PETER STOCKMANN. There is no need. Indeed, to some extent I was forced to do so—for my own sake. I always hoped that, if I helped to improve your financial position, I should be able to keep some check on you.

DR. STOCKMANN. What!! Then it was only for your own sake—!

PETER STOCKMANN. Up to a certain point, yes. It is painful for a man in an official position to have his nearest relative compromising himself time after time.

DR. STOCKMANN. And do you consider that I do that?

PETER STOCKMANN. Yes, unfortunately, you do, without even being aware of it. You have a restless, pugnacious, rebellious disposition. And then there is that disastrous propensity of yours to want to write about every sort of possible and impossible thing. The moment an idea comes into your head, you must needs go and write a newspaper article or a whole pamphlet about it.

Dr. Stockmann. Well, but is it not the duty of a citizen to let the public share in any new ideas he may have?

Peter Stockmann. Oh, the public doesn't require any new ideas. The public is best served by the good, old-established ideas it already has.

Dr. Stockmann. And that is your honest opinion?

Peter Stockmann. Yes, and for once I must talk frankly to you. Hitherto I have tried to avoid doing so, because I know how irritable you are; but now I must tell you the truth, Thomas. You have no conception what an amount of harm you do yourself by your impetuosity. You complain of the authorities, you even complain of the government—you are always pulling them to pieces; you insist that you have been neglected and persecuted. But what else can such a cantankerous man as you expect?

Dr. Stockmann. What next! Cantankerous, am I?

Peter Stockmann. Yes, Thomas, you are an extremely cantankerous man to work with—I know that to my cost. You disregard everything that you ought to have consideration for. You seem completely to forget that it is me you have to thank for your appointment here as medical officer to the Baths—

Dr. Stockmann. I was entitled to it as a matter of course!—I and nobody else! I was the first person to see that the town could be made into a flourishing watering-place, and I was the only one who saw it at that time. I had to fight single-handed in support of the idea for many years; and I wrote and wrote—

Peter Stockmann. Undoubtedly. But things were not ripe for the scheme then—though, of course, you could not judge of that in your out-of-the-way corner up north. But as soon as the opportune moment came I—and the others—took the matter into our hands—

Dr. Stockmann. Yes, and made this mess of all my beautiful plan. It is pretty obvious now what clever fellows you were!

Peter Stockmann. To my mind the whole thing only seems to mean that you are seeking another outlet for your combativeness. You want to pick a quarrel with your superiors—an old habit of yours. You cannot put up with any authority over you. You look askance at anyone who occupies a superior official position; you regard him as a personal enemy, and then any stick is good enough to beat him with. But now I have called your attention to the fact that the town's interests are at stake—and, incidentally, my own too. And therefore I must tell you, Thomas, that you will find me inexorable with regard to what I am about to require you to do.

Dr. Stockmann. And what is that?

Peter Stockmann. As you have been so indiscreet as to speak of this delicate matter to outsiders, despite the fact that you ought to have treated it as entirely official and confidential, it is obviously impossible to hush it up now. All sorts of rumours will get about directly, and everybody who has a grudge against us will take care to embellish these rumours. So it will be necessary for you to refute them publicly.

Dr. Stockmann. I! How? I don't understand.

Peter Stockmann. What we shall expect is that, after making further investigations, you will come to the conclusion that the matter is not by any means as dangerous or as critical as you imagined in the first instance.

Dr. Stockmann. Oho!—so that is what you expect!

Peter Stockmann. And, what is more, we shall expect you to make public profession of your confidence in the Committee and in their readiness to consider fully and conscientiously what steps may be necessary to remedy any possible defects.

Dr. Stockmann. But you will never be able to do that by patching and tinkering at it—never! Take my word for it, Peter; I mean what I say, as deliberately and emphatically as possible.

Peter Stockmann. As an officer under the Committee, you have no right to any individual opinion.

Dr. Stockmann (*amazed*). No right?

Peter Stockmann. In your official capacity, no. As a private person, it is quite another matter. But as a subordinate member of the staff of the Baths, you have no right to express any opinion which runs contrary to that of your superiors.

Dr. Stockmann. This is too much! I, a doctor, a man of science, have no right to—!

Peter Stockmann. The matter in hand is not simply a scientific one. It is a complicated matter, and has its economic as well as its technical side.

Dr. Stockmann. I don't care what it is! I intend to be free to express my opinion on any subject under the sun.

Peter Stockmann. As you please—but not on any subject concerning the Baths. That we forbid.

Dr. Stockmann (*shouting*). You forbid—! You! A pack of—

Peter Stockmann. *I* forbid it—I, your chief; and if I forbid it, you have to obey.

Dr. Stockmann (*controlling himself*). Peter—if you were not my brother—

Petra (*throwing open the door*). Father, you shan't stand this!

Mrs. Stockmann (*coming in after her*). Petra, Petra!

Peter Stockmann. Oh, so you have been eavesdropping.

Mrs. Stockmann. You were talking so loud, we couldn't help—

Petra. Yes, I was listening.

Peter Stockmann. Well, after all, I am very glad—

Dr. Stockmann (*going up to him*). You were saying something about forbidding and obeying?

Peter Stockmann. You obliged me to take that tone with you.

Dr. Stockmann. And so I am to give myself the lie, publicly?

Peter Stockmann. We consider it absolutely necessary that you should make some such public statement as I have asked for.

Dr. Stockmann. And if I do not—obey?

PETER STOCKMANN. Then we shall publish a statement ourselves to reassure the public.

DR. STOCKMANN. Very well; but in that case I shall use my pen against you. I stick to what I save said; I will show that I am right and that you are wrong. And what will you do then?

PETER STOCKMANN. Then I shall not be able to prevent your being dismissed.

DR. STOCKMANN. What—?

PETRA. Father—dismissed!

MRS. STOCKMANN. Dismissed!

PETER STOCKMANN. Dismissed from the staff of the Baths. I shall be obliged to propose that you shall immediately be given notice, and shall not be allowed any further participation in the Baths' affairs.

DR. STOCKMANN. You would dare to do that!

PETER STOCKMANN. It is you that are playing the daring game.

PETRA. Uncle, that is a shameful way to treat a man like father!

MRS. STOCKMANN. Do hold your tongue, Petra!

PETER STOCKMANN (*looking at* PETRA). Oh, so we volunteer our opinions already, do we? Of course. (*To* MRS. STOCKMANN) Katherine, I imagine you are the most sensible person in this house. Use any influence you may have over your husband, and make him see what this will entail for his family as well as—

DR. STOCKMANN. My family is my own concern and nobody else's!

PETER STOCKMANN. —for his own family, as I was saying, as well as for the town he lives in.

DR. STOCKMANN. It is I who have the real good of the town at heart! I want to lay bare the defects that sooner or later must come to the light of day. I will show whether I love my native town.

PETER STOCKMANN. You, who in your blind obstinacy want to cut off the most important source of the town's welfare?

DR. STOCKMANN. The source is poisoned, man! Are you mad? We are making our living by retailing filth and corruption! The whole of our flourishing municipal life derives its sustenance from a lie!

PETER STOCKMANN. All imagination—or something even worse. The man who can throw out such offensive insinuations about his native town must be an enemy of our community.

DR. STOCKMANN (*going up to him*). Do you dare to—!

MRS. STOCKMANN (*throwing herself between them*). Thomas!

PETRA (*catching her father by the arm*). Don't lose your temper, father!

PETER STOCKMANN. I will not expose myself to violence. Now you have had a warning; so reflect on what you owe to yourself and your family. Good-bye. (*Goes out.*)

DR. STOCKMANN (*walking up and down*). Am I to put up with such treatment as this? In my own house, Katherine! What do you think of that!

MRS. STOCKMANN. Indeed it is both shameful and absurd, Thomas—

PETRA. If only I could give uncle a piece of my mind—

DR. STOCKMANN. It is my own fault. I ought to have flown out at him long ago!—shown my teeth!—bitten! To hear him call me an enemy to our community! Me! I shall not take that lying down, upon my soul!

MRS. STOCKMANN. But, dear Thomas, your brother has power on his side—

DR. STOCKMANN. Yes, but I have right on mine, I tell you.

MRS. STOCKMANN. Oh yes, right—right. What is the use of having right on your side if you have not got might?

PETRA. Oh, mother—how can you say such a thing!

DR. STOCKMANN. Do you imagine that in a free country it is no use having right on your side? You are absurd, Katherine. Besides, haven't I got the liberal-minded, independent press to lead the way, and the compact majority behind me? That is might enough, I should think!

MRS. STOCKMANN. But, good heavens, Thomas, you don't mean to—?

DR. STOCKMANN. Don't mean to what?

MRS. STOCKMANN. To set yourself up in opposition your brother.

DR. STOCKMANN. In God's name, what else do you suppose I should do but take my stand on right and truth?

PETRA. Yes, I was just going to say that.

MRS. STOCKMANN. But it won't do you any earthly good. If they won't do it, they won't.

DR. STOCKMANN. Oho, Katherine! Just give me time, and you will see how I will carry the war into their camp.

MRS. STOCKMANN. Yes, you carry the war into their camp, and you get your dismissal—that is what you will do.

DR. STOCKMANN. In any case I shall have done my duty towards the public—towards the community. I, who am called its enemy!

MRS. STOCKMANN. But towards your family, Thomas? Towards your own home! Do you think that is doing your duty towards those you have to provide for?

PETRA. Ah, don't think always first of us, mother.

MRS. STOCKMANN. Oh, it is easy for you to talk; you are able to shift for yourself, if need be. But remember the boys, Thomas; and think a little, too, of yourself, and of me—

DR. STOCKMANN. I think you are out of your senses, Katherine! If I were to be such a miserable coward as to go on my knees to Peter and his damned crew, do you suppose I should ever know an hour's peace of mind all my life afterwards?

MRS. STOCKMANN. I don't know anything about that; but God preserve us from the peace of mind we shall have, all the same, if you go on defying him! You will find yourself again without the means of subsistence, with no income to count upon. I should think we had had enough of that in the old days. Remember that, Thomas; think what that means.

Dr. Stockmann (*collecting himself with a struggle and clenching his fist*). And this is what this slavery can bring upon a free, honorable man! Isn't it horrible, Katherine?

Mrs. Stockmann. Yes, it is sinful to treat you so, it is perfectly true. But, good heavens, one has to put up with so much injustice in this world.—There are the boys, Thomas! Look at them! What is to become of them? Oh, no, no, you can never have the heart—.

(Ejlif *and* Morten *have come in while she was speaking, with their school books in their hands.*)

Dr. Stockmann. The boys—! (*Recovers himself suddenly.*) No, even if the whole world goes to pieces, I will never bow my neck to this yoke! (*Goes towards his room.*)

Mrs. Stockmann (*following him*). Thomas—what are you going to do!

Dr. Stockmann (*at his door*). I mean to have the right to look my sons in the face when they are grown men. (*Goes into his room.*)

Mrs. Stockmann (*bursting into tears*). God help us all!

Petra. Father is splendid! He will not give in.

(*The boys look on in amazement;* Petra *signs to them not to speak.*)

ACT III

Scene. *The editorial office of the* People's Messenger. *The entrance door is on the left-hand side of the back wall; on the right-hand side is another door with glass panels through which the printing-room can be seen. Another door in the right-hand wall. In the middle of the room is a large table covered with papers, newspapers and books. In the foreground on the left a window, before which stand a desk and a high stool. There are a couple of easy chairs by the table, and other chairs standing along the wall. The room is dingy and uncomfortable; the furniture is old, the chairs stained and torn. In the printing-room the compositors are seen at work, and a printer is working a hand-press.* Hovstad *is sitting at the desk, writing.* Billing *comes in from the right with* Dr. Stockmann's *manuscript in his hand.*

Billing. Well, I must say!

Hovstad (*still writing*). Have you read it through?

Billing (*laying the MS. on the desk*). Yes, indeed I have.

Hovstad. Don't you think the Doctor hits them pretty hard?

Billing. Hard? Bless my soul, he's crushing! Every word falls like—how shall I put it?—like the blow of a sledgehammer.

HOVSTAD. Yes, but they are not the people to throw up the sponge at the first blow.

BILLING. That is true; and for that reason we must strike blow upon blow until the whole of this aristocracy tumbles to pieces. As I sat in there reading this, I almost seemed to see a revolution in being.

HOVSTAD (*turning round*). Hush!—Speak so that Aslaksen cannot hear you.

BILLING (*lowering his voice*). Aslaksen is a chicken-hearted chap, a coward; there is nothing of the man in him. But this time you will insist on your own way, won't you? You will put the Doctor's article in?

HOVSTAD. Yes, and if the Mayor doesn't like it—

BILLING. That will be the devil of a nuisance.

HOVSTAD. Well, fortunately we can turn the situation to good account, whatever happens. If the Mayor will not fall in with the Doctor's project, he will have all the small tradesmen down on him—the whole of the Householders' Association and the rest of them. And if he does fall in with it, he will fall out with the whole crowd of large shareholders in the Baths, who up to now have been his most valuable supporters—

BILLING. Yes, because they will certainly have to fork out a pretty penny—

HOVSTAD. Yes, you may be sure they will. And in this way the ring will be broken up, you see, and then in every issue of the paper we will enlighten the public on the Mayor's incapability on one point and another, and make it clear that all the positions of trust in the town, the whole control of municipal affairs, ought to be put in the hands of the Liberals.

BILLING. That is perfectly true! I see it coming—I see it coming; we are on the threshold of a revolution!

(*A knock is heard at the door.*)

HOVSTAD. Hush! (*Calls out*) Come in! (DR. STOCKMANN *comes in by the street door.* HOVSTAD *goes to meet him.*) Ah, it is you, Doctor! Well?

DR. STOCKMANN. You may set to work and print it, Mr. Hovstad!

HOVSTAD. Has it come to that, then?

BILLING. Hurrah!

DR. STOCKMANN. Yes, print away. Undoubtedly it has come to that Now they must take what they get. There is going to be a fight in the town, Mr. Billing!

BILLING. War to the knife, I hope! We will get our knives to their throats, Doctor!

DR. STOCKMANN. This article is only a beginning. I have already got four or five more sketched out in my head. Where is Aslaksen?

BILLING (*calls into the printing-room*). Aslaksen, just come here for a minute!

HOVSTAD. Four or five more articles, did you say? On the same subject?

Dr. Stockmann. No—far from it, my dear fellow. No, they are about quite another matter. But they all spring from the question of the water-supply and the drainage. One thing leads to another, you know. It is like beginning to pull down an old house, exactly.

Billing. Upon my soul, it's true; you find you are not done till you have pulled all the old rubbish down.

Aslaksen (*coming in*). Pulled down? You are not thinking of pulling down the Baths surely, Doctor?

Hovstad. Far from it, don't be afraid.

Dr. Stockmann. No, we meant something quite different. Well, what do you think of my article, Mr. Hovstad?

Hovstad. I think it is simply a masterpiece—

Dr. Stockmann. Do you really think so? Well, I am very pleased, very pleased.

Hovstad. It is so clear and intelligible. One need have no special knowledge to understand the bearing of it. You will have every enlightened man on your side.

Aslaksen. And every prudent man too, I hope?

Billing. The prudent and the imprudent—almost the whole town.

Aslaksen. In that case we may venture to print it.

Dr. Stockmann. I should think so!

Hovstad. We will put it in to-morrow morning.

Dr. Stockmann. Of course—you must not lose a single day. What I wanted to ask you, Mr. Aslaksen, was if you would supervise the printing of it yourself.

Aslaksen. With pleasure.

Dr. Stockmann. Take care of it as if it were a treasure! No misprints—every word is important. I will look in again a little later; perhaps you will be able to let me see a proof. I can't tell you how eager I am to see it in print, and see it burst upon the public—

Billing. Burst upon them—yes, like a flash of lightning!

Dr. Stockmann. —and to have it submitted to the judgment of my intelligent fellow-townsmen. You cannot imagine what I have gone through to-day. I have been threatened first with one thing and then with another; they have tried to rob me of my most elementary rights as a man—

Billing. What! Your rights as a man!

Dr. Stockmann. —they have tried to degrade me, to make a coward of me, to force me to put personal interests before my most sacred convictions—

Billing. That is too much—I'm damned if it isn't.

Hovstad. Oh, you mustn't be surprised at anything from that quarter.

Dr. Stockmann. Well, they will get the worst of it with me; they may assure themselves of that. I shall consider the "People's Messenger" my sheet-anchor now, and every single day I will bombard them with one article after another, like bomb-shells—

Aslaksen. Yes, but—

Billing. Hurrah!—it is war, it is war!

Dr. Stockmann. I shall smite them to the ground—I shall crush them—I shall break down all their defences, before the eyes of the honest public! That is what I shall do!

Aslaksen. Yes, but in moderation, Doctor—proceed with moderation—

Billing. Not a bit of it, not a bit of it! Don't spare the dynamite!

Dr. Stockmann. Because it is not merely a question of water-supply and drains now, you know. No—it is the whole of our social life that we have got to purify and disinfect—

Billing. Spoken like a deliverer!

Dr. Stockmann. All the incapables must be turned out, you understand—and that in every walk of life! Endless vistas have opened themselves to my mind's eye to-day. I cannot see it all quite clearly yet, but I shall in time. Young and vigorous standard-bearers—those are what we need and must seek, my friends; we must have new men in command at all our outposts.

Billing. Hear, hear!

Dr. Stockmann. We only need to stand by one another, and it will all be perfectly easy. The revolution will be launched like a ship that runs smoothly off the stocks. Don't you think so?

Hovstad. For my part I think we have now a prospect of getting the municipal authority into the hands where it should lie.

Aslaksen. And if only we proceed with moderation, I cannot imagine that there will be any risk.

Dr. Stockmann. Who the devil cares whether there is any risk or not! What I am doing, I am doing in the name of truth and for the sake of my conscience.

Hovstad. You are a man who deserves to be supported, Doctor.

Aslaksen. Yes, there is no denying that the Doctor is a true friend to the town—a real friend to the community, that he is.

Billing. Take my word for it, Aslaksen, Dr. Stockmann is a friend of the people.

Aslaksen. I fancy the Householders' Association will make use of that expression before long.

Dr. Stockmann (*affected, grasps their hands*). Thank you, thank you, my dear staunch friends. It is very refreshing to me to hear you say that; my brother called me something quite different. By Jove, he shall have it back, with interest! But now I must be off to see a poor devil—. I will come back, as I said. Keep a very careful eye on the manuscript, Aslaksen, and don't for worlds leave out any of my notes of exclamation! Rather put one or two more in! Capital, capital! Well, good-bye for the present—good-bye, good-bye!

(*They show him to the door, and bow him out.*)

HOVSTAD. He may prove an invaluably useful man to us.

ASLAKSEN. Yes, so long as he confines himself to this matter of the Baths. But if he goes farther afield, I don't think it would be advisable to follow him.

HOVSTAD. Hm!—that all depends—

BILLING. You are so infernally timid, Aslaksen!

ASLAKSEN. Timid? Yes, when it is a question of the local authorities, I am timid, Mr. Billing; it is a lesson I have learnt in the school of experience, let me tell you. But try me in higher politics, in matters that concern the government itself, and then see if I am timid.

BILLING. No, you aren't, I admit. But this is simply contradicting yourself.

ASLAKSEN. I am a man with a conscience, and that is the whole matter. If you attack the government, you don't do the community any harm, anyway; those fellows pay no attention to attacks, you see—they go on just as they are, in spite of them. But *local* authorities are different; they *can* be turned out, and then perhaps you may get an ignorant lot into office who may do irreparable harm to the householders and everybody else.

HOVSTAD. But what of the education of citizens by self-government—don't you attach any importance to that?

ASLAKSEN. When a man has interests of his own to protect, he cannot think of everything, Mr. Hovstad.

HOVSTAD. Then I hope I shall never have interests of my own to protect!

BILLING. Hear, hear!

ASLAKSEN (*with a smile*). Hm! (*Points to the desk*) Mr. Sheriff Stensgaard was your predecessor at that editorial desk.

BILLING (*spitting*). Bah! That turncoat.

HOVSTAD. I am not a weathercock—and never will be.

ASLAKSEN. A politician should never be too certain of anything, Mr. Hovstad. And as for you, Mr. Billing, I should think it is time for you to be taking in a reef or two in your sails, seeing that you are applying for the post of secretary to the Bench.

BILLING. I—!

HOVSTAD. Are you, Billing?

BILLING. Well, yes—but you must clearly understand I am doing it only to annoy the bigwigs.

ASLAKSEN. Anyhow, it is no business of mine. But if I am to be accused of timidity and of inconsistency in my principles, this is what I want to point out: my political past is an open book. I have never changed, except perhaps to become a little more moderate, you see. My heart is still with the people; but I don't deny that my reason has a certain bias towards the authorities—the local ones, I mean. (*Goes into the printing-room.*)

BILLING. Oughtn't we to try and get rid of him, Hovstad?

HOVSTAD. Do you know anyone else who will advance the money for our paper and printing bill?

BILLING. It is an infernal nuisance that we don't possess some capital to trade on.

HOVSTAD (*sitting down at his desk*). Yes, if we only had that, then—

BILLING. Suppose you were to apply to Dr. Stockmann?

HOVSTAD (*turning over some papers*). What is the use? He has got nothing.

BILLING. No, but he has got a warm man in the background, old Morten Kiil—"the Badger," as they call him.

HOVSTAD (*writing*). Are you so sure *he* has got anything?

BILLING. Good Lord, of course he has! And some of it must come to the Stockmanns. Most probably he will do something for the children, at all events.

HOVSTAD (*turning half round*). Are you counting on that?

BILLING. Counting on it? Of course I am not counting on anything.

HOVSTAD. That is right. And I should not count on the secretaryship to the Bench either, if I were you; for I can assure you—you won't get it.

BILLING. Do you think I am not quite aware of that? My object is precisely *not* to get it. A slight of that kind stimulates a man's fighting power—it is like getting a supply of fresh bile—and I am sure one needs that badly enough in a hole-and-corner place like this, where it is so seldom anything happens to stir one up.

HOVSTAD (*writing*). Quite so, quite so.

BILLING. Ah, I shall be heard of yet!—Now I shall go and write the appeal to the Householders' Association. (*Goes into the room on the right.*)

HOVSTAD (*sitting at his desk, biting his penholder, says slowly*). Hm!—that's it, is it? (*A knock is heard*) Come in! (PETRA *comes in by the outer door.* HOVSTAD *gets up.*) What, you!—here?

PETRA. Yes, you must forgive me—

HOVSTAD (*pulling a chair forward*). Won't you sit down?

PETRA. No, thank you; I must go again in a moment.

HOVSTAD. Have you come with a message from your father, by any chance?

PETRA. No, I have come on my own account. (*Takes a book out of her coat pocket*) Here is the English story.

HOVSTAD. Why have you brought it back?

PETRA. Because I am not going to translate it.

HOVSTAD. But you promised me faithfully—

PETRA. Yes, but then I had not read it. I don't suppose you have read it either?

HOVSTAD. No, you know quite well I don't understand English; but—

PETRA. Quite so. That is why I wanted to tell you that you must find something else. (*Lays the book on the table*) You can't use this for the "People's Messenger."

HOVSTAD. Why not?

PETRA. Because it conflicts with all your opinions.

HOVSTAD. Oh, for that matter—

PETRA. You don't understand me. The burden of this story is that there is a supernatural power that looks after the so-called good people in this world and makes everything happen for the best in their case—while all the so-called bad people are punished.

HOVSTAD. Well, but that is all right. That is just what our readers want.

PETRA. And are you going to be the one to give it to them? For myself, I do not believe a word of it. You know quite well that things do not happen so in reality.

HOVSTAD. You are perfectly right; but an editor cannot always act as he would prefer. He is often obliged to bow to the wishes of the public in unimportant matters. Politics are the most important thing in life—for a newspaper, anyway; and if I want to carry my public with me on the path that leads to liberty and progress, I must not frighten them away. If they find a moral tale of this sort in the serial at the bottom of the page, they will be all the more ready to read what is printed above it; they feel more secure, as it were.

PETRA. For shame! You would never go and set a snare like that for your readers; you are not a spider!

HOVSTAD (*smiling*). Thank you for having such a good opinion of me. No; as a matter of fact that is Billing's idea and not mine.

PETRA. Billing's!

HOVSTAD. Yes; anyway he propounded that theory here one day. And it is Billing who is so anxious to have that story in the paper; I don't know anything about the book.

PETRA. But how can Billing, with his emancipated views—

HOVSTAD. Oh, Billing is a many-sided man. He is applying for the post of secretary to the Bench, too, I hear.

PETRA. I don't believe it, Mr. Hovstad. How could he possibly bring himself to do such a thing?

HOVSTAD. Ah, you must ask him that.

PETRA. I should never have thought it of him.

HOVSTAD (*looking more closely at her*). No? Does it really surprise you so much?

PETRA. Yes. Or perhaps not altogether. Really, I don't quite know—

Hovstad. We journalists are not much worth, Miss Stockmann.

Petra. Do you really mean that?

Hovstad. I think so sometimes.

Petra. Yes, in the ordinary affairs of everyday life, perhaps; I can understand that. But now, when you have taken a weighty matter in hand—

Hovstad. This matter of your father's, you mean?

Petra. Exactly. It seems to me that now you must feel you are a man worth more than most.

Hovstad. Yes, to-day I do feel something of that sort.

Petra. Of course you do, don't you? It is a splendid vocation you have chosen—to smooth the way for the march of unappreciated truths, and new and courageous lines of thought. If it were nothing more than because you stand fearlessly in the open and take up the cause of an injured man—

Hovstad. Especially when that injured man is—ahem!—I don't rightly know how to—

Petra. When that man is so upright and so honest, you mean?

Hovstad (*more gently*). Especially when he is your father, I meant.

Petra (*suddenly checked*). *That?*

Hovstad. Yes, Petra—Miss Petra.

Petra. Is it *that,* that is first and foremost with you? Not the matter itself? Not the truth?—not my father's big generous heart?

Hovstad. Certainly—of course—that too.

Petra. No, thank you; you have betrayed yourself, Mr. Hovstad, and now I shall never trust you again in anything.

Hovstad. Can you really take it so amiss in me that it is mostly for your sake—?

Petra. What I am angry with you for, is for not having been honest with my father. You talked to him as if the truth and the good of the community were what lay nearest to your heart. You have made fools of both my father and me. You are not the man you made yourself out to be. And that I shall never forgive you—never!

Hovstad. You ought not to speak so bitterly, Miss Petra—least of all now.

Petra. Why not now, especially?

Hovstad. Because your father cannot do without my help.

Petra (*looking him up and down*). Are you that sort of man too? For shame!

Hovstad. No, no, I am not. This came upon me so unexpectedly—you must believe that.

Petra. I know what to believe. Good-bye.

Aslaksen (*coming from the printing-room, hurriedly and with an air of mystery*). Damnation, Hovstad!—(*Sees* Petra) Oh, this is awkward—

Petra. There is the book; you must give it to some one else. (*Goes towards the door.*)

HOVSTAD (*following her*). But, Miss Stockmann—

PETRA. Good-bye. (*Goes out.*)

ASLAKSEN. I say—Mr. Hovstad—

HOVSTAD. Well, well!—what is it?

ASLAKSEN. The Mayor is outside in the printing-room.

HOVSTAD. The Mayor, did you say?

ASLAKSEN. Yes, he wants to speak to you. He came in by the back door—didn't want to be seen, you understand.

HOVSTAD. What can he want? Wait a bit—I will go myself. (*Goes to the door of the printing-room, opens it, bows and invites* PETER STOCKMANN *in*) Just see, Aslaksen, that no one—

ASLAKSEN. Quite so. (*Goes into the printing-room.*)

PETER STOCKMANN. You did not expect to see me here, Mr. Hovstad.

HOVSTAD. No, I confess I did not.

PETER STOCKMANN (*looking round*). You are very snug in here—very nice indeed.

HOVSTAD. Oh—

PETER STOCKMANN. And here I come, without any notice, to take up your time!

HOVSTAD. By all means, Mr. Mayor. I am at your service. But let me relieve you of your— (*Takes* STOCKMANN'S *hat and stick and puts them on a chair.*) Won't you sit down?

PETER STOCKMANN (*sitting down by the table*). Thank you. (HOVSTAD *sits down.*) I have had an extremely annoying experience to-day, Mr. Hovstad.

HOVSTAD. Really? Ah well, I expect with all the various business you have to attend to—

PETER STOCKMANN. The Medical Officer of the Baths is responsible for what happened to-day.

HOVSTAD. Indeed? The Doctor?

PETER STOCKMANN. He has addressed a kind of report to the Baths Committee on the subject of certain supposed defects in the Baths.

HOVSTAD. Has he indeed?

PETER STOCKMANN. Yes—has he not told you? I thought he said—

HOVSTAD. Ah, yes—it is true he did mention something about—

ASLAKSEN (*coming from the printing-room*). I ought to have that copy—

HOVSTAD (*angrily*). Ahem!—there it is on the desk.

ASLAKSEN (*taking it*). Right.

PETER STOCKMANN. But look there—that is the thing I was speaking of!

ASLAKSEN. Yes, that is the Doctor's article, Mr. Mayor.

HOVSTAD. Oh, is *that* what you were speaking about?

PETER STOCKMANN. Yes, that is it. What do you think of it?

HOVSTAD. Oh, I am only a layman—and I have only taken a very cursory glance at it.

PETER STOCKMANN. But you are going to print it?

HOVSTAD. I cannot very well refuse a distinguished man—

ASLAKSEN. I have nothing to do with editing the paper, Mr. Mayor—

PETER STOCKMANN. I understand.

ASLAKSEN. I merely print what is put into my hands.

PETER STOCKMANN. Quite so.

ASLAKSEN. And so I must— (*Moves off towards the printing-room.*)

PETER STOCKMANN. No, but wait a moment, Mr. Aslaksen. You will allow me, Mr. Hovstad?

HOVSTAD. If you please, Mr. Mayor.

PETER STOCKMANN. You are a discreet and thoughtful man, Mr. Aslaksen.

ASLAKSEN. I am delighted to hear you think so, sir.

PETER STOCKMANN. And a man of very considerable influence.

ASLAKSEN. Chiefly among the small tradesmen, sir.

PETER STOCKMANN. The small tax-payers are the majority—here as everywhere else.

ASLAKSEN. That is true.

PETER STOCKMANN. And I have no doubt you know the general trend of opinion among them, don't you?

ASLAKSEN. Yes, I think I may say I do, Mr. Mayor.

PETER STOCKMANN. Yes. Well, since there is such a praiseworthy spirit of self-sacrifice among the less wealthy citizens of our town—

ASLAKSEN. What?

HOVSTAD. Self-sacrifice?

PETER STOCKMANN. It is pleasing evidence of a public-spirited feeling, extremely pleasing evidence. I might almost say I hardly expected it. But you have a closer knowledge of public opinion than I.

ASLAKSEN. But, Mr. Mayor—

PETER STOCKMANN. And indeed it is no small sacrifice that the town is going to make.

HOVSTAD. The town?

ASLAKSEN. But I don't understand. Is it the Baths—?

PETER STOCKMANN. At a provisional estimate, the alterations that the Medical Officer asserts to be desirable will cost somewhere about twenty thousand pounds.

ASLAKSEN. That is a lot of money, but—

PETER STOCKMANN. Of course it will be necessary to raise a municipal loan.

HOVSTAD (*getting up*). Surely you never mean that the town must pay—?

Aslaksen. Do you mean that it must come out of the municipal funds?—out of the ill-filled pockets of the small tradesmen?

Peter Stockmann. Well, my dear Mr. Aslaksen, where else is the money to come from?

Aslaksen. The gentlemen who own the Baths ought to provide that.

Peter Stockmann. The proprietors of the Baths are not in a position to incur any further expense.

Aslaksen. Is that absolutely certain, Mr. Mayor?

Peter Stockmann. I have satisfied myself that it is so. If the town wants these very extensive alterations, it will have to pay for them.

Aslaksen. But, damn it all—I beg your pardon—this is quite another matter, Mr. Hovstad!

Hovstad. It is, indeed.

Peter Stockmann. The most fatal part of it is that we shall be obliged to shut the Baths for a couple of years.

Hovstad. Shut them? Shut them altogether?

Aslaksen. For two years?

Peter Stockmann. Yes, the work will take as long as that—at least.

Aslaksen. I'm damned if we will stand that, Mr. Mayor! What are we householders to live upon in the meantime?

Peter Stockmann. Unfortunately, that is an extremely difficult question to answer, Mr. Aslaksen. But what would you have us do? Do you suppose we shall have a single visitor in the town, if we go about proclaiming that our water is polluted, that we are living over a plague spot, that the entire town—

Aslaksen. And the whole thing is merely imagination?

Peter Stockmann. With the best will in the world, I have not been able to come to any other conclusion.

Aslaksen. Well then I must say it is absolutely unjustifiable of Dr. Stockman—I beg your pardon, Mr. Mayor—

Peter Stockmann. What you say is lamentably true, Mr. Aslaksen. My brother has, unfortunately, always been a headstrong man.

Aslaksen. After this, do you mean to give him your support, Mr. Hovstad?

Hovstad. Can you suppose for a moment that I—?

Peter Stockmann. I have drawn up a short *résumé* of the situation as it appears from a reasonable man's point of view. In it I have indicated how certain possible defects might suitably be remedied without outrunning the resources of the Baths Committee.

Hovstad. Have you got it with you, Mr. Mayor?

Peter Stockmann (*fumbling in his pocket*). Yes, I brought it with me in case you should—

Aslaksen. Good Lord, there he is!

Peter Stockmann. Who? My brother?

HOVSTAD. Where? Where?

ASLAKSEN. He has just gone through the printing-room.

PETER STOCKMANN. How unlucky! I don't want to meet him here, and I had still several things to speak to you about.

HOVSTAD (*pointing to the door on the right*). Go in there for the present.

PETER STOCKMANN. But—?

HOVSTAD. You will only find Billing in there.

ASLAKSEN. Quick, quick, Mr. Mayor—he is just coming.

PETER STOCKMANN. Yes, very well; but see that you get rid of him quickly. (*Goes out through the door on the right, which* ASLAKSEN *opens for him and shuts after him.*)

HOVSTAD. Pretend to be doing something, Aslaksen.

(*Sits down and writes.* ASLAKSEN *begins foraging among a heap of newspapers that are lying on a chair.*)

DR. STOCKMANN (*coming in from the printing-room*). Here I am again. (*Puts down his hat and stick.*)

HOVSTAD (*writing*). Already, Doctor? Hurry up with what we were speaking about, Aslaksen. We are very pressed for time to-day.

DR. STOCKMANN (*to* ASLAKEN). No proof for me to see yet, I hear.

ASLAKSEN (*without turning round*). You couldn't expect it yet, Doctor.

DR. STOCKMANN. No, no; but I am impatient, as you can understand. I shall not know a moment's peace of mind till I see it in print.

HOVSTAD. Hm!—it will take a good while yet, won't it, Aslaksen?

ASLAKSEN. Yes, I am almost afraid it will.

DR. STOCKMANN. All right, my dear friends; I will come back. I do not mind coming back twice if necessary. A matter of such great importance —the welfare of the town at stake—it is no time to shirk trouble. (*Is just going, but stops and comes back.*) Look here—there is one thing more I want to speak to you about.

HOVSTAD. Excuse me, but could it not wait till some other time?

DR. STOCKMANN. I can tell you in half a dozen words. It is only this. When my article is read to-morrow and it is realised that I have been quietly working the whole winter for the welfare of the town—

HOVSTAD. Yes, but, Doctor—

DR. STOCKMANN. I know what you are going to say. You don't see how on earth it was any more than my duty—my obvious duty as a citizen. Of course it wasn't; I know that as well as you. But my fellow-citizens, you know—! Good Lord, think of all the good souls who think so highly of me—!

ASLAKSEN. Yes, our townsfolk have had a very high opinion of you so far, Doctor.

DR. STOCKMANN. Yes, and that is just why I am afraid they—. Well, this is the point; when this reaches them, especially the poorer classes, and sounds in their ears like a summons to take the town's affairs into their own hands for the future—

Hovstad (*getting up*). Ahem! Doctor, I won't conceal from you the fact—

Dr. Stockmann. Ah!—I knew there was something in the wind! But I won't hear a word of it. If anything of that sort is being set on foot—

Hovstad. Of what sort?

Dr. Stockmann. Well, whatever it is—whether it is a demonstration in my honour, or a banquet, or a subscription list for some presentation to me—whatever it is, you must promise me solemnly and faithfully to put a stop to it. You too, Mr. Aslaksen; do you understand?

Hovstad. You must forgive me, Doctor, but sooner or later we must tell you the plain truth—

(*He is interrupted by the entrance of* Mrs. Stockmann, *who comes in from the street door.*)

Mrs. Stockmann (*seeing her husband*). Just as I thought!

Hovstad (*going towards her*). You too, Mrs. Stockmann?

Dr. Stockmann. What on earth do *you* want here, Katherine?

Mrs. Stockmann. I should think you know very well what I want.

Hovstad. Won't you sit down? Or perhaps—

Mrs. Stockmann. No, thank you; don't trouble. And you must not be offended at my coming to fetch my husband; I am the mother of three children, you know.

Dr. Stockmann. Nonsense!—we know all about that.

Mrs. Stockmann. Well, one would not give you credit for much thought for your wife and children to-day; if you had had that, you would not have gone and dragged us all into misfortune.

Dr. Stockmann. Are you out of your senses, Katherine! Because a man has a wife and children, is he not to be allowed to proclaim the truth—is he not to be allowed to be an actively useful citizen—is he not to be allowed to do a service to his native town!

Mrs. Stockmann. Yes, Thomas—in reason.

Aslaksen. Just what I say. Moderation is everything.

Mrs. Stockmann. And that is why you wrong us, Mr. Hovstad, in enticing my husband away from his home and making a dupe of him in all this.

Hovstad. I certainly am making a dupe of no one—

Dr. Stockmann. Making a dupe of me! Do you suppose *I* should allow myself to be duped!

Mrs. Stockmann. It is just what you do. I know quite well you have more brains than anyone in the town, but you are extremely easily duped, Thomas. (*To* Hovstad) Please to realise that he loses his post at the Baths if you print what he has written—

Aslaksen. What!

Hovstad. Look here, Doctor—

Dr. Stockmann (*laughing*). Ha—ha!—just let them try! No, no—they will take good care not to. I have got the compact majority behind me, let me tell you!

Mrs. Stockmann. Yes, that is just the worst of it—your having any such horrid thing behind you.

Dr. Stockmann. Rubbish, Katherine!—Go home and look after your house and leave me to look after the community. How can you be so afraid, when I am so confident and happy? (*Walks up and down, rubbing his hands.*) Truth and the People will win the fight, you may be certain! I see the whole of the broad-minded middle class marching like a victorious army—! (*Stops beside a chair*) What the deuce is that lying there?

Aslaksen. Good Lord!

Hovstad. Ahem!

Dr. Stockmann. Here we have the topmost pinnacle of authority! (*Takes the Mayor's official hat carefully between his finger-tips and holds it up in the air.*)

Mrs. Stockmann. The Mayor's hat!

Dr. Stockmann. And here is the staff of office too. How in the name of all that's wonderful—?

Hovstad. Well, you see—

Dr. Stockmann. Oh, I understand. He has been here trying to talk you over. Ha—ha!—he made rather a mistake there! And as soon as he caught sight of me in the printing-room—. (*Bursts out laughing.*) Did he run away, Mr. Aslaksen?

Aslaksen (*hurriedly*). Yes, he ran away, Doctor.

Dr. Stockmann. Ran away without his stick or his—. Fiddlesticks! Peter doesn't run away and leave his belongings behind him. But what the deuce have you done with him? Ah!—in there, of course. Now you shall see, Katherine.

Mrs. Stockmann. Thomas—please don't—!

Aslaksen. Don't be rash, Doctor.

(Dr. Stockmann *has put on the Mayor's hat and taken his stick in his hand. He goes up to the door, opens it and stands with his hand to his hat at the salute.* Peter Stockmann *comes in, red with anger.* Billing *follows him.*)

Peter Stockmann. What does this tomfoolery mean?

Dr. Stockmann. Be respectful, my good Peter. I am the chief authority in the town now. (*Walks up and down.*)

Mrs. Stockmann (*almost in tears*). Really, Thomas!

Peter Stockmann (*following him about*). Give me my hat and stick.

Dr. Stockmann (*in the same tone as before*). If you are chief constable, let me tell you that I am the Mayor—I am the master of the whole town, please understand!

PETER STOCKMANN. Take off my hat, I tell you. Remember it is part of an official uniform.

DR. STOCKMANN. Pooh! Do you think the newly awakened lion-hearted people are going to be frightened by an official hat? There is going to be a revolution in the town to-morrow, let me tell you. You thought you could turn me out; but now I shall turn you out—turn you out of all your various offices. Do you think I cannot? Listen to me. I have triumphant social forces behind me. Hovstad and Billing will thunder in the "People's Messenger," and Aslaksen will take the field at the head of the whole Householders' Association—

ASLAKSEN. That I won't, Doctor.

DR. STOCKMANN. Of course you will—

PETER STOCKMANN. Ah!—may I ask then if Mr. Hovstad intends to join this agitation?

HOVSTAD. No, Mr. Mayor.

ASLAKSEN. No, Mr. Hovstad is not such a fool as to go and ruin his paper and himself for the sake of an imaginary grievance.

DR. STOCKMANN (*looking round him*). What does this mean?

HOVSTAD. You have represented your case in a false light, Doctor, and therefore I am unable to give you my support.

BILLING. And after what the Mayor was so kind as to tell me just now, I—

DR. STOCKMANN. A false light! Leave that part of it to me. Only print my article; I am quite capable of defending it.

HOVSTAD. I am not going to print it. I cannot and will not and dare not print it.

DR. STOCKMANN. You dare not? What nonsense!—you are the editor; and an editor controls his paper, I suppose!

ASLAKSEN. No, it is the subscribers, Doctor.

PETER STOCKMANN. Fortunately, yes.

ASLAKSEN. It is public opinion—the enlightened public—householders and people of that kind; they control the newspapers.

DR. STOCKMANN (*composedly*). And I have all these influences against me?

ASLAKSEN. Yes, you have. It would mean the absolute ruin of the community if your article were to appear.

DR. STOCKMANN. Indeed.

PETER STOCKMANN. My hat and stick, if you please. (DR. STOCKMANN *takes off the hat and lays it on the table with the stick.* PETER STOCKMANN *takes them up.*) Your authority as mayor has come to an untimely end.

DR. STOCKMANN. We have not got to the end yet. (*To* HOVSTAD)

Then it is quite impossible for you to print my article in the "People's Messenger"?

HOVSTAD. Quite impossible—out of regard for your family as well.

MRS. STOCKMANN. You need not concern yourself about his family, thank you, Mr. Hovstad.

PETER STOCKMANN (*taking a paper from his pocket*). It will be sufficient, for the guidance of the public, if this appears. It is an official statement. May I trouble you?

HOVSTAD (*taking the paper*). Certainly; I will see that it is printed.

DR. STOCKMANN. But not mine. Do you imagine that you can silence me and stifle the truth! You will not find it so easy as you suppose. Mr. Aslaksen, kindly take my manuscript at once and print it as a pamphlet—at my expense. I will have four hundred copies—no, five—six hundred.

ASLAKSEN. If you offered me its weight in gold, I could not lend my press for any such purpose, Doctor. It would be flying in the face of public opinion. You will not get it printed anywhere in the town.

DR. STOCKMANN. Then give it me back.

HOVSTAD (*giving him the MS.*). Here it is.

DR. STOCKMANN (*taking his hat and stick*). It shall be made public all the same. I will read it out at a mass meeting of the townspeople. All my fellow-citizens shall hear the voice of truth!

PETER STOCKMANN. You will not find any public body in the town that will give you the use of their hall for such a purpose.

ASLAKSEN. Not a single one, I am certain.

BILLING. No, I'm damned if you will find one.

MRS. STOCKMANN. But this is too shameful! Why should every one turn against you like that?

DR. STOCKMANN (*angrily*). I will tell you why. It is because all the men in this town are old women—like you; they all think of nothing but their families, and never of the community.

MRS. STOCKMANN (*putting her arm into his*). Then I will show them that an—an old woman can be a man for once. I am going to stand by you, Thomas!

DR. STOCKMANN. Bravely said, Katherine! It shall be made public—as I am a living soul! If I can't hire a hall, I shall hire a drum, and parade the town with it and read it at every street-corner.

PETER STOCKMANN. You are surely not such an arrant fool as that!

DR. STOCKMANN. Yes, I am.

ASLAKSEN. You won't find a single man in the whole town to go with you.

BILLING. No, I'm damned if you will.

MRS. STOCKMANN. Don't give in, Thomas. I will tell the boys to go with you.

DR. STOCKMANN. That is a splendid idea!

MRS. STOCKMANN. Morten will be delighted; and Ejlif will do whatever he does.

DR. STOCKMANN. Yes, and Petra!—and you too, Katherine!

MRS. STOCKMANN. No, I won't do that; but I will stand at the window and watch you, that's what I will do.

DR. STOCKMANN (*puts his arms round her and kisses her*). Thank you, my dear! Now you and I are going to try a fall, my fine gentlemen! I am going to see whether a pack of cowards can succeed in gagging a patriot who wants to purify society!

(*He and his wife go out by the street door.*)

PETER STOCKMANN (*shaking his head seriously*). Now he has sent *her* out of her senses, too.

ACT IV

SCENE. *A big old-fashioned room in* CAPTAIN HORSTER'S *house. At the back folding-doors, which are standing open, lead to an ante-room. Three windows in the left-hand wall. In the middle of the opposite wall a platform has been erected. On this is a small table with two candles, a water-bottle and glass, and a bell. The room is lit by lamps placed between the windows. In the foreground on the left there is a table with candles and a chair. To the right is a door and some chairs standing near it. The room is nearly filled with a crowd of townspeople of all sorts, a few women and schoolboys being amongst them. People are still streaming in from the back, and the room is soon filled.*

1ST CITIZEN (*meeting another*). Hullo, Lamstad! You here too?

2ND CITIZEN. I go to every public meeting, I do.

3RD CITIZEN. Brought your whistle too, I expect!

2ND CITIZEN. I should think so. Haven't you?

3RD CITIZEN. Rather! And old Evensen said he was going to bring a cow-horn, he did.

2ND CITIZEN. Good old Evensen!

(*Laughter among the crowd.*)

4TH CITIZEN (*coming up to them*). I say, tell me what is going on here to-night.

2ND CITIZEN. Dr. Stockmann is going to deliver an address attacking the Mayor.

4TH CITIZEN. But the Mayor is his brother.

1ST CITIZEN. That doesn't matter; Dr. Stockmann's not the chap to be afraid.

3RD CITIZEN. But he is in the wrong; it said so in the "People's Messenger."

2ND CITIZEN. Yes, I expect he must be in the wrong this time, because neither the Householders' Association nor the Citizens' Club would lend him their hall for his meeting.

1ST CITIZEN. He couldn't even get the loan of the hall at the Baths.

2ND CITIZEN. No, I should think not.

A MAN (*in another part of the crowd*). I say—who are we to back up in this?

ANOTHER MAN (*beside him*). Watch Aslaksen, and do as he does.

BILLING (*pushing his way through the crowd, with a writing-case under his arm*). Excuse me, gentlemen—do you mind letting me through? I am reporting for the "People's Messenger." Thank you very much! (*He sits down at the table on the left.*)

A WORKMAN. Who was that?

2ND WORKMAN. Don't you know him? It's Billing, who writes for Aslaksen's paper.

(CAPTAIN HORSTER *brings in* MRS. STOCKMANN *and* PETRA *through the door on the right.* EJLIF *and* MORTEN *follow them in.*)

HORSTER. I thought you might all sit here; you can slip out easily from here, if things get too lively.

MRS. STOCKMANN. Do you think there will be a disturbance?

HORSTER. One can never tell—with such a crowd. But sit down, and don't be uneasy.

MRS. STOCKMANN (*sitting down*). It was extremely kind of you to offer my husband the room.

HORSTER. Well, if nobody else would—

PETRA (*who has sat down beside her mother*). And it was a plucky thing to do, Captain Horster.

HORSTER. Oh, it is not such a great matter as all that.

(HOVSTAD *and* ASLAKSEN *make their way through the crowd.*)

ASLAKSEN (*going up to* HORSTER). Has the Doctor not come yet?

HORSTER. He is waiting in the next room.

(*Movement in the crowd by the door at the back.*)

HOVSTAD. Look—here comes the Mayor!

BILLING. Yes, I'm damned if he hasn't come after all!

(PETER STOCKMANN *makes his way gradually through the crowd, bows courteously and takes up a position by the wall on the left. Shortly afterwards* DR. STOCKMANN *comes in by the right-hand door. He is dressed in a black frock-coat, with a white tie. There is a little feeble applause, which is hushed down. Silence is obtained.*)

Dr. Stockmann (*in an undertone*). How do you feel, Katherine?

Mrs. Stockmann. All right, thank you. (*Lowering her voice*) Be sure not to lose your temper, Thomas.

Dr. Stockmann. Oh, I know how to control myself. (*Looks at his watch, steps on to the platform and bows.*) It is a quarter past—so I will begin. (*Takes his MS. out of his pocket.*)

Aslaksen. I think we ought to elect a chairman first.

Dr. Stockmann. No, it is quite unnecessary.

Some of the Crowd. Yes—yes!

Peter Stockmann. I certainly think, too, that we ought to have a chairman.

Dr. Stockmann. But I have called this meeting to deliver a lecture, Peter.

Peter Stockmann. Dr. Stockmann's lecture may possibly lead to a considerable conflict of opinion.

Voices in the Crowd. A chairman! A chairman!

Hovstad. The general wish of the meeting seems to be that a chairman should be elected.

Dr. Stockmann (*restraining himself*). Very well—let the meeting have its way.

Aslaksen. Will the Mayor be good enough to undertake the task?

Three Men (*clapping their hands*). Bravo! Bravo!

Peter Stockmann. For various reasons, which you will easily understand, I must beg to be excused. But fortunately we have amongst us a man who I think will be acceptable to you all. I refer to the President of the Householders' Association, Mr. Aslaksen.

Several Voices. Yes—Aslaksen! Bravo Aslaksen!

(Dr. Stockmann *takes up his MS. and walks up and down the platform.*)

Aslaksen. Since my fellow-citizens choose to entrust me with this duty, I cannot refuse. (*Loud applause.* Aslaksen *mounts the platform.*)

Billing (*writing*). "Mr. Aslaksen was elected with enthusiasm."

Aslaksen. And now, as I am in this position, I should like to say a few brief words. I am a quiet and peaceable man, who believes in discreet moderation, and—and—in moderate discretion. All my friends can bear witness to that.

Several Voices. That's right! That's right, Aslaksen!

Aslaksen. I have learnt in the school of life and experience that moderation is the most valuable virtue a citizen can possess—

Peter Stockmann. Hear, hear!

ASLAKSEN. —And moreover that discretion and moderation are what enable a man to be of most service to the community. I would therefore suggest to our esteemed fellow-citizen, who has called this meeting, that he should strive to keep strictly within the bounds of moderation.

A MAN (*by the door*). Three cheers for the Moderation Society!

A VOICE. Shame!

SEVERAL VOICES. Sh!—Sh!

ASLAKSEN. No interruptions, gentlemen, please! Does anyone wish to make any remarks?

PETER STOCKMANN. Mr. Chairman.

ASLAKSEN. The Mayor will address the meeting.

PETER STOCKMANN. In consideration of the close relationship in which, as you all know, I stand to the present Medical Officer of the Baths, I should have preferred not to speak this evening. But my official position with regard to the Baths and my solicitude for the vital interests of the town compel me to bring forward a motion. I venture to presume that there is not a single one of our citizens present who considers it desirable that unreliable and exaggerated accounts of the sanitary condition of the Baths and the town should be spread abroad.

SEVERAL VOICES. No, no! Certainly not! We protest against it!

PETER STOCKMANN. Therefore I should like to propose that the meeting should not permit the Medical Officer either to read or to comment on his proposed lecture.

DR. STOCKMANN (*impatiently*). Not permit—! What the devil—!

MRS. STOCKMANN (*coughing*). Ahem!—ahem!

DR. STOCKMANN (*collecting himself*). Very well. Go ahead!

PETER STOCKMANN. In my communication to the "People's Messenger," I have put the essential facts before the public in such a way that every fair-minded citizen can easily form his own opinion. From it you will see that the main result of the Medical Officer's proposals—apart from their constituting a vote of censure on the leading men of the town—would be to saddle the ratepayers with an unnecessary expenditure of at least some thousands of pounds.

(*Sounds of disapproval among the audience, and some cat-calls.*)

ASLAKSEN (*ringing his bell*). Silence, please, gentlemen! I beg to support the Mayor's motion. I quite agree with him that there is something behind this agitation started by the Doctor. He talks about the Baths; but it is a revolution he is aiming at—he wants to get the administration of the town put into new hands. No one doubts the honesty of the Doctor's intentions—no one will suggest that there can be any two opinions as to that. I myself am a believer in self-government for the people, provided it does not fall too heavily on the ratepayers. But that would be the case here; and that is why I will see Dr. Stockmann damned—I beg your pardon—before

I go with him in the matter. You can pay too dearly for a thing sometimes; that is my opinion.

(*Loud applause on all sides.*)

Hovstad. I, too, feel called upon to explain my position. Dr. Stockmann's agitation appeared to be gaining a certain amount of sympathy at first, so I supported it as impartially as I could. But presently we had reason to suspect that we had allowed ourselves to be misled by misrepresentation of the state of affairs—

Dr. Stockmann. Misrepresentation—!

Hovstad. Well, let us say a not entirely trustworthy representation. The Mayor's statement has proved that. I hope no one here has any doubt as to my liberal principles; the attitude of the "People's Messenger" towards important political questions is well known to every one. But the advice of experienced and thoughtful men has convinced me that in purely local matters a newspaper ought to proceed with a certain caution.

Aslaksen. I entirely agree with the speaker.

Hovstad. And, in the matter before us, it is now an undoubted fact that Dr. Stockmann has public opinion against him. Now, what is an editor's first and most obvious duty, gentlemen? Is it not to work in harmony with his readers? Has he not received a sort of tacit mandate to work persistently and assiduously for the welfare of those whose opinions he represents? Or is it possible I am mistaken in that?

Voices (*from the crowd*). No, no! You are quite right!

Hovstad. It has cost me a severe struggle to break with a man in whose house I have been lately a frequent guest—a man who till to-day has been able to pride himself on the undivided goodwill of his fellow-citizens—a man whose only, or at all events whose essential, failing is that he is swayed by his heart rather than his head.

A Few Scattered Voices. That is true! Bravo, Stockmann!

Hovstad. But my duty to the community obliged me to break with him. And there is another consideration that impels me to oppose him, and, as far as possible, to arrest him on the perilous course he has adopted; that is, consideration for his family—

Dr. Stockmann. Please stick to the water-supply and drainage!

Hovstad. —consideration, I repeat, for his wife and his children for whom he has made no provision.

Morten. Is that us, mother?

Mrs. Stockmann. Hush!

Aslaksen. I will now put the Mayor's proposition to the vote.

Dr. Stockmann. There is no necessity! To-night I have no intention of dealing with all that filth down at the Baths. No; I have something quite different to say to you.

Peter Stockmann (*aside*). What is coming now?

A DRUNKEN MAN (*by the entrance door*). I am a ratepayer! And therefore I have a right to speak too! And my entire—firm—inconceivable opinion is—

A NUMBER OF VOICES. Be quiet, at the back there!

OTHERS. He is drunk! Turn him out! (*They turn him out.*)

DR. STOCKMANN. Am I allowed to speak?

ASLAKSEN (*ringing his bell*). Dr. Stockmann will address the meeting.

DR. STOCKMANN. I should like to have seen anyone, a few days ago, dare to attempt to silence me as has been done to-night! I would have defended my sacred rights as a man, like a lion! But now it is all one to me; I have something of even weightier importance to say to you.

(*The crowd presses nearer to him,* MORTEN KIIL *conspicuous among them.*)

DR. STOCKMANN (*continuing*). I have thought and pondered a great deal, these last few days—pondered over such a variety of things that in the end my head seemed too full to hold them—

PETER STOCKMANN (*with a cough*). Ahem!

DR. STOCKMANN. —but I got them clear in my mind at last, and then I saw the whole situation lucidly. And that is why I am standing here to-night. I have a great revelation to make to you, my fellow-citizens! I will impart to you a discovery of a far wider scope than the trifling matter that our water-supply is poisoned and our medicinal Baths are standing on pestiferous soil.

A NUMBER OF VOICES (*shouting*). Don't talk about the Baths! We won't hear you! None of that!

DR. STOCKMANN. I have already told you that what I want to speak about is the great discovery I have made lately—the discovery that all the sources of our *moral* life are poisoned and that the whole fabric of our civic community is founded on the pestiferous soil of falsehood.

VOICES OF DISCONCERTED CITIZENS. What is that he says?

PETER STOCKMANN. Such an insinuation—!

ASLAKSEN (*with his hand on his bell*). I call upon the speaker to moderate his language.

DR. STOCKMANN. I have always loved my native town as a man only can love the home of his youthful days. I was not old when I went away from here; and exile, longing and memories cast, as it were, an additional halo over both the town and its inhabitants. (*Some clapping and applause.*) And there I stayed, for many years, in a horrible hole far away up north. When I came into contact with some of the people that lived scattered about among the rocks, I often thought it would have been more service to the poor half-starved creatures if a veterinary doctor had been sent up there, instead of a man like me. (*Murmurs among the crowd.*)

BILLING (*laying down his pen*). I'm damned if I have ever heard—!

HOVSTAD. It is an insult to a respectable population!

DR. STOCKMANN. Wait a bit! I do not think anyone will charge me with having forgotten my native town up there. I was like one of the eider-ducks brooding on its nest, and what I hatched was—the plans for these Baths. (*Applause and protests.*) And then when fate at last decreed for me the great happiness of coming home again—I assure you, gentlemen, I thought I had nothing more in the world to wish for. Or rather, there was one thing I wished for—eagerly, untiringly, ardently—and that was to be able to be of service to my native town and the good of the community.

PETER STOCKMANN (*looking at the ceiling*). You chose a strange way of doing it—ahem!

DR. STOCKMANN. And so, with my eyes blinded to the real facts, I revelled in happiness. But yesterday morning—no, to be precise, it was yesterday afternoon—the eyes of my mind were opened wide, and the first thing I realised was the colossal stupidity of the authorities—.

(*Uproar, shouts and laughter.* MRS. STOCKMANN *coughs persistently.*)

PETER STOCKMANN. Mr. Chairman!

ASLAKSEN (*ringing his bell*). By virtue of my authority—!

DR. STOCKMANN. It is a petty thing to catch me up on a word, Mr. Aslaksen. What I mean is only that I got scent of the unbelievable piggishness our leading men had been responsible for down at the Baths. I can't stand leading men at any price!—I have had enough of such people in my time. They are like billy-goats in a young plantation; they do mischief everywhere. They stand in a free man's way, whichever way he turns, and what I should like best would be to see them exterminated like any other vermin—. (*Uproar.*)

PETER STOCKMANN. Mr. Chairman, can we allow such expressions to pass?

ASLAKSEN (*with his hand on his bell*). Doctor—!

DR. STOCKMANN. I cannot understand how it is that I have only now acquired a clear conception of what these gentry are, when I had almost daily before my eyes in this town such an excellent specimen of them—my brother Peter—slow-witted and hide-bound in prejudice—.

(*Laughter, uproar and hisses.* MRS. STOCKMANN *sits coughing assiduously.* ASLAKSEN *rings his bell violently.*)

THE DRUNKEN MAN (*who has got in again*). Is it me he is talking about? My name's Petersen, all right—but devil take me if I—

ANGRY VOICES. Turn out that drunken man! Turn him out. (*He is turned out again.*)

PETER STOCKMANN. Who was that person?

1ST CITIZEN. I don't know who he is, Mr. Mayor.

2ND CITIZEN. He doesn't belong here.

3RD CITIZEN. I expect he is a navvy from over at (*the rest is inaudible*).

ASLAKSEN. He had obviously had too much beer.—Proceed, Doctor; but please strive to be moderate in your language.

DR. STOCKMANN. Very well, gentlemen, I will say no more about our leading men. And if anyone imagines, from what I have just said, that my object is to attack these people this evening, he is wrong—absolutely wide of the mark. For I cherish the comforting conviction that these parasites—all these venerable relics of a dying school of thought—are most admirably paving the way for their own extinction; they need no doctor's help to hasten their end. Nor is it folk of that kind who constitute the most pressing danger to the community. It is not they who are most instrumental in poisoning the sources of our moral life and infecting the ground on which we stand. It is not they who are the most dangerous enemies of truth and freedom amongst us.

SHOUTS (*from all sides*). Who then? Who is it? Name! Name!

DR. STOCKMANN. You may depend upon it I shall name them! That is precisely the great discovery I made yesterday. (*Raises his voice.*) The most dangerous enemy of truth and freedom amongst us is the compact majority—yes, the damned compact Liberal majority—that is it! Now you know!

(*Tremendous uproar. Most of the crowd are shouting, stamping and hissing. Some of the older men among them exchange stolen glances and seem to be enjoying themselves.* MRS. STOCKMANN *gets up, looking anxious.* EJLIF *and* MORTEN *advance threateningly upon some schoolboys who are playing pranks.* ASLAKSEN *rings his bell and begs for silence.* HOVSTAD *and* BILLING *both talk at once, but are inaudible. At last quiet is restored.*)

ASLAKSEN. As chairman, I call upon the speaker to withdraw the ill-considered expressions he has just used.

DR. STOCKMANN. Never, Mr. Aslaksen! It is the majority in our community that denies me my freedom and seeks to prevent my speaking the truth.

HOVSTAD. The majority always has right on its side.

BILLING. And truth too, by God!

DR. STOCKMANN. The majority *never* has right on its side. Never, I say! That is one of these social lies against which an independent, intelligent man must wage war. Who is it that constitute the majority of the population in a country? Is it the clever folk or the stupid? I don't imagine you will dispute the fact that at present the stupid people are in an absolutely overwhelming majority all the world over. But, good Lord!—you can never pretend that it is right that the stupid folk should govern the clever ones! (*Uproar and cries.*) Oh, yes—you can shout me down, I know! but you cannot answer me. The majority has *might* on its side—unfortunately; but *right* it has *not*. I am in the right—I and a few other scattered individuals. The minority is always in the right. (*Renewed uproar.*)

HOVSTAD. Aha!—so Dr. Stockmann has become an aristocrat since the day before yesterday!

DR. STOCKMANN. I have already said that I don't intend to waste a word on the puny, narrow-chested, short-winded crew whom we are leaving astern. Pulsating life no longer concerns itself with them. I am thinking of the few, the scattered few amongst us, who have absorbed new and vigorous truths. Such men stand, as it were, at the outposts, so far ahead that the compact majority has not yet been able to come up with them; and there they are fighting for truths that are too newly-born into the world of consciousness to have any considerable number of people on their side as yet.

HOVSTAD. So the Doctor is a revolutionary now!

DR. STOCKMANN. Good heavens—of course I am, Mr. Hovstad! I propose to raise a revolution against the lie that the majority has the monopoly of the truth. What sort of truths are they that the majority usually supports? They are truths that are of such advanced age that they are beginning to break up. And if a truth is as old as that, it is also in a fair way to become a lie, gentlemen. (*Laughter and mocking cries.*) Yes, believe me or not, as you like; but truths are by no means as long-lived as Methuselah—as some folk imagine. A normally constituted truth lives, let us say, as a rule seventeen or eighteen, or at most twenty years; seldom longer. But truths as aged as that are always worn frightfully thin, and nevertheless it is only then that the majority recognises them and recommends them to the community as wholesome moral nourishment. There is no great nutritive value in that sort of fare, I can assure you; and, as a doctor, I ought to know. These "majority truths" are like last year's cured meat—like rancid, tainted ham; and they are the origin of the moral scurvy that is rampant in our communities.

ASLAKSEN. It appears to me that the speaker is wandering a long way from his subject.

PETER STOCKMANN. I quite agree with the Chairman.

DR. STOCKMANN. Have you gone clean out of your senses, Peter? I am sticking as closely to my subject as I can; for my subject is precisely this, that it is the masses, the majority—this infernal compact majority—that poisons the sources of our moral life and infects the ground we stand on.

HOVSTAD. And all this because the great, broad-minded majority of the people is prudent enough to show deference only to well-ascertained and well-approved truths?

DR. STOCKMANN. Ah, my good Mr. Hovstad, don't talk nonsense about well-ascertained truths! The truths of which the masses now approve are the very truths that the fighters at the outposts held to in the days of our grandfathers. We fighters at the outposts nowadays no longer approve of them; and I do not believe there is any other well-ascertained truth except this, that no community can live a healthy life if it is nourished only on such old marrowless truths.

HOVSTAD. But instead of standing there using vague generalities, it would be interesting if you would tell us what these old marrowless truths are, that we are nourished on. (*Applause from many quarters.*)

DR. STOCKMANN. Oh, I could give you a whole string of such abominations; but to begin with I will confine myself to one well-approved truth, which at bottom is a foul lie, but upon which nevertheless Mr. Hovstad and the "People's Messenger" and all the "Messenger's" supporters are nourished.

HOVSTAD. And that is—?

DR. STOCKMANN. That is, the doctrine you have inherited from your forefathers and proclaim thoughtlessly far and wide—the doctrine that the public, the crowd, the masses are the essential part of the population—that they constitute the People—that the common folk, the ignorant and incomplete element in the community, have the same right to pronounce judgment and to approve, to direct and to govern, as the isolated, intellectually superior personalities in it.

BILLING. Well, damn me if ever I—

HOVSTAD (*at the same time, shouting out*). Fellow-citizens, take good note of that!

A NUMBER OF VOICES (*angrily*). Oho!—we are not the People! Only the superior folks are to govern, are they!

A WORKMAN. Turn the fellow out, for talking such rubbish!

ANOTHER. Out with him!

ANOTHER (*calling out*). Blow your horn, Evensen! (*A horn is blown loudly, amidst hisses and an angry uproar.*)

DR. STOCKMANN (*when the noise has somewhat abated*). Be reasonable! Can't you stand hearing the voice of truth for once? I don't in the least expect you to agree with me all at once; but I must say I did expect Mr. Hovstad to admit I was right, when he had recovered his composure a little. He claims to be a freethinker—

VOICES (*in murmurs of astonishment*). Freethinker, did he say? Is Hovstad a freethinker?

HOVSTAD (*shouting*). Prove it, Dr. Stockmann! When have I said so in print?

DR. STOCKMANN (*reflecting*). No, confound it, you are right!—you have never had the courage to. Well, I won't put you in a hole, Mr. Hovstad. Let us say it is I that am the freethinker, then. I am going to prove to you, scientifically, that the "People's Messenger" leads you by the nose in a shameful manner when it tells you that you—that the common people, the crowd, the masses are the real essence of the People. That is only a newspaper lie, I tell you! The common people are nothing more than the raw material of which a People is made. (*Groans, laughter and uproar.*) Well, isn't that the case? Isn't there an enormous difference between a well-bred and an ill-bred strain of animals? Take, for instance, a common barn-door hen. What sort of eating do you get from a shrivelled-up old scrag of a fowl like that? Not much, do you! And what sort of eggs does it lay? A fairly good crow or a raven can lay pretty nearly as good an egg. But take a well-bred Spanish or Japanese hen, or a good pheasant or a turkey—then you will see the difference. Or take the case of dogs, with whom we humans are on such intimate terms. Think first of an ordinary common cur—I mean one of the horrible, coarse-haired, low-bred curs that do nothing but run about the streets and befoul the walls of the houses. Compare one of these curs with a poodle whose sires for many generations have been bred in a gentleman's house, where they have had the best of food and had the opportunity of hearing soft voices and music. Do you not think that the poodle's brain is developed to quite a different degree from that of the cur? Of course it is. It is puppies of well-bred poodles like that, that showmen train to do incredibly clever tricks—things that a common cur could never learn to do even if it stood on its head. (*Uproar and mocking cries.*)

A CITIZEN (*calls out*). Are you going to make out we are dogs, now?

ANOTHER CITIZEN. We are not animals, Doctor!

DR. STOCKMANN. Yes, but bless my soul, we *are*, my friend! It is true we are the finest animals anyone could wish for; but, even amongst us, exceptionally fine animals are rare. There is a tremendous difference between poodle-men and cur-men. And the amusing part of it is, that Mr. Hovstad quite agrees with me as long as it is a question of four-footed animals—

HOVSTAD. Yes, it is true enough as far as they are concerned.

DR. STOCKMANN. Very well. But as soon as I extend the principle and apply it to two-legged animals, Mr. Hovstad stops short. He no longer dares to think independently, or to pursue his ideas to their logical conclusion; so he turns the whole theory upside down and proclaims in the "People's Messenger" that it is the barn-door hens and street curs that are the finest specimens in the menagerie. But that is always the way, as long as a man retains the traces of common origin and has not worked his way up to intellectual distinction.

HOVSTAD. I lay no claim to any sort of distinction. I am the son of humble countryfolk, and I am proud that the stock I come from is rooted deep among the common people he insults.

VOICES. Bravo, Hovstad! Bravo! Bravo!

DR. STOCKMANN. The kind of common people I mean are not only to be found low down in the social scale; they crawl and swarm all around us—even in the highest social positions. You have only to look at your own fine, distinguished Mayor! My brother Peter is every bit as plebeian as anyone that walks in two shoes— (*Laughter and hisses.*)

PETER STOCKMANN. I protest against personal allusions of this kind.

DR. STOCKMANN (*imperturbably*). —and that, not because he is, like myself, descended from some old rascal of a pirate from Pomerania or thereabouts—because that is who we are descended from—

PETER STOCKMANN. An absurd legend. I deny it!

DR. STOCKMANN. —but because he thinks what his superiors think and holds the same opinions as they. People who do that are, intellectually speaking, common people; and that is why my magnificent brother Peter is in reality so very far from any distinction—and consequently also so far from being liberal-minded.

PETER STOCKMANN. Mr. Chairman—!

HOVSTAD. So it is only the distinguished men that are liberal-minded in this country? We are learning something quite new! (*Laughter.*)

DR. STOCKMANN. Yes, that is part of my new discovery too. And another part of it is that broad-mindedness is almost precisely the same thing as morality. That is why I maintain that it is absolutely inexcusable in the "People's Messenger" to proclaim, day in and day out, the false doctrine that it is the masses, the crowd, the compact majority that have the monopoly of broad-mindedness and morality—and that vice and corruption and every kind of intellectual depravity are the result of culture, just as all the filth that is draining into our Baths is the result of the tanneries up at Mölledal! (*Uproar and interruptions.* DR. STOCKMANN *is undisturbed, and goes on, carried away by his ardour, with a smile.*) And yet this same "People's Messenger" can go on preaching that the masses ought to be elevated to higher conditions of life! But, bless my soul, if the "Messenger's" teaching is to be depended upon, this very raising up the masses would mean nothing more or less than setting them straightway upon the paths of depravity! Happily the theory that culture demoralises is only an old falsehood that our forefathers believed in and we have inherited. No, it is ignorance, poverty, ugly conditions of life that do the devil's work! In a house which does not get aired and swept every day—my wife Katherine maintains that the floor ought to be scrubbed as well, but that is a debatable question—in such a house, let me tell you, people will lose within two or three years the power of thinking or acting in a moral manner. Lack of oxygen weakens the conscience. And there must be a plentiful lack of oxygen in very many houses in this town, I should think, judging from the fact that the whole compact majority can be unconscientious enough to wish to build the town's prosperity on a quagmire of falsehood and deceit.

ASLAKSEN. We cannot allow such a grave accusation to be flung at a citizen community.

A CITIZEN. I move that the Chairman direct the speaker to sit down.

VOICES (*angrily*). Hear, hear! Quite right! Make him sit down!

DR. STOCKMANN (*losing his self-control*). Then I will go and shout the truth at every street corner! I will write it in other towns' newspapers! The whole country shall know what is going on here!

HOVSTAD. It almost seems as if Dr. Stockmann's intention were to ruin the town.

DR. STOCKMANN. Yes, my native town is so dear to me that I would rather ruin it than see it flourishing upon a lie.

ASLAKSEN. This is really serious.

(Uproar and cat-calls. MRS. STOCKMANN *coughs, but to no purpose; her husband does not listen to her any longer.)*

HOVSTAD *(shouting above the din).* A man must be a public enemy to wish to ruin a whole community!

DR. STOCKMANN *(with growing fervour).* What does the destruction of a community matter, if it lives on lies! It ought to be razed to the ground, I tell you! All who live by lies ought to be exterminated like vermin! You will end by infecting the whole country; you will bring about such a state of things that the whole country will deserve to be ruined. And if things come to that pass, I shall say from the bottom of my heart: Let the whole country perish, let all these people be exterminated!

VOICES *(from the crowd).* That is talking like an out-and-out enemy of the people!

BILLING. There sounded the voice of the people, by all that's holy!

THE WHOLE CROWD *(shouting).* Yes, yes! He is an enemy of the people! He hates his country! He hates his own people!

ASLAKSEN. Both as a citizen and as an individual, I am profoundly disturbed by what we have had to listen to. Dr. Stockmann has shown himself in a light I should never have dreamed of. I am unhappily obliged to subscribe to the opinion which I have just heard my estimable fellow-citizens utter; and I propose that we should give expression to that opinion in a resolution. I propose a resolution as follows: "This meeting declares that it considers Dr. Thomas Stockmann, Medical Officer of the Baths, to be an enemy of the people."

(A storm of cheers and applause. A number of men surround the DOCTOR *and hiss him.* MRS. STOCKMANN *and* PETRA *have got up from their seats.* MORTEN *and* EJLIF *are fighting the other schoolboys for hissing; some of their elders separate them.)*

DR. STOCKMANN *(to the men who are hissing him).* Oh, you fools! I tell you that—

ASLAKSEN *(ringing his bell).* We cannot hear you now, Doctor. A formal vote is about to be taken; but, out of regard for personal feelings, it shall be by ballot and not verbal. Have you any clean paper, Mr. Billings?

BILLING. I have both blue and white here.

ASLAKSEN *(going to him).* That will do nicely; we shall get on more quickly that way. Cut it up into small strips—yes, that's it. *(To the meeting.)* Blue means no; white means yes. I will come round myself and collect votes.

(PETER STOCKMANN *leaves the hall.* ASLAKSEN *and one or two others go round the room with the slips of paper in their hats.*)

1ST CITIZEN (*to* HOVSTAD). I say, what has come to the Doctor? What are we to think of it?

HOVSTAD. Oh, you know how headstrong he is.

2ND CITIZEN (*to* BILLING). Billing, you go to their house—have you ever noticed if the fellow drinks?

BILLING. Well I'm hanged if I know what to say. There are always spirits on the table when you go.

3RD CITIZEN. I rather think he goes quite off his head sometimes.

1ST CITIZEN. I wonder if there is any madness in his family?

BILLING. I shouldn't wonder if there were.

4TH CITIZEN. No, it is nothing more than sheer malice; he wants to get even with somebody for something or other.

BILLING. Well certainly he suggested a rise in his salary on one occasion lately, and did not get it.

THE CITIZENS (*together*). Ah!—then it is easy to understand how it is!

THE DRUNKEN MAN (*who has got amongst the audience again*). I want a blue one, I do! And I want a white one too!

VOICES. It's that drunken chap again! Turn him out!

MORTEN KIIL (*going up to* DR. STOCKMANN). Well, Stockmann, do you see what these monkey tricks of yours lead to?

DR. STOCKMANN. I have done my duty.

MORTEN KIIL. What was that you said about the tanneries at Mölledal?

DR. STOCKMANN. You heard well enough. I said they were the source of all the filth.

MORTEN KIIL. My tannery too?

DR. STOCKMANN. Unfortunately your tannery is by far the worst.

MORTEN KIIL. Are you going to put that in the papers?

DR. STOCKMANN. I shall conceal nothing.

MORTEN KIIL. That may cost you dear, Stockmann. (*Goes out.*)

A STOUT MAN (*going up to* CAPTAIN HORSTER, *without taking any notice of the ladies*). Well, Captain, so you lend your house to enemies of the people?

HORSTER. I imagine I can do what I like with my own possessions, Mr. Vik.

THE STOUT MAN. Then you can have no objection to my doing the same with mine.

HORSTER. What do you mean, sir?

THE STOUT MAN. You shall hear from me in the morning. (*Turns his back on him and moves off.*)

PETRA. Was that not your owner, Captain Horster?

HORSTER. Yes, that was Mr. Vik the ship-owner.

Aslaksen (*with the voting-papers in his hands, gets up on to the platform and rings his bell*). Gentlemen, allow me to announce the result. By the votes of every one here except one person—

A Young Man. That is the drunk chap!

Aslaksen. By the votes of every one here except a tipsy man, this meeting of citizens declares Dr. Thomas Stockmann to be an enemy of the people. (*Shouts and applause.*) Three cheers for our ancient and honourable citizen community! (*Renewed applause.*) Three cheers for our able and energetic Mayor, who has so loyally suppressed the promptings of family feeling! (*Cheers.*) The meeting is dissolved. (*Gets down.*)

Billing. Three cheers for the Chairman!

The Whole Crowd. Three cheers for Aslaksen! Hurrah!

Dr. Stockmann. My hat and coat, Petra! Captain, have you room on your ship for passengers to the New World?

Horster. For you and yours we will make room, Doctor.

Dr. Stockmann (*as* Petra *helps him into his coat*). Good. Come, Katherine! Come, boys!

Mrs. Stockmann (*in an undertone*). Thomas, dear, let us go out by the back way.

Dr. Stockmann. No back ways for me, Katherine. (*Raising his voice.*) You will hear more of this enemy of the people, before he shakes the dust off his shoes upon you! I am not so forgiving as a certain Person; I do not say: "I forgive you, for ye know not what ye do."

Aslaksen (*shouting*). That is a blasphemous comparison, Dr. Stockmann!

Billing. It is, by God! It's dreadful for an earnest man to listen to.

A Coarse Voice. Threatens us now, does he!

Other Voices (*excitedly*). Let's go and break his windows! Duck him in the fjord!

Another Voice. Blow your horn, Evensen! Pip, pip!

(*Horn-blowing, hisses and wild cries.* Dr. Stockmann *goes out through the hall with his family,* Horster *elbowing a way for them.*)

The Whole Crowd (*howling after them as they go*). Enemy of the People! Enemy of the People!

Billing (*as he puts his papers together*). Well, I'm damned if I go and drink toddy with the Stockmanns to-night!

(*The crowd press towards the exit. The uproar continues outside; shouts of* "Enemy of the People!" *are heard from without.*)

ACT V

Scene. Dr. Stockmann's *study. Bookcases, and cabinets containing specimens, line the walls. At the back is a door leading to the hall; in the foreground on the left, a door leading to the sitting-room. In the right-hand wall are two windows, of which all the panes are broken. The* DOCTOR'S *desk, littered with books and papers, stands in the middle of the room, which is in disorder. It is morning.* DR. STOCKMANN *in dressing-gown, slippers and a smoking-cap, is bending down and raking with an umbrella under one of the cabinets. After a little while he rakes out a stone.*

DR. STOCKMANN (*calling through the open sitting-room door*). Katherine, I have found another one.

MRS. STOCKMANN (*from the sitting-room*). Oh, you will find a lot more yet, I expect.

DR. STOCKMANN (*adding the stone to a heap of others on the table*). I shall treasure these stones as relics. Ejlif and Morten shall look at them every day, and when they are grown up they shall inherit them as heirlooms. (*Rakes about under a bookcase.*) Hasn't—what the deuce is her name—the girl, you know—hasn't she been to fetch the glazier yet?

MRS. STOCKMANN (*coming in*). Yes, but he said he didn't know if he would be able to come to-day.

DR. STOCKMANN. You will see he won't dare to come.

MRS. STOCKMANN. Well, that is just what Randine thought—that he didn't dare to, on account of the neighbours. (*Calls into the sitting-room.*) What is it you want, Randine? Give it to me. (*Goes in, and comes out again directly.*) Here is a letter for you, Thomas.

DR. STOCKMANN. Let me see it. (*Opens and reads it.*) Ah!—of course.

MRS. STOCKMANN. Who is it from?

DR. STOCKMANN. From the landlord. Notice to quit.

MRS. STOCKMANN. Is it possible? Such a nice man—

DR. STOCKMANN (*looking at the letter*). Does not dare do otherwise, he says. Doesn't like doing it, but dares not do otherwise—on account of his fellow-citizens—out of regard for public opinion. Is in a dependent position—dares not offend certain influential men—

MRS. STOCKMANN. There, you see, Thomas!

DR. STOCKMANN. Yes, yes, I see well enough; the whole lot of them in the town are cowards; not a man among them dares do anything for fear of the others. (*Throws the letter on to the table.*) But it doesn't matter to us, Katherine. We are going to sail away to the New World, and—

MRS. STOCKMANN. But, Thomas, are you sure we are well advised to take this step?

DR. STOCKMANN. Are you suggesting that I should stay here, where they have pilloried me as an enemy of the people—branded me—broken my windows! And just look here, Katherine—they have torn a great rent in my black trousers too!

MRS. STOCKMANN. Oh, dear—and they are the best pair you have got!

DR. STOCKMANN. You should never wear your best trousers when you go out to fight for freedom and truth. It is not that I care so much about the trousers, you know; you can always sew them up again for me. But that the common herd should dare to make this attack on me, as if they were my equals—that is what I cannot, for the life of me, swallow!

MRS. STOCKMANN. There is no doubt they have behaved very ill to you, Thomas; but is that sufficient reason for our leaving our native country for good and all?

DR. STOCKMANN. If we went to another town, do you suppose we should not find the common people just as insolent as they are here? Depend upon it, there is not much to choose between them. Oh, well, let the curs snap—that is not the worst part of it. The worst is that, from one end of this country to the other, every man is the slave of his Party. Although, as far as that goes, I daresay it is not much better in the free West either; the compact majority, and liberal public opinion, and all that infernal old bag of tricks are probably rampant there too. But there things are done on a larger scale, you see. They may kill you, but they won't put you to death by slow torture. They don't squeeze a free man's soul in a vice, as they do here. And, if need be, one can live in solitude. (*Walks up and down.*) If only I knew where there was a virgin forest or a small South Sea island for sale, cheap—

MRS. STOCKMANN. But think of the boys, Thomas.

DR. STOCKMANN (*standing still*). What a strange woman you are, Katherine! Would you prefer to have the boys grow up in a society like this? You saw for yourself last night that half the population are out of their minds; and if the other half have not lost their senses, it is because they are mere brutes, with no sense to lose.

MRS. STOCKMANN. But, Thomas dear, the imprudent things you said had something to do with it, you know.

DR. STOCKMANN. Well, isn't what I said perfectly true? Don't they turn every idea topsy-turvy? Don't they make a regular hotch-potch of right and wrong? Don't they say that the things I know are true, are lies? The craziest part of it all is the fact of these "liberals," men of full age, going about in crowds imagining that they are the broad-minded party! Did you ever hear anything like it, Katherine!

MRS. STOCKMANN. Yes, yes, it's mad enough of them, certainly; but— (PETRA *comes in from the sitting-room*). Back from school already?

PETRA. Yes. I have been given notice of dismissal.

MRS. STOCKMANN. Dismissal?

DR. STOCKMANN. You too?

PETRA. Mrs. Busk gave me my notice; so I thought it was best to go at once.

DR. STOCKMANN. You were perfectly right, too!

MRS. STOCKMANN. Who would have thought Mrs. Busk was a woman like that!

PETRA. Mrs. Busk isn't a bit like that, mother; I saw quite plainly how it hurt her to do it. But she didn't dare do otherwise, she said; and so I got my notice.

Dr. Stockmann (*laughing and rubbing his hands*). She didn't dare do otherwise, either! It's delicious!

Mrs. Stockmann. Well, after the dreadful scenes last night—

Petra. It was not only that. Just listen to this, father!

Dr. Stockmann. Well?

Petra. Mrs. Busk showed me no less than three letters she received this morning—

Dr. Stockmann. Anonymous, I suppose?

Petra. Yes.

Dr. Stockmann. Yes, because they didn't dare to risk signing their names, Katherine!

Petra. And two of them were to the effect that a man who has been our guest here, was declaring last night at the Club that my views on various subjects are extremely emancipated—

Dr. Stockmann. You did not deny that, I hope?

Petra. No, you know I wouldn't. Mrs. Busk's own views are tolerably emancipated, when we are alone together; but now that this report about me is being spread, she dare not keep me on any longer.

Mrs. Stockmann. And some one who had been a guest of ours! That shows you the return you get for your hospitality, Thomas!

Dr. Stockmann. We won't live in such a disgusting hole any longer. Pack up as quickly as you can, Katherine; the sooner we can get away, the better.

Mrs. Stockmann. Be quiet—I think I hear some one in the hall. See who it is, Petra.

Petra (*opening the door*). Oh, it's you, Captain Horster! Do come in.

Horster (*coming in*). Good morning. I thought I would just come in and see how you were.

Dr. Stockmann (*shaking his hand*). Thanks—that is really kind of you.

Mrs. Stockmann. And thank you, too, for helping us through the crowd, Captain Horster.

Petra. How did you manage to get home again?

Horster. Oh, somehow or other. I am fairly strong, and there is more sound than fury about these folk.

Dr. Stockmann. Yes, isn't their swinish cowardice astonishing? Look here, I will show you something! There are all the stones they have thrown through my windows. Just look at them! I'm hanged if there are more than two decently large bits of hardstone in the whole heap; the rest are nothing but gravel—wretched little things. And yet they stood out there bawling and swearing that they would do me some violence; but as for *doing* anything—you don't see much of that in this town.

HORSTER. Just as well for you this time, doctor!

DR. STOCKMANN. True enough. But it makes one angry all the same; because if some day it should be a question of a national fight in real earnest, you will see that public opinion will be in favour of taking to one's heels, and the compact majority will turn tail like a flock of sheep, Captain Horster. That is what is so mournful to think of; it gives me so much concern, that—. No, devil take it, it is ridiculous to care about it! They have called me an enemy of the people, so an enemy of the people let me be!

MRS. STOCKMANN. You will never be that, Thomas.

DR. STOCKMANN. Don't swear to that, Katherine. To be called an ugly name may have the same effect as a pin-scratch in the lung. And that hateful name—I can't get quit of it. It is sticking here in the pit of my stomach, eating into me like a corrosive acid. And no magnesia will remove it.

PETRA. Bah—you should only laugh at them, father.

HORSTER. They will change their minds some day, Doctor.

MRS. STOCKMANN. Yes, Thomas, as sure as you are standing here.

DR. STOCKMANN. Perhaps, when it is too late. Much good may it do them! They may wallow in their filth then and rue the day when they drove a patriot into exile. When do you sail, Captain Horster?

HORSTER. Hm!—that was just what I had come to speak about—

DR. STOCKMANN. Why, has anything gone wrong with the ship?

HORSTER. No; but what has happened is that I am not to sail in it.

PETRA. Do you mean that you have been dismissed from your command?

HORSTER (*smiling*). Yes, that's just it.

PETRA. You too.

MRS. STOCKMANN. There, you see, Thomas!

DR. STOCKMANN. And that for the truth's sake! Oh, if I had thought such a thing possible—

HORSTER. You mustn't take it to heart; I shall be sure to find a job with some ship-owner or other, elsewhere.

DR. STOCKMANN. And that is this man Vik—a wealthy man, independent of every one and everything—! Shame on him!

HORSTER. He is quite an excellent fellow otherwise; he told me himself he would willingly have kept me on, if only he had dared—

DR. STOCKMANN. But he didn't dare? No, of course not.

HORSTER. It is not such an easy matter, he said, for a party man—

DR. STOCKMANN. The worthy man spoke the truth. A party is like a sausage machine; it mashes up all sorts of heads together into the same mincemeat—fatheads and blockheads, all in one mash!

MRS. STOCKMANN. Come, come, Thomas dear!

PETRA (*to* HORSTER). If only you had not come home with us, things might not have come to this pass.

HORSTER. I do not regret it.

PETRA (*holding out her hand to him*). Thank you for that!

HORSTER (*to* DR. STOCKMANN). And so what I came to say was that if you are determined to go away, I have thought of another plan—

DR. STOCKMANN. That's splendid!—if only we can get away at once.

MRS. STOCKMANN. Hush—wasn't that some one knocking?

PETRA. That is uncle, surely.

DR. STOCKMANN. Aha! (*Calls out.*) Come in!

MRS. STOCKMANN. Dear Thomas, promise me definitely—

(PETER STOCKMANN *comes in from the hall.*)

PETER STOCKMANN. Oh, you are engaged. In that case, I will—

DR. STOCKMANN. No, no, come in.

PETER STOCKMANN. But I wanted to speak to you alone.

MRS. STOCKMANN. We will go into the sitting-room in the meanwhile.

HORSTER. And I will look in again later.

DR. STOCKMANN. No, go in there with them, Captain Horster; I want to hear more about—

HORSTER. Very well, I will wait, then. (*He follows* MRS. STOCKMANN *and* PETRA *into the sitting-room.*)

DR. STOCKMANN. I daresay you find it rather draughty here to-day. Put your hat on.

PETER STOCKMANN. Thank you, if I may. (*Does so.*) I think I caught cold last night; I stood and shivered—

DR. STOCKMANN. Really? I found it warm enough.

PETER STOCKMANN. I regret that it was not in my power to prevent those excesses last night.

DR. STOCKMANN. Have you anything particular to say to me besides that?

PETER STOCKMANN (*taking a big letter from his pocket*). I have this document for you, from the Baths Committee.

DR. STOCKMANN. My dismissal?

PETER STOCKMANN. Yes, dating from to-day. (*Lays the letter on the table.*) It gives us pain to do it; but, to speak frankly, we dared not do otherwise on account of public opinion.

DR. STOCKMANN (*smiling*). Dared not? I seem to have heard that word before, to-day.

PETER STOCKMANN. I must beg you to understand your position clearly. For the future you must not count on any practice whatever in the town.

DR. STOCKMANN. Devil take the practice! But why are you so sure of that?

PETER STOCKMANN. The Householders' Association is circulating a list from house to house. All right-minded citizens are being called upon to give up employing you; and I can assure you that not a single head of a family will risk refusing his signature. They simply dare not.

Dr. Stockmann. No, no; I don't doubt it. But what then?

Peter Stockmann. If I might advise you, it would be best to leave the place for a little while—

Dr. Stockmann. Yes, the propriety of leaving the place *has* occurred to me.

Peter Stockmann. Good. And then, when you have had six months to think things over, if, after mature consideration, you can persuade yourself to write a few words of regret, acknowledging your error—

Dr. Stockmann. I might have my appointment restored to me, do you mean?

Peter Stockmann. Perhaps. It is not at all impossible.

Dr. Stockmann. But what about public opinion, then? Surely you would not dare to do it on account of public feeling.

Peter Stockmann. Public opinion is an extremely mutable thing. And, to be quite candid with you, it is a matter of great importance to us to have some admission of that sort from you in writing.

Dr. Stockmann. Oh, that's what you are after, is it! I will just trouble you to remember what I said to you lately about foxy tricks of that sort!

Peter Stockmann. Your position was quite different then. At that time you had reason to suppose you had the whole town at your back—

Dr. Stockmann. Yes, and now I feel I have the whole town *on* my back—(*flaring up*) I would not do it if I had the devil and his dam on my back—! Never—never, I tell you!

Peter Stockmann. A man with a family has no right to behave as you do. You have no right to do it, Thomas.

Dr. Stockmann. I have no right! There is only one single thing in the world a free man has no right to do. Do you know what that is?

Peter Stockmann. No.

Dr. Stockmann. Of course you don't, but I will tell you. A free man has no right to soil himself with filth; he has no right to behave in a way that would justify his spitting in his own face.

Peter Stockmann. This sort of thing sounds extremely plausible, of course; and if there were no other explanation for your obstinacy—. But as it happens that there is.

Dr. Stockmann. What do you mean?

Peter Stockmann. You understand very well what I mean. But, as your brother and as a man of discretion, I advise you not to build too much upon expectations and prospects that may so very easily fail you.

Dr. Stockmann. What in the world is all this about?

Peter Stockmann. Do you really ask me to believe that you are ignorant of the terms of Mr. Kiil's will?

Dr. Stockmann. I know that the small amount he possesses is to go to an institution for indigent old work-people. How does that concern me?

PETER STOCKMANN. In the first place, it is by no means a small amount that is in question. Mr. Kiil is a fairly wealthy man.

DR. STOCKMANN. I had no notion of that!

PETER STOCKMANN. Hm!—hadn't you really? Then I suppose you had no notion, either, that a considerable portion of his wealth will come to your children, you and your wife having a life-rent of the capital. Has he never told you so?

DR. STOCKMANN. Never, on my honour! Quite the reverse; he has consistently done nothing but fume at being so unconscionably heavily taxed. But are you perfectly certain of this, Peter?

PETER STOCKMANN. I have it from an absolutely reliable source.

DR. STOCKMANN. Then, thank God, Katherine is provided for—and the children too! I must tell her this at once— (*Calls out.*) Katherine, Katherine!

PETER STOCKMANN (*restraining him*). Hush, don't say a word yet!

MRS. STOCKMANN (*opening the door*). What is the matter?

DR. STOCKMANN. Oh, nothing, nothing; you can go back. (*She shuts the door.* DR. STOCKMANN *walks up and down in his excitement.*) Provided for!—Just think of it, we are all provided for! And for life! What a blessed feeling it is to know one is provided for!

PETER STOCKMANN. Yes, but that is just exactly what you are not. Mr. Kiil can alter his will any day he likes.

DR. STOCKMANN. But he won't do that, my dear Peter. The "Badger" is much too delighted at my attack on you and your wise friends.

PETER STOCKMANN (*starts and looks intently at him*). Ah, that throws a light on various things.

DR. STOCKMANN. What things?

PETER STOCKMANN. I see that the whole thing was a combined manoeuvre on your part and his. These violent, reckless attacks that you have made against the leading men of the town, under the pretence that it was in the name of truth—

DR. STOCKMANN. What about them?

PETER STOCKMANN. I see that they were nothing else than the stipulated price for that vindictive old man's will.

DR. STOCKMANN (*almost speechless*). Peter—you are the most disgusting plebeian I have ever met in all my life.

PETER STOCKMANN. All is over between us. Your dismissal is irrevocable—we have a weapon against you now. (*Goes out.*)

DR. STOCKMANN. For shame! For shame! (*Calls out.*) Katherine, you must have the floor scrubbed after him! Let—what's her name—devil take it, the girl who has always got soot on her nose—

MRS. STOCKMANN (*in the sitting-room*). Hush, Thomas, be quiet!

PETRA (*coming to the door*). Father, grandfather is here, asking if he may speak to you alone.

Dr. Stockmann. Certainly he may. (*Going to the door.*) Come in, Mr. Kiil. (Morten Kiil *comes in.* Dr. Stockmann *shuts the door after him.*) What can I do for you? Won't you sit down?

Morten Kiil. I won't sit. (*Looks around.*) You look very comfortable here to-day, Thomas.

Dr. Stockmann. Yes, don't we!

Morten Kiil. Very comfortable—plenty of fresh air. I should think you have got enough to-day of that oxygen you were talking about yesterday. Your conscience must be in splendid order to-day, I should think.

Dr. Stockmann. It is.

Morten Kiil. So I should think. (*Taps his chest.*) Do you know what I have got here?

Dr. Stockmann. A good conscience, too, I hope.

Morten Kiil. Bah!—No, it is something better than that. (*He takes a thick pocket-book from his breast-pocket, opens it, and displays a packet of papers.*)

Dr. Stockmann (*looking at him in astonishment*). Shares in the Baths?

Morten Kiil. They were not difficult to get to-day.

Dr. Stockmann. And you have been buying—?

Morten Kiil. As many as I could pay for.

Dr. Stockmann. But, my dear Mr. Kiil—consider the state of the Baths' affairs!

Morten Kiil. If you behave like a reasonable man, you can soon set the Baths on their feet again.

Dr. Stockmann. Well, you can see for yourself that I have done all I can, but—. They are all mad in this town!

Morten Kiil. You said yesterday that the worst of this pollution came from my tannery. If that is true, then my grandfather and my father before me, and I myself, for many years past, have been poisoning the town like three destroying angels. Do you think I am going to sit quiet under that reproach?

Dr. Stockmann. Unfortunately, I am afraid you will have to.

Morten Kiil. No, thank you. I am jealous of my name and reputation. They call me "the Badger," I am told. A badger is a kind of pig, I believe; but I am not going to give them the right to call me that. I mean to live and die a clean man.

Dr. Stockmann. And how are you going to set about it?

Morten Kiil. You shall cleanse me, Thomas.

Dr. Stockmann. I!

Morten Kiil. Do you know what money I have bought these shares with? No, of course you can't know—but I will tell you. It is the money that Katherine and Petra and the boys will have when I am gone. Because I have been able to save a little bit after all, you know.

Dr. Stockmann (*flaring up*). And you have gone and taken Katherine's money for *this!*

Morten Kiil. Yes, the whole of the money is invested in the Baths now. And now I just want to see whether you are quite stark, staring mad, Thomas! If you still make out that these animals and other nasty things of that sort come from my tannery, it will be exactly as if you were to flay broad strips of skin from Katherine's body, and Petra's, and the boys'; and no decent man would do that—unless he were mad.

Dr. Stockmann (*walking up and down*). Yes, but I *am* mad; I *am* mad!

Morten Kiil. You cannot be so absurdly mad as all that, when it is a question of your wife and children.

Dr. Stockmann (*standing still in front of him*). Why couldn't you consult me about it, before you went and bought all that trash?

Morten Kiil. What is done cannot be undone.

Dr. Stockmann (*walks about uneasily*). If only I were not so certain about it—! But I am absolutely convinced that I am right.

Morten Kiil (*weighing the pocket-book in his hand*). If you stick to your mad idea, this won't be worth much, you know. (*Puts the pocket-book in his pocket.*)

Dr. Stockmann. But, hang it all! it might be possible for science to discover some prophylactic, I should think—or some antidote of some kind—

Morten Kiil. To kill these animals, do you mean?

Dr. Stockmann. Yes, or to make them innocuous.

Morten Kiil. Couldn't you try some rat's-bane?

Dr. Stockmann. Don't talk nonsense! They all say it is only imagination, you know. Well, let it go at that! Let them have their own way about it! Haven't the ignorant, narrow-minded curs reviled me as an enemy of the people?—and haven't they been ready to tear the clothes off my back too?

Morten Kiil. And broken all your windows to pieces!

Dr. Stockmann. And then there is my duty to my family. I must talk it over with Katherine; she is great on those things.

Morten Kiil. That is right; be guided by a reasonable woman's advice.

Dr. Stockmann (*advancing towards him*). To think you could do such a preposterous thing! Risking Katherine's money in this way, and putting me in such a horribly painful dilemma! When I look at you, I think I see the devil himself—.

Morten Kiil. Then I had better go. But I must have an answer from you before two o'clock—yes or no. If it is no, the shares go to a charity, and that this very day.

Dr. Stockmann. And what does Katherine get?

Morten Kiil. Not a halfpenny. (*The door leading to the hall opens, and* Hovstad *and* Aslaksen *make their apeparance.*) Look at those two!

Dr. Stockmann (*staring at them*). What the devil!—have *you* actually the face to come into my house?

HOVSTAD. Certainly.

ASLAKSEN. We have something to say to you, you see.

MORTEN KIIL (*in a whisper*). Yes or no—before two o'clock.

ASLAKSEN (*glancing at* HOVSTAD). Aha!

(MORTEN KIIL *goes out.*)

DR. STOCKMANN. Well, what do you want with me? Be brief.

HOVSTAD. I can quite understand that you are annoyed with us for our attitude at the meeting yesterday—

DR. STOCKMANN. Attitude, do you call it? Yes, it was a charming attitude! I call it weak, womanish—damnably shameful!

HOVSTAD. Call it what you like, we could not do otherwise.

DR. STOCKMANN. You *dared* not do otherwise—isn't that it?

HOVSTAD. Well, if you like to put it that way.

ASLAKSEN. But why did you not let us have word of it beforehand?—just a hint to Mr. Hovstad or to me?

DR. STOCKMANN. A hint? Of what?

ASLAKSEN. Of what was behind it all.

DR. STOCKMANN. I don't understand you in the least.

ASLAKSEN (*with a confidential nod*). Oh, yes, you do, Dr. Stockmann.

HOVSTAD. It is no good making a mystery of it any longer.

DR. STOCKMANN (*looking first at one of them and then at the other*). What the devil do you both mean?

ASLAKSEN. May I ask if your father-in-law is not going round the town buying up all the shares in the Baths?

DR. STOCKMANN. Yes, he has been buying Baths' shares to-day; but—

ASLAKSEN. It would have been more prudent to get some one else to do it—some one less nearly related to you.

HOVSTAD. And you should not have let your name appear in the affair. There was no need for anyone to know that the attack on the Baths came from you. You ought to have consulted me, Dr. Stockmann.

DR. STOCKMANN (*looks in front of him; then a light seems to dawn on him and he says in amazement*). Are such things conceivable? Are such things possible?

ASLAKSEN (*with a smile*). Evidently they are. But it is better to use a little *finesse,* you know.

HOVSTAD. And it is much better to have several persons in a thing of that sort; because the responsibility of each individual is lessened, when there are others with him.

DR. STOCKMANN (*composedly*). Come to the point, gentlemen. What do you want?

ASLAKSEN. Perhaps Mr. Hovstad had better—

HOVSTAD. No, you tell him, Aslaksen.

ASLAKSEN. Well, the fact is that, now we know the bearings of the whole affair, we think we might venture to put the "People's Messenger" at your disposal.

DR. STOCKMANN. Do you dare do that now? What about public opinion? Are you not afraid of a storm breaking upon our heads?

HOVSTAD. We will try to weather it.

ASLAKSEN. And you must be ready to go off quickly on a new tack, Doctor. As soon as your invective has done its work—

DR. STOCKMANN. Do you mean, as soon as my father-in-law and I have got hold of the shares at a low figure?

HOVSTAD. Your reasons for wishing to get the control of the Baths are mainly scientific, I take it.

DR. STOCKMANN. Of course; it was for scientific reasons that I persuaded the old "Badger" to stand in with me in the matter. So we will tinker at the conduit-pipes a little, and dig up a little bit of the shore, and it shan't cost the town a sixpence. That will be all right—eh?

HOVSTAD. I think so—if you have the "People's Messenger" behind you.

ASLAKSEN. The Press is a power in a free community, Doctor.

DR. STOCKMANN. Quite so. And so is public opinion. And you, Mr. Aslaksen—I suppose you will be answerable for the Householders' Association?

ASLAKSEN. Yes, and for the Temperance Society. You may rely on that.

DR. STOCKMANN. But, gentlemen—I really am ashamed to ask the question—but, what return do you—?

HOVSTAD. We should prefer to help you without any return whatever, believe me. But the "People's Messenger" is in rather a shaky condition; it doesn't go really well; and I should be very unwilling to suspend the paper now, when there is so much work to do here in the political way.

DR. STOCKMANN. Quite so; that would be a great trial to such a friend of the people as you are. (*Flares up.*) But I am an enemy of the people, remember! (*Walks about the room.*) Where have I put my stick? Where the devil is my stick?

HOVSTAD. What's that?

ASLAKSEN. Surely you never mean—?

DR. STOCKMANN (*standing still*). And suppose I don't give you a single penny of all I get out of it? Money is not very easy to get out of us rich folk, please to remember!

HOVSTAD. And you please to remember that this affair of the shares can be represented in two ways!

DR. STOCKMANN. Yes, and you are just the man to do it. If I don't come to the rescue of the "People's Messenger," you will certainly take an evil view of the affair; you will hunt me down, I can well imagine—pursue me—try to throttle me as a dog does a hare.

HOVSTAD. It is a natural law; every animal must fight for its own livelihood.

ASLAKSEN. And get its food where it can, you know.

DR. STOCKMANN (*walking about the room*). Then you go and look for yours in the gutter; because I am going to show you which is the strongest animal of us three! (*Finds an umbrella and brandishes it above his head.*) Ah, now—!

HOVSTAD. You are surely not going to use violence!

ASLAKSEN. Take care what you are doing with that umbrella.

DR. STOCKMANN. Out of the window with you, Mr. Hovstad!

HOVSTAD (*edging to the door*). Are you quite mad!

DR. STOCKMANN. Out of the window, Mr. Aslaksen! Jump, I tell you! You will have to do it, sooner or later.

ASLAKSEN (*running round the writing-table*). Moderation, Doctor—I am a delicate man—I can stand so little— (*Calls out.*) Help, help!

(MRS. STOCKMANN, PETRA *and* HORSTER *come in from the sitting-room.*)

MRS. STOCKMANN. Good gracious, Thomas! What is happening?

DR. STOCKMANN (*brandishing the umbrella*). Jump out, I tell you! Out into the gutter!

HOVSTAD. An assault on an unoffending man! I call you to witness, Captain Horster. (*Hurries out through the hall.*)

ASLAKSEN (*irresolutely*). If only I knew the way about here—. (*Steals out through the sitting-room.*)

MRS. STOCKMANN (*holding her husband back*). Control yourself, Thomas!

DR. STOCKMANN (*throwing down the umbrella*). Upon my soul, they have escaped after all.

MRS. STOCKMANN. What did they want you to do?

DR. STOCKMANN. I will tell you later on; I have something else to think about now. (*Goes to the table and writes something on a calling-card.*) Look there, Katherine; what is written there?

MRS. STOCKMANN. Three big No's; what does that mean?

DR. STOCKMANN. I will tell you that too, later on. (*Holds out the card to* PETRA.) There, Petra; tell sooty-face to run over to the "Badger's" with that, as quickly as she can. Hurry up!

(PETRA *takes the card and goes out to the hall.*)

DR. STOCKMANN. Well, I think I have had a visit from every one of the devil's messengers to-day! But now I am going to sharpen my pen till they can feel its point; I shall dip it in venom and gall; I shall hurl my ink-pot at their heads!

MRS. STOCKMANN. Yes, but we are going away, you know, Thomas.

(PETRA *comes back.*)

DR. STOCKMANN. Well?

PETRA. She has gone with it.

DR. STOCKMANN. Good.—Going away, did you say? No, I'll be hanged if we are going away! We are going to stay where we are, Katherine!

PETRA. Stay here?

MRS. STOCKMANN. Here, in the town?

DR. STOCKMANN. Yes, here. This is the field of battle—this is where the fight will be. This is where I shall triumph! As soon as I have had my trousers sewn up I shall go out and look for another house. We must have a roof over our heads for the winter.

HORSTER. That you shall have in my house.

DR. STOCKMANN. Can I?

HORSTER. Yes, quite well. I have plenty of room, and I am almost never at home.

MRS. STOCKMANN. How good of you, Captain Horster!

PETRA. Thank you!

DR. STOCKMANN (*grasping his hand*). Thank you, thank you! That is one trouble over! Now I can set to work in earnest at once. There is an endless amount of things to look through here, Katherine! Luckily I shall have all my time at my disposal; because I have been dismissed from the Baths, you know.

MRS. STOCKMANN (*with a sigh*). Oh, yes, I expected that.

DR. STOCKMANN. And they want to take my practice away from me, too. Let them! I have got the poor people to fall back upon, anyway—those that don't pay anything; and, after all, they need me most, too. But, by Jove, they will have to listen to me; I shall preach to them in season and out of season, as it says somewhere.

MRS. STOCKMANN. But, dear Thomas, I should have thought events had showed you what use it is to preach.

DR. STOCKMANN. You are really ridiculous, Katherine. Do you want me to let myself be beaten off the field by public opinion and the compact majority and all that devilry? No, thank you! And what I want to do is so simple and clear and straightforward. I only want to drum into the heads of these curs the fact that the liberals are the most insidious enemies of freedom—that party programmes strangle every young and vigorous truth—that considerations of expediency turn morality and justice upside down—and that they will end by making life here unbearable. Don't you think, Captain Horster, that I ought to be able to make people understand that?

HORSTER. Very likely; I don't know much about such things myself.

DR. STOCKMANN. Well, look here—I will explain! It is the party leaders that must be exterminated. A party leader is like a wolf, you see—like a voracious wolf. He requires a certain number of smaller victims to prey upon every year, if he is to live. Just look at Hovstad and Aslaksen! How many smaller victims have they not put an end to—or at any rate maimed and mangled until they are fit for nothing except to be householders or subscribers to the "People's Messenger"! (*Sits down on the edge of the table.*) Come here, Katherine—look how beautifully the sun shines to-day! And this lovely spring air I am drinking in!

Mrs. Stockmann. Yes, if only we could live on sunshine and spring air, Thomas.

Dr. Stockmann. Oh, you will have to pinch and save a bit—then we shall get along. That gives me very little concern. What is much worse is that I know of no one who is liberal-minded and high-minded enough to venture to take up my work after me.

Petra. Don't think about that, father; you have plenty of time before you.—Hullo, here are the boys already!

(Ejlif *and* Morten *come in from the sitting-room.*)

Mrs. Stockmann. Have you got a holiday?

Morten. No; but we were fighting with the other boys between lessons—

Ejlif. That isn't true; it was the other boys were fighting with us.

Morten. Well, and then Mr. Rörlund said we had better stay at home for a day or two.

Dr. Stockmann (*snapping his fingers and getting up from the table*). I have it! I have it, by Jove! You shall never set foot in the school again!

The Boys. No more school!

Mrs. Stockmann. But, Thomas—

Dr. Stockmann. Never, I say. I will educate you myself; that is to say, you shan't learn a blessed thing—

Morten. Hooray!

Dr. Stockmann. —but I will make liberal-minded and high-minded men of you. You must help me with that, Petra.

Petra. Yes, father, you may be sure I will.

Dr. Stockmann. And my school shall be in the room where they insulted me and called me an enemy of the people. But we are too few as we are; I must have at least twelve boys to begin with.

Mrs. Stockmann. You will certainly never get them in this town.

Dr. Stockmann. We shall. (*To the boys.*) Don't you know any street urchins—regular ragamuffins—?

Morten. Yes, father, I know lots!

Dr. Stockmann. That's capital! Bring me some specimens of them. I am going to experiment with curs, just for once; there may be some exceptional heads amongst them.

Morten. And what are we going to do, when you have made liberal-minded and high-minded men of us?

Dr. Stockmann. Then you shall drive all the wolves out of the country, my boys!

(Ejlif *looks rather doubtful about it;* Morten *jumps about crying* "Hurrah!")

Mrs. Stockmann. Let us hope it won't be the wolves that will drive you out of the country, Thomas.

Dr. Stockmann. Are you out of your mind, Katherine? Drive me out! Now—when I am the strongest man in the town!

Mrs. Stockmann. The strongest—now?

Dr. Stockmann. Yes, and I will go so far as to say that now I am the strongest man in the whole world.

Morten. I say!

Dr. Stockmann (*lowering his voice*). Hush! You mustn't say anything about it yet; but I have made a great discovery.

Mrs. Stockmann. Another one?

Dr. Stockmann. Yes. (*Gathers them round him, and says confidentially*) It is this, let me tell you—that the strongest man in the world is he who stands most alone.

Mrs. Stockmann (*smiling and shaking her head*). Oh, Thomas, Thomas!

Petra (*encouragingly, as she grasps her father's hands*). Father!

QUESTIONS

1. Dr. Stockmann and his brother are early established as character foils. In what different ways are they contrasted? How does each help to bring out the character of the other?

2. Is Dr. Stockmann's desire to publish the truth about the Baths purely altruistic? Why is he so happy to learn, in Act I, that the Baths are polluted? Is he in any respect like his brother?

3. How astute is Dr. Stockmann in foreseeing the consequences of his discovery? in judging the characters of other people? How would you characterize him as a political man? Trace the stages of his political education. What does he learn in Act II? in Act III? in Act IV? in Act V? To what degree does he change during the course of the play?

4. Morten Kiil says, in Act II, "It is better never to trust anybody; you may find you have been made a fool of before you know where you are." In what respects are Kiil and Dr. Stockmann character foils? Who is shrewder? Who is more admirable?

5. Which of the following adjectives can be accurately applied to Dr. Stockmann's impromptu speech in Act IV: *courageous, intemperate, arrogant, foolish, large-minded, wise?* Support your answer.

6. What purpose is served by the characterization of Dr. Stockmann, in Act I, as a man who likes good things—roast beef, hot toddy, good company?

7. How are we to take Dr. Stockmann's discovery at the end of the play: "the strongest man in the world is he who stands most alone." In terms of the play, is it true?

8. It has been said that "Politics makes strange bedfellows." In this play, what are the respective alignments and relationships between Dr. Stockmann, Peter Stockmann, Hovstad and Billing, and Aslaksen (a) after Dr. Stockmann announces his discovery, (b) at the end of the play? What interests are represented by each of these men?

9. In Act III, Dr. Stockmann asks his wife, "Because a man has a wife and children is he not allowed to tell the truth?" The question poses a real moral dilemma. What answer does Peter Stockmann make to it? What answer to it is implied by the play? Is Dr. Stockmann the only character put under pressure by threats against another member of his family?

10. Evaluate, in terms of the action of the play, Dr. Stockmann's assertion that "The most dangerous enemy to truth and freedom . . . is the compact majority." What other assertions does he make about majorities? Is this play antidemocratic in theme? Why or why not?

11. Hovstad expresses at least three attitudes toward the function of a newspaper: (a) that "truth should be the first consideration" (Act II), (b) that a newspaper should carry the public "on the path that leads to liberty and progress" (Act III), and (c) that "an editor's first and most obvious duty" is "to work in harmony with his readers" (Act IV). In what order does Hovstad honor these three principles? In what order does Ibsen, as judged by the action of the play, rank them?

12. Of Dr. Stockmann's principal antagonists—Peter Stockmann, Hovstad, Billing, Aslaksen, Morton Kiil—which is the most powerful? Which is the second most powerful? Which is most corrupt? What are the chief characterizing qualities of each?

13. Where do Mrs. Stockmann's loyalties lie? Does she change during the course of the play? Is she more, or less, far-sighted than her husband?

14. Mark each of the following statements made by characters in the play as true or false. If the statement is false, explain whether its falseness springs from misjudgment, lack of self-knowledge, or an out-and-out lie: (a) Dr. Stockmann: "I shall smite them to the ground—I shall crush them—I shall break down all their defenses before the eyes of the honest public!" (Act III). (b) Hovstad: "I am not a weathercock—and never will be" (Act III). (c) Billing (of his application for the post of secretary to the Bench): "You must clearly understand I am doing it only to annoy the bigwigs. . . . My object is precisely *not* to get it" (Act III). (d) Hovstad (of the idea that an editor is often obliged to bow to the wishes of the public in unimportant matters): "No; as a matter of fact, that is Billing's idea and not

mine. . . . And it is Billing who is so anxious to have that story in the paper" (Act III). (e) ASLAKSEN: "I have nothing to do with editing the paper, Mr. Mayor" (Act III). (f) PETER STOCKMANN: "The proprietors of the Baths are not in a position to incur any further expense" (Act III). (g) DR. STOCKMANN (in reply to his wife's injunction "Be sure not to lose your temper, Thomas"): "Oh, I know how to control myself" (Act IV). (h) PETER STOCKMANN: "In my communication to the *People's Messenger* I have put the essential facts before the public in such a way that every fair-minded citizen can easily form his own opinion" (Act IV).

15. What advantage does Ibsen's realistic technique have for his particular subject matter? How does he make clear that a character is speaking differently from what he thinks or feels? Or does he always? What would the effect on the tone of the play have been, had Ibsen used asides?

Federico García Lorca

BLOOD WEDDING

CHARACTERS

The Mother
The Bride
The Mother-in-Law
Leonardo's Wife
The Servant Woman
The Neighbor Woman
Young Girls
Leonardo
The Bridegroom
The Bride's Father
The Moon
Death (*as a* Beggar Woman)
Woodcutters
Young men

ACT ONE

SCENE I

A room painted yellow.

Bridegroom (*entering*). Mother.

Mother. What?

Bridegroom. I'm going.

Mother. Where?

Bridegroom. To the vineyard. (*He starts to go.*)

Mother. Wait.

Bridegroom. You want something?

Mother. Your breakfast, son.

Bridegroom. Forget it. I'll eat grapes. Give me the knife.

Mother. What for?

Bridegroom (*laughing*). To cut the grapes with.

Mother (*muttering as she looks for the knife*). Knives, knives. Cursed be all knives, and the scoundrel who invented them.

Bridegroom. Let's talk about something else.

MOTHER. And guns and pistols and the smallest little knife—and even hoes and pitchforks.

BRIDEGROOM. All right.

MOTHER. Everything that can slice a man's body. A handsome man, full of young life, who goes out to the vineyards or to his own olive groves—his own because he's inherited them . . .

BRIDEGROOM (*lowering his head*). Be quiet.

MOTHER. . . . and then that man doesn't come back. Or if he does come back it's only for someone to cover him over with a palm leaf or a plate of rock salt so he won't bloat. I don't know how you dare carry a knife on your body—or how I let this serpent (*she takes a knife from a kitchen chest*) stay in the chest.

BRIDEGROOM. Have you had your say?

MOTHER. If I lived to be a hundred I'd talk of nothing else. First your father; to me he smelled like a carnation and I had him for barely three years. Then your brother. Oh, is it right—how can it be—that a small thing like a knife or a pistol can finish off a man—a bull of a man? No, I'll never be quiet. The months pass and the hopelessness of it stings in my eyes and even to the roots of my hair.

BRIDEGROOM (*forcefully*). Let's quit this talk!

MOTHER. No. No. Let's not quit this talk. Can anyone bring me your father back? Or your brother? Then there's the jail. What do they mean, jail? They eat there, smoke there, play music there! My dead men choking with weeds, silent, turning to dust. Two men like two beautiful flowers. The killers in jail, carefree, looking at the mountains.

BRIDEGROOM. Do you want me to go kill them?

MOTHER. No . . . If I talk about it it's because . . . Oh, how can I help talking about it, seeing you go out that door? It's . . . I don't like you to carry a knife. It's just that . . . that I wish you wouldn't go out to the fields.

BRIDEGROOM (*laughing*). Oh, come now!

MOTHER. I'd like it if you were a woman. Then you wouldn't be going out to the arroyo now and we'd both of us embroider flounces and little woolly dogs.

BRIDEGROOM (*he puts his arm around his mother and laughs*). Mother, what if I should take you with me to the vineyards?

MOTHER. What would an old lady do in the vineyards? Were you going to put me down under the young vines?

BRIDEGROOM (*lifting her in his arms*). Old lady, old lady—you little old, little old lady!

MOTHER. Your father, he used to take me. That's the way with men of good stock; good blood. Your grandfather left a son on every corner. That's what I like. Men, men; wheat, wheat.

BRIDEGROOM. And I, Mother?

MOTHER. You, what?

BRIDEGROOM. Do I need to tell you again?

MOTHER (*seriously*). Oh!

BRIDEGROOM. Do you think it's bad?

MOTHER. No.

BRIDEGROOM. Well, then?

MOTHER. I don't really know. Like this, suddenly, it always surprises me. I know the girl is good. Isn't she? Well-behaved. Hard working. Kneads her bread, sews her skirts, but even so when I say her name I feel as though someone had hit me on the forehead with a rock.

BRIDEGROOM. Foolishness.

MOTHER. More than foolishness. I'll be left alone. Now only you are left me—I hate to see you go.

BRIDEGROOM. But you'll come with us.

MOTHER. No. I can't leave your father and brother here alone. I have to go to them every morning and if I go away it's possible one of the Félix family, one of the killers, might die—and they'd bury him next to ours. And that'll never happen! Oh, no! That'll never happen! Because I'd dig them out with my nails and, all by myself, crush them against the wall.

BRIDEGROOM (*sternly*). There you go again.

MOTHER. Forgive me. (*pause*) How long have you known her?

BRIDEGROOM. Three years. I've been able to buy the vineyard.

MOTHER. Three years. She used to have another sweetheart, didn't she?

BRIDEGROOM. I don't know. I don't think so. Girls have to look at what they'll marry.

MOTHER. Yes. I looked at nobody. I looked at your father, and when they killed him I looked at the wall in front of me. One woman with one man, and that's all.

BRIDEGROOM. You know my girl's good.

MOTHER. I don't doubt it. All the same, I'm sorry not to have known what her mother was like.

BRIDEGROOM. What difference does it make now?

MOTHER (*looking at him*). Son.

BRIDEGROOM. What is it?

MOTHER. That's true! You're right! When do you want me to ask for her?

BRIDEGROOM (*happily*). Does Sunday seem all right to you?

MOTHER (*seriously*). I'll take her the bronze earrings, they're very old —and you buy her . . .

BRIDEGROOM. You know more about that . . .

MOTHER. . . . you buy her some open-work stockings—and for you, two suits—three! I have no one but you now!

BRIDEGROOM. I'm going. Tomorrow I'll go see her.

MOTHER. Yes, yes—and see if you can make me happy with six grandchildren—or as many as you want, since your father didn't live to give them to me.

BRIDEGROOM. The first-born for you!

MOTHER. Yes, but have some girls. I want to embroider and make lace, and be at peace.

BRIDEGROOM. I'm sure you'll love my wife.

MOTHER. I'll love her. (*She starts to kiss him but changes her mind.*) Go on. You're too big now for kisses. Give them to your wife. (*Pause. To herself*) When she is your wife.

BRIDEGROOM. I'm going.

MOTHER. And that land around the little mill—work it over. You've not taken good care of it.

BRIDEGROOM. You're right. I will.

MOTHER. God keep you.

(*The son goes out. The* MOTHER *remains seated—her back to the door. A* NEIGHBOR WOMAN *with a 'kerchief on her head appears in the door.*)

Come in.

NEIGHBOR. How are you?

MOTHER. Just as you see me.

NEIGHBOR. I came down to the store and stopped in to see you. We live so far away!

MOTHER. It's twenty years since I've been up to the top of the street.

NEIGHBOR. You're looking well.

MOTHER. You think so?

NEIGHBOR. Things happen. Two days ago they brought in my neighbor's son with both arms sliced off by the machine. (*She sits down.*)

MOTHER. Rafael?

NEIGHBOR. Yes. And there you have him. Many times I've thought your son and mine are better off where they are—sleeping, resting—not running the risk of being left helpless.

MOTHER. Hush. That's all just something thought up—but no consolation.

NEIGHBOR (*sighing*). Ay!

MOTHER (*sighing*). Ay!

(*Pause.*)

NEIGHBOR (*sadly*). Where's your son?

MOTHER. He went out.

NEIGHBOR. He finally bought the vineyard!

MOTHER. He was lucky.

NEIGHBOR. Now he'll get married.

MOTHER (*as though reminded of something, she draws her chair near the* NEIGHBOR). Listen.

NEIGHBOR (*in a confidential manner*). Yes. What is it?

MOTHER. You know my son's sweetheart?

NEIGHBOR. A good girl!

MOTHER. Yes, but . . .

NEIGHBOR. But who knows her really well? There's nobody. She lives out there alone with her father—so far away—fifteen miles from the nearest house. But she's a good girl. Used to being alone.

MOTHER. And her mother?

NEIGHBOR. Her mother I *did* know. Beautiful. Her face glowed like a saint's—but *I* never liked her. She didn't love her husband.

MOTHER (*sternly*). Well, what a lot of things certain people know!

NEIGHBOR. I'm sorry. I didn't mean to offend—but it's true. Now, whether she was decent or not nobody said. That wasn't discussed. She was haughty.

MOTHER. There you go again!

NEIGHBOR. You asked me.

MOTHER. I wish no one knew anything about them—either the live one or the dead one—that they were like two thistles no one even names but cuts off at the right moment.

NEIGHBOR. You're right. Your son is worth a lot.

MOTHER. Yes—a lot. That's why I look after him. They told me the girl had a sweetheart some time ago.

NEIGHBOR. She was about fifteen. He's been married two years now—to a cousin of hers, as a matter of fact. But nobody remembers about their engagement.

MOTHER. How do you remember it?

NEIGHBOR. Oh, what questions you ask!

MOTHER. We like to know all about the things that hurt us. Who was the boy?

NEIGHBOR. Leonardo.

MOTHER. What Leonardo?

NEIGHBOR. Leonardo Félix.

MOTHER. Félix!

NEIGHBOR. Yes, but—how is Leonardo to blame for anything? He was eight years old when those things happened.

MOTHER. That's true. But I hear that name—Félix—and it's all the same. (*Muttering*) Félix, a slimy mouthful. (*She spits.*) It makes me spit—spit so I won't kill!

NEIGHBOR. Control yourself. What good will it do?

MOTHER. No good. But you see how it is.

NEIGHBOR. Don't get in the way of your son's happiness. Don't say anything to him. You're old. So am I. It's time for you and me to keep quiet.

MOTHER. I'll say nothing to him.

NEIGHBOR (*kissing her*). Nothing.

MOTHER (*calmly*). Such things . . . !

NEIGHBOR. I'm going. My men will soon be coming in from the fields.

MOTHER. Have you ever known such a hot sun?

NEIGHBOR. The children carrying water out to the reapers are black with it. Goodbye, woman.

MOTHER. Goodbye. (*The* MOTHER *starts toward the door at the left. Halfway there she stops and slowly crosses herself.*)

SCENE II

A room painted rose with copperware and wreaths of common flowers. In the center of the room is a table with a tablecloth. It is morning.

LEONARDO'S MOTHER-IN-LAW *sits in one corner holding a child in her arms and rocking it. His* WIFE *is in the other corner mending stockings.*

MOTHER-IN-LAW. Lullaby, my baby
once there was a big horse
who didn't like water.
The water was black there
under the branches.
When it reached the bridge
it stopped and it sang.
Who can say, my baby,
what the stream holds
with its long tail
in its green parlor?

WIFE (*softly*). Carnation, sleep and dream,
the horse won't drink from the stream.

MOTHER-IN-LAW. My rose, asleep now lie,
the horse is starting to cry.
His poor hooves were bleeding,
his long mane was frozen,
and deep in his eyes
stuck a silvery dagger.
Down he went to the river,
Oh, down he went down!
And his blood was running,
Oh, more than the water.

WIFE. Carnation, sleep and dream,
the horse won't drink from the stream.

MOTHER-IN-LAW. My rose, asleep now lie,
the horse is starting to cry.

WIFE. He never did touch

the dank river shore
though his muzzle was warm
and with silvery flies.
So, to the hard mountains
he could only whinny
just when the dead stream
covered his throat.
Ay-y-y, for the big horse
who didn't like water!
Ay-y-y, for the snow-wound
big horse of the dawn!

MOTHER-IN-LAW. Don't come in! Stop him
and close up the window
with branches of dreams
and a dream of branches

WIFE. My baby is sleeping.

MOTHER-IN-LAW. My baby is quiet.

WIFE. Look, horse, my baby
has him a pillow.

MOTHER-IN-LAW. His cradle is metal.

WIFE. His quilt a fine fabric.

MOTHER-IN-LAW. Lullaby, my baby.

WIFE. Ay-y-y, for the big horse
who didn't like water!

MOTHER-IN-LAW. Don't come near, don't come in!
Go away to the mountains
and through the grey valleys,
that's where your mare is.

WIFE (*looking at the baby*). My baby is sleeping.

MOTHER-IN-LAW. My baby is resting.

WIFE (*softly*). Carnation, sleep and dream,
The horse won't drink from the stream.

MOTHER-IN-LAW (*getting up, very softly*). My rose, asleep now lie
for the horse is starting to cry.

(*She carries the child out.* LEONARDO *enters.*)

LEONARDO. Where's the baby?

WIFE. He's sleeping.

LEONARDO. Yesterday he wasn't well. He cried during the night.

WIFE. Today he's like a dahlia. And you? Were you at the blacksmith's?

LEONARDO. I've just come from there. Would you believe it? For more than two months he's been putting new shoes on the horse and they're always coming off. As far as I can see he pulls them off on the stones.

WIFE. Couldn't it just be that you use him so much?

LEONARDO. No. I almost never use him.

WIFE. Yesterday the neighbors told me they'd seen you on the far side of the plains.

LEONARDO. Who said that?

WIFE. The women who gather capers. It certainly surprised me. Was it you?

LEONARDO. No. What would I be doing there, in that wasteland?

WIFE. That's what I said. But the horse was streaming sweat.

LEONARDO. Did you see him?

WIFE. No. Mother did.

LEONARDO. Is she with the baby?

WIFE. Yes. Do you want some lemonade?

LEONARDO. With good cold water.

WIFE. And then you didn't come to eat!

LEONARDO. I was with the wheat weighers. They always hold me up.

WIFE (*very tenderly, while she makes the lemonade*). Did they pay you a good price?

LEONARDO. Fair.

WIFE. I need a new dress and the baby a bonnet with ribbons.

LEONARDO (*getting up*). I'm going to take a look at him.

WIFE. Be careful. He's asleep.

MOTHER-IN-LAW (*coming in*). Well! Who's been racing the horse that way? He's down there, worn out, his eyes popping from their sockets as though he'd come from the ends of the earth.

LEONARDO (*acidly*). I have.

MOTHER-IN-LAW. Oh, excuse me! He's your horse.

WIFE (*timidly*). He was at the wheat buyers.

MOTHER-IN-LAW. He can burst for all of me!

(*She sits down. Pause.*)

WIFE. Your drink. Is it cold?

LEONARDO. Yes.

WIFE. Did you hear they're going to ask for my cousin?

LEONARDO. When?

WIFE. Tomorrow. The wedding will be within a month. I hope they're going to invite us.

LEONARDO (*gravely*). I don't know.

MOTHER-IN-LAW. His mother, I think, wasn't very happy about the match.

LEONARDO. Well, she may be right. She's a girl to be careful with.

WIFE. I don't like to have you thinking bad things about a good girl.

MOTHER-IN-LAW (*meaningfully*). If he does, it's because he knows her. Didn't you know he courted her for three years?

LEONARDO. But I left her. (*To his* WIFE.) Are you going to cry now? Quit that! (*He brusquely pulls her hands away from her face.*) Let's go see the baby.

(*They go in with their arms around each other. A* GIRL *appears. She is happy. She enters running.*)

GIRL. Señora.

MOTHER-IN-LAW. What is it?

GIRL. The groom came to the store and he's bought the best of everything they had.

MOTHER-IN-LAW. Was he alone?

GIRL. No. With his mother. Stern, tall. (*She imitates her.*) And such extravagance!

MOTHER-IN-LAW. They have money.

GIRL. And they bought some open-work stockings! Oh, such stockings! A woman's dream of stockings! Look: a swallow here (*she points to her ankle*) a ship here (*she points to her calf*) and here (*she points to her thigh*) a rose!

MOTHER-IN-LAW. Child!

GIRL. A rose with the seeds and the stem! Oh! All in silk.

MOTHER-IN-LAW. Two rich families are being brought together.

(LEONARDO *and his* WIFE *appear.*)

GIRL. I came to tell you what they're buying.

LEONARDO (*loudly*). We don't care.

WIFE. Leave her alone.

MOTHER-IN-LAW. Leonardo, it's not that important.

GIRL. Please excuse me. (*She leaves, weeping.*)

MOTHER-IN-LAW. Why do you always have to make trouble with people?

LEONARDO. I didn't ask for your opinion. (*He sits down.*)

MOTHER-IN-LAW. Very well.

(*Pause.*)

WIFE (*to* LEONARDO). What's the matter with you? What idea've you got boiling there inside your head? Don't leave me like this, not knowing anything.

LEONARDO. Stop that.

WIFE. No. I want you to look at me and tell me.

LEONARDO. Let me alone. (*He rises.*)

WIFE. Where are you going, love?

LEONARDO (*sharply*). Can't you shut up?

MOTHER-IN-LAW (*energetically, to her daughter*). Be quiet!

(LEONARDO *goes out.*)

The baby! (*She goes into the bedroom and comes out again with the baby in her arms. The* WIFE *has remained standing, unmoving.*)

MOTHER-IN-LAW. His poor hooves were bleeding,
his long mane was frozen,
and deep in his eyes
stuck a silvery dagger.
Down he went to the river,
Oh, down he went down!
And his blood was running,
Oh, more than the water.

WIFE (*turning slowly, as though dreaming*). Carnation, sleep and dream,
the horse is drinking from the stream.

MOTHER-IN-LAW. My rose, asleep now lie
the horse is starting to cry.

WIFE. Lullaby, my baby.

MOTHER-IN-LAW. Ay-y-y, for the big horse
who didn't like water!

WIFE (*dramatically*). Don't come near, don't come in!
Go away to the mountains!
Ay-y-y, for the snow-wound,
big horse of the dawn!

MOTHER-IN-LAW (*weeping*). My baby is sleeping . . .

WIFE (*weeping, as she slowly moves closer*). My baby is resting . . .

MOTHER-IN-LAW. Carnation, sleep and dream,
the horse won't drink from the stream.

WIFE (*weeping, and leaning on the table*). My rose, asleep now lie,
the horse is starting to cry.

SCENE III

Interior of the cave where the BRIDE *lives. At the back is a cross of large rose colored flowers. The round doors have lace curtains with rose colored ties. Around the walls, which are of a white and hard material, are round fans, blue jars, and little mirrors.*

SERVANT. Come right in . . .

(*She is very affable, full of humble hypocrisy. The* BRIDEGROOM *and his* MOTHER *enter. The* MOTHER *is dressed in black satin and wears a lace mantilla; the* BRIDEGROOM *in black corduroy with a great golden chain.*)

Won't you sit down? They'll be right here.

(*She leaves. The* MOTHER *and son are left sitting motionless as statues. Long pause.*)

MOTHER. Did you wear the watch?

BRIDEGROOM. Yes. (*He takes it out and looks at it.*)

MOTHER. We have to be back on time. How far away these people live!

BRIDEGROOM. But this is good land.

MOTHER. Good; but much too lonesome. A four-hour trip and not one house, not one tree.

BRIDEGROOM. This is the wasteland.

MOTHER. Your father would have covered it with trees.

BRIDEGROOM. Without water?

MOTHER. He would have found some. In the three years we were married he planted ten cherry trees, (*remembering*) those three walnut trees by the mill, a whole vineyard and a plant called Jupiter which had scarlet flowers—but it dried up.

(*Pause.*)

BRIDEGROOM (*referring to the* BRIDE). She must be dressing.

(*The* BRIDE'S FATHER *enters. He is very old, with shining white hair. His head is bowed. The* MOTHER *and the* BRIDEGROOM *rise. They shake hands in silence.*)

FATHER. Was it a long trip?

MOTHER. Four hours.

(*They sit down.*)

FATHER. You must have come the longest way.

MOTHER. I'm too old to come along the cliffs by the river.

BRIDEGROOM. She gets dizzy.

(*Pause.*)

FATHER. A good hemp harvest.

BRIDEGROOM. A really good one.

FATHER. When I was young this land didn't even grow hemp. We've had to punish it, even weep over it, to make it give us anything useful.

MOTHER. But now it does. Don't complain. I'm not here to ask you for anything.

FATHER (*smiling*). You're richer than I. Your vineyards are worth a fortune. Each young vine a silver coin. But—do you know?—what bothers me is that our lands are separated. I like to have everything together. One thorn I have in my heart, and that's the little orchard there, stuck in between my fields—and they won't sell it to me for all the gold in the world.

BRIDEGROOM. That's the way it always is.

FATHER. If we could just take twenty teams of oxen and move your vineyards over here, and put them down on the hillside, how happy I'd be!

Mother. But why?

Father. What's mine is hers and what's yours is his. That's why. Just to see it all together. How beautiful it is to bring things together!

Bridegroom. And it would be less work.

Mother. When I die, you could sell ours and buy here, right alongside.

Father. Sell, sell? Bah! Buy, my friend, buy everything. If I had had sons I would have bought all this mountainside right up to the part with the stream. It's not good land, but strong arms can make it good, and since no people pass by, they don't steal your fruit and you can sleep in peace.

(*Pause.*)

Mother. You know what I'm here for.

Father. Yes.

Mother. And?

Father. It seems all right to me. They have talked it over.

Mother. My son has money and knows how to manage it.

Father. My daughter too.

Mother. My son is handsome. He's never known a woman. His good name cleaner than a sheet spread out in the sun.

Father. No need to tell you about my daughter. At three, when the morning star shines, she prepares the bread. She never talks: soft as wool, she embroiders all kinds of fancy work and she can cut a strong cord with her teeth.

Mother. God bless her house.

Father. May God bless it.

(*The* Servant *appears with two trays. One with drinks and the other with sweets.*)

Mother (*to the son*). When would you like the wedding?

Bridegroom. Next Thursday.

Father. The day on which she'll be exactly twenty-two years old.

Mother. Twenty-two! My oldest son would be that age if he were alive. Warm and manly as he was, he'd be living now if men hadn't invented knives.

Father. One mustn't think about that.

Mother. Every minute. Always a hand on your breast.

Father. Thursday, then? Is that right?

Bridegroom. That's right.

Father. You and I and the bridal couple will go in a carriage to the church which is very far from here; the wedding party on the carts and horses they'll bring with them.

Mother. Agreed.

(*The* SERVANT *passes through.*)

FATHER. Tell her she may come in now. (*To the* MOTHER) I shall be much pleased if you like her.

(*The* BRIDE *appears. Her hands fall in a modest pose and her head is bowed.*)

MOTHER. Come here. Are you happy?

BRIDE. Yes, señora.

FATHER. You shouldn't be so solemn. After all, she's going to be your mother.

BRIDE. I'm happy. I've said "yes" because I wanted to.

MOTHER. Naturally. (*She takes her by the chin.*) Look at me.

FATHER. She resembles my wife in every way.

MOTHER. Yes? What a beautiful glance! Do you know what it is to be married, child?

BRIDE (*seriously*). I do.

MOTHER. A man, some children and a wall two yards thick for everything else.

BRIDEGROOM. Is anything else needed?

MOTHER. No. Just that you all live—that's it! Live long!

BRIDE. I'll know how to keep my word.

MOTHER. Here are some gifts for you.

BRIDE. Thank you.

FATHER. Shall we have something?

MOTHER. Nothing for me. (*To the* SON) But you?

BRIDEGROOM. Yes, thank you.

(*He takes one sweet, the* BRIDE *another.*)

FATHER (*to the* BRIDEGROOM). Wine?

MOTHER. He doesn't touch it.

FATHER. All the better.

(*Pause. All are standing.*)

BRIDEGROOM (*to the* BRIDE). I'll come tomorrow.

BRIDE. What time?

BRIDEGROOM. Five.

BRIDE. I'll be waiting for you.

BRIDEGROOM. When I leave your side I feel a great emptiness, and something like a knot in my throat.

BRIDE. When you are my husband you won't have it any more.

BRIDEGROOM. That's what I tell myself.

MOTHER. Come. The sun doesn't wait. (*To the* FATHER) Are we agreed on everything?

FATHER. Agreed.

MOTHER (*to the* SERVANT). Goodbye, woman.

SERVANT. God go with you!

(*The* MOTHER *kisses the* BRIDE *and they begin to leave in silence.*)

MOTHER (*at the door*). Goodbye, daughter.

(*The* BRIDE *answers with her hand.*)

FATHER. I'll go out with you.

(*They leave.*)

SERVANT. I'm bursting to see the presents.

BRIDE (*sharply*). Stop that!

SERVANT. Oh, child, show them to me.

BRIDE. I don't want to.

SERVANT. At least the stockings. They say they're all open work. Please!

BRIDE. I said no.

SERVANT. Well, my Lord. All right then. It looks as if you didn't want to get married.

BRIDE (*biting her hand in anger*). Ay-y-y!

SERVANT. Child, child! What's the matter with you? Are you sorry to give up your queen's life? Don't think of bitter things. Have you any reason to? None. Let's look at the presents. (*She takes the box.*)

BRIDE (*holding her by the wrists*). Let go.

SERVANT. Ay-y-y, girl!

BRIDE. Let go, I said.

SERVANT. You're stronger than a man.

BRIDE. Haven't I done a man's work? I wish I were.

SERVANT. Don't talk like that.

BRIDE. Quiet, I said. Let's talk about something else.

(*The light is fading from the stage. Long pause.*)

SERVANT. Did you hear a horse last night?

BRIDE. What time?

SERVANT. Three.

BRIDE. It might have been a stray horse—from the herd.

SERVANT. No. It carried a rider.

BRIDE. How do you know?

SERVANT. Because I saw him. He was standing by your window. It shocked me greatly.

BRIDE. Maybe it was my fiancé. Sometimes he comes by at that time.

SERVANT. No.

BRIDE. You saw him?

SERVANT. Yes.
BRIDE. Who was it?
SERVANT. It was Leonardo.
BRIDE (*strongly*). Liar! You liar! Why should he come here?
SERVANT. He came.
BRIDE. Shut up! Shut your cursed mouth.

(*The sound of a horse is heard.*)

SERVANT (*at the window*). Look. Lean out. Was it Leonardo.
BRIDE. It was!

ACT TWO

SCENE I

The entrance hall of the BRIDE'S *house. A large door in the back. It is night. The* BRIDE *enters wearing ruffled white petticoats full of laces and embroidered bands, and a sleeveless white bodice. The* SERVANT *is dressed the same way.*

SERVANT. I'll finish combing your hair out here.
BRIDE. It's too warm to stay in there.
SERVANT. In this country it doesn't even cool off at dawn.

(*The* BRIDE *sits on a low chair and looks into a little hand mirror. The* SERVANT *combs her hair.*)

BRIDE. My mother came from a place with lots of trees—from a fertile country.
SERVANT. And she was so happy!
BRIDE. But she wasted away here.
SERVANT. Fate.
BRIDE. As we're all wasting away here. The very walls give off heat. Ay-y-y! Don't pull so hard.
SERVANT. I'm only trying to fix this wave better. I want it to fall over your forehead.

(*The* BRIDE *looks at herself in the mirror.*)

How beautiful you are! Ay-y-y! (*She kisses her passionately.*)
BRIDE (*seriously*). Keep right on combing.
SERVANT (*combing*). Oh, lucky you—going to put your arms around a man; and kiss him; and feel his weight.
BRIDE. Hush.
SERVANT. And the best part will be when you'll wake up and you'll feel him at your side and when he caresses your shoulders with his breath, like a little nightingale's feather.

BRIDE (*sternly*). Will you be quiet.

SERVANT. But, child! What *is* a wedding? A wedding is just that and nothing more. Is it the sweets—or the bouquets of flowers? No. It's a shining bed and a man and a woman.

BRIDE. But you shouldn't talk about it.

SERVANT. Oh, *that's* something else again. But fun enough too.

BRIDE. Or bitter enough.

SERVANT. I'm going to put the orange blossoms on from here to here, so the wreath will shine out on top of your hair. (*She tries on the sprigs of orange blossom.*)

BRIDE (*looking at herself in the mirror*). *Give it to me.* (*She takes the wreath, looks at it and lets her head fall in discouragement.*)

SERVANT. Now what's the matter?

BRIDE. Leave me alone.

SERVANT. This is no time for you to start feeling sad. (*Encouragingly*) Give me the wreath.

(*The* BRIDE *takes the wreath and hurls it away.*)

Child! You're just asking God to punish you, throwing the wreath on the floor like that. Raise your head! Don't you want to get married? Say it. You can still withdraw.

(*The* BRIDE *rises.*)

BRIDE. Storm clouds. A chill wind that cuts through my heart. Who hasn't felt it?

SERVANT. You love your sweetheart, don't you?

BRIDE. I love him.

SERVANT. Yes, yes. I'm sure you do.

BRIDE. But this is a very serious step.

SERVANT. You've got to take it.

BRIDE. I've already given my word.

SERVANT. I'll put on the wreath.

BRIDE (*she sits down*). Hurry. They should be arriving by now.

SERVANT. They've already been at least two hours on the way.

BRIDE. How far is it from here to the church?

SERVANT. Five leagues by the stream, but twice that by the road.

(*The* BRIDE *rises and the* SERVANT *grows excited as she looks at her.*)

SERVANT. Awake, O Bride, awaken,
On your wedding morning waken!
The world's rivers may all
Bear along your bridal Crown!

BRIDE (*smiling*). Come now.

SERVANT (*enthusiastically kissing her and dancing around her*). Awake,
with the fresh bouquet
of flowering laurel.
Awake,
by the trunk and branch
of the laurels!

(*The banging of the front door latch is heard.*)

BRIDE. Open the door! That must be the first guests.

(*She leaves. The* SERVANT *opens the door.*)

SERVANT (*in astonishment*). You!
LEONARDO. Yes, me. Good morning.
SERVANT. The first one!
LEONARDO. Wasn't I invited?
SERVANT. Yes.
LEONARDO. That's why I'm here.
SERVANT. Where's your wife?
LEONARDO. I came on my horse. She's coming by the road.
SERVANT. Didn't you meet anyone?
LEONARDO. I *passed* them on my horse.
SERVANT. You're going to kill that horse with so much racing.
LEONARDO. When he dies, he's dead!

(*Pause.*)

SERVANT. Sit down. Nobody's up yet.
LEONARDO. Where's the bride?
SERVANT. I'm just on my way to dress her.
LEONARDO. The bride! She ought to be happy!
SERVANT (*changing the subject*). How's the baby?
LEONARDO. What baby?
SERVANT. Your son.
LEONARDO (*remembering, as though in a dream*). Ah!
SERVANT. Are they bringing him?
LEONARDO. No.

(*Pause. Voices sing distantly.*)

VOICES. Awake, O Bride, awaken,
On your wedding morning waken!
LEONARDO. Awake, O Bride, awaken,
On your wedding morning waken!
SERVANT. It's the guests. They're still quite a way off.
LEONARDO. The bride's going to wear a big wreath, isn't she? But it ought not to be so large. One a little smaller would look better on her. Has

the groom already brought her the orange blossom that must be worn on the breast?

BRIDE (*appearing, still in petticoats and wearing the wreath*). He brought it.

SERVANT (*sternly*). Don't come out like that.

BRIDE. What does it matter? (*Seriously*) Why do you ask if they brought the orange blossom? Do you have something in mind?

LEONARDO. Nothing. What would I have in mind? (*Drawing near her*) You, you know me; you know I don't. Tell me so. What have I ever meant to you? Open your memory, refresh it. But two oxen and an ugly little hut are almost nothing. That's the thorn.

BRIDE. What have you come here to do?

LEONARDO. To see your wedding.

BRIDE. Just as I saw yours!

LEONARDO. Tied up by you, done with your two hands. Oh, they can kill me but they can't spit on me. But even money, which shines so much, spits sometimes.

BRIDE. Liar!

LEONARDO. I don't want to talk. I'm hot-blooded and I don't want to shout so all these hills will hear me

BRIDE. My shouts would be louder.

SERVANT. You'll have to stop talking like this. (*To the* BRIDE) You don't have to talk about what's past. (*The* SERVANT *looks around uneasily at the doors.*)

BRIDE. She's right. I shouldn't even talk to you. But it offends me to the soul that you come here to watch me, and spy on my wedding, and ask about the orange blossom with something on your mind. Go and wait for your wife at the door.

LEONARDO. But, can't you and I even talk?

SERVANT (*with rage*). No! No, you can't talk.

LEONARDO. Ever since I got married I've been thinking night and day about whose fault it was, and every time I think about it, out comes a new fault to eat up the old one; but always there's a fault left!

BRIDE. A man with a horse knows a lot of things and can do a lot to ride roughshod over a girl stuck out in the desert. But I have my pride. And that's why I'm getting married. I'll lock myself in with my husband and then I'll have to love him above everyone else.

LEONARDO. Pride won't help you a bit. (*He draws near to her.*)

BRIDE. Don't come near me!

LEONARDO. To burn with desire and keep quiet about it is the greatest punishment we can bring on ourselves. What good was pride to me—and not seeing you, and letting you lie awake night after night? No good! It only served to bring the fire down on me! You think that time heals and walls hide things, but it isn't true, it isn't true! When things get that deep inside you there isn't anybody can change them.

BRIDE (*trembling*). I can't listen to you. I can't listen to your voice. It's as though I'd drunk a bottle of anise and fallen asleep wrapped in a quilt of roses. It pulls me along, and I know I'm drowning—but I go on down.

SERVANT (*seizing* LEONARDO *by the lapels*). You've got to go right now!

LEONARDO. This is the last time I'll ever talk to her. Don't you be afraid of anything.

BRIDE. And I know I'm crazy and I know my breast rots with longing; but here I am—calmed by hearing him, by just seeing him move his arms.

LEONARDO. I'd never be at peace if I didn't tell you these things. I got married. Now you get married.

SERVANT. But she *is* getting married!

(*Voices are heard singing, nearer.*)

VOICES. Awake, O Bride, awaken,
On your wedding morning waken!

BRIDE. Awake, O Bride, awaken, (*She goes out, running toward her room.*)

SERVANT. The people are here now. (*To* LEONARDO) Don't you come near her again.

LEONARDO. Don't worry. (*He goes out to the left. Day begins to break.*)

FIRST GIRL (*entering*). Awake, O Bride, awaken,
the morning you're to marry;
sing round and dance round;
balconies a wreath must carry.

VOICES. Bride, awaken!

SERVANT (*creating enthusiasm*). Awake,
with the green bouquet
of love in flower.
Awake,
by the trunk and the branch
of the laurels!

SECOND GIRL (*entering*). Awake,
with her long hair,
snowy sleeping gown,
patent leather boots with silver—
her forehead jasmines crown.

SERVANT. Oh, shepherdess,
the moon begins to shine!

FIRST GIRL. Oh, gallant,
leave your hat beneath the vine!

FIRST YOUNG MAN (*entering, holding his hat on high*). Bride, awaken,
for over the fields

the wedding draws nigh
with trays heaped with dahlias
and cakes piled high.

VOICES. Bride, awaken!

SECOND GIRL. The bride
has set her white wreath in place
and the groom
ties it on with a golden lace.

SERVANT. By the orange tree,
sleepless the bride will be.

THIRD GIRL (*entering*). By the citron vine,
gifts from the groom will shine.

(*Three* GUESTS *come in.*)

FIRST YOUTH. Dove, awaken!
In the dawn
shadowy bells are shaken.

GUEST. The bride, the white bride
today a maiden,
tomorrow a wife.

FIRST GIRL. Dark one, come down
trailing the train of your silken gown.

GUEST. Little dark one, come down,
cold morning wears a dewy crown.

FIRST GUEST. Awaken, wife, awake,
orange blossoms the breezes shake.

SERVANT. A tree I would embroider her
with garnet sashes wound,
And on each sash a cupid,
with "Long Live" all around.

VOICES. Bride, awaken.

FIRST YOUTH. The morning you're to marry!

GUEST. The morning you're to marry
how elegant you'll seem;
worthy, mountain flower,
of a captain's dream.

FATHER (*entering*). A captain's wife
the groom will marry.
He comes with his oxen the treasure to carry!

THIRD GIRL. The groom
is like a flower of gold.
When he walks,
blossoms at his feet unfold.

SERVANT. Oh, my lucky girl!

SECOND YOUTH. Bride, awaken.
SERVANT. Oh, my elegant girl!
FIRST GIRL. Through the windows
hear the wedding shout.
SECOND GIRL. Let the bride come out.
FIRST GIRL. Come out, come out!
SERVANT. Let the bells
ring and ring out clear!
FIRST YOUTH. For here she comes!
For now she's near!
SERVANT. Like a bull, the wedding
is arising here!

(The BRIDE *appears. She wears a black dress in the style of 1900, with a bustle and large train covered with pleated gauzes and heavy laces. Upon her hair, brushed in a wave over her forehead, she wears an orange blossom wreath. Guitars sound. The* GIRLS *kiss the* BRIDE.)

THIRD GIRL. What scent did you put on your hair?
BRIDE (*laughing*). None at all.
SECOND GIRL (*looking at her dress*). This cloth is what you can't get.
FIRST YOUTH. Here's the groom!
BRIDEGROOM. Salud!
FIRST GIRL (*putting a flower behind his ear*). The groom
is like a flower of gold.
SECOND GIRL. Quiet breezes
from his eyes unfold.

(*The* GROOM *goes to the* BRIDE.)

BRIDE. Why did you put on those shoes?
BRIDEGROOM. They're gayer than the black ones.
LEONARDO'S WIFE (*entering and kissing the* BRIDE). Salud!

(*They all speak excitedly.*)

LEONARDO (*entering as one who performs a duty*). The morning you're to marry
We give you a wreath to wear.
LEONARDO'S WIFE. So the fields may be made happy
with the dew dropped from your hair!
MOTHER (*to the* FATHER). Are those people here, too?
FATHER. They're part of the family. Today is a day of forgiveness!
MOTHER. I'll put up with it, but I don't forgive.
BRIDEGROOM. With your wreath, it's a joy to look at you!
BRIDE. Let's go to the church quickly.
BRIDEGROOM. Are you in a hurry?

BRIDE. Yes. I want to be your wife right now so that I can be with you alone, not hearing any voice but yours.

BRIDEGROOM. That's what I want!

BRIDE. And not seeing any eyes but yours. And for you to hug me so hard, that even though my dead mother should call me, I wouldn't be able to draw away from you.

BRIDEGROOM. My arms are strong. I'll hug you for forty years without stopping.

BRIDE (*taking his arm, dramatically*). Forever!

FATHER. Quick now! Round up the teams and carts! The sun's already out.

MOTHER. And go along carefully! Let's hope nothing goes wrong.

(*The great door in the background opens.*)

SERVANT (*weeping*). As you set out from your house,
oh, maiden white,
remember you leave shining
with a star's light.

FIRST GIRL. Clean of body, clean of clothes
from her home to church she goes.

(*They start leaving.*)

SECOND GIRL. Now you leave your home
for the church!

SERVANT. The wind sets flowers
on the sands.

THIRD GIRL. Ah, the white maid!

SERVANT. Dark winds are the lace
of her mantilla.

(*They leave. Guitars, castanets and tambourines are heard.* LEONARDO *and his* WIFE *are left alone.*)

WIFE. Let's go.

LEONARDO. Where?

WIFE. To the church. But not on your horse. You're coming with me.

LEONARDO. In the cart?

WIFE. Is there anything else?

LEONARDO. I'm not the kind of man to ride in a cart.

WIFE. Nor I the wife to go to a wedding without her husband. I can't stand any more of this!

LEONARDO. Neither can I!

WIFE. And why do you look at me that way? With a thorn in each eye.

LEONARDO. Let's go!

WIFE. I don't know what's happening. But I think, and I don't want to think. One thing I do know. I'm already cast off by you. But I have a son. And another coming. And so it goes. My mother's fate was the same. Well, I'm not moving from here.

(*Voices outside.*)

VOICES. As you set out from your home
and to the church go
remember you leave shining
with a star's glow.
WIFE (*weeping*). Remember you leave shining
with a star's glow!
I left my house like that too. They could have stuffed the whole countryside in my mouth. I was that trusting.
LEONARDO (*rising*). Let's go!
WIFE. But you with me!
LEONARDO. Yes. (*pause*) Start moving!

(*They leave.*)

VOICES. As you set out from your home
and to the church go,
remember you leave shining
with a star's glow.

SCENE II

The exterior of the BRIDE'*s Cave Home, in white gray and cold blue tones. Large cactus trees. Shadowy and silver tones. Panoramas of light tan tablelands, everything hard like a landscape in popular ceramics.*

SERVANT (*arranging glasses and trays on a table*). A-turning,
the wheel was a-turning
and the water was flowing,
for the wedding night comes.
May the branches part
and the moon be arrayed
at her white balcony rail.
(*In a loud voice*) Set out the tablecloths! (*In a pathetic voice*)
A-singing,
bride and groom were singing
and the water was flowing
for their wedding night comes.
Oh, rime-frost, flash!—
and almonds bitter
fill with honey!

(*In a loud voice*) Get the wine ready! (*In a poetic tone*)
Elegant girl,
most elegant in the world,
see the way the water is flowing,
for your wedding night comes.
Hold your skirts close in
under the bridegroom's wing
and never leave your house,
for the Bridegroom is a dove
with his breast a firebrand
and the fields wait for the whisper
of spurting blood.
A-turning
the wheel was a-turning
and the water was flowing
and your wedding night comes.
Oh, water, sparkle!

MOTHER (*entering*). At last!

FATHER. Are we the first ones?

SERVANT. No. Leonardo and his wife arrived a while ago. They drove like demons. His wife got here dead with fright. They made the trip as though they'd come on horseback.

FATHER. That one's looking for trouble. He's not of good blood.

MOTHER. What blood would you expect him to have? His whole family's blood. It comes down from his great grandfather, who started in killing, and it goes on down through the whole evil breed of knife wielding and false smiling men.

FATHER. Let's leave it at that!

SERVANT. But how can she leave it at that?

MOTHER. It hurts me to the tips of my veins. On the forehead of all of them I see only the hand with which they killed what was mine. Can you really see me? Don't I seem mad to you? Well, it's the madness of not having shrieked out all my breast needs to. Always in my breast there's a shriek standing tiptoe that I have to beat down and hold in under my shawls. But the dead are carried off and one has to keep still. And then, people find fault. (*She removes her shawl.*)

FATHER. Today's not the day for you to be remembering these things.

MOTHER. When the talk turns on it, I have to speak. And more so today. Because today I'm left alone in my house.

FATHER. But with the expectation of having someone with you.

MOTHER. That's my hope: grandchildren.

(*They sit down.*)

FATHER. I want them to have a lot of them. This land needs hands that aren't hired. There's a battle to be waged against weeds, the thistles, the big rocks that come from one doesn't know where. And those hands have to be the owner's, who chastises and dominates, who makes the seeds grow. Lots of sons are needed.

MOTHER. And some daughters! Men are like the wind! They're forced to handle weapons. Girls never go out into the street.

FATHER (*happily*). I think they'll have both.

MOTHER. My son will cover her well. He's of good seed. His father could have had many sons with me.

FATHER. What I'd like is to have all this happen in a day. So that right away they'd have two or three boys.

MOTHER. But it's not like that. It takes a long time. That's why it's so terrible to see one's own blood spilled out on the ground. A fountain that spurts for a minute, but costs us years. When I got to my son, he lay fallen in the middle of the street. I wet my hands with his blood and licked them with my tongue—because it was my blood. You don't know what that's like. In a glass and topaze shrine I'd put the earth moistened by his blood.

FATHER. Now you must hope. My daughter is wide-hipped and your son is strong.

MOTHER. That's why I'm hoping.

(They rise.)

FATHER. Get the wheat trays ready!

SERVANT. They're all ready.

LEONARDO'S WIFE (*entering*). May it be for the best!

MOTHER. Thank you.

LEONARDO. Is there going to be a celebration?

FATHER. A small one. People can't stay long.

SERVANT. Here they are!

(GUESTS *begin entering in gay groups. The* BRIDE *and* BRIDEGROOM *come in arm-in-arm.* LEONARDO *leaves.*)

BRIDEGROOM. There's never been a wedding with so many people!

BRIDE (*sullen*). Never.

FATHER. It was brilliant.

MOTHER. Whole branches of families came.

BRIDEGROOM. People who never went out of the house.

MOTHER. Your father sowed well, and now you're reaping it.

BRIDEGROOM. There were cousins of mine whom I no longer knew.

MOTHER. All the people from the seacoast.

BRIDEGROOM (*happily*). They were frightened of the horses.

(They talk.)

MOTHER (*to the* BRIDE). What are you thinking about?

BRIDE. I'm not thinking about anything.

MOTHER. Your blessings weigh heavily.

(*Guitars are heard.*)

BRIDE. Like lead.

MOTHER (*stern*). But they shouldn't weigh so. Happy as a dove you ought to be.

BRIDE. Are you staying here tonight?

MOTHER. No. My house is empty.

BRIDE. You ought to stay!

FATHER (*to the* MOTHER). Look at the dance they're forming. Dances of the far away seashore.

(LEONARDO *enters and sits down. His* WIFE *stands rigidly behind him.*)

MOTHER. They're my husband's cousins. Stiff as stones at dancing.

FATHER. It makes me happy to watch them. What a change for this house! (*He leaves.*)

BRIDEGROOM (*to the* BRIDE). Did you like the orange blossom?

BRIDE (*looking at him fixedly*). Yes.

BRIDEGROOM. It's all of wax. It will last forever. I'd like you to have had them all over your dress.

BRIDE. No need of that.

(LEONARDO *goes off to the right.*)

FIRST GIRL. Let's go and and take out your pins.

BRIDE (*to the* BRIDEGROOM). I'll be right back.

LEONARDO'S WIFE. I hope you'll be happy with my cousin!

BRIDEGROOM. I'm sure I will.

LEONARDO'S WIFE. The two of you here; never going out; building a home. I wish I could live far away like this, too!

BRIDEGROOM. Why don't you buy land? The mountainside is cheap and children grow up better.

LEONARDO'S WIFE. We don't have any money. And at the rate we're going . . . !

BRIDEGROOM. Your husband is a good worker.

LEONARDO'S WIFE. Yes, but he likes to fly around too much; from one thing to another. He's not a patient man.

SERVANT. Aren't you having anything? I'm going to wrap up some wine cakes for your mother. She likes them so much.

BRIDEGROOM. Put up three dozen for her.

LEONARDO'S WIFE. No, no. A half-dozen's enough for her!

BRIDEGROOM. But today's a day!

LEONARDO'S WIFE (*to the* SERVANT). Where's Leonardo?

BRIDEGROOM. He must be with the guests.

LEONARDO'S WIFE. I'm going to go see. (*She leaves.*)

SERVANT (*looking off at the dance*). That's beautiful there.

BRIDEGROOM. Aren't you dancing?

SERVANT. No one will ask me.

(*Two* GIRLS *pass across the back of the stage; during this whole scene the background should be an animated crossing of figures.*)

BRIDEGROOM (*happily*). They just don't know anything. Lively old girls like you dance better than the young ones.

SERVANT. Well! Are you tossing me a compliment, boy? What a family yours is! Men among men! As a little girl I saw your grandfather's wedding. What a figure! It seemed as if a mountain were getting married.

BRIDEGROOM. I'm not as tall.

SERVANT. But there's the same twinkle in your eye. Where's the girl?

BRIDEGROOM. Taking off her wreath.

SERVANT. Ah! Look. For midnight, since you won't be sleeping, I have prepared ham for you, and some large glasses of old wine. On the lower shelf of the cupboard. In case you need it.

BRIDEGROOM (*smiling*). I won't be eating at midnight.

SERVANT (*slyly*). If not you, maybe the bride. (*She leaves.*)

FIRST YOUTH (*entering*). You've got to come have a drink with us!

BRIDEGROOM. I'm waiting for the bride.

SECOND YOUTH. You'll have her at dawn!

FIRST YOUTH. That's when it's best!

SECOND YOUTH. Just for a minute.

BRIDEGROOM. Let's go.

(*They leave. Great excitement is heard. The* BRIDE *enters. From the opposite side two* GIRLS *come running to meet her.*)

FIRST GIRL. To whom did you give the first pin; me or this one?

BRIDE. I don't remember.

FIRST GIRL. To me, you gave it to me here.

SECOND GIRL. To me, in front of the altar.

BRIDE (*uneasily, with a great inner struggle*). I don't know anything about it.

FIRST GIRL. It's just that I wish you'd . . .

BRIDE (*interrupting*). Nor do I care. I have a lot to think about.

SECOND GIRL. Your pardon.

(LEONARDO *crosses at the rear of the stage.*)

BRIDE (*she sees* LEONARDO). And this is an upsetting time.

FIRST GIRL. We wouldn't know anything about that!

BRIDE. You'll know about it when your time comes. This step is a very hard one to take.

FIRST GIRL. Has she offended you?

BRIDE. No. You must pardon me.

SECOND GIRL. What for? But *both* the pins are good for getting married, aren't they?

BRIDE. Both of them.

FIRST GIRL. Maybe now one will get married before the other.

BRIDE. Are you so eager?

SECOND GIRL (*shyly*). Yes.

BRIDE. Why?

FIRST GIRL. Well . . .

(*She embraces the* SECOND GIRL. *Both go running off. The* BRIDEGROOM *comes in very slowly and embraces the* BRIDE *from behind.*)

BRIDE (*in sudden fright*). Let go of me!

BRIDEGROOM. Are you frightened of me?

BRIDE. Ay-y-y! It's you?

BRIDEGROOM. Who else would it be? (*pause*) Your father or me.

BRIDE. That's true!

BRIDEGROOM. Of course, your father would have hugged you more gently.

BRIDE (*darkly*). Of course!

BRIDEGROOM (*embracing her strongly and a little bit brusquely*). Because he's old.

BRIDE (*curtly*). Let me go!

BRIDEGROOM. Why? (*He lets her go.*)

BRIDE. Well . . . the people. They can see us.

(*The* SERVANT *crosses at the back of the stage again without looking at the* BRIDE *and* BRIDEGROOM.)

BRIDEGROOM. What of it? It's consecrated now.

BRIDE. Yes, but let me be . . . Later.

BRIDEGROOM. What's the matter with you? You look frightened!

BRIDE. I'm all right. Don't go.

(LEONARDO'S WIFE *enters.*)

LEONARDO'S WIFE. I don't mean to intrude . . .

BRIDEGROOM. What is it?

LEONARDO'S WIFE. Did my husband come through here?

BRIDEGROOM. No.

LEONARDO'S WIFE. Because I can't find him, and his horse isn't in the stable either.

BRIDEGROOM (*happily*). He must be out racing it.

(*The* WIFE *leaves, troubled. The* SERVANT *enters.*)

SERVANT. Aren't you two proud and happy with so many good wishes?

BRIDEGROOM. I wish it were over with. The bride is a little tired.

SERVANT. That's no way to act, child.

BRIDE. It's as though I'd been struck on the head.

SERVANT. A bride from these mountains must be strong. (*To the* BRIDEGROOM) You're the only one who can cure her, because she's yours (*She goes running off.*)

BRIDEGROOM (*embracing the* BRIDE). Let's go dance a little. (*He kisses her.*)

BRIDE (*worried*). No. I'd like to stretch out on my bed a little.

BRIDEGROOM. I'll keep you company.

BRIDE. Never! With all these people here? What would they say? Let me be quiet for a moment.

BRIDEGROOM. Whatever you say! But don't be like that tonight!

BRIDE (*at the door*). I'll be better tonight.

BRIDEGROOM. That's what I want.

(*The* MOTHER *appears.*)

MOTHER. Son.

BRIDEGROOM. Where've you been?

MOTHER. Out there—in all that noise. Are you happy?

BRIDEGROOM. Yes.

MOTHER. Where's your wife?

BRIDEGROOM. Resting a little. It's a bad day for brides!

MOTHER. A bad day? The only good one. To me it was like coming into my own.

(*The* SERVANT *enters and goes toward the* BRIDE*'s room.*)

Like the breaking of new ground; the planting of new trees.

BRIDEGROOM. Are you going to leave?

MOTHER. Yes. I ought to be at home.

BRIDEGROOM. Alone.

MOTHER. Not alone. For my head is full of things: of men, and fights.

BRIDEGROOM. But now the fights are no longer fights.

(*The* SERVANT *enters quickly; she disappears at the rear of the stage, running.*)

MOTHER. While you live, you have to fight.

BRIDEGROOM. I'll always obey you!

MOTHER. Try to be loving with your wife, and if you see she's acting foolish or touchy, caress her in a way that will hurt her a little: a strong hug, a bite and then a soft kiss. Not so she'll be angry, but just so she'll feel you're the man, the boss, the one who gives orders. I learned that from your father. And since you don't have him, I have to be the one to tell you about these strong defenses.

Bridegroom. I'll always do as you say.

Father (*entering*). Where's my daughter?

Bridegroom. She's inside.

(*The* Father *goes to look for her.*)

First Girl. Get the bride and groom! We're going to dance a round!

First Youth (*to the* Bridegroom). You're going to lead it.

Father (*entering*). She's not there.

Bridegroom. No?

Father. She must have gone up to the railing.

Bridegroom. I'll go see! (*He leaves. A hubbub of excitement and guitars is heard.*)

First Girl. They've started it already! (*She leaves.*)

Bridegroom (*entering*). She isn't there.

Mother (*uneasily*). Isn't she?

Father. But where could she have gone?

Servant (*entering*). But where's the girl, where is she?

Mother (*seriously*). That we don't know.

(*The* Bridegroom *leaves. Three* Guests *enter.*)

Father (*dramatically*). But, isn't she in the dance?

Servant. She's not in the dance.

Father (*with a start*). There are a lot of people. Go look!

Servant. I've already looked.

Father (*tragically*). Then where is she?

Bridegroom (*entering*). Nowhere. Not anywhere.

Mother (*to the* Father). What does this mean? Where is your daughter?

(Leonardo's Wife *enters.*)

Leonardo's Wife. They've run away! They've run away! She and Leonardo. On the horse. With their arms around each other, they rode off like a shooting star!

Father. That's not true! Not my daughter!

Mother. Yes, your daughter! Spawn of a wicked mother, and he, he too. But now she's my son's wife!

Bridegroom (*entering*). Let's go after them! Who has a horse?

Mother. Who has a horse? Right away! Who has a horse? I'll give him all I have—my eyes, my tongue even . . .

Voice. Here's one.

Mother (*to the* Son). Go! After them! (*He leaves with two young men.*) No. Don't go. Those people kill quickly and well . . . but yes, run, and I'll follow!

Father. It couldn't be my daughter. Perhaps she's thrown herself in the well.

Mother. Decent women throw themselves in water; not that one! But now she's my son's wife. Two groups. There are two groups here. (*They all enter.*) My family and yours. Everyone set out from here. Shake the dust from your heels! We'll go help my son. (*The people separate into two groups.*) For he has his family: his cousins from the sea, and all who came from inland. Out of here! On all roads. The hour of blood has come again. Two groups! You with yours and I with mine. After them! After them!

ACT THREE

SCENE I

A forest. It is nighttime. Great moist tree trunks. A dark atmosphere. Two violins are heard. Three Woodcutters *enter.*

First Woodcutter. And have they found them?

Second Woodcutter. No. But they're looking for them everywhere.

Third Woodcutter. They'll find them.

Second Woodcutter. Sh-h-h!

Third Woodcutter. What?

Second Woodcutter. They seem to be coming closer on all the roads at once.

First Woodcutter. When the moon comes out they'll see them.

Second Woodcutter. They ought to let them go.

First Woodcutter. The world is wide. Everybody can live in it.

Third Woodcutter. But they'll kill them.

Second Woodcutter. You have to follow your passion. They did right to run away.

First Woodcutter. They were deceiving themselves but at the last blood was stronger.

Third Woodcutter. Blood!

First Woodcutter. You have to follow the path of your blood.

Second Woodcutter. But blood that sees the light of day is drunk up by the earth.

First Woodcutter. What of it? Better dead with the blood drained away than alive with it rotting.

Third Woodcutter. Hush!

First Woodcutter. What? Do you hear something?

Third Woodcutter. I hear the crickets, the frogs, the night's ambush.

First Woodcutter. But not the horse.

Third Woodcutter. No.

FIRST WOODCUTTER. By now he must be loving her.

SECOND WOODCUTTER. Her body for him; his body for her.

THIRD WOODCUTTER. They'll find them and they'll kill them.

FIRST WOODCUTTER. But by then they'll have mingled their bloods. They'll be like two empty jars, like two dry arroyos.

SECOND WOODCUTTER. There are many clouds and it would be easy for the moon not to come out.

THIRD WOODCUTTER. The bridegroom will find them with or without the moon. I saw him set out. Like a raging star. His face the color of ashes. He looked the fate of all his clan.

FIRST WOODCUTTER. His clan of dead men lying in the middle of the street.

SECOND WOODCUTTER. There you have it!

THIRD WOODCUTTER. You think they'll be able to break through the circle?

SECOND WOODCUTTER. It's hard to. There are knives and guns for ten leagues 'round.

THIRD WOODCUTTER. He's riding a good horse.

SECOND WOODCUTTER. But he's carrying a woman.

FIRST WOODCUTTER. We're close by now.

SECOND WOODCUTTER. A tree with forty branches. We'll soon cut it down.

THIRD WOODCUTTER. The moon's coming out now. Let's hurry.

(From the left shines a brightness.)

FIRST WOODCUTTER. O rising moon!
Moon among the great leaves.

SECOND WOODCUTTER. Cover the blood with jasmines!

FIRST WOODCUTTER. O lonely moon!
Moon among the great leaves.

SECOND WOODCUTTER. Silver on the bride's face.

THIRD WOODCUTTER. O evil moon!
Leave for their love a branch in shadow.

FIRST WOODCUTTER. O sorrowing moon!
Leave for their love a branch in shadow.

(They go out. The MOON *appears through the shining brightness at the left. The* MOON *is a young woodcutter with a white face. The stage takes on an intense blue radiance.)*

MOON. Round swan in the river
and a cathedral's eye,
false dawn on the leaves,
they'll not escape; these things am I!
Who is hiding? And who sobs

in the thornbrakes of the valley?
The moon sets a knife
abandoned in the air
which being a leaden threat
yearns to be blood's pain.
Let me in! I come freezing
down to walls and windows!
Open roofs, open breasts
where I may warm myself!
I'm cold! My ashes
of somnolent metals
seek the fire's crest
on mountains and streets.
But the snow carries me
upon its mottled back
and pools soak me
in their water, hard and cold.
But this night there will be
red blood for my cheeks,
and for the reeds that cluster
at the wide feet of the wind.
Let there be neither shadow nor bower,
and then they can't get away!
O let me enter a breast
where I may get warm!
A heart for me!
Warm! That will spurt
over the mountains of my chest;
let me come in, oh let me! (*To the branches*)
I want no shadows. My rays
must get in everywhere,
even among the dark trunks I want
the whisper of gleaming lights,
so that this night there will be
sweet blood for my cheeks,
and for the reeds that cluster
at the wide feet of the wind.
Who is hiding? Out, I say!
No! They will not get away!
I will light up the horse
with a fever bright as diamonds.

(He disappears among the trunks, and the stage goes back to its dark lighting. An OLD WOMAN *comes out completely covered by thin green cloth.*

She is barefooted. Her face can barely be seen among the folds. This character does not appear in the cast.)

BEGGAR WOMAN. That moon's going away, just when they's near.
They won't get past here. The river's whisper
and the whispering tree trunks will muffle
the torn flight of their shrieks.
It has to be here, and soon. I'm worn out.
The coffins are ready, and white sheets
wait on the floor of the bedroom
for heavy bodies with torn throats.
Let not one bird awake, let the breeze,
gathering their moans in her skirt,
fly with them over black tree tops
or bury them in soft mud. (*Impatiently!*)
Oh, that moon! That moon!

(*The* MOON *appears. The intense blue light returns.*)

MOON. They're coming. One band through the ravine and the other along the river. I'm going to light up the boulders. What do you need?

BEGGAR WOMAN. Nothing.

MOON. The wind blows hard now, with a double edge.

BEGGAR WOMAN. Light up the waistcoat and open the buttons; the knives will know the path after that.

MOON. But let them be a long time a-dying. So the blood
will slide its delicate hissing between my fingers.
Look how my ashen valleys already are waking
in longing for this fountain of shuddering gushes!

BEGGAR WOMAN. Let's not let them get past the arroyo. Silence!

MOON. There they come! (*He goes. The stage is left dark.*)

BEGGAR WOMAN. Quick! Lots of light! Do you hear me? They can't get away!

(*The* BRIDEGROOM *and the* FIRST YOUTH *enter. The* BEGGAR WOMAN *sits down and covers herself with her cloak.*)

BRIDEGROOM. This way.

FIRST YOUTH. You won't find them.

BRIDEGROOM (*angrily*). Yes, I'll find them.

FIRST YOUTH. I think they've taken another path.

BRIDEGROOM. No. Just a moment ago I felt the galloping.

FIRST YOUTH. It could have been another horse.

BRIDEGROOM (*intensely*). Listen to me. There's only one horse in the whole world, and this one's it. Can't you understand that? If you're going to follow me, follow me without talking.

FIRST YOUTH. It's only that I want to . . .

BRIDEGROOM. Be quiet. I'm sure of meeting them there. Do you see this arm? Well, it's not my arm. It's my brother's arm, and my father's, and that of all the dead ones in my family. And it has so much strength that it can pull this tree up by the roots, if it wants to. And let's move on, because here I feel the clenched teeth of all my people in me so that I can't breathe easily.

BEGGAR WOMAN (*whining*). Ay-y-y!

FIRST YOUTH. Did you hear that?

BRIDEGROOM. You go that way and then circle back.

FIRST YOUTH. This is a hunt.

BRIDEGROOM. A hunt. The greatest hunt there is.

(*The* YOUTH *goes off. The* BRIDEGROOM *goes rapidly to the left and stumbles over the* BEGGAR WOMAN, *Death.*)

BEGGAR WOMAN. Ay-y-y!

BRIDEGROOM. What do you want?

BEGGAR WOMAN. I'm cold.

BRIDEGROOM. Which way are you going?

BEGGAR WOMAN (*always whining like a beggar*). Over there, far away . . .

BRIDEGROOM. Where are you from?

BEGGAR WOMAN. Over there . . . very far away.

BRIDEGROOM. Have you seen a man and a woman running away on a horse?

BEGGAR WOMAN (*awakening*). Wait a minute . . . (*She looks at him.*) Handsome young man. (*She rises.*) But you'd be much handsomer sleeping.

BRIDEGROOM. Tell me; answer me. Did you see them?

BEGGAR WOMAN. Wait a minute . . . What broad shoulders! How would you like to be laid out on them and not have to walk on the soles of your feet which are so small?

BRIDEGROOM (*shaking her*). I asked you if you saw them! Have they passed through here?

BEGGAR WOMAN (*energetically*). No. They haven't passed; but they're coming from the hill. Don't you hear them?

BRIDEGROOM. No.

BEGGAR WOMAN. Do you know the road?

BRIDEGROOM. I'll go, whatever it's like!

BEGGAR WOMAN. I'll go along with you. I know this country.

BRIDEGROOM (*impatiently*). Well, let's go! Which way?

BEGGAR WOMAN (*dramatically*). This way!

(*They go rapidly out. Two violins, which represent the forest, are heard distantly. The* WOODCUTTERS *return. They have their axes on their shoulders. They move slowly among the tree trunks.*)

First Woodcutter. O rising death!
Death among the great leaves.

Second Woodcutter. Don't open the gush of blood!

First Woodcutter. O lonely death!
Death among the dried leaves.

Third Woodcutter. Don't lay flowers over the wedding!

Second Woodcutter. O sad death!
Leave for their love a green branch.

First Woodcutter. O evil death!
Leave for their love a branch of green!

(They go out while they are talking. Leonardo *and the* Bride *appear.)*

Leonardo. Hush!

Bride. From here I'll go on alone.
You go now! I want you to turn back.

Leonardo. Hush, I said!

Bride. With your teeth, with your hands, anyway you can,
take from my clean throat
the metal of this chain,
and let me live forgotten
back there in my house in the ground.
And if you don't want to kill me
as you would kill a tiny snake,
set in my hands, a bride's hands,
the barrel of your shotgun.
Oh, what lamenting, what fire,
sweeps upward through my head!
What glass splinters are stuck in my tongue!

Leonardo. We've taken the step now; hush!
because they're close behind us,
and I must take you with me.

Bride. Then it must be by force!

Leonardo. By force? Who was it first
went down the stairway?

Bride. I went down it.

Leonardo. And who was it put
a new bridle on the horse?

Bride. I myself did it. It's true.

Leonardo. And whose were the hands
strapped spurs to my boots?

Bride. The same hands, these that are yours,
but which when they see you would like
to break the blue branches
and sunder the purl of your veins.
I love you! I love you! But leave me!

For if I were able to kill you
I'd wrap you 'round in a shroud
with the edges bordered in violets.
Oh, what lamenting, what fire,
sweeps upward through my head!

LEONARDO. What glass splinters are stuck in my tongue!
Because I tried to forget you
and put a wall of stone
between your house and mine.
It's true. You remember?
And when I saw you in the distance
I threw sand in my eyes.
But I was riding a horse
and the horse went straight to your door.
And the silver pins of your wedding
turned my red blood black.
And in me our dream was choking
my flesh with its poisoned weeds.
Oh, it isn't my fault—
the fault is the earth's—
and this fragrance that you exhale
from your breasts and your braids.

BRIDE. Oh, how untrue! I want
from you neither bed nor food,
yet there's not a minute each day
that I don't want to be with you,
because you drag me, and I come,
then you tell me to go back
and I follow you,
like chaff blown on the breeze.
I have left a good, honest man,
and all his people,
with the wedding feast half over
and wearing my bridal wreath.
But you are the one will be punished.
and that I don't want to happen.
Leave me alone now! You run away!
There is no one who will defend you.

LEONARDO. The birds of early morning
are calling among the trees.
The night is dying
on the stone's ridge.
Let's go to a hidden corner
where I may love you forever,
for to me the people don't matter,

nor the venom they throw on us. (*He embraces her strongly.*)

BRIDE. And I'll sleep at your feet,
to watch over your dreams.
Naked, looking over the fields,
as though I were a bitch.
Because that's what I am! Oh, I look at you
and your beauty sears me.

LEONARDO. Fire is stirred by fire.
The same tiny flame
will kill two wheat heads together.
Let's go!

BRIDE. Where are you taking me?

LEONARDO. Where they cannot come,
these men who surround us.
Where I can look at you!

BRIDE (*sarcastically*). Carry me with you from fair to fair,
a shame to clean women,
so that people will see me
with my wedding sheets
on the breeze like banners.

LEONARDO. I, too, would want to leave you
if I thought as men should.
But wherever you go, I go.
You're the same. Take a step. Try.
Nails of moonlight have fused
my waist and your chains.

(*This whole scene is violent, full of great sensuality.*)

BRIDE. Listen!

LEONARDO. They're coming.

BRIDE. Run!
It's fitting that I should die here,
with water over my feet,
with thorns upon my head.
And fitting the leaves should mourn me,
a woman lost and virgin.

LEONARDO. Be quiet. Now they're appearing.

BRIDE. Go now!

LEONARDO. Quiet. Don't let them hear us.

(*The* BRIDE *hesitates.*)

BRIDE. Both of us!

LEONARDO (*embracing her*).
Any way you want!
If they separate us, it will be

because I am dead.
BRIDE. And I dead too.

(They go out in each other's arms. The MOON *appears very slowly. The stage takes on a strong blue light. The two violins are heard. Suddenly two long, ear-splitting shrieks are heard, and the music of the two violins is cut short. At the second shriek the* BEGGAR WOMAN *appears and stands with her back to the audience. She opens her cape and stands in the center of the stage like a great bird with immense wings. The* MOON *halts. The curtain comes down in absolute silence.)*

SCENE II

THE FINAL SCENE. *A white dwelling with arches and thick walls. To the right and left, are white stairs. At the back, a great arch and a wall of the same color. The floor also should be shining white. This simple dwelling should have the monumental feeling of a church. There should not be a single gray nor any shadow, not even what is necessary for perspective.*

Two GIRLS *dressed in dark blue are winding a red skein.*

FIRST GIRL. Wool, red wool,
what would you make?
SECOND GIRL. Oh, jasmine for dresses,
fine wool like glass.
At four o'clock born,
at ten o'clock dead.
A thread from this wool yarn,
a chain 'round your feet
a knot that will tighten
the bitter white wreath.
LITTLE GIRL (*singing*). Were you at the wedding?
FIRST GIRL. No.
LITTLE GIRL. Well, neither was I!
What could have happened
'midst the shoots of the vineyards?
What could have happened
'neath the branch of the olive?
What really happened
that no one came back?
Were you at the wedding?
SECOND GIRL. We told you once, no.
LITTLE GIRL (*leaving*). Well, neither was I!
SECOND GIRL. Wool, red wool,
what would you sing?
FIRST GIRL. Their wounds turning waxen

balm-myrtle for pain.
Asleep in the morning,
and watching at night.

LITTLE GIRL (*in the doorway*). And then, the thread stumbled
on the flinty stones,
but mountains, blue mountains,
are letting it pass.
Running, running, running,
and finally to come
to stick in a knife blade,
to take back the bread. (*She goes out.*)

SECOND GIRL. Wool, red wool,
what would you tell?

FIRST GIRL. The lover is silent,
crimson the groom,
at the still shoreline
I saw them laid out. (*She stops and looks at the skein.*)

LITTLE GIRL (*appearing in the doorway*). Running, running, running,
the thread runs to here.
All covered with clay
I feel them draw near.
Bodies stretched stiffly
in ivory sheets!

(*The* WIFE *and* MOTHER-IN-LAW *of* LEONARDO *appear. They are anguished.*)

FIRST GIRL. Are they coming yet?

MOTHER-IN-LAW (*harshly*). We don't know.

SECOND GIRL. What can you tell us about the wedding?

FIRST GIRL. Yes, tell me.

MOTHER-IN-LAW (*curtly*). Nothing.

LEONARDO'S WIFE. I want to go back and find out all about it.

MOTHER-IN-LAW (*sternly*). You, back to your house.
Brave and alone in your house.
To grow old and to weep.
But behind closed doors.
Never again. Neither dead nor alive.
We'll nail up our windows
and let rains and nights
fall on the bitter weeds.

LEONARDO'S WIFE. What could have happened?

MOTHER-IN-LAW. It doesn't matter what.
Put a veil over your face.
Your children are yours,

that's all. On the bed
put a cross of ashes
where his pillow was. (*They go out.*)

BEGGAR WOMAN (*at the door*). A crust of bread, little girls.

LITTLE GIRL. Go away!

(*The* GIRLS *huddle close together.*)

BEGGAR WOMAN. Why?

LITTLE GIRL. Because you whine; go away!

FIRST GIRL. Child!

BEGGAR WOMAN. I might have asked for your eyes! A cloud of birds is following me. Will you have one?

LITTLE GIRL. I want to get away from here!

SECOND GIRL (*to the* BEGGAR WOMAN). Don't mind her!

FIRST GIRL. Did you come by the road through the arroyo?

BEGGAR WOMAN. I came that way!

FIRST GIRL (*timidly*). Can I ask you something?

BEGGAR WOMAN. I saw them: they'll be here soon; two torrents
still at last, among the great boulders,
two men at the horse's feet.

FIRST GIRL. Hush, old woman, hush!

BEGGAR WOMAN. Crushed flowers for eyes, and their teeth
Two dead men in the night's splendor. (*With pleasure*) Dead, yes, dead.
two fistfuls of hard-frozen snow.
Both of them fell, and the Bride returns
with bloodstains on her skirt and hair.
And they come covered with two sheets
carried on the shoulders of two tall boys.
That's how it was; nothing more. What was fitting.
Over the golden flower, dirty sand.

(*She goes. The* GIRLS *bow their heads and start going out rhythmically.*)

FIRST GIRL. Dirty sand.

SECOND GIRL. Over the golden flower.

LITTLE GIRL. Over the golden flower
they're bringing the dead from the arroyo.
Dark the one,
dark the other.
What shadowy nightingale flies and weeps
over the golden flower!

(*She goes. The stage is left empty. The* MOTHER *and a* NEIGHBOR *woman appear. The* NEIGHBOR *is weeping.*)

MOTHER. Hush.

NEIGHBOR. I can't.

MOTHER. Hush, I said. (*At the door*) Is there nobody here? (*She puts her hands to her forehead.*) My son ought to answer me. But now my son is an armful of shrivelled flowers. My son is a fading voice beyond the mountains now. (*With rage, to the* NEIGHBOR) Will you shut up? I want no wailing in this house. Your tears are only tears from your eyes, but when I'm alone mine will come—from the soles of my feet, from my roots—burning more than blood.

NEIGHBOR. You come to my house; don't you stay here.

MOTHER. I want to be here. Here. In peace. They're all dead now: and at midnight I'll sleep, sleep without terror of guns or knives. Other mothers will go to their windows, lashed by rain, to watch for their sons' faces. But not I. And of my dreams I'll make a cold ivory dove that will carry camellias of white frost to the graveyard. But no; not graveyard, not graveyard: the couch of earth, the bed that shelters them and rocks them in the sky (*A woman dressed in black enters, goes toward the right, and there kneels. To the* NEIGHBOR) Take your hands from your face. We have terrible days ahead. I want to see no one. The earth and I. My grief and I. And these four walls. Ay-y-y! Ay-y-y! (*She sits down, overcome.*)

NEIGHBOR. Take pity on yourself!

MOTHER (*pushing back her hair*). I must be calm. (*She sits down.*) Because the neighbor women will come and I don't want them to see me so poor. So poor! A woman without even one son to hold to her lips.

(*The* BRIDE *appears. She is without her wreath and wears a black shawl.*)

NEIGHBOR (*with rage, seeing the* BRIDE). Where are you going?

BRIDE. I'm coming here.

MOTHER (*to the* NEIGHBOR). Who is it?

NEIGHBOR. Don't you recognize her?

MOTHER. That's why I asked who it was. Because I don't want to recognize her, so I won't sink my teeth in her throat. You snake! (*She moves wrathfully on the* BRIDE, *then stops. To the* NEIGHBOR) Look at her! There she is, and she's crying, while I stand here calmly and don't tear her eyes out. I don't understand myself. Can it be I didn't love my son? But, where's his good name? Where is it now? Where is it? (*She beats the* BRIDE, *who drops to the floor.*)

NEIGHBOR. For God's sake! (*She tries to separate them.*)

BRIDE (*to the* NEIGHBOR). Let her; I came here so she'd kill me and they'd take me away with them. (*To the* MOTHER) But not with her hands; with grappling hooks, with a sickle—and with force—until they break on my bones. Let her! I want her to know I'm clean, that I may be crazy, but that they can bury me without a single man ever having seen himself in the whiteness of my breasts.

MOTHER. Shut up, shut up; what do I care about that?

BRIDE. Because I ran away with the other one; I ran away! (*With anguish*) You would have gone, too. I was a woman burning with desire, full of sores inside and out, and your son was a little bit of water from which I hoped for children, land, health; but the other one was a dark river, choked with brush, that brought near me the undertone of its rushes and its whispered song. And I went along with your son who was like a little boy of cold water—and the other sent against me hundreds of birds who got in my way and left white frost on my wounds, my wounds of a poor withered woman, of a girl caressed by fire. I didn't want to; remember that! I didn't want to. Your son was my destiny and I have not betrayed him, but the other one's arm dragged me along like the pull of the sea, like the head toss of a mule, and he would have dragged me always, always, always—even if I were an old woman and all your son's sons held me by the hair!

(*A* NEIGHBOR *enters.*)

MOTHER. She is not to blame; nor am I! (*Sarcastically*) Who is, then? It's a delicate, lazy, sleepless woman who throws away an orange blossom wreath and goes looking for a piece of bed warmed by another woman!

BRIDE. Be still! Be still! Take your revenge on me; here I am! See how soft my throat is; it would be less work for you than cutting a dahlia in your garden. But never that! Clean, clean as a new-born little girl. And strong enough to prove it to you. Light the fire. Let's stick our hands in; you, for your son, I, for my body. *You'll* draw yours out first.

(*Another* NEIGHBOR *enters.*)

MOTHER. But what does your good name matter to me? What does your death matter to me? What does anything about anything matter to me? Blesséd be the wheat stalks, because my sons are under them; blesséd be the rain, because it wets the face of the dead. Blesséd be God, who stretches us out together to rest.

(*Another* NEIGHBOR *enters.*)

BRIDE. Let me weep with you.

MOTHER. Weep. But at the door.

(*The* GIRL *enters. The* BRIDE *stays at the door. The* MOTHER *is at the center of the stage.*)

LEONARDO'S WIFE (*entering and going to the left*). He was a beautiful horseman,
now he's a heap of snow.
He rode to fairs and mountains
and women's arms.
Now, the night's dark moss

crowns his forehead.

MOTHER. A sunflower to your mother,
a mirror of the earth.
Let them put on your breast
the cross of bitter rosebay;
and over you a sheet
of shining silk;
between your quiet hands
let water form its lament.

WIFE. Ay-y-y, four gallant boys
come with tired shoulders!

BRIDE. Ay-y-y, four gallant boys
carry death on high!

MOTHER. Neighbors.

LITTLE GIRL (*at the door*). They're bringing them now.

MOTHER. It's the same thing.
Always the cross, the cross.

WOMEN. Sweet nails,
cross adored,
sweet name
of Christ our Lord.

BRIDE. May the cross protect both the quick and the dead.

MOTHER. Neighbors: with a knife,
with a little knife,
on their appointed day, between two and three,
these two men killed each other for love.
With a knife,
with a tiny knife
that barely fits the hand,
but that slides in clean
through the astonished flesh
and stops at the place
where trembles, enmeshed,
the dark root of a scream.

BRIDE. And this is a knife,
a tiny knife
that barely fits the hand;
fish without scales, without river,
so that on their appointed day, between two and three,
with this knife,
two men are left stiff,
with their lips turning yellow.

MOTHER. And it barely fits the hand
but it slides in clean

through the astonished flesh
and stops there, at the place
where trembles enmeshed
the dark root of a scream.

(*The* NEIGHBORS, *kneeling on the floor, sob.*)

QUESTIONS

1. Who is the protagonist of this tragedy—the mother? the bridegroom? Leonardo Félix? the bride? Why is only one of the characters given a name?

2. The external conflicts of the play are strong. In which characters are there also internal conflicts? What forces conflict in each? What are the two chief conflicting forces in the play? Does the play favor one force over the other?

3. Reconstruct the past history of Leonardo and the bride. Why did they not marry? Why did Leonardo marry someone else?

4. Reconstruct the past history of the bride's mother and father. Of what importance is this material to the play? Why is it included?

5. Explain the motivations in or attitudes toward the marriage of each of the following: the mother, the father, the servant, the bridegroom, the bride, Leonardo.

6. The setting of the play is a district in rural Spain. How much does the play reveal about the customs, mores, and culture of this society? What do you learn about its economy, family relationships, courtship and marriage customs, morality, and religious beliefs?

7. Where does the play place responsibility for the tragedy? What force or forces does the play assert to be dominant in human life? Could the tragedy have been averted?

8. The language of the play consists of prose dialogue, verse dialogue, and song. At what points is verse dialogue used? Why? What function is served by the songs? Are the three kinds of language sharply separated, or do they blend into each other? Compare the quality of the prose dialogue with that in Ibsen's play. What function does language serve in each play?

9. Contrast the directions in this play regarding settings with those in Ibsen's play. How do you explain the difference? What purpose do the settings serve in each play?

10. In Act II, Scene 2, the wedding celebration, there is a great deal of coming and going, entering and exiting, by all the characters. Does this serve a utilitarian or a poetic purpose? Explain. Contrast with the use of exits and entrances in Act III of Ibsen's play.

11. What function is served by the three woodcutters in Act III, Scene 1? In what scenes do other characters serve a similar purpose?

12. Does the personification of the moon in Act III come as a shock? Why or why not? What would have happened to Ibsen's play had a similar scene been introduced into it?

13. In the scene in the forest, García Lorca directs the use of two violins. For what effect? Would background music be appropriate for Ibsen's play?

14. Why is the beggar woman not listed in the cast of characters? Since she is identified as death only in a stage direction, which the audience would not see, how is her role made clear? Could an audience identify it?

15. What symbolic meanings are suggested by each of the following? (a) the lullaby about the big horse (Act I, Scene 2), (b) the fact that the bride lives in a cave house, (c) Leonardo's horse, (d) blood, (e) the moon, (f) the red skein (Act III, Scene 2).

CHAPTER THREE

Tragedy and Comedy

The two masks of drama—one with the corners of its mouth turned down, the other with the corners of its mouth turned up—are familiar everywhere. Derived from masks actually worn by the actors in ancient Greek plays, they symbolize the two principal modes of drama. Indeed, just as life gravitates between tears and laughter, they seem to imply that all drama is divided between tragedy and comedy.

But drama is an ancient literary form; in its development from the beginnings to the present it has produced a rich variety of plays. Can all these plays be classified under two terms? If our answer to this question is Yes, we must define the terms very broadly. If our answer is No, then how many terms do we need, and where do we stop? Polonius, in *Hamlet,* says of a visiting troupe of players that they can act either "tragedy, comedy, history, pastoral, pastoral-comical, historical-pastoral, tragical-historical, tragical-comical-historical-pastoral, scene individable, or poem unlimited." Like Polonius himself, his list seems ridiculous. Moreover, even if we adopted these terms, and more, could we be sure that they would accurately classify all plays or that a new play, written tomorrow, would not demand a totally new category?

The discussion that follows proceeds on four assumptions. First, perfect definitions and an airtight system of classification are impossible. There exist no views of tragedy and comedy that have not been challenged and no classification system that unequivocally provides for all examples. Second, it is quite unnecessary that we classify each play we read or see. The most important questions to ask about a play are not "Is this a tragedy?" or "Is this a comedy?" but "Does this play furnish an enjoyable, valid, and significant experience?" Third, the quality of experience furnished by a play, however, may be partially dependent on our perception of its relationship to earlier literary forms, and therefore familiarity with traditional notions of tragedy and comedy is important for our understanding and appreciation of plays. Many of the conventions used in specific plays have been determined by the kind of play the author felt himself to be writing. Other plays have been written in deliberate defiance of these conventions. Fourth, whether or not tragedy and comedy be taken as the two all-inclusive dramatic modes, they are certainly, as symbolized by the masks, the two principal ones, and useful points, therefore, from which to begin discussion.

The popular distinctions between comedy and tragedy are fairly simple: comedy is funny; tragedy is sad. Comedy has a happy ending, tragedy an unhappy one. The typical ending for comedy is a marriage; the typical ending for tragedy is a death. There is some truth in these notions, but only some. Some plays called comedies make no attempt to be funny. Successful tragedies, though they involve suffering and sadness, do not leave the spectator depressed. Some funny plays have sad endings: they send the viewer away with a lump in the throat. A few plays usually classified as tragedies do not have unhappy endings but conclude with the protagonist's triumph. In short, the popular distinctions are unreliable. Though we need not entirely abandon them, we must take a more complex view. Let us begin with tragedy.

The first great theorist of dramatic art was Aristotle, whose discussion of tragedy in *Poetics* has dominated critical thought ever since. A very brief summary of Aristotle's view will be helpful.

A tragedy, so Aristotle wrote, is the imitation in dramatic form of an action that is serious and complete, with incidents arousing pity and fear wherewith it effects a catharsis of such emotions. The language used is pleasurable and throughout is appropriate to the situation in which it is used. The chief characters are noble personages ("better than ourselves," says Aristotle), and the actions they perform are noble actions. The plot involves a change in the protagonist's fortune, in which he falls from happiness to misery. The protagonist is not a perfectly good man nor yet a bad man; his misfortune is brought upon him not by vice and depravity but by some error of judgment. A good tragic plot has organic unity: the events follow not just *after* one another but *because* of one another. The best tragic plots involve a reversal (a change from one state of things within the play to its opposite) or a discovery (a change from ignorance to knowledge) or both.

In the account that follows, we will not attempt to delineate the boundaries of tragedy nor necessarily to describe it at its greatest. Instead, we will describe a common understanding of tragedy as a point of departure for further discussion. Nor shall we enter into the endless controversies over what Aristotle meant by "catharsis" or over which of his statements are meant to apply to all tragedies and which only to the best ones. The important thing is that Aristotle had important insights into the nature of some of the greatest tragedies and that, rightly or wrongly interpreted, his conceptions are the basis for a kind of archetypal notion of tragedy that has dominated critical thought. What are the central features of that archetype?

1. The tragic hero is a man of noble stature. He has a greatness about him. He is not an ordinary man but one of outstanding quality. In Greek and in Shakespearean tragedy, he is usually a prince or a king. We may, if we wish, set down this predilection of former times for kings as tragic heroes as an undemocratic prejudice that regarded some men to be of nobler "blood" than others—pre-eminent by virtue of their aristocratic birth. But it is only partially that. We may with equal validity regard the hero's kingship as the symbol rather than as the cause of his greatness. He is great not primarily by virtue of his kingship but by his possession of extraordinary powers, by qualities of passion or aspiration or nobility of mind. The tragic hero's kingship is also a symbol of his initial good fortune, the mark of his high position. If the hero's fall is to arouse in us the emotions of pity and fear, it must be a fall from a height.

2. Though the tragic hero is pre-eminently great, he is not perfect. Combined with his strength, there is usually a weakness. Aristotle says that his fall is caused by "some error of judgment," and probably he meant no more than that. Critical tradition, however, has most frequently interpreted this error of judgment as a flaw in character—the so-called tragic flaw. With all his great qualities, the tragic hero is usually afflicted with some fault of character such as inordinate ambition, quickness to anger, a tendency to jealousy, or overweening pride. This flaw in his character leads to his downfall.

3. The hero's downfall, therefore, is partially his own fault, the result of his own free choice, not the result of pure accident or villainy or some overriding malignant fate. Accident, villainy, or fate may contribute to the downfall but only as cooperating agents: they are not alone responsible. The combination of the hero's greatness and his responsibility for his own downfall is what entitles us to describe his down-

fall as tragic rather than as merely pathetic. In common speech these two adjectives are often confused. If a father of ten children is accidentally killed at a street corner, the event, strictly speaking, is pathetic, not tragic. When a weak man succumbs to his weakness and comes to a bad end, the event should be called pathetic, not tragic. The tragic event involves a fall from greatness, brought about, at least partially, by the agent's free action.

4. Nevertheless, the hero's misfortune is not wholly deserved. The punishment exceeds the crime. We do not come away from tragedy with the feeling that "He got what he had coming to him" but rather with the sad sense of a waste of human potential. For what most impresses us about the tragic hero is not his weakness but his greatness. He is, in a sense, "larger than life," or, as Aristotle said, "better than ourselves." He reveals to us the dimensions of human possibility. He is a person mainly admirable, and his fall therefore fills us with pity and fear.

5. Yet the tragic fall is not pure loss. Though it may result in the protagonist's death, it involves, before his death, some increase in awareness, some gain in self-knowledge—as Aristotle puts it, some "discovery" —a change from ignorance to knowledge. On the level of plot, the discovery may be merely learning the truth about some fact or situation of which the protagonist was ignorant, but on the level of character it is accompanied or followed by a significant insight, a fuller self-knowledge, an increase not only in knowledge but in wisdom. Not unusually this increase in wisdom involves some sort of reconciliation with the universe or with the protagonist's situation. He exits not cursing his fate but accepting it and acknowledging that it is to some degree just.

6. Though it arouses solemn emotions—pity and fear, says Aristotle, but compassion and awe might be better terms—tragedy, when well performed, does not leave its audience in a state of depression. Though we cannot be sure what Aristotle meant by his term catharsis, some sort of emotional release at the end is a common experience of those who witness great tragedies on the stage. They have been greatly moved by pity, fear, and associated emotions, but they are not left emotionally beaten down or dejected. Instead, there may be a feeling almost of exhilaration. This feeling is a response to the tragic action. With the fall of the hero and his gain in wisdom or self-knowledge, there is, besides the appalling sense of human waste, a fresh recognition of human greatness, a sense that human life has unrealized potentialities. Though the hero may be defeated, he at least has dared greatly, and he gains understanding from his defeat.

Is the comic mask laughing or smiling? The question is more important than may at first appear, for usually we laugh *at* someone but smile *with* someone. The laugh expresses recognition of some absurdity in human behavior; the smile expresses pleasure in someone's company or good fortune.

The comic mask may be interpreted both ways. Comedy, Northrop Frye has said, lies between satire and romance. Historically, there have been two chief kinds of comedy—scornful comedy and romantic comedy, laughing comedy and smiling comedy. Of the two, scornful or satiric comedy is the oldest and probably still the most dominant.

The most essential difference between tragedy and comedy, particularly scornful comedy, is in their depiction of human nature. Where tragedy emphasizes human greatness, comedy delineates human weakness. Where tragedy celebrates human freedom, comedy points up human limitation. Wherever men fail to measure up to their own resolutions or to their own self-conceptions, wherever they are guilty of hypocrisy, vanity, or folly, wherever they fly in the face of good sense and rational behavior, comedy exhibits their absurdity and invites us to laugh at them. Where tragedy tends to say, with Shakespeare's Hamlet, "What a piece of work is man! how noble in reason! how infinite in faculty! in form and moving how express and admirable! in action how like an angel! in apprehension how like a god!" comedy says, with Shakespeare's Puck, "Lord, what fools these mortals be!"

Because comedy exposes human folly, its function is partly critical and corrective. Where tragedy challenges us with a vision of human possibility, comedy reveals to us a spectacle of human ridiculousness that it makes us want to avoid. No doubt, we should not exaggerate this function of comedy. We go to the theater primarily for enjoyment, not to receive lessons in personality or character development. Nevertheless, laughter may be educative at the same time that it is enjoyable. The comedies of Aristophanes and Molière, of Ben Jonson and Congreve, are, first of all, good fun, but, secondly, they are antidotes for human folly.

Romantic or smiling comedy, as opposed to scornful comedy, and as exemplified by many plays of Shakespeare—*As You Like It, Twelfth Night, The Merchant of Venice, The Tempest,* for instance—puts its emphasis upon sympathetic rather than ridiculous characters. These characters—likeable, not given up to folly or vanity—are placed in various kinds of difficulties from which, at the end of the play, they are rescued, attaining their ends or having their good fortunes restored. Though different from the protagonists of scornful comedy, however, these characters are not the commanding or lofty figures that tragic heroes are. They are sensible and good rather than noble, aspiring, and grand. They do not strike us with awe as the tragic hero does. They do not so challengingly test the limits of human possibility. In short, they move in a smaller world. Romantic comedies, therefore, do not occupy a different universe from satiric comedies; they simply lie at opposite sides of the same territory. The romantic comedy, moreover, though its protagonists are sympathetic, has usually a number of lesser characters whose folly is held up to ridicule. The satiric comedy, on the other hand, frequently has minor characters—often a pair of young lovers—who are sympathetic and likeable. The difference between the two kinds of comedy may be only a matter of whether we laugh at the primary or at the secondary characters.

There are other differences between comedy and tragedy. The norms of comedy are primarily social. Where tragedy tends to isolate the tragic hero and emphasize his uniqueness, comedy puts its protagonists always in the midst of a group and emphasizes their commonness. Where the tragic hero possesses an overpowering individuality, so that his play is often named after him (for example, *Antigone, Othello*), the comic protagonist tends to be a type, and his play is often named for the type (for example, *The Misanthrope, The Brute*). We judge the tragic hero by absolute moral standards, by how far he soars above society. We judge the comic protagonist by social standards, by how well he adjusts to society and conforms to the expectations of the group.

Finally, comic plots are less likely than tragic plots to exhibit the high degree of organic unity—of logical cause-and-effect progression—that Aristotle required of tragedy. Plausibility, in fact, is not usually the central characteristic of a comic plot. Unlikely coincidences, improbable disguises, mistaken identities—these are the stuff of which comedy is made; and, as long as they make us laugh and, at at the same time, help to illuminate human nature and human folly, we need not greatly care. Not that plausibility is no longer important—only that other things are more important, and these other things are often achieved by the most outrageous violations of probability.

Particularly is this true as regards the comic ending. Conventionally, comedies have a happy ending, but the emphasis here is on *conventionally*. The happy ending is, indeed, a *convention* of comedy, which is to say that a comedy ends happily because comedies end happily—that is the nature of the form—not necessarily because a happy ending is a plausible outcome of the events that have preceded. The greatest masters of comedy—Aristophanes, Shakespeare, Molière—have often been extremely arbitrary in the manner in which they achieved their endings. The accidental discovery of a lost will, rescue by an act of divine intervention (*deus ex machina*), the sudden reform of a mean-spirited person into a friendly person—such devices have been used by the greatest comic writers. And, even where the ending is achieved more plausibly, comedy asks us to forget for the time being that in actuality life has no endings, except for death. Marriage, which provides the ending for so many comedies, is really a beginning. The marriage agreement at the end of Chekhov's play *The Brute* delights us because the reversal from the beginning has been so complete. We need not mar our delight by asking how long a marriage between such opposite and obstinate temperaments is likely to be happy.

And now, though we do not wish to imitate the folly of Polonius, it is well that we learn two additional terms: melodrama and farce. In the two-part classification suggested by the two symbolic masks, melodrama belongs with tragedy and farce with comedy, but the differences are sufficient to make the two new terms useful.

Melodrama, like tragedy, attempts to arouse feelings of fear and pity, but it does so ordinarily through cruder means. The conflict is an over-simplified one between good and evil depicted in terms of black and white. Plot is emphasized at the expense of characterization. Sensational incidents provide the staple of the plot. The young mother and her baby are evicted into a howling storm by the villain holding the mortgage. The heroine is tied to the railroad tracks as the express train approaches. Most important, good finally triumphs over evil, and the ending is happy. Typically, at the end, the hero marries the heroine; villainy is foiled or crushed. Melodrama may, of course, have different degrees of power and subtlety; it is not always as crude as its crudest examples. But, in it, moral issues are typically over-simplified, and good is finally triumphant. Melodrama does not provide the complex insights of tragedy. It is typically escapist rather than interpretive.

Farce, more consistently than comedy, is aimed at arousing explosive laughter. But again the means are cruder. The conflicts are violent and usually at the physical level. Plot is emphasized at the expense of characterization, improbable situations and coincidence at the expense of articulated plot. Absurdity replaces plausibility. Coarse wit, practical jokes, and physical action are staples. Characters trip over benches, insult each other, run into walls, knock each other down, get into brawls. Performed with gusto, farce may be hilariously funny. Psychologically, it may boost our spirits and purge us of hostility and aggression. In content, however, like melodrama, it is escapist rather than interpretive.

Now we have four classifications—tragedy, comedy, melodrama, farce—the latter two as appendages of the former. But none of these classifications is rigid. They blend into each other and are incapable of exact definition. If we take them over-seriously, the tragic mask may laugh, and the comic mask weep.

TOPICS FOR DISCUSSION

1. *An Enemy of the People* has been referred to, by at least one critic, as "a satiric comedy." Is this an accurate description? How does the play differ from comedy as popularly conceived? Does it have a happy ending? Is Dr. Stockmann the kind of hero you would most expect to find in satiric comedy, romantic comedy, or tragedy? Why?
2. How does *Blood Wedding* differ from an Aristotelian tragedy?
3. *Everyman* is often referred to as a tragedy. In what respects does it resemble the classical conception of tragedy? (See page 1083.) In what respects does it differ?

Sophocles

ANTIGONE

The plots of Greek tragedies were based on legends with which Greek audiences were more or less familiar (as, for example, American audiences would be familiar with the major events in an historical play based on the life of Lincoln). These plays often owed much of their impact to the audience's previous knowledge of the characters and their fate, which enabled the playwright to make powerful use of dramatic irony and allusion. In addition, much of the audience's delight came from seeing how the playwright worked out the details of the story. The purpose of this introductory note, therefore, is to supply such information as the play's first audiences might be presumed to have had.

Oedipus, King of Thebes, upon learning that he had unwittingly killed his own father, Laius, and married his mother, Jocasta, gouged out his eyes and went into exile. After making the same discovery, Jocasta hanged herself. Left behind were two sons, Eteocles and Polynices, and two daughters, Antigone and Ismene. The sons quarreled over the throne, and, as a result, Polynices was driven into exile. Allying himself with six other Greek princes, Polynices then formed an army—the Argives—and marched upon Thebes to recover the kingship. During the battle that ensued, the two brothers, engaged in single combat, killed one another. This left Creon, their uncle, brother of Jocasta, to ascend the throne. Creon's first official act was to forbid the burial of Polynices—on pain of death. It is at this point that the action of the play begins, for Antigone, who is betrothed to Creon's son, Haemon, opposes the decree. To fully understand the play, we must realize that, to the Greeks, a proper burial with all of the appropriate ceremonies was a matter of grave importance. Creon's decree was thus contrary to solemn unwritten laws that any Greek audience would acknowledge and respect.

The play was first performed in Athens about 442 B.C. In the present version, the translators use spellings for the proper names that are closer to the original Greek than the more familiar Anglicized spellings used in this note.

CHARACTERS

ANTIGONE, *daughter of Oedipus and Jocasta*
ISMENE, *sister of Antigone*
CREON, *King of Thebes, uncle of Antigone*
EURYDICE, *wife of Creon*
HAIMON, *son of Creon*
TEIRESIAS, *a prophet*
A SENTRY
A MESSENGER
CHORUS OF THEBAN ELDERS
CHORAGOS, *leader of the Chorus*
SERVANTS, GUARDS

SCENE. *Before the palace of* CREON, *King of Thebes. A central double door and two lateral doors. A platform extends the length of the façade, and from this platform three steps lead down into the "orchestra," or chorus-ground.*

TIME. *Dawn of the day after the repulse of the Argive army from the assault on Thebes.*

PROLOGUE

(ANTIGONE *and* ISMENE *enter from the central door of the Palace.*)

ANTIGONE. Ismene, dear sister,
You would think that we had already suffered enough
For the curse on Oedipus:
I cannot imagine any grief
That you and I have not gone through. And now—
Have they told you of the new decree of our King Creon?
ISMENE. I have heard nothing: I know
That two sisters lost two brothers, a double death
In a single hour; and I know that the Argive army
Fled in the night; but beyond this nothing.
ANTIGONE. I thought so. And that is why I wanted you
To come out here with me. There is something we must do.
ISMENE. Why do you speak so strangely?
ANTIGONE. Listen, Ismene:
Creon buried our brother Eteocles
With military honors, gave him a soldier's funeral,
And it was right that he should; but Polyneices,
Who fought as bravely and died as miserably,—
They say that Creon has sworn
No one shall bury him, no one mourn for him,

But his body must lie in the fields, a sweet treasure
For carrion birds to find as they search for food.
That is what they say, and our good Creon is coming here
To announce it publicly; and the penalty—
Stoning to death in the public square!
There it is,
And now you can prove what you are:
A true sister, or a traitor to your family.

ISMENE. Antigone, you are mad! What could I possibly do?

ANTIGONE. You must decide whether you will help me or not.

ISMENE. I do not understand you. Help you in what?

ANTIGONE. Ismene, I am going to bury him. Will you come?

ISMENE. Bury him! You have just said the new law forbids it.

ANTIGONE. He is my brother. And he is your brother, too.

ISMENE. But think of the danger! Think what Creon will do!

ANTIGONE. Creon is not strong enough to stand in my way.

ISMENE. Ah sister!
Oedipus died, everyone hating him
For what his own search brought to light, his eyes
Ripped out by his own hand; and Iocaste died,
His mother and wife at once: she twisted the cords
That strangled her life; and our two brothers died,
Each killed by the other's sword. And we are left:
But oh, Antigone,
Think how much more terrible than these
Our own death would be if we should go against Creon
And do what he has forbidden! We are only women,
We cannot fight with men, Antigone!
The law is strong, we must give in to the law
In this thing, and in worse. I beg the Dead
To forgive me, but I am helpless: I must yield
To those in authority. And I think it is dangerous business
To be always meddling.

ANTIGONE. If that is what you think,
I should not want you, even if you asked to come.
You have made your choice, you can be what you want to be.
But I will bury him; and if I must die,
I say that this crime is holy: I shall lie down
With him in death, and I shall be as dear
To him as he to me.
It is the dead,
Not the living, who make the longest demands:
We die for ever . . .
You may do as you like,

Since apparently the laws of the gods mean nothing to you.

ISMENE. They mean a great deal to me; but I have no strength
To break laws that were made for the public good.

ANTIGONE. That must be your excuse, I suppose. But as for me,
I will bury the brother I love.

ISMENE. Antigone,
I am so afraid for you!

ANTIGONE. You need not be:
You have yourself to consider, after all.

ISMENE. But no one must hear of this, you must tell no one!
I will keep it a secret, I promise!

ANTIGONE. Oh, tell it! Tell everyone!
Think how they'll hate you when it all comes out
If they learn that you knew about it all the time!

ISMENE. So fiery! You should be cold with fear.

ANTIGONE. Perhaps. But I am doing only what I must.

ISMENE. But can you do it? I say that you cannot.

ANTIGONE. Very well: when my strength gives out, I shall do no more.

ISMENE. Impossible things should not be tried at all.

ANTIGONE. Go away, Ismene:
I shall be hating you soon, and the dead will too,
For your words are hateful. Leave me my foolish plan:
I am not afraid of the danger; if it means death,
It will not be the worst of deaths—death without honor.

ISMENE. Go then, if you feel that you must.
You are unwise,
But a loyal friend indeed to those who love you. (*Exit into the Palace.*)

(ANTIGONE *goes off, L.*)

(*Enter the* CHORUS.)

PÁRADOS[1]

[1] Párados: the song or ode chanted by the chorus on their entry. It is accompanied by dancing and music played on a flute. The chorus, in this play, represents elders of the city of Thebes. They remain on stage (on a lower level than the principal actors) for the remainder of the play. The choral odes and dances serve to separate one scene from another (there was no curtain in Greek theater) as well as to comment on the action, reinforce the emotion, and interpret the situation. The chorus also performs dance movements during certain portions of the scenes themselves. *Strophe* and *antistrophe* are terms denoting the movement and counter-movement of the chorus from one side of their playing area to the other. When the chorus participates in dialogue with the other characters, their lines are spoken by the Choragos, their leader.

STROPHE 1

Chorus. Now the long blade of the sun, lying
Level east to west, touches with glory
Thebes of the Seven Gates. Open, unlidded
Eye of golden day! O marching light
Across the eddy and rush of Dirce's stream,
Striking the white shields of the enemy
Thrown headlong backward from the blaze of morning!
Choragos. Polyneices their commander
Roused them with windy phrases,
He the wild eagle screaming
Insults above our land,
His wings their shields of snow,
His crest their marshalled helms.

ANTISTROPHE 1

Chorus. Against our seven gates in a yawning ring
The famished spears came onward in the night;
But before his jaws were sated with our blood,
Or pinefire took the garland of our towers,
He was thrown back; and as he turned, great Thebes—
No tender victim for his noisy power—
Rose like a dragon behind him, shouting war.
Choragos. For God hates utterly
The bray of bragging tongues;
And when he beheld their smiling,
Their swagger of golden helms,
The frown of his thunder blasted
Their first man from our walls.

STROPHE 2

Chorus. We heard his shout of triumph high in the air
Turn to a scream; far out in a flaming arc
He fell with his windy torch, and the earth struck him.
And others storming in fury no less than his
Found stock of death in the dusty joy of battle.
Choragos. Seven captains at seven gates
Yielded their clanging arms to the god
That bends the battle-line and breaks it.
These two only, brothers in blood,
Face to face in matchless rage,
Mirroring each the other's death,
Clashed in long combat.

ANTISTROPHE 2

CHORUS. But now in the beautiful morning of victory
Let Thebes of the many chariots sing for joy!
With hearts for dancing we'll take leave of war:
Our temples shall be sweet with hymns of praise,
And the long night shall echo with our chorus.

SCENE I

CHORAGOS. But now at last our new King is coming:
Creon of Thebes, Menoikeus' son.
In this auspicious dawn of his reign
What are the new complexities
That shifting Fate has woven for him?
What is his counsel? Why has he summoned
The old men to hear him?

(*Enter* CREON *from the Palace, C. He addresses the* CHORUS *from the top step.*)

CREON. Gentlemen: I have the honor to inform you that our Ship of State, which recent storms have threatened to destroy, has come safely to harbor at last, guided by the merciful wisdom of Heaven. I have summoned you here this morning because I know that I can depend upon you: your devotion to King Laïos was absolute; you never hesitated in your duty to our late ruler Oedipus; and when Oedipus died, your loyalty was transferred to his children. Unfortunately, as you know, his two sons, the princes Eteocles and Polyneices, have killed each other in battle; and I, as the next in blood, have succeeded to the full power of the throne.

I am aware, of course, that no Ruler can expect complete loyalty from his subjects until he has been tested in office. Nevertheless, I say to you at the very outset that I have nothing but contempt for the kind of Governor who is afraid, for whatever reason, to follow the course that he knows is best for the State; and as for the man who sets private friendship above the public welfare—I have no use for him, either. I call God to witness that if I saw my country headed for ruin, I should not be afraid to speak out plainly; and I need hardly remind you that I would never have any dealings with an enemy of the people. No one values friendship more highly than I; but we must remember that friends made at the risk of wrecking our Ship are not real friends at all.

These are my principles, at any rate, and that is why I have made the following decision concerning the sons of Oedipus: Eteocles, who died as a man should die, fighting for his country, is to be buried with full military honors, with all the ceremony that is usual when the greatest heroes die; but his brother Polyneices, who broke his exile to come back with fire and sword against his native city and the shrines of his father's gods, whose one idea was to spill the blood of his blood and sell his own people into slavery—Polyneices, I say, is to have no burial: no man is to touch him or say the least prayer for him; he shall lie on the plain, unburied; and the birds and the scavenging dogs can do with him whatever they like.

This is my command, and you can see the wisdom behind it. As long as I am King, no traitor is going to be honored with the loyal man. But whoever shows by word and deed that he is on the side of the State—he shall have my respect while he is living, and my reverence when he is dead.

CHORAGOS. If that is your will, Creon son of Menoikeus,
You have the right to enforce it: we are yours.

CREON. That is my will. Take care that you do your part.

CHORAGOS. We are old men: let the younger ones carry it out.

CREON. I do not mean that: the sentries have been appointed.

CHORAGOS. Then what is it that you would have us do?

CREON. You will give no support to whoever breaks this law.

CHORAGOS. Only a crazy man is in love with death!

CREON. And death it is; yet money talks, and the wisest
Have sometimes been known to count a few coins too many.

(*Enter* SENTRY *from L.*)

SENTRY. I'll not say that I'm out of breath from running, King, because every time I stopped to think about what I have to tell you, I felt like going back. And all the time a voice kept saying, "You fool, don't you know you're walking straight into trouble?"; and then another voice: "Yes, but if you let somebody else get the news to Creon first, it will be even worse than that for you!" But good sense won out, at least I hope it was good sense, and here I am with a story that makes no sense at all; but I'll tell it anyhow, because, as they say, what's going to happen's going to happen, and—

CREON. Come to the point. What have you to say?

SENTRY. I did not do it. I did not see who did it. You must not punish me for what someone else has done.

CREON. A comprehensive defense! More effective, perhaps,
If I knew its purpose. Come: what is it?

SENTRY. A dreadful thing . . . I don't know how to put it—

CREON. Out with it!

SENTRY. Well, then;
The dead man—
Polyneices—

(*Pause. The* SENTRY *is overcome, fumbles for words.* CREON *waits impassively.*)

out there—
someone—

New dust on the slimy flesh!

(*Pause. No sign from* CREON.)

Someone has given it burial that way, and
Gone . . .

(*Long pause.* CREON *finally speaks with deadly control.*)

CREON. And the man who dared do this?

SENTRY. I swear I
Do not know! You must believe me!
Listen:
The ground was dry, not a sign of digging, no,
Not a wheeltrack in the dust, no trace of anyone.
It was when they relieved us this morning: and one of them,
The corporal, pointed to it.
There it was,
The strangest—
Look:
The body, just mounded over with light dust: you see?
Not buried really, but as if they'd covered it
Just enough for the ghost's peace. And no sign
Of dogs or any wild animal that had been there.

And then what a scene there was! Every man of us
Accusing the other: we all proved the other man did it,
We all had proof that we could not have done it.
We were ready to take hot iron in our hands,
Walk through fire, swear by all the gods,
It was not I!
I do not know who it was, but it was not I!

(CREON'*s rage has been mounting steadily, but the* SENTRY *is too intent upon his story to notice it.*)

And then, when this came to nothing, someone said
A thing that silenced us and made us stare
Down at the ground: you had to be told the news,
And one of us had to do it! We threw the dice,
And the bad luck fell to me. So here I am,
No happier to be here than you are to have me:
Nobody likes the man who brings bad news.

CHORAGOS. I have been wondering, King: can it be that the gods have done this?

CREON (*furiously*). Stop!
Must you doddering wrecks

Go out of your heads entirely? "The gods!"
Intolerable!
The gods favor this corpse? Why? How had he served them?
Tried to loot their temples, burn their images,
Yes, and the whole State, and its laws with it!
Is it your senile opinion that the gods love to honor bad men?
A pious thought!—
No, from the very beginning
There have been those who have whispered together,
Stiff-necked anarchists, putting their heads together,
Scheming against me in alleys. These are the men,
And they have bribed my own guard to do this thing.
(*Sententiously.*) Money!
There's nothing in the world so demoralizing as money.
Down go your cities,
Homes gone, men gone, honest hearts corrupted,
Crookedness of all kinds, and all for money!
(*To* SENTRY) But you—!
I swear by God and by the throne of God,
The man who has done this thing shall pay for it!
Find that man, bring him here to me, or your death
Will be the least of your problems: I'll string you up
Alive, and there will be certain ways to make you
Discover your employer before you die;
And the process may teach you a lesson you seem to have missed:
The dearest profit is sometimes all too dear:
That depends on the source. Do you understand me?
A fortune won is often misfortune.

SENTRY. King, may I speak?
CREON. Your very voice distresses me.
SENTRY. Are you sure that it is my voice, and not your conscience?
CREON. By God, he wants to analyze me now!
SENTRY. It is not what I say, but what has been done, that hurts you.
CREON. You talk too much.
SENTRY. Maybe; but I've done nothing.
CREON. Sold your soul for some silver: that's all you've done.
SENTRY. How dreadful it is when the right judge judges wrong!
CREON. Your figures of speech
May entertain you now; but unless you bring me the man,
You will get little profit from them in the end.

(*Exit* CREON *into the Palace.*)

SENTRY. "Bring me the man"—!
I'd like nothing better than bringing him the man!

But bring him or not, you have seen the last of me here.
At any rate, I am safe!

(*Exit* Sentry.)

ODE I

STROPHE 1

Chorus. Numberless are the world's wonders, but none
More wonderful than man; the stormgray sea
Yields to his prows, the huge crests bear him high;
Earth, holy and inexhaustible, is graven
With shining furrows where his plows have gone
Year after year, the timeless labor of stallions.

ANTISTROPHE 1

The lightboned birds and beasts that cling to cover,
The lithe fish lighting their reaches of dim water,
All are taken, tamed in the net of his mind;
The lion on the hill, the wild horse windy-maned,
Resign to him; and his blunt yoke has broken
The sultry shoulders of the mountain bull.

STROPHE 2

Words also, and thought as rapid as air,
He fashions to his good use; statecraft is his,
And his the skill that deflects the arrows of snow,
The spears of winter rain: from every wind
He has made himself secure—from all but one:
In the late wind of death he cannot stand.

ANTISTROPHE 2

O clear intelligence, force beyond all measure!
O fate of man, working both good and evil!
When the laws are kept, how proudly his city stands!
When the laws are broken, what of his city then?
Never may the anárchic man find rest at my hearth,
Never be it said that my thoughts are his thoughts.

SCENE II

(*Re-enter* Sentry, *leading* Antigone.)

Choragos. What does this mean? Surely this captive woman
Is the Princess, Antigone. Why should she be taken?

SENTRY. Here is the one who did it! We caught her
In the very act of burying him.—Where is Creon?
CHORAGOS. Just coming from the house.

(*Enter* CREON, C.)

CREON. What has happened?
Why have you come back so soon?
SENTRY (*expansively*). O King,
A man should never be too sure of anything: I would have sworn
That you'd not see me here again: your anger
Frightened me so, and the things you threatened me with;
But how could I tell then
That I'd be able to solve the case so soon?

No dice-throwing this time: I was only too glad to come!

Here is this woman. She is the guilty one:
We found her trying to bury him.
Take her, then; question her; judge her as you will.
I am through with the whole thing now, and glád óf it.
CREON. But this is Antigone! Why have you brought her here?
SENTRY. She was burying him, I tell you!
CREON (*severely*). Is this the truth?
SENTRY. I saw her with my own eyes. Can I say more?
CREON. The details: come, tell me quickly!
SENTRY. It was like this:
After those terrible threats of yours, King,
We went back and brushed the dust away from the body.
The flesh was soft by now, and stinking,
So we sat on a hill to windward and kept guard.
No napping this time! We kept each other awake.
But nothing happened until the white round sun
Whirled in the center of the round sky over us:
Then, suddenly,
A storm of dust roared up from the earth, and the sky
Went out, the plain vanished with all its trees
In the stinging dark. We closed our eyes and endured it.
The whirlwind lasted a long time, but it passed;
And then we looked, and there was Antigone!
I have seen
A mother bird come back to a stripped nest, heard
Her crying bitterly a broken note or two
For the young ones stolen. Just so, when this girl
Found the bare corpse, and all her love's work wasted,
She wept, and cried on heaven to damn the hands

That had done this thing.
And then she brought more dust
And sprinkled wine three times for her brother's ghost.

We ran and took her at once. She was not afraid,
Not even when we charged her with what she had done.
She denied nothing.
And this was a comfort to me,
And some uneasiness: for it is a good thing
To escape from death, but it is no great pleasure
To bring death to a friend.
Yet I always say
There is nothing so comfortable as your own safe skin!

CREON (*slowly, dangerously*). And you, Antigone,
You with your head hanging—do you confess this thing?

ANTIGONE. I do. I deny nothing.

CREON (*to* SENTRY). You may go. (*Exit* SENTRY.)
(*To* ANTIGONE) Tell me, tell me briefly:
Had you heard my proclamation touching this matter?

ANTIGONE. It was public. Could I help hearing it?

CREON. And yet you dared defy the law.

ANTIGONE. I dared.
It was not God's proclamation. That final Justice
That rules the world below makes no such laws.
Your edict, King, was strong,
But all your strength is weakness itself against
The immortal unrecorded laws of God.
They are not merely now: they were, and shall be,
Operative for ever, beyond man utterly.

I knew I must die, even without your decree:
I am only mortal. And if I must die
Now, before it is my time to die,
Surely this is no hardship: can anyone
Living, as I live, with evil all about me,
Think Death less than a friend? This death of mine
Is of no importance; but if I had left my brother
Lying in death unburied, I should have suffered.
Now I do not.
You smile at me. Ah Creon,
Think me a fool, if you like; but it may well be
That a fool convicts me of folly.

CHORAGOS. Like father, like daughter: both headstrong, deaf to reason!
She has never learned to yield.

CREON. She has much to learn.
The inflexible heart breaks first, the toughest iron
Cracks first, and the wildest horses bend their necks
At the pull of the smallest curb.
Pride? In a slave?
This girl is guilty of a double insolence,
Breaking the given laws and boasting of it.
Who is the man here,
She or I, if this crime goes unpunished?
Sister's child, or more than sister's child,
Or closer yet in blood—she and her sister
Win bitter death for this!
(*To* SERVANTS) Go, some of you,
Arrest Ismene. I accuse her equally.
Bring her: you will find her sniffling in the house there.

Her mind's a traitor: crimes kept in the dark
Cry for light, and the guardian brain shudders;
But how much worse than this
Is brazen boasting of barefaced anarchy!
ANTIGONE. Creon, what more do you want than my death?
CREON. Nothing.
That gives me everything.
ANTIGONE. Then I beg you: kill me.
This talking is a great weariness: your words
Are distasteful to me, and I am sure that mine
Seem so to you. And yet they should not seem so:
I should have praise and honor for what I have done.
All these men here would praise me
Were their lips not frozen shut with fear of you.
(*Bitterly.*) Ah the good fortune of kings,
Licensed to say and do whatever they please!
CREON. You are alone here in that opinion.
ANTIGONE. No, they are with me. But they keep their tongues in leash.
CREON. Maybe. But you are guilty, and they are not.
ANTIGONE. There is no guilt in reverence for the dead.
CREON. But Eteocles—was he not your brother too?
ANTIGONE. My brother too.
CREON. And you insult his memory?
ANTIGONE (*softly*). The dead man would not say that I insult it.
CREON. He would: for you honor a traitor as much as him.
ANTIGONE. His own brother, traitor or not, and equal in blood.
CREON. He made war on his country. Eteocles defended it.
ANTIGONE. Nevertheless, there are honors due all the dead.

CREON. But not the same for the wicked as for the just.
ANTIGONE. Ah Creon, Creon,
Which of us can say what the gods hold wicked?
CREON. An enemy is an enemy, even dead.
ANTIGONE. It is my nature to join in love, not hate.
CREON (*finally losing patience*). Go join them, then; if you must have your love,
Find it in hell!
CHORAGOS. But see, Ismene comes:

(*Enter* ISMENE, *guarded.*)

Those tears are sisterly, the cloud
That shadows her eyes rains down gentle sorrow.
CREON. You too, Ismene,
Snake in my ordered house, sucking my blood
Stealthily—and all the time I never knew
That these two sisters were aiming at my throne!
Ismene,
Do you confess your share in this crime, or deny it?
Answer me.
ISMENE. Yes, if she will let me say so. I am guilty.
ANTIGONE (*coldly*). No, Ismene. You have no right to say so.
You would not help me, and I will not have you help me.
ISMENE. But now I know what you meant; and I am here
To join you, to take my share of punishment.
ANTIGONE. The dead man and the gods who rule the dead
Know whose act this was. Words are not friends.
ISMENE. Do you refuse me, Antigone? I want to die with you:
I too have a duty that I must discharge to the dead.
ANTIGONE. You shall not lessen my death by sharing it.
ISMENE. What do I care for life when you are dead?
ANTIGONE. Ask Creon. You're always hanging on his opinions.
ISMENE. You are laughing at me. Why, Antigone?
ANTIGONE. It's a joyless laughter, Ismene.
ISMENE. But can I do nothing?
ANTIGONE. Yes. Save yourself. I shall not envy you.
There are those who will praise you; I shall have honor, too.
ISMENE. But we are equally guilty!
ANTIGONE. No more, Ismene.
You are alive, but I belong to Death.
CREON (*to the* CHORUS). Gentlemen, I beg you to observe these girls:
One has just now lost her mind; the other,
It seems, has never had a mind at all.
ISMENE. Grief teaches the steadiest minds to waver, King.

CREON. Yours certainly did, when you assumed guilt with the guilty!
ISMENE. But how could I go on living without her?
CREON. You are.
She is already dead.
ISMENE. But your own son's bride!
CREON. There are places enough for him to push his plow.
I want no wicked women for my sons!
ISMENE. O dearest Haimon, how your father wrongs you!
CREON. I've had enough of your childish talk of marriage!
CHORAGOS. Do you really intend to steal this girl from your son?
CREON. No; Death will do that for me.
CHORAGOS. Then she must die?
CREON (*ironically*). You dazzle me.
—But enough of this talk!
(*To* GUARDS.) You, there, take them away and guard them well:
For they are but women, and even brave men run
When they see Death coming.

(*Exeunt* ISMENE, ANTIGONE, *and* GUARDS.)

ODE II

STROPHE 1

CHORUS. Fortunate is the man who has never tasted God's vengeance!
Where once the anger of heaven has struck, that house is shaken
For ever: damnation rises behind each child
Like a wave cresting out of the black northeast,
When the long darkness under sea roars up
And bursts drumming death upon the windwhipped sand.

ANTISTROPHE 1

I have seen this gathering sorrow from time long past
Loom upon Oedipus' children: generation from generation
Takes the compulsive rage of the enemy god.
So lately this last flower of Oedipus' line
Drank the sunlight! but now a passionate word
And a handful of dust have closed up all its beauty.

STROPHE 2

What mortal arrogance
Transcends the wrath of Zeus?
Sleep cannot lull him, nor the effortless long months
Of the timeless gods: but he is young for ever,

And his house is the shining day of high Olympos.
All that is and shall be,
And all the past, is his.
No pride on earth is free of the curse of heaven.

ANTISTROPHE 2

The straying dreams of men
May bring them ghosts of joy:
But as they drowse, the waking embers burn them;
Or they walk with fíxed éyes, as blind men walk.
But the ancient wisdom speaks for our own time:
Fate works most for woe
With Folly's fairest show.
Man's little pleasure is the spring of sorrow.

SCENE III

CHORAGOS. But here is Haimon, King, the last of all your sons.
Is it grief for Antigone that brings him here,
And bitterness at being robbed of his bride?

(*Enter* HAIMON.)

CREON. We shall soon see, and no need of diviners.
—Son,
You have heard my final judgment on that girl:
Have you come here hating me, or have you come
With deference and with love, whatever I do?
HAIMON. I am your son, father. You are my guide.
You make things clear for me, and I obey you.
No marriage means more to me than your continuing wisdom.
CREON. Good. That is the way to behave: subordinate
Everything else, my son, to your father's will.
That is what a man prays for, that he may get
Sons attentive and dutiful in his house,
Each one hating his father's enemies,
Honoring his father's friends. But if his sons
Fail him, if they turn out unprofitably,
What has he fathered but trouble for himself
And amusement for the malicious?
So you are right
Not to lose your head over this woman.
Your pleasure with her would soon grow cold, Haimon,
And then you'd have a hellcat in bed and elsewhere.
Let her find her husband in Hell!

Of all the people in this city, only she
Has had contempt for my law and broken it.
Do you want me to show myself weak before the people?
Or to break my sworn word? No, and I will not.
The woman dies.
I suppose she'll plead "family ties." Well, let her.
If I permit my own family to rebel,
How shall I earn the world's obedience?
Show me the man who keeps his house in hand,
He's fit for public authority.
                                        I'll have no dealings
With law-breakers, critics of the government:
Whoever is chosen to govern should be obeyed—
Must be obeyed, in all things, great and small,
Just and unjust! O Haimon,
The man who knows how to obey, and that man only,
Knows how to give commands when the time comes.
You can depend on him, no matter how fast
The spears come: he's a good soldier, he'll stick it out.

Anarchy, anarchy! Show me a greater evil!
This is why cities tumble and the great houses rain down,
This is what scatters armies!

No, no: good lives are made so by discipline.
We keep the laws then, and the lawmakers,
And no woman shall seduce us. If we must lose,
Let's lose to a man, at least! Is a woman stronger than we?
    CHORAGOS. Unless time has rusted my wits,
What you say, King, is said with point and dignity.
    HAIMON (*boyishly earnest*). Father:
Reason is God's crowning gift to man, and you are right
To warn me against losing mine. I cannot say—
I hope that I shall never want to say!—that you
Have reasoned badly. Yet there are other men
Who can reason, too; and their opinions might be helpful.
You are not in a position to know everything
That people say or do, or what they feel:
Your temper terrifies them—everyone
Will tell you only what you like to hear.
But I, at any rate, can listen; and I have heard them
Muttering and whispering in the dark about this girl.
They say no woman has ever, so unreasonably,
Died so shameful a death for a generous act:
"She covered her brother's body. Is this indecent?

She kept him from dogs and vultures. Is this a crime?
Death?—She should have all the honor that we can give her!"

This is the way they talk out there in the city.
You must believe me:
Nothing is closer to me than your happiness.
What could be closer? Must not any son
Value his father's fortune as his father does his?
I beg you, do not be unchangeable:
Do not believe that you alone can be right.
The man who thinks that,
The man who maintains that only he has the power
To reason correctly, the gift to speak, the soul—
A man like that, when you know him, turns out empty.

It is not reason never to yield to reason!

In flood time you can see how some trees bend,
And because they bend, even their twigs are safe,
While stubborn trees are torn up, roots and all.
And the same thing happens in sailing:
Make your sheet fast, never slacken—and over you go,
Head over heels and under: and there's your voyage.
Forget you are angry! Let yourself be moved!
I know I am young; but please let me say this:
The ideal condition
Would be, I admit, that men should be right by instinct;
But since we are all too likely to go astray,
The reasonable thing is to learn from those who can teach.

CHORAGOS. You will do well to listen to him, King,
If what he says is sensible. And you, Haimon,
Must listen to your father.—Both speak well.

CREON. You consider it right for a man of my years and experience
To go to school to a boy?

HAIMON. It is not right
If I am wrong. But if I am young, and right,
What does my age matter?

CREON. You think it right to stand up for an anarchist?

HAIMON. Not at all. I pay no respect to criminals.

CREON. Then she is not a criminal?

HAIMON. The City would deny it, to a man.

CREON. And the City proposes to teach me how to rule?

HAIMON. Ah. Who is it that's talking like a boy now?

CREON. My voice is the one voice giving orders in this City!

HAIMON. It is no City if it takes orders from one voice.

CREON. The State is the King!
HAIMON. Yes, if the State is a desert.

(*Pause.*)

CREON. This boy, it seems, has sold out to a woman.
HAIMON. If you are a woman: my concern is only for you.
CREON. So? Your "concern"! In a public brawl with your father!
HAIMON. How about you, in a public brawl with justice?
CREON. With justice, when all that I do is within my rights?
HAIMON. You have no right to trample on God's right.
CREON (*completely out of control*). Fool, adolescent fool! Taken in by a woman!
HAIMON. You'll never see me taken in by anything vile.
CREON. Every word you say is for her!
HAIMON (*quickly, darkly*). And for you.
And for me. And for the gods under the earth.
CREON. You'll never marry her while she lives.
HAIMON. Then she must die.—But her death will cause another.
CREON. Another?
Have you lost your senses? Is this an open threat?
HAIMON. There is no threat in speaking to emptiness.
CREON. I swear you'll regret this superior tone of yours!
You are the empty one!
HAIMON. If you were not my father,
I'd say you were perverse.
CREON. You girlstruck fool, don't play at words with me!
HAIMON. I am sorry. You prefer silence.
CREON. Now, by God—!
I swear, by all the gods in heaven above us,
You'll watch it, I swear you shall!
(*To the* SERVANTS) Bring her out!
Bring the woman out! Let her die before his eyes!
Here, this instant, with her bridegroom beside her!
HAIMON. Not here, no; she will not die here, King.
And you will never see my face again.
Go on raving as long as you've a friend to endure you.

(*Exit* HAIMON.)

CHORAGOS. Gone, gone.
Creon, a young man in a rage is dangerous!
CREON. Let him do, or dream to do, more than a man can.
He shall not save these girls from death.
CHORAGOS. These girls?
You have sentenced them both?

CREON. No, you are right.
I will not kill the one whose hands are clean.
CHORAGOS. But Antigone?
CREON (*somberly*). I will carry her far away
Out there in the wilderness, and lock her
Living in a vault of stone. She shall have food,
As the custom is, to absolve the State of her death.
And there let her pray to the gods of hell:
They are her only gods:
Perhaps they will show her an escape from death,
Or she may learn,
though late,
That piety shown the dead is pity in vain.

(*Exit* CREON.)

ODE III

STROPHE

CHORUS. Love, unconquerable
Waster of rich men, keeper
Of warm lights and all-night vigil
In the soft face of a girl:
Sea-wanderer, forest-visitor!
Even the pure Immortals cannot escape you,
Any mortal man, in his one day's dusk,
Trembles before your glory.

ANTISTROPHE

Surely you swerve upon ruin
The just man's consenting heart,
As here you have made bright anger
Strike between father and son—
And none has conquered but Love!
A girl's glánce wórking the will of heaven:
Pleasure to her alone who mocks us,
Merciless Aphrodite.[2]

SCENE IV

(*As* ANTIGONE *enters guarded.*)

[2]Aphrodite: goddess of love

CHORAGOS. But I can no longer stand in awe of this,
Nor, seeing what I see, keep back my tears.
Here is Antigone, passing to that chamber
Where all find sleep at last.

STROPHE 1

ANTIGONE. Look upon me, friends, and pity me
Turning back at the night's edge to say
Good-by to the sun that shines for me no longer;
Now sleepy Death
Summons me down to Acheron,[3] that cold shore:
There is no bridesong there, nor any music.
CHORUS. Yet not unpraised, not without a kind of honor,
You walk at last into the underworld;
Untouched by sickness, broken by no sword.
What woman has ever found your way to death?

ANTISTROPHE 1

ANTIGONE. How often I have heard the story of Niobe,[4]
Tantalos' wretched daughter, how the stone
Clung fast about her, ivy-close: and they say
The rain falls endlessly
And sifting soft snow; her tears are never done.
I feel the loneliness of her death in mine.
CHORUS. But she was born of heaven, and you
Are woman, woman-born. If her death is yours,
A mortal woman's, is this not for you
Glory in our world and in the world beyond?

STROPHE 2

ANTIGONE. You laugh at me. Ah, friends, friends,
Can you not wait until I am dead? O Thebes,
O men many-charioted, in love with Fortune,
Dear springs of Dirce, sacred Theban grove,
Be witnesses for me, denied all pity,
Unjustly judged! and think a word of love
For her whose path turns

[3] Acheron: a river in Hades

[4] Niobe: an early queen of Thebes who, grief stricken over the death of her children, was turned by Zeus into a statue—a stone from which tears continued to flow.

Under dark earth, where there are no more tears.
CHORUS. You have passed beyond human daring and come at last
Into a place of stone where Justice sits.
I cannot tell
What shape of your father's guilt appears in this.

ANTISTROPHE 2

ANTIGONE. You have touched it at last: that bridal bed
Unspeakable, horror of son and mother mingling:
Their crime, infection of all our family!
O Oedipus, father and brother!
Your marriage strikes from the grave to murder mine.
I have been a stranger here in my own land:
All my life
The blasphemy of my birth has followed me.
CHORUS. Reverence is a virtue, but strength
Lives in established law: that must prevail.
You have made your choice,
Your death is the doing of your conscious hand.

EPODE

ANTIGONE. Then let me go, since all your words are bitter,
And the very light of the sun is cold to me.
Lead me to my vigil, where I must have
Neither love nor lamentation; no song, but silence.

(CREON *interrupts impatiently*.)

CREON. If dirges and planned lamentations could put off death,
Men would be singing for ever.
(*To the* SERVANTS) Take her, go!
You know your orders: take her to the vault
And leave her alone there. And if she lives or dies;
That's her affair, not ours; our hands are clean.
ANTIGONE. O tomb, vaulted bride-bed in eternal rock,
Soon I shall be with my own again
Where Persephone[5] welcomes the thin ghosts underground:
And I shall see my father again, and you, mother,
And dearest Polyneices—
dearest indeed
To me, since it was my hand

[5] Persephone: queen of the underworld

That washed him clean and poured the ritual wine:
And my reward is death before my time!

And yet, as men's hearts know, I have done no wrong,
I have not sinned before God. Or if I have,
I shall know the truth in death. But if the guilt
Lies upon Creon who judged me, then, I pray,
May his punishment equal my own.

CHORAGOS. O passionate heart,
Unyielding, tormented still by the same winds!

CREON. Her guards shall have good cause to regret their delaying.

ANTIGONE. Ah! That voice is like the voice of death!

CREON. I can give you no reason to think you are mistaken.

ANTIGONE. Thebes, and you my fathers' gods,
And rulers of Thebes, you see me now, the last
Unhappy daughter of a line of kings,
Your kings, led away to death. You will remember
Because I would not transgress the laws of heaven.
What things I suffer, and at what men's hands,
(*To the* GUARDS, *simply*) Come: let us wait no longer.

(*Exit* ANTIGONE, *L., guarded.*)

ODE IV

STROPHE 1

CHORUS. All Danae's[6] beauty was locked away
In a brazen cell where the sunlight could not come:
A small room, still as any grave, enclosed her.
Yet she was a princess too,
And Zeus in a rain of gold poured love upon her.
O child, child,
No power in wealth or war
Or tough sea-blackened ships
Can prevail against untiring Destiny!

ANTISTROPHE 1

And Dryas' son[7] also, that furious king,
Bore the god's prisoning anger for his pride:

6 Danae: Danae was imprisoned by her father in a bronze chamber to prevent her from having a lover, but Zeus visited her in a golden shower and fathered her son, Perseus.

7 Dryas' son: Lycurgus, King of Thrace, for attempting to suppress the worship of Dionysus, was driven mad by the god and imprisoned in a cave.

Sealed up by Dionysos in deaf stone,
His madness died among echoes.
So at the last he learned what dreadful power
His tongue had mocked:
For he had profaned the revels,
And fired the wrath of the nine
Implacable Sisters[8] that love the sound of the flute.

STROPHE 2

And old men tell a half-remembered tale[9]
Of horror done where a dark ledge splits the sea
And a double surf beats on the gráy shóres:
How a king's new woman, sick
With hatred for the queen he had imprisoned,
Ripped out his two sons' eyes with her bloody hands
While grinning Ares[10] watched the shuttle plunge
Four times: four blind wounds crying for revenge,

ANTISTROPHE 2

Crying, tears and blood mingled.—Piteously born,
Those sons whose mother was of heavenly birth!
Her father was the god of the North Wind
And she was cradled by gales,
She raced with young colts on the glittering hills
And walked untrammeled in the open light:
But in her marriage deathless Fate found means
To build a tomb like yours for all her joy.

SCENE V

(*Enter blind* Teiresias,[11] *led by a boy. The opening speeches of* Teiresias *should be in singsong contrast to the realistic lines of* Creon.)

Teiresias. This is the way the blind man comes, Princes, Princes,
Lock-step, two heads lit by the eyes of one.

Creon. What new thing have you to tell us, old Teiresias?

[8] Sisters: the nine Muses

[9] tale: Phineus, King of Thrace, after having two sons by his first wife, Cleopatra, daughter of Boreas, god of the North Wind, imprisoned her and married again. His second wife blinded Cleopatra's two sons.

[10] Ares: the home of Ares, god of war, was in Thrace.

[11] Teiresias: a prophet who foretold the future by listening to the cries of birds and interpreting other signs and omens.

TEIRESIAS. I have much to tell you: listen to the prophet, Creon.
CREON. I am not aware that I have ever failed to listen.
TEIRESIAS. Then you have done wisely, King, and ruled well.
CREON. I admit my debt to you. But what have you to say?
TEIRESIAS. This, Creon: you stand once more on the edge of fate.
CREON. What do you mean? Your words are a kind of dread.
TEIRESIAS. Listen, Creon:
I was sitting in my chair of augury, at the place
Where the birds gather about me. They were all a-chatter,
As is their habit, when suddenly I heard
A strange note in their jangling, a scream, a
Whirring fury; I knew that they were fighting,
Tearing each other, dying
In a whirlwind of wings clashing. And I was afraid.
I began the rites of burnt-offering at the altar,
But Hephaistos[12] failed me: instead of bright flame,
There was only the sputtering slime of the fat thigh-flesh
Melting: the entrails dissolved in gray smoke,
The bare bone burst from the welter. And no blaze!

This was a sign from heaven. My boy described it,
Seeing for me as I see for others.

I tell you, Creon, you yourself have brought
This new calamity upon us. Our hearths and altars
Are stained with the corruption of dogs and carrion birds
That glut themselves on the corpse of Oedipus' son.
The gods are deaf when we pray to them, their fire
Recoils from our offering, their birds of omen
Have no cry of comfort, for they are gorged
With the thick blood of the dead.
O my son,
These are no trifles! Think: all men make mistakes,
But a good man yields when he knows his course is wrong,
And repairs the evil. The only crime is pride.

Give in to the dead man, then: do not fight with a corpse—
What glory is it to kill a man who is dead?
Think, I beg you:
It is for your own good that I speak as I do.
You should be able to yield for your own good.

CREON. It seems that prophets have made me their especial province.
All my life long

12 Hephaistos: god of fire

I have been a kind of butt for the dull arrows
Of doddering fortune-tellers!
No, Teiresias:
If your birds—if the great eagles of God himself
Should carry him stinking bit by bit to heaven,
I would not yield. I am not afraid of pollution:
No man can defile the gods.
Do what you will,
Go into business, make money, speculate
In India gold or that synthetic gold from Sardis,
Get rich otherwise than by my consent to bury him.
Teiresias, it is a sorry thing when a wise man
Sells his wisdom, lets out his words for hire!

TEIRESIAS. Ah Creon! Is there no man left in the world—

CREON. To do what?—Come, let's have the aphorism!

TEIRESIAS. No man who knows that wisdom outweighs any wealth?

CREON. As surely as bribes are baser than any baseness.

TEIRESIAS. You are sick, Creon! You are deathly sick!

CREON. As you say: it is not my place to challenge a prophet.

TEIRESIAS. Yet you have said my prophecy is for sale.

CREON. The generation of prophets has always loved gold.

TEIRESIAS. The generation of kings has always loved brass.

CREON. You forget yourself! You are speaking to your King.

TEIRESIAS. I know it. You are a king because of me.

CREON. You have a certain skill; but you have sold out.

TEIRESIAS. King, you will drive me to words that—

CREON. Say them, say them!
Only remember: I will not pay you for them.

TEIRESIAS. No, you will find them too costly.

CREON. No doubt. Speak:
Whatever you say, you will not change my will.

TEIRESIAS. Then take this, and take it to heart!
The time is not far off when you shall pay back
Corpse for corpse, flesh of your own flesh.
You have thrust the child of this world into living night,
You have kept from the gods below the child that is theirs:
The one in a grave before her death, the other,
Dead, denied the grave. This is your crime:
And the Furies and the dark gods of Hell
Are swift with terrible punishment for you.
Do you want to buy me now, Creon?
Not many days,
And your house will be full of men and women weeping,

And curses will be hurled at you from far
Cities grieving for sons unburied, left to rot
Before the walls of Thebes.

These are my arrows, Creon: they are all for you.

(*To* Boy) But come, child: lead me home.
Let him waste his fine anger upon younger men.
Maybe he will learn at last
To control a wiser tongue in a better head.

(*Exit* Teiresias.)

Choragos. The old man has gone, King, but his words
Remain to plague us. I am old, too,
But I cannot remember that he was ever false.
Creon. That is true. . . . It troubles me.
Oh it is hard to give in! but it is worse
To risk everything for stubborn pride.
Choragos. Creon: take my advice.
Creon. What shall I do?
Choragos. Go quickly: free Antigone from her vault
And build a tomb for the body of Polyneices.
Creon. You would have me do this?
Choragos. Creon, yes!
And it must be done at once: God moves
Swiftly to cancel the folly of stubborn men.
Creon. It is hard to deny the heart! But I
Will do it: I will not fight with destiny.
Choragos. You must go yourself, you cannot leave it to others.
Creon. I will go.
—Bring axes, servants:
Come with me to the tomb. I buried her, I
Will set her free.
Oh, quickly!
My mind misgives—
The laws of the gods are mighty, and a man must serve them
To the last day of his life!

(*Exit* Creon.)

PAEAN[13]

STROPHE 1

[13] Paean: here, a hymn of invocation petitioning a god for healing

CHORAGOS. God of many names[14]
CHORUS. O Iacchos
son
of Kadmeian Sémele
O born of the Thunder!
Guardian of the West
Regent
of Eleusis' plain
O Prince of maenad Thebes
and the Dragon Field by rippling Ismenos:

ANTISTROPHE 1

CHORAGOS. God of many names
CHORUS. the flame of torches
flares on our hills
the nymphs of Iacchos
dance at the spring of Castalia:

from the vine-close mountain
come ah come in ivy:
Evohé evohé! sings through the streets of Thebes

STROPHE 2

CHORAGOS. God of many names
CHORUS. Iacchos of Thebes
heavenly Child
of Sémele bride of the Thunderer!
The shadow of plague is upon us:
come
with clement feet
oh come from Parnasos
down the long slopes
across the lamenting water

ANTISTROPHE 2

CHORAGOS. Io Fire! Chorister of the throbbing stars!
O purest among the voices of the night!

[14] God . . . names: Iacchos, the god of wine, son of Zeus and Semele, also known as Bacchos and Dionysos. Dionysian rites were performed on the plain of Eleusis, west of Athens. The priestesses of Dionysos, known as *Maenads,* celebrated the festivals of their god with frenzied dances, shouting "Evohé!" and "Io!"—cries of rapture. Mount Parnasos was sacred to Dionysos; the spring of Castalia, sacred to the Muses, was beside it.

Thou son of God, blaze for us!
Chorus. Come with choric rapture of circling Maenads
Who cry *Io Iacche!*
God of many names!

ÉXODOS[15]

(*Enter* Messenger, L.)

Messenger. Men of the line of Kadmos,[16] you who live
Near Amphion's[17] citadel:
I cannot say
Of any condition of human life "This is fixed,
This is clearly good, or bad." Fate raises up,
And Fate casts down the happy and unhappy alike:
No man can foretell his Fate.
Take the case of Creon:
Creon was happy once, as I count happiness:
Victorious in battle, sole governor of the land,
Fortunate father of children nobly born.
And now it has all gone from him! Who can say
That a man is still alive when his life's joy fails?
He is a walking dead man. Grant him rich,
Let him live like a king in his great house:
If his pleasure is gone, I would not give
So much as the shadow of smoke for all he owns.
Choragos. Your words hint at sorrow: what is your news for us?
Messenger. They are dead. The living are guilty of their death.
Choragos. Who is guilty? Who is dead? Speak!
Messenger. Haimon.
Haimon is dead; and the hand that killed him
Is his own hand.
Choragos. His father's? or his own?
Messenger. His own, driven mad by the murder his father had done.
Choragos. Teiresias, Teiresias, how clearly you saw it all!
Messenger. This is my news: you must draw what conclusions you can from it.
Choragos. But look: Eurydice, our Queen:
Has she overheard us?

[15] Éxodos: final scene
[16] Kadmos: father of Semele, he was the founder and first king of Thebes, and he built the upper part of the city.
[17] Amphion: a gifted musician who built the lower city to the sound of his lyre.

(*Enter* EURYDICE *from the Palace, C.*)

EURYDICE. I have heard something, friends:
As I was unlocking the gate of Pallas'[18] shrine,
For I needed her help today, I heard a voice
Telling of some new sorrow. And I fainted
There at the temple with all my maidens about me.
But speak again: whatever it is, I can bear it:
Grief and I are no strangers.

MESSENGER. Dearest Lady,
I will tell you plainly all that I have seen.
I shall not try to comfort you: what is the use,
Since comfort could lie only in what is not true?
The truth is always best.
I went with Creon
To the outer plain where Polyneices was lying,
No friend to pity him, his body shredded by dogs.
We made our prayers in that place to Hecate[19]
And Pluto,[20] that they would be merciful. And we bathed
The corpse with holy water, and we brought
Fresh-broken branches to burn what was left of it,
And upon the urn we heaped up a towering barrow
Of the earth of his own land.
When we were done, we ran
To the vault where Antigone lay on her couch of stone.
One of the servants had gone ahead,
And while he was yet far off he heard a voice
Grieving within the chamber, and he came back
And told Creon. And as the King went closer,
The air was full of wailing, the words lost,
And he begged us to make all haste. "Am I a prophet?"
He said, weeping, "And must I walk this road,
The saddest of all that I have gone before?
My son's voice calls me on. Oh quickly, quickly!
Look through the crevice there, and tell me
If it is Haimon, or some deception of the gods!"
We obeyed; and in the cavern's farthest corner
We saw her lying:
She had made a noose of her fine linen veil
And hanged herself. Haimon lay beside her,
His arms about her waist, lamenting her,

[18] Pallas: Athena, goddess of wisdom
[19] Hecate: goddess of the underworld
[20] Pluto: god of the underworld

His love lost under ground, crying out
That his father had stolen her away from him.
When Creon saw him the tears rushed to his eyes
And he called to him: "What have you done, child? Speak to me.
What are you thinking that makes your eyes so strange?
O my son, my son, I come to you on my knees!"
But Haimon spat in his face. He said not a word,
Staring—
        And suddenly drew his sword
And lunged. Creon shrank back, the blade missed; and the boy,
Desperate against himself, drove it half its length
Into his own side, and fell. And as he died
He gathered Antigone close in his arms again,
Choking, his blood bright red on her white cheek.
And now he lies dead with the dead, and she is his
At last, his bride in the houses of the dead.

(*Exit* EURYDICE *into the Palace.*)

CHORAGOS. She has left us without a word. What can this mean?
MESSENGER. It troubles me, too; yet she knows what is best,
Her grief is too great for public lamentation,
And doubtless she has gone to her chamber to weep
For her dead son, leading her maidens in his dirge.
CHORAGOS. It may be so: but I fear this deep silence.

(*Pause.*)

MESSENGER. I will see what she is doing. I will go in.

(*Exit* MESSENGER *into the Palace.*)

(*Enter* CREON *with attendants, bearing* HAIMON'S *body.*)

CHORAGOS. But here is the King himself: oh look at him,
Bearing his own damnation in his arms.
CREON. Nothing you say can touch me any more.
My own blind heart has brought me
From darkness to final darkness. Here you see
The father murdering, the murdered son—
And all my civic wisdom!

Haimon my son, so young, so young to die,
I was the fool, not you; and you died for me.
CHORAGOS. That is the truth; but you were late in learning it.
CREON. This truth is hard to bear. Surely a god
Has crushed me beneath the hugest weight of heaven.

And driven me headlong a barbaric way
To trample out the thing I held most dear.

The pains that men will take to come to pain!

(*Enter* MESSENGER *from the Palace.*)

MESSENGER. The burden you carry in your hands is heavy,
But it is not all: you will find more in your house.
CREON. What burden worse than this shall I find there?
MESSENGER. The Queen is dead.
CREON. O port of death, deaf world,
Is there no pity for me? And you, Angel of evil,
I was dead, and your words are death again.
Is it true, boy? Can it be true?
Is my wife dead? Has death bred death?
MESSENGER. You can see for yourself.

(*The doors are opened, and the body of* EURYDICE *is disclosed within.*)

CREON. Oh pity!
All true, all true, and more than I can bear!
O my wife, my son!
MESSENGER. She stood before the altar, and her heart
Welcomed the knife her own hand guided,
And a great cry burst from her lips for Megareus[21] dead,
And for Haimon dead, her sons; and her last breath
Was a curse for their father, the murderer of her sons.
And she fell, and the dark flowed in through her closing eyes.
CREON. O God, I am sick with fear.
Are there no swords here? Has no one a blow for me?
MESSENGER. Her curse is upon you for the deaths of both.
CREON. It is right that it should be. I alone am guilty.
I know it, and I say it. Lead me in,
Quickly, friends.
I have neither life nor substance. Lead me in.
CHORAGOS. You are right, if there can be right in so much wrong.
The briefest way is best in a world of sorrow.
CREON. Let it come,
Let death come quickly, and be kind to me.
I would not ever see the sun again.
CHORAGOS. All that will come when it will; but we, meanwhile,
Have much to do. Leave the future to itself.

[21] Megareus: during the siege of Thebes, Creon's son Megareus sacrificed himself to appease the wrath of the gods.

CREON. All my heart was in that prayer!
CHORAGOS. Then do not pray any more: the sky is deaf.
CREON. Lead me away. I have been rash and foolish.
I have killed my son and my wife.
I look for comfort; my comfort lies here dead.
Whatever my hands have touched has come to nothing.
Fate has brought all my pride to a thought of dust.

(As CREON *is being led into the house, the* CHORAGOS *advances and speaks directly to the audience.)*

CHORAGOS. There is no happiness where there is no wisdom;
No wisdom but in submission to the gods.
Big words are always punished,
And proud men in old age learn to be wise.

QUESTIONS

1. By the end of Scene II, the central conflict of the play is fully defined. What is it? Is it of purely historical interest, or is it a conflict that can be related to vital issues of today? To what extent may it be identified with modern ideas of "law and order" and "civil disobedience"?

2. From what theory of kingship does Creon act? To what extent is his theory supported or opposed by other characters in the play, such as the Chorus and Haimon? Can we make any inferences about the legitimacy of Creon's rule in Sophocles's eyes?

3. Is the conflict between Antigone and Creon one of good versus evil, or one of contradictory ideas about good? What is Creon's motivation in refusing to allow Polyneices to receive a proper burial? Is it a worthy motivation? Are the considerations involved in Creon's decision of historical interest alone, or are they also of vital interest today? How do they relate to the decisions that any victorious party or nation must make after a civil or international conflict? How do they relate to ideas about punishment in general?

4. What is Antigone's motivation in defying Creon's edict? Is it a worthy one? Discuss.

5. Discuss Antigone's character. What do her defiance of Creon, her behavior toward Ismene, and the attitudes of Ismene and Haimon toward her reveal about her character? How does Sophocles want us to feel toward her? Is she a virtuous and innocent victim, or does she, like Creon, have a tragic flaw? (Among critics, there has been much disagreement about this.)

6. Discuss Creon's character. Assuming that in issuing his decree, Creon acts out of genuine conviction as to what is best for the city, does he exhibit any defects of character in making that decision or in carrying it out? At what points in the action do flaws in his character become apparent? At what points,

and why, does he change? In the Exodos, why does he bury Polyneices *before* going to free Antigone? What is it that he learns too late?

7. What kind of person is Ismene? Why does she refuse to help Antigone at first? Why does she change later on? What is her role in the play?

8. In Scene III, in what conflict of loyalties is Haimon caught? What is his attitude toward his father? How does he handle his conflict? What is his role in the play?

9. What function does Teiresias serve in the play?

10. In the conflict between Antigone and Creon, with which side does the Chorus sympathize? If we regard the Chorus as a character, what kind of character is it? Is it a static or developing character? How does it change? Does it speak for Sophocles at any point in the play?

11. Relate the subject matter of each of the Odes and of the Paean to the dramatic action.

12. Critics have disagreed as to whether Antigone or Creon is the protagonist of the play. What arguments can be advanced for each point of view? To what extent does each character fulfill Aristotle's requirements for a tragic hero?

13. For an audience familiar with the outcome of the play, which of Creon's speeches exhibit dramatic irony—that is, which have a different or larger meaning for the audience than for Creon himself?

William Shakespeare

OTHELLO

CHARACTERS

DUKE OF VENICE
BRABANTIO, *a Senator*
OTHER SENATORS
GRATIANO, *brother to Brabantio*
LODOVICO, *kinsman to Brabantio*
OTHELLO, *a noble Moor in the service of the Venetian state*
CASSIO, *his lieutenant*
IAGO, *his ancient*
MONTANO, *Othello's predecessor in the government of Cyprus*
RODERIGO, *a Venetian gentleman*
CLOWN, *servant to Othello*
DESDEMONA, *daughter to Brabantio and wife to Othello*
EMILIA, *wife to Iago*
BIANCA, *mistress to Cassio*
SAILOR, MESSENGER, HERALD, OFFICERS, GENTLEMEN, MUSICIANS, *and* ATTENDANTS

SCENE. *Venice; a seaport in Cyprus.*

ACT I

SCENE I. Venice. A street.

Enter RODERIGO *and* IAGO.

RODERIGO. Tush, never tell me. I take it much unkindly
That thou, Iago, who hast had my purse
As if the strings were thine, shouldst know of this.
IAGO. 'Sblood, but you will not hear me.
If ever I did dream of such a matter,
Abhor me.
RODERIGO. Thou told'st me thou didst hold him in thy hate.
IAGO. Despise me if I do not. Three great ones of the city,
In personal suit to make me his Lieutenant,
Off-capped to him. And, by the faith of man,
I know my price, I am worth no worse a place.
But he, as loving his own pride and purposes,

Evades them, with a bombast circumstance
Horribly stuffed with epithets of war.
And, in conclusion,
Nonsuits° my mediators, for, "Certes," says he,
"I have already chose my officer."
And what was he?
Forsooth, a great arithmetician,°
One Michael Cassio, a Florentine,
A fellow almost damned in a fair wife,°
That never set a squadron in the field,
Nor the division of a battle knows
More than a spinster, unless the bookish theoric,
Wherein the toged Consuls° can propose
As masterly as he—mere prattle without practice
Is all his soldiership. But he, sir, had the election.
And I, of whom his eyes had seen the proof
At Rhodes, at Cyprus, and on other grounds
Christian and heathen, must be beleed° and calmed
By debitor and creditor. This countercaster,°
He, in good time,° must his Lieutenant be,
And I—God bless the mark!—his Moorship's Ancient.°

RODERIGO. By Heaven, I rather would have been his hangman.

IAGO. Why, there's no remedy. 'Tis the course of service,
Preferment goes by letter and affection,
And not by old gradation,° where each second
Stood heir to the first. Now, sir, be judge yourself
Whether I in any just term am affined°
To love the Moor.

RODERIGO. I would not follow him, then.

IAGO. Oh, sir, content you,
I follow him to serve my turn upon him.
We cannot all be masters, nor all masters
Cannot be truly followed. You shall mark

16. Nonsuits: rejects the petition of. **19. arithmetician:** Contemporary books on military tactics are full of elaborate diagrams and numerals to explain military formations. Cassio is a student of such books. **21. almost . . . wife:** A much-disputed phrase. There is an Italian proverb, "You have married a fair wife? You are damned." If Iago has this in mind, he means by *almost* that Cassio is about to marry. **25. toged Consuls:** councilors in togas [L.P.]. **30. beleed:** placed on the lee (or unfavorable) side. **31. countercaster:** calculator (repeating the idea of arithmetician). Counters were used in making calculations. **32. in . . . time:** A phrase expressing indignation. **33. Ancient:** ensign, the third officer in the company of which Othello is Captain and Cassio Lieutenant. **36–37. Preferment . . . gradation:** promotion comes through private recommendation and favoritism and not by order of seniority. **39. affined:** tied by affection.

Many a duteous and knee-crooking knave
That doting on his own obsequious bondage
Wears out his time, much like his master's ass,
For naught but provender, and when he's old, cashiered.
Whip me such honest knaves. Others there are
Who, trimmed in forms and visages of duty,
Keep yet their hearts attending on themselves,
And throwing but shows of service on their lords
Do well thrive by them, and when they have lined their coats
Do themselves homage. These fellows have some soul,
And such a one do I profess myself. For, sir,
It is as sure as you are Roderigo,
Were I the Moor, I would not be Iago.
In following him, I follow but myself.
Heaven is my judge, not I for love and duty,
But seeming so, for my peculiar° end.
For when my outward action doth demonstrate
The native act and figure of my heart
In compliment extern, 'tis not long after
But I will wear my heart upon my sleeve
For daws to peck at. I am not what I am.

RODERIGO. What a full fortune does the thick-lips owe°
If he can carry 't thus!°

IAGO. Call up her father,
Rouse him. Make after him, poison his delight,
Proclaim him in the streets. Incense her kinsmen,
And though he in a fertile climate dwell,
Plague him with flies. Though that his joy be joy,
Yet throw such changes of vexation on 't
As it may lose some color.

RODERIGO. Here is her father's house, I'll call aloud.

IAGO. Do, with like timorous° accent and dire yell
As when, by night and negligence, the fire
Is spied in populous cities.

RODERIGO. What ho, Brabantio! Signior Brabantio, ho!

IAGO. Awake! What ho, Brabantio! Thieves! Thieves! Thieves!
Look to your house, your daughter and your bags!°
Thieves! Thieves!

(BRABANTIO *appears above, at a window.*)

BRABANTIO. What is the reason of this terrible summons?
What is the matter there?

60. peculiar: personal [L.P.]. **66. owe:** own. **67. carry't thus:** i.e., bring off this marriage. **75. timorous:** terrifying. **80. bags:** moneybags.

RODERIGO. Signior, is all your family within?
IAGO. Are your doors locked?
BRABANTIO. Why, wherefore ask you this?
IAGO. 'Zounds, sir, you're robbed. For shame, put on your gown,
Your heart is burst, you have lost half your soul.
Even now, now, very now, an old black ram
Is tupping your white ewe. Arise, arise,
Awake the snorting° citizens with the bell,
Or else the Devil° will make a grandsire of you.
Arise, I say.
BRABANTIO. What, have you lost your wits?
RODERIGO. Most reverend signior, do you know my voice?
BRABANTIO. Not I. What are you?
RODERIGO. My name is Roderigo.
BRABANTIO. The worser welcome.
I have charged thee not to haunt about my doors.
In honest plainness thou hast heard me say
My daughter is not for thee, and now, in madness,
Being full of supper and distempering draughts,
Upon malicious bravery° dost thou come
To start° my quiet.
RODERIGO. Sir, sir, sir—
BRABANTIO. But thou must needs be sure
My spirit and my place have in them power
To make this bitter to thee.
RODERIGO. Patience, good sir.
BRABANTIO. What tell'st thou me of robbing? This is Venice,
My house is not a grange.°
RODERIGO. Most grave Brabantio,
In simple and pure soul I come to you.

IAGO. 'Zounds, sir, you are one of those that will not serve God if the Devil bid you. Because we come to do you service and you think we are ruffians, you'll have your daughter covered with a Barbary° horse, you'll have your nephews° neigh to you, you'll have coursers for cousins,° and jennets° for germans.°

BRABANTIO. What profane wretch art thou?

IAGO. I am one, sir, that comes to tell you your daughter and the Moor are now making the beast with two backs.

BRABANTIO. Thou art a villain.
IAGO. You are—a Senator.

90. snorting: snoring. **91. Devil:** The Devil in old pictures and woodcuts was represented as black. **100. bravery:** defiance. **101. start:** startle. **106. grange:** lonely farm. **110. Barbary:** Moorish. **111. nephews:** grandsons. **cousins:** near relations. **112. jennets:** Moorish ponies. **germans:** kinsmen.

Brabantio. This thou shalt answer. I know thee, Roderigo.
Roderigo. Sir, I will answer anything. But I beseech you
If 't be your pleasure and most wise consent,
As partly I find it is, that your fair daughter,
At this odd-even° and dull watch o' the night,
Transported with no worse nor better guard
But with a knave of common hire, a gondolier,
To the gross clasps of a lascivious Moor—
If this be known to you, and your allowance,°
We then have done you bold and saucy wrongs.
But if you know not this, my manners tell me
We have your wrong rebuke. Do not believe
That from the sense of all civility
I thus would play and trifle with your reverence.
Your daughter, if you have not given her leave,
I say again, hath made a gross revolt,
Tying her duty, beauty, wit, and fortunes
In an extravagant° and wheeling° stranger
Of here and everywhere. Straight satisfy yourself.
If she be in her chamber or your house,
Let loose on me the justice of the state
For thus deluding you.
Brabantio. Strike on the tinder,° ho!
Give me a taper!° Call up all my people!
This accident is not unlike my dream.
Belief of it oppresses me already.
Light, I say! Light!

(*Exit above.*)

Iago. Farewell, for I must leave you.
It seems not meet, nor wholesome to my place,°
To be produced—as if I stay I shall—
Against the Moor. For I do know the state,
However this may gall him with some check,
Cannot with safety cast° him. For he's embarked
With such loud reason to the Cyprus wars,
Which even now stand in act, that, for their souls,
Another of his fathom they have none
To lead their business. In which regard,
Though I do hate him as I do Hell pains,

121. odd-even: about midnight. **125. your allowance:** by your permission. **134. extravagant:** vagabond. **wheeling:** wandering. **138. tinder:** the primitive method of making fire, used before the invention of matches. **139. taper:** candle. **144. place:** i.e., as Othello's officer. **148. cast:** dismiss from service.

Yet for necessity of present life
I must show out a flag and sign of love,
Which is indeed but sign. That you shall surely find him,
Lead to the Sagittary° the raisèd search,
And there will I be with him. So farewell. (*Exit.*)

(*Enter, below,* BRABANTIO, *in his nightgown, and* SERVANTS *with torches.*)

BRABANTIO. It is too true an evil. Gone she is,
And what's to come of my despisèd time
Is naught but bitterness. Now, Roderigo,
Where didst thou see her? Oh, unhappy girl!
With the Moor, say'st thou? Who would be a father!
How didst thou know 'twas she? Oh, she deceives me
Past thought! What said she to you? Get more tapers.
Raise all my kindred. Are they married, think you?

RODERIGO. Truly, I think they are.

BRABANTIO. Oh Heaven! How got she out? Oh, treason of the blood!
Fathers, from hence trust not your daughters' minds
By what you see them act. Are there not charms°
By which the property° of youth and maidhood
May be abused?° Have you not read, Roderigo,
Of some such thing?

RODERIGO. Yes, sir, I have indeed.

BRABANTIO. Call up my brother. Oh, would you had had her!
Some one way, some another. Do you know
Where we may apprehend her and the Moor?

RODERIGO. I think I can discover him, if you please
To get good guard and go along with me.

BRABANTIO. Pray you, lead on. At every house I'll call,
I may command° at most. Get weapons, ho!
And raise some special officers of night.
On, good Roderigo, I'll deserve your pains.°

(*Exeunt.*)

SCENE II. Another street.

Enter OTHELLO, IAGO, *and* ATTENDANTS *with torches.*

157. Sagittary: presumably some building in Venice, not identified, used as a meeting place for the Council. **170. charms:** magic spells. **171. property:** nature. **172. abused:** deceived. **180. command:** find supporters. **182. deserve . . . pains:** reward your labor.

IAGO. Though in the trade of war I have slain men,
Yet do I hold it very stuff o' the conscience
To do no contrivèd murder. I lack iniquity
Sometimes to do me service. Nine or ten times
I had thought to have yerked him here under the ribs.

OTHELLO. 'Tis better as it is.

IAGO. Nay, but he prated
And spoke such scurvy and provoking terms
Against your honor
That, with the little godliness I have,
I did full hard forbear him. But I pray you, sir,
Are you fast married? Be assured of this,
That the Magnifico is much beloved,
And hath in his effect a voice potential
As double as° the Duke's. He will divorce you,
Or put upon you what restraint and grievance
The law, with all his might to enforce it on,
Will give him cable.

OTHELLO. Let him do his spite.
My services which I have done the signiory°
Shall outtongue his complaints. 'Tis yet to know—
Which, when I know that boasting is an honor,
I shall promulgate—I fetch my life and being
From men of royal siege, and my demerits°
May speak unbonneted to as proud a fortune
As this that I have reached. For know, Iago,
But that I love the gentle Desdemona,
I would not my unhousèd° free condition
Put into circumscription and confine
For the sea's worth. But look! What lights come yond?

IAGO. Those are the raisèd father and his friends.
You were best go in.

OTHELLO. Not I, I must be found.
My parts, my title, and my perfect° soul
Shall manifest me rightly. Is it they?

IAGO. By Janus, I think no.

(*Enter* CASSIO, *and certain* OFFICERS *with torches.*)

OTHELLO. The servants of the Duke, and my Lieutenant.
The goodness of the night upon you, friends!
What is the news?

13–14. potential . . . as: twice as powerful as. **18. signiory:** state of Venice. **22. demerits:** deserts. **26. unhousèd:** unmarried. **31. perfect:** ready.

CASSIO. The Duke does greet you, General
And he requires your haste-posthaste appearance,
Even on the instant.
OTHELLO. What is the matter, think you?
CASSIO. Something from Cyprus, as I may divine.
It is a business of some heat. The galleys
Have sent a dozen sequent messengers
This very night at one another's heels,
And many of the consuls, raised and met,
Are at the Duke's already. You have been hotly called for
When, being not at your lodging to be found,
The Senate hath sent about three several° quests
To search you out.
OTHELLO. 'Tis well I am found by you.
I will but spend a word here in the house
And go with you. (*Exit.*)
CASSIO. Ancient, what makes he here?
IAGO. Faith, he tonight hath boarded a land carrack.°
If it prove lawful prize, he's made forever.
CASSIO. I do not understand.
IAGO. He's married.
CASSIO. To who?

(*Re-enter* OTHELLO.)

IAGO. Marry, to—Come, Captain, will you go?
OTHELLO. Have with you.
CASSIO. Here comes another troop to seek for you.
IAGO. It is Brabantio. General, be advised,
He comes to bad intent.
(*Enter* BRABANTIO, RODERIGO, *and* OFFICERS *with torches and weapons.*)

OTHELLO. Holloa! Stand there!
RODERIGO. Signior, it is the Moor.
BRABANTIO. Down with him, thief!

(*They draw on both sides.*)

IAGO. You, Roderigo! Come, sir, I am for you.
OTHELLO. Keep up° your bright swords, for the dew will rust them.
Good signior, you shall more command with years
Than with your weapons.

46. several: separate. **50. carrack:** the largest type of Spanish merchant ship.
59. Keep up: sheathe.

BRABANTIO. O thou foul thief, where hast thou stowed my daughter?
Damned as thou art, thou hast enchanted her.
For I'll refer me to all things of sense
If she in chains of magic were not bound,
Whether a maid so tender, fair, and happy,
So opposite to marriage that she shunned
The wealthy curlèd darlings of our nation,
Would ever have, to incur a general mock,
Run from her guardage° to the sooty bosom
Of such a thing as thou, to fear, not to delight.
Judge me the world if 'tis not gross in sense
That thou hast practiced on her with foul charms,
Abused her delicate youth with drugs or minerals
That weaken motion.° I'll have 't disputed on,°
'Tis probable, and palpable to thinking.
I therefore apprehend and do attach° thee
For an abuser of the world, a practicer
Of arts inhibited and out of warrant.°
Lay hold upon him. If he do resist,
Subdue him at his peril.
OTHELLO. Hold your hands,
Both you of my inclining and the rest.
Were it my cue to fight, I should have known it
Without a prompter. Where will you that I go
To answer this your charge?
BRABANTIO. To prison, till fit time
Of law and course of direct session
Call thee to answer.
OTHELLO. What if I do obey?
How may the Duke be therewith satisfied,
Whose messengers are here about my side
Upon some present business of the state
To bring me to him?
FIRST OFFICER. 'Tis true, most worthy signior.
The Duke's in Council, and your noble self
I am sure is sent for.
BRABANTIO. How! The Duke in Council!
In this time of the night! Bring him away.
Mine's not an idle cause. The Duke himself,
Or any of my brothers of the state,
Cannot but feel this wrong as 'twere their own.

70. **guardage:** guardianship. 75. **motion:** sense. **disputed on:** argued in the law courts [L.P.]. 77. **attach:** arrest. 79. **inhibited . . . warrant:** forbidden and illegal [L.P.].

For if such actions may have passage free,
Bondslaves and pagans shall our statesmen be.

(*Exeunt.*)

SCENE III. A council chamber.

The DUKE *and* SENATORS *sitting at a table,* OFFICERS *attending.*

DUKE. There is no composition° in these news°
That gives them credit.
FIRST SENATOR. Indeed they are disproportioned.
My letters say a hundred and seven galleys.
DUKE. And mine, a hundred and forty.
SECOND SENATOR. And mine, two hundred.
But though they jump not on a just account°—
As in these cases, where the aim reports,°
'Tis oft with difference—yet do they all confirm
A Turkish fleet, and bearing up to Cyprus.
DUKE. Nay, it is possible enough to judgment.
I do not so secure me in the error,°
But the main article° I do approve
In fearful° sense.
SAILOR (*within*). What ho! What ho! What ho!
FIRST OFFICER. A messenger from the galleys.

(*Enter* SAILOR.)

DUKE. Now, what's the business
SAILOR. The Turkish preparation makes for Rhodes.
So was I bid report here to the state.
By Signior Angelo.
DUKE. How say you by this change?
FIRST SENATOR. This cannot be,
By no assay of reason. 'Tis a pageant
To keep us in false gaze. When we consider
The importancy of Cyprus to the Turk,
And let ourselves again but understand
That as it more concerns the Turk than Rhodes,
So may he with more facile question bear it,°

1. composition: agreement. **news:** reports. **5. jump . . . account:** do not agree with an exact estimate. **6. aim reports:** i.e., intelligence reports of an enemy's intention often differ in the details. **10. I . . . error:** I do not consider myself free from danger, because the reports may not all be accurate. **11. main article:** general report. **12. fearful:** to be feared. **23. with . . . it:** take it more easily.

For that it stands not in such warlike brace
But altogether lacks the abilities
That Rhodes is dressed in—if we make thought of this,
We must not think the Turk is so unskillful
To leave that latest which concerns him first,
Neglecting an attempt of ease and gain
To wake and wage a danger profitless.

DUKE. Nay, in all confidence, he's not for Rhodes.

FIRST OFFICER. Here is more news.

(*Enter a* MESSENGER.)

MESSENGER. The Ottomites,° Reverend and Gracious,
Steering with due course toward the isle of Rhodes,
Have there injointed° them with an after-fleet.°

FIRST SENATOR. Aye, so I thought. How many, as you guess?

MESSENGER. Of thirty sail. And now they do restem°
Their backward course, bearing with frank appearance
Their purposes toward Cyprus. Signior Montano,
Your trusty and most valiant servitor,
With his free duty recommends° you thus,
And prays you to believe him.

DUKE. 'Tis certain then for Cyprus.
Marcus Luccicos, is not he in town?

FIRST SENATOR. He's now in Florence.

DUKE. Write from us to him, post-posthaste dispatch.

FIRST SENATOR. Here comes Brabantio and the valiant Moor.

(*Enter* BRABANTIO, OTHELLO, IAGO, RODERIGO, *and* OFFICERS.)

DUKE. Valiant Othello, we must straight employ you
Against the general enemy Ottoman.
(*To* BRABANTIO) I did not see you. Welcome, gentle signior,
We lacked your counsel and your help tonight.

BRABANTIO. So did I yours. Good your Grace, pardon me,
Neither my place nor aught I heard of business
Hath raised me from my bed, nor doth the general care
Take hold on me. For my particular° grief
Is of so floodgate and o'erbearing nature
That it engluts and swallows other sorrows,
And it is still itself.

DUKE. Why, what's the matter?

BRABANTIO. My daughter! Oh, my daughter!

33. Ottomites: Turks. **35. injointed:** joined. **after-fleet:** second fleet. **37. restem:** steer again. **41. recommends:** advises [L.P.]. **55. particular:** personal.

ALL. Dead?
BRABANTIO. Aye, to me.
She is abused, stol'n from me and corrupted
By spells and medicines bought of mountebanks.
For nature so preposterously to err,
Being not deficient, blind, or lame of sense,
Sans witchcraft could not.
DUKE. Whoe'er he be that in this foul proceeding
Hath thus beguiled your daughter of herself
And you of her, the bloody book of law
You shall yourself read in the bitter letter
After your own sense—yea, though our proper° son
Stood in your action.
BRABANTIO. Humbly I thank your Grace.
Here is the man, this Moor, whom now, it seems,
Your special mandate for the state affairs
Hath hither brought.
ALL. We are very sorry for 't.
DUKE (*to* OTHELLO). What in your own part can you say to this?
BRABANTIO. Nothing but this is so.
OTHELLO. Most potent, grave, and reverend signiors,
My very noble and approved good masters,
That I have ta'en away this old man's daughter,
It is most true—true, I have married her.
The very head and front of my offending
Hath this extent, no more. Rude am I in my speech,
And little blest with the soft phrase of peace.
For since these arms of mine had seven years' pith
Till now some nine moons wasted, they have used
Their dearest action in the tented field.
And little of this great world can I speak,
More than pertains to feats of broil and battle,
And therefore little shall I grace my cause
In speaking for myself. Yet, by your gracious patience,
I will a round unvarnished tale deliver
Of my whole course of love—what drugs, what charms,
What conjuration and what mighty magic—
For such proceeding I am charged withal—
I won his daughter.
BRABANTIO. A maiden never bold,
Of spirit so still and quiet that her motion
Blushed at herself, and she—in spite of nature,

69. proper: own.

Of years, of country, credit,° everything—
To fall in love with what she feared to look on!
It is a judgment maimed and most imperfect
That will confess perfection so could err
Against all rules of nature, and must be driven
To find out practices of cunning Hell
Why this should be. I therefore vouch again
That with some mixtures powerful o'er the blood,
Or with some dram conjured to this effect,
He wrought upon her.

DUKE. To vouch this is no proof
Without more certain and more overt test
Than these thin habits and poor likelihoods
Of modern seeming do prefer against him.

FIRST SENATOR. But, Othello, speak.
Did you by indirect and forcèd courses
Subdue and poison this young maid's affections?
Or came it by request, and such fair question
As soul to soul affordeth?

OTHELLO. I do beseech you
Send for the lady to the Sagittary,
And let her speak of me before her father.
If you do find me foul in her report,
The trust, the office I do hold of you,
Not only take away, but let your sentence
Even fall upon my life.

DUKE. Fetch Desdemona hither.

OTHELLO. Ancient, conduct them, you best know the place.

(*Exeunt* IAGO *and* ATTENDANTS.)

And till she come, as truly as to Heaven
I do confess the vices of my blood,
So justly to your grave ears I'll present
How I did thrive in this fair lady's love
And she in mine.

DUKE. Say it, Othello.

OTHELLO. Her father loved me, oft invited me,
Still questioned me the story of my life
From year to year, the battles, sieges, fortunes,
That I have passed.
I ran it through, even from my boyish days
To the very moment that he bade me tell it.

97. credit: reputation.

Wherein I spake of most disastrous chances,
Of moving accidents by flood and field,
Of hairbreadth 'scapes i' the imminent deadly breach,
Of being taken by the insolent foe
And sold to slavery, of my redemption thence,
And portance in my travels' history.
Wherein of antres° vast and deserts idle,
Rough quarries, rocks, and hills whose heads touch heaven,
It was my hint to speak—such was the process.
And of the cannibals that each other eat,
The anthropophagi,° and men whose heads
Do grow beneath their shoulders. This to hear
Would Desdemona seriously incline.
But still the house affairs would draw her thence,
Which ever as she could with haste dispatch,
She'd come again, and with a greedy ear
Devour up my discourse. Which I observing,
Took once a pliant hour and found good means
To draw from her a prayer of earnest heart
That I would all my pilgrimage dilate,
Whereof by parcels she had something heard,
But not intentively. I did consent,
And often did beguile her of her tears
When I did speak of some distressful stroke
That my youth suffered. My story being done,
She gave me for my pains a world of sighs.
She swore, in faith, 'twas strange, 'twas passing strange,
'Twas pitiful, 'twas wondrous pitiful.
She wished she had not heard it, yet she wished
That Heaven had made her° such a man. She thanked me,
And bade me, if I had a friend that loved her,
I should but teach him how to tell my story
And that would woo her. Upon this hint I spake.
She loved me for the dangers I had passed,
And I loved her that she did pity them.
This only is the witchcraft I have used.
Here comes the lady, let her witness it.

(*Enter* DESDEMONA, IAGO, *and* ATTENDANTS.)

DUKE. I think this tale would win my daughter too.
Good Brabantio,
Take up this mangled matter at the best.°

139. antres: caves. **143. anthropophagi:** cannibals. **162. her:** for her. **172. Take . . . best:** make the best settlement you can of this confused business.

Men do their broken weapons rather use
Than their bare hands.
BRABANTIO. I pray you hear her speak.
If she confess that she was half the wooer,
Destruction on my head if my bad blame
Light on the man! Come hither, gentle mistress.
Do you perceive in all this noble company
Where most you owe obedience?
DESDEMONA. My noble Father,
I do perceive here a divided duty.
To you I am bound for life and education,
My life and education both do learn me
How to respect you, you are the lord of duty,
I am hitherto your daughter. But here's my husband,
And so much duty as my mother showed
To you, preferring you before her father
So much I challenge that I may profess
Due to the Moor my lord.
BRABANTIO. God be with you! I have done.
Please it your Grace, on to the state affairs.
I had rather to adopt a child than get° it.
Come hither, Moor.
I here do give thee that with all my heart
Which, but thou hast already, with all my heart
I would keep from thee. For your sake, jewel,
I am glad at soul I have no other child,
For thy escape would teach me tyranny,
To hang clogs on them. I have done, my lord.
DUKE. Let me speak like yourself, and lay a sentence°
Which, as a grise° or step, may help these lovers
Into your favor.
When remedies are past, the griefs are ended
By seeing the worst, which late on hopes depended.
To mourn a mischief that is past and gone
Is the next way to draw new mischief on.
What cannot be preserved when fortune takes,
Patience her injury a mockery makes.
The robbed that smiles steals something from the thief.
He robs himself that spends a bootless grief.
BRABANTIO. So let the Turk of Cyprus us beguile,
We lose it not so long as we can smile.
He bears the sentence well that nothing bears

190. get: beget. **198. sentence:** proverbial saying. **199. grise:** degree.

But the free comfort which from thence he hears.
But he bears both the sentence and the sorrow
That, to pay grief, must of poor patience borrow.
These sentences, to sugar or to gall,
Being strong on both sides, are equivocal.
But words are words. I never yet did hear
That the bruised heart was piercèd through the ear.
I humbly beseech you, proceed to the affairs of state.

DUKE. The Turk with a most mighty preparation makes for Cyprus. Othello, the fortitude of the place is best known to you, and though we have there a substitute° of most allowed sufficiency, yet opinion, a sovereign mistress of effects, throws a more safer voice on you. You must therefore be content to slubber° the gloss of your new fortunes with this more stubborn and boisterous expedition.

OTHELLO. The tyrant custom, most grave Senators,
Hath made the flinty and steel couch of war
My thrice-driven bed of down. I do agnize°
A natural and prompt alacrity
I find in hardness, and do undertake
These present wars against the Ottomites.
Most humbly therefore bending to your state,
I crave fit disposition for my wife,
Due reference of place and exhibition,°
With such accommodation and besort°
As levels with her breeding.

DUKE. If you please,
Be 't at her father's.

BRABANTIO. I'll not have it so.

OTHELLO. Nor I.

DESDEMONA. Nor I. I would not there reside,
To put my father in impatient thoughts
By being in his eye. Most gracious Duke,
To my unfolding lend your prosperous° ear,
And let me find a charter in your voice
To assist my simpleness.

DUKE. What would you, Desdemona?

DESDEMONA. That I did love the Moor to live with him,
My downright violence and storm of fortunes
May trumpet to the world. My heart's subdued
Even to the very quality° of my lord.
I saw Othello's visage in his mind,

222. substitute: deputy commander. **224. slubber:** tarnish. **228. agnize:** confess. **234. exhibition:** allowance. **235. besort:** attendants. **241. prosperous:** favorable. **248. quality:** profession.

And to his honors and his valiant parts
Did I my soul and fortunes consecrate.
So that, dear lords, if I be left behind,
A moth of peace, and he go to the war,
The rites for which I love him are bereft me,
And I a heavy interim shall support
By his dear absence. Let me go with him.
OTHELLO. Let her have your voices.
Vouch with me, Heaven, I therefore beg it not
To please the palate of my appetite,
Nor to comply with heat—the young affects
In me defunct°—and proper satisfaction,
But to be free and bounteous to her mind.°
And Heaven defend your good souls, that you think
I will your serious and great business scant
For she is with me. No, when light-winged toys
Of feathered Cupid seel° with wanton dullness
My speculative and officed instruments,°
That my disports° corrupt and taint my business,
Let housewives make a skillet of my helm,
And all indign° and base adversities
Make head against my estimation!°
DUKE. Be it as you shall privately determine,
Either for her stay or going. The affair cries haste,
And speed must answer 't. You must hence tonight.
DESDEMONA. Tonight, my lord?
DUKE. This night.
OTHELLO. With all my heart.
DUKE. At nine i' the morning here we'll meet again.
Othello, leave some officer behind,
And he shall our commission bring to you,
With such things else of quality and respect
As doth import you.
OTHELLO. So please your Grace, my Ancient,
A man he is of honesty and trust.
To his conveyance I assign my wife,
With what else needful your good grace shall think
To be sent after me.
DUKE. Let it be so.

260–61. young . . . defunct: in me the passion of youth is dead. **262. to . . . mind:** Othello repeats Desdemona's claim that this is a marriage of minds. **266. seel:** close up. **267. speculative . . . instruments:** powers of sight and action; i.e., my efficiency as your general. **268. disports:** amusements. **270. indign:** unworthy. **271. estimation:** reputation.

Good night to everyone. (*To* Brabantio) And, noble signior,
If virtue no delighted beauty lack,
Your son-in-law is far more fair than black.

First Senator. Adieu, brave Moor. Use Desdemona well.

Brabantio. Look to her, Moor, if thou hast eyes to see.
She has deceived her father, and may thee.

(*Exeunt* Duke, Senators, Officers, *etc.*)

Othello. My life upon her faith! Honest Iago,
My Desdemona must I leave to thee.
I prithee, let thy wife attend on her,
And bring them after in the best advantage.
Come, Desdemona, I have but an hour
Of love, of worldly matters and direction,
To spend with thee. We must obey the time.

(*Exeunt* Othello *and* Desdemona.)

Roderigo. Iago!

Iago. What say'st thou, noble heart?

Roderigo. What will I do, thinkest thou?

Iago. Why, go to bed and sleep.

Roderigo. I will incontinently° drown myself.

Iago. If thou dost, I shall never love thee after. Why, thou silly gentleman!

Roderigo. It is silliness to live when to live is torment, and then have we a prescription to die when death is our physician.

Iago. Oh, villainous! I have looked upon the world for four times seven years, and since I could distinguish betwixt a benefit and an injury I never found man that knew how to love himself. Ere I would say I would drown myself for the love of a guinea hen, I would change my humanity with a baboon.

Roderigo. What should I do? I confess it is my shame to be so found, but it is not in my virtue to amend it.

Iago. Virtue! A fig! 'Tis in ourselves that we are thus or thus. Our bodies are gardens, to the which our wills are gardeners. So that if we will plant nettles or sow lettuce, set hyssop and weed up thyme, supply it with one gender of herbs or distract it with many, either to have it sterile with idleness or manured with industry—why, the power and corrigible° authority of this lies in our wills. If the balance of our lives had not one scale of reason to poise another of sensuality, the blood and baseness of our natures would conduct us to most preposterous conclusions. But we have reason to cool our raging motions, our carnal stings, our unbitted lusts, whereof

302. incontinently: immediately. **318. corrigible:** correcting, directing.

I take this that you call love to be a sect or scion.°

RODERIGO. It cannot be.

IAGO. It is merely a lust of the blood and a permission of the will. Come, be a man. Drown thyself! Drown cats and blind puppies. I have professed me thy friend, and I confess me knit to thy deserving with cables of perdurable toughness. I could never better stead thee than now. Put money in thy purse, follow thou the wars, defeat thy favor with an usurped beard°—I say put money in thy purse. It cannot be that Desdemona should long continue her love to the Moor—put money in thy purse—nor he his to her. It was a violent commencement, and thou shalt see an answerable sequestration°—put but money in thy purse. These Moors and changeable in their wills.—Fill thy purse with money. The food that to him now is as luscious as locusts shall be to him shortly as bitter as coloquintida. She must change for youth. When she is sated with his body, she will find the error of her choice. She must have change, she must—therefore put money in thy purse. If thou wilt needs damn thyself, do it a more delicate way than drowning. Make all the money thou canst. If sanctimony and a frail vow betwixt an erring° barbarian and a supersubtle Venetian be not too hard for my wits and all the tribe of Hell, thou shalt enjoy her—therefore make money. A pox of drowning thyself! It is clean out of the way. Seek thou rather to be hanged in compassing thy joy than to be drowned and go without her.

RODERIGO. Wilt thou be fast to my hopes if I depend on the issue?

IAGO. Thou art sure of me. Go, make money. I have told thee often, and I retell thee again and again, I hate the Moor. My cause is hearted,° thine hath no less reason. Let us be conjunctive in our revenge against him. If thou canst cuckold him thou dost thyself a pleasure, me a sport. There are many events in the womb of time, which will be delivered. Traverse, go, provide thy money. We will have more of this tomorrow. Adieu.

RODERIGO. Where shall we meet i' the morning?

IAGO. At my lodging.

RODERIGO. I'll be with thee betimes.

IAGO. Go to, farewell. Do you hear, Roderigo?

RODERIGO. What say you?

IAGO. No more of drowning, do you hear?

RODERIGO. I am changed. I'll go sell all my land. (*Exit.*)

IAGO. Thus do I ever make my fool my purse,
For I mine own gained knowledge should profane

323. sect or scion: Both words mean a slip taken from a tree and planted to produce a new growth. **329. defeat . . . beard:** disguise your face by growing a beard. **332–33. answerable sequestration:** corresponding separation; i.e., reaction. **339. Make . . . canst:** turn all you can into ready cash. **340. erring:** vagabond. **347. hearted:** heartfelt.

If I would time expend with such a snipe
But for my sport and profit. I hate the Moor,
And it is thought abroad that 'twixt my sheets
He has done my office. I know not if 't be true,
But I for mere suspicion in that kind
Will do as if for surety. He holds me well,
The better shall my purpose work on him.
Cassio's a proper° man. Let me see now,
To get his place, and to plume up my will
In double knavery—How, how?—Let's see.—
After some time, to abuse Othello's ear
That he is too familiar with his wife.
He hath a person and a smooth dispose
To be suspected,° framed to make women false.
The Moor is of a free and open nature
That thinks men honest that but seem to be so,
And will as tenderly be led by the nose
As asses are.
I have 't. It is engendered. Hell and night
Must bring this monstrous birth to the world's light. (*Exit.*)

ACT II

SCENE I. A seaport in Cyprus. An open place near the wharf.

Enter MONTANO *and two* GENTLEMEN.

MONTANO. What from the cape can you discern at sea?
FIRST GENTLEMAN. Nothing at all. It is a high-wrought flood.
I cannot 'twixt the heaven and the main
Descry a sail.
MONTANO. Methinks the wind hath spoke aloud at land,
A fuller blast ne'er shook our battlements.
If it hath ruffianed so upon the sea,
What ribs of oak, when mountains melt on them,
Can hold the mortise? What shall we hear of this?
SECOND GENTLEMAN. A segregation° of the Turkish fleet.
For do but stand upon the foaming shore,
The chidden billow seems to pelt the clouds,
The wind-shaked surge, with high and monstrous mane,
Seems to cast water on the burning Bear,
And quench the guards of the ever-fixèd Pole.
I never did like molestation view

369. proper: handsome. **374–75. He . . . suspected:** an easy way with him that is naturally suspected.

Act II, Sc. i: 10. segregation: separation.

On the enchafèd flood.
MONTANO. If that the Turkish fleet
Be not ensheltered and embayed, they are drowned.
It is impossible to bear it out.

(*Enter a* THIRD GENTLEMAN.)

THIRD GENTLEMAN. News, lads! Our wars are done.
The desperate tempest hath so banged the Turks
That their designment halts. A noble ship of Venice
Hath seen a grievous wreck and sufferance°
On most part of their fleet.
MONTANO. How! Is this true?
THIRD GENTLEMAN. The ship is here put in,
A Veronesa. Michael Cassio,
Lieutenant to the warlike Moor Othello,
Is come on shore, the Moor himself at sea,
And is in full commission here for Cyprus.
MONTANO. I am glad on 't. 'Tis a worthy governor.
THIRD GENTLEMAN. But this same Cassio, though he speak of comfort
Touching the Turkish loss, yet he looks sadly
And prays the Moor be safe, for they were parted
With foul and violent tempest.
MONTANO. Pray Heavens he be,
For I have served him, and the man commands
Like a full soldier. Let's to the seaside, ho!
As well to see the vessel that's come in
As to throw out our eyes for brave Othello,
Even till we make the main and the aerial blue
An indistinct regard.
THIRD GENTLEMAN. Come, let's do so.
For every minute is expectancy
Of more arrivance.

(*Enter* CASSIO.)

CASSIO. Thanks, you the valiant of this warlike isle
That so approve the Moor! Oh, let the heavens
Give him defense against the elements,
For I have lost him on a dangerous sea.
MONTANO. Is he well shipped?
CASSIO. His bark is stoutly timbered, and his pilot
Of very expert and approved allowance.
Therefore my hopes, not surfeited to death,
Stand in bold cure.

23. sufferance: damage.

(*A cry within: "A sail, a sail, a sail!" Enter a* FOURTH GENTLEMAN.)

CASSIO. What noise?
FOURTH GENTLEMAN. The town is empty. On the brow o' the sea
Stand ranks of people, and they cry "A sail!"
CASSIO. My hopes do shape him for the governor.

(*Guns heard.*)

SECOND GENTLEMAN. They do discharge their shot of courtesy.
Our friends, at least.
CASSIO. I pray you, sir, go forth,
And give us truth who 'tis that is arrived.
SECOND GENTLEMAN. I shall. (*Exit.*)
MONTANO. But, good Lieutenant, is your General wived?
CASSIO. Most fortunately. He hath achieved a maid
That paragons description and wild fame,
One that excels the quirks of blazoning pens
And in the essential vesture of creation
Does tire the ingener.°

(*Re-enter* SECOND GENTLEMAN.)

How now! Who has put in?
SECOND GENTLEMAN. 'Tis one Iago, Ancient to the General.
CASSIO. He has had most favorable and happy speed.
Tempests themselves, high seas, and howling winds,
The guttered rocks, and congregated sands,
Traitors ensteeped to clog the guiltless keel,
As having sense of beauty, do omit
Their mortal nature, letting go safely by
The divine Desdemona.
MONTANO. What is she?
CASSIO. She that I spake of, our great Captain's captain,
Left in the conduct of the bold Iago,
Whose footing here anticipates our thoughts
A sennight's speed. Great Jove, Othello guard,
And swell his sail with thine own powerful breath,
That he may bless this bay with his tall ship,
Make love's quick pants in Desdemona's arms,
Give renewed fire to our extincted spirits,
And bring all Cyprus comfort.

(*Enter* DESDEMONA, EMILIA, IAGO, RODERIGO, *and* ATTENDANTS.)

63–65. One . . . ingener: one that is too good for the fancy phrases (*quirks*) of painting pens (i.e., poets) and in her absolute perfection wearies the artist (i.e., the painter). (Cassio is full of gallant phrases and behavior, in contrast to Iago's bluntness.) **ingener**: inventor.

Oh, behold,
The riches of the ship is come on shore!
Ye men of Cyprus, let her have your knees.
Hail to thee, lady! And the grace of Heaven,
Before, behind thee, and on every hand,
Enwheel thee round!

DESDEMONA. I thank you, valiant Cassio.
What tidings can you tell me of my lord?

CASSIO. He is not yet arrived, nor know I aught
But that he's well and will be shortly here.

DESDEMONA. Oh, but I fear—How lost you company?

CASSIO. The great contention of the sea and skies
Parted our fellowship.—But hark! A sail.

(*A cry within: "A sail, a sail!" Guns heard.*)

SECOND GENTLEMAN. They give their greeting to the citadel.
This likewise is a friend.

CASSIO. See for the news.

(*Exit* GENTLEMAN.)

Good Ancient, you are welcome. (*To* EMILIA) Welcome, mistress.
Let it not gall your patience, good Iago,
That I extend my manners. 'Tis my breeding
That gives me this bold show of courtesy. (*Kissing her.*)

IAGO. Sir, would she give you so much of her lips
As of her tongue she oft bestows on me,
You'd have enough.

DESDEMONA. Alas, she has no speech.

IAGO. In faith, too much,
I find it still when I have list° to sleep.
Marry, before your ladyship, I grant,
She puts her tongue a little in her heart
And chides with thinking.

EMILIA. You have little cause to say so.

IAGO. Come on, come on. You are pictures° out of doors,
Bells° in your parlors, wildcats in your kitchens,
Saints in your injuries,° devils being offended,
Players in your housewifery, and housewives in your beds.

DESDEMONA. Oh, fie upon thee, slanderer!

IAGO. Nay, it is true, or else I am a Turk.
You rise to play, and go to bed to work.

104. list: desire. **109. pictures:** i.e., painted and dumb. **110. Bells:** i.e., ever clacking. **111. Saints . . . injuries:** saints when you hurt anyone else.

EMILIA. You shall not write my praise.

IAGO. No, let me not.

DESDEMONA. What wouldst thou write of me if thou shouldst praise me?

IAGO. O gentle lady, do not put me to 't,
For I am nothing if not critical.

DESDEMONA. Come on, assay.°—There's one gone to the harbor?

IAGO. Aye, madam.

DESDEMONA. I am not merry, but I do beguile
The thing I am by seeming otherwise.
Come, how wouldst thou praise me?

IAGO. I am about it, but indeed my invention
Comes from my pate as birdlime does from frieze°—
It plucks out brains and all. But my Muse labors,
And thus she is delivered.
If she be fair and wise, fairness and wit,
The one's for use, the other useth it.

DESDEMONA. Well praised! How if she be black and witty?

IAGO. If she be black, and thereto have a wit,
She'll find a white° that shall her blackness fit.

DESDEMONA. Worse and worse.

EMILIA. How if fair and foolish?

IAGO. She never yet was foolish that was fair,
For even her folly helped her to an heir.

DESDEMONA. These are old fond paradoxes to make fools laugh i' the alehouse. What miserable praise hast thou for her that's foul and foolish?

IAGO. There's none so foul, and foolish thereunto,
But does foul pranks which fair and wise ones do.

DESDEMONA. Oh, heavy ignorance! Thou praisest the worst best. But what praise couldst thou bestow on a deserving woman indeed, one that in the authority of her merit did justly put on the vouch of very malice itself?°

IAGO. She that was ever fair and never proud,
Had tongue at will° and yet was never loud,
Never lacked gold and yet went never gay,
Fled from her wish and yet said "Now I may."
She that, being angered, her revenge being nigh,
Bade her wrong stay and her displeasure fly.
She that in wisdom never was so frail
To change the cod's head for the salmon's tail.°

120. assay: try. **125–26. my . . . frieze:** my literary effort (*invention*) is as hard to pull out of my head as frieze (cloth with a nap) stuck to birdlime. **133. white:** with a pun on *wight* (l. 156), man, person. **143–45. one . . . itself:** one so deserving that even malice would declare her good. **147. tongue . . . will:** a ready flow of words. **153. To . . . tail:** to prefer the tail end of a good thing to the head of a poor thing.

She could think and ne'er disclose her mind,
See suitors following and not look behind.
She was a wight, if ever such wight were—

DESDEMONA. To do what?

IAGO. To suckle fools and chronicle small beer.°

DESDEMONA. Oh, most lame and impotent conclusion! Do not learn of him, Emilia, though he be thy husband. How say you, Cassio? Is he not a most profane and liberal° counselor?

CASSIO. He speaks home, madam. You may relish him more in the soldier than in the scholar.

IAGO (*aside*). He takes her by the palm. Aye, well said, whisper. With as little a web as this will I ensnare as great a fly as Cassio. Aye, smile upon her, do, I will gyve thee in thine own courtship. You say true, 'tis so indeed. If such tricks as these strip you out of your Lieutenantry, it had been better you had not kissed your three fingers° so oft, which now again you are most apt to play the sir° in. Very good, well kissed! An excellent courtesy! 'Tis so indeed. Yet again your fingers to your lips? Would they were clyster pipes° for your sake! (*Trumpet within.*) The Moor! I know the trumpet.

CASSIO. 'Tis truly so.

DESDEMONA. Let's meet him and receive him.

CASSIO. Lo where he comes!

(*Enter* OTHELLO *and* ATTENDANTS.)

OTHELLO. O my fair warrior!°

DESDEMONA. My dear Othello!

OTHELLO. It gives me wonder great as my content
To see you here before me. O my soul's joy!
If after every tempest come such calms,
May the winds blow till they have wakened death!
And let the laboring bark climb hills of seas
Olympus-high, and duck again as low
As Hell's from Heaven! If it were now to die,
'Twere now to be most happy, for I fear
My soul hath her content so absolute
That not another comfort like to this
Succeeds in unknown fate.

DESDEMONA. The Heavens forbid
But that our loves and comforts should increase,
Even as our days do grow!

158. chronicle . . . beer: write a whole history about trifles (*small beer* thin drink). **161. liberal:** gross. **168. kissed . . . fingers:** a gesture of gallantry. **169. play . . . sir:** act the fine gentleman. **171. clyster pipes:** an enema syringe. **176. warrior:** because she is a soldier's wife.

OTHELLO. Amen to that, sweet powers!
I cannot speak enough of this content.
It stops me here,° it is too much of joy.
And this, and this, the greatest discords be (*Kissing her*)
That e'er our hearts shall make!

IAGO (*aside*). Oh, you are well tuned now,
But I'll set down the pegs° that make this music,
As honest as I am.

OTHELLO. Come, let us to the castle.
News, friends. Our wars are done, the Turks are drowned.
How does my old acquaintance of this isle?
Honey, you shall be well desired in Cyprus,
I have found great love amongst them. O my sweet,
I prattle out of fashion, and I dote
In mine own comforts. I prithee, good Iago,
Go to the bay and disembark my coffers.°
Bring thou the master° to the citadel.
He is a good one, and his worthiness
Does challenge much respect. Come, Desdemona,
Once more well met at Cyprus.

(*Exeunt all but* IAGO *and* RODERIGO.)

IAGO. Do thou meet me presently at the harbor. Come hither. If thou beest valiant—as they say base men being in love have then a nobility in their natures more than is native to them—list me. The Lieutenant tonight watches on the court of guard. First, I must tell thee this. Desdemona is directly in love with him.

RODERIGO. With him! Why, 'tis not possible.

IAGO. Lay thy finger thus,° and let thy soul be instructed. Mark me with what violence she first loved the Moor, but for bragging and telling her fantastical lies. And will she love him still for prating? Let not thy discreet heart think it. Her eye must be fed, and what delight shall she have to look on the Devil? When the blood is made dull with the act of sport, there should be, again to inflame it and to give satiety a fresh appetite, loveliness in favor,° sympathy in years, manners, and beauties, all which the Moor is defective in. Now, for want of these required conveniences, her delicate tenderness will find itself abused, begin to heave the gorge, disrelish and abhor the Moor. Very nature will instruct her in it and compel her to some second choice. Now, sir, this granted—as it is a most pregnant and unforced position°—who stands so eminently in the degree of this fortune

191. here: i.e., in the heart. **194. set . . . pegs:** i.e., make you sing in a different key. A stringed instrument was tuned by the pegs. **202. coffers:** trunks. **203. master:** captain of the ship. **213. thus:** i.e., on the lips. **219. favor:** face. **223–24. pregnant . . . position:** very significant and probable argument.

as Cassio does? A knave very voluble, no further conscionable° than in putting on the mere form of civil and humane seeming° for the better compassing of his salt° and most hidden loose affection? Why, none, why, none. A slipper° and subtle knave, a finder-out of occasions, that has an eye can stamp and counterfeit advantages,° though true advantage never present itself. A devilish knave! Besides, the knave is handsome, young, and hath all those requisites in him that folly and green minds look after. A pestilent complete knave, and the woman hath found him already.

RODERIGO. I cannot believe that in her. She's full of most blest condition.°

IAGO. Blest fig's-end!° The wine she drinks is made of grapes. If she had been blest, she would never have loved the Moor. Blest pudding! Didst thou not see her paddle with the palm of his hand? Didst not mark that?

RODERIGO. Yes, that I did, but that was just courtesy.

IAGO. Lechery, by this hand, an index and obscure prologue to the history of lust and foul thoughts. They met so near with their lips that their breaths embraced together. Villainous thoughts, Roderigo! When these mutualities so marshal the way, hard at hand comes the master and main exercise, the incorporate° conclusion. Pish! But, sir, be you ruled by me. I have brought you from Venice. Watch you tonight. For the command, I'll lay't upon you. Cassio knows you not. I'll not be far from you. Do you find some occasion to anger Cassio, either by speaking too loud, or tainting° his discipline, or from what other curse you please which the time shall more favorably minister.

RODERIGO. Well.

IAGO. Sir, he is rash and very sudden in choler,° and haply may strike at you. Provoke him, that he may, for even out of that will I cause these of Cyprus to mutiny, whose qualification shall come into no true taste again but by the displanting of Cassio. So shall you have a shorter journey to your desires by the means I shall then have to prefer° them, and the impediment most profitably removed without the which there were no expectation of our prosperity.

RODERIGO. I will do this, if I can bring it to any opportunity.

IAGO. I warrant thee. Meet me by and by at the citadel. I must fetch his necessaries ashore. Farewell.

RODERIGO. Adieu. (*Exit.*)

IAGO. That Cassio loves her, I do well believe it.
That she loves him, 'tis apt and of great credit.
The Moor, howbeit that I endure him not,
Is of a constant, loving, noble nature,

225. no . . . conscionable: who has no more conscience. **226. humane seeming:** courteous appearance. **227. salt:** lecherous. **228. slipper:** slippery. **229. stamp . . . advantages:** forge false opportunities. **234. condition:** disposition. **235. fig's-end:** nonsense [L.P.]. **243. incorporate:** bodily. **246. tainting:** disparaging. **250. choler:** anger. **254. prefer:** promote.

And I dare think he'll prove to Desdemona
A most dear husband. Now, I do love her too,
Not out of absolute lust, though peradventure
I stand accountant for as great a sin.
But partly led to diet° my revenge
For that I do suspect the lusty Moor
Hath leaped into my seat. The thought whereof
Doth like a poisonous mineral gnaw my inwards.
And nothing can or shall content my soul
Till I am evened with him, wife for wife.
At least into a jealousy so strong
Or failing so, yet that I put the Moor
That judgment cannot cure. Which thing to do,
If this poor trash of Venice, whom I trash
For his quick hunting,° stand the putting-on,
I'll have our Michael Cassio on the hip,
Abuse him to the Moor in the rank garb°—
For I fear Cassio with my nightcap too—
Make the Moor thank me, love me, and reward me
For making him egregiously an ass
And practicing upon his peace and quiet
Even to madness. 'Tis here, but yet confused.
Knavery's plain face is never seen till used. (*Exit.*)

SCENE II. A street.

Enter a HERALD *with a proclamation,* PEOPLE *following.*

HERALD. It is Othello's pleasure, our noble and valiant General, that upon certain tidings now arrived, importing the mere perdition° of the Turkish fleet, every man put himself into triumph°—some to dance, some to make bonfires, each man to what sport and revels his addiction leads him. For, besides these beneficial news, it is the celebration of his nuptial. So much was his pleasure should be proclaimed. All offices° are open, and there is full liberty of feasting from this present hour of five till the bell have told eleven. Heaven bless the isle of Cyprus and our noble General Othello!

(*Exeunt.*)

SCENE III. A hall in the castle.

Enter OTHELLO, DESDEMONA, CASSIO, *and* ATTENDANTS.

269. diet: feed. **278–79. trash . . . hunting:** hold back from outrunning the pack. [L.P.]. **281. rank garb:** gross manner; i.e., by accusing him of being Desdemona's lover.

Sc. ii. 2. mere perdition: absolute destruction. **3. triumph:** celebrate. **6. offices:** the kitchen and buttery—i.e., free food and drink for all.

OTHELLO. Good Michael, look you to the guard tonight.
Let's teach ourselves that honorable stop,
Not to outsport discretion.

CASSIO. Iago hath direction what to do,
But notwithstanding with my personal eye
Will I look to 't.

OTHELLO. Iago is most honest.
Michael, good night. Tomorrow with your earliest
Let me have speech with you. Come, my dear love,
The purchase made, the fruits are to ensue—
That profit's yet to come 'tween me and you.
Good night.

(*Exeunt* OTHELLO, DESDEMONA, *and* ATTENDANTS. *Enter* IAGO.)

CASSIO. Welcome, Iago. We must to the watch.

IAGO. Not this hour, Lieutenant, 'tis not yet ten o' the clock. Our General cast° us thus early for the love of his Desdemona, who let us not therefore blame. He hath not yet made wanton the night with her, and she is sport for Jove.

CASSIO. She's a most exquisite lady.

IAGO. And, I'll warrant her, full of game

CASSIO. Indeed she's a most fresh and delicate creature.

IAGO. What an eye she has! Methinks it sounds a parley to provocation.

CASSIO. An inviting eye, and yet methinks right modest.

IAGO. And when she speaks, is it not an alarum to love?

CASSIO. She is indeed perfection.

IAGO. Well, happiness to their sheets! Come, Lieutenant, I have a stoup of wine, and here without are a brace of Cyprus gallants that would fain have a measure to the health of black Othello.

CASSIO. Not tonight, good Iago. I have very poor and unhappy brains for drinking. I could well wish courtesy would invent some other custom of entertainment.

IAGO. Oh, they are our friends. But one cup—I'll drink for you.

CASSIO. I have drunk but one cup tonight, and that was craftily qualified too, and behold what innovation it makes here. I am unfortunate in the infirmity, and dare not task my weakness with any more.

IAGO. What, man! 'Tis a night of revels. The gallants desire it.

CASSIO. Where are they?

IAGO. Here at the door. I pray you call them in.

CASSIO. I'll do 't, but it dislikes me. (*Exit.*)

IAGO. If I can fasten but one cup upon him,

14. cast: dismissed.

With that which he hath drunk tonight already
He'll be as full of quarrel and offense
As my young mistress' dog. Now my sick fool Roderigo,
Whom love hath turned almost the wrong side out,
To Desdemona hath tonight caroused
Potations pottle-deep, and he's to watch.
Three lads of Cyprus, noble swelling spirits
That hold their honors in a wary distance,°
The very elements° of this warlike isle,
Have I tonight flustered with flowing cups,
And they watch too. Now, 'mongst this flock of drunkards,
Am I to put our Cassio in some action
That may offend the isle. But here they come.
If consequence do but approve my dream,
My boat sails freely, both with wind and stream.

(*Re-enter* CASSIO, *with him* MONTANO *and* GENTLEMEN, SERVANTS *following with wine.*)

CASSIO. 'Fore God, they have given me a rouse already.

MONTANO. Good faith, a little one—not past a pint, as I am a soldier.

IAGO. Some wine, ho! (*Sings*)

"And let me the cannikin clink, clink,
And let me the cannikin clink.
A soldier's a man,
A life's but a span.°
Why, then let a soldier drink."

Some wine, boys!

CASSIO. 'Fore God, an excellent song.

IAGO. I learned it in England, where indeed they are most potent in potting.° Your Dane, your German, and your swag-bellied Hollander—Drink, ho!—are nothing to your English.

CASSIO. Is your Englishman so expert in his drinking?

IAGO. Why, he drinks you with facility your Dane dead drunk, he sweats not to overthrow your Almain, he gives your Hollander a vomit° ere the next pottle can be filled.

CASSIO. To the health of our General!

MONTANO. I am for it, Lieutenant, and I'll do you justice.

IAGO. O sweet England! (*Sings*)

"King Stephen was a worthy peer,
His breeches cost him but a crown.

47. hold . . . distance: "have a chip on their shoulders." **48. very elements:** typical specimens. **61. span:** lit., the measure between the thumb and little finger of the outstretched hand; about 9 inches. **66. potting:** drinking. **70. gives . . . vomit:** drinks as much as will make a Dutchman throw up.

He held them sixpence all too dear,
With that he called the tailor lown.°

"He was a wight of high renown,
And thou art but of low degree.
'Tis pride that pulls the country down.
Then take thine auld cloak about thee."

Some wine, ho!

CASSIO. Why, this is a more exquisite song than the other.

IAGO. Will you hear 't again?

CASSIO. No, for I hold him to be unworthy of his place that does those things. Well, God's above all, and there be souls must be saved and there be souls must not be saved.

IAGO. It's true, good Lieutenant.

CASSIO. For mine own part—no offense to the General, nor any man of quality—I hope to be saved.

IAGO. And so do I too, Lieutenant.

CASSIO. Aye, but, by your leave, not before me. The Lieutenant is to be saved before the Ancient. Let's have no more of this, let's to our affairs. God forgive us our sins! Gentlemen, let's look to our business. Do not think, gentlemen, I am drunk. This is my Ancient, this is my right hand and this is my left. I am not drunk now, I can stand well enough and speak well enough.

ALL. Excellent well.

CASSIO. Why, very well, then, you must not think then that I am drunk. (*Exit.*)

MONTANO. To the platform, masters. Come, let's set the watch.

IAGO. You see this fellow that is gone before.
He is a soldier fit to stand by Caesar
And give direction. And do but see his vice.
'Tis to his virtue a just equinox,
The one as long as the other. 'Tis pity of him.
I fear the trust Othello puts him in
On some odd time of his infirmity
Will shake this island.

MONTANO. But is he often thus?

IAGO. 'Tis evermore the prologue to his sleep.
He'll watch the horologe a double set,°
If drink rock not his cradle.

MONTANO. It were well
The General were put in mind of it.
Perhaps he sees it not, or his good nature

78. lown: lout. **112. watch . . . set:** stay awake the clock twice round.

Prizes the virtue that appears in Cassio
And looks not on his evils. Is not this true?

(*Enter* RODERIGO.)

IAGO (*aside to him*). How now, Roderigo! I pray you, after the Lieutenant. Go.

(*Exit* RODERIGO.)

MONTANO. And 'tis great pity that the noble Moor
Should hazard such a place as his own second
With one of an ingraft infirmity.
It were an honest action to say
So to the Moor.
IAGO. Not I, for this fair island.
I do love Cassio well, and would do much
To cure him of this evil—But, hark! What noise?

(*A cry within: "Help! Help!" Re-enter* CASSIO, *driving in* RODERIGO.)

CASSIO. 'Zounds! You rogue! You rascal!
MONTANO. What's the matter, Lieutenant?
CASSIO. A knave teach me my duty!
But I'll beat the knave into a wicker bottle.
RODERIGO. Beat me!
CASSIO. Dost thou prate, rogue? (*Striking* RODERIGO.)
MONTANO. Nay, good Lieutenant, (*staying him*)
I pray you, sir, hold your hand.
CASSIO. Let me go, sir,
Or I'll knock you o'er the mazzard.
MONTANO. Come, come, you're drunk.
CASSIO. Drunk!

(*They fight.*)

IAGO (*aside to* RODERIGO). Away, I say. Go out and cry a mutiny.

(*Exit* RODERIGO.)

Nay, good Lieutenant! God's will, gentlemen!
Help, ho!—Lieutenant—sir—Montano—sir—
Help, masters!—Here's a goodly watch indeed!

(*A bell rings.*)

Who's that that rings the bell?—Diablo, ho!
The town will rise. God's will, Lieutenant, hold—
You will be shamed forever.

(*Re-enter* OTHELLO *and* ATTENDANTS.)

OTHELLO. What is the matter here?
MONTANO. 'Zounds, I bleed still, I am hurt to the death. (*Faints.*)
OTHELLO. Hold, for your lives!
IAGO. Hold, ho! Lieutenant—sir—Montano—gentlemen—
Have you forgot all sense of place and duty?
Hold! The General speaks to you. Hold, hold, for shame!
OTHELLO. Why, how now, ho! From whence ariseth this?
Are we turned Turks, and to ourselves do that
Which Heaven hath forbid the Ottomites?
For Christian shame, put by this barbarous brawl.
He that stirs next to carve for his own rage
Holds his soul light, he dies upon his motion.
Silence that dreadful bell. It frights the isle
From her propriety. What is the matter, masters?
Honest Iago, that look'st dead with grieving,
Speak, who began this? On thy love, I charge thee.
IAGO. I do not know. Friends all but now, even now,
In quarter and in terms like bride and groom
Devesting them for bed. And then, but now,
As if some planet had unwitted men,
Swords out, and tilting one at other's breast
In opposition bloody. I cannot speak
Any beginning to this peevish odds,
And would in action glorious I had lost
Those legs that brought me to a part of it!
OTHELLO. How comes it, Michael, you are thus forgot?°
CASSIO. I pray you, pardon me, I cannot speak.
OTHELLO. Worthy Montano, you were wont be civil.
The gravity and stillness of your youth
The world hath noted, and your name is great
In mouths of wisest censure.° What's the matter
That you unlace your reputation thus,
And spend your rich opinion° for the name
Of a night brawler? Give me answer to it.
MONTANO. Worthy Othello, I am hurt to danger.
Your officer, Iago, can inform you—
While I spare speech, which something now offends me—
Of all that I do know. Nor know I aught
By me that's said or done amiss this night,
Unless self-charity° be sometimes a vice,

166. are . . . forgot: have so forgotten yourself. **171. censure:** judgment. **173. opinion:** reputation [L.P.]. **180. self-charity:** love for oneself.

And to defend ourselves it be a sin
When violence assails us.
OTHELLO. Now, by Heaven,
My blood begins my safer guides to rule,
And passion, having my best judgment collied,°
Assays to lead the way. If I once stir,
Or do but lift this arm, the best of you
Shall sink in my rebuke. Give me to know
How this foul rout began, who set it on,
And he that is approved° in this offense,
Though he had twinned with me, both at a birth,
Shall lose me. What! In a town of war,
Yet wild, the people's hearts brimful of fear,
To manage private and domestic quarrel,
In night, and on the court and guard of safety!
'Tis monstrous. Iago, who began 't?
MONTANO. If partially affined, or leagued in office,
Thou dost deliver more or less than truth,
Thou art no soldier.
IAGO. Touch me not so near.
I had rather have this tongue cut from my mouth
Than it should do offense to Michael Cassio.
Yet I persuade myself to speak the truth
Shall nothing wrong him. Thus it is, General.
Montano and myself being in speech,
There comes a fellow crying out for help,
And Cassio following him with determined sword
To execute upon him. Sir, this gentleman
Steps in to Cassio and entreats his pause.
Myself the crying fellow did pursue,
Lest by his clamor—as it so fell out—
The town might fall in fright. He, swift of foot,
Outran my purpose, and I returned the rather
For that I heard the clink and fall of swords,
And Cassio high in oath, which till tonight
I ne'er might say before. When I came back—
For this was brief—I found them close together,
At blow and thrust, even as again they were
When you yourself did part them.
More of this matter cannot I report.
But men are men, the best sometimes forget
Though Cassio did some little wrong to him,

184. collied: darkened. **189. approved:** proved guilty.

As men in rage strike those that wish them best,
Yet surely Cassio, I believe, received
From him that fled some strange indignity,
Which patience could not pass.

OTHELLO. I know, Iago,
Thy honesty and love doth mince this matter,
Making it light to Cassio. Cassio, I love thee,
But never more be officer of mine.

(*Re-enter* DESDEMONA, *attended.*)

Look, if my gentle love be not raised up!
I'll make thee an example.

DESDEMONA. What's the matter?

OTHELLO. All's well now, sweeting. Come away to
bed. (*To* MONTANO, *who is led off*)
Sir, for your hurts, myself will be your surgeon.
Lead him off.
Iago, look with care about the town,
And silence those whom this vile brawl distracted.
Come, Desdemona. 'Tis the soldiers' life
To have their balmy slumbers waked with strife.

(*Exeunt all but* IAGO *and* CASSIO.)

IAGO. What, are you hurt, Lieutenant?

CASSIO. Aye, past all surgery.

IAGO. Marry, Heaven forbid!

CASSIO. Reputation, reputation, reputation! Oh, I have lost my reputation! I have lost the immortal part of myself, and what remains is bestial. My reputation, Iago, my reputation!

IAGO. As I am an honest man, I thought you had received some bodily wound. There is more sense in that than in reputation. Reputation is an idle and most false imposition, oft got without merit and lost without deserving. You have lost no reputation at all unless you repute yourself such a loser. What, man! There are ways to recover the General again. You are but now cast in his mood,° a punishment more in policy° than in malice—even so as one would beat his offenseless dog to affright an imperious lion.° Sue to him again and he's yours.

CASSIO. I will rather sue to be despised than to deceive so good a commander with so slight, so drunken, and so indiscreet an officer. Drunk? And speak parrot?° And squabble? Swagger? Swear? And discourse fustian

248. cast . . . mood: dismissed because he is in a bad mood. **in policy:** i.e., because he must appear to be angry before the Cypriots. **249–50. even . . . lion:** a proverb meaning that when the lion sees the dog beaten, he will know what is coming to him. **253. speak parrot:** babble.

with one's own shadow? O thou invisible spirit of wine, if thou has no name to be known by, let us call thee devil!

IAGO. What was he that you followed with your sword? What had he done to you?

CASSIO. I know not.

IAGO. Is 't possible?

CASSIO. I remember a mass of things, but nothing distinctly—a quarrel, but nothing wherefore. Oh God, that men should put an enemy in their mouths to steal away their brains! That we should, with joy, pleasance, revel, and applause, transform ourselves into beasts!

IAGO. Why, but you are now well enough. How came you thus recovered?

CASSIO. It hath pleased the devil drunkenness to give place to the devil wrath. One unperfectness shows me another, to make me frankly despise myself.

IAGO. Come, you are too severe a moraler. As the time, the place, and the condition of this country stands, I could heartily wish this had not befallen. But since it is as it is, mend it for your own good.

CASSIO. I will ask him for my place again, he shall tell me I am a drunkard! Had I as many mouths as Hydra, such an answer would stop them all. To be now a sensible man, by and by a fool, and presently a beast! Oh, strange! Every inordinate cup is unblest, and the ingredient is a devil.

IAGO. Come, come, good wine is a good familiar creature, if it be well used. Exclaim no more against it. And, good Lieutenant, I think you think I love you.

CASSIO. I have well approved it, sir. I drunk!

IAGO. You or any man living may be drunk at some time, man. I'll tell you what you shall do. Our General's wife is now the General. I may say so in this respect, for that he hath devoted and given up himself to the contemplation, mark, and denotement of her parts and graces. Confess yourself freely to her, importune her help to put you in your place again. She is of so free, so kind, so apt, so blessed a disposition, she holds it a vice in her goodness not to do more than she is requested. This broken joint between you and her husband entreat her to splinter° and, my fortunes against any lay° worth naming, this crack of your love shall grow stronger than it was before.

CASSIO. You advise me well.

IAGO. I protest, in the sincerity of love and honest kindness.

CASSIO. I think it freely, and betimes in the morning I will beseech the virtuous Desdemona to undertake for me. I am desperate of my fortunes if they check me here.

288. splinter: put in splints. **289. lay:** bet.

IAGO. You are in the right. Good night, Lieutenant, I must to the watch.

CASSIO. Good night, honest Iago. (*Exit.*)

IAGO. And what's he then that says I play the villain?
When this advice is free I give and honest,
Probal° to thinking, and indeed the course
To win the Moor again? For 'tis most easy
The inclining Desdemona to subdue
In any honest suit. She's framed as fruitful
As the free elements. And then for her
To win the Moor, were 't to renounce his baptism,
All seals and symbols of redeemèd sin,
His soul is so enfettered to her love
That she may make, unmake, do what she list,
Even as her appetite shall play the god
With his weak function.° How am I then a villain
To counsel Cassio to this parallel course,
Directly to his good? Divinity of Hell!
When devils will the blackest sins put on,
They do suggest at first with heavenly shows,
As I do now. For whiles this honest fool
Plies Desdemona to repair his fortunes,
And she for him pleads strongly to the Moor,
I'll pour this pestilence into his ear,
That she repeals° him for her body's lust.
And by how much she strives to do him good,
She shall undo her credit with the Moor.
So will I turn her virtue into pitch,
And out of her own goodness make the net
That shall enmesh them all.

(*Enter* RODERIGO.)

How now, Roderigo!

RODERIGO. I do follow here in the chase, not like a hound that hunts but one that fills up the cry. My money is almost spent, I have been tonight exceedingly well cudgeled, and I think the issue will be I shall have so much experience for my pains and so, with no money at all and a little more wit, return again to Venice.

IAGO. How poor are they that have not patience!
What wound did ever heal but by degrees?
Thou know'st we work by wit and not by witchcraft,
And wit depends on dilatory Time.

301. Probal: probable. **310. function:** intelligence. **320. repeals:** calls back.

Does't not go well? Cassio hath beaten thee,
And thou by that small hurt hast cashiered Cassio.
Though other things grow fair against the sun,
Yet fruits that blossom first will first be ripe.
Content thyself awhile. By the mass, 'tis morning.
Pleasure and action make the hours seem short.
Retire thee, go where thou art billeted.
Away, I say. Thou shalt know more hereafter.
Nay, get thee gone.

(*Exit* RODERIGO.)

Two things are to be done:
My wife must move for Cassio to her mistress,
I'll set her on,
Myself the while to draw the Moor apart
And bring him jump when he may Cassio find
Soliciting his wife. Aye, that's the way.
Dull not device by coldness and delay. (*Exit.*)

ACT III

SCENE I. Before the castle.

Enter CASSIO *and some* MUSICIANS.

CASSIO. Masters, play here, I will content your pains°—
Something that's brief, and bid "Good morrow, General."°

(*Music. Enter* CLOWN.)

CLOWN. Why, masters, have your instruments been in Naples, that they speak i' the nose thus?

FIRST MUSICIAN. How, sir, how?

CLOWN. Are these, I pray you, wind instruments?

FIRST MUSICIAN. Aye, marry are they, sir.

CLOWN. Oh, thereby hangs a tail.

FIRST MUSICIAN. Whereby hangs a tale, sir?

CLOWN. Marry, sir, by many a wind instrument that I know. But, masters, here's money for you. And the General so likes your music that he desires you, for love's sake, to make no more noise with it.

FIRST MUSICIAN. Well, sir, we will not.

1. **content . . . pains:** reward your labor. 2. **bid . . . General:** It was a common custom to play or sing a song beneath the bedroom window of a distinguished guest or of a newly wedded couple on the morning after their wedding night.

CLOWN. If you have any music that may not be heard, to 't again. But, as they say, to hear music the General does not greatly care.

FIRST MUSICIAN. We have none such, sir.

CLOWN. Then put up your pipes in your bag, for I'll away. Go, vanish into air, away!

(*Exeunt* MUSICIANS.)

CASSIO. Dost thou hear, my honest friend?

CLOWN. No, I hear not your honest friend, I hear you.

CASSIO. Prithee keep up thy quillets.° There's a poor piece of gold for thee. If the gentlewoman that attends the General's wife be stirring, tell her there's one Cassio entreats her a little favor of speech. Wilt thou do this?

CLOWN. She is stirring, sir. If she will stir hither, I shall seem to notify unto her.

CASSIO. Do, good my friend.

(*Exit* CLOWN. *Enter* IAGO.)

In happy time, Iago.
IAGO. You have not been abed, then?
CASSIO. Why, no, the day had broke
Before we parted. I have made bold, Iago,
To send in to your wife. My suit to her
Is that she will to virtuous Desdemona
Procure me some access.
IAGO. I'll send her to you presently,
And I'll devise a mean to draw the Moor
Out of the way, that your convérse and business
May be more free.
CASSIO. I humbly thank you for 't.

(*Exit* IAGO.)

I never knew
A Florentine more kind and honest.

(*Enter* EMILIA.)

EMILIA. Good morrow, good Lieutenant. I am sorry
For your displeasure, but all will sure be well.
The General and his wife are talking of it,
And she speaks for you stoutly. The Moor replies
That he you hurt is of great fame in Cyprus
And great affinity,° and that in wholesome wisdom
He might not but refuse you. But he protests he loves you,

21. keep . . . quillets: put away your wisecracks. **43. affinity:** kindred.

And needs no other suitor but his likings
To take the safest occasion by the front
To bring you in again.

CASSIO. Yet I beseech you
If you think fit, or that it may be done,
Give me advantage of some brief discourse
With Desdemona alone.

EMILIA. Pray you, come in.
I will bestow you where you shall have time
To speak your bosom freely.

CASSIO. I am much bound to you.

(*Exeunt.*)

SCENE II. A room in the castle.

Enter OTHELLO, IAGO, *and* GENTLEMEN.

OTHELLO. These letters give, Iago, to the pilot,
And by him do my duties to the Senate.
That done, I will be walking on the works.
Repair there to me.

IAGO. Well, my good lord, I'll do 't.

OTHELLO. This fortification, gentlemen, shall we see 't?

GENTLEMEN. We'll wait upon your lordship.

(*Exeunt.*)

SCENE III. The garden of the castle.

Enter DESDEMONA, CASSIO, *and* EMILIA.

DESDEMONA. Be thou assured, good Cassio, I will do
All my abilities in thy behalf.

EMILIA. Good madam, do. I warrant it grieves my husband
As if the case were his.

DESDEMONA. Oh, that's an honest fellow. Do not doubt, Cassio,
But I will have my lord and you again
As friendly as you were.

CASSIO. Bounteous madam,
Whatever shall become of Michael Cassio,
He's never anything but your true servant.

DESDEMONA. I know 't. I thank you. You do love my lord.
You have known him long, and be you well assured

He shall in strangeness stand no farther off
Than in a politic distance.°

CASSIO. Aye, but, lady,
That policy may either last so long,
Or feed upon such nice and waterish diet,
Or breed itself so out of circumstance,
That, I being absent and my place supplied,
My General will forget my love and service.

DESDEMONA. Do not doubt° that. Before Emilia here
I give thee warrant of thy place.° Assure thee,
If I do vow a friendship, I'll perform it
To the last article. My lord shall never rest.
I'll watch him tame and talk him out of patience,
His bed shall seem a school, his board a shrift.°
I'll intermingle every thing he does
With Cassio's suit. Therefore be merry, Cassio,
For thy solicitor shall rather die
Than give thy cause away.

(*Enter* OTHELLO *and* IAGO, *at a distance.*)

EMILIA. Madam, here comes my lord.

CASSIO. Madam, I'll take my leave.

DESDEMONA. Nay, stay and hear me speak.

CASSIO. Madam, not now. I am very ill at ease,
Unfit for mine own purposes.

DESDEMONA. Well, do your discretion.

(*Exit* CASSIO.)

IAGO. Ha! I like not that.

OTHELLO. What dost thou say?

IAGO. Nothing, my lord. Or if—I know not what.

OTHELLO. Was not that Cassio parted from my wife?

IAGO. Cassio, my lord! No, sure, I cannot think it,
That he would steal away so guilty-like,
Seeing you coming.

OTHELLO. I do believe 'twas he.

DESDEMONA. How now, my lord!
I have been talking with a suitor here,
A man that languishes in your displeasure.

OTHELLO. Who is 't you mean?

12–13. He . . . distance: i.e., his apparent coldness to you shall only be so much as his official position demands for reasons of policy. **19. doubt:** fear. **20. give . . . place:** guarantee that you will be restored to your position. **24. shrift:** place of confession [L.P.].

DESDEMONA. Why, your Lieutenant, Cassio. Good my lord,
If I have any grace or power to move you,
His present reconciliation take.°
For if he be not one that truly loves you,
That errs in ignorance and not in cunning,
I have no judgment in an honest face.
I prithee call him back.
OTHELLO. Went he hence now?
DESDEMONA. Aye, sooth, so humbled
That he hath left part of his grief with me,
To suffer with him. Good love, call him back.
OTHELLO. Not now, sweet Desdemona, some other time.
DESDEMONA. But shall 't be shortly?
OTHELLO. The sooner, sweet, for you.
DESDEMONA. Shall 't be tonight at supper?
OTHELLO. No, not tonight.
DESDEMONA. Tomorrow dinner then?
OTHELLO. I shall not dine at home.
I meet the captains at the citadel.
DESDEMONA. Why, then tomorrow night or Tuesday morn,
On Tuesday noon, or night, on Wednesday morn.
I prithee name the time, but let it not
Exceed three days. In faith, he's penitent,
And yet his trespass, in our common reason—
Save that, they say, the wars must make examples
Out of their best—is not almost° a fault
To incur a private check.° When shall he come?
Tell me, Othello. I wonder in my soul
What you would ask me that I should deny,
Or stand so mammering° on. What! Michael Cassio,
That came a-wooing with you, and so many a time
When I have spoke of you dispraisingly
Hath ta'en your part—to have so much to do
To bring him in! Trust me, I could do much—
OTHELLO. Prithee, no more. Let him come when he will.
I will deny thee nothing.
DESDEMONA. Why, this is not a boon.
'Tis as I should entreat you wear your gloves,
Or feed on nourishing dishes, or keep you warm,
Or sue to you to do a peculiar profit
To your own person. Nay, when I have a suit

48. His . . . take: accept his immediate apology and forgive him. **67. almost:** hardly. **68. check:** rebuke. **71. mammering:** hesitating.

Wherein I mean to touch your love indeed,
It shall be full of poise and difficult weight,
And fearful to be granted.
OTHELLO. I will deny thee nothing.
Whereon I do beseech thee grant me this,
To leave me but a little to myself.
DESDEMONA. Shall I deny you? No. Farewell, my lord.
OTHELLO. Farewell, my Desdemona. I'll come to thee straight.
DESDEMONA. Emilia, come. Be as your fancies teach you.
Whate'er you be, I am obedient.

(*Exeunt* DESDEMONA *and* EMILIA.)

OTHELLO. Excellent wretch! Perdition catch my soul
But I do love thee! And when I love thee not,
Chaos is come again.
IAGO. My noble lord—
OTHELLO. What dost thou say, Iago?
IAGO. Did Michael Cassio, when you wooed my lady,
Know of your love?
OTHELLO. He did, from first to last. Why dost thou ask?
IAGO. But for a satisfaction of my thought,
No further harm.
OTHELLO. Why of thy thought, Iago?
IAGO. I did not think he had been acquainted with her.
OTHELLO. Oh yes, and went between us very oft.
IAGO. Indeed!
OTHELLO. Indeed! Aye, indeed. Discern'st thou aught in that?
Is he not honest?
IAGO. Honest, my lord!
OTHELLO. Honest! Aye, honest.
IAGO. My lord, for aught I know.
OTHELLO. What dost thou think?
IAGO. Think, my lord!
OTHELLO. Think, my lord! By Heaven, he echoes me
As if there were some monster in his thought
Too hideous to be shown. Thou dost mean something.
I heard thee say even now thou likedst not that
When Cassio left my wife. What didst not like?
And when I told thee he was of my counsel
In my whole course of wooing, thou criedst "Indeed!"
And didst contract and purse thy brow together
As if thou then hadst shut up in thy brain
Some horrible conceit. If thou dost love me,
Show me thy thought.
IAGO. My lord, you know I love you.

OTHELLO. I think thou dost,
And for I know thou'rt full of love and honesty
And weigh'st thy words before thou givest them breath,
Therefore these stops of thine fright me the more.
For such things in a false disloyal knave
Are tricks of custom, but in a man that's just
They're close delations,° working from the heart,
That passion cannot rule.

IAGO. For Michael Cassio,
I dare be sworn I think that he is honest.

OTHELLO. I think so too.

IAGO. Men should be what they seem,
Or those that be not, would they might seem none!°

OTHELLO. Certain, men should be what they seem.

IAGO. Why, then I think Cassio's an honest man.

OTHELLO. Nay, yet there's more in this.
I prithee speak to me as to thy thinkings,
As thou dost ruminate, and give thy worst of thoughts
The worst of words.

IAGO. Good my lord, pardon me.
Though I am bound to every act of duty,
I am not bound to that all slaves are free to.
Utter my thoughts? Why, say they are vile and false,
As where's that palace whereinto foul things
Sometimes intrude not? Who has a breast so pure
But some uncleanly apprehensions
Keep leets° and law days, and in session sit
With meditations lawful?

OTHELLO. Thou dost conspire against thy friend, Iago,
If thou but think'st him wronged and makest his ear
A stranger to thy thoughts.

IAGO. I do beseech you—
Though I perchance am vicious in my guess,
As, I confess, it is my nature's plague
To spy into abuses, and oft my jealousy°
Shapes faults that are not—that your wisdom yet,
From one that so imperfectly conceits,°
Would take no notice, nor build yourself a trouble
Out of his scattering and unsure observance.°
It were not for your quiet nor your good,

124. close delations: concealed accusations. **128. seem none:** i.e., not seem to be honest men. **141. leets:** courts. **148. jealousy:** suspicion. **150. conceits:** conceives. **152. observance:** observation.

Nor for my manhood, honesty, or wisdom,
To let you know my thoughts.
OTHELLO. What dost thou mean?
IAGO. Good name in man and woman, dear my lord,
Is the immediate jewel of their souls.
Who steals my purse steals trash—'tis something, nothing,
'Twas mine, 'tis his, and has been slave to thousands—
But he that filches from me my good name
Robs me of that which not enriches him
And makes me poor indeed.
OTHELLO. By Heaven, I'll know thy thoughts.
IAGO. You cannot if my heart were in your hand,
Nor shall not whilst 'tis in my custody.
OTHELLO. Ha!
IAGO. Oh, beware, my lord, of jealousy.
It is the green-eyed monster which doth mock
The meat it feeds on. That cuckold lives in bliss
Who, certain of his fate, loves not his wronger.°
But, oh, what damnèd minutes tells he o'er
Who dotes, yet doubts, suspects, yet strongly loves!
OTHELLO. Oh, misery!
IAGO. Poor and content is rich, and rich enough,
But riches fineless° is as poor as winter
To him that ever fears he shall be poor.
Good Heaven, the souls of all my tribe defend
From jealousy!
OTHELLO. Why, why is this?
Think'st thou I'd make a life of jealousy,
To follow still the changes of the moon
With fresh suspicions? No, to be once in doubt
Is once to be resolved.° Exchange me for a goat
When I shall turn the business of my soul
To such exsufflicate and blown surmises,
Matching thy inference.° 'Tis not to make me jealous
To say my wife is fair, feeds well, loves company,
Is free of speech, sings, plays, and dances well.
Where virtue is, these are more virtuous.
Nor from mine own weak merits will I draw

168–69. That . . . wronger: i.e., the cuckold who hates his wife and knows her falseness is not tormented by suspicious jealousy. **174. fineless:** limitless. **180–81. to . . . resolved:** whenever I find myself in doubt I at once seek out the truth. **182–84. When . . . inference:** when I shall allow that which concerns me most dearly to be influenced by such trifling suggestions as yours. **exsufflicate:** blown up like a bubble.

The smallest fear or doubt of her revolt,
For she had eyes, and chose me. No, Iago,
I'll see before I doubt, when I doubt, prove,
And on the proof, there is no more but this—
Away at once with love or jealousy!

IAGO. I am glad of it, for now I shall have reason
To show the love and duty that I bear you
With franker spirit. Therefore, as I am bound,
Receive it from me. I speak not yet of proof.
Look to your wife. Observe her well with Cassio.
Wear your eye thus, not jealous nor secure.
I would not have your free and noble nature
Out of self-bounty° be abused, look to 't.
I know our country disposition well.
In Venice° they do let Heaven see the pranks
They dare not show their husbands. Their best conscience
Is not to leave 't undone, but keep 't unknown.

OTHELLO. Dost thou say so?

IAGO. She did deceive her father, marrying you,
And when she seemed to shake and fear your looks,
She loved them most.

OTHELLO. And so she did.

IAGO. Why, go to, then.
She that so young could give out such a seeming
To seel° her father's eyes up close as oak—
He thought 'twas witchcraft—but I am much to blame.
I humbly do beseech you of your pardon
For too much loving you.

OTHELLO. I am bound to thee forever.

IAGO. I see this hath a little dashed your spirits.

OTHELLO. Not a jot, not a jot.

IAGO. I' faith, I fear it has.
I hope you will consider what is spoke
Comes from my love, but I do see you're moved.
I am to pray you not to strain my speech
To grosser issues nor to larger reach
Than to suspicion.

OTHELLO. I will not.

IAGO. Should you do so, my lord,
My speech should fall into such vile success
As my thoughts aim not at. Cassio's my worthy friend.—

201. self-bounty: natural goodness. **203. In Venice:** Venice was notorious for its loose women; the Venetian courtesans were among the sights of Europe and were much commented upon by travelers. **211. seel:** blind.

My lord, I see you're moved.
OTHELLO. No, not much moved.
I do not think but Desdemona's honest.°
IAGO. Long live she so! And long live you to think so!
OTHELLO. And yet, how nature erring from itself—
IAGO. Aye, there's the point. As—to be bold with you—
Not to affect° many proposed matches
Of her own clime, complexion, and degree,
Whereto we see in all things nature tends°—
Foh! One may smell in such a will most rank,°
Foul disproportion, thoughts unnatural.
But pardon me. I do not in position
Distinctly speak of her, though I may fear
Her will, recoiling to her better judgment,
May fall to match° you with her country forms,°
And happily° repent.
OTHELLO. Farewell, farewell.
If more thou dost perceive, let me know more.
Set on thy wife to observe. Leave me, Iago.
IAGO (*going*). My lord, I take my leave.
OTHELLO. Why did I marry? This honest creature doubtless
Sees and knows more, much more, than he unfolds.
IAGO (*returning*). My lord, I would I might entreat your honor
To scan this thing no further. Leave it to time.
Though it be fit that Cassio have his place,
For sure he fills it up with great ability,
Yet if you please to hold him off awhile,
You shall by that perceive him and his means.
Note if your lady strain his entertainment°
With any strong or vehement importunity—
Much will be seen in that. In the meantime,
Let me be thought too busy in my fears—
As worthy cause I have to fear I am—
And hold her free, I do beseech your Honor.
OTHELLO. Fear not my government.°
IAGO. I once more take my leave. (*Exit.*)
OTHELLO. This fellow's of exceeding honesty,

226. honest: When applied to Desdemona, "honest" means "chaste," but applied to Iago it has the modern meaning of "open and sincere." **230. affect:** be inclined to. **232. in . . . tends:** i.e., a woman naturally marries a man of her own country, color, and rank. **233. will . . . rank:** desire most lustful. **238. match:** compare. **country forms:** the appearance of her countrymen; i.e., white men. **239. happily:** haply, by chance. **251. strain . . . entertainment:** urge you to receive him. **257. government:** self-control.

And knows all qualities, with a learned spirit,
Of human dealings. If I do prove her haggard,
Though that her jesses were my dear heartstrings,
I'd whistle her off and let her down the wind
To prey at fortune.° Haply, for I am black
And have not those soft parts of conversation
That chamberers° have, or for I am declined
Into the vale of years—yet that's not much—
She's gone, I am abused, and my relief
Must be to loathe her. Oh, curse of marriage,
That we can call these delicate creatures ours,
And not their appetites! I had rather be a toad
And live upon the vapor of a dungeon
Than keep a corner in the thing I love
For others' uses. Yet, 'tis the plague of great ones,
Prerogatived are they less than the base.
'Tis destiny unshunnable, like death.
Even then this forkèd plague° is fated to us
When we do quicken.° Desdemona comes.

(*Re-enter* DESDEMONA *and* EMILIA.)

If she be false, oh, then Heaven mocks itself!
I'll not believe 't.

DESDEMONA. How now, my dear Othello!
Your dinner, and the generous° islanders
By you invited, do attend your presence.

OTHELLO. I am to blame.

DESDEMONA. Why do you speak so faintly?
Are you not well?

OTHELLO. I have a pain upon my forehead here.

DESDEMONA. Faith, that's with watching,° 'twill away again.
Let me but bind it hard, within this hour
It will be well.

OTHELLO. Your napkin° is too little,

(*He puts the handkerchief from him, and she drops it.*)

Let it alone. Come, I'll go in with you.

DESDEMONA. I am very sorry that you are not well.

261–64. If . . . fortune: Othello keeps up the imagery of falconry throughout. He means: If I find that she is wild, I'll whistle her off the game and let her go where she will, for she's not worth keeping. **haggard:** a wild hawk. **jesses:** the straps attached to a hawk's legs. **266. chamberers:** playboys. **277. forkèd plague:** i.e., to be a cuckold. **278. quicken:** stir in our mother's womb. **281. generous:** noble [L.P.]. **286. watching:** lack of sleep. **288. napkin:** handkerchief.

(*Exeunt* OTHELLO *and* DESDEMONA.)

EMILIA. I am glad I have found this napkin.
This was her first remembrance from the Moor.
My wayward° husband hath a hundred times
Wooed me to steal it, but she so loves the token,
For he conjured° her she should ever keep it,
That she reserves it evermore about her
To kiss and talk to. I'll have the work ta'en out,°
And give 't Iago. What he will do with it
Heaven knows, not I.
I nothing but to please his fantasy.°

(*Re-enter* IAGO.)

IAGO. How now! What do you here alone?
EMILIA. Do not you chide, I have a thing for you.
IAGO. A thing for me? It is a common thing—
EMILIA. Ha!
IAGO. To have a foolish wife.
EMILIA. Oh, is that all? What will you give me now
For that same handkerchief?
IAGO. What handkerchief?
EMILIA. What handkerchief!
Why, that the Moor first gave to Desdemona,
That which so often you did bid me steal.
IAGO. Hast stol'n it from her?
EMILIA. No, faith, she let it drop by negligence,
And, to the advantage, I being here took 't up.
Look, here it is.
IAGO. A good wench. Give it me.
EMILIA. What will you do with 't, that you have been so earnest
To have me filch it?
IAGO (*snatching it*). Why, what's that to you?
EMILIA. If 't be not for some purpose of import,
Give 't me again. Poor lady, she'll run mad
When she shall lack it.
IAGO. Be not acknown on 't,° I have use for it.
Go, leave me.

(*Exit* EMILIA.)

I will in Cassio's lodging lose this napkin,
And let him find it. Trifles light as air

293. wayward: unaccountable. **295. conjured:** begged with an oath. **297. work . . . out:** pattern copied. **300. fantasy:** whim. **321. Be . . . 't:** know nothing about it.

Are to the jealous confirmations strong
As proofs of Holy Writ. This may do something.
The Moor already changes with my poison.
Dangerous conceits are in their natures poisons,
Which at the first are scarce found to distaste,
But with a little act upon the blood
Burn like the mines of sulphur. I did say so.°
Look where he comes!

(*Re-enter* OTHELLO.)

Not poppy,° nor mandragora,°
Nor all the drowsy syrups of the world,
Shall ever medicine thee to that sweet sleep
Which thou owedst° yesterday,

OTHELLO. Ha! Ha! False to me?

IAGO. Why, how now, General! No more of that.

OTHELLO. Avaunt! Be gone! Thou hast set me on the rack.
I swear 'tis better to be much abused
Than but to know 't a little.

IAGO. How now, my lord!

OTHELLO. What sense had I of her stol'n hours of lust?
I saw 't not, thought it not, it harmed not me.
I slept the next night well, was free and merry.
I found not Cassio's kisses on her lips.
He that is robbed, not wanting° what is stol'n,
Let him not know 't and he's not robbed at all.

IAGO. I am sorry to hear this.

OTHELLO. I had been happy if the general camp,
Pioners° and all, had tasted her sweet body,
So I had nothing known. Oh, now forever
Farewell the tranquil mind! Farewell content!
Farewell the plumèd troop and the big wars
That make ambition virtue! Oh, farewell,
Farewell the neighing steed and the shrill trump,
The spirit-stirring drum, the ear-piercing fife,
The royal banner and all quality,
Pride, pomp, and circumstance of glorious war!
And, O you mortal engines, whose rude throats
The immortal Jove's dread clamors counterfeit,
Farewell! Othello's occupation's gone!

331. **I . . . so:** As Iago says this, Othello is seen approaching, with all the signs of his agitation outwardly visible. 332. **poppy:** opium. **mandragora:** called also mandrake, a root used as a drug to bring sleep. 335. **owedst:** owned. 344. **wanting:** missing. 348. **Pioners:** pioneers, the lowest type of soldier.

IAGO. Is 't possible, my lord?
OTHELLO. Villain, be sure thou prove my love a whore,
Be sure of it, give me the ocular proof.
Or by the worth of man's eternal soul,
Thou hadst been better have been born a dog
Than answer my waked wrath!
IAGO. Is 't come to this?
OTHELLO. Make me to see 't, or at the least so prove it
That the probation° bear no hinge nor loop
To hang a doubt on, or woe upon thy life!
IAGO. My noble lord—
OTHELLO. If thou dost slander her and torture me,
Never pray more, abandon all remorse.°
On horror's head horrors accumulate,
Do deeds to make Heaven weep, all earth amazed,
For nothing canst thou to damnation add
Greater than that.
IAGO. Oh, grace! Oh, Heaven defend me!
Are you a man? Have you a soul or sense?
God be wi' you, take mine office. O wretched fool,
That livest to make thine honesty a vice!
O monstrous world! Take note, take note, O world,
To be direct and honest is not safe.
I thank you for this profit, and from hence
I'll love no friend, sith° love breeds such offense.
OTHELLO. Nay, stay. Thou shouldst be honest.
IAGO. I should be wise, for honesty's a fool,
And loses that it works for.
OTHELLO. By the world,
I think my wife be honest, and think she is not.
I think that thou art just, and think thou art not.
I'll have some proof. Her name, that was as fresh
As Dian's° visage, is now begrimed and black
As mine own face. If there be cords, or knives,
Poison, or fire, or suffocating streams,
I'll not endure it. Would I were satisfied!
IAGO. I see, sir, you are eaten up with passion.
I do repent me that I put it to you.
You would be satisfied?
OTHELLO. Would! Nay, I will.
IAGO. And may, but, how? How satisfied, my lord?

367. probation: proof. **371. remorse:** pity. **382. sith:** since. **389. Dian:** Diana, goddess of chastity.

Would you, the supervisor,° grossly gape on?
Behold her topped?

OTHELLO. Death and damnation! Oh!

IAGO. It were a tedious difficulty, I think,
To bring them to that prospect. Damn them then,
If ever mortal eyes do see them bolster°
More than their own! What then? How then?
What shall I say? Where's satisfaction?
It is impossible you should see this,
Were they as prime° as goats, as hot as monkeys,
As salt° as wolves in pride,° and fools as gross
As ignorance made drunk. But yet I say
If imputation° and strong circumstances,
Which lead directly to the door of truth,
Will give you satisfaction, you may have 't.

OTHELLO. Give me a living reason she's disloyal.

IAGO. I do not like the office.
But sith I am entered in this cause so far,
Pricked to 't by foolish honesty and love,
I will go on. I lay with Cassio lately,
And being troubled with a raging tooth,
I could not sleep.
There are a kind of men so loose of soul
That in their sleeps will mutter their affairs.
One of this kind is Cassio.
In sleep I heard him say "Sweet Desdemona,
Let us be wary, let us hide our loves."
And then, sir, would he gripe° and wring my hand,
Cry "O sweet creature!" and then kiss me hard,
As if he plucked up kisses by the roots
That grew upon my lips. Then laid his leg
Over my thigh, and sighed and kissed, and then
Cried "Cursed fate that gave thee to the Moor!"

OTHELLO. Oh, monstrous! Monstrous!

IAGO. Nay, this was but his dream.

OTHELLO. But this denoted a foregone conclusion.
'Tis a shrewd doubt,° though it be but a dream.

IAGO. And this may help to thicken other proofs
That do demónstrate thinly.

OTHELLO. I'll tear her all to pieces.

397. **supervisor:** looker-on. 401. **bolster:** sleep together. 405. **prime:** lustful. 406. **salt:** eager. **pride:** in heat. 408. **imputation:** probability. 423. **gripe:** grip. 431. **shrewd doubt:** bitter suspicion.

IAGO. Nay, but be wise. Yet we see nothing done.
She may be honest yet. Tell me but this:
Have you not sometimes seen a handkerchief
Spotted with strawberries in your wife's hand?
OTHELLO. I gave her such a one, 'twas my first gift.
IAGO. I know not that. But such a handkerchief—
I am sure it was your wife's—did I today
See Cassio wipe his beard with.
OTHELLO. If it be that—
IAGO. If it be that, or any that was hers,
It speaks against her with the other proofs.
OTHELLO. Oh, that the slave had forty thousand lives!
One is too poor, too weak, for my revenge.
Now do I see 'tis true. Look here, Iago,
All my fond love thus do I blow to Heaven—
'Tis gone.
Arise, black Vengeance, from thy hollow cell!
Yield up, O Love, thy crown and hearted throne
To tyrannous hate! Swell, bosom, with thy fraught,°
For 'tis of aspics'° tongues!
IAGO. Yet be content.
OTHELLO. Oh, blood, blood, blood!
IAGO. Patience, I say. Your mind perhaps may change.
OTHELLO. Never, Iago. Like to the Pontic Sea,
Whose icy current and compulsive course
Ne'er feels retiring ebb but keeps due on
To the Propontic and the Hellespont;
Even so my bloody thoughts, with violent pace,
Shall ne'er look back, ne'er ebb to humble love,
Till that capable° and wide revenge
Swallow them up. Now, by yond marble Heaven,
In the due reverence of a sacred vow (*Kneels.*)
I here engage my words.
IAGO. Do not rise yet. (*Kneels.*)
Witness, you ever burning lights above,
You elements that clip° us round about,
Witness that here Iago doth give up
The execution of his wit, hands, heart,
To wronged Othello's service! Let him command,
And to obey shall be in me remorse,°

451. fraught: freight. **452. aspics':** asps'. **461. capable:** comprehensive. **466. clip:** embrace. **470. remorse:** solemn obligation.

What bloody business ever.

(*They rise.*)

OTHELLO. I greet thy love,
Not with vain thanks, but with acceptance bounteous,
And will upon the instant put thee to 't.
Within these three days let me hear thee say
That Cassio's not alive.

IAGO. My friend is dead. 'Tis done at your request.
But let her live.

OTHELLO. Damn her, lewd minx! Oh, damn her!
Come, go with me apart. I will withdraw,
To furnish me with some swift means of death
For the fair devil. Now art thou my Lieutenant.

IAGO. I am your own forever.

(*Exeunt.*)

SCENE IV. Before the castle.

Enter DESDEMONA, EMILIA, *and* CLOWN.

DESDEMONA. Do you know, sirrah, where Lieutenant Cassio lies?

CLOWN. I dare not say he lies anywhere.

DESDEMONA. Why, man?

CLOWN. He's a soldier, and for one to say a soldier lies is stabbing.

DESDEMONA. Go to. Where lodges he?

CLOWN. To tell you where he lodges is to tell you where I lie.

DESDEMONA. Can anything be made of this?

CLOWN. I know not where he lodges, and for me to devise a lodging, and say he lies here or he lies there, were to lie in mine own throat.

DESDEMONA. Can you inquire him out and be edified by report?°

CLOWN. I will catechize the world for him; that is, make questions and by them answer.

DESDEMONA. Seek him, bid him come hither. Tell him I have moved my lord on his behalf and hope all will be well.

CLOWN. To do this is within the compass of man's wit, and therefore I will attempt the doing it. (*Exit.*)

DESDEMONA. Where should I lose that handkerchief, Emilia?

EMILIA. I know not, madam.

DESDEMONA. Believe me, I had rather have lost my purse
Full of crusados. And, but my noble Moor
Is true of mind and made of no such baseness
As jealous creatures are, it were enough

10. edified . . . report: enlightened by the information. Desdemona speaks with mock pomposity.

To put him to ill thinking.
EMILIA. Is he not jealous?
DESDEMONA. Who, he? I think the sun where he was born
Drew all such humors from him.
EMILIA. Look where he comes.
DESDEMONA. I will not leave him now till Cassio
Be called to him.

(*Enter* OTHELLO.)

How is 't with you, my lord?
OTHELLO. Well, my good lady. (*Aside*) Oh, hardness to dissemble!
How do you, Desdemona?
DESDEMONA. Well, my good lord.
OTHELLO. Give me your hand. This hand is moist,° my lady.
DESDEMONA. It yet has felt no age nor known no sorrow.
OTHELLO. This argues fruitfulness and liberal heart.
Hot, hot, and moist—this hand of yours requires
A sequester from liberty, fasting and prayer,
Much castigation, exercise devout.
For here's a young and sweating devil here,
That commonly rebels. 'Tis a good hand,
A frank one.
DESDEMONA. You may indeed say so,
For 'twas that hand that gave away my heart.
OTHELLO. A liberal° hand. The hearts of old gave hands,
But our new heraldry is hands, not hearts.°
DESDEMONA. I cannot speak of this. Come now, your promise.
OTHELLO. What promise, chuck?°
DESDEMONA. I have sent to bid Cassio come speak with you.
OTHELLO. I have a salt and sorry rheum offends me.
Lend me thy handkerchief.
DESDEMONA. Here, my lord.
OTHELLO. That which I gave you.
DESDEMONA. I have it not about me.
OTHELLO. Not?
DESDEMONA. No indeed, my lord.
OTHELLO. That's a fault. That handkerchief
Did an Egyptian to my mother give.
She was a charmer, and could almost read
The thoughts of people. She told her while she kept it

30. moist: a hot moist palm was believed to show desire. **40. liberal:** overgenerous. **40–41. The . . . hearts:** once love and deeds went together, but now it is all deeds (i.e., faithlessness) and no love. **43. chuck:** a term of affection, but not the kind of word with which a person of Othello's dignity would normally address his wife. He is beginning to treat her with contemptuous familiarity.

'Twould make her amiable and subdue my father
Entirely to her love, but if she lost it
Or made a gift of it, my father's eye
Should hold her loathed and his spirits should hunt
After new fancies. She dying gave it me,
And bid me, when my fate would have me wive,
To give it her. I did so. And take heed on 't,
Make it a darling like your precious eye.
To lose 't or give 't away were such perdition
As nothing else could match.

DESDEMONA. It 't possible?

OTHELLO. 'Tis true. There's magic in the web of it.
A sibyl that had numbered in the world
The sun to course two hundred compasses
In her prophetic fury sewed the work.
The worms were hallowed that did breed the silk,
And it was dyed in mummy which the skillful
Conserved° of maidens' hearts.

DESDEMONA. Indeed! Is 't true?

OTHELLO. Most veritable, therefore look to 't well.

DESDEMONA. Then would to God that I had never seen 't.

OTHELLO. Ha! Wherefore?

DESDEMONA. Why do you speak so startlingly and rash?

OTHELLO. Is 't lost? Is 't gone? Speak, is it out o' the way?

DESDEMONA. Heaven bless us!

OTHELLO. Say you?

DESDEMONA. It is not lost, but what an if it were?

OTHELLO. How!

DESDEMONA. I say it is not lost.

OTHELLO. Fetch 't, let me see it.

DESDEMONA. Why, so I can, sir, but I will not now.
This is a trick to put me from my suit.
Pray you let Cassio be received again.

OTHELLO. Fetch me the handkerchief. My mind misgives.

DESDEMONA. Come, come,
You'll never meet a more sufficient man.

OTHELLO. The handkerchief!

DESDEMONA. I pray talk me of Cassio.

OTHELLO. The handkerchief!

DESDEMONA. A man that all his time
Hath founded his good fortunes on your love,
Shared dangers with you—

69. Conserved: prepared.

OTHELLO. The handkerchief!
DESDEMONA. In sooth, you are to blame.
OTHELLO. Away! (*Exit.*)
EMILIA. Is not this man jealous?
DESDEMONA. I ne'er saw this before.
Sure there's some wonder in this handkerchief.
I am most unhappy in the loss of it.
EMILIA. 'Tis not a year or two shows us a man.°
They are all but stomachs and we all but food.
They eat us hungerly, and when they are full
They belch us. Look you, Cassio and my husband.

(*Enter* CASSIO *and* IAGO.)

IAGO. There is no other way, 'tis she must do 't.
And, lo, the happiness!° Go and impórtune her.
DESDEMONA. How now, good Cassio! What's the news with you?
CASSIO. Madam, my former suit. I do beseech you
That by your virtuous means I may again
Exist, and be a member of his love
Whom I with all the office of my heart
Entirely honor. I would not be delayed.
If my offense be of such mortal kind
That nor my service past nor present sorrows
Nor purposed merit in futurity
Can ransom me into his love again,
But to know so must be my benefit.
So shall I clothe me in a forced content
And shut myself up in some other course
To Fortune's alms.
DESDEMONA. Alas, thrice-gentle Cassio!
My advocation° is not now in tune.
My lord is not my lord, nor should I know him
Were he in favor° as in humor altered.
So help me every spirit sanctified,
As I have spoken for you all my best
And stood within the blank° of his displeasure
For my free speech! You must awhile be patient.
What I can do I will, and more I will
Than for myself I dare. Let that suffice you.

97. 'Tis . . . man: it does not take a couple of years for us to discover the nature of a man; i.e., he soon shows his real nature. **102. And . . . happiness:** what good luck, here she is. **117. advocation:** advocacy. **119. favor:** face [L.P.]. **122. blank:** aim.

IAGO. Is my lord angry?
EMILIA. He went hence but now,
And certainly in strange unquietness.
IAGO. Can he be angry? I have seen the cannon
When it hath blown his ranks into the air,
And, like the Devil, from his very arm
Puffed his own brother, and can he be angry?
Something of moment then. I will go meet him.
There's matter in 't indeed if he be angry.
DESDEMONA. I prithee do so.

(*Exit* IAGO.)

Something sure of state,
Either from Venice, or some unhatched practice
Made demonstrable here in Cyprus to him,
Hath puddled his clear spirit. And in such cases
Men's natures wrangle with inferior things,
Though great ones are their object. 'Tis even so,
For let our finger ache and it indues
Our other healthful members even to that sense
Of pain. Nay, we must think men are not gods,
Nor of them look for such observancy
As fits the bridal.° Beshrew me much, Emilia,
I was, unhandsome warrior° as I am,
Arraigning his unkindness with my soul,
But now I find I had suborned the witness,°
And he's indicted falsely.
EMILIA. Pray Heaven it be state matters, as you think,
And no conception nor no jealous toy°
Concerning you.
DESDEMONA. Alas the day, I never gave him cause!
EMILIA. But jealous souls will not be answered so.
They are not ever jealous for the cause,
But jealous for they are jealous 'Tis a monster
Begot upon itself, born on itself.
DESDEMONA. Heaven keep that monster from Othello's mind!
EMILIA. Lady, amen.
DESDEMONA. I will go seek him. Cassio, walk hereabout.
If I do find him fit, I'll move your suit,
And seek to effect it to my uttermost.

144. bridal: honeymoon. **145. unhandsome warrior:** clumsy soldier. Desdemona continually thinks of herself as Othello's companion in arms. Cf. I.iii249 ff. **147. suborned . . . witness:** corrupted the evidence; i.e., it is my fault, not his. **150. jealous toy:** silly suspicion.

CASSIO. I humbly thank your ladyship.

(*Exeunt* DESDEMONA *and* EMILIA. *Enter* BIANCA.)

BIANCA. Save you, friend Cassio!
CASSIO. What make you from home?
How is it with you, my most fair Bianca?
I' faith, sweet love, I was coming to your house.
BIANCA. And I was going to your lodging, Cassio.
What, keep a week away? Seven days and nights?
Eightscore eight hours? And lovers' absent hours,
More tedious than the dial eightscore times?
Oh, weary reckoning!
CASSIO. Pardon me, Bianca.
I have this while with leaden thoughts been pressed,
But I shall in a more continuate time
Strike off this score of absence. Sweet Bianca,

(*Giving her* DESDEMONA'S *handkerchief*)

Take me this work out.
BIANCA. O' Cassio, whence came this?
This is some token from a newer friend.
To the felt absence now I feel a cause.
Is 't come to this? Well, well.
CASSIO. Go to, woman!
Throw your vile guesses in the Devil's teeth,
From whence you have them. You are jealous now
That this is from some mistress, some remembrance.
No, by my faith, Bianca.
BIANCA. Why, whose is it?
CASSIO. I know not, sweet. I found it in my chamber.
I like the work well. Ere it be demanded—
As like enough it will—I'd have it copied.
Take it, and do 't, and leave me for this time.
BIANCA. Leave you! Wherefore?
CASSIO. I do attend here on the General,
And think it no addition,° nor my wish,
To have him see me womaned.°
BIANCA. Why, I pray you?
CASSIO. Not that I love you not.
BIANCA. But that you do not love me.
I pray you bring me on the way a little,
And say if I shall see you soon at night.

188. addition: honor. **189. womaned:** with a girl.

CASSIO. 'Tis but a little way that I can bring you,
For I attend here. But I'll see you soon.
BIANCA. 'Tis very good, I must be circumstanced.°

(*Exeunt.*)

ACT IV

SCENE I. Cyprus. Before the castle.

Enter OTHELLO *and* IAGO.

IAGO. Will you think so?
OTHELLO. Think so, Iago!
IAGO. What,
To kiss in private?
OTHELLO. An unauthorized kiss.
IAGO. Or to be naked with her friend in bed
An hour or more, not meaning any harm?
OTHELLO. Naked in bed, Iago, and not mean harm!
It is hypocrisy against the Devil.
They that mean virtuously and yet do so,
The Devil their virtue tempts and they tempt Heaven.
IAGO. So they do nothing, 'tis a venial° slip.
But if I give my wife a handkerchief—
OTHELLO. What then?
IAGO. Why, then, 'tis hers, my lord, and being hers,
She may, I think, bestow 't on any man.
OTHELLO. She is protectress of her honor too.
May she give that?
IAGO. Her honor is an essence that's not seen.
They have it very oft that have it not.
But for the handkerchief—
OTHELLO. By Heaven, I would most gladly have forgot it.
Thou said'st—oh, it comes o'er my memory,
As doth the raven o'er the infected house,°
Boding to all—he had my handkerchief.
IAGO. Aye, what of that?
OTHELLO. That's not so good now.
IAGO. What,
If I had said I had seen him do you wrong?
Or heard him say—as knaves be such abroad,

195. circumstanced: put off.
Act iv, Sc. 1. 9. venial: pardonable. **21. As . . . house:** i.e., as a bird of prey waits for its victim to die.

Who having, by their own importunate suit,
Or voluntary dotage of some mistress,
Convincèd or supplied° them, cannot choose
But they must blab—

OTHELLO. Hath he said anything?

IAGO. He hath, my lord, but be you well assured,
No more, than he'll unswear.

OTHELLO. What hath he said?

IAGO. Faith, that he did—I know not what he did.

OTHELLO. What? What?

IAGO. Lie—

OTHELLO. With her?

IAGO. With her, on her, what you will.

OTHELLO. Lie° with her! Lie on her!—We say lie on her when they belie her.—Lie with her! 'Zounds, that's fulsome!° Handkerchief—confessions—handkerchief!—To confess, and be hanged for his labor. First to be hanged, and then to confess. I tremble at it. Nature would not invest herself in such shadowing passion without some instruction.° It is not words that shake me thus. Pish! Noses, ears, and lips. Is 't possible?—Confess?—Handkerchief?—Oh, devil! (*Falls in a trance.*)

IAGO. Work on,
My medicine, work! Thus credulous fools are caught,
And many worthy and chaste dames even thus,
All guiltless, meet reproach. What ho! My lord!
My lord, I say! Othello!

(*Enter* CASSIO.)

How now, Cassio!

CASSIO. What's the matter?

IAGO. My lord is fall'n into an epilepsy.
This is his second fit, he had one yesterday.

CASSIO. Rub him about the temples.

IAGO. No, forbear,
The lethargy° must have his quiet course.
If not, he foams at mouth and by and by
Breaks out to savage madness. Look, he stirs.
Do you withdraw yourself a little while,
He will recover straight. When he is gone,
I would on great occasion speak with you.

(*Exit* CASSIO.)

28. Convincèd or supplied: overcome or satisfied their desires. **35–41. Lie . . . devil:** Othello breaks into incoherent muttering before he falls down in a fit. **36. fulsome:** disgusting. **38–39. Nature . . . instruction:** nature would not fill me with such overwhelming emotion unless there was some cause. **51. lethargy:** epileptic fit.

How is it, General? Have you not hurt your head?°
OTHELLO. Dost thou mock me?
IAGO. I mock you! No, by Heaven.
Would you would bear your fortune like a man!
OTHELLO. A hornèd man's a monster and a beast.
IAGO. There's many a beast, then, in a populous city,
And many a civil monster.
OTHELLO. Did he confess it?
IAGO. Good sir, be a man.
Think every bearded fellow that's but yoked°
May draw with you.° There's millions now alive
That nightly lie in those unproper beds
Which they dare swear peculiar.° Your case is better.
Oh, 'tis the spite of Hell, the Fiend's archmock,
To lip° a wanton in a secure couch°
And to suppose her chaste! No, let me know,
And knowing what I am, I know what she shall be.
OTHELLO. Oh, thou art wise, 'tis certain.
IAGO. Stand you awhile apart,
Confine yourself but in a patient list.°
Whilst you were here o'erwhelmèd with your grief—
A passion most unsuiting such a man—
Cassio came hither. I shifted him away,
And laid good 'scuse upon your ecstasy,°
Bade him anon return and here speak with me,
The which he promisèd. Do but encave yourself,
And mark the fleers, the gibes, and notable scorns,
That dwell in every region of his face.
For I will make him tell the tale anew,
Where, how, how oft, how long ago, and when
He hath and is again to cope° your wife.
I say but mark his gesture. Marry, patience,
Or I shall say you are all in all in spleen,
And nothing of a man.
OTHELLO. Dost thou hear, Iago?
I will be found most cunning in my patience,
But—dost thou hear?—most bloody.
IAGO. That's not amiss,
But yet keep time in all. Will you withdraw?

57. Have . . . head: With brutal cynicism Iago asks whether Othello is suffering from cuckold's headache. **64. yoked:** married. **65. draw . . . you:** be your yoke fellow **66–67. That . . . peculiar:** that lie nightly in beds which they believe are their own but which others have shared. **69. lip:** kiss. **secure couch:** lit., a carefree bed; i.e., a bed which has been used by the wife's lover, but secretly. **73. patient list:** confines of patience. **77. ecstasy:** fit. **84. cope:** encounter.

(OTHELLO *retires.*)

Now will I question Cassio of Bianca,
A housewife° that by selling her desires
Buys herself bread and clothes. It is a creature
That dotes on Cassio, as 'tis the strumpet's plague
To beguile many and be beguiled by one.
He, when he hears of her, cannot refrain
From the excess of laughter. Here he comes.

(*Re-enter* CASSIO.)

As he shall smile, Othello shall go mad,
And his unbookish° jealousy must construe
Poor Cassio's smiles, gestures, and light behavior
Quite in the wrong. How do you now, Lieutenant?

CASSIO. The worser that you give me the addition°
Whose want even kills me.

IAGO. Ply Desdemona well, and you are sure on 't.
Now, if this suit lay in Bianca's power,
How quickly should you speed!

CASSIO. Alas, poor caitiff!°

OTHELLO. Look how he laughs already!

IAGO. I never knew a woman love man so.

CASSIO. Alas, poor rogue! I think, i' faith, she loves me.

OTHELLO. Now he denies it faintly and laughs it out.

IAGO. Do you hear, Cassio?

OTHELLO. Now he impórtunes him
To tell it o'er. Go to. Well said, well said.

IAGO. She gives it out that you shall marry her.
Do you intend it?

CASSIO. Ha, ha, ha!

OTHELLO. Do you triumph, Roman?° Do you triumph?

CASSIO. I marry her! What, a customer! I prithee bear some charity to my wit. Do not think it so unwholesome. Ha, ha, ha!

OTHELLO. So, so, so, so. They laugh that win.

IAGO. Faith, the cry goes that you shall marry her.

CASSIO. Prithee say true.

IAGO. I am a very villain else.

OTHELLO. Have you scored° me? Well.

CASSIO. This is the monkey's own giving out. She is persuaded I

92. housewife: hussy. **99. unbookish:** unlearned. **102. addition:** title (Lieutenant) which he has lost. **106. caitiff:** wretch. **116. triumph, Roman:** The word "triumph" suggests "Roman" because the Romans celebrated their victories with triumphs, elaborate shows, and processions. **123. scored:** marked, as with a blow from a whip.

will marry her out of her own love and flattery, not out of my promise.

OTHELLO. Iago beckons me, now he begins the story.

CASSIO. She was here even now. She haunts me in every place. I was the other day talking on the sea bank with certain Venetians, and thither comes the bauble, and, by this hand, she falls me thus about my neck—

OTHELLO. Crying "O dear Cassio!" as it were. His gesture imports it.

CASSIO. So hangs and lolls and weeps upon me, so hales and pulls me. Ha, ha, ha!

OTHELLO. Now he tells how she plucked him to my chamber. Oh, I see that nose of yours, but not that dog I shall throw it to.

CASSIO. Well, I must leave her company.

IAGO. Before me!° Look where she comes.

CASSIO. 'Tis such another fitchew!° Marry, a perfumed one.

(*Enter* BIANCA.)

What do you mean by this haunting of me?

BIANCA. Let the Devil and his dam haunt you! What did you mean by that same handkerchief you gave me even now? I was a fine fool to take it. I must take out the work? A likely piece of work, that you should find it in your chamber and not know who left it there! This is some minx's token, and I must take out the work? There, give it your hobbyhorse. Wheresoever you had it, I'll take out no work on 't.

CASSIO. How now, my sweet Bianca! How now! How now!

OTHELLO. By Heaven, that should be my handkerchief!

BIANCA. An° you'll come to supper tonight, you may. An you will not, come when you are next prepared for. (*Exit.*)

IAGO. After her, after her.

CASSIO. Faith, I must, she'll rail i' the street else.

IAGO. Will you sup there?

CASSIO. Faith, I intend so.

IAGO. Well, I may chance to see you, for I would very fain speak with you.

CASSIO. Prithee, come, will you?

IAGO. Go to. Say no more.

(*Exit* CASSIO.)

OTHELLO (*advancing*). How shall I murder him, Iago?

IAGO. Did you perceive how he laughed at his vice?

OTHELLO. Oh, Iago!

IAGO. And did you see the handkerchief?

OTHELLO. Was that mine?

IAGO. Yours, by this hand. And to see how he prizes the foolish

137. **Before me:** by my soul. 138. **fitchew:** polecat. 148. **An:** if.

woman your wife! She gave it him, and he hath given it his whore.

OTHELLO. I would have him nine years a-killing. A fine woman! A fair woman! A sweet woman!

IAGO. Nay, you must forget that.

OTHELLO. Aye, let her rot, and perish, and be damned tonight, for she shall not live. No, my heart is turned to stone, I strike it and it hurts my hand. Oh, the world hath not a sweeter creature. She might lie by an emperor's side, and command him tasks.

IAGO. Nay, that's not your way.°

OTHELLO. Hang her! I do but say what she is, so delicate with her needle, an admirable musician—oh, she will sing the savageness out of a bear—of so high and plenteous wit and invention—

IAGO. She's the worse for all this.

OTHELLO. Oh, a thousand thousand times. And then, of so gentle a condition!

IAGO. Aye, too gentle.

OTHELLO. Nay, that's certain. But yet the pity of it, Iago! O Iago, the pity of it, Iago!

IAGO. If you are so fond over her iniquity, give her patent to offend, for if it touch not you, it comes near nobody.

OTHELLO. I will chop her into messes. Cuckold me!

IAGO. Oh, 'tis foul in her.

OTHELLO. With mine officer!

IAGO. That's fouler.

OTHELLO. Get me some poison, Iago, this night. I'll not expostulate with her, lest her body and beauty unprovide my mind again. This night, Iago.

IAGO. Do it not with poison, strangle her in her bed, even the bed she hath contaminated.

OTHELLO. Good, good. The justice of it pleases. Very good.

IAGO. And for Cassio, let me be his undertaker.°
You shall hear more by midnight.

OTHELLO. Excellent good. (*A trumpet within.*) What trumpet is that same?

IAGO. Something from Venice, sure. 'Tis Lodovico
Come from the Duke. And see, your wife is with him.

(*Enter* LODOVICO, DESDEMONA, *and* ATTENDANTS.)

LODOVICO. God save the worthy General!

OTHELLO. With all my heart, sir.

LODOVICO. The Duke and Senators of Venice greet you. (*Gives him a letter.*)

171. Nay . . . way: i.e., don't get soft thoughts about her. **192. be . . . undertaker:** undertake to manage his business. In Shakespeare's plays the word does *not* mean "mortician."

OTHELLO. I kiss the instrument of their pleasures. (*Opens the letter, and reads.*)

DESDEMONA. And what's the news, good Cousin Lodovico?

IAGO. I am very glad to see you, signior.
Welcome to Cyprus.

LODOVICO. I thank you. How does Lieutenant Cassio?

IAGO. Lives, sir.

DESDEMONA. Cousin, there's fall'n between him and my lord
An unkind breach, but you shall make all well.

OTHELLO. Are you sure of that?

DESDEMONA. My lord?

OTHELLO (*reads*). "This fail you not to do, as you will—"

LODOVICO. He did not call, he's busy in the paper.
Is there division 'twixt my lord and Cassio?

DESDEMONA. A most unhappy one. I would do much
To atone° them, for the love I bear to Cassio.

OTHELLO. Fire and brimstone!

DESDEMONA. My lord?

OTHELLO. Are you wise?°

DESDEMONA. What, is he angry?

LODOVICO. Maybe the letter moved him,
For, as I think, they do command him home,
Deputing Cassio in his government.

DESDEMONA. By my troth, I am glad on 't.

OTHELLO. Indeed!

DESDEMONA. My lord?

OTHELLO. I am glad to see you mad.

DESDEMONA. Why, sweet Othello?

OTHELLO. Devil! (*Striking her.*)

DESDEMONA. I have not deserved this.

LODOVICO. My lord, this would not be believed in Venice.
Though I should swear I saw 't. 'Tis very much.
Make her amends, she weeps.

OTHELLO. O devil, devil!
If that the earth could teem with a woman's tears,
Each drop she falls would prove a crocodile.°
Out of my sight!

DESDEMONA. I will not stay to offend you. (*Going.*)

LODOVICO. Truly, an obedient lady.
I do beseech your lordship, call her back.

214. atone: reconcile. **215. Are . . . wise:** i.e., in saying you bear love to Cassio. **226–27. If . . . crocodile:** If the earth could breed from woman's tears, each tear that she lets fall would become a crocodile. It was believed that the crocodile would cry and sob to attract the sympathetic passer-by, who was then snapped up.

OTHELLO. Mistress!
DESDEMONA. My lord?
OTHELLO. What would you with her, sir?
LODOVICO. Who, I, my lord?
OTHELLO. Aye, you did wish that I would make her turn.
Sir, she can turn and turn, and yet go on
And turn again. And she can weep, sir, weep.
And she's obedient, as you say, obedient,
Very obedient. Proceed you in your tears.
Concerning this, sir—oh, well-painted passion!°—
I am commanded home. Get you away.
I'll send for you anon. Sir, I obey the mandate,
And will return to Venice. Hence, avaunt!

(*Exit* DESDEMONA.)

Cassio shall have my place. And, sir, tonight,
I do entreat that we may sup together.
You are welcome, sir, to Cyprus. Goats and monkeys! (*Exit.*)
LODOVICO. Is this the noble Moor whom our full Senate
Call all-in-all sufficient? This the nature
Whom passion could not shake? Whose solid virtue
The shot of accident nor dart of chance
Could neither graze nor pierce?
IAGO. He is much changed.
LODOVICO. Are his wits safe? Is he not light of brain?
IAGO. He's that he is. I may not breathe my censure°
What he might be. If what he might he is not,
I would to Heaven he were!
LODOVICO. What, strike his wife!
IAGO. Faith, that was not so well, yet would I knew
That stroke would prove the worst!
LODOVICO. Is it his use?
Or did the letters work upon his blood,
And new-create this fault?
IAGO. Alas, alas!
It is not honesty in me to speak
What I have seen and known. You shall observe him,
And his own courses will denote him so
That I may save my speech. Do but go after,
And mark how he continues.
LODOVICO. I am sorry that I am deceived in him.

(*Exeunt.*)

239. well-painted passion: emotion [L.P.]. **252. censure:** opinion [L.P.].

SCENE II. A room in the castle.

Enter OTHELLO *and* EMILIA.

OTHELLO. You have seen nothing, then?
EMILIA. Nor ever heard, nor ever did suspect.
OTHELLO. Yes, you have seen Cassio and she together.
EMILIA. But then I saw no harm, and then I heard
Each syllable that breath made up between them.
OTHELLO. What, did they never whisper?
EMILIA. Never, my lord.
OTHELLO. Nor send you out o' the way?
EMILIA. Never.
OTHELLO. To fetch her fan, her gloves, her mask, nor nothing?
EMILIA. Never, my lord.
OTHELLO. That's strange.
EMILIA. I durst, my lord, to wager she is honest,
Lay down my soul at stake. If you think other,
Remove your thought, it doth abuse your bosom.
If any wretch have put this in your head,
Let Heaven requite it with the serpent's curse!
For if she be not honest, chaste, and true,
There's no man happy, the purest of their wives
Is foul as slander.
OTHELLO. Bid her come hither. Go.

(*Exit* EMILIA.)

She says enough. Yet she's a simple bawd
That cannot say as much. This is a subtle whore,
A closet lock and key of villainous secrets.
And yet she'll kneel and pray, I have seen her do 't.

(*Enter* DESDEMONA *with* EMILIA.)

DESDEMONA. My lord, what is your will?
OTHELLO. Pray, chuck, come hither.
DESDEMONA. What is your pleasure?
OTHELLO. Let me see your eyes.
Look in my face.
DESDEMONA. What horrible fancy's this?
OTHELLO (*to* EMILIA). Some of your function,° mistress.
Leave procreants alone and shut the door,
Cough, or cry hem, if anybody come.

27. Some . . . function: get about your business; i.e., prostitution. Othello pretends that Emilia is keeper of a brothel and Desdemona one of the women.

Your mystery,° your mystery. Nay, dispatch.

(*Exit* Emilia.)

Desdemona. Upon my knees, what doth your speech import?
I understand a fury in your words,
But not the words.

Othello. Why, what art thou?

Desdemona. Your wife, my lord, your true and loyal wife.

Othello. Come, swear it, damn thyself,
Lest, being like one of Heaven,° the devils themselves
Should fear to seize thee. Therefore be double-damned.
Swear thou art honest.

Desdemona. Heaven doth truly know it.

Othello. Heaven truly knows that thou art false as Hell.

Desdemona. To whom, my lord? With whom? How am I false?

Othello. O Desdemona! Away! Away! Away!

Desdemona. Alas the heavy day! Why do you weep?
Am I the motive of these tears, my lord?
If haply you my father do suspect
An instrument of this your calling-back,
Lay not your blame on me. If you have lost him,
Why, I have lost him too.

Othello. Had it pleased Heaven
To try me with affliction, had they rained
All kinds of sores and shames on my bare head,
Steeped me in poverty to the very lips,
Given to captivity me and my utmost hopes,
I should have found in some place of my soul
A drop of patience. But, alas, to make me
A fixèd figure for the time of scorn
To point his slow unmoving finger at!
Yet could I bear that too, well, very well.
But there where I have garnered up my heart,
Where either I must live or bear no life,
The fountain from the which my current runs
Or else dries up—to be discarded thence!
Or keep it as a cistern for foul toads
To knot and gender in! Turn thy complexion there,
Patience, thou young and rose-lipped cherubin—
Aye, there, look grim as Hell!

Desdemona. I hope my noble lord esteems me honest.

30. mystery: profession. **36. being . . . Heaven:** because you look like an angel.

OTHELLO. Oh, aye, as summer flies are in the shambles,°
That quicken even with blowing.° O thou weed,
Who art so lovely fair and smell'st so sweet
That the sense aches at thee, would thou hadst ne'er been born!
DESDEMONA. Alas, what ignorant sin have I committed?
OTHELLO. Was this fair paper,° this most goodly book,
Made to write "whore" upon? What committed!
Committed! O thou public commoner!°
I should make very forges of my cheeks
That would to cinders burn up modesty
Did I but speak thy deeds. What committed!
Heaven stops the nose at it, and the moon winks.
The bawdy wind, that kisses all it meets,
Is hushed within the hollow mine of earth
And will not hear it. What committed!
Impudent strumpet!
DESDEMONA. By Heaven, you do me wrong.
OTHELLO. Are not you a strumpet?
DESDEMONA. No, as I am a Christian.
If to preserve this vessel for my lord
From any other foul unlawful touch
Be not to be a strumpet, I am none.
OTHELLO. What, not a whore?
DESDEMONA. No, as I shall be saved.
OTHELLO. Is 't possible?
DESDEMONA. Oh, Heaven forgive us!
OTHELLO. I cry you mercy, then.
I took you for that cunning whore of Venice
That married with Othello. (*Raising his voice*) You, mistress,
That have the office opposite to Saint Peter,
And keep the gate of Hell!

(*Re-enter* EMILIA.)

You, you, aye, you!
We have done our course, there's money for your pains.
I pray you turn the key, and keep our counsel. (*Exit.*)
EMILIA. Alas, what does this gentleman conceive?
How do you, madam? How do you, my good lady?
DESDEMONA. Faith, half-asleep.
EMILIA. Good madam, what's the matter with my lord?
DESDEMONA. With who?

66. shambles: slaughterhouse. **67. quicken . . . blowing:** come to life as soon as the eggs are laid. **71. fair paper:** i.e., her white body. **73. public commoner:** one who offers herself to all comers.

EMILIA. Why, with my lord, madam.
DESDEMONA. Who is thy lord?
EMILIA. He that is yours, sweet lady.
DESDEMONA. I have none. Do not talk to me, Emilia.
I cannot weep, nor answer have I none
But what should go by water.° Prithee tonight
Lay on my bed my wedding sheets. Remember,
And call thy husband hither.
EMILIA. Here's a change indeed! (*Exit.*)
DESDEMONA. 'Tis meet I should be used so, very meet.
How have I been behaved that he might stick
The small'st opinion on my least misuse?°

(*Re-enter* EMILIA *with* IAGO.)

IAGO. What is your pleasure, madam? How is 't with you?
DESDEMONA. I cannot tell. Those that do teach young babes
Do it with gentle means and easy tasks.
He might have chid me so, for, in good faith,
I am a child to chiding.
IAGO. What's the matter, lady?
EMILIA. Alas, Iago, my lord hath so bewhored her,
Thrown such despite and heavy terms upon her,
As true hearts cannot bear.
DESDEMONA. Am I that name, Iago?
IAGO. What name, fair lady?
DESDEMONA. Such as she says my lord did say I was.
EMILIA. He called her whore. A beggar in his drink
Could not have laid such terms upon his callet.°
IAGO. Why did he so?
DESDEMONA. I do not know. I am sure I am none such.
IAGO. Do not weep, do not weep. Alas the day!
EMILIA. Hath she forsook so many noble matches,
Her father and her country and her friends,
To be called whore? Would it not make one weep?
DESDEMONA. It is my wretched fortune.
IAGO. Beshrew him for 't!
How comes this trick upon him?
DESDEMONA. Nay, Heaven doth know.
EMILIA. I will be hanged if some eternal villain,
Some busy and insinuating rogue,
Some cogging, cozening slave, to get some office,

104. go . . . water: be expressed in tears. **109. misuse:** mistake. **121. callet:** moll.

Have not devised this slander. I'll be hanged else.
IAGO. Fie, there is no such man, it is impossible.
DESDEMONA. If any such there be, Heaven pardon him!
EMILIA. A halter pardon him! And Hell gnaw his bones!
Why should he call her whore? Who keeps her company?
What place? What time? What form? What likelihood?
The Moor's abused by some most villainous knave,
Some base notorious knave, some scurvy fellow.
O Heaven, that such companions° Thou'dst unfold,°
And put in every honest hand a whip
To lash the rascals naked through the world
Even from the east to the west!
IAGO. Speak withindoor.°
EMILIA. Oh, fie upon them! Some such squire he was
That turned your wit the seamy side without,
And made you to suspect me with the Moor.
IAGO. You are a fool. Go to.°
DESDEMONA. O good Iago,
What shall I do to win my lord again?
Good friend, go to him, for, by this light of Heaven,
I know not how I lost him. Here I kneel.
If e'er my will did trespass 'gainst his love
Either in discourse of thought or actual deed,
Or that mine eyes, mine ears, or any sense
Delighted them in any other form,
Or that I do not yet, and ever did,
And ever will, though he do shake me off
To beggarly divorcement, love him dearly,
Comfort forswear me! Unkindness may do much,
And his unkindness may defeat my life,
But never taint my love. I cannot say "whore,"
It doth abhor me now I speak the word.
To do the act that might the addition° earn
Not the world's mass of vanity° could make me.
IAGO. I pray you be content, 'tis but his humor.
The business of the state does him offense,
And he does chide with you.
DESDEMONA. If 'twere no other—
IAGO. 'Tis but so, I warrant. (*Trumpets within.*)
Hark how these instruments summon to supper!
The messengers of Venice stay the meat.°

141. **companions**: low creatures. **unfold**: bring to light. 144. **Speak withindoor**: don't shout so loud that all the street will hear you. 148. **Go to**: an expression of derision. 163. **addition**: title. 164. **vanity**: i.e., riches. 170. **meat**: serving of supper.

Go in, and weep not, all things shall be well.

(*Exeunt* Desdemona *and* Emilia. *Enter* Roderigo.)

How now, Roderigo!

Roderigo. I do not find that thou dealest justly with me.

Iago. What in the contrary?

Roderigo. Every day thou daffest me with some device, Iago, and rather, as it seems to me now, keepest from me all conveniency than suppliest me with the least advantage of hope. I will indeed no longer endure it, nor am I yet persuaded to put up in peace what already I have foolishly suffered.

Iago. Will you hear me, Roderigo?

Roderigo. Faith, I have heard too much, for your words and performances are no kin together.

Iago. You charge me most unjustly.

Roderigo. With naught but truth. I have wasted myself out of my means. The jewels you have had from me to deliver to Desdemona would half have corrupted a votarist.° You have told me she hath received them, and returned me expectations and comforts of sudden respect and acquaintance, but I find none.

Iago. Well, go to, very well.

Roderigo. Very well! Go to! I cannot go to, man, nor 'tis not very well. By this hand, I say 'tis very scurvy, and begin to find myself fopped in it.

Iago. Very well.

Roderigo. I tell you 'tis not very well. I will make myself known to Desdemona. If she will return me my jewels, I will give over my suit and repent my unlawful solicitation. If not, assure yourself I will seek satisfaction of you.

Iago. You have said now.°

Roderigo. Aye, and said nothing but what I protest intendment of doing.

Iago. Why, now I see there's mettle in thee, and even from this instant do build on thee a better opinion than ever before. Give me thy hand, Roderigo. Thou hast taken against me a most just exception, but yet I protest I have dealt most directly in thy affair.

Roderigo. It hath not appeared.

Iago. I grant indeed it hath not appeared, and your suspicion is not without wit and judgment. But, Roderigo, if thou hast that in thee indeed which I have greater reason to believe now than ever—I mean purpose, courage, and valor—this night show it. If thou the next night following

186. votarist: nun. **198. You . . . now:** or in modern slang, "Oh yeah."

enjoy not Desdemona, take me from this world with treachery and devise engines° for my life.

RODERIGO. Well, what is it? Is it within reason and compass?

IAGO. Sir, there is especial commission come from Venice to depute Cassio in Othello's place.

RODERIGO. Is that true? Why, then Othello and Desdemona return again to Venice.

IAGO. Oh, no. He goes into Mauritania, and takes away with him the fair Desdemona, unless his abode be lingered here by some accident. Wherein none can be so determinate as the removing of Cassio.

RODERIGO. How do you mean, "removing of" him?

IAGO. Why, by making him uncapable of Othello's place, knocking out his brains.

RODERIGO. And that you would have me to do?

IAGO. Aye, if you dare do yourself a profit and a right. He sups tonight with a harlotry,° and thither will I go to him. He knows not yet of his honorable fortune. If you will watch his going thence, which I will fashion to fall out between twelve and one, you may take him at your pleasure. I will be near to second your attempt, and he shall fall between us. Come, stand not amazed at it, but go along with me. I will show you such a necessity in his death that you shall think yourself bound to put it on him. It is now high suppertime, and the night grows to waste. About it.

RODERIGO. I will hear further reason for this.

IAGO. And you shall be satisfied.

(*Exeunt.*)

SCENE III. Another room in the castle.

Enter OTHELLO, LODOVICO, DESDEMONA, EMILIA, *and* ATTENDANTS.

LODOVICO. I do beseech you, sir, trouble yourself no further.

OTHELLO. Oh, pardon me, 'twill do me good to walk.

LODOVICO. Madam, good night. I humbly thank your ladyship.

DESDEMONA. Your Honor is most welcome.

OTHELLO. Will you walk, sir?
Oh—Desdemona—

DESDEMONA. My lord?

OTHELLO. Get you to bed on the instant, I will be returned forthwith. Dismiss your attendant there. Look it be done.

DESDEMONA. I will, my lord.

(*Exeunt* OTHELLO, LODOVICO, *and* ATTENDANTS.)

211. engines: instruments of torture. **225. harlotry:** harlot.

EMILIA. How goes it now? He looks gentler than he did.
DESDEMONA. He says he will return incontinent.°
He hath commanded me to go to bed,
And bade me to dismiss you.
EMILIA. Dismiss me!
DESDEMONA. It was his bidding, therefore, good Emilia,
Give me my nightly wearing, and adieu.
We must not now displease him.
EMILIA. I would you had never seen him!
DESDEMONA. So would not I. My love doth so approve him
That even his stubbornness, his checks, his frowns—
Prithee, unpin me—have grace and favor in them.
EMILIA. I have laid those sheets you bade me on the bed.
DESDEMONA. All's one. Good faith, how foolish are our minds!
If I do die before thee, prithee shroud me
In one of those same sheets.
EMILIA. Come, come, you talk.
DESDEMONA. My mother had a maid called Barbara.
She was in love, and he she loved proved mad
And did forsake her. She had a song of "willow"°—
An old thing 'twas, but it expressed her fortune,
And she died singing it. That song tonight
Will not go from my mind. I have much to do
But to go hang my head all at one side
And sing it like poor Barbara. Prithee, dispatch.
EMILIA. Shall I go fetch your nightgown?
DESDEMONA. No, unpin me here.
This Lodovico is a proper man.
EMILIA. A very handsome man.
DESDEMONA. He speaks well.

EMILIA. I know a lady in Venice would have walked barefoot to Palestine for a touch of his nether lip.

DESDEMONA (*singing*).
"The poor soul sat sighing by a sycamore tree,
Sing all a green willow.
Her hand on her bosom, her head on her knee,
Sing willow, willow, willow.
The fresh streams ran by her, and murmured her moans,
Sing willow, willow, willow.
Her salt tears fell from her, and softened the stones—"
Lay by these—(*singing*)
"Sing willow, willow, willow"

11. incontinent: immediately. **27. willow**: the emblem of the forlorn lover.

Prithee, hie thee, he'll come anon.—(*singing*)

"Sing all a green willow must be my garland.
Let nobody blame him, his scorn I approve—"

Nay, that's not next. Hark! Who is 't that knocks?

EMILIA. It's the wind.

DESDEMONA (*singing*).

"I called my love false love, but what said he then?
Sing willow, willow, willow.
If I court moe° women, you'll couch with moe men."

So get thee gone, good night. Mine eyes do itch.
Doth that bode weeping?

EMILIA. 'Tis neither here nor there.

DESDEMONA. I have heard it said so. Oh, these men, these men!
Dost thou in conscience think—tell me, Emilia—
That there be women do abuse their husbands
In such gross kind?

EMILIA. There be some such, no question.

DESDEMONA. Wouldst thou do such a deed for all the world?

EMILIA. Why, would not you?

DESDEMONA. No, by this heavenly light!

EMILIA. Nor I neither by this heavenly light. I might do 't as well i' the dark.

DESDEMONA. Wouldst thou do such a deed for all the world?

EMILIA. The world's a huge thing. It is a great price
For a small vice.

DESDEMONA. In troth, I think thou wouldst not.

EMILIA. In troth, I think I should, and undo 't when I had done. Marry, I would not do such a thing for a joint ring,° nor for measures of lawn,° nor for gowns, petticoats, nor caps, nor any petty exhibition;° but for the whole world—why, who would not make her husband a cuckold to make him a monarch? I should venture Purgatory for 't.

DESDEMONA. Beshrew me if I would do such a wrong
For the whole world.

EMILIA. Why, the wrong is but a wrong i' the world, and having the world for your labor, 'tis a wrong in your own world and you might quickly make it right.

DESDEMONA. I do not think there is any such woman.

EMILIA. Yes, a dozen, and as many to the vantage as would store the world they played for. But I do think it is their husbands' faults

55. moe: more. **71–72. joint ring:** ring made in two pieces, a lover's gift. **measures of lawn:** lengths of finest lawn, or as a modern woman would say, "sheer nylon." **petty exhibition:** small allowance of money.

If wives do fall. Say that they slack their duties
And pour our treasures into foreign laps,
Or else break out in peevish jealousies,
Throwing restraint upon us, or say they strike us,
Or scant our former having in despite,°
Why, we have galls,° and though we have some grace,
Yet have we some revenge. Let husbands know
Their wives have sense like them. They see and smell
And have their palates both for sweet and sour,
As husbands have. What is it that they do
When they change us for others? Is it sport?
I think it is. And doth affection breed it?
I think it doth. Is 't frailty that thus errs?
It is so too. And have not we affections,
Desires for sport, and frailty, as men have?
Then let them use us well. Else let them know
The ills we do, their ills instruct us so.

DESDEMONA. Good night, good night. Heaven me such uses send,
Not to pick bad from bad, but by bad mend!

(*Exeunt.*)

ACT V

SCENE I. Cyprus. A street.

Enter IAGO *and* RODERIGO.

IAGO. Here, stand behind this bulk, straight will he come.
Wear thy good rapier bare, and put it home.
Quick, quick, fear nothing, I'll be at thy elbow.
It makes us, or it mars us. Think on that,
And fix most firm thy resolution.

RODERIGO. Be near at hand, I may miscarry in 't.

IAGO. Here, at thy hand. Be bold, and take thy stand. (*Retires.*)

RODERIGO. I have no great devotion to the deed,
And yet he hath given me satisfying reasons.
'Tis but a man gone. Forth, my sword. He dies.

IAGO. I have rubbed this young quat° almost to the sense,°
And he grows angry. Now, whether he kill Cassio,
Or Cassio him, or each do kill the other,

88. scant . . . despite: for spite cut down our allowance. **89. galls:** bile, the cause of bitterness.

Act V, Sc. i. 11. quat: pimple. **sense:** quick.

Every way makes my gain. Live Roderigo,
He calls me to a restitution large
Of gold and jewels that I bobbed from him
As gifts to Desdemona.
It must not be. If Cassio do remain,
He hath a daily beauty in his life
That makes me ugly,° and besides, the Moor
May unfold me to him. There stand I in much peril.
No, he must die. Be 't so. I hear him coming.

(*Enter* CASSIO.)

RODERIGO. I know his gait, 'tis he. Villain, thou diest! (*Makes a pass at* CASSIO.)

CASSIO. That thrust had been mine enemy indeed
But that my coat is better than thou know'st.
I will make proof of thine. (*Draws, and wounds* RODERIGO.)

RODERIGO. Oh, I am slain!

(IAGO *from behind wounds* CASSIO *in the leg, and exit.*)

CASSIO. I am maimed for ever. Help, ho! Murder! Murder! (*Falls.*)

(*Enter* OTHELLO.)

OTHELLO. The voice of Cassio. Iago keeps his word.

RODERIGO. Oh, villain that I am!

OTHELLO. It is even so.

CASSIO. Oh, help, ho! Light! A surgeon!

OTHELLO. 'Tis he. O brave Iago, honest and just,
That hast such noble sense of thy friend's wrong!
Thou teachest me. Minion,° your dear lies dead,
And your unblest fate hies. Strumpet, I come!
Forth of my heart those charms, thine eyes, are blotted.
Thy bed lust-stained shall with lust's blood be spotted. (*Exit.*)

(*Enter* LODOVICO *and* GRATIANO.)

CASSIO. What ho! No watch?° No passage?° Murder! Murder!

GRATIANO. 'Tis some mischance, the cry is very direful.

CASSIO. Oh, help!

LODOVICO. Hark!

RODERIGO. Oh, wretched villain!

LODOVICO. Two or three groan. It is a heavy° night.
These may be counterfeits. Let's think 't unsafe

19–20. He . . . ugly: by comparison with him I am a poor thing. Iago is conscious of his lack of social graces. **33. Minion:** darling, in a bad sense. **37. watch:** police. **No passage:** nobody passing. **42. heavy:** thick.

To come in to the cry without more help.

RODERIGO. Nobody come? Then shall I bleed to death.

LODOVICO. Hark!

(*Re-enter* IAGO, *with a light.*)

GRATIANO. Here's one comes in his shirt, with light and weapons.

IAGO. Who's there? Whose noise is this that cries on murder?

LODOVICO. We do not know.

IAGO. Did not you hear a cry?

CASSIO. Here, here! For Heaven's sake, help me!

IAGO. What's the matter?

GRATIANO. This is Othello's Ancient, as I take it.

LODOVICO. The same indeed, a very valiant fellow.

IAGO. What are you here that cry so grievously?

CASSIO. Iago? Oh, I am spoiled, undone by villains! Give me some help.

IAGO. Oh me, Lieutenant! What villains have done this?

CASSIO. I think that one of them is hereabout,
And cannot make away.

IAGO. Oh, treacherous villains!
(*To* LODOVICO *and* GRATIANO) What are you there?
Come in and give some help.

RODERIGO. Oh, help me here!

CASSIO. That's one of them.

IAGO. Oh, murderous slave! Oh, villain! (*Stabs* RODERIGO.)

RODERIGO. Oh, damned Iago! Oh, inhuman dog!

IAGO. Kill men i' the dark! Where be these bloody thieves?
How silent is this town! Ho! Murder! Murder!
What may you be? Are you of good or evil?

LODOVICO. As you shall prove us, praise us.

IAGO. Signior Lodovico?

LODOVICO. He, sir.

IAGO. I cry you mercy. Here's Cassio hurt by villains.

GRATIANO. Cassio!

IAGO. How is 't, brother?

CASSIO. My leg is cut in two.

IAGO. Marry, Heaven forbid!
Light, gentlemen. I'll bind it with my shirt.

(*Enter* BIANCA.)

BIANCA. What is the matter, ho? Who is 't that cried?

IAGO. Who is 't that cried!

BIANCA. Oh, my dear Cassio! My sweet Cassio! Oh, Cassio, Cassio, Cassio!

IAGO. Oh, notable strumpet, Cassio, may you suspect
Who they should be that have thus mangled you?

CASSIO. No.

GRATIANO. I am sorry to find you thus. I have been to seek you.

IAGO. Lend me a garter. So. Oh, for a chair,
To bear him easily hence!

BIANCA. Alas, he faints! Oh, Cassio, Cassio, Cassio!

IAGO. Gentlemen all, I do suspect this trash
To be a party in this injury.
Patience awhile, good Cassio. Come, come,
Lend me a light. Know we this face or no?
Alas, my friend and my dear countryman
Roderigo? No—yes, sure. Oh Heaven! Roderigo.

GRATIANO. What, of Venice?

IAGO. Even he, sir. Did you know him?

GRATIANO. Know him! Aye.

IAGO. Signior Gratiano? I cry you gentle pardon.
These bloody accidents must excuse my manners,
That so neglected you.

GRATIANO. I am glad to see you.

IAGO. How do you, Cassio? Oh, a chair, a chair!

GRATIANO. Roderigo!

IAGO. He, he, 'tis he. (*A chair brought in*) Oh, that's well said, the chair.
Some good man bear him carefully from hence.
I'll fetch the General's surgeon. (*To* BIANCA) For you, mistress,
Save you your labor. He that lies slain here, Cassio,
Was my dear friend. What malice was between you?

CASSIO. None in the world, nor do I know the man.

IAGO (*to* BIANCA). What, look you pale? Oh, bear him out o' the air.

(CASSIO *and* RODERIGO *are borne off.*)

Stay you, good gentlemen. Look you pale, mistress?
Do you perceive the gastness of her eye?
Nay, if you stare, we shall hear more anon.
Behold her well, I pray you look upon her.
Do you see, gentlemen? Nay, guiltiness will speak,
Though tongues were out of use.

(*Enter* EMILIA.)

EMILIA. 'Las, what's the matter? What's the matter, husband?

IAGO. Cassio hath here been set on in the dark

By Roderigo, and fellows that are 'scaped.
He's almost slain, and Roderigo dead.

EMILIA. Alas, good gentlemen! Alas, good Cassio!

IAGO. This is the fruit of whoring. Prithee, Emilia,
Go know of Cassio where he supped tonight.
What, do you shake at that?

BIANCA. He supped at my house, but I therefore shake not.

IAGO. Oh, did he so? I charge you, go with me.

EMILIA. Fie, fie upon thee, strumpet!

BIANCA. I am no strumpet, but of life as honest
As you that thus abuse me.

EMILIA. As I! Foh! Fie upon thee!

IAGO. Kind gentlemen, let's go see poor Cassio dressed.°
Come, mistress, you must tell 's another tale.
Emilia, run you to the citadel,
And tell my lord and lady what hath happed!
Will you go on? I pray. (*Aside*) This is the night
That either makes me or fordoes me quite.

(*Exeunt.*)

SCENE II. A bedchamber in the castle. DESDEMONA *in bed asleep, a light burning.*

Enter OTHELLO.

OTHELLO. It is the cause,° it is the cause, my soul.
Let me not name it to you, you chaste stars!
It is the cause. Yet I'll not shed her blood,
Nor scar that whiter skin of hers than snow
And smooth as monumental alabaster.
Yet she must die, else she'll betray more men.
Put out the light, and then put out the light.
If I quench thee, thou flaming minister,°
I can again thy former light restore,
Should I repent me. But once put out thy light,
Thou cunning'st° pattern of excelling nature,
I know not where is that Promethean heat
That can thy light relume. When I have plucked the rose,

123. dressed: i.e., his wound dressed.

Sc. ii. 1. It . . . cause: The meaning of the opening lines of this speech has been much discussed. The *cause* is Desdemona's supposed faithlessness; Othello, at this moment, sees himself as embodied vengeance, the venger of man betrayed by woman. **8. minister:** servant. **11. cunning'st:** most skillfully made.

I cannot give it vital growth again,
It needs must wither. I'll smell it on the tree. (*Kissing her*)
Ah, balmy breath, that dost almost persuade
Justice to break her sword! One more, one more.
Be thus when thou art dead, and I will kill thee,
And love thee after. One more, and this the last.
So sweet was ne'er so fatal. I must weep,
But they are cruel tears. This sorrow's heavenly,
It strikes where it doth love. She wakes.

DESDEMONA. Who's there? Othello?

OTHELLO. Aye, Desdemona.

DESDEMONA. Will you come to bed, my lord?

OTHELLO. Have you prayed tonight, Desdemona?

DESDEMONA. Aye, my lord.

OTHELLO. If you bethink yourself of any crime
Unreconciled as yet to Heaven and grace,
Solicit for it straight.

DESDEMONA. Alas, my lord, what may you mean by that?

OTHELLO. Well, do it, and be brief. I will walk by.
I would not kill thy unpreparèd spirit.
No, Heaven forfend! I would not kill thy soul.

DESDEMONA. Talk you of killing?

OTHELLO. Aye, I do.

DESDEMONA. Then Heaven have mercy on me!

OTHELLO. Amen, with all my heart!

DESDEMONA. If you say so, I hope you will not kill me.

OTHELLO. Hum!

DESDEMONA. And yet I fear you, for you are fatal then
When your eyes roll so. Why I should fear I know not,
Since guiltiness I know not, but yet I feel I fear.

OTHELLO. Think on thy sins.

DESDEMONA. They are loves I bear to you.

OTHELLO. Aye, and for that thou diest.

DESDEMONA. That death's unnatural that kills for loving.
Alas, why gnaw you so your nether lip?
Some bloody passion shakes your very frame.
These are portents, but yet I hope, I hope,
They do not point on me.

OTHELLO. Peace, and be still!

DESDEMONA. I will so. What's the matter?

OTHELLO. That handkerchief which I so loved and gave thee
Thou gavest to Cassio.

DESDEMONA. No, by my life and soul!

Send for the man, and ask him.
OTHELLO. Sweet soul, take heed,
Take heed of perjury, thou art on thy deathbed.
DESDEMONA. Aye, but not yet to die.
OTHELLO. Yes, presently.°
Therefore confess thee freely of thy sin,
For to deny each article with oath
Cannot remove nor choke the strong conception
That I do groan withal. Thou art to die.
DESDEMONA. Then Lord have mercy on me!
OTHELLO. I say amen.
DESDEMONA. And have you mercy too! I never did
Offend you in my life, never loved Cassio
But with such general warranty of Heaven
As I might love. I never gave him token.
OTHELLO. By Heaven, I saw my handkerchief in 's hand.
O perjured woman! Thou dost stone° my heart,
And makest me call what I intend to do
A murder, which I thought a sacrifice.
I saw the handkerchief.
DESDEMONA. He found it, then,
I never gave it him. Send for him hither.
Let him confess a truth.
OTHELLO. He hath confessed.
DESDEMONA. What, my lord?
OTHELLO. That he hath used thee.
DESDEMONA. How? Unlawfully?
OTHELLO. Aye.
DESDEMONA. He will not say so.
OTHELLO. No, his mouth is stopped.
Honest Iago hath ta'en order for 't.
DESDEMONA. Oh, my fear interprets! What, is he dead?
OTHELLO. Had all his hairs been lives, my great revenge
Had stomach for them all.
DESDEMONA. Alas, he is betrayed, and I undone!
OTHELLO. Out, strumpet! Weep'st thou for him to my face?
DESDEMONA. Oh, banish me, my lord, but kill me not!
OTHELLO. Down, strumpet!
DESDEMONA. Kill me tomorrow, let me live tonight!
OTHELLO. Nay, if you strive—
DESDEMONA. But half an hour!
OTHELLO. Being done, there is no pause.

54. presently: at once. **65. stone:** turn to stone.

DESDEMONA. But while I say one prayer!

OTHELLO. It is too late. (*He stifles her.*)

EMILIA (*within*). My lord, my lord! What ho! My lord, my lord!

OTHELLO. What noise is this? Not dead? Not yet quite dead?
I that am cruel am yet merciful,
I would not have thee linger in thy pain.
So, so.

EMILIA (*within*). What ho! My lord, my lord!

OTHELLO. Who's there?

EMILIA (*within*). Oh, good my lord, I would speak a word with you!

OTHELLO. Yes, 'tis Emilia. By and by. She's dead.
'Tis like she comes to speak of Cassio's death.
The noise was here. Ha! No more moving?
Still as the grave. Shall she come in? Were 't good?
I think she stirs again. No. What's best to do?
If she come in, she'll sure speak to my wife.
My wife! My wife! My wife! I have no wife.
Oh, insupportable! Oh, heavy hour!
Methinks it should be now a huge eclipse
Of sun and moon, and that the affrighted globe
Should yawn° at alteration.

EMILIA (*within*). I do beseech you
That I may speak with you, O good my lord!

OTHELLO. I had forgot thee. Oh, come in, Emilia.
Soft, by and by. Let me the curtains° draw.
Where art thou? (*Unlocks the door.*)

(*Enter* EMILIA.)

What's the matter with thee now?

EMILIA. Oh, my good lord, yonder 's foul murders done!

OTHELLO. What, now?

EMILIA. But now, my lord.

OTHELLO. It is the very error of the moon.
She comes more nearer earth than she was wont
And makes men mad.

EMILIA. Cassio, my lord, hath killed a young Venetian
Called Roderigo.

OTHELLO. Roderigo killed!
And Cassio killed!

EMILIA. No, Cassio is not killed.

OTHELLO. Not Cassio killed! Then murder's out of tune,

104. yawn: gape [L.P.]. **107. curtains:** i.e., of the bed.

And sweet revenge grows harsh.
DESDEMONA. Oh, falsely, falsely murdered!
EMILIA. Alas, what cry is that?
OTHELLO. That! What?
EMILIA. Out and alas! That was my lady's voice.
Help! Help, ho! Help! O lady, speak again!
Sweet Desdemona! O sweet mistress, speak!
DESDEMONA. A guiltless death I die.
EMILIA. Oh, who hath done this deed?
DESDEMONA. Nobody, I myself. Farewell.
Commend me to my kind lord. Oh, farewell! (*Dies.*)
OTHELLO. Why, how should she be murdered?
EMILIA. Alas, who knows?
OTHELLO. You heard her say herself it was not I.
EMILIA. She said so. I must needs report the truth.
OTHELLO. She's like a liar gone to burning Hell.
'Twas I that killed her.
EMILIA. Oh, the more angel she,
And you the blacker devil!
OTHELLO. She turned to folly, and she was a whore.
EMILIA. Thou dost belie her, and thou art a devil.
OTHELLO. She was false as water.
EMILIA. Thou art rash as fire to say
That she was false. Oh, she was heavenly true!
OTHELLO. Cassio did top her, ask thy husband else.
Oh, I were damned beneath all depth in Hell
But that I did proceed upon just grounds
To this extremity. Thy husband knew it all.
EMILIA. My husband!
OTHELLO. Thy husband.
EMILIA. That she was false to wedlock?
OTHELLO. Aye, with Cassio. Nay, had she been true,
If Heaven would make me such another world
Of one entire and perfect chrysolite,
I'd not have sold her for it.
EMILIA. My husband!
OTHELLO. Aye, 'twas he that told me first.
An honest man he is, and hates the slime
That sticks on filthy deeds.
EMILIA. My husband!
OTHELLO. What needs this iteration, woman? I say thy husband.
EMILIA. Oh, mistress, villainy hath made mocks with love!
My husband say that she was false!
OTHELLO. He, woman.

I say thy husband. Dost understand the word?
My friend, thy husband, honest, honest Iago.

EMILIA. If he say so, may his pernicious soul
Rot half a grain a day! He lies to the heart.
She was too fond of her most filthy bargain.

OTHELLO. Ha!

EMILIA. Do thy worst.
This deed of thine is no more worthy Heaven
Than thou wast worthy her.

OTHELLO. Peace, you were best.

EMILIA. Thou hast not half that power to do me harm
As I have to be hurt. O gull! O dolt!
As ignorant as dirt! Thou hast done a deed—
I care not for thy sword, I'll make thee known,
Though I lost twenty lives. Help! Help, ho! Help!
The Moor hath killed my mistress! Murder! Murder!

(*Enter* MONTANO, GRATIANO, IAGO, *and others.*)

MONTANO. What is the matter? How now, General!

EMILIA. Oh, are you come, Iago? You have done well,
That men must lay their murders on your neck.

GRATIANO. What is the matter?

EMILIA. Disprove this villain, if thou be'st a man.
He says thou told'st him that his wife was false.
I know thou didst not, thou'rt not such a villain.
Speak, for my heart is full.

IAGO. I told him what I thought, and told no more
Than what he found himself was apt and true.

EMILIA. But did you ever tell him she was false?

IAGO. I did.

EMILIA. You told a lie, an odious, damnèd lie,
Upon my soul, a lie, a wicked lie!
She false with Cassio! Did you say with Cassio?

IAGO. With Cassio, mistress. Go to, charm your tongue.°

EMILIA. I will not charm my tongue, I am bound to speak.
My mistress here lies murdered in her bed.

ALL. Oh, Heavens forfend!

EMILIA. And your reports have set the murder on.

OTHELLO. Nay, stare not, masters. It is true indeed.

GRATIANO. 'Tis a strange truth.

MONTANO. Oh, monstrous act!

EMILIA. Villainy, villainy, villainy!

187. charm . . . tongue: be silent.

I think upon 't. I think I smell 't. Oh, villainy!
I thought so then.° I'll kill myself for grief.
Oh, villainy, villainy!
IAGO. What, are you mad? I charge you, get you home.
EMILIA. Good gentlemen, let me have leave to speak.
'Tis proper I obey him, but not now.
Perchance, Iago, I will ne'er go home.
OTHELLO. Oh! Oh! Oh! (*Falling on the bed.*)
EMILIA. Nay, lay thee down and roar,
For thou hast killed the sweetest innocent
That e'er did lift up eye.
OTHELLO (*rising*). Oh, she was foul!
I scarce did know you, Uncle. There lies your niece,
Whose breath indeed these hands have newly stopped.
I know this act shows horrible and grim.
GRATIANO. Poor Desdemona! I am glad thy father's dead.
Thy match was mortal to him, and pure grief
Shore his old thread in twain. Did he live now,
This sight would make him do a desperate turn—
Yea, curse his better angel from his side,
And fall to reprobation.°
OTHELLO. 'Tis pitiful, but yet Iago knows
That she with Cassio hath the act of shame
A thousand times committed. Cassio confessed it.
And she did gratify his amorous works
With that recognizance and pledge of love
Which I first gave her, I saw it in his hand.
It was a handkerchief, an antique token
My father gave my mother.
EMILIA. Oh, Heaven! Oh, heavenly powers!
IAGO. 'Zounds! Hold your peace.
EMILIA. 'Twill out, 'twill out. I peace!
No, I will speak as liberal as the north.°
Let Heaven and men and devils, let them all,
All, all, cry shame against me, yet I'll speak.
IAGO. Be wise, and get you home.
EMILIA. I will not.

(IAGO *offers to stab* EMILIA.)

GRATIANO. Fie!
Your sword upon a woman!

196. I . . . then: i.e., I suspected this earlier—as for example when Iago took the handkerchief. **213. reprobation:** damnation; i.e., by self-murder. **224. liberal . . . north:** as freely as the north wind, which is loud and bitter.

EMILIA. O thou dull Moor! That handkerchief thou speak'st of
I found by fortune and did give my husband,
For often with a solemn earnestness,
More than indeed belonged to such a trifle,
He begged of me to steal it.
IAGO. Villainous whore!
EMILIA. She give it Cassio! No, alas, I found it,
And I did give 't my husband.
IAGO. Filth, thou liest!
EMILIA. By Heaven, I do not, I do not, gentlemen.
Oh, murderous coxcomb! What should such a fool
Do with so good a wife?
OTHELLO. Are there no stones° in Heaven
But what serve for the thunder? Precious villain!

(*He runs at* IAGO. IAGO, *from behind, stabs* EMILIA, *and exit.*)

GRATIANO. The woman falls. Sure, he hath killed his wife.
EMILIA. Aye, aye. Oh, lay me by my mistress' side.
GRATIANO. He's gone, but his wife's killed.
MONTANO. 'Tis a notorious villain. Take you this weapon,
Which I have here recovered from the Moor.
Come, guard the door without, let him not pass,
But kill him rather. I'll after that same villain,
For 'tis a damnèd slave.

(*Exeunt all but* OTHELLO *and* EMILIA.)

OTHELLO. I am not valiant neither.
But every puny whipster gets my sword.
But why should honor outlive honesty?
Let it go all.
EMILIA. What did thy song bode, lady?
Hark, canst thou hear me? I will play the swan,
And die in music. (*Singing.*)
"Willow, willow, willow."
Moor, she was chaste. She loved thee, cruel Moor,
So come my soul to bliss as I speak true.
So speaking as I think, I die, I die. (*Dies.*)
OTHELLO. I have another weapon in this chamber.
It is a sword of Spain, the ice brook's temper.—
Oh, here it is. Uncle, I must come forth.
GRATIANO (*within*). If thou attempt it, it will cost thee dear.
Thou hast no weapon, and perforce must suffer.

238. stones: thunderbolts.

OTHELLO. Look in upon me then, and speak with me,
Or, naked° as I am, I will assault thee.

(*Re-enter* GRATIANO.)

GRATIANO. What is the matter?
OTHELLO. Behold, I have a weapon,
A better never did itself sustain
Upon a soldier's thigh. I have seen the day
That with this little arm and this good sword
I have made my way through more impediments
Than twenty times your stop. But, oh, vain boast!
Who can control his fate? 'Tis not so now.
Be not afraid, though you do see me weaponed.
Here is my journey's end, here is my butt°
And very sea mark of my utmost sail.
Do you go back dismayed? 'Tis a lost fear.
Man but a rush° against Othello's breast,
And he retires. Where should Othello go?
Now, how dost thou look now? O ill-starred wench!
Pale as thy smock! When we shall meet at compt,°
This look of thine will hurl my soul from Heaven
And fiends will snatch at it. Cold, cold, my girl!
Even like thy chastity. Oh, cursèd slave!
Whip me, ye devils,
From the possession of this heavenly sight!
Blow me about in winds! Roast me in sulphur!
Wash me in steep-down gulfs of liquid fire!
O Desdemona! Desdemona! Dead!
Oh! Oh! Oh!

(*Enter* LODOVICO, MONTANO, CASSIO *carried in a chair, and* OFFICERS *with* IAGO, *prisoner.*)

LODOVICO. Where is this rash and most unfortunate man?
OTHELLO. That's he that was Othello. Here I am.
LODOVICO. Where is that viper? Bring the villain forth.
OTHELLO. I look down toward his feet,° but that's a fable.
If that thou be'st a devil, I cannot kill thee. (*Wounds* IAGO.)
LODOVICO. Wrench his sword from him.
IAGO. I bleed, sir, but not killed.
OTHELLO. I am not sorry neither. I'd have thee live,
For, in my sense, 'tis happiness to die.

262. naked: unarmed. **271. butt:** aim. **274. Man . . . rush:** attack with only a reed. **277. compt:** account; i.e., the Day of Judgment. **290. toward . . . feet:** i.e., to see if he has the cloven hoof of a devil.

LODOVICO. O thou Othello, that wert once so good,
Fall'n in the practice° of a damnèd slave,
What shall be said to thee?
OTHELLO. Why, anything.
An honorable murderer, if you will,
For naught did I in hate, but all in honor.
LODOVICO. This wretch hath part confessed his villainy.
Did you and he consent in Cassio's death?
OTHELLO. Aye.
CASSIO. Dear General, I never gave you cause.
OTHELLO. I do believe it, and I ask your pardon.
Will you, I pray, demand that demidevil
Why he hath thus ensnared my soul and body?
IAGO. Demand me nothing. What you know, you know.
From this time forth I never will speak word.
LODOVICO. What, not to pray?
GRATIANO. Torments will ope your lips.
OTHELLO. Well, thou dost best.
LODOVICO. Sir, you shall understand what hath befall'n,
Which, as I think, you know not. Here is a letter
Found in the pocket of the slain Roderigo,
And here another. The one of them imports
The death of Cassio to be undertook
By Roderigo.
OTHELLO. Oh, villain!
CASSIO. Most heathenish and most gross!
LODOVICO. Now here's another discontented paper,
Found in his pocket too. And this, it seems,
Roderigo meant to have sent this damnèd villain
But that, belike, Iago in the interim
Came in and satisfied him.
OTHELLO. Oh, the pernicious caitiff!
How came you, Cassio, by that handkerchief
That was my wife's?
CASSIO. I found it in my chamber.
And he himself confessed but even now
That there he dropped it for a special purpose
Which wrought to his desire.
OTHELLO. O fool! Fool! Fool!
CASSIO. There is besides in Roderigo's letter
How he upbraids Iago, that he made him
Brave° me upon the watch, whereon it came

296. Fall'n . . . practice: destroyed by the plotting. **330. Brave:** insult.

That I was cast.° And even but now he spake
After long seeming dead, Iago hurt him,
Iago set him on.
LODOVICO. You must forsake this room, and go with us.
Your power and your command is taken off,
And Cassio rules in Cyprus. For this slave,
If there be any cunning cruelty
That can torment him much and hold him long,°
It shall be his. You shall close prisoner rest
Till that the nature of your fault be known
To the Venetian state. Come, bring away.
OTHELLO. Soft you, a word or two before you go.
I have done the state some service, and they know 't.
No more of that. I pray you, in your letters,
When you shall these unlucky deeds relate,
Speak of me as I am, nothing extenuate,
Nor set down aught in malice. Then must you speak
Of one that loved not wisely but too well,
Of one not easily jealous, but, being wrought,
Perplexed in the extreme, of one whose hand,
Like the base Indian, threw a pearl away
Richer than all his tribe—of one whose subdued eyes,
Albeit unusèd to the melting mood,
Drop tears as fast as the Arabian trees
Their medicinal gum. Set you down this,
And say besides that in Aleppo once,
Where a malignant and a turbaned Turk
Beat a Venetian and traduced the state,
I took by the throat the circumcisèd dog
And smote him, thus. (*Stabs himself.*)
LODOVICO. Oh, bloody period!
GRATIANO. All that's spoke is marred.
OTHELLO. I kissed thee ere I killed thee. No way but this,
Killing myself, to die upon a kiss. (*Falls on the bed, and dies.*)
CASSIO. This did I fear, but thought he had no weapon.
For he was great of heart.
LODOVICO (*to* IAGO). O Spartan° dog,
More fell° than anguish, hunger, or the sea!
Look on the tragic loading of this bed,
This is thy work. The object poisons sight,
Let it be hid.° Gratiano, keep the house,

331. cast: dismissed. **338. long:** i.e., in dying. **366. Spartan:** i.e., hardhearted. **367. fell:** cruel. **370. Let . . . hid:** At these words the curtains are closed across the inner stage (or chamber, if this scene was acted aloft), concealing all three bodies.

And seize upon the fortunes of the Moor,
For they succeed on you. To you, Lord Governor,
Remains the censure of this hellish villain,
The time, the place, the torture.
Oh, enforce it!
Myself will straight aboard, and to the state
This heavy act with heavy heart relate.

(*Exeunt.*)

QUESTIONS

1. In what ways is Othello, in the first two acts, shown to be a person of extraordinary quality?

2. Is Othello a person jealous "by nature"? Does he show any disposition to jealousy in the first two acts? What does he say about himself in his final soliloquy? Would he make a good comic hero? (There has been much critical controversy over the psychological probability of Othello's being roused so quickly to such a high pitch of jealousy in Act III. Some have explained it by attributing a predisposition to jealousy in Othello; others have attributed it to the almost superhuman Machiavellian cleverness of Iago, which would have taken in any husband. In general, however, Shakespeare was less interested in psychological consistency and the subtle tracing of motivation—which are modern interests—than he was in theatrical effectiveness and the orchestration of emotions. Perhaps the question we should properly ask is not "How probable is Othello's jealousy?" but "How vital and effective has Shakespeare rendered it?")

3. Who is more naturally suspicious of human nature—Othello or Iago?

4. Is something of Othello's nobility manifested even in the scale of his jealousy? How does he respond to his conviction that Desdemona has been unfaithful to him? Would a lesser man have responded in the same way? Why or why not?

5. How does Othello's final speech reestablish his greatness?

6. What are Iago's motivations in his actions toward Othello, Cassio, and Roderigo? What is his philosophy? How does his technique of handling Roderigo differ from his technique in handling Othello and Cassio? Why?

7. In rousing Othello's suspicions against Desdemona (III, iii) Iago uses the same technique, in part, that he had used with Othello in inculpating Cassio (II, iii) and that he later uses with Lodovico in inculpating Othello (IV, ii). What is this technique? Why is it effective?

8. What opinions of Iago, before his exposure, are expressed by Othello, Desdemona, Cassio, and Lodovico? Is Othello the only one taken in by him? Does his own wife think him capable of villainy?

9. Though Othello is the protagonist, the majority of the soliloquies and asides are given to Iago. Why?

10. The difference between Othello and Desdemona that Iago plays on most is that of color, and, reading the play today, we may be tempted to see the play as being centrally about race relations. However, only one other character, besides Othello, makes much of this difference in color. Which one? Is this character sympathetically portrayed? What attitude toward Othello himself, and his marriage, is taken by the Duke, Cassio, Lodovico, Emilia, Desdemona herself? What differences between Othello and Desdemona, besides color, are used by Iago to undermine Othello's confidence in Desdemona's fidelity? What differences does Othello himself take into account?

11. What are Desdemona's principal character traits? In what ways are she and Emilia character foils? Is she entirely discreet in pleading Cassio's case to Othello? Why or why not? Why does she lie about the handkerchief (III, iv)?

12. Like Sophocles in *Antigone,* Shakespeare makes extensive use of dramatic irony in this play. Point out effective examples.

13. Unlike *Antigone* and *Blood Wedding, Othello* utilizes comedy. For what purposes is it used? What larger difference in effect between *Othello* and these other tragedies does this use of comedy contribute to?

14. As much responsible as any other quality for the original popularity and continued vitality of *Othello* is its poetry. What are some of the prominent characteristics of that poetry (language, imagery, rhythm)? What speeches are particularly memorable or effective? Though most of the play is written in blank verse, some passages are written in rhymed iambic pentameter couplets and others in prose. Can you suggest any reasons for Shakespeare's use of these other mediums?

15. How would the effect of the play have been different if Othello had died *before* discovering Desdemona's innocence?

Molière

THE MISANTHROPE

CHARACTERS

ALCESTE, *in love with Célimène*
PHILINTE, *Alceste's friend*
ORONTE, *in love with Célimène*
CÉLIMÈNE, *Alceste's beloved*
ELIANTE, *Célimène's cousin*
ARSINOÉ, *a friend of Célimène's*
ACASTE } *marquesses*
CLITANDRE } *marquesses*
BASQUE, *Célimène's servant*
A GUARD *of the Marshalsea*
DUBOIS, *Alceste's valet*

The scene throughout is in Célimène's house at Paris.

ACT I

SCENE I

PHILINTE. Now, what's got into you?
ALCESTE (*seated*). Kindly leave me alone.
PHILINTE. Come, come, what is it? This lugubrious tone . . .
ALCESTE. Leave me, I said; you spoil my solitude.
PHILINTE. Oh, listen to me, now, and don't be rude.
ALCESTE. I choose to be rude, Sir, and to be hard of hearing.
PHILINTE. These ugly moods of yours are not endearing;
Friends though we are, I really must insist . . .

ALCESTE (*abruptly rising*). Friends? Friends, you say? Well, cross me off your list.
I've been your friend till now, as you well know;
But after what I saw a moment ago
I tell you flatly that our ways must part.
I wish no place in a dishonest heart.
PHILINTE. Why, what have I done, Alceste? Is this quite just?
ALCESTE. My God, you ought to die of self-disgust.
I call your conduct inexcusable, Sir,
And every man of honor will concur.
I see you almost hug a man to death,
Exclaim for joy until you're out of breath,
And supplement these loving demonstrations
With endless offers, vows, and protestations;
Then when I ask you "Who was that?" I find
That you can barely bring his name to mind!
Once the man's back is turned, you cease to love him,
And speak with absolute indifference of him!
By God, I say it's base and scandalous
To falsify the heart's affections thus;
If I caught myself behaving in such a way,
I'd hang myself for shame, without delay.
PHILINTE. It hardly seems a hanging matter to me;
I hope that you will take it graciously
If I extend myself a slight reprieve,
And live a little longer, by your leave.
ALCESTE. How dare you joke about a crime so grave?
PHILINTE. What crime? How else are people to behave?
ALCESTE. I'd have them be sincere, and never part
With any word that isn't from the heart.
PHILINTE. When someone greets us with a show of pleasure,
It's but polite to give him equal measure,
Return his love the best that we know how,
And trade him offer for offer, vow for vow.
ALCESTE. No, no, this formula you'd have me follow,
However fashionable, is false and hollow,
And I despise the frenzied operations
Of all these barterers of protestations,
These lavishers of meaningless embraces,
These utterers of obliging commonplaces,
Who court and flatter everyone on earth
And praise the fool no less than the man of worth.
Should you rejoice that someone fondles you,
Offers his love and service, swears to be true,

And fills your ears with praises of your name,
When to the first damned fop he'll say the same?
No, no: no self-respecting heart would dream
Of prizing so promiscuous an esteem;
However high the praise, there's nothing worse
Than sharing honors with the universe.
Esteem is founded on comparison:
To honor all men is to honor none.
Since you embrace this indiscriminate vice,
Your friendship comes at far too cheap a price;
I spurn the easy tribute of a heart
Which will not set the worthy man apart:
I choose, Sir, to be chosen; and in fine,
The friend of mankind is no friend of mine.
PHILINTE. But in polite society, custom decrees
That we show certain outward courtesies . . .
ALCESTE. Ah, no! we should condemn with all our force
Such false and artificial intercourse.
Let men behave like men; let them display
Their inmost hearts in everything they say;
Let the heart speak, and let our sentiments
Not mask themselves in silly compliments.
PHILINTE. In certain cases it would be uncouth
And most absurd to speak the naked truth;
With all respect for your exalted notions,
It's often best to veil one's true emotions.
Wouldn't the social fabric come undone
If we were wholly frank with everyone?
Suppose you met with someone you couldn't bear;
Would you inform him of it then and there?
ALCESTE. Yes.
PHILINTE. Then you'd tell old Emilie it's pathetic
The way she daubs her features with cosmetic
And plays the gay coquette at sixty-four?
ALCESTE. I would.
PHILINTE. And you'd call Dorilas a bore,
And tell him every ear at court is lame
From hearing him brag about his noble name?
ALCESTE. Precisely.
PHILINTE. Ah, you're joking.
ALCESTE. *Au contraire:*
In this regard there's none I'd choose to spare.
All are corrupt; there's nothing to be seen
In court or town but aggravates my spleen.

I fall into deep gloom and melancholy
When I survey the scene of human folly,
Finding on every hand base flattery,
Injustice, fraud, self-interest, treachery . . .
Ah, it's too much; mankind has grown so base,
I mean to break with the whole human race.

PHILINTE. This philosophic rage is a bit extreme;
You've no idea how comical you seem;
Indeed, we're like those brothers in the play
Called *School for Husbands,* one of whom was prey . . .[1]

ALCESTE. Enough, now! None of your stupid similes.

PHILINTE. Then let's have no more tirades, if you please.
The world won't change, whatever you say or do;
And since plain speaking means so much to you,
I'll tell you plainly that by being frank
You've earned the reputation of a crank,
And that you're thought ridiculous when you rage
And rant against the manners of the age.

ALCESTE. So much the better; just what I wish to hear.
No news could be more grateful to my ear.
All men are so detestable in my eyes,
I should be sorry if they thought me wise.

PHILINTE. Your hatred's very sweeping, is it not?

ALCESTE. Quite right: I hate the whole degraded lot.

PHILINTE. Must all poor human creatures be embraced,
Without distinction, by your vast distaste?
Even in these bad times, there are surely a few . . .

ALCESTE. No, I include all men in one dim view:
Some men I hate for being rogues; the others
I hate because they treat the rogues like brothers,
And, lacking a virtuous scorn for what is vile,
Receive the villain with a complaisant smile.
Notice how tolerant people choose to be
Toward that bold rascal who's at law with me.
His social polish can't conceal his nature;
One sees at once that he's a treacherous creature;
No one could possibly be taken in
By those soft speeches and that sugary grin.

[1] *School* . . . prey: *School for Husbands* is an earlier play by Molière. The chief characters are two brothers, one of whom, puritanical and suspicious, mistrusts the fashions and customs of the world, shuts up his ward and fiancée to keep her from infection by them, and is outwitted and betrayed by her. The other, more amiable and easy going, allows his ward a free reign and is rewarded with her love.

The whole world knows the shady means by which
The low-brow's grown so powerful and rich,
And risen to a rank so bright and high
That virtue can but blush, and merit sigh.
Whenever his name comes up in conversation,
None will defend his wretched reputation;
Call him knave, liar, scoundrel, and all the rest,
Each head will nod, and no one will protest.
And yet his smirk is seen in every house,
He's greeted everywhere with smiles and bows,
And when there's any honor that can be got
By pulling strings, he'll get it, like as not.
My God! It chills my heart to see the ways
Men come to terms with evil nowadays;
Sometimes, I swear, I'm moved to flee and find
Some desert land unfouled by humankind.

PHILINTE. Come, let's forget the follies of the times
And pardon mankind for its petty crimes;
Let's have an end of rantings and of railings,
And show some leniency toward human failings.
This world requires a pliant rectitude;
Too stern a virtue makes one stiff and rude;
Good sense views all extremes with detestation,
And bids us to be noble in moderation.
The rigid virtues of the ancient days
Are not for us; they jar with all our ways
And ask of us too lofty a perfection.
Wise men accept their times without objection,
And there's no greater folly, if you ask me,
Than trying to reform society.
Like you, I see each day a hundred and one
Unhandsome deeds that might be better done,
But still, for all the faults that meet my view,
I'm never known to storm and rave like you.
I take men as they are, or let them be,
And teach my soul to bear their frailty;
And whether in court or town, whatever the scene,
My phlegm's as philosophic as your spleen.

ALCESTE. This phlegm which you so eloquently commend,
Does nothing ever rile it up, my friend?
Suppose some man you trust should treacherously
Conspire to rob you of your property,
And do his best to wreck your reputation?
Wouldn't you feel a certain indignation?

Philinte. Why, no. These faults of which you so complain
Are part of human nature, I maintain,
And it's no more a matter for disgust
That men are knavish, selfish and unjust,
Than that the vulture dines upon the dead,
And wolves are furious, and apes ill-bred.
Alceste. Shall I see myself betrayed, robbed, torn to bits,
And not . . . Oh, let's be still and rest our wits.
Enough of reasoning, now. I've had my fill.
Philinte. Indeed, you would do well, Sir, to be still.
Rage less at your opponent, and give some thought
To how you'll win this lawsuit that he's brought.
Alceste. I assure you I'll do nothing of the sort.
Philinte. Then who will plead your case before the court?
Alceste. Reason and right and justice will plead for me.
Philinte. Oh, Lord. What judges do you plan to see?
Alceste. Why, none. The justice of my cause is clear.
Philinte. Of course, man; but there's politics to fear . . .
Alceste. No, I refuse to lift a hand. That's flat.
I'm either right, or wrong.
Philinte. Don't count on that.
Alceste. No, I'll do nothing.
Philinte. Your enemy's influence
Is great, you know . . .
Alceste. That makes no difference.
Philinte. It will; you'll see.
Alceste. Must honor bow to guile?
If so, I shall be proud to lose the trial.
Philinte. Oh, really . . .
Alceste. I'll discover by this case
Whether or not men are sufficiently base
And impudent and villainous and perverse
To do me wrong before the universe.
Philinte. What a man!
Alceste. Oh, I could wish, whatever the cost,
Just for the beauty of it, that my trial were lost.
Philinte. If people heard you talking so, Alceste,
They'd split their sides. Your name would be a jest.
Alceste. So much the worse for jesters.
Philinte. May I enquire
Whether this rectitude you so admire,
And these hard virtues you're enamored of
Are qualities of the lady whom you love?
It much surprises me that you, who seem

To view mankind with furious disesteem,
Have yet found something to enchant your eyes
Amidst a species which you so despise.
And what is more amazing, I'm afraid,
Is the most curious choice your heart has made.
The honest Eliante is fond of you,
Arsinoé, the prude, admires you too;
And yet your spirit's been perversely led
To choose the flighty Célimène instead,
Whose brittle malice and coquettish ways
So typify the manners of our days.
How is it that the traits you most abhor
Are bearable in this lady you adore?
Are you so blind with love that you can't find them?
Or do you contrive, in her case, not to mind them?

ALCESTE. My love for that young widow's not the kind
That can't perceive defects; no, I'm not blind.
I see her faults, despite my ardent love,
And all I see I fervently reprove.
And yet I'm weak; for all her falsity,
That woman knows the art of pleasing me,
And though I never cease complaining of her,
I swear I cannot manage not to love her.
Her charm outweighs her faults; I can but aim
To cleanse her spirit in my love's pure flame.

PHILINTE. That's no small task; I wish you all success.
You think then that she loves you?

ALCESTE. Heavens, yes!
I wouldn't love her did she not love me.

PHILINTE. Well, if her taste for you is plain to see,
Why do these rivals cause you such despair?

ALCESTE. True love, Sir, is possessive, and cannot bear
To share with all the world. I'm here today
To tell her she must send that mob away.

PHILINTE. If I were you, and had your choice to make,
Eliante, her cousin, would be the one I'd take;
That honest heart, which cares for you alone,
Would harmonize far better with your own.

ALCESTE. True, true: each day my reason tells me so;
But reason doesn't rule in love, you know.

PHILINTE. I fear some bitter sorrow is in store;
This love . . .

SCENE II[2]

ORONTE (*to* ALCESTE). The servants told me at the door
That Eliante and Célimène were out,
But when I heard, dear Sir, that you were about,
I came to say, without exaggeration,
That I hold you in the vastest admiration,
And that it's always been my dearest desire
To be the friend of one I so admire.
I hope to see my love of merit requited,
And you and I in friendship's bond united.
I'm sure you won't refuse—if I may be frank—
A friend of my devotedness—and rank. (*During this speech of* ORONTE'S, ALCESTE *is abstracted, and seems unaware that he is being spoken to. He only breaks off his reverie when* ORONTE *says*)
It was for you, if you please, that my words were intended.

ALCESTE. For me, Sir?

ORONTE. Yes, for you. You're not offended?

ALCESTE. By no means. But this much surprises me . . .
The honor comes most unexpectedly . . .

ORONTE. My high regard should not astonish you;
The whole world feels the same. It is your due.

ALCESTE. Sir . . .

ORONTE. Why, in all the State there isn't one
Can match your merits; they shine, Sir, like the sun.

ALCESTE. Sir . . .

ORONTE. You are higher in my estimation
Than all that's most illustrious in the nation.

ALCESTE. Sir . . .

ORONTE. If I lie, may heaven strike me dead!
To show you that I mean what I have said,
Permit me, Sir, to embrace you most sincerely,
And swear that I will prize our friendship dearly.
Give me your hand. And now, Sir, if you choose,
We'll make our vows.

ALCESTE. Sir . . .

ORONTE. What! You refuse?

ALCESTE. Sir, it's a very great honor you extend:

[2] Scene II: In English and in most modern plays, a scene is a continuous section of the action in one setting, and acts are not usually divided into scenes unless there is a shift in setting or a shift in time. In older French drama, however, a scene is any portion of the play involving one group of characters, and a new scene begins, without interruption of the action, whenever any important character enters or exits.

But friendship is a sacred thing, my friend;
It would be profanation to bestow
The name of friend on one you hardly know.
All parts are better played when well-rehearsed;
Let's put off friendship, and get acquainted first.
We may discover it would be unwise
To try to make our natures harmonize.
ORONTE. By heaven! You're sagacious to the core;
This speech has made me admire you even more.
Let time, then, bring us closer day by day;
Meanwhile, I shall be yours in every way.
If, for example, there should be anything
You wish at court, I'll mention it to the King.
I have his ear, of course; it's quite well known
That I am much in favor with the throne.
In short, I am your servant. And now, dear friend,
Since you have such fine judgment, I intend
To please you, if I can, with a small sonnet
I wrote not long ago. Please comment on it,
And tell me whether I ought to publish it.
ALCESTE. You must excuse me, Sir; I'm hardly fit
To judge such matters.
ORONTE. Why not?
ALCESTE. I am, I fear,
Inclined to be unfashionably sincere.
ORONTE. Just what I ask; I'd take no satisfaction
In anything but your sincere reaction.
I beg you not to dream of being kind.
ALCESTE. Since you desire it, Sir, I'll speak my mind.
ORONTE. *Sonnet*. It's a sonnet . . . *Hope* . . . The poem's addressed
To a lady who wakened hopes within my breast.
Hope . . . this is not the pompous sort of thing,
Just modest little verses, with a tender ring.
ALCESTE. Well, we shall see.
ORONTE. *Hope* . . . I'm anxious to hear
Whether the style seems properly smooth and clear,
And whether the choice of words is good or bad.
ALCESTE. We'll see, we'll see.
ORONTE. Perhaps I ought to add
That it took me only a quarter-hour to write it.
ALCESTE. The time's irrelevant, Sir: kindly recite it.
ORONTE (*reading*). Hope comforts us awhile, t'is true,
Lulling our cares with careless laughter,
And yet such joy is full of rue,

My Phyllis, if nothing follows after.

PHILINTE. I'm charmed by this already; the style's delightful.

ALCESTE (*sotto voce, to* PHILINTE). How can you say that? Why, the thing is frightful.

ORONTE. Your fair face smiled on me awhile,
But was it kindness so to enchant me?
'Twould have been fairer not to smile,
If hope was all you meant to grant me.

PHILINTE. What a clever thought! How handsomely you phrase it!

ALCESTE (*sotto voce, to* PHILINTE). You know the thing is trash. How dare you praise it?

ORONTE. If it's to be my passion's fate
Thus everlastingly to wait,
Then death will come to set me free:
For death is fairer than the fair;
Phyllis, to hope is to despair
When one must hope eternally.

PHILINTE. The close is exquisite—full of feeling and grace.

ALCESTE (*sotto voce, aside*). Oh, blast the close; you'd better close your face
Before you send your lying soul to hell.

PHILINTE. I can't remember a poem I've liked so well.

ALCESTE (*sotto voce, aside*). Good Lord!

ORONTE (*to* PHILINTE). I fear you're flattering me a bit.

PHILINTE. Oh, no!

ALCESTE (*sotto voce, aside*). What else d'you call it, you hypocrite?

ORONTE (*to* ALCESTE). But you, Sir, keep your promise now: don't shrink
From telling me sincerely what you think.

ALCESTE. Sir, these are delicate matters; we all desire
To be told that we've the true poetic fire.
But once, to one whose name I shall not mention,
I said, regarding some verse of his invention,
That gentlemen should rigorously control
That itch to write which often afflicts the soul;
That one should curb the heady inclination
To publicize one's little avocation;
And that in showing off one's works of art
One often plays a very clownish part.

SERIOUS poet wouldn't HAVE someone READ

ORONTE. Are you suggesting in a devious way
That I ought not . . .

ALCESTE. Oh, that I do not say.
Further, I told him that no fault is worse
Than that of writing frigid, lifeless verse,
And that the merest whisper of such a shame

Suffices to destroy a man's good name.
ORONTE. D'you mean to say my sonnet's dull and trite?
ALCESTE. I don't say that. But I went on to cite
Numerous cases of once-respected men
Who came to grief by taking up the pen.
ORONTE. And am I like them? Do I write so poorly?
ALCESTE. I don't say that. But I told this person, "Surely
You're under no necessity to compose;
Why you should wish to publish, heaven knows.
There's no excuse for printing tedious rot
Unless one writes for bread, as you do not.
Resist temptation, then, I beg of you;
Conceal your pastimes from the public view;
And don't give up, on any provocation,
Your present high and courtly reputation,
To purchase at a greedy printer's shop
The name of silly author and scribbling fop."
These were the points I tried to make him see.
ORONTE. I sense that they are also aimed at me;
But now—about my sonnet—I'd like to be told . . .
ALCESTE. Frankly, that sonnet should be pigeonholed.
You've chosen the worst models to imitate.
The style's unnatural. Let me illustrate:

For example, Your fair face smiled on me awhile,
Followed by, 'Twould have been fairer not to smile!
Or this: such joy is full of rue;
Or this: For death is fairer than the fair;
Or, Phyllis, to hope is to despair
When one must hope eternally!

This artificial style, that's all the fashion,
Has neither taste, nor honesty, nor passion;
It's nothing but a sort of wordy play,
And nature never spoke in such a way.
What, in this shallow age, is not debased?
Our fathers, though less refined, had better taste;
I'd barter all that men admire today
For one old love-song I shall try to say:

If the King had given me for my own
Paris, his citadel,
And I for that must leave alone
Her whom I love so well,
I'd say then to the Crown,

Take back your glittering town;
My darling is more fair, I swear,
My darling is more fair.

The rhyme's not rich, the style is rough and old,
But don't you see that it's the purest gold
Beside the tinsel nonsense now preferred,
And that there's passion in its every word?

If the King had given me for my own
Paris, his citadel,
And I for that must leave alone
Her whom I love so well,
I'd say then to the Crown,
Take back your glittering town;
My darling is more fair, I swear,
My darling is more fair.

There speaks a loving heart. (*To* PHILINTE) You're laughing, eh?
Laugh on, my precious wit. Whatever you say,
I hold that song's worth all the bibelots
That people hail today with ah's and oh's.
ORONTE. And I maintain my sonnet's very good.
ALCESTE. It's not at all surprising that you should.
You have your reasons; permit me to have mine
For thinking that you cannot write a line.
ORONTE. Others have praised my sonnet to the skies.
ALCESTE. I lack their art of telling pleasant lies.
ORONTE. You seem to think you've got no end of wit.
ALCESTE. To praise your verse, I'd need still more of it.
ORONTE. I'm not in need of your approval, Sir.
ALCESTE. That's good; you couldn't have it if you were.
ORONTE. Come now, I'll lend you the subject of my sonnet;
I'd like to see you try to improve upon it.
ALCESTE. I might, by chance, write something just as shoddy;
But then I wouldn't show it to everybody.
ORONTE. You're most opinionated and conceited.
ALCESTE. Go find your flatterers, and be better treated.
ORONTE. Look here, my little fellow, pray watch your tone.
ALCESTE. My great big fellow, you'd better watch your own.
PHILINTE (*stepping between them*). Oh, please, please, gentlemen!
This will never do.
ORONTE. The fault is mine, and I leave the field to you.
I am your servant, Sir, in every way.
ALCESTE. And I, Sir, am your most abject valet.

SCENE III

PHILINTE. Well, as you see, sincerity in excess
Can get you into a very pretty mess;
Oronte was hungry for appreciation . . .
ALCESTE. Don't speak to me.
PHILINTE. What?
ALCESTE. No more conversation.
PHILINTE. Really, now . . .
ALCESTE. Leave me alone.
PHILINTE. If I . . .
ALCESTE. Out of my sight!
PHILINTE. But what . . .
ALCESTE. I won't listen.
PHILINTE. But . . .
ALCESTE. Silence!
PHILINTE. Now, is it polite . . .
ALCESTE. By heaven, I've had enough. Don't follow me.
PHILINTE. Ah, you're just joking. I'll keep you company.

ACT II

SCENE I

ALCESTE. Shall I speak plainly, Madam? I confess
Your conduct gives me infinite distress,
And my resentment's grown too hot to smother.
Soon, I foresee, we'll break with one another.
If I said otherwise, I should deceive you;
Sooner or later, I shall be forced to leave you,
And if I swore that we shall never part,
I should misread the omens of my heart.
CÉLIMÈNE. You kindly saw me home, it would appear,
So as to pour invectives in my ear.
ALCESTE. I've no desire to quarrel. But I deplore
Your inability to shut the door
On all these suitors who beset you so.
There's what annoys me, if you care to know.
CÉLIMÈNE. Is it my fault that all these men pursue me?
Am I to blame if they're attracted to me?
And when they gently beg an audience,
Ought I to take a stick and drive them hence?
ALCESTE. Madam, there's no necessity for a stick;
A less responsive heart would do the trick.

Of your attractiveness I don't complain;
But those your charms attract, you then detain
By a most melting and receptive manner,
And so enlist their hearts beneath your banner.
It's the agreeable hopes which you excite
That keep these lovers round you day and night;
Were they less liberally smiled upon,
That sighing troop would very soon be gone.
But tell me, Madam, why it is that lately
This man Clitandre interests you so greatly?
Because of what high merits do you deem
Him worthy of the honor of your esteem?
Is it that your admiring glances linger
On the splendidly long nail of his little finger?
Or do you share the general deep respect
For the blond wig he chooses to affect?
Are you in love with his embroidered hose?
Do you adore his ribbons and his bows?
Or is it that this paragon bewitches
Your tasteful eye with his vast German breeches?
Perhaps his giggle, or his falsetto voice,
Makes him the latest gallant of your choice?

CÉLIMÈNE. You're much mistaken to resent him so.
Why I put up with him you surely know:
My lawsuit's very shortly to be tried,
And I must have his influence on my side.

ALCESTE. Then lose your lawsuit, Madam, or let it drop;
Don't torture me by humoring such a fop.

CÉLIMÈNE. You're jealous of the whole world, Sir.

ALCESTE. That's true,
Since the whole world is well-received by you.

CÉLIMÈNE. That my good nature is so unconfined
Should serve to pacify your jealous mind;
Were I to smile on one, and scorn the rest,
Then you might have some cause to be distressed.

ALCESTE. Well, if I mustn't be jealous, tell me, then,
Just how I'm better treated than other men.

CÉLIMÈNE. You know you have my love. Will that not do?

ALCESTE. What proof have I that what you say is true?

CÉLIMÈNE. I would expect, Sir, that my having said it
Might give the statement a sufficient credit.

ALCESTE. But how can I be sure that you don't tell
The selfsame thing to other men as well?

CÉLIMÈNE. What a gallant speech! How flattering to me!

What a sweet creature you make me out to be!
Well then, to save you from the pangs of doubt,
All that I've said I hereby cancel out;
Now, none but yourself shall make a monkey of you:
Are you content?
Alceste. Why, why am I doomed to love you?
I swear that I shall bless the blissful hour
When this poor heart's no longer in your power!
I make no secret of it: I've done my best
To exorcise this passion from my breast;
But thus far all in vain; it will not go;
It's for my sins that I must love you so.
Célimène. Your love for me is matchless, Sir; that's clear.
Alceste. Indeed, in all the world it has no peer;
Words can't describe the nature of my passion,
And no man ever loved in such a fashion.
Célimène. Yes, it's a brand-new fashion, I agree:
You show your love by castigating me,
And all your speeches are enraged and rude.
I've never been so furiously wooed.
Alceste. Yet you could calm that fury, if you chose.
Come, shall we bring our quarrels to a close?
Let's speak with open hearts, then, and begin . . .

SCENE II

Célimène. What is it?
Basque. Acaste is here.
Célimène. Well, send him in.

SCENE III

Alceste. What! Shall we never be alone at all?
You're always ready to receive a call,
And you can't bear, for ten ticks of the clock,
Not to keep open house for all who knock.
Célimène. I couldn't refuse him: he'd be most put out.
Alceste. Surely that's not worth worrying about.
Célimène. Acaste would never forgive me if he guessed
That I consider him a dreadful pest.
Alceste. If he's a pest, why bother with him then?
Célimène. Heavens! One can't antagonize such men;
Why, they're the chartered gossips of the court,

And have a say in things of every sort.
One must receive them, and be full of charm;
They're no great help, but they can do you harm,
And though your influence be ever so great,
They're hardly the best people to alienate.
ALCESTE. I see, dear lady, that you could make a case
For putting up with the whole human race;
These friendships that you calculate so nicely . . .

SCENE IV

BASQUE. Madam, Clitandre is here as well.
ALCESTE. Precisely.
CÉLIMÈNE. Where are you going?
ALCESTE. Elsewhere.
CÉLIMÈNE. Stay.
ALCESTE. No, no.
CÉLIMÈNE. Stay, Sir.
ALCESTE. I can't.
CÉLIMÈNE. I wish it.
ALCESTE. No, I must go.
I beg you, Madam, not to press the matter;
You know I have no taste for idle chatter.
CÉLIMÈNE. Stay: I command you.
ALCESTE. No, I cannot stay.
CÉLIMÈNE. Very well; you have my leave to go away.

SCENE V

ELIANTE (*to* CÉLIMÈNE). The Marquesses have kindly come to call.
Were they announced?
CÉLIMÈNE. Yes. Basque, bring chairs for all. (BASQUE *provides the chairs, and exits. To* ALCESTE)
You haven't gone?
ALCESTE. No; and I shan't depart
Till you decide who's foremost in your heart.
CÉLIMÈNE. Oh, hush.
ALCESTE. It's time to choose; take them, or me.
CÉLIMÈNE. You're mad.
ALCESTE. I'm not, as you shall shortly see.
CÉLIMÈNE. Oh?
ALCESTE. You'll decide.
CÉLIMÈNE. You're joking now, dear friend.

ALCESTE. No, no; you'll choose; my patience is at an end.

CLITANDRE. Madam, I come from court, where poor Cléonte
Behaved like a perfect fool, as is his wont.
Has he no friend to counsel him, I wonder,
And teach him less unerringly to blunder?

CÉLIMÈNE. It's true, the man's a most accomplished dunce;
His gauche behavior charms the eye at once;
And every time one sees him, on my word,
His manner's grown a trifle more absurd.

ACASTE. Speaking of dunces, I've just now conversed
With old Damon, who's one of the very worst;
I stood a lifetime in the broiling sun
Before his dreary monologue was done.

CÉLIMÈNE. Oh, he's a wondrous talker, and has the power
To tell you nothing hour after hour:
If, by mistake, he ever came to the point,
The shock would put his jawbone out of joint.

ELIANTE (*to* PHILINTE). The conversation takes its usual turn,
And all our dear friends' ears will shortly burn.

CLITANDRE. Timante's a character, Madam.

CÉLIMÈNE. Isn't he, though?
A man of mystery from top to toe,
Who moves about in a romantic mist
On secret missions which do not exist.
His talk is full of eyebrows and grimaces;
How tired one gets of his momentous faces;
He's always whispering something confidential
Which turns out to be quite inconsequential;
Nothing's too slight for him to mystify;
He even whispers when he says "good-by."

ACASTE. Tell us about Géralde.

CÉLIMÈNE. That tiresome ass.
He mixes only with the titled class,
And fawns on dukes and princes, and is bored
With anyone who's not at least a lord.
The man's obsessed with rank, and his discourses
Are all of hounds and carriages and horses;
He uses Christian names with all the great,
And the word Milord, with him, is out of date.

CLITANDRE. He's very taken with Bélise, I hear.

CÉLIMÈNE. She is the dreariest company, poor dear.
Whenever she comes to call, I grope about
To find some topic which will draw her out,
But, owing to her dry and faint replies,

The conversation wilts, and droops, and dies.
In vain one hopes to animate her face
By mentioning the ultimate commonplace;
But sun or shower, even hail or frost
Are matters she can instantly exhaust.
Meanwhile her visit, painful though it is,
Drags on and on through mute eternities,
And though you ask the time, and yawn, and yawn,
She sits there like a stone and won't be gone.

ACASTE. Now for Adraste.

CÉLIMÈNE. Oh, that conceited elf
Has a gigantic passion for himself;
He rails against the court, and cannot bear it
That none will recognize his hidden merit;
All honors given to others give offense
To his imaginary excellence.

CLITANDRE. What about young Cléon? His house, they say,
Is full of the best society, night and day.

CÉLIMÈNE. His cook has made him popular, not he:
It's Cléon's table that people come to see.

ELIANTE. He gives a splendid dinner, you must admit.

CÉLIMÈNE. But must he serve himself along with it?
For my taste, he's a most insipid dish
Whose presence sours the wine and spoils the fish.

PHILINTE. Damis, his uncle, is admired no end.
What's your opinion, Madam?

CÉLIMÈNE. Why, he's my friend.

PHILINTE. He seems a decent fellow, and rather clever.

CÉLIMÈNE. He works too hard at cleverness, however.
I hate to see him sweat and struggle so
To fill his conversation with bons mots.
Since he's decided to become a wit
His taste's so pure that nothing pleases it;
He scolds at all the latest books and plays,
Thinking that wit must never stoop to praise,
That finding fault's a sign of intellect,
That all appreciation is abject,
And that by damning everything in sight
One shows oneself in a distinguished light.
He's scornful even of our conversations:
Their trivial nature sorely tries his patience;
He folds his arms, and stands above the battle,
And listens sadly to our childish prattle.

ACASTE. Wonderful, Madam! You've hit him off precisely.

CLITANDRE. No one can sketch a character so nicely.
ALCESTE. How bravely, Sirs, you cut and thrust at all
These absent fools, till one by one they fall:
But let one come in sight, and you'll at once
Embrace the man you lately called a dunce,
Telling him in a tone sincere and fervent
How proud you are to be his humble servant.
CLITANDRE. Why pick on us? Madame's been speaking, Sir,
And you should quarrel, if you must, with her.
ALCESTE. No, no, by God, the fault is yours, because
You lead her on with laughter and applause,
And make her think that she's the more delightful
The more her talk is scandalous and spiteful.
Oh, she would stoop to malice far, far less
If no such claque approved her cleverness.
It's flatterers like you whose foolish praise
Nourishes all the vices of these days.
PHILINTE. But why protest when someone ridicules
Those you'd condemn, yourself, as knaves or fools?
CÉLIMÈNE. Why, Sir? Because he loves to make a fuss.
You don't expect him to agree with us,
When there's an opportunity to express
His heaven-sent spirit of contrariness?
What other people think, he can't abide;
Whatever they say, he's on the other side;
He lives in deadly terror of agreeing;
'Twould make him seem an ordinary being.
Indeed, he's so in love with contradiction,
He'll turn against his most profound conviction
And with a furious eloquence deplore it,
If only someone else is speaking for it.
ALCESTE. Go on, dear lady, mock me as you please;
You have your audience in ecstasies.
PHILINTE. But what she says is true: you have a way
Of bridling at whatever people say;
Whether they praise or blame, your angry spirit
Is equally unsatisfied to hear it.
ALCESTE. Men, Sir, are always wrong, and that's the reason
That righteous anger's never out of season;
All that I hear in all their conversation
Is flattering praise or reckless condemnation.
CÉLIMÈNE. But . . .
ALCESTE. No, no, Madam, I am forced to state
That you have pleasures which I deprecate,

And that these others, here, are much to blame
For nourishing the faults which are your shame.
CLITANDRE. I shan't defend myself, Sir; but I vow
I'd thought this lady faultless until now.
ACASTE. I see her charms and graces, which are many;
But as for faults, I've never noticed any.
ALCESTE. I see them, Sir; and rather than ignore them,
I strenuously criticize her for them.
The more one loves, the more one should object
To every blemish, every least defect.
Were I this lady, I would soon get rid
Of lovers who approved of all I did,
And by their slack indulgence and applause
Endorsed my follies and excused my flaws.
CÉLIMÈNE. If all hearts beat according to your measure,
The dawn of love would be the end of pleasure;
And love would find its perfect consummation
In ecstasies of rage and reprobation.
ELIANTE. Love, as a rule, affects men otherwise,
And lovers rarely love to criticize.
They see their lady as a charming blur,
And find all things commendable in her.
If she has any blemish, fault, or shame,
They will redeem it by a pleasing name.
The pale-faced lady's lily-white, perforce;
The swarthy one's a sweet brunette, of course;
The spindly lady has a slender grace;
The fat one has a most majestic pace;
The plain one, with her dress in disarray,
They classify as *beauté négligée;*
The hulking one's a goddess in their eyes,
The dwarf, a concentrate of Paradise;
The haughty lady has a noble mind;
The mean one's witty, and the dull one's kind;
The chatterbox has liveliness and verve,
The mute one has a virtuous reserve.
So lovers manage, in their passion's cause,
To love their ladies even for their flaws.
ALCESTE. But I still say . . .
CÉLIMÈNE. I think it would be nice
To stroll around the gallery once or twice.
What! You're not going, Sirs?
CLITANDRE and ACASTE. No, Madam, no.
ALCESTE. You seem to be in terror lest they go.

Do what you will, Sirs; leave, or linger on,
But I shan't go till after you are gone.

ACASTE. I'm free to linger, unless I should perceive
Madame is tired, and wishes me to leave.

CLITANDRE. And as for me, I needn't go today
Until the hour of the King's *coucher*.

CÉLIMÈNE (*to* ALCESTE). You're joking, surely?

ALCESTE. Not in the least; we'll see
Whether you'd rather part with them, or me.

SCENE VI

BASQUE (*to* ALCESTE). Sir, there's a fellow here who bids me state
That he must see you, and that it can't wait.

ALCESTE. Tell him that I have no such pressing affairs.

BASQUE. It's a long tailcoat that this fellow wears,
With gold all over.

CÉLIMÈNE (*to* ALCESTE). You'd best go down and see.
Or—have him enter.

SCENE VII

ALCESTE (*confronting the guard*). Well, what do you want with me?
Come in, Sir.

GUARD. I've a word, Sir, for your ear.

ALCESTE. Speak it aloud, Sir; I shall strive to hear.

GUARD. The Marshals have instructed me to say
You must report to them without delay.

ALCESTE. Who? Me, Sir?

GUARD. Yes, Sir; you.

ALCESTE. But what do they want?

PHILINTE (*to* ALCESTE). To scotch your silly quarrel with Oronte.

CÉLIMÈNE (*to* PHILINTE). What quarrel?

PHILINTE. Oronte and he have fallen out
Over some verse he spoke his mind about;
The Marshals wish to arbitrate the matter.

ALCESTE. Never shall I equivocate or flatter!

PHILINTE. You'd best obey their summons; come, let's go.

ALCESTE. How can they mend our quarrel, I'd like to know?
Am I to make a cowardly retraction,
And praise those jingles to his satisfaction?

I'll not recant; I've judged that sonnet rightly.
It's bad.
PHILINTE. But you might say so more politely. . . .
ALCESTE. I'll not back down; his verses make me sick.
PHILINTE. If only you could be more politic!
But come, let's go.
ALCESTE. I'll go, but I won't unsay
A single word.
PHILINTE. Well, let's be on our way.
ALCESTE. Till I am ordered by my lord the King
To praise that poem, I shall say the thing
Is scandalous, by God, and that the poet
Ought to be hanged for having the nerve to show it. (*To* CLITANDRE *and* ACASTE, *who are laughing*)
By heaven, Sirs, I really didn't know
That I was being humorous.
CÉLIMÈNE. Go, Sir, go;
Settle your business.
ALCESTE. I shall, and when I'm through,
I shall return to settle things with you.

ACT III

SCENE I

CLITANDRE. Dear Marquess, how contented you appear;
All things delight you, nothing mars your cheer.
Can you, in perfect honesty, declare
That you've a right to be so debonair?
ACASTE. By Jove, when I survey myself, I find
No cause whatever for distress of mind.
I'm young and rich; I can in modesty
Lay claim to an exalted pedigree;
And owing to my name and my condition
I shall not want for honors and position.
Then as to courage, that most precious trait,
I seem to have it, as was proved of late
Upon the field of honor, where my bearing,
They say, was very cool and rather daring.
I've wit, of course; and taste in such perfection
That I can judge without the least reflection,
And at the theater, which is my delight,
Can make or break a play on opening night,

And lead the crowd in hisses or bravos,
And generally be known as one who knows.
I'm clever, handsome, gracefully polite;
My waist is small, my teeth are strong and white;
As for my dress, the world's astonished eyes
Assure me that I bear away the prize.
I find myself in favor everywhere,
Honored by men, and worshiped by the fair;
And since these things are so, it seems to me
I'm justified in my complacency.

CLITANDRE. Well, if so many ladies hold you dear,
Why do you press a hopeless courtship here?

ACASTE. Hopeless, you say? I'm not the sort of fool
That likes his ladies difficult and cool.
Men who are awkward, shy, and peasantish
May pine for heartless beauties, if they wish,
Grovel before them, bear their cruelties,
Woo them with tears and sighs and bended knees,
And hope by dogged faithfulness to gain
What their poor merits never could obtain.
For men like me, however, it makes no sense
To love on trust, and foot the whole expense.
Whatever any lady's merits be,
I think, thank God, that I'm as choice as she;
That if my heart is kind enough to burn
For her, she owes me something in return;
And that in any proper love affair
The partners must invest an equal share.

CLITANDRE. You think, then, that our hostess favors you?

ACASTE. I've reason to believe that that is true.

CLITANDRE. How did you come to such a mad conclusion?
You're blind, dear fellow. This is sheer delusion.

ACASTE. All right, then: I'm deluded and I'm blind.

CLITANDRE. Whatever put the notion in your mind?

ACASTE. Delusion.

CLITANDRE. What persuades you that you're right?

ACASTE. I'm blind.

CLITANDRE. But have you any proofs to cite?

ACASTE. I tell you I'm deluded.

CLITANDRE. Have you, then,
Received some secret pledge from Célimène?

ACASTE. Oh, no: she scorns me.

CLITANDRE. Tell me the truth, I beg.

ACASTE. She just can't bear me.
CLITANDRE. Ah, don't pull my leg.
Tell me what hope she's given you, I pray.
ACASTE. I'm hopeless, and it's you who win the day.
She hates me thoroughly, and I'm so vexed
I mean to hang myself on Tuesday next.
CLITANDRE. Dear Marquess, let us have an armistice
And make a treaty. What do you say to this?
If ever one of us can plainly prove
That Célimène encourages his love,
The other must abandon hope, and yield,
And leave him in possession of the field.
ACASTE. Now, there's a bargain that appeals to me;
With all my heart, dear Marquess, I agree.
But hush.

SCENE II

CÉLIMÈNE. Still here?
CLITANDRE. 'Twas love that stayed our feet.
CÉLIMÈNE. I think I heard a carriage in the street.
Whose is it? D'you know?

SCENE III

BASQUE. Arsinoé is here,
Madame.
CÉLIMÈNE. Arsinoé, you say? Oh, dear.
BASQUE. Eliante is entertaining her below.
CÉLIMÈNE. What brings the creature here, I'd like to know?
ACASTE. They say she's dreadfully prudish, but in fact
I think her piety . . .
CÉLIMÈNE. It's all an act.
At heart she's worldly, and her poor success
In snaring men explains her prudishness.
It breaks her heart to see the beaux and gallants
Engrossed by other women's charms and talents,
And so she's always in a jealous rage
Against the faulty standards of the age.
She lets the world believe that she's a prude
To justify her loveless solitude,
And strives to put a brand of moral shame
On all the graces that she cannot claim.

But still she'd love a lover; and Alceste
Appears to be the one she'd love the best.
His visits here are poison to her pride;
She seems to think I've lured him from her side;
And everywhere, at court or in the town,
The spiteful, envious woman runs me down.
In short, she's just as stupid as can be,
Vicious and arrogant in the last degree,
And . . .

SCENE IV

CÉLIMÈNE. Ah! What happy chance has brought you here?
I've thought about you ever so much, my dear.

ARSINOÉ. I've come to tell you something you should know.

CÉLIMÈNE. How good of you to think of doing so!

(CLITANDRE *and* ACASTE *go out, laughing.*)

SCENE V

ARSINOÉ. It's just as well those gentlemen didn't tarry.

CÉLIMÈNE. Shall we sit down?

ARSINOÉ. That won't be necessary.
Madam, the flame of friendship ought to burn
Brightest in matters of the most concern,
And as there's nothing which concerns us more
Than honor, I have hastened to your door
To bring you, as your friend, some information
About the status of your reputation.
I visited, last night, some virtuous folk,
And, quite by chance, it was of you they spoke;
There was, I fear, no tendency to praise
Your light behavior and your dashing ways.
The quantity of gentlemen you see
And your by now notorious coquetry
Were both so vehemently criticized
By everyone, that I was much surprised.
Of course, I needn't tell you where I stood;
I came to your defense as best I could,
Assured them you were harmless, and declared
Your soul was absolutely unimpaired.
But there are some things, you must realize,

One can't excuse, however hard one tries,
And I was forced at last into conceding
That your behavior, Madam, is misleading,
That it makes a bad impression, giving rise
To ugly gossip and obscene surmise,
And that if you were more *overtly* good,
You wouldn't be so much misunderstood.
Not that I think you've been unchaste—no! no!
The saints preserve me from a thought so low!
But mere good conscience never did suffice:
One must avoid the outward show of vice.
Madam, you're too intelligent, I'm sure,
To think my motives anything but pure
In offering you this counsel—which I do
Out of a zealous interest in you.

CÉLIMÈNE. Madam, I haven't taken you amiss;
I'm very much obliged to you for this;
And I'll at once discharge the obligation
By telling you about *your* reputation.
You've been so friendly as to let me know
What certain people say of me, and so
I mean to follow your benign example
By offering you a somewhat similar sample.
The other day, I went to an affair
And found some most distinguished people there
Discussing piety, both false and true.
The conversation soon came round to you.
Alas! Your prudery and bustling zeal
Appeared to have a very slight appeal.
Your affectation of a grave demeanor,
Your endless talk of virtue and of honor,
The aptitude of your suspicious mind
For finding sin where there is none to find,
Your towering self-esteem, that pitying face
With which you contemplate the human race,
Your sermonizings and your sharp aspersions
On people's pure and innocent diversions—
All these were mentioned, Madam, and, in fact,
Were roundly and concertedly attacked.
"What good," they said, "are all these outward shows,
When everything belies her pious pose?
She prays incessantly; but then, they say,
She beats her maids and cheats them of their pay;
She shows her zeal in every holy place,

But still she's vain enough to paint her face;
She holds that naked statues are immoral,
But with a naked *man* she'd have no quarrel."
Of course, I said to everybody there
That they were being viciously unfair;
But still they were disposed to criticize you,
And all agreed that someone should advise you
To leave the morals of the world alone,
And worry rather more about your own.
They felt that one's self-knowledge should be great
Before one thinks of setting others straight;
That one should learn the art of living well
Before one threatens other men with hell,
And that the Church is best equipped, no doubt,
To guide our souls and root our vices out.
Madam, you're too intelligent, I'm sure,
To think my motives anything but pure
In offering you this counsel—which I do
Out of a zealous interest in you.

ARSINOÉ. I dared not hope for gratitude, but I
Did not expect so acid a reply;
I judge, since you've been so extremely tart,
That my good counsel pierced you to the heart.

CÉLIMÈNE. Far from it, Madam. Indeed, it seems to me
We ought to trade advice more frequently.
One's vision of oneself is so defective
That it would be an excellent corrective.
If you are willing, Madam, let's arrange
Shortly to have another frank exchange
In which we'll tell each other, *entre nous*,
What you've heard tell of me, and I of you.

ARSINOÉ. Oh, people never censure you, my dear;
It's me they criticize. Or so I hear.

CÉLIMÈNE. Madam, I think we either blame or praise
According to our taste and length of days.
There is a time of life for coquetry,
And there's a season, too, for prudery.
When all one's charms are gone, it is, I'm sure,
Good strategy to be devout and pure:
It makes one seem a little less forsaken.
Some day, perhaps, I'll take the road you've taken:
Time brings all things. But I have time aplenty,
And see no cause to be a prude at twenty.

ARSINOÉ. You give your age in such a gloating tone

That one would think I was an ancient crone;
We're not so far apart, in sober truth,
That you can mock me with a boast of youth!
Madam, you baffle me. I wish I knew
What moves you to provoke me as you do.
CÉLIMÈNE. For my part, Madam, I should like to know
Why you abuse me everywhere you go.
Is it my fault, dear lady, that your hand
Is not, alas, in very great demand?
If men admire me, if they pay me court
And daily make me offers of the sort
You'd dearly love to have them make to you,
How can I help it? What would you have me do?
If what you want is lovers, please feel free
To take as many as you can from me.
ARSINOÉ. Oh, come. D'you think the world is losing sleep
Over that flock of lovers which you keep,
Or that we find it difficult to guess
What price you pay for their devotedness?
Surely you don't expect us to suppose
Mere merit could attract so many beaux?
It's not your virtue that they're dazzled by;
Nor is it virtuous love for which they sigh.
You're fooling no one, Madam; the world's not blind;
There's many a lady heaven has designed
To call men's noblest, tenderest feelings out,
Who has no lovers dogging her about;
From which it's plain that lovers nowadays
Must be acquired in bold and shameless ways,
And only pay one court for such reward
As modesty and virtue can't afford.
Then don't be quite so puffed up, if you please,
About your tawdry little victories;
Try, if you can, to be a shade less vain,
And treat the world with somewhat less disdain.
If one were envious of your amours,
One soon could have a following like yours;
Lovers are no great trouble to collect
If one prefers them to one's self-respect.
CÉLIMÈNE. Collect them then, my dear; I'd love to see
You demonstrate that charming theory;
Who knows, you might . . .
ARSINOÉ. Now, Madam, that will do;
It's time to end this trying interview.

My coach is late in coming to your door,
Or I'd have taken leave of you before.
CÉLIMÈNE. Oh, please don't feel that you must rush away;
I'd be delighted, Madam, if you'd stay.
However, lest my conversation bore you,
Let me provide some better company for you;
This gentleman, who comes most apropos,
Will please you more than I could do, I know.

SCENE VI

CÉLIMÈNE. Alceste, I have a little note to write
Which simply must go out before tonight;
Please entertain *Madame;* I'm sure that she
Will overlook my incivility.

SCENE VII

ARSINOÉ. Well, Sir, our hostess graciously contrives
For us to chat until my coach arrives;
And I shall be forever in her debt
For granting me this little tête-à-tête.
We women very rightly give our hearts
To men of noble character and parts,
And your especial merits, dear Alceste,
Have roused the deepest sympathy in my breast.
Oh, how I wish they had sufficient sense
At court, to recognize your excellence!
They wrong you greatly, Sir. How it must hurt you
Never to be rewarded for your virtue!
ALCESTE. Why, Madam, what cause have I to feel aggrieved?
What great and brilliant thing have I achieved?
What service have I rendered to the King
That I should look to him for anything?
ARSINOÉ. Not everyone who's honored by the State
Has done great services. A man must wait
Till time and fortune offer him the chance.
Your merit, Sir, is obvious at a glance,
And . . .
ALCESTE. Ah, forget my merit; I'm not neglected.
The court, I think, can hardly be expected
To mine men's souls for merit, and unearth
Our hidden virtues and our secret worth.

ARSINOÉ. *Some* virtues, though, are far too bright to hide;
Yours are acknowledged, Sir, on every side.
Indeed, I've heard you warmly praised of late
By persons of considerable weight.

ALCESTE. This fawning age has praise for everyone,
And all distinctions, Madam, are undone.
All things have equal honor nowadays,
And no one should be gratified by praise.
To be admired, one only need exist,
And every lackey's on the honors list.

ARSINOÉ. I only wish, Sir, that you had your eye
On some position at court, however high;
You'd only have to hint at such a notion
For me to set the proper wheels in motion;
I've certain friendships I'd be glad to use
To get you any office you might choose.

ALCESTE. Madam, I fear that any such ambition
Is wholly foreign to my disposition.
The soul God gave me isn't of the sort
That prospers in the weather of a court.
It's all too obvious that I don't possess
The virtues necessary for success.
My one great talent is for speaking plain;
I've never learned to flatter or to feign;
And anyone so stupidly sincere
Had best not seek a courtier's career.
Outside the court, I know, one must dispense
With honors, privilege, and influence;
But still one gains the right, foregoing these,
Not to be tortured by the wish to please.
One needn't live in dread of snubs and slights,
Nor praise the verse that every idiot writes,
Nor humor silly Marquesses, nor bestow
Politic sighs on Madam So-and-So.

ARSINOÉ. Forget the court, then; let the matter rest.
But I've another cause to be distressed
About your present situation, Sir.
It's to your love affair that I refer.
She whom you love, and who pretends to love you,
Is, I regret to say, unworthy of you.

ALCESTE. Why, Madam! Can you seriously intend
To make so grave a charge against your friend?

ARSINOÉ. Alas, I must. I've stood aside too long
And let that lady do you grievous wrong;

But now my debt to conscience shall be paid:
I tell you that your love has been betrayed.
ALCESTE. I thank you, Madam; you're extremely kind.
Such words are soothing to a lover's mind.
ARSINOÉ. Yes, though she *is* my friend, I say again
You're very much too good for Célimène.
She's wantonly misled you from the start.
ALCESTE. You may be right; who knows another's heart?
But ask yourself if it's the part of charity
To shake my soul with doubts of her sincerity.
ARSINOÉ. Well, if you'd rather be a dupe than doubt her,
That's your affair. I'll say no more about her.
ALCESTE. Madam, you know that doubt and vague suspicion
Are painful to a man in my position;
It's most unkind to worry me this way
Unless you've some real proof of what you say.
ARSINOÉ. Sir, say no more: all doubt shall be removed,
And all that I've been saying shall be proved.
You've only to escort me home, and there
We'll look into the heart of this affair.
I've ocular evidence which will persuade you
Beyond a doubt, that Célimène's betrayed you.
Then, if you're saddened by that revelation,
Perhaps I can provide some consolation.

ACT IV

SCENE I

PHILINTE. Madam, he acted like a stubborn child;
I thought they never would be reconciled;
In vain we reasoned, threatened, and appealed;
He stood his ground and simply would not yield.
The Marshals, I feel sure, have never heard
An argument so splendidly absurd.
"No, gentlemen," said he, "I'll not retract.
His verse is bad: extremely bad, in fact.
Surely it does the man no harm to know it.
Does it disgrace him, not to be a poet?
A gentleman may be respected still,
Whether he writes a sonnet well or ill.
That I dislike his verse should not offend him;
In all that touches honor, I commend him;

He's noble, brave, and virtuous—but I fear
He can't in truth be called a sonneteer.
I'll gladly praise his wardrobe; I'll endorse
His dancing, or the way he sits a horse;
But, gentlemen, I cannot praise his rhyme.
In fact, it ought to be a capital crime
For anyone so sadly unendowed
To write a sonnet, and read the thing aloud."
At length he fell into a gentler mood
And, striking a concessive attitude,
He paid Oronte the following courtesies:
"Sir, I regret that I'm so hard to please,
And I'm profoundly sorry that your lyric
Failed to provoke me to a panegyric."
After these curious words, the two embraced,
And then the hearing was adjourned—in haste.

ELIANTE. His conduct has been very singular lately;
Still, I confess that I respect him greatly.
The honesty in which he takes such pride
Has—to my mind—its noble, heroic side.
In this false age, such candor seems outrageous;
But I could wish that it were more contagious.

PHILINTE. What most intrigues me in our friend Alceste
Is the grand passion that rages in his breast.
The sullen humors he's compounded of
Should not, I think, dispose his heart to love;
But since they do, it puzzles me still more
That he should choose your cousin to adore.

ELIANTE. It does, indeed, belie the theory
That love is born of gentle sympathy,
And that the tender passion must be based
On sweet accords of temper and of taste.

PHILINTE. Does she return his love, do you suppose?

ELIANTE. Ah, that's a difficult question, Sir. Who knows?
How can we judge the truth of her devotion?
Her heart's a stranger to its own emotion.
Sometimes it thinks it loves, when no love's there;
At other times it loves quite unaware.

PHILINTE. I rather think Alceste is in for more
Distress and sorrow than he's bargained for;
Were he of my mind, Madam, his affection
Would turn in quite a different direction,
And we would see him more responsive to
The kind regard which he receives from you.

ELIANTE. Sir, I believe in frankness, and I'm inclined,
In matters of the heart, to speak my mind.
I don't oppose his love for her; indeed,
I hope with all my heart that he'll succeed,
And were it in my power, I'd rejoice
In giving him the lady of his choice.
But if, as happens frequently enough
In love affairs, he meets with a rebuff—
If Célimène should grant some rival's suit—
I'd gladly play the role of substitute;
Nor would his tender speeches please me less
Because they'd once been made without success.
PHILINTE. Well, Madam, as for me, I don't oppose
Your hopes in this affair; and heaven knows
That in my conversations with the man
I plead your cause as often as I can.
But if those two should marry, and so remove
All chance that he will offer you his love,
Then I'll declare my own, and hope to see
Your gracious favor pass from him to me.
In short, should you be cheated of Alceste,
I'd be most happy to be second best.
ELIANTE. Philinte, you're teasing.
PHILINTE. Ah, Madam, never fear;
No words of mine were ever so sincere,
And I shall live in fretful expectation
Till I can make a fuller declaration.

SCENE II

ALCESTE. Avenge me, Madam! I must have satisfaction,
Or this great wrong will drive me to distraction!
ELIANTE. Why, what's the matter? What's upset you so?
ALCESTE. Madam, I've had a mortal, mortal blow.
If Chaos repossessed the universe,
I swear I'd not be shaken any worse.
I'm ruined . . . I can say no more . . . My soul . . .
ELIANTE. Do try, Sir, to regain your self-control.
ALCESTE. Just heaven! Why were so much beauty and grace
Bestowed on one so vicious and so base?
ELIANTE. Once more, Sir, tell us . . .
ALCESTE. My world has gone to wrack;
I'm—I'm betrayed; she's stabbed me in the back:

Yes, Célimène (who would have thought it of her?)
Is false to me, and has another lover.
ELIANTE. Are you quite certain? Can you prove these things?
PHILINTE. Lovers are prey to wild imaginings
And jealous fancies. No doubt there's some mistake . . .
ALCESTE. Mind your own business, Sir, for heaven's sake.
(*To* ELIANTE) Madam, I have the proof that you demand
Here in my pocket, penned by her own hand.
Yes, all the shameful evidence one could want
Lies in this letter written to Oronte—
Oronte! whom I felt sure she couldn't love,
And hardly bothered to be jealous of.
PHILINTE. Still, in a letter, appearances may deceive;
This may not be so bad as you believe.
ALCESTE. Once more I beg you, Sir, to let me be;
Tend to your own affairs; leave mine to me.
ELIANTE. Compose yourself; this anguish that you feel . . .
ALCESTE. Is something, Madam, you alone can heal.
My outraged heart, beside itself with grief,
Appeals to you for comfort and relief.
Avenge me on your cousin, whose unjust
And faithless nature has deceived my trust;
Avenge a crime your pure soul must detest.
ELIANTE. But how, Sir?
ALCESTE. Madam, this heart within my breast
Is yours; pray take it; redeem my heart from her,
And so avenge me on my torturer.
Let her be punished by the fond emotion,
The ardent love, the bottomless devotion,
The faithful worship which this heart of mine
Will offer up to yours as to a shrine.
ELIANTE. You have my sympathy, Sir, in all you suffer;
Nor do I scorn the noble heart you offer;
But I suspect you'll soon be mollified,
And this desire for vengeance will subside.
When some beloved hand has done us wrong
We thirst for retribution—but not for long;
However dark the deed that she's committed,
A lovely culprit's very soon acquitted.
Nothing's so stormy as an injured lover,
And yet no storm so quickly passes over.
ALCESTE. No, Madam, no—this is no lovers' spat;
I'll not forgive her; it's gone too far for that;
My mind's made up; I'll kill myself before

I waste my hopes upon her any more.
Ah, here she is. My wrath intensifies.
I shall confront her with her tricks and lies,
And crush her utterly, and bring you then
A heart no longer slave to Célimène.

SCENE III

ALCESTE (*aside*). Sweet heaven, help me to control my passion.

CÉLIMÈNE (*aside, to* ALCESTE). Oh, Lord. Why stand there staring in that fashion?
And what d'you mean by those dramatic sighs,
And that malignant glitter in your eyes?

ALCESTE. I mean that sins which cause the blood to freeze
Look innocent beside your treacheries;
That nothing Hell's or Heaven's wrath could do
Ever produced so bad a thing as you.

CÉLIMÈNE. Your compliments were always sweet and pretty.

ALCESTE. Madam, it's not the moment to be witty.
No, blush and hang your head; you've ample reason,
Since I've the fullest evidence of your treason.
Ah, this is what my sad heart prophesied;
Now all my anxious fears are verified;
My dark suspicion and my gloomy doubt
Divined the truth, and now the truth is out.
For all your trickery, I was not deceived;
It was my bitter stars that I believed.
But don't imagine that you'll go scot-free;
You shan't misuse me with impunity.
I know that love's irrational and blind;
I know the heart's not subject to the mind,
And can't be reasoned into beating faster;
I know each soul is free to choose its master;
Therefore had you but spoken from the heart,
Rejecting my attentions from the start,
I'd have no grievance, or at any rate
I could complain of nothing but my fate.
Ah, but so falsely to encourage me—
That was a treason and a treachery
For which you cannot suffer too severely,
And you shall pay for that behavior dearly.
Yes, now I have no pity, not a shred;
My temper's out of hand; I've lost my head;

Shocked by the knowledge of your double-dealings,
My reason can't restrain my savage feelings;
A righteous wrath deprives me of my senses,
And I won't answer for the consequences.
CÉLIMÈNE. What does this outburst mean? Will you please explain?
Have you, by any chance, gone quite insane?
ALCESTE. Yes, yes, I went insane the day I fell
A victim to your black and fatal spell,
Thinking to meet with some sincerity
Among the treacherous charms that beckoned me.
CÉLIMÈNE. Pooh. Of what treachery can you complain?
ALCESTE. How sly you are, how cleverly you feign!
But you'll not victimize me any more.
Look: here's a document you've seen before.
This evidence, which I acquired today,
Leaves you, I think, without a thing to say.
CÉLIMÈNE. Is this what sent you into such a fit?
ALCESTE. You should be blushing at the sight of it.
CÉLIMÈNE. Ought I to blush? I truly don't see why.
ALCESTE. Ah, now you're being bold as well as sly;
Since there's no signature, perhaps you'll claim . . .
CÉLIMÈNE. I wrote it, whether or not it bears my name.
ALCESTE. And you can view with equanimity
This proof of your disloyalty to me!
CÉLIMÈNE. Oh, don't be so outrageous and extreme.
ALCESTE. You take this matter lightly, it would seem.
Was it no wrong to me, no shame to you,
That you should send Oronte this billet-doux?
CÉLIMÈNE. Oronte! Who said it was for him?
ALCESTE. Why, those
Who brought me this example of your prose.
But what's the difference? If you wrote the letter
To someone else, it pleases me no better.
My grievance and your guilt remain the same.
CÉLIMÈNE. But need you rage, and need I blush for shame,
If this was written to a *woman* friend?
ALCESTE. Ah! Most ingenious. I'm impressed no end;
And after that incredible evasion
Your guilt is clear. I need no more persuasion.
How dare you try so clumsy a deception?
D'you think I'm wholly wanting in perception?
Come, come, let's see how brazenly you'll try
To bolster up so palpable a lie:
Kindly construe this ardent closing section

As nothing more than sisterly affection!
Here, let me read it. Tell me, if you dare to,
That this is for a woman . . .
CÉLIMÈNE. I don't care to.
What right have you to badger and berate me,
And so highhandedly interrogate me?
ALCESTE. Now, don't be angry; all I ask of you
Is that you justify a phrase or two . . .
CÉLIMÈNE. No, I shall not. I utterly refuse,
And you may take those phrases as you choose.
ALCESTE. Just show me how this letter could be meant
For a woman's eyes, and I shall be content.
CÉLIMÈNE. No, no, it's for Oronte; you're perfectly right.
I welcome his attentions with delight,
I prize his character and his intellect,
And everything is just as you suspect.
Come, do your worst now; give your rage free rein;
But kindly cease to bicker and complain.
ALCESTE (*aside*). Good God! Could anything be more inhuman?
Was ever a heart so mangled by a woman?
When I complain of how she has betrayed me,
She bridles, and commences to upbraid me!
She tries my tortured patience to the limit;
She won't deny her guilt; she glories in it!
And yet my heart's too faint and cowardly
To break these chains of passion, and be free,
To scorn her as it should, and rise above
This unrewarded, mad, and bitter love.
(*To* CÉLIMÈNE) Ah, traitress, in how confident a fashion
You take advantage of my helpless passion,
And use my weakness for your faithless charms
To make me once again throw down my arms!
But do at least deny this black transgression;
Take back that mocking and perverse confession;
Defend this letter and your innocence,
And I, poor fool, will aid in your defense.
Pretend, pretend, that you are just and true,
And I shall make myself believe in you.
CÉLIMÈNE. Oh, stop it. Don't be such a jealous dunce,
Or I shall leave off loving you at once.
Just why should I *pretend*? What could impel me
To stoop so low as that? And kindly tell me
Why, if I loved another, I shouldn't merely
Inform you of it, simply and sincerely!
I've told you where you stand, and that admission

Should altogether clear me of suspicion;
After so generous a guarantee,
What right have you to harbor doubts of me?
Since women are (from natural reticence)
Reluctant to declare their sentiments,
And since the honor of our sex requires
That we conceal our amorous desires,
Ought any man for whom such laws are broken
To question what the oracle has spoken?
Should he not rather feel an obligation
To trust that most obliging declaration?
Enough, now. Your suspicions quite disgust me;
Why should I love a man who doesn't trust me?
I cannot understand why I continue,
Fool that I am, to take an interest in you.
I ought to choose a man less prone to doubt,
And give you something to be vexed about.
ALCESTE. Ah, what a poor enchanted fool I am;
These gentle words, no doubt, were all a sham;
But destiny requires me to entrust
My happiness to you, and so I must.
I'll love you to the bitter end, and see
How false and treacherous you dare to be.
CÉLIMÈNE. No, you don't really love me as you ought.
ALCESTE. I love you more than can be said or thought;
Indeed, I wish you were in such distress
That I might show my deep devotedness.
Yes, I could wish that you were wretchedly poor,
Unloved, uncherished, utterly obscure;
That fate had set you down upon the earth
Without possessions, rank, or gentle birth;
Then, by the offer of my heart, I might
Repair the great injustice of your plight;
I'd raise you from the dust, and proudly prove
The purity and vastness of my love.
CÉLIMÈNE. This is a strange benevolence indeed!
God grant that I may never be in need . . .
Ah, here's Monsieur Dubois, in quaint disguise.

SCENE IV

ALCESTE. Well, why this costume? Why those frightened eyes?
What ails you?

DUBOIS. Well, Sir, things are most mysterious.
ALCESTE. What do you mean?
DUBOIS. I fear they're very serious.
ALCESTE. What?
DUBOIS. Shall I speak more loudly?
ALCESTE. Yes; speak out.
DUBOIS. Isn't there someone here, Sir?
ALCESTE. Speak, you lout!
Stop wasting time.
DUBOIS. Sir, we must slip away.
ALCESTE. How's that?
DUBOIS. We must decamp without delay.
ALCESTE. Explain yourself.
DUBOIS. I tell you we must fly.
ALCESTE. What for?
DUBOIS. We mustn't pause to say good-by.
ALCESTE. Now what d'you mean by all of this, you clown?
DUBOIS. I mean, Sir, that we've got to leave this town.
ALCESTE. I'll tear you limb from limb and joint from joint
If you don't come more quickly to the point.
DUBOIS. Well, Sir, today a man in a black suit,
Who wore a black and ugly scowl to boot,
Left us a document scrawled in such a hand
As even Satan couldn't understand.
It bears upon your lawsuit, I don't doubt;
But all hell's devils couldn't make it out.
ALCESTE. Well, well, go on. What then? I fail to see
How this event obliges us to flee.
DUBOIS. Well, Sir: an hour later, hardly more,
A gentleman who's often called before
Came looking for you in an anxious way.
Not finding you, he asked me to convey
(Knowing I could be trusted with the same)
The following message . . . Now, what *was* his name?
ALCESTE. Forget his name, you idiot. What did he say?
DUBOIS. Well, it was one of your friends, Sir, anyway.
He warned you to begone, and he suggested
That if you stay, you may well be arrested.
ALCESTE. What? Nothing more specific? Think, man, think!
DUBOIS. No, Sir. He had me bring him pen and ink,
And dashed you off a letter which, I'm sure,
Will render things distinctly less obscure.
ALCESTE. Well—let me have it!
CÉLIMÈNE. What *is* this all about?

ALCESTE. God knows; but I have hopes of finding out.
How long am I to wait, you blitherer?

DUBOIS (*after a protracted search for the letter*). I must have left it on your table, Sir.

ALCESTE. I ought to . . .

CÉLIMÈNE. No, no, keep your self-control;
Go find out what's behind his rigmarole.

ALCESTE. It seems that fate, no matter what I do,
Has sworn that I may not converse with you;
But, Madam, pray permit your faithful lover
To try once more before the day is over.

ACT V

SCENE I

ALCESTE. No, it's too much. My mind's made up, I tell you.

PHILINTE. Why should this blow, however hard, compel you . . .

ALCESTE. No, no, don't waste your breath in argument;
Nothing you say will alter my intent;
This age is vile, and I've made up my mind
To have no further commerce with mankind.
Did not truth, honor, decency, and the laws
Oppose my enemy and approve my cause?
My claims were justified in all men's sight;
I put my trust in equity and right;
Yet, to my horror and the world's disgrace,
Justice is mocked, and I have lost my case!
A scoundrel whose dishonesty is notorious
Emerges from another lie victorious!
Honor and right condone his brazen fraud,
While rectitude and decency applaud!
Before his smirking face, the truth stands charmed,
And virtue conquered, and the law disarmed!
His crime is sanctioned by a court decree!
And not content with what he's done to me,
The dog now seeks to ruin me by stating
That I composed a book now circulating,
A book so wholly criminal and vicious
That even to speak its title is seditious!
Meanwhile Oronte, my rival, lends his credit
To the same libelous tale, and helps to spread it!
Oronte! a man of honor and of rank,
With whom I've been entirely fair and frank;

Who sought me out and forced me, willy-nilly,
To judge some verse I found extremely silly;
And who, because I properly refused
To flatter him, or see the truth abused,
Abets my enemy in a rotten slander!
There's the reward of honesty and candor!
The man will hate me to the end of time
For failing to commend his wretched rhyme!
And not this man alone, but all humanity
Do what they do from interest and vanity;
They prate of honor, truth, and righteousness,
But lie, betray, and swindle nonetheless.
Come then: man's villainy is too much to bear;
Let's leave this jungle and this jackal's lair.
Yes! treacherous and savage race of men,
You shall not look upon my face again.

PHILINTE. Oh, don't rush into exile prematurely;
Things aren't as dreadful as you make them, surely.
It's rather obvious, since you're still at large,
That people don't believe your enemy's charge.
Indeed, his tale's so patently untrue
That it may do more harm to him than you.

ALCESTE. Nothing could do that scoundrel any harm:
His frank corruption is his greatest charm,
And, far from hurting him, a further shame
Would only serve to magnify his name.

PHILINTE. In any case, his bald prevarication
Has done no injury to your reputation,
And you may feel secure in that regard.
As for your lawsuit, it should not be hard
To have the case reopened, and contest
This judgment . . .

ALCESTE. No, no, let the verdict rest.
Whatever cruel penalty it may bring,
I wouldn't have it changed for anything.
It shows the times' injustice with such clarity
That I shall pass it down to our posterity
As a great proof and signal demonstration
Of the black wickedness of this generation.
It may cost twenty thousand francs; but I
Shall pay their twenty thousand, and gain thereby
The right to storm and rage at human evil,
And send the race of mankind to the devil.

PHILINTE. Listen to me . . .
ALCESTE. Why? What can you possibly say?
Don't argue, Sir; your labor's thrown away.
Do you propose to offer lame excuses
For men's behavior and the times' abuses?
PHILINTE. No, all you say I'll readily concede:
This is a low, dishonest age indeed;
Nothing but trickery prospers nowadays,
And people ought to mend their shabby ways.
Yes, man's a beastly creature; but must we then
Abandon the society of men?
Here in the world, each human frailty
Provides occasion for philosophy,
And that is virtue's noblest exercise;
If honesty shone forth from all men's eyes,
If every heart were frank and kind and just,
What could our virtues do but gather dust
(Since their employment is to help us bear
The villainies of men without despair)?
A heart well-armed with virtue can endure . . .
ALCESTE. Sir, you're a matchless reasoner, to be sure;
Your words are fine and full of cogency;
But don't waste time and eloquence on me.
My reason bids me go, for my own good.
My tongue won't lie and flatter as it should;
God knows what frankness it might next commit,
And what I'd suffer on account of it.
Pray let me wait for Célimène's return
In peace and quiet. I shall shortly learn,
By her response to what I have in view,
Whether her love for me is feigned or true.
PHILINTE. Till then, let's visit Eliante upstairs.
ALCESTE. No, I am too weighed down with somber cares.
Go to her, do; and leave me with my gloom
Here in the darkened corner of this room.
PHILINTE. Why, that's no sort of company, my friend;
I'll see if Eliante will not descend.

SCENE II

ORONTE. Yes, Madam, if you wish me to remain
Your true and ardent lover, you must deign
To give me some more positive assurance.

All this suspense is quite beyond endurance.
If your heart shares the sweet desires of mine,
Show me as much by some convincing sign;
And here's the sign I urgently suggest:
That you no longer tolerate Alceste,
But sacrifice him to my love, and sever
All your relations with the man forever.
CÉLIMÈNE. Why do you suddenly dislike him so?
You praised him to the skies not long ago.
ORONTE. Madam, that's not the point. I'm here to find
Which way your tender feelings are inclined.
Choose, if you please, between Alceste and me,
And I shall stay or go accordingly.
ALCESTE (*emerging from the corner*). Yes, Madam, choose; this gentleman's demand
Is wholly just, and I support his stand.
I too am true and ardent; I too am here
To ask you that you make your feelings clear.
No more delays, now; no equivocation;
The time has come to make your declaration.
ORONTE. Sir, I've no wish in any way to be
An obstacle to your felicity.
ALCESTE. Sir, I've no wish to share her heart with you;
That may sound jealous, but at least it's true.
ORONTE. If, weighing us, she leans in your direction . . .
ALCESTE. If she regards you with the least affection . . .
ORONTE. I swear I'll yield her to you there and then.
ALCESTE. I swear I'll never see her face again.
ORONTE. Now, Madam, tell us what we've come to hear.
ALCESTE. Madam, speak openly and have no fear.
ORONTE. Just say which one is to remain your lover.
ALCESTE. Just name one name, and it will all be over.
ORONTE. What! Is it possible that you're undecided?
ALCESTE. What! Can your feelings possibly be divided?
CÉLIMÈNE. Enough: this inquisition's gone too far:
How utterly unreasonable you are!
Not that I couldn't make the choice with ease;
My heart has no conflicting sympathies;
I know full well which one of you I favor,
And you'd not see me hesitate or waver.
But how can you expect me to reveal
So cruelly and bluntly what I feel?
I think it altogether too unpleasant

To choose between two men when both are present;
One's heart has means more subtle and more kind
Of letting its affections be divined,
Nor need one be uncharitably plain
To let a lover know he loves in vain.
ORONTE. No, no, speak plainly; I for one can stand it.
I beg you to be frank.
ALCESTE. And I demand it.
The simple truth is what I wish to know,
And there's no need for softening the blow.
You've made an art of pleasing everyone,
But now your days of coquetry are done:
You have no choice now, Madam, but to choose,
For I'll know what to think if you refuse;
I'll take your silence for a clear admission
That I'm entitled to my worst suspicion.
ORONTE. I thank you for this ultimatum, Sir,
And I may say I heartily concur.
CÉLIMÈNE. Really, this foolishness is very wearing:
Must you be so unjust and overbearing?
Haven't I told you why I must demur?
Ah, here's Eliante; I'll put the case to her.

SCENE III

CÉLIMÈNE. Cousin, I'm being persecuted here
By these two persons, who, it would appear,
Will not be satisfied till I confess
Which one I love the more, and which the less,
And tell the latter to his face that he
Is henceforth banished from my company.
Tell me, has ever such a thing been done?
ELIANTE. You'd best not turn to me; I'm not the one
To back you in a matter of this kind:
I'm all for those who frankly speak their mind.
ORONTE. Madam, you'll search in vain for a defender.
ALCESTE. You're beaten, Madam, and may as well surrender.
ORONTE. Speak, speak, you must; and end this awful strain.
ALCESTE. Or don't, and your position will be plain.
ORONTE. A single word will close this painful scene.
ALCESTE. But if you're silent, I'll know what you mean.

SCENE IV

ACASTE (*to* CÉLIMÈNE). Madam, with all due deference, we two
Have come to pick a little bone with you.

CLITANDRE (*to* ORONTE *and* ALCESTE). I'm glad you're present, Sirs; as you'll soon learn,
Our business here is also your concern.

ARSINOÉ (*to* CÉLIMÈNE). Madam, I visit you so soon again
Only because of these two gentlemen,
Who came to me indignant and aggrieved
About a crime too base to be believed.
Knowing your virtue, having such confidence in it,
I couldn't think you guilty for a minute,
In spite of all their telling evidence;
And, rising above our little difference,
I've hastened here in friendship's name to see
You clear yourself of this great calumny.

ACASTE. Yes, Madam, let us see with what composure
You'll manage to respond to this disclosure.
You lately sent Clitandre this tender note.

CLITANDRE. And this one, for Acaste, you also wrote.

ACASTE (*to* ORONTE *and* ALCESTE). You'll recognize this writing Sirs, I think;
The lady is so free with pen and ink
That you must know it all too well, I fear.
But listen: this is something you should hear.

"How absurd you are to condemn my lightheartedness in society, and to accuse me of being happiest in the company of others. Nothing could be more unjust; and if you do not come to me instantly and beg pardon for saying such a thing, I shall never forgive you as long as I live. Our big bumbling friend the Viscount . . ."

What a shame that he's not here.

"Our big bumbling friend the Viscount, whose name stands first in your complaint, is hardly a man to my taste; and ever since the day I watched him spend three-quarters of an hour spitting into a well, so as to make circles in the water, I have been unable to think highly of him. As for the little Marquess . . ."

In all modesty, gentlemen, that is I.

"As for the little Marquess, who sat squeezing my

hand for such a long while yesterday, I find him in all respects the most trifling creature alive; and the only things of value about him are his cape and his sword. As for the man with the green ribbons . . ."

(*To* ALCESTE) It's your turn now, Sir.

"As for the man with the green ribbons, he amuses me now and then with his bluntness and his bearish ill-humor; but there are many times indeed when I think him the greatest bore in the world. And as for the sonneteer . . ."

(*To* ORONTE) Here's your helping.

"And as for the sonneteer, who has taken it into his head to be witty, and insists on being an author in the teeth of opinion, I simply cannot be bothered to listen to him, and his prose wearies me quite as much as his poetry. Be assured that I am not always so well-entertained as you suppose; that I long for your company, more than I dare to say, at all these entertainments to which people drag me; and that the presence of those one loves is true and perfect seasoning to all one's pleasures."

CLITANDRE. And now for me.

"Clitandre, whom you mention, and who so pesters me with his saccharine speeches, is the last man on earth for whom I could feel any affection. He is quite mad to suppose that I love him, and so are you, to doubt that you are loved. Do come to your senses; exchange your suppositions for his; and visit me as often as possible, to help me bear the annoyance of his unwelcome attentions."

It's a sweet character that these letters show,
And what to call it, Madam, you well know.
Enough. We're off to make the world acquainted
With this sublime self-portrait that you've painted.
ACASTE. Madam, I'll make you no farewell oration;
No, you're not worthy of my indignation.
Far choicer hearts than yours, as you'll discover,
Would like this little Marquess for a lover.

SCENE V

Oronte. So! After all those loving letters you wrote,
You turn on me like this, and cut my throat!
And your dissembling, faithless heart, I find,
Has pledged itself by turns to all mankind!
How blind I've been! But now I clearly see;
I thank you, Madam, for enlightening me.
My heart is mine once more, and I'm content;
The loss of it shall be your punishment.
(*To* Alceste) Sir, she is yours; I'll seek no more to stand
Between your wishes and this lady's hand.

SCENE VI

Arsinoé (*to* Célimène). Madam, I'm forced to speak. I'm far too stirred
To keep my counsel, after what I've heard.
I'm shocked and staggered by your want of morals.
It's not my way to mix in others' quarrels;
But really, when this fine and noble spirit,
This man of honor and surpassing merit,
Laid down the offering of his heart before you,
How *could* you . . .
Alceste. Madam, permit me, I implore you,
To represent myself in this debate.
Don't bother, please, to be my advocate.
My heart, in any case, could not afford
To give your services their due reward;
And if I chose, for consolation's sake,
Some other lady, t'would not be you I'd take.
Arsinoé. What makes you think you could, Sir? And how dare you
Imply that I've been trying to ensnare you?
If you can for a moment entertain
Such flattering fancies, you're extremely vain.
I'm not so interested as you suppose
In Célimène's discarded gigolos.
Get rid of that absurd illusion, do.
Women like me are not for such as you.
Stay with this creature, to whom you're so attached;
I've never seen two people better matched.

SCENE VII

ALCESTE (*to* CÉLIMÈNE). Well, I've been still throughout this exposé,
Till everyone but me has said his say.
Come, have I shown sufficient self-restraint?
And may I now . . .
CÉLIMÈNE. Yes, make your just complaint.
Reproach me freely, call me what you will;
You've every right to say I've used you ill.
I've wronged you, I confess it; and in my shame
I'll make no effort to escape the blame.
The anger of those others I could despise;
My guilt toward you I sadly recognize.
Your wrath is wholly justified, I fear;
I know how culpable I must appear,
I know all things bespeak my treachery,
And that, in short, you've grounds for hating me.
Do so; I give you leave.
ALCESTE. Ah, traitress—how,
How should I cease to love you, even now?
Though mind and will were passionately bent
On hating you, my heart would not consent.
(*To* ELIANTE *and* PHILINTE) Be witness to my madness, both of you;
See what infatuation drives one to;
But wait; my folly's only just begun,
And I shall prove to you before I'm done
How strange the human heart is, and how far
From rational we sorry creatures are.
(*To* CÉLIMÈNE) Woman, I'm willing to forget your shame,
And clothe your treacheries in a sweeter name;
I'll call them youthful errors, instead of crimes,
And lay the blame on these corrupting times.
My one condition is that you agree
To share my chosen fate, and fly with me
To that wild, trackless solitary place
In which I shall forget the human race.
Only by such a course can you atone
For those atrocious letters; by that alone
Can you remove my present horror of you,
And make it possible for me to love you.
CÉLIMÈNE. What! *I* renounce the world at my young age,
And die of boredom in some hermitage?
ALCESTE. Ah, if you really loved me as you ought,
You wouldn't give the world a moment's thought;

Must you have me, and all the world beside?
CÉLIMÈNE. Alas, at twenty one is terrified
Of solitude. I fear I lack the force
And depth of soul to take so stern a course.
But if my hand in marriage will content you,
Why, there's a plan which I might well consent to,
And . . .
ALCESTE. No, I detest you now. I could excuse
Everything else, but since you thus refuse
To love me wholly, as a wife should do,
And see the world in me, as I in you,
Go! I reject your hand, and disenthrall
My heart from your enchantments, once for all.

SCENE VIII

ALCESTE (*to* ELIANTE). Madam, your virtuous beauty has no peer,
Of all this world, you only are sincere;
I've long esteemed you highly, as you know;
Permit me ever to esteem you so,
And if I do not now request your hand,
Forgive me, Madam, and try to understand.
I feel unworthy of it; I sense that fate
Does not intend me for the married state,
That I should do you wrong by offering you
My shattered heart's unhappy residue,
And that in short . . .
ELIANTE. Your argument's well taken:
Nor need you fear that I shall feel forsaken.
Were I to offer him this hand of mine,
Your friend Philinte, I think, would not decline.
PHILINTE. Ah, Madam, that's my heart's most cherished goal,
For which I'd gladly give my life and soul.
ALCESTE (*to* ELIANTE *and* PHILINTE). May you be true to all you now profess,
And so deserve unending happiness.
Meanwhile, betrayed and wronged in everything,
I'll flee this bitter world where vice is king,
And seek some spot unpeopled and apart
Where I'll be free to have an honest heart.
PHILINTE. Come, Madam, let's do everything we can
To change the mind of this unhappy man.

QUESTIONS

1. How does the argument between Alceste and Philinte in the opening scene state the play's major thematic conflict? Which of the two philosophies expressed is the more idealistic? Which more realistic? Is either or are both of them extreme?

2. What are the attitudes of Célimène, Eliante, and Arsinoé toward Alceste? Do they respect him? Why or why not?

3. *The Misanthrope* is generally acknowledged to be one of the world's greatest comedies, but, at the same time, it is an atypical one, both in its hero and in its ending. In what ways does Alceste approach the stature of a tragic hero? In what way is the ending unlike a comic ending?

4. Alceste is in conflict with social convention, with social injustice, and with Célimène. Does he discriminate between them as to their relative importance? Discuss.

5. Are there any indications in the opening scene that the motivations behind Alceste's hatred of social convention are not as unmixed as he thinks them?

6. Alceste declares himself not blind to Célimène's faults. Is he blind in any way about his relationship with Célimène? If so, what does his blindness spring from?

7. What do Alceste's reasons for refusing to appeal his law suit (Act V, Scene i) and his wish that Célimène were "Unloved, uncherished, utterly obscure" so that he might raise her "from the dust" (Act IV, Scene iii) tell us about his character?

8. What are Célimène's good qualities? What are her bad ones? In what ways are she and Alceste foils? Might Célimène have been redeemed had Alceste been able to accept her without taking her from society?

9. How is the gossip session between Acaste, Clitandre, and Célimène (Act II, Scene v) a double-edged satire? Which of Célimène's satirical portraits is the finest? How accurate is Célimène's portrait of Alceste himself?

10. Which is the more scathingly satirized—Alceste, or the society in which he lives? Why?

11. What character in the play most nearly represents a desirable norm of social behavior? Why?

12. What characteristics keep Alceste from being a tragic hero? What keeps the ending from being a tragic ending?

13. The verse of Molière's play is quite different in kind and quality from García Lorca's. Insofar as they can be judged in translation, what are the major differences? What relation is there between the poetic style of each play and its subject matter?

14. Compare *The Misanthrope* and *An Enemy of the People* as plays dealing with conflict between an individual and his society. How are the characters of Alceste and Dr. Stockmann similar? How are they different? Which is portrayed by his creator with the greater sympathy? Why?

15. Are politeness and hypocrisy the same thing? If not, distinguish between them.

George Bernard Shaw

CANDIDA

ACT I

A fine morning in October 1894 in the north east quarter of London, a vast district miles away from the London of Mayfair and St. James's, and much less narrow, squalid, fetid and airless in its slums. It is strong in unfashionable middle class life: wide-streeted; myriad-populated; well served with ugly iron urinals, Radical clubs, and tram lines carrying a perpetual stream of yellow cars; enjoying in its main thoroughfares the luxury of grass-grown "front gardens" untrodden by the foot of man save as to the path from the gate to the hall door; blighted by a callously endured monotony of miles and miles of unlovely brick houses, black iron railings, stony pavements, slated roofs, and respectably ill dressed or disreputably worse dressed people, quite accustomed to the place, and mostly plodding uninterestedly about somebody else's work. The little energy and eagerness that crop up shew themselves in cockney cupidity and business "push." Even the policemen and the chapels are not infrequent enough to break the monotony. The sun is shining cheerfully: there is no fog; and though the smoke effectually prevents anything, whether faces and hands or bricks and mortar, from looking fresh and clean, it is not hanging heavily enough to trouble a Londoner.

This desert of unattractiveness has its oasis. Near the outer end of the Hackney Road is a park of 217 acres, fenced in, not by railings, but by a wooden paling, and containing plenty of greensward, trees, a lake for bathers, flower beds which are triumphs of the admired cockney art of carpet gardening, and a sandpit, originally imported from the seaside for the delight of children, but speedily deserted on its becoming a natural vermin preserve for all the petty fauna of Kingsland, Hackney, and Hoxton. A bandstand, an unfurnished forum for religious, anti-religious, and political orators, cricket pitches, a gymnasium, and an old fashioned stone kiosk are among its attractions. Wherever the prospect is bounded by trees or rising green grounds, it is a pleasant place. Where the ground stretches flat to the grey palings, with bricks and mortar, sky signs, crowded chimneys and smoke beyond, the prospect makes it desolate and sordid.

The best view of Victoria Park is commanded by the front window of St. Dominic's Parsonage, from which not a brick is visible. The parsonage is semi-detached, with a front garden and a porch. Visitors go up the flight of steps to the porch: tradespeople and members of the family go down by a door under the steps to the basement, with a breakfast room, used for all meals, in front, and the kitchen at the back. Upstairs, on the level of the hall door, is the drawingroom, with its large plate glass window looking out

 First performed in 1895.

on the park. In this, the only sittingroom that can be spared from the children and the family meals, the parson, the Reverend James Mavor Morell, *does his work. He is sitting in a strong round backed revolving chair at the end of a long table, which stands across the window, so that he can cheer himself with a view of the park over his left shoulder. At the opposite end of the table, adjoining it, is a little table only half as wide as the other, with a typewriter on it. His typist is sitting at this machine, with her back to the window. The large table is littered with pamphlets, journals, letters, nests of drawers, an office diary, postage scales and the like. A spare chair for visitors having business with the parson is in the middle, turned to his end. Within reach of his hand is a stationery case, and a photograph in a frame. The wall behind him is fitted with bookshelves, on which an adept eye can measure the parson's casuistry and divinity by Maurice's Theological Essays and a complete set of Browning's poems, and the reformer's politics by a yellow backed Progress and Poverty, Fabian Essays, A Dream of John Ball, Marx's Capital, and half a dozen other literary landmarks in Socialism. Facing him on the other side of the room, near the typewriter, is the door. Further down opposite the fireplace, a bookcase stands on a cellaret, with a sofa near it. There is a generous fire burning; and the hearth, with a comfortable armchair and a black japanned flower-painted coal scuttle at one side, a miniature chair for children on the other, a varnished wooden mantelpiece, with neatly moulded shelves, tiny bits of mirror let into the panels, a travelling clock in a leather case (the inevitable wedding present), and on the wall above a large autotype of the chief figure in Titian's Assumption of the Virgin, is very inviting. Altogether the room is the room of a good housekeeper, vanquished, as far as the table is concerned, by an untidy man, but elsewhere mistress of the situation. The furniture, in its ornamental aspect, betrays the style of the advertised "drawingroom suite" of the pushing suburban furniture dealer; but there is nothing useless or pretentious in the room, money being too scarce in the house of an east end parson to be wasted on snobbish trimmings.*

The Reverend James Mavor Morell *is a Christian Socialist clergyman of the Church of England, and an active member of the Guild of St Matthew and the Christian Social Union. A vigorous, genial, popular man of forty, robust and goodlooking, full of energy, with pleasant, hearty, considerate manners, and a sound unaffected voice, which he uses with the clean athletic articulation of a practised orator, and with a wide range and perfect command of expression. He is a first rate clergyman, able to say what he likes to whom he likes, to lecture people without setting himself up against them, to impose his authority on them without humiliating them, and, on occasion, to interfere in their business without impertinence. His well-spring of enthusiasm and sympathetic emotion has never run dry for a moment: he still eats and sleeps heartily enough to win the daily battle between exhaustion and recuperation triumphantly. Withal, a great baby, pardonably vain of his powers and unconsciously pleased with himself. He has a healthy complexion: good forehead, with the brows somewhat blunt, and the eyes bright and eager, mouth resolute but not particularly well cut, and a substantial nose, with the mobile spreading nostrils of the dramatic orator, void, like all his features, of subtlety.*

The typist, Miss Proserpine Garnett, *is a brisk little woman of about 30, of the lower middle class, neatly but cheaply dressed in a black merino skirt and a blouse, notably pert and quick of speech, and not very civil in her manner, but sensitive and affectionate. She is clattering away busily at her machine whilst* Morell *opens the last of his morning's letters. He realizes its contents with a comic groan of despair.*

Proserpine. Another lecture?

Morell. Yes. The Hoxton Freedom Group wants me to address them on Sunday morning (*he lays great emphasis on Sunday, this being the unreasonable part of the business*). What are they?

Proserpine. Communist Anarchists, I think.

Morell. Just like Anarchists not to know that they cant have a parson on Sunday! Tell them to come to church if they want to hear me: it will do them good. Say I can come on Mondays and Thursdays only. Have you the diary there?

Proserpine (*taking up the diary*). Yes.

Morell. Have I any lecture for next Monday?

Proserpine (*referring to diary*). Tower Hamlets Radical Club.

Morell. Well, Thursday then?

Proserpine. English Land Restoration League.

Morell. What next?

Proserpine. Guild of St Matthew on Monday. Independent Labor Party, Greenwich Branch, on Thursday. Monday, Social-Democratic Federation, Mile End Branch. Thursday, first Confirmation class. (*Impatiently*) Oh, I'd better tell them you cant come. Theyre only half a dozen ignorant and conceited costermongers without five shillings between them.

Morell (*amused*). Ah; but you see theyre near relatives of mine.

Proserpine (*staring at him*). Relatives of yours!

Morell. Yes: we have the same father—in Heaven.

Proserpine (*relieved*). Oh, is that all?

Morell (*with a sadness which is a luxury to a man whose voice expresses it so finely*). Ah, you dont believe it. Everybody says it: nobody believes it: nobody. (*Briskly, getting back to business*) Well, well! Come, Miss Proserpine: cant you find a date for the costers? What about the 25th? That was vacant the day before yesterday.

Proserpine (*referring to diary*). Engaged. The Fabian Society.

Morell. Bother the Fabian Society! Is the 28th gone too?

Proserpine. City dinner. Youre invited to dine with the Founders' Company.

MORELL. Thatll do: I'll go to the Hoxton Group of Freedom instead. (*She enters the engagement in silence, with implacable disparagement of the Hoxton Anarchists in every line of her face.* MORELL *bursts open the cover of a copy of The Church Reformer, which has come by post, and glances through Mr Stewart Headlam's leader and the Guild of St Matthew news. These proceedings are presently enlivened by the appearance of* MORELL'S *curate, the* REVEREND ALEXANDER MILL, *a young gentleman gathered by* MORELL *from the nearest University settlement, whither he had come from Oxford to give the east end of London the benefit of his university training. He is a conceitedly well intentioned, enthusiastic, immature novice, with nothing positively unbearable about him except a habit of speaking with his lips carefully closed a full half inch from each corner for the sake of a finicking articulation and a set of university vowels, this being his chief means so far of bringing his Oxford refinement (as he calls his habits) to bear on Hackney vulgarity.* MORELL, *whom he has won over by a doglike devotion, looks up indulgently from The Church Reformer, and remarks*) Well, Lexy? Late again, as usual!

LEXY. I'm afraid so. I wish I could get up in the morning.

MORELL (*exulting in his own energy*). Ha! Ha! (*Whimsically*) Watch and pray, Lexy: watch and pray.

LEXY. I know. (*Rising wittily to the occasion*) But how can I watch and pray when I am asleep? Isnt that so, Miss Prossy? (*He makes for the warmth of the fire.*)

PROSERPINE (*sharply*). Miss Garnett, if you please.

LEXY. I beg your pardon. Miss Garnett.

PROSERPINE. Youve got to do all the work today.

LEXY (*on the hearth*). Why?

PROSERPINE. Never mind why. It will do you good to earn your supper before you eat it, for once in a way, as I do. Come! dont dawdle. You should have been off on your rounds half an hour ago.

LEXY (*perplexed*). Is she in earnest, Morell?

MORELL (*in the highest spirits: his eyes dancing*). Yes. *I* am going to dawdle today.

LEXY. You! You dont know how.

MORELL (*rising*). Ha! ha! Dont I? I'm going to have this morning all to myself. My wife's coming back: she's due here at 11.45.

LEXY (*surprised*). Coming back already! with the children? I thought they were to stay to the end of the month.

MORELL. So they are: she's only coming up for two days, to get some flannel things for Jimmy, and to see how we're getting on without her.

LEXY (*anxiously*). But, my dear Morell, if what Jimmy and Fluffy had was scarlatina, do you think it wise—

MORELL. Scarlatina! Rubbish! it was German measles. I brought it into the house myself from the Pycroft Street school. A parson is like a doctor, my boy: he must face infection as a soldier must face bullets. (*He claps* LEXY *manfully on the shoulders.*) Catch the measles if you can, Lexy: she'll nurse you; and what a piece of luck that will be for you! Eh?

Lexy (*smiling uneasily*). It's so hard to understand you about Mrs Morell—

Morell (*tenderly*). Ah, my boy, get married: get married to a good woman; and then youll understand. Thats a foretaste of what will be best in the Kingdom of Heaven we are trying to establish on earth. That will cure you of dawdling. An honest man feels that he must pay Heaven for every hour of happiness with a good spell of hard unselfish work to make others happy. We have no more right to consume happiness without producing it than to consume wealth without producing it. Get a wife like my Candida; and youll always be in arrear with your repayment. (*He pats* Lexy *affectionately and moves to leave the room.*)

Lexy. Oh, wait a bit: I forgot. (Morell *halts and turns with the door knob in his hand*) Your father-in-law is coming round to see you.

(Morell, *surprised and not pleased, shuts the door again, with a complete change of manner.*)

Morell. Mr. Burgess?

Lexy. Yes. I passed him in the park, arguing with somebody. He asked me to let you know that he was coming.

Morell (*half incredulous*). But he hasnt called here for three years. Are you sure, Lexy? Youre not joking, are you?

Lexy (*earnestly*). No sir, really.

Morell (*thoughtfully*). Hm! Time for him to take another look at Candida before she grows out of his knowledge. (*He resigns himself to the inevitable, and goes out.*)

(Lexy *looks after him with beaming worship.* Miss Garnett, *not being able to shake* Lexy, *relieves her feelings by worrying the typewriter.*)

Lexy. What a good man! What a thorough loving soul he is! (*He takes* Morell*'s place at the table, making himself very comfortable as he takes out a cigaret.*)

Proserpine (*impatiently, pulling the letter she has been working at off the typewriter and folding it*). Oh, a man ought to be able to be fond of his wife without making a fool of himself about her.

Lexy (*shocked*). Oh, Miss Prossy!

Proserpine (*snatching at the stationery case for an envelope, in which she encloses the letter as she speaks*). Candida here, and Candida there, and Candida everywhere! (*She licks the envelope*) It's enough to drive anyone out of their *senses* (*thumping the envelope to make it stick*) to hear a woman raved about in that absurd manner merely because she's got good hair and a tolerable figure.

Lexy (*with reproachful gravity*). I think her extremely beautiful, Miss

Garnett. (*He takes the photograph up; looks at it; and adds, with even greater impressiveness*) extremely beautiful. How fine her eyes are!

PROSERPINE. Her eyes are not a bit better than mine: now! (*He puts down the photograph and stares austerely at her.*) And you know very well you think me dowdy and second rate enough.

LEXY (*rising majestically*). Heaven forbid that I should think of any of God's creatures in such a way! (*He moves stiffly away from her across the room to the neighborhood of the bookcase.*)

PROSERPINE (*sarcastically*). Thank you. Thats very nice and comforting.

LEXY (*saddened by her depravity.*) I had no idea you had any feeling against Mrs Morell.

PROSERPINE (*indignantly*). I have no feeling against her. She's very nice, very good-hearted: I'm very fond of her, and can appreciate her real qualities far better than any man can. (*He shakes his head sadly. She rises and comes at him with intense pepperiness*) You dont believe me? You think I'm jealous? Oh, what a knowledge of the human heart you have, Mr Lexy Mill! How well you know the weaknesses of Woman, dont you? It must be so nice to be a man and have a fine penetrating intellect instead of mere emotions like us, and to know that the reason we dont share your amorous delusions is that we're all jealous of one another! (*She abandons him with a toss of her shoulders, and crosses to the fire to warm her hands.*)

LEXY. Ah, if you women only had the same clue to Man's strength that you have to his weakness, Miss Prossy, there would be no Woman Question.

PROSERPINE (*over her shoulder, as she stoops, holding her hands to the blaze*). Where did you hear Morell say that? You didnt invent it yourself: youre not clever enough.

LEXY. Thats quite true. I am not ashamed of owing him that, as I owe him so many other spiritual truths. He said it at the annual conference of the Women's Liberal Federation. Allow me to add that though they didnt appreciate it, I, a mere man, did. (*He turns to the bookcase again, hoping that this may leave her crushed.*)

PROSERPINE (*putting her hair straight at a panel of mirror in the mantelpiece*). Well, when you talk to me, give me your own ideas, such as they are, and not his. You never cut a poorer figure than when you are trying to imitate him.

LEXY (*stung*). I try to follow his example, not to imitate him.

PROSERPINE (*coming at him again on her way back to her work*). Yes, you do: you *imitate* him. Why do you tuck your umbrella under your left arm instead of carrying it in your hand like anyone else? Why do you walk with your chin stuck out before you, hurrying along with that eager look in your eyes? you! who never get up before half past nine in the morning. Why do you say "knoaledge" in church, though you always say "knolledge" in private conversation! Bah! do you think I dont know? (*She goes back to the typewriter.*) Here! come and set about your work: weve wasted enough time for one morning. Here's copy of the diary for today. (*She hands him a memorandum.*)

LEXY (*deeply offended*). Thank you.

(*He takes it and stands at the table with his back to her, reading it. She begins to transcribe her shorthand notes on the typewriter without troubling herself about his feelings*).

(*The door opens; and* MR BURGESS *enters unannounced. He is a man of sixty, made coarse and sordid by the compulsory selfishness of petty commerce, and later on softened into sluggish bumptiousness by overfeeding and commercial success. A vulgar ignorant guzzling man, offensive and contemptuous to people whose labor is cheap, respectful to wealth and rank, and quite sincere and without rancor or envy in both attitudes. The world has offered him no decently paid work except that of a sweater; and he has become, in consequence, somewhat hoggish. But he has no suspicion of this himself, and honestly regards his commercial prosperity as the inevitable and socially wholesome triumph of the ability, industry, shrewdness, and experience in business of a man who in private is easygoing, affectionate, and humorously convivial to a fault. Corporeally he is podgy, with a snoutish nose in the centre of a flat square face, a dust colored beard with a patch of grey in the centre under his chin, and small watery blue eyes with a plaintively sentimental expression, which he transfers easily to his voice by his habit of pompously intoning his sentences.*)

BURGESS (*stopping on the threshold, and looking round*). They told me Mr Morell was here.

PROSERPINE (*rising*). I'll fetch him for you.

BURGESS (*staring disappointedly at her*). Youre not the same young lady as hused to typewrite for him?

PROSERPINE. No.

BURGESS (*grumbling on his way to the hearthrug*). No: she was young-er. (MISS GARNETT *stares at him; then goes out, slamming the door.*) Startin on your rounds, Mr Mill?

LEXY (*folding his memorandum and pocketing it*). Yes: I must be off presently.

BURGESS (*momentously*). Dont let me detain you, Mr. Mill. What I come about is *private* between me and Mr Morell.

LEXY (*huffily*). I have no intention of intruding, I am sure, Mr Burgess. *Good* morning.

BURGESS (*patronizingly*). Oh, good morning to you.

(MORELL *returns as* LEXY *is making for the door.*)

MORELL (*to* LEXY). Off to work?

LEXY. Yes, sir.

MORELL. Take my silk handkerchief and wrap your throat up. Theres a cold wind. Away with you.

(LEXY, *more than consoled for* BURGESS'*s rudeness, brightens up and goes out.*)

BURGESS. Spoilin your korates as usu'l, James. Good mornin. When I pay a man, an' 'is livin depens on me, I keep him in 'is place.

MORELL (*rather shortly*). I always keep my curates in their places as my helpers and comrades. If you get as much work out of your clerks and warehousemen as I do out of my curates, you must be getting rich pretty fast. Will you take your old chair. (*He points with curt authority to the armchair beside the fireplace; then takes the spare chair from the table and sits down at an unfamiliar distance from his visitor.*)

BURGESS (*without moving*). Just the same as hever, James!

MORELL. When you last called—it was about three years ago, I think—you said the same thing a little more frankly. Your exact words then were "Just as big a fool as ever, James!"

BURGESS (*soothingly*). Well, praps I did; but (*with conciliatory cheerfulness*) I meant no hoffence by it. A clorgyman is privileged to be a bit of a fool, you know: it's ony becomin in 'is profession that he should. Anyhow, I come here, not to rake up hold differences, but to let bygones be bygones. (*Suddenly becoming very solemn, and approaching* MORELL) James: three years ago, you done me a hill turn. You done me hout of a contrac; an when I gev you arsh words in my natral disappointment, you turned my daughrter again me. Well, Ive come to hact the part of a Kerischin. (*Offering his hand*) I forgive you, James.

MORELL (*starting up*). Confound your impudence!

BURGESS (*retreating, with almost lachrymose deprecation of this treatment*). Is that becomin language for a clorgyman, James? And you so particlar, too!

MORELL (*hotly*). No, sir: it is not becoming language for a clergyman. I used the wrong word. I should have said damn your impudence: thats what St Paul or any honest priest would have said to you. Do you think I have forgotten that tender of yours for the contract to supply clothing to the workhouse?

BURGESS (*in a paroxysm of public spirit*). I hacted in the hinterest of the ratepayers, James. It was the lowest tender: you carnt deny that.

MORELL. Yes, the lowest, because you paid worse wages than any other employer—starvation wages—aye, worse than starvation wages—to the women who made the clothing. Your wages would have driven them to the streets to keep body and soul together. (*Getting angrier and angrier*) Those women were my parishioners. I shamed the Guardians out of accepting your tender: I shamed the ratepayers out of letting them do it: I shamed everybody but you. (*Boiling over*) How dare you, sir, come here and offer to forgive me, and talk about your daughter, and—

BURGESS. Heasy, James! heasy! heasy! Dont git hinto a fluster about nothink. Ive howned I was wrong.

MORELL. Have you? I didnt hear you.

BURGESS. Of course I did. I hown it now. Come: I harsk your pardon for the letter I wrote you. Is that enough?

MORELL (*snapping his fingers*). Thats nothing. Have you raised the wages?

BURGESS (*triumphantly*). Yes.

MORELL. What!

BURGESS (*unctuously*). Ive turned a moddle hemployer. I dont hemploy no women now: theyre all sacked; and the work is done by machinery. Not a man 'as less than sixpence a *h*our; and the skilled ands gits the Trade Union rate. (*Proudly*) What ave you to say to me now?

MORELL (*overwhelmed*). Is it possible! Well, theres more joy in heaven over one sinner that repenteth!—(*Going to* BURGESS *with an explosion of apologetic cordiality*) My dear Burgess: how splendid of you! I most heartily beg your pardon for my hard thoughts. (*Grasping his hand*) And now, dont you feel the better for the change? Come! confess! youre happier. You look happier.

BURGESS (*ruefully*). Well, praps I do. I spose I must, since you notice it. At all events, I git my contrax assepted by the County Council. (*Savagely*)They dussent ave no-think to do with me unless I paid fair wages: curse em for a parcel o meddlin fools!

MORELL (*dropping his hand, utterly discouraged*). So that was why you raised the wages! (*He sits down moodily.*)

BURGESS (*severely, in spreading, mounting tones*). Woy helse should I do it? What does it lead to but drink and huppishness in workin men? (*He seats himself magisterially in the easy chair.*) It's hall very well for you, James: it gits you hinto the papers and makes a great man of you; but you never think of the arm you do, puttin money into the pockets of workin men that they dunno ow to spend, and takin it from people that might be makin a good huse on it.

MORELL (*with a heavy sigh, speaking with cold politeness*). What is your business with me this morning? I shall not pretend to believe that you are here merely out of family sentiment.

BURGESS (*obstinately*). Yes I ham: just family sentiment and nothink helse.

MORELL (*with weary calm*). I dont believe you.

BURGESS (*rising threateningly*). Dont say that to me again, James Mavor Morell.

MORELL (*unmoved*). I'll say it just as often as may be necessary to convince you that it's true. I dont believe you.

Burgess (*collapsing into an abyss of wounded feeling*). Oh, well, if voure detormined to be hunfriendly, I spose I'd better go. (*He moves reluctantly towards the door.* Morell *makes no sign. He lingers.*) I didnt hexpect to find a hunforgivin spirit in you, James. (Morell *still not responding, he takes a few more reluctant steps doorwards. Then he comes back, whining.*) We huseter git on well enough, spite of our different hopinions. Woy are you so changed to me? I give you my word I come here in peeorr [pure] frenliness, not wishin to be hon bad terms with my hown daughrter's usban. Come, James: be a Kerischin, and shake ands. (*He puts his hand sentimentally on* Morell's *shoulder.*)

Morell (*looking up at him thoughtfully*). Look here, Burgess. Do you want to be as welcome here as you were before you lost that contract?

Burgess. I do, James. I do—honest.

Morell. Then why dont you behave as you did then?

Burgess (*cautiously removing his hand*). Ow d'y' mean?

Morell. I'll tell you. You thought me a young fool then.

Burgess (*coaxingly*). No I didnt, James. I—

Morell (*cutting him short*). Yes, you did. And I thought you an old scoundrel.

Burgess (*most vehemently deprecating this gross self-accusation on* Morell's *part*). No you didnt, James. Now you do yourself a hinjustice.

Morell. Yes I did. Well, that did not prevent our getting on very well together. God made you what I call a scoundrel as He made me what you call a fool. (*The effect of this observation on* Burgess *is to remove the keystone of his moral arch. He becomes bodily weak, and, with his eyes fixed on* Morell *in a helpless stare, puts out his hand apprehensively to balance himself, as if the floor had suddenly sloped under him.* Morell *proceeds, in the same tone of quiet conviction*) It was not for me to quarrel with His handiwork in the one case more than in the other. So long as you come here honestly as a self-respecting, thorough, convinced scoundrel, justifying your scoundrelism and proud of it, you are welcome. But (*and now* Morell's *tone becomes formidable; and he rises and strikes the back of the chair for greater emphasis*) I wont have you here snivelling about being a model employer and a converted man when youre only an apostate with your coat turned for the sake of a County Council contract. (*He nods at him to enforce the point; then goes to the hearth-rug, where he takes up a comfortably commanding position with his back to the fire, and continues*) No: I like a man to be true to himself, even in wickedness. Come now: either take your hat and go; or else sit down and give me a good scoundrelly reason for wanting to be friends with me. (Burgess, *whose emotions have subsided sufficiently to be expressed by a dazed grin, is relieved by this concrete proposition. He ponders it for a moment, and then, slowly and very modestly, sits down in the chair* Morell *has just left.*) Thats right. Now out with it.

Burgess (*chuckling in spite of himself*). Well, you orr a queer bird,

James, and no mistake. But (*almost enthusiastically*) one carnt elp likin you: besides, as I said afore, of course one dont take hall a clorgyman says seriously, or the world couldnt go on. Could it now? (*He composes himself for graver discourse, and, turning his eyes on* MORELL, *proceeds with dull seriousness*) Well, I dont mind tellin you, since it's your wish we should be free with one another, that I did think you a bit of a fool once; but I'm beginnin to think that praps I was be'ind the times a bit.

MORELL (*exultant*). Aha! Youre finding that out at last, are you?

BURGESS (*portentously*). Yes: times 'as changed mor'n I could a believed. Five yorr [year] ago, no sensible man would a thought o takin hup with your hidears. I hused to wonder you was let preach at all. Why, I know a clorgyman what 'as bin kep hout of his job for yorrs by the Bishop o London, although the pore feller's not a bit more religious than you are. But today, if hennyone was to horffer to bet me a thousan pound that youll hend by bein a bishop yourself, I dussent take the bet. (*Very impressively*) You and your crew are getting hinfluential: I can see that. Theyll ave to give you somethink someday, if it's honly to stop your mouth. You ad the right instinc arter all, James: the line you took is the payin line in the long run for a man o your sort.

MORELL (*offering his hand with thorough decision*). Shake hands, Burgess. Now youre talking honestly. I dont think theyll make me a bishop; but if they do, I'll introduce you to the biggest jobbers I can get to come to my dinner parties.

BURGESS (*who has risen with a sheepish grin and accepted the hand of friendship*). You will ave your joke, James. Our quarrel's made up now, ain it?

A WOMAN'S VOICE. Say yes, James.

(Startled, they turn quickly and find that CANDIDA *has just come in, and is looking at them with an amused maternal indulgence which is her characteristic expression. She is a woman of 33, well built, well nourished, likely, one guesses, to become matronly later on, but now quite at her best, with the double charm of youth and motherhood. Her ways are those of a woman who has found that she can always manage people by engaging their affection, and who does so frankly and instinctively without the smallest scruple. So far, she is like any other pretty woman who is just clever enough to make the most of her sexual attractions for trivially selfish ends; but* CANDIDA'S *serene brow, courageous eyes, and well set mouth and chin signify largeness of mind and dignity of character to ennoble her cunning in the affections. A wise-hearted observer, looking at her, would at once guess that whoever had placed the Virgin of the Assumption over her hearth did so because he fancied some spiritual resemblance between them, and yet would not suspect either her husband or herself of any such idea, or indeed of any concern with the art of Titian.*

(*Just now she is in bonnet and mantle, carrying a strapped rug with her umbrella stuck through it, a handbag, and a supply of illustrated papers.*)

MORELL (*shocked at his remissness*). Candida! Why—(*he looks at his watch, and is horrified to find it so late*). My darling! (*Hurrying to her and seizing the rug strap, pouring forth his remorseful regrets all the time*) I intended to meet you at the train. I let the time slip. (*Flinging the rug on the sofa*) I was so engrossed by—(*returning to her*)—I forgot—oh! (*he embraces her with penitent emotion*).

BURGESS (*a little shamefaced and doubtful of his reception*). How orr you, Candy? (*She, still in* MORELL's *arms, offers him her cheek, which he kisses.*) James and me is come to a nunnerstannin. A *h*onorable unnerstannin. Ain we, James?

MORELL (*impetuously*). Oh bother your understanding! youve kept me late for Candida. (*With compassionate fervor*) My poor love: how did you manage about the luggage? How—

CANDIDA (*stopping him and disengaging herself*). There! there! there! I wasnt alone. Eugene has been down with us; and we travelled together.

MORELL (*pleased*). Eugene!

CANDIDA. Yes: he's struggling with my luggage, poor boy. Go out, dear, at once; or he'll pay for the cab; and I dont want that. (MORELL *hurries out.* CANDIDA *puts down her handbag; then takes off her mantle and bonnet and puts them on the sofa with the rug, chatting meanwhile.*) Well, papa: how are you getting on at home?

BURGESS. The ouse aint worth livin in since you left it, Candy. I wish youd come round and give the gurl a talkin to. Who's this Eugene thats come with you?

CANDIDA. Oh, Eugene's one of James discoveries. He found him sleeping on the Embankment last June. Havnt you noticed our new picture (*pointing to the Virgin*)? He gave us that.

BURGESS (*incredulously*). Garn! D'you mean to tell me—your hown father—that cab touts or such like, orf the Embankment, buys pictures like that? (*Severely*) Dont deceive me, Candy: it's a 'Igh Church picture; and James chose it hisself.

CANDIDA. Guess again. Eugene isnt a cab tout.

BURGESS. Then what is he? (*Sarcastically*) A nobleman, I spose.

CANDIDA (*nodding delightedly*). Yes. His uncle's a peer! A real live earl.

BURGESS (*not daring to believe such good news*). No!

CANDIDA. Yes. He had a seven day bill for £55 in his pocket when James found him on the Embankment. He thought he couldnt get any money for it until the seven days were up; and he was too shy to ask for credit. Oh, he's a dear boy! We are very fond of him.

BURGESS (*pretending to belittle the aristocracy, but with his eyes gleam-*

ing). Hm! I thort you wouldnt git a hearl's nevvy visitin in Victawriar Pawrk unless he were a bit of a flat. (*Looking again at the picture*) Of course I dont old with that picture, Candy; but still it's a 'igh class fust rate work of ort: I can see that. Be sure you hintrodooce me to im, Candy. (*He looks at his watch anxiously*) I can ony stay about two minutes.

(MORELL *comes back with* EUGENE, *whom* BURGESS *contemplates moist-eyed with enthusiasm. He is a strange, shy youth of eighteen, slight, effeminate, with a delicate childish voice, and a hunted tormented expression and shrinking manner that shew the painful sensitiveness of very swift and acute apprehensiveness in youth, before the character has grown to its full strength. Miserably irresolute, he does not know where to stand or what to do. He is afraid of* BURGESS, *and would run away into solitude if he dared; but the very intensity with which he feels a perfectly commonplace position comes from excessive nervous force; and his nostrils, mouth, and eyes betray a fiercely petulant wilfulness, as to the bent of which his brow, already lined with pity, is reassuring. He is so uncommon as to be almost unearthly; and to prosaic people there is something noxious in this unearthliness, just as to poetic people there is something angelic in it. His dress is anarchic. He wears an old blue serge jacket, unbuttoned, over a woollen lawn tennis shirt, with a silk handkerchief for a cravat, trousers matching the jacket, and brown canvas shoes. In these garments he has apparently lain in the heather and waded through the waters; and there is no evidence of his having ever brushed them.*

(*As he catches sight of a stranger on entering, he stops, and edges along the wall on the opposite side of the room.*)

MORELL (*as he enters*). Come along: you can spare us quarter of an hour at all events. This is my father-in-law. Mr Burgess—Mr Marchbanks.

MARCHBANKS (*nervously backing against the bookcase*). Glad to meet you, sir.

BURGESS (*crossing to him with great heartiness, whilst* MORELL *joins* CANDIDA *at the fire*). Glad to meet you, I'm shore, Mr Morchbanks. (*Forcing him to shake hands*) Ow do you find yoreself this weather? Ope you aint lettin James put no foolish ideas into your ed?

MARCHBANKS. Foolish ideas? Oh, you mean Socialism? No.

BURGESS. Thats right. (*Again looking at his watch*) Well, I must go now: there's no elp for it. Yore not comin my way, orr you, Mr Morchbanks?

MARCHBANKS. Which way is that?

BURGESS. Victawriar Pawrk Station. Theres a city train at 12.25.

MORELL. Nonsense. Eugene will stay to lunch with us, I expect.

MARCHBANKS (*anxiously excusing himself*). No—I—I—

BURGESS. Well, well, I shornt press you: I bet youd rather lunch with Candy. Some night, I ope, youll come and dine with me at my club, the Freeman Founders in Nortn Folgit. Come: say you will!

MARCHBANKS. Thank you, Mr. Burgess. Where is Norton? Down in Surrey, isnt it?

(BURGESS, *inexpressibly tickled, begins to splutter with laughter.*)

CANDIDA (*coming to the rescue*). Youll lose your train, papa, if you dont go at once. Come back in the afternoon and tell Mr Marchbanks where to find the club.

BURGESS (*roaring with glee*). Down in Surrey! Har, har! thats not a bad one. Well, I never met a man as didnt know Nortn Folgit afore. (*Abashed at his own noisiness*) Goodbye, Mr Morchbanks: I know yore too ighbred to take my pleasantry in bad part. (*He again offers his hand.*)

MARCHBANKS (*taking it with a nervous jerk*). Not at all.

BURGESS. Bye, bye, Candy. I'll look in again later on. So long, James.

MORELL. Must you go?

BURGESS. Dont stir. (*He goes out with unabated heartiness.*)

MORELL. Oh, I'll see you off. (*He follows him.*)

(EUGENE *stares after them apprehensively, holding his breath until* BURGESS *disappears.*)

CANDIDA (*laughing*). Well, Eugene? (*He turns with a start, and comes eagerly towards her, but stops irresolutely as he meets her amused look.*) What do you think of my father?

MARCHBANKS. I—I hardly know him yet. He seems to be a very nice old gentleman.

CANDIDA (*with gentle irony*). And youll go to the Freeman Founders to dine with him, wont you?

MARCHBANKS (*miserably, taking it quite seriously*). Yes, if it will please you.

CANDIDA (*touched*). Do you know, you are a very nice boy, Eugene, with all your queerness. If you had laughed at my father I shouldnt have minded; but I like you ever so much better for being nice to him.

MARCHBANKS. Ought I to have laughed? I noticed that he said something funny; but I am so ill at ease with strangers; and I never can see a joke. I'm very sorry. (*He sits down on the sofa, his elbows on his knees and his temples between his fists, with an expression of hopeless suffering.*)

CANDIDA (*bustling him goodnaturedly*). Oh come! You great baby, you! You are worse than usual this morning. Why were you so melancholy as we came along in the cab?

MARCHBANKS. Oh, that was nothing. I was wondering how much I ought to give the cabman. I know it's utterly silly; but you dont know how dreadful such things are to me—how I shrink from having to deal with strange people. (*Quickly and reassuringly*) But it's all right. He beamed all over and touched his hat when Morell gave him two shillings. I was on the point of offering him ten.

(MORELL *comes back with a few letters and newspapers which have come by the midday post.*)

CANDIDA. Oh, James dear, he was going to give the cabman ten shillings! ten shillings for a three minutes drive! Oh dear!

MORELL (*at the table, glancing through the letters*). Never mind her, Marchbanks. The overpaying instinct is a generous one: better than the underpaying instinct, and not so common.

MARCHBANKS (*relapsing into dejection*). No: cowardice, incompetence. Mrs Morell's quite right.

CANDIDA. Of course she is. (*She takes up her hand-bag*) And now I must leave you to James for the present. I suppose you are too much of a poet to know the state a woman finds her house in when she's been away for three weeks. Give me my rug. (EUGENE *takes the strapped rug from the couch, and gives it to her. She takes it in her left hand, having the bag in her right.*) Now hang my cloak across my arm. (*He obeys.*) Now my hat. (*He puts it into the hand which has the bag.*) Now open the door for me. (*He hurries before her and opens the door.*) Thanks. (*She goes out; and* MARCHBANKS *shuts the door.*)

MORELL (*still busy at the table*). Youll stay to lunch, Marchbanks, of course.

MARCHBANKS (*scared*). I mustnt. (*He glances quickly at* MORELL, *but at once avoids his frank look, and adds, with obvious disingenuousness*) I mean I cant.

MORELL. You mean you wont.

MARCHBANKS (*earnestly*). No: I should like to, indeed. Thank you very much. But—but—

MORELL. But—but—but—but—Bosh! If youd like to stay, stay. If youre shy, go and take a turn in the park and write poetry until half past one; and then come in and have a good feed.

MARCHBANKS. Thank you, I should like that very much. But I really mustnt. The truth is, Mrs Morell told me not to. She said she didnt think youd ask me to stay to lunch, but that I was to remember, if you did, that you didnt really want me to. (*Plaintively*) She said I'd understand; but I dont. Please dont tell her I told you.

MORELL (*drolly*). Oh, is that all? Wont my suggestion that you should take a turn in the park meet the difficulty?

MARCHBANKS. How?

MORELL (*exploding good-humoredly*). Why, you duffer—(*But this boisterousness jars himself as well as* EUGENE. *He checks himself*) No: I wont put it in that way. (*He comes to* EUGENE *with affectionate seriousness*) My dear lad: in a happy marriage like ours, there is something very sacred in the return of the wife to her home. (MARCHBANKS *looks quickly at him, half anticipating his meaning.*) An old friend or a truly noble and sympathetic soul is not in the way on such occasions; but a chance visitor is. (*The hunted horror-stricken expression comes out with sudden vividness in* EUGENE'*s face as he understands.* MORELL, *occupied with his own thoughts, goes on without noticing this*) Candida thought I would rather not have you here; but she was wrong. I'm very fond of you, my boy; and I should like you to see for yourself what a happy thing it is to be married as I am.

MARCHBANKS. Happy! Your marriage! You think that! You believe that!

MORELL (*buoyantly*). I know it, my lad. Larochefoucauld said that there are convenient marriages but no delightful ones. You dont know the comfort of seeing through and through a thundering liar and rotten cynic like that fellow. Ha! ha! Now, off with you to the park, and write your poem. Half past one, sharp, mind: we never wait for anybody.

MARCHBANKS (*wildly*). No: stop: you shant. I'll force it into the light.

MORELL (*puzzled*). Eh? Force what?

MARCHBANKS. I must speak to you. There is something that must be settled between us.

MORELL (*with a whimsical glance at his watch*). Now?

MARCHBANKS (*passionately*). Now. Before you leave this room. (*He retreats a few steps, and stands as if to bar* MORELL'*s way to the door.*)

MORELL (*without moving, and gravely, perceiving now that there is something serious the matter*). I'm not going to leave it, my dear boy: I thought you were. (EUGENE, *baffled by his firm tone, turns his back on him, writhing with anger.* MORELL *goes to him and puts his hand on his shoulder strongly and kindly, disregarding his attempt to shake it off.*) Come: sit down quietly; and tell me what it is. And remember: we are friends, and need not fear that either of us will be anything but patient and kind to the other, whatever we may have to say.

MARCHBANKS (*twisting himself round on him*). Oh, I am not forgetting myself: I am only (*covering his face desperately with his hands*) full of horror. (*Then, dropping his hands, and thrusting his face forward fiercely at* MORELL, *he goes on threateningly*) You shall see whether this is a time for patience and kindness. (MORELL, *firm as a rock, looks indulgently at him.*) Dont look at me in that self-complacent way. You think yourself stronger than I am; but I shall stagger you if you have a heart in your breast.

MORELL (*powerfully confident*). Stagger me, my boy. Out with it.

MARCHBANKS. First—

MORELL. First?

MARCHBANKS. I love your wife.

(MORELL *recoils, and, after staring at him for a moment in utter amazement, bursts into uncontrollable laughter.* EUGENE *is taken aback, but not disconcerted; and he soon becomes indignant and contemptuous.*)

MORELL (*sitting down to have his laugh out*). Why, my dear child, of course you do. Everybody loves her: they cant help it. I like it. But (*looking up jocosely at him*) I say, Eugene: do you think yours is a case to be talked about? Youre under twenty: she's over thirty. Doesnt it look rather too like a case of calf love?

MARCHBANKS (*vehemently*). You dare say that of her! You think that way of the love she inspires! It is an insult to her!

MORELL (*rising quickly, in an altered tone*). To her! Eugene: take care. I have been patient. I hope to remain patient. But there are some things I wont allow. Dont force me to shew you the indulgence I should shew to a child. Be a man.

MARCHBANKS (*with a gesture as if sweeping something behind him*). Oh, let us put aside all that cant. It horrifies me when I think of the doses of it she has had to endure in all the weary years during which you have selfishly and blindly sacrificed her to minister to your self-sufficiency: you! (*turning on him*) who have not one thought—one sense—in common with her.

MORELL (*philosophically*). She seems to bear it pretty well. (*Looking him straight in the face*) Eugene, my boy: you are making a fool of yourself: a very great fool of yourself. Theres a piece of wholesome plain speaking for you. (*He knocks in the lesson with a nod in his old way, and posts himself on the hearth-rug, holding his hands behind him to warm them.*)

MARCHBANKS. Oh, do you think I dont know all that? Do you think that the things people make fools of themselves about are any less real and true than the things they behave sensibly about? (MORELL'*s gaze wavers for the first time. He forgets to warm his hands, and stands listening, startled and thoughtful.*) They are more true: they are the only things that are true. You are very calm and sensible and moderate with me because you can see that I am a fool about your wife; just as no doubt that old man who was here just now is very wise over your Socialism, because he sees that you are a fool about it. (MORELL'*s perplexity deepens markedly.* EUGENE *follows up his advantage, plying him fiercely with questions*) Does that prove you wrong? Does your complacent superiority to me prove that *I* am wrong?

MORELL. Marchbanks: some devil is putting these words into your mouth. It is easy—terribly easy—to shake a man's faith in himself. To take advantage of that to break a man's spirit is devil's work. Take care of what you are doing. Take care.

MARCHBANKS (*ruthlessly*). I know. I'm doing it on purpose. I told you I should stagger you.

(*They confront one another threateningly for a moment. Then* MORELL *recovers his dignity.*)

MORELL (*with noble tenderness*). Eugene: listen to me. Some day, I hope and trust, you will be a happy man like me. (EUGENE *chafes intolerantly, repudiating the worth of his happiness.* MORELL, *deeply insulted, con-*

trols himself with fine forbearance, and continues steadily, with great artistic beauty of delivery) You will be married; and you will be working with all your might and valor to make every spot on earth as happy as your own home. You will be one of the makers of the Kingdom of Heaven on earth; and—who knows—you may be a master builder where I am only a humble journeyman; for dont think, my boy, that I cannot see in you, young as you are, promise of higher powers than I can ever pretend to. I well know that it is in the poet that the holy spirit of man—the god within him—is most god-like. It should make you tremble to think of that—to think that the heavy burthen and great gift of a poet may be laid upon you.

MARCHBANKS *(unimpressed and remorseless, his boyish crudity of assertion telling sharply against* MORELL'S *oratory)*. It does not make me tremble. It is the want of it in others that makes me tremble.

MORELL *(redoubling his force of style under the stimulus of his genuine feeling and* EUGENE'S *obduracy)*. Then help to kindle it in them—in *me*—not to extinguish it. In the future, when you are as happy as I am, I will be your true brother in the faith. I will help you to believe that God has given us a world that nothing but our own folly keeps from being a paradise. I will help you to believe that every stroke of your work is sowing happiness for the great harvest that all—even the humblest— shall one day reap. And last, but trust me, not least, I will help you to believe that your wife loves you and is happy in her home. We need such help, Marchbanks: we need it greatly and always. There are so many things to make us doubt, if once we let our understanding be troubled. Even at home, we sit as if in camp, encompassed by a hostile army of doubts. Will you play the traitor and let them in on me?

MARCHBANKS *(looking round wildly)*. Is it like this for her here always? A woman, with a great soul, craving for reality, truth, freedom; and being fed on metaphors, sermons, stale perorations, mere rhetoric. Do you think a woman's soul can live on your talent for preaching?

MORELL *(stung)*. Marchbanks: you make it hard for me to control myself. My talent is like yours insofar as it has any real worth at all. It is the gift of finding words for divine truth.

MARCHBANKS *(impetuously)*. It's the gift of the gab, nothing more and nothing less. What has your knack of fine talking to do with the truth, any more than playing the organ has? Ive never been in your church; but Ive been to your political meetings; and Ive seen you do whats called rousing the meeting to enthusiasm: that is, you excited them until they behaved exactly as if they were drunk. And their wives looked on and saw what fools they were. Oh, it's an old story: youll find it in the Bible. I imagine King David, in his fits of enthusiasm, was very like you. *(Stabbing him with the words)* "But his wife despised him in her heart."

MORELL *(wrathfully)*. Leave my house. Do you hear? *(He advances on him threateningly.)*

MARCHBANKS (*shrinking back against the couch*). Let me alone. Dont touch me. (MORELL *grasps him powerfully by the lapel of his coat: he cowers down on the sofa and screams passionately*) Stop, Morell: if you strike me, I'll kill myself: I wont bear it. (*Almost in hysterics*) Let me go. Take your hand away.

MORELL (*with slow emphatic scorn*). You little snivelling cowardly whelp. (*He releases him*) Go, before you frighten yourself into a fit.

MARCHBANKS (*on the sofa, gasping, but relieved by the withdrawal of* MORELL'*s hand*). I'm not afraid of you: it's you who are afraid of me.

MORELL (*quietly, as he stands over him*). It looks like it, doesnt it?

MARCHBANKS (*with petulant vehemence*). Yes it does. (MORELL *turns away contemptuously.* EUGENE *scrambles to his feet and follows him*) You think because I shrink from being brutally handled—because (*with tears in his voice*) I can do nothing but cry with rage when I am met with violence—because I cant lift a heavy trunk down from the top of a cab like you—because I cant fight you for your wife as a drunken navvy would: all that makes you think I'm afraid of you. But youre wrong. If I havnt got what you call British pluck, I havnt British cowardice either: I'm not afraid of a clergyman's ideas. I'll fight your ideas. I'll rescue her from her slavery to them. I'll pit my own ideas against them. You are driving me out of the house because you darent let her choose between your ideas and mine. You are afraid to let me see her again. (MORELL, *angered, turns suddenly on him. He flies to the door in involuntary dread*) Let me alone, I say. I'm going.

MORELL (*with cold scorn*). Wait a moment: I am not going to touch you: dont be afraid. When my wife comes back she will want to know why you have gone. And when she finds that you are never going to cross our threshold again, she will want to have that explained too. Now I dont wish to distress her by telling her that you have behaved like a blackguard.

MARCHBANKS (*coming back with renewed vehemence*). You shall. You must. If you give any explanation but the true one, you are a liar and a coward. Tell her what I said; and how you were strong and manly, and shook me as a terrier shakes a rat; and how I shrank and was terrified; and how you called me a snivelling little whelp and put me out of the house. If you dont tell her, I will: I'll write it to her.

MORELL (*puzzled*). Why do you want her to know this?

MARCHBANKS (*with lyric rapture*). Because she will understand me, and know that I understand her. If you keep back one word of it from her—if you are not ready to lay the truth at her feet as I am—then you will know to the end of your days that she really belongs to me and not to you. Goodbye. (*Going.*)

MORELL (*terribly disquieted*). Stop: I will not tell her.

MARCHBANKS (*turning near the door*). Either the truth or a lie you must tell her, if I go.

MORELL (*temporizing*). Marchbanks: it is sometimes justifiable—

MARCHBANKS (*cutting him short*). I know: to lie. It will be useless. Goodbye, Mr. Clergyman.

(*As he turns finally to the door, it opens and* CANDIDA *enters in her housekeeping dress.*)

CANDIDA. Are you going, Eugene? (*Looking more observantly at him*) Well, dear me, just look at you, going out into the street in that state! You are a poet, certainly. Look at him, James! (*She takes him by the coat, and brings him forward, shewing him to* MORELL) Look at his collar! Look at his tie! look at his hair! One would think somebody had been throttling you. (EUGENE *instinctively tries to look round at* MORELL; *but she pulls him back*) Here! Stand still. (*She buttons his collar; ties his neckerchief in a bow; and arranges his hair.*) There! Now you look so nice that I think youd better stay to lunch after all, though I told you you mustnt. It will be ready in half an hour. (*She puts a final touch to the bow. He kisses her hand*) Dont be silly.

MARCHBANKS. I want to stay, of course; unless the reverend gentleman your husband has anything to advance to the contrary.

CANDIDA. Shall he stay, James, if he promises to be a good boy and help me to lay the table?

MORELL (*shortly*). Oh yes, certainly: he had better. (*He goes to the table and pretends to busy himself with his papers there.*)

MARCHBANKS (*offering his arm to* CANDIDA). Come and lay the table. (*She takes it. They go to the door together. As they pass out he adds*) I am the happiest of mortals.

MORELL. So was I—an hour ago.

ACT II

The same day later in the afternoon. The same room. The chair for visitors has been replaced at the table. MARCHBANKS, *alone and idle, is trying to find out how the typewriter works. Hearing someone at the door, he steals guiltily away to the window and pretends to be absorbed in the view.* MISS GARNETT, *carrying the notebook in which she takes down* MORELL'*s letters in shorthand from his dictation, sits down at the typewriter and sets to work transcribing them, much too busy to notice* EUGENE. *When she begins the second line she stops and stares at the machine. Something wrong evidently.*

PROSERPINE. Bother! You've been meddling with my typewriter, Mr Marchbanks; and theres not the least use in your trying to look as if you hadnt.

MARCHBANKS (*timidly*). I'm very sorry, Miss Garnett. I only tried to make it write. (*Plaintively*) But it wouldnt.

PROSERPINE. Well, youve altered the spacing.

MARCHBANKS (*earnestly*). I assure you I didnt. I didnt indeed. I only turned a little wheel. It gave a sort of click.

PROSERPINE. Oh, now I understand. (*She restores the spacing, talking volubly all the time*) I suppose you thought it was a sort of barrel-organ. Nothing to do but turn the handle, and it would write a beautiful love letter for you straight off, eh?

MARCHBANKS (*seriously*). I suppose a machine could be made to write love letters. Theyre all the same, arnt they?

PROSERPINE (*somewhat indignantly: any such discussion, except by way of pleasantry, being outside her code of manners*) How do I know? Why do you ask me?

MARCHBANKS. I beg your pardon. I thought clever people—people who can do business and write letters and that sort of thing—always had to have love affairs to keep them from going mad.

PROSERPINE (*rising, outraged*). Mr Marchbanks! (*She looks severely at him, and marches majestically to the bookcase.*)

MARCHBANKS (*approaching her humbly*). I hope I havnt offended you. Perhaps I shouldnt have alluded to your love affairs.

PROSERPINE (*plucking a blue book from the shelf and turning sharply on him*). I havnt any love affairs. How dare you say such a thing? The idea! (*She tucks the book under her arm, and is flouncing back to her machine when he addresses her with awakened interest and sympathy.*)

MARCHBANKS. Really! Oh, then you are shy, like me.

PROSERPINE. Certainly I am not shy. What do you mean?

MARCHBANKS (*secretly*). You must be: that is the reason there are so few love affairs in the world. We all go about longing for love: it is the first need of our natures, the first prayer of our hearts; but we dare not utter our longing: we are too shy. (*Very earnestly*) Oh, Miss Garnett, what would you not give to be without fear, without shame—

PROSERPINE (*scandalized*). Well, upon my word!

MARCHBANKS (*with petulant impatience*). Ah, dont say those stupid things to me: they dont deceive me: what use are they? Why are you afraid to be your real self with me? I am just like you.

PROSERPINE. Like me! Pray are you flattering me or flattering yourself? I dont feel quite sure which. (*She again tries to get back to her work.*)

MARCHBANKS (*stopping her mysteriously*). Hush! I go about in search of love; and I find it in unmeasured stores in the bosoms of others. But when I try to ask for it, this horrible shyness strangles me; and I stand dumb, or worse than dumb, saying meaningless things: foolish lies. And I see the affection I am longing for given to dogs and cats and pet birds, because they come and ask it. (*Almost whispering*) It must be asked for: it is like a ghost: it cannot speak unless it is first spoken to. (*At his usual pitch, but with deep melancholy*) All the love in the world is longing to speak; only it dare not, because it is shy! shy! shy! That is the world's tragedy. (*With a deep sigh he sits in the visitors' chair and buries his face in his hands.*)

PROSERPINE (*amazed, but keeping her wits about her: her point of honor in encounters with strange young men*). Wicked people get over that shyness occasionally, dont they?

MARCHBANKS (*scrambling up almost fiercely*). Wicked people means people who have no love: therefore they have no shame. They have the power to ask love because they dont need it: they have the power to offer it because they have none to give. (*He collapses into his seat, and adds, mournfully*) But we, who *have* love, and long to mingle it with the love of others: we cannot utter a word. (*Timidly*) You find that, dont you?

PROSERPINE. Look here: if you dont stop talking like this, I'll leave the room, Mr Marchbanks: I really will. It's not proper.

(*She resumes her seat at the typewriter, opening the blue book and preparing to copy a passage from it.*)

MARCHBANKS (*hopelessly*). Nothing thats worth saying is proper. (*He rises, and wanders about the room in his lost way.*) I cant understand you, Miss Garnett. What am I to talk about?

PROSERPINE (*snubbing him*). Talk about indifferent things. Talk about the weather.

MARCHBANK. Would you talk about indifferent things if a child were by, crying bitterly with hunger?

PROSERPINE. I suppose not.

MARCHBANKS. Well: *I* cant talk about indifferent things with my heart crying out bitterly in its hunger.

PROSERPINE. Then hold your tongue.

MARCHBANKS. Yes: that is what it always comes to. We hold our tongues. Does that stop the cry of your heart? for it does cry: doesnt it? It must, if you have a heart.

PROSERPINE (*suddenly rising with her hand pressed on her heart*). Oh, it's no use trying to work while you talk like that. (*She leaves her little table and sits on the sofa. Her feelings are keenly stirred*) It's no business of yours whether my heart cries or not; but I have a mind to tell you, for all that.

MARCHBANKS. You neednt. I know already that it must.

PROSERPINE. But mind! if you ever say I said so, I'll deny it.

MARCHBANKS (*compassionately*). Yes, I know. And so you havnt the courage to tell him?

PROSERPINE (*bouncing up*). Him! Who?

MARCHBANKS. Whoever he is. The man you love. It might be anybody. The curate, Mr Mill, perhaps.

PROSERPINE (*with disdain*). Mr. Mill!!! A fine man to break my heart about, indeed! I'd rather have you than Mr Mill.

MARCHBANKS (*recoiling*). No, really: I'm very sorry; but you mustnt think of that. I—

PROSERPINE (*testily, going to the fire-place and standing at it with her back to him*). Oh, dont be frightened: it's not you. It's not any one particular person.

MARCHBANKS. I know. You feel that you could love anybody that offered—

PROSERPINE (*turning, exasperated*). Anybody that offered! No, I do not. What do you take me for?

MARCHBANKS (*discouraged*). No use. You wont make me real answers: only those things that everybody says. (*He strays to the sofa and sits down disconsolately.*)

PROSERPINE (*nettled at what she takes to be a disparagement of her manners by an aristocrat*). Oh well, if you want original conversation, youd better go and talk to yourself.

MARCHBANKS. That is what all poets do: they talk to themselves but out loud; and the world overhears them. But it's horribly lonely not to hear someone else talk sometimes.

PROSERPINE. Wait until Mr Morell comes. *He'll* talk to you. (MARCHBANKS *shudders*) Oh, you neednt make wry faces over him: he can talk better than you. (*With temper*) He'd talk your little head off. (*She is going back angrily to her place, when he, suddenly enlightened, springs up and stops her.*)

MARCHBANKS. Ah! I understand now.

PROSERPINE (*reddening*). What do you understand?

MARCHBANKS. Your secret. Tell me: is it really and truly possible for a woman to love him?

PROSERPINE (*as if this were beyond all bounds*). Well!!

MARCHBANKS (*passionately*). No: answer me. I want to know: I *must* know. *I* can't understand it. I can see nothing in him but words, pious resolutions, what people call goodness. You cant love that.

PROSERPINE (*attempting to snub him by an air of cool propriety*). I simply dont know what youre talking about. I dont understand you.

MARCHBANKS (*vehemently*). You do. You lie.

PROSERPINE. Oh!

MARCHBANKS. You do understand; and you *know*. (*Determined to have an answer*) Is it possible for a woman to love him?

PROSERPINE (*looking him straight in the face*). Yes. (*He covers his face with his hands*) Whatever is the matter with you! (*He takes down his hands. Frightened at the tragic mask presented to her, she hurries past him at the utmost possible distance, keeping her eyes on his face until he turns from her and goes to the child's chair beside the hearth, where he sits in the deepest dejection. As she approaches the door, it opens and* BURGESS *enters. Seeing him, she ejaculates*) Praise heaven! here's somebody (*and feels safe enough to resume her place at her table. She puts a fresh sheet of paper into the typewriter as* Burgess *crosses to* Eugene).

Burgess (*bent on taking care of the distinguished visitor*). Well: so this is the way they leave you to yoreself, Mr Morchbanks. Ive come to keep you company. (Marchbanks *looks up at him in consternation, which is quite lost on him.*) James is receivin a deppitation in the dinin room; and Candy is hupstairs heducating of a young stitcher gurl she's hinterested in. (*Condolingly*) You must find it lonesome here with no one but the typist to talk to. (*He pulls round the easy chair, and sits down.*)

Proserpine (*highly incensed*). He'll be all right now that he has the advantage of *your* polished conversation: thats one comfort, anyhow. (*She begins to typewrite with clattering asperity.*)

Burgess (*amazed at her audacity*). Hi was not addressin myself to you, young woman, that I'm awerr of.

Proserpine. Did you ever see worse manners, Mr Marchbanks?

Burgess (*with pompous severity*). Mr Morchbanks is a gentleman, and knows his place, which is more than some people do.

Proserpine (*fretfully*). It's well you and I are not ladies and gentlemen: I'd talk to you pretty straight if Mr Marchbanks wasnt here. (*She pulls the letter out of the machine so crossly that it tears.*) There! now I've spoiled this letter! have to be done all over again! Oh, I cant contain myself: silly old fathead!

Burgess (*rising, breathless with indignation*). Ho! I'm a silly ole fat'ead, am I? Ho, indeed (*gasping*)! Hall right, my gurl! Hall right. You just wait till I tell that to yore hemployer. Youll see. I'll teach you: see if I dont.

Proserpine (*conscious of having gone too far*) I—

Burgess (*cutting her short*). No: youve done it now. No huse a-talkin to me. I'll let you know who I am. (Proserpine *shifts her paper carriage with a defiant bang, and disdainfully goes on with her work.*) Dont you take no notice of her, Mr Morchbanks. She's beneath it. (*He loftily sits down again.*)

Marchbanks (*miserably nervous and disconcerted*). Hadnt we better change the subject? I—I dont think Miss Garnett meant anything.

Proserpine (*with intense conviction*). Oh, didn't I though, *just!*

Burgess. I wouldnt demean myself to take notice on her.

(*An electric bell rings twice.*)

Proserpine (*gathering up her note-book and papers*). Thats for me. (*She hurries out.*)

Burgess (*calling after her*). Oh, we can spare you. (*Somewhat relieved by the triumph of having the last word, and yet half inclined to try to improve on it, he looks after her for a moment; then subsides into his seat by* Eugene, *and addresses him very confidentially*) Now we're alone, Mr Morchbanks, let me give you a friendly int that I wouldnt give to heverybody. Ow long ave you known my son-in-law James ere?

MARCHBANKS. I dont know. I never can remember dates. A few months, perhaps.

BURGESS. Ever notice hennythink queer about him?

MARCHBANKS. I dont think so.

BURGESS (*impressively*). No more you wouldnt. Thats the danger on it. Well, he's mad.

MARCHBANKS. Mad!

BURGESS. Mad as a Morch 'are. You take notice on him and youll see.

MARCHBANKS (*uneasily*). But surely that is only because his opinions—

BURGESS (*touching him on the knee with his forefinger, and pressing it to hold his attention*). Thats the same what I hused to think, Mr Morchbanks. Hi thought long enough that it was only his hopinions; though, mind you, hopinions becomes vurry serious things when people takes to hactin on em as e does. But thats not what I go on. (*He looks round to make sure that they are alone, and bends over to* EUGENE*'s ear*) What do you think he sez to me this mornin in this very room?

MARCHBANKS. What?

BURGESS. He sez to me—this is as sure as we're setting here now—he sez "I'm a fool," he sez; "and yore a scounderl." Me a scounderl, mind you! And then shook ands with me on it, as if it was to my credit! Do you mean to tell me as that man's sane?

MORELL (*outside, calling to* PROSERPINE *as he opens the door*). Get all their names and addresses, Miss Garnett.

PROSERPINE (*in the distance*). Yes, Mr Morell.

(MORELL *comes in, with the deputation's documents in his hands.*)

BURGESS (*aside to* MARCHBANKS). Yorr he is. Just keep your heye on im and see. (*Rising momentously*) I'm sorry, James, to ave to make a complaint to you. I dont want to do it; but I feel I oughter, as a matter o right and dooty.

MORELL. Whats the matter?

BURGESS. Mr Morchbanks will bear me hout: he was a witness. (*Very solemnly*) Yore young woman so far forgot herself as to call me a silly ole fat'ead.

MORELL (*with tremendous heartiness*). Oh, now, isnt that *exactly* like Prossy? She's so frank: she cant contain herself! Poor Prossy! Ha! ha!

BURGESS (*trembling with rage*). And do you hexpec me to put up with it from the like of er?

MORELL. Pooh, nonsense! you cant take any notice of it. Never mind. (*He goes to the cellaret and puts the papers into one of the drawers.*)

BURGESS. Oh, Hi dont mind. Hi'm above it. But is it *right?* thats what I want to know. Is it right?

MORELL. Thats a question for the Church, not for the laity. Has it done you any harm? thats the question for you, eh? Of course it hasnt. Think no more of it. (*He dismisses the subject by going to his place at the table and setting to work at his correspondence.*)

BURGESS (*aside to* MARCHBANKS). What did I tell you? Mad as a atter. (*He goes to the table and asks, with the sickly civility of a hungry man*) When's dinner, James?

MORELL. Not for a couple of hours yet.

BURGESS (*with plaintive resignation*). Gimme a nice book to read over the fire, will you, James: thur's a good chap.

MORELL. What sort of book? A good one?

BURGESS (*with almost a yell of remonstrance*). Nah-oo! Summat pleasant, just to pass the time. (MORELL *takes an illustrated paper from the table and offers it. He accepts it humbly*) Thank yer, James. (*He goes back to the big chair at the fire, and sits there at his ease, reading.*)

MORELL (*as he writes*). Candida will come to entertain you presently. She has got rid of her pupil. She is filling the lamps.

MARCHBANKS (*starting up in the wildest consternation*). But that will soil her hands. I cant bear that, Morell: it's a shame. I'll go and fill them. (*He makes for the door.*)

MORELL. Youd better not. (MARCHBANKS *stops irresolutely*) She'd only set you to clean my boots, to save me the trouble of doing it myself in the morning.

BURGESS (*with grave disapproval*). Dont you keep a servant now, James?

MORELL. Yes; but she isnt a slave; and the house looks as if I kept three. That means that everyone has to lend a hand. It's not a bad plan: Prossy and I can talk business after breakfast while we're washing up. Washing up's no trouble when there are two people to do it.

MARCHBANKS (*tormentedly*). Do you think every woman is as coarse-grained as Miss Garnett?

BURGESS (*emphatically*). Thats quite right, Mr Morchbanks: thats *quite* right. She *is* corsegrained.

MORELL (*quietly and significantly*). Marchbanks!

MARCHBANKS. Yes?

MORELL. How many servants does your father keep?

MARCHBANKS (*pettishly*). Oh, I dont know. (*He moves to the sofa, as if to get as far as possible from* MORELL'*s questioning, and sits down in great agony of spirit, thinking of the paraffin.*)

MORELL (*very gravely*). So many that you dont know! (*More aggressively*) When theres anything coarsegrained to be done, you just ring the bell and throw it on to somebody else, eh?

MARCHBANKS. Oh, dont torture me. You dont even ring the bell. But your wife's beautiful fingers are dabbling in paraffin oil while you sit here comfortably preaching about it: everlasting preaching! preaching! words! words! words!

BURGESS (*intensely appreciating this retort*). Har, har! Devil a better! (*Radiantly*) Ad you there, James, straight.

(CANDIDA *comes in, well aproned, with a reading lamp trimmed, filled, and ready for lighting. She places it on the table near* MORELL, *ready for use.*)

CANDIDA (*brushing her finger tips together with a slight twitch of her nose*). If you stay with us, Eugene, I think I will hand over the lamps to you.

MARCHBANKS. I will stay on condition that you hand over all the rough work to me.

CANDIDA. Thats very gallant; but I think I should like to see how you do it first. (*Turning to* MORELL) James: youve not been looking after the house properly.

MORELL. What have I done—or not done—my love?

CANDIDA (*with serious vexation*). My own particular pet scrubbing brush has been used for blackleading. (*A heart-breaking wail bursts from* MARCHBANKS. BURGESS *looks round, amazed.* CANDIDA *hurries to the sofa.*) Whats the matter? Are you ill, Eugene?

MARCHBANKS. No: not ill. Only horror! horror! horror! (*He bows his head on his hands.*)

BURGESS (*shocked*). What! Got the orrors, Mr Morchbanks! Oh, thats bad, at your age. You must leave it off grajally.

CANDIDA (*reassured*). Nonsense, papa! It's only poetic horror, isnt it, Eugene (*petting him*)?

BURGESS (*abashed*). Oh, poetic orror, is it? I beg your pordon, I'm shore (*He turns to the fire again, deprecating his hasty conclusion.*)

CANDIDA. What is it, Eugene? the scrubbing brush? (*He shudders*) Well, there! never mind. (*She sits down beside him.*) Wouldnt you like to present me with a nice new one, with an ivory back inlaid with mother-of-pearl?

MARCHBANKS (*softly and musically, but sadly and longingly*). No, not a scrubbing brush, but a boat: a tiny shallop to sail away in, far from the world, where the marble floors are washed by the rain and dried by the sun; where the south wind dusts the beautiful green and purple carpets. Or a chariot! to carry us up into the sky, where the lamps are stars, and dont need to be filled with paraffin oil every day.

MORELL (*harshly*). And where there is nothing to do but be idle, selfish, and useless.

CANDIDA (*jarred*). Oh, James! how could you spoil it all?

MARCHBANKS (*firing up*). Yes, to be idle, selfish, and useless: that is, to be beautiful and free and happy: hasnt every man desired that with all his soul for the woman he loves? Thats my ideal: whats yours, and that of all the dreadful people who live in these hideous rows of houses? Sermons and scrubbing brushes! With you to preach the sermon and your wife to scrub.

CANDIDA (*quaintly*). He cleans the boots, Eugene. You will have to clean them to-morrow for saying that about him.

MARCHBANKS. Oh, dont talk about boots! Your feet should be beautiful on the mountains.

CANDIDA. My feet would not be beautiful on the Hackney Road without boots.

BURGESS (*scandalized*). Come, Candy! dont be vulgar. Mr Morchbanks aint accustomed to it. Youre giving him the orrors again. I mean the poetic ones.

(MORELL *is silent. Apparently he is busy with his letters: really he is puzzling with misgiving over his new and alarming experience that the surer he is of his moral thrusts, the more swiftly and effectively* EUGENE *parries them. To find himself beginning to fear a man whom he does not respect afflicts him bitterly.*)

(MISS GARNETT *comes in with a telegram.*)

PROSERPINE (*handing the telegram to* MORELL). Reply paid. The boy's waiting. (*To* CANDIDA, *coming back to her machine and sitting down*) Maria is ready for you now in the kitchen, Mrs Morell. (CANDIDA *rises.*) The onions have come.

MARCHBANKS (*convulsively*). Onions!

CANDIDA. Yes, onions. Not even Spanish ones: nasty little red onions. You shall help me to slice them. Come along.

(*She catches him by the wrist and runs out, pulling him after her.* BURGESS *rises in consternation, and stands aghast on the hearth-rug, staring after them.*)

BURGESS. Candy didnt oughter andle a hearl's nevvy like that. It's goin too fur with it. Lookee ere, James: do e often git taken queer like that?

MORELL (*shortly, writing a telegram*). I dont know.

BURGESS (*sentimentally*). He talks very pretty. I awlus had a turn for a bit of poetry. Candy takes arter me that-a-way. Huseter make me tell er fairy stories when she was ony a little kiddy not that igh (*indicating a stature of two feet or thereabouts*).

MORELL (*preoccupied*). Ah, indeed. (*He blots the telegram and goes out.*)

PROSERPINE. Used you to make the fairy stories up out of your own head?

(BURGESS, *not deigning to reply, strikes an attitude of the haughtiest disdain on the hearth-rug.*)

PROSERPINE (*calmly*). I should never have supposed you had it in you. By the way, I'd better warn you, since youve taken such a fancy to Mr Marchbanks. He's mad.

BURGESS. Mad! What! Im too!!

PROSERPINE. Mad as a March hare. He did frighten me, I can tell you, just before you came in that time. Havnt you noticed the queer things he says?

BURGESS. So thats what the poetic orrors means. Blame me if it didnt come into my ed once or twyst that he was a bit horff 'is chump! (*He crosses the room to the door, lifting up his voice as he goes.*) Well, this is a pretty sort of asylum for a man to be in, with no one but you to take care of him!

PROSERPINE (*as he passes her*). Yes, what a dreadful thing it would be if anything happened to *you!*

BURGESS (*loftily*). Dont you haddress no remorks to me. Tell your hemployer that Ive gone into the gorden for a smoke.

PROSERPINE (*mocking*). Oh!

(*Before* BURGESS *can retort,* MORELL *comes back.*)

BURGESS (*sentimentally*). Goin for a turn in the gording to smoke, James.

MORELL (*brusquely*). Oh, all right, all right. (BURGESS *goes out pathetically in the character of a weary old man.* MORELL *stands at the table, turning over his papers, and adding, across to* PROSERPINE, *half humorously, half absently*) Well, Miss Prossy, why have you been calling my father-in-law names?

PROSERPINE (*blushing fiery red, and looking quickly up at him, half scared, half reproachful*). I—(*She bursts into tears.*)

MORELL (*with tender gaiety, leaning across the table towards her, and consoling her*). Oh, come! come! come! Never mind, Pross: he *is* a silly old fathead, isn't he?

(*With an explosive sob, she makes a dash at the door, and vanishes, banging it.* MORELL, *shaking his head resignedly, sighs, and goes wearily to his chair, where he sits down and sets to work, looking old and careworn.*

(CANDIDA *comes in. She has finished her household work and taken off the apron. She at once notices his dejected appearance, and posts herself quietly at the visitors' chair, looking down at him attentively. She says nothing.*)

MORELL (*looking up, but with his pen raised ready to resume his work*). Well? Where is Eugene?

CANDIDA. Washing his hands in the scullery under the tap. He will make an excellent cook if he can only get over his dread of Maria.

MORELL (*shortly*). Ha! No doubt. (*He begins writing again.*)

CANDIDA (*going nearer, and putting her hand down softly on his to stop him as she says*). Come here, dear. Let me look at you. (*He drops his pen and yields himself to her disposal. She makes him rise, and brings him a little away from the table, looking at him critically all the time.*) Turn your face to the light. (*She places him facing the window*) My boy is not well. Has he been overworking?

MORELL. Nothing more than usual.

CANDIDA. He looks very pale, and grey, and wrinkled, and old. (*His melancholy deepens; and she attacks it with wilful gaiety*) Here: (*pulling him towards the easy chair*) youve done enough writing for to-day. Leave Prossy to finish it. Come and talk to me.

MORELL. But—

CANDIDA (*insisting*). Yes, I *must* be talked to. (*She makes him sit down, and seats herself on the carpet beside his knee*) Now (*patting his hand*) youre beginning to look better already. Why must you go out every night lecturing and talking? I hardly have one evening a week with you. Of course what you say is all very true; but it does no good: they dont mind what you say to them one little bit. They think they agree with you; but whats the use of their agreeing with you if they go and do just the opposite of what you tell them the moment your back is turned? Look at our congregation at St Dominic's! Why do they come to hear you talking about Christianity every Sunday? Why, just because theyve been so full of business and money-making for six days that they want to forget all about it and have a rest on the seventh; so that they can go back fresh and make money harder than ever! You positively help them at it instead of hindering them.

MORELL (*with energetic seriousness*). You know very well, Candida, that I often blow them up soundly for that. And if there is nothing in their churchgoing but rest and diversion, why dont they try something more amusing? more self-indulgent? There must be some good in the fact that they prefer St Dominic's to worse places on Sundays.

CANDIDA. Oh, the worse places arnt open; and even if they were, they darent be seen going to them. Besides, James dear, you preach so splendidly that it's as good as a play for them. Why do you think the women are so enthusiastic?

MORELL (*shocked*). Candida!

CANDIDA. Oh, *I* know. You silly boy: you think it's your Socialism and your religion; but if it were that, theyd do what you tell them instead of only coming to look at you. They all have Prossy's complaint.

MORELL. Prossy's complaint! What do you mean, Candida?

CANDIDA. Yes, Prossy, and all the other secretaries you ever had. Why does Prossy condescend to wash up the things, and to peel potatoes and abase herself in all manner of ways for six shillings a week less than she used to get in a city office? She's in love with you, James: thats the reason. Theyre all in love with you. And you are in love with preaching because you do it so beautifully. And you think it's all enthusiasm for the kingdom of Heaven on earth; and so do they. You dear silly!

MORELL. Candida: what dreadful! what soul-destroying cynicism! Are you jesting? Or—can it be?—are you jealous?

CANDIDA (*with curious thoughtfulness*). Yes, I feel a little jealous sometimes.

MORELL (*incredulously*). Of Prossy?

CANDIDA (*laughing*). No, no, no, no. Not jealous *of* anybody. Jealous *for* somebody else, who is not loved as he ought to be.

MORELL. Me?

CANDIDA. You! Why, youre spoiled with love and worship: you get far more than is good for you. No: I mean Eugene.

MORELL (*startled*). Eugene!

CANDIDA. It seems unfair that all the love should go to you, and none to him; although he needs it so much more than you do. (*A convulsive movement shakes him in spite of himself.*) Whats the matter? Am I worrying you?

MORELL (*hastily*). Not at all. (*Looking at her with troubled intensity*) You know that I have perfect confidence in you, Candida.

CANDIDA. You vain thing! Are you so sure of your irresistible attractions?

MORELL. Candida; you are shocking me. I never thought of my attractions. I thought of your goodness, of your purity. That is what I confide in.

CANDIDA. What a nasty uncomfortable thing to say to me! Oh, you are a clergyman, James: a thorough clergyman!

MORELL (*turning away from her, heart-stricken*). So Eugene says.

CANDIDA (*with lively interest, leaning over to him with her arms on his knee*). Eugene's always right. He's a wonderful boy: I have grown fonder and fonder of him all the time I was away. Do you know, James, that though he has not the least suspicion of it himself, he is ready to fall madly in love with me?

MORELL (*grimly*). Oh, he has no suspicion of it himself, hasnt he?

CANDIDA. Not a bit. (*She takes her arms from his knee, and turns thoughtfully, sinking into a more restful attitude with her hands in her lap*) Some day he will know: when he is grown up and experienced, like you. And he will know that I must have known. I wonder what he will think of me then.

MORELL. No evil, Candida. I hope and trust, no evil.

CANDIDA (*dubiously*). That will depend.

MORELL (*bewildered*). Depend!

CANDIDA (*looking at him*). Yes: it will depend on what happens to him. (*He looks vacantly at her.*) Dont you see? It will depend on how he comes to learn what love really is. I mean on the sort of woman who will teach it to him.

MORELL (*quite at a loss*). Yes. No. I dont know what you mean.

CANDIDA (*explaining*). If he learns it from a good woman, then it will be all right: he will forgive me.

MORELL. Forgive?

CANDIDA. But suppose he learns it from a bad woman, as so many men do, especially poetic men, who imagine all women are angels! Suppose he only discovers the value of love when he has thrown it away and degraded himself in his ignorance! Will he forgive me then, do you think?

MORELL. Forgive you for what?

CANDIDA (*realizing how stupid he is, and a little disappointed, though quite tenderly so*). Dont you understand? (*He shakes his head. She turns to him again, so as to explain with the fondest intimacy*) I mean, will he forgive me for not teaching him myself? For abandoning him to the bad women for the sake of my goodness, of my purity, as you call it? Ah, James, how little you understand me, to talk of your confidence in my goodness and purity! I would give them both to poor Eugene as willingly as I would give my shawl to a beggar dying of cold, if there were nothing else to restrain me. Put your trust in my love for you, James; for if that went, I should care very little for your sermons: mere phrases that you cheat yourself and others with every day. (*She is about to rise.*)

MORELL. *His* words!

CANDIDA (*checking herself quickly in the act of getting up*). Whose words?

MORELL. Eugene's.

CANDIDA (*delighted*). He is always right. He understands you; he understands me; he understands Prossy; and you, darling, you understand nothing. (*She laughs, and kisses him to console him. He recoils as if stabbed, and springs up.*)

MORELL. How can you bear to do that when—Oh, Candida (*with anguish in his voice*) I had rather you had plunged a grappling iron into my heart than given me that kiss.

CANDIDA (*amazed*). My dear: whats the matter?

MORELL (*frantically waving her off*). Dont touch me.

CANDIDA. James!!!

(*They are interrupted by the entrance of* MARCHBANKS *with* BURGESS, *who stop near the door, staring.*)

MARCHBANKS (*aside to her*). It is your cruelty. I hate cruelty. It is a horrible thing to see one person make another suffer.

CANDIDA (*petting him ironically*). Poor boy! have I been cruel? Did I make it slice nasty little red onions?

MARCHBANKS (*earnestly*). Oh, stop, stop: I dont mean myself. You have made him suffer frightfully. I feel his pain in my own heart. I know that it is not your fault: it is something that must happen; but dont make light of it. I shudder when you torture him and laugh.

CANDIDA (*incredulously*). *I* torture James! Nonsense, Eugene: how you exaggerate! Silly! (*She rises and goes to the table, a little troubled*) Dont work any more, dear. Come and talk to us.

MORELL (*affectionately but bitterly*). Ah no: *I* cant talk. I can only preach.

CANDIDA (*caressing his hand*). Well, come and preach.

BURGESS (*strongly remonstrating*). Aw no, Candy. 'Ang it all!

(LEXY MILL *comes in, anxious and important.*)

LEXY (*hastening to shake hands with* CANDIDA). How do you do, Mrs Morell? So glad to see you back again.

CANDIDA. Thank you, Lexy. You know Eugene, dont you?

LEXY. Oh yes. How do you do, Marchbanks?

MARCHBANKS. Quite well, thanks.

LEXY (*to* MORELL). Ive just come from the Guild of St Matthew. They are in the greatest consternation about your telegram.

CANDIDA. What did you telegraph about, James?

LEXY (*to* CANDIDA). He was to have spoken for them tonight. Theyve taken the large hall in Mare Street and spent a lot of money on posters. Morell's telegram was to say he couldnt come. It came on them like a thunderbolt.

CANDIDA (*surprised, and beginning to suspect something wrong*). Given up an engagement to speak!

MARCHBANKS. Is anything the matter?

MORELL (*deadly white, putting an iron constraint on himself*). Nothing but this: that either you were right this morning, or Candida is mad.

BURGESS (*in loudest protest*). What! Candy mad too! Oh, come! come! come! (*He crosses the room to the fireplace, protesting as he goes, and knocks the ashes out of his pipe on the bars.*)

(MORELL *sits down at his table desperately, leaning forward to hide his face, and interlacing his fingers rigidly to keep them steady.*)

CANDIDA (*to* MORELL, *relieved and laughing*). Oh, youre only shocked! Is that all? How conventional all you unconventional people are! (*She sits gaily on the arm of the chair.*)

BURGESS. Come: be'ave yourself, Candy. Whatll Mr Morchbanks think of you?

CANDIDA. This comes of James teaching me to think for myself, and never to hold back out of fear of what other people may think of me. It works beautifully as long as I think the same things as he does. But now! because I have just thought something different! look at him! Just look! (*She points to* MORELL, *greatly amused.*)

(EUGENE *looks, and instantly presses his hand on his heart, as if some pain had shot through it. He sits down on the sofa like a man witnessing a tragedy.*)

BURGESS (*on the hearth-rug*). Well, James, you certnly haint as himpressive lookin as usu'l.

MORELL (*with a laugh which is half a sob*). I suppose not. I beg all your pardons: I was not conscious of making a fuss. (*Pulling himself together*) Well, well, well, well, well! (*He sets to work at his papers again with resolute cheerfulness.*)

CANDIDA (*going to the sofa and sitting beside* MARCHBANKS, *still in a bantering humor*). Well, Eugene: why are you so sad. Did the onions make you cry?

BURGESS. Fust time in his life, I'll bet. Ain it, Candy?

LEXY (*to* MORELL). They decided to send an urgent telegram to you asking whether you could not change your mind. Have you received it?

MORELL (*with restrained impatience*). Yes, yes: I got it.

LEXY. It was reply paid.

MORELL. Yes, I know. I answered it. I cant go.

CANDIDA. But why, James?

MORELL (*almost fiercely*). Because I dont choose. These people forget that I am a man: they think I am a talking machine to be turned on for their pleasure every evening of my life. May I not have *one* night at home, with my wife, and my friends?

(*They are all amazed at this outburst, except* EUGENE. *His expression remains unchanged.*)

CANDIDA. Oh, James, you mustnt mind what I said about that. And if you dont go youll have an attack of bad conscience to-morrow.

LEXY (*intimidated, but urgent*). I know, of course, that they make the most unreasonable demands on you. But they have been telegraphing all over the place for another speaker; and they can get nobody but the President of the Agnostic League.

MORELL (*promptly*). Well, an excellent man. What better do they want?

LEXY. But he always insists so powerfully on the divorce of Socialism from Christianity. He will undo all the good we have been doing. Of course you know best; but—(*he shrugs his shoulders and wanders to the hearth beside* BURGESS).

CANDIDA (*coaxingly*). Oh, *do* go, James. We'll all go.

BURGESS (*grumblingly*). Look 'ere, Candy! I say! Let's stay at home by the fire, comfortable. He wont need to be more'n a couple-o-hour away.

CANDIDA. Youll be just as comfortable at the meeting. We'll all sit on the platform and be great people.

EUGENE (*terrified*). Oh please dont let us go on the platform. No: everyone will stare at us: I couldnt. I'll sit at the back of the room.

CANDIDA. Dont be afraid. Theyll be too busy looking at James to notice you.

MORELL. Prossy's complaint, Candida! Eh?

CANDIDA (*gaily*). Yes: Prossy's complaint.

BURGESS (*mystified*). Prossy's complaint! What are you talkin about, James?

MORELL (*not heeding him, rises; goes to the door; and holds it open, calling in a commanding tone*). Miss Garnett.

PROSERPINE (*in the distance*). Yes, Mr Morell. Coming.

(*They all wait, except* BURGESS, *who turns stealthily to* LEXY.)

BURGESS. Listen ere, Mr Mill. Whats Prossy's complaint? Whats wrong with er?

LEXY (*confidentially*). Well, I dont exactly know; but she spoke very strangely to me this morning. I'm afraid she's a little out of her mind sometimes.

BURGESS (*overwhelmed*). Why, it must be catchin! Four in the same ouse!

PROSERPINE (*appearing on the threshold*). What is it, Mr Morell?

MORELL. Telegraph to the Guild of St Matthew that I am coming.

PROSERPINE (*surprised*). Dont they expect you?

MORELL (*peremptorily*). Do as I tell you.

(PROSERPINE, *frightened, sits down at her typewriter, and obeys.* MORELL, *now unaccountably resolute and forceful, goes across to* BURGESS. CANDIDA *watches his movements with growing wonder and misgiving.*)

MORELL. Burgess: you dont want to come.

BURGESS. Oh, dont put it like that, James. It's ony that it aint Sunday, you know.

MORELL. I'm sorry. I thought you might like to be introduced to the chairman. He's on the Works Committee of the County Council, and has some influence in the matter of contracts. (BURGESS *wakes up at once.*) Youll come?

BURGESS (*with enthusiasm*). Cawrse I'll come, James. Aint it awlus a pleasure to ear you!

MORELL (*turning to* PROSSY). I shall want you to take some notes at the meeting, Miss Garnett, if you have no other engagement. (*She nods, afraid to speak.*) You are coming, Lexy, I suppose?

LEXY. Certainly.

CANDIDA. We're all coming, James.

MORELL. No: you are not coming; and Eugene is not coming. You will stay here and entertain him—to celebrate your return home. (EUGENE *rises, breathless.*)

CANDIDA. But, James—

MORELL (*authoritatively*). I insist. You do not want to come; and he does not want to come. (CANDIDA *is about to protest.*) Oh, dont concern yourselves: I shall have plenty of people without you: your chairs will be wanted by unconverted people who have never heard me before.

CANDIDA (*troubled*). Eugene: wouldnt you like to come?

MORELL. I should be afraid to let myself go before Eugene: he is so critical of sermons. (*Looking at him*) He knows I am afraid of him: he told me as much this morning. Well, I shall shew him how much afraid I am by leaving him here in your custody, Candida.

MARCHBANKS (*to himself, with vivid feeling*). Thats brave. Thats beautiful.

CANDIDA (*with anxious misgiving*). But—but—Is anything the matter, James? (*Greatly troubled*) I cant understand—

MORELL (*taking her tenderly in his arms and kissing her on the forehead*). Ah, I thought it was *I* who couldnt understand, dear.

ACT III

Past ten in the evening. The curtains are drawn, and the lamps lighted. The typewriter is in its case: the large table has been cleared and tidied: everything indicates that the day's work is over.

CANDIDA *and* MARCHBANKS *are sitting by the fire. The reading lamp is on the mantelshelf above* MARCHBANKS, *who is in the small chair, reading aloud. A little pile of manuscripts and a couple of volumes of poetry are on the carpet beside him.* CANDIDA *is in the easy chair. The poker, a light brass one, is upright in her hand. Leaning back and looking intently at the point of it, with her feet stretched towards the blaze, she is in a waking dream, miles away from her surroundings and completely oblivious of Eugene.*

MARCHBANKS (*breaking off in his recitation*). Every poet that ever lived has put that thought into a sonnet. He must: he cant help it. (*He looks to her for assent, and notices her absorption in the poker*) Havnt you been listening? (*No response*) Mrs Morell!

CANDIDA (*starting*). Eh?

MARCHBANKS. Havnt you been listening?

CANDIDA (*with a guilty excess of politeness*). Oh yes. It's very nice. Go on, Eugene. I'm longing to hear what happens to the angel.

MARCHBANKS (*letting the manuscript drop from his hand to the floor*). I beg your pardon for boring you.

CANDIDA. But you are not boring me, I assure you. *Please* go on. Do, Eugene.

MARCHBANKS. I finished the poem about the angel quarter of an hour ago. Ive read you several things since.

CANDIDA (*remorsefully*). I'm so sorry, Eugene. I think the poker must have hypnotized me. (*She puts it down.*)

MARCHBANKS. It made me horribly uneasy.

CANDIDA. Why didnt you tell me? I'd have put it down at once.

MARCHBANKS. I was afraid of making you uneasy too. It looked as if it were a weapon. If I were a hero of old I should have laid my drawn sword between us. If Morell had come in he would have thought you had taken up the poker because there was no sword between us.

CANDIDA (*wondering*). What? (*With a puzzled glance at him*) I cant quite follow that. Those sonnets of yours have perfectly addled me. Why should there be a sword between us?

MARCHBANKS (*evasively*). Oh, never mind. (*He stoops to pick up the manuscript.*)

CANDIDA. Put that down again, Eugene. There are limits to my appetite for poetry: even your poetry. Youve been reading to me for more than two hours, ever since James went out. I want to talk.

MARCHBANKS (*rising, scared*). No: I mustnt talk. (*He looks round him in his lost way, and adds, suddenly*) I think I'll go out and take a walk in the park. (*He makes for the door.*)

CANDIDA. Nonsense: it's closed long ago. Come and sit down on the hearth-rug, and talk moonshine as you usually do. I want to be amused. Dont you want to?

MARCHBANKS (*half in terror, half enraptured*). Yes.

CANDIDA. Then come along. (*She moves her chair back a little to make room.*)

(*He hesitates; then timidly stretches himself on the hearth-rug, face upwards, and throws back his head across her knees, looking up at her.*)

MARCHBANKS. Oh, Ive been so miserable all the evening, because I was doing right. Now I'm doing wrong; and I'm happy.

CANDIDA (*tenderly amused at him*). Yes: I'm sure you feel a great grown-up wicked deceiver. Quite proud of yourself, arnt you?

MARCHBANKS (*raising his head quickly and turning a little to look round at her*). Take care. I'm ever so much older than you, if you only knew. (*He turns quite over on his knees, with his hands clasped and his arms on her lap, and speaks with growing impulse, his blood beginning to stir.*) May I say some wicked things to you?

CANDIDA (*without the least fear or coldness, and with perfect respect for his passion, but with a touch of her wise-hearted maternal humor*). No. But you may say anything you really and truly feel. Anything at all, no matter what it is. I am not afraid, so long as it is your real self that speaks, and not a mere attitude: a gallant attitude, or a wicked attitude, or even a poetic attitude. I put you on your honor and truth. Now say whatever you want to.

MARCHBANKS (*the eager expression vanishing utterly from his lips and nostrils as his eyes light up with pathetic spirituality*). Oh, now I cant say anything: all the words I know belong to some attitude or other—all except one.

CANDIDA. What one is that?

MARCHBANKS (*softly, losing himself in the music of the name*). Candida, Candida, Candida, Candida, Candida. I must say that now, because you have put me on my honor and truth; and I never think or feel Mrs Morell: it is always Candida.

CANDIDA. Of course. And what have you to say to Candida?

MARCHBANKS. Nothing but to repeat your name a thousand times. Dont you feel that every time is a prayer to you?

CANDIDA. Doesnt it make you happy to be able to pray?

MARCHBANKS. Yes, very happy.

CANDIDA. Well, that happiness is the answer to your prayer. Do you want anything more?

MARCHBANKS. No: I have come into heaven, where want is unknown.

(MORELL *comes in. He halts on the threshold, and takes in the scene at a glance.*)

MORELL (*grave and self-contained*). I hope I dont disturb you.

(CANDIDA *starts up violently, but without the smallest embarrassment, laughing at herself.* EUGENE, *capsized by her sudden movement, recovers himself without rising, and sits on the rug hugging his ankles, also quite unembarrassed.*)

CANDIDA. Oh, James how you startled me! I was so taken up with Eugene that I didnt hear your latchkey. How did the meeting go off? Did you speak well?

MORELL. I have never spoken better in my life.

CANDIDA. That was first rate! How much was the collection?

MORELL. I forgot to ask.

CANDIDA (*to* EUGENE). He must have spoken splendidly, or he would never have forgotten that. (*To* MORELL) Where are all the others?

MORELL. They left long before I could get away: I thought I should never escape. I believe they are having supper somewhere.

CANDIDA (*in her domestic business tone*). Oh, in that case, Maria may go to bed. I'll tell her. (*She goes out to the kitchen.*)

MORELL (*looking sternly down at* MARCHBANKS). Well?

MARCHBANKS (*squatting grotesquely on the hearth-rug, and actually at ease with* MORELL: *even impishly humorous*). Well?

MORELL. Have you anything to tell me?

MARCHBANKS. Only that I have been making a fool of myself here in private whilst you have been making a fool of yourself in public.

MORELL. Hardly in the same way, I think.

MARCHBANKS (*eagerly, scrambling up*). The very, very *very* same way. I have been playing the Good Man. Just like you. When you began your heroics about leaving me here with Candida—

MORELL (*involuntarily*). Candida!

MARCHBANKS. Oh yes: Ive got that far. But dont be afraid. Heroics are infectious: I caught the disease from you. I swore not to say a word in your absence that I would not have said a month ago in your presence.

MORELL. Did you keep your oath?

MARCHBANKS (*suddenly perching himself on the back of the easy chair*). It kept itself somehow until about ten minutes ago. Up to that moment I went on desperately reading to her—reading my own poems—anybody's poems—to stave off a conversation. I was standing outside the gate of Heaven, and refusing to go in. Oh, you cant think how heroic it was, and how uncomfortable! Then—

MORELL (*steadily controlling his suspense*). Then?

MARCHBANKS (*prosaically slipping down into a quite ordinary attitude on the seat of the chair*). Then she couldnt bear being read to any longer.

MORELL. And you approached the gate of Heaven at last?

MARCHBANKS. Yes.

MORELL. Well? (*Fiercely*) Speak, man: have you no feeling for me?

MARCHBANKS (*softly and musically*). Then she became an angel; and there was a flaming sword that turned every way, so that I couldnt go in; for I saw that gate was really the gate of Hell.

MORELL (*triumphantly*). She repulsed you!

MARCHBANKS (*rising in wild scorn*). No, you fool: if she had done that I should never have seen that I was in Heaven already. Repulsed me! You think that would have saved us! virtuous indignation! Oh, you are not worthy to live in the same world with her. (*He turns away contemptuously to the other side of the room.*)

MORELL (*who has watched him quietly without changing his place*). Do you think you make yourself more worthy by reviling me, Eugene?

MARCHBANKS. Here endeth the thousand and first lesson. Morell: I dont think much of your preaching after all: I believe I could do it better myself. The man I want to meet is the man that Candida married.

MORELL. The man that—? Do you mean me?

MARCHBANKS. I dont mean the Reverend James Mavor Morell, moralist and windbag. I mean the real man that the Reverend James must have hidden somewhere inside his black coat: the man that Candida loved. You cant make a woman like Candida love you by merely buttoning your collar at the back instead of in front.

MORELL (*boldly and steadily*). When Candida promised to marry me,

I was the same moralist and windbag you now see. I wore my black coat; and my collar was buttoned behind instead of in front. Do you think she would have loved me any the better for being insincere in my profession?

MARCHBANKS (*on the sofa, hugging his ankles*). Oh, she forgave you, just as she forgives me for being a coward, and a weakling, and what you call a snivelling little whelp and all the rest of it. (*Dreamily*) A woman like that has divine insight: she loves our souls, and not our follies and vanities and illusions, nor our collars and coats, nor any other of the rags and tatters we are rolled up in. (*He reflects on this for an instant; then turns intently to question* MORELL) What I want to know is how you got past the flaming sword that stopped me.

MORELL. Perhaps because I was not interrupted at the end of ten minutes.

MARCHBANKS (*taken aback*). What!

MORELL. Man can climb to the highest summits; but he cannot dwell there long.

MARCHBANKS (*springing up*). It's false: there can he dwell for ever, and there only. It's in the other moments that he can find no rest, no sense of the silent glory of life. Where would you have me spend my moments, if not on the summits?

MORELL. In the scullery, slicing onions and filling lamps.

MARCHBANKS. Or in the pulpit, scrubbing cheap earthenware souls?

MORELL. Yes, that too. It was there that I earned my golden moment, and the right, in that moment, to ask her to love me. *I* did not take the moment on credit; nor did I use it to steal another man's happiness.

MARCHBANKS (*rather disgustedly, trotting back towards the fireplace*). I have no doubt you conducted the transaction as honestly as if you were buying a pound of cheese. (*He stops on the brink of the hearth-rug, and adds, thoughtfully, to himself, with his back turned to* MORELL) I could only go to her as a beggar.

MORELL (*starting*). A beggar dying of cold! asking for her shawl!

MARCHBANKS (*turning, surprised*). Thank you for touching up my poetry. Yes, if you like: a beggar dying of cold, asking for her shawl.

MORELL (*excitedly*). And she refused. Shall I tell you why she refused? I *can* tell you, on her own authority. It was because of—

MARCHBANKS. She didnt refuse.

MORELL. Not!

MARCHBANKS. She offered me all I chose to ask for: her shawl, her wings, the wreath of stars on her head, the lilies in her hand, the crescent moon beneath her feet—

MORELL (*seizing him*). Out with the truth, man: my wife is my wife: I want no more of your poetic fripperies. I know well that if I have lost her love and you have gained it, no law will bind her.

MARCHBANKS (*quaintly, without fear or resistance*). Catch me by the shirt collar, Morell: she will arrange it for me afterwards as she did this morning. (*With quiet rapture*) I shall feel her hands touch me.

MORELL. You young imp, do you know how dangerous it is to say that to me? Or (*with a sudden misgiving*) has something made you brave?

MARCHBANKS. I'm not afraid now. I disliked you before: that was why I shrank from your touch. But I saw today—when she tortured you—that you love her. Since then I have been your friend: you may strangle me if you like.

MORELL (*releasing him*). Eugene: if that is not a heartless lie—if you have a spark of human feeling left in you—will you tell me what has happened during my absence?

MARCHBANKS. What happened! Why, the flaming sword (MORELL *stamps with impatience*)—Well, in plain prose, I love her so exquisitely that I wanted nothing more than the happiness of being in such love. And before I had time to come down from the highest summits, *you* came in.

MORELL (*suffering deeply*). So it is still unsettled. Still the misery of doubt.

MARCHBANKS. Misery! I am the happiest of men. I desire nothing now but her happiness. (*In a passion of sentiment*) Oh, Morell, let us both give her up. Why should she have to choose between a wretched little nervous disease like me, and a pig-headed parson like you? Let us go on a pilgrimage, you to the east and I to the west, in search of a worthy lover for her: some beautiful archangel with purple wings—

MORELL. Some fiddlestick! Oh, if she is mad enough to leave me for you, who will protect her? who will help her? who will work for her? who will be a father to her children? (*He sits down distractedly on the sofa, with his elbows on his knees and his head propped on his clenched fists.*)

MARCHBANKS (*snapping his fingers wildly*). She does not ask those silly questions. It is she who wants somebody to protect, to help, to work for: somebody to give her children to protect, to help and to work for. Some grown up man who has become as a little child again. Oh, you fool, you fool, you triple fool! I am the man, Morell: I am the man. (*He dances about excitedly, crying*) You don't understand what a woman is. Send for her, Morell: send for her and let her choose between—(*The door opens and* CANDIDA *enters. He stops as if petrified.*)

CANDIDA (*amazed, on the threshold*). What on earth are you at, Eugene?

MARCHBANKS (*oddly*). James and I are having a preaching match; and he is getting the worst of it.

(CANDIDA *looks quickly round at* MORELL. *Seeing that he is distressed, she hurries down to him, greatly vexed.*)

CANDIDA. You have been annoying him. Now I wont have it, Eugene: do you hear? (*She puts her hand on* MORELL*'s shoulder, and quite forgets* *her wifely tact in her anger*) My boy shall not be worried: I will protect him.

MORELL (*rising proudly*). Protect!

CANDIDA (*not heeding him: to* EUGENE). What have you been saying?

MARCHBANKS (*appalled*). Nothing. I—

CANDIDA. Eugene! Nothing?

MARCHBANKS (*piteously*). I mean—I—I'm very sorry. I wont do it again: indeed I wont. I'll let him alone.

MORELL (*indignantly, with an aggressive movement towards* EUGENE). Let me alone! You young—

CANDIDA (*stopping him*). Sh!—no: let me deal with him, James.

MARCHBANKS. Oh, youre not angry with me, are you?

CANDIDA (*severely*). Yes I am: very angry. I have a good mind to pack you out of the house.

MORELL (*taken aback by* CANDIDA'*s vigor, and by no means relishing the position of being rescued by her from another man*). Gently, Candida, gently. I am able to take care of myself.

CANDIDA (*petting him*). Yes, dear: of course you are. But you mustnt be annoyed and made miserable.

MARCHBANKS (*almost in tears, turning to the door*). I'll go.

CANDIDA. Oh, you neednt go: I cant turn you out at this time of night. (*Vehemently*) Shame on you! For shame!

MARCHBANKS (*desperately*). But what have I done?

CANDIDA. I know what you have done: as well as if I had been here all the time. Oh, it was unworthy! You are like a child: you cannot hold your tongue.

MARCHBANKS. I would die ten times over sooner than give you a moment's pain.

CANDIDA (*with infinite contempt for this puerility*). Much good your dying would do me!

MORELL. Candida, my dear: this altercation is hardly quite seemly. It is a matter between two men; and I am the right person to settle it.

CANDIDA. Two men! Do you call that a man? (*To* EUGENE) You bad boy!

MARCHBANKS (*gathering a whimsically affectionate courage from the scolding*). If I am to be scolded like a boy, I must make a boy's excuse. He began it. And he's bigger than I am.

CANDIDA (*losing confidence a little as her concern for* MORELL'*s dignity takes the alarm*). That cant be true. (*To* MORELL) You didnt begin it, James, did you?

MORELL (*contemptuously*). No.

MARCHBANKS (*indignant*). Oh!

MORELL (*to* EUGENE). *You* began it: this morning. (CANDIDA, *instantly connecting this with his mysterious allusion in the afternoon to something told him by* EUGENE *in the morning, looks at him with quick suspicion.*

MORELL *proceeds, with the emphasis of offended superiority*) But your other point is true. I am certainly the bigger of the two, and, I hope, the stronger, Candida. So you had better leave the matter in my hands.

CANDIDA (*again soothing him*). Yes, dear; but—(*troubled*) I dont understand about this morning.

MORELL (*gently snubbing her*). You need not understand, my dear.

CANDIDA. But James, I (*the street bell rings*)—Oh bother! Here they all come. (*She goes out to let them in.*)

MARCHBANKS (*running to* MORELL). Oh, Morell, isnt it dreadful? She's angry with us: she hates me. What shall I do?

MORELL (*with quaint desperation, walking up and down the middle of the room*). Eugene: my head is spinning round. I shall begin to laugh presently.

MARCHBANKS (*following him anxiously*). No, no: she'll think Ive thrown you into hysterics. Dont laugh.

(*Boisterous voices and laughter are heard approaching.* LEXY MILL, *his eyes sparkling, and his bearing denoting unwonted elevation of spirit, enters with* BURGESS, *who is greasy and self-complacent, but has all his wits about him.* MISS GARNETT, *with her smartest hat and jacket on, follows them; but though her eyes are brighter than before, she is evidently a prey to misgiving. She places herself with her back to her typewriting table, with one hand on it to steady herself, passing the other across her forehead as if she were a little tired and giddy.* MARCHBANKS *relapses into shyness and edges away into the corner near the window, where* MORELL'*s books are.*)

LEXY (*exhilarated*). Morell: I *must* congratulate you. (*Grasping his hand*) What a noble, splendid, inspired address you gave us! You surpassed yourself.

BURGESS. So you did, James. It fair kep me awake to the lars' word. Didnt it, Miss Gornett?

PROSERPINE (*worriedly*). Oh, I wasnt minding you: I was trying to make notes. (*She takes out her note-book, and looks at her stenography, which nearly makes her cry.*)

MORELL. Did I go too fast, Pross?

PROSERPINE. Much too fast. You know I cant do more than ninety words a minute. (*She relieves her feelings by throwing her note-book angrily beside her machine, ready for use next morning.*)

MORELL (*soothingly*). Oh well, well, never mind, never mind, never mind. Have you all had supper?

LEXY. Mr Burgess has been kind enough to give us a really splendid supper at the Belgrave.

BURGESS (*with effusive magnanimity*). Dont mention it, Mr Mill. (*Modestly*) Youre arty welcome to my little treat.

PROSERPINE. We had champagne. I never tasted it before. I feel quite giddy.

MORELL (*surprised*). A champagne supper! That was very handsome. Was it my eloquence that produced all this extravagance?

LEXY (*rhetorically*). Your eloquence, and Mr Burgess's goodness of heart. (*With a fresh burst of exhilaration*) And what a very fine fellow the chairman is, Morell! He came to supper with us.

MORELL (*with long drawn significance, looking at* BURGESS). O-o-o-h! the chairman. *Now* I understand.

(BURGESS *covers with a deprecatory cough a lively satisfaction with his own diplomatic cunning.* LEXY *folds his arms and leans against the head of the sofa in a high-spirited attitude after nearly losing his balance.* CANDIDA *comes in with glasses, lemons, and a jug of hot water on a tray.*)

CANDIDA. Who will have some lemonade? You know our rules: total abstinence. (*She puts the tray on the table, and takes up the lemon squeezer, looking enquiringly round at them.*)

MORELL. No use, dear. Theyve all had champagne. Pross has broken her pledge.

CANDIDA (*to* PROSERPINE). You dont mean to say youve been drinking champagne!

PROSERPINE (*stubbornly*). Yes I do. I'm only a beer teetotaller, not a champagne teetotaller. I don't like beer. Are there any letters for me to answer, Mr Morell?

MORELL. No more to-night.

PROSERPINE. Very well. Goodnight, everybody.

LEXY (*gallantly*). Had I not better see you home, Miss Garnett?

PROSERPINE. No thank you. I shant trust myself with anybody tonight. I wish I hadnt taken any of that stuff. (*She takes uncertain aim at the door; dashes at it; and barely escapes without disaster.*)

BURGESS (*indignantly*). Stuff indeed! That girl dunno what champagne is! Pommery and Greeno at twelve and six a bottle. She took two glasses amost straight horff.

MORELL (*anxious about her*). Go and look after her, Lexy.

LEXY (*alarmed*). But if she should really be—Suppose she began to sing in the street, or anything of that sort.

MORELL. Just so: she may. Thats why youd better see her safely home.

CANDIDA. Do, Lexy: theres a good fellow. (*She shakes his hand and pushes him gently to the door.*)

LEXY. It's evidently my duty to go. I hope it may not be necessary. Goodnight, Mrs Morell. (*To the rest*) Goodnight. (*He goes.* CANDIDA *shuts the door.*)

BURGESS. He was gushin with hextra piety hisself arter two sips. People carnt drink like they huseter. (*Bustling across to the hearth*) Well, James: it's time to lock up. Mr Morchbanks: shall I ave the pleasure of your company for a bit o the way ome?

MARCHBANKS (*affrightedly*). Yes: I'd better go. (*He hurries towards the door; but* CANDIDA *places herself before it, barring his way.*)

CANDIDA (*with quiet authority*). You sit down. Youre not going yet.

MARCHBANKS (*quailing*). No: I—I didnt mean to. (*He sits down abjectly on the sofa.*)

CANDIDA. Mr Marchbanks will stay the night with us, papa.

BURGESS. Oh well, I'll say goodnight. So long, James. (*He shakes hands with* MORELL, *and goes over to* EUGENE) Make em give you a night-light by your bed, Mr Morchbanks: itll comfort you if you wake up in the night with a touch of that complaint of yores. Goodnight.

MARCHBANKS. Thank you: I will. Goodnight, Mr. Burgess. (*They shake hands.* BURGESS *goes to the door.*)

CANDIDA (*intercepting* MORELL, *who is following* BURGESS). Stay here, dear: I'll put on papa's coat for him. (*She goes out with* BURGESS.)

MARCHBANKS (*rising and stealing over to* MORELL). Morell: theres going to be a terrible scene. Arnt you afraid?

MORELL. Not in the least.

MARCHBANKS. I never envied you your courage before. (*He puts his hand appealingly on* MORELL'S *forearm*) Stand by me, wont you?

MORELL (*casting him off resolutely*). Each for himself, Eugene. She must choose between us now.

(CANDIDA *returns.* EUGENE *creeps back to the sofa like a guilty schoolboy.*)

CANDIDA (*between them, addressing* EUGENE). Are you sorry?

MARCHBANKS (*earnestly*). Yes. Heartbroken.

CANDIDA. Well then, you are forgiven. Now go off to bed like a good little boy: I want to talk to James about you.

MARCHBANKS (*rising in great consternation*). Oh, I cant do that, Morell. I must be here. I'll not go away. Tell her.

CANDIDA (*her suspicions confirmed*). Tell me what? (*His eyes avoid hers furtively. She turns and mutely transfers the question to* MORELL.)

MORELL (*bracing himself for the catastrophe*). I have nothing to tell her, except (*here his voice deepens to a measured and mournful tenderness*) that she is my greatest treasure on earth—if she is really mine.

CANDIDA (*coldly, offended by his yielding to his orator's instinct and treating her as if she were the audience at the Guild of St Matthew*). I am sure Eugene can say no less, if that is all.

MARCHBANKS (*discouraged*). Morell: she's laughing at us.

MORELL (*with a quick touch of temper*). There is nothing to laugh at. Are you laughing at us, Candida?

CANDIDA (*with quiet anger*). Eugene is very quick-witted, James. I hope I am going to laugh; but I am not sure that I am not going to be very angry. (*She goes to the fireplace, and stands there leaning with her arms on the mantelpiece, and her foot on the fender, whilst* EUGENE *steals to* MORELL *and plucks him by the sleeve.*)

MARCHBANKS (*whispering*). Stop, Morell. Dont let us say anything.

MORELL (*pushing* EUGENE *away without deigning to look at him*). I hope you dont mean that as a threat, Candida.

CANDIDA (*with emphatic warning*). Take care, James. Eugene: I asked you to go. Are you going?

MORELL (*putting his foot down*). He shall not go. I wish him to remain.

MARCHBANKS. I'll go. I'll do whatever you want. (*He turns to the door.*)

CANDIDA. Stop! (*He obeys.*) Didnt you hear James say he wished you to stay? James is master here. Dont you know that?

MARCHBANKS (*flushing with a young poet's rage against tyranny*). By what right is he master?

CANDIDA (*quietly*). Tell him, James.

MORELL (*taken aback*). My dear: I dont know of any right that makes me master. I assert no such right.

CANDIDA (*with infinite reproach*). You dont know! Oh, James! James! (*To* EUGENE, *musingly*) I wonder do you understand, Eugene! (*He shakes his head helplessly, not daring to look at her.*) No: youre too young. Well, I give you leave to stay: to stay and learn. (*She comes away from the hearth and places herself between them*) Now, James! whats the matter? Come: tell me.

MARCHBANKS (*whispering tremulously across to him*). Dont.

CANDIDA. Come. Out with it!

MORELL (*slowly*). I meant to prepare your mind carefully, Candida, so as to prevent misunderstanding.

CANDIDA. Yes, dear: I am sure you did. But never mind: I shant misunderstand.

MORELL. Well—er— (*he hesitates, unable to find the long explanation which he supposed to be available*).

CANDIDA. Well?

MORELL (*blurting it out baldly*). Eugene declares that you are in love with him.

MARCHBANKS (*frantically*). No, no, no, no, never. I did not, Mrs Morell: it's not true. I said I loved you. I said I understood you, and that he couldnt. And it was not after what passed there before the fire that I spoke: it was not, on my word. It was this morning.

CANDIDA (*enlightened*). This morning!

MARCHBANKS. Yes. (*He looks at her, pleading for credence, and then adds simply*) That was what was the matter with my collar.

CANDIDA. Your collar? (*Suddenly taking in his meaning she turns to* MORELL, *shocked*) Oh, James: did you—(*she stops*)?

MORELL (*ashamed*). You know, Candida, that I have a temper to struggle with. And he said (*shuddering*) that you despised me in your heart.

CANDIDA (*turning quickly on* EUGENE). Did you say that?

MARCHBANKS (*terrified*). No.

CANDIDA (*almost fiercely*). Then James has just told me a falsehood. Is that what you mean?

MARCHBANKS. No, no: I—I—(*desperately*) it was David's wife. And it wasnt at home: it was when she saw him dancing before all the people.

MORELL (*taking the cue with a debater's adroitness*). Dancing before all the people, Candida; and thinking he was moving their hearts by his mission when they were only suffering from—Prossy's complaint. (*She is about to protest: he raises his hand to silence her*) Dont try to look indignant, Candida—

CANDIDA. Try!

MORELL (*continuing*). Eugene was right. As you told me a few hours after, he is always right. He said nothing that you did not say better yourself. He is the poet, who sees everything; and I am the poor parson, who understands nothing.

CANDIDA (*remorsefully*). Do you mind what is said by a foolish boy, because I said something like it in jest?

MORELL. That foolish boy can speak with the inspiration of a child and the cunning of a serpent. He has claimed that you belong to him and not to me; and, rightly or wrongly, I have come to fear that it may be true. I will not go about tortured with doubts and suspicions. I will not live with you and keep a secret from you. I will not suffer the intolerable degradation of jealousy. We have agreed—he and I—that you shall choose between us now. I await your decision.

CANDIDA (*slowly recoiling a step, her heart hardened by his rhetoric in spite of the sincere feeling behind it*). Oh! I am to choose, am I? I suppose it is quite settled that I must belong to one or the other.

MORELL (*firmly*). Quite. You must choose definitely.

MARCHBANKS (*anxiously*). Morell: you dont understand. She means that she belongs to herself.

CANDIDA (*turning on him*). I mean that, and a good deal more, Master Eugene, as you will both find out presently. And pray, my lords and masters, what have you to offer for my choice? I am up for auction, it seems. What do you bid, James?

MORELL (*reproachfully*). Cand—(*He breaks down: his eyes and throat fill with tears: the orator becomes a wounded animal*) I can't speak—

CANDIDA (*impulsively going to him*). Ah, dearest—

MARCHBANKS (*in wild alarm*). Stop: it's not fair. You mustnt shew her that you suffer, Morell. I am on the rack too; but I am not crying.

MORELL (*rallying all his forces*). Yes: you are right. It is not for pity that I am bidding. (*He disengages himself from* CANDIDA.)

CANDIDA (*retreating, chilled*). I beg your pardon, James: I did not mean to touch you. I am waiting to hear your bid.

MORELL (*with proud humility*). I have nothing to offer you but my strength for your defence, my honesty for your surety, my ability and industry for your livelihood, and my authority and position for your dignity. That is all it becomes a man to offer to a woman.

CANDIDA (*quite quietly*). And you, Eugene? What do you offer?

MARCHBANKS. My weakness. My desolation. My heart's need.

CANDIDA (*impressed*). Thats a good bid, Eugene. Now I know how to make my choice.

(*She pauses and looks curiously from one to the other, as if weighing them.* MORELL, *whose lofty confidence has changed into heartbreaking dread at* EUGENE'*s bid, loses all power of concealing his anxiety.* EUGENE, *strung to the highest tension, does not move a muscle.*)

MORELL (*in a suffocated voice: the appeal bursting from the depths of his anguish*). Candida!

MARCHBANKS (*aside, in a flash of contempt*). Coward!

CANDIDA (*significantly*). I give myself to the weaker of the two.

(EUGENE *divines her meaning at once: his face whitens like steel in a furnace.*)

MORELL (*bowing his head with the calm of collapse*). I accept your sentence, Candida.

CANDIDA. Do *you* understand, Eugene?

MARCHBANKS. Oh, I feel I'm lost. He cannot bear the burden.

MORELL (*incredulously, raising his head and voice with comic abruptness*). Do you mean *me*, Candida?

CANDIDA (*smiling a little*). Let us sit and talk comfortably over it like three friends. (*To* MORELL) Sit down, dear. (MORELL, *quite lost, takes the chair from the fireside: the children's chair.*) Bring me that chair, Eugene. (*She indicates the easy chair. He fetches it silently, even with something like cold strength, and places it next* MORELL, *a little behind him. She sits down. He takes the visitor's chair himself, and sits, inscrutable. When they are all settled she begins, throwing a spell of quietness on them by her calm, sane, tender tone*) You remember what you told me about yourself, Eugene: how nobody has cared for you since your old nurse died: how those clever fashionable sisters and successful brothers of yours were your mother's and father's pets: how miserable you were at Eton: how your father is trying to starve you into returning to Oxford: how you have had to live without comfort or welcome or refuge: always lonely, and nearly always disliked and misunderstood, poor boy!

MARCHBANKS (*faithful to the nobility of his lot*). I had my books. I had Nature. And at last I met you.

CANDIDA. Never mind that just at present. Now I want you to look at this other boy here: *my* boy! spoiled from his cradle. We go once a fortnight to see his parents. You should come with us, Eugene, to see the pictures of the hero of that household. James as a baby! the most wonderful of all babies. James holding his first school prize, won at the ripe age of eight! James as the captain of his eleven! James in his first frock coat! James under all sorts of glorious circumstances! You know how strong he is (I hope he didnt hurt you): how clever he is: how happy. (*With deepening gravity*) Ask James's mother and his three sisters what it cost to save James the trouble of doing anything but be strong and clever and happy. Ask *me* what it costs to be James's mother and three sisters and wife and mother to his children all in one. Ask Prossy and Maria how troublesome the house is even when we have no visitors to help us to slice the onions. Ask the tradesmen who want to worry James and spoil his beautiful sermons who it is that puts them off. When there is money to give, he gives it: when there is money to refuse, I refuse it. I build a castle of comfort and indulgence and love for him, and stand sentinel always to keep little vulgar cares out. I make him master here, though he does not know it, and could not tell you a moment ago how it came to be so. (*With sweet irony*) And when he thought I might go away with you, his only anxiety was—what should become of *me!* And to tempt me to stay he offered me (*leaning forward to stroke his hair caressingly at each phrase*) *his* strength for *my* defence! his industry for my livelihood! his dignity for my position! his—(*relenting*) ah, I am mixing up your beautiful cadences and spoiling them, am I not, darling? (*She lays her cheek fondly against his.*)

MORELL (*quite overcome, kneeling beside her chair and embracing her with boyish ingenuousness*). It's all true, every word. What I am you have made me with the labor of your hands and the love of your heart. You are my wife, my mother, my sisters: you are the sum of all loving care to me.

CANDIDA (*in his arms, smiling, to* EUGENE). Am I *your* mother and sisters to you, Eugene?

MARCHBANKS (*rising with a fierce gesture of disgust*). Ah, never. Out, then, into the night with me!

CANDIDA (*rising quickly*). You are not going like that, Eugene?

MARCHBANKS (*with the ring of a man's voice—no longer a boy's—in the words*). I know the hour when it strikes. I am impatient to do what must be done.

MORELL (*who has also risen*). Candida: dont let him do anything rash.

CANDIDA (*confident, smiling at* EUGENE). Oh, there is no fear. He has learnt to live without happiness.

MARCHBANKS. I no longer desire happiness: life is nobler than that. Parson James: I give you my happiness with both hands. I love you because you have filled the heart of the woman I loved. Goodbye. (*He goes towards the door.*)

CANDIDA. One last word. (*He stops, but without turning to her. She goes to him*) How old are you, Eugene?

MARCHBANKS. As old as the world now. This morning I was eighteen.

CANDIDA. Eighteen! Will you, for my sake, make a little poem out of the two sentences I am going to say to you? And will you promise to repeat it to yourself whenever you think of me?

MARCHBANKS (*without moving*). Say the sentences.

CANDIDA. When I am thirty, she will be forty-five. When I am sixty, she will be seventy-five.

MARCHBANKS (*turning to her*). In a hundred years, we shall be the same age. But I have a better secret than that in my heart. Let me go now. The night outside grows impatient.

CANDIDA. Goodbye. (*She takes his face in her hands; and as he divines her intention and falls on his knees, she kisses his forehead. Then he flies out into the night. She turns to* MORELL, *holding out her arms to him*) Ah, James!

(*They embrace. But they do not know the secret in the poet's heart.*)

QUESTIONS

1. Morell, at the beginning of the play, regards himself, and is regarded by other people, as a strong man. What reasons are there for this? What are the evidences of his strength?

2. What illusions about himself and his marriage is Morell shown to be under during the course of the play? By what stages and by what means is his self-confidence undermined? What does he learn about himself before the end of the play?

3. Marchbanks, at the beginning of the play, seems the weaker of the two main male characters. In what kinds of matters is he weak? Does he have any strengths? What effect does he have on Prossy and Morell? Why?

4. What illusions is Marchbanks under at the beginning of the play? What does he learn about Candida, about marriage, and about himself during the course of the play? What is the significance of his going out alone "into the night" at the end of the play? Are we to feel sorry for him?

5. In the final stage direction, Shaw raises a question for readers that he does not raise for spectators: What is "the secret in the poet's heart"?

6. What kind of person is Candida? What kind of things does she value? What kind of things bore her? On what qualities does she rely for controlling other people? Why is she a good wife for Morell? Would she make a good wife for Marchbanks?

7. Does Marchbanks really come close to winning Candida's affections away from Morell? Does Candida really auction herself off in Act III? Where does the main conflict in the play lie?

8. Who is the strongest character in the play? Why?

9. *Candida* has been frequently admired for its tight dramatic construction. In what ways is the construction effective?

10. One critic has written of *Candida*: "The plot is the same as that of *Othello*, the awakening of doubt in a husband's mind as to the fidelity of his wife." In what other respects is *Candida* like *Othello*? In what important ways is it different? Why is one tragedy and the other comedy? To what extent does *Candida* confirm or fail to confirm the ideas about comedy expressed in the preceding chapter?

11. *The Stronger, An Enemy of the People,* and *Candida* all have something to say about what constitutes strength. Do they say the same thing or different things? Discuss.

Plays for Further Reading

Lorraine Hansberry

A RAISIN IN THE SUN

To Mama: in gratitude for the dream

CHARACTERS

Ruth Younger
Travis Younger
Walter Lee Younger (*Brother*)
Beneatha Younger
Lena Younger (*Mama*)
Joseph Asagai
George Murchison
Karl Lindner
Bobo
Moving Men

The action of the play is set in Chicago's Southside, sometime between World War II and the present.

ACT I

SCENE I. *Friday morning*
SCENE II. *The following morning*

ACT II

SCENE I. *Later, the same day*
SCENE II. *Friday night, a few weeks later*
SCENE III. *Saturday, moving day, one week later*

ACT III

An hour later

What happens to a dream deferred?
Does it dry up
Like a raisin in the sun?
Or fester like a sore—

And then run?
Does it stink like rotten meat?
Or crust and sugar over—
Like a syrupy sweet?

Maybe it just sags
Like a heavy load.

Or does it explode?

Langston Hughes[1]

ACT I

SCENE I. *The* YOUNGER *living room would be a comfortable and well-ordered room if it were not for a number of indestructible contradictions to this state of being. Its furnishings are typical and undistinguished and their primary feature now is that they have clearly had to accommodate the living of too many people for too many years—and they are tired. Still, we can see that at some time, a time probably no longer remembered by the family (except perhaps for* MAMA*), the furnishings of this room were actually selected with care and love and even hope—and brought to this apartment and arranged with taste and pride.*

That was a long time ago. Now the once loved pattern of the couch upholstery has to fight to show itself from under acres of crocheted doilies and couch covers which have themselves finally come to be more important than the upholstery. And here a table or a chair has been moved to disguise the worn places in the carpet; but the carpet has fought back by showing its weariness, with depressing uniformity, elsewhere on its surface.

Weariness has, in fact, won in this room. Everything has been polished, washed, sat on, used, scrubbed too often. All pretenses but living itself have long since vanished from the very atmosphere of this room.

Moreover, a section of this room, for it is not really a room unto itself, though the landlord's lease would make it seem so, slopes backward to provide a small kitchen area, where the family prepares the meals that are eaten in the living room proper, which must also serve as dining room. The single window that has been provided for these "two" rooms is located in this kitchen area. The sole natural light the family may enjoy in the course of a day is only that which fights its way through this little window.

At left, a door leads to a bedroom which is shared by MAMA *and her daughter,* BENEATHA. *At right, opposite, is a second room (which in the be-*

[1] From "Dream Deferred." Copyright 1951 by Langston Hughes. Reprinted from *The Panther and the Lash* by Langston Hughes, by permission of Alfred A. Knopf, Inc.

ginning of the life of this apartment was probably a breakfast room), which serves as a bedroom for WALTER *and his wife,* RUTH.

Time: Sometime between World War II and the present.

Place: Chicago's Southside.

At rise: It is morning dark in the living room. TRAVIS *is asleep on the make-down bed at center. An alarm clock sounds from within the bedroom at right, and presently* RUTH *enters from that room and closes the door behind her. She crosses sleepily toward the window. As she passes her sleeping son she reaches down and shakes him a little. At the window she raises the shade and a dusky Southside morning light comes in feebly. She fills a pot with water and puts it on to boil. She calls to the boy, between yawns, in a slightly muffled voice.*

RUTH *is about thirty. We can see that she was a pretty girl, even exceptionally so, but now it is apparent that life has been little that she expected, and disappointment has already begun to hang in her face. In a few years, before thirty-five even, she will be known among her people as a "settled woman."*

She crosses to her son and gives him a good, final, rousing shake.

RUTH. Come on now, boy, it's seven thirty! (*Her son sits up at last, in a stupor of sleepiness.*) I say hurry up, Travis! You ain't the only person in the world got to use a bathroom! (*The child, a sturdy, handsome little boy of ten or eleven, drags himself out of the bed and almost blindly takes his towels and "today's clothes" from drawers and a closet and goes out to the bathroom, which is in an outside hall and which is shared by another family or families on the same floor.* RUTH *crosses to the bedroom door at right and opens it and calls in to her husband.*) Walter Lee! . . . It's after seven thirty! Lemme see you do some waking up in there now! (*She waits.*) You better get up from there, man! It's after seven thirty I tell you. (*She waits again.*) All right, you just go ahead and lay there and next thing you know Travis be finished and Mr. Johnson'll be in there and you'll be fussing and cussing round here like a mad man! And be late too! (*She waits, at the end of patience.*) Walter Lee—it's time for you to get up!

(*She waits another second and then starts to go into the bedroom, but is apparently satisfied that her husband has begun to get up. She stops, pulls the door to, and returns to the kitchen area. She wipes her face with a moist cloth and runs her fingers through her sleep-disheveled hair in a vain effort and ties an apron around her housecoat. The bedroom door at right opens and her husband stands in the doorway in his pajamas, which are rumpled and mismated. He is a lean, intense young man in his middle thirties, inclined to quick nervous movements and erratic speech habits—and always in his voice there is a quality of indictment.*)

WALTER. Is he out yet?

RUTH. What you mean *out?* He ain't hardly got in there good yet.

WALTER (*wandering in, still more oriented to sleep than to a new day*). Well, what was you doing all that yelling for if I can't even get in there yet? (*Stopping and thinking*) Check coming today?

RUTH. They *said* Saturday and this is just Friday and I hopes to God you ain't going to get up here first thing this morning and start talking to me 'bout no money—'cause I 'bout don't want to hear it.

WALTER. Something the matter with you this morning?

RUTH. No—I'm just sleepy as the devil. What kind of eggs you want?

WALTER. Not scrambled. (RUTH *starts to scramble eggs.*) Paper come? (RUTH *points impatiently to the rolled up* Tribune *on the table, and he gets it and spreads it out and vaguely reads the front page.*) Set off another bomb yesterday.

RUTH (*maximum indifference*). Did they?

WALTER (*looking up*). What's the matter with you?

RUTH. Ain't nothing the matter with me. And don't keep asking me that this morning.

WALTER. Ain't nobody bothering you. (*Reading the news of the day absently again*) Say Colonel McCormick is sick.

RUTH (*affecting tea-party interest*). Is he now? Poor thing.

WALTER (*sighing and looking at his watch*). Oh, me. (*He waits.*) Now what is that boy doing in that bathroom all this time? He just going to have to start getting up earlier. I can't be being late to work on account of him fooling around in there.

RUTH (*turning on him*). Oh, no he ain't going to be getting up no earlier no such thing! It ain't his fault that he can't get to bed no earlier nights 'cause he got a bunch of crazy good-for-nothing clowns sitting up running their mouths in what is supposed to be his bedroom after ten o'clock at night. . . .

WALTER. That's what you mad about, ain't it? The things I want to talk about with my friends just couldn't be important in your mind, could they?

(*He rises and finds a cigarette in her handbag on the table and crosses to the little window and looks out, smoking and deeply enjoying this first one.*)

RUTH (*almost matter of factly, a complaint too automatic to deserve emphasis*). Why you always got to smoke before you eat in the morning?

WALTER (*at the window*). Just look at 'em down there. . . . Running and racing to work . . . (*he turns and faces his wife and watches her a moment at the stove, and then, suddenly*) You look young this morning, baby.

RUTH (*indifferently*). Yeah?

WALTER. Just for a second—stirring them eggs. It's gone now—just for a second it was—you looked real young again. (*Then, drily*) It's gone now—you look like yourself again.

Ruth. Man, if you don't shut up and leave me alone.

Walter (*looking out to the street again*). First thing a man ought to learn in life is not to make love to no colored woman first thing in the morning. You all some evil people at eight o'clock in the morning.

(Travis *appears in the hall doorway, almost fully dressed and quite wide awake now, his towels and pajamas across his shoulders. He opens the door and signals for his father to make the bathroom in a hurry.*)

Travis (*watching the bathroom*). Daddy, come on!

(Walter *gets his bathroom utensils and flies out to the bathroom.*)

Ruth. Sit down and have your breakfast, Travis.

Travis. Mama, this is Friday. (*Gleefully*) Check coming tomorrow, huh?

Ruth. You get your mind off money and eat your breakfast.

Travis (*eating*). This is the morning we supposed to bring the fifty cents to school.

Ruth. Well, I ain't got no fifty cents this morning.

Travis. Teacher say we have to.

Ruth. I don't care what teacher say. I ain't got it. Eat your breakfast, Travis.

Travis. I *am* eating.

Ruth. Hush up now and just eat!

(*The boy gives her an exasperated look for her lack of understanding, and eats grudgingly.*)

Travis. You think Grandmama would have it?

Ruth. No! And I want you to stop asking your grandmother for money, you hear me?

Travis (*outraged*). Gaaaleee! I don't ask her, she just gimme it sometimes!

Ruth. Travis Willard Younger—I got too much on me this morning to be—

Travis. Maybe Daddy—

Ruth. *Travis!*

(*The boy hushes abruptly. They are both quiet and tense for several seconds.*)

Travis (*presently*). Could I maybe go carry some groceries in front of the supermarket for a little while after school then?

Ruth. Just hush, I said. (Travis *jabs his spoon into his cereal bowl viciously, and rests his head in anger upon his fists.*) If you through eating, you can get over there and make up your bed.

(The boy obeys stiffly and crosses the room, almost mechanically, to the bed and more or less carefully folds the covering. He carries the bedding into his mother's room and returns with his books and cap.)

TRAVIS (*sulking and standing apart from her unnaturally*). I'm gone.

RUTH (*looking up from the stove to inspect him automatically*). Come here. (*He crosses to her and she studies his head.*) If you don't take this comb and fix this here head, you better! (TRAVIS *puts down his books with a great sigh of oppression, and crosses to the mirror. His mother mutters under her breath about his "slubbornness."*) 'Bout to march out of here with that head looking just like chickens slept in it! I just don't know where you get your slubborn ways. . . . And get your jacket, too. Looks chilly out this morning.

TRAVIS (*with conspicuously brushed hair and jacket*). I'm gone.

RUTH. Get carfare and milk money—(*waving one finger*)—and not a single penny for no caps, you hear me?

TRAVIS (*with sullen politeness*). Yes'm.

(He turns in outrage to leave. His mother watches after him as in his frustration he approaches the door almost comically. When she speaks to him, her voice has become a very gentle tease.)

RUTH (*mocking; as she thinks he would say it*). Oh, Mama makes me so mad sometimes, I don't know what to do! (*She waits and continues to his back as he stands stock-still in front of the door.*) I wouldn't kiss that woman good-bye for nothing in this world this morning! (*The boy finally turns around and rolls his eyes at her, knowing the mood has changed and he is vindicated; he does not, however, move toward her yet.*) Not for nothing in this world! (*She finally laughs aloud at him and holds out her arms to him and we see that it is a way between them, very old and practiced. He crosses to her and allows her to embrace him warmly but keeps his face fixed with masculine rigidity. She holds him back from her presently and looks at him and runs her fingers over the features of his face. With utter gentleness—*) Now—whose little old angry man are you?

TRAVIS (*the masculinity and gruffness start to fade at last*). Aw gaalee —Mama . . .

RUTH (*mimicking*). Aw—gaaaaalleeeee, Mama! (*She pushes him, with rough playfulness and finality, toward the door.*) Get on out of here or you going to be late.

TRAVIS (*in the face of love, new aggressiveness*). Mama, could I *please* go carry groceries?

RUTH. Honey, it's starting to get so cold evenings.

WALTER (*coming in from the bathroom and drawing a make-believe gun from a make-believe holster and shooting at his son*). What is it he wants to do?

RUTH. Go carry groceries after school at the supermarket.

WALTER. Well, let him go . . .

TRAVIS (*quickly, to the ally*). I *have* to—she won't gimme the fifty cents. . . .

WALTER (*to his wife only*). Why not?

RUTH (*simply, and with flavor*). 'Cause we don't have it.

WALTER (*to* RUTH *only*). What you tell the boy things like that for? (*Reaching down into his pants with a rather important gesture*) Here, son—

(*He hands the boy the coin, but his eyes are directed to his wife's.* TRAVIS *takes the money happily.*)

TRAVIS. Thanks, Daddy.

(*He starts out.* RUTH *watches both of them with murder in her eyes.* WALTER *stands and stares back at her with defiance, and suddenly reaches into his pocket again on an afterthought.*)

WALTER (*without even looking at his son, still staring hard at his wife*). In fact, here's another fifty cents. . . . Buy yourself some fruit today—or take a taxicab to school or something!

TRAVIS. Whoopee—

(*He leaps up and clasps his father around the middle with his legs, and they face each other in mutual appreciation; slowly* WALTER LEE *peeks around the boy to catch the violent rays from his wife's eyes and draws his head back as if shot.*)

WALTER. You better get down now—and get to school, man.

TRAVIS (*at the door*). O.K. Good-bye. (*He exits.*)

WALTER (*after him, pointing with pride*). That's *my* boy. (*She looks at him in disgust and turns back to her work.*) You know what I was thinking 'bout in the bathroom this morning?

RUTH. No.

WALTER. How come you always try to be so pleasant!

RUTH. What is there to be pleasant 'bout!

WALTER. You want to know what I was thinking 'bout in the bathroom or not!

RUTH. I know what you thinking 'bout.

WALTER (*ignoring her*). 'Bout what me and Willy Harris was talking about last night.

RUTH (*immediately—a refrain*). Willy Harris is a good-for-nothing loud mouth.

WALTER. Anybody who talks to me has got to be a good-for-nothing loud mouth, ain't he? And what you know about who is just a good-for-nothing loud mouth? Charlie Atkins was just a "good-for-nothing loud mouth" too, wasn't he! When he wanted me to go in the dry-cleaning business with him. And now—he's grossing a hundred thousand a year. A hundred thousand dollars a year! You still call *him* a loud mouth!

Ruth (*bitterly*). Oh, Walter Lee. . . . (*She folds her head on her arms over the table.*)

Walter (*rising and coming to her and standing over her*). You tired, ain't you? Tired of everything. Me, the boy, the way we live—this beat-up hole—everything. Ain't you? (*She doesn't look up, doesn't answer.*) So tired—moaning and groaning all the time, but you wouldn't do nothing to help, would you? You couldn't be on my side that long for nothing, could you?

Ruth. Walter, please leave me alone.

Walter. A man needs for a woman to back him up. . . .

Ruth. Walter—

Walter. Mama would listen to you. You know she listen to you more than she do me and Bennie. She think more of you. All you have to do is just sit down with her when you drinking your coffee one morning and talking 'bout things like you do and—(*he sits down beside her and demonstrates graphically what he thinks her methods and tone should be*)—you just sip your coffee, see, and say easy like that you been thinking 'bout that deal Walter Lee is so interested in, 'bout the store and all, and sip some more coffee, like what you saying ain't really that important to you— And the next thing you know, she be listening good and asking you questions and when I come home—I can tell her the details. This ain't no fly-by-night proposition, baby. I mean we figured it out, me and Willy and Bobo.

Ruth (*with a frown*). Bobo?

Walter. Yeah. You see, this little liquor store we got in mind cost seventy-five thousand and we figured the initial investment on the place be 'bout thirty thousand, see. That be ten thousand each. Course, there's a couple of hundred you got to pay so's you don't spend your life just waiting for them clowns to let your license get approved—

Ruth. You mean graft?

Walter (*frowning impatiently*). Don't call it that. See there, that just goes to show you what women understand about the world. Baby, don't *nothing* happen for you in this world 'less you pay *somebody* off!

Ruth. Walter, leave me alone! (*She raises her head and stares at him vigorously—then says, more quietly*) *Eat* your eggs, they gonna be cold.

Walter (*straightening up from her and looking off*). That's it. There you are. Man say to his woman: I got me a dream. His woman say: Eat your eggs. (*Sadly, but gaining in power*) Man say: I got to take hold of this here world, baby! And a woman will say: Eat your eggs and go to work. (*Passionately now*) Man say: I got to change my life, I'm choking to death, baby! And his woman say—(*in utter anguish as he brings his fists down on his thighs*)—Your eggs is getting cold!

Ruth (*softly*). Walter, that ain't none of our money.

Walter (*not listening at all or even looking at her*). This morning, I was lookin' in the mirror and thinking about it. . . . I'm thirty-five years old; I been married eleven years and I got a boy who sleeps in the living room—(*very, very quietly*)—and all I got to give him is stories about how rich white people live. . . .

RUTH. Eat your eggs, Walter.

WALTER. *Damn my eggs . . . damn all the eggs that ever was!*

RUTH. Then go to work.

WALTER (*looking up at her*). See—I'm trying to talk to you 'bout myself—(*shaking his head with the repetition*)—and all you can say is eat them eggs and go to work.

RUTH (*wearily*). Honey, you never say nothing new. I listen to you every day, every night and every morning, and you never say nothing new. (*Shrugging*) So you would rather *be* Mr. Arnold than be his chauffeur. So—I would *rather* be living in Buckingham Palace.

WALTER. That is just what is wrong with the colored woman in this world. . . . Don't understand about building their men up and making 'em feel like they somebody. Like they can do something.

RUTH (*drily, but to hurt*). There *are* colored men who do things.

WALTER. No thanks to the colored woman.

RUTH. Well, being a colored woman, I guess I can't help myself none.

(*She rises and gets the ironing board and sets it up and attacks a huge pile of rough-dried clothes, sprinkling them in preparation for the ironing and then rolling them into tight fat balls.*)

WALTER (*mumbling*). We one group of men tied to a race of women with small minds.

(*His sister* BENEATHA *enters. She is about twenty, as slim and intense as her brother. She is not as pretty as her sister-in-law, but her lean, almost intellectual face has a handsomeness of its own. She wears a bright-red flannel nightie, and her thick hair stands wildly about her head. Her speech is a mixture of many things; it is different from the rest of the family's insofar as education has permeated her sense of English—and perhaps the Midwest rather than the South has finally—at last—won out in her inflection; but not altogether, because over all of it is a soft slurring and transformed use of vowels which is the decided influence of the Southside. She passes through the room without looking at either* RUTH *or* WALTER *and goes to the outside door and looks, a little blindly, out to the bathroom. She sees that it has been lost to the Johnsons. She closes the door with a sleepy vengeance and crosses to the table and sits down a little defeated.*)

BENEATHA. I am going to start timing those people.

WALTER. You should get up earlier.

BENEATHA (*her face in her hands. She is still fighting the urge to go back to bed*). Really—would you suggest dawn? Where's the paper?

WALTER (*pushing the paper across the table to her as he studies her almost clinically, as though he has never seen her before*). You a horrible-looking chick at this hour.

BENEATHA (*drily*). Good morning, everybody.

WALTER (*senselessly*). How is school coming?

BENEATHA (*in the same spirit*). Lovely. Lovely. And you know, biology is the greatest. (*Looking up at him*) I dissected something that looked just like you yesterday.

WALTER. I just wondered if you've made up your mind and everything.

BENEATHA (*gaining in sharpness and impatience*). And what did I answer yesterday morning—and the day before that?

RUTH (*from the ironing board, like someone disinterested and old*). Don't be so nasty, Bennie.

BENEATHA (*still to her brother*). And the day before that and the day before that!

WALTER (*defensively*). I'm interested in you. Something wrong with that? Ain't many girls who decide—

WALTER *and* BENEATHA (*in unison*). —"to be a doctor."

(*Silence.*)

WALTER. Have we figured out yet just exactly how much medical school is going to cost?

RUTH. Walter Lee, why don't you leave that girl alone and get out of here to work?

BENEATHA (*exits to the bathroom and bangs on the door*). Come on out of there, please! (*She comes back into the room.*)

WALTER (*looking at his sister intently*). You know the check is coming tomorrow.

BENEATHA (*turning on him with a sharpness all her own*). That money belongs to Mama, Walter, and it's for her to decide how she wants to use it. I don't care if she wants to buy a house or a rocket ship or just nail it up somewhere and look at it. It's hers. Not ours—*hers*.

WALTER (*bitterly*). Now ain't that fine! You just got your mother's interest at heart, ain't you, girl? You such a nice girl—but if Mama got that money she can always take a few thousand and help you through school too—can't she?

BENEATHA. I have never asked anyone around here to do anything for me!

WALTER. No! And the line between asking and just accepting when the time comes is big and wide—ain't it!

BENEATHA (*with fury*). What do you want from me, Brother—that I quit school or just drop dead, which!

WALTER. I don't want nothing but for you to stop acting holy 'round here. Me and Ruth done made some sacrifices for you—why can't you do something for the family?

RUTH. Walter, don't be dragging me in it.

WALTER. You are in it—Don't you get up and go work in somebody's kitchen for the last three years to help put clothes on her back?

RUTH. Oh, Walter—that's not fair. . . .

WALTER. It ain't that nobody expects you to get on your knees and say thank you, Brother; thank you, Ruth; thank you, Mama—and thank you, Travis, for wearing the same pair of shoes for two semesters—

BENEATHA (*dropping to her knees*). Well—I *do*—all right?—thank everybody . . . and forgive me for ever wanting to be anything at all . . . forgive me, forgive me!

RUTH. Please stop it! Your mama'll hear you.

WALTER. Who the hell told you you had to be a doctor? If you so crazy 'bout messing 'round with sick people—then go be a nurse like other women—or just get married and be quiet. . . .

BENEATHA. Well—you finally got it said. . . . It took you three years but you finally got it said. Walter, give up; leave me alone—it's Mama's money.

WALTER. *He was my father, too!*

BENEATHA. So what? He was mine, too—and Travis' grandfather—but the insurance money belongs to Mama. Picking on me is not going to make her give it to you to invest in any liquor stores—(*underbreath, dropping into a chair*)—and I for one say, God bless Mama for that!

WALTER (*to* RUTH). See—did you hear? Did you hear!

RUTH. Honey, please go to work.

WALTER. Nobody in this house is ever going to understand me.

BENEATHA. Because you're a nut.

WALTER. Who's a nut?

BENEATHA. You—you are a nut. Thee is mad, boy.

WALTER (*looking at his wife and his sister from the door, very sadly*). The world's most backward race of people, and that's a fact.

BENEATHA (*turning slowly in her chair*). And then there are all those prophets who would lead us out of the wilderness—(WALTER *slams out of the house.*)—into the swamps!

RUTH. Bennie, why you always gotta be pickin' on your brother? Can't you be a little sweeter sometimes? (*Door opens.* WALTER *walks in.*)

WALTER (*to* RUTH). I need some money for carfare.

RUTH (*looks at him, then warms; teasing, but tenderly*). Fifty cents? (*She goes to her bag and gets money.*) Here, take a taxi.

(WALTER *exits.* MAMA *enters. She is a woman in her early sixties, full-bodied and strong. She is one of those women of a certain grace and beauty who wear it so unobtrusively that it takes a while to notice. Her dark-brown face is surrounded by the total whiteness of her hair, and, being a woman who has adjusted to many things in life and overcome many more, her face is full of strength. She has, we can see, wit and faith of a kind that keep her eyes lit and full of interest and expectancy. She is, in a word, a beautiful woman. Her bearing is perhaps most like the noble bearing of the women of the Hereros of Southwest Africa—rather as if she imagines that as she walks she still bears a basket or a vessel upon her head. Her speech, on the other hand, is as careless as her carriage is precise—she is inclined to slur everything—but her voice is perhaps not so much quiet as simply soft.)*

MAMA. Who that 'round here slamming doors at this hour?

(She crosses through the room, goes to the window, opens it, and brings in a feeble little plant growing doggedly in a small pot on the window sill. She feels the dirt and puts it back out.)

RUTH. That was Walter Lee. He and Bennie was at it again.

MAMA. My children and they tempers. Lord, if this little old plant don't get more sun than it's been getting it ain't never going to see spring again. (*She turns from the window.*) What's the matter with you this morning, Ruth? You looks right peaked. You aiming to iron all them things? Leave some for me. I'll get to 'em this afternoon. Bennie honey, it's too drafty for you to be sitting 'round half dressed. Where's your robe?

BENEATHA. In the cleaners.

MAMA. Well, go get mine and put it on.

BENEATHA. I'm not cold, Mama, honest.

MAMA. I know—but you so thin. . . .

BENEATHA (*irritably*). Mama, I'm not cold.

MAMA (*seeing the make-down bed as* TRAVIS *has left it*). Lord have mercy, look at that poor bed. Bless his heart—he tries, don't he? (*She moves to the bed* TRAVIS *has sloppily made up.*)

RUTH. No—he don't half try at all 'cause he knows you going to come along behind him and fix everything. That's just how come he don't know how to do nothing right now—you done spoiled that boy so.

MAMA. Well—he's a little boy. Ain't supposed to know 'bout housekeeping. My baby, that's what he is. What you fix for his breakfast this morning?

RUTH (*angrily*). I feed my son, Lena!

MAMA. I ain't meddling—(*underbreath; busy-bodyish*) I just noticed all last week he had cold cereal, and when it starts getting this chilly in the fall a child ought to have some hot grits or something when he goes out in the cold—

RUTH (*furious*). I gave him hot oats—is that all right!

MAMA. I ain't meddling. (*Pause.*) Put a lot of nice butter on it? (RUTH *shoots her an angry look and does not reply.*) He likes lots of butter.

RUTH (*exasperated*). Lena—

MAMA (*to* BENEATHA. MAMA *is inclined to wander conversationally sometimes*). What was you and your brother fussing 'bout this morning?

BENEATHA. It's not important, Mama.

(*She gets up and goes to look out at the bathroom, which is apparently free, and she picks up her towels and rushes out.*)

MAMA. What was they fighting about?

RUTH. Now you know as well as I do.

MAMA (*shaking her head*). Brother still worrying his self sick about that money?

RUTH. You know he is.

MAMA. You had breakfast?

RUTH. Some coffee.

MAMA. Girl, you better start eating and looking after yourself better. You almost thin as Travis.

RUTH. Lena—

MAMA. Un-hunh?

RUTH. What are you going to do with it?

MAMA. Now don't you start, child. It's too early in the morning to be talking about money. It ain't Christian.

RUTH. It's just that he got his heart set on that store—

MAMA. You mean that liquor store that Willy Harris want him to invest in?

RUTH. Yes—

MAMA. We ain't no business people, Ruth. We just plain working folks.

RUTH. Ain't nobody business people till they go into business. Walter Lee say colored people ain't never going to start getting ahead till they start gambling on some different kinds of things in the world—investments and things.

MAMA. What done got into you, girl? Walter Lee done finally sold you on investing.

RUTH. No. Mama, something is happening between Walter and me. I don't know what it is—but he needs something—something I can't give him any more. He needs this chance, Lena.

MAMA (*frowning deeply*). But liquor, honey—

RUTH. Well—like Walter say—I spec people going to always be drinking themselves some liquor.

MAMA. Well—whether they drinks it or not ain't none of my business. But whether I go into business selling it to 'em *is*, and I don't want that on my ledger this late in life. (*Stopping suddenly and studying her daughter-in-law*) Ruth Younger, what's the matter with you today? You look like you could fall over right there.

RUTH. I'm tired.

MAMA. Then you better stay home from work today.

RUTH. I can't stay home. She'd be calling up the agency and screaming at them, "My girl didn't come in today—send me somebody! My girl didn't come in!" Oh, she just have a fit. . . .

MAMA. Well, let her have it. I'll just call her up and say you got the flu—

RUTH (*laughing*). Why the flu?

MAMA. 'Cause it sounds respectable to 'em. Something white people get, too. They know 'bout the flu. Otherwise they think you been cut up or something when you tell 'em you sick.

RUTH. I got to go in. We need the money.

MAMA. Somebody would of thought my children done all but starved to death the way they talk about money here late. Child, we got a great big old check coming tomorrow.

RUTH (*sincerely, but also self-righteously*). Now that's your money. It ain't got nothing to do with me. We all feel like that—Walter and Bennie and me—even Travis.

MAMA (*thoughtfully, and suddenly very far away*). Ten thousand dollars—

RUTH. Sure is wonderful.

MAMA. Ten thousand dollars.

RUTH. You know what you should do, Miss Lena? You should take yourself a trip somewhere. To Europe or South America or someplace—

MAMA (*throwing up her hands at the thought*). Oh, child!

RUTH. I'm serious. Just pack up and leave! Go on away and enjoy yourself some. Forget about the family and have yourself a ball for once in your life—

MAMA (*drily*). You sound like I'm just about ready to die. Who'd go with me? What I look like wandering 'round Europe by myself?

RUTH. Shoot—these here rich white women do it all the time. They don't think nothing of packing up they suitcases and piling on one of them big steamships and—swoosh!—they gone, child.

MAMA. Something always told me I wasn't no rich white woman.

RUTH. Well—what are you going to do with it then?

MAMA. I ain't rightly decided. (*Thinking. She speaks now with emphasis.*) Some of it got to be put away for Beneatha and her schoolin'—and ain't nothing going to touch that part of it. Nothing. (*She waits several seconds, trying to make up her mind about something, and looks at* RUTH *a little tentatively before going on.*) Been thinking that we maybe could meet the notes on a little old two-story somewhere, with a yard where Travis could play in the summertime, if we use part of the insurance for a down payment and everybody kind of pitch in. I could maybe take on a little day work again, few days a week—

RUTH (*studying her mother-in-law furtively and concentrating on her *ironing, anxious to encourage without seeming to*). Well, Lord knows, we've put enough rent into this here rat trap to pay for four houses by now. . . .

MAMA (*looking up at the words "rat trap" and then looking around and leaning back and sighing—in a suddenly reflective mood—*). "Rat trap"—yes, that's all it is. (*Smiling*) I remember just as well the day me and Big Walter moved in here. Hadn't been married but two weeks and wasn't planning on living here no more than a year. (*She shakes her head at the dissolved dream.*) We was going to set away, little by little, don't you know, and buy a little place out in Morgan Park. We had even picked out the house. (*Chuckling a little*) Looks right dumpy today. But Lord, child, you should know all the dreams I had 'bout buying that house and fixing it up and making me a little garden in the back—(*She waits and stops smiling.*) And didn't none of it happen. (*Dropping her hands in a futile gesture*)

RUTH (*keeps her head down, ironing*). Yes, life can be a barrel of disappointments, sometimes.

MAMA. Honey, Big Walter would come in here some nights back then and slump down on that couch there and just look at the rug, and look at me and look at the rug and then back at me—and I'd know he was down then . . . really down. (*After a second very long and thoughtful pause; she is seeing back to times that only she can see.*) And then, Lord, when I lost that baby—little Claude—I almost thought I was going to lose Big Walter too. Oh, that man grieved hisself! He was one man to love his children.

RUTH. Ain't nothin' can tear at you like losin' your baby.

MAMA. I guess that's how come that man finally worked hisself to death like he done. Like he was fighting his own war with this here world that took his baby from him.

RUTH. He sure was a fine man, all right. I always liked Mr. Younger.

MAMA. Crazy 'bout his children! God knows there was plenty wrong with Walter Younger—hard-headed, mean, kind of wild with women—plenty wrong with him. But he sure loved his children. Always wanted them to have something—be something. That's where Brother gets all these notions, I reckon. Big Walter used to say, he'd get right wet in the eyes sometimes, lean his head back with the water standing in his eyes and say, "Seem like God didn't see fit to give the black man nothing but dreams—but He did give us children to make them dreams seem worth while." (*She smiles.*) He could talk like that, don't you know.

RUTH. Yes, he sure could. He was a good man, Mr. Younger.

MAMA. Yes, a fine man—just couldn't never catch up with his dreams, that's all.

(BENEATHA *comes in, brushing her hair and looking up to the ceiling, where the sound of a vacuum cleaner has started up.*)

BENEATHA. What could be so dirty on that woman's rugs that she has to vacuum them every single day?

RUTH. I wish certain young women 'round here who I could name would take inspiration about certain rugs in a certain apartment I could also mention.

BENEATHA (*shrugging*). How much cleaning can a house need, for Christ's sakes.

MAMA (*not liking the Lord's name used thus*). Bennie!

RUTH. Just listen to her—just listen!

BENEATHA. Oh, God!

MAMA. If you use the Lord's name just one more time—

BENEATHA (*a bit of a whine*). Oh, Mama—

RUTH. Fresh—just fresh as salt, this girl!

BENEATHA (*drily*). Well—if the salt loses its savor—

MAMA. Now that will do. I just ain't going to have you 'round here reciting the scriptures in vain—you hear me?

BENEATHA. How did I manage to get on everybody's wrong side by just walking into a room?

RUTH. If you weren't so fresh—

BENEATHA. Ruth, I'm twenty years old.

MAMA. What time you be home from school today?

BENEATHA. Kind of late. (*With enthusiasm*) Madeline is going to start my guitar lessons today.

(MAMA *and* RUTH *look up with the same expression.*)

MAMA. Your *what* kind of lessons?

BENEATHA. Guitar.

RUTH. Oh, Father!

MAMA. How come you done taken it in your mind to learn to play the guitar?

BENEATHA. I just want to, that's all.

MAMA (*smiling*). Lord, child, don't you know what to do with yourself? How long it going to be before you get tired of this now—like you got tired of that little play-acting group you joined last year? (*Looking at* RUTH) And what was it the year before that?

RUTH. The horseback-riding club for which she bought that fifty-five-dollar riding habit that's been hanging in the closet ever since!

MAMA (*to* BENEATHA). Why you got to flit so from one thing to another, baby?

BENEATHA (*sharply*). I just want to learn to play the guitar. Is there anything wrong with that?

MAMA. Ain't nobody trying to stop you. I just wonders sometimes why you has to flit so from one thing to another all the time. You ain't never done nothing with all that camera equipment you brought home—

BENEATHA. I don't flit! I—I experiment with different forms of expression—

RUTH. Like riding a horse?

BENEATHA. —People have to express themselves one way or another.

MAMA. What is it you want to express?

BENEATHA (*angrily*). Me! (MAMA *and* RUTH *look at each other and burst into raucous laughter.*) Don't worry—I don't expect you to understand.

MAMA (*to change the subject*). Who you going out with tomorrow night?

BENEATHA (*with displeasure*). George Murchison again.

MAMA (*pleased*). Oh—you getting a little sweet on him?

RUTH. You ask me, this child ain't sweet on nobody but herself—(*Underbreath*) Express herself!

(*They laugh.*)

BENEATHA. Oh—I like George all right, Mama. I mean I like him enough to go out with him and stuff, but—

RUTH (*for devilment*). What does *and stuff* mean?

BENEATHA. Mind your own business.

MAMA. Stop picking at her now, Ruth. (*A thoughtful pause, and then a suspicious sudden look at her daughter as she turns in her chair for emphasis*) What *does* it mean?

BENEATHA (*wearily*). Oh, I just mean I couldn't ever really be serious about George. He's—he's so shallow.

RUTH. Shallow—what do you mean he's shallow? He's *rich!*

MAMA. Hush, Ruth.

BENEATHA. I know he's rich. He knows he's rich, too.

RUTH. Well—what other qualities a man got to have to satisfy you, little girl?

BENEATHA. You wouldn't even begin to understand. Anybody who married Walter could not possibly understand.

MAMA (*outraged*). What kind of way is that to talk about your brother?

BENEATHA. Brother is a flip—let's face it.

MAMA (*to* RUTH, *helplessly*). What's a flip?

RUTH (*glad to add kindling*). She's saying he's crazy.

BENEATHA. Not crazy. Brother isn't really crazy yet—he—he's an elaborate neurotic.

MAMA. Hush your mouth!

BENEATHA. As for George. Well. George looks good—he's got a beautiful car and he takes me to nice places and, as my sister-in-law says, he is probably the richest boy I will ever get to know and I even like him sometimes—but if the Youngers are sitting around waiting to see if their little Bennie is going to tie up the family with the Murchisons, they are wasting their time.

RUTH. You mean you wouldn't marry George Murchison if he asked you someday? That pretty, rich thing? Honey, I knew you was odd—

BENEATHA. No I would not marry him if all I felt for him was what I feel now. Besides, George's family wouldn't really like it.

MAMA. Why not?

BENEATHA. Oh, Mama—The Murchisons are honest-to-God-real-*live*-rich colored people, and the only people in the world who are more snobbish than rich white people are rich colored people. I thought everybody knew that. I've met Mrs. Murchison. She's a scene!

MAMA. You must not dislike people 'cause they well off, honey.

BENEATHA. Why not? It makes just as much sense as disliking people 'cause they are poor, and lots of people do that.

RUTH (*a wisdom-of-the-ages manner. To* MAMA). Well, she'll get over some of this—

BENEATHA. Get over it? What are you talking about, Ruth? Listen, I'm going to be a doctor. I'm not worried about who I'm going to marry yet—if I ever get married.

MAMA *and* RUTH. *If!*

MAMA. Now, Bennie—

BENEATHA. Oh, I probably will . . . but first I'm going to be a doctor, and George, for one, still thinks that's pretty funny. I couldn't be bothered with that, I am going to be a doctor and everybody around here better understand that!

MAMA (*kindly*). 'Course you going to be a doctor, honey, God willing.

BENEATHA (*drily*). God hasn't got a thing to do with it.

MAMA. Beneatha—that just wasn't necessary.

BENEATHA. Well—neither is God. I get sick of hearing about God.

MAMA. Beneatha!

BENEATHA. I mean it! I'm just tired of hearing about God all the time. What has He got to do with anything? Does He pay tuition?

MAMA. You 'bout to get your fresh little jaw slapped!

RUTH. That's just what she needs, all right!

BENEATHA. Why? Why can't I say what I want to around here, like everybody else?

MAMA. It don't sound nice for a young girl to say things like that—you wasn't brought up that way. Me and your father went to trouble to get you and Brother to church every Sunday.

BENEATHA. Mama, you don't understand. It's all a matter of ideas, and God is just one idea I don't accept. It's not important, I am not going out and be immoral or commit crimes because I don't believe in God. I don't even think about it. It's just that I get tired of Him getting credit for all the things the human race achieves through its own stubborn effort. There simply is no blasted God—there is only man and it is he who makes miracles!

(MAMA *absorbs this speech, studies her daughter and rises slowly and crosses to* BENEATHA *and slaps her powerfully across the face. After, there is only silence and the daughter drops her eyes from her mother's face, and* MAMA *is very tall before her.*)

MAMA. Now—you say after me, in my mother's house there is still God. (*There is a long pause and* BENEATHA *stares at the floor wordlessly.* MAMA *repeats the phrase with precision and cool emotion.*) In my mother's house there is still God.

BENEATHA. In my mother's house there is still God.

(*A long pause*)

MAMA (*walking away from* BENEATHA, *too disturbed for triumphant posture. Stopping and turning back to her daughter*). There are some ideas we ain't going to have in this house. Not long as I am at the head of this family.

BENEATHA. Yes, ma'am.

(MAMA *walks out of the room.*)

RUTH (*almost gently, with profound understanding*). You think you a woman, Bennie—but you still a little girl. What you did was childish—so you got treated like a child.

BENEATHA. I see. (*Quietly*) I also see that everybody thinks it's all right for Mama to be a tyrant. But all the tyranny in the world will never put a God in the heavens! (*She picks up her books and goes out.*)

RUTH (*goes to* MAMA'*s door*). She said she was sorry.

MAMA (*coming out, going to her plant*). They frightens me, Ruth. My children.

RUTH. You got good children, Lena. They just a little off sometimes—but they're good.

MAMA. No—there's something come down between me and them that don't let us understand each other and I don't know what it is. One done almost lost his mind thinking 'bout money all the time and the other done commence to talk about things I can't seem to understand in no form or fashion. What is it that's changing, Ruth?

RUTH (*soothingly, older than her years*). Now . . . you taking it all too seriously. You just got strong-willed children and it takes a strong woman like you to keep 'em in hand.

MAMA (*looking at her plant and sprinkling a little water on it*). They spirited all right, my children. Got to admit they got spirit—Bennie and Walter. Like this little old plant that ain't never had enough sunshine or nothing—and look at it. . . .

(*She has her back to* RUTH, *who has had to stop ironing and lean against something and put the back of her hand to her forehead.*)

RUTH (*trying to keep* MAMA *from noticing*). You . . . sure . . . loves that little old thing, don't you? . . .

MAMA. Well, I always wanted me a garden like I used to see sometimes at the back of the houses down home. This plant is close as I ever got to having one. (*She looks out of the window as she replaces the plant.*) Lord, ain't nothing as dreary as the view from this window on a dreary day, is there? Why ain't you singing this morning, Ruth? Sing that "No Ways Tired." That song always lifts me up so—(*She turns at last to see that* RUTH *has slipped quietly into a chair, in a state of semiconsciousness.*) Ruth! Ruth honey—what's the matter with you . . . Ruth!

CURTAIN

SCENE II. *It is the following morning; a Saturday morning, and house cleaning is in progress at the* YOUNGERS. *Furniture has been shoved hither and yon and* MAMA *is giving the kitchen-area walls a washing down.* BENEATHA, *in dungarees, with a handkerchief tied around her face, is spraying insecticide into the cracks in the walls. As they work, the radio is on and a Southside disc-jockey program is inappropriately filling the house with a rather exotic saxophone blues.* TRAVIS, *the sole idle one, is leaning on his arms, looking out of the window.*

TRAVIS. Grandmama, that stuff Bennie is using smells awful. Can I go downstairs, please?

MAMA. Did you get all them chores done already? I ain't see you doing much.

TRAVIS. Yes'm—finished early. Where did Mama go this morning?

MAMA (*looking at* BENEATHA). She had to go on a little errand.

TRAVIS. Where?

MAMA. To tend to her business.

TRAVIS. Can I go outside then?

MAMA. Oh, I guess so. You better stay right in front of the house, though . . . and keep a good lookout for the postman.

TRAVIS. Yes'm. (*He starts out and decides to give his* AUNT BENEATHA *a good swat on the legs as he passes her.*) Leave them poor little old cockroaches alone, they ain't bothering you none.

(*He runs as she swings the spray gun at him both viciously and playfully.* WALTER *enters from the bedroom and goes to the phone.*)

MAMA. Look out there, girl, before you be spilling some of that stuff on that child!

TRAVIS (*teasing*). That's right—look out now! (*He exits.*)

BENEATHA (*drily*). I can't imagine that it would hurt him—it has never hurt the roaches.

MAMA. Well, little boys' hides ain't as tough as Southside roaches.

WALTER (*into phone*). Hello—Let me talk to Willy Harris.

MAMA. You better get over there behind the bureau. I seen one marching out of there like Napoleon yesterday.

WALTER. Hello. Willy? It ain't come yet. It'll be here in a few minutes. Did the lawyer give you the papers?

BENEATHA. There's really only one way to get rid of them, Mama—

MAMA. How?

BENEATHA. Set fire to this building.

WALTER. Good. Good. I'll be right over.

BENEATHA. Where did Ruth go, Walter?

WALTER. I don't know. (*He exits abruptly.*)

BENEATHA. Mama, where did Ruth go?

MAMA (*looking at her with meaning*). To the doctor, I think.

BENEATHA. The doctor? What's the matter? (*They exchange glances.*) You don't think—

MAMA (*with her sense of drama*). Now I ain't saying what I think. But I ain't never been wrong 'bout a woman neither.

(*The phone rings.*)

BENEATHA (*at the phone*). Hay-lo . . . (*Pause, and a moment of recognition*) Well—when did you get back! . . . And how was it? . . . Of course I've missed you—in my way. . . . This morning? No . . . house cleaning and all that and Mama hates it if I let people come over when the house is like this. . . . You *have?* Well, that's different. . . . What is it—Oh, what the hell, come on over. . . . Right, see you then. (*She hangs up.*)

MAMA (*who has listened vigorously, as is her habit*). Who is that you inviting over here with this house looking like this? You ain't got the pride you was born with!

BENEATHA. Asagai doesn't care how houses look, Mama—he's an intellectual.

MAMA. *Who?*

BENEATHA. Asagai—Joseph Asagai. He's an African boy I met on campus. He's been studying in Canada all summer.

MAMA. What's his name?

BENEATHA. Asagai, Joseph. Ah-sah-guy . . . He's from Nigeria.

MAMA. Oh, that's the little country that was founded by slaves way back. . . .

BENEATHA. No, Mama—that's Liberia.

MAMA. I don't think I never met no African before.

BENEATHA. Well, do me a favor and don't ask him a whole lot of ignorant questions about Africans. I mean, do they wear clothes and all that—

MAMA. Well, now, I guess if you think we so ignorant 'round here maybe you shouldn't bring your friends here—

BENEATHA. It's just that people ask such crazy things. All anyone seems to know about when it comes to Africa is Tarzan—

MAMA (*indignantly*). Why should I know anything about Africa?

BENEATHA. Why do you give money at church for the missionary work?

MAMA. Well, that's to help save people.

BENEATHA. You mean to save them from *heathenism*—

MAMA (*innocently*). Yes.

BENEATHA. I'm afraid they need more salvation from the British and the French.

(RUTH *comes in forlornly and pulls off her coat with dejection. They both turn to look at her.*)

RUTH (*dispiritedly*). Well, I guess from all the happy faces—everybody knows.

BENEATHA. You pregnant?

MAMA. Lord have mercy, I sure hope it's a little old girl. Travis ought to have a sister.

(BENEATHA *and* RUTH *give her a hopeless look for this grandmotherly enthusiasm.*)

BENEATHA. How far along are you?

RUTH. Two months.

BENEATHA. Did you mean to? I mean did you plan it or was it an accident?

MAMA. What do you know about planning or not planning?

BENEATHA. Oh, Mama.

RUTH (*wearily*). She's twenty years old, Lena.

BENEATHA. Did you plan it, Ruth?

RUTH. Mind your own business.

BENEATHA. It is my business—where is he going to live, on the *roof?* (*There is silence following the remark as the three women react to the sense of it.*) Gee—I didn't mean that, Ruth, honest. Gee, I don't feel like that at all. I—I think it is wonderful.

RUTH (*dully*). Wonderful.

BENEATHA. Yes—really.

MAMA (*looking at* RUTH, *worried*). Doctor say everything going to be all right?

RUTH (*far away*). Yes—she says everything is going to be fine. . . .

MAMA (*immediately suspicious*). "She"—What doctor you went to?

(RUTH *folds over, near hysteria.*)

MAMA (*worriedly hovering over* RUTH). Ruth honey—what's the matter with you—you sick?

(RUTH *has her fists clenched on her thighs and is fighting hard to suppress a scream that seems to be rising in her.*)

BENEATHA. What's the matter with her, Mama?

MAMA (*working her fingers in* RUTH'S *shoulder to relax her*). She be all right. Women gets right depressed sometimes when they get her way. (*Speaking softly, expertly, rapidly*) Now you just relax. That's right . . . just lean back, don't think 'bout nothing at all . . . nothing at all—

RUTH. I'm all right. . . .

(*The glassy-eyed look melts and then she collapses into a fit of heavy sobbing. The bell rings.*)

BENEATHA. Oh, my God—that must be Asagai.

MAMA (*to* RUTH). Come on now, honey. You need to lie down and rest awhile . . . then have some nice hot food.

(*They exit,* RUTH'S *weight on her mother-in-law.* BENEATHA, *herself profoundly disturbed, opens the door to admit a rather dramatic-looking young man with a large package.*)

ASAGAI. Hello, Alaiyo—

BENEATHA (*holding the door open and regarding him with pleasure*). Hello . . . (*Long pause*) Well—come in. And please excuse everything. My mother was very upset about my letting anyone come here with the place like this.

ASAGAI (*coming into the room*). You look disturbed too. . . . Is something wrong?

BENEATHA (*still at the door, absently*). Yes . . . we've all got acute ghetto-itus. (*She smiles and comes toward him, finding a cigarette and sitting.*) So—sit down! How was Canada?

ASAGAI (*a sophisticate*). Canadian.

BENEATHA (*looking at him*). I'm very glad you are back.

ASAGAI (*looking back at her in turn*). Are you really?

BENEATHA. Yes—very.

ASAGAI. Why—you were quite glad when I went away. What happened?

BENEATHA. You went away.

ASAGAI. Ahhhhhhhh.

BENEATHA. Before—you wanted to be so serious before there was time.

ASAGAI. How much time must there be before one knows what one feels?

BENEATHA (*stalling this particular conversation. Her hands pressed together, in a deliberately childish gesture*). What did you bring me?

ASAGAI (*handing her the package*). Open it and see.

BENEATHA (*eagerly opening the package and drawing out some records and the colorful robes of a Nigerian woman*). Oh, Asagai! . . . You got them for me! . . . How beautiful . . . and the records too! (*She lifts out the robes and runs to the mirror with them and holds the drapery up in front of herself.*)

ASAGAI (*coming to her at the mirror*). I shall have to teach you how to drape it properly. (*He flings the material about her for the moment and stands back to look at her.*) Ah—*Oh-pay-gay-day, oh-gbah-mu-shay.* (*A Yoruba exclamation for admiration*) You wear it well . . . very well . . . mutilated hair and all.

BENEATHA (*turning suddenly*). My hair—what's wrong with my hair?

ASAGAI (*shrugging*). Were you born with it like that?

BENEATHA (*reaching up to touch it*). No . . . of course not. (*She looks back to the mirror, disturbed.*)

ASAGAI (*smiling*). How then?

BENEATHA. You know perfectly well how . . . as crinkly as yours . . . that's how.

ASAGAI. And it is ugly to you that way?

BENEATHA (*quickly*). Oh, no—not ugly . . . (*More slowly, apologetically*) But it's so hard to manage when it's, well—raw.

ASAGAI. And so to accommodate that—you mutilate it every week?

BENEATHA. It's not mutilation!

ASAGAI (*laughing aloud at her seriousness*). Oh . . . please! I am only teasing you because you are so very serious about these things. (*He stands back from her and folds his arms across his chest as he watches her pulling at her hair and frowning in the mirror.*) Do you remember the first time you met me at school? . . . (*He laughs.*) You came up to me and you said—and I thought you were the most serious little thing I had ever seen—you said: (*He imitates her.*) "Mr. Asagai—I want very much to talk with you. About Africa. You see, Mr. Asagai, I am looking for my *identity!*" (*He laughs.*)

BENEATHA (*turning to him, not laughing*). Yes—(*Her face is quizzical, profoundly disturbed.*)

ASAGAI (*still teasing and reaching out and taking her face in his hands and turning her profile to him*). Well . . . it is true that this is not so much a profile of a Hollywood queen as perhaps a queen of the Nile—(*A mock dismissal of the importance of the question*) But what does it matter? Assimilationism is so popular in your country.

BENEATHA (*wheeling, passionately, sharply*). I am not an assimilationist!

ASAGAI (*the protest hangs in the room for a moment and* ASAGAI *studies her, his laughter fading*). Such a serious one. (*There is a pause.*) So—you like the robes? You must take excellent care of them—they are from my sister's personal wardrobe.

BENEATHA (*with incredulity*). You—you sent all the way home—for me?

ASAGAI (*with charm*). For you—I would do much more. . . . Well, that is what I came for. I must go.

BENEATHA. Will you call me Monday?

ASAGAI. Yes . . . We have a great deal to talk about. I mean about identity and time and all that.

BENEATHA. Time?

ASAGAI. Yes. About how much time one needs to know what one feels.

BENEATHA. You never understood that there is more than one kind of feeling which can exist between a man and a woman—or, at least, there should be.

ASAGAI (*shaking his head negatively but gently*). No. Between a man and a woman there need be only one kind of feeling. I have that for you. . . . Now even . . . right this moment. . . .

BENEATHA. I know—and by itself—it won't do. I can find that anywhere.

ASAGAI. For a woman it should be enough.

BENEATHA. I know—because that's what it says in all the novels that men write. But it isn't. Go ahead and laugh—but I'm not interested in being someone's little episode in America or—(*with feminine vengeance*)—one of them! (ASAGAI *has burst into laughter again.*) That's funny as hell, huh!

ASAGAI. It's just that every American girl I have known has said that to me. White—black—in this you are all the same. And the same speech, too!

BENEATHA (*angrily*). Yuk, yuk, yuk!

ASAGAI. It's how you can be sure that the world's most liberated women are not liberated at all. You all talk about it too much!

(MAMA *enters and is immediately all social charm because of the presence of a guest.*)

BENEATHA. Oh—Mama—this is Mr. Asagai.

MAMA. How do you do?

ASAGAI (*total politeness to an elder*). How do you do, Mrs. Younger. Please forgive me for coming at such an outrageous hour on a Saturday.

MAMA. Well, you are quite welcome. I just hope you understand that our house don't always look like this. (*Chatterish*) You must come again. I would love to hear all about—(*not sure of the name*)—your country. I think it's so sad the way our American Negroes don't know nothing about Africa 'cept Tarzan and all that. And all that money they pour into these churches when they ought to be helping you people over there drive out them French and Englishmen done taken away your land.

(The mother flashes a slightly superior look at her daughter upon completion of the recitation.)

ASAGAI (*taken aback by this sudden and acutely unrelated expression of sympathy*). Yes . . . yes. . . .

MAMA (*smiling at him suddenly and relaxing and looking him over*). How many miles is it from here to where you come from?

ASAGAI. Many thousands.

MAMA (*looking at him as she would* WALTER). I bet you don't half look after yourself, being away from your mama either. I spec you better come 'round here from time to time and get yourself some decent home-cooked meals. . . .

ASAGAI (*moved*). Thank you. Thank you very much. (*They are all quiet, then—*) Well . . . I must go. I will call you Monday, Alaiyo.

MAMA. What's that he call you?

ASAGAI. Oh—"Alaiyo." I hope you don't mind. It is what you would call a nickname, I think. It is a Yoruba word. I am a Yoruba.

MAMA (*looking at* BENEATHA). I—I thought he was from—

ASAGAI (*understanding*). Nigeria is my country. Yoruba is my tribal origin—

BENEATHA. You didn't tell us what Alaiyo means . . . for all I know, you might be calling me Little Idiot or something. . . .

ASAGAI. Well . . . let me see . . . I do not know how just to explain it. . . . The sense of a thing can be so different when it changes languages.

BENEATHA. You're evading.

ASAGAI. No—really it is difficult. . . . (*Thinking*) It means . . . it means One for Whom Bread—Food—Is Not Enough. (*He looks at her.*) Is that all right?

BENEATHA (*understanding, softly*). Thank you.

MAMA (*looking from one to the other and not understanding any of it*). Well . . . that's nice. . . . You must come see us again—Mr.—

ASAGAI. Ah-sah-guy . . .

MAMA. Yes . . . Do come again.

ASAGAI. Good-bye. (*He exits.*)

MAMA (*after him*). Lord, that's a pretty thing just went out here! (*Insinuatingly, to her daughter*) Yes, I guess I see why we done commence to get so interested in Africa 'round here. Missionaries my aunt Jenny! (*She exits.*)

BENEATHA. Oh, Mama! . . .

(She picks up the Nigerian dress and holds it up to her in front of the mirror again. She sets the headdress on haphazardly and then notices her hair again and clutches at it and then replaces the headdress and frowns at herself. Then she starts to wriggle in front of the mirror as she thinks a Nigerian woman might. TRAVIS *enters and regards her.)*

TRAVIS. You cracking up?

BENEATHA. Shut up.

(She pulls the headdress off and looks at herself in the mirror and clutches at her hair again and squinches her eyes as if trying to imagine something. Then, suddenly, she gets her raincoat and kerchief and hurriedly prepares for going out.)

MAMA *(coming back into the room)*. She's resting now. Travis, baby, run next door and ask Miss Johnson to please let me have a little kitchen cleanser. This here can is empty as Jacob's kettle.

TRAVIS. I just come in.

MAMA. Do as you told. *(He exits and she looks at her daughter.)* Where you going?

BENEATHA *(halting at the door)*. To become a queen of the Nile!

(She exits in a breathless blaze of glory. RUTH *appears in the bedroom doorway.)*

MAMA. Who told you to get up?

RUTH. Ain't nothing wrong with me to be lying in no bed for. Where did Bennie go?

MAMA *(drumming her fingers)*. Far as I could make out—to Egypt. (RUTH *just looks at her.)* What time is it getting to?

RUTH. Ten twenty. And the mailman going to ring that bell this morning just like he done every morning for the last umpteen years.

(TRAVIS *comes in with the cleanser can.)*

TRAVIS. She say to tell you that she don't have much.

MAMA *(angrily)*. Lord, some people I could name sure is tight-fisted! *(Directing her grandson)* Mark two cans of cleanser down on the list there. If she that hard up for kitchen cleanser, I sure don't want to forget to get her none!

RUTH. Lena—maybe the woman is just short on cleanser—

MAMA *(not listening)*. —Much baking powder as she done borrowed from me all these years, she could of done gone into the baking business!

(The bell sounds suddenly and sharply and all three are stunned—serious and silent—mid-speech. In spite of all the other conversations and distractions of the morning, this is what they have been waiting for, even TRAVIS, *who looks helplessly from his mother to his grandmother.* RUTH *is the first to come to life again.)*

RUTH *(to* TRAVIS*)*. *Get down them steps, boy!*

(TRAVIS *snaps to life and flies out to get the mail.)*

MAMA (*her eyes wide, her hand to her breast*). You mean it done really come?

RUTH (*excitedly*). Oh, Miss Lena!

MAMA (*collecting herself*). Well . . . I don't know what we all so excited about 'round here for. We known it was coming for months.

RUTH. That's a whole lot different from having it come and being able to hold it in your hands . . . a piece of paper worth ten thousand dollars. . . . (TRAVIS *bursts back into the room. He holds the envelope high above his head, like a little dancer, his face is radiant and he is breathless. He moves to his grandmother with sudden slow ceremony and puts the envelope into her hands. She accepts it, and then merely holds it and looks at it.*) Come on! Open it . . . Lord have mercy, I wish Walter Lee was here!

TRAVIS. Open it, Grandmama!

MAMA (*staring at it*). Now you all be quiet. It's just a check.

RUTH. *Open it. . . .*

MAMA (*still staring at it*). Now don't act silly. . . . We ain't never been no people to act silly 'bout no money—

RUTH (*swiftly*). We ain't never had none before—*open it!*

(MAMA *finally makes a good strong tear and pulls out the thin blue slice of paper and inspects it closely. The boy and his mother study it raptly over* MAMA'*s shoulders.*)

MAMA. *Travis!* (*She is counting off with doubt.*) Is that the right number of zeros.

TRAVIS. Yes'm . . . ten thousand dollars. Gaalee, Grandmama, you rich.

MAMA (*She holds the check away from her, still looking at it. Slowly her face sobers into a mask of unhappiness*). Ten thousand dollars. (*She hands it to* RUTH.) Put it away somewhere, Ruth. (*She does not look at* RUTH; *her eyes seem to be seeing something somewhere very far off.*) Ten thousand dollars they give you. Ten thousand dollars.

TRAVIS (*to his mother, sincerely*). What's the matter with Grandmama —don't she want to be rich?

RUTH (*distractedly*). You go on out and play now, baby. (TRAVIS *exits.* MAMA *starts wiping dishes absently, humming intently to herself.* RUTH *turns to her, with kind exasperation.*) You're gone and got yourself upset.

MAMA (*not looking at her*). I spec if it wasn't for you all . . . I would just put that money away or give it to the church or something.

RUTH. Now what kind of talk is that. Mr. Younger would just be plain mad if he could hear you talking foolish like that.

MAMA (*stopping and staring off*). Yes . . . he sure would. (*Sighing*) We got enough to do with that money, all right. (*She halts then, and turns and looks at her daughter-in-law hard;* RUTH *avoids her eyes and* MAMA *wipes her hands with finality and starts to speak firmly to* RUTH.) Where did you go today, girl?

RUTH. To the doctor.

MAMA (*impatiently*). Now, Ruth . . . you know better than that. Old Doctor Jones is strange enough in his way but there ain't nothing 'bout him make somebody slip and call him "she"—like you done this morning.

RUTH. Well, that's what happened—my tongue slipped.

MAMA. You went to see that woman, didn't you?

RUTH (*defensively, giving herself away*). What woman you talking about?

MAMA (*angrily*). That woman who—

(WALTER *enters in great excitement.*)

WALTER. Did it come?

MAMA (*quietly*). Can't you give people a Christian greeting before you start asking about money?

WALTER (*to* RUTH). Did it come? (RUTH *unfolds the check and lays it quietly before him, watching him intently with thoughts of her own.* WALTER *sits down and grasps it close and counts off the zeros.*) Ten thousand dollars— (*He turns suddenly, frantically to his mother and draws some papers out of his breast pocket.*) Mama—look. Old Willy Harris put everything on paper—

MAMA. Son—I think you ought to talk to your wife. . . . I'll go on out and leave you alone if you want—

WALTER. I can talk to her later— Mama, look—

MAMA. Son—

WALTER. WILL SOMEBODY PLEASE LISTEN TO ME TODAY!

MAMA (*quietly*). I don't 'low no yellin' in this house, Walter Lee, and you know it— (WALTER *stares at them in frustration and starts to speak several times.*) And there ain't going to be no investing in no liquor stores. I don't aim to have to speak on that again.

(*A long pause*)

WALTER. Oh—so you don't aim to have to speak on that again? So *you* have decided. . . . (*Crumpling his papers*) Well, *you* tell that to my boy tonight when you put him to sleep on the living-room couch. . . . (*Turning to* MAMA *and speaking directly to her*) Yeah—and tell it to my wife, Mama, tomorrow when she has to go out of here to look after somebody else's kids. And tell it to *me*, Mama, every time we need a new pair of curtains and I have to watch *you* go out and work in somebody's kitchen. Yeah, you tell me then!

(WALTER *starts out.*)

RUTH. Where you going?

WALTER. I'm going out!

RUTH. Where?

WALTER. Just out of this house somewhere—

RUTH (*getting her coat*). I'll come too.

WALTER. I don't want you to come!

RUTH. I got something to talk to you about, Walter.

WALTER. That's too bad.

MAMA (*still quietly*). Walter Lee— (*She waits and he finally turns and looks at her.*) Sit down.

WALTER. I'm a grown man, Mama.

MAMA. Ain't nobody said you wasn't grown. But you still in my house and my presence. And as long as you are—you'll talk to your wife civil. Now sit down.

RUTH (*suddenly*). Oh, let him go on out and drink himself to death! He makes me sick to my stomach! (*She flings her coat against him.*)

WALTER (*violently*). And you turn mine too, baby! (RUTH *goes into their bedroom and slams the door behind her.*) That was my greatest mistake—

MAMA (*still quietly*). Walter, what is the matter with you?

WALTER. Matter with me? Ain't nothing the matter with *me!*

MAMA. Yes there is. Something eating you up like a crazy man. Something more than me not giving you this money. The past few years I been watching it happen to you. You get all nervous acting and kind of wild in the eyes— (WALTER *jumps up impatiently at her words.*) I said sit there now, I'm talking to you!

WALTER. Mama—I don't need no nagging at me today.

MAMA. Seem like you getting to a place where you always tied up in some kind of knot about something. But if anybody ask you 'bout it you just yell at 'em and bust out the house and go out and drink somewheres. Walter Lee, people can't live with that. Ruth's a good, patient girl in her way—but you getting to be too much. Boy, don't make the mistake of driving that girl away from you.

WALTER. Why—what she do for me?

MAMA. She loves you.

WALTER. Mama—I'm going out. I want to go off somewhere and be by myself for a while.

MAMA. I'm sorry 'bout your liquor store, son. It just wasn't the thing for us to do. That's what I want to tell you about—

WALTER. I got to go out, Mama— (*He rises.*)

MAMA. It's dangerous, son.

WALTER. What's dangerous?

MAMA. When a man goes outside his home to look for peace.

WALTER (*beseechingly*). Then why can't there never be no peace in this house then?

MAMA. You done found it in some other house?

WALTER. No—there ain't no woman! Why do women always think

there's a woman somewhere when a man gets restless. (*Coming to her*) Mama—Mama—I want so many things. . . .

MAMA. Yes, son—

WALTER. I want so many things that they are driving me kind of crazy. . . . Mama—look at me.

MAMA. I'm looking at you. You a good-looking boy. You got a job, a nice wife, a fine boy and—

WALTER. A job. (*Looks at her*) Mama, a job? I open and close car doors all day long. I drive a man around in his limousine and I say, "Yes, sir; no, sir; very good, sir; shall I take the Drive, sir?" Mama, that ain't no kind of job . . . that ain't nothing at all. (*Very quietly*) Mama, I don't know if I can make you understand.

MAMA. Understand what, baby?

WALTER (*quietly*). Sometimes it's like I can see the future stretched out in front of me—just plain as day. The future, Mama. Hanging over there at the edge of my days. Just waiting for me—a big, looming blank space—full of *nothing*. Just waiting for *me*. (*Pause*) Mama—sometimes when I'm downtown and I pass them cool, quiet-looking restaurants where them white boys are sitting back and talking 'bout things . . . sitting there turning deals worth millions of dollars . . . sometimes I see guys don't look much older than me—

MAMA. Son—how come you talk so much 'bout money?

WALTER (*with immense passion*). Because it is life, Mama!

MAMA (*quietly*). Oh— (*Very quietly*) So now it's life. Money is life. Once upon a time freedom used to be life—now it's money. I guess the world really do change. . . .

WALTER. No—it was always money, Mama. We just didn't know about it.

MAMA. No . . . something has changed. (*She looks at him.*) You something new, boy. In my time we was worried about not being lynched and getting to the North if we could and how to stay alive and still have a pinch of dignity too. . . . Now here come you and Beneatha—talking 'bout things we ain't never even thought about hardly, me and your daddy. You ain't satisfied or proud of nothing we done. I mean that you had a home; that we kept you out of trouble till you was grown; that you don't have to ride to work on the back of nobody's streetcar—You my children—but how different we done become.

WALTER. You just don't understand, Mama, you just don't understand.

MAMA. Son—do you know your wife is expecting another baby? (WALTER *stands, stunned, and absorbs what his mother has said.*) That's what she wanted to talk to you about. (WALTER *sinks down into a chair.*) This ain't for me to be telling—but you ought to know. (*She waits.*) I think Ruth is thinking 'bout getting rid of that child.

WALTER (*slowly understanding*). No—no—Ruth wouldn't do that.

MAMA. When the world gets ugly enough—a woman will do anything for her family. *The part that's already living.*

WALTER. You don't know Ruth, Mama, if you think she would do that.

(RUTH *opens the bedroom door and stands there a little limp.*)

RUTH (*beaten*). Yes I would too, Walter. (*Pause*) I gave her a five-dollar down payment.

(*There is total silence as the man stares at his wife and the mother stares at her son.*)

MAMA (*presently*). Well— (*Tightly*) Well—son, I'm waiting to hear you say something. . . . I'm waiting to hear how you be your father's son. Be the man he was. . . . (*Pause*) Your wife say she going to destroy your child. And I'm waiting to hear you talk like him and say we a people who give children life, not who destroys them— (*She rises.*) I'm waiting to see you stand up and look like your daddy and say we done give up one baby to poverty and that we ain't going to give up nary another one. . . . I'm waiting.

WALTER. Ruth—

MAMA. If you a son of mine, tell her! (WALTER *turns, looks at her and can say nothing. She continues, bitterly.*) You . . . you are a disgrace to your father's memory. Somebody get me my hat.

CURTAIN

ACT II

SCENE I.

Time: Later the same day.

At rise: RUTH *is ironing again. She has the radio going. Presently* BENEATHA'*s bedroom door opens and* RUTH'*s mouth falls and she puts down the iron in fascination.*

RUTH. What have we got on tonight!

BENEATHA (*emerging grandly from the doorway so that we can see her thoroughly robed in the costume* ASAGAI *brought*). You are looking at what a well-dressed Nigerian woman wears— (*She parades for* RUTH, *her hair completely hidden by the headdress; she is coquettishly fanning herself with an ornate oriental fan, mistakenly more like Butterfly than any Nigerian that ever was.*) Isn't it beautiful? (*She promenades to the radio and, with an arrogant flourish, turns off the good loud blues that is playing.*) Enough of this assimilationist junk! (RUTH *follows her with her eyes as she goes to the phonograph and puts on a record and turns and waits ceremoniously for the music to come up. Then, with a shout—*) OCOMOGOSIAY!

(RUTH *jumps. The music comes up, a lovely Nigerian melody.* BENEATHA *listens, enraptured, her eyes far away—"back to the past." She begins to dance.* RUTH *is dumfounded.*)

RUTH. What kind of dance is that?

BENEATHA. A folk dance.

RUTH (*Pearl Bailey*). What kind of folks do that, honey?

BENEATHA. It's from Nigeria. It's a dance of welcome.

RUTH. Who you welcoming?

BENEATHA. The men back to the village.

RUTH. Where they been?

BENEATHA. How should I know—out hunting or something. Anyway, they are coming back now. . . .

RUTH. Well, that's good.

BENEATHA (*with the record*).

Alundi, alundi
Alundi alunya
Jop pu a jeepua
Ang gu sooooooooo

Ai yai yae . . .
Ayehaye—alundi . . .

(WALTER *comes in during this performance; he has obviously been drinking. He leans against the door heavily and watches his sister, at first with distaste. Then his eyes look off—"back to the past"—as he lifts both his fists to the roof, screaming.*)

WALTER. YEAH . . . AND ETHIOPIA STRETCH FORTH HER HANDS AGAIN! . . .

RUTH (*drily, looking at him*). Yes—and Africa sure is claiming her own tonight. (*She gives them both up and starts ironing again.*)

WALTER (*all in a drunken, dramatic shout*). Shut up! . . . I'm digging them drums . . . them drums move me! . . . (*He makes his weaving way to his wife's face and leans in close to her.*) In my *heart of hearts*—(*he thumps his chest*)—I am much warrior!

RUTH (*without even looking up*). In your heart of hearts you are much drunkard.

WALTER (*coming away from her and starting to wander around the room, shouting*). Me and Jomo . . . (*Intently, in his sister's face. She has stopped dancing to watch him in this unknown mood.*) That's my man, Kenyatta. (*Shouting and thumping his chest*) FLAMING SPEAR! HOT DAMN! (*He is suddenly in possession of an imaginary spear and actively spearing enemies all over the room.*) OCOMOGOSIAY . . . THE LION IS WAKING . . . OWIMOWEH! (*He pulls his shirt open and leaps up on a table and gestures with his spear. The bell rings.* RUTH *goes to answer.*)

BENEATHA (*to encourage* WALTER, *thoroughly caught up with this side of him*). OCOMOGOSIAY, FLAMING SPEAR!

WALTER (*on the table, very far gone, his eyes pure glass sheets. He sees what we cannot, that he is a leader of his people, a great chief, a descendant of Chaka, and that the hour to march has come.*) Listen, my black brothers—

BENEATHA. OCOMOGOSIAY!

WALTER. —Do you hear the waters rushing against the shores of the coastlands—

BENEATHA. OCOMOGOSIAY!

WALTER. —Do you hear the screeching of the cocks in yonder hills beyond where the chiefs meet in council for the coming of the mighty war—

BENEATHA. OCOMOGOSIAY!

WALTER. —Do you hear the beating of the wings of the birds flying low over the mountains and the low places of our land—

(RUTH *opens the door.* GEORGE MURCHISON *enters.*)

BENEATHA. OCOMOGOSIAY!

WALTER. —Do you hear the singing of the women, singing the war songs of our fathers to the babies in the great houses . . . singing the sweet war songs? OH, DO YOU HEAR, MY BLACK BROTHERS!

BENEATHA (*completely gone*). We hear you, Flaming Spear—

WALTER. Telling us to prepare for the greatness of the time— (*To* GEORGE) Black Brother! (*He extends his hand for the fraternal clasp.*)

GEORGE. Black Brother, hell!

RUTH (*having had enough, and embarrassed for the family*). Beneatha, you got company—what's the matter with you? Walter Lee Younger, get down off that table and stop acting like a fool. . . .

(WALTER *comes down off the table suddenly and makes a quick exit to the bathroom.*)

RUTH. He's had a little to drink. . . . I don't know what her excuse is.

GEORGE (*to* BENEATHA). Look honey, we're going *to* the theater—we're not going to be *in* it . . . so go change, huh?

RUTH. You expect this boy to go out with you looking like that?

BENEATHA (*looking at* GEORGE). That's up to George. If he's ashamed of his heritage—

GEORGE. Oh, don't be so proud of yourself, Bennie—just because you look eccentric.

BENEATHA. How can something that's natural be eccentric?

GEORGE. That's what being eccentric means—being natural. Get dressed.

BENEATHA. I don't like that, George.

RUTH. Why must you and your brother make an argument out of everything people say?

BENEATHA. Because I hate assimilationist Negroes!

RUTH. Will somebody please tell me what assimila-whoever means!

GEORGE. Oh, it's just a college girl's way of calling people Uncle Toms —but that isn't what it means at all.

RUTH. Well, what does it mean?

BENEATHA (*cutting* GEORGE *off and staring at him as she replies to* RUTH). It means someone who is willing to give up his own culture and submerge himself completely in the dominant, and in this case, *oppressive* culture!

GEORGE. Oh, dear, dear, dear! Here we go! A lecture on the African past! On our Great West African Heritage! In one second we will hear all about the great Ashanti empires; the great Songhay civilizations; and the great sculpture of Bénin—and then some poetry in the Bantu—and the whole monologue will end with the word *heritage!* (*Nastily*) Let's face it, baby, your heritage is nothing but a bunch of raggedy-assed spirituals and some grass huts!

BENEATHA. *Grass huts!* (RUTH *crosses to her and forcibly pushes her toward the bedroom.*) See there . . . you are standing there in your splendid ignorance talking about people who were the first to smelt iron on the face of the earth! (RUTH *is pushing her through the door.*) The Ashanti were performing surgical operations when the English—(RUTH *pulls the door to, with* BENEATHA *on the other side, and smiles graciously at* GEORGE. BENEATHA *opens the door and shouts the end of the sentence defiantly at* GEORGE)—were still tattooing themselves with blue dragons. . . . (*She goes back inside.*)

RUTH. Have a seat, George. (*They both sit.* RUTH *folds her hands rather primly on her lap, determined to demonstrate the civilization of the family.*) Warm, ain't it? I mean for September. (*Pause*) Just like they always say about Chicago weather: If it's too hot or cold for you, just wait a minute and it'll change. (*She smiles happily at this cliché of clichés.*) Everybody say it's got to do with them bombs and things they keep setting off. (*Pause*) Would you like a nice cold beer?

GEORGE. No, thank you. I don't care for beer. (*He looks at his watch.*) I hope she hurries up.

RUTH. What time is the show?

GEORGE. It's an eight-thirty curtain. That's just Chicago, though. In New York standard curtain time is eight forty. (*He is rather proud of this knowledge.*)

RUTH (*properly appreciating it*). You get to New York a lot?

GEORGE (*offhand*). Few times a year.

RUTH. Oh—that's nice. I've never been to New York.

(WALTER *enters. We feel he has relieved himself, but the edge of unreality is still with him.*)

WALTER. New York ain't got nothing Chicago ain't. Just a bunch of hustling people all squeezed up together—being "Eastern." (*He turns his face into a screw of displeasure.*)

GEORGE. Oh—you've been?

WALTER. *Plenty* of times.

RUTH (*shocked at the lie*). Walter Lee Younger!

WALTER (*staring her down*). Plenty! (*Pause*) What we got to drink in this house? Why don't you offer this man some refreshment? (*To* GEORGE) They don't know how to entertain people in this house, man.

GEORGE. Thank you—I don't really care for anything.

WALTER (*feeling his head; sobriety coming*). Where's Mama?

RUTH. She ain't come back yet.

WALTER (*looking* MURCHISON *over from head to toe, scrutinizing his carefully casual tweed sports jacket over cashmere V-neck sweater over soft eyelet shirt and tie, and soft slacks, finished off with white buckskin shoes*). Why all you college boys wear them fairyish-looking white shoes?

RUTH. Walter Lee!

(GEORGE MURCHISON *ignores the remark.*)

WALTER (*to* RUTH). Well, they look crazy as hell—white shoes, cold as it is.

RUTH (*crushed*). You have to excuse him—

WALTER. No he don't! Excuse me for what? What you always excusing me for! I'll excuse myself when I needs to be excused! (*A pause*) They look as funny as them black knee socks Beneatha wears out of here all the time.

RUTH. It's the college *style,* Walter.

WALTER. Style, hell. She looks like she got burnt legs or something!

RUTH. Oh, Walter—

WALTER (*an irritable mimic*). Oh, Walter! Oh, Walter! (*To* MURCHISON) How's your old man making out? I understand you all going to buy that big hotel on the Drive? (*He finds a beer in the refrigerator, wanders over to* MURCHISON, *sipping and wiping his lips with the back of his hand, and straddling a chair backwards to talk to the other man.*) Shrewd move. Your old man is all right, man. (*Tapping his head and half winking for emphasis*) I mean he knows how to operate. I mean he thinks *big,* you know what I mean, I mean for a *home,* you know? But I think he's kind of running out of ideas now. I'd like to talk to him. Listen, man, I got some plans that could turn this city upside down. I mean I think like he does. *Big.* Invest big, gamble big, hell, lose *big* if you have to, you know what I mean. It's hard to find a man on this whole Southside who understands my kind of thinking—you dig? (*He scrutinizes* MURCHISON *again, drinks his beer, squints his eyes and leans in close, confidential, man to man.*) Me and you ought to sit down and talk sometimes, man. Man, I got me some ideas. . . .

MURCHISON (*with boredom*). Yeah—sometimes we'll have to do that, Walter.

WALTER (*understanding the indifference, and offended*). Yeah—well, when you get the time, man. I know you a busy little boy.

RUTH. Walter, please—

WALTER (*bitterly, hurt*). I know ain't nothing in this world as busy as you colored college boys with your fraternity pins and white shoes. . . .

RUTH (*covering her face with humiliation*). Oh, Walter Lee—

WALTER. I see you all all the time—with the books tucked under your arms—going to your (*British A—a mimic*) "clahsses." And for what! What the hell you learning over there? Filling up your heads—(*counting off on his fingers*)—with the sociology and the psychology—but they teaching you how to be a man? How to take over and run the world? They teaching you how to run a rubber plantation or a steel mill? Naw—just to talk proper and read books and wear white shoes. . . .

GEORGE (*looking at him with distaste, a little above it all*). You're all wacked up with bitterness, man.

WALTER (*intently, almost quietly, between the teeth, glaring at the boy*). And you—ain't you bitter, man? Ain't you just about had it yet? Don't you see no stars gleaming that you can't reach out and grab? You happy?—You contented son-of-a-bitch—you happy? You got it made? Bitter? Man, I'm a volcano. Bitter? Here I am a giant—surrounded by ants! Ants who can't even understand what it is the giant is talking about.

RUTH (*passionately and suddenly*). Oh, Walter—ain't you with nobody!

WALTER (*violently*). No! 'Cause ain't nobody with me! Not even my own mother!

RUTH. Walter, that's a terrible thing to say!

(BENEATHA *enters, dressed for the evening in a cocktail dress and earrings.*)

GEORGE. Well—hey, you look great.

BENEATHA. Let's go, George. See you all later.

RUTH. Have a nice time.

GEORGE. Thanks. Good night. (*To* WALTER, *sarcastically*) Good night, *Prometheus.* (BENEATHA *and* GEORGE *exit.*)

WALTER (*to* RUTH). Who is Prometheus?

RUTH. I don't know. Don't worry about it.

WALTER (*in fury, pointing after* GEORGE). See there—they get to a point where they can't insult you man to man—they got to go talk about something ain't nobody never heard of!

RUTH. How do you know it was an insult? (*To humor him*) Maybe Prometheus is a nice fellow.

WALTER. Prometheus! I bet there ain't even no such thing! I bet that simple-minded clown—

RUTH. Walter— (*She stops what she is doing and looks at him.*)

WALTER (*yelling*). Don't start!

RUTH. Start what?

WALTER. Your nagging! Where was I? Who was I with? How much money did I spend?

RUTH (*plaintively*). Walter Lee—why don't we just try to talk about it. . . .

WALTER (*not listening*). I been out talking with people who understand me. People who care about the things I got on my mind.

RUTH (*wearily*). I guess that means people like Willy Harris.

WALTER. Yes, people like Willy Harris.

RUTH (*with a sudden flash of impatience*). Why don't you all just hurry up and go into the banking business and stop talking about it!

WALTER. Why? You want to know why? 'Cause we all tied up in a race of people that don't know how to do nothing but moan, pray and have babies!

(*The line is too bitter even for him and he looks at her and sits down.*)

RUTH. Oh, Walter . . . (*Softly*) Honey, why can't you stop fighting me?

WALTER (*without thinking*). Who's fighting you? Who even cares about you?

(*This line begins the retardation of his mood.*)

RUTH. Well— (*She waits a long time, and then with resignation starts to put away her things.*) I guess I might as well go on to bed. . . . (*More or less to herself*) I don't know where we lost it . . . but we have. . . . (*Then, to him*) I—I'm sorry about this new baby, Walter. I guess maybe I better go on and do what I started . . . I guess I just didn't realize how bad things was with us . . . I guess I just didn't really realize— (*She starts out to the bedroom and stops.*) You want some hot milk?

WALTER. Hot milk?

RUTH. Yes—hot milk.

WALTER. Why hot milk?

RUTH. 'Cause after all that liquor you come home with you ought to have something hot in your stomach.

WALTER. I don't want no milk.

RUTH. You want some coffee then?

WALTER. No, I don't want no coffee. I don't want nothing hot to drink. (*Almost plaintively*) Why you always trying to give me something to eat?

RUTH (*standing and looking at him helplessly*). What else can I give you, Walter Lee Younger?

(*She stands and looks at him and presently turns to go out again. He lifts his head and watches her going away from him in a new mood which began to emerge when he asked her "Who cares about you?"*)

Walter. It's been rough, ain't it, baby? (*She hears and stops but does not turn around and he continues to her back.*) I guess between two people there ain't never as much understood as folks generally thinks there is. I mean like between me and you— (*She turns to face him.*) How we gets to the place where we scared to talk softness to each other. (*He waits, thinking hard himself.*) Why you think it got to be like that? (*He is thoughtful, almost as a child would be.*) Ruth, what is it gets into people ought to be close?

Ruth. I don't know, honey. I think about it a lot.

Walter. On account of you and me, you mean? The way things are with us. The way something done come down between us.

Ruth. There ain't so much between us, Walter. . . . Not when you come to me and try to talk to me. Try to be with me . . . a little even.

Walter (*total honesty*). Sometimes . . . sometimes . . . I don't even know how to try.

Ruth. Walter—

Walter. Yes?

Ruth (*coming to him, gently and with misgiving, but coming to him*). Honey . . . life don't have to be like this. I mean sometimes people can do things so that things are better. . . . You remember how we used to talk when Travis was born . . . about the way we were going to live . . . the kind of house . . . (*She is stroking his head.*) Well, it's all starting to slip away from us. . . .

(Mama *enters, and* Walter *jumps up and shouts at her.*)

Walter. Mama, where have you been?

Mama. My—them steps is longer than they used to be. Whew! (*She sits down and ignores him.*) How you feeling this evening, Ruth?

(Ruth *shrugs, disturbed some at having been prematurely interrupted and watching her husband knowingly.*)

Walter. Mama, where have you been all day?

Mama (*still ignoring him and leaning on the table and changing to more comfortable shoes*). Where's Travis?

Ruth. I let him go out earlier and he ain't come back yet. Boy, is he going to get it!

Walter. Mama!

Mama (*as if she has heard him for the first time*). Yes, son?

Walter. Where did you go this afternoon?

Mama. I went downtown to tend to some business that I had to tend to.

Walter. What kind of business?

Mama. You know better than to question me like a child, Brother.

Walter (*rising and bending over the table*). Where were you, Mama? (*Bringing his fists down and shouting*) Mama, you didn't go do something with that insurance money, something crazy?

(*The front door opens slowly, interrupting him, and* Travis *peeks his head in, less than hopefully.*)

Travis (*to his mother*). Mama, I—

Ruth. "Mama I" nothing! You're going to get it, boy! Get on in that bedroom and get yourself ready!

Travis. But I—

Mama. Why don't you all never let the child explain hisself.

Ruth. Keep out of it now, Lena.

(Mama *clamps her lips together, and* Ruth *advances toward her son menacingly.*)

Ruth. A thousand times I have told you not to go off like that—

Mama (*holding out her arms to her grandson*). Well—at least let me tell him something. I want him to be the first one to hear. . . . Come here, Travis. (*The boy obeys, gladly.*) Travis—(*she takes him by the shoulder and looks into his face*)—you know that money we got in the mail this morning?

Travis. Yes'm—

Mama. Well—what you think your grandmama gone and done with that money?

Travis. I don't know, Grandmama.

Mama (*putting her finger on his nose for emphasis*). She went out and she bought you a house! (*The explosion comes from* Walter *at the end of the revelation and he jumps up and turns away from all of them in a fury.* Mama *continues, to* Travis) You glad about the house? It's going to be yours when you get to be a man.

Travis. Yeah—I always wanted to live in a house.

Mama. All right, gimme some sugar then—(Travis *puts his arms around her neck as she watches her son over the boy's shoulder. Then, to* Travis, *after the embrace*) Now when you say your prayers tonight, you thank God and your grandfather—'cause it was him who give you the house—in his way.

Ruth (*taking the boy from* Mama *and pushing him toward the bedroom*). Now you get out of here and get ready for your beating.

Travis. Aw, Mama—

Ruth. Get on in there—(*Closing the door behind him and turning radiantly to her mother-in-law*) So you went and did it!

Mama (*quietly, looking at her son with pain*). Yes, I did.

Ruth (*raising both arms classically*). *Praise God!* (*Looks at* Walter *a moment, who says nothing. She crosses rapidly to her husband.*) Please, honey—let me be glad . . . you be glad too. (*She has laid her hands on his shoulders, but he shakes himself free of her roughly, without turning to face her.*) Oh, Walter . . . a home . . . a home. (*She comes back to* Mama.) Well—where is it? How big is it? How much it going to cost?

MAMA. Well—

RUTH. When we moving?

MAMA (*smiling at her*). First of the month.

RUTH (*throwing back her head with jubilance*). *Praise God!*

MAMA (*tentatively, still looking at her son's back turned against her and* RUTH). It's—it's a nice house too. . . . (*She cannot help speaking directly to him. An imploring quality in her voice, her manner, makes her almost like a girl now.*) Three bedrooms—nice big one for you and Ruth. . . . Me and Beneatha still have to share our room, but Travis have one of his own—and (*with difficulty*) I figure if the—new baby—is a boy, we could get one of them double-decker outfits. . . . And there's a yard with a little patch of dirt where I could maybe get to grow me a few flowers. . . . And a nice big basement. . . .

RUTH. Walter honey, be glad—

MAMA (*still to his back, fingering things on the table*). 'Course I don't want to make it sound fancier than it is. . . . It's just a plain little old house—but it's made good and solid—and it will be *ours*. Walter Lee—it makes a difference in a man when he can walk on floors that belong to *him*. . . .

RUTH. Where is it?

MAMA (*frightened at this telling*). Well—well—it's out there in Clybourne Park—

(RUTH'*s radiance fades abruptly, and* WALTER *finally turns slowly to face his mother with incredulity and hostility.*)

RUTH. Where?

MAMA (*matter-of-factly*). Four o six Clybourne Street, Clybourne Park.

RUTH. Clybourne Park? Mama, there ain't no colored people living in Clybourne Park.

MAMA (*almost idiotically*). Well, I guess there's going to be some now.

WALTER (*bitterly*). So that's the peace and comfort you went out and bought for us today!

MAMA (*raising her eyes to meet his finally*). Son—I just tried to find the nicest place for the least amount of money for my family.

RUTH (*trying to recover from the shock*). Well—well—'course I ain't one never been 'fraid of no crackers, mind you—but—well, wasn't there no other houses nowhere?

MAMA. Them houses they put up for colored in them areas way out all seem to cost twice as much as other houses. I did the best I could.

RUTH (*struck senseless with the news, in its various degrees of goodness and trouble, she sits a moment, her fists propping her chin in thought, and then she starts to rise, bringing her fists down with vigor, the radiance spreading from cheek to cheek again*). Well—well!—All I can say is—if this is my time in life—*my time*—to say good-bye—(*and she builds with momentum as she starts to circle the room with an exuberant, almost tearfully happy release*)—to these Goddamned cracking walls!—(*she pounds the walls*)—and these marching *roaches!*—(*she wipes at an imaginary army of marching roaches*)—and this cramped little closet which ain't now or never was no kitchen! . . . then I say it loud and good, *Hallelujah! and good-bye misery. . . . I don't never want to see your ugly face again!* (*She laughs joyously, having practically destroyed the apartment, and flings her arms up and lets them come down happily, slowly, reflectively, over her abdomen, aware for the first time perhaps that the life therein pulses with happiness and not despair.*) Lena?

MAMA (*moved, watching her happiness*). Yes, honey?

RUTH (*looking off*). Is there—is there a whole lot of sunlight?

MAMA (*understanding*). Yes, child, there's a whole lot of sunlight.

(*Long pause*)

RUTH (*collecting herself and going to the door of the room* TRAVIS *is in*). Well—I guess I better see 'bout Travis. (*To* MAMA) Lord, I sure don't feel like whipping nobody today! (*She exits.*)

MAMA (*the mother and son are left alone now and the mother waits a long time, considering deeply, before she speaks*). Son—you—you understand what I done, don't you? (WALTER *is silent and sullen.*) I—I just seen my family falling apart today . . . just falling to pieces in front of my eyes. . . . We couldn't of gone on like we was today. We was going backwards 'stead of forwards—talking 'bout killing babies and wishing each other was dead. . . . When it gets like that in life—you just got to do something different, push on out and do something bigger. . . . (*She waits.*) I wish you say something, son . . . I wish you'd say how deep inside you you think I done the right thing—

WALTER (*crossing slowly to his bedroom door and finally turning there and speaking measuredly*). What you need me to say you done right for? *You* the head of this family. You run our lives like you want to. It was your money and you did what you wanted with it. So what you need for me to say it was all right for? (*Bitterly, to hurt her as deeply as he knows is possible*) So you butchered up a dream of mine—you—who always talking 'bout your children's dreams. . . .

MAMA. Walter Lee—

(*He just closes the door behind him.* MAMA *sits alone, thinking heavily.*)

CURTAIN

SCENE II.

Time: Friday night, a few weeks later.

At rise: Packing crates mark the intention of the family to move. BENEATHA *and* GEORGE *come in, presumably from an evening out again.*

GEORGE. O.K. . . . O.K., whatever you say. . . . (*They both sit on the couch. He tries to kiss her. She moves away.*) Look, we've had a nice evening; let's not spoil it, huh? . . .

(*He again turns her head and tries to nuzzle in and she turns away from him, not with distaste but with momentary lack of interest; in a mood to pursue what they were talking about.*)

BENEATHA. I'm *trying* to talk to you.

GEORGE. We always talk.

BENEATHA. Yes—and I love to talk.

GEORGE (*exasperated; rising*). I know it and I don't mind it sometimes . . . I want you to cut it out, see—The moody stuff, I mean. I don't like it. You're a nice-looking girl . . . all over. That's all you need, honey, forget the atmosphere. Guys aren't going to go for the atmosphere—they're going to go for what they see. Be glad for that. Drop the Garbo routine. It doesn't go with you. As for myself, I want a nice—(*groping*)—simple (*thoughtfully*) —sophisticated girl . . . not a poet—O.K.?

(*She rebuffs him again and he starts to leave.*)

BENEATHA. Why are you angry?

GEORGE. Because this is stupid! I don't go out with you to discuss the nature of "quiet desperation" or to hear all about your thoughts—because the world will go on thinking what it thinks regardless—

BENEATHA. Then why read books? Why go to school?

GEORGE (*with artificial patience, counting on his fingers*). It's simple. You read books—to learn facts—to get grades—to pass the course—to get a degree. That's all—it has nothing to do with thoughts.

(*A long pause*)

BENEATHA. I see. (*A longer pause as she looks at him*) Good night, George.

(GEORGE *looks at her a little oddly, and starts to exit. He meets* MAMA *coming in.*)

GEORGE. Oh—hello, Mrs. Younger.

MAMA. Hello, George, how you feeling?

GEORGE. Fine—fine, how are you?

MAMA. Oh, a little tired. You know them steps can get you after a day's work. You all have a nice time tonight?

GEORGE. Yes—a fine time. Well, good night.

MAMA. Good night. (*He exits.* MAMA *closes the door behind her.*) Hello, honey. What you sitting like that for?

BENEATHA. I'm just sitting.

MAMA. Didn't you have a nice time?

BENEATHA. No.

MAMA. No? What's the matter?

BENEATHA. Mama, George is a fool—honest. (*She rises.*)

MAMA (*hustling around unloading the packages she has entered with. She stops*). Is he, baby?

BENEATHA. Yes.

(BENEATHA *makes up* TRAVIS' *bed as she talks.*)

MAMA. You sure?

BENEATHA. Yes.

MAMA. Well—I guess you better not waste your time with no fools.

(BENEATHA *looks up at her mother, watching her put groceries in the refrigerator. Finally she gathers up her things and starts into the bedroom. At the door she stops and looks back at her mother.*)

BENEATHA. Mama—

MAMA. Yes, baby—

BENEATHA. Thank you.

MAMA. For what?

BENEATHA. For understanding me this time.

(*She exits quickly and the mother stands, smiling a little, looking at the place where* BENEATHA *just stood.* RUTH *enters.*)

RUTH. Now don't you fool with any of this stuff, Lena—

MAMA. Oh, I just thought I'd sort a few things out.

(*The phone rings.* RUTH *answers.*)

RUTH (*at the phone*). Hello—Just a minute. (*Goes to the door*) Walter, it's Mrs. Arnold. (*Waits. Goes back to the phone. Tense*) Hello. Yes, this is his wife speaking . . . He's lying down now. Yes . . . well, he'll be in tomorrow. He's been very sick. Yes—I know we should have called, but we were so sure he'd be able to come in today. Yes—yes, I'm very sorry. Yes . . . Thank you very much. (*She hangs up.* WALTER *is standing in the doorway of the bedroom behind her.*) That was Mrs. Arnold.

WALTER (*indifferently*). Was it?

RUTH. She said if you don't come in tomorrow that they are getting a new man. . . .

WALTER. Ain't that sad—ain't that crying sad.

RUTH. She said Mr. Arnold has had to take a cab for three days. . . . Walter, you ain't been to work for three days! (*This is a revelation to her.*) Where you been, Walter Lee Younger? (WALTER *looks at her and starts to laugh.*) You're going to lose your job.

WALTER. That's right . . .

RUTH. Oh, Walter, and with your mother working like a dog every day—

WALTER. That's sad too—Everything is sad.

MAMA. What you been doing for these three days, son?

WALTER. Mama—you don't know all the things a man what got leisure can find to do in this city. . . . What's this—Friday night? Well—Wednesday I borrowed Willy Harris' car and I went for a drive . . . just me and myself and I drove and drove . . . Way out . . . way past South Chicago, and I parked the car and I sat and looked at the steel mills all day long. I just sat in the car and looked at them big black chimneys for hours. Then I drove back and I went to the Green Hat. (*Pause*) And Thursday—Thursday I borrowed the car again and I got in it and I pointed it the other way and I drove the other way—for hours—way, way up to Wisconsin, and I looked at the farms. I just drove and looked at the farms. Then I drove back and I went to the Green Hat. (*Pause*) And today—today I didn't get the car. Today I just walked. All over the South side. And I looked at the Negroes and they looked at me and finally I just sat down on the curb at Thirty-ninth and South Parkway and I just sat there and watched the Negroes go by. And then I went to the Green Hat. You all sad? You all depressed? And you know where I am going right now—

(RUTH *goes out quietly.*)

MAMA. Oh, Big Walter, is this the harvest of our days?

WALTER. You know what I like about the Green Hat? (*He turns the radio on and a steamy, deep blues pours into the room.*) I like this little cat they got there who blows a sax. . . . He blows. He talks to me. He ain't but 'bout five feet tall and he's got a conked head and his eyes is always closed and he's all music—

MAMA (*rising and getting some papers out of her handbag*). Walter—

WALTER. And there's this other guy who plays the piano . . . and they got a sound. I mean they can work on some music. . . . They got the best little combo in the world in the Green Hat. . . . You can just sit there and drink and listen to them three men play and you realize that don't nothing matter worth a damn, but just being there—

MAMA. I've helped do it to you, haven't I, son? Walter, I been wrong.

WALTER. Naw—you ain't never been wrong about nothing, Mama.

MAMA. Listen to me, now. I say I been wrong, son. That I been doing to you what the rest of the world been doing to you. (*She stops and he looks up slowly at her and she meets his eyes pleadingly.*) Walter—what you ain't never understood is that I ain't got nothing, don't own nothing, ain't never really wanted nothing that wasn't for you. There ain't nothing as precious to me. . . . There ain't nothing worth holding on to, money, dreams, nothing else—if it means—if it means it's going to destroy my boy. (*She puts her papers in front of him and he watches her without speaking or moving.*) I paid the man thirty-five hundred dollars down on the house. That leaves sixty-five hundred dollars. Monday morning I want you to take this money and take three thousand dollars and put it in a savings account for Beneatha's medical schooling. The rest you put in a checking account—with your name on it. And from now on any penny that come out of it or that go in it is for you to look after. For you to decide. (*She drops her hands a little helplessly.*) It ain't much, but it's all I got in the world and I'm putting it in your hands. I'm telling you to be the head of this family from now on like you supposed to be.

WALTER (*stares at the money*). You trust me like that, Mama?

MAMA. I ain't never stop trusting you. Like I ain't never stop loving you.

(*She goes out, and* WALTER *sits looking at the money on the table as the music continues in its idiom, pulsing in the room. Finally, in a decisive gesture, he gets up, and, in mingled joy and desperation, picks up the money. At the same moment,* TRAVIS *enters for bed.*)

TRAVIS. What's the matter, Daddy? You drunk?

WALTER (*sweetly, more sweetly than we have ever known him*). No, Daddy ain't drunk. Daddy ain't going to never be drunk again. . . .

TRAVIS. Well, good night, Daddy.

(*The* FATHER *has come from behind the couch and leans over, embracing his son.*)

WALTER. Son, I feel like talking to you tonight.

TRAVIS. About what?

WALTER. Oh, about a lot of things. About you and what kind of man you going to be when you grow up. . . . Son—son, what do you want to be when you grow up?

TRAVIS. A bus driver.

WALTER (*laughing a little*). A what? Man, that ain't nothing to want to be!

TRAVIS. Why not?

WALTER. 'Cause, man—it ain't big enough—you know what I mean.

TRAVIS. I don't know then. I can't make up my mind. Sometimes Mama asks me that too. And sometimes when I tell her I just want to be like you—she says she don't want me to be like that and sometimes she says she does. . . .

WALTER (*gathering him up in his arms*). You know what, Travis? In seven years you going to be seventeen years old. And things is going to be very different with us in seven years, Travis. . . . One day when you are seventeen I'll come home—home from my office downtown somewhere—

TRAVIS. You don't work in no office, Daddy.

WALTER. No—but after tonight. After what your daddy gonna do tonight, there's going to be offices—a whole lot of offices. . . .

TRAVIS. What you gonna do tonight, Daddy?

WALTER. You wouldn't understand yet, son, but your daddy's gonna make a transaction . . . a business transaction that's going to change our lives. . . . That's how come one day when you 'bout seventeen years old I'll come home and I'll be pretty tired, you know what I mean, after a day of conferences and secretaries getting things wrong the way they do . . . 'cause an executive's life is hell, man—(*The more he talks, the farther away he gets.*) And I'll pull the car up on the driveway . . . just a plain black Chrysler, I think, with white walls—no—black tires. More elegant. Rich people don't have to be flashy . . . though I'll have to get something a little sportier for Ruth—maybe a Cadillac convertible to do her shopping in. . . . And I'll come up the steps to the house and the gardener will be clipping away at the hedges and he'll say, "Good evening, Mr. Younger." And I'll say, "Hello, Jefferson, how are you this evening?" And I'll go inside and Ruth will come downstairs and meet me at the door and we'll kiss each other and she'll take my arm and we'll go up to your room to see you sitting on the floor with the catalogues of all the great schools in America around you. . . . All the great schools in the world! And—and I'll say, all right son—it's your seventeenth birthday, what is it you've decided? . . . Just tell me where you want to go to school and you'll *go*. Just tell me, what it is you want to be—and you'll *be* it. . . . Whatever you want to be—Yessir! (*He holds his arms open for* TRAVIS.) You just name it, son . . . (TRAVIS *leaps into them.*) and I hand you the world!

(WALTER*'s voice has risen in pitch and hysterical promise and on the last line he lifts* TRAVIS *high.*)

BLACKOUT

SCENE III.

Time: Saturday, moving day, one week later.

Before the curtain rises, RUTH*'s voice, a strident, dramatic church alto cuts through the silence.*

It is, in the darkness a triumphant surge, a penetrating statement of expectation: "Oh, Lord, I don't feel no ways tired! Children, oh, glory hallelujah!"

As the curtain rises we see that RUTH *is alone in the living room, finishing up the family's packing. It is moving day. She is nailing crates and tying cartons.* BENEATHA *enters, carrying a guitar case, and watches her exuberant sister-in-law.*

RUTH. Hey!

BENEATHA (*putting away the case*). Hi.

RUTH (*pointing at a package*). Honey—look in that package there and see what I found on sale this morning at the South Center. (RUTH *gets up and moves to the package and draws out some curtains.*) Lookahere—hand-turned hems!

BENEATHA. How do you know the window size out there?

RUTH (*who hadn't thought of that*). Oh—Well, they bound to fit something in the whole house. Anyhow, they was too good a bargain to pass up. (RUTH *slaps her head, suddenly remembering something.*) Oh, Bennie—I meant to put a special note on that carton over there. That's your mamma's good china and she wants 'em to be very careful with it.

BENEATHA. I'll do it.

(BENEATHA *finds a piece of paper and starts to draw large letters on it.*)

RUTH. You know what I'm going to do soon as I get in that new house?

BENEATHA. What?

RUTH. Honey—I'm going to run me a tub of water up to here. . . . (*With her fingers practically up to her nostrils*) And I'm going to get in it—and I am going to sit . . . and sit . . . and sit in that hot water and the first person who knocks to tell *me* to hurry up and come out—

BENEATHA. Gets shot at sunrise.

RUTH (*laughing happily*). You said it, sister! (*Noticing how large* BENEATHA *is absent-mindedly making the note*) Honey, they ain't going to read that from no airplane.

BENEATHA (*laughing herself*). I guess I always think things have more emphasis if they are big, somehow.

RUTH (*looking up at her and smiling*). You and your brother seem to have that as a philosophy of life. Lord, that man—done changed so 'round here. You know—you know what we did last night? Me and Walter Lee?

BENEATHA. What?

RUTH (*smiling to herself*). We went to the movies. (*Looking at* BENEATHA *to see if she understands*) We went to the movies. You know the last time me and Walter went to the movies together?

BENEATHA. No.

RUTH. Me neither. That's how long it been. (*Smiling again*) But we went last night. The picture wasn't much good, but that didn't seem to matter. We went—and we held hands.

BENEATHA. Oh, Lord!

RUTH. We held hands—and you know what?

BENEATHA. What?

RUTH. When we come out of the show it was late and dark and all the stores and things was closed up . . . and it was kind of chilly and there wasn't many people on the streets . . . and we was still holding hands, me and Walter.

BENEATHA. You're killing me.

(WALTER *enters with a large package. His happiness is deep in him; he cannot keep still with his new-found exuberance. He is singing and wiggling and snapping his fingers. He puts his package in a corner and puts a phonograph record, which he has brought in with him, on the record player. As the music comes up he dances over to* RUTH *and tries to get her to dance with him. She gives in at last to his raunchiness and in a fit of giggling allows herself to be drawn into his mood and together they deliberately burlesque an old social dance of their youth.*)

BENEATHA (*regarding them a long time as they dance, then drawing in her breath for a deeply exaggerated comment which she does not particularly mean*). Talk about—olddddddddd-fashionedddddd—Negroes!

WALTER (*stopping momentarily*). What kind of Negroes?

(*He says this in fun. He is not angry with her today, nor with anyone. He starts to dance with his wife again.*)

BENEATHA. Old-fashioned.

WALTER (*as he dances with* RUTH). You know, when these *New Negroes* have their convention—(*pointing at his sister*)—that is going to be the chairman of the Committee on Unending Agitation. (*He goes on dancing, then stops.*) Race, race, race! . . . Girl, I do believe you are the first person in the history of the entire human race to successfully brainwash yourself. (BENEATHA *breaks up and he goes on dancing. He stops again, enjoying his tease.*) Damn, even the N double A C P takes a holiday sometimes! (BENEATHA *and* RUTH *laugh. He dances with* RUTH *some more and starts to laugh and stops and pantomimes someone over an operating table.*) I can just see that chick someday looking down at some poor cat on an operating table before she starts to slice him, saying . . . (*pulling his sleeves back maliciously*) "By the way, what are your views on civil rights down there? . . ."

(*He laughs at her again and starts to dance happily. The bell sounds.*)

BENEATHA. Sticks and stones may break my bones but . . . words will never hurt me!

(BENEATHA *goes to the door and opens it as* WALTER *and* RUTH *go on with the clowning.* BENEATHA *is somewhat surprised to see a quiet-looking middle-aged white man in a business suit holding his hat and a briefcase in his hand and consulting a small piece of paper.*)

MAN. Uh—how do you do, miss. I am looking for a Mrs.—(*he looks at the slip of paper*) Mrs. Lena Younger?

BENEATHA (*smoothing her hair with slight embarrassment*). Oh—yes, that's my mother. Excuse me. (*She closes the door and turns to quiet the *other two.*) Ruth! Brother! Somebody's here. (*Then she opens the door. The man casts a curious quick glance at all of them.*) Uh—come in please.

MAN (*coming in*). Thank you.

BENEATHA. My mother isn't here just now. Is it business?

MAN. Yes . . . well, of a sort.

WALTER (*freely, the Man of the House*). Have a seat. I'm Mrs. Younger's son. I look after most of her business matters.

(RUTH *and* BENEATHA *exchange amused glances.*)

MAN (*regarding* WALTER, *and sitting*). Well—My name is Karl Lindner . . .

WALTER (*stretching out his hand*). Walter Younger. This is my wife—(RUTH *nods politely*)—and my sister.

LINDNER. How do you do.

WALTER (*amiably, as he sits himself easily on a chair, leaning with interest forward on his knees and looking expectantly into the newcomer's face*). What can we do for you, Mr. Lindner!

LINDNER (*some minor shuffling of the hat and briefcase on his knees*). Well—I am a representative of the Clybourne Park Improvement Association—

WALTER (*pointing*). Why don't you sit your things on the floor?

LINDNER. Oh—yes. Thank you. (*He slides the briefcase and hat under the chair.*) And as I was saying—I am from the Clybourne Park Improvement Association and we have had it brought to our attention at the last meeting that you people—or at least your mother—has bought a piece of residential property at—(*he digs for the slip of paper again*)—four o six Clybourne Street. . . .

WALTER. That's right. Care for something to drink? Ruth, get Mr. Lindner a beer.

LINDNER (*upset for some reason*). Oh—no, really. I mean thank you very much, but no thank you.

RUTH (*innocently*). Some coffee?

LINDNER. Thank you, nothing at all.

(BENEATHA *is watching the man carefully.*)

LINDNER. Well, I don't know how much you folks know about our organization. (*He is a gentle man; thoughtful and somewhat labored in his manner.*) It is one of those community organizations set up to look after—oh, you know, things like block upkeep and special projects and we also have what we call our New Neighbors Orientation Committee. . . .

BENEATHA (*drily*). Yes—and what do they do?

LINDNER (*turning a little to her and then returning the main force to* WALTER). Well—it's what you might call a sort of welcoming committee, I guess. I mean they, we, I'm the chairman of the committee—go around and see the new people who move into the neighborhood and sort of give them the lowdown on the way we do things out in Clybourne Park.

BENEATHA (*with appreciation of the two meanings, which escape* RUTH *and* WALTER). Un-huh.

LINDNER. And we also have the category of what the association calls—(*he looks elsewhere*)—uh—special community problems. . . .

BENEATHA. Yes—and what are some of those?

WALTER. Girl, let the man talk.

LINDNER (*with understated relief*). Thank you. I would sort of like to explain this thing in my own way. I mean I want to explain to you in a certain way.

WALTER. Go ahead.

LINDNER. Yes. Well. I'm going to try to get right to the point. I'm sure we'll all appreciate that in the long run.

BENEATHA. Yes.

LINDNER. Well—

WALTER. Be still now!

LINDNER. Well—

RUTH (*still innocently*). Would you like another chair—you don't look comfortable.

LINDNER (*more frustrated than annoyed*). No, thank you very much. Please. Well—to get right to the point I—(*a great breath, and he is off at last*) I am sure you people must be aware of some of the incidents which have happened in various parts of the city when colored people have moved into certain areas—(BENEATHA *exhales heavily and starts tossing a piece of fruit up and down in the air.*) Well—because we have what I think is going to be a unique type of organization in American community life—not only do we deplore that kind of thing—but we are trying to do something about it. (BENEATHA *stops tossing and turns with a new and quizzical interest to the man.*) We feel—(*gaining confidence in his mission because of the interest in the faces of the people he is talking to*)—we feel that most of the trouble in this world, when you come right down to it—(*he hits his knee for emphasis*)—most of the trouble exists because people just don't sit down and talk to each other.

RUTH (*nodding as she might in church, pleased with the remark*). You can say that again, mister.

LINDNER (*more encouraged by such affirmation*). That we don't try hard enough in this world to understand the other fellow's problem. The other guy's point of view.

RUTH. Now that's right.

(BENEATHA *and* WALTER *merely watch and listen with genuine interest.*)

LINDNER. Yes—that's the way we feel out in Clybourne Park. And that's why I was elected to come here this afternoon and talk to you people. Friendly like, you know, the way people should talk to each other and see if we couldn't find some way to work this thing out. As I say, the whole business is a matter of *caring* about the other fellow. Anybody can see that you are a nice family of folks, hard-working and honest I'm sure. (BENEATHA *frowns slightly, quizzically, her head tilted regarding him.*) Today everybody knows what it means to be on the outside of *something*. And of course, there is always somebody who is out to take the advantage of people who don't always understand.

WALTER. What do you mean?

LINDNER. Well—you see our community is made up of people who've worked hard as the dickens for years to build up that little community. They're not rich and fancy people; just hard-working, honest people who don't really have much but those little homes and a dream of the kind of community they want to raise their children in. Now, I don't say we are perfect and there is a lot wrong in some of the things they want. But you've got to admit that a man, right or wrong, has the right to want to have the neighborhood he lives in a certain kind of way. And at the moment the overwhelming majority of our people out there feel that people get along better, take more of a common interest in the life of the community, when they share a common background. I want you to believe me when I tell you that race prejudice simply doesn't enter into it. It is a matter of the people of Clybourne Park believing, rightly or wrongly, as I say, that for the happiness of all concerned that our Negro families are happier when they live in their *own* communities.

BENEATHA (*with a grand and bitter gesture*). This, friends, is the Welcoming Committee!

WALTER (*dumbfounded, looking at* LINDNER). Is this what you came marching all the way over here to tell us?

LINDNER. Well, now we've been having a fine conversation. I hope you'll hear me all the way through.

WALTER (*tightly*). Go ahead, man.

LINDNER. You see—in the face of all things I have said, we are prepared to make your family a very generous offer. . . .

BENEATHA. Thirty pieces and not a coin less!

WALTER. Yeah?

LINDNER (*putting on his glasses and drawing a form out of the briefcase*). Our association is prepared, through the collective effort of our people, to buy the house from you at a financial gain to your family.

RUTH. Lord have mercy, ain't this the living gall!

WALTER. All right, you through?

LINDNER. Well, I want to give you the exact terms of the financial arrangement—

WALTER. We don't want to hear no exact terms of no arrangements. I want to know if you got any more to tell us 'bout getting together?

LINDNER (*taking off his glasses*). Well—I don't suppose that you feel. . . .

WALTER. Never mind how I feel—you got any more to say 'bout how people ought to sit down and talk to each other? . . . Get out of my house, man. (*He turns his back and walks to the door.*)

LINDNER (*looking around at the hostile faces and reaching and assembling his hat and briefcase*). Well—I don't understand why you people are reacting this way. What do you think you are going to gain by moving into a neighborhood where you just aren't wanted and where some elements —well—people can get awful worked up when they feel that their whole way of life and everything they've ever worked for is threatened.

WALTER. Get out.

LINDNER (*at the door, holding a small card*). Well—I'm sorry it went like this.

WALTER. Get out.

LINDNER (*almost sadly, regarding* WALTER). You just can't force people to change their hearts, son.

(*He turns and puts his card on a table and exits.* WALTER *pushes the door to with stinging hatred, and stands looking at it.* RUTH *just sits and* BENEATHA *just stands. They say nothing.* MAMA *and* TRAVIS *enter.*)

MAMA. Well—this all the packing got done since I left out of here this morning. I testify before God that my children got all the energy of the dead. What time the moving men due?

BENEATHA. Four o'clock. You had a caller, Mama. (*She is smiling, teasingly.*)

MAMA. Sure enough—who?

BENEATHA (*her arms folded saucily*). The Welcoming Committee.

(WALTER *and* RUTH *giggle.*)

MAMA (*innocently*). Who?

BENEATHA. The Welcoming Committee. They said they're sure going to be glad to see you when you get there.

WALTER (*devilishly*). Yeah, they said they can't hardly wait to see your face.

(*Laughter.*)

MAMA (*sensing their facetiousness*). What's the matter with you all?

WALTER. Ain't nothing the matter with us. We just telling you 'bout the gentleman who came to see you this afternoon. From the Clybourne Park Improvement Association.

MAMA. What he want?

RUTH (*in the same mood as* BENEATHA *and* WALTER). To welcome you, honey.

WALTER. He said they can't hardly wait. He said the one thing they don't have, that they just *dying* to have out there is a fine family of colored people! (*To* RUTH *and* BENEATHA) Ain't that right!

RUTH *and* BENEATHA (*mockingly*). Yeah! He left his card in case—

(*They indicate the card, and* MAMA *picks it up and throws it on the floor—understanding and looking off as she draws her chair up to the table on which she has put her plant and some sticks and some cord.*)

MAMA. Father, give us strength. (*Knowingly—and without fun*) Did he threaten us?

BENEATHA. Oh—Mama—they don't do it like that any more. He talked Brotherhood. He said everybody ought to learn how to sit down and hate each other with good Christian fellowship.

(*She and* WALTER *shake hands to ridicule the remark.*)

MAMA (*sadly*). Lord, protect us. . . .

RUTH. You should hear the money those folks raised to buy the house from us. All we paid and then some.

BENEATHA. What they think we going to do—eat 'em?

RUTH. No, honey, marry 'em.

MAMA (*shaking her head*). Lord, Lord, Lord. . . .

RUTH. Well—that's the way the crackers crumble. Joke.

BENEATHA (*laughingly noticing what her mother is doing*). Mama, what are you doing?

MAMA. Fixing my plant so it won't get hurt none on the way. . . .

BENEATHA. Mama, you going to take *that* to the new house?

MAMA. Un-huh—

BENEATHA. That raggedy-looking old thing?

MAMA (*stopping and looking at her*). It expresses *me*.

RUTH (*with delight, to* BENEATHA). So there, Miss Thing!

(WALTER *comes to* MAMA *suddenly and bends down behind her and squeezes her in his arms with all his strength. She is overwhelmed by the suddenness of it and, though delighted, her manner is like that of* RUTH *with* TRAVIS.)

MAMA. Look out now, boy! You make me mess up my thing here!

WALTER (*his face lit, he slips down on his knees beside her, his arms still about her*). Mama . . . you know what it means to climb up in the chariot?

MAMA (*gruffly, very happy*). Get on away from me now. . . .

RUTH (*near the gift-wrapped package, trying to catch* WALTER'S *eye*). Psst—

WALTER. What the old song say, Mama. . . .

RUTH. Walter— Now? (*She is pointing at the package.*)

WALTER (*speaking the lines, sweetly, playfully, in his mother's face*).

I got wings . . . you got wings . . .
All God's children got wings . . .

MAMA. Boy—get out of my face and do some work. . . .

WALTER.

When I get to heaven gonna put on my wings.
Gonna fly all over God's heaven . . .

BENEATHA (*teasingly, from across the room*). Everybody talking 'bout heaven ain't going there!

WALTER (*to* RUTH, *who is carrying the box across to them*). I don't know, you think we ought to give her that. . . . Seems to me she ain't been very appreciative around here.

MAMA (*eying the box, which is obviously a gift*). What is that?

WALTER (*taking it from* RUTH *and putting it on the table in front of* MAMA). Well—what you all think? Should we give it to her?

RUTH. Oh—she was pretty good today.

MAMA. I'll good you— (*She turns her eyes to the box again.*)

BENEATHA. Open it, Mama.

(*She stands up, looks at it, turns and looks at all of them, and then presses her hands together and does not open the package.*)

WALTER (*sweetly*). Open it, Mama. It's for you. (MAMA *looks in his eyes. It is the first present in her life without its being Christmas. Slowly she opens her package and lifts out, one by one, a brand-new sparkling set of gardening tools.* WALTER *continues, prodding*) Ruth made up the note—read it . . .

MAMA (*picking up the card and adjusting her glasses*). "To our own Mrs. Miniver—Love from Brother, Ruth and Beneatha." Ain't that lovely. . . .

TRAVIS (*tugging at his father's sleeve*). Daddy, can I give her mine now?

WALTER. All right, son. (TRAVIS *flies to get his gift.*) Travis didn't want to go in with the rest of us, Mama. He got his own. (*Somewhat amused*) We don't know what it is. . . .

TRAVIS (*racing back in the room with a large hatbox and putting it in front of his grandmother*). Here!

MAMA. Lord have mercy, baby. You done gone and bought your grandmother a hat?

TRAVIS (*very proud*). Open it!

(*She does and lifts out an elaborate, but very elaborate, wide gardening hat, and all the adults break up at the sight of it.*)

RUTH. Travis, honey, what is that?

TRAVIS (*who thinks it is beautiful and appropriate*). It's a gardening hat! Like the ladies always have on in the magazines when they work in their gardens.

BENEATHA (*giggling fiercely*). Travis—we were trying to make Mama Mrs. Miniver—not Scarlett O'Hara!

MAMA (*indignantly*). What's the matter with you all! This here is a beautiful hat! (*Absurdly*) I always wanted me one just like it!

(*She pops it on her head to prove it to her grandson, and the hat is ludicrous and considerably oversized.*)

RUTH. Hot dog! Go, Mama!

WALTER (*doubled over with laughter*). I'm sorry, Mama—but you look like you ready to go out and chop you some cotton sure enough!

(*They all laugh except* MAMA, *out of deference to* TRAVIS' *feelings.*)

MAMA (*gathering the boy up to her*). Bless your heart—this is the prettiest hat I ever owned— (WALTER, RUTH, *and* BENEATHA *chime in noisily, festively and insincerely congratulating* TRAVIS *on his gift.*) What are we all standing around here for? We ain't finished packin' yet. Bennie, you ain't packed one book.

(*The bell rings.*)

BENEATHA. That couldn't be the movers . . . it's not hardly two good yet—

(BENEATHA *goes into her room.* MAMA *starts for door.*)

WALTER (*turning, stiffening*). Wait—wait—I'll get it. (*He stands and looks at the door.*)

MAMA. You expecting company, son?

WALTER (*just looking at the door*). Yeah—yeah. . . .

(MAMA *looks at* RUTH, *and they exchange innocent and unfrightened glances.*)

MAMA (*not understanding*). Well, let them in, son.

BENEATHA (*from her room*). We need some more string.

MAMA. Travis—you run to the hardware and get me some string cord.

(MAMA *goes out and* WALTER *turns and looks at* RUTH. TRAVIS *goes to a dish for money.*)

RUTH. Why don't you answer the door, man?

WALTER (*suddenly bounding across the floor to her*). 'Cause sometimes it hard to let the future begin! (*Stooping down in her face*)

I got wings! You got wings!
All God's children got wings!

(*He crosses to the door and throws it open. Standing there is a very slight little man in a not too prosperous business suit and with haunted frightened eyes and a hat pulled down tightly, brim up, around his forehead.* TRAVIS *passes between the men and exits.* WALTER *leans deep in the man's face, still in his jubilance.*)

When I get to heaven gonna put on my wings.
Gonna fly all over God's heaven . . .

(*The little man just stares at him.*)

Heaven—

(*Suddenly he stops and looks past the little man into the empty hallway.*) Where's Willy, man?

BOBO. He ain't with me.

WALTER (*not disturbed*). Oh—come on in. You know my wife.

BOBO (*dumbly, taking off his hat*). Yes—h'you, Miss Ruth.

RUTH (*quietly, a mood apart from her husband already, seeing* BOBO). Hello, Bobo.

WALTER. You right on time today. . . . Right on time. That's the way! (*He slaps* BOBO *on his back.*) Sit down . . . lemme hear.

(RUTH *stands stiffly and quietly in back of them, as though somehow she senses death, her eyes fixed on her husband.*)

BOBO (*his frightened eyes on the floor, his hat in his hands*). Could I please get a drink of water, before I tell you about it, Walter Lee?

(WALTER *does not take his eyes off the man.* RUTH *goes blindly to the tap and gets a glass of water and brings it to* BOBO.

WALTER. There ain't nothing wrong, is there?

BOBO. Lemme tell you—

WALTER. Man—didn't nothing go wrong?

BOBO. Lemme tell you—Walter Lee. (*Looking at* RUTH *and talking to her more than to* WALTER) You know how it was. I got to tell you how it was. I mean first I got tell you how it was all the way . . . I mean about the money I put in, Walter Lee. . . .

WALTER (*with taut agitation now*). What about the money you put in?

BOBO. Well—it wasn't much as we told you—me and Willy—(*He stops.*) I'm sorry, Walter. I got a bad feeling about it. I got a real bad feeling about it. . . .

WALTER. Man, what you telling me about all this for? . . . Tell me what happened in Springfield. . . .

BOBO. Springfield.

RUTH (*like a dead woman*). What was supposed to happen in Springfield?

BOBO (*to her*). This deal that me and Walter went into with Willy—Me and Willy was going to go down to Springfield and spread some money 'round so's we wouldn't have to wait so long for the liquor license. . . . That's what we were going to do. Everybody said that was the way you had to do, you understand, Miss Ruth?

WALTER. Man—what happened down there?

BOBO (*a pitiful man, near tears*). I'm trying to tell you, Walter.

WALTER (*screaming at him suddenly*). THEN TELL ME, GODDAMMIT . . . WHAT'S THE MATTER WITH YOU?

BOBO. Man . . . I didn't go to no Springfield, yesterday.

WALTER (*halted, life hanging in the moment*). Why not?

BOBO (*the long way, the hard way to tell*). 'Cause I didn't have no reasons to. . . .

WALTER. Man, what are you talking about!

BOBO. I'm talking about the fact that when I got to the train station yesterday morning—eight o'clock like we planned . . . Man—*Willy didn't never show up.*

WALTER. Why . . . where was he . . . where is he?

BOBO. That's what I'm trying to tell you . . . I don't know . . . I waited six hours . . . I called his house . . . and I waited . . . six hours . . . I waited in that train station six hours . . . (*Breaking into tears*) That was all the extra money I had in the world. . . . (*Looking up at* WALTER *with the tears running down his face*) Man, *Willy is gone.*

WALTER. Gone, what you mean Willy is gone? Gone where? You mean he went by himself. You mean he went off to Springfield by himself—to take care of getting the license—(*Turns and looks anxiously at* RUTH) You mean maybe he didn't want too many people in on the business down there? (*Looks to* RUTH *again, as before*) You know Willy got his own ways. (*Looks back to* BOBO) Maybe you was late yesterday and he just went on down there without you. Maybe—maybe—he's been callin' you at home tryin' to tell you what happened or something. Maybe—maybe—he just got sick. He's somewhere—he's got to be somewhere. We just got to find him—me and you got to find him. (*Grabs* BOBO *senselessly by the collar and starts to shake him*) We got to!

BOBO (*in sudden angry, frightened agony*). What's the matter with you, Walter! *When a cat take off with your money he don't leave you no maps!*

WALTER (*turning madly, as though he is looking for* WILLY *in the very room*). Willy! . . . Willy . . . don't do it. . . . Please don't do it. . . . Man, not with that money . . . Man, please, not with that money . . . Oh, God . . . Don't let it be true. . . . (*He is wandering around, crying out for* WILLY *and looking for him or perhaps for help from God.*) Man . . . I trusted you . . . Man, I put my life in your hands. . . . (*He starts to crumple down on the floor as* RUTH *just covers her face in horror.* MAMA *opens the door and comes into the room, with* BENEATHA *behind her.*) Man . . . (*He starts to pound the floor with his fists, sobbing wildly.*) *That money is made out of my father's flesh. . . .*

BOBO (*standing over him helplessly*). I'm sorry, Walter. . . . (*Only* WALTER'S *sobs reply.* BOBO *puts on his hat.*) I had my life staked on this deal, too. . . . (*He exits.*)

MAMA (*to* WALTER). Son—(*She goes to him, bends down to him, talks to his bent head.*) Son . . . Is it gone? Son, I gave you sixty-five hundred dollars. Is it gone? All of it? Beneatha's money too?

WALTER (*lifting his head slowly*). Mama . . . I never . . . went to the bank at all. . . .

MAMA (*not wanting to believe him*). You mean . . . your sister's school money . . . you used that too . . . Walter? . . .

WALTER. Yessss! . . . All of it. . . . It's all gone. . . .

(*There is total silence.* RUTH *stands with her face covered with her hands;* BENEATHA *leans forlornly against a wall, fingering a piece of red ribbon from the mother's gift.* MAMA *stops and looks at her son without recognition and then, quite without thinking about it, starts to beat him senselessly in the face.* BENEATHA *goes to them and stops it.*)

BENEATHA. Mama!

(MAMA *stops and looks at both of her children and rises slowly and wanders vaguely, aimlessly away from them.*)

MAMA. I seen . . . him . . . night after night . . . come in . . . and look at that rug . . . and then look at me . . . the red showing in his eyes . . . the veins moving in his head. . . . I seen him grow thin and old before he was forty . . . working and working and working like somebody's old horse . . . killing himself . . . and you—you give it all away in a day. . . .

BENEATHA. Mama—

MAMA. Oh, God . . . (*She looks up to Him.*) Look down here—and show me the strength.

BENEATHA. Mama—

MAMA (*folding over*). Strength . . .

BENEATHA (*plaintively*). Mama . . .

MAMA. Strength!

CURTAIN

ACT III

An hour later.

At curtain, there is a sullen light of gloom in the living room, gray light not unlike that which began the first scene of Act I. At left we can see WALTER *within his room, alone with himself. He is stretched out on the bed, his shirt out and open, his arms under his head. He does not smoke, he does not cry out, he merely lies there, looking up at the ceiling, much as if he were alone in the world.*

In the living room BENEATHA *sits at the table, still surrounded by the now almost ominous packing crates. She sits looking off. We feel that this is a mood struck perhaps an hour before, and it lingers now, full of the empty sound of profound disappointment. We see on a line from her brother's bedroom the sameness of their attitudes. Presently the bell rings and* BENEATHA *rises without ambition or interest in answering. It is* ASAGAI, *smiling broadly, striding into the room with energy and happy expectation and conversation.*

ASAGAI. I came over . . . I had some free time. I thought I might help with the packing. Ah, I like the look of packing crates! A household in preparation for a journey! It depresses some people . . . but for me . . . it is another feeling. Something full of the flow of life, do you understand? Movement, progress . . . It makes me think of Africa.

BENEATHA. Africa!

ASAGAI. What kind of a mood is this? Have I told you how deeply you move me?

BENEATHA. He gave away the money, Asagai. . . .

ASAGAI. Who gave away what money?

BENEATHA. The insurance money. My brother gave it away.

ASAGAI. Gave it away?

BENEATHA. He made an investment! With a man even Travis wouldn't have trusted.

ASAGAI. And it's gone?

BENEATHA. Gone!

ASAGAI. I'm very sorry. . . . And you, now?

BENEATHA. Me? . . . Me? . . . Me I'm nothing. . . . Me. When I was very small . . . we used to take our sleds out in the wintertime and the only hills we had were the ice-covered stone steps of some houses down the street. And we used to fill them in with snow and make them smooth and slide down them all day . . . and it was very dangerous you know . . . far too steep . . . and sure enough one day a kid named Rufus came down too fast and hit the sidewalk . . . and we saw his face just split open right there in front of us. . . . And I remember standing there looking at his bloody open face thinking that was the end of Rufus. But the ambulance came and they took him to the hospital and they fixed the broken bones and they sewed it all up . . .

and the next time I saw Rufus he just had a little line down the middle of his face. . . . I never got over that. . . .

(WALTER *sits up, listening on the bed. Throughout this scene it is important that we feel his reaction at all times, that he visibly respond to the words of his sister and* ASAGAI.)

ASAGAI. What?

BENEATHA. That was what one person could do for another, fix him up—sew up the problem, make him all right again. That was the most marvelous thing in the world. . . . I wanted to do that. I always thought it was the one concrete thing in the world that a human being could do. Fix up the sick, you know—and make them whole again. This was truly being God. . . .

ASAGAI. You wanted to be God?

BENEATHA. No—I wanted to cure. It used to be so important to me. I wanted to cure. It used to matter. I used to care. I mean about people and how their bodies hurt. . . .

ASAGAI. And you've stopped caring?

BENEATHA. Yes—I think so.

ASAGAI. Why?

(WALTER *rises, goes to the door of his room and is about to open it, then stops and stands listening, leaning on the door jamb.*)

BENEATHA. Because it doesn't seem deep enough, close enough to what ails mankind—I mean this thing of sewing up bodies or administering drugs. Don't you understand? It was a child's reaction to the world. I thought that doctors had the secret to all the hurts. . . . That's the way a child sees things—or an idealist.

ASAGAI. Children see things very well sometimes—and idealists even better.

BENEATHA. I know that's what you think. Because you are still where I left off—you still care. This is what you see for the world, for Africa. You with the dreams of the future will patch up all Africa—you are going to cure the Great Sore of colonialism with Independence—

ASAGAI. Yes!

BENEATHA. Yes—and you think that one word is the penicillin of the human spirit: "Independence!" But then what?

ASAGAI. That will be the problem for another time. First we must get there.

BENEATHA. And where does it end?

ASAGAI. End? Who even spoke of an end? To life? To living?

BENEATHA. An end to misery!

ASAGAI (*smiling*). You sound like a French intellectual.

BENEATHA. No! I sound like a human being who just had her future taken right out of her hands! While I was sleeping in my bed in there, things were happening in this world that directly concerned me—and nobody asked me, consulted me—they just went out and did things—and changed my life. Don't you see there isn't any real progress, Asagai, there is only one large circle that we march in, around and around, each of us with our own little picture—in front of us—our own little mirage that we think is the future.

Asagai. That is the mistake.

Beneatha. What?

Asagai. What you just said—about the circle. It isn't a circle—it is simply a long line—as in geometry, you know, one that reaches into infinity. And because we cannot see the end—we also cannot see how it changes. And it is very odd but those who see the changes are called "idealists"—and those who cannot, or refuse to think, they are the "realists." It is very strange, and amusing too, I think.

Beneatha. You—you are almost religious.

Asagai. Yes . . . I think I have the religion of doing what is necessary in the world—and of worshipping man—because he is so marvelous, you see.

Beneatha. Man is foul! And the human race deserves its misery!

Asagai. You see: *you* have become the religious one in the old sense. Already, and after such a small defeat, you are worshipping despair.

Beneatha. From now on, I worship the truth—and the truth is that people are puny, small and selfish. . . .

Asagai. Truth? Why is it that you despairing ones always think that only you have the truth? I never thought to see *you* like that. You! Your brother made a stupid, childish mistake—and you are grateful to him. So that now you can give up the ailing human race on account of it. You talk about what good is struggle; what good is anything? Where are we all going? And why are we bothering?

Beneatha. *And you cannot answer it!* All your talk and dreams about Africa and Independence. Independence and then what? What about all the crooks and petty thieves and just plain idiots who will come into power to steal and plunder the same as before—only now they will be black and do it in the name of the new Independence— You cannot answer that.

Asagai (*shouting over her*). *I live the answer!* (*Pause.*) In my village at home it is the exceptional man who can even read a newspaper . . . or who ever *sees* a book at all. I will go home and much of what I will have to say will seem strange to the people of my village. . . . But I will teach and work and things will happen, slowly and swiftly. At times it will seem that nothing changes at all . . . and then again . . . the sudden dramatic events which make history leap into the future. And then quiet again. Retrogression even. Guns, murder, revolution. And I even will have moments when I wonder if the quiet was not better than all that death and hatred. But I will look about my village at the illiteracy and disease and ignorance and I will not wonder long. And perhaps . . . perhaps I will be a great man. . . . I mean perhaps I will hold on to the substance of truth and find my way always with the right course . . . and perhaps for it I will be butchered in my bed some night by the servants of the empire. . . .

BENEATHA. *The martyr!*

ASAGAI. . . . or perhaps I shall live to be a very old man, respected and esteemed in my new nation. . . . And perhaps I shall hold office and this is what I'm trying to tell you, Alaiyo; perhaps the things I believe now for my country will be wrong and outmoded, and I will not understand and do terrible things to have things my way or merely to keep my power. Don't you see that there will be young men and women, not British soldiers then, but my own black countrymen . . . to step out of the shadows some evening and slit my then useless throat? Don't you see they have always been there . . . that they always will be. And that such a thing as my own death will be an advance? They who might kill me even . . . actually replenish me!

BENEATHA. Oh, Asagai, I know all that.

ASAGAI. Good! Then stop moaning and groaning and tell me what you plan to do.

BENEATHA. Do?

ASAGAI. I have a bit of a suggestion.

BENEATHA. What?

ASAGAI (*rather quietly for him*). That when it is all over—that you come home with me—

BENEATHA (*slapping herself on the forehead with exasperation born of misunderstanding*). Oh—Asagai—at this moment you decide to be romantic!

ASAGAI (*quickly understanding the misunderstanding*). My dear, young creature of the New World—I do not mean across the city—I mean across the ocean; home—to Africa.

BENEATHA (*slowly understanding and turning to him with murmured amazement*). To—to Nigeria?

ASAGAI. Yes! . . . (*Smiling and lifting his arms playfully*) Three hundred years later the African Prince rose up out of the seas and swept the maiden back across the middle passage over which her ancestors had come—

BENEATHA (*unable to play*). Nigeria?

ASAGAI. Nigeria. Home. (*Coming to her with genuine romantic flippancy*) I will show you our mountains and our stars; and give you cool drinks from gourds and teach you the old songs and the ways of our people—and, in time, we will pretend that—(*very softly*)—you have only been away for a day—

(*She turns her back to him, thinking. He swings her around and takes her full in his arms in a long embrace which proceeds to passion.*)

BENEATHA (*pulling away*). You're getting me all mixed up—

ASAGAI. Why?

BENEATHA. Too many things—too many things have happened today. I must sit down and think. I don't know what I feel about anything right this minute. (*She promptly sits down and props her chin on her fist.*)

ASAGAI (*charmed*). All right, I shall leave you. No—don't get up. (*Touching her, gently, sweetly*) Just sit awhile and think. . . . Never be afraid to sit awhile and think. (*He goes to door and looks at her.*) How often I have looked at you and said, "Ah—so this is what the New World hath finally wrought. . . ."

(*He exits.* BENEATHA *sits on alone. Presently* WALTER *enters from his room and starts to rummage through things, feverishly looking for something. She looks up and turns in her seat.*)

BENEATHA (*hissingly*). Yes—just look at what the New World hath wrought! . . . Just look! (*She gestures with bitter disgust.*) There he is! *Monsieur le petit bourgeois noir*—himself! There he is—Symbol of a Rising Class! Entrepreneur! Titan of the system! (WALTER *ignores her completely and continues frantically and destructively looking for something and hurling things to floor and tearing things out of their place in his search.* BENEATHA *ignores the eccentricity of his actions and goes on with the monologue of insult.*) Did you dream of yachts on Lake Michigan, Brother? Did you see yourself on that Great Day sitting down at the Conference Table, surrounded by all the mighty bald-headed men in America? All halted, waiting, breathless, waiting for your pronouncements on industry? Waiting for you—Chairman of the Board? (WALTER *finds what he is looking for—a small piece of white paper—and pushes it in his pocket and puts on his coat and rushes out without ever having looked at her. She shouts after him.*) I look at you and I see the final triumph of stupidity in the world!

(*The door slams and she returns to just sitting again.* RUTH *comes quickly out of* MAMA*'s room.*)

RUTH. Who was that?
BENEATHA. Your husband.
RUTH. Where did he go?
BENEATHA. Who knows—maybe he has an appointment at U.S. Steel.
RUTH (*anxiously, with frightened eyes*). You didn't say nothing bad to him, did you?
BENEATHA. Bad? Say anything bad to him? No—I told him he was a sweet boy and full of dreams and everything is strictly peachy keen, as the ofay kids say!

(MAMA *enters from her bedroom. She is lost, vague, trying to catch hold, to make some sense of her former command of the world, but it still eludes her. A sense of waste overwhelms her gait; a measure of apology rides on her shoulders. She goes to her plant, which has remained on the table, looks at it, picks it up and takes it to the window sill and sits it outside, and she stands and looks at it a long moment. Then she closes the window, straightens her body with effort and turns around to her children.*)

MAMA. Well—ain't it a mess in here, though? (*A false cheerfulness, a beginning of something*) I guess we all better stop moping around and get some work done. All this unpacking and everything we got to do. (RUTH *raises her head slowly in response to the sense of the line; and* BENEATHA *in similar manner turns very slowly to look at her mother.*) One of you all better call the moving people and tell 'em not to come.

RUTH. Tell 'em not to come?

MAMA. Of course, baby. Ain't no need in 'em coming all the way here and having to go back. They charges for that too. (*She sits down, fingers to her brow, thinking.*) Lord, ever since I was a little girl, I always remembers people saying, "Lena—Lena Eggleston, you aims too high all the time. You needs to slow down and see life a little more like it is. Just slow down some." That's what they always used to say down home—"Lord, that Lena Eggleston is a high-minded thing. She'll get her due one day!"

RUTH. No, Lena. . . .

MAMA. Me and Big Walter just didn't never learn right.

RUTH. Lena, no! We gotta go. Bennie—tell her. . . . (*She rises and crosses to* BENEATHA *with her arms outstretched.* BENEATHA *doesn't respond.*) Tell her we can still move . . . the notes ain't but a hundred and twenty-five a month. We got four grown people in this house—we can work. . . .

MAMA (*to herself*). Just aimed too high all the time—

RUTH (*turning and going to* MAMA *fast—the words pouring out with urgency and desperation*). Lena—I'll work. . . . I'll work twenty hours a day in all the kitchens in Chicago. . . . I'll strap my baby on my back if I have to and scrub all the floors in America and wash all the sheets in America if I have to—but we got to move. . . . We got to get out of here. . . .

(MAMA *reaches out absently and pats* RUTH'S *hand.*)

MAMA. No—I see things differently now. Been thinking 'bout some of the things we could do to fix this place up some. I seen a second-hand bureau over on Maxwell Street just the other day that could fit right there. (*She points to where the new furniture might go.* RUTH *wanders away from her.*) Would need some new handles on it and then a little varnish and then it look like something brand-new. And—we can put up them new curtains in the kitchen. . . . Why this place be looking fine. Cheer us all up so that we forget trouble ever came. . . . (*To* RUTH) And you could get some nice screens to put up in your room round the baby's bassinet. . . . (*She looks at both of them, pleadingly.*) Sometimes you just got to know when to give up some things . . . and hold on to what you got.

(WALTER *enters from the outside, looking spent and leaning against the door, his coat hanging from him.*)

MAMA. Where you been, son?

WALTER (*breathing hard*). Made a call.

MAMA. To who, son?

WALTER. To The Man.

MAMA. What man, baby?

WALTER. The Man, Mama. Don't you know who The Man is?

RUTH. Walter Lee?

WALTER. *The Man.* Like the guys in the streets say—The Man. Captain Boss—Mistuh Charley . . . Old Captain Please Mr. Bossman . . .

BENEATHA (*suddenly*). Lindner!

WALTER. That's right! That's good. I told him to come right over.

BENEATHA (*fiercely, understanding*). For what? What do you want to see him for!

WALTER (*looking at his sister*). We going to do business with him.

MAMA. What you talking 'bout, son?

WALTER. Talking 'bout life, Mama. You all always telling me to see life like it is. Well—I laid in there on my back today . . . and I figured it out. Life just like it is. Who gets and who don't get. (*He sits down with his coat on and laughs.*) Mama, you know it's all divided up. Life is. Sure enough. Between the takers and the "tooken." (*He laughs.*) I've figured it out finally. (*He looks around at them.*) Yeah. Some of us always getting "tooken." (*He laughs.*) People like Willy Harris, they don't never get "tooken." And you know why the rest of us do? 'Cause we all mixed up. Mixed up bad. We get to looking 'round for the right and the wrong; and we worry about it and cry about it and stay up nights trying to figure out 'bout the wrong and the right of things all the time. . . . And all the time, man, them takers is out there operating, just taking and taking. Willy Harris? Shoot—Willy Harris don't even count. He don't even count in the big scheme of things. But I'll say one thing for old Willy Harris . . . he's taught me something. He's taught me to keep my eye on what counts in this world. Yeah—(*shouting out a little*) Thanks, Willy!

RUTH. What did you call that man for, Walter Lee?

WALTER. Called him to tell him to come on over to the show. Gonna put on a show for the man. Just what he wants to see. You see, Mama, the man came here today and he told us that them people out there where you want us to move—well they so upset they willing to pay us not to move out there. (*He laughs again.*) And—and oh, Mama—you would of been proud of the way me and Ruth and Bennie acted. We told him to get out . . . Lord have mercy! We told the man to get out. Oh, we was some proud folks this afternoon, yeah. (*He lights a cigarette.*) We were still full of that old-time stuff. . . .

RUTH (*coming toward him slowly*). You talking 'bout taking them people's money to keep us from moving in that house?

WALTER. I ain't just talking 'bout it, baby—I'm telling you that's what's going to happen.

BENEATHA. Oh, God! Where is the bottom! Where is the real honest-to-God bottom so he can't go any farther!

WALTER. See—that's old stuff. You and that boy that was here today. You all want everybody to carry a flag and a spear and sing some marching songs, huh? You wanna spend your life looking into things and trying to find the right and the wrong part, huh? Yeah. You know what's going to happen to that boy someday—he'll find himself sitting in a dungeon, locked in forever—and the takers will have the key! Forget it, baby! There ain't no causes—there ain't nothing but taking in this world, and he who takes most is smartest—and it don't make a damn bit of difference *how*.

MAMA. You making something inside me cry, son. Some awful pain inside me.

WALTER. Don't cry, Mama. Understand. That white man is going to walk in that door able to write checks for more money than we ever had. It's important to him and I'm going to help him . . . I'm going to put on the show, Mama.

MAMA. Son—I come from five generations of people who was slaves and sharecroppers—but ain't nobody in my family never let nobody pay 'em no money that was a way of telling us we wasn't fit to walk the earth. We ain't never been that poor. (*Raising her eyes and looking at him*) We ain't never been that dead inside.

BENEATHA. Well—we are dead now. All the talk about dreams and sunlight that goes on in this house. All dead.

WALTER. What's the matter with you all! I didn't make this world! It was give to me this way! Hell, yes, I want me some yachts someday! Yes, I want to hang some real pearls 'round my wife's neck. Ain't she supposed to wear no pearls? Somebody tell me—tell me, who decides which women is suppose to wear pearls in this world. I tell you I am a *man*—and I think my wife should wear some pearls in this world!

(*This last line hangs a good while and* WALTER *begins to move about the room. The word "Man" has penetrated his consciousness; he mumbles it to himself repeatedly between strange agitated pauses as he moves about.*)

MAMA. Baby, how you going to feel on the inside?

WALTER. Fine! . . . Going to feel fine . . . a man. . . .

MAMA. You won't have nothing left then, Walter Lee.

WALTER (*coming to her*). I'm going to feel fine, Mama. I'm going to look that son-of-a-bitch in the eyes and say—(*he falters*)—and say, "All right, Mr. Lindner—(*he falters even more*)—that's your neighborhood out there. You got the right to keep it like you want. You got the right to have it like you want. Just write the check and—the house is yours." And, and I am going to say— (*His voice almost breaks.*) And you—you people just put the money in my hand and you won't have to live next to this bunch of stinking niggers! . . . (*He straightens up and moves away from his mother, walking around the room.*) Maybe—maybe I'll just get down on my black knees. . . . (*He does so;* RUTH *and* BENNIE *and* MAMA *watch him in frozen horror.*) Captain, Mistuh, Bossman. (*He starts crying.*) A-hee-hee-hee! (*Wringing his hands in profoundly anguished imitation*) Yasssssuh! Great White Father, just gi' ussen de money, fo' God's sake, and we's ain't gwine come out deh and dirty up yo' white folks neighborhood. . . .

(*He breaks down completely, then gets up and goes into the bedroom.*)

BENEATHA. That is not a man. That is nothing but a toothless rat.

MAMA. Yes—death done come in this here house. (*She is nodding, slowly, reflectively.*) Done come walking in my house. On the lips of my children. You what supposed to be my beginning again. You—what supposed to be my harvest. (*To* BENEATHA) You—you mourning your brother?

BENEATHA. He's no brother of mine.

MAMA. What you say?

BENEATHA. I said that that individual in that room is no brother of mine.

MAMA. That's what I thought you said. You feeling like you better than he is today? (BENEATHA *does not answer.*) Yes? What you tell him a minute ago? That he wasn't a man? Yes? You give him up for me? You done wrote his epitaph too—like the rest of the world? Well, who give you the privilege?

BENEATHA. Be on my side for once! You saw what he just did, Mama! You saw him—down on his knees. Wasn't it you who taught me—to despise any man who would do that. Do what he's going to do.

MAMA. Yes—I taught you that. Me and your daddy. But I thought I taught you something else too . . . I thought I taught you to love him.

BENEATHA. Love him? There is nothing left to love.

MAMA. There is always something left to love. And if you ain't learned that, you ain't learned nothing. (*Looking at her*) Have you cried for that boy today? I don't mean for yourself and for the family 'cause we lost the money. I mean for him; what he been through and what it done to him. Child, when do you think is the time to love somebody the most; when they done good and made things easy for everybody? Well then, you ain't through learning—because that ain't the time at all. It's when he's at his lowest and can't believe in hisself 'cause the world done whipped him so. When you starts measuring somebody, measure him right, child, measure him right. Make sure you done taken into account what hills and valleys he come through before he got to wherever he is.

(TRAVIS *bursts into the room at the end of the speech, leaving the door open.*)

TRAVIS. Grandmama—the moving men are downstairs! The truck just pulled up.

MAMA (*turning and looking at him*). Are they, baby? They downstairs?

(*She sighs and sits.* LINDNER *appears in the doorway. He peers in and knocks lightly, to gain attention, and comes in. All turn to look at him.*)

LINDNER (*hat and briefcase in hand*). Uh—hello . . .

(RUTH *crosses mechanically to the bedroom door and opens it and lets it swing open freely and slowly as the lights come up on* WALTER *within, still in his coat, sitting at the far corner of the room. He looks up and out through the room to* LINDNER.)

RUTH. He's here.

(*A long minute passes and* WALTER *slowly gets up.*)

LINDNER (*coming to the table with efficiency, putting his briefcase on the table and starting to unfold papers and unscrew fountain pens*). Well, I certainly was glad to hear from you people. (WALTER *has begun the trek out of the room, slowly and awkwardly, rather like a small boy, passing the back of his sleeve across his mouth from time to time.*) Life can really be so much simpler than people let it be most of the time. Well—with whom do I negotiate? You, Mrs. Younger, or your son here? (MAMA *sits with her hands folded on her lap and her eyes closed as* WALTER *advances.* TRAVIS *goes close to* LINDNER *and looks at the papers curiously.*) Just some official papers, sonny.

RUTH. Travis, you go downstairs.

MAMA (*opening her eyes and looking into* WALTER'*s*). No. Travis, you stay right here. And you make him understand what you doing, Walter Lee. You teach him good. Like Willy Harris taught you. You show where our five generations done come to. Go ahead, son—

WALTER (*looks down into his boy's eyes.* TRAVIS *grins at him merrily and* WALTER *draws him beside him with his arm lightly around his shoulders*). Well, Mr. Lindner. (BENEATHA *turns away.*) We called you—(*there is a profound, simple groping quality in his speech*)—because, well, me and my family—(*He looks around and shifts from one foot to the other.*) Well—we are very plain people. . . .

LINDNER. Yes—

WALTER. I mean—I have worked as a chauffeur most of my life—and my wife here, she does domestic work in people's kitchens. So does my mother. I mean—we are plain people. . . .

LINDNER. Yes, Mr. Younger—

WALTER (*really like a small boy, looking down at his shoes and then up at the man*). And—uh—well, my father, well, he was a laborer most of his life.

LINDNER (*absolutely confused*). Uh, yes—

WALTER (*looking down at his toes once again*). My father almost beat a man to death once because this man called him a bad name or something, you know what I mean?

LINDNER. No, I'm afraid I don't.

WALTER (*finally straightening up*). Well, what I mean is that we come from people who had a lot of pride. I mean—we are very proud people. And that's my sister over there and she's going to be a doctor—and we are very proud—

LINDNER. Well—I am sure that is very nice, but—

WALTER (*starting to cry and facing the man eye to eye*). What I am telling you is that we called you over here to tell you that we are very proud and that this is—this is my son, who makes the sixth generation of our family in this country, and that we have all thought about your offer and we have decided to move into our house because my father—my father—he earned it. (MAMA *has her eyes closed and is rocking back and forth as though she were in church, with her head nodding the amen yes.*) We don't want to make no trouble for nobody or fight no causes—but we will try to be good neighbors. That's all we got to say. (*He looks the man absolutely in the eyes.*) We don't want your money. (*He turns and walks away from the man.*)

LINDNER (*looking around at all of them*). I take it then that you have decided to occupy.

BENEATHA. That's what the man said.

LINDNER (*to* MAMA *in her reverie*). Then I would like to appeal to you, Mrs. Younger. You are older and wiser and understand things better I am sure. . . .

MAMA (*rising*). I am afraid you don't understand. My son said we was going to move and there ain't nothing left for me to say. (*Shaking her head with double meaning*) You know how these young folks is nowadays, mister. Can't do a thing with 'em. Good-bye.

LINDNER (*folding up his materials*). Well—if you are that final about it. . . . There is nothing left for me to say. (*He finishes. He is almost ignored by the family, who are concentrating on* WALTER LEE. *At the door* LINDNER *halts and looks around.*) I sure hope you people know what you're doing. (*He shakes his head and exits.*)

RUTH (*looking around and coming to life*). Well, for God's sake—if the moving men are here—LET'S GET THE HELL OUT OF HERE!

MAMA (*into action*). Ain't it the truth! Look at all this here mess. Ruth, put Travis' good jacket on him. . . . Walter Lee, fix your tie and tuck your shirt in, you look just like somebody's hoodlum. Lord have mercy, where is my plant? (*She flies to get it amid the general bustling of the family, who are deliberately trying to ignore the nobility of the past moment.*) You all start on down. . . . Travis child, don't go empty-handed. . . . Ruth, where did I put that box with my skillets in it? I want to be in charge of it myself. . . . I'm going to make us the biggest dinner we ever ate tonight. . . . Beneatha, what's the matter with them stockings? Pull them things up, girl. . . .

(*The family starts to file out as two moving men appear and begin to carry out the heavier pieces of furniture, bumping into the family as they move about.*)

BENEATHA. Mama, Asagai—asked me to marry him today and go to Africa—

MAMA (*in the middle of her getting-ready activity*). He did? You ain't old enough to marry nobody—(*Seeing the moving men lifting one of her chairs precariously*) Darling, that ain't no bale of cotton, please handle it so we can sit in it again. I had that chair twenty-five years. . . .

(*The movers sigh with exasperation and go on with their work.*)

BENEATHA (*girlishly and unreasonably trying to pursue the conversation*). To go to Africa, Mama—be a doctor in Africa. . . .

MAMA (*distracted*). Yes, baby—

WALTER. Africa! What he want you to go to Africa for?

BENEATHA. To practice there. . . .

WALTER. Girl, if you don't get all them silly ideas out your head! You better marry yourself a man with some loot. . . .

BENEATHA (*angrily, precisely as in the first scene of the play*). What have you got to do with who I marry!

WALTER. Plenty. Now I think George Murchison—

(*He and* BENEATHA *go out yelling at each other vigorously;* BENEATHA *is heard saying that she would not marry* GEORGE MURCHISON *if he were Adam and she were Eve, etc. The anger is loud and real till their voices diminish.* RUTH *stands at the door and turns to* MAMA *and smiles knowingly.*)

MAMA (*fixing her hat at last*). Yeah—they something all right, my children. . . .

RUTH. Yeah—they're something. Let's go, Lena.

MAMA (*stalling, starting to look around at the house*). Yes—I'm coming. Ruth—

RUTH. Yes?

MAMA (*quietly, woman to woman*). He finally come into his manhood today, didn't he? Kind of like a rainbow after the rain. . . .

RUTH (*biting her lip lest her own pride explode in front of* MAMA). Yes, Lena.

(WALTER's *voice calls for them raucously.*)

MAMA (*waving* RUTH *out vaguely*). All right, honey—go on down. I be down directly.

(RUTH *hesitates, then exits.* MAMA *stands, at last alone in the living room, her plant on the table before her as the lights start to come down. She looks around at all the walls and ceilings and suddenly, despite herself, while the children call below, a great heaving thing rises in her and she puts her fist to her mouth, takes a final desperate look, pulls her coat about her, pats her hat and goes out. The lights dim down. The door opens and she comes back in, grabs her plant, and goes out for the last time.*)

CURTAIN

Arthur Miller

DEATH OF A SALESMAN

CHARACTERS

WILLY LOMAN
LINDA
BIFF
HAPPY
BERNARD
THE WOMAN
HOWARD WAGNER
JENNY
STANLEY
MISS FORSYTHE
LETTA
CHARLEY
UNCLE BEN

THE PLACE. *Willy Loman's house and yard and various places he visits in the New York and Boston of today.*

Throughout the play, in the stage directions, left and right mean stage left and stage right.

ACT I

A melody is heard, played upon a flute. It is small and fine, telling of grass and trees and the horizon. The curtain rises.

Before us is the Salesman's house. We are aware of towering, angular shapes behind it, surrounding it on all sides. Only the blue light of the sky falls upon the house and forestage; the surrounding area shows an angry glow of orange. As more light appears, we see a solid vault of apartment houses around the small, fragile-seeming home. An air of the dream clings to the place, a dream rising out of reality. The kitchen at center seems actual enough, for there is a kitchen table with three chairs, and a refrigerator. But no other fixtures are seen. At the back of the kitchen there is a draped entrance, which leads to the living-room. To the right of the kitchen, on a level raised two feet, is a bedroom furnished only with a brass bedstead and a straight chair. On a shelf over the bed a silver athletic trophy stands. A window opens onto the apartment house at the side.

Behind the kitchen, on a level raised six and a half feet, is the boys' bedroom, at present barely visible. Two beds are dimly seen, and at the back of the room a dormer window. (This bedroom is above the unseen living-room.) At the left a stairway curves up to it from the kitchen.

The entire setting is wholly or, in some places, partially transparent. The roof-line of the house is one-dimensional; under and over it we see the apartment buildings. Before the house lies an apron, curving beyond the forestage into the orchestra. This forward area serves as the back yard as well as the locale of all WILLY's *imaginings and of his city scenes. Whenever the action is in the present the actors observe the imaginary wall-lines, entering the house only through its door at the left. But in the scenes of the past these boundaries are broken, and characters enter or leave a room by stepping "through" a wall onto the forestage.*

From the right, WILLY LOMAN, *the Salesman, enters, carrying two large sample cases. The flute plays on. He hears but is not aware of it. He is past sixty years of age, dressed quietly. Even as he crosses the stage to the doorway of the house, his exhaustion is apparent. He unlocks the door, comes into the kitchen, and thankfully lets his burden down, feeling the soreness of his palms. A word-sigh escapes his lips—it might be "Oh, boy, oh, boy." He closes the door, then carries his cases out into the living-room, through the draped kitchen doorway.*

LINDA, *his wife, has stirred in her bed at the right. She gets out and puts on a robe, listening. Most often jovial, she has developed an iron repression of her exceptions to* WILLY's *behavior—she more than loves him, she admires him, as though his mercurial nature, his temper, his massive dreams and little cruelties, served her only as sharp reminders of the turbulent longings within him, longings which she shares but lacks the temperament to utter and follow to their end.*

LINDA (*hearing* WILLY *outside the bedroom, calls with some trepidation*). Willy!

WILLY. It's all right. I came back.

LINDA. Why? What happened? (*Slight pause*) Did something happen, Willly?

WILLY. No, nothing happened.

LINDA. You didn't smash the car, did you?

WILLY (*with casual irritation*). I said nothing happened. Didn't you hear me?

LINDA. Don't you feel well?

WILLY. I'm tired to the death. (*The flute has faded away. He sits on the bed beside her, a little numb.*) I couldn't make it. I just couldn't make it, Linda.

LINDA (*very carefully, delicately*). Where were you all day? You look terrible.

WILLY. I got as far as a little above Yonkers. I stopped for a cup of coffee. Maybe it was the coffee.

LINDA. What?

WILLY (*after a pause*). I suddenly couldn't drive any more. The car kept going off onto the shoulder, y'know?

LINDA (*helpfully*). Oh. Maybe it was the steering again. I don't think Angelo knows the Studebaker.

WILLY. No, it's me, it's me. Suddenly I realize I'm goin' sixty miles an hour and I don't remember the last five minutes. I'm—I can't seem to—keep my mind to it.

LINDA. Maybe it's your glasses. You never went for your new glasses.

WILLY. No, I see everything. I came back ten miles an hour. It took me nearly four hours from Yonkers.

LINDA (*resigned*). Well, you'll just have to take a rest, Willy, you can't continue this way.

WILLY. I just got back from Florida.

LINDA. But you didn't rest your mind. Your mind is overactive, and the mind is what counts, dear.

WILLY. I'll start out in the morning. Maybe I'll feel better in the morning. (*She is taking off his shoes.*) These goddam arch supports are killing me.

LINDA. Take an aspirin. Should I get you an aspirin? It'll soothe you.

WILLY (*with wonder*). I was driving along, you understand? And I was fine. I was even observing the scenery. You can imagine, me looking at scenery, on the road every week of my life. But it's so beautiful up there, Linda, the trees are so thick, and the sun is warm. I opened the windshield and just let the warm air bathe over me. And then all of a sudden I'm goin' off the road! I'm tellin' ya, I absolutely forgot I was driving. If I'd've gone the other way over the white line I might've killed somebody. So I went on again—and five minutes later I'm dreamin' again, and I nearly—(*He presses two fingers against his eyes.*) I have such thoughts, I have such strange thoughts.

LINDA. Willy, dear. Talk to them again. There's no reason why you can't work in New York.

WILLY. They don't need me in New York. I'm the New England man. I'm vital in New England.

LINDA. But you're sixty years old. They can't expect you to keep traveling every week.

WILLY. I'll have to send a wire to Portland. I'm supposed to see Brown and Morrison tomorrow morning at ten o'clock to show the line. Goddammit, I could sell them! (*He starts putting on his jacket.*)

LINDA (*taking the jacket from him*). Why don't you go down to the place tomorrow and tell Howard you've simply got to work in New York? You're too accommodating, dear.

WILLY. If old man Wagner was alive I'd a been in charge of New York now! That man was a prince, he was a masterful man. But that boy of his, that Howard, he don't appreciate. When I went north the first time, the Wagner Company didn't know where New England was!

LINDA. Why don't you tell those things to Howard, dear?

WILLY (*encouraged*). I will, I definitely will. Is there any cheese?

LINDA. I'll make you a sandwich.

WILLY. No, go to sleep. I'll take some milk. I'll be up right away. The boys in?

LINDA. They're sleeping. Happy took Biff on a date tonight.

WILLY (*interested*). That so?

LINDA. It was so nice to see them shaving together, one behind the other, in the bathroom. And going out together. You notice? The whole house smells of shaving lotion.

WILLY. Figure it out. Work a lifetime to pay off a house. You finally own it, and there's nobody to live in it.

LINDA. Well, dear, life is a casting off. It's always that way.

WILLY. No, no, some people—some people accomplish something. Did Biff say anything after I went this morning?

LINDA. You shouldn't have criticized him, Willy, especially after he just got off the train. You mustn't lose your temper with him.

WILLY. When the hell did I lose my temper? I simply asked him if he was making any money. Is that a criticism?

LINDA. But, dear, how could he make any money?

WILLY (*worried and angered*). There's such an undercurrent in him. He became a moody man. Did he apologize when I left this morning?

LINDA. He was crestfallen, Willy. You know how he admires you. I think if he finds himself, then you'll both be happier and not fight any more.

WILLY. How can he find himself on a farm? Is that a life? A farmhand? In the beginning, when he was young, I thought, well, a young man, it's good for him to tramp around, take a lot of different jobs. But it's more than ten years now and he has yet to make thirty-five dollars a week!

LINDA. He's finding himself, Willy.

WILLY. Not finding yourself at the age of thirty-four is a disgrace!

LINDA. Shh!

WILLY. The trouble is he's lazy, goddammit!

LINDA. Willy, please!

WILLY. Biff is a lazy bum!

LINDA. They're sleeping. Get something to eat. Go on down.

WILLY. Why did he come home? I would like to know what brought him home.

LINDA. I don't know. I think he's still lost, Willy. I think he's very lost.

WILLY. Biff Loman is lost. In the greatest country in the world a young man with such—personal attractiveness, gets lost. And such a hard worker. There's one thing about Biff—he's not lazy.

LINDA. Never.

WILLY (*with pity and resolve*). I'll see him in the morning; I'll have a nice talk with him. I'll get him a job selling. He could be big in no time. My God! Remember how they used to follow him around in high school? When he smiled at one of them their faces lit up. When he walked down the street . . . (*He loses himself in reminiscences.*)

LINDA (*trying to bring him out of it*). Willy, dear, I got a new kind of American-type cheese today. It's whipped.

WILLY. Why do you get American when I like Swiss?

LINDA. I just thought you'd like a change—

WILLY. I don't want a change! I want Swiss cheese. Why am I always being contradicted?

LINDA (*with a covering laugh*). I thought it would be a surprise.

WILLY. Why don't you open a window in here, for God's sake?

LINDA (*with infinite patience*). They're all open, dear.

WILLY. The way they boxed us in here. Bricks and windows, windows and bricks.

LINDA. We should've bought the land next door.

WILLY. The street is lined with cars. There's not a breath of fresh air in the neighborhood. The grass don't grow any more, you can't raise a carrot in the back yard. They should've had a law against apartment houses. Remember those two beautiful elm trees out there? When I and Biff hung the swing between them?

LINDA. Yeah, like being a million miles from the city.

WILLY. They should've arrested the builder for cutting those down. They massacred the neighborhood. (*Lost*) More and more I think of those days, Linda. This time of year it was lilac and wisteria. And then the peonies would come out, and the daffodils. What fragrance in this room!

LINDA. Well, after all, people had to move somewhere.

WILLY. No, there's more people now.

LINDA. I don't think there's more people. I think—

WILLY. There's more people! That's what's ruining this country! Population is getting out of control. The competition is maddening! Smell the stink from that apartment house! And another one on the other side . . . How can they whip cheese?

(*On* WILLY*'s last line, Biff and Happy raise themselves up in their beds, listening.*)

LINDA. Go down, try it. And be quiet.

WILLY (*turning to* LINDA, *guiltily*). You're not worried about me, are you, sweetheart?

BIFF. What's the matter?

HAPPY. Listen!

LINDA. You've got too much on the ball to worry about.

WILLY. You're my foundation and my support, Linda.

LINDA. Just try to relax, dear. You make mountains out of molehills.

WILLY. I won't fight with him any more. If he wants to go back to Texas, let him go.

LINDA. He'll find his way.

WILLY. Sure. Certain men just don't get started till later in life. Like Thomas Edison, I think. Or B. F. Goodrich. One of them was deaf. (*He starts for the bedroom doorway.*) I'll put my money on Biff.

LINDA. And Willy—if it's warm Sunday we'll drive in the country. And we'll open the windshield, and take lunch.

WILLY. No, the windshields don't open on the new cars.

LINDA. But you opened it today.

WILLY. Me? I didn't. (*He stops.*) Now isn't that peculiar! Isn't that a remarkable—(*He breaks off in amazement and fright as the flute is heard distantly.*)

LINDA. What, darling?

WILLY. That is the most remarkable thing.

LINDA. What, dear?

WILLY. I was thinking of the Chevvy. (*Slight pause*) Nineteen twenty-eight . . . when I had that red Chevvy—(*Breaks off*) That's funny? I coulda sworn I was driving that Chevvy today.

LINDA. Well, that's nothing. Something must've reminded you.

WILLY. Remarkable. Ts. Remember those days? The way Biff used to simonize that car? The dealer refused to believe there was eighty thousand miles on it. (*He shakes his head.*) Heh! (*To* LINDA) Close your eyes, I'll be right up. (*He walks out of the bedroom.*)

HAPPY (*to* BIFF). Jesus, maybe he smashed up the car again!

LINDA (*calling after* WILLY). Be careful on the stairs, dear! The cheese is on the middle shelf! (*She turns, goes over to the bed, takes his jacket, and goes out of the bedroom.*)

(*Light has risen on the boys' room. Unseen,* WILLY *is heard talking to himself, "Eighty thousand miles," and a little laugh.* BIFF *gets out of bed, comes downstage a bit, and stands attentively.* BIFF *is two years older than his brother* HAPPY, *well built, but in these days bears a worn air and seems less self-assured. He has succeeded less, and his dreams are stronger and less acceptable than* HAPPY'S. HAPPY *is tall, powerfully made. Sexuality is like a visible color on him, or a scent that many women have discovered. He, like his brother, is lost, but in a different way, for he has never allowed himself to turn his face toward defeat and is thus more confused and hard-skinned, although seemingly more content.*)

HAPPY (*getting out of bed*). He's going to get his license taken away if he keeps that up. I'm getting nervous about him, y'know, Biff?

BIFF. His eyes are going.

HAPPY. No, I've driven with him. He sees all right. He just doesn't keep his mind on it. I drove into the city with him last week. He stops at a green light and then it turns red and he goes. (*He laughs.*)

BIFF. Maybe he's color-blind.

HAPPY. Pop? Why he's got the finest eye for color in the business. You know that.

BIFF (*sitting down on his bed*). I'm going to sleep.

HAPPY. You're not still sour on Dad, are you, Biff?

BIFF. He's all right, I guess.

WILLY (*underneath them, in the living-room*). Yes, sir, eighty thousand miles—eighty-two thousand!

BIFF. You smoking?

HAPPY (*holding out a pack of cigarettes*). Want one?

BIFF (*taking a cigarette*). I can never sleep when I smell it.

WILLY. What a simonizing job, heh!

HAPPY (*with deep sentiment*). Funny, Biff, y'know? Us sleeping in here again? The old beds. (*He pats his bed affectionately.*) All the talk that went across those two beds, huh? Our whole lives.

BIFF. Yeah. Lotta dreams and plans.

HAPPY (*with a deep and masculine laugh*). About five hundred women would like to know what was said in this room.

(*They share a soft laugh.*)

BIFF. Remember that big Betsy something—what the hell was her name—over on Bushwick Avenue?

HAPPY (*combing his hair*). With the collie dog!

BIFF. That's the one. I got you in there, remember?

HAPPY. Yeah, that was my first time—I think. Boy, there was a pig! (*They laugh, almost crudely.*) You taught me everything I know about women. Don't forget that.

BIFF. I bet you forgot how bashful you used to be. Especially with girls.

HAPPY. Oh, I still am, Biff.

BIFF. Oh, go on.

HAPPY. I just control it, that's all. I think I got less bashful and you got more so. What happened, Biff? Where's the old humor, the old confidence? (*He shakes* BIFF's *knee.* BIFF *gets up and moves restlessly about the room.*) What's the matter?

BIFF. Why does Dad mock me all the time?

HAPPY. He's not mocking you, he—

BIFF. Everything I say there's a twist of mockery on his face. I can't get near him.

HAPPY. He just wants you to make good, that's all. I wanted to talk to you about Dad for a long time, Biff. Something's—happening to him. He —talks to himself.

BIFF. I noticed that this morning. But he always mumbled.

HAPPY. But not so noticeable. It got so embarrassing I sent him to Florida. And you know something? Most of the time he's talking to you.

BIFF. What's he say about me?

HAPPY. I can't make it out.

BIFF. What's he say about me?

HAPPY. I think the fact that you're not settled, that you're still kind of up in the air . . .

BIFF. There's one or two other things depressing him, Happy.

HAPPY. What do you mean?

BIFF. Never mind. Just don't lay it all to me.

HAPPY. But I think if you just got started—I mean—is there any future for you out there?

BIFF. I tell ya, Hap, I don't know what the future is. I don't know—what I'm supposed to want.

HAPPY. What do you mean?

BIFF. Well, I spent six or seven years after high school trying to work myself up. Shipping clerk, salesman, business of one kind or another. And it's a measly manner of existence. To get on that subway on the hot mornings in summer. To devote your whole life to keeping stock, or making phone calls, or selling or buying. To suffer fifty weeks of the year for the sake of a two-week vacation, when all you really desire is to be outdoors, with your shirt off. And always to have to get ahead of the next fella. And still—that's how you build a future.

HAPPY. Well, you really enjoy it on a farm? Are you content out there?

BIFF (*with rising agitation*). Hap, I've had twenty or thirty different kinds of jobs since I left home before the war, and it always turns out the same. I just realized it lately. In Nebraska when I herded cattle, and the Dakotas, and Arizona, and now in Texas. It's why I came home now, I guess, because I realized it. This farm I work on, it's spring there now, see? And they've got about fifteen new colts. There's nothing more inspiring or—beautiful than the sight of a mare and a new colt. And it's cool there now, see? Texas is cool now, and it's spring. And whenever spring comes to where I am, I suddenly get the feeling, my God, I'm not gettin' anywhere! What the hell am I doing, playing around with horses, twenty-eight dollars a week! I'm thirty-four years old, I oughta be makin' my future. That's when I come running home. And now, I get here, and I don't know what to do with my-self. (*After a pause*) I've always made a point of not wasting my life, and everytime I come back here I know that all I've done is to waste my life.

HAPPY. You're a poet, you know that, Biff? You're a—you're an idealist!

BIFF. No, I'm mixed up very bad. Maybe I oughta get married. Maybe

I oughta get stuck into something. Maybe that's my trouble. I'm like a boy. I'm not married, I'm not in business, I just—I'm like a boy. Are you content, Hap? You're a success, aren't you? Are you content?

HAPPY. Hell, no!

BIFF. Why? You're making money, aren't you?

HAPPY (*moving about with energy, expressiveness*). All I can do now is wait for the merchandise manager to die. And suppose I get to be merchandise manager? He's a good friend of mine, and he just built a terrific estate on Long Island. And he lived there about two months and sold it, and now he's building another one. He can't enjoy it once it's finished. And I know that's just what I would do. I don't know what the hell I'm workin' for. Sometimes I sit in my apartment—all alone. And I think of the rent I'm paying. And it's crazy. But then, it's what I always wanted. My own apartment, a car, and plenty of women. And still, goddammit, I'm lonely.

BIFF (*with enthusiasm*). Listen, why don't you come out West with me?

HAPPY. You and I, heh?

BIFF. Sure, maybe we could buy a ranch. Raise cattle, use our muscles. Men built like we are should be working out in the open.

HAPPY (*avidly*). The Loman Brothers, heh?

BIFF (*with vast affection*). Sure, we'd be known all over the counties!

HAPPY (*enthralled*). That's what I dream about, Biff. Sometimes I want to just rip my clothes off in the middle of the store and outbox that goddam merchandise manager. I mean I can outbox, outrun, and outlift anybody in that store, and I have to take orders from those common, petty sons-of-bitches till I can't stand it any more.

BIFF. I'm tellin' you, kid, if you were with me I'd be happy out there.

HAPPY (*enthused*). See, Biff, everybody around me is so false that I'm constantly lowering my ideals . . .

BIFF. Baby, together we'd stand up for one another, we'd have someone to trust.

HAPPY. If I were around you—

BIFF. Hap, the trouble is we weren't brought up to grub for money. I don't know how to do it.

HAPPY. Neither can I!

BIFF. Then let's go!

HAPPY. The only thing is—what can you make out there?

BIFF. But look at your friend. Builds an estate and then hasn't the peace of mind to live in it.

HAPPY. Yeah, but when he walks into the store the waves part in front of him. That's fifty-two thousand dollars a year coming through the revolving door, and I got more in my pinky finger than he's got in his head.

BIFF. Yeah, but you just said—

HAPPY. I gotta show some of those pompous, self-important executives over there that Hap Loman can make the grade. I want to walk into the store the way he walks in. Then I'll go with you, Biff. We'll be together yet, I swear. But take those two we had tonight. Now weren't they gorgeous creatures?

BIFF. Yeah, yeah, most gorgeous I've had in years.

HAPPY. I get that any time I want, Biff. Whenever I feel disgusted. The only trouble is, it gets like bowling or something. I just keep knockin' them over and it doesn't mean anything. You still run around a lot?

BIFF. Naa. I'd like to find a girl—steady, somebody with substance.

HAPPY. That's what I long for.

BIFF. Go on! You'd never come home.

HAPPY. I would! Somebody with character, with resistance! Like Mom, y'know? You're gonna call me a bastard when I tell you this. That girl Charlotte I was with tonight is engaged to be married in five weeks. (*He tries on his new hat.*)

BIFF. No kiddin'!

HAPPY. Sure, the guy's in line for the vice-presidency of the store. I don't know what gets into me, maybe I just have an overdeveloped sense of competition or something, but I went and ruined her, and furthermore I can't get rid of her. And he's the third executive I've done that to. Isn't that a crummy characteristic? And to top it all, I go to their weddings! (*Indignantly, but laughing*) Like I'm not supposed to take bribes. Manufacturers offer me a hundred-dollar bill now and then to throw an order their way. You know how honest I am, but it's like this girl, see. I hate myself for it. Because I don't want the girl, and, still, I take it and—I love it!

BIFF. Let's go to sleep.

HAPPY. I guess we didn't settle anything, heh?

BIFF. I just got one idea that I think I'm going to try.

HAPPY. What's that?

BIFF. Remember Bill Oliver?

HAPPY. Sure, Oliver is very big now. You want to work for him again?

BIFF. No, but when I quit he said something to me. He put his arm on my shoulder, and he said, "Biff, if you ever need anything, come to me."

HAPPY. I remember that. That sounds good.

BIFF. I think I'll go to see him. If I could get ten thousand or even seven or eight thousand dollars I could buy a beautiful ranch.

HAPPY. I bet he'd back you. 'Cause he thought highly of you, Biff. I mean, they all do. You're well liked, Biff. That's why I say to come back here, and we both have the apartment. And I'm tellin' you, Biff, any babe you want . . .

BIFF. No, with a ranch I could do the work I like and still be something. I just wonder though. I wonder if Oliver still thinks I stole that carton of basketballs.

HAPPY. Oh, he probably forgot that long ago. It's almost ten years.

You're too sensitive. Anyway, he didn't really fire you.

BIFF. Well, I think he was going to. I think that's why I quit. I was never sure whether he knew or not. I know he thought the world of me, though. I was the only one he'd let lock up the place.

WILLY (*below*). You gonna wash the engine, Biff?

HAPPY. Shh!

(BIFF *looks at* HAPPY, *who is gazing down, listening.* WILLY *is mumbling in the parlor.*)

HAPPY. You hear that?

(*They listen.* WILLY *laughs warmly.*)

BIFF (*growing angry*). Doesn't he know Mom can hear that?

WILLY. Don't get your sweater dirty, Biff!

(*A look of pain crosses* BIFF'*s face.*)

HAPPY. Isn't that terrible? Don't leave again, will you? You'll find a job here. You gotta stick around. I don't know what to do about him, it's getting embarrassing.

WILLY. What a simonizing job!

BIFF. Mom's hearing that!

WILLY. No kiddin', Biff, you got a date? Wonderful!

HAPPY. Go on to sleep. But talk to him in the morning, will you?

BIFF (*reluctantly getting into bed*). With her in the house. Brother!

HAPPY (*getting into bed*). I wish you'd have a good talk with him.

(*The light on their room begins to fade.*)

BIFF (*to himself in bed*). That selfish, stupid . . .

HAPPY. Sh . . . Sleep, Biff.

(*Their light is out. Well before they have finished speaking,* WILLY'*s form is dimly seen below in the darkened kitchen. He opens the refrigerator, searches in there, and takes out a bottle of milk. The apartment houses are fading out, and the entire house and surroundings become covered with leaves. Music insinuates itself as the leaves appear.*)

WILLY. Just wanna be careful with those girls, Biff, that's all. Don't make any promises. No promises of any kind. Because a girl, y'know, they always believe what you tell 'em, and you're very young, Biff, you're too young to be talking seriously to girls.

(*Light rises on the kitchen.* WILLY, *talking, shuts the refrigerator door and comes downstage to the kitchen table. He pours milk into a glass. He is totally immersed in himself, smiling faintly.*)

WILLY. Too young entirely, Biff. You want to watch your schooling first. Then when you're all set, there'll be plenty of girls for a boy like you.

(*He smiles broadly at a kitchen chair.*) That so? The girls pay for you? (*He laughs.*) Boy, you must really be makin' a hit.

(Willy *is gradually addressing—physically—a point offstage, speaking through the wall of the kitchen, and his voice has been rising in volume to that of a normal conversation.*)

Willy. I been wondering why you polish the car so careful. Ha! Don't leave the hubcaps, boys. Get the chamois to the hubcaps. Happy, use newspaper on the windows, it's the easiest thing. Show him how to do it, Biff! You see, Happy? Pad it up, use it like a pad. That's it, that's it, good work. You're doin' all right, Hap. (*He pauses, then nods in approbation for a few seconds, then looks upward.*) Biff, first thing we gotta do when we get time is clip that big branch over the house. Afraid it's gonna fall in a storm and hit the roof. Tell you what. We get a rope and sling her around, and then we climb up there with a couple of saws and take her down. Soon as you finish the car, boys, I wanna see ya. I got a surprise for you, boys.

Biff (*offstage*). Whatta ya got, Dad?

Willy. No, you finish first. Never leave a job till you're finished—remember that. (*Looking toward the "big trees"*) Biff, up in Albany I saw a beautiful hammock. I think I'll buy it next trip, and we'll hang it right between those two elms. Wouldn't that be something? Just swingin' there under those branches. Boy, that would be . . .

(*Young* Biff *and Young* Happy *appear from the direction* Willy *was addressing.* Happy *carries rags and a pail of water.* Biff, *wearing a sweater with a block "S," carries a football.*)

Biff (*pointing in the direction of the car offstage*). How's that, Pop, professional?

Willy. Terrific. Terrific job, boys. Good work, Biff.

Happy. Where's the surprise, Pop?

Willy. In the back seat of the car.

Happy. Boy! (*He runs off.*)

Biff. What is it, Dad? Tell me, what'd you buy?

Willy (*laughing, cuffs him*). Never mind, something I want you to have.

Biff (*turns and starts off*). What is it, Hap?

Happy (*offstage*). It's a punching bag!

Biff. Oh, Pop!

Willy. It's got Gene Tunney's signature on it!

(Happy *runs onstage with a punching bag.*)

Biff. Gee, how'd you know we wanted a punching bag?

Willy. Well, it's the finest thing for the timing.

Happy (*lies down on his back and pedals with his feet*). I'm losing weight, you notice, Pop?

WILLY (*to* HAPPY). Jumping rope is good too.

BIFF. Did you see the new football I got?

WILLY (*examining the ball*). Where'd you get a new ball?

BIFF. The coach told me to practice my passing.

WILLY. That so? And he gave you the ball, heh?

BIFF. Well, I borrowed it from the locker room. (*He laughs confidentially.*)

WILLY (*laughing with him at the theft*). I want you to return that.

HAPPY. I told you he wouldn't like it!

BIFF (*angrily*). Well, I'm bringing it back!

WILLY (*stopping the incipient argument, to* HAPPY). Sure, he's gotta practice with a regulation ball, doesn't he? (*To* BIFF) Coach'll probably congratulate you on your initiative!

BIFF. Oh, he keeps congratulating my initiative all the time, Pop.

WILLY. That's because he likes you. If somebody else took that ball there'd be an uproar. So what's the report, boys, what's the report?

BIFF. Where'd you go this time, Dad? Gee, we were lonesome for you.

WILLY (*pleased, puts an arm around each boy and they come down to the apron*). Lonesome, heh?

BIFF. Missed you every minute.

WILLY. Don't say? Tell you a secret, boys. Don't breathe it to a soul. Someday I'll have my own business, and I'll never have to leave home any more.

HAPPY. Like Uncle Charley, heh?

WILLY. Bigger than Uncle Charley! Because Charley is not—liked. He's liked, but he's not—well liked.

BIFF. Where'd you go this time, Dad?

WILLY. Well, I got on the road, and I went north to Providence. Met the Mayor.

BIFF. The Mayor of Providence!

WILLY. He was sitting in the hotel lobby.

BIFF. What'd he say?

WILLY. He said, "Morning!" And I said, "You got a fine city here, Mayor." And then he had coffee with me. And then I went to Waterbury. Waterbury is a fine city. Big clock city, the famous Waterbury clock. Sold a nice bill there. And then Boston—Boston is the cradle of the Revolution. A fine city. And a couple of other towns in Mass., and on to Portland and Bangor and straight home!

BIFF. Gee, I'd love to go with you sometime, Dad.

WILLY. Soon as summer comes.

HAPPY. Promise?

WILLY. You and Hap and I, and I'll show you all the towns. America is full of beautiful towns and fine, upstanding people. And they know me, boys, they know me up and down New England. The finest people. And when I bring you fellas up, there'll be open sesame for all of us, 'cause one thing, boys: I have friends. I can park my car in any street in New England, and the cops protect it like their own. This summer, heh?

BIFF *and* HAPPY (*together*). Yeah! You bet!

WILLY. We'll take our bathing suits.

HAPPY. We'll carry your bags, Pop!

WILLY. Oh, won't that be something! Me comin' into the Boston stores with you boys carryin' my bags. What a sensation!

(BIFF *is prancing around, practicing passing the ball.*)

WILLY. You nervous, Biff, about the game?

BIFF. Not if you're gonna be there.

WILLY. What do they say about you in school, now that they made you captain?

HAPPY. There's a crowd of girls behind him everytime the classes change.

BIFF (*taking* WILLY's *hand*). This Saturday, Pop, this Saturday—just for you, I'm going to break through for a touchdown.

HAPPY. You're supposed to pass.

BIFF. I'm takin' one play for Pop. You watch me, Pop, and when I take off my helmet, that means I'm breakin' out. Then you watch me crash through that line!

WILLY (*kisses* BIFF). Oh, wait'll I tell this in Boston!

(BERNARD *enters in knickers. He is younger than* BIFF, *earnest and loyal, a worried boy.*)

BERNARD. Biff, where are you? You're supposed to study with me today.

WILLY. Hey, looka Bernard. What're you lookin' so anemic about, Bernard?

BERNARD. He's gotta study, Uncle Willy. He's got Regents next week.

HAPPY (*tauntingly, spinning* BERNARD *around*). Let's box, Bernard!

BERNARD. Biff! (*He gets away from* HAPPY.) Listen, Biff, I heard Mr. Birnbaum say that if you don't start studyin' math he's gonna flunk you, and you won't graduate. I heard him!

WILLY. You better study with him, Biff. Go ahead now.

BERNARD. I heard him!

BIFF. Oh, Pop, you didn't see my sneakers! (*He holds up a foot for* WILLY *to look at.*)

WILLY. Hey, that's a beautiful job of printing!

BERNARD (*wiping his glasses*). Just because he printed University of Virginia on his sneakers doesn't mean they've got to graduate him. Uncle Willy!

WILLY (*angrily*). What're you talking about? With scholarships to three universities they're gonna flunk him?

BERNARD. But I heard Mr. Birnbaum say—

WILLY. Don't be a pest, Bernard! (*To his boys*) What an anemic!

BERNARD. Okay, I'm waiting for you in my house, Biff.

(BERNARD *goes off. The* LOMANS *laugh.*)

WILLY. Bernard is not well liked, is he?

BIFF. He's liked, but he's not well liked.

HAPPY. That's right, Pop.

WILLY. That's just what I mean. Bernard can get the best marks in school, y'understand, but when he gets out in the business world, y'understand, you are going to be five times ahead of him. That's why I thank Almighty God you're both built like Adonises. Because the man who makes an appearance in the business world, the man who creates personal interest, is the man who gets ahead. Be liked and you will never want. You take me, for instance. I never have to wait in line to see a buyer. "Willy Loman is here!" That's all they have to know, and I go right through.

BIFF. Did you knock them dead, Pop?

WILLY. Knocked 'em cold in Providence, slaughtered 'em in Boston.

HAPPY (*on his back, pedaling again*). I'm losing weight, you notice, Pop?

(LINDA *enters, as of old, a ribbon in her hair, carrying a basket of washing.*)

LINDA (*with youthful energy*). Hello, dear!

WILLY. Sweetheart!

LINDA. How'd the Chevvy run?

WILLY. Chevrolet, Linda, is the greatest car ever built. (*To the* BOYS) Since when do you let your mother carry wash up the stairs?

BIFF. Grab hold there, boy!

HAPPY. Where to, Mom?

LINDA. Hang them up on the line. And you better go down to your friends, Biff. The cellar is full of boys. They don't know what to do with themselves.

BIFF. Ah, when Pop comes home they can wait!

WILLY (*laughs appreciatively*). You better go down and tell them what to do, Biff.

BIFF. I think I'll have them sweep out the furnace room.

WILLY. Good work, Biff.

BIFF (*goes through wall-line of kitchen to doorway at back and calls down*). Fellas! Everybody sweep out the furnace room! I'll be right down!

VOICES. All right! Okay, Biff.

BIFF. George and Sam and Frank, come out back! We're hangin' up the wash! Come on, Hap, on the double! (*He and* HAPPY *carry out the basket.*)

LINDA. The way they obey him!

WILLY. Well, that's training, the training. I'm tellin' you, I was sellin' thousands and thousands, but I had to come home.

LINDA. Oh, the whole block'll be at that game. Did you sell anything?

WILLY. I did five hundred gross in Providence and seven hundred gross in Boston.

LINDA. No! Wait a minute, I've got a pencil. (*She pulls pencil and paper out of her apron pocket.*) That makes your commission . . . Two hundred—my God! Two hundred and twelve dollars!

WILLY. Well, I didn't figure it yet, but . . .

LINDA. How much did you do?

WILLY. Well, I—I did—about a hundred and eighty gross in Providence. Well, no—it came to—roughly two hundred gross on the whole trip.

LINDA (*without hesitation*). Two hundred gross. That's . . . (*She figures.*)

WILLY. The trouble was that three of the stores were half closed for inventory in Boston. Otherwise I woulda broke records.

LINDA. Well, it makes seventy dollars and some pennies. That's very good.

WILLY. What do we owe?

LINDA. Well, on the first there's sixteen dollars on the refrigerator—

WILLY. Why sixteen?

LINDA. Well, the fan belt broke, so it was a dollar eighty.

WILLY. But it's brand new.

LINDA. Well, the man said that's the way it is. Till they work themselves in, y'know.

(*They move through the wall-line into the kitchen.*)

WILLY. I hope we didn't get stuck on that machine.

LINDA. They got the biggest ads of any of them!

WILLY. I know, it's a fine machine. What else?

LINDA. Well, there's nine-sixty for the washing machine. And for the vacuum cleaner there's three and a half due on the fifteenth. Then the roof, you got twenty-one dollars remaining.

WILLY. It don't leak, does it?

LINDA. No, they did a wonderful job. Then you owe Frank for the carburetor.

WILLY. I'm not going to pay that man! That goddam Chevrolet, they ought to prohibit the manufacture of that car!

LINDA. Well, you owe him three and a half. And odds and ends, comes to around a hundred and twenty dollars by the fifteenth.

WILLY. A hundred and twenty dollars! My God, if business don't pick up I don't know what I'm gonna do!

LINDA. Well, next week you'll do better.

WILLY. Oh, I'll knock 'em dead next week. I'll go to Hartford. I'm very well liked in Hartford. You know, the trouble is, Linda, people don't seem to take to me.

(*They move onto the forestage.*)

LINDA. Oh, don't be foolish.

WILLY. I know it when I walk in. They seem to laugh at me.

LINDA. Why? Why would they laugh at you? Don't talk that way, Willy.

(WILLY *moves to the edge of the stage.* LINDA *goes into the kitchen and starts to darn stockings.*)

WILLY. I don't know the reason for it, but they just pass me by. I'm not noticed.

LINDA. But you're doing wonderful, dear. You're making seventy to a hundred dollars a week.

WILLY. But I gotta be at it ten, twelve hours a day. Other men—I don't know—they do it easier. I don't know why—I can't stop myself—I talk too much. A man oughta come in with a few words. One thing about Charley. He's a man of few words, and they respect him.

LINDA. You don't talk too much, you're just lively.

WILLY (*smiling*). Well, I figure, what the hell, life is short, a couple of jokes. (*To himself*) I joke too much! (*The smile goes.*)

LINDA. Why? You're—

WILLY. I'm fat. I'm very—foolish to look at, Linda. I didn't tell you, but Christmas time I happened to be calling on F. H. Stewarts, and a salesman I know, as I was going in to see the buyer I heard him say something about—walrus. And I—I cracked him right across the face. I won't take that. I simply will not take that. But they do laugh at me. I know that.

LINDA. Darling . . .

WILLY. I gotta overcome it. I know I gotta overcome it. I'm not dressing to advantage, maybe.

LINDA. Willy, darling, you're the handsomest man in the world—

WILLY. Oh, no, Linda.

LINDA. To me you are. (*Slight pause*) The handsomest.

(*From the darkness is heard the laughter of a woman.* WILLY *doesn't turn to it, but it continues through* LINDA'S *lines.*)

LINDA. And the boys, Willy. Few men are idolized by their children the way you are.

(*Music is heard as behind a scrim, to the left of the house,* THE WOMAN, *dimly seen, is dressing.*)

WILLY (*with great feeling*). You're the best there is, Linda, you're a pal, you know that? On the road—on the road I want to grab you sometimes and just kiss the life outa you.

(The laughter is loud now, and he moves into a brightening area at the left, where THE WOMAN *has come from behind the scrim and is standing, putting on her hat, looking into a "mirror" and laughing.)*

WILLY. 'Cause I get so lonely—especially when business is bad and there's nobody to talk to. I get the feeling that I'll never sell anything again, that I won't make a living for you, or a business, a business for the boys. *(He talks through* THE WOMAN's *subsiding laughter;* THE WOMAN *primps at the "mirror.")* There's so much I want to make for—

THE WOMAN. Me? You didn't make me, Willy. I picked you.

WILLY *(pleased)*. You picked me?

THE WOMAN *(who is quite proper-looking,* WILLY's *age)*. I did. I've been sitting at that desk watching all the salesmen go by, day in, day out. But you've got such a sense of humor, and we do have such a good time together, don't we?

WILLY. Sure, sure. *(He takes her in his arms.)* Why do you have to go now?

THE WOMAN. It's two o'clock . . .

WILLY. No, come on in! *(He pulls her.)*

THE WOMAN. . . . my sisters'll be scandalized. When'll you be back?

WILLY. Oh, two weeks about. Will you come up again?

THE WOMAN. Sure thing. You do make me laugh. It's good for me. *(She squeezes his arm, kisses him.)* And I think you're a wonderful man.

WILLY. You picked me, heh?

THE WOMAN. Sure. Because you're so sweet. And such a kidder.

WILLY. Well, I'll see you next time I'm in Boston.

THE WOMAN. I'll put you right through to the buyers.

WILLY *(slapping her bottom)*. Right. Well, bottoms up!

THE WOMAN *(slaps him gently and laughs)*. You just kill me, Willy. *(He suddenly grabs her and kisses her roughly.)* You kill me. And thanks for the stockings. I love a lot of stockings. Well, good night.

WILLY. Good night. And keep your pores open!

THE WOMAN. Oh, Willy!

(THE WOMAN *bursts out laughing, and* LINDA's *laughter blends in.* THE WOMAN *disappears into the dark. Now the area at the kitchen table brightens.* LINDA *is sitting where she was at the kitchen table, but now is mending a pair of her silk stockings.)*

LINDA. You are, Willy. The handsomest man. You've got no reason to feel that—

WILLY *(coming out of* THE WOMAN's *dimming area and going over to* LINDA). I'll make it all up to you, Linda, I'll—

LINDA. There's nothing to make up, dear. You're doing fine, better than—

WILLY (*noticing her mending*). What's that?

LINDA. Just mending my stockings. They're so expensive—

WILLY (*angrily, taking them from her*). I won't have you mending stockings in this house! Now throw them out!

(LINDA *puts the stockings in her pocket.*)

BERNARD (*entering on the run*). Where is he? If he doesn't study!

WILLY (*moving to the forestage, with great agitation*). You'll give him the answers!

BERNARD. I do, but I can't on a Regents! That's a state exam! They're liable to arrest me!

WILLY. Where is he? I'll whip him, I'll whip him!

LINDA. And he'd better give back that football, Willy, it's not nice.

WILLY. Biff! Where is he? Why is he taking everything?

LINDA. He's too rough with the girls, Willy. All the mothers are afraid of him!

WILLY. I'll whip him!

BERNARD. He's driving the car without a license!

(THE WOMAN's *laugh is heard.*)

WILLY. Shut up!

LINDA. All the mothers—

WILLY. Shut up!

BERNARD (*backing quietly away and out*). Mr. Birnbaum says he's stuck up.

WILLY. Get outa here!

BERNARD. If he doesn't buckle down he'll flunk math! (*He goes off.*)

LINDA. He's right, Willy, you've gotta—

WILLY (*exploding at her*). There's nothing the matter with him! You want him to be a worm like Bernard? He's got spirit, personality . . .

(*As he speaks,* LINDA, *almost in tears, exits into the living-room.* WILLY *is alone in the kitchen, wilting and staring. The leaves are gone. It is night again, and the apartment houses look down from behind.*)

WILLY. Loaded with it. Loaded! What is he stealing? He's giving it back, isn't he? Why is he stealing? What did I tell him? I never in my life told him anything but decent things.

(HAPPY *in pajamas has come down the stairs;* WILLY *suddenly becomes aware of* HAPPY's *presence.*)

HAPPY. Let's go now, come on.

WILLY (*sitting down at the kitchen table*). Huh! Why did she have to wax the floors herself? Everytime she waxes the floors she keels over. She knows that!

HAPPY. Shh! Take it easy. What brought you back tonight?

WILLY. I got an awful scare. Nearly hit a kid in Yonkers. God! Why didn't I go to Alaska with my brother Ben that time! Ben! That man was a genius, that man was success incarnate! What a mistake! He begged me to go.

HAPPY. Well, there's no use in—

WILLY. You guys! There was a man started with the clothes on his back and ended up with diamond mines!

HAPPY. Boy, someday I'd like to know how he did it.

WILLY. What's the mystery? The man knew what he wanted and went out and got it! Walked into a jungle, and comes out, the age of twenty-one, and he's rich! The world is an oyster, but you don't crack it open on a mattress.

HAPPY. Pop, I told you I'm gonna retire you for life.

WILLY. You'll retire me for life on seventy goddam dollars a week? And your women and your car and your apartment, and you'll retire me for life! Christ's sake, I couldn't get past Yonkers today! Where are you guys, where are you? The woods are burning! I can't drive a car!

(CHARLEY *has appeared in the doorway. He is a large man, slow of speech, laconic, immovable. In all he says, despite what he says, there is pity, and, now, trepidation. He has a robe over pajamas, slippers on his feet. He enters the kitchen.*)

CHARLEY. Everything all right?

HAPPY. Yeah, Charley, everything's . . .

WILLY. What's the matter?

CHARLEY. I heard some noise. I thought something happened. Can't we do something about the walls? You sneeze in here, and in my house hats blow off.

HAPPY. Let's go to bed, Dad. Come on.

(CHARLEY *signals to* HAPPY *to go.*)

WILLY. You go ahead, I'm not tired at the moment.

HAPPY (*to* WILLY). Take it easy, huh? (*He exits.*)

WILLY. What're you doin' up?

CHARLEY (*sitting down at the kitchen table opposite* WILLY). Couldn't sleep good. I had a heartburn.

WILLY. Well, you don't know how to eat.

CHARLEY. I eat with my mouth.

WILLY. No, you're ignorant. You gotta know about vitamins and things like that.

CHARLEY. Come on, let's shoot. Tire you out a little.

WILLY (*hesitantly*). All right. You got cards?

CHARLEY (*taking a deck from his pocket*). Yeah, I got them. Someplace. What is it with those vitamins?

WILLY (*dealing*). They build up your bones. Chemistry.

CHARLEY. Yeah, but there's no bones in a heartburn.

WILLY. What are you talkin' about? Do you know the first thing about it?

CHARLEY. Don't get insulted.

WILLY. Don't talk about something you don't know anything about.

(*They are playing. Pause.*)

CHARLEY. What're you doin' home?

WILLY. A little trouble with the car.

CHARLEY. Oh. (*Pause*) I'd like to take a trip to California.

WILLY. Don't say.

CHARLEY. You want a job?

WILLY. I got a job, I told you that. (*After a slight pause*) What the hell are you offering me a job for?

CHARLEY. Don't get insulted.

WILLY. Don't insult me.

CHARLEY. I don't see no sense in it. You don't have to go on this way.

WILLY. I got a good job. (*Slight pause*) What do you keep comin' in here for?

CHARLEY. You want me to go?

WILLY (*after a pause, withering*). I can't understand it. He's going back to Texas again. What the hell is that?

CHARLEY. Let him go.

WILLY. I got nothin' to give him, Charley, I'm clean, I'm clean.

CHARLEY. He won't starve. None a them starve. Forget about him.

WILLY. Then what have I got to remember?

CHARLEY. You take it too hard. To hell with it. When a deposit bottle is broken you don't get your nickel back.

WILLY. That's easy enough for you to say.

CHARLEY. That ain't easy for me to say.

WILLY. Did you see the ceiling I put up in the living-room?

CHARLEY. Yeah, that's a piece of work. To put up a ceiling is a mystery to me. How do you do it?

WILLY. What's the difference?

CHARLEY. Well, talk about it.

WILLY. You gonna put up a ceiling?

CHARLEY. How could I put up a ceiling?

WILLY. Then what the hell are you bothering me for?

CHARLEY. You're insulted again.

WILLY. A man who can't handle tools is not a man. You're disgusting.

CHARLEY. Don't call me disgusting, Willy.

(UNCLE BEN, *carrying a valise and an umbrella, enters the forestage from around the right corner of the house. He is a stolid man, in his sixties, with a mustache and an authoritative air. He is utterly certain of his destiny, and there is an aura of far places about him. He enters exactly as* WILLY *speaks.*)

WILLY. I'm getting awfully tired, Ben.

(BEN'S *music is heard.* BEN *looks around at everything.*)

CHARLEY. Good, keep playing; you'll sleep better. Did you call me Ben?

(BEN *looks at his watch.*)

WILLY. That's funny. For a second there you reminded me of my brother Ben.

BEN. I only have a few minutes.

(*He strolls, inspecting the place.* WILLY *and* CHARLEY *continue playing.*)

CHARLEY. You never heard from him again, heh? Since that time?

WILLY. Didn't Linda tell you? Couple of weeks ago we got a letter from his wife in Africa. He died.

CHARLEY. That so.

BEN (*chuckling*). So this is Brooklyn, eh?

CHARLEY. Maybe you're in for some of his money.

WILLY. Naa, he had seven sons. There's just one opportunity I had with that man . . .

BEN. I must make a train, William. There are several properties I'm looking at in Alaska.

WILLY. Sure, sure! If I'd gone with him to Alaska that time, everything would've been totally different.

CHARLEY. Go on, you'd froze to death up there.

WILLY. What're you talking about?

BEN. Opportunity is tremendous in Alaska, William. Surprised you're not up there.

WILLY. Sure, tremendous.

CHARLEY. Heh?

WILLY. There was the only man I ever met who knew the answers.

CHARLEY. Who?

BEN. How are you all?

WILLY (*taking a pot, smiling*). Fine, fine.

CHARLEY. Pretty sharp tonight.

BEN. Is Mother living with you?

WILLY. No, she died a long time ago.

CHARLEY. Who?

BEN. That's too bad. Fine specimen of a lady, Mother.

WILLY (*to* CHARLEY). Heh?

BEN. I'd hoped to see the old girl.

CHARLEY. Who died?

BEN. Heard anything from Father, have you?

WILLY (*unnerved*). What do you mean, who died?

CHARLEY (*taking a pot*). What're you talkin' about?

BEN (*looking at his watch*). William, it's half-past eight!

WILLY (*as though to dispel his confusion he angrily stops* CHARLEY'S *hand*). That's my build!

CHARLEY. I put the ace—

WILLY. If you don't know how to play the game I'm not gonna throw my money away on you!

CHARLEY (*rising*). It was my ace, for God's sake!

WILLY. I'm through, I'm through!

BEN. When did Mother die?

WILLY. Long ago. Since the beginning you never knew how to play cards.

CHARLEY (*picks up the cards and goes to the door*). All right! Next time I'll bring a deck with five aces.

WILLY. I don't play that kind of game!

CHARLEY (*turning to him*). You ought to be ashamed of yourself!

WILLY. Yeah?

CHARLEY. Yeah! (*He goes out.*)

WILLY (*slamming the door after him*). Ignoramus!

BEN (*as* WILLY *comes toward him through the wall-line of the kitchen*). So you're William.

WILLY (*shaking* BEN'S *hand*). Ben! I've been waiting for you so long! What's the answer? How did you do it?

BEN. Oh, there's a story in that.

(LINDA *enters the forestage, as of old, carrying the wash basket.*)

LINDA. Is this Ben?

BEN (*gallantly*). How do you do, my dear.

LINDA. Where've you been all these years? Willy's always wondered why you—

WILLY (*pulling* BEN *away from her impatiently*). Where is Dad? Didn't you follow him? How did you get started?

BEN. Well, I don't know how much you remember.

WILLY. Well, I was just a baby, of course, only three or four years old—

BEN. Three years and eleven months.

WILLY. What a memory, Ben!

BEN. I have many enterprises, William, and I have never kept books.

WILLY. I remember I was sitting under the wagon in—was it Nebraska?

BEN. It was South Dakota, and I gave you a bunch of wild flowers.

WILLY. I remember you walking away down some open road.

BEN (*laughing*). I was going to find Father in Alaska.

WILLY. Where is he?

BEN. At that age I had a very faulty view of geography, William. I discovered after a few days that I was heading due south, so instead of Alaska, I ended up in Africa.

LINDA. Africa!

WILLY. The Gold Coast!

BEN. Principally diamond mines.

LINDA. Diamond mines!

BEN. Yes, my dear. But I've only a few minutes—

WILLY. No! Boys! Boys! (YOUNG BIFF *and* HAPPY *appear.*) Listen to this. This is your Uncle Ben, a great man! Tell my boys, Ben!

BEN. Why, boys, when I was seventeen I walked into the jungle, and when I was twenty-one I walked out. (*He laughs.*) And by God I was rich.

WILLY (*to the boys*). You see what I been talking about? The greatest things can happen!

BEN (*glancing at his watch*). I have an appointment in Ketchikan Tuesday week.

WILLY. No, Ben! Please tell about Dad. I want my boys to hear. I want them to know the kind of stock they spring from. All I remember is a man with a big beard, and I was in Mamma's lap, sitting around a fire, and some kind of high music.

BEN. His flute. He played the flute.

WILLY. Sure, the flute, that's right!

(*New music is heard, a high, rollicking tune.*)

BEN. Father was a very great and a very wild-hearted man. We would start in Boston, and he'd toss the whole family into the wagon, and then he'd drive the team right across the country; through Ohio, and Indiana, Michigan, Illinois, and all the Western states. And we'd stop in the towns and sell the flutes that he'd made on the way. Great inventor, Father. With one gadget he made more in a week than a man like you could make in a lifetime.

WILLY. That's just the way I'm bringing them up, Ben—rugged, well liked, all-around.

BEN. Yeah? (*To* BIFF) Hit that, boy—hard as you can. (*He pounds his stomach.*)

BIFF. Oh, no, sir!

BEN (*taking boxing stance*). Come on, get to me! (*He laughs.*)

WILLY. Go to it, Biff! Go ahead, show him!

BIFF. Okay! (*He cocks his fists and starts in.*)

LINDA (*to* WILLY). Why must he fight, dear?

BEN (*sparring with* BIFF). Good boy! Good boy!

WILLY. How's that, Ben, heh?

HAPPY. Give him the left, Biff!

LINDA. Why are you fighting?

BEN. Good boy! (*Suddenly comes in, trips* BIFF, *and stands over him, the point of his umbrella poised over* BIFF'*s eye.*)

LINDA. Look out, Biff!

BIFF. Gee!

BEN (*patting* BIFF'*s knee*). Never fight fair with a stranger, boy. You'll never get out of the jungle that way. (*Taking* LINDA'*s hand and bowing*) It was an honor and a pleasure to meet you, Linda.

LINDA (*withdrawing her hand coldly, frightened*). Have a nice—trip.

BEN (*to* WILLY). And good luck with your—what do you do?

WILLY. Selling.

BEN. Yes. Well . . . (*He raises his hand in farewell to all.*)

WILLY. No, Ben, I don't want you to think . . . (*He takes* BEN'*s arm to show him.*) It's Brooklyn, I know, but we hunt too.

BEN. Really, now.

WILLY. Oh, sure, there's snakes and rabbits and—that's why I moved out here. Why, Biff can fell any one of these trees in no time! Boys! Go right over to where they're building the apartment house and get some sand. We're gonna rebuild the entire front stoop right now! Watch this, Ben!

BIFF. Yes, sir! On the double, Hap!

HAPPY (*as he and* BIFF *run off*). I lost weight, Pop, you notice?

(CHARLEY *enters in knickers, even before the boys are gone.*)

CHARLEY. Listen, if they steal any more from that building the watchman'll put the cops on them!

LINDA (*to* WILLY). Don't let Biff . . .

(BEN *laughs lustily.*)

WILLY. You shoulda seen the lumber they brought home last week. At least a dozen six-by-tens worth all kinds a money.

CHARLEY. Listen, if that watchman—

WILLY. I gave them hell, understand. But I got a couple of fearless characters there.

CHARLEY. Willy, the jails are full of fearless characters.

BEN (*clapping* WILLY *on the back, with a laugh at* CHARLEY). And the stock exchange, friend!

WILLY (*joining in* BEN'*s laughter*). Where are the rest of your pants?

CHARLEY. My wife bought them.

WILLY. Now all you need is a golf club and you can go upstairs and go to sleep. (*To* BEN) Great athlete! Between him and his son Bernard they can't hammer a nail!

BERNARD (*rushing in*). The watchman's chasing Biff!

WILLY (*angrily*). Shut up! He's not stealing anything!

LINDA (*alarmed, hurrying off left*). Where is he? Biff, dear! (*She exits.*)

WILLY (*moving toward the left, away from* BEN). There's nothing wrong. What's the matter with you?

BEN. Nervy boy. Good!

WILLY (*laughing*). Oh, nerves of iron, that Biff!

CHARLEY. Don't know what it is. My New England man comes back and he's bleedin', they murdered him up there.

WILLY. It's contacts, Charley, I got important contacts!

CHARLEY (*sarcastically*). Glad to hear it, Willy. Come in later, we'll shoot a little casino. I'll take some of your Portland money. (*He laughs at* WILLY *and exits.*)

WILLY (*turning to* BEN). Business is bad, it's murderous. But not for me, of course.

BEN. I'll stop by on my way back to Africa.

WILLY (*longingly*). Can't you stay a few days? You're just what I need, Ben, because I—I have a fine position here, but I—well, Dad left when I was such a baby and I never had a chance to talk to him and I still feel—kind of temporary about myself.

BEN. I'll be late for my train.

(*They are at opposite ends of the stage.*)

WILLY. Ben, my boys—can't we talk? They'd go into the jaws of hell for me, but I—

BEN. William, you're being first-rate with your boys. Outstanding, manly chaps!

WILLY (*hanging on to his words*). Oh, Ben, that's good to hear! Because sometimes I'm afraid that I'm not teaching them the right kind of—Ben, how should I teach them?

BEN (*giving great weight to each word, and with a certain vicious audacity*). William, when I walked into the jungle, I was seventeen. When I walked out I was twenty-one. And, by God, I was rich! (*He goes off into darkness around the right corner of the house.*)

WILLY. . . . was rich! That's just the spirit I want to imbue them with! To walk into a jungle! I was right! I was right! I was right!

(BEN *is gone, but* WILLY *is still speaking to him as* LINDA, *in nightgown and robe, enters the kitchen, glances around for* WILLY, *then goes to the door of the house, looks out and sees him. Comes down to his left. He looks at her.*)

LINDA. Willy, dear? Willy?

WILLY. I was right!

LINDA. Did you have some cheese? (*He can't answer.*) It's very late, darling. Come to bed, heh?

WILLY (*looking straight up*). Gotta break your neck to see a star in this yard.

LINDA. You coming in?

WILLY. Whatever happened to that diamond watch fob? Remember? When Ben came from Africa that time? Didn't he give me a watch fob with a diamond in it?

LINDA. You pawned it, dear. Twelve, thirteen years ago. For Biff's radio correspondence course.

WILLY. Gee, that was a beautiful thing. I'll take a walk.

LINDA. But you're in your slippers.

WILLY (*starting to go around the house at the left*). I was right! I was! (*Half to* LINDA, *as he goes, shaking his head*) What a man! There was a man worth talking to. I was right!

LINDA (*calling after* WILLY). But in your slippers, Willy!

(WILLY *is almost gone when* BIFF, *in his pajamas, comes down the stairs and enters the kitchen.*)

BIFF. What is he doing out there?

LINDA. Sh!

BIFF. God Almighty, Mom, how long has he been doing this?

LINDA. Don't, he'll hear you.

BIFF. What the hell is the matter with him?

LINDA. It'll pass by morning.

BIFF. Shouldn't we do anything?

LINDA. Oh, my dear, you should do a lot of things, but there's nothing to do, so go to sleep.

(HAPPY *comes down the stairs and sits on the steps.*)

HAPPY. I never heard him so loud, Mom.

LINDA. Well, come around more often; you'll hear him. (*She sits down at the table and mends the lining of* WILLY'*s jacket.*)

BIFF. Why didn't you ever write me about this, Mom?

LINDA. How would I write to you? For over three months you had no address.

BIFF. I was on the move. But you know I thought of you all the time. You know that, don't you, pal?

LINDA. I know, dear, I know. But he likes to have a letter. Just to know that there's still a possibility for better things.

BIFF. He's not like this all the time, is he?

LINDA. It's when you come home he's always the worst.

BIFF. When I come home?

LINDA. When you write you're coming, he's all smiles, and talks about the future, and—he's just wonderful. And then the closer you seem to come, the more shaky he gets, and then, by the time you get here, he's arguing, and he seems angry at you. I think it's just that maybe he can't bring himself to—to open up to you. Why are you so hateful to each other? Why is that?

BIFF (*evasively*). I'm not hateful, Mom.

LINDA. But you no sooner come in the door than you're fighting!

BIFF. I don't know why. I mean to change. I'm tryin', Mom, you understand?

LINDA. Are you home to stay now?

BIFF. I don't know. I want to look around, see what's doin'.

LINDA. Biff, you can't look around all your life, can you?

BIFF. I just can't take hold, Mom. I can't take hold of some kind of a life.

LINDA. Biff, a man is not a bird, to come and go with the springtime.

BIFF. Your hair . . . (*He touches her hair.*) Your hair got so gray.

LINDA. Oh, it's been gray since you were in high school. I just stopped dyeing it, that's all.

BIFF. Dye it again, will ya? I don't want my pal looking old. (*He smiles.*)

LINDA. You're such a boy! You think you can go away for a year and . . . You've got to get it into your head now that one day you'll knock on this door and there'll be strange people here—

BIFF. What are you talking about? You're not even sixty, Mom.

LINDA. But what about your father?

BIFF (*lamely*). Well, I meant him too.

HAPPY. He admires Pop.

LINDA. Biff, dear, if you don't have any feeling for him, then you can't have any feeling for me.

BIFF. Sure I can, Mom.

LINDA. No. You can't just come to see me, because I love him. (*With a threat, but only a threat, of tears*) He's the dearest man in the world to me, and I won't have anyone making him feel unwanted and low and blue. You've got to make up your mind now, darling, there's no leeway any more. Either he's your father and you pay him that respect, or else you're not to come here. I know he's not easy to get along with—nobody knows that better than me—but . . .

WILLY (*from the left, with a laugh*). Hey, hey, Biffo!

BIFF (*starting to go out after* WILLY). What the hell is the matter with him?

(HAPPY *stops him.*)

LINDA. Don't—don't go near him!

BIFF. Stop making excuses for him! He always, always wiped the floor with you. Never had an ounce of respect for you.

HAPPY. He's always had respect for—

BIFF. What the hell do you know about it?

HAPPY (*surlily*). Just don't call him crazy!

BIFF. He's got no character—Charley wouldn't do this. Not in his own house—spewing out that vomit from his mind.

HAPPY. Charley never had to cope with what he's got to.

BIFF. People are worse off than Willy Loman. Believe me, I've seen them.

LINDA. Then make Charley your father, Biff. You can't do that, can you? I don't say he's a great man. Willy Loman never made a lot of money. His name was never in the paper. He's not the finest character that ever lived. But he's a human being, and a terrible thing is happening to him. So attention must be paid. He's not to be allowed to fall into his grave like an old dog. Attention, attention must be finally paid to such a person. You called him crazy—

BIFF. I didn't mean—

LINDA. No, a lot of people think he's lost his—balance. But you don't have to be very smart to know what his trouble is. The man is exhausted.

HAPPY. Sure!

LINDA. A small man can be just as exhausted as a great man. He works for a company thirty-six years this March, opens up unheard-of territories to their trademark, and now in his old age they take his salary away.

HAPPY (*indignantly*). I didn't know that, Mom.

LINDA. You never asked, my dear! Now that you get your spending money someplace else you don't trouble your mind with him.

HAPPY. But I gave you money last—

LINDA. Christmas time, fifty dollars! To fix the hot water it cost ninety-seven fifty! For five weeks he's been on straight commission, like a beginner, an unknown!

BIFF. Those ungrateful bastards!

LINDA. Are they any worse than his sons? When he brought them business, when he was young, they were glad to see him. But now his old friends, the old buyers that loved him so and always found some order to hand him in a pinch—they're all dead, retired. He used to be able to make six, seven calls a day in Boston. Now he takes his valises out of the car and puts them back and takes them out again and he's exhausted. Instead of walking he talks now. He drives seven hundred miles, and when he gets there no one knows him any more, no one welcomes him. And what goes through a man's mind, driving seven hundred miles home without having earned a cent? Why shouldn't he talk to himself? Why? When he has to go to Charley and borrow fifty dollars a week and pretend to me that it's his pay? How long can that go on? How long? You see what I'm sitting here and waiting for? And you tell me he has no character? The man who never worked a day but for your benefit? When does he get the medal for that? Is this his reward—to turn around at the age of sixty-three and find his sons, who he loved better than his life, one aphilandering bum—

HAPPY. Mom!

LINDA. That's all you are, my baby! (*To* BIFF) And you! What happened to the love you had for him? You were such pals! How you used to talk to him on the phone every night! How lonely he was till he could come home to you!

BIFF. All right, Mom. I'll live here in my room, and I'll get a job. I'll keep away from him, that's all.

LINDA. No, Biff. You can't stay here and fight all the time.

BIFF. He threw me out of this house, remember that.

LINDA. Why did he do that? I never knew why.

BIFF. Because I know he's a fake and he doesn't like anybody around who knows!

LINDA. Why a fake? In what way? What do you mean?

BIFF. Just don't lay it all at my feet. It's between me and him—that's all I have to say. I'll chip in from now on. He'll settle for half my pay check. He'll be all right. I'm going to bed. (*He starts for the stairs.*)

LINDA. He won't be all right.

BIFF (*turning on the stairs, furiously*). I hate this city and I'll stay here. Now what do you want?

LINDA. He's dying, Biff.

(HAPPY *turns quickly to her, shocked.*)

BIFF (*after a pause*). Why is he dying?

LINDA. He's been trying to kill himself.

BIFF (*with great horror*). How?

LINDA. I live from day to day.

BIFF. What're you talking about?

LINDA. Remember I wrote you that he smashed up the car again? In February?

BIFF. Well?

LINDA. The insurance inspector came. He said that they have evidence. That all these accidents in the last year—weren't—weren't—accidents.

HAPPY. How can they tell that? That's a lie.

{ LINDA. It seems there's a woman . . . (*She takes a breath as*)
{ BIFF (*sharply but contained*). What woman?

LINDA (*simultaneously*). . . . and this woman . . .

LINDA. What?

BIFF. Nothing. Go ahead.

LINDA. What did you say?

BIFF. Nothing. I just said what woman?

HAPPY. What about her?

LINDA. Well, it seems she was walking down the road and saw his car. She says that he wasn't driving fast at all, and that he didn't skid. She says he came to that little bridge, and then deliberately smashed into the railing, and it was only the shallowness of the water that saved him.

BIFF. Oh, no, he probably just fell asleep again.

LINDA. I don't think he fell asleep.

BIFF. Why not?

LINDA. Last month . . . (*With great difficulty*) Oh, boys, it's so hard to say a thing like this! He's just a big stupid man to you, but I tell you there's more good in him than in many other people. (*She chokes, wipes her eyes.*) I was looking for a fuse. The lights blew out, and I went down the cellar. And behind the fuse box—it happened to fall out—was a length of rubber pipe—just short.

HAPPY. No kidding?

LINDA. There's a little attachment on the end of it. I knew right away. And sure enough, on the bottom of the water heater there's a new little nipple on the gas pipe.

HAPPY (*angrily*). That—jerk.

BIFF. Did you have it taken off?

LINDA. I'm—I'm ashamed to. How can I mention it to him? Every day I go down and take away that little rubber pipe. But, when he comes home, I put it back where it was. How can I insult him that way? I don't know what to do. I live from day to day, boys. I tell you, I know every thought in his mind. It sounds so old-fashioned and silly, but I tell you he put his whole life into you and you've turned your backs on him. (*She is bent over in the chair, weeping, her face in her hands.*) Biff, I swear to God! Biff, his life is in your hands!

HAPPY (*to* BIFF). How do you like that damned fool!

BIFF (*kissing her*). All right, pal, all right. It's all settled now. I've been remiss. I know that, Mom. But now I'll stay, and I swear to you, I'll apply myself. (*Kneeling in front of her, in a fever of self-reproach*) It's just—you see, Mom, I don't fit in business. Not that I won't try. I'll try, and I'll make good.

HAPPY. Sure you will. The trouble with you in business was you never tried to please people.

BIFF. I know, I—

HAPPY. Like when you worked for Harrison's. Bob Harrison said you were tops, and then you go and do some damn fool thing like whistling whole songs in the elevator like a comedian.

BIFF (*against* HAPPY). So what? I like to whistle sometimes.

HAPPY. You don't raise a guy to a responsible job who whistles in the elevator!

LINDA. Well, don't argue about it now.

HAPPY. Like when you'd go off and swim in the middle of the day instead of taking the line around.

BIFF (*his resentment rising*). Well, don't you run off? You take off sometimes, don't you? On a nice summer day?

HAPPY. Yeah, but I cover myself!

LINDA. Boys!

HAPPY. If I'm going to take a fade the boss can call any number where I'm supposed to be and they'll swear to him that I just left. I'll tell you something that I hate to say, Biff, but in the business world some of them think you're crazy.

BIFF (*angered*). Screw the business world!

HAPPY. All right, screw it! Great, but cover yourself!

LINDA. Hap, Hap!

BIFF. I don't care what they think! They've laughed at Dad for years, and you know why? Because we don't belong in this nuthouse of a city! We should be mixing cement on some open plain, or—or carpenters. A carpenter is allowed to whistle!

(WILLY *walks in from the entrance of the house, at left.*)

WILLY. Even your grandfather was better than a carpenter. (*Pause. They watch him.*) You never grew up. Bernard does not whistle in the elevator, I assure you.

BIFF (*as though to laugh* WILLY *out of it*). Yeah, but you do, Pop.

WILLY. I never in my life whistled in an elevator! And who in the business world thinks I'm crazy?

BIFF. I didn't mean it like that, Pop. Now don't make a whole thing out of it, will ya?

WILLY. Go back to the West! Be a carpenter, a cowboy, enjoy yourself!

LINDA. Willy, he was just saying—

WILLY. I heard what he said!

HAPPY (*trying to quiet* WILLY). Hey, Pop, come on now . . .

WILLY (*continuing over* HAPPY's *line*). They laugh at me, heh? Go to Filene's, go to the Hub, go to Slattery's, Boston. Call out the name Willy Loman and see what happens! Big shot!

BIFF. All right, Pop.

WILLY. Big!

BIFF. All right!

WILLY. Why do you always insult me?

BIFF. I didn't say a word. (*To* LINDA) Did I say a word?

LINDA. He didn't say anything, Willy.

WILLY (*going to the doorway of the living-room*). All right, good night, good night.

LINDA. Willy, dear, he just decided . . .

WILLY (*to* BIFF). If you get tired hanging around tomorrow, paint the ceiling I put up in the living-room.

BIFF. I'm leaving early tomorrow.

HAPPY. He's going to see Bill Oliver, Pop.

WILLY (*interestedly*). Oliver? For what?

BIFF (*with reserve, but trying, trying*). He always said he'd stake me. I'd like to go into business, so maybe I can take him up on it.

LINDA. Isn't that wonderful?

WILLY. Don't interrupt. What's wonderful about it? There's fifty men in the City of New York who'd stake him. (*To* BIFF) Sporting goods?

BIFF. I guess so. I know something about it and—

WILLY. He knows something about it! You know sporting goods better than Spalding, for God's sake! How much is he giving you?

BIFF. I don't know, I didn't even see him yet, but—

WILLY. Then what're you talkin' about?

BIFF (*getting angry*). Well, all I said was I'm gonna see him, that's all!

WILLY (*turning away*). Ah, you're counting your chickens again.

BIFF (*starting left for the stairs*). Oh, Jesus, I'm going to sleep!

WILLY (*calling after him*). Don't curse in this house!

BIFF (*turning*). Since when did you get so clean?

HAPPY (*trying to stop them*). Wait a . . .

WILLY. Don't use that language to me! I won't have it!

HAPPY (*grabbing* BIFF, *shouts*). Wait a minute! I got an idea. I got a feasible idea. Come here, Biff, let's talk this over now, let's talk some sense here. When I was down in Florida last time, I thought of a great idea to sell sporting goods. It just came back to me. You and I, Biff—we have a line, the Loman Line. We train a couple of weeks, and put on a couple of exhibitions, see?

WILLY. That's an idea!

HAPPY. Wait! We form two basketball teams, see? Two water-polo teams. We play each other. It's a million dollars' worth of publicity. Two brothers, see? The Loman Brothers. Displays in the Royal Palms—all the hotels. And banners over the ring and the basketball court: "Loman Brothers." Baby, we could sell sporting goods!

WILLY. That is a one-million-dollar idea!

LINDA. Marvelous!

BIFF. I'm in great shape as far as that's concerned.

HAPPY. And the beauty of it is, Biff, it wouldn't be like a business. We'd be out playin' ball again . . .

BIFF (*enthused*). Yeah, that's . . .

WILLY. Million-dollar . . .

Happy. And you wouldn't get fed up with it, Biff. It'd be the family again. There'd be the old honor, and comradeship, and if you wanted to go off for a swim or somethin'—well, you'd do it! Without some smart cooky gettin' up ahead of you!

Willy. Lick the world! You guys together could absolutely lick the civilized world.

Biff. I'll see Oliver tomorrow. Hap, if we could work that out . . .

Linda. Maybe things are beginning to—

Willy (*wildly enthused, to* Linda). Stop interrupting! (*To* Biff) But don't wear sport jacket and slacks when you see Oliver.

Biff. No, I'll—

Willy. A business suit, and talk as little as possible, and don't crack any jokes.

Biff. He did like me. Always liked me.

Linda. He loved you!

Willy (*to* Linda). Will you stop! (*To* Biff) Walk in very serious. You are not applying for a boy's job. Money is to pass. Be quiet, fine, and serious. Everybody likes a kidder, but nobody lends him money.

Happy. I'll try to get some myself, Biff. I'm sure I can.

Willy. I see great things for you kids, I think your troubles are over. But remember, start big and you'll end big. Ask for fifteen. How much you gonna ask for?

Biff. Gee, I don't know—

Willy. And don't say "Gee." "Gee" is a boy's word. A man walking in for fifteen thousand dollars does not say "Gee!"

Biff. Ten, I think, would be top though.

Willy. Don't be so modest. You always started too low. Walk in with a big laugh. Don't look worried. Start off with a couple of your good stories to lighten things up. It's not what you say, it's how you say it—because personality always wins the day.

Linda. Oliver always thought the highest of him—

Willy. Will you let me talk?

Biff. Don't yell at her, Pop, will ya?

Willy (*angrily*). I was talking, wasn't I?

Biff. I don't like you yelling at her all the time, and I'm tellin' you, that's all.

Willy. What're you, takin' over this house?

Linda. Willy—

Willy (*turning on her*). Don't take his side all the time, goddammit!

Biff (*furiously*). Stop yelling at her!

Willy (*suddenly pulling on his cheek, beaten down, guilt ridden*). Give my best to Bill Oliver—he may remember me. (*He exits through the living-room doorway.*)

Linda (*her voice subdued*). What'd you have to start that for? (Biff *turns away.*) You see how sweet he was as soon as you talked hopefully? (*She goes over to* BIFF.) Come up and say good night to him. Don't let him go to bed that way.

HAPPY. Come on, Biff, let's buck him up.

LINDA. Please, dear. Just say good night. It takes so little to make him happy. Come. (*She goes through the living-room doorway, calling upstairs from within the living-room.*) Your pajamas are hanging in the bathroom, Willy!

HAPPY (*looking toward where* LINDA *went out*). What a woman! They broke the mold when they made her. You know that, Biff?

BIFF. He's off salary. My God, working on commission!

HAPPY. Well, let's face it: he's no hot-shot selling man. Except that sometimes, you have to admit, he's a sweet personality.

BIFF (*deciding*). Lend me ten bucks, will ya? I want to buy some new ties.

HAPPY. I'll take you to a place I know. Beautiful stuff. Wear one of my striped shirts tomorrow.

BIFF. She got gray. Mom got awful old. Gee, I'm gonna go in to Oliver tomorrow and knock him for a—

HAPPY. Come on up. Tell that to Dad. Let's give him a whirl. Come on.

BIFF (*steamed up*). You know, with ten thousand bucks, boy!

HAPPY (*as they go into the living-room*). That's the talk, Biff, that's the first time I've heard the old confidence out of you! (*From within the living-room, fading off*) You're gonna live with me, kid, and any babe you want just say the word . . . (*The last lines are hardly heard. They are mounting the stairs to their parents' bedroom.*)

LINDA (*entering her bedroom and addressing* WILLY, *who is in the bathroom. She is straightening the bed for him*). Can you do anything about the shower? It drips.

WILLY (*from the bathroom*). All of a sudden everything falls to pieces! Goddam plumbing, oughta be sued, those people. I hardly finished putting it in and the thing . . . (*His words rumble off.*)

LINDA. I'm just wondering if Oliver will remember him. You think he might?

WILLY (*coming out of the bathroom in his pajamas*). Remember him? What's the matter with you, you crazy? If he'd've stayed with Oliver he'd be on top by now! Wait'll Oliver gets a look at him. You don't know the average caliber any more. The average young man today—(*he is getting into bed*)—is got a caliber of zero. Greatest thing in the world for him was to bum around.

(BIFF *and* HAPPY *enter the bedroom. Slight pause.*)

WILLY (*stops short, looking at* BIFF). Glad to hear it, boy.

HAPPY. He wanted to say good night to you, sport.

WILLY (*to* BIFF). Yeah. Knock him dead, boy. What'd you want to tell me?

BIFF. Just take it easy, Pop. Good night. (*He turns to go.*)

WILLY (*unable to resist*). And if anything falls off the desk while you're talking to him—like a package or something—don't you pick it up. They have office boys for that.

LINDA. I'll make a big breakfast—

WILLY. Will you let me finish? (*To* BIFF) Tell him you were in the business in the West. Not farm work.

BIFF. All right, Dad.

LINDA. I think everything—

WILLY (*going right through her speech*). And don't undersell yourself. No less than fifteen thousand dollars.

BIFF (*unable to bear him*). Okay. Good night, Mom. (*He starts moving.*)

WILLY. Because you got a greatness in you, Biff, remember that. You got all kinds of greatness . . .

(*He lies back, exhausted.* BIFF *walks out.*)

LINDA (*calling after* BIFF). Sleep well, darling!

HAPPY. I'm gonna get married, Mom. I wanted to tell you.

LINDA. Go to sleep, dear.

HAPPY (*going*). I just wanted to tell you.

WILLY. Keep up the good work. (HAPPY *exits.*) God . . . remember that Ebbets Field game? The championship of the city?

LINDA. Just rest. Should I sing to you?

WILLY. Yeah. Sing to me. (LINDA *hums a soft lullaby.*) When that team came out—he was the tallest, remember?

LINDA. Oh, yes. And in gold.

(BIFF *enters the darkened kitchen, takes a cigarette, and leaves the house. He comes downstage into a golden pool of light. He smokes, staring at the night.*)

WILLY. Like a young god. Hercules—something like that. And the sun, the sun all around him. Remember how he waved to me? Right up from the field, with the representatives of three colleges standing by? And the buyers I brought, and the cheers when he came out—Loman, Loman, Loman! God Almighty, he'll be great yet. A star like that, magnificent, can never really fade away!

(*The light on* WILLY *is fading. The gas heater begins to glow through the kitchen wall, near the stairs, a blue flame beneath red coils.*)

LINDA (*timidly*). Willy dear, what has he got against you?

WILLY. I'm so tired. Don't talk any more.

(BIFF *slowly returns to the kitchen. He stops, stares toward the heater.*)

LINDA. Will you ask Howard to let you work in New York?

WILLY. First thing in the morning. Everything'll be all right.

(BIFF *reaches behind the heater and draws out a length of rubber tubing. He is horrified and turns his head toward* WILLY'S *room, still dimly lit, from which the strains of* LINDA'S *desperate but monotonous humming rise.*)

WILLY (*staring through the window into the moonlight*). Gee, look at the moon moving between the buildings!

(BIFF *wraps the tubing around his hand and quickly goes up the stairs.*)

ACT II

Music is heard, gay and bright. The curtain rises as the music fades away. WILLY, *in shirt sleeves, is sitting at the kitchen table, sipping coffee, his hat in his lap.* LINDA *is filling his cup when she can.*

WILLY. Wonderful coffee. Meal in itself.

LINDA. Can I make you some eggs?

WILLY. No. Take a breath.

LINDA. You look so rested, dear.

WILLY. I slept like a dead one. First time in months. Imagine, sleeping till ten on a Tuesday morning. Boys left nice and early, heh?

LINDA. They were out of here by eight o'clock.

WILLY. Good work!

LINDA. It was so thrilling to see them leaving together. I can't get over the shaving lotion in this house!

WILLY (*smiling*). Mmm—

LINDA. Biff was very changed this morning. His whole attitude seemed to be hopeful. He couldn't wait to get downtown to see Oliver.

WILLY. He's heading for a change. There's no question, there simply are certain men that take longer to get—solidified. How did he dress?

LINDA. His blue suit. He's so handsome in that suit. He could be a—anything in that suit!

(WILLY *gets up from the table.* LINDA *holds his jacket for him.*)

WILLY. There's no question, no question at all. Gee, on the way home tonight I'd like to buy some seeds.

LINDA (*laughing*). That'd be wonderful. But not enough sun gets back there. Nothing'll grow any more.

WILLY. You wait, kid, before it's all over we're gonna get a little place out in the country, and I'll raise some vegetables, a couple of chickens . . .

LINDA. You'll do it yet, dear.

(WILLY *walks out of his jacket.* LINDA *follows him.*)

WILLY. And they'll get married, and come for a weekend. I'd build a little guest house. 'Cause I got so many fine tools, all I'd need would be a little lumber and some peace of mind.

LINDA (*joyfully*). I sewed the lining . . .

WILLY. I would build two guest houses, so they'd both come. Did he decide how much he's going to ask Oliver for?

LINDA (*getting him into the jacket*). He didn't mention it, but I imagine ten or fifteen thousand. You going to talk to Howard today?

WILLY. Yeah. I'll put it to him straight and simple. He'll just have to take me off the road.

LINDA. And, Willy, don't forget to ask for a little advance, because we've got the insurance premium. It's the grace period now.

WILLY. That's a hundred . . .?

LINDA. A hundred and eight, sixty-eight. Because we're a little short again.

WILLY. Why are we short?

LINDA. Well, you had the motor job on the car . . .

WILLY. That goddam Studebaker!

LINDA. And you got one more payment on the refrigerator . . .

WILLY. But it just broke again!

LINDA. Well, it's old, dear.

WILLY. I told you we should've bought a well-advertised machine. Charley bought a General Electric and it's twenty years old and it's still good, that son-of-a-bitch.

LINDA. But, Willy—

WILLY. Whoever heard of a Hastings refrigerator? Once in my life I would like to own something outright before it's broken! I'm always in a race with the junkyard! I just finished paying for the car and it's on its last legs. The refrigerator consumes belts like a goddam maniac. They time those things. They time them so when you finally paid for them, they're used up.

LINDA (*buttoning up his jacket as he unbuttons it*). All told, about two hundred dollars would carry us, dear. But that includes the last payment on the mortgage. After this payment, Willy, the house belongs to us.

WILLY. It's twenty-five years!

LINDA. Biff was nine years old when we bought it.

WILLY. Well, that's a great thing. To weather a twenty-five year mortgage is—

LINDA. It's an accomplishment.

WILLY. All the cement, the lumber, the reconstruction I put in this house! There ain't a crack to be found in it any more.

LINDA. Well, it served its purpose.

WILLY. What purpose? Some stranger'll come along, move in, and that's that. If only Biff would take this house, and raise a family . . . (*He starts to go.*) Good-by, I'm late.

LINDA (*suddenly remembering*). Oh, I forgot! You're supposed to meet them for dinner.

WILLY. Me?

LINDA. At Frank's Chop House on Forty-eighth near Sixth Avenue.

WILLY. Is that so! How about you?

LINDA. No, just the three of you. They're gonna blow you to a big meal!

WILLY. Don't say! Who thought of that?

LINDA. Biff came to me this morning, Willy, and he said, "Tell Dad, we want to blow him to a big meal." Be there six o'clock. You and your two boys are going to have dinner.

WILLY. Gee whiz! That's really somethin'. I'm gonna knock Howard for a loop, kid. I'll get an advance, and I'll come home with a New York job. Goddammit, now I'm gonna do it!

LINDA. Oh, that's the spirit, Willy!

WILLY. I will never get behind a wheel the rest of my life!

LINDA. It's changing, Willy, I can feel it changing!

WILLY. Beyond a question. G'by, I'm late. (*He starts to go again.*)

LINDA (*calling after him as she runs to the kitchen table for a handkerchief*). You got your glasses?

WILLY (*feels for them, then comes back in*). Yeah, yeah, got my glasses.

LINDA (*giving him the handkerchief*). And a handkerchief.

WILLY. Yeah, handkerchief.

LINDA. And your saccharine?

WILLY. Yeah, my saccharine.

LINDA. Be careful on the subway stairs.

(*She kisses him, and a silk stocking is seen hanging from her hand.* WILLY *notices it.*)

WILLY. Will you stop mending stockings? At least while I'm in the house. It gets me nervous. I can't tell you. Please.

(LINDA *hides the stocking in her hand as she follows* WILLY *across the forestage in front of the house.*)

LINDA. Remember, Frank's Chop House.

WILLY (*passing the apron*). Maybe beets would grow out there.

LINDA (*laughing*). But you tried so many times.

WILLY. Yeah. Well, don't work hard today. (*He disappears around the right corner of the house.*)

LINDA. Be careful!

(*As* WILLY *vanishes,* LINDA *waves to him. Suddenly the phone rings. She runs across the stage and into the kitchen and lifts it.*)

LINDA. Hello? Oh, Biff! I'm so glad you called, I just . . . Yes, sure, I just told him. Yes, he'll be there for dinner at six o'clock, I didn't forget. Listen, I was just dying to tell you. You know that little rubber pipe I told you about? That he connected to the gas heater? I finally decided to go down the cellar this morning and take it away and destroy it. But it's gone! Imagine? He took it away himself, it isn't there! (*She listens.*) When? Oh, then you took it. Oh—nothing, it's just that I'd hoped he'd taken it away himself. Oh, I'm not worried, darling, because this morning he left in such high spirits, it was like the old days! I'm not afraid any more. Did Mr. Oliver see you? . . . Well, you wait there then. And make a nice impression on him, darling. Just don't perspire too much before you see him. And have a nice time with Dad. He may have big news too! . . . That's right, a New York job. And be sweet to him tonight, dear. Be loving to him. Because he's only a little boat looking for a harbor. (*She is trembling with sorrow and joy.*) Oh, that's wonderful, Biff, you'll save his life. Thanks, darling. Just put your arm around him when he comes into the restaurant. Give him a smile. That's the boy . . . Good-by, dear . . . You got your comb? . . . That's fine. Good-by, Biff dear.

(*In the middle of her speech,* HOWARD WAGNER, *thirty-six, wheels on a small typewriter table on which is a wire-recording machine and proceeds to plug it in. This is on the left forestage. Light slowly fades on* LINDA *as it rises on* HOWARD. HOWARD *is intent on threading the machine and only glances over his shoulder as* WILLY *appears.*)

WILLY. Pst! Pst!

HOWARD. Hello, Willy, come in.

WILLY. Like to have a little talk with you, Howard.

HOWARD. Sorry to keep you waiting. I'll be with you in a minute.

WILLY. What's that, Howard?

HOWARD. Didn't you ever see one of these? Wire recorder.

WILLY. Oh. Can we talk a minute?

HOWARD. Records things. Just got delivery yesterday. Been driving me crazy, the most terrific machine I ever saw in my life. I was up all night with it.

WILLY. What do you do with it?

HOWARD. I bought it for dictation, but you can do anything with it. Listen to this. I had it home last night. Listen to what I picked up. The first one is my daughter. Get this. (*He flicks the switch and "Roll Out the Barrel" is heard being whistled.*) Listen to that kid whistle.

WILLY. That is lifelike, isn't it?

HOWARD. Seven years old. Get that tone.

WILLY. Ts, ts. Like to ask a little favor if you . . .

(The whistling breaks off, and the voice of HOWARD's *daughter is heard.)*

HIS DAUGHTER. "Now you, Daddy."

HOWARD. She's crazy for me! *(Again the same song is whistled.)* That's me! Ha! *(He winks.)*

WILLY. You're very good!

(The whistling breaks off again. The machine runs silent for a moment.)

HOWARD. Sh! Get this now, this is my son.

HIS SON. "The capital of Alabama is Montgomery; the capital of Arizona is Phoenix; the capital of Arkansas is Little Rock; the capital of California is Sacramento . . ." *(and on, and on).*

HOWARD *(holding up five fingers.)* Five years old, Willy!

WILLY. He'll make an announcer some day!

HIS SON *(continuing).* "The capital . . ."

HOWARD. Get that—alphabetical order! *(The machine breaks off suddenly.)* Wait a minute. The maid kicked the plug out.

WILLY. It certainly is a—

HOWARD. Sh, for God's sake!

HIS SON. "It's nine o'clock, Bulova watch time. So I have to go to sleep."

WILLY. That really is—

HOWARD. Wait a minute! The next is my wife.

(They wait.)

HOWARD'S VOICE. "Go on, say something." *(Pause)* "Well, you gonna talk?"

HIS WIFE. "I can't think of anything."

HOWARD'S VOICE. "Well, talk—it's turning."

HIS WIFE *(shyly, beaten).* "Hello." *(Silence)* "Oh, Howard, I can't talk into this . . ."

HOWARD *(snapping the machine off).* That was my wife.

WILLY. That is a wonderful machine. Can we—

HOWARD. I tell you, Willy, I'm gonna take my camera, and my bandsaw, and all my hobbies, and out they go. This is the most fascinating relaxation I ever found.

WILLY. I think I'll get one myself.

HOWARD. Sure, they're only a hundred and a half. You can't do without it. Supposing you wanna hear Jack Benny, see? But you can't be at home at that hour. So you tell the maid to turn the radio on when Jack Benny comes on, and this automatically goes on with the radio . . .

WILLY. And when you come home you . . .

HOWARD. You can come home twelve o'clock, one o'clock, any time you like, and you get yourself a Coke and sit yourself down, throw the switch, and there's Jack Benny's program in the middle of the night!

WILLY. I'm definitely going to get one. Because lots of time I'm on the road, and I think to myself, what I must be missing on the radio!

HOWARD. Don't you have a radio in the car?

WILLY. Well, yeah, but who ever thinks of turning it on?

HOWARD. Say, aren't you supposed to be in Boston?

WILLY. That's what I want to talk to you about, Howard. You got a minute? (*He draws a chair in from the wing.*)

HOWARD. What happened? What're you doing here?

WILLY. Well . . .

HOWARD. You didn't crack up again, did you?

WILLY. Oh, no. No . . .

HOWARD. Geez, you had me worried there for a minute. What's the trouble?

WILLY. Well, tell you the truth, Howard. I've come to the decision that I'd rather not travel any more.

HOWARD. Not travel! Well, what'll you do?

WILLY. Remember, Christmas time, when you had the party here? You said you'd try to think of some spot for me here in town.

HOWARD. With us?

WILLY. Well, sure.

HOWARD. Oh, yeah, yeah. I remember. Well, I couldn't think of anything for you, Willy.

WILLY. I tell ya, Howard. The kids are all grown up, y'know. I don't need much any more. If I could take home—well, sixty-five dollars a week, I could swing it.

HOWARD. Yeah, but Willy, see I—

WILLY. I tell ya why, Howard. Speaking frankly and between the two of us, y'know—I'm just a little tired.

HOWARD. Oh, I could understand that, Willy. But you're a road man, Willy, and we do a road business. We've only got a half-dozen salesmen on the floor here.

WILLY. God knows, Howard, I never asked a favor of any man. But I was with the firm when your father used to carry you in here in his arms.

HOWARD. I know that, Willy, but—

WILLY. Your father came to me the day you were born and asked me what I thought of the name of Howard, may he rest in peace.

HOWARD. I appreciate that, Willy, but there just is no spot here for you. If I had a spot I'd slam you right in, but I just don't have a single solitary spot.

(*He looks for his lighter.* WILLY *has picked it up and gives it to him. Pause.*)

WILLY (*with increasing anger*). Howard, all I need to set my table is fifty dollars a week.

HOWARD. But where am I going to put you, kid?

WILLY. Look, it isn't a question of whether I can sell merchandise, is it?

HOWARD. No, but it's a business, kid, and everybody, gotta pull his own weight.

WILLY (*desperately*). Just let me tell you a story, Howard—

HOWARD. 'Cause you gotta admit, business is business.

WILLY (*angrily*). Business is definitely business, but just listen for a minute. You don't understand this. When I was a boy—eighteen, nineteen—I was already on the road. And there was a question in my mind as to whether selling had a future for me. Because in those days I had a yearning to go to Alaska. See, there were three gold strikes in one month in Alaska, and I felt like going out. Just for the ride, you might say.

HOWARD (*barely interested*). Don't say.

WILLY. Oh, yeah, my father lived many years in Alaska. He was an adventurous man. We've got quite a little streak of self-reliance in our family. I thought I'd go out with my older brother and try to locate him, and maybe settle in the North with the old man. And I was almost decided to go, when I met a salesman in the Parker House. His name was Dave Singleman. And he was eighty-four years old, and he'd drummed merchandise in thirty-one states. And old Dave, he'd go up to his room, y'understand, put on his green velvet slippers—I'll never forget—and pick up his phone and call the buyers, and without ever leaving his room, at the age of eighty-four, he made his living. And when I saw that, I realized that selling was the greatest career a man could want. 'Cause what could be more satisfying than to be able to go, at the age of eighty-four, into twenty or thirty different cities, and pick up a phone, and be remembered and loved and helped by so many different people? Do you know? when he died—and by the way he died the death of a salesman, in his green velvet slippers in the smoker of the New York, New Haven and Hartford, going into Boston—when he died, hundreds of salesmen and buyers were at his funeral. Things were sad on a lotta trains for months after that. (*He stands up.* HOWARD *has not looked at him.*) In those days there was personality in it, Howard. There was respect, and comradeship, and gratitude in it. Today, it's all cut and dried, and there's no chance for bringing friendship to bear—or personality. You see what I mean? They don't know me any more.

HOWARD (*moving away, to the right*). That's just the thing, Willy.

WILLY. If I had forty dollars a week—that's all I'd need. Forty dollars, Howard.

HOWARD. Kid, I can't take blood from a stone, I—

WILLY (*desperation is on him now*). Howard, the year Al Smith was nominated, your father came to me and—

HOWARD (*starting to go off*). I've got to see some people, kid.

WILLY (*stopping him*). I'm talking about your father! There were promises made across this desk! You mustn't tell me you've got people to see —I put thirty-four years into this firm, Howard, and now I can't pay my insurance! You can't eat the orange and throw the peel away—a man is not a piece of fruit! (*After a pause*) Now pay attention. Your father—in 1928 I had a big year. I averaged a hundred and seventy dollars a week in commissions.

HOWARD (*impatiently*). Now, Willy, you never averaged—

WILLY (*banging his hand on the desk*). I averaged a hundred and seventy dollars a week in the year of 1928! And your father came to me—or rather, I was in the office here—it was right over this desk—and he put his hand on my shoulder—

HOWARD (*getting up*). You'll have to excuse me, Willy, I gotta see some people. Pull yourself together. (*Going out*) I'll be back in a little while.

(*On* HOWARD's *exit, the light on his chair grows very bright and strange.*)

WILLY. Pull myself together! What the hell did I say to him? My God, I was yelling at him! How could I! (WILLY *breaks off, staring at the light, which occupies the chair, animating it. He approaches this chair, standing across the desk from it.*) Frank, Frank, don't you remember what you told me that time? How you put your hand on my shoulder, and Frank . . . (*He leans on the desk and as he speaks the dead man's name he accidentally switches on the recorder, and instantly*)

HOWARD'S SON. ". . . of New York is Albany. The capital of Ohio is Cincinnati, the capital of Rhode Island is . . ." (*The recitation continues.*)

WILLY (*leaping away with fright, shouting*). Ha! Howard! Howard! Howard!

HOWARD (*rushing in*). What happened?

WILLY (*pointing at the machine, which continues nasally, childishly, with the capital cities*). Shut it off! Shut it off!

HOWARD (*pulling the plug out*). Look, Willy . . .

WILLY (*pressing his hands to his eyes*). I gotta get myself some coffee. I'll get some coffee . . .

(WILLY *starts to walk out.* HOWARD *stops him.*)

HOWARD (*rolling up the cord*). Willy, look . . .

WILLY. I'll go to Boston.

HOWARD. Willy, you can't go to Boston for us.

WILLY. Why can't I go?

HOWARD. I don't want you to represent us. I've been meaning to tell you for a long time now.

WILLY. Howard, are you firing me?

HOWARD. I think you need a good long rest, Willy.

WILLY. Howard—

HOWARD. And when you feel better, come back, and we'll see if we can work something out.

WILLY. But I gotta earn money, Howard. I'm in no position to—

HOWARD. Where are your sons? Why don't your sons give you a hand?

WILLY. They're working on a very big deal.

HOWARD. This is no time for false pride, Willy. You go to your sons and you tell them that you're tired. You've got two great boys, haven't you?

WILLY. Oh, no question, no question, but in the meantime . . .

HOWARD. Then that's that, heh?

WILLY. All right, I'll go to Boston tomorrow.

HOWARD. No, no.

WILLY. I can't throw myself on my sons. I'm not a cripple!

HOWARD. Look, kid, I'm busy this morning.

WILLY (*grasping* HOWARD's *arm*). Howard, you've got to let me go to Boston!

HOWARD (*hard, keeping himself under control*). I've got a line of people to see this morning. Sit down, take five minutes, and pull yourself together, and then go home, will ya? I need the office, Willy. (*He starts to go, turns, remembering the recorder, starts to push off the table holding the recorder.*) Oh, yeah. Whenever you can this week, stop by and drop off the samples. You'll feel better, Willy, and then come back and we'll talk. Pull yourself together, kid, there's people outside.

(HOWARD *exits, pushing the table off left.* WILLY *stares into space, exhausted. Now the music is heard*—BEN's *music*—*first distantly, then closer, closer. As* WILLY *speaks,* BEN *enters from the right. He carries valise and umbrella.*)

WILLY. Oh, Ben, how did you do it? What is the answer? Did you wind up the Alaska deal already?

BEN. Doesn't take much time if you know what you're doing. Just a short business trip. Boarding ship in an hour. Wanted to say good-by.

WILLY. Ben, I've got to talk to you.

BEN (*glancing at his watch*). Haven't the time, William.

WILLY (*crossing the apron to* BEN). Ben, nothing's working out. I don't know what to do.

BEN. Now, look here, William. I've bought timberland in Alaska and I need a man to look after things for me.

WILLY. God, timberland! Me and my boys in those grand outdoors!

BEN. You've a new continent at your doorstep, William. Get out of these cities, they're full of talk and time payments and courts of law. Screw on your fists and you can fight for a fortune up there.

WILLY. Yes, yes! Linda, Linda!

(LINDA *enters as of old, with the wash.*)

LINDA. Oh, you're back?

BEN. I haven't much time.

WILLY. No, wait! Linda, he's got a proposition for me in Alaska.

LINDA. But you've got—(*To* BEN) He's got a beautiful job here.

WILLY. But in Alaska, kid, I could—

LINDA. You're doing well enough, Willy!

BEN (*to* LINDA). Enough for what, my dear?

LINDA (*frightened of* BEN *and angry at him*). Don't say those things to him! Enough to be happy right here, right now. (*To* WILLY, *while* BEN *laughs*) Why must everybody conquer the world? You're well liked, and the boys love you, and someday—(*to* BEN)—why, old man Wagner told him just the other day that if he keeps it up he'll be a member of the firm, didn't he, Willy?

WILLY. Sure, sure. I am building something with this firm, Ben, and if a man is building something he must be on the right track, mustn't he?

BEN. What are you building? Lay your hand on it. Where is it?

WILLY (*hesitantly*). That's true, Linda, there's nothing.

LINDA. Why? (*To* BEN) There's a man eighty-four years old—

WILLY. That's right, Ben, that's right. When I look at that man I say, what is there to worry about?

BEN. Bah!

WILLY. It's true, Ben. All he has to do is go into any city, pick up the phone, and he's making his living and you know why?

BEN (*picking up his valise*). I've got to go.

WILLY (*holding* BEN *back*). Look at this boy!

(BIFF, *in his high school sweater, enters carrying suitcase.* HAPPY *carries* BIFF'S *shoulder guards, gold helmet, and football pants.*)

WILLY. Without a penny to his name, three great universities are begging for him, and from there the sky's the limit, because it's not what you do, Ben. It's who you know and the smile on your face! It's contacts, Ben, contacts! The whole wealth of Alaska passes over the lunch table at the Commodore Hotel, and that's the wonder, the wonder of this country, that a man can end with diamonds here on the basis of being liked! (*He turns to* BIFF) And that's why when you get out on that field today, it's important. Because thousands of people will be rooting for you and loving you. (*To* BEN, *who has again begun to leave*) And Ben! when he walks into a business office his name will sound out like a bell and all the doors will open to him! I've seen it, Ben, I've seen it a thousand times! You can't feel it with your hand like timber, but it's there!

BEN. Good-by, William.

WILLY. Ben, am I right? Don't you think I'm right? I value your advice.

BEN. There's a new continent at your doorstep, William. You could walk out rich. Rich! (*He is gone.*)

WILLY. We'll do it here, Ben! You hear me? We're gonna do it hear!

(YOUNG BERNARD *rushes in. The gay music of the boys is heard.*)

BERNARD. Oh, gee, I was afraid you left already!

WILLY. Why? What time is it?

BERNARD. It's half-past one!

WILLY. Well, come on, everybody! Ebbets Field next stop! Where's the pennants? (*He rushes through the wall-line of the kitchen and out into the living-room.*)

LINDA (*to* BIFF). Did you pack fresh underwear?

BIFF (*who has been limbering up*). I want to go!

BERNARD. Biff, I'm carrying your helmet, ain't I?

HAPPY. No, I'm carrying the helmet.

BERNARD. Oh, Biff, you promised me.

HAPPY. I'm carrying the helmet.

BERNARD. How am I going to get in the locker room?

LINDA. Let him carry the shoulder guards. (*She puts her coat and hat on in the kitchen.*)

BERNARD. Can I, Biff? 'Cause I told everybody I'm going to be in the locker room.

HAPPY. In Ebbets Field it's the clubhouse.

BERNARD. I meant the clubhouse, Biff!

HAPPY. Biff!

BIFF (*grandly, after a slight pause*). Let him carry the shoulder guards.

HAPPY (*as he gives* BERNARD *the shoulder guards*). Stay close to us now.

(WILLY *rushes in with the pennants.*)

WILLY (*handing them out*). Everybody wave when Biff comes out on the field. (HAPPY *and* BERNARD *run off.*) You set now, boy?

(*The music has died away.*)

BIFF. Ready to go, Pop. Every muscle is ready.

WILLY (*at the edge of the apron*). You realize what this means?

BIFF. That's right, Pop.

WILLY (*feeling* BIFF'S *muscles*). You're comin' home this afternoon captain of the All-Scholastic Championship Team of the City of New York.

BIFF. I got it, Pop. And remember, pal, when I take off my helmet, that touchdown is for you.

WILLY. Let's go! (*He is starting out, with his arm around* BIFF, *when* CHARLEY *enters, as of old, in knickers.*) I got no room for you, Charley.

CHARLEY. Room? For what?

WILLY. In the car.

CHARLEY. You goin' for a ride? I wanted to shoot some casino.

WILLY (*furiously*). Casino! (*Incredulously*) Don't you realize what today is?

LINDA. Oh, he knows, Willy. He's just kidding you.

WILLY. That's nothing to kid about!

CHARLEY. No, Linda, what's goin' on?

LINDA. He's playing in Ebbets Field.

CHARLEY. Baseball in this weather?

WILLY. Don't talk to him. Come on, come on! (*He is pushing them out.*)

CHARLEY. What a minute, didn't you hear the news?

WILLY. What?

CHARLEY. Don't you listen to the radio? Ebbets Field just blew up.

WILLY. You go to hell! (CHARLEY *laughs. Pushing them out*) Come on, come on! We're late.

CHARLEY (*as they go*). Knock a homer, Biff, knock a homer!

WILLY (*the last to leave, turning to* CHARLEY). I don't think that was funny, Charley. This is the greatest day of his life.

CHARLEY. Willy, when are you going to grow up?

WILLY. Yeah, heh? When this game is over, Charley, you'll be laughing out of the other side of your face. They'll be calling him another Red Grange. Twenty-five thousand a year.

CHARLEY (*kidding*). Is that so?

WILLY. Yeah, that's so.

CHARLEY. Well, then, I'm sorry, Willy. But tell me something.

WILLY. What?

CHARLEY. Who is Red Grange?

WILLY. Put up your hands. Goddam you, put up your hands!

(CHARLEY, *chuckling, shakes his head and walks away, around the left corner of the stage.* WILLY *follows him. The music rises to a mocking frenzy.*)

WILLY. Who the hell do you think you are, better than everybody else? You don't know everything, you big, ignorant, stupid . . . Put up your hands!

(*Light rises, on the right side of the forestage, on a small table in the reception room of* CHARLEY'*s office. Traffic sounds are heard.* BERNARD, *now mature, sits whistling to himself. A pair of tennis rackets and an overnight bag are on the floor beside him.*)

WILLY (*offstage*). What are you walking away for? Don't walk away! If you're going to say something say it to my face! I know you laugh at me behind my back. You'll laugh out of the other side of your goddam face after this game. Touchdown! Touchdown! Eighty thousand people! Touchdown! Right between the goal posts.

(BERNARD *is a quiet, earnest, but self-assured young man.* WILLY'*s voice is coming from right upstage now.* BERNARD *lowers his feet off the table and listens.* JENNY, *his father's secretary, enters.*)

JENNY (*distressed*). Say, Bernard, will you go out in the hall?

BERNARD. What is that noise? Who is it?

JENNY. Mr. Loman. He just got off the elevator.

BERNARD (*getting up*). Who's he arguing with?

JENNY. Nobody. There's nobody with him. I can't deal with him any more, and your father gets all upset everytime he comes. I've got a lot of typing to do, and your father's waiting to sign it. Will you see him?

WILLY (*entering*). Touchdown! Touch—(*He sees* JENNY.) Jenny, Jenny, good to see you. How're ya? Workin'? Or still honest?

JENNY. Fine. How've you been feeling?

WILLY. Not much any more, Jenny. Ha, Ha! (*He is surprised to see the rackets.*)

BERNARD. Hello, Uncle Willy.

WILLY (*almost shocked*). Bernard! Well, look who's here! (*He comes quickly, guiltily, to* BERNARD *and warmly shakes his hand.*)

BERNARD. How are you? Good to see you.

WILLY. What are you doing here?

BERNARD. Oh, just stopped by to see Pop. Get off my feet till my train leaves. I'm going to Washington in a few minutes.

WILLY. Is he in?

BERNARD. Yes, he's in his office with the accountant. Sit down.

WILLY (*sitting down*). What're you going to do in Washington?

BERNARD. Oh, just a case I've got there, Willy.

WILLY. That so? (*Indicating the rackets*) You going to play tennis there?

BERNARD. I'm staying with a friend who's got a court.

WILLY. Don't say. His own tennis court. Must be fine people, I bet.

BERNARD. They are, very nice. Dad tells me Biff's in town.

WILLY (*with a big smile*). Yeah, Biff's in. Working on a very big deal, Bernard.

BERNARD. What's Biff doing?

WILLY. Well, he's been doing very big things in the West. But he decided to establish himself here. Very big. We're having dinner. Did I hear your wife had a boy?

BERNARD. That's right. Our second.

WILLY. Two boys! What do you know!

BERNARD. What kind of a deal has Biff got?

WILLY. Well, Bill Oliver—very big sporting goods man—he wants Biff very badly. Called him in from the West. Long distance, carte blanche, special deliveries. Your friends have their own private tennis court?

BERNARD. You still with the old firm, Willy?

WILLY (*after a pause*). I'm—I'm overjoyed to see how you made the grade, Bernard, overjoyed. It's an encouraging thing to see a young man really—really—Looks very good for Biff—very—(*He breaks off, then*) Bernard—(*He is so full of emotion, he breaks off again.*)

BERNARD. What is it, Willy?

WILLY (*small and alone*). What—what's the secret?

BERNARD. What secret?

WILLY. How—how did you? Why didn't he ever catch on?

BERNARD. I wouldn't know that, Willy.

WILLY (*confidentially, desperately*). You were his friend, his boyhood friend. There's something I don't understand about it. His life ended after that Ebbets Field game. From the age of seventeen nothing good ever happened to him.

BERNARD. He never trained himself for anything.

WILLY. But he did, he did. After high school he took so many correspondence courses. Radio mechanics; television; God knows what, and never made the slightest mark.

BERNARD (*taking off his glasses*). Willy, do you want to talk candidly?

WILLY (*rising, faces* BERNARD). I regard you as a very brilliant man, Bernard. I value your advice.

BERNARD. Oh, the hell with the advice, Willy. I couldn't advise you. There's just one thing I've always wanted to ask you. When he was supposed to graduate, and the math teacher flunked him—

WILLY. Oh, that son-of-a-bitch ruined his life.

BERNARD. Yeah, but, Willy, all he had to do was go to summer school and make up that subject.

WILLY. That's right, that's right.

BERNARD. Did you tell him not to go to summer school?

WILLY. Me? I begged him to go. I ordered him to go!

BERNARD. Then why wouldn't he go?

WILLY. Why? Why! Bernard, that question has been trailing me like a ghost for the last fifteen years. He flunked the subject, and laid down and died like a hammer hit him!

BERNARD. Take it easy, kid.

WILLY. Let me talk to you—I got nobody to talk to. Bernard, Bernard, was it my fault? Y'see? It keeps going around in my mind, maybe I did something to him. I got nothing to give him.

BERNARD. Don't take it so hard.

WILLY. Why did he lay down? What is the story there? You were his friend!

BERNARD. Willy, I remember, it was June, and our grades came out. And he'd flunked math.

WILLY. That son-of-a-bitch!

BERNARD. No, it wasn't right then. Biff just got very angry, I remember, and he was ready to enroll in summer school.

WILLY (*surprised*). He was?

BERNARD. He wasn't beaten by it at all. But then, Willy, he disappeared from the block for almost a month. And I got the idea that he'd gone up to New England to see you. Did he have a talk with you then?

(WILLY *stares in silence.*)

BERNARD. Willy?

WILLY (*with a strong edge of resentment in his voice*). Yeah, he came to Boston. What about it?

BERNARD. Well, just that when he came back—I'll never forget this, it always mystifies me. Because I thought so well of Biff, even though he'd always taken advantage of me. I loved him, Willy, y'know? And he came back after that month and took his sneakers—remember those sneakers with "University of Virginia" printed on them? He was so proud of those, wore them every day. And he took them down in the cellar, and burned them up in the furnace. We had a fist fight. It lasted at least half an hour. Just the two of us, punching each other down the cellar, and crying right through it. I've often thought of how strange it was that I knew he'd given up his life. What happened in Boston, Willy?

(WILLY *looks at him as at an intruder.*)

BERNARD. I just bring it up because you asked me.

WILLY (*angrily*). Nothing. What do you mean, "What happened?" What's that go to do with anything?

BERNARD. Well, don't get sore.

WILLY. What are you trying to do, blame it on me? If a boy lays down is that my fault?

BERNARD. Now, Willy, don't get—

WILLY. Well, don't—don't talk to me that way! What does that mean, "What happened?"

(CHARLEY *enters. He is in his vest, and he carries a bottle of bourbon.*)

CHARLEY. Hey, you're going to miss that train. (*He waves the bottle.*)

BERNARD. Yeah, I'm going. (*He takes the bottle.*) Thanks, Pop. (*He picks up his rackets and bag.*) Good-by, Willy, and don't worry about it. You know, "If at first you don't succeed . . ."

WILLY. Yes, I believe in that.

BERNARD. But sometimes, Willy, it's better for a man just to walk away.

WILLY. Walk away?

BERNARD. That's right.

WILLY. But if you can't walk away?

BERNARD (*after a slight pause*). I guess that's when it's tough. (*Extending his hand*) Good-by, Willy.

WILLY (*shaking* BERNARD's *hand*). Good-by, boy.

CHARLEY (*an arm on* BERNARD'S *shoulder*). How do you like this kid? Gonna argue a case in front of the Supreme Court.

BERNARD (*protesting*). Pop!

WILLY (*genuinely shocked, pained, and happy*). No! The Supreme Court!

BERNARD. I gotta run. 'By, Dad!

CHARLEY. Knock 'em dead, Bernard!

(BERNARD *goes off*.)

WILLY (*as* CHARLEY *takes out his wallet*). The Supreme Court! And he didn't even mention it!

CHARLEY (*counting out money on the desk*). He don't have to—he's gonna do it.

WILLY. And you never told him what to do, did you? You never took any interest in him.

CHARLEY. My salvation is that I never took any interest in anything. There's some money—fifty dollars. I got an accountant inside.

WILLY. Charley, look . . . (*With difficulty*) I got my insurance to pay. If you can manage it—I need a hundred and ten dollars.

(CHARLEY *doesn't reply for a moment; merely stops moving*.)

WILLY. I'd draw it from my bank but Linda would know, and I . . .

CHARLEY. Sit down, Willy.

WILLY (*moving toward the chair*). I'm keeping an account of everything, remember. I'll pay every penny back. (*He sits*.)

CHARLEY. Now listen to me, Willy.

WILLY. I want you to know I appreciate . . .

CHARLEY (*sitting down on the table*). Willy, what're you doin'? What the hell is goin' on in your head?

WILLY. Why? I'm simply . . .

CHARLEY. I offered you a job. You can make fifty dollars a week. And I won't send you on the road.

WILLY. I've got a job.

CHARLEY. Without pay? What kind of a job is a job without pay? (*He rises*.) Now, look, kid, enough is enough. I'm no genius but I know when I'm being insulted.

WILLY. Insulted!

CHARLEY. Why don't you want to work for me?

WILLY. What's the matter with you? I've got a job.

CHARLEY. Then what're you walkin' in here every week for?

WILLY (*getting up*). Well, if you don't want me to walk in here—

CHARLEY. I am offering you a job.

WILLY. I don't want your goddam job!

CHARLEY. When the hell are you going to grow up?

WILLY (*furiously*). You big ignoramus, if you say that to me again I'll rap you one! I don't care how big you are! (*He's ready to fight.*)

(*Pause.*)

CHARLEY (*kindly, going to him*). How much do you need, Willy?

WILLY. Charley, I'm strapped. I'm strapped. I don't know what to do. I was just fired.

CHARLEY. Howard fired you?

WILLY. That snotnose. Imagine that? I named him. I named him Howard.

CHARLEY. Willy, when're you gonna realize that them things don't mean anything? You named him Howard, but you can't sell that. The only thing you got in this world is what you can sell. And the funny thing is that you're a salesman, and you don't know that.

WILLY. I've always tried to think otherwise, I guess. I always felt that if a man was impressive, and well liked, that nothing—

CHARLEY. Why must everybody like you? Who liked J. P. Morgan? Was he impressive? In a Turkish bath he'd look like a butcher. But with his pockets on he was very well liked. Now listen, Willy, I know you don't like me, and nobody can say I'm in love with you, but I'll give you a job because—just for the hell of it, put it that way. Now what do you say?

WILLY. I—I just can't work for you, Charley.

CHARLEY. What're you, jealous of me?

WILLY. I can't work for you, that's all, don't ask me why.

CHARLEY (*angered, takes out more bills*). You been jealous of me all your life, you damned fool! Here, pay your insurance. (*He puts the money in* WILLY'*s hand.*)

WILLY. I'm keeping strict accounts.

CHARLEY. I've got some work to do. Take care of yourself. And pay your insurance.

WILLY (*moving to the right*). Funny, y'know? After all the highways, and the trains, and the appointments, and the years, you end up worth more dead than alive.

CHARLEY. Willy, nobody's worth nothin' dead. (*After a slight pause*) Did you hear what I said? (WILLY *stands still, dreaming.*) Willy!

WILLY. Apologize to Bernard for me when you see him. I didn't mean to argue with him. He's a fine boy. They're all fine boys, and they'll end up big—all of them. Someday they'll all play tennis together. Wish me luck, Charley. He saw Bill Oliver today.

CHARLEY. Good luck.

WILLY (*on the verge of tears*). Charley, you're the only friend I got. Isn't that a remarkable thing? (*He goes out.*)

CHARLEY. Jesus!

(Charley *stares after him a moment and follows. All light blacks out. Suddenly raucous music is heard, and a red glow rises behind the screen at right.* Stanley, *a young waiter, appears, carrying a table, followed by* Happy, *who is carrying two chairs.*)

Stanley (*putting the table down*). That's all right, Mr. Loman, I can handle it myself. (*He turns and takes the chairs from* Happy *and places them at the table.*)

Happy (*glancing around*). Oh, this is better.

Stanley. Sure, in the front there you're in the middle of all kinds a noise. Whenever you got a party, Mr. Loman, you just tell me and I'll put you back here. Y'know, there's a lotta people they don't like it private, because when they go out they like to see a lotta action around them because they're sick and tired to stay in the house by theirself. But I know you, you ain't from Hackensack. You know what I mean?

Happy (*sitting down*). So how's it coming, Stanley?

Stanley. Ah, it's a dog's life. I only wish during the war they'd a took me in the Army. I coulda been dead by now.

Happy. My brother's back, Stanley.

Stanley. Oh, he come back, heh? From the Far West.

Happy. Yeah, big cattle man, my brother, so treat him right. And my father's coming too.

Stanley. Oh, your father too!

Happy. You got a couple of nice lobsters?

Stanley. Hundred per cent, big.

Happy. I want them with the claws.

Stanley. Don't worry, I don't give you no mice. (Happy *laughs.*) How about some wine? It'll put a head on the meal.

Happy. No. You remember, Stanley, that recipe I brought you from overseas? With the champagne in it?

Stanley. Oh, yeah, sure. I still got it tacked up yet in the kitchen. But that'll have to cost a buck apiece anyways.

Happy. That's all right.

Stanley. What'd you, hit a number or somethin'?

Happy. No, it's a little celebration. My brother is—I think he pulled off a big deal today. I think we're going into business together.

Stanley. Great! That's the best for you. Because a family business, you know what I mean?—that's the best.

Happy. That's what I think.

Stanley. 'Cause what's the difference? Somebody steals? It's in the family. Know what I mean? (*Sotto voce*) Like this bartender here. The boss is goin' crazy what kinda leak he's got in the cash register. You put it in but it don't come out.

Happy (*raising his head*). Sh!

STANLEY. What?

HAPPY. You notice I wasn't lookin' right or left, was I?

STANLEY. No.

HAPPY. And my eyes are closed.

STANLEY. So what's the—?

HAPPY. Strudel's comin'.

STANLEY (*catching on, looks around*). Ah, no, there's no—

(*He breaks off as a furred, lavishly dressed girl enters and sits at the next table. Both follow her with their eyes.*)

STANLEY. Geez, how'd ya know?

HAPPY. I got radar or something. (*Staring directly at her profile*) Oooooooo . . . Stanley.

STANLEY. I think that's for you, Mr. Loman.

HAPPY. Look at that mouth. Oh, God. And the binoculars.

STANLEY. Geez, you got a life, Mr. Loman.

HAPPY. Wait on her.

STANLEY (*going to the* GIRL'*s table*). Would you like a menu, ma'am?

GIRL. I'm expecting someone, but I'd like a—

HAPPY. Why don't you bring her—excuse me, miss, do you mind? I sell champagne, and I'd like you to try my brand. Bring her a champagne, Stanley.

GIRL. That's awfully nice of you.

HAPPY. Don't mention it. It's all company money. (*He laughs.*)

GIRL. That's a charming product to be selling, isn't it?

HAPPY. Oh, gets to be like everything else. Selling is selling, y'know.

GIRL. I suppose.

HAPPY. You don't happen to sell, do you?

GIRL. No, I don't sell.

HAPPY. Would you object to a compliment from a stranger? You ought to be on a magazine cover.

GIRL (*looking at him a little archly*). I have been.

(STANLEY *comes in with a glass of champagne.*)

HAPPY. What'd I say before, Stanley? You see? She's a cover girl.

STANLEY. Oh, I could see, I could see.

HAPPY (*to the* GIRL). What magazine?

GIRL. Oh, a lot of them. (*She takes the drink.*) Thank you.

HAPPY. You know what they say in France, don't you? "Champagne is the drink of the complexion"—Hya, Biff!

(BIFF *has entered and sits with* HAPPY.)

BIFF. Hello, kid. Sorry I'm late.

HAPPY. I just got here. Uh, Miss—?

GIRL. Forsythe.

HAPPY. Miss Forsythe, this is my brother.

BIFF. Is Dad here?

HAPPY. His name is Biff. You might've heard of him. Great football player.

GIRL. Really? What team?

HAPPY. Are you familiar with football?

GIRL. No, I'm afraid I'm not.

HAPPY. Biff is quarterback with the New York Giants.

GIRL. Well, that is nice, isn't it? (*She drinks.*)

HAPPY. Good health.

GIRL. I'm happy to meet you.

HAPPY. That's my name. Hap. It's really Harold, but at West Point they called me Happy.

GIRL (*now really impressed*). Oh, I see. How do you do? (*She turns her profile.*)

BIFF. Isn't Dad coming?

HAPPY. You want her?

BIFF. Oh, I could never make that.

HAPPY. I remember the time that idea would never come into your head. Where's the old confidence, Biff?

BIFF. I just saw Oliver—

HAPPY. Wait a minute. I've got to see that old confidence again. Do you want her? She's on call.

BIFF. Oh, no. (*He turns to look at the* GIRL.)

HAPPY. I'm telling you. Watch this. (*Turning to the* GIRL) Honey? (*She turns to him.*) Are you busy?

GIRL. Well, I am . . . but I could make a phone call.

HAPPY. Do that, will you, honey? And see if you can get a friend. We'll be here for a while. Biff is one of the greatest football players in the country.

GIRL (*standing up*). Well, I'm certainly happy to meet you.

HAPPY. Come back soon.

GIRL. I'll try.

HAPPY. Don't try, honey, try hard.

(*The* GIRL *exits.* STANLEY *follows, shaking his head in bewildered admiration.*)

HAPPY. Isn't that a shame now? A beautiful girl like that? That's why I can't get married. There's not a good woman in a thousand. New York is loaded with them, kid!

BIFF. Hap, look—

HAPPY. I told you she was on call!

BIFF (*strangely unnerved*). Cut it out, will ya? I want to say something to you.

HAPPY. Did you see Oliver?

BIFF. I saw him all right. Now look, I want to tell Dad a couple of things and I want you to help me.

HAPPY. What? Is he going to back you?

BIFF. Are you crazy? You're out of your goddam head, you know that?

HAPPY. Why? What happened?

BIFF (*breathlessly*). I did a terrible thing today, Hap. It's been the strangest day I ever went through. I'm all numb, I swear.

HAPPY. You mean he wouldn't see you?

BIFF. Well, I waited six hours for him, see? All day. Kept sending my name in. Even tried to date his secretary so she'd get me to him, but no soap.

HAPPY. Because you're not showin' the old confidence, Biff. He remembered you, didn't he?

BIFF (*stopping* HAPPY *with a gesture*). Finally, about five o'clock, he comes out. Didn't remember who I was or anything. I felt like such an idiot, Hap.

HAPPY. Did you tell him my Florida idea?

BIFF. He walked away. I saw him for one minute. I got so mad I could've torn the walls down! How the hell did I ever get the idea I was a salesman there? I even believed myself that I'd been a salesman for him! And then he gave me one look and—I realized what a ridiculous lie my whole life has been! We've been talking in a dream for fifteen years. I was a shipping clerk.

HAPPY. What'd you do?

BIFF (*with great tension and wonder*). Well, he left, see. And the secretary went out. I was all alone in the waiting-room. I don't know what came over me, Hap. The next thing I know I'm in his office—paneled walls, everything. I can't explain it. I—Hap, I took his fountain pen.

HAPPY. Geez, did he catch you?

BIFF. I ran out. I ran down all eleven flights. I ran and ran and ran.

HAPPY. That was an awful dumb—what'd you do that for?

BIFF (*agonized*). I don't know, I just—wanted to take something, I don't know. You gotta help me, Hap, I'm gonna tell Pop.

HAPPY. You crazy? What for?

BIFF. Hap, he's got to understand that I'm not the man somebody lends that kind of money to. He thinks I've been spiting him all these years and it's eating him up.

HAPPY. That's just it. You tell him something nice.

BIFF. I can't.

HAPPY. Say you got a lunch date with Oliver tomorrow.

BIFF. So what do I do tomorrow?

HAPPY. You leave the house tomorrow and come back at night and say Oliver is thinking it over. And he thinks it over for a couple of weeks, and gradually it fades away and nobody's the worse.

BIFF. But it'll go on forever!

HAPPY. Dad is never so happy as when he's looking forward to something!

(WILLY *enters.*)

HAPPY. Hello, scout!

WILLY. Gee, I haven't been here in years!

(STANLEY *has followed* WILLY *in and sets a chair for him.* STANLEY *starts off but* HAPPY *stops him.*)

HAPPY. Stanley!

(STANLEY *stands by, waiting for an order.*)

BIFF (*going to* WILLY *with guilt, as to an invalid*). Sit down, Pop. You want a drink?

WILLY. Sure, I don't mind.

BIFF. Let's get a load on.

WILLY. You look worried.

BIFF. N-no. (*To* STANLEY) Scotch all around. Make it doubles.

STANLEY. Doubles, right. (*He goes.*)

WILLY. You had a couple already, didn't you?

BIFF. Just a couple, yeah.

WILLY. Well, what happened, boy? (*Nodding affirmatively, with a smile*) Everything go all right?

BIFF (*takes a breath, then reaches out and grasps* WILLY's *hand*). Pal . . . (*He is smiling bravely, and* WILLY *is smiling too.*) I had an experience today.

HAPPY. Terrific, Pop.

WILLY. That so? What happened?

BIFF (*high, slightly alcoholic, above the earth*). I'm going to tell you everything from first to last. It's been a strange day. (*Silence. He looks around, composes himself as best he can, but his breath keeps breaking the rhythm of his voice.*) I had to wait quite a while for him, and—

WILLY. Oliver?

BIFF. Yeah, Oliver. All day, as a matter of cold fact. And a lot of—instances—facts, Pop, facts about my life came back to me. Who was it, Pop? Who ever said I was a salesman with Oliver?

WILLY. Well, you were.

BIFF. No, Dad, I was a shipping clerk.

WILLY. But you were practically—

BIFF (*with determination*). Dad, I don't know who said it first, but I was never a salesman for Bill Oliver.

WILLY. What're you talking about?

BIFF. Let's hold on to the facts tonight, Pop. We're not going to get anywhere bullin' around. I was a shipping clerk.

WILLY (*angrily*). All right, now listen to me—

BIFF. Why don't you let me finish?

WILLY. I'm not interested in stories about the past or any crap of that kind because the woods are burning, boys, you understand? There's a big blaze going on all around. I was fired today.

BIFF (*shocked*). How could you be?

WILLY. I was fired, and I'm looking for a little good news to tell your mother, because the woman has waited and the woman has suffered. The gist of it is that I haven't got a story left in my head, Biff. So don't give me a lecture about facts and aspects. I am not interested. Now what've you got to say to me?

(STANLEY *enters with three drinks. They wait until he leaves.*)

WILLY. Did you see Oliver?

BIFF. Jesus, Dad!

WILLY. You mean you didn't go up there?

HAPPY. Sure he went up there.

BIFF. I did. I—saw him. How could they fire you?

WILLY (*on the edge of his chair*). What kind of a welcome did he give you?

BIFF. He won't even let you work on commission?

WILLY. I'm out! (*Driving*) So tell me, he gave you a warm welcome?

HAPPY. Sure, Pop, sure!

BIFF (*driven*). Well, it was kind of—

WILLY. I was wondering if he'd remember you. (*To* HAPPY) Imagine, man doesn't see him for ten, twelve years and gives him that kind of a welcome!

HAPPY. Damn right!

BIFF (*trying to return to the offensive*). Pop look—

WILLY. You know why he remembered you, don't you? Because you impressed him in those days.

BIFF. Let's talk quietly and get this down to the facts, huh?

WILLY (*as though* BIFF *had been interrupting*). Well, what happened? It's great news, Biff. Did he take you into his office or'd you talk in the waiting-room?

BIFF. Well, he came in, see, and—

WILLY (*with a big smile*). What'd he say? Betcha he threw his arm around you.

BIFF. Well, he kinda—

WILLY. He's a fine man. (*To* HAPPY) Very hard man to see, y'know.

HAPPY (*agreeing*). Oh, I know.

WILLY (*to* BIFF). Is that where you had the drinks?

BIFF. Yeah, he gave me a couple of—no, no!

HAPPY (*cutting in*). He told him my Florida idea.

WILLY. Don't interrupt. (*To* BIFF) How'd he react to the Florida idea?

BIFF. Dad, will you give me a minute to explain?

WILLY. I've been waiting for you to explain since I sat down here! What happened? He took you into his office and what?

BIFF. Well—I talked. And—and he listened, see.

WILLY. Famous for the way he listens, y'know. What was his answer?

BIFF. His answer was—(*He breaks off, suddenly angry.*)Dad, you're not letting me tell you what I want to tell you!

WILLY (*accusing, angered*). You didn't see him, did you?

BIFF. I did see him!

WILLY. What'd you insult him or something? You insulted him, didn't you?

BIFF. Listen, will you let me out of it, will you just let me out of it!

HAPPY. What the hell!

WILLY. Tell me what happened!

BIFF (*to* HAPPY). I can't talk to him!

(*A single trumpet note jars the ear. The light of green leaves stains the house, which holds the air of night and a dream.* YOUNG BERNARD *enters and knocks on the door of the house.*)

YOUNG BERNARD (*frantically*). Mrs. Loman, Mrs. Loman!

HAPPY. Tell him what happened!

BIFF (*to* HAPPY). Shut up and leave me alone!

WILLY. No, no! You had to go and flunk math!

BIFF. What math? What're you talking about?

YOUNG BERNARD. Mrs. Loman, Mrs. Loman!

(LINDA *appears in the house, as of old.*)

WILLY (*wildly*). Math, math, math!

BIFF. Take it easy, Pop!

YOUNG BERNARD. Mrs. Loman!

WILLY (*furiously*). If you hadn't flunked you'd've been set by now!

BIFF. Now, look, I'm gonna tell you what happened, and you're going to listen to me.

YOUNG BERNARD. Mrs. Loman!

BIFF. I waited six hours—

HAPPY. What the hell are you saying?

BIFF. I kept sending in my name but he wouldn't see me. So finally he . . . (*He continues unheard as light fades low on the restaurant.*)

YOUNG BERNARD. Biff flunked math!

LINDA. No!

YOUNG BERNARD. Birnbaum flunked him! They won't graduate him!

LINDA. But they have to. He's gotta go to the university. Where is he? Biff! Biff!

YOUNG BERNARD. No, he left. He went to Grand Central.

LINDA. Grand—You mean he went to Boston!

YOUNG BERNARD. Is Uncle Willy in Boston?

LINDA. Oh, maybe Willy can talk to the teacher. Oh, the poor, poor boy!

(*Light on house area snaps out.*)

BIFF (*at the table, now audible, holding up a gold fountain pen*). . . . so I'm washed up with Oliver, you understand? Are you listening to me?

WILLY (*at a loss*). Yeah, sure. If you hadn't flunked—

BIFF. Flunked what? What're you talking about?

WILLY. Don't blame everything on me! I didn't flunk math—you did! What pen?

HAPPY. That was awful dumb, Biff, a pen like that is worth—

WILLY (*seeing the pen for the first time*). You took Oliver's pen?

BIFF (*weakening*). Dad, I just explained it to you.

WILLY. You stole Bill Oliver's fountain pen!

BIFF. I didn't exactly steal it! That's just what I've been explaining to you!

HAPPY. He had it in his hand and just then Oliver walked in, so he got nervous and stuck it in his pocket!

WILLY. My God, Biff!

BIFF. I never intended to do it, Dad!

OPERATOR'S VOICE. Standish Arms, good evening!

WILLY (*shouting*). I'm not in my room!

BIFF (*frightened*). Dad, what's the matter? (*He and* HAPPY *stand up.*)

OPERATOR. Ringing Mr. Loman for you!

WILLY. I'm not there, stop it!

BIFF (*horrified, gets down on one knee before* WILLY). Dad, I'll make good, I'll make good. (WILLY *tries to get to his feet.* BIFF *holds him down.*) Sit down now.

WILLY. No, you're no good, you're no good for anything.

BIFF. I am, Dad, I'll find something else, you understand? Now don't worry about anything. (*He holds up* WILLY'S *face.*) Talk to me, Dad.

OPERATOR. Mr. Loman does not answer. Shall I page him?

WILLY (*attempting to stand, as though to rush and silence the* OPERATOR). No, no, no!

HAPPY. He'll strike something, Pop.

WILLY. No, no . . .

BIFF (*desperately, standing over* WILLY). Pop, listen! Listen to me! I'm telling you something good. Oliver talked to his partner about the

Florida idea. You listening? He—he talked to his partner, and he came to me . . . I'm going to be all right, you hear? Dad, listen to me, he said it was just a question of the amount!

WILLY. Then you . . . got it?

HAPPY. He's gonna be terrific, Pop!

WILLY (*trying to stand*). Then you got it, haven't you? You got it! You got it!

BIFF (*agonized, holds* WILLY *down*). No, no. Look, Pop. I'm supposed to have lunch with them tomorrow. I'm just telling you this so you'll know that I can still make an impression, Pop. And I'll make good somewhere, but I can't go tomorrow, see?

WILLY. Why not? You simply—

BIFF. But the pen, Pop!

WILLY. You give it to him and tell him it was an oversight!

HAPPY. Sure, have lunch tomorrow!

BIFF. I can't say that—

WILLY. You were doing a crossword puzzle and accidentally used his pen!

BIFF. Listen, kid, I took those balls years ago, now I walk in with his fountain pen? That clinches it, don't you see? I can't face him like that! I'll try elsewhere.

PAGE'S VOICE. Paging Mr. Loman!

WILLY. Don't you want to be anything?

BIFF. Pop, how can I go back?

WILLY. You don't want to be anything, is that what's behind it?

BIFF (*now angry at* WILLY *for not crediting his sympathy*). Don't take it that way! You think it was easy walking into that office after what I'd done to him? A team of horses couldn't have dragged me back to Bill Oliver!

WILLY. Then why'd you go?

BIFF. Why did I go? Why did I go! Look at you! Look at what's become of you!

(*Off left,* THE WOMAN *laughs.*)

WILLY. Biff, you're going to go to that lunch tomorrow, or—

BIFF. I can't go. I've got no appointment!

HAPPY. Biff, for . . . !

WILLY. Are you spiting me?

BIFF. Don't take it that way! Goddammit!

WILLY (*strikes* BIFF *and falters away from the table*). You rotten little louse! Are you spiting me?

THE WOMAN. Someone's at the door, Willy!

BIFF. I'm no good, can't you see what I am?

HAPPY (*separating them*). Hey, you're in a restaurant! Now cut it out, both of you! (*The* GIRLS *enter.*) Hello, girls, sit down.

(THE WOMAN *laughs, off left.*)

MISS FORSYTHE. I guess we might as well. This is Letta.

THE WOMAN. Willy, are you going to wake up?

BIFF (*ignoring* WILLY). How're ya, miss, sit down. What do you drink?

MISS FORSYTHE. Letta might not be able to stay long.

LETTA. I gotta get up very early tomorrow. I got jury duty. I'm so excited! Were you fellows ever on a jury?

BIFF. No, but I been in front of them! (*The* GIRLS *laugh.*) This is my father.

LETTA. Isn't he cute? Sit down with us, Pop.

HAPPY. Sit him down, Biff!

BIFF (*going to him*). Come on, slugger, drink us under the table. To hell with it! Come on, sit down, pal.

(*On* BIFF's *last insistence,* WILLY *is about to sit.*)

THE WOMAN (*now urgently*). Willy, are you going to answer the door!

(THE WOMAN's *call pulls* WILLY *back. He starts right, befuddled.*)

BIFF. Hey, where are you going?

WILLY. Open the door.

BIFF. The door?

WILLY. The washroom . . . the door . . . where's the door?

BIFF (*leading* WILLY *to the left*). Just go straight down.

(WILLY *moves left.*)

THE WOMAN. Willy, Willy, are you going to get up, get up, get up, get up?

(WILLY *exits left.*)

LETTA. I think it's sweet you bring your daddy along.

MISS FORSYTHE. Oh, he isn't really your father!

BIFF (*at left, turning to her resentfully*). Miss Forsythe, you've just seen a prince walk by. A fine, troubled prince. A hard-working, unappreciated prince. A pal, you understand? A good companion. Always for his boys.

LETTA. That's so sweet.

HAPPY. Well, girls, what's the program? We're wasting time. Come on, Biff. Gather round. Where would you like to go?

BIFF. Why don't you do something for him?

HAPPY. Me!

BIFF. Don't you give a damn for him, Hap?

HAPPY. What're you talking about? I'm the one who—

BIFF. I sense it, you don't give a good goddam about him. (*He takes the rolled-up hose from his pocket and puts it on the table in front of* HAPPY.) Look what I found in the cellar, for Christ's sake. How can you bear to let it go on?

HAPPY. Me? Who goes away? Who runs off and—

BIFF. Yeah, but he doesn't mean anything to you. You could help him—I can't! Don't you understand what I'm talking about? He's going to kill himself, don't you know that?

HAPPY. Don't I know it! Me!

BIFF. Hap, help him! Jesus . . . help him . . . Help me, help me, I can't bear to look at his face! (*Ready to weep, he hurries out, up right.*)

HAPPY (*starting after him*). Where are you going?

MISS FORSYTHE. What's he so mad about?

HAPPY. Come on, girls, we'll catch up with him.

MISS FORSYTHE (*as* HAPPY *pushes her out*). Say, I don't like that temper of his!

HAPPY. He's just a little overstrung, he'll be all right!

WILLY (*off left, as* THE WOMAN *laughs*). Don't answer! Don't answer!

LETTA. Don't you want to tell your father—

HAPPY. No, that's not my father. He's just a guy. Come on, we'll catch Biff, and, honey, we're going to paint this town! Stanley, where's the check! Hey, Stanley!

(*They exit.* STANLEY *looks toward left.*)

STANLEY (*calling to* HAPPY *indignantly*). Mr. Loman! Mr. Loman!

(STANLEY *picks up a chair and follows them off. Knocking is heard off left.* THE WOMAN *enters, laughing.* WILLY *follows her. She is in a black slip; he is buttoning his shirt. Raw, sensuous music accompanies their speech.*)

WILLY. Will you stop laughing? Will you stop?

THE WOMAN. Aren't you going to answer the door? He'll wake the whole hotel.

WILLY. I'm not expecting anybody.

THE WOMAN. Whyn't you have another drink, honey, and stop being so damn self-centered?

WILLY. I'm so lonely.

THE WOMAN. You know you ruined me, Willy? From now on, whenever you come to the office, I'll see that you go right through to the buyers. No waiting at my desk any more, Willy. You ruined me.

WILLY. That's nice of you to say that.

THE WOMAN. Gee, you are self-centered! Why so sad? You are the saddest, self-centeredest soul I ever did see-saw. (*She laughs. He kisses her.*) Come on inside, drummer boy. It's silly to be dressing in the middle of the night. (*As knocking is heard*) Aren't you going to answer the door?

WILLY. They're knocking on the wrong door.

THE WOMAN. But I felt the knocking. And he heard us talking in here. Maybe the hotel's on fire!

WILLY (*his terror rising*). It's a mistake.

THE WOMAN. Then tell him to go away!

WILLY. There's nobody there.

THE WOMAN. It's getting on my nerves, Willy. There's somebody standing out there and it's getting on my nerves!

WILLY (*pushing her away from him*). All right, stay in the bathroom here, and don't come out. I think there's a law in Massachusetts about it, so don't come out. It may be that new room clerk. He looked very mean. So don't come out. It's a mistake, there's no fire.

(*The knocking is heard again. He takes a few steps away from her, and she vanishes into the wing. The light follows him, and now he is facing* YOUNG BIFF, *who carries a suitcase.* BIFF *steps toward him. The music is gone.*)

BIFF. Why didn't you answer?

WILLY. Biff! What are you doing in Boston?

BIFF. Why didn't you answer? I've been knocking for five minutes, I called you on the phone—

WILLY. I just heard you. I was in the bathroom and had the door shut. Did anything happen home?

BIFF. Dad—I let you down.

WILLY. What do you mean?

BIFF. Dad . . .

WILLY. Biffo, what's this about? (*Putting his arm around* BIFF) Come on, let's go downstairs and get you a malted.

BIFF. Dad, I flunked math.

WILLY. Not for the term?

BIFF. The term. I haven't got enough credits to graduate.

WILLY. You mean to say Bernard wouldn't give you the answers?

BIFF. He did, he tried, but I only got a sixty-one.

WILLY. And they wouldn't give you four points.

BIFF. Birnbaum refused absolutely. I begged him, Pop, but he won't give me those points. You gotta talk to him before they close the school. Because if he saw the kind of man you are, and you just talked to him in your way, I'm sure he'd come through for me. The class came right before practice, see, and I didn't go enough. Would you talk to him? He'd like you, Pop. You know the way you could talk.

WILLY. You're on. We'll drive right back.

BIFF. Oh, Dad, good work! I'm sure he'll change it for you!

WILLY. Go downstairs and tell the clerk I'm checkin' out. Go right down.

BIFF. Yes, sir! See, the reason he hates me, Pop—one day he was late for class so I got up at the blackboard and imitated him. I crossed my eyes and talked with a lithp.

WILLY (*laughing*). You did? The kids like it?

BIFF. They nearly died laughing!

WILLY. Yeah? What'd you do?

BIFF. The thquare root of thixthy twee is . . . (WILLY *bursts out laughing;* BIFF *joins him.*) And in the middle of it he walked in!

(WILLY *laughs and* THE WOMAN *joins in offstage.*)

WILLY (*without hesitation*). Hurry downstairs and—

BIFF. Somebody in there?

WILLY. No, that was next door.

(THE WOMAN *laughs offstage.*)

BIFF. Somebody got in your bathroom!

WILLY. No, it's the next room, there's a party—

THE WOMAN (*enters, laughing. She lisps this*). Can I come in? There's something in the bathtub, Willy, and it's moving!

(WILLY *looks at* BIFF, *who is staring open-mouthed and horrified at* THE WOMAN.)

WILLY. Ah—you better go back to your room. They must be finished painting by now. They're painting her room so I let her take a shower here. Go back, go back . . . (*He pushes her.*)

THE WOMAN (*resisting*). But I've got to get dressed, Willy, I can't—

WILLY. Get out of here! Go back, go back . . . (*Suddenly striving for the ordinary*) This is Miss Francis, Biff, she's a buyer. They're painting her room. Go back, Miss Francis, go back . . .

THE WOMAN. But my clothes, I can't go out naked in the hall!

WILLY (*pushing her offstage*). Get outa here! Go back, go back!

(BIFF *slowly sits down on his suitcase as the argument continues offstage.*)

THE WOMAN. Where's my stockings? You promised me stockings, Willy!

WILLY. I have no stockings here!

THE WOMAN. You had two boxes of size nine sheers for me, and I want them!

WILLY. Here, for God's sake, will you get outa here!

THE WOMAN (*enters holding a box of stockings*). I just hope there's nobody in the hall. That's all I hope. (*To* BIFF) Are you football or baseball?

BIFF. Football.

THE WOMAN (*angry, humiliated*). That's me too. G'night. (*She snatches her clothes from* WILLY *and walks out.*)

WILLY (*after a pause*). Well, better get going. I want to get to the school first thing in the morning. Get my suits out of the closet. I'll get my valise. (BIFF *doesn't move.*) What's the matter? (BIFF *remains motionless, tears falling.*) She's a buyer. Buys for J. H. Simmons. She lives down the hall—they're painting. You don't imagine—(*He breaks off. After a pause*) Now listen, pal, she's just a buyer. She sees merchandise in her room and they have to keep it looking just so . . . (*Pause. Assuming command*) All right, get my suits. (BIFF *doesn't move.*) Now stop crying and do as I say. I gave you an order. Biff, I gave you an order! Is that what you do when I give you an order? How dare you cry! (*Putting his arm around* BIFF) Now look, Biff, when you grow up you'll understand about these things. You mustn't—you mustn't overemphasize a thing like this. I'll see Birnbaum first thing in the morning.

BIFF. Never mind.

WILLY (*getting down beside* BIFF). Never mind! He's going to give you those points. I'll see to it.

BIFF. He wouldn't listen to you.

WILLY. He certainly will listen to me. You need those points for the U. of Virginia.

BIFF. I'm not going there.

WILLY. Heh? If I can't get him to change that mark you'll make it up in summer school. You've got all summer to—

BIFF (*his weeping breaking from him*). Dad . . .

WILLY (*infected by it*). Oh, my boy . . .

BIFF. Dad . . .

WILLY. She's nothing to me, Biff. I was lonely, I was terribly lonely.

BIFF. You—you gave her Mama's stockings! (*His tears break through and he rises to go.*)

WILLY (*grabbing for* BIFF). I gave you an order!

BIFF. Don't touch me, you—liar!

WILLY. Apologize for that!

BIFF. You fake! You phony little fake! You fake! (*Overcome, he turns quickly and weeping fully goes out with his suitcase.* WILLY *is left on the floor on his knees.*)

WILLY. I gave you an order! Biff, come back here or I'll beat you! Come back here! I'll whip you!

(STANLEY *comes quickly in from the right and stands in front of* WILLY.)

WILLY (*shouts at* STANLEY). I gave you an order . . .

STANLEY. Hey, let's pick it up, pick it up, Mr. Loman. (*He helps* WILLY *to his feet.*) Your boys left with the chippies. They said they'll see you home.

(*A second waiter watches some distance away.*)

WILLY. But we were supposed to have dinner together.

(*Music is heard,* WILLY'S *theme.*)

STANLEY. Can you make it?

WILLY. I'll—sure, I can make it. (*Suddenly concerned about his clothes*) Do I—I look all right?

STANLEY. Sure, you look all right. (*He flicks a speck off* WILLY'S *lapel.*)

WILLY. Here—here's a dollar.

STANLEY. Oh, your son paid me. It's all right.

WILLY (*putting it in* STANLEY'S *hand*). No, take it. You're a good boy.

STANLEY. Oh, no, you don't have to . . .

WILLY. Here's some more, I don't need it any more. (*After a slight pause*) Tell me—is there a seed store in the neighborhood?

STANLEY. Seeds? You mean like to plant?

(*As* WILLY *turns,* STANLEY *slips the money back into his jacket pocket.*)

WILLY. Yes. Carrots, peas . . .

STANLEY. Well, there's hardware stores on Sixth Avenue, but it may be too late now.

WILLY (*anxiously*). Oh, I'd better hurry. I've got to get some seeds. (*He starts off to the right.*) I've got to get some seeds, right away. Nothing's planted. I don't have a thing in the ground.

(WILLY *hurries out as the light goes down.* STANLEY *moves over to the right after him, watches him off. The other waiter has been staring at* WILLY.)

STANLEY (*to the waiter*). Well, whatta you looking at?

(*The waiter picks up the chairs and moves off right.* STANLEY *takes the table and follows him. The light fades on this area. There is a long pause, the sound of the flute coming over. The light gradually rises on the kitchen, which is empty.* HAPPY *appears at the door of the house, followed by* BIFF. HAPPY *is carrying a large bunch of long-stemmed roses. He enters the kitchen, looks around for* LINDA. *Not seeing her, he turns to* BIFF, *who is just outside the house door, and makes a gesture with his hands, indicating "Not here, I guess." He looks into the living-room and freezes. Inside,* LINDA, *unseen, is seated,* WILLY'S *coat on her lap. She rises ominously and quietly and moves toward* HAPPY, *who backs up into the kitchen, afraid.*)

HAPPY. Hey, what're you doing up? (LINDA *says nothing but moves toward him implacably.*) Where's Pop? (*He keeps backing to the right, and now* LINDA *is in full view in the doorway to the living-room.*) Is he sleeping?

LINDA. Where were you?

HAPPY (*trying to laugh it off*). We met two girls, Mom, very fine types. Here, we brought you some flowers. (*Offering them to her*) Put them in your room, Ma.

(*She knocks them to the floor at* BIFF'*s feet. He has now come inside and closed the door behind him. She stares at* BIFF, *silent.*)

HAPPY. Now what'd you do that for? Mom, I want you to have some flowers—

LINDA (*cutting* HAPPY *off, violently to* BIFF). Don't you care whether he lives or dies?

HAPPY (*going to the stairs*). Come upstairs, Biff.

BIFF (*with a flare of disgust, to* HAPPY). Go away from me! (*To* LINDA) What do you mean, lives or dies? Nobody's dying around here, pal.

LINDA. Get out of my sight! Get out of here!

BIFF. I wanna see the boss.

LINDA. You're not going near him!

BIFF. Where is he? (*He moves into the living-room and* LINDA *follows.*)

LINDA (*shouting after* BIFF). You invite him for dinner. He looks forward to it all day—(BIFF *appears in his parents' bedroom, looks around, and exits*)—and then you desert him there. There's no stranger you'd do that to!

HAPPY. Why? He had a swell time with us. Listen, when I—(LINDA *comes back into the kitchen*)—desert him I hope I don't outlive the day!

LINDA. Get out of here!

HAPPY. Now look, Mom . . .

LINDA. Did you have to go to women tonight? You and your lousy rotten whores!

(BIFF *re-enters the kitchen.*)

HAPPY. Mom, all we did was follow Biff around trying to cheer him up! (*To* BIFF) Boy, what a night you gave me!

LINDA. Get out of here, both of you, and don't come back! I don't want you tormenting him any more. Go on now, get your things together! (*To* BIFF) You can sleep in his apartment. (*She starts to pick up the flowers and stops herself.*) Pick up this stuff, I'm not your maid any more. Pick it up, you bum, you!

(HAPPY *turns his back to her in refusal.* BIFF *slowly moves over and gets down on his knees, picking up the flowers.*)

LINDA. You're a pair of animals! Not one, not another living soul would have had the cruelty to walk out on that man in a restaurant!

BIFF (*not looking at her*). Is that what he said?

LINDA. He didn't have to say anything. He was so humiliated he nearly limped when he came in.

HAPPY. But, Mom, he had a great time with us—

BIFF (*cutting him off violently*). Shut up!

(*Without another word,* HAPPY *goes upstairs.*)

LINDA. You! You didn't even go in to see if he was all right!

BIFF (*still on the floor in front of* LINDA, *the flowers in his hand; with self-loathing*). No. Didn't. Didn't do a damned thing. How do you like that, heh? Left him babbling in a toilet.

LINDA. You louse. You . . .

BIFF. Now you hit it on the nose! (*He gets up, throws the flowers in the wastebasket.*) The scum of the earth, and you're looking at him!

LINDA. Get out of here!

BIFF. I gotta talk to the boss, Mom. Where is he?

LINDA. You're not going near him. Get out of this house!

BIFF (*with absolute assurance, determination*). No. We're gonna have an abrupt conversation, him and me.

LINDA. You're not talking to him!

(*Hammering is heard from outside the house, off right.* BIFF *turns toward the noise.*)

LINDA (*suddenly pleading*). Will you please leave him alone?

BIFF. What's he doing out there?

LINDA. He's planting the garden!

BIFF (*quietly*). Now? Oh, my God!

(BIFF *moves outside,* LINDA *following. The light dies down on them and comes up on the center of the apron as* WILLY *walks into it. He is carrying a flashlight, a hoe, and a handful of seed packets. He raps the top of the hoe sharply to fix it firmly, and then moves to the left, measuring off the distance with his foot. He holds the flashlight to look at the seed packets, reading off the instructions. He is in the blue of night.*)

WILLY. Carrots . . . quarter-inch apart. Rows . . . one-foot rows. (*He measures it off.*) One foot. (*He puts down a package and measures off.*) Beets. (*He puts down another package and measures again.*) Lettuce. (*He reads the package, puts it down.*) One foot—(*He breaks off as* BEN *appears at the right and moves slowly down to him.*) What a proposition, ts, ts. Terrific, terrific. 'Cause she's suffered, Ben, the woman has suffered. You understand me? A man can't go out the way he came in. Ben, a man has got to add up to something. You can't, you can't—(BEN *moves toward him as though to interrupt.*) You gotta consider, now. Don't answer so quick. Remember, it's a guaranteed twenty-thousand-dollar proposition. Now look,

Ben, I want you to go through the ins and outs of this thing with me. I've got nobody to talk to, Ben, and the woman has suffered, you hear me?

BEN (*standing still, considering*). What's the proposition?

WILLY. It's twenty thousand dollars on the barrelhead. Guaranteed, gilt-edged, you understand?

BEN. You don't want to make a fool of yourself. They might not honor the policy.

WILLY. How can they dare refuse? Didn't I work like a coolie to meet every premium on the nose? And now they don't pay off? Impossible!

BEN. It's called a cowardly thing, William.

WILLY. Why? Does it take more guts to stand here the rest of my life ringing up a zero?

BEN (*yielding*). That's a point, William. (*He moves, thinking, turns.*) And twenty thousand—that *is* something one can feel with the hand, it is there.

WILLY (*now assured, with rising power*). Oh, Ben, that's the whole beauty of it! I see it like a diamond, shining in the dark, hard and rough, that I can pick up and touch in my hand. Not like—like an appointment! This would not be another damned-fool appointment, Ben, and it changes all the aspects. Because he thinks I'm nothing, see, and so he spites me. But the funeral—(*Straightening up*) Ben, that funeral will be massive! They'll come from Maine, Massachusetts, Vermont, New Hampshire! All the old-timers with the strange license plates—that boy will be thunder-struck, Ben, because he never realized—I am known! Rhode Island, New York, New Jersey—I am known, Ben, and he'll see it with his eyes once and for all. He'll see what I am, Ben! He's in for a shock, that boy!

BEN (*coming down to the edge of the garden*). He'll call you a coward.

WILLY (*suddenly fearful*). No, that would be terrible.

BEN. Yes. And a damned fool.

WILLY. No, no, he mustn't, I won't have that! (*He is broken and desperate.*)

BEN. He'll hate you, William.

(*The gay music of the boys is heard.*)

WILLY. Oh, Ben, how do we get back to all the great times? Used to be so full of light, and comradeship, the sleigh-riding in winter and the ruddiness on his cheeks. And always some kind of good news coming up, always something nice coming up ahead. And never even let me carry the valises in the house, and simonizing, simonizing that little red car! Why, why can't I give him something and not have him hate me?

BEN. Let me think about it. (*He glances at his watch.*) I still have a little time. Remarkable proposition, but you've got to be sure you're not making a fool of yourself.

(BEN *drifts off upstage and goes out of sight.* BIFF *comes down from the left.*)

WILLY (*suddenly conscious of* BIFF, *turns and looks up at him, then begins picking up the packages of seeds in confusion*). Where the hell is that seed? (*Indignantly*) You can't see nothing out here! They boxed in the whole goddam neighborhood!

BIFF. There are people all around here. Don't you realize that?

WILLY. I'm busy. Don't bother me.

BIFF (*taking the hoe from* WILLY). I'm saying good-by to you, Pop. (WILLY *looks at him, silent, unable to move.*) I'm not coming back any more.

WILLY. You're not going to see Oliver tomorrow?

BIFF. I've got no appointment, Dad.

WILLY. He put his arms around you, and you've got no appointment?

BIFF. Pop, get this now, will you? Every time I've left it's been a fight that sent me out of here. Today I realized something about myself and I tried to explain it to you and I—I think I'm just not smart enough to make any sense out of it for you. To hell with whose fault it is or anything like that. (*He takes* WILLY's *arm.*) Let's just wrap it up, heh? Come on in, we'll tell Mom. (*He gently tries to pull* WILLY *to left.*)

WILLY (*frozen, immobile, with guilt in his voice*). No, I don't want to see her.

BIFF. Come on!

(*He pulls again, and* WILLY *tries to pull away.*)

WILLY (*highly nervous*). No, no, I don't want to see her.

BIFF (*tries to look into* WILLY's *face, as if to find the answer there.*) Why don't you want to see her?

WILLY (*more harshly now*). Don't bother me, will you?

BIFF. What do you mean, you don't want to see her? You don't want them calling you yellow do you? This isn't your fault; it's me, I'm a bum. Now come inside! (WILLY *strains to get away.*) Did you hear what I said to you?

(WILLY *pulls away and quickly goes by himself into the house.* BIFF *follows.*)

LINDA (*to* WILLY). Did you plant, dear?

BIFF (*at the door, to* LINDA). All right, we had it out. I'm going and I'm not writing any more.

LINDA (*going to* WILLY *in the kitchen*). I think that's the best way, dear. 'Cause there's no use drawing it out, you'll just never get along.

(WILLY *doesn't respond.*)

BIFF. People ask where I am and what I'm doing, you don't know, and you don't care. That way it'll be off your mind and you can start brightening up again. All right? That clears it, doesn't it? (WILLY *is silent, and* BIFF *goes to him.*) You gonna wish me luck, scout? (*He extends his hand.*) What do you say?

LINDA. Shake his hand, Willy.

WILLY (*turning to her, seething with hurt*). There's no necessity to mention the pen at all, y'know.

BIFF (*gently*). I've got no appointment, Dad.

WILLY (*erupting fiercely*). He put his arm around . . . ?

BIFF. Dad, you're never going to see what I am, so what's the use of arguing? If I strike oil I'll send you a check. Meantime forget I'm alive.

WILLY (*to* LINDA). Spite, see?

BIFF. Shake hands, Dad.

WILLY. Not my hand.

BIFF. I was hoping not to go this way.

WILLY. Well, this is the way you're going. Good-by.

(BIFF *looks at him a moment, then turns sharply and goes to the stairs.*)

WILLY (*stops him with:*) May you rot in hell if you leave this house!

BIFF (*turning*). Exactly what is it that you want from me?

WILLY. I want you to know, on the train, in the mountains, in the valleys, wherever you go, that you cut down your life for spite!

BIFF. No, no.

WILLY. Spite, spite, is the word of your undoing! And when you're down and out, remember what did it. When you're rotting somewhere beside the railroad tracks, remember, and don't you dare blame it on me!

BIFF. I'm not blaming it on you!

WILLY. I won't take the rap for this, you hear?

(HAPPY *comes down the stairs and stands on the bottom step, watching.*)

BIFF. That's just what I'm telling you!

WILLY (*sinking into a chair at the table, with full accusation*). You're trying to put a knife in me—don't think I don't know what you're doing!

BIFF. All right, phony! Then let's lay it on the line. (*He whips the rubber tube out of his pocket and puts it on the table.*)

HAPPY. You crazy—

LINDA. Biff! (*She moves to grab the hose, but* BIFF *holds it down with his hand.*)

BIFF. Leave it there! Don't move it!

WILLY (*not looking at it*). What is that?

BIFF. You know goddam well what that is.

WILLY (*caged, wanting to escape*). I never saw that.

BIFF. You saw it. The mice didn't bring it into the cellar! What is this supposed to do, make a hero out of you? This supposed to make me sorry for you?

WILLY. Never heard of it.

BIFF. There'll be no pity for you, you hear it? No pity!

WILLY (*to* LINDA). You hear the spite!

BIFF. No, you're going to hear the truth—what you are and what I am!

LINDA. Stop it!

WILLY. Spite!

HAPPY (*coming down toward* BIFF). You cut it now!

BIFF (*to* HAPPY). The man don't know who we are! The man is gonna know! (*To* WILLY) We never told the truth for ten minutes in this house!

HAPPY. We always told the truth!

BIFF (*turning on him*). You big blow, are you the assistant buyer? You're one of the two assistants to the assistant, aren't you?

HAPPY. Well, I'm practically—

BIFF. You're practically full of it! We all are! And I'm through with it. (*To* WILLY) Now hear this, Willy, this is me.

WILLY. I know you!

BIFF. You know why I had no address for three months? I stole a suit in Kansas City and I was in jail. (*To* LINDA, *who is sobbing*) Stop crying. I'm through with it.

(LINDA *turns away from them, her hands covering her face.*)

WILLY. I suppose that's my fault!

BIFF. I stole myself out of every good job since high school!

WILLY. And whose fault is that?

BIFF. And I never got anywhere because you blew me so full of hot air I could never stand taking orders from anybody! That's whose fault it is!

WILLY. I hear that!

LINDA. Don't, Biff!

BIFF. It's goddam time you heard that! I had to be boss big shot in two weeks, and I'm through with it!

WILLY. Then hang yourself! For spite, hang yourself!

BIFF. No! Nobody's hanging himself, Willy! I ran down eleven flights with a pen in my hand today. And suddenly I stopped, you hear me? And in the middle of that office building, do you hear this? I stopped in the middle of that building and I saw—the sky. I saw the things that I love in this world. The work and the food and time to sit and smoke. And I looked at the pen and said to myself, what the hell am I grabbing this for? Why am I trying to become what I don't want to be? What am I doing in an office, making a contemptuous, begging fool of myself, when all I want is out there, waiting for me the minute I say I know who I am! Why can't I say that, Willy?

(*He tries to make* WILLY *face him, but* WILLY *pulls away and moves to the left.*)

WILLY (*with hatred, threateningly*). The door of your life is wide open!

BIFF. Pop! I'm a dime a dozen, and so are you!

WILLY (*turning on him now in an uncontrolled outburst*). I am not a dime a dozen! I am Willy Loman, and you are Biff Loman!

(BIFF *starts for* WILLY, *but is blocked by* HAPPY. *In his fury,* BIFF *seems on the verge of attacking his father.*)

BIFF. I am not a leader of men, Willy, and neither are you. You were never anything but a hard-working drummer who landed in the ash can like all the rest of them! I'm one dollar an hour, Willy! I tried seven states and couldn't raise it. A buck an hour! Do you gather my meaning? I'm not bringing home any prizes any more, and you're going to stop waiting for me to bring them home!

WILLY (*directly to* BIFF). You vengeful, spiteful mutt!

(BIFF *breaks from* HAPPY. WILLY, *in fright, starts up the stairs.* BIFF *grabs him.*)

BIFF (*at the peak of his fury*). Pop, I'm nothing! I'm nothing, Pop. Can't you understand that? There's no spite in it any more. I'm just what I am, that's all.

(BIFF'S *fury has spent itself, and he breaks down, sobbing, holding on to* WILLY, *who dumbly fumbles for* BIFF'S *face.*)

WILLY (*astonished*). What're you doing? What're you doing? (*To* LINDA) Why is he crying?

BIFF (*crying, broken*). Will you let me go, for Christ's sake? Will you take that phony dream and burn it before something happens? (*Struggling to contain himself, he pulls away and moves to the stairs.*) I'll go in the morning. Put him—put him to bed. (*Exhausted,* BIFF *moves up the stairs to his room.*)

WILLY (*after a long pause, astonished, elevated*). Isn't that—isn't that remarkable? Biff—he likes me!

LINDA. He loves you, Willy!

HAPPY (*deeply moved*). Always did, Pop.

WILLY. Oh, Biff! (*Staring wildly*) He cried! Cried to me. (*He is choking with his love, and now cries out his promise.*) That boy—that boy is going to be magnificent!

(BEN *appears in the light just outside the kitchen.*)

BEN. Yes, outstanding, with twenty thousand behind him.

LINDA (*sensing the racing of his mind, fearfully, carefully*). Now come to bed, Willy. It's all settled now.

WILLY (*finding it difficult not to rush out of the house*). Yes, we'll sleep. Come on. Go to sleep, Hap.

BEN. And it does take a great kind of a man to crack the jungle.

(In accents of dread, BEN's *idyllic music starts up.)*

HAPPY *(his arm around* LINDA*).* I'm getting married, Pop, don't forget it. I'm changing everything. I'm gonna run that department before the year is up. You'll see, Mom. *(He kisses her.)*

BEN. The jungle is dark but full of diamonds, Willy.

(WILLY *turns, moves, listening to* BEN.)

LINDA. Be good. You're both good boys, just act that way, that's all.

HAPPY. 'Night, Pop. *(He goes upstairs.)*

LINDA *(to* WILLY*).* Come, dear.

BEN *(with greater force).* One must go in to fetch a diamond out.

WILLY *(to* LINDA, *as he moves slowly along the edge of the kitchen, toward the door).* I just want to get settled down, Linda. Let me sit alone for a little.

LINDA *(almost uttering her fear).* I want you upstairs.

WILLY *(taking her in his arms).* In a few minutes, Linda. I couldn't sleep right now. Go on, you look awful tired. *(He kisses her.)*

BEN. Not like an appointment at all. A diamond is rough and hard to the touch.

WILLY. Go on now. I'll be right up.

LINDA. I think this is the only way, Willy.

WILLY. Sure, it's the best thing.

BEN. Best thing!

WILLY. The only way. Everything is gonna be—go on, kid, get to bed. You look so tired.

LINDA. Come right up.

WILLY. Two minutes.

(LINDA *goes into the living-room, then reappears in her bedroom.* WILLY *moves just outside the kitchen door.)*

WILLY. Loves me. *(Wonderingly)* Always loved me. Isn't that a remarkable thing? Ben, he'll worship me for it!

BEN *(with promise).* It's dark there, but full of diamonds.

WILLY. Can you imagine that magnificence with twenty thousand dollars in his pocket?

LINDA *(calling from her room).* Willy! Come up!

WILLY *(calling into the kitchen).* Yes! Yes. Coming! It's very smart, you realize that, don't you, sweetheart? Even Ben sees it. I gotta go, baby. 'By! 'By! *(Going over to* BEN, *almost dancing)* Imagine? When the mail comes he'll be ahead of Bernard again!

BEN. A perfect proposition all around.

WILLY. Did you see how he cried to me? Oh, if I could kiss him, Ben!

BEN. Time, William, time!

WILLY. Oh, Ben, I always knew one way or another we were gonna make it, Biff and I!

BEN (*looking at his watch*). The boat. We'll be late. (*He moves slowly off into the darkness.*)

WILLY (*elegiacally, turning to the house*). Now when you kick off, boy, I want a seventy-yard boot, and get right down the field under the ball, and when you hit, hit low and hit hard, because it's important, boy. (*He swings around and faces the audience.*) There's all kinds of important people in the stands, and the first thing you know . . . (*Suddenly realizing he is alone*) Ben! Ben, where do I . . . ? (*He makes a sudden movement of search.*) Ben, how do I . . . ?

LINDA (*calling*). Willy, you coming up?

WILLY (*uttering a gasp of fear, whirling about as if to quiet her*). Sh! (*He turns around as if to find his way; sounds, faces, voices, seem to be swarming in upon him and he flicks at them, crying*) Sh! Sh! (*Suddenly music, faint and high, stops him. It rises in intensity, almost to an unbearable scream. He goes up and down on his toes, and rushes off around the house.*) Shhh!

LINDA. Willy?

(*There is no answer.* LINDA *waits.* BIFF *gets up off his bed. He is still in his clothes.* HAPPY *sits up.* BIFF *stands listening.*)

LINDA (*with real fear*). Willy, answer me! Willy!

(*There is the sound of a car starting and moving away at full speed.*)

LINDA. No!

BIFF (*rushing down the stairs*). Pop!

(*As the car speeds off, the music crashes down in a frenzy of sound, which becomes the soft pulsation of a single cello string.* BIFF *slowly returns to his bedroom. He and* HAPPY *gravely don their jackets.* LINDA *slowly walks out of her room. The music has developed into a dead march. The leaves of day are appearing over everything.* CHARLEY *and* BERNARD, *somberly dressed, appear and knock on the kitchen door.* BIFF *and* HAPPY *slowly descend the stairs to the kitchen as* CHARLEY *and* BERNARD *enter. All stop a moment when* LINDA, *in clothes of mourning, bearing a little bunch of roses, comes through the draped doorway into the kitchen. She goes to* CHARLEY *and takes his arm. Now all move toward the audience, through the wall-line of the kitchen. At the limit of the apron,* LINDA *lays down the flowers, kneels, and sits back on her heels. All stare down at the grave.*)

REQUIEM

CHARLEY. It's getting dark, Linda.

(LINDA *doesn't react. She stares at the grave.*)

BIFF. How about it, Mom? Better get some rest, heh? They'll be closing the gate soon.

(LINDA *makes no move. Pause.*)

HAPPY (*deeply angered*). He had no right to do that. There was no necessity for it. We would've helped him.

CHARLEY (*grunting*). Hmmm.

BIFF. Come along, Mom.

LINDA. Why didn't anybody come?

CHARLEY. It was a very nice funeral.

LINDA. But where are all the people he knew? Maybe they blame him.

CHARLEY. Naa. It's a rough world, Linda. They wouldn't blame him.

LINDA. I can't understand it. At this time especially. First time in thirty-five years we were just about free and clear. He only needed a little salary. He was even finished with the dentist.

CHARLEY. No man only needs a little salary.

LINDA. I can't understand it.

BIFF. There were a lot of nice days. When he'd come home from a trip; or on Sundays, making the stoop; finishing the cellar; putting on the new porch; when he built the extra bathroom; and put up the garage. You know something, Charley, there's more of him in that front stoop than in all the sales he ever made.

CHARLEY. Yeah. He was a happy man with a batch of cement.

LINDA. He was so wonderful with his hands.

BIFF. He had the wrong dreams. All, all, wrong.

HAPPY (*almost ready to fight* BIFF). Don't say that!

BIFF. He never knew who he was.

CHARLEY (*stopping* HAPPY's *movement and reply. To* BIFF). Nobody dast blame this man. You don't understand: Willy was a salesman. And for a salesman, there is no rock bottom to the life. He don't put a bolt to a nut, he don't tell you the law or give you medicine. He's a man way out there in the blue, riding on a smile and a shoestring. And when they start not smiling back—that's an earthquake. And then you get yourself a couple of spots on your hat, and you're finished. Nobody dast blame this man. A salesman is got to dream, boy. It comes with the territory.

BIFF. Charley, the man didn't know who he was.

HAPPY (*infuriated*). Don't say that!

BIFF. Why don't you come with me, Happy?

HAPPY. I'm not licked that easily. I'm staying right in this city, and I'm gonna beat this racket! (He looks at BIFF, *his chin set.*) The Loman Brothers!

BIFF. I know who I am, kid.

HAPPY. All right, boy. I'm gonna show you and everybody else that Willy Loman did not die in vain. He had a good dream. It's the only dream you can have—to come out number-one man. He fought it out here, and this is where I'm gonna win it for him.

BIFF (*with a hopeless glance at* HAPPY, *bends toward his mother*). Let's go, Mom.

LINDA. I'll be with you in a minute. Go on, Charley. (*He hesitates.*) I want to, just for a minute. I never had a chance to say good-by.

(CHARLEY *moves away, followed by* HAPPY. BIFF *remains a slight distance up and left of* LINDA. *She sits there, summoning herself. The flute begins, not far away, playing behind her speech.*)

LINDA. Forgive me, dear. I can't cry. I don't know what it is, but I can't cry. I don't understand it. Why did you ever do that? Help me, Willy, I can't cry. It seems to me that you're just on another trip. I keep expecting you. Willy, dear, I can't cry. Why did you do it? I search and search and I search, and I can't understand it, Willy. I made the last payment on the house today. Today, dear. And there'll be nobody home. (*A sob rises in her throat.*) We're free and clear. (*Sobbing more fully, released*) We're free. (BIFF *comes slowly toward her.*) We're free . . . We're free . . .

(BIFF *lifts her to her feet and moves out up right with her in his arms.* LINDA *sobs quietly.* BERNARD *and* CHARLEY *come together and follow them, followed by* HAPPY. *Only the music of the flute is left on the darkening stage as over the house the hard towers of the apartment buildings rise into sharp focus, and the curtain falls.*)

Edward Albee

THE SANDBOX

A Brief Play, in Memory of My Grandmother (1876–1959)

PLAYERS

THE YOUNG MAN, 25, *a good-looking, well-built boy in a bathing suit*
MOMMY, 55, *a well-dressed, imposing woman*
DADDY, 60, *a small man; gray, thin*
GRANDMA, 86, *a tiny, wizened woman with bright eyes*
THE MUSICIAN, *no particular age, but young would be nice*

NOTE. *When, in the course of the play,* MOMMY *and* DADDY *call each other by these names, there should be no suggestion of regionalism. These names are of empty affection and point up the pre-senility and vacuity of their characters.*

THE SCENE. *A bare stage, with only the following: Near the footlights, far stage-right, two simple chairs set side by side, facing the audience; near the footlights, far stage-left, a chair facing stage-right with a music stand before it; farther back, and stage-center, slightly elevated and raked, a large child's sandbox with a toy pail and shovel; the background is the sky, which alters from brightest day to deepest night.*

At the beginning, it is brightest day; the YOUNG MAN *is alone on stage to the rear of the sandbox, and to one side. He is doing calisthenics; he does calisthenics until quite at the very end of the play. These calisthenics, employing the arms only, should suggest the beating and fluttering of wings. The* YOUNG MAN *is, after all, the Angel of Death.*

MOMMY *and* DADDY *enter from stage-left,* MOMMY *first.*

MOMMY (*motioning to* DADDY). Well, here we are; this is the beach.

DADDY (*whining*). I'm cold.

MOMMY (*dismissing him with a little laugh*). Don't be silly; it's as warm as toast. Look at that nice young man over there: *he* doesn't think it's cold. (*Waves to the* YOUNG MAN) Hello.

YOUNG MAN (*with an endearing smile*). Hi!

MOMMY (*looking about*). This will do perfectly . . . don't you think so, Daddy? There's sand there . . . and the water beyond. What do you think, Daddy?

DADDY (*vaguely*). Whatever you say, Mommy.

MOMMY (*with the same little laugh*). Well, of course . . . whatever I say. Then, it's settled, is it?

DADDY (*shrugs*). She's *your* mother, not mine.

MOMMY. *I* know she's my mother. What do you take me for? (*A pause*) All right, now; let's get on with it. (*She shouts into the wings, stage-left*) You! Out there! You can come in now.

(*The* MUSICIAN *enters, seats himself in the chair, stage-left, places music on the music stand, is ready to play.* MOMMY *nods approvingly.*)

MOMMY. Very nice; very nice. Are you ready, Daddy? Let's go get Grandma.

DADDY. Whatever you say, Mommy.

MOMMY (*leading the way out, stage-left*). Of course, whatever I say. (*To the* MUSICIAN) You can begin now.

(*The* MUSICIAN *begins playing;* MOMMY *and* DADDY *exit; the* MUSICIAN, *all the while playing, nods to the* YOUNG MAN.)

YOUNG MAN (*with the same endearing smile*). Hi!

(*After a moment,* MOMMY *and* DADDY *re-enter, carrying* GRANDMA. *She is borne in by their hands under her armpits; she is quite rigid; her legs are drawn up; her feet do not touch the ground; the expression on her ancient face is that of puzzlement and fear.*)

DADDY. Where do we put her?

MOMMY (*the same little laugh*). Wherever I say, of course. Let me see . . . well . . . all right, over there . . . in the sandbox. (*Pause*) Well, what are you waiting for, Daddy? . . . The sandbox!

(*Together they carry* GRANDMA *over to the sandbox and more or less dump her in.*)

GRANDMA (*righting herself to a sitting position; her voice a cross between a baby's laugh and cry*). Ahhhhhh! Graaaaa!

DADDY (*dusting himself*). What do we do now?

MOMMY (*to the* MUSICIAN). You can stop now. (*The* MUSICIAN *stops.*) (*Back to* DADDY) What do you mean, what do we do now? We go over there and sit down, of course. (*To the* YOUNG MAN) Hello there.

YOUNG MAN (*again smiling*). Hi!

(MOMMY *and* DADDY *move to the chairs, stage-right, and sit down. A pause.*)

GRANDMA (*same as before*). Ahhhhhh! Ah-haaaaaa! Graaaaaa!

DADDY. Do you think . . . do you think she's . . . comfortable?

MOMMY (*impatiently*). How would I know?

DADDY (*pause*). What do we do now?

MOMMY (*as if remembering*). We . . . wait. We . . . sit here . . . and we wait . . . that's what we do.

DADDY (*after a pause*). Shall we talk to each other?

MOMMY (*with that little laugh; picking something off her dress*). Well, *you* can talk, if you want to . . . if you can think of anything to *say* . . . if you can think of anything *new*.

DADDY (*thinks*). No . . . I suppose not.

MOMMY (*with a triumphant laugh*). Of course not!

GRANDMA (*banging the toy shovel against the pail*). Haaaaaa! Ah-haaaaaa!

MOMMY (*out over the audience*). Be quiet, Grandma . . . just be quiet, and wait.

(GRANDMA *throws a shovelful of sand at* MOMMY.)

MOMMY (*still out over the audience*). She's throwing sand at me! You stop that, Grandma; you stop throwing sand at Mommy! (*To* DADDY) She's throwing sand at me.

(DADDY *looks around at* GRANDMA, *who screams at him.*)

GRANDMA. GRAAAAA!

MOMMY. Don't look at her. Just . . . sit here . . . be very still . . . and wait. (*To the* MUSICIAN) You . . . uh . . . you go ahead and do whatever it is you do.

(*The* MUSICIAN *plays.* MOMMY *and* DADDY *are fixed, staring out beyond the audience.* GRANDMA *looks at them, looks at the* MUSICIAN, *looks at the sandbox, throws down the shovel.*)

GRANDMA. Ah-haaaaaa! Graaaaaa! (*Looks for reaction; gets none. Now . . . directly to the audience*) Honestly! What a way to treat an old woman! Drag her out of the house . . . stick her in a car . . . bring her out here from the city . . . dump her in a pile of sand . . . and leave her here to set. I'm eighty-six years old! I was married when I was seventeen. To a farmer. He died when I was thirty. (*To the* MUSICIAN) Will you stop that, please? (*The* MUSICIAN *stops playing.*) I'm a feeble old woman . . . how do you expect anybody to hear me over that peep! peep! peep! (*To herself*) There's no respect around here. (*To the* YOUNG MAN) There's no respect around here!

YOUNG MAN (*same smile*). Hi!

GRANDMA (*after a pause, a mild double-take, continues, to the audience*). My husband died when I was thirty (*indicates* MOMMY), and I had to raise that big cow over there all by my lonesome. You can imagine what *that was like*. Lordy! (*To the* YOUNG MAN) Where'd they get *you?*

YOUNG MAN. Oh . . . I've been around for a while.

GRANDMA. I'll bet you have! Heh, heh, heh. Will you look at you!

YOUNG MAN (*flexing his muscles*). Isn't that something? (*Continues his calisthenics.*)

GRANDMA. Boy, oh boy; I'll say. Pretty good.

YOUNG MAN (*sweetly*). I'll say.

GRANDMA. Where ya from?

YOUNG MAN. Southern California.

GRANDMA (*nodding*). Figgers; figgers. What's your name, honey?

YOUNG MAN. I don't know . . .

GRANDMA (*to the audience*). Bright, too!

YOUNG MAN. I mean . . . I mean, they haven't given me one yet . . . the studio . . .

GRANDMA (*giving him the once-over*). You don't say . . . you don't say. Well . . . uh, I've got to talk some more . . . don't you go 'way.

YOUNG MAN. Oh, no

GRANDMA (*turning her attention back to the audience*). Fine; fine. (*Then, once more, back to the* YOUNG MAN) You're . . . you're an actor, hunh?

YOUNG MAN (*beaming*). Yes. I am.

GRANDMA (*to the audience again; shrugs*). I'm smart that way. *Anyhow,* I had to raise . . . *that* over there all by my lonesome; and what's next to her there . . . that's what she married. Rich? I tell you . . . money, money, money. They took me off the *farm* . . . which was real decent of them . . . and they moved me into the big town house with *them* . . . fixed a nice place for me under the stove . . . gave me an army blanket . . . and my own dish . . . my very own dish! So, what have I got to complain about? Nothing, of course. I'm not complaining. (*She looks up at the sky, shouts to someone off stage*) Shouldn't it be getting dark now, dear?

(*The lights dim; night comes on. The* MUSICIAN *begins to play; it becomes deepest night. There are spots on all the players, including the* YOUNG MAN, *who is, of course, continuing his calisthenics.*)

DADDY (*stirring*). It's nighttime.

MOMMY. Shhhh. Be still . . . wait.

DADDY (*whining*). It's so hot.

MOMMY. Shhhhhh. Be still . . . wait.

GRANDMA (*to herself*). That's better. Night. (*To the* MUSICIAN) Honey, do you play all through this part? (*The* MUSICIAN *nods.*) Well, keep it nice and soft; that's a good boy. (*The* MUSICIAN *nods again; plays softly.*) That's nice.

(*There is an off-stage rumble.*)

DADDY (*starting*). What was that?

MOMMY (*beginning to weep*). It was nothing.

DADDY. It was . . . it was . . . thunder . . . or a wave breaking . . . or something.

MOMMY (*whispering, through her tears*). It was an off-stage rumble . . . and you know what *that* means . . .

DADDY. I forget . . .

MOMMY (*barely able to talk*). It means the time has come for poor Grandma . . . and I can't bear it!

DADDY (*vacantly*). I . . . I suppose you've got to be brave.

GRANDMA (*mocking*). That's right, kid; be brave. You'll bear up; you'll get over it.

(*Another off-stage rumble . . . louder.*)

MOMMY. Ohhhhhhhhhh . . . poor Grandma . . . poor Grandma . . .

GRANDMA (*to* MOMMY). I'm fine! I'm all right! It hasn't happened yet!

(*A violent off-stage rumble. All the lights go out, save the spot on the* YOUNG MAN; *the* MUSICIAN *stops playing.*)

MOMMY. Ohhhhhhhhh . . . Ohhhhhhhhhh . . .

(*Silence.*)

GRANDMA. Don't put the lights up yet . . . I'm not ready; I'm not quite ready. (*Silence*) All right, dear . . . I'm about done.

(*The lights come up again, to brightest day; the* MUSICIAN *begins to play.* GRANDMA *is discovered, still in the sandbox, lying on her side, propped up on an elbow, half covered, busily shoveling sand over herself.*)

GRANDMA (*muttering*). I don't know how I'm supposed to do anything with this goddam toy shovel . . .

DADDY. Mommy! It's daylight!

MOMMY (*brightly*). So it is! Well! Our long night is over. We must put away our tears, take off our mourning . . . and face the future. It's our duty.

GRANDMA (*still shoveling; mimicking*). . . . take off our mourning . . . face the future . . . Lordy!

(MOMMY *and* DADDY *rise, stretch.* MOMMY *waves to the* YOUNG MAN.)

YOUNG MAN (*with that smile*). Hi!

(GRANDMA *plays dead.* (!) MOMMY *and* DADDY *go over to look at her; she is a little more than half buried in the sand; the toy shovel is in her hands, which are crossed on her breast.*)

MOMMY (*before the sandbox; shaking her head*). Lovely! It's . . . it's hard to be sad . . . she looks . . . so happy. (*With pride and conviction*) It pays to do things well. (*To the* MUSICIAN) All right, you can stop now, if you want to. I mean, stay around for a swim, or something; it's all right with us. (*She sighs heavily*) Well, Daddy . . . off we go.

Daddy. Brave Mommy!
Mommy. Brave Daddy!

(*They exit, stage-left.*)

Grandma (*after they leave; lying quite still*). It pays to do things well . . . Boy, oh boy! (*She tries to sit up*) . . . well, kids . . . (*but she finds she can't*) . . . I . . . I can't get up. I . . . I can't move . . .

(*The* Young Man *stops his calisthenics, nods to the* Musician, *walks over to* Grandma, *kneels down by the sandbox.*)

Grandma. I . . . can't move . . .
Young Man. Shhhhh . . . be very still . . .
Grandma. I . . . I can't move . . .
Young Man. Uh . . . ma'am; I . . . I have a line here.
Grandma. Oh, I'm sorry, sweetie; you go right ahead.
Young Man. I am . . . uh . . .
Grandma. Take your time, dear.
Young Man (*prepares; delivers the line like a real amateur*). I am the Angel of Death. I am . . . uh . . . I am come for you.
Grandma. What . . . wha . . . (*then, with resignation*) . . . ohhhh . . . ohhhh, I see.

(*The* Young Man *bends over, kisses* Grandma *gently on the forehead.*)

Grandma (*her eyes closed, her hands folded on her breast again, the shovel between her hands, a sweet smile on her face*). Well . . . that was very nice, dear . . .
Young Man (*still kneeling*). Shhhhh . . . be still . . .
Grandma. What I meant was . . . you did that very well, dear . . .
Young Man (*blushing*). . . . oh . . .
Grandma. No; I mean it. You've got that . . . you've got a quality.
Young Man (*with his endearing smile*). Oh . . . thank you; thank you very much . . . ma'am.
Grandma (*slowly; softly—as the* Young Man *puts his hands on top of* Grandma*'s*). You're . . . you're welcome . . . dear.

(*Tableau. The* Musician *continues to play as the curtain slowly comes down.*)

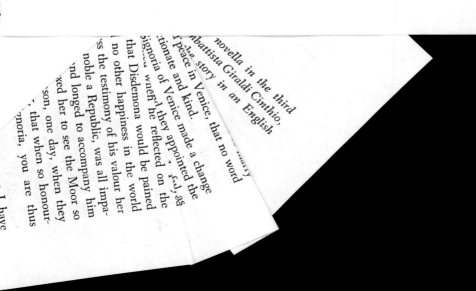

received is disturbed by the love I bear you; for I see that of necessity one of two things must happen; either that I take you with me, to encounter the perils of the sea, or, to save you from this danger, I must leave you here in Venice. The first could not be otherwise than serious to me, for all the toil you would have to bear, and every danger that might befall you, would cause me extreme anxiety and pain. Yet, were I to leave you behind me, I should be hateful to myself, since in parting from you I should part from my own life."

Disdemona, on hearing this, replied, "My husband, what thoughts ... these that wander through your mind? Why let such things distu... I will accompany you whithersoe'er you go, were it to pass throu... now to cross the water in a safe and well-provided ship: if ind... toils and perils to encounter, I will share them wit... should think you loved me little, were ... ing me to bear you co... favour w... that he... likewise taken ... lady; and being of ... spent the greater part of ...

In the same Company the... the Moor was much affectioned. H... how much her husband valued him, show... ness, which was all very grateful to the Mo... regardless of the faith that he had pledged his wife, ... ship, fidelity, and obligation which he owed ... love with Disdemona...

of his ill success was that Disdemona loved the Captain of the troop; and he pondered how to remove him from her sight. The love which he had borne the lady now changed into the bitterest hate; and, having failed in his purposes, he devoted all his thoughts to plot the death of the Captain of the troop, and to divert the affection of the Moor from Disdemona. After revolving in his mind various schemes, all alike wicked, he at length resolved to accuse her of unfaithfulness to her husband, and to represent the Captain as her paramour. But knowing the singular love the Moor bore to Disdemona, and the friendship which he had for the Captain, he was well aware that, unless he practised an artful fraud upon the Moor, it were impossible to make him give ear to either accusation: wherefore he resolved to wait, until time and circumstance should open a path for him to engage in his foul project.

Not long afterwards, it happened that the Captain, having drawn his sword upon a soldier of the guard, and struck him, the Moor deprived him of his rank; whereat Disdemona was deeply grieved, and endeavoured again and again to reconcile her husband to the man. This the Moor told to the wicked Ensign, and how his wife importuned him so much about the Captain, that he feared he should be forced at last to receive him back to service. Upon this hint the Ensign resolved to act, and began to work his web of intrigue; "Perchance," said he, "the lady Disdemona may have good reason to look kindly on him."

"And wherefore?" said the Moor.

"Nay, I would not step 'twixt man and wife," replied the Ensign; "but let your eyes be witness to themselves."

In vain the Moor went on to question the officer—he would proceed no further; nevertheless his words left a sharp stinging thorn in the Moor's heart, who could think of nothing else, trying to guess their meaning, and lost in melancholy. And one day, when his wife had been endeavouring to pacify his anger toward the Captain, and praying him not to be unmindful of ancient services and friendship, for one small fault, especially since peace had been made between the Captain and the soldier he had struck, the Moor was angered, and exclaimed, "Great cause have you, Disdemona, to care so anxiously about this man! Is he a brother, or your kinsman, that he should be so near your heart?"

The lady, with all gentleness and humility, replied, "Be not angered, my dear lord; I have no other cause to bid me speak, than sorrow that I see you lose so dear a friend as, by your own words, this Captain has been to you: nor has he done so grave a fault, that you should bear him so much enmity. Nay, but you Moors are of so hot a nature, that every little trifle moves you to anger and revenge."

Still more enraged at these words, the Moor replied, "I could bring proofs—by heaven it mocks belief! but for the wrongs I have endured, revenge must satisfy my wrath."

Disdemona, in astonishment and fright, seeing her husband's anger kindled against her, so contrary to his wont, said humbly and with timidness, "None save a good intent has led me thus to speak with you, my lord; but to give cause no longer for offence, I'll never speak a word more on the subject."

The Moor, observing the earnestness with which his wife again pleaded for the Captain, began to guess the meaning of the Ensign's words; and in deep melancholy he went to seek that villain, and induce him to speak more openly of what he knew. Then the Ensign, who was bent upon injuring the unhappy lady, after feigning at first great reluctance to say aught that might displease the Moor, at length pretended to yield to his entreaties, and said, "I can't deny, it pains me to the soul to be thus forced to say what needs must be more hard to hear than any other grief; but since you will it so, and that the regard I owe your honour compels me to confess the truth, I will no longer refuse to satisfy your questions and my duty. Know then, that for no other reason is your lady vext to see the Captain in disfavour, than for the pleasure that she has in his company whenever he comes to your house, and all the more since she has taken an aversion to your blackness."

These words went straight to the Moor's heart; but in order to hear more (now that he believed true all that the Ensign had told him), he replied, with a fierce glance, "By heavens, I scarce can hold this hand from plucking out that tongue of thine, so bold, which dares to speak such slander of my wife!"

"Captain," replied the Ensign, "I looked for such reward, for these my faithful offices—none else; but since my duty, and the jealous care I bear your honour, have carried me thus far, I do repeat, so stands the truth, as you have heard it from these lips: and if the lady Disdemona hath, with a false show of love for you, blinded your eyes to what you should have seen, this is no argument but that I speak the truth. Nay, this same Captain told it me himself, like one whose happiness is incomplete until he can declare it to another: and, but that I feared your anger, I should have given him, when he told it me, his merited reward, and slain him. But since informing you, of what concerns more you than any other man, brings me so undeserved a recompense, would I had held my peace, since silence might have spared me your displeasure."

Then the Moor, burning with indignation and anguish, said, "Make thou these eyes self-witnesses of what thou tell'st, or on thy life I'll make thee wish thou hadst been born without a tongue."

"An easy task it would have been," replied the villain, "when he was used to visit at your house; but now, that you have banished him, not for just cause, but for more frivolous pretext, it will be hard to prove the truth. Still I do not forgo the hope, to make you witness of that which you will not credit from my lips."

Thus they parted. The wretched Moor, struck to the heart as by a barbed dart, returned to his home, and awaited the day when the Ensign should disclose to him the truth which was to make him miserable to the end of his days. But the evil-minded Ensign was, on his part, not less troubled by the chastity which he knew the lady Disdemona observed inviolate; and it seemed to him impossible to discover a means of making the Moor believe what he had falsely told him; and turning the matter over in his thoughts, in various ways, the villain resolved on a new deed of guilt.

Disdemona often used to go, as I have already said, to visit the Ensign's wife, and remained with her a good part of the day. Now the Ensign observed, that she carried about with her a handkerchief, which he knew the Moor had given her, finely embroidered in the Moorish fashion, and which was precious to Disdemona, nor less so to the Moor. Then he conceived the plan, of taking this kerchief from her secretly, and thus laying the snare for her final ruin. The Ensign had a little daughter, a child three years of age who was much loved by Disdemona; and one day, when the unhappy lady had gone to pay a visit at the house of this vile man, he took the little child up in his arms, and carried her to Disdemona, who took her, and pressed her to her bosom; whilst at the same instant this traitor, who had extreme dexterity of hand, drew the kerchief from her sash so cunningly, that she did not notice him, and overjoyed he took his leave of her.

Disdemona, ignorant of what had happened, returned home, and, busied with other thoughts, forgot the handkerchief. But a few days afterwards looking for it, and not finding it, she was in alarm, lest the Moor should ask her for it, as he oft was wont to do. Meanwhile the wicked Ensign, seizing a fit opportunity, went to the Captain of the troop, and with crafty malice left the handkerchief at the head of his bed, without his discovering the trick; until the following morning, when, on his getting out of bed, the handkerchief fell upon the floor, and he set his foot upon it. And not being able to imagine how it had come into his house, knowing that it belonged to Disdemona, he resolved to give it her; and waiting until the Moor had gone from home, he went to the back door, and knocked. It seemed as if fate conspired with the Ensign to work the death of the unhappy Disdemona. Just at that time the Moor returned home, and hearing a knocking at the back door, he went to the window, and in a rage exclaimed, "Who knocks there?" The Captain, hearing the Moor's voice, and fearing lest he should come downstairs and attack him, took to flight without answering a word. The Moor went down, and opening the door, hastened into the street, and looked about, but in vain. Then returning into the house, in great anger, he demanded of his wife who it was that had knocked at the door. Disdemona replied, as was true, that she did not know: but the Moor said, "It seemed to me the Captain."

"I know not," answered Disdemona, "whether it was he, or another person."

The Moor restrained his fury, great as it was, wishing to do nothing before consulting the Ensign, to whom he hastened instantly, and told him all that had passed, praying him to gather from the Captain all he could respecting the affair. The Ensign, overjoyed at the occurrence, promised the Moor to do as he requested; and one day he took occasion to speak with the Captain, when the Moor was so placed that he could see and hear them as they conversed. And whilst talking to him of every other subject than of Disdemona, he kept laughing all the time aloud; and feigning astonishment, he made various movements with his head and hands, as if listening to some tale of marvel. As soon as the Moor saw the Captain depart, he went up to the Ensign, to hear what he had said to him. And the Ensign, after long entreaty, at length said, "He has hidden from me nothing, and has told me that he has been used to visit your wife whenever you went from home, and that on the last occasion she gave him this handkerchief, which you presented to her when you married her."

The Moor thanked the Ensign, and it seemed now clear to him that, should he find Disdemona not to have the handkerchief, it was all true that the Ensign had told to him. One day, therefore, after dinner, in conversation with his wife on various subjects, he asked her for the kerchief. The unhappy lady, who had been in great fear of this, grew red as fire at this demand; and to hide the scarlet of her cheeks, which was closely noted by the Moor, she ran to a chest, and pretended to seek the handkerchief: and after hunting for it a long time, she said, "I know not how it is—I cannot find it—can you perchance have taken it?"

"If I had taken it," said the Moor, "why should I ask it of you? but you will look better another time."

On leaving the room, the Moor fell to meditating how he should put his wife to death, and likewise the Captain of the troop, so that their death should not be laid to his charge. And as he ruminated over this day and night, he could not prevent his wife's observing that he was not the same toward her as he had been wont; and she said to him again and again, "What is the matter? what troubles you? how comes it that you, who were the most light-hearted man in the world, are now so melancholy?"

The Moor feigned various reasons in reply to his wife's questioning, but she was not satisfied; and, although conscious that she had given the Moor no cause, by act or deed, to be so troubled, yet she feared that he might have grown wearied of her; and she would say to the Ensign's wife, "I know not what to say of the Moor; he used to be all love toward me; but within these few days he has become another man; and much I fear, that I shall prove a warning to young girls not to marry against the wishes of their parents, and that the Italian ladies may learn from me not to wed a man whom nature and habitude of life estrange from us. But as I know the Moor is on such terms of friendship with your husband, and communicates to him all his affairs, I pray you, if you have heard from him aught that you may tell me of, fail not to befriend me." And as she said this, she wept bitterly.

The Ensign's wife, who knew the whole truth (her husband wishing to make use of her to compass the death of Disdemona), but could never consent to such a project, dared not, from fear of her husband, disclose a single circumstance: all she said was, "Beware lest you give any cause of suspicion to your husband, and show to him by every means your fidelity and love."

"Indeed I do so," replied Disdemona; "but it is all of no avail."

Meanwhile the Moor sought in every way to convince himself of what he fain would have found untrue; and he prayed the Ensign to contrive that he might see the handkerchief in the possession of the Captain. This was a difficult matter to the wicked Ensign, nevertheless he promised to use every means to satisfy the Moor of the truth of what he said.

Now the Captain had a wife at home, who worked the most marvellous embroidery upon lawn; and seeing the handkerchief which belonged to the Moor's wife, she resolved, before it was returned to her, to work one like it. As she was engaged in this task, the Ensign observed her standing at a window, where she could be seen by all passers-by in the street; and he pointed her out to the Moor, who was now perfectly convinced of his wife's guilt. Then he arranged with the Ensign to slay Disdemona, and the Captain of the troop, treating them as it seemed they both deserved. And the Moor prayed the Ensign that he would kill the Captain, promising eternal gratitude to him. But the Ensign at first refused to undertake so dangerous a task, the Captain being a man of equal skill and courage; until at length, after much entreating, and being richly paid, the Moor prevailed on him to promise to attempt the deed.

Having formed this resolution, the Ensign, going out one dark night, sword in hand, met the Captain, on his way to visit a courtesan, and struck him a blow on his right thigh, which cut off his leg, and felled him to the earth. Then the Ensign was on the point of putting an end to his life, when the Captain, who was a courageous man, and used to the sight of blood and death, drew his sword, and, wounded as he was, kept on his defence, exclaiming with a loud voice, "I'm murdered!" Thereupon the Ensign, hearing the people come running up, with some of the soldiers who were lodged thereabouts, took to his heels, to escape being caught; then turning about again, he joined the crowd, pretending to have been attracted by the noise. And when he saw the Captain's leg cut off, he judged that, if not already dead, the blow must at all events end his life; and whilst in his heart he was rejoiced at this, he yet feigned to compassionate the Captain as he had been his brother.

The next morning the tidings of this affair spread through the whole city, and reached the ears of Disdemona; whereat she, who was kind-hearted and little dreamed that any ill would betide her, evinced the greatest grief at the calamity. This served but to confirm the Moor's suspicions, and he went to seek for the Ensign, and said to him, "Do you know, that ass my wife is in such grief at the Captain's accident, that she is well-nigh gone mad."

"And what could you expect, seeing he is her very soul?" replied the Ensign.

"Ay, soul forsooth!" exclaimed the Moor; "I'll draw the soul from out her body: call me no man, if that I fail to shut the world upon this wretch."

Then they consulted of one means and another—poison and daggers—to kill poor Disdemona, but could resolve on nothing. At length the Ensign said, "A plan comes to my mind, which will give you satisfaction, and raise cause for no suspicion—it is this: the house in which you live is very old, and the ceiling of your chamber has many cracks; I propose we take a stocking, filled with sand, and beat Disdemona with it till she dies; thus will her body bear no signs of violence. When she is dead, we can pull down a portion of the ceiling, and thus make it seem as if a rafter falling on her head had killed the lady. Suspicion can not rest on you, since all men will impute her death to accident."

This cruel counsel pleased the Moor, and he only waited for a fitting time to execute the plot. One night, when he and Disdemona had retired to bed, the Ensign, whom the Moor had concealed in a closet which opened into the chamber, raised a noise in the closet, according to a concerted plan; whereat the Moor said to his wife, "Did you not hear that noise?"

"Indeed I heard it," she replied.

"Rise," said the Moor, "and see what 'tis."

The unhappy Disdemona rose from bed, and the instant she approached the closet, out rushed the Ensign, and being strong and of stout nerve, he beat her cruelly with the bag of sand across her back; upon which Disdemona fell to the ground, scarce able to draw her breath: but with the little voice she had left, she called upon the Moor for aid. But the Moor, leaping from bed, exclaimed, "Thou wickedest of women, thus has thy falseness found its just reward—the recompense to wives, who counterfeiting love, place horns upon their husbands' brows."

The wretched lady, hearing these words, and feeling that she was near her end (for the Ensign had given her another blow), appealed to the justice of Heaven, since justice here had failed her, in proof of her fidelity and truth; and as she was thus calling Heaven to witness, the wicked Ensign inflicted a third blow, under which she sank lifeless on the floor.

Then the Ensign and the Moor, laying Disdemona on the bed, and wounding her head, pulled down part of the ceiling of the chamber, as they had arranged; whereupon the Moor began to call aloud for help, exclaiming that the house was falling. Hearing this uproar, the neighbors all came running up, and there found Disdemona lying dead beneath a rafter—a sight which, from the good life of that poor lady, did fill all hearts with sorrow.

On the following day Disdemona was buried, followed to the grave by the universal grief of the people. But Heaven, the just regarder of all hearts, willed not that so wicked a deed should go unpunished. Ere long the Moor, whom Disdemona had loved more than her own life, began to feel such sorrow at her loss, that he went wandering about, as one bereft of reason, searching in every part of the house. And reflecting in his thoughts that the Ensign had been the cause that he had lost, with Disdemona, all joy in life, he conceived so deep a hatred to that wicked man, he could not bear to set eyes on him; and had it not been for his fear of the inviolable justice of the Signoria of Venice, he would have slain him openly. But being unable to do this with safety, he deprived him of his rank, and would not allow him to remain in his Company; whereat such an enmity arose between the two, that no greater or more deadly can be imagined.

The Ensign, that wickedest of all bad men, now turned his thoughts to injuring the Moor; and seeking out the Captain, whose wound was by this time healed, and who went about with a wooden leg, in place of the one that had been cut off, he said to him, " 'Tis time you should be avenged for your lost limb; and if you will come with me to Venice, I'll tell you who the malefactor is, whom I dare not mention to you here, for many reasons, and I will bring you proofs."

The Captain of the troop, whose anger returned fiercely, but without knowing why, thanked the Ensign, and went with him to Venice. On arriving there, the Ensign told him that it was the Moor who had cut off his leg, on account of the suspicion he had formed of Disdemona's conduct with him; and for that reason he had slain her, and then spread the report that the ceiling had fallen and killed her. Upon hearing which, the Captain accused the Moor to the Signoria, both of having cut off his leg and killed his wife, and called the Ensign to witness the truth of what he said. The Ensign declared both charges to be true, for that the Moor had disclosed to him the whole plot, and had tried to persuade him to perpetrate both crimes; and that having afterwards killed his wife, out of jealousy he had conceived, he had narrated to him the manner in which he had perpetrated her death.

The Signori of Venice, when they heard of the cruelty inflicted by a barbarian upon a lady of their city, commanded that the Moor's arms should be pinioned in Cyprus, and he be brought to Venice, where with many tortures they sought to draw from him the truth. But the Moor, bearing with unyielding courage all the torment, denied the whole charge so resolutely, that no confession could be drawn from him. But although, by his constancy and firmness, he escaped death, he was, after being confined for several days in prison, condemned to perpetual banishment, in which he was eventually slain by the kinsfolk of Disdemona, as he merited. The Ensign returned to his own country, and following up his wonted villainy, he accused one of his companions of having sought to persuade him to kill an enemy of his, who was a man of noble rank; whereupon this person was arrested, and put to the torture; but when he denied the truth of what his accuser had declared, the Ensign himself was likewise tortured, to make him prove the truth of his accusation; and he was tortured so that his body ruptured, upon which he was removed from prison and taken home, where he died a miserable death. Thus did Heaven avenge the innocence of Disdemona; and all these events were narrated by the Ensign's wife, who was privy to the whole, after his death, as I have told them here.

Index of Topics

Index of Authors, Titles, and First Lines

Authors' names appear in capitals, titles of poems in italics, and first lines of poems in roman type. Numbers in roman type indicate the page of the selection, and italic numbers indicate discussion of the poem.

7 8 9 0 1 2 3
I J